INSIDE JUSTICE

www.amplifypublishing.com

Inside Justice: Secrecy at Work

For more information, please contact:
Amplify Publishing, an imprint of Amplify Publishing Group
620 Herndon Parkway, Suite 220
Herndon, VA 20170
info@mascotbooks.com

Library of Congress Control Number: 2022918489

CPSIA Code: PRV0623A
ISBN-13: 978-1-63755-638-2

Printed in the United States

This book is lovingly dedicated to:

My daughter Emily, who taught me that secrecy can be the least courageous path and who now lives a life of openness as a model for others to follow, and

My daughter Lindsay, who gained so much insight early in life as to be forever wise beyond her years.

INSIDE JUSTICE
SECRECY at WORK

Government Secrecy About JFK, MLK, RFK, Lies and Spies,
Mysteries and Histories, Leaks and Secrecy Techniques,
Corruption and Conspiracies, "Neither Confirming Nor Denying,"
Personal Privacy, High-Tech Surveillance, National Security,
Hillary Clinton's Emails, Watergate, Whitewater and Other Scandals
— Plus the Complete and Up-to-Date Lowdown on UFOs

DANIEL J. METCALFE

CONTENTS

Foreword

By *Stephen I. Vladeck*
Charles Alan Wright Chair in Federal Courts, University of Texas School of Law

No one else could have written this book. I say that not only because so much of what follows is Dan Metcalfe's personal memoir of his remarkable, three-decades-plus career inside the Department of Justice, but because that career gave Dan unique insights into—and understandings of—the labyrinthine laws, internal procedures, and political norms governing governmental information and secrecy that may never be surpassed. Indeed, even though we were only colleagues for a few years, and taught together only once, I can safely say that I've learned more about the law and politics of secrecy from Dan Metcalfe than from anyone else I've ever known. Readers of this fascinating book will be able to say the same.

One of the most important lessons Dan taught me is that, although there are a number of laws and regulations governing when governmental information can—and can't—be secret, the "law" of government secrecy is far more than just (and often entirely unrelated to) the text on those pages. Different constituencies *within* the government have their own norms, traditions, and institutional politics affecting how they approach the broader question of when information should be withheld and when it should be shared, and it's hard for outside observers to even begin to appreciate how much interoffice politics and personalities can complicate matters even within the same administration. That's why one of the richest things about this book is how, in the stories Dan recounts and the battles he re-litigates, a sense emerges of the challenges any government faces in grappling with a national security state—and the weight of inertia that so often pushes against those who might otherwise strive for greater transparency and accountability for prior government deeds and misdeeds, to say nothing of the additional obstacles created by those in the government whose motives may be less pure.

And for as long as I've known Dan, one of the things I've admired about him most is that he's a straight shooter. That will make for some awkward reading in some places—for those who don't share his assessment of specific figures or scandals. But there's a lesson there, too, and one that is too often lost upon contemporary commentators: reasonable people can often look at the same two sets of data and come away with profoundly different conclusions about what they mean and why they matter. If anything, that's part of why it's so *vital* that transparency be the norm, and secrecy be the exception. Our democratic structures are able to function at their best when we know as much as we reasonably can about what the government is doing, and are able to have as full-throated a public debate over its wisdom and legality as the circumstances will allow. Some of that understanding could be said to have constitutional underpinnings, but even if it doesn't, it ought to be an uncontroversial principle of basic good governance.

There's an old, rhyming Russian proverb that President Ronald Reagan (who was taught it by Suzanne Massie) popularized in American circles in the 1980s: "доверяй, но проверяй." In English, it translates most closely—albeit, sans rhyme—to "trust, but verify." Reagan deployed it most frequently in reference to negotiations over the reduction of strategic nuclear weapons. But perhaps the biggest takeaway of Dan's book—and, indeed, his career—is that we ought not to be shy about directing that same principled skepticism toward ourselves and our own government institutions. Ultimately, the book is a remarkable capstone to a remarkable career, and we would all do well to heed its many lessons.

Austin, Texas
March 2023

Preface

"There is not a crime, there is not a dodge, there is not a trick, there is not a swindle, there is not a vice which [sic] does not live by secrecy."

-- Joseph Pulitzer (née Pulitzer József), publisher, philanthropist, journalist, lawyer, and politician, 1847-1911

This book was inspired by the many family members, friends, and close colleagues who so persistently told me that I "ought to write a book" about the extraordinary work that I was privileged to have done during my 30-year career at the United States Department of Justice from 1971-2007.[1] I even had a book agent tell me from a more professional standpoint during my first year of "retirement" in 2007[2] that I "definitely had a book in me."[3]

But by the middle of that year, not long after leaving the Justice Department as a former Trial Attorney and longtime "component head,"[4] there were several things that diverted me from this. First, there were the ongoing scandals of Attorney General Alberto R. Gonzales, in which I became increasingly embroiled (i.e., in its sometimes rabid media coverage) inasmuch as I had been such an outspoken critic of his in interviews given to *Legal Times* and other media outlets upon my leaving the Department; the continued controversy and media frenzy about him did not abate until well after his own departure later that year.[5]

Then there was fact that I was becoming a law professor as of the Fall 2007 semester, with responsibility for designing and implementing the two new courses that I would be teaching at American University's Washington College of Law -- a responsibility that, having always known that I someday would teach law, I took very seriously. And related to that, there was the unique academic "secrecy center" (the Collaboration on Government Secrecy, or "CGS," for short) that I was launching at my law school, as the first of its kind at any law school in the world,[6] ancillary to my teaching. CGS "took off," as they say, in August of 2007 and its development was increasingly time-consuming as it continued to grow over the course of the next seven years.

So those are my excuses (among several others that need not be dwelt upon here) for not following through on this enterprise until becoming quarantined together with my housemate Sharon in mid-2020. But once I did do so, I soon realized that it afforded me the opportunity to write a relatively unabashed memoir of sorts,[7] but more importantly to at the same time educate its readers about government secrecy (including "pseudosecrecy"), about the operation of the Freedom of Information Act, the Federal Records Act, and the Privacy Act of 1974, and about the inner workings of the Department of Justice in what I trust is an interesting fashion.[8] Of this, the reader will have to be the judge.

*   *   *   *   *

Looking back, my professional career path (from age 19 to beyond age 65) seems quite improbable, even implausible, but it did indeed happen that way. And along the way, as it happened, I witnessed the dramatic growth of the Justice Department -- and the rest of the Federal Government as well -- from "pre-Watergate" idealism to post-9/11 realism, from one major scandal to the next, and from the crimes of Nixon appointees to the criminal incompetence of Attorney General Alberto Gonzales in the presidential administration of George W. Bush.

It was much more than I ever thought I might see. But when you work in the business of governmentwide secrecy policy -- especially at a high level, with only political appointees above you, and for a long time -- you see much more than you ever imagined was possible. And some of what you see, and get deeply involved in, are things that are so highly sensitive, about individuals as well as government functioning, that they must remain secret even after the passage of many years' time. If nothing else, my conscience requires that.

So some of this book's "stories" can be told only in an anonymized, masked, or otherwise limited fashion, for reasons that I will try to make clear in each case. Those particular chapters (twelve or thirteen in total, depending upon how one wants to count them) have been crafted with particular care, lest more be disclosed in these pages than ought to be. Suffice to say here that there are several people still living whose lives would be damaged if I did otherwise. And in almost all such cases, they deserve not to be harmed.

But by the same token, this book will not shy from "naming names" with respect (read: disrespect, actually) to people who in my view certainly deserve to be so mentioned -- former Attorney General Alberto R. Gonzales; former Principal Deputy Associate Attorney General (and now Associate Supreme Court Justice) Neil M. Gorsuch; former Senator John C. Danforth; former Deputy Assistant Attorney General (and later Solicitor General) Noel J. Francisco; former Deputy Assistant Attorney General (and now Circuit Court Judge) Gregory G. Katsas; former Chief of Staff to the Deputy Attorney General (and now Postal Service worker) Michael J. Elston; former World Bank Vice President and General Counsel Anne-Marie Leroy; Senior Federal Circuit Court Judge Evan J. Wallach;[9] former State Department Under Secretary for Management Patrick F. Kennedy; and even lesser Justice Department officials such as former Assistant Attorney General Stephen J. Markman; former Assistant Attorney General John R. Bolton; FBI FOIA Chief David M. Hardy; and former Acting Associate Attorney General Philip J. Perry (then-Vice President Dick Cheney's son-in-law) fall into this ill-repute category, to name a few.

Also, for both clarity and continuity, I have tried to organize this book's chapters as chronologically as possible.[10] In a couple of instances, though, this goal was not quite achievable, partly because so many subjects overlapped in time. For this, I used the years of presidential administrations -- from Nixon to Ford to Carter to Reagan to "Bush 41" to Clinton to "Bush 43" and lastly to Obama -- as rough guideposts.[11] I trust that this chronological structure, with cross-references from one chapter to another, as well as endnotes throughout, will serve to convey as much information as possible. Indeed, that is a goal.

And I have scrupulously "scrubbed" this book's contents, just as I used to do with the many written things that I regularly reviewed for others at the Justice Department and sometimes for other agencies[12] -- for accuracy, clarity, and effectiveness, but not so much for "political correctness." So any factual error in it, as the saying goes, is therefore entirely mine, only mine, and actually doubly mine -- but I warn anyone who thinks I made one that, by definition, "I was there," and that I kept darn good notes, of course.

Prologue

"Secrecy, being an instrument of conspiracy, ought never to be the system of a regular government."

-- Jeremy Bentham, English philosopher and legal scholar, 1748-1832

"The very word secrecy is repugnant in a free and open society; and we are as a people inherently and historically opposed to secret societies, to secret oaths, and to secret proceedings."

-- President John Fitzgerald Kennedy (1917-1963), Speech Before the American Newspaper Publishers Association, April 27, 1961

On Sunday, January 7, 2007, I spent my last day at the United States Department of Justice putting the finishing touches on a list of items that I was leaving behind upon my retirement from the Department after more than 30 years of federal service. Actually, it had been more than 35 years since I had first walked into the Main Justice Building in 1971, but my tenure there was interrupted by a few things: Finishing college, finishing law school, working for a big law firm for a summer,[1] and clerking for a federal judge for a year. I had worked long and hard at all of this, especially during my last five-plus years at the Department when I was working in "post-9/11" mode.[2]

And I had topped this all off during the preceding week by working during two consecutive weekends, on New Year's Day, on the national day of mourning for former President Gerald R. Ford, and for four "unofficial" days subsequent to my actual retirement date, which had been the previous Wednesday. Even at that, I still found myself scrambling to finish all that I wanted to do before leaving the position that I had held for more than 25 years.

One of my deputies, Janice Galli McLeod, had kindly agreed to come in to our office that Sunday so that I could leave some "stream of consciousness" things such as recommendations, advice, cautions, directions, reminders, and follow-ups on the many matters that were pending at the time, lest anything "fall through the cracks" once I was unofficially as well as officially gone. Janice had been a "pool secretary" in a previous life and she graciously indulged my rapid-fire dictation toward this end. She also memorized the locations of the many work files that I had spent days organizing for her.

I must say that I had mixed feelings that day. On one hand, I was both sad and a bit melancholy to be leaving what I had truly considered to be "the best job in the world"; else I would not have remained in it for so many years.[3] But on the other hand, I knew that retiring then would allow me in a timely way to commence doing something that I had always known I would someday do -- teach law. And it would put an end to the extreme embarrassment of working under Attorney General Alberto R. Gonzales in the Administration of President George W. Bush.[4]

On balance, though, I knew that I had accomplished about as much as possible, perhaps even then some, in my time at the Justice Department -- from intern to law clerk to Trial Attorney to office director-cum-"component head" to career Senior Executive Service member. Indeed, looking back that day, I had an enormous feeling of satisfaction about all of this, including the wide variety of high-level matters that I had managed to be involved in, sometimes as a matter of sheer happenstance, sometimes by taking every opportunity that came along.

It felt good to have been able to do so many things, so successfully, during a single career in government service. And I had a strong feeling that they had the makings of an interesting and, to those with any interest in government secrecy or transparency, even educational book.

It took a while for that to emerge, more than 15 years, but here it is.

Introduction

"O, what may man within him hide, though angel on the outward side!"

-- William Shakespeare, *Measure for Measure*, 1604

Secrecy is as old as human civilization itself. In fact, depending upon how one defines "civilization," it arguably is older. And based on centuries upon centuries of empirical evidence, it appears to be entirely fundamental to human nature.

Imagine, if you will, the earliest human who could be referred to as such. With needs and activities as primitive as could be, he hunts and/or gathers in order to sustain himself. And as we imagine him, the closest that he has come to a secret was when he might have hidden from some prehistoric creature that saw him as prey. While he might have "secreted" himself at such times in order to survive, though, he made no "secret" of any real information, in relation to another person, in doing so.

But picture that caveman once he started interacting with other humans, even in the most basic of ways. One day, no doubt, he ventured from his cave to discover some danger nearby -- let's say in the form of a ferocious beast that might attack the occupants of his cave at night. He might have decided to try to kill such a beast, in a pre-emptive strike, or he might well have chosen to retreat to his cave, vowing within himself to defend the cave from any attack, if the need were to arise, as the best option.

Not being alone in that cave, however, this caveman now would have another decision to make, a distinctly social one: Does he tell his cavemate(s) about the newly discovered threat (through whatever form of communication he could use) or does he refrain from doing that? Doing so could have advantages and it could have disadvantages. Not an easy choice, but one that inevitably had to have been first made.

The intended example here, of course, is the very first caveman who chose *not* to tell anyone else -- for fear of causing that other caveperson undue anxiety, if for no other reason. Let us imagine, for simplicity's sake, that this caveman shared his immediate existence (i.e., his cave) with just one other person, a cavewoman. It is not hard to imagine some caveman deciding to keep such information from his mate in order to, in his mind, best "protect" her (i.e., from that anxiety). Such paternalism seems to be inherently human.

Then, putting aside for the moment the wisdom of such a choice, and assuming on the basis of human nature that at at least some point in prehistoric (or pre-Paleolithic) times that choice certainly *was* first made, the following question arises: "Was that the first secret?" Some people, including many of my students over the years, might at first think so.[1] The better answer, though, is: "No, not really."

To be sure, that primitive situation involves *information* (i.e., the sighting of a particular danger nearby)[2] that is being withheld (at least implicitly, through affirmative noncommunication) by one human from another (as opposed to the solitary act of hiding oneself from a predator). But that entire enterprise is purely internal to one person. In other words, no one else knows of even the *fact* of it, i.e., the abstract fact of its very existence as such,[3] let alone its content. Indeed, it is no different in character (significance aside) than the merest thought that any one person ever has that is expressed to no one else.[4] As such, it is no more of a "secret" than that.

But picture that caveman in a slightly more "civilized" setting (if it even amounts to "civilization"), one that must have come into existence at some point in time or another. Instead of sharing that cave just with his mate, they now have someone else in there with them as well, likely two someones -- for a total of two cavemen (Caveman #1 and Caveman #2) and two cavewomen (who, reflective of the misogyny of the times, are not given numbers) -- together forming the earliest beginnings of what we might call "society."

And now let us imagine that it was *both* cavemen who together discovered that nearby threat one day. Suddenly, our cavemen's choices are not so simple, are they? Assuming that both cavemen agree to not immediately fight the beast and to withdraw to their cave instead, they now have a more complex matter of social interaction between the two of them as to how to handle their newly acquired joint knowledge. Most simply put, in modern parlance, they have to decide "what to tell the wives."[5]

Assuming that these two cavemen are likeminded about what choice to make in that regard (which is, by the way, an essential element of secrecy),[6] let us next imagine that they jointly decide (just as that caveman alone did in the most basic example) to spare "the wives" from anxiety about what the cavemen now know by keeping this significant new information to themselves. Yes, they have created, and in fact are already implementing, a true secret.[7]

In this example, the two cavemen will keep this knowledge to themselves (at least for a time, if not forever) and they both will behave accordingly in relation to their mates in order to maintain that secrecy. If either cavewoman somehow asks, in effect, "How was your day, dear?" she will be met with a lie, an evasion, or some other form of rudimentary prevarication that manages to maintain the secrecy at hand.[8]

As such, each of the two cavemen guards the secret not only by refraining from communicating that information affirmatively, but also by withholding it (or, where necessary, by "covering it up") upon any direct inquiry from any other person who is not also "in on it." And at an only slightly more sophisticated level, this also necessarily involves conducting any subsequent social interaction with other potential cavepersons in such a way as to not reveal it *indirectly* either -- i.e., avoiding any words or behavior from which a person in the dark could surmise even in general that "something is up."[9]

Indeed, in the implementation of even this most basic of secrecy regimes (as distinct from more modern and sophisticated secrecy regimes), our first caveman, perhaps being more experienced in such matters, might even seek to instruct the second caveman (who perhaps is less bright, in a "Barney Rubble" sort of way) on how best to keep their secret from their mates. After all, this first caveman is relying on the other guy to not slip up and unduly alarm either of the cavewomen -- because discovery of the secret by the other guy's mate would inevitably lead to his own mate learning it in turn.

In short, he has a stake in the other guy's ability to keep a secret, which is a vital element of secrecy.[10] So he guides this other guy, and perhaps even "practices" sample dialogues with him, accordingly. And with some luck, or whatever passed for it back in those days, the secret would remain safe -- and perhaps so would the cave.

Sooner or later, though, without any doubt whatsoever, some poor bugger of a second caveman (as the British would call him, with a stiff upper lip), somehow or the other, somewhere or another, must have been the first to really screw this up.[11]

Thus was born the first "leak" of secret information.[12] It would not take much. Just some hapless fellow who was ill-equipped by dint of experience, temperament, and/or prehistoric wit to keep something significant -- even its abstract existence, let alone its underlying details -- from his mate. And before you know it, the details come tumbling out, "the wives" compare notes, and then the recriminations begin.[13]

"How dare you keep something so significant from us!" -- or some outraged communication to that effect -- is the reaction. To which the only arguably viable reply can be, variously, "I did it for your own good," "I did it only to spare you grief about something I thought I could handle myself," or the ever-popular "We did it to protect you, dear." Notice that this last formulation, in addition to using the blame-sharing "we," explicitly employs the concept of protection from the information itself, or from the pain expected to be caused by that information's disclosure, without evident regard for protection from the actual underlying danger.

*　*　*　*　*

This all goes to the very heart of what human civilization is: People joined together for common survival and, if all goes well, "historical advancement," whatever that means at the time. And a big part of this is the understanding that the strong and able will protect the weak and infirm -- which fundamentally means that those who are protected must rely on those stronger leaders for their security, even if that involves sacrificing their own "independence" (read: "civil liberties"), one might say, in the bargain.

At bottom, this is what government is all about -- some form of agreement or understanding, even if only tacit, between the governors and the governed, in which at least some benefit flows to the individual in exchange for at least some acquiescence to the process of being governed. Call it a "social compact," call it nonresistance to a dictator, call it citizenship in a democracy, it basically is the same: At the most fundamental level, people say, "Okay, I'll go along, just so long as you keep me safe."

And no small part of that, in any advanced society (whatever that means), is government secrecy -- the idea that in order to best keep its people both safe and feeling secure (the latter being an entirely subjective but no less vital element here), a government will not tell everyone everything that is known.[14] One reason for this is basic paternalism: Like the cavemen (or their many descendants), who do not want to "worry the wives," governments tend to act as if ordinary folks "can't handle" cataclysmic or even potentially disastrous news and are best shielded from it. Implicit in this is the notion that government officials are far better equipped to be "in the know" than is the general populace that they serve.

Another, closely related reason lies likewise within a second basic aspect of human nature: Government officials tend to become proprietary about the information with which they are entrusted. Put simply, they are inclined to think of it as "their" information after a while, making them disinclined to part with it, even to one of their constituents. It even can become, cynically observed, a source of their "power." Is this feeling legitimate? No, it is not. But when one views governmental functioning as just an extension or macrocosm of basic human behavior, it is not surprising at all.

A third, more practical reason for government secrecy is that information disclosure (i.e., secrecy's opposite) can be quite risky. One might posit that a government can and should communicate all but its most sensitive internal information to the citizens (read: "the public") for whom (at least in a democracy) that government "works." Such an idea, "warm and fuzzy" as it is, just sounds good.

But when there exist other people (i.e., "foreigners," who might harm the citizenry), from whom all would agree the information *should* be kept secret, then how is a government to ensure that any disclosure to its own citizenry does not in turn arm those foreign others with harmful knowledge as well?[15] The answer to that, even from early caveman days, is that it cannot.

Imagine this, for example: An extension of the "caveman" setting reaches the point of societal development at which we have a small community, let's call it Community #1, under a benevolent leader, that is living as peaceably as can be. And imagine further that a nearby similar community, Community #2, shares a common marketplace with Community #1 but is more warlike in nature and menacingly threatens the safety and security of Community #1. No one knows exactly why; they just do. (This hypothetical thus flows from another aspect of human nature: militaristic aggression, which is known to flare up in some individuals as well as in some societies.)

So realizing this, and fearing that as peaceful folks they are not likely to be able to successfully defend themselves if attacked, the people of Community #1 build an impenetrable wall surrounding them in order to ensure that the people of Community #2 can't surreptitiously attack them. But in the next big rainstorm, part of that wall collapses, in a far corner of the community hidden from view, and it is expected that it will take at least several days for it to be rebuilt.

Now, does Community #1's leader announce this development to the entire community, sharing knowledge of this vulnerability with them one and all? On one hand, some community members might think, "The people have a right to know!" And this popular proclamation resonates long and loud among the members of that community.

But on the other hand, doesn't their leader have to worry about the possibility that knowledge of this critical vulnerability might find its way during the next marketplace gathering to the hostile people of Community #2? Such a thing is easily feared, given how rumors can fly, and the weight of such responsibility can hang heavily upon whoever is in charge. So one can easily imagine that one day, in the course of man's development from cave to metropolis, but most likely very early on, this sort of thing happened for the very first time. And its conundrum had to be confronted by some unfortunate leader of a Community #1.

And so it is that some limitations on government information disclosure, commensurate with the information's sensitivity in context of security risk, are born. And once born, of course, government secrecy regimes tend to become more and more complex (not to mention entrenched) as time goes by, as potential adversaries become more threatening and/or savvy, and as the world becomes an increasingly more complicated place -- complicated as in . . . Pearl Harbor, nuclear fission and fusion, the Cold War, and "9/11," for example -- and potentially even COVID-19.[16] And what is more, such regimes self-perpetuate (not to mention propagate) over time.

What this breeds, almost inevitably, is the very real possibility (one might say likelihood) of a government getting "carried away" with secrecy, beyond bounds that most members of its citizenry would (i.e., *if* they knew of them) see as reasonable.[17] Such a "secrecy gap," between what is done by a government in the populace's name and that public's awareness of it, lies both in public perception (including misperception) and in firm reality. In other words, sometimes it is accurately understood but sometimes it is not.[18]

A correctly perceived manifestation of this "secrecy gap," though, is the situation in which a government decides to withhold information from the public for what is stated (ideally gently, without evident arrogance) to be the public's "own good," lest its disclosure cause harm.[19] To be sure, since the horrific attacks of September 11, 2001, the Federal Government undeniably has viewed the sensitivity of its information anew, "through a post-9/11 lens," to coin a phrase (which I did),[20] toward possible greater information nondisclosure (see Chapter Thirty-Six). This really should not be surprising either.

So when the Federal Bureau of Investigation and the Department of Homeland Security look at records containing the security details of toxic chemical plants, for example,[21] they see information that they think could be used by terrorists to create a disaster, especially if those records directly reveal security vulnerabilities.[22] But when those who live in nearby neighborhoods consider this, they might well be just as apt to think that such information *should* be disclosed -- on the optimistic premise that disclosure to the public is more likely to lead to quicker vulnerability repair (i.e., purely on a "squeaky wheel" basis) and that they ultimately would be safer at the end of the day.[23] Or, they might say, at least they would be armed with the knowledge with which to move elsewhere. Quite a conflict.

What this readily comes down to, not unlike with that first caveman and his mate (and all the more so with the leader of Community #1), is the question of how a government's officials ought to decide what is best kept secret from its citizens, even when acting purely on its citizens' behalves. While the roots of this question are ancient, and surely are embedded deeply in what we think of as human nature,[24] it is only in the last 80 years -- i.e., since the run-up to World War II and most especially during the past 20 years, since 9/11 -- that this has become a matter of great and urgent public concern. Indeed, all misperceptions aside, the "secrecy gap" between government and the governed has grown to critical proportions, with no good end in sight.[25]

* * * * *

This book aims to cover a combination of things. First and foremost, it will explore the many aspects of "government secrecy" (and its nemesis, "leaks") from the "inside," in a way that is, ideally, both comprehensive and uniquely incisive.[26] It will both analyze secrecy, as a growing area of law and public administration, and at the same time discuss it in so basic a way as to be clear and understandable to the average reader (read: "legal layperson") who wants to know more about how his or her government operates. Particular cases in this subject area, as well as personal experiences with the players and issues involved, will facilitate its doing so.

And in so doing, it will necessarily convey the essence of a professional life spent within the United States Department of Justice,[27] from intern to top career executive positions, through no fewer than eleven presidential administrations (counting each presidential term), under more than a dozen attorneys general,[28] and with respect to such key governmental functions as policy development, policy dissemination, statutory interpretation, legal advice, litigation, administrative adjudication, legislative negotiation, international relations, emergency planning, high-level decisionmaking, and organizational management.

Further, and most topically, it will examine the Federal Government's handling of "secrecy"[29] up to and including the Bush 43 second presidential term (and some aspects of President Barack Obama's as well)[30] -- for "at the end of the day," as the expression goes, government secrecy has much to do with where America now stands in 2023 as it recovers from the chaotic and dangerously aberrational presidential term of Donald J. Trump.

* * * * *

The Freedom Information Act (abbreviated as "FOIA," as in "It's good FOIA"), is a federal law that, generally speaking, affords public access to records that are maintained by the agencies of the executive branch[31] of the Federal Government.[32] Enacted in 1966, made effective a year later on July 4, 1967, and amended several times since then, it provides the legal basis for hundreds of thousands of "FOIA requests" each year, many of which embody strong disagreements between agencies and members of the public, often highly controversial ones that then proceed to what sometimes are "high-profile" litigation cases.[33]

The basic mechanics of the Act are simple: A FOIA requester[34] makes a formal written request (known as a "FOIA request"[35]) for "reasonably described" records maintained by an agency of the executive branch, and the agency conducts a "reasonable" search for them. Then, assuming there is no barrier having to do with fees or any other procedural matter, any and all responsive records (originally in only paper or microfilm form, more recently in some electronic form) are "processed" for disclosure[36] -- meaning that the possible applicability of the FOIA's 14 disclosure exemptions is considered.[37]

Finally, if all goes well from both the agency and requester perspective, any nonexempt records (or nonexempt portions of them) are sent to the requester by mail, or nowadays sometimes electronically.[38] At that point, the FOIA requester either can sit satisfied with what has been done, or he, she, or it can appeal that action to a higher-level agency authority in what is known as an "administrative appeal."

To be sure, the processes of FOIA administration do involve some additional surrounding aspects, such as the adequacy of the agency's record search; the payment of fees charged (primarily for record search and duplication); the possible waiver of such fees on a "public interest" basis; the determination of a requester's possible entitlement to some limitation of fees by dint of his, her, or its requester status; the timeliness of agency responses;[39] the possible agency use of a principle colloquially known as "Glomarization" in exceptional cases (see Chapter Seventeen); and the possible agency use of an even more exotic record "exclusion" in certain extremely exceptional cases (see Chapter Eighteen).

And underneath all of this, animating all but the very simplest of FOIA requests, are persistent issues of national security, business confidentiality, personal privacy, law enforcement sensitivity (now including what is called "homeland security" sensitivity), and agency privilege.[40] Matters of national security (read: classified information) are covered by FOIA Exemption 1, business confidentiality by Exemption 4, agency privilege by Exemption 5, personal privacy by Exemption 6 and Exemption 7(C), ongoing law enforcement investigations and proceedings by Exemption 7(A), confidential law enforcement sources by Exemption 7(D), and various other secondary subject areas are covered by other exemptions as well.[41] To federal agencies, this is the very heart of the FOIA.[42]

The FOIA is administered on a decentralized basis. Each federal department and agency (sometimes at the "sub-agency" level) maintains at least one principal "FOIA Office" through which it handles its own FOIA requests. One department, the Department of Justice, has long held the responsibility of overseeing this disclosure regime on a governmentwide basis; it has the duty of "encouraging" compliance with the Act by all agencies of the executive branch[43] -- through such activities as statutory interpretation, policy development, the issuance of governmentwide FOIA policy guidance, and the vigorous training of all government FOIA personnel on subjects of proper FOIA administration, and the support of FOIA litigation at all levels -- all of which are undertaken by the Office of Information and Privacy (see Chapter Twenty).[44] Supportive of this is the fact that the Justice Department holds nearly sole authority (i.e., with only very limited exception) for defending federal agencies in court if they are sued.[45]

* * * * *

When the Freedom of Information Act was enacted in 1966, it became only the third "openness-in-government" law in the world, after one that was enacted in Sweden (and later devolved to Finland) exactly 200 years earlier. Now, there are more than 100 nations and international governing bodies that have such an open government law, due largely to the prompt proliferation of such laws in the wake of the Soviet Union's collapse in the early 1990s and then the recognition that such disclosure regimes can serve as a strong deterrent to government corruption as of the turn of the century.

Because any dissatisfied FOIA "requester" can file a lawsuit in federal court to challenge any FOIA-related agency action, there have been an estimated 10,000 FOIA lawsuits filed thus far, with more than 30 of them ultimately adjudicated through decisions issued by the United States Supreme Court. Without a doubt, the most significant of these is the Supreme Court's landmark *Reporters Committee* decision, issued in 1989,[46] which established several vital principles for the balancing of personal-privacy interests against any qualifying public interest in disclosure under the FOIA's two privacy exemptions, Exemptions 6 and Exemption 7(C), which by far are the FOIA exemptions most frequently invoked.[47]

Hundreds of thousands of FOIA requests are filed with more than 100 federal departments and agencies each year, with less than two percent of FOIA requests proceeding to the administrative appeal stage and only 0.1 percent of FOIA requests becoming the subjects of litigation. The cost of all of this is now nearly half a billion dollars each year, far more than was ever imagined when the impact of the law was envisioned by Congress and interested members of the public upon the FOIA's enactment.

From almost its inception, however, the FOIA generally has been grossly underfunded by Congress,[48] resulting in large "backlogs" of pending FOIA requests at many agencies, particularly agencies with law enforcement, national security, or international responsibilities that maintain records of much greater-than-average complexity and sensitivity. This situation alone can be the cause of considerable, intractable conflict between requesters and agencies, leading to periodic legislative "reform" efforts that seem to reach fruition roughly every ten years.[49]

There also is the increasing difficulty of achieving optimal government transparency in a post-9/11 world, especially in areas of public controversy that are probed by the media. While journalists or other media representatives make up only a surprisingly small percentage of FOIA requesters,[50] the most striking use of the FOIA is when it contemporaneously compels the disclosure of records pertaining to matters of government "scandal," including the files of internal agency investigations, where a controversy over the very handling of a FOIA request itself can add "fuel to a fire."

This was especially so during the presidency of President Bill Clinton, but the subsequent Administrations of Presidents George W. Bush and Barack H. Obama were continually plagued by disclosure issues as well.[51] More than anything else, the steps taken by the Federal Government in the wake of 9/11 have spawned intense FOIA activity at, and subsequent criticism of, many federal agencies.

This basic description of the Freedom of Information Act, together with that which is contained in the immediately following chapter, should serve to inform an understanding of the various chapters of this book and, as such, is best presented preliminarily toward that end. Additionally, there exists another closely related (and partly overlapping) statute, the Privacy Act of 1974, which is best understood in relation to the coverage and operation of the FOIA. It is addressed in its own chapter, Chapter Fourteen.

CHAPTER ONE

Government Secrecy
and Transparency

"Sunlight is said to be the best of disinfectants, electric light the most efficient policeman."

-- Louis D. Brandeis, "What Publicity Can Do," *Harper's Weekly*, 1913

". . . governmental secrecy is incompatible with democracy."

-- Professor Donald C. Rowat, "The Problem of Administrative Secrecy," 32 *Int'l Rev. Admin. Sci.* 99 (1966)

Government transparency is a relatively recent phenomenon, not nearly as old as government secrecy itself, and it is something that certainly could not exist without its opposite to begin with. Indeed, secrecy and transparency are but two sides of the same coin, especially when it comes to the tendency of governments to not share information with those who are governed, a propensity that is multi-faceted and strong.

On one side of this coin -- government secrecy -- are such things as "national security classification," "official secrets," the "state secrets privilege," law enforcement (read: now also homeland security) secrecy, privacy, and the like. In non-democratic forms of government, which is to say nearly all that existed until about 250 years ago, a better way of describing it would be as "the status quo," or "just how things are." Until not so very long ago, the ordinary relationship between governors and the governed included little if any official information disclosure -- and certainly none "as of right." So in order to consider transparency in government one must view it as a modern exception to government secrecy and understand it in relation to the fundamental nature of "secrecy" itself.

Secrecy is inherent in human nature. Put any three people together and it is likely that sooner or later, for one reason or another, two of them will be keeping a secret from the third.[1] Within families, for instance, there are all sorts of reasons for which secrets are kept, very often between parent and child, with siblings and other relatives thrown in for good measure, out of natural feelings of protectiveness and paternalism (hopefully not resentment).

Governments, as macrocosms of this, are naturally both protective and paternalistic toward their own populations,[2] tending to feel that that have very good reasons not to disclose information that could bring them (or some person) harm. Government officials, in addition to feeling personally proprietary about the sensitive records with which they work, have to be very mindful that sharing information with their citizens necessarily means also making it available to "outsiders" who might use it to harm the citizenry with whom it is shared. And nothing breeds government secrecy better than war.

The obverse side of the "secrecy/transparency" coin is known by several names, all meaning the same basic thing: Freedom of information (sometimes abbreviated as "FOI"), openness-in-government (or "government openness"), open records, open meetings, record "access," sunshine-in-government, and even the "right to know" (abbreviated as "RTK"). Worldwide (and also in the United States, within the past 20 years or so), the term most commonly used for this is "government transparency,"[3] and the movement of both governments and even some government-like institutions to be more "transparent" has strongly taken hold.

Some might say that a government is already being "transparent" in some sense when it tells its citizenry anything at all about what it does, or has done, in its name. But such voluntary government disclosures -- reports designed for public consumption, press releases, press conferences, prepared statements, public congressional testimony (read: to the extent voluntary), and the like -- are of only limited utility in bridging the information gap between the governed and their governors.

To any populace concerned about what its government does, this is a "transparency" all too easily manufactured, going only so far in fostering public trust. Rather, true transparency occurs when a government determines to bind itself, through the force of law, to the principle that its citizenry can seek access to particular existing records and is entitled to obtain them unless that government properly withholds them according to established standards of information nondisclosure. That is what the Freedom of Information Act is all about.

* * * * *

The man widely regarded by scholars as the "father" (read: grandfather) of government transparency came to prominence in the latter half of the eighteenth century. So no, it was not James Madison, a framer of the U.S. Constitution and author of the Federalist Papers on whose birth date "Freedom of Information

Day" is now celebrated annually in the United States.[4] Rather, it was a relatively obscure legislator in the Kingdom of Sweden, the land that gave the world the concept of "ombudsman" as well. There, remarkably, one man single-handedly spawned a movement that two centuries later began to grip the world.

Anders Chydenius was that transparency genius.[5] Born in what is now part of Finland, he was a true Renaissance man, both a clergyman and a doctor, as well as a strong proponent of the Enlightenment Movement that swept Northern Europe during his time. And a part of his philosophy, more than that of anyone else by far, was that a government works best when it shares as much information as possible with its people.

In 1765, in one of those rare confluences of history, Chydenius was elected to the Swedish Parliament (known as the "Riksdag") just at the time at which his liberal political party became the majority party of that body. And even though only a novice, "back-bench" legislator, he aggressively used that position to persuade his peers that "freedom of information" was an idea worth accepting and promptly implementing through legislation. Thus, in 1766, the world's first "freedom of information act" was born.

As remarkable as this achievement was, Anders Chydenius was not without a source of inspiration. Indeed, in the archives of his work in Finland,[6] one can find evidence of his familiarity with the governing principles of the Tang Dynasty during 7th-century China, most particularly during the reign of Emperor Taizong (626-49 A.D.), whose relative enlightenment toward his people and the processes of governing stood markedly apart for his time.

Today, as transparency advances even in modern-day Communist China, of all places, those promoting the concept there can take some national pride in this little-known antecedent.[7] It is not known whether Chydenius looked back even farther in time, to the birth of democracy in ancient Greece, but he could have. And had he done so, he would have seen that the literacy and the rare degree of government openness that existed in that cradle of democracy, especially in Athens, set the stage for acceptance of his singular vision throughout the world.[8]

Yes, the most basic character of government transparency is as a pillar of the democratic ideal. Democracy means citizen participation in government, and representative democracy means that citizens hold the right to choose their leaders, through elections in which they vote based upon what they know (or nowadays, what they think they know). Democratic governance thus premises an informed electorate, first and foremost, which in turn is most heavily fostered by the public disclosure of government information. So, too, is the ability of the citizenry to hold government officials accountable for their actions once they are in office likewise an essential part of democracy.

So as of the end of the 1700s, Sweden stood singularly as the world's shining example of government transparency, just as its opposite, government secrecy, was beginning to emerge in some particular, rather than more general, contexts.[9] In the nascent democracy of the United States of America, for example, this can be seen in what was the biggest secret of the Revolutionary War -- America's entreaties with France for its crucial aid against the British (see Chapter Forty-Nine) -- and then in the delicate negotiations of the Jay Treaty with the King of England over the terms of U.S. independence.[10]

In both cases, these government secrets were so highly sensitive that President George Washington kept them from even the people's representatives in Congress.[11] This became the earliest American precedent for what today would be called the invocation of "Executive Privilege," i.e., when the president refuses to provide requested information to Congress (see Chapter Twenty-Two).

Nearly a century later, as America was torn by its Civil War, government secrecy surfaced again as an absolute necessity in the form of military operational "intelligence" and "counterintelligence," with spies on both sides of that conflict seeking to gain advantages through covert activity. So Washington, D.C., though little more than a muddy swamp at the beginning of that war, became a center of espionage, at the very border of North and South, with secret dealings abounding.

Even President Abraham Lincoln himself provided a key chapter to government secrecy's development when he decided personally to employ "secret agents" to ascertain troop and fortification strengths throughout the South during the Civil War. This led most famously (at least to lawyers and law students who study the case) to the first decision of the United States Supreme Court to consider the nature and significance of government secrecy. In it, the Supreme Court ruled that any such "contract for intelligence services," assuming that it was made by President Lincoln and dutifully fulfilled, was simply unenforceable in court, because of its very nature as something to be kept secret in the national interest.[12]

Indeed, the Supreme Court's decision in the 1875 case of *Totten v. United States* not only resolved the status of the particular "secret" government activity that was involved in the case, it became a precedent for government secrecy cases in the future. Most significantly, it served as the wellspring for a distinct legal concept that arose and then quickly flourished a century later: Freedom of Information Act "Glomarization," an analytical principle that refers to a government's inability to either confirm or deny the existence of a particular document without thereby causing harm (see Chapter Seventeen). *Totten* stands as the first in an ultimately long line of court cases that today continue to define the contours of secrecy and transparency both in the United States and around the world.

By the beginning of the 20th century, though, there still were only isolated instances of notorious government secrecy, no government secrecy regimes per se (other than England's "Official Secrets Act," which traces back to 1889), and (except in Sweden) nothing to be counterpoised against that by way of a government transparency policy. And when the Nation of Finland was formally established in 1919, it carried with it the transparency tradition that had formed when it was part of the Swedish Kingdom (before its dominance by Imperial Russia) and became the second officially "transparent" country in the world.

Speaking of upheaval in Europe during that time, the outbreak of World War I saw a further impetus toward secrecy -- both military secrecy and war-related espionage -- to a greater degree. New means of warfighting called for limiting the availability of information about them, while relatively new forms of records -- such as sophisticated photographs -- led to strict military censorship. And it was during this time that the world's longest-enduring national secret (unless those of Vatican City are counted) was born -- of all things, the formula for "invisible ink," which believe it or not was not formally "declassified" by the Government of the United States until the year 2011.[13]

But it was the run-up to and advent of World War II that truly ushered in the modern era of secrecy at the governmental level, thereby setting the stage for government transparency to be counterpoised against it, or not, as the case may be. And as was the case with previous wars, it was the quest for military "intelligence information" (read: counterintelligence), only this time on a much larger scale, that then fueled government secrecy -- even the world's second formal secrecy regime (read: after that of England and its colonies).[14]

President Franklin D. Roosevelt was most responsible for this, beginning with the extended lead-in to the U.S.'s involvement in what became known as World War II. Less remembered in the wake of that second war to end all wars is that for several years in the late 1930s and nearly the first two full years of the 1940s, the U.S. actually teetered on the brink of fully involving itself in the war that Germany already was waging successfully in Europe. Indeed, the very fact that isolationist forces within the U.S. were so pervasive and strong made the need for current and comprehensive intelligence about the war raging in Europe all the more vital to President Roosevelt.

And gaining "signals intelligence," through which the plans and details of the military operations of adversaries might immediately be learned, became an imperative for him -- which was the seminal factor underlying the birth of a true government secrecy regime in the United States. So the U.S. began intense code-breaking and signals intelligence efforts in the late 1930s (based upon predecessor work done in the 1920s[15]), which were carried out with such secrecy that at times different parts of the U.S. military were unaware of what the others were doing -- and as a result they had difficulty integrating one another's intelligence information.[16]

For its part, Great Britain saw it as essential to its own survival that it persuade the U.S. to enter the war, and it saw the information that it could gain through its more established signals intelligence apparatus as vital to that cause. So it created what was then the most secretive government enterprise ever, on an estate known (read: not publicly) as "Bletchley Park" (see Chapter Forty-Nine), in which it gathered the most brilliant code-breaker minds available in an intense effort to break Germany's military codes (read: the "Enigma" code, first and foremost) as quickly as possible.[17] Of course, the absolute secrecy required for such an enterprise stems from the fact that code-breaking is fully successful only if it is achieved without knowledge of that success by the other side.[18]

And back on the other side of what the British back then (and sometimes now) called "the pond," the United States set up its own version of Bletchley Park (not that it officially knew of it) named "Arlington Hall," which concentrated on what was called the "Pacific Theater" of the war while Bletchley Park concentrated on the "Atlantic Theater." This code-breaking enterprise was located on the campus of what had been the Arlington Hall Junior College for Women, a private school in Arlington, Virginia, just outside of Washington, D.C. It was led by renowned cryptologist William F. Friedman,[19] whose team proceeded to break the infamous "PURPLE" cypher used by the Japanese just prior to the bombing at Pearl Harbor.[20] Eventually, the leaders of the Arlington Hall team visited with their Bletchley Park counterparts and they exchanged cryptographic techniques. All of this was done, of course, with the utmost secrecy.[21]

Indeed, with the advent of World War II, nearly everything changed. And if the development of what was then "modern technology" -- electronics, radar, telecommunications systems, precision photography, and equipment used for cryptography -- had both enabled and necessitated the growth of modern secrecy, then the invention of the atomic bomb (read: nuclear fission) propelled it into the future with a sudden bang. Nothing in the history of secrecy in any form -- neither military operations nor Bletchley Park -- compared to what became known as the "Manhattan Project" based in Los Alamos, New Mexico, as of 1943, and what it achieved to bring that war to an end two years later (read: also an estimated two years earlier than otherwise) (see Chapter Forty-Nine).

In the immediate aftermath of World War II, government secrecy abounded and government transparency was nowhere to be found. In the United States, government leaders became focused on protecting "atomic secrets" not from Germany but from the Soviet Union, an enterprise that began with the absorption of Europe's key nuclear scientists, even before the war's end, in a secret program called "Operation Paperclip." Great Britain, fresh off of its spectacular cryptology successes of the war, was committed to maintaining its code-breaking superiority and keeping its signals intelligence capabilities from the hands of Soviets as well.

So both nations, the U.S. and the U.K., became intensely concerned with their vulnerability to post-war espionage, and with good reason, due to the strongly idealistic strains of communist sympathy in Western society. East versus West, spy vs. spy, communism versus capitalism, the watchwords of post-war Europe and the United States bespoke the fact that a modern age of government secrecy had exploded onto the world stage almost as abruptly as the bombs dropped on Japan.

Indeed, the years and decades immediately following 1945 became filled with many indicia and milestones of government secrecy. In the United States, President Harry S. Truman issued the first executive order providing for the "classification" and protection of certain government records on "national security" grounds.[22] Congress, for its part, passed a law establishing a separate secrecy regime for records pertaining to "atomic energy."[23] And much of America became very suspicious of alleged "Communist sympathizers" whom, it was feared, might aid the Soviet Union in its growing ideological (and nuclear) standoff against the United States. It was a very intense Cold War that had begun, and extreme government secrecy was the order of the day.

It was against this backdrop that a counter-movement (odd as it at first was) developed in the United States. Ordinarily, when one thinks of government transparency, as counterpoised against government secrecy, one imagines government records or information being made available to the public, a benefit (of sorts) given by the governors to the governed. But the genesis of transparency in the U.S. was something only roughly akin to that: The desire by majority-party legislators, born of frustration, to obtain access to records of the executive branch that were being withheld from them by officials of the opposing political party.

This came about because in the United States, unlike in a parliamentary democracy such as the U.K. and its Commonwealth progeny,[24] the legislative and executive branches of government are not necessarily in the hands of the same political party. This meant that during the two terms of President Dwight D. Eisenhower, a Republican, the executive branch could be held by one political party with both bodies of Congress, the Senate and the House of Representatives, held by the other.

And this is exactly what became the case as of January 1955 when both the

House and the Senate obtained Democratic majorities that lasted for the remaining six years of the Eisenhower presidency. During this time, tensions quickly began to grow between the Democrats and Republicans in Congress, especially in the House, over executive branch efforts to frustrate the Democratic majority's access to federal agency records that House Members said they needed in order to help them govern. By the end of that year, this frustration created growing pressure toward the formation of a new House subcommittee to address this freshly perceived problem.

Thus the first major government transparency law in the world (with due apologies to Sweden and Finland) was born not out of some lofty vision of government openness as a pillar of democracy, nor even as an access mechanism designed to inform the public (at least not directly) about what its Federal Government was "up to." Rather, it was conceived as a "left-hand/right-hand" maneuver within the Federal Government itself, an attempted cure for rising tensions among politicians over their own access to government records.

Regardless of this origin, however, this formal consideration of the need for freedom of information in the U.S. soon took firm hold, due largely to the personal tenaciousness of a single legislator, quite reminiscent of Anders Chydenius nearly two centuries earlier. That legislator, John E. Moss, a Democrat from California, was somewhat of a "back-bencher" himself, but he became frustrated with the Eisenhower Administration executive branch's refusal to provide what he considered to be basic information to Members of Congress.

And when the Democrats took control of the House in 1955, Congressman Moss, like Anders Chydenius, persuaded his leadership to take action on the matter. This led to the creation of a special subcommittee on government information, chaired by Congressman Moss, and to a decade of hearings and legislative development that culminated in enactment of the Freedom of Information Act in 1966.[25] Thus was born the world's third national transparency law, one so sure to shock the culture of American bureaucracy that Congress gave it an effective date of one full year after enactment.[26]

Even at that, the Freedom of Information Act likely would not have been signed into law by President Lyndon B. Johnson but for the intense pressure of media groups, which historically are open government's strongest supporters.[27] Then-White House Press Secretary Billy D. "Bill" Moyers was later able to describe President Johnson's reluctance to sign this groundbreaking bill into law; he said that LBJ did so "kicking and screaming"[28] and only upon heavy last-minute pressure from media groups.[29]

* * * * *

Then, believe it or not, after 15 additional years -- i.e., as of when the Office of Information and Privacy ("OIP," as it was known internationally) was created in 1981 -- that worldwide openness-in-government number still stood at only three. (Yes, only three, and that third transparency law, our FOIA, was not yet a strong law.) But this finally began to change, and then to accelerate, in the years and decades that followed.

It was in 1981 that I learned that among the Department of Justice's FOIA-related responsibilities was that of hosting "foreign visitors" in order to assist them, one and all, with their nascent efforts to establish freedom-of-information policies and regimes in other countries of the world. In fact, it was (and is) official U.S. policy, reiterated by the Department of State from one presidential administration to the next,[30] that we do so -- and the Office of Information and Privacy met that responsibility with both vigor and unparalleled expertise.[31] And in time, government secrecy worldwide became something to be counterbalanced by transparency.[32]

First, three former Commonwealth nations -- Australia, New Zealand, and Canada -- doubled that number to six in 1982 and 1983, as the start of a growing trend among parliamentary democracies around the world. Then the break-up of the Soviet Union in the early 1990s, which of course dramatically affected all of what soon became the former "Communist bloc" countries, greatly swelled that number, as did the newly realized use of transparency to fight corruption near the century's end, which ultimately swept through South America, Asia, Central America, and, to a disappointing lesser extent, the continent of Africa.

And by the time I retired from teaching in 2017, that number had exceeded 100 nations, with more on the way. Yes, the close to four decades between those years (read: from 1981 to 2017) saw a veritable explosion of government transparency activity around the world and I was in a position, first at the Justice Department[33] and then as an academic in "retirement," to play a central role in much of it.

* * * * *

The very first nation to send a delegation of "foreign visitors" to the Office of Information and Privacy to learn about the enactment, operation, and implementation of our Freedom of Information Act was Japan, in late 1981, with many more to follow. In fact, over the next two decades, year after year, more visitors came from there than from any other nation. And it seemed as if each year, I would hear them proudly proclaim that, "within the next year," Japan would have its own version of such a law.[34] But it kept not happening. Finally, at the request of the Japanese Government itself, and under the auspices of our Department of State, I traveled to and throughout Japan in 1998 in an effort to spur that enactment, which finally occurred in 1999.[35]

There also was China. In a true marvel and mystery of government openness, China roared onto the world stage of international transparency in the mid-2000s, just in time for the Tokyo Olympics in 2008. In fact, that was the point: The SARS epidemic in 2003 had spawned exceptional mistrust of China's central government by its citizens and, even for a Communist-ruled nation, this created a government incentive toward having at least some openness in government (read: lest those national leaders suddenly find themselves surrounded by two million flash-mob "strollers" in Tiananmen Square).[36]

Also, as in Japan, there was growing favoritism toward that openness in China's provinces.[37] This led to a nascent national transparency regime being launched in 2008 and it also led to a series of bilateral academic conferences conducted under the joint sponsorship of the Chinese National Government and the National Committee on U.S.-China Relations, under the leadership of Professor Jerome A. Cohen, who was a legend in that academic field.

We held our first such event, named the "Inaugural Sino-American Conference on the Rule of Law and Human Rights" (believe it or not), in Nantong, China, in December of 2009.[38] And as a U.S. member of these delegations, I served as the principal expert on the United States' legal structure for transparency. Originally, this subject constituted only a quarter of the total two-day program, but as time went on, this became closer to about 40% of it. Today, I think it is fair to say, even as China's overall stance toward the United States has hardened since then (read: and vice-versa), that it is only inevitable that the country that many of us grew up thinking of as the closed-society "Red China" will (even if very slowly) edge itself closer and closer to the international transparency community in time.[39]

The nation that by dint of its history (read: with the Official Secrets Act) was nearly the least likely to establish a freedom-of-information regime (read: after China, Russia, and perhaps Albania) was the United Kingdom (by which is meant England, Wales, and Northern Ireland, to the exclusion of Scotland and Ireland).[40] However, after many years of groundwork (read: with one government "white paper" after another), and with much "campaigning" by civil society groups,[41] the British Parliament enacted the U.K.'s own "Freedom of Information Act" (likewise called "the FOIA," for short) in 2000, which enjoyed a record-setting five-year implementation period.[42] During that time, OIP provided consultation assistance to the British Government several times in London, at the request of its then-Lord Chancellor's Office, including through a detailed 10-point set of recommendations that I developed especially for it.

Whilst it is closely connected to the United Kingdom, Scotland has its own

Freedom of Information Act,[43] which was enacted by the Scottish Parliament (known as "Hollyrood," after the Edinburgh palace area in which it meets) in 2002 and it likewise became effective in 2005. Its implementation, too, was led by its own Office of the Information Commissioner, in St. Andrews (read: the birthplace of golf and a lovely place to stay), which was first led by Information Commissioner Kevin H. Dunion OBE, who worked with very able assistance from the University of Dundee (read: comparable to University College London aiding the U.K. Government).

That university's law school, by the way, became the second one in the world to establish an academic center like the one that I had created at American University's Washington College of Law two years earlier (see Chapter Forty-Two).[44] Ancillary to my work for UCL, I visited Scotland several times from 2008-2015 to "preach FOIA" and advise the bonny good folks there on implementation matters.[45]

So whether driven by the worldwide movement toward greater democracy or the desire to use government openness as a tool for combating government (and indirect private-sector[46]) corruption, or both, more and more countries are seeing the value of FOIA-like laws and very naturally look to the United States, foremost among other nations, as a model of long standing to be followed.[47] While the U.S.'s standing on the world stage certainly began to suffer greatly during the Administration of George W. Bush during 2001-2009, and it hit its absolute nadir during that of President Donald J. Trump from 2017-2021, there is good reason for it to again be a model for other nations to follow.

Whereas that all began with the United States being a model for the initial adoption for transparency laws in the 1980s, it has progressed to those laws' implementation and refinement with the passage of time. Indeed, as more and more national government members of the international transparency community now move toward the latter, the extensive U.S. experience with amending its Freedom of Information Act many times over during the course of the past 50 years can inform those processes as well.

In sum, the past four decades have seen enormous growth in the subject area of "international transparency," as scores of nations around the world, covering all continents save Antarctica,[48] have developed, enacted, implemented, and refined FOIA-like laws at their national-government levels based largely on the U.S.'s experience with its own Freedom of Information Act.[49] And as this is now closely coordinated more and more in a worldwide fashion, as a potent antidote to all forms of government secrecy, the stage is now set for it to serve as a global pillar of democracy (and tool against corruption) for decades to come.

* * * * *

The FOIA was greatly strengthened in 1974, as part a major government reform effort that swept the U.S. in the wake of the "Watergate" scandal under President Richard M. Nixon, and it was joined by its major companion statute, the Privacy Act of 1974, which among other privacy protections also made additional information available to individuals from their own government files (see Chapter Fourteen).

A key part of this reform was the removal of the FOIA's categorical exemption of all law enforcement records, such as those held in the voluminous files of the Federal Bureau of Investigation (read: the "FBI" or "the Bureau"), so that only portions of those files could be withheld where specifically necessary to protect informants, personal privacy, ongoing law enforcement activities, and secret law enforcement techniques.[50] Yes, notorious FBI Director J. Edgar Hoover did not within his lifetime have to worry about transparency at the FBI, but soon after he died that changed dramatically.[51]

Indeed, it can fairly be said that the FOIA in its original form, in effect during the late 1960s and early 1970s, was a relatively weak law that only began the process of creating a major "culture shift" in the halls of government agencies. The very idea that any member of the public could compel federal agency employees to search for particular records and analyze them for their sensitivity, by force of law, was difficult to accept, to say the least. And to say that there was much resistance to the FOIA in its early days, despite what the law required, is no overstatement. Only the fact that FOIA requesters could go to court to enforce their access rights and overcome that resistance made a difference.

But slowly and surely, the entrenched attitudes of the past began to yield to the law's firm dictates, especially when court decision after court decision came down in requesters' favor, admonishing agencies to search more capably, to apply the Act's exemptions more responsibly, and to wield their imposition of fees less heavy-handedly. More intractable, however, was the problem of persistent agency untimeliness, with the largest of them -- especially the nation's intelligence, law enforcement, and diplomatic agencies -- often operating with large backlogs of pending requests. Yes, transparency is expensive, and at many agencies there never seemed to be enough resources to permit compliance with the FOIA's ten-day (or now twenty-day) response deadlines.

Meanwhile, though, especially after the FOIA's strengthening in 1974, other nations of the world began looking to it as both an inspiration and a model for the possible development of their own transparency laws. In the early 1980s, when the Commonwealth Nations of Canada, Australia, and New Zealand enacted FOIAs of their own in quick succession, bringing the world's total to six, that led the way.[52] Soon enough, delegations from around the world began arriving at the Department of Justice to study the operation of the FOIA here as a model transparency law. Japan was first, with delegations of government officials and academics predicting that they would have a version of the FOIA enacted by the mid-1980s. (Ultimately, it took Japan until the year 1999 to do so, mirroring and even exceeding John Moss's decade-long effort to bring the FOIA to fruition in the U.S.)

From 1981 on, nearly 100 nations sent representatives to the United States in efforts to enact (and then better implement) their own transparency laws,[53] and U.S. FOIA officials (read: from the Office of Information and Privacy) began traveling to other countries toward that end -- as it became official U.S. policy to promote transparency overseas. And as the count of nations with FOIA-like laws grew during the late 1980s, from six to more than 25, there suddenly was a dramatic geopolitical development that caused that number to soar: The Berlin Wall fell.

Indeed, that dramatic event had an enormous effect on the development of international transparency. Soon, with the implosion of the Soviet Union, there were many former Soviet Socialist Republics that were eager to become democracies as quickly as possible. And having a FOIA became a highly prized emblem of democracy for these emerging nations. A case in point: Within a single week during that decade, the Office of Information and Privacy received delegations from both Slovakia and Slovenia that were racing to draft their FOIA-like laws; each one, keenly aware of the other, declared with national pride that it, not the other nation, would be the first of their neighbors to reach enactment.

This surge in the growth of transparency worldwide continued apace through the 1990s. Of even greater significance, though, was the fact that it was soon followed by an even stronger causative factor: The firm recognition, near the end of the millennium, that transparency can be a very powerful tool with which to combat corruption. To be sure, it has never been a secret that transparency fights corruption, and it does so in two major ways.

First, and most obviously, it is a very potent means by which the media, "civil society" watchdog groups, and even ordinary citizens can unearth evidence of government corruption that already has occurred. More subtly, though, it also is a highly effective means of deterring corrupt acts that otherwise would occur in the future. All it takes is for word to get around that the corrupt conduct of one government official was exposed through use of the FOIA for any official even thinking about such conduct to start thinking twice about doing the same.[54]

Then all of a sudden it was as if the governments of certain regions of the world -- Central America, South America, Asia, and to a relatively small degree

Africa -- realized that FOIA laws can hold much more practical value than just serving as a foundation for democracy. The quintessential example of this is China, where democracy is far from an animating factor (read: very far) but the need for the national government to deal with the rampant corruption that exists there (or at least appear to be taking steps to do so) is undeniable. So, despite the fact that having a FOIA there would have been unimaginable not so very long ago, even China now has nascent transparency laws at both the national and provincial levels.[55]

But in Africa, where widespread corruption has been the norm, especially as to the operation of what are called the "extractive industries," transparency did not proliferate nearly as quickly as many (myself included) had expected. In fact, even today, not much more than a handful of countries on that continent have viable (read: truly viable) transparency regimes, with South Africa haltingly leading the way.[56]

In Nigeria, for instance, the prospects for enactment brightened and dimmed for many years until in 2011 a minimally effective FOIA law made it through its national legislature. Uganda and Angola enacted such laws, but thus far they stand as largely unimplemented shells that do not yet qualify as viable transparency regimes. And in Tanzania, the most recent African nation to join the club, it still remains to be seen whether its new law will truly take hold. Generally speaking, there is more room in Africa than anywhere else in the world for the international fight against corruption to benefit from government transparency.[57] And with that, there is reason to hope that the influence of the World Bank will aid this sooner rather than later (see Chapter Forty-Four).

There is no doubt that the growth of transparency worldwide suffered significantly when the United States lost much standing on the world stage during the presidency of George W. Bush. This occurred as a general matter with the U.S. military presence in Iraq and Afghanistan in the wake of the 9/11 attacks,[58] and it also flowed more specifically from the exceptional secrecy that characterized the junior Bush's presidency in multiple respects from 2001-2009. Unfortunately, during those years it became increasingly difficult for the United States to advocate for international transparency and by 2008 it no longer stood as much of a model in the eyes of the world.

The year 2009, however, brought the seeds of change for the better. In the U.S., the simple fact that the Bush Administration would be ending after eight long years held great promise for restoration of the U.S.'s role as a world leader, both on international matters in general and as to matters of government transparency in particular. And the fact that Bush was being replaced by a president who had quite openly campaigned on a specific platform of having much less secrecy than his predecessor meant a great deal.

To be sure, President Barack Obama had much to contend with as he entered office: Three wars (in Iraq, in Afghanistan, and the "Global War on Terror" that Bush had declared); an economy that had "cratered" largely due to government opacity, if not mendacity (which spawned its own pressure for financial "bail-out transparency"); a surge in the activities of pirates off the eastern coast of Africa; and a well-earned lack of Federal Government credibility (to put it mildly) both domestically and on the world stage.

Yet President Obama made good on his campaign promise, at least at the very outset, with stunning declarations about how his administration would be "the most transparent one ever." The fact that these lofty policy goals soon ran aground domestically on the hard practicalities of governing in a post-9/11 world only slightly diminished the luster they carried internationally. By late 2010, in fact, Obama was in a position to take a major step toward re-asserting the U.S.'s position of leadership on transparency worldwide -- and he did so at no less a forum than the United Nations General Assembly. On September 23, 2010, he called upon all nations of the world to take positive steps within the next year toward greater transparency, whether they yet had such a regime or not.

This suggested that 2011 would be nothing short of a banner year for international transparency, in one fashion or another, but before that year could even begin there was a distinct setback. The Obama Administration, encouraged by positive reaction to Obama's U.N. speech, quickly decided (albeit in secret) that it would follow that success with a bold step directed at the region of the world most in need of reform -- Africa.

The idea was that when President Obama undertook a planned state visit to India in November of 2010 the two nations would enter into not only a first-of-its-kind bilateral agreement on transparency in general, but also one that would be aimed specifically at bringing greater transparency to the continent of Africa. However, at the very last minute (read: almost the last second), as Obama was literally about to sign this agreement in New Delhi, it suddenly collapsed, devolving down to an agreement that mentioned Africa not at all.[59]

India had in many ways been a perfect choice for such an unprecedented partnership. It had joined the international transparency community in 2005, with a strong "Right-to-Know" law that applied at both the national and local levels. Together with Japan, Mexico, and the United Kingdom, it was arguably the biggest success story of that decade, with a technological bent that was second to none. And most significantly, it had become a leader on the world stage as part of the "BRIC" coalition, which positioned it to play a credible role towards Africa.[60]

But therein lay the problem, apparently, because after leading the U.S. State Department to believe that it was willing to join the U.S. in a bilateral effort aimed at improving transparency in Africa, India abruptly decided that the joint initiative with the U.S. was fine but the Africa part was not. And this left the Obama Administration's State Department with much less of a "build-on" to Obama's U.N. speech than it had hoped for.

Hence, a replacement was needed, some formal association of the U.S. with other nations to develop transparency laws (read: create them, where still needed; amend them, where necessary; and further refine them, where improvements in implementation could be made). That replacement was the development of what soon became widely known as the "Open Government Partnership" (or "OGP," for short), the preliminary details of which were (with no small irony) kept from public view for several months. (Yes, it was "secrecy about transparency," an ironic sub-category.) Formally launched in September 2011, in connection with the U.N.'s General Assembly meeting that year, OGP stood as the U.S.'s own answer to the dramatic challenge that President Obama had raised the year before.

And with a worldwide membership of several dozen nations, including some that had yet even to enact a transparency law, the OGP became a forum for nations to work together on transparency improvements of all kinds. It was not long before nations such as Brazil, Indonesia, and Norway distinguished themselves as OGP leaders, demonstrating their willingness and capability to join together with the United States in such efforts. And in a clever OGP innovation, the "civil society" organizations of its member nations came to participate in parallel fashion as well.[61]

Today, this development holds enormous potential for taking international transparency to a new level -- just as post-war modernization, the fall of the Soviet Union, and the emergence of government openness as a powerful anti-corruption tool did in the 20th century -- despite its early growing pains. Regardless of its immediate successes or failures, the Open Government Partnership will go down in history as the first coordinated effort among nations of the world to replace secrecy with transparency as much as can be.

As for the future of government transparency, it does indeed look bright,[62] especially when one considers where it stood just 50 years ago (not to mention up to 200 years ago, save for in Sweden).[63] Today, more than 100 nations of the world have a viable FOIA-type regime operating at the national level, with an additional four dozen nations standing poised, to one degree or another, to join the international transparency community before long. So doubtless the day will come when nearly all of the nations on Earth allow their citizens (if not anyone in the world) to make "FOIA requests" for the records of their national governments.

In other words, from both an historical and an international perspective, it is now quite clear that government transparency is here to stay.

CHAPTER TWO
Privacy as Secrecy

"The intensity and complexity of life, attendant upon advancing civilization, have rendered necessary some retreat from the world, and man, under the refining influence of culture, has become more sensitive to publicity, so that solitude and privacy have become more essential to the individual. . . . The right is lost only when the author himself communicates his production to the public -- in other words, publishes it."

-- Samuel D. Warren II and future Supreme Court Justice Louis D. Brandeis, "The Right to Privacy," *Harvard Law Review*, December 15, 1890, defining the newly recognized right as "the right to be let alone"

Although it is not often expressed as such, privacy actually is a big part of secrecy.[1] The protection of personal privacy is a strongly held societal value in the United States and even more so in most of Europe, where there is an historic interest in what over there is called "human rights privacy." But privacy, as a concept writ large, did not exist until about 130 years ago, when two young scholars essentially established it in a law review article published in 1890.

In this groundbreaking piece of legal scholarship, titled "The Right to Privacy" and published in the *Harvard Law Review*, Professor Samuel D. Warren and future Supreme Court Justice Louis D. Brandeis set the foundation for personal privacy by identifying and advocating the "right of the individual to be let alone."[2] They argued that this right derives from "the common law, [which] in its eternal youth, grows to meet the new demands of society," and that it is "fundamental."[3] This analysis became the touchstone of modern conceptions of privacy law, as societal demands and sudden advances in technology drove them forward throughout the 20th century.[4]

These technological advances -- from sophisticated file systems to database development to full-blown computerization -- inevitably led to the maintenance of information about individuals by government agencies.[5] This grew more extensive in the first half of the 20th century as national governments became regulatory states, collecting more and more individual-based information. And for the vast bulk of such information that was deemed "personal" and "private" in modern societies, there arose the idea that privacy should be the basis for its own new category of government secrecy.

Indeed, by the middle of the 20th century, when secrecy first became a counterpoint to government transparency, the protection of personal-privacy rights, in a way that would have made Warren and Brandeis proud,[6] was a fully formed societal value that became enshrined in statutory form.[7] Hence, two exemptions from disclosure under the Freedom of Information Act, Exemptions 6 and 7(C), provided strong personal-privacy protection, just as Warren and Brandeis envisioned 75 years earlier.[8]

This came to the fore in 1989 when the United States Supreme Court issued what is quite arguably its most significant Freedom of Information Act decision ever. In *United States Department of Justice v. Reporters Committee for Freedom of the Press*, the Supreme Court dealt with the sensitivity of an individual's criminal-history information that (if it existed) was of very old vintage. That information was contained (or not) in an FBI "rap sheet" database derived from public records (read: "police blotter" entries) that went back many decades, but the individual involved was still alive, so the question presented was whether he still retained privacy protection.[9]

In answering this question with a resounding "yes" in this landmark case, the Supreme Court took the occasion to set forth several key privacy principles that together brought about a new, modern regime of broad privacy protection, one that effectively expanded the realm of government secrecy along with it. Simply put, whatever information was now to be withheld as broadly exempt from disclosure under the FOIA's privacy exemptions, under their traditional "balancing" process,[10] would now be kept secret from the public.

The starting point for the Court's analysis is the existence of a personal-privacy interest held by an identifiable, non-deceased individual.[11] Given the case's facts, it first observed that "a strong privacy interest inheres in the nondisclosure of compiled computerized information,"[12] which it said certainly applies to "information about private citizens that is accumulated in various governmental files."[13] This is especially so, the Court emphasized, in the case of "records that the Government happens to be storing."[14]

And as to the dual facts that the type of "rap sheet" information at issue was once publicly available but that this was so many decades ago, the Supreme Court envisaged a brand-new privacy-protection concept for it, that of "practical obscurity."[15] Its idea was that even though such information could have been viewed by the public bit by bit in the past, it probably no longer could, plus so much time had passed since it may have been viewed that the very "passage of time rendered it private."[16] This itself broadened the scope of personal privacy and thus, too, its zone of secrecy.

In tandem with this, moreover, the Supreme Court also sharply delimited the scope of the "public interest" to be balanced against privacy interests in FOIA decisionmaking. It declared that henceforth the only such "public interests" to be considered in that balancing process would be limited to whether disclosure would serve the "core purpose" of the Act -- i.e., showing the "operations or activities of the government, sometimes stated as "what the government is up to." This had a further effect of broadening the realm of privacy protection.

Thirdly, the Supreme Court in *Reporters Committee* encouraged agencies to engage in what it called "categorical balancing" in favor of nondisclosure. What this means is that if an agency is dealing with large volumes of documents that contain information of possible privacy sensitivity, it may withhold such information "across the board" without having to make individualized balancing determinations on it. As the Court phrased it, "categorical decisions may be appropriate and individual circumstances disregarded when a case fits into a genus in which the balance characteristically tips in one direction." This approach eases an agency's FOIA burden[17] and leads to greater withholding of information (and, hence, greater secrecy) on privacy grounds.

All told, these modern principles of personal-privacy protection brought about a "sea change" in privacy law.[18] It was my responsibility to distill them from what the Supreme Court had written in *Reporters Committee* and formulate clear guidelines for agencies to follow in implementing it. This took the form of written policy guidance, extensive training, and case-by-case advice on privacy-protection issues through OIP's "FOIA Counselor Service." Indeed, in the years following *Reporters Committee*'s issuance in 1989, as the realm of privacy secrecy became broader and broader, this was a top priority for the Office of Information and Privacy -- and for me.[19]

So to take this discussion full circle, privacy is indeed a big part of government secrecy, and this is so in many ways and instances. Beyond what is covered in this chapter, there are other major aspects of privacy protection for personal information in government files, computerized information systems, and electronic databases.[20] One of them is privacy "Glomarization" (see Chapter Seventeen). Another is law enforcement privacy protection in general (see Chapter Thirteen). And a third is found in the Privacy Act of 1974 (see Chapter Fourteen), which works in conjunction with the broadened scope of privacy under *Reporters Committee* to prohibit disclosure, and mandate secrecy, in many instances.[21]

CHAPTER THREE
"Survivor Privacy"

"Remember, when you are dead, you do not know you are dead. It is only [sic] painful for others."

-- Actor/comedian Ricky D. Gervais, Twitter tweet, October 30, 2013

"One of your first clients died today, dear." Thus I was greeted upon my return home from another long day at the Justice Department. It was January 30, 2006, and I had been working 75-hour weeks literally ever since 9/11, the day that I had shut down my office even before the third plane struck the Pentagon because I saw women hurriedly fleeing the White House by carrying their shoes from my office window two blocks away.

The "client" that my wife was referring to was only an indirect one, of course, because in my 30-year career at the United States Department of Justice -- first as a teenage intern, then as a first-year law student in the extended Attorney General's Office, then as a Trial Attorney for several years, and ultimately as head of one of the Department's 40 distinct components for more than 25 years,[1] my true client had been the people of the United States. Yes, it had always been a distinct honor and privilege to appear in court by saying, "Daniel J. Metcalfe of the Department of Justice, Your Honor, on behalf of the United States."

Usually, my more specific client would be a federal agency -- for me most commonly the Federal Bureau of Investigation, the Central Intelligence Agency, or the National Security Agency, in my area of specialization, though I did represent other agencies as well: the Commerce Department in a constitutional challenge; the Housing and Urban Development Department in a class action; the National Mediation Board in a statutory jurisdiction case that I handled also in the court of appeals; and the Department of State in a novel lawsuit under the Privacy Act, for instance. Being a Trial Attorney at the United States Department of Justice can provide the opportunity to specialize in one type of litigation or another yet at the same time afford a breadth of experience with different types of cases, as well.

But in cases filed against the Federal Government under the Freedom of Information Act (or "FOIA," as in "It's good FOIA," which we sometimes would say),[2] the case was always about information -- information most commonly in "record" form, either generated by or obtained by a federal agency within the executive branch that someone (literally "any person," in the words of the statute), as a FOIA requester, was trying to obtain and have disclosed to the public. And among such cases, there very often were ones that involved items of personal information or records, sometimes extremely sensitive ones, where the issue would require the delicate balancing of personal-privacy interests against the public interest in disclosure.[3]

Where this was so, where the personal-privacy interests of individuals were at stake, especially individuals whose names were contained for one reason or another in law enforcement files, the Justice Department owed a duty to such persons to responsibly protect those interests, by withholding information from the public to the full extent of the law.[4] And that law, found in the FOIA's two personal-privacy exemptions and the case law evolving under them, was applied by agencies to many thousands of FOIA requests each year and by courts in the hundreds of FOIA cases that are adjudicated there.

In this case, the one well remembered on the day of her death, the "client" in that sense, was Coretta Scott King, widow of the assassinated Dr. Martin Luther King, Jr., and the case was one in which an aggressive FOIA requester had sought complete disclosure of the Justice Department's extensive investigative files on his assassination. And as a young Justice Department Trial Attorney in 1977, it was my responsibility to defend the Department's withholding, whatever it might turn out to be,[5] of much of the information in those law enforcement files.

And doing that, as far as I was concerned, required my making sure that I was entirely confident that all of the information withheld from public disclosure in the case as exempt under the FOIA was correctly withheld -- which in turn meant that for many parts of these investigatory files I decided exactly which record segments, no matter how small, were to be withheld. So this was no ordinary case. It called for extraordinary treatment, as a matter of both the public interest and the potential interests of the King family, and I was determined to take every pain necessary to handle it as such.

One major reason for this is that by the late 1970s it had become clear that Martin Luther King had been a long-term victim of the FBI. It was well documented by then that FBI Director J. Edgar Hoover absolutely despised Dr. King for what Hoover thought to be King's "two-faced philandering" while acting as a "minister of God."[6] This was atop Hoover's view of King as a rabble-rousing demagogue who threatened the peace with his demonstrations. And to Hoover, King was a dangerous Communist pawn, owing largely to his association with a liberal attorney by the name of Stanley D. Levison.[7]

So King became a major target of an existing FBI operation that it called "COINTELPRO," which was an acronym for "counterintelligence program," a series of covert and illegal projects conducted by it from 1956 to the mid-1970s aimed at surveilling, infiltrating, discrediting, and disrupting domestic political organizations across the Nation.[8] In King's case, this amounted to almost constant surveillance of his activities over the course of several years, which of course led to the creation of voluminous FBI files. And the most intrusive of that surveillance was with what the Bureau called "coverage" of him through "techs" -- which meant electronic surveillance ("ELSUR," to King's close companions) within his home, offices, meeting places, and hotel rooms, especially the latter.

Bluntly put, the FBI managed to record King's conversations, and those of persons with him, during many of his activities, including those of a sexual nature.[9] These latter encounters involved women other than his wife, and many of the surveillance recordings were extremely explicit, about as explicit as could be imagined. Many, but not all, of them were made in hotel rooms occupied by King, most often at the Willard Hotel in Washington, D.C.,[10] as he spent much of his time away from his family, "on the road."[11]

So when it came to "processing" the parts of these investigatory files that contained such intimate information, I was presented with a novel legal question, to be sure. To begin with, the state of the law at that time was that a person's privacy interests were extinguished upon death -- period, full stop. I could not lawfully withhold any of that information, no matter how intimate, in order to protect the privacy interests of King, because he had none; he was dead.

But it seemed to me that in a truly extraordinary case such as this, I at least arguably had a duty to consider the possibility of withholding the information in order to protect the personal-privacy interests of King's wife and children, if such interests could be said to exist under the law. Unfortunately, there was nothing in the language of the FOIA's privacy exemptions that spoke to this at all, nor did there exist any federal case law whatsoever at that time providing legal support for such a thing.[12] That had to figure heavily in my thinking.

Nevertheless, I kept coming back to my thought that Coretta Scott King was purely a "victim" of these exceptional circumstances, twice over in fact, in that her husband had so recklessly betrayed her and then the FBI had so callously -- and perhaps unlawfully[13] -- worsened the situation by recording King's adultery in the audio sense and then further recording the details of it in its files, so why should she pay a price for that? This, I thought, created acute privacy interests, far greater in magnitude than are ordinarily seen.[14]

Plus, I thought, there were the King children to consider, the youngest of whom was only fourteen years old at the time.[15] Did they deserve to have the intimate, surreptitiously recorded details of their father's indiscretions made public through the disclosure of official government files? I didn't think so. And what I thought, in the scheme of things, is what mattered.

Indeed, as a practical matter, this decision was left entirely to me, inasmuch as I would be the one to defend any novel withholding theory in court, explaining why the judge in the case, Judge Gerhard A. Gesell, should "make new law" by ruling in my favor on it.[16] And that "new law," as I labeled it, was the concept of "survivor privacy" -- the idea that in the case of information that is exceptionally sensitive, it can be withheld under one of the FOIA's privacy exemptions even if the subject of the information is deceased, in order to protect the privacy interests of one or more of the decedent's survivors.

Yet the fact that there was little or no direct legal support for this privacy concept also loomed large. As noted, the language of the FOIA's two privacy exemptions said nothing about the circumstance of death, nor did they in any way advert to any privacy interests of survivors. Neither did the "legislative history" underlying Exemption 6 (from the 1960s) or Exemption 7(C) (from 1974) provide even any arguable support for taking such a position; such a circumstance was not at all envisioned by Congress even 3½ years beforehand during the processes of developing the FOIA's 1974 amendments.

But I began employing this concept in my processing of the records anyway. Working on the first-generation copies of them, I withheld all information that revealed King's infidelities, either directly or indirectly,[17] deleting both paragraphs and smaller segments of the records with consistent precision, so as not to withhold too much information in any instance. You could say that I was taking a so-called "Goldilocks" approach, being careful not to withhold either too much or too little as I went along.

To do so, I used what back then we called an "El Marko" pen, which was much like the highlighter pens that are in use today. It covered words with a thick brown ink that still could be read through, but when photocopied (preferably with a Kodak copier, for best results) it came out impenetrably (read: at the time) black. My other tool was a little bottle of ammonia, which could be used to restore parts of segments that were "browned out" if upon reflection I thought that a bit more of them could safely be disclosed; just the slightest touch of that would do the trick, though I did get several drops of it on my desk's green felt blotter.[18]

By the time I completed this process, and re-read every last bit of what I had done just to be doubly sure, I was ready to craft a summary judgment motion. In doing so, I gave heavy treatment to the other parts of the case -- the information withheld under Exemptions 1, 2, 7(D), 7(E), and also the "ordinary" aspects of Exemption 7(C) -- but freely acknowledged that my El Marko pen had swept up information necessary to protect the privacy interests of King's wife and children. I made what was in effect a bare policy argument for that, emphasizing that they were the innocent victims of the FBI's surveillance overreaching and that surely the FOIA was not intended to punish someone such as them twice over.

A few weeks after filing this, as well as a reply brief in further support of my motion, I received a call from a woman whom I knew as "Judge Brown"[19] telling me that Judge Gesell wanted to see me in his courtroom that morning. Thankful that I always dressed for court because "you never know," I arrived there to find my opposing counsel nervously wondering what was up, as this was not at all the usual procedure for a case. But Judge Gesell promptly took the Bench, ordered us to remain standing, side by side, each of us territorially grabbing our side of the lectern, and grilled us for almost two hours on the details of the case.

This was entirely fine with me, as I relished being able to have a rough-and-tumble give-and-take with my opposing counsel (whom I knew well) while I also answered the judge's questions at the same time. As far as I'm concerned as an oral advocate, I much prefer having an entirely free-wheeling opportunity to address whatever concerns might be on the judge's mind, as well as a full chance to explain why my opponent's points are either weak or not at all well taken. And as for the novel "survivor privacy" part of the case, this format allowed me to make a passionate argument for it while I watched the judge to gauge his receptivity to it. He certainly did seem to be quite receptive, from where I stood.

And that is the way Judge Gesell ruled when he granted the Government's motion for summary judgment a few weeks later. He granted judgment to the FBI as to all of the information withheld in the case, including on some tricky issues of confidential source protection in different contexts, and he ruled in the FBI's favor on all of the privacy issues presented as well. Most significantly, Judge Gesell accepted the need to protect "the privacy of Dr. King's family,"[20] the first federal judge to do such a thing. In so doing, he put the novel concept of survivor privacy "on the map," so to speak.[21]

* * * * *

Over the following years, in the Civil Division and then at OIP, I made the FOIA folks at all federal agencies aware of this new "survivor" basis for affording privacy protection under the FOIA. But at the same time, I urged them to use it for only information of exceptional sensitivity, as was the case with the King family.[22] In other words, we reserved it for particularly sensitive, often graphic, personal details where nondisclosure would spare surviving family members from further mental anguish and pain.

And so this new principle was applied during the 1980s and 1990s in several instances (only some of which proceeded to court), mostly to situations involving death -- e.g., to autopsy reports and photos, to the medical records of a small child, to the contents of a suicide note, to President Kennedy's post-mortem photographs and x-rays, to inmate injury reports, and even to the identities of individuals who died from experimental radiation exposure. Although almost all of these incidents involved the element of death, not all of them did, and it was not a prerequisite.

The most significant and well known of these cases was one that involved the audio recording of the last words of the crew of the Space Shuttle *Challenger*, who died within two minutes of launch on January 28. 1986, when the shuttle exploded. Although the full transcript of that 73-second voice recording was released by NASA, *The New York Times* pressed under the FOIA for release of the recording itself, taking the bold position that the FOIA's primary privacy exemption, Exemption 6, was technically unavailable to NASA regardless of any "survivor privacy" sensitivity.

And when the D.C. Circuit Court of Appeals rejected that pro-disclosure position, by a narrow 6-5 majority in an *en banc* decision, the case was left for the district court on remand to consider applying the "survivor privacy" principle to the extraordinary facts of the case. And apply it, it did. The district court ruled that "the privacy interest asserted on behalf of the *Challenger* families is a valid and substantial one." Most significantly, in so ruling it declared that "[e]xposure to the voice of a beloved family member immediately prior to that family member's death is what would cause the *Challenger* families pain . . . a disruption of their peace of mind."[23]

But the "survivor privacy" concept was not completely entrenched in FOIA case law, because while it was firmly accepted by two courts of appeals,[24] it could always be rejected by others, as it was yet to be dispositively adopted by the United States Supreme Court. Until Deputy White House Counsel Vincent W. Foster, Jr., decided to kill himself on the six-month anniversary of the Clinton Administration, that is.

Vince Foster was a close friend of President Bill Clinton and Hillary Rodham Clinton who for many years worked as a partner in the Rose Law Firm in Little Rock, Arkansas, together with Hillary and the firm's managing partner, Webster L. "Webb" Hubbell (who went on to briefly become the chief justice of the Arkansas

Supreme Court). When President Clinton was elected and came to Washington on January 20, 1993, he brought both Webb and Vince with him, the former to work in the Justice Department and the latter to work in the Office of the White House Counsel.[25] There, Vince began working on a series of unusually challenging, high-stress matters.

Exactly six months later, on a Tuesday afternoon, July 20, 1993, Vince casually thanked his secretary for bringing him lunch, told her that he would be "right back,"[26] left the White House in the middle of the day, drove his car to Fort Marcy Park on the Virginia side of the Potomac River, and took his own life with an antique firearm that had been in his family for generations. To the shock of his family and coworkers, it turned out that Vince had been suffering from chronic clinical depression, which appeared to have been exacerbated by one of many Clinton Administration scandals (known as "Travelgate"), in which he had become entangled during the weeks leading up to his death.[27]

Vince's body was found later that afternoon laying on a grassy berm in the park, face up, gun in hand. Fort Marcy Park, which is primarily a river overlook off of the George Washington Memorial Parkway, is administered by the National Park Service, part of the Department of the Interior, which meant that its Park Police had jurisdiction over an investigation.[28] Park Police officers investigated the surrounding area and took many "death scene" photographs, several of which showed Vince's full face and, because his mouth was the bullet's point of entry, some blood, but not a profusion of it, was shown as well.

It certainly looked like suicide, especially as evidence accumulated about Vince's recent deep depression, exacerbated during his White House tenure, that he had largely kept to himself. And it turned out that he had reached out to his doctor to obtain a prescription for anti-depressant medication shortly before his death. Atop that, a so-called "suicide note" was found at the bottom of his briefcase in his office, torn into 27 pieces, stating among other things that "here [in Washington] ruining people is considered sport."[29]

Vince Foster's death quickly became the object of much speculation and conspiracy-laden theorizing, fueled by the Whitewater-related scandals of the Clinton Administration,[30] and as it became emmeshed in other White House controversies, it ultimately was the subject of no fewer than five separate official investigations, including two conducted by Congress and those undertaken by two successive independent counsels investigating White House-related matters more generally.

This in turn inevitably led to the filing of multiple FOIA requests for records pertaining to these investigations, principally those held by the FBI, the Office of the Independent Counsel, and the National Park Service. One requester, Accuracy in Media, Inc. (in this case known quite unfortunately by the acronym "AIM"), specifically sought copies of the photographs that were taken of Vince's body by the Park Police at the place of his death.

The National Park Service, as the parent agency of the Park Police and custodian of the records at that time, withheld these photographs under Exemption 7(C) of the FOIA on the basis of their exceptional sensitivity and consequent ability to injure the personal-privacy interests of Vince's surviving family.[31] After AIM brought a FOIA lawsuit, this withholding was soon upheld when the Court of Appeals for the D.C. Circuit readily found that Exemption 7(C) applied to the five photographs on a "survivor privacy" basis, a ruling that ordinarily would have put an end to the matter.

The controversy was perpetuated, however, because one of Accuracy in Media's counsel in its case, former Judicial Watch attorney Allan J. Favish, had perhaps anticipatorily filed his own FOIA request, this time with the Office of the Independent Counsel, for the same photographs.[32] He brought a lawsuit for the photographs in the Central District of California, after taking up residence there, claiming that he intended to serve an "overriding public interest" through his own further personal investigation of the circumstances surrounding Vince's death.[33] And so the case was litigated once again, this time in California.

After ruling that Favish was himself not precluded from his own pursuit of the photographs in California even though his former client (with whom we unsuccessfully argued he had "privity," meaning that they should be legally viewed as one) had lost a judgment as to them in Washington, D.C.,[34] the California district court and then in turn the Court of Appeals for the Ninth Circuit proceeded to rule mightily in his favor. These courts had little regard for the applicability of the "survivor privacy" principle and they decided that four of the photographs should be disclosed to Favish on "overriding public interest" grounds, notwithstanding the precedent of the prior D.C. Circuit decision protecting them. This left "survivor privacy" very much in doubt as a legal precedent, with three circuit courts of appeals split on it.[35]

So then the question presented to those of us at the Department of Justice who cared about the "survivor privacy" principle, as well as to others, was whether the Government should take the *Favish* loss up to the Supreme Court. A decision on this -- the filing of what is called a *certiorari* petition -- is made by the Solicitor General of the United States ("the SG," to those who work with him or her) under strict procedural standards, including first and foremost whether there is "a conflict in the circuits."[36] There was no question but that the case qualified for Supreme Court review by those standards; no better circuit conflict could exist than one in which two circuit courts issued diametrically opposite rulings on whether the very same records had to be disclosed.

But obtaining Solicitor General authorization for the filing of a *certiorari* petition in this case was not the "slam dunk" that we had expected it to be.[37] The first step on this path, traditionally, was the filing of a petition for rehearing "with suggestion for rehearing *en banc*," in this case with the Ninth Circuit, even though there was absolutely no reason to think that it would be granted.[38] But without disclosing too much detail about Solicitor General's Office ("OSG," to those who practice appellate law) decisionmaking, I can say that the filing of an *en banc* petition nearly was not authorized, owing to concerns about the fact that Vince Foster had killed himself in such a "public place."[39]

Indeed, it took some heavy "lobbying" by several interested parties within the confines of the Solicitor General's Office and elsewhere to preserve the possibility of "going for *cert.*" in the Supreme Court through the filing of that predicate Ninth Circuit rehearing petition. But that rehearing petition was eventually authorized and filed and it was promptly denied, just as had been expected.[40] So the ability to file a petition for *certiorari* in the *Favish* case was preserved and the next step was getting the Solicitor General to authorize that.

From the perspective of the Federal Government's side of a case, there are three critical steps to gaining reversal of an adverse appellate court ruling. The first is the Solicitor General authorizing the filing of a *certiorari* petition asking the Supreme Court to review that adverse decision. The second is getting a "grant" of that petition, based upon what is referred to as the "certworthiness" of the case. And the third, of course, is obtaining a favorable decision from the Court after the Government's position in the case is fully briefed and then presented at an oral argument.

It is said in the halls of the Main Justice Building that the most difficult step of these three is not the last one or even the second. Rather, it is getting the Solicitor General, who has to keep the "big picture" of federal litigation in mind, to agree that it is best in the scheme of things to "take that issue up" and to do so at that particular time. And then there also is the matter of the Solicitor General's "capital," so to speak, as what is called the "Tenth Justice," in the currency of his or her credibility with the Court.

In other words, when the Solicitor General represents to the Supreme Court of the United States that accepting a case for review is truly warranted, that is something that resonates with the Court unlike the representations of any other party. Therefore, within the culture and tradition of the Office of the Solicitor General, together with that of the Supreme Court itself, it carries a weight that should never be wielded lightly.[41]

So having obtained the Solicitor General's authorization for seeking Ninth Circuit rehearing turned out to be quite another thing from getting his authorization to "go for *cert*."[42] That same "suicide location" factor still plagued the case, and we also were up against the standard SG's Office long-term viewpoint of "let's wait for a better case."[43] But then another large factor soon entered the landscape of the case, in the form of the Foster family, which primarily consisted of Vince's widow Elizabeth (also known as "Lisa"), his three children, his mother, and his sister Sheila.

Led by Vince's widow Lisa and his sister Sheila Foster Anthony,[44] the Foster family took the exceptional step of intervening in the *Favish* case for the purposes of advocating their personal-privacy interests on appeal. They even filed their own *certiorari* petition in the Supreme Court at an early juncture. This led to a meeting in the Solicitor General's Office at which the Foster family's counsel was given the opportunity to make a case for *certiorari* on the family's behalf, in a most collegial manner. Usually, this is a courtesy afforded by the Solicitor General to the federal agency client involved, but we kept making the point that this was hardly the usual case, and this meeting certainly helped advance the *certiorari* cause.

Ultimately, this cause prevailed when Solicitor General Ted Olsen finally authorized a *certiorari* petition's filing.[45] And with that, Assistant to the Solicitor General Pattie Millett began writing that *certiorari* petition, knowing that the stakes were high not only for the Foster family but for the "survivor privacy" principle as well.[46] Simply put, Pattie is the best brief writer I have ever seen, with a style and analytical cogency beyond compare. Today, as a member of the D.C. Circuit, she employs that skill to "*cert*.-proof" her panel decisions in a way that only a few appellate practitioners truly understand.[47]

Yet Pattie also is by nature as collegial as they come,[48] willing to be receptive to ideas and potential edits that are suggested by her colleagues. She knew that I had given birth to the idea of "survivor privacy" on my ammonia-stained desk blotter 25 years earlier and she allowed me to heavily participate in her drafting of the *cert*. petition and the reply brief in support of *certiorari*, not that they needed much help at all.

Next came the good news that *cert*. was granted. Most of us were not really surprised by that, given the strength of the petition, but it was a relief to know that the Department of Justice would have the opportunity to argue against the Ninth Circuit's cavalier reasoning and overturn its aberrant disclosure order. As well, we would be able to vindicate the Foster family's legitimate personal-privacy interests and bring them some peace of mind (as opposed to its opposite), which is what the "survivor privacy" concept is all about.

However, there were three more vital steps remaining in order to achieve that. The first was what is called the "opening brief," in which the *certiorari* petition's discussion of the case's merits would be greatly expanded. Then, as the petitioner, we would be filing a "reply brief" that would explain to the Court why Favish's respondent's brief (and the points made in amici briefs) lacked merit. And ultimately, the case would be set down for oral argument, which sometimes is the key to a Supreme Court case's success.

Pattie's merits briefs in the case were strong and powerful. They surveyed the history and development of the "survivor privacy" principle in FOIA case law over the previous 25 years, from the Martin Luther King case at its birth to its subsequent application to autopsy reports, medical records, and even the post-mortem x-rays of JFK's body.[49] And they placed emphasis on the traditional rights of family members to have "control" of a loved one's body (and by extension any images of it) so that they could grieve a death in the way in which they chose, according to the contours of their own culture, customs, and family traditions.

But Pattie wanted more, "some hook," she would say, that would grab the Justices by the heart and make it viscerally impossible for them to rule otherwise. I took that request very seriously, knowing that Pattie's instinct for such things is superb and wanting to continue to provide as much support as possible in this cause that we had been pursuing with great zeal. So I tasked the sharpest law clerk in OIP to search for something that could work like that, predicting that if such a thing existed, it would most likely be in state case law, not necessarily cases decided at the federal level.

And sure enough, we came up with a state court case in which the facts were perfect for Pattie's use. It involved a young woman's rapist and murderer, who as an inmate sought a copy of her death-scene photographs, i.e., depicting how he had left her body, from different angles. And bless his dark heart, he actually admitted that he was seeking those photographs so that he could tape them to the wall above his prison bed. As I said to Pattie, can you imagine hearing of such a thing if you were a parent of that young woman?

Well, Pattie made much of that vivid image, both in what she wrote and then in what she said as she presented oral argument in the case. Sitting behind her in the Supreme Court courtroom,[50] I could feel the power of her arguments and her passion for the interests of Vince Foster's family. And this seemed to have quite an impact on the Justices as well, as they asked questions that showed sympathy to our side of the case. Suffice to say that when the argument was over, everyone, even "über cautious" Pattie, felt that she had carried the day.

Less than four months later (which is relatively quick for the Supreme Court), this certainly turned out to be the case -- a landmark case, in fact. On March 30, 2004, the Court handed down a unanimous decision in favor of the Government (and the Foster family) that explicitly and at great length adopted the principle of "survivor privacy" once and for all. Writing for the Court, Justice Anthony M. Kennedy immediately turned to the paramount issue in the case,[51] holding that "[the] FOIA recognizes surviving family members' right[s] to personal privacy with respect to their close relative's death-scene images."[52] And in so holding, he declared that Exemption 7(C) is broad enough to protect surviving families' "own privacy rights against public intrusions long deemed impermissible under the common law and in our cultural traditions."[53]

Justice Kennedy's opinion prominently cited the seminal "survivor privacy" case involving the family of Martin Luther King, as well as the subsequent ones involving the tragic deaths of the astronauts on the Space Shuttle *Challenger* and the assassination of President Kennedy.[54] At bottom, he emphasized that the "survivor privacy" concept rests on the propriety of protecting survivors, in cases of extraordinary sensitivity, from "disruption [to] their peace of mind" or, he elaborated, to their "own peace of mind and tranquility."[55]

The Court next dealt with Favish's arguments that no privacy interest should be found to exist in this case because Vince was a high-level public official or because some photographs roughly similar to the ones at issue (but less graphic) had entered the public domain. Justice Kennedy gave relative short shrift to these arguments and handily dispatched both of them in no uncertain terms with a flat declaration: "Neither the deceased's former status as a public official, nor the fact that other pictures had been made public, detracts from the weighty privacy interests involved."

Likewise, the Court's decision shows that the occurrence of an event in a public place is not much of a disqualifying factor for privacy protection under the FOIA, and no more so in an exceptional "survivor privacy" case. One atypical aspect of the *Favish* case is that Vince's suicide occurred on national parkland, which is how the United States Park Police came to take and possess the death-scene photographs that were being contested. The facts that his suicide occurred "in public," that the photographs were of course taken in that public place, and that perhaps anyone else could have done likewise had Vince's body been discovered there under different circumstances, all gave rise to the question of whether the photographs were as entitled to protection as they would have been had they been taken at the site of a suicide in a private, or at least less public, place.

And as was observed above, this was enough of a question that it for some time stood as a hurdle to the pursuit of further appeal in the Office of the Solicitor General.[56] The way in which Pattie and I had viewed this element of the case is that it was a good illustration of the wise adage, "don't let the perfect be the enemy of the good." It therefore was quite significant that those particular facts, too, did not detract from the Court's valuation of those "weighty privacy interests." The fact that Vince in his anguish had chosen to take his life in a public park (rather than in the privacy of his home, or even his own backyard), where anyone walking nearby easily could have seen what the photographs depicted, ultimately did not slow the Supreme Court down one bit.

On the other side of the ledger, the Court was unmistakably influenced by the prospect of inmates jailed for murder plus rape or child molestation being able to obtain raw photographs of their victims for "gruesome" display on the walls of their prison cells -- a real-world possibility that was pointedly emphasized by the Government at the Supreme Court level. Fully appreciating Pattie's potent argument along those lines,[57] Justice Kennedy said: "We are advised by the Government that child molesters, rapists, murderers, and other violent criminals often make FOIA requests for autopsies, photographs, and records of their deceased victims. Our holding ensures that the privacy interests of surviving family members would allow the Government to deny these gruesome requests in appropriate cases."[58]

Justice Kennedy then deepened his analysis of the issue with a few more words about the "exploitation" potential in the case, including by the media.[59] He spoke first in general of the "unwarranted public exploitation" of FOIA-disclosed records. And as to "survivor privacy" cases like the one before the Court, he expressed great concern about "attempts to exploit pictures of the deceased family member's remains for public[ation] purposes." Writing for the unanimous Court, Justice Kennedy then concluded by characterizing the vital interests of the Foster family members as their being "secure [in] their own refuge from [what recently has become] a sensation-seeking culture[,] for their own peace of mind and tranquility."

In sum, the "survivor privacy" principle for personal-privacy protection was born of necessity with the family of Martin Luther King, as I struggled for perfection on my ammonia-stained blotter. Then, I was very fortunate to be so heavily involved with it more than twenty-five years later in *Favish*, when it finally was presented to and adopted by the United States Supreme Court.[60] And now "survivor privacy" is an entirely solid part of the FOIA landscape, as it stands firmly available for use in appropriate (albeit by definition exceptional) cases.

CHAPTER FOUR

From Scrub Pines
to Washington Times

"I'm just thinking, here I am a slave who touched a star who then made him a demigod. I have to be the luckiest bastard who ever lived."

-- Sherrilyn Woodward (a.k.a. Sherrilyn McQueen and Kinley MacGregor, formerly Sherrilyn Kenyon), *Dance With the Devil*, 2003

No small amount of luck was involved; that should be acknowledged at the outset. Indeed, it was never expected that someone of my background and location would even aspire to work on a national-level stage, let alone actually reach one so quickly and completely. Yet within the span of a relatively few short years, with one thing leading to another, I traveled from small-town pines to big-city times at the United States Department of Justice in Washington, D.C. Then, for more than a quarter-century, from one presidential administration to the next,[1] I was in a position to create, develop, and implement government information policy -- "disclosure policy," as we called it under Attorney General Janet Reno, but "secrecy" during most other times -- for the entire executive branch of the Government of the United States.

I grew up in the middle of Long Island, New York, among a generation of families that strove to escape what for them was the harshness of life on New York City's streets. To our young post-World War II parents, there was nothing more important than reaching up to grab the lowest rung of the middle class by "getting out of the City" to a house somewhere on Long Island, where the kids could have grass instead of pavement as their backyards.

Yes, to us New York City was "the City," a densely populated place to pull yourself out of if you possibly could, and we were on "the Island," with thousands of lucky others who managed to get away with the minimal upward mobility that home ownership afforded. It was a concrete-to-tree-lined-street version of the "American dream."

Not everyone made it, of course. Nearly all of us had friends and relatives still "stuck in the City," families whose parents were continuing to save up with hopes of making such a move. They came like foreign visitors from the old neighborhoods of Brooklyn and Queens, speaking of their long trips "out to the Island" but looking longingly at the stretches of woods and lawns that they saw when they arrived. We hosted some of their children for weeks at a time, in our own version of New York City's "fresh air fund," sharing life "out in the country" with cousins whose summers would otherwise be nonstop heat and grime.

But even a family that managed to "make it" by living "out on the Island" did not necessarily get to stay there. For many families, like my own, that jump was one made on the very thinnest of margins -- an economic risk that was desperately sought but not always well taken.

By its very nature, the growth of home ownership after World War II, fueled by the GI Bill, involved the stretching of family finances in every way possible toward that goal, with modest success achieved much, but not all, of the time. When my family moved to a house on Long Island in 1960, in fact, it was at the expense of the previous owner, a father of four who had defaulted on his "GI loan" and then had to tell his kids that they were being evicted from their home.

So it was that my brothers and sister and I were raised on Long Island during the 1960s. The place where we lived, Brentwood, actually was neither a village nor a town. Rather, it was simply defined by its school district, which grew rapidly with the construction of one new housing development after another, as the scrub-pine woods of that part of Suffolk County were torn down as quickly as buyers could be found for the thousands of small houses that replaced them.

In fact, on that part of Long Island, about 35 miles east of the New York City line, the population growth that occurred during the late 1950s and the 1960s was so explosive that Brentwood suddenly became the sixth-largest school district in all of New York State, behind only cities such as Albany, Buffalo, Syracuse, and of course New York City itself.

As the eldest of five children in a family there, I knew early on that my parents had just barely afforded our modest house, and that my father's income, gained at the expense of a seventy-mile round trip to JFK (née Idlewild) Airport every day, was just enough to keep us safely in Brentwood rather than back in Queens. By the time the fourth child began to come along, my family's situation was such that this strained its finances to the near-breaking point. So my father began working a second job as a cabdriver, my mother took on day-care work during her pregnancy, and I began to do the best that I could to help out -- through an after-school paper route at the age of 12.

This was the genesis of the work ethic that I wound up taking with me to

Washington seven years later. Before getting there, though, I made it my business to gain as much personal experience as was possible in the place in which I lived. With dual motivation, I kept that paper route until age sixteen, becoming the top newspaper carrier on my part of Long Island and making modest but vital contributions to the family's finances. And although at the time there was not much else around that a young teenager could do, I took full advantage of two developmental activities that were locally available -- organizing a series of youth bowling leagues over several seasons and then precociously managing a Little League team for five years in support of my two younger brothers.[2] In fact, it was not long after becoming the youngest New York State Little League manager ever at age 15 that I started hearing the other managers and coaches say, "That damn kid's gonna be a lawyer someday!" -- which was as much a complaint as it was a prediction (read: not at all a compliment), I knew, perhaps because I always had a copy of the rulebook handy to wield against them.

The point is that these things gave me exceptional experience, both in being organized and in being responsible, given where I lived. But when it came time to get that first real job at age sixteen -- the legal minimum for holding "working papers," as they were then called -- Brentwood had relatively little to offer. To be sure, it was not quite as bad as living in a coal-mining town in which you either followed your father and grandfather down into the mines or else you left town altogether, but it was not far from it.

On that part of Long Island, midway between its north and south shores, there were only two local "industries," such as they were, at the time. The first consisted of mental institutions, of which Brentwood and adjacent Central Islip had far more than their share. The second was that Brentwood was the central location of the Sisters of St. Joseph, a centuries-old teaching order of Catholic nuns that had established its headquarters there long before the housing developers arrived. With an enormous European-style "mother house," several ancillary convents, a long-term academy, and a brand-new old-age home for retired nuns, its huge complex stood as an employment location of choice for local men and boys. So at age sixteen I "entered the convent," so to speak, not to leave it until I was midway through college more than three years later.[3]

The subject of college, I should explain, was another borderline matter -- and it loomed large for me. With four younger siblings coming up behind me for many years (amounting to an 18½-year span from me to my youngest brother), I knew all along that there would be absolutely no family money available for my college years. In fact, no Metcalfe in our entire extended family had ever obtained a college degree, and it was clear to one and all that if I were to become the first to do so I would have to do it almost entirely on my own.[4] However, this turned out to be a good thing, I believe, because it greatly deepened the independence and resourcefulness that would serve me so very well later on.

So I inevitably fell into the only good option that was available to me, both academically and financially: I became a low-cost "commuter" student at the State University of New York at Stony Brook, a relatively new university that had opened up only fifteen miles from Brentwood. This was a very lucky thing. First, it was lucky in the sense that it was not so many years earlier that there had been no such state university campus on Long Island at all, let alone one within viable commuting distance from where I lived.

Furthermore, even in its relatively few years of existence by then, SUNY at Stony Brook had quickly become recognized as the premier school of New York State's university system. Most significantly for me, moreover, Stony Brook had a solid political science department, with faculty members who were beginning to strongly embrace what was called "the internship concept" as a means of fostering government service.

Indeed, Stony Brook was recognized as just about the best college that a graduate of Brentwood High School could hope to attend back in the 1960s, academically speaking. Of my high school graduating class of nearly a thousand, no more than a small percentage went on to college anywhere, at least not directly out of high school, and I can recall no one gaining admission to a school with a better academic standing. And of those who did get to go to college, a relatively large group of us either lived at or commuted to what we nicknamed "the Brook."

As one of that group of thirteen Brentwood High graduates, I felt lucky to be there, even with the pervasive construction sites, the extremely large class sizes, and the university's well-earned reputation for "tough grading." That latter aspect took its toll, all right: After the first year, none of the other twelve managed to make the dean's list, which required a 3.0 average, while I posted just a 3.3.[5] Even our high school class valedictorian, who had earned a singular reputation for studying nonstop, soon fell by the wayside within Stony Brook's heavy "counterculture" environment.

In sum, I felt by the end of my second year of college that I already had beaten the odds in many ways. I had taken full advantage of what was available to me where I grew up (having been fortunate even to be there in the first place), I had managed to attend the best college that I could possibly have hoped to attend (by working nearly full-time at the convent while going to school), and I had raised my cumulative grade point average to more than 3.6 in anticipation of applying to highly competitive law schools.[6] All in all, I had had the good fortune to piece together a good combination of circumstances for someone whose starting point was what mine had been. Yet I was about to get even luckier, very much so, in a "right place, right time" sort of way.

Fortunately for me, New York's state university system had for several years maintained a special academic program that took college seniors to Washington, D.C., for a semester, and during my sophomore year I learned that Stony Brook was about to participate in this program for the first time the following fall. It was called the "Washington Semester Program," operating out of SUNY Brockport, and Stony Brook was to be allotted just three slots in it for the Fall 1971 semester, slots that were intended to go to three rising seniors, with no guarantee of the school's participation beyond that.

That is when I learned a bit about the power of oral advocacy and ardent persuasion, as I had the nerve to press the political science faculty to let me represent the school as one of those three students even though I would be only a junior during that coming year. Through some combination of brazen persistence, academic credentials, and no doubt at least a little bit of luck, this long shot succeeded: I was selected for that program together with two seniors, and I soon found myself saving up for what I knew would have to be a very frugal semester in Washington, D.C., during the fall of my junior year. What I did not know, at least not more than aspirationally, was that that single step would set the stage for my entire professional life.

Washington, D.C., was "where the action was" as far as I was concerned. I was very interested in law and government, but living on Long Island had made me more than a little cynical about the type of politics that infused local government there. And state-level government was far removed from us, located as it was beyond the City and then further "up north" in Albany. But Washington attracted me as a place where problems were solved, on a national or even global scale, and where young people heeded President John F. Kennedy's still-recent call to service akin to the way in which the generation before us went off to fight World War II. Or so it seemed to me, at age nineteen, when I ventured off to it.

CHAPTER FIVE
Internship Days

"I got an internship at a nudist camp. I'm doing it for the exposure."

-- Old internship joke, circa 1970s

The Washington Semester Program had existed for several semesters by the time I joined it in 1971, with a standard number of 40 students who lived in an old hotel at the base of Capitol Hill where, it was said, Lyndon Johnson had gotten his start by winning a congressional aide association election almost four decades earlier.[1] Its basic structure was that all 40 students attended evening classes and related events,[2] but a third of them could compete to work in full-time internships during the semester, which were arranged through the program's staff with either House or Senate offices. I succeeded in becoming one of the 13 interns, whom I was sure would gain the best experience in the program, and soon the other 12 sought and obtained internships on what we all then knowingly called "the Hill."[3]

I readily made myself the odd man out, however, because I had it in my head that the place for me was the United States Department of Justice, a place where it seemed lawyers did great things such as fight organized crime and stand up to Southern racism. The problem with this, though, was that the Department of Justice actually had no such personnel category as "academic intern" in those days.[4] By all rights, that ought to have been a showstopper.

But my being ignorant of this actually proved to be a lucky break for me, because undeterred by that barrier I slipped right into the "Main Justice Building" on Pennsylvania Avenue (which you actually could surreptitiously do in those days), wandered the halls, and zeroed in on a part of the Justice Department that I had learned was working on an especially big law enforcement project at that time. Before anyone really knew any better, I had managed to talk my way into an "intern slot" there (not that such a thing really existed, mind you), in the National Institute of Law Enforcement and Criminal Justice, which was the research arm of the Law Enforcement Assistance Administration ("LEAA," for short), a major Justice Department component located on Indiana Avenue just three blocks away.

This sounds highly implausible by current governmental standards, I know. But Washington, D.C., was still a much sleepier Southern town back then. The occasional anti-war demonstration or civil rights march aside, tight security was still a thing of the future. Prospective interns and adventurous tourists alike could take their own tours of the Capitol Building, for example, walking through it unchallenged from top to bottom.[5] Other federal office buildings had security that sometimes was no more than nominal. Only the White House itself was beyond reach,[6] and even there President Richard M. Nixon had just begun to barricade himself from what soon would be known collectively as "Watergate." Little did I know that that massive scandal would propel me, in my own small way, forward in government.

All I knew then, though, was that I wanted more than anything to have an internship at the United States Department of Justice, which I idealistically thought was responsible more than any other government agency for what was good, and ought to be made better, in America. Yes, Attorney General-then-Senator Robert F. Kennedy had picked up where his brother had left off in my mind, and his assassination just three years earlier had only deepened the idealism with which I was proceeding. So when I found myself standing before a surprised personnel officer at LEAA, I quickly argued that academic interns were just the thing that the Department of Justice needed, that I should get right down to work, and that we should let "Main Justice" figure out the "bureaucratic niceties" of the arrangement later on.

This relatively junior Justice Department official for some reason took a chance on me -- and when years later he himself rose to become the Department's director of personnel, I was able to kid him that his successful Justice career was launched at the same time as my own. But back then, all we knew was that I could just walk down the hall, introduce myself as someone willing to work forty or more hours a week on whatever was needed, and proceed to "intern" as hard and as well as I was able. And the fact that it was no more complicated than that, at least at first, did not amaze me nearly as much as it should have, given that this was a major part of the executive branch of the Federal Government that I had wandered into. Thus it was that I went directly from a convent kitchen to the United States Department of Justice while still a teenager.

One more entry in the "right place at the right time" scorebook: It just so happened that the reason why that amenable personnel officer was at LEAA in the first place, as a temporary "detailee," was that that part of the Justice Department was at the time undergoing a massive build-up as part of President Nixon's war on "street crime." Indeed, it was said in LEAA's hallways, apocryphal or not, that under recent legislation its budget was now growing at a rate greater than that of any governmental entity since the Napoleonic Empire. And the National Institute of Law Enforcement and Criminal Justice, in particular, just so happened to be beginning work on what was to be called the "1972/1973 LEAA Impact Plan," a comprehensive plan for spending hundreds of millions of dollars across the full gamut of law enforcement-related programs under Congress's 1968 Safe Streets Act. And this was due to be completed within about three months, i.e., during the exact time period that my internship would encompass.

So I found myself joining a staff that was scrambling mightily to rapidly develop and assemble what essentially was to be a "recipe book" for how the Federal Government, all fifty states, and the District of Columbia would spend their new law enforcement and crime-deterrence dollars most wisely and modernly during the coming years. It was a perfect environment for me. I was given a small office, some initial assignments from attorneys and Ph.D. subject-matter experts who perhaps did not yet know that I was only a college junior, and it was "sink or swim" from day one. I swam.

In fact, one of my clearest recollections of that hectic time was when I suddenly realized, about two weeks into this ersatz internship, that in my own way I actually could "keep up with" these seasoned government professionals as I labored to learn their subject areas and help them craft their high-profile plan. And almost as significantly, they seemed to think so, too.[7]

This is where I have to admit that I had a big advantage over some of them: I could write, both well and fast, which fit perfectly with the tasks at hand. And I could edit, too, because for some reason proofreading and scanning text has always come exceptionally easily to me.[8] (Almost as naturally as splitting infinitives or writing sentence fragments does.) And thirdly, sometimes as importantly, I was not at all shy about picking up the phone to call whoever needed to be contacted around the country about the latest technology for fingerprint recognition or the most effective means of crime deterrence, for example. Soon I was relied upon by this staff to do things that I later learned were far beyond what interns (or the like) ordinarily get to do -- but that was entirely fine with me. I enjoyed being regarded as nearly "indispensable."

What this all added up to was an extremely rare (and probably *ultra vires*) opportunity for someone of my background to learn firsthand about high-level government functioning and be able to make a significant contribution in the bargain. Partway through my tenure there, the senior personnel folks over at

Main Justice finally caught up to my presence and for a few nervous days I was told that the Justice Department was going to have to either pay me, as a salaried temporary employee, or send me packing. I made my preference between these two options loudly known, as might be imagined, but was constrained by the fact that a firm element of my internship program was that we interns, like so many of our numbers on Capitol Hill in those days, were mere "volunteers."

Fortunately, the people for whom I had worked so hard and well by that point went to the mat for me, and somehow -- I never learned exactly how -- I just managed to stay on.[9] In retrospect, of course, I realize that this almost certainly would not have been possible had I attempted such a thing anywhere within the Justice Department's headquarters building, or with any Department component that was not expanding so quickly that it could barely keep track of all of its new personnel.

So that is how it was that I spent my twentieth birthday on a Saturday,[10] helping to meet LEAA's deadline for completion of an unprecedented nationwide crime-fighting plan. It covered a wide range of law enforcement-related matters, from the newest "hardware" that was so popular with local sheriffs to new correctional theories (born of the then-recent Attica prison uprising) to even such "soft" areas as decriminalization and pre-trial diversion.

Amazingly, I actually wound up authoring about ten percent of the 400-page final document, having developed my own particular areas of expertise, and also contributing by carefully proofreading (plus what I came to call "scrubbing") the entire plan. To someone who just a few months earlier had "retired" from three and a half years of working in a convent kitchen and five years of managing Little League baseball, this sure seemed like big-time success to me.

Indeed, it was more than enough to make me hooked on government service in general and on working for the Department of Justice in particular, which is exactly what internships are supposed to do. Simply put, I could not wait to get back to Washington once the internship ended, and I would have considered transferring to a college there had I the means to do so. But I found that as things sometimes do in Washington, as one thing tends to lead to another, my internship led to my next Justice Department position two years later, this time as a paid law clerk in what was then part of the Office of the Attorney General.

CHAPTER SIX
Back on Long Island

"Life is what happens to you while you're busy making other plans."

-- John Lennon, in the song "Beautiful Boy" on the *Double Fantasy* album (1980)

Before being able to return to Washington, though, I had to do several things: I had to go back to Long Island and write two very lengthy papers about my internship experience in order to receive full academic credit for that semester; I had to finish my last three semesters of college in order to graduate;[1] I had to gain admission to a law school in Washington; and I had to somehow earn enough money so that I could afford to go away to law school at all. Oh, and not get drafted, as I had drawn what seemed like a very-less-than-lucky number -- number 98 -- in the national draft lottery for the Vietnam War.[2] Again, the odds were not in my favor.

But now I had some extraordinary practical experience under my belt, not to mention some truly professional writing experience, so such things no longer seemed quite so daunting. Once back on Long Island, I quickly concluded that I should build on this experience by continuing to work full-time, in a professional legal setting if at all possible, so that I could start saving the "big bucks" that law school would require (just in case I didn't get drafted and have to enlist upon college graduation).

I luckily found such a job, with a law firm in the county seat of neighboring Nassau County, simply by sending my shiny new resume out to literally every law firm within a twenty-five-mile radius (which meant to the west, toward the City, because there wasn't much to the north, south, or east), and I was able to negotiate full-time work hours that permitted me to take all of my classes at Stony Brook in the very late afternoon or at night. That job held me for the next twenty months,[3] right up until the time that I returned to Washington, and it allowed me both to finish college with a flexible schedule and to save several thousands of dollars even while contributing room and board at home.

Those savings still were not enough to fund three years of law school, however. Luckily, though, I was awarded a huge academic scholarship at the Washington-area law school of my choice, the National Law Center at The George Washington University, and I actually managed to negotiate a special student loan deal there, as part of my Trustee Scholar package, that enabled me to obtain a full student loan to begin with and then to earn interest on my declining savings balance as the law school years passed.[4] It was a fabulous deal, for which I was very thankful that the pre-law advisor at Stony Brook had stressed the importance of a high grade-point average, which in my case had led to several straight 4.0 semesters.[5]

Yet this all was very nearly for naught, as the Nixon Administration announced that the draft for the Vietnam War would not end until the *end* of June 1973, the very month in which college seniors graduating that year like myself would lose their college deferments. My mother, for one, was fearfully convinced that Nixon would not cut the draft off until the round number 100 was reached, in which case I would have had to at least defer law school, probably lose my scholarship, and either be drafted for two years or (as I had made alternative arrangements to do) enlist for three.[6]

But again, I lucked out, big time: The draft, which did indeed last throughout the month of June before the authority for it expired, did not continue up to number 100 as feared. Rather, it magically ended at number ninety-five, three digits to the good for me rather than two to the bad.[7] And with that, everything that I had worked for suddenly fell into place.

That's when I got lucky with another piece of the picture in Washington. Back at the Justice Department, much had happened since I had left it at the end of 1971. The discovery of Richard Nixon's "Watergate plumbers" had spawned a host of related scandals that threatened to topple his presidency, so much so that he was forced to name Elliot L. Richardson, a man of unquestionable integrity,[8] as his next attorney general, in place of two disgraced predecessors,[9] in the spring of 1973.

Then Attorney General Richardson, as luck would have it, named the LEAA office director for whom I had worked, Martin B. Danziger, to head a newly created Office of Criminal Justice (later to be called the Office of Legal Policy) within the larger Office of the Attorney General. And when Marty and his assistants (with whom I had kept in touch)[10] learned that I was coming back to Washington to attend law school there in August of 1973, well, it was in so many ways a perfect match.

CHAPTER SEVEN

Back to Washington

"Before my term has ended, we shall have to test anew whether a nation organized and governed such as ours can endure. The outcome is by no means certain."

-- President John Fitzgerald Kennedy (1917-1963), annual message to Congress on the State of the Union, January 30, 1961

Once I began law school, I still had need for earnings during the academic year, and it sure was nice being back at the Justice Department and getting paid a law clerk's salary there, this time working fully "on the books." Most significantly, of course, it also afforded me the chance to work at the highest levels of the Department, even if as a lowly first-year law student. Indeed, my rare internship in 1971 quickly turned into a rarer-still career opportunity in 1973, given what Attorney General Elliott Richardson, Marty Danziger, and others were aiming to do. So I threw myself headlong into Justice Department work again, despite the fact that I was supposed to be spending almost all of my time learning to be a lawyer.[1]

Yes, it was very rewarding. A highlight came when I got to work on a Justice Department reorganization plan (a nonrecord copy of which I still have)[2] that would have created a new number three position at the Department, that of associate attorney general, which was badly needed (see the Epilogue).[3] Ironically, that plan was due to be finalized with Attorney General Richardson in a meeting scheduled for the week of October 15th, 1973, but I kept hearing during that week that this was being delayed due a rare "back-up" of matters competing for Attorney General Richardson's attention in the wake of his nonstop personal work on the plea agreement for Vice President Spiro T. Agnew a week earlier,[4] plus the plea agreement of former White House Counsel John W. Dean III, and his attention to increasingly delicate negotiations between White House lawyers and Special Prosecutor Archibald Cox, Jr. Evidently, he was in almost constant contact with the White House (mostly through White House Chief of Staff Alexander M. Haig, Jr., and White House Special Counsel J. Fred Buzhardt, Jr.) during that entire time.

These things did not bring an end to that week, however, and indeed it would turn out to be several years before the position of associate attorney general ultimately was established during the Carter Administration in 1977.[5] This was due to what immediately came to be called the "Saturday Night Massacre," the infamous event in which Nixon effectively "fired" both Attorney General Richardson and Deputy Attorney General William D. Ruckelshaus in a desperate attempt to forestall his own demise at the hands of Watergate Special Prosecutor Archibald Cox, Jr. -- an event that shook the country then and reverberates still to this day.

Indeed, on the evening of Saturday, October 20, 1973, White House correspondents dramatically reported from the edge of the White House's North Lawn that Nixon had just taken steps so radical that a "constitutional crisis" seemed to be at hand.[6] With these actions, the Justice Department fell into the hands of its then-third-ranking official, Solicitor General Robert H. Bork, who as acting attorney general immediately did what Richardson and Ruckelshaus had refused to do -- fire Special Prosecutor Cox in order to prevent him from further pressing for disclosure of Oval Office tape recordings (the ones that ultimately led to Nixon's resignation) as part of Cox's "Watergate" investigations.

Because of my Justice Department position, I certainly had a greater-than-average interest in all of this. First, I heard CBS News White House correspondent Dan Rather breathlessly announce on TV that at the Justice Department the Offices of the Attorney General and Deputy Attorney General were now "sealed," along with all Special Prosecutor's offices. That meant that, at age twenty-one, I was to be the junior-most member of the Department's professional staff locked out of his office due to "Watergate" in the following days. Not quite what I had expected when making the jump to that level just weeks earlier.

Also, inasmuch as I lived just two blocks from the White House at the time, half-way between it and GW Law School, I found myself immediately drawn to the White House gate at the northwestern edge of the North Lawn, arriving just a few minutes after the dramatic announcement. When I arrived there, the media area alongside the north end of West Executive Drive was still lit up with very heavy activity, but the public sidewalk on the other side of the perimeter fence was entirely bare, which was strikingly incongruous. Indeed, the whole situation seemed utterly surreal. I remember meeting some tourists from Oregon who just happened to be walking by and explaining to them what a momentous thing it was that had just happened. They asked me questions as if I were some veteran expert on how the government worked, or might not work if it now fell apart.

Before I knew it, a small crowd started gathering around us, with more and more questions being raised, and then it became the nucleus of what turned into a spontaneous street demonstration of hundreds of people, complete with dancers in Nixon masks and television coverage of its own. I said to myself that I certainly had wanted to leave Long Island for the center of American government, but this was not exactly what I had had in mind.

During the following week, after a felicitous Monday holiday,[7] morale at the Justice Department was at an all-time low, to say the least. The Department had become highly politicized during the past couple of years, even to the point of harboring criminal conduct, but Elliot Richardson had been widely viewed as its savior. Throughout the Department, I knew, there had been strong hope that his tenure as attorney general would erase the stain of his immediate predecessors, no matter what happened at the White House level above.

However, within the Attorney General's and Deputy Attorney General's Offices in particular, it now was as if we had suffered a double death in the family, a smaller-scale version of the John F. Kennedy Assassination, with the two people we all were counting on to repair the Department's reputation now gone. And rightly or wrongly, there was much anger at Acting Attorney General Bork for doing Nixon's dirty work after others had refused Nixon as a matter of principle.[8] I remember being part of a small group of junior staff members (all of them senior to me) who had the somber task of sorting through the many bags of angry mail that soon arrived on the massive table in the attorney general's conference room.[9] It was a dismal time.

Meanwhile, though, I had my own priorities to focus on. Even with all the resources that I had mustered in the form of savings, scholarship, and loans, money was still very tight for me, as well as for my family. I had managed to buy a good, safe car for all the commuting between home, law firm, and Stony Brook during my last two college years -- a brand-new $2000 Ford Maverick, the sturdy "Volkswagen Beetle" of its time -- but this was needed for my next two brothers coming up behind me, so it became a family donation. With this asset lost to Brentwood, it was all the more important that I take full advantage of my Justice Department employment as much as I could. So I worked as many days and hours as was physically possible during the "post-massacre" months, even though I was supposed to be learning first-year law.

Another lucky break for me: GW Law School back then had an atypical academic schedule in which its first-year students took their first-semester exams after Christmas, not before as elsewhere. This enabled me to work nearly full-time through the month of December, "banking" hours in such a way that they piled up toward exam time. I even benefited from the "extra" two full days that federal employees enjoyed that year when Nixon -- in a spasm of guilt, no doubt -- declared both Monday, December 24 and Monday, December 31 to be federal holidays.

I wasn't quite as thankful to him as my mother had been for his ending the draft at number 95 six months earlier, but it was a big help. And when with the aid of a top-notch study group[10] my last-minute cramming yielded second-in-the-class grades, the picture was complete. In fact, the same approach yielded the exact same academic result for the spring semester, as well, which positioned me for all sorts of good things to come (though I dropped to third in the class after the third semester).

Throughout the Justice Department, though, it was clear that things would never be the same in the wake of Attorney General Richardson's resignation. People began leaving left and right (mostly left), as if some idealistic crusade had come to an end, and it seemed like the entire government was numbly waiting for the next big shoe to drop. Congressman Gerald R. Ford, Jr., was named by Nixon to replace Agnew as vice president, then approved by both Houses of Congress as the Constitution required, and we needed a new attorney general as well.

When that turned out to be Senator William B. Saxbe -- a Republican from Ohio most famous for remarking that Nixon's 1973 "Watergate" stance was much akin to that of the bordello piano player who claimed that he "didn't know what was going on in the rooms upstairs"[11] -- you could hear a collective groan on the Fourth and Fifth Floors of Main Justice. Yet as a "member of the club" (i.e., a senator), Senator Saxbe no doubt appealed to Nixon as being easily confirmable even in that volatile political environment. But as a very conservative attorney general replacement, however, he struck the people in my office as a far cry from Elliot Richardson.[12]

Indeed, after Saxbe was confirmed as attorney general in early 1974,[13] so many people left the Attorney General's Office and Deputy Attorney General's Office so quickly that I suddenly found myself "trading up" offices along the 4500 and 4200 Corridors of the building, to the point at which, for a good stretch of time, I actually had an extremely large office (later to become the personal office of the Assistant Attorney General for Legal Policy) all to myself.

And it was in the rear doorway of that office, coincidentally, that I stood in February of 1974 and heard a very senior attorney in the office next door receive an offer from Assistant Attorney General for Legal Counsel Robert G. Dixon, Jr., to head up a new Freedom of Information Act policy office that AAG Dixon was at that time first planning to establish.[14] Little did I imagine, when that attorney confided to me that he was declining to go ahead with that offer for personal reasons (which I mistook as connected to the fact that he was gay), that I myself would be offered that very position (and more) just seven years later, in early 1981. It was not that I couldn't see myself as a long-term Justice Department employee, because by then I was hell-bent on being nothing less. It was just that, still not long from the scrub pines of Long Island, and notwithstanding my very lucky Justice Department experiences up to that point, it would have taken one hell of an optimistic imagination to envision something such as that.

CHAPTER EIGHT
The Lure of Capitol Hill

"I found my thrill, on Capitol Hill."

-- Antoine "Fats" Domino, singing to President Bill Clinton at the White House when awarded the Presidential Medal of Freedom, October 26, 1998

Back on Long Island, though, something was brewing that became serious enough to actually make me leave the Justice Department for a time. Across the Nation, the political landscape was in many places infused with strong anti-Nixon sentiment and had evolved to the point at which a whole new generation of politicians were lining up to, in effect, storm Washington. (Politically, I mean, not the other way.) One of them was a young Suffolk County legislator, Thomas J. Downey, who was considering taking on my local congressman, a rather colorless Nixon supporter who had been in Congress for many undistinguished years.

I learned of this from a friend and on my next trip back there I met with Tom and his nascent group of political advisors, who at that point were few in number but passionate in their anti-Nixon spirit. I, too, had that spirit -- due to what Nixon had done to the Justice Department before my very eyes -- and to make a short story even shorter, I soon signed up to be Tom's "man in Washington" for his electoral campaign, volunteering for all that I could do there in support of his upcoming battle. Like so many young people who come to Washington and get caught up in swirl of national government and politics, I had suddenly found something that seemed bigger to me than even my own financial circumstances.

Fortunately for me, though, it was at just about that time that the director of my Justice Department team, Marty Danziger, saw the handwriting on Mr. Saxbe's wall and secured a very good nongovernment position as executive director of the United Mine Workers Welfare and Retirement Fund. Not only did I have the opportunity to go with Marty as a law clerk there, but I learned that I could put in evening hours adjudicating mine workers' retirement-eligibility appeals for even greater pay. So with some very delicate timing due to Hatch Act restrictions on political activity by "current federal employees" (for which I do know the statute of limitations definitely has run),[1] I made the shift from Justice Department law clerk to private-sector law-clerk-cum-political-operative on the side.

Tom Downey was three years older than me (and still is), but he had been elected to the newly created Suffolk County Legislature at the startling age of 22, not long after graduating from Cornell University. He was experienced, telegenic, politically connected through his grandmother in the Town of Babylon, and as I saw it with my new-found Washington "sophistication" he had a darn good chance of defeating that incumbent in what was shaping up to be an extraordinary congressional election year.

Juggling both my new job with Marty and my law school classes as well, I began setting up a full week of meetings for Tom with as many helpful people in Washington as possible, holding him out as one of a new generation of young politician who was aiming to be both an anti-Nixon standard bearer and the next Congress's youngest member. Perhaps due to the tenor of the times, this was not nearly as difficult, even for a political neophyte such as myself, as one might think it would be. It took not much more than some aggressive telephone calls to whoever I thought, based upon what I then knew of Washington, would be most compatible with the "youth campaign" that Tom was about to run.

The idea was that we would kick off Tom's campaign with several energetic days in Washington before he applied himself in earnest back on Long Island where the voters were, both to educate him on national-level issues (such as the then-emerging "energy crisis") and to establish some preliminary credibility for him as more than just a young local-level guy.[2] As it turned out, what I managed to schedule for him during that week yielded even greater benefits in the form of practical advice from those who preceded him on how best to accomplish what he was trying to do.

Toward that end, I scheduled him for meetings with Senator Joe Biden, who not long before had won election to the Senate at the remarkable age of twenty-nine (turning thirty shortly before being sworn in); Congressman (later Senator) Donald W. Riegle, Jr., who had won a House seat in his late twenties and then literally "wrote the book" on the subject (*O Congress*); Congressman (later Senator) John Breaux, who in meeting with us described himself as having been "the baby of the 93rd Congress" at age twenty-eight; and several others.[3]

Young Democrats one and all, they were amazingly receptive to Tom and his campaign. Senator Biden's office manager still was his father-in-law at that time (after his wife and daughter had been tragically killed in an auto accident between the time of his election and his swearing in a year earlier), and both he and Senator Biden could not have been more gracious to us. They gave us several tips on how to deal with the "age issue"[4] and they also familiarized Tom with a brand of "retail politics" that came to serve him well in many elections yet to come.

Congressman Riegel stressed the importance of union support, which had been key for him in his Michigan district and would be important to Tom as his biggest campaign contributor thus far had been the International Ladies Garment Workers of America, courtesy of his politically active grandmother. Several of our contacts advised on how best to tap the votes of senior citizens, who were an emerging voting bloc at the time. And the staff of Senator Richard C. "Dick" Clark of Iowa described how he had just won an upset election through the then-novel method of "walking the state" from end to end. The highlight, perhaps, was when Congressman Breaux spontaneously took us to breakfast at the Democratic Club on the Hill, where Tom readily saw himself fitting in quite nicely.[5]

To make a long story short (or at least a bit shorter), this Washington week in the spring of 1974 was successful beyond anyone's expectations. It broadened Tom's horizons, just as living and working in Washington had greatly broadened mine. It further energized him for what he was about to attempt -- not that Tom was a low-energy guy to begin with, far from it. And it also provided contacts that would serve him well between then and the election in November.[6]

In November, Tom went on to win the election, becoming the youngest Member of the 94th Congress and ultimately serving for eight more congressional terms, from 1975-1993. I continued to assist him throughout that first campaign, with whatever I could do in Washington to help him with issues important to the voters back home, and I received a firm promise from him (on the steps of the Capitol in front of several witnesses, no less) that I would be his first Supreme Court appointment in the event of his election as president somewhere down the road. (Yes, we both were young.) I took that promise gladly -- and later on when Tom became very good friends with another young congressman, Albert A. Gore, Jr., it became slightly less theoretical.[7] Those were heady times, especially in Washington, when almost anything, good or bad, seemed possible.[8]

CHAPTER NINE

Law School

"If Moses had gone to . . . Law School and spent three years working on the Hill, he would have written the Ten Commandments with three exceptions and a saving clause."

-- Charles Langbridge Morgan, President of PEN International, 1954

Back from the campaign trail in the second half of 1974, I focused on building upon my legal credentials. What seemed to be most important at that time was earning an academic record in law school that would serve me well in the future. I was able to earn good money with Marty Danziger that summer writing appeals procedures for the Mine Workers Fund, so that was covered, and my Justice Department career was "on hold" due to Hatch Act restrictions given my continued work for Tom Downey, so for the first time since I began law school I had the luxury of making academics a priority.

Fortunately, my first-year law school record of second in the class earned me a full-tuition scholarship upgrade and then my academic standing during the second year (of third in the class) carried that forward through graduation. But I had learned that the academic credential that seemed to matter most was service on the school's law review, for which I was promptly selected, and then it was a matter of "getting published" as a student law review author as quickly as possible, which was a distinction.

This is where, once again, I was very fortunate: I latched onto a case that, as it later turned out, was heading for the United States Supreme Court. Without going into full legal detail, the summer of 1974 was a highly unusual time for the Court. Rather than ending its Term in June as it almost invariably did, the Court stayed in session into July that year[1] in order to handle one of its biggest cases ever, the "Nixon tapes" case, which the Court decided in late July and which prompted Nixon's resignation two weeks later.

At the same time, the Court belatedly handed down its decision in a big racial discrimination case on "inter-district" school busing in Detroit, which it decided by a slender 5-4 margin in an opinion written by Chief Justice Warren E. Burger, but with Justice Potter Stewart writing a pivotal fifth-vote concurrence. This case, *Milliken v. Bradley*, was being both hailed and decried by many legal observers as establishing distinct new limits on all such "inter-district" anti-discrimination remedies.

Barely a month later, in a housing discrimination case out of Chicago, *Gautreaux v. Chicago Housing Authority*, the Seventh Circuit Court of Appeals applied this fresh Supreme Court precedent in a very particular way. This decision was authored by Retired Associate Supreme Court Justice Tom C. Clark, whom Lyndon Johnson had effectively forced off of the Supreme Court years earlier by creating a conflict of interest when he appointed his son Ramsey as attorney general;[2] ever since, Justice Clark had been "sitting by designation" in circuit court cases around the country, which was how he happened to be the author of this Seventh Circuit decision in August of 1974. And in this decision, by a margin of 2-1, he approved a broad remedy for housing discrimination that he said was consistent even with the seemingly restrictive new majority rule for such things that had just been set forth in *Milliken*.

This decision therefore was noteworthy in multiple respects, and I wrote an analysis of it that proposed the novel theory that retired Justice Clark was in a unique position to craft a legal approach based upon his special insight into Justice Stewart's *Milliken* concurrence, having sat on the Supreme Court alongside him for many years.[3] My prediction, in effect, was that Justice Clark's broad housing discrimination remedy in the Chicago *Gautreaux* case was cast in such a way as to survive any Supreme Court review of it -- and could actually serve to halt any Burger Court retreat from remedying discrimination twenty years after *Brown v. Board of Education* -- because he accurately "read between the lines" of Justice Stewart's crucial concurring opinion in the *Milliken* case.

At the same time that I was working on my law review analysis of this decision during the fall of 1974, the Justice Department of course had to decide whether to seek Supreme Court review of it, as Justice Clark had ruled so firmly against the Government and his Seventh Circuit panel, by the same 2-1 margin, had by then denied rehearing. This necessarily required the Solicitor General to decide whether to take the calculated risk of raising Justice Clark's analysis, atop the case's particular fact pattern, to the level of the Supreme Court for its consideration -- which we all knew could possibly lead to an immediate retrenchment from *Milliken* given the nuanced nature of Justice Clark's opinion.

Knowing my way quite well through Main Justice's corridors, I was able to connect with the Justice Department attorneys who were working on that very question, in parallel fashion, and we actually "traded notes" a bit on the case to our mutual benefit. As far as I was concerned, the case surely was important enough to warrant Supreme Court review so that this new modified theory of remedial anti-discrimination could be tested -- which (only coincidentally, of course) would have the immediate effect of making my law review analysis even more significant in turn. So I effectively lobbied for the Solicitor General to authorize such a Government appeal (by a petition process known as *certiorari*), through an appellate attorney who as it happened was in a position to strongly influence that outcome -- and this actually worked.[4]

In fact, as it turned out, everything fell perfectly into place: My law review analysis was published in the first publication volume possible in January 1975; the Solicitor General decided to risk asking for Supreme Court review of the issue; the Supreme Court granted that *certiorari* petition for review; and then after oral argument[5] the Supreme Court ultimately decided the case with a unanimous decision (*sub nom. Hills v. Gautreaux*) that was written by Justice Stewart, in which he upheld Justice Clark's decision along the very lines that I had suggested more than a year earlier in my published work.[6]

This law review credential, which was earned in no small part through leveraging my early Justice Department experience, then enabled me to earn "big bucks" for what turned out to be the only time in my legal career.[7] For law students, at least back then, summer employment amounted to two very different things: After the first law school year, a law student generally would be lucky just to get any paying legal job whatsoever in order to gain practical experience. But after the second year, law students can be "summer associates" at law firms of substantial size, earning nearly full attorney salaries for three months as they are courted by those firms with a strong eye toward their recruitment.[8]

I found myself very well positioned for this and had my choice of several big Washington law firms for which to work during the summer of 1975. I chose the law firm of Arnold & Porter ("A&P," to its clients), not so much because it had a reputation for *pro bono*, public service-oriented work (which it certainly did, especially after publication of the book *Gideon's Trumpet*),[9] as for the fact that it had just taken the lead among D.C. law firms by raising its Summer Associate salary to the munificent sum of $300 per week -- which for me was a princely wage (oxymoronically speaking) at the time.

In fact, the knowledge that I would be earning so much during that coming summer[10] allowed me the luxury of spending most of the Spring 1975 semester performing my own "*pro bono*" work. As a student holding full-tuition Trustee Scholar status, I felt obliged to "give back" to the law school community if reasonably possible. So in addition to running the school's day-long process of class registration for the Dean's Office, which I was asked by the deans to do based on my law review position and track record of organizational activity, I found something that I thought also was institutionally important -- tutoring a blind law student.

I had learned from an assistant to the school's associate dean (whom we students suspected effectively ran the school) that it had admitted two sightless students to the class behind mine and that one had thrived in the first semester with strong economic support from her family while the other, an orphan, had not. When I casually asked what the school was doing to help the second student, who was in danger of flunking out if she did not do well enough in the spring, the answer was "uh, well, not much."[11]

So I took it upon myself to nobly do whatever I could to prevent this student from flunking out in the spring as she nearly had in the previous fall, knowing that by the school's strict rules -- which I learned were not in any way relaxed in her case, despite her large handicap -- she needed a higher-than-passing grade average in her three spring classes in order to offset her minimal performance in the fall. Soon I was devoting more hours to this poor student's subjects, for which I myself had crammed with last-minute studying just a year or so earlier, than I was spending on the second-year classes of my own. I quickly found truth in the old adage that you don't really know a subject until you can teach it to someone else, but I must admit that it was more of a challenge than I had naïvely thought it would be to try to do this with a student who was, after all, blind.

By the end of that semester, with me placing full priority on her success as her exam deadlines neared, both she and I thought that we had succeeded and that she would be able to make the grade. However, it did not work out that way, due to the fact that one of her professors, notorious for being absent-minded,[12] failed in his own commitment to submit his exam for pre-test Braille transcription -- which meant that the first hours of that exam were spent by this student on the basic task of "Brailling" rather than on substantive question answering. Though she did well enough on her other exams, this poor student did flunk out, by a small but undeniable margin -- and to this day, for what it's worth, I regard this as the first (and, I thought then, biggest) failure of my legal career.[13]

My primary point in all of this is that I do not think I would have been able to accomplish any of it without first having been able to take advantage of the opportunities that so fortuitously had already come my way, despite my own odds, especially those two rare stretches of early government service. There was just something about having been at the Justice Department, and having found myself able to make relatively sophisticated contributions there, that gave me the confidence to do more than I had ever dreamt was possible back on Long Island. So I capped off my law school days with a leading position on the law review's editorial board, was designated by the school's deans and placement office as the school's top candidate for federal judicial clerkships, and then spent my first year out of law school immersing myself in litigation as a clerk to a federal district court judge.

I had received several offers to clerk at the appellate-court level, but I knew enough about how federal judicial clerkships worked (and just as importantly about the "rough and tumble" law that I wanted to practice) that I knew a district court clerkship would be best for me. And this judgment turned out to be exactly "spot on," as my British friends would say, with respect to both the clerkship that I chose and the particular litigation position in which I applied what I learned during it.

The judge for whom I clerked, District Court Judge Oliver Gasch, was a true "Southern gentleman" who, having been born and raised in "the South" (by which I mean the northwest quadrant of the District of Columbia) was as courtly and gracious as they came. He just loved the fact that he and my then-fiancée (i.e., my second one) had graduated from the same university: He was Princeton, class of '28, back when Debbie could not have attended that school; she was Princeton, class of '72, one of the first women to graduate from there. (They used to share stories about Princeton's annual "P-rade," a 19th-century tradition that took place as the highlight of the university's reunion weekend each year.)

Judge Gasch had just turned 70 when I began to clerk for him in June of 1976 and he often regaled me (especially while giving me a lift home many evenings, as he lived just a few blocks from me off of upper Connecticut Avenue) with stories of his young bachelor days, when he would square dance with Eleanor Roosevelt and "cut a mean figure around town."[14] He was "pure D.C.," through and through.

After a stint at the D.C. Corporation Counsel's Office (what is now the Office of the D.C. Attorney General), he became the Principal Assistant United States Attorney for the District of Columbia and then the United States Attorney during the entire Eisenhower Administration. He then had the good fortune of being president of the D.C. Bar just as President Lyndon B. Johnson (in a spasm of bipartisanship) was looking for a Republican to appoint to the District Court for the District of Columbia in 1965.

Most noteworthy for my purposes, though, was the fact that Judge Gasch had practiced law prior to the advent of "newfangled" statutes (as he called them) such as Title VII, the Labor Management Relations Act, and of course the Freedom of Information Act coming onto the scene. He didn't like those cases; actually, he didn't much care for handling any civil litigation cases at all. Rather, he liked trying criminal cases, which were an especially big part of the docket due to the District of Columbia's particular jurisdictional status, and after nearly eight years of leading the United States Attorney's Office, he knew that area of the law and criminal trial practice cold.

So clerking in Judge Gasch's chambers meant that you would get minimal exposure to criminal matters (for which he did not really need a clerk),[15] but you would be left pretty much to your own devices to independently deal with the civil side of his docket in all respects.[16] Really. So it was an unbeatable legal experience in civil litigation. Yes, Judge Gasch would always read his civil opinions before signing them, but at least in my case his review of them largely took the form of his unsplitting my infinitives. (Yes, I did shamelessly put some extra ones in there for effect.)

As for the substance of the cases (and we had some big ones, including a precedent-setting case under the FOIA), although Judge Gasch was a staunch conservative and I was an unabashed liberal, we only once disagreed on the proper outcome of a case during my entire clerkship year. (I would like to think that this was because we both were "following the law," as Attorney General Janet Reno later would say.)

And as to that one case, Judge Gasch and I eventually agreed on just one thing: That we would "hold it over" for the next year's law clerk to handle. Well, two successive clerks later, he decided that case as his gut (rather than the law) told him, whereupon he was promptly reversed by the court of appeals.[17]

CHAPTER TEN

Return to the Justice Department

"It's good FOIA."

-- The author, in "The Nature of Government Secrecy," 2009, and in a keynote address given at the Library of Congress at its 25th Annual Forum on Federal Information Policies on September 12, 2008

It sometimes is said that there are two basic types of judicial clerkships -- a pedagogical one in which the clerk largely absorbs the judge's knowledge and practical wisdom through that year-long, osmosis-like association; and a more activist one in which the clerk is put in a "sink or swim" situation, having to quickly rise to his or her fullest potential, in a way that makes him or her almost (or so it might seem) as effective as the judge. I had chosen a federal judge who offered clerkships very much of the latter variety, far more than most other judges, knowing that I could thrive in such an environment. And as before, I swam.

Again, I was poised to do so based upon my prior government experience, including direct legal experience during my second tour of duty at the Department of Justice. And again this worked out marvelously, because by the end of that clerkship year I knew the processes of civil litigation (in which I was far more interested by then than criminal law) about as well as was possible within that relatively short period of time. And with that knowledge, I knew that the Justice Department position in which I very much wanted to start my true legal career was that of an Assistant United States Attorney (known as an "AUSA"), as a fast-paced litigator representing the government in dozens of lawsuits at a time, sometimes more than could be humanly handled,[1] in that same federal courthouse down the hall.

Only this time I could not just fast-talk myself into that Justice Department position "just down the hall." Rather, the Civil Division of the Office of the United States Attorney for the District of Columbia (not to be confused with the Civil Division of the Justice Department at "Main Justice") had a very firm rule at the time (and probably still does) that it would not hire new attorneys right out of law school or even once they had completed a judicial clerkship. To the folks there, with a rule that likely went back several decades, more experience was required to be even a "brand-new" AUSA. There was just no getting around it; I was stymied by a branch of my former two-time employer.

So I did the next-best thing: I decided to become an "Attorney General's Honors Program" attorney in the Department's Civil Division at Main Justice, where I would have full-time litigation responsibilities right from the start and actually could be overseeing AUSAs "out in the field" in one of the areas of specialized subject-matter expertise that were held by the attorneys at Main Justice. And there were many such subject-matter areas from which to choose, once you were selected for the program and began to maneuver a bit.

On its face, perhaps, this could be viewed as an even better job, at least for someone working in Washington, but I knew full well that the major advantage that government service holds for a young attorney is the opportunity to quickly hold enormous amounts of responsibility, atop skill-development opportunities, with large caseloads.[2] Generally speaking, this is simply more so in United States Attorneys' Offices (much the same as it is in the busy offices of local district attorneys), or at Main Justice, than anywhere else in the Federal Government.

Yet once again, I got amazingly lucky, and in a way that no one could have possibly foreseen. It just so happened that when I joined the Justice Department's Civil Division as an Honors Program attorney in the fall of 1977, there was a sudden need for new attorneys in its recently created litigation section that dealt with government information and privacy litigation -- cases brought against the Federal Government under the Freedom of Information Act ("FOIA," to its friends) and the Privacy Act of 1974. Both of these statutes were "public interest" offspring of the "Watergate" era, in that one had been enacted and the other had been greatly revitalized in the immediate aftermath of that enormous scandal three years earlier.[3]

Anyway, the extensive amendments that Congress made to the FOIA (over President Ford's veto) near the end of 1974 had "put teeth" into that law in many important procedural respects -- through firm time deadlines, annual reporting requirements, *in camera* inspection, and fee restrictions on agencies, among other things -- and they had also, for the first time, realistically extended the law's reach both to law enforcement records and (in large part) to the records of intelligence agencies.

This made the extensive files of the Federal Bureau of Investigation and the Central Intelligence Agency, in particular, fresh targets for contentious Freedom of Information Act requests brought by members of public-interest groups and others who, in the immediate wake of "Watergate," wanted to "turn the federal government inside out" through record disclosures as a catalyst for sustained government reform.[4] And FOIA requests beget FOIA litigation. Larger and larger numbers of these FOIA disputes, many of them encompassing highly controversial subject areas and very sensitive records, began reaching federal court.

By the mid-1970s, the Justice Department was straining to cope with these rapidly increasing numbers of high-profile FOIA lawsuits, which made its litigation clients (mostly the FBI and the CIA, but also other law enforcement and intelligence agencies) most uneasy. So the Department created a new litigation section within its Civil Division to specialize in handling those cases, with highly concentrated effort, both directly and through expert supervision of AUSAs "out in the field." That's where I came in. And that's where, once again, I got very lucky with the circumstances that existed at the time of my arrival for this third tour of duty at Justice.[5]

You see, not only was there this near-overnight explosion of activity in this particular area of federal litigation, but the Civil Division section formed to handle it, named the "Information and Privacy Section," suddenly experienced an enormous turnover in its attorney ranks -- some called it a "mass evacuation" -- in the months just prior and subsequent to my arrival. Due to a combination of extraordinary circumstances that could not briefly be described here,[6] two-thirds of the section's dozen attorneys transferred to other parts of the Civil Division and were replaced by a cohort of eight newly hired young Trial Attorneys, of which I was one. Of this group, oddly, I was the only one with any significant litigation experience, albeit as a judicial clerk; I also was the only "nonminority."

Yes, of this cohort of eight newly hired attorneys there were four women, two African-American men, an Hispanic man, and myself -- and as a group we were thrust into a litigation section that was, to put it mildly, in extreme turmoil. But that turmoil, born largely of that new section chief's controversial replacement of her predecessor, almost immediately yielded extraordinary opportunities for me, as a young attorney, to gain exceptionally strong and fast litigation experience -- in much the same way as I was able to gain exceptional experience at the Justice Department previously as an intern and then again as a "one L."[7]

Only this time, this included being able to "hit the ground running" not only for myself with my own cases, but also by assisting most of the other new section attorneys with the all-important rules, procedural requirements, strategy, and other basic "nuts and bolts" of the litigation process, and actually becoming a "mentor," in effect, to several of them.[8] Again, this might seem implausible, but it was true.

Simply put, I had the good fortune of becoming a relatively "senior" Trial Attorney in that part of the Civil Division from almost the very outset -- and, as such, I soon had my pick of the many pending cases that were handed off by the many departing attorneys, not to mention of the newly filed ones that were continuing to swell the section's caseload. Before long, never once turning anything down, I was responsible for major cases involving the records of the Martin Luther King, Jr. Assassination, the JFK Assassination,[9] the CIA, the National Security Agency ("NSA," to the few who then knew much about it), and abuses of the FBI by the Nixon White House, to name only a few.

Atop those, among many others, was a case in which a public interest group sought the records of the six major investigations of the Watergate Special Prosecution Force, which totaled more than a half-million document pages, and a series of cases through which the American Civil Liberties Union challenged suspected covert activities of the CIA on targeted American campuses. These cases all were destined to become leading precedents in the development of case law under the FOIA, which was still in its relative infancy at the time, and I handled them with great care accordingly.[10]

So practically before I knew it, working hard and well to take maximum advantage of yet another "right place/right time" opportunity, I was immersed in the intricacies of government secrecy litigation -- from such issues as confidential source protection to exceptional personal-privacy protection to law enforcement legitimacy and to the new concept of refusal to confirm or deny the existence of any records reflecting certain national security-related activities -- and I quickly became a leading government expert on nearly all aspects of this emerging area of the law.

This held great appeal to me, for multiple reasons. First, by taking cases that by dint of both novelty and complexity kept me working literally nonstop for weeks on end,[11] I was getting the full advantage of the intensive "AUSA-type" litigation experience that I originally had sought. And when one of those FOIA cases proceeded to a rare multiple-day trial in San Francisco in 1978, with extensive pre-trial depositions, that counterpart experience was complete.

Even more significantly, though, I soon concluded that this relatively new area of law, which had kicked into high gear just shortly before I started practicing it, was an absolutely fascinating one -- in no small part due to the key element of recordkeeping in virtually all government functioning. Put another way, every big FOIA case back then involved not only compelling legal issues of statutory interpretation (most of which were issues of "first impression"), but also underlying fact patterns that were extremely compelling in and of themselves -- from assassinations to assignations to things that were covert for good reason. And all such things were reduced to writing.

Indeed, the very contents of the records sought in such cases, and the particular government activities that were reflected in them, were some of the most sensitive that could be imagined.[12] And it was quite a challenge to find ways to defend the application of what were still very general provisions of law (usually somewhat vaguely worded disclosure exemptions) to highly sensitive information, which often required a good deal of creativity -- or even to reach a considered judgment sometimes that some of the information being withheld ought to be disclosed. To me, that challenge was irresistibly compelling and, as will be seen below, it was not easily left behind.

CHAPTER ELEVEN

The White House "Name Check" Case

"The ends of criminal justice would be defeated if judgments were to be founded on a partial or speculative presentation of the facts."

-- Warren E. Burger, Chief Justice of the United States, in United States v. Nixon, July 24, 1974

A high-visibility case that I just could not turn down (read: actually, I grabbed it) was *Abramson v. FBI*, a case involving the Nixon White House's use (read: abuse) of the extensive "name check" system that had long been in use at the FBI. This case had been pending only briefly at the time I picked it up from another Information and Privacy Section attorney, and was somewhat in a state of disarray, but I was entirely comfortable doing so because that attorney, Nicki L. Koutsis, was the same one with whom I took another case to trial in San Francisco at about the same time. Plus, although I certainly could not know it for sure at the time, it had the makings of a case that would resonate in the FOIA world even beyond its own confines.[1]

Abramson was a case brought by Howard Abramson, a free-lance journalist[2] who had somehow "gotten wind" (as reporters do) that one of Richard Nixon's two principal henchman at the time, White House Domestic Affairs Director John D. Ehrlichman, had fraudulently dipped into the FBI's files back in the late 1960s and early 1970s in order to obtain "derogatory information" (known within the Bureau as "derog") on some of Nixon's "severest critics" for purely (read: impurely) political purposes. I knew that such a case, especially given the tenor of the times, would necessarily require an exhaustive self-examination by the Bureau of its entire "name check" system.

Now Ehrlichman was already serving a lengthy prison sentence for his craven role as a principal architect of President Nixon's "Watergate" scandals, so it was not difficult to imagine that he had in fact done what Howard Abramson was alleging. The question was whether the Bureau actually still maintained records documenting this and -- more importantly -- how we would handle the great sensitivity of any such records given that the individuals involved had by definition already been "victimized" by Nixon's White House in conjunction with the FBI. This was exceptionally challenging, all the more so because the case unavoidably carried what was then called the "aura of Watergate" by several judges on the District Court for the District of Columbia.

So in order to even begin to formulate any possible defense of the case, I made it my business to "camp out" at FBI Headquarters for a while, where I ungently interrogated the long-term head of the Bureau's "name check" system. This fellow, who had been in charge of "running name checks" for quite some time by then,[3] reluctantly allowed as how the Bureau had indeed compiled its "derog" on nearly a dozen such file subjects (read: victims), in tidy "summaries" that were "cooperatively" transmitted to the White House upon Ehrlichman's request. More specifically, there were 63 pages of such "name check" summaries that contained derogatory information, culled from existing FBI files, on a total of 11 public figures.[4]

This was an enormous violation of personal-privacy interests, a subject that had been growing increasingly unpopular with the public, and with Congress, particularly in the wake of the information abuses committed as part of the "Watergate" scandals not long prior to this. In fact, it was exactly this sort of "political action" that Congress sought to prevent in enacting the Privacy Act of 1974 (see Chapter Fourteen).

Knowing that we really had no choice but to make this sad fact public,[5] I had the Bureau prepare a verifiably complete set of all such FBI-to-White House transmissions, together with all related records about them, including all information transmitted, for an unsparing review.[6] And that review, once completed,[7] became the foundation of both the case's defense and the public statements that the Bureau made about what had happened. However, that litigation defense was not so easily formulated. Rather, I had to deal with an entirely novel and highly problematic pair of legal issues in this case.

To be sure, the FOIA, as amended three years earlier, afforded a great deal of personal-privacy protection in law enforcement files through its new Exemption 7(C). But the Act's amended language, as a threshold requirement to even reach that privacy protection,[8] covered only "investigatory records compiled for law enforcement purposes," with the words "records" and "compiled" standing as analytical stumbling blocks against us. Here, the sensitive information at issue was not compiled for legitimate law enforcement purposes when it was put together as a package (read: in summary form) for delivery to the White House; nor was it freshly "compiled" (as opposed to "recompiled") at that point.

The first of these barriers was that the Act explicitly referred to "records," not "information," in the new threshold language of Exemption 7.[9] But it seemed only to make good sense to interpret "record" broadly and pragmatically, so as to logically encompass its component of "information" -- especially in a case in which the individuals whose information was at stake now faced the prospect of being victimized twice over.

The second was the word "compiled," which is not quite the same as what actually happened with the derogatory information we were dealing with; that information had been "recompiled." Indeed, in what was then an unprecedented way, the records at issue had admittedly been compiled (read: recompiled) for political purposes, i.e., the Nixon White House's improper purpose of using them against its "enemies."[10] So under an ordinary interpretation of the statute, the individuals whose personal-privacy interests were at stake would not be entitled to have their information withheld from public disclosure, merely because the Bureau had acceded to an improper White House request. "Not right," I thought.

Indeed, that rigid view seemed to me to turn the FOIA on its head, so to speak, not to mention that it would be downright unfair to the individuals involved, who were after all victims of government misconduct in the first place; in rough parlance, they were at risk of being screwed twice over.[11] So I fashioned a novel defense to the case, an analytical path if you will, that was aimed at both defending my client agency and avoiding such an unfair result. And it focused directly on those two "stumbling block" words, "records" and "compiled," taking them head-on.

I prepared a motion for summary judgment that argued that the Bureau was entitled to use Exemption 7(C) despite these two statutory words. This motion contended that although the records in the case (read: the "derog" summaries) admittedly had been compiled for other-than-legitimate law enforcement purposes, that was actually a "recompilation" of the *information* contained within them. In other words, the information was *originally* compiled by the FBI for proper law enforcement purposes (within the Bureau's broad statutory mandate for such things) even though it later was "recompiled" for other purposes in the records created at Ehrlichman's request. And that original compilation, I argued, is what really mattered.

In other words, in "status-quo/change" terms, any information originally compiled for law enforcement purposes does not *lose* its Exemption 7 protection when subsequently recompiled into a new document for purposes other than law enforcement. And that was exactly what had happened here, as was attested to by FBI Special Agent Jerry R. Donahoe, so therefore the word "compiled" was not a proper barrier.[12]

Further, the summary judgment motion argued that what was at issue in the case actually was *information*, albeit aggregated in record form, as that was what the Bureau had in fact culled out of its files and summarized for Ehrlichman. It would be "exalting form over substance," I said, to dwell on Congress's use of the word "record" where, as a practical matter, agencies can summarize existing information in the exceptional way in which the Bureau did in that case. In sum, I argued, the case was about information, although recompiled for an illegitimate purpose, that had been compiled by the Bureau for a legitimate (read: just barely) purpose in the first place.

This case was pending before District Court Judge Charles E. Richey, a Nixon patronage appointee to the Bench who had a well-deserved reputation for neither intelligence nor judicial temperament.[13] He held an oral argument on the motion at which he seemed unable to grasp the unorthodox nature of the case, though it was hard to tell for sure. But then he issued a decision firmly in the Government's favor that held that the individuals whose information was at stake in the case were indeed entitled to the personal-privacy protection of Exemption 7(C).

When a decision in your favor is handed down by a District Court, there is a natural tendency to celebrate as if it were permanent. It might not be so, however, depending first on whether the party on the other side decides to appeal, which can be done in any case if that party chooses to do so. And if that favorable decision is appealed -- which in this case was almost a foregone conclusion in that I knew that neither Howard Abramson nor his attorney (and wife) Sharon Nelson Abramson was of the type to give up -- then that lower court victory, and the issues that are "resolved" in it, must be defended all over again.

This aptly describes what happened in *Abramson*. Judge Richey's decision was not handed down until late November of 1979, at which point I was "up to my hubcaps" in a slew (read: lots) of other high-profile cases, and when I looked at the D.C. Circuit's briefing schedule for the *Abramson* appeal I knew that I'd best not try to squeeze something such as that into my "110%" schedule during that time period. So someone in Civil Appellate handled it, which was the heavy default arrangement anyway, and he did just a fine job on it. But we lost. Big time.[14]

This is where this narrative should pause for a word or two about federal judges. They are "political" appointees, for the most part, in that they all are appointed by a president and confirmed (almost without exception) by the Senate.[15] And as such, they can be, sometimes, less than reliable in their consistency, their objectivity, and their ability to shed their ideological biases when they consider a policy-laden case. Generally speaking, they are regarded as either conservative or "progressive" (read: "liberal," until just recently) and, in government cases, either "pro-government" or not.

Here's an example: When I was clerking and then beginning to litigate, there were nine judges on the D.C. Circuit. And of the nine, it was widely agreed that three of them were conservative, three were liberal, and the other three were pretty much "down the middle." So when the three-judge panel members for a case were announced, those of us who watched such things would pretty much be able to predict the case's outcome on that basis alone.

Now did that "thumbnail prediction" always hold as accurate? No, of course not. But it certainly did work particularly well for FOIA cases back then. And it also worked quite well for cases decided by the United States Supreme Court, especially when the Court maintained what was viewed as a "4-4-1" split, with Justice Potter Stewart seen as in the middle for most types of cases and issues, during much of the 1970s. In fact, the very thing that I wrote about in law school for my law review publication was the quintessential example of this (see Chapter Nine).

As it happened, the D.C. Circuit panel that heard *Abramson* on appeal had three "card-carrying liberals" (read: not "pro-government") on it, one of whom, Circuit Court Judge Harry T. Edwards, had just months earlier been appointed to that court from academia. And as it turned out, the circuit judge who wrote the D.C. Circuit's opinion reversing Judge Richey in *Abramson* was Judge Edwards,[16] and from the oral argument it seemed as if he was looking to "make his mark" with the case.

In that opinion, Judge Edwards took the somewhat muddled legal analysis that appeared in Judge Richey's ruling and applied an analysis of his own to it that gave little or no credence to what the Government was arguing. The coin of his realm, so to speak, was "documents," not "information," and he carried that idea throughout his entire analysis of the case. And even though Judge Edwards at times seemed to implicitly accept the "compiled/recompiled" dynamic, that did nothing to avail the Government's side of the issue as he kept coming back to his view of the "recompiled" information as "distinct" from what was originally compiled when it was viewed in "record" form.

To make a long story shorter, Judge Edwards's opinion seemed to recognize the privacy sensitivity of the derogatory information at issue in the case, but that was of little moment to him because he could not get beyond Exemption 7's "law enforcement threshold." And the reason for that was that he evidently could see no equivalence between the "records" that the statute speaks of and the "information" that was involved in the case. Furthermore, his opinion did not recognize that such information could be "compiled" -- originally -- and then "recompiled" later on, as was indeed the case in *Abramson*.[17] So he reversed Judge Richey's ruling and ordered the derogatory information disclosed.

Well, this was a "kick in the head" to the Government, because we felt a heavy obligation to the 11 individuals involved not to let them pay the price for John Ehrlichman's perfidy. It surely was not their fault that Ehrlichman had acted as deceitfully as he had, nor that the Bureau (no doubt as a matter of obsequious White House pandering) had simply "gone along."[18] But the only way that we could protect them at that point was to persuade the Supreme Court to reverse Judge Edwards' decision.

Chapter Three discusses the process of getting Supreme Court reversal of an adverse appellate court decision in connection with the *Favish* case and the issue of "survivor privacy." Almost the exact same process, with its underlying dynamics, applied in *Abramson*. For those of us who thought it was worth trying to gain reversal, we knew that the first step -- perhaps even the most difficult one -- was to persuade the Solicitor General to authorize the filing of a *certiorari* petition to begin with.

This was complicated by the fact that there was no "conflict in the circuits" on the threshold Exemption 7 issue presented; Exemption 7 as amended had not been in existence long enough for that by that point. And it also was complicated (read: greatly undermined) by the fact that the Civil Division, through its Appellate Staff, actually recommended *against cert*. -- for reasons that I must say I never fully understood -- which ordinarily would be fatal. Nevertheless, those of us who thought otherwise weighed in very heavily in the Solicitor General's Office[19] and I was able to get the FBI to push strongly for *cert*. as well.

So sure enough, the filing of a *certiorari* petition was authorized, despite the fact that it was not the unanimous recommendation. This was very much due to the efforts of Deputy Solicitor General Kenneth S. Geller, who not only supported the authorization of a *certiorari* petition, he decided to handle the case before the Supreme Court himself. Ken filed a *certiorari* petition that emphasized the great significance (read: great harm) of the D.C. Circuit's ruling below to the emerging case law that was interpreting the language of the 1974 FOIA Amendments, as well as of any decision issued by the circuit of "universal venue" under the FOIA.

And on June 15, 1981, the Supreme Court did grant *certiorari* in the case, leading to the briefing of it during the remainder of that year.[20] This was quite significant, in the scheme of things, because it was one of the first instances of the Supreme Court granting *certiorari* in a FOIA case partly on the basis of the D.C. Circuit "universal venue" factor.[21] And it also was only the second time in more than seven years that the Court took the opportunity to construe the language of the 1974 FOIA Amendments.

Then the case was argued before the Court, on January 11, 1982. At that argument -- which at times was a bit muddled itself as the Court struggled with the "record versus information" issue and especially the "compiled versus recompiled" one -- Ken strongly attacked what he called Judge Edwards's "mechanical and excessively literal" approach. He forcefully argued that a case such as this did not call for a "formalistic, literalistic focus on particular pieces of paper," but rather on what the information at issue was all about. Ken actually went so far as to call Judge Edwards's approach "senseless," which had several of us silently cheering in the Supreme Court Bar section of the courtroom.

The Supreme Court wound up echoing that very sentiment when it handed down its decision in *Abramson* on May 24, 1982. I remember well that on that day, having moved from the Civil Division to the Office of Information and Privacy the previous fall, I was having a one-on-one, hard-nosed legislation negotiation meeting with John D. Podesta, Jr., who then was working as a powerful congressional aide to Senator Patrick J. Leahy (D-VT), the key senator on FOIA reform, when I received the good news.[22]

It was a 5-4 decision, much to the surprise of many, with the majority opinion written by Justice Byron R. "Whizzer" White and dissenting opinions written by Justices Harry A. Blackmun and Justice Sandra Day O'Connor.[23] The four justices who joined Justice White to constitute the case's majority were Chief Justice Warren E. Burger and Justices Lewis F. Powell, Jr., William H. Rehnquist, and John Paul Stevens. Justices William J. Brennan, Jr., and Thurgood Marshall each joined one of the two dissents,

Justice White's majority opinion grappled with both the "compiled" question and the "record" one, but focused primarily on the former, with its use of the words "summarized" or "reproduced" as a stand-in for it.[24] It did so because it implicitly assumed that the unit of analysis in the case was "information," not a record or a document. This was evident right from the start when it articulated the "question presented" in the case as whether "information contained in records compiled for law enforcement purposes [can] lose that exempt status."

From that starting point, Justice White examined how the D.C. Circuit's view of the case would operate in actual practice, in comparison with how the Government's view would work, with respect to "identical information." He found that the D.C. Circuit's approach to the case's rare fact pattern, when extrapolated to other possible fact patterns, "makes little sense," just as Ken Geller had said at oral argument. By contrast, the Government's approach, Justice White found, not only was a plausible interpretation of the statute, it "more accurately reflects the intention of Congress" in the 1974 Amendments.

Accordingly, Justice White stated for the Court's majority: "We hold that information initially contained in a record made for law enforcement purposes continues to meet the threshold requirements of Exemption 7 where that recorded information is reproduced or summarized in a new document prepared for a non-law enforcement purpose."[25] And although he oddly shied away from any form of the word "compiled" by using the word "made" in this holding, the result was still the same: The Government prevailed, even if by a narrow majority.[26]

Lastly, what can be viewed as the final chapter of the case[27] was written by Congress four years later. In the 1986 FOIA Amendments, when Congress greatly "reformed" Exemption 7, it did so with an unmistakable eye toward the *Abramson* case. It broadened Exemption 7's threshold language by adding the words "or information" to it.[28] And it made it explicitly clear in the underlying legislative reports that when it did so it was embracing *Abramson*'s outcome. So it was that the case that I "picked up" in a "state of disarray" in late 1977 became the basis of both a lasting Supreme Court precedent and the codification of my analysis and argument in it more than eight years down the road.

CHAPTER TWELVE

The Big Watergate FOIA Case

"It is better to risk saving a guilty person than to condemn an innocent one."

-- François-Marie Arouet (Voltaire), 1694-1778

At an "Annual Freedom of Information Day" program that I conducted at the Washington College of Law in 2009, I had the pleasure of hosting both a senator with whom I had worked on FOIA reform legislation after his election to the Senate in 1974 (see Chapter Forty-Two) and a former Member of Congress whom I had helped get elected as the youngest Member of the 94th Congress in that same year (see Chapter Eight) thirty-five years earlier. Speaking at this program, they nostalgically referred to one another as fellow "Watergate babies," having entered Congress at such relatively young ages (i.e., 34 and 26, respectively) soon after that scandal reached its peak with President Richard M. Nixon's resignation in August of 1974.[1]

Well, I, too, think of myself as somewhat of a "Watergate baby," given that I was at the Justice Department as a first-year law student/law clerk in 1973 at the time of the "Saturday Night Massacre"[2] and carried over in what was part of the Attorney General's Office well into 1974 (see Chapter Seven). And then I went on to handle (read: at both the district court and court of appeals levels) the biggest Freedom of Information Act case ever to deal with "Watergate" records.

These records were those of the "Watergate Special Prosecution Force" ("WSPF," to its non-indictees), which was established by newly named Watergate Special Prosecutor Archibald Cox, Jr., in May of 1973. The "Force" (which was with them) slowly wrapped its arms around all aspects of the burgeoning scandal, absorbing and further developing the investigative work already done by the FBI, the Department of Justice's Criminal Division, and the local U.S. Attorney's Office. And as summer turned to fall that year, it zeroed in on the increasingly evident culpability of President Nixon himself.

Then, on October 20, 1973, Nixon knowingly concluded that he could not comply with Special Prosecutor Cox's latest court-supported subpoenas -- for audiotapes of presidential conversations made in the Oval Office -- so he decided to have him fired instead. Except that under the terms of Cox's appointment (to which Nixon had acceded in a weak moment), only Attorney General Elliot L. Richardson could fire Cox.

So on the evening of Saturday, October 20, Nixon ordered Attorney General Richardson to fire Cox. Richardson, having given Cox a commitment to not do so merely on a presidential order, refused to do so, choosing to resign instead, as did Deputy Attorney General William D. Ruckelshaus, as well. Only when the Justice Department's third-in-command, Solicitor General Robert H. Bork, agreed to fire Cox himself did the evening end. Many thought that that would be the end for all "Watergate-related" investigative and prosecutorial efforts.

But the intense public reaction to what Nixon had done -- some called it a "constitutional crisis" -- was so universally negative that Nixon, who by this point was just hanging by a thread, was forced to have Acting Attorney General Bork appoint a replacement special prosecutor -- recent American Bar Association President Leonidas "Leon" Jaworski -- just 11 days later. And because of Nixon's wounded public standing (read: the "Saturday Night Massacre" proved to be a self-inflicted wound), Jaworski was actually given even more independence than Cox had had.

With that, new Special Prosecutor Jaworski retained the entire staff of the Watergate Special Prosecution Force, which went on to conduct wide-ranging investigations and prosecutions of "Watergate-related" activities for the next 3½ years, long after Nixon himself resigned in August of 1974. And this involved the creation of hundreds of thousands of investigative and prosecutorial records, all of which, upon the expiration of the Special Prosecutor's Office in June of 1977 were by operation of law transferred into the custody of the National Archives and Records Service ("NARS," to historians, or "the National Archives," or simply "the Archives," to those of us who worked at "Main Justice" just next door), which back then was part of the General Services Administration ("GSA," to its statutory "ascertainers").[3]

The "Watergate scandal" spawned a few relatively small FOIA cases dealing with particular aspects of it. But the *Fund for Constitutional Government v. National Archives & Records Service* case,[4] which encompassed more than a half-million pages of the six major investigations conducted by the Watergate Special Prosecution Force,[5] was by far the biggest and most consequential -- if I do say so myself, because I inherited responsibility for defending this case soon after arriving in the Justice Department's Civil Division in 1977. In fact, it was already well on its way to becoming one of the leading early precedents in the entire FOIA realm by that time.

Now here is where one of the FOIA's "dirty little secrets" comes to the fore: Of necessity, the Act works (read: functions viably) only if FOIA requesters are willing to pay for "their" copies of the requested records.[6] By that, I mean much more than that the Act authorizes the charging of fees and that agencies impose them. Rather, I mean that it really costs nothing for a FOIA requester to put a large number of an agency's records "on the hook" under the Act,[7] whereas in many cases (read: where it is handling highly sensitive law enforcement records) it can cost that agency enormous sums in resource expenditures to "process" those records for public disclosure. So, as a practical matter (read: self-defense), an agency will not engage in such an expensive endeavor unless the requester is interested enough to follow through with payment for it. Else the Act is subject to easy abuse.

If you think about it, this just makes good sense. When a FOIA requester seeks a voluminous set of records and none of them is exempt, then it costs the agency relatively little to comply with that request and there is little or no problem. But what if the agency were to possess an enormous set of sensitive records that would have to be "processed" (read: individually reviewed for the application of FOIA exemptions) for any disclosure? And what if the requester of those records simply said, in effect, "No, I don't want to pay for my own copy of those records as processed, I just want the agency to process them and place them in its FOIA reading room so that any member of the public can see them."

Well, that is essentially what Bill Dobrovir and Andra Oakes said in the *Fund for Constitutional Government* case; they wanted to force my client to expend all of the resources required for processing hundreds of thousands of pages of WSPF records, at enormous cost, just because they asked for that to be done under the FOIA. Never mind that these records had come to the National Archives merely as a records custodian. Never mind that the Archives had had to create a specialized staff to deal with them. And never mind that, in a "sample run," the Archives had determined that it took an average of two hours per page to do this.[8] This is the FOIA issue that was presented in that case before we could even get to the applicability of the FOIA's law enforcement exemptions (not to mention FOIA Exemption 5 and the issue of grand jury secrecy) to the requested WSPF files.

Fortunately for the Government, the judge before whom the case was being litigated was a pragmatic veteran of government service himself. District Court Judge Thomas Aquinas Flannery (bless his soul) had been an assistant U.S attorney in the District of Columbia for more than a dozen years (working under the judge for whom I clerked, Oliver Gasch, when he was the United States Attorney) and then was the United States Attorney himself before being nominated to the Bench by Nixon in 1971. He was smart, even-tempered, and above all had a wealth of government experience upon which to draw.

So the plaintiff's counsel and I began negotiations over how the Archives would handle their client's FOIA request. For my part, I was intent on achieving a result that would impose the least amount of administrative burden on my client, especially given that its potential burden vulnerability with such a FOIA request was nothing short of staggering.[9] But I soon realized that I had an advantage in this: The plaintiff, for its part, was most eager to challenge the agency's record deletions, thinking that they could readily be overcome in court.[10]

We therefore reached the agreement that we would "hold" the threshold issue of how many records would be processed until after we first litigated the agency's deletions on the records that could most readily be handled. These were the "closing memoranda," or their functional equivalents, for each of the six major investigations involved. This allowed the plaintiff's counsel to get their early opportunity in court (which I certainly did not mind), but most importantly it allowed me to "kick the can down the road" on the threatening burden issue that quite understandably most concerned my client (and by extension, other agencies as well).

So in the summer of 1978, my client team and I applied four different exemptions to those six closing memoranda -- Exemption 3 (in two respects), Exemption 5, Exemption 7(C), and Exemption 7(D) -- prepared affidavits justifying all deletions within them, and filed a motion for summary judgment as to all information withheld.[11] And in response, Dobrovir and Oakes challenged all but the Exemption 7(D) deletions, which fairly well protected confidential law enforcement sources, but they surprisingly made their lengthiest arguments on the subject of grand jury secrecy, not personal privacy.

Judge Flannery ruled broadly in the Government's favor, however, upholding deletions made pursuant to Exemptions 7(C) and 7(D), Exemption 5 (under the deliberative process privilege), and Exemption 3 (to protect tax-return information as well as matters occurring before a grand jury). As to the latter, he concluded that "policy considerations involved in maintaining grand jury secrecy" required those deletions. And as to the deliberative process privilege, he observed that it was "tailor-made" for the situation in which a prosecutor assesses the information being compiled before a final prosecutorial decision is made.

As to matters of personal privacy, our summary judgment motion set forth several broad principles of personal-privacy protection that Judge Flannery firmly embraced. He recognized that by their very nature, these prosecution memoranda (read: "pross memos," which is what prosecutors call them) contained many types of information about individuals who were investigated, but in the end, were not prosecuted at all: allegations, assessments, suppositions, or speculations of wrongdoing; summaries of statements and interviews regarding their activities; and information relating to the decision to prosecute or not to prosecute and therefore reflecting on the culpability of the individuals mentioned.

And at the outer edges, he said, the memoranda also contained discussions of individuals who were not themselves subjects of the investigation nor otherwise publicly associated with it, but whose privacy was nevertheless at stake. In all such instances, Judge Flannery reasoned, disclosure would subject the named individuals "to public embarrassment and ridicule" and would place them "in the position of having to defend [their] conduct without the benefit of a formal judicial proceeding."

As has been observed time and again (see Chapters Two and Eleven), once a favorable decision is handed down and you would bet your last dollar it will be appealed by the other side, you get less excited about it and just regard it as "Round One" in the case. A special "plus factor" in this case, though, was that after Judge Flannery ruled, the plaintiff did not proceed to press my Archives team to begin processing more records.[12] Rather, it merely noticed an appeal, almost as if it did not want any processing done until it had had a chance to reverse Judge Flannery's rulings on the standards to be applied.

So the *Fund for Constitutional Government* case headed for "Round Two" in the D.C. Circuit Court of Appeals. This time, unlike in the *Abramson* case (see Chapter Eleven), I had no time obstacle to handling the case on appeal that I could not overcome. And I had every intention of personally ensuring that the precedent-setting rulings that we had obtained from Judge Flannery more than survived appeal.

On appeal, the issues were briefed on both sides as if our lives depended on it. This time, Dobrovir and Oakes had the benefit of having more intellectual firepower for that purpose, in the form of young Erwin Chemerinsky,[13] but that meant that they devoted much time, space (read: in their briefs), and energy on arguments that in my view were marginal at best (and dangerous at worst). For instance, they tried to import tort law into the realm of the FOIA by contending that anyone who arguably was a "public figure" was not entitled to receive personal-privacy protection under Exemption 7(C).

In a similar vein, they also argued that high-level government and corporate officials, even when acting in their personal rather than their official capacities, were likewise unentitled to the protection of that FOIA exemption -- categorically. And they asked the D.C. Circuit to lay down a firm FOIA rule to the effect that individuals considered for criminal prosecution should be "hung out to dry" even when the prosecutor decides, for any of myriad reasons, not to proceed with any prosecution at all.

I realized that if the D.C. Circuit accepted any of this, especially as the leading circuit court of appeals for the FOIA,[14] then the protective scope of Exemption 7(C) would be greatly diminished, perhaps for years to come. (This was still only 1980, mind you, when FOIA case law, particularly at the appellate level, was both sparse and relatively young.) So I took these arguments head-on, demonstrating why and how they were utterly unrealistic in the real world of federal prosecutorial decisionmaking.

In the district court below, I had had the advantage of having a former United States Attorney hear the case, bringing his perspective to bear on such things. So as I was writing the appellee's brief, I took his perspective on the issues, arguing why his view of the case ought to be upheld. And that is when I received word of a gigantic "gift" in the case: When the D.C. Circuit panel for the case was announced, I saw that it included a judge from the district court who would be sitting "by designation"[15] -- former United States Attorney Oliver Gasch!

Now, one might think that I was happy just to be arguing a case before a judge whom I knew so well -- he actually winked at my wife Debbie as she entered the courtroom -- but in my mind that paled next to the fact that Judge Gasch, like Judge Flannery before him, brought experience as a United States Attorney to the case. He knew (and I knew that he knew) how cases actually develop in federal prosecutors' offices, how in big investigations many people are scrutinized for possible prosecutable conduct, and how some of them simply get "caught up" in an investigation without ever having done anything that rises to a prosecutable level. And how it sometimes, especially in an exceptionally big case, turns out that many of them are just flat-out innocent of any wrongdoing whatsoever.

So that is how I argued the case, when on November 3, 1980, the time came for it. For the privacy part of the case, I argued as if it was only Judge Gasch on the Bench, by making what amounted to a plea on behalf of all those individuals who are mentioned or worse in "pross memos," who simply do not deserve to have their names sullied and bandied about in public, without having any public forum in which they could clear their names and restore their reputations. And for the grand jury secrecy part of the case, I argued that my opponents were espousing an unrealistic view of how grand juries (and federal prosecutors) actually operate.

This all paid off big-time when it turned out that not only did we receive a big win in our favor, but Judge Gasch was the author of the Court's opinion. That opinion, issued in June of 1981, upheld Judge Flannery on both the personal privacy and grand jury secrecy parts of the case,[16] firmly rejecting all of the arguments that had been made by the team of Dobrovir, Oakes, and Chemerinsky to the contrary. And it vindicated all the hard work that had been put into the case by my own litigation-support team at the Archives.

First, Judge Gasch put to rest the notion that "public figures" (or high-level government or corporate officials) should not receive the benefits of Exemption 7(C)'s privacy protections. Emphasizing the status of the individuals involved who were investigated but were never subsequently indicted,"[17] he broadly declared that "revelation of the fact that [any] individual has been investigated for suspected criminal activity represents a significant intrusion on that individual's privacy cognizable under Exemption 7(C)."

Moreover, he then made the even deeper point that "[t]he degree of intrusion *is indeed potentially augmented by* the fact[s] that the individual is a well-known figure and the investigation [is] one which attracts as much national attention as those conducted by the WSPF." As such, he established a basis for the Government position that a case's notoriety can actually cut in favor of *nondisclosure* in the public-interest balancing of interests required under Exemption 7(C), not the other way around.

In fact, Judge Gasch observed, "[t]here can be no clearer example of an unwarranted invasion of personal privacy than to release to the public that another individual was the subject of an FBI investigation." Doing so, he recognized, "would produce the unwarranted result of placing the named individuals in the position of having to defend their conduct in the public forum outside of the procedural protections normally afforded the accused in criminal proceedings." Their interests in avoiding that, he declared, "cannot be overridden by a general public curiosity."

Over the years, the D.C. Circuit's *Fund for Constitutional Government* decision has withstood the test of time as one of the FOIA's leading precedents, for more than four decades now, still cited for its authoritative force even today.[18] There are few if any such decisions in any appellate court, and on any FOIA issue, about which that can be said.

CHAPTER THIRTEEN

Law Enforcement Privacy Protection

"Which office do I go to to get my reputation back?"

-- Former Secretary of Labor Raymond J. Donovan, upon his acquittal, May 25, 1987

As is described immediately above, in a particularly vital section of the 1974 FOIA Amendments Congress took what originally was a categorical exemption from disclosure for all law enforcement files and replaced it with, among other things, more specific exemption protection for the types of sensitive personal-privacy information that can exist in such files. This laid the groundwork for "law enforcement privacy protection," under FOIA Exemption 7(C), as a distinct realm of government secrecy and a major part of the administration of the Freedom of Information Act.

This exemption area includes all of the particular personal details that one would expect to find in records compiled for law enforcement purposes: The personal characteristics of investigatory subjects,[1] their background information, aspects of their conduct, opinions (especially prosecutorial ones) expressed about them, and evidence compiled against them are all part of this, as are other sensitive personal details that such persons ordinarily would not want or expect to be made public -- unless that person is prosecuted and they properly become public through that prosecution, of course.

But before the sensitivity of such things is considered, the predominant question under Exemption 7(C) is whether an individual will be publicly identified as involved in a law enforcement investigation at all, as a threshold matter. In other words, if it is appropriate to withhold even the abstract fact that someone is (or was) of investigatory interest to an agency of federal law enforcement, then that will (read: analytically) prevent the Federal Government from making public that overarching fact.[2]

This means that Exemption 7(C)'s prohibition against "an unwarranted invasion of personal privacy" can sweep quite broadly, almost as much as the categorical file exemption (read: Exemption 7, before it was amended) that it replaced. And it makes the very status of any individual who is named in law enforcement records a key initial consideration for how those records will be processed for disclosure under the FOIA.

This in turn brings prominently into play some basic principles about law enforcement privacy protection. Most basic is that any revelation of the fact that an individual is being (or has been) investigated for suspected criminal activity represents a significant intrusion on that individual's privacy interests cognizable under Exemption 7(C). Stated another way, there can be no clearer example of an unwarranted invasion of personal privacy than to disclose to the public that someone is or was the subject of an FBI (or other type of law enforcement) investigation. The means that federal law enforcement agencies must withhold the names of individuals who are investigated for suspected criminal activity but are never subsequently indicted or otherwise charged.[3]

Indeed, as the district court judge in the *Fund for Constitutional Government* case discussed in the immediately preceding chapter observed, to do otherwise would subject the named individuals to "public embarrassment and ridicule" and would place them "in the position of having to defend [their] conduct without the benefit of a formal judicial proceeding." Moreover, any such defense would by definition be in a public forum outside of the procedural protections normally afforded the accused in criminal proceedings.[4]

Furthermore, the degree of privacy invasion occasioned by public disclosure of this threshold fact is potentially augmented (read: not at all diminished) if the individual is a "public figure," including both government and private-sector officials. As such, most notably, the "tort standard" commonly applicable in libel and other defamation cases simply does not apply.

And speaking of the "degree of privacy invasion" involved, these principles include recognition of the fact that, beyond those of investigatory subjects, the names of all sorts of people are contained in raw investigatory files -- from witnesses to potential witnesses to cooperating information providers to people who refuse to provide information to relatives to "known associates" to mere bystanders and to individuals initially "mixed up" with other people. Indeed, the mere fact that the name of any such person, or anyone else for that matter, appears in a law enforcement file is highly sensitive and if disclosed, even in general, can be stigmatizing. This is the very basis for the now-universal use of what we in the early 1980s started referring to as "privacy Glomarization" (see Chapter Seventeen).

Lastly, for purposes of the "balancing of interests" that is undertaken to implement Exemption 7(C)'s "unwarranted invasion" standard (read: what is called the "public interest balancing" test), this personal-privacy interest cannot be overridden by any general public curiosity in a matter. Indeed, as the United States Supreme Court emphasized in its *Favish* decision (see Chapter Three), it would take a distinct, non-conjectural public interest in disclosure to "warrant" such a result.

What this all adds up to is that everyone has the right to be investigated (or even considered for possible investigation) by federal law enforcement agencies (including inspectors general, professional responsibility offices, and other ethics offices for federal employees) without having that very fact become known to anyone who does not have a legitimate "need to know" about the agency's investigatory interest in him or her.[5] All sorts of people are investigated for all sorts of things all the time, but that does not mean that they should be "outed" as such.

Indeed, they are entitled to have that take place "behind closed doors" -- without damage to personal reputation, professional standing, and these days through ubiquitous bandying about on social media -- unless and until an investigation "pans out" in the form of an indictment or the preferral of criminal (or in some cases civil enforcement) charges. Another, less elegant way of expressing this is: "You just do not ever leak the name of the subject of an investigation!"[6] Rather, one should carefully guard its secrecy.

These basic principles are routinely taught to federal investigators, federal prosecutors, and federal FOIA officers alike.[7] And they are followed universally, almost without exception,[8] for the benefit of both members of the public and law enforcement agencies as well. But every now and then, much more so in relatively recent years than previously, there have been departures from the rule. And some of them have been, in my view, utterly atrocious, such as the one in 2002 in which it became painfully obvious that Attorney General John D. Ashcroft just "never got the memo."

This prime example is the case of Dr. Steven J. Hatfill, who regrettably came to be known as the "Anthrax Killer." Lest it be forgotten, just a week after the horrors of September 11, 2001, we experienced another tragic, ongoing security threat in the form of envelopes containing the deadly substance anthrax that were mailed to several high-profile targets, which as it continued for weeks on end managed to terrorize Americans anew. Beginning on September 18, what turned out to be a total of seven letter envelopes containing anthrax spores were received by several news media offices and by two Democrat Senators, killing five people and seriously infecting 17 others.

These anthrax attacks came in two waves, exactly three weeks apart. The first set of envelopes all had a Trenton, New Jersey, postmark dated September 18, 2001. Five letters were believed to have been mailed at that time, to NBC News, ABC News, CBS News, the *New York Post* in New York City, and to the *National Enquirer* publication at American Media, Inc., located in Boca Raton, Florida. Two more anthrax letters, bearing the same Trenton postmark, were dated October 9, a full 21 days after the first mailing.[9] These letters were addressed to Democratic Senators Thomas A. Daschle and Patrick J. Leahy of South Dakota and Vermont. The Daschle letter was opened by an aide of his on October 15, whereupon mail service throughout the Federal Government was sharply curtailed or shut down.[10] The unopened Leahy letter was discovered in an impounded mailbag on November 16.[11]

All told, 22 people developed anthrax infections, 11 of whom contracted the especially life-threatening inhalational variety. Five died of inhalational anthrax: An employee of American Media; two employees of the Brentwood mail facility in Washington, D.C., where anthrax spores seemed to have had exceptional motility; and two people whose source of exposure was never determined, a resident of the Bronx who worked in Manhattan and a 94-year-old widow who lived in Oxford, Connecticut.[12]

All across the country, but especially on the East Coast, people suddenly feared opening their mail, most particularly any received at Federal Government offices in Washington, D.C. And all of this soon spurred a nationwide manhunt for the heinous perpetrator(s), whom experts said must have had rare proficiency in working with that deadly substance in order to manage to do such a sophisticated thing.

Dr. Hatfill was a physician and biological weapons expert who worked at a Defense Department facility known as Fort Detrick, in Frederick, Maryland (just down the road from where my parents lived at the time and across the street from where my youngest brother lives now). He had the misfortune of being one of few people in the world who possessed the access, experience, and skill to work with anthrax spores that scientists said would have been required in order to achieve such terrible results. And as with other such anthrax experts, he soon fell under relatively routine investigatory suspicion (read: internally within the FBI) as a possible perpetrator of these attacks, only in his case the suspicions grew greater and greater as he was investigated further.

In August of 2002, under much public pressure to solve the crime and take the killer "off the streets," Attorney General John Ashcroft blithely yet pointedly labeled Hatfill a "person of interest" in the FBI's anthrax investigation at a press conference held in Newark, New Jersey.[13] By all accounts, this phrase had never previously been used by any law enforcement authority until it was irresponsibly coined by an officer of the King County Sheriff's Office, at the outset of her career, during the investigation of a murderer known as the "Green River Killer" in 1986.[14] The person identified by her as a "person of interest" in that case turned out to be completely innocent of the serial murders being investigated and was later awarded $30,000 as a settlement of his lawsuit against three Seattle area news organizations. In my view, it was the sheriff's office that was most culpable for that.

But this phrase was used by Ashcroft, over and over and seemingly quite routinely,[15] when he was under that growing public pressure to find the anthrax perpetrator and relieve the public's fear of what he (read: the perpetrator) had been doing. In other words, he (read: Ashcroft) was doing the sort of thing that politicians do do -- respond to public pressure -- he just did it to the wrong guy at the wrong time.[16]

Dr. Hatfill, as it turned out, was not the "Anthrax Killer." He just was a victim of, *inter alia*, an awful combination of circumstances -- from large coincidences to small flukes in his background -- that made it look superficially like he was in fact that person. Which is what indeed does happen within the realm of law enforcement sometimes, as is often reflected in literature: The person who seems "dead solid perfect" as the killer near the beginning of the book or movie turns out to be not in fact guilty; rather, it's some other guy.

Well, in this case it turned out (read: eventually) that there actually was "another guy," -- a different military scientist at Fort Detrick by the name of Dr. Bruce E. Ivins -- who years later (read: not until 2008), just before he committed suicide, was suspected by the FBI to be the sole perpetrator of the anthrax attacks, though some people, based upon some contradictory evidence, thought otherwise. So where did that leave poor Dr. Steven Hatfill, having been identified by no less a law enforcement authority than the Nation's attorney general as the prime (read: only) suspect in the case, which as a practical matter meant "the perpetrator" in the public's eyes?

Well, it left him with having had his life greatly shattered, both personally and professionally, and with having undergone years (read: almost six of them) of public suspicion and law enforcement harassment (read: from his perspective, not from the FBI's), to say the least. Or as one of his attorneys, Victor M. Glasberg, put it at the time: "Steve's life has been devastated by a drumbeat of innuendo, implication, and speculation. We have a frightening public attack on an individual who, guilty or not, should not be exposed to this type of public opprobrium based on speculation."[17]

That pretty well sums up the underpinning for this law enforcement privacy principle, I think, except for one additional thing: On June 27, 2008, the United States Department of Justice announced that it was settling Steven Hatfill's Privacy Act lawsuit for $4.6 million (atop undisclosed settlements of his parallel suits against several news organizations), as it officially exonerated him of any involvement in the anthrax attacks.[18]

* * * * *

Now the sad case of Richard A. Jewell was another matter. The late Richard A. Jewell, ironically, was a very patriotic man. Not the sharpest knife in the drawer, by any means, but he was civic-minded, diligent at work, and quite easy-going, perhaps to a fault. And he got himself entangled in one of the most high-profile manhunts in American history, in which he was suddenly branded with the label "Olympic Park Bomber."

This all started on the evening of July 27, 1996, when a huge pipe bomb (read: actually only one of three pipes that were packaged together) exploded at Centennial Olympic Park in Atlanta during the 1996 Summer Olympic Games. One person was killed by the blast directly, one died of a heart attack running to the scene, and 111 people were injured. And there was no doubt but that the death and injury toll would have been much, much higher were it not for the alertly prescient efforts of a security guard at the scene -- Richard Jewell.

Jewell was the one who noticed the abandoned bomb bag (read: "field pack" or knapsack) underneath a bench alongside of an NBC broadcast tower well before the blast. He alerted local police, who after a period of disbelief called in their bomb squad. The bomb was briefly examined, while Jewell took the initiative of warning everyone in the tower to evacuate. And then he warned everyone on the ground to move as far away from the bench as quickly as they could; he was still in the process of herding them away when the bomb exploded.

Initially, of course, Jewell was hailed as a hero for what he had done, both for alertly discovering the bomb and for so diligently and selflessly moving nearby spectators to safety. For example, NBC's Katie Couric, who was on site covering the Olympics, said in interviewing him: "You were in the right place at the right time and you did the right thing, Richard."

Jewell, a rather hapless fellow still living with his mother at age 33, went home to tell her about what had happened and to see himself interviewed on television, where he was remarkably humble about his accomplishment. This might have been because his first or second thought after the explosion was that it could possibly lead to him obtaining a long-sought job in law enforcement somewhere.

Indeed, the media coverage of the incident was especially strong, partly because so many foreign media outlets were present in Atlanta at the time for Olympics coverage. And as a "human interest" story as well as "security" one, it proceeded to resonate around the world. This turned out to be very unfortunate for Richard Jewell.

As for the Olympic Games themselves, the local "powers that were" (read: primarily the International Olympic Committee) quickly decided that they should go on, that it was sufficiently "safe" for both the athletes and the spectators to return to all Olympic venues. But this placed even greater pressure on all law enforcement agencies (read: mostly the FBI) to "catch the bomber" before he or she might strike again.[19]

That pressure was the downfall of Richard Jewell, because it converted the FBI's relatively routine review of Jewell's candidacy for "perpetrator" in the case (read: along the lines of "the butler did it" or "always suspect the husband") into an intense focus on him as maybe the easy key to readily solving it. This strong pressure was personified by FBI Director Louis J. Freeh, a considerably intense man, who evidently wanted the Bureau to solve the case "sooner rather than later" and injected himself into the day-to-day handling of it -- much more intensively than is perhaps "normal" for an FBI director.[20]

So the FBI Special Agents working the case immediately "profiled" Jewell (read: they applied the psychological analysis methods that had been pioneered at the FBI Academy) and it was not long before they reached the easy preliminary conclusion that he matched the classic "lone bomber" profile almost across the board, with a "hero complex" diagnosis thrown in for good measure.[21] And no one outside of law enforcement circles knew anything about this, of course, which is how it should have been.

But then came a "blast" unlike that of any mere pipe bomb: Somebody leaked to a reporter for *The Atlanta Journal-Constitution* ("*AJC,*" to its rapt readers) the facts that the FBI already had an individual of investigatory "focus" in the case and that he was none other than "hero-turned-villain" (read: my words, not the *AJC*'s) Richard A. Jewell.[22] This leaker is dramatically depicted in the Clint Eastwood-directed film *Richard Jewell* as an experienced FBI Special Agent named "Tom Shaw," as he was slyly enticed into doing this by scoop-hungry *AJC* reporter Kathy Scruggs.[23]

And of course all hell broke loose onto the head of Richard Jewell, as a "media circus" ensued. First he was a hero, but then, in a flash, the media called him a suspect and he became a public spectacle. Every aspect of his life, from the most mundane to the more embarrassing, was dragged through the court of public opinion. Reporters and television crews were camped out at his doorstep morning, noon, and night for days on end, taking a particular toll on his mother. Only by virtue of Jewell's optimistic (read: naïve) personality did he make it through the long ordeal of being reviled and mocked in the media for such a lengthy period of time, not to mention being actively investigated by the FBI.[24] It seemed that despite all of this, all that had happened to him and was continuing to happen to him, he continued to maintain a fundamental faith that the American system of justice would eventually exonerate him.

And it did, eventually. On October 26, 1996, eighty-eight days after his name was leaked, the Department of Justice, speaking for the FBI, declared that Jewell was no longer a person of any investigative interest to it.[25] But no direct apology was forthcoming, just a general statement of regret about the leak involved. The following summer, though, many months too late, Attorney General Janet Reno expressed her own regret over the damning leak. Speaking with her usual candor and succinctness, she said: "I'm very sorry it happened. I think we owe him an apology."[26]

Jewell finally obtained savvy counsel (read: much savvier than himself) who assisted him in seeking some vindication through litigation. He did not sue the FBI, accepting the belated apology from Attorney General Janet Reno instead,[27] but he did sue a number of media outlets that continuously proliferated his "story," sometimes by going to great lengths (read: very arguably overboard) for the entertainment of their audiences. He filed libel and defamation lawsuits against CNN, NBC News, *The Atlanta Journal-Constitution*, and *The New York Post*.

The outcomes of these cases were perhaps best predicted by late-night TV host Jay Leno, who had mercilessly ridiculed Jewell (and even also his mother) seemingly nonstop since the bombing took place. On his "Tonight Show" for October 28, 1996, Leno apologized to Jewell for making him the butt of those jokes and for calling him the "Una-doofus" (read: in reference to the Unabomber). "We did make fun of the guy, and now it turns out the FBI has nothing," acknowledged Leno, who went on to joke that his apology "has nothing to do with the fact if he wins his lawsuit with NBC he'll be my new boss."[28]

Indeed, Jewell reached an out-of-court settlement with NBC for more than a half-million dollars, based primarily on something that veteran anchor Tom Brokaw had said about him, which took him well down that road. For its part, CNN agreed to pay both Richard and Bobi Jewell a tidy sum for what it had done to them. And *The New York Post* is believed to have secretly settled the Jewells suit against it likewise.

As for *The Atlanta Journal-Constitution,* the media outlet that started it all, it wound up not having to pay Richard Jewell a dime -- and not just because he died before their protracted litigation came to fruition. The case reached Georgia's appellate courts, including its supreme court, leading ultimately to a Georgia Court of Appeals decision in the newspaper's favor. It concluded that "because the articles in their entirety were substantially true at the time they were published -- even though the investigators' suspicions were ultimately deemed unfounded," Jewell (and then his estate) had no legal recourse against that newspaper.

In an interview in 2006, a year before he died, however, Richard Jewell was reported to say that the lawsuits were "not about money"; the "vast majority" of it "went to lawyers or taxes," he said. To him, he stressed, "the lawsuits were about clearing [his] name" -- which is, after all, what the very idea of "law enforcement privacy protection" is all about.[29]

* * * * *

As bad as the cases of Hatfill and Jewell were, as examples of how *not* to protect law enforcement privacy, the case of Brandon Mayfield was in a way even worse. His very sad and corrupted story began with one of the two major "follow-on" terrorism events to occur in the wake of 9/11 -- the train bombings in Madrid in 2004.[30] And whereas both the Hatfill and Jewell fact patterns were each plagued with a group of particular circumstances that led to facile initial conclusions of their guilt (read: "It's just gotta be this guy; look at all these little things combined together."), Brandon Mayfield's case was triggered by one enormous thing: His fingerprints were mistakenly determined to be a match for fingerprints found in connection with the Madrid train bombings.

Those bombings occurred on March 11, 2004 (hence the sobriquet "M-11" used for it in Spain), with ten bombs exploding within a three-minute span on four different trains. The blasts killed 191 people in total and wounded an estimated 1600, and it was officially determined that they were perpetrated by eight militants associated with al-Qaeda, with crucial aid from a retired Spanish miner who sold the explosives to the terrorists but did not participate beyond that.

As part of their investigation of all this, Spanish law enforcement authorities came across a plastic bag containing detonation devices that were firmly believed to be connected to the explosives used. From this bag, they lifted a total of eight latent fingerprints that they then circulated worldwide through Interpol, which in turn led to their being "possibly matched" by the FBI through its vast fingerprint database. And that "possible match" (read: one of 20, as it turned out) was with Brandon Mayfield, a civil liberties attorney living near Portland, Oregon, whose prints had been taken when he was a platoon leader in the Army. Also, he is Muslim.

In addition to his religious beliefs, Mayfield was married to an Egyptian woman (which is why he converted to Islam); he just a year earlier had provided *pro bono* legal support to a member of the "Portland Seven," a group of Muslims convicted of trying to travel to Afghanistan to help the Taliban; he worshipped at the same mosque as some of that group; and he sometimes was perceived to be "acting suspiciously" while Special Agents from the FBI's Portland Field Office surveilled his every movement (as well as those of his wife and their three children) for several weeks.[31] To those FBI Special Agents "working the case," this appeared to add up to a "slam dunk" case,[32] just as with Hatfill two years earlier and with Jewell in 1996 (which itself perhaps should have warned them that something other than Mayfield was amiss).[33]

So in May of 2004, almost two months after the Madrid bombings, Mayfield was arrested by the FBI, which held him as a "material witness" to that crime, and had him in custody for a period of more than two weeks. (During this time, his family members were not told where he was being held. Early on, though, both he and his family were told that he was being held as a "primary suspect" on offenses that were punishable by death and that the FBI had in fact made a "100% match" of his fingerprints with the fingerprints from the Madrid bombing.) The very first part of this custodial time period was arguably "legitimate," but the remainder of it was cleverly (read: perniciously) engineered (no pun intended) by the Bureau.

And here is what sets this case apart: The Bureau had reached the point at which, despite what it had anticipated, it was simply unable to gather any concrete corroborating evidence against Mayfield (read: enough to legitimately continue to hold him in custody), so it devised a plan by which it leaked (read: to reporters, under promises of confidentiality, ostensibly) Mayfield's name as a "Madrid bombing suspect" and then, when news of this circulated widely and the expected public reaction set in, it proceeded to "offer" him the option of staying in jail because by then he truly needed "protective custody." Outrageous![34]

All that time, moreover, the FBI did a wholly inadequate job on following through with Mayfield's fingerprint "match." Had the FBI done so, and not so firmly accepted what its own laboratory analysts said only preliminarily,[35] even the zealous Special Agents of the Portland Field Office doubtless would not have moved forward as they did.[36] Indeed, even before they arrested Mayfield, Spain's law enforcement authorities had concluded that, though the fingerprints were "similar," they viewed Mayfield's as a "negative match."[37] A lot of good that did him.

To top all of this off, it was not long before the Spanish authorities matched the bombing fingerprints "conclusively" to those of the actual terrorist, Algerian national Ouhane Daoud. Inexcusably, Brandon Mayfield was not released from custody until the day after this happened -- and even at that, adding insult to injury, he remained under a spurious gag order about the whole matter for another five days.

Eventually (read: inevitably), the FBI grudgingly admitted its mistakes and apologized to both Brandon Mayfield and his family members for what it had done to them, claiming that it all was just due to "an extremely unusual confluence of events." Notably, however, the Bureau did not offer any damages settlement to him at that time.

So in response, Mayfield filed several lawsuits over the invasions of his privacy, including one for blatant violation of his Privacy Act rights in connection with the FBI's contrived "leak," pointing out that the FBI had "turned his life upside down" through its sheer (read: intentional or willful) negligence (see Chapter Fourteen) and its evident bias toward Muslims.[38] And the fact that he was a seasoned litigator doubtless added to the acuteness of his claims.[39]

This led to a settlement in the amount of $2,000,000, which is much less than the Government had to pay to Steven Hatfill, of course, but then again, Hatfill's period of privacy abuse lasted much, much longer. And this settlement, signed by the Court on November 29, 2006, called for a more formal, written apology from the Department of Justice for all that the FBI had done to the Mayfield family. But it fell far short of meeting its obligations to provide proper "law enforcement privacy protection" for all persons, no matter what their backgrounds might be.

* * * * *

Although these three cases -- Hatfill, Jewel, and Mayfield -- are the best bad examples of federal agencies breaching "law enforcement privacy" that I can remember,[40] this does not mean that there are no others,[41] some of which are competitive in their own ways but involve individuals who, for one reason or another, are not the type of individuals who sue their government.[42] Former Army General David H. Petraeus, who retired from the Army to be director of the Central Intelligence Agency, became one such privacy victim in 2012.

General Petraeus was a married four-star Army officer who got caught up (read: if that's what they're calling it these days) in a sexual relationship with his "biographer" (read: that's definitely what they're calling it these days) and made the further, extra-legal mistake of providing her (read: Paula D. Broadwell, whose name has since entered the public domain) with documents that contained much classified information. During 2011, Petraeus gave her several notebooks in which during his military career he had amassed information that included the identities of covert officers, military code words, and descriptions of war strategy, intelligence capabilities, and diplomatic talks, as well as information learned through White House National Security Council meetings. He knew better, of course, and this constituted very serious wrongdoing.

And while Petraeus was under FBI investigation for this, with the affair known by neither his wife nor the general public, somebody (read: probably at the FBI) leaked this to *The New York Times*, which promptly did what it does: It published the story, including the fact that prosecutors (read: both in the FBI and at Main Justice) had recommended that felony charges be brought against him.[43] That caused quite a stir in several quarters, as might be imagined.

In response, Petraeus did what philandering husbands (not to mention CIA directors) often do: He flatly denied the allegations and he even brazenly stated that he had no interest in any sort of a plea deal about them. Most unfortunately for him, this even included lying to the FBI,[44] which as many television viewers know, one simply does not do, as it is a felony.[45]

Ultimately, under enormous public pressure (not to mention political pressure from the White House, just prior to the 2012 presidential election), Petraeus resigned as CIA director, admitted his wrongdoing, apologized for it by expressing "deep regret" (read: of course), and proceeded to negotiate one hell of a good plea deal in which he pled guilty to just one little misdemeanor charge of "mishandling classified information" (read: apparently that's what they *are* calling what Petraeus did these days). This development in the case left both the military and the legal communities astonished, as it constituted extremely light treatment, even for a CIA director.[46]

Moreover, when it came time for him to be sentenced, the prosecutors generously recommended that Petraeus receive only a $40,000 fine and two years of probation. On April 23, 2013, though, a federal judge sentenced him to that two years of probation but more than doubled the fine to $100,000. That latter part was perhaps a nominal recognition of the fact that Petraeus had, in effect, "gotten away with murder."[47]

At the bottom of all of this, however, was the fact that -- like Steven Hatfill, Richard Jewell, and Brandon Mayfield -- David Petraeus was still grievously victimized by a wrongful government disclosure of law enforcement information that, "by all that's right and holy" (read: as mandated by the Privacy Act), ought to have been kept secret unless and until he was publicly prosecuted. Or, less legally speaking, in his own version of "sex, drugs, and rock 'n roll" (see Chapter Twenty-Five), Petraeus got screwed not only by his biographer-cum-paramour, but also by the person(s) who leaked the details of his situation to *The New York Times*.

But the distinctive thing about General Petraeus was that although he was unquestionably victimized and damaged (read: both professionally and in his marriage)[48] by a government leak, very much unlike his fellow "leakees" he most certainly did not seek compensation for his harm, under the Privacy Act or otherwise. Rather, he evidently was not inclined to sue the very government that had lifted him to such heights in the first place. Nevertheless, his circumstances (and those of another general, discussed immediately below) well illustrate the damage that can be done to an individual when a law enforcement agency fails to provide appropriate protection of its investigatory information.

*　*　*　*　*

Another such victim was General John R. Allen, another four-star general, who was a close colleague of General Petraeus and with whom he shared having a quite unusual "email friendship" (read: at the total magnitude of tens of thousands of exchanges) with a "military groupie/socialite" by the name of Jill Kelley (née Gilberte Khawam), who frequently entertained senior military officers from nearby MacDill Air Force Base (the home base of both Petraeus and Allen) at lavish parties held in her luxurious Tampa home. Now this is where the whole story (read: as to both generals, Petraeus and Allen) gets even more "dense."

You see, even though Jill Kelley was happily married to a local oncology surgeon (read: named Scott, the "nice guy" of the piece), she nevertheless carried on what could most charitably be described as a "highly flirtatious" (read: and in its own way, highly successful) social relationship with General Petraeus (and somewhat less so with General Allen), word of which somehow reached Petraeus's biographer/paramour -- the aforementioned Paula Broadwell, who was a respected academic, a West Point graduate, and a lieutenant colonel in the U.S. Army Reserves -- even hundreds of miles away.

And in an unmistakably jealous reaction to someone whom she evidently saw as a potential romantic rival, Colonel Broadwell then sent threatening email messages -- many, many of them -- to Jill Kelley, warning her to "stay away" from David Petraeus. Even Kelley's husband Scott received some such emails, all of which alarmed the hell out of them both because they could not imagine from whence they came.[49] These email messages were sent beginning in mid-May of 2012 and they continued for a period of months.

So, what did Jill Kelley do? She decided to consult with another social acquaintance of hers (read: apparently, there was a long list), who happened to be a Special Agent of the FBI, and she then brought him into her confidence (read: as another aspect of "secrecy").[50] This fellow, veteran FBI Special Agent Frederick W. Humphries II, aggressively took this as her making a "cyber-stalking" complaint and proceeded to actively (read: zealously) pursue it within the FBI. After a while, dissatisfied with his own agency's lack of progress on the case, Humphries rashly took the wrongful step of disclosing information about the case to a Member of

Congress, then-House Majority Leader Eric Cantor. Whatever happened to it after that step remains unknown.

So back to General Allen. He, like Jill Kelley, began receiving anonymous email messages (read: from Broadwell), only his warned him to "stay away" from Jill Kelley (read: same language, but not exactly the same threat). Unbeknownst to him, he had by then become involved in this FBI investigation because he, too, had been a very active email correspondent of Jill Kelley's, though not of the same magnitude as Petraeus, and he therefore came under suspicion of, generally stated (pun intended), committing "some sort of wrongdoing." Now this was fine, insofar as it went, except that this sensitive "law enforcement fact" was wrongfully made known to the media as well. And it was reported to the public, much to General Allen's personal and professional embarrassment.

How this exactly came about has never been conclusively and officially determined. But what *was* well known by the Department of Defense press corps is that during a return flight from Hawaii on November 13, 2012, Secretary of Defense Leon E. Panetta's general counsel, who was aboard, received a direct communication from the FBI about the Allen/Petraeus/Kelley emails, whereupon Defense Secretary Panetta was immediately informed. And by the time that plane landed, the reporters aboard it were fully informed of General Allen's situation (and perhaps that of General Petraeus also, though he had by then resigned as DCI).

Hence, in Secretary of Defense Panetta, we had another agency head, this time of cabinet rank, and someone with vast Federal Government experience, who apparently "didn't get the memo"[51] about the protection of such sensitive law enforcement information, not to mention of individuals under the Privacy Act of 1974. Not to worry, though, as General Allen, like General Petraeus, was not the type to sue his own government for damages.[52]

CHAPTER FOURTEEN
The Privacy Act

"No one likes to see a government folder with his name on it."

-- Stephen King, *Firestarter*, 1980

Among the Office of Information and Privacy's major responsibilities was to administer the Department of Justice's implementation of the Privacy Act of 1974, that "sister" statute to the Freedom of Information Act that Congress enacted in its burst of "post-Watergate" fervor near the end of that year.[1] Unlike the FOIA, for which the Attorney General holds governmentwide policy responsibility under the law, such responsibility for the Privacy Act was given to another federal agency, the Office of Management and Budget ("OMB," to its many detractors) within the Executive Office of the President ("EOP," to its high-level inhabitants), perhaps because the Justice Department was smart enough to avoid it.[2] But by the end of the first Reagan term, OMB started to fall down on the job on this, and the Justice Department (read: OIP) soon began picking up the Privacy Act slack for it across the Federal Government.[3]

The Privacy Act is a privacy-protection and government record disclosure statute that in addition to affording first-party access to records about individuals regulates the Federal Government's collection, maintenance, use, and disclosure of information about individuals (which is sometimes referred to as "fair information practices"). It took effect on September 27, 1975, as the first such comprehensive privacy-protection law enacted anywhere in the world. (In other words, the U.S. was out ahead of Scandinavia on this one.)

With respect to access to government records, the Privacy Act heavily overlaps the FOIA, though in contrast to that statute it affords rights only to United States citizens (plus persons holding lawful permanent residency, known as "LPRs"), and it applies only to records about such individuals that are located within formal "systems of records" maintained by executive branch agencies. Record retrieval according to an individual's name or personal identifier is a key jurisdictional element of it as well.[4]

Consequently, if access to a record is properly requested under the Privacy Act as well as under the FOIA, it can be withheld only if it is exempt from disclosure under both statutes. Generally speaking, and apart from the Privacy Act's special systemwide exemptions for all records of the Central Intelligence Agency and certain types of law enforcement files, the Privacy Act's access exemptions are narrower than those of FOIA: They do not include business information, most privileged information, and (ironically) information the disclosure of which would invade another person's personal-privacy interests.[5]

The heart of the Privacy Act, though, is the additional rights and protections that it provides to the individuals to whom particular agency records pertain. The first of these is a disclosure prohibition[6] that bars agencies from disclosing Privacy Act-protected information -- that is, records within systems of records that are retrieved[7] through use of a citizen's or LPR's name or identifier -- without that individual's written consent or unless one of several distinct disclosure-prohibition exceptions applies.

The major such exceptions to this prohibition are disclosures properly made within an agency; disclosures that are required by a FOIA request that the agency has received; disclosure to a congressional committee; disclosure in compliance with a federal court order; and a disclosure made in accordance with a specific "routine use" of that information, compatible with the purpose for which the information was obtained (for example, routine Justice Department sharing of judicial nominations information with the White House), that formally has been established (i.e., in a published "systems notice") for that "system of records."[8]

Notwithstanding its many exceptions, this statutory disclosure prohibition makes government agencies quite vulnerable to "wrongful disclosure" lawsuits that are brought by individuals who are the subjects of "leaks." There have been several high-profile such cases over the years, such as the ones brought by former CIA case officer Valerie E. Plame Wilson, anthrax investigation "person of interest" Steven J. Hatfill, accused Madrid train bomber Brandon Mayfield, Centennial Olympic Park bombing suspect Richard A. Jewell (see Chapter Thirteen), and former Assistant United States Attorney Richard G. Convertino.[9]

Another similar one is described in the Acknowledgments, as one in which I assisted the Department's Civil Division and its client the Office of Professional Responsibility in obtaining a successful Privacy Act judgment against a former Justice Department attorney who complained of the Department's referral of professional misconduct allegations against her to the District of Columbia and Maryland bar authorities in 1995. This was after that attorney made a blatant, admitted leak of internal information to my good friend Michael R. Isikoff at *Newsweek*.[10]

Next is the right to request amendment of records, correction of records, and/or expungement/expunction of records based on a showing that they are not accurate, relevant, timely, or complete. Agencies are required to have formal administrative processes by which individuals can obtain such relief, which can be advantageously preceded by the individual obtaining access to the records (in whole or in part), through a Privacy Act access request, in order to learn their contents.[11]

Also, as an alternative to amendment and correction, a dissatisfied individual is entitled to submit a brief counterstatement to a record, which the agency is required to attach to it (either physically or electronically) so that the challenged record will not be used or disseminated elsewhere without that accompaniment. And in all cases, an individual can request an accounting of any subsequent record dissemination.

Then there are the Privacy Act's "fair information practices" provisions, which largely pertain to the collection and maintenance of personal information. As for the former, agencies are required, wherever practicable, to collect such information from the individual directly, rather than from third-party sources, and to notify individuals whenever they are asked to supply personal information to the government of the consequences of doing so or not doing so, as the case may be.

There also is a provision, found in an uncodified section of the Act, that makes it unlawful for an agency to "deny to any individual any right, benefit, or privilege provided by law because of such individual's refusal to disclose his social security account number," except for inclusion in any record system that was established prior to its effective date of January 1, 1975. I litigated a precedent-setting case brought just three years after that date, *Benoit Otis Brookins II v. United States Department of State*, in which a young foreign service officer, standing on some principal, refused to provide his social security number in connection with a routine request for a "travel advance." I remember tracing the State Department's authority to maintain such information in a record system established during World War II, which provided the basis for a favorable district court judgment that was then upheld by the D.C. Circuit Court of Appeals.

As for record maintenance, the Privacy Act has two provisions that even after forty-five years remain relatively little known but that nevertheless contain potent agency obligations. The first, found in subsection (e)(5) of the Act, requires agencies to "maintain all records which are used by the agency in making any determination about any individual with such accuracy, relevance, timeliness, and completeness as is reasonably necessary to assure [sic] fairness to the individual in the determination."

The second, which is found in subsection (e)(7) of the Act and is potentially even broader in its sweep, commands that an agency shall "maintain no record describing how any individual exercises rights guaranteed by the First Amendment [to the U.S. Constitution] unless expressly authorized by statute," consented to by that individual, or deemed relevant to "an authorized law enforcement activity." Together, these two obscure provisions protect an individual's expressive and associational activities from being used against him or her by the Federal Government.

These provisions mean, for example, that when considering an applicant for a career employment position, a federal hiring official cannot indulge in the now-commonplace private-sector practice of "doing an Internet search" on that applicant and then jotting down on the application any pertinent (including derogatory) information found.[12] Indeed, such a step, taken as part of a corrupt hiring scheme during the George W. Bush Administration, became the basis of more than $500,000 in damages and attorney's fees that were paid by the Federal Government in the case of *Gerlich v. United States Department of Justice* in 2014 (see Chapter Forty-Three).

Civil damages are indeed available as a strong enforcement and deterrent mechanism under the Privacy Act, wherever a violation of its disclosure prohibition or of a "fair information practices" provision is shown to have been "intentional or willful" and to have had a demonstrable "adverse effect" on an individual. And as with the FOIA, court-awarded attorney's fees are available to successful Privacy Act litigants as well.

Beyond that, the Privacy Act has an even more powerful enforcement mechanism: It contains criminal penalties, at the misdemeanor level, that can be imposed against federal employees for willful violation of its provisions (except for its access and amendment provisions, which operate much like the FOIA). There have been more than a dozen such criminal prosecutions over the years, most often where the violator acted with a commercial motive, and OIP has regularly made good use of these examples for their *in terrorem* effect in its Privacy Act training.

Lastly, the Privacy Act is long overdue for legislative reform and updating, especially considering that it was drafted by Congress quite hurriedly in the wake of President Nixon's resignation in 1974 and contains both inconsistences and an outdated focus on information in paper (rather than electronic) form. Over the years, it has been amended significantly only once -- by the insertion of several "computer matching" provisions in 1988. The FOIA, by comparison, has been amended many times since 1974. Indeed, congressional oversight of the Privacy Act's governmentwide implementation has suffered from gross inattention since the mid-1980s, and most observers agree that it is long past time for it to be overhauled.[13]

CHAPTER FIFTEEN
The "Solo Source" Case

"Two communist soldiers are standing by the Berlin Wall during the Cold War.
Soldier 1: 'Are you thinking what I'm thinking?'
Soldier 2: 'Yes, I am.'
Soldier 1: 'Then I'll have to arrest you.'"

-- Old Cold War joke, circa 1960s

During the 1960s, the Federal Bureau of Investigation managed to pull off one of the most spectacular intelligence coups against the Kremlin (at least on American soil, which is where the Bureau operated) that anyone at the FBI (and eventually elsewhere) had ever seen. The target of this was the Communist Party of the United States ("CPUSA," to its American comrades), an organization that was perfectly legal -- it even fielded candidates in presidential elections -- but which unquestionably operated as a tool of the Soviet Union in the United States.

And the FBI had a rare motive for doing so, one having to do with two extremely valuable intelligence sources (though in "Bureau speak," they were "informants") who had operated precariously, but with enormous success, as high-level CPUSA members, as well as effective "double agents" for the FBI, since 1952. The first of these, Morris H. Childs (née Moishe Chilovsky), was a very highly valued member of the CPUSA's top leadership.

Beginning in the 1950s, Morris Childs acted as a secret courier on behalf of the American Communist Party, briefing Soviet officials on political affairs in the United States and carrying funds from Moscow to New York City and elsewhere to support the American Communist movement. Over the course of two decades of activity in this role, he played a major part in the clandestine transfer of nearly $30 million in Soviet subsidies to the American Communist movement, traveling dozens of times between the United States and Moscow.[1] This held enormous value to the CPUSA and gave him a leading "place at the table" of its leadership. He became both executive secretary of the New York Communist Party and a high-ranking member of the CPUSA's National Committee.[2]

Likewise, Morris's younger brother Jakob "Jack" Childs was also a high-ranking CPUSA official, due in no small part to the fact that he, like his brother, was very close to longtime CPUSA General Secretary Gus Hall (née Arvo Kustaa Halberg). While he had long operated in his older brother's shadow, Jack Childs was instrumental to launching Morris's CPUSA career when the latter was in ill health in the very early 1950s, though he never was the natural-born leader that Morris was. But the fact that he was such a close confidante of CPUSA leader Gus Hall, having been a personal aide to others in that position, carried him a long way in the organization.

Jack Childs was the first of the brothers to be recruited as an FBI informant,[3] as he was the less doctrinaire of the two, but then through him the Bureau soon recruited his brother Morris, as well. Their "handler" was FBI Special Agent Carl N. Freyman, who was only in his late 30s at the time and was looking to the future with the Childs brothers, especially Morris, who seemed to him to have strong "career" potential for rising on the American Communist scene, although he had a heart condition at the time. He also was the more intellectual of the two brothers, so Special Agent Freyman based his recruitment "pitch" to him partly on that.

It was not long before both Childs brothers were firmly in the FBI's embrace,[4] although for the first several years they provided the Bureau with "informant reports" that were less valuable than those of later years. But in those later years, as of the late 1950s, all through the 1960s, as well as the 1970s, into the 1980s, as Morris's CPUSA career blossomed,[5] he provided invaluable information to the FBI about both CPUSA and Kremlin activity.[6] This was a fantastic success.[7] And with a not-so-subtle wink to the fact that the Bureau had two persons named Childs informing for it, it drolly code-named them the "Solo Sources," with their overall activities dubbed "Operation Solo."[8]

However, in time, there arose a potential downside to this. One of the things about having a long-term informant (or "mole") well placed within a tight-knit organization with a solid institutional memory (such as the CPUSA, not to mention the Kremlin) is that he or she can become a victim of his or her own success. That was the risk that the Childs brothers certainly faced as the years went by -- and the FBI was rightly concerned about it.

By 1964, at a time of heightened espionage between the United States and the Soviet Union (i.e., not long after the Cuban Missile Crisis), the FBI's anxiety about this reached its peak. It had enjoyed what had seemed to it to be two "leaks" of sensitive information that it feared might hint to the CPUSA that there could be an informant in its midsts, particularly in connection with its secret Soviet subsidies. Because of the perceived loyalty of its high-level staff, it was difficult for the CPUSA to imagine that it did have such an informant (much less two) on the inside, but the Bureau increasingly feared that it was just "tempting fate" on its Solo Sources with the passage of time.[9]

So someone at the Bureau (exactly who is lost in the mists of time) had the brilliant idea of trying to take the pressure off of the Childs brothers by getting the CPUSA leadership to believe that it did indeed have an informant in its midsts, but that it was someone else, not either of the Solo Sources. To achieve this, the FBI employed what was known as a "snitch jacket" operation,[10] which involved using a false document that firmly made it appear that a "someone else" at the CPUSA was a Bureau informant. And they carefully selected William Albertson to be that "someone."[11]

The next step was to create a false informant document that would be adequate -- more than adequate, the Bureau wanted -- to the task. Fortunately, the FBI prides itself on having the best forgers this side of the European art markets practically on stand-by for this sort of thing. And it had its best forger prepare a bogus "informant report" in Albertson's handwriting that even he couldn't readily recognize as fake.[12] As a last touch, the report was prepared on the type of paper that was used by Albertson with a ballpoint pen of the type that he was known to use.

After that, all that remained was for the fake report to be placed in a location in which it could be credibly discovered by one of Albertson's colleagues -- i.e., under circumstances firmly indicating that it was Albertson who had fatefully misplaced it there. And the Bureau soon came up with a more-than-plausible scenario for that.

On July 5, 1964, the Bureau learned that the next day Albertson would be commuting with one of his CPUSA colleagues. Later that night, it broke into that car and left the forged document on the front seat where Albertson sat. The next day, of course, that CPUSA employee discovered the document, recognized it for what it was, and immediately brought it to Gus Hall.

This succeeded brilliantly, exactly as planned. The forged document completely convinced Hall and other senior CPUSA officials that it was Albertson who was the feared FBI informant. Albertson vehemently denied this, of course, very understandably so, but in the face of such an "informant report" he simply was not believed. And so he was unceremoniously expelled on the spot.

The CPUSA naturally thought that by taking this immediate action it had eliminated the informant threat that it had perceived (which is exactly what the Bureau had hoped for, of course), so it soon went back to "business as usual," except without Albertson.[13] And the Childs brothers (who ironically were well positioned to observe and report all of this from the "inside")[14] were able to continue in their roles, undisturbed and unthreatened, until old age forced their retirement more than a dozen years later.[15]

Indeed, the Childs brothers carried on just as they had been, with great success for both the CPUSA (ostensibly) and the FBI. Throughout the late 1960s and well into the 1970s, Morris and Jack traveled around the world as international CPUSA operatives.[16] During the early 1960s, they were able to pass along first-hand information about work for the CPUSA done in the early 1950s by a former secret Communist named Stanley D. Levison[17] -- who had gone on to become a mentor to Dr. Martin Luther King, Jr., which in turn became J. Edgar Hoover's rationale for subsequently classifying so much of the Bureau's information on King and perhaps further explained how deeply his hatred for King ran (see Chapter Three).[18]

This entire FBI operation was a masterstroke, from the Bureau's perspective, something to go down in the annals of FBI successes as one of its greatest and cleverest (if not the cleverest) counterintelligence operations of all time. First and foremost, it crucially protected the safety (read: lives) of both of the Childs brothers, allowing their interconnected covers to survive even in the face of the growing circumstantial evidence that had begun to encircle them.

What is more, in one "swell foop," as they would say, it functionally disabled a highly valued Cold War opponent who had in fact been a very effective and loyal member of the CPUSA. I remember reading an FBI report on the operation stating that Albertson was chosen for this partly because he was one of the most "efficient" and "capable" people that the CPUSA had, a hardworking, highly effective party leader, who together with his wife Lillie seemed to be model CPUSA members.

Ordinarily, the secret of the Solo Sources (i.e., even their very existence) would have remained buried within the bowels of the FBI perhaps forever, as was its policy and practice with its informants, all the more so if they were national security sources (see Chapter Sixteen, for example). Not even the Bureau's ostensible overlords in Main Justice (on different floors, until 1975) would have known about it: There was no real "need to know." And with that, the dazzling success of "L'Affaire Albertson" would have remained hidden as well.

But that's where the Freedom of Information Act, in tandem with the "law of unintended consequences," came into play. In 1975, after the effective date of the 1974 FOIA Amendments, which in effect subjected the FBI to the FOIA for the first time, there were a few journalists and historians who jumped at that chance to make some high-impact FOIA request to it "right out of the box." One of the most persistent (as well as perspicacious) of these early FOIA requesters was NBC Legal Correspondent Carl Stern.[19] Oh, and did I say that he was lucky?

Yes, Carl was lucky, indeed, because he benefited from the fact that the Bureau's handling of its FOIA requests in those early, mid-1970s days was, in a word, shoddy. After the 1974 FOIA Amendments became effective as of February 1975, it took nearly three years before the Bureau managed to truly "get up to speed" on properly implementing them, in no small part because it was genuinely "deluged" with both first-party (read: by individuals for records about themselves) and third-party (read: for records about others or other subjects) access requests. And one of the best (read: worst) examples of that was what led, inexorably, to the Solo Sources' disclosure.

You see, Carl had made an early FOIA request for any existing FBI records reflecting its efforts to disrupt white supremacy groups (called "white hate" groups at the time). To the Bureau's credit, it didn't take all that long for Carl to receive a FOIA response from it. But when he did, when such records were released to him (even though mostly in heavily redacted form), he found that one of the documents mistakenly was on another subject altogether -- "disruption of the CPUSA."[20]

And that document, dated January 6, 1965, made direct reference to the FBI's success in having a CPUSA official "expelled," carefully deleting the name of that official at the document's beginning.[21] But one appearance of that name near the end of the document, "Albertson," was carelessly overlooked, presumably in haste, and was left in.[22] This in turn led to FOIA requests being made for the FBI's "Albertson's file," which could not be categorically withheld on the basis of Albertson's privacy because he was by then dead, but which were nevertheless broadly withheld (for the time being) on other grounds.[23]

And then an American Civil Liberties Union attorney by the name of Frank Donner, who headed the ACLU's Project on Political Surveillance, got involved on Lillie Albertson's behalf. He showed her what had been disclosed by the FBI to other FOIA requesters and advised her to make a FOIA (and Privacy Act) request herself. So she did so, in mid-1976, and she quickly followed that up with a FOIA (and Privacy Act) lawsuit that I personally handled, involving no less than 70,000 pages of records.[24] And not long thereafter, in 1977, she additionally filed an administrative damages claim against the Federal Government under the Federal Tort Claims Act ("FTCA," to its claimants).

Ordinarily, tort claims under the FTCA would be handled by the Civil Division's Torts Branch (in anticipation of possible litigation), and especially important FOIA matters anticipated to proceed to litigation would in exceptional cases be overseen by the Civil Division's Federal Programs Branch, into which the former Information and Privacy Section had been merged in 1978. While there wasn't exactly a ton of institutional experience with this sort of thing, inasmuch as the latter of the two statutes was relatively new, let's just say that the wisdom of having a single Civil Division Trial Attorney handle both things together had not yet arrived.

But this matter (which was not yet a "case" per se) was far from ordinary, and not just because it contained both types of claims.[25] The Civil Division's Assistant Attorney General, Barbara Allen Babcock, who knew my work quite well, decided that I would handle not only the FOIA aspect of the matter but the related tort claim in it as well,[26] which in 1978 made the assignment almost unique.[27] I was more than willing to do so, as I recognized this as one of those rare, "one-of-a-kind" cases, and also in that I had several highly experienced friends in the Torts Branch to whom I could turn in double-checking my strategy in handling that part of the case.

I also had one more key asset to deploy: My good friend Freddi Lipstein. Freddi was even by then already a "grizzled veteran" of the Civil Division's Appellate Staff; she was its leading appellate litigator of all types of national-security cases. So she had been "read into" the "Solo Source" classification compartment in advance, in anticipation of Lillie Albertson's FOIA case eventually "going up" on appeal. I had come to know her well in connection with other national-security matters and knew that she could help if I wanted to try to settle the tort claim in the case.

And as it turned out, I did. As I remember it, I had little difficulty in persuading the FBI to release many thousands of newly processed or reprocessed pages of records in proper response to Lillie Albertson's long-pending FOIA request. This did not happen overnight, mind you, but I put the process for this (and for its disclosure standards, on an exceptional "public interest" basis) well on track for eventual completion.

The other part of it all, though, the Federal Tort Claims Act administrative claim, was another matter entirely. I made it my business to read everything I could on this sad episode -- including internal FBI memos even if they were to or from FBI Director J. Edgar Hoover, as well as everything that still remained classified at that time -- which I pretty much had to do in order to be sure that we were making proper exemption-applicability decisions for the FOIA part of the case anyway.

And having done so, certainly more than anyone at Main Justice (i.e., not the FBI) had, I could not help but come to the conclusion that both William and

Lillie Albertson had been acutely victimized by the FBI's extraordinary action, even though (and actually all the more so because) the operation had been such a spectacular success.[28] Indeed, their lives had been completely ruined by what the FBI achieved at their expense; one could fairly say that the Bureau's degree of success had been directly proportional to the depth of what they suffered as a direct result of it.

I knew that such a conclusion, even during the liberal Carter Administration, would not at all sit well with the leadership of my biggest client, nor would it with the residual "hard liners" at Main Justice. But I also knew that I could not in good conscience recommend any response to Lillie Albertson's administrative claim under the FTCA that included the invocation of any threshold procedural defense. (Even the good folks (read: the good attorneys who were over there) in the Torts Branch were "spring-loaded" to erect such defenses, one might say.[29])

So I leveraged the unique position that I was in as the AAG-designated over-seer of "all things Albertson" and began the slow, highly deliberate process of internally advocating that the tort claim be settled, through a substantial award of damages under the FTCA. It simply seemed to me that the tort claim ought not be defended and that a substantial settlement amount, of as much as $100,000, I thought, was warranted.[30] And in negotiations with Lillie Albertson's very ca-pable ACLU counsel (whom I knew well, having litigated against them before), I suggested that I might be able gain the necessary high-level approval of such a settlement if I could assure everyone in Department that it would be accepted if offered.

This is how it can work in government settlement negotiations: The first-line government attorney negotiating a matter does not have the final authority to bind the Government to what is therefore only tentatively agreed upon -- with that "final settlement authority" existing several levels up the supervisory chain, as opposed to there usually being only one such approval level at most, i.e., the client, above the plaintiff's counsel. That way, any settlement figure or term is far closer to a "final" one on the plaintiff's side than on the defendant's. And the Government routinely tries to leverage this dynamic to its advantage; a skilled Government attorney can succeed in doing that more often than not.

So in this case, by playing "good cop" rather than "bad cop," at least at first, I was able to get Lillie Albertson's hopes up at a settlement level of my choosing, one that, if she agreed to it, I could honestly say that on that basis I hoped to have it approved. I spent much time and effort laying the groundwork for reaching such a settlement, which I thought truly would have been in both sides' inter-ests.[31] And I had every reason to believe that Lillie Albertson would at this point agree to accept my proposed amount,[32] especially if I could accompany it with an impressive further disclosure of records responsive to her longstanding FOIA request, which I knew I could.[33]

There turned out to be a problem with this, however: The director of the Torts Branch, being a "hard liner" beyond compare, kept making one objection to settlement after another,[34] over extended periods of time, so that my own "time" ran out due to my leaving the Civil Division for OIP. So I had to leave the matter unsettled, with only my strong recommendation that it be settled at $100,000 as I had set it up to be. (At least I was leaving Freddi Lipstein to play a primary role in it upon my departure.)

Well, this was not to be. I left the Civil Division for OIP at the end of October 1981, and this settlement issue dragged on not just for months, but for years afterward.[35] Many, many years, in fact, until the Department finally in late 1989 approved a settlement of the tort claim -- for the sum of $170,000.[36] And I recall being quite certain that that higher dollar amount had little to do with inflation. (Freddie Lipstein, I should add, continued with her involvement in the matter; I have little doubt but that without her strong efforts, the settlement would have taken even longer and been even costlier.[37])

CHAPTER SIXTEEN

The Truly One-of-a-Kind Case

"A lie has no legs, but a scandal has wings."

-- English historian Thomas Fuller, 1608-1661

Any litigator will tell you that even in the most fascinating of subject-matter areas, his or her cases will become to some degree repetitive, perhaps even dull or relatively mundane, after a while. Indeed, the very nature of our legal system, with its use of the doctrine of *stare decisis* to decide court cases on the basis of judicial precedent, practically guarantees this. Trial attorneys in all types of courts and locations are often on the lookout for any exceptionally different case that will give them a new and different professional challenge.

So I was quite excited to get a brand-new case that seemed as if it might be a truly "one-of-a-kind" one in 1979. And with the way in which this case developed, with an underlying premise that without the slightest doubt was unlike that of any case that ever came before it, it became nothing less than that during the following year.

This case was filed as a Privacy Act "wrongful disclosure" lawsuit, by an individual who alleged, through counsel, that he had been grievously "harmed" by the FBI.[1] He claimed that the Bureau had mistakenly and irresponsibly identified him as a "confidential informant" when it responded to a FOIA request filed by a local reporter. And I soon learned that this indeed had occurred, due to a clerical-type mistake, when the FBI had rushed its FOIA "processing" in a massive attempt to meet a "deluge" of FOIA requests one summer, through something that it had somewhat glibly named "Project Onslaught."[2]

It was during that "onslaught" period that certain sensitive FBI records had been "processed" (i.e., reviewed for the application of the FOIA's relatively new law enforcement exemptions) in response to that reporter's FOIA request, which had required the careful deletion of certain portions of them. In short, the fact was that the plaintiff's name *had* been mentioned in one of these records, accurately so, and that it should have been withheld in all such document locations as exempt. But very regrettably it was overlooked in one location and as a result had been disclosed to the reporter in that one spot.[3] The expression "haste makes waste" has never had more apt applicability.

So this plaintiff, on the face of his Complaint, asserted that he had been wrongly identified as an FBI informant, that in fact his well-known reputation in his community was the polar opposite of such a thing, and that he clearly was the victim of some outrageous FBI scheme, not unlike its notorious "COINTELPRO" operations, to besmirch and defame him through an official-looking indication that he had informed on others (including in less-than-casual circumstances) to the FBI. Therefore, he indignantly demanded that the FBI issue a formal apology to him, his family, and his associates; that it immediately expunge this "false" record; and that the Bureau, under the Justice Department's redemptive supervision,[4] take other remedial steps as warranted.

The primary problem here was that the document in itself actually *was* accurate, that this plaintiff indeed had been a confidential FBI source (an extremely successful one, over a period of many years, in fact), and that both he and the Bureau (through his FBI "handler") had thus far managed to keep this a deep secret from anyone who was not situated at the highest levels of the Department. And as if that were not enough, much of what he had informed on had to do with things that connected, at least indirectly, to matters overseas -- which meant that he actually was a "national security source," with a file as long as your arm that accordingly was heavily classified.

Now one might think that the very last thing that such an FBI informant would want to do is file a lawsuit that greatly imperiled the dark secret that he and the Bureau had so effectively succeeded in protecting. But I learned that in this case, there was a good reason for this particular source doing so. One of his close relatives was a law student who was personally outraged by what the FBI had quite apparently done to him.

And that close relative, together with others, had applied relentless pressure on him to sue the FBI in order to "restore his good name" (and by extension their own) once they learned of the FBI's "mistaken" disclosure.[5] Unfortunately, this relative was at the time studying under a civil liberties law professor who was ready and willing to do exactly that, almost as a "cultural" thing, because this outraged him, too. (Yes, this professor was male, but I do not regard that as identifying either.)

Under these circumstances, this plaintiff/informant woefully explained,[6] he was deathly afraid that any substantial resistance to suing the FBI on his part would dangerously arouse suspicions about him, within both his family and his "community," sooner or later.[7] Once his alleged (and "documented") source status was publicized, he really had no choice but to sue, he explained -- with the hope and trust that the FBI would well understand that and somehow or another find a way to protect him.

I learned this not over the phone, given the classified nature of what was involved, but by virtue of a face-to-face meeting that I was able to have when I quite coincidently had a trial and subsequent hearings in the very city in which the FBI's longtime "handler" of this source, Special Agent James M. Fox, then lived.[8] So it was that I sat in a bar in San Francisco one afternoon and heard the most amazing tale of how this situation came to be.[9]

And part of what I heard, and paid especially close attention to, was that this particular national security source had dangerously operated in an environment the remnants of which (as of 1979) made it quite foreseeable that his life (and, ironically,[10] even the lives of his close family members who had clamored for him to bring suit) would be at risk if the "wrong people," even now (read: then, more than a decade later), were to learn that he had so brazenly managed to fool them (or in some cases their predecessors) in such a way, so badly, and for so long. Yes, it was still a very serious matter even after all these years.[11]

Therefore, it was simply out of the question for the Bureau to suddenly abandon this source's dark secret[12] just because it had made an egregious FOIA-processing error and, for his part, he had been pressured to bring this lawsuit.[13] But that did not mean that we were prepared to just "play along" by conceding the suit. Surely, I thought, I could somehow manage to avoid such a result yet still protect this source and his family. Indeed, after taking a creative step that relied on the judge in the case's willingness to trust me, I found a way of bringing this lawsuit to a viable conclusion -- a "safe landing," we called it -- with relatively little risk.

But I will not elaborate on this any further here,[14] except that I can safely say that this case's denouement involved my flying to the city where the case had been filed, carrying a thick pile of documents that I had to lock up in a "class six container" in the local FBI field office overnight, and then sitting across from a judge in his chambers for nearly two hours straight while that judge chain-smoked his way through viewing every page of that document pile before ruling.[15]

CHAPTER SEVENTEEN
"Glomarization"

"We can neither confirm nor deny that this is our first tweet."

-- Opening lines in the CIA's first (noncovert) Twitter account, June 6, 2014

Another nondisclosure concept that we developed in the 1970s was the legal position that, under certain exceptional circumstances, an agency could neither confirm nor deny the very existence of any record responsive to a particular FOIA request without causing harm cognizable under a FOIA exemption. An inevitable analytical development under any FOIA-like disclosure regime, this is something that I consistently referred to as "Glomarization," so dubbed after the name of a U.S. submarine-retrieval ship (the *Glomar Explorer*) that was the focus of the first instance in which the need for taking such an extraordinary legal position arose.

"Glomarization" -- as a concept, a principle, or a response to a request for information disclosure -- did not exist before the mid-1970s. While there were some scant instances of private-sector spokespersons using the phrase "we neither confirm nor deny" in order to fend off pointed questions from journalists earlier in the 20th century, it was not until the Central Intelligence Agency ("CIA," to its many impatient FOIA requesters) first employed it in connection with "Project Azorian" in 1975 that very idea of it actually sprang to life.

"Project Azorian" was a secret U.S. plan to clandestinely raise a Soviet nuclear submarine, the *K-129*, that had exploded and sunk to a depth of more than three miles in the Pacific Ocean in the late 1960s, with an eye toward exploiting its technology and secret information. It involved locating that submarine somewhere northwest of Hawaii (near the International Dateline), constructing a first-of-its-kind "submarine-retrieval vessel" (named the *Glomar Explorer*), and deploying it to recover a targeted section of the sunken sub, which contained both nuclear torpedoes and perhaps codebooks, with a "cover story" that kept the Soviet navy at bay. When this was achieved, seemingly without Soviet knowledge, the CIA saw it as a great success; much like the FBI's view of its "Albertson operation" ten years earlier (see Chapter Fifteen), the CIA viewed this as one of the greatest intelligence coups of the Cold War.

The "secret" of this extraordinary enterprise was multi-layered. First, there were the very facts that the *Glomar Explorer* had been built by the United States as a submarine-retrieval vessel and, further, that it had been deployed. (For this, the CIA had concocted a "cover story" about a billionaire -- back when that was really saying something -- and manganese nodules.[1]) Then there was the fact that the attempted retrieval of the Soviet submarine had been successful (i.e., that the sub had been raised from the ocean floor). And last, but far from least, was the fact that that submarine had yielded much of its "treasure trove" of technology and related technical information, as the U.S. had hoped.[2]

This last fact was most important, for a reason that goes to the very heart of secrecy, at least as it is used in a "Spy versus Spy" dynamic.[3] To consider this, think of the formidable World War II German cryptography system known as the "Enigma" machine that the British codebreakers at Bletchley Park, England, were finally able to "break" and then replicate (see Chapter Forty-Nine). This was an enormous achievement, one that required that team's nonstop devotion and concentration, above all else, to accomplish.

But when those codebreakers finally achieved that -- at the very moment that they did so -- their greatest priority *instantly* shifted to ensuring that their German counterparts did not learn that they had just done so, lest much of the value of what they had done be lost. In other words, what they had accomplished was much more significant and valuable to the Allied Forces if the very secret of it could be scrupulously maintained, for as long as possible.

So, too, was the bottom-line secret of "Project Azorian" and the *Glomar Explorer* operation. What the U.S. military and Intelligence Community gained from it was all the more potent by dint of the fact that, like Germany's "Enigma" creators during World War II, the Soviets seemingly had no idea that its sunken submarine had been raised and plundered. Consequently, the CIA (together with its military partners) had an extraordinarily powerful motivation to maintain this secrecy for as long as it could.[4]

Well, it turned out that this secrecy did not last for nearly as long as was hoped. And this was in no small part so because of the Freedom of Information Act ("FOIA," to those affected by it). Had this all occurred just a short time earlier, the Federal Government's desired degree and length of secrecy would not have been threatened by the FOIA's potential applicability. But those days ended in the mid-1970s, once the FOIA was amended (over President Gerald R. Ford's veto) and its provisions became readily available for use by journalists and public-interest groups in cases such as this.

Indeed, the entire timing of this whole situation was itself quite remarkable. The targeted submarine sank to the bottom of the Pacific Ocean in March of 1968. And after the Soviets for some reason failed to locate it on the ocean floor, the U.S. Navy did, later in 1968. This was seen as presenting a rare opportunity for the U.S. to study Soviet nuclear missile technology and possibly recover cryptographic materials (coincidentally), *if* the CIA and its military partners could accomplish the unprecedented feat of raising that submarine. So it was that the construction of the *Glomar Explorer* was begun in late 1972, with it completed in June of 1974. And this brand-new specialized vessel was immediately deployed, during the month of July 1974, into early August.

During that same time, President Richard M. Nixon (who had of course personally approved the entire plan) finally resigned from the presidency, leading directly to Congress's major amendments of the FOIA in November of that momentous year (see the Glossary). And then those amendments took effect on February 19, 1975, at just about the exact same time that there appeared to be a "leak" about the *Glomar Explorer* to the media. (Sometimes things just work out that way.)

That suspected "leak," as it turned out, was far from a complete one, partly due to how layered the *Glomar Explorer* secret actually was.[5] As noted above, it involved both *The Los Angeles Times* and *The New York Times*, mostly the latter, but also nearly a dozen other news outlets, and it led to a period of successful media suppression.

In February of 1975, *New York Times* investigative reporter Seymour M. "Sy" Hersh (who had won a Pulitzer Prize a few years earlier for exposing the Mỹ Lai Massacre)[6] apparently learned enough about the *Glomar Explorer* enterprise that he was able to prepare an article about it. But as it was to do years later with the CIA's undersea surveillance operation called "Ivy Bells" (see Chapter Forty-Nine)[7] and many years later with NSA's "Stellar Wind" secret surveillance program (see the Introduction), *The New York Times* held off on publishing Hersh's article until the month of March.[8] And by that point, the "story," for media purposes, quickly had become focused on the efforts that the CIA reportedly had made to forestall any publication more than on the raising of the sub.[9]

And that is where and when the Freedom of Information Act came in. On March 21, 1975, a journalist working for *Rolling Stone Magazine* by the name of Harriet Ann Phillippi (later known as "Hank Phillippi Ryan") made a FOIA request for any records related to any attempts that had been made by the CIA to "persuade" the news media to not publish or broadcast anything about the *Glomar Explorer*.

So in its denial of the FOIA request, the CIA set forth what was the first "Glomarization" response by a federal agency. It did so by stating that "[w]e can neither confirm nor deny the existence of the information requested," a position that the CIA promptly upheld on administrative appeal.[10] This led to the seminal FOIA case of *Phillippi v. CIA*, Civil Action No. 75-1265 (D.D.C. 1975), which was filed two months later and came before District Court Judge Oliver Gasch (coincidentally, the judge for whom I was to begin clerking the following year).

In *Philippi*, the Department of Justice defended the CIA's "neither confirm nor deny" position (which is what it was called at the outset) with a motion for summary judgment that was supported by a limited defense on the public record of the case but with the proferring of two sealed affidavits, one classified "secret" and the other "top secret." Judge Gasch decided to consider the two sealed affidavits, *in camera*, as a basis for adjudicating the CIA's dispositive motion.

On December 1, 1975, Judge Gasch granted the CIA's motion for summary judgment, ruling that "any materials which the defendants may have" (read: ["might have"]) would, if they actually existed, be exempt from FOIA disclosure under Exemptions 1 and 3 of the Act. He made it clear that in so ruling he was relying upon the contents of the CIA's two *in camera* affidavits, the propriety of which soon became a threshold procedural issue in the case. Indeed, plaintiff Phillippi, supported by very able counsel, immediately took that ruling up to the D.C. Circuit Court of Appeals.

Meanwhile, on an entirely separate track, a closely related FOIA litigation case, *Military Audit Project v. Bush*, Civil Action No. 75-2103 (D.D.C., filed Apr. 3, 1975),[11] had been brought before another judge, District Court Judge Gerhard A. Gesell, who three years later would be the judge in the Martin Luther King case involving another novel FOIA issue, "survivor privacy" (see Chapter Three). The plaintiff in the *Military Audit* case had sought "the contract" and construction-related documents for a submarine-retrieval vessel, which approached the CIA's *Glomar Explorer* secret from a slightly different angle than did Harriet Phillippi.

Judge Gesell, unlike Judge Gasch, was not immediately receptive to the CIA's "neither confirm nor deny" position (to say the least), even after the CIA filed three high-level affidavits, two of them *in camera*, and he scheduled an *in camera* hearing on the matter in mid-June of 1976, for which he refused the sly request of plaintiff's counsel that he be allowed to attend. Although the prospect of such a hearing posed a foreseeable threat to *Glomar Explorer* secrecy, the CIA in *Military Audit* simply urged Judge Gesell to follow the same approach that Judge Gasch had taken in the earlier *Phillippi* case, which by then had been argued before the D.C. Circuit and was awaiting a decision on appeal.[12]

For his part, different than Judge Gasch, Judge Gesell stated that he wanted a better public declaration before considering the two declarations *in camera*. In response, the defendants filed two additional affidavits, one by the CIA's Deputy Director for Science and Technology Carl E. Duckett (who, it later was publicly learned, was arguably the "mastermind" of the operation) and a second one by Assistant to the President for National Security Affairs Brent Scowcroft (who likely was the operation's true authorizing official).

Then on June 15, 1976, the CIA tried to satisfy Judge Gesell with an affidavit from CIA Director George H.W. Bush, though it mostly addressed the secrecy of the CIA's budget. So on June 30, Judge Gesell once again denied the CIA motion and set another date for an *in camera* proceeding. He also refused to certify the question for an interlocutory appeal (which was different from what the CIA obtained in a subsequent case discussed below), whereupon the CIA then had to resort to filing a petition for a writ of mandamus in the court of appeals,[13] together with an attempted appeal notwithstanding Judge Gesell's denial of interlocutory certification. But on October 1, 1976, the court of appeals denied the mandamus petition and dismissed the appeal.

Upon remand to the district court, the Justice Department finally "pulled out all the stops." It submitted no fewer than eight classified affidavits *in camera* and it also proffered the classified testimony of additional witnesses. In response, Judge Gesell agreed to hear such *in camera* testimony, and he did so, whereupon he ultimately ruled in the CIA's favor. On October 26, 1976, he issued an order stating that he was dismissing the case for the reasons that were stated to him *in camera*.

This ruling was appealed, of course, but during the pendency of that appeal, the CIA's position in the case changed, enough for it to move the court of appeals to remand the case back down to the district court for disposition accordingly. This change in litigation position clearly resulted from a shift in the perception of national security interests that occurred when the Carter Administration took over from the Ford Administration, as described below. At this point, the Government acknowledged that the *Glomar Explorer* was owned by the United States and that it had been on a mission related to United States national security.[14]

On November 16, 1976, the D.C. Circuit issued its decision in *Phillippi v. CIA*, reversing Judge Gasch on procedural grounds. It held that he had erred in permitting the CIA to submit *in camera* affidavits fully explaining its position without first having the agency state its nondisclosure rationale in as much detail as possible on the public record.[15] Most significantly, though, the court of appeals endorsed the analytical viability of the "neither confirm nor deny" defense, at least at the conceptual level, which was itself a major development in FOIA case law.

Things changed dramatically, however, because the Ford Administration gave way to the Carter Administration in January of 1977. Up to that point in time, notwithstanding the bits of *Glomar Explorer* information that had reached the public domain,[16] the Justice Department's legal position on the CIA's behalf in *Phillippi* and *Military Audit* had been a firm, unyielding "neither confirm nor deny" defense in both cases. And most to the point, this position was taken not only at the CIA's fervent urging but also with the full support of Brent Scowcroft, who was President Ford's national security advisor.[17]

But this was not the same when Dr. Zbigniew K. Brzezinski replaced Scowcroft as National Security Advisor to President Jimmy Carter. Indeed, this was a big change. And the change in leadership at the Department of Justice doubtless was a factor as well. So, too, was the fact that both Judge Gesell in the *Military Audit* case as well as the D.C. Circuit in the *Phillippi* case were pushing back on the Justice Department's legal position, straining it to its limits.

So for whatever reason or combination of reasons, the Government actually retreated from its "Glomarization" position in these two seminal "Glomarization" cases in early 1977, which of course served to immediately defuse the potential explosiveness of both cases.[18] And accordingly, they both proceeded to be more "ordinary" FOIA cases that dealt with national security exemption applicability to admittedly existing records.[19]

In sum, this all meant that the very idea of using "Glomarization" in exceptional FOIA cases had been accepted judicially in the abstract -- by the D.C. Circuit in the *Phillippi* case -- but it was not yet applied dispositively in the actual adjudication of any case. So this newly important FOIA principle was a delicate one, for which its reception and ideal implementation by the courts in the first cases (read: the first half-dozen or so, especially within the D.C. Circuit) to apply it would be crucial.

And that is where and when I came in. When I arrived in the Department of Justice's Civil Division in the fall of 1977, the CIA was still very much in the process (read: throes) of adjusting to the Ford-to-Carter changes that had occurred that year. Some public-interest organizations were more than happy to help it make that adjustment, very much in a pro-disclosure direction, of course. And one, the American Civil Liberties Union ("ACLU," to it contributors), came up with a nationwide, coordinated plan to do so through use of the FOIA.

This plan involved the student newspapers of many American colleges and universities. The ACLU decided, as a matter of strategy, that it should make a concerted effort through them to bring to light the CIA's activities undertaken in connection with such academic institutions, which were publicly known to cover a wide range of (but not necessarily all) such things. So the ACLU aggressively coordinated a series of student FOIA requests, 125 of them in total, for any CIA record pertaining to any activity connected in any way to each individual campus.

The CIA, for its part, was not quite sure how to handle these entirely unprecedented, well-coordinated FOIA requests.[20] So it did what it did best with its FOIA requests at the time: It placed those requests in its growing "FOIA backlog," which gave it some time to figure out how best to handle them.[21] Which meant that these "university" requests (which is what we called them) soon became "ripe" for lawsuits to be filed on top of them.

The first of these "university" FOIA lawsuits was filed by Nathan Gardels, editor-in-chief of the *Daily Bruin*, the student newspaper at the University of California (Los Angeles), otherwise known as UCLA. I personally handled this case, *Gardels v. CIA*, both at the district court level and on Gardels' appeal of the district court's judgment in favor of the CIA in the D.C. Circuit Court of Appeals. With this came the other such court cases that the ACLU filed: *Medoff v. CIA*, from Fairleigh Dickenson University in the District of New Jersey; *Daily Orange v. CIA*, from Syracuse University in the Northern District of New York; *Kapsa v. CIA*, from Ohio State University in the Southern District of Ohio; and *Daily Pennsylvanian v. CIA*, from the University of Pennsylvania in the Eastern District of Pennsylvania.

All told, these five FOIA litigation cases were carefully chosen by the ACLU to be the leading edge of its campaign to pressure the CIA on its university-related activities both nationwide and around the world. And with this, beginning with the *Gardels* case in the District Court for the District of Columbia, the CIA and I had to no less carefully formulate exactly what position we would take on them, both at the administrative level and in court, which was something entirely novel.[22] And given the nature of the CIA's activities in this realm, this meant considering the possible deployment of what was then the brand-new FOIA-defense concept of "Glomarization."

My starting point in this analysis was in learning the activities that the CIA did in fact engage in in connection with colleges and universities. It had done things of that nature for many years by then, necessarily leading to the creation and the maintenance of many records. Some such things, such as recruitment, for example, were out in the open, with no general need to withheld most information contained in records about it.

But other things, such as the use of willing university professors and other academics for information-gathering purposes while travelling overseas, was by their nature quite secret. And their effectiveness would be impaired, in any particular case, by *any* FOIA disclosure about them (read: either of records about them or of even their existence), let alone on the ACLU's attempted nationwide scale.

This boiled down to our concluding that the CIA engaged in two types of university-related activities -- overt and covert -- with the fact that the former was undertaken on a particular campus being not really a secret, which meant that the CIA's records pertaining to that required no special protection. By that I mean nothing beyond the ordinary application of FOIA exemptions to their particularly sensitive portions.

But the latter category of activity, due to its inherently covert nature, was a different story. Yes, the CIA could publicly acknowledge that it engaged in covert university-related activity *in general*, somewhere and sometimes, but it would be another thing entirely for it to admit to that in connection with any academic institution in particular. And we had little doubt that if we were to do so, we could expect very active efforts, by student groups at a minimum, to discover and expose any covert sources on those campuses.[23]

Indeed, the very fact that the CIA engaged in such activity (the scope of which *we* defined) in connection with any particular college or university was something that itself had to be kept secret -- a secret that existed at the level of being an abstract fact -- which meant that the records of such covert activity could not even be acknowledged to exist without causing harm. Yes, the very *existence* of such records pertaining to a named academic institution had to be maintained as a classified abstract fact.

At this point in the FOIA's development, neither agencies nor courts had been dealing with anything as sophisticated as an "abstract fact."[24] But we knew that we had to do so, for the first time other than for the *Glomar Explorer*, in dealing with these targeted university cases. And we knew that in order to successfully do so we had to make this novel degree of FOIA sophistication as simple as possible to describe.[25] So we began to divide all CIA university-related records, conceptually, into two distinct categories, "overt records" and "covert records."

This bifurcation is what carried the day. It allowed the CIA to say, in response to any and all of the 125 "university" FOIA requests, that it was processing its "overt records" (if any existed) in the ordinary course, for "regular" FOIA disclosure. But as to the possible existence of any "covert records" created within the context of a particular academic setting, it was neither confirming nor denying that. Yes, we applied "Glomarization" for that distinct, yet entirely hypothetical, part of each university FOIA request.[26] And we did so consistently, regardless of what reality actually was in any given case.[27]

So this is the legal position that I defended in court, beginning with the *Gardels* case in early 1978.[28] My agency counsel at the CIA and I knew that it was vital that we prevail in our use of "Glomarization" in that case because it was a first -- the first of all of the "university cases" to be litigated and, even more importantly, the first "Glomarization" case to be fully adjudicated as well. So we "pulled out all the stops," so to speak, and brought in several high-ranking intelligence officials to attest to the essence of our case, including two successive deputy directors of the CIA.

What these agency witnesses explained to the Court, in general, is how the CIA had long (read: for nearly 30 years, by that point) accepted the voluntary assistance of prominent (read: patriotic) members of the academic community who dealt with their counterparts in other countries and often traveled overseas in doing so. The information that they gathered for the CIA through such academic contacts was often invaluable, but they could not do so if they were known (or even suspected, actually) to be "working with the CIA." (This was especially so after its "post-Watergate" revelations.) And the key part of this is that the public identification of their particular academic institution as having an (read: any) affiliation with the CIA would make them suspect, in many foreigners' eyes, just on that basis alone.

Hence, if the CIA were to be forced through the FOIA to disclose where (read: whether or not) it had such an affiliation, the usefulness of these valuable "intelligence sources" would be severely compromised. It was on that basis, primarily, that the CIA needed to apply the new "Glomarization" defense to the ACLU's widespread, targeted FOIA requests. And this defense was grounded in both national security classification and the CIA's special statutory authority for protecting its "intelligence sources and methods."

Unfortunately, the *Gardels* case was being heard by District Court Judge June L. Green, who had until recently then been one of only six female judges in the entire federal judicial system (see Chapter Three), but (and entirely unrelated to that) was not known for her judicial acumen. Indeed, the judge for whom I had then just clerked (i.e., less than a year earlier), District Court Judge Oliver Gasch, had been appointed to the Court at the same time as Judge Green, knew her well, and warned me that if I ever had a case before her I should, shall we say, try to avoid speaking polysyllabically.

Perhaps sensing an advantage in drawing Judge Green on the case, Gardels' ACLU counsel aggressively moved for an order compelling the CIA to file what was called a "*Vaughn* index" itemizing any withheld records (read: something that is incompatible with a "Glomarization" position). And then, practically on the eve of a scheduled oral argument on that motion, Judge Green inexplicably decided that *in camera* inspection was the means by which she wanted to adjudicate the case. What is more, she ordered that that be undertaken within so short a period of time (i.e., just a matter of days) that at least theoretically it would have been logistically impossible to undertake it if there actually *were* existing documents in the case.

In short, Judge Green's *sua sponte* order, which senselessly sought the *in camera* submission of "the documents" in the case, was utterly antithetical to the very *nature* of a "Glomarization" case. And as such, at least in my view, it actually constituted a dispositive order against the CIA's position, not merely the interim procedural order governing the means of the case's adjudication that Judge Green evidently thought it to be. As a practical matter, it was as if she had issued a final ruling in Nathan Gardels' favor.

This is something that called for urgent action, no holds barred, even over the weekend that happened to directly follow.[29] So I immediately prepared a lengthy motion (read: motion with a lengthy supporting brief) for reconsideration of Judge Green's *in camera* inspection order and, taking no chances given the timing involved, I also filed a motion in the alternative (with a lengthy supporting brief) for the certification of her order for interlocutory appeal.[30] And the latter motion in and of itself took the alternative position that her order, in context, was "appealable as of right" even if Judge Green (or in turn the court of appeals) did not deem it to be "certifiable."[31]

To her credit, Judge Green did grant one of those alternative motions, the certification one under 28 U.S.C. § 1292(b) -- which had the effect of "staying" her misguided *in camera* inspection order and getting the CIA "out from under the gun," so to say, pending a timely and less precipitous review of the matter by the court of appeals. In short, the "Glomarization" crisis spawned by Judge Green (perhaps inadvertently) was averted, for at least the time being.

But this is where I have to admit to there having been an internal "wrinkle" to this success that a few days later was rather pointedly, and quite properly, brought to my attention. This came in the form of a summons to the office of someone who had just been promoted to the position of deputy solicitor general and who was destined to become chief judge of the Seventh Circuit Court of Appeals.

Yes, newly minted Deputy Solicitor General Frank H. Easterbrook had noticed Judge Green's order certifying the *Gardels* case for interlocutory appeal and was wondering how on earth I could move for such an order without the Solicitor General first authorizing such an appeal in case the motion were to be granted. A fair question, indeed, even if it was only a technical (read: no, not really so "technical") matter of internal Department of Justice procedure.

I well remember standing "on the carpet" in his office and summoning up the only two defenses I could think of.[32] First, there were exigent circumstances involved, given the full import and hellacious timing of Judge Green's *in camera* inspection order. Second, I was operating within the Civil Division's "Information and Privacy Section," where supervisory assistance was virtually nonexistent at the time and, well, I just did not know that I needed Solicitor General authorization to take such a step in district court. (On second thought, maybe I raised the second of these two "defenses" first, which would have made more sense.)

Well, neither of these defenses seemed to satisfy Frank Easterbrook, but there was nothing to be done. Given that Judge Green had certified the case for interlocutory appeal, the Solicitor General then authorized the filing of a motion atop that in the appellate court, that motion was in turn granted, and the issue -- i.e., the propriety (read: basic common sense) of the issuance of an *in camera* inspection order in a "Glomarization" case -- was elevated well above Judge Green.

And when the D.C. Circuit promptly reversed that order (read: agreeing with my litigation position) and sent the case back down to be properly adjudicated on its merits, I had the opportunity to advocate the CIA's position on those merits of the case without constraint. To my ACLU opposing counsel, of course, this meant that he would fight tooth and nail to win the case however he could on the merits. And that meant that he would seek to depose each of my three high-level experts: Deputy CIA Director John F. Blake;[33] Don I. Wortman, CIA Deputy Director for Administration; and Michel C. Oksenberg, a senior member of the National Security Council staff and Professor of Political Science (and China studies) at the University of Michigan.[34]

We battled over that, as might be imagined, based upon the CIA's position that it had already met its "*Phillippi* obligation" of providing a detailed public explanation, though I ultimately had to acquiesce to those depositions being held, but only as provided for by Rule 31 of the Federal Rules of Civil Procedure, i.e., "on written questions." And on that basis, there was no longer any concern (read: great concern) about the witnesses, highly experienced as they were, inadvertently saying something that afterward could be characterized as somehow divulging the "abstract fact" that was the very *corpus* of the case.

Those depositions were taken over the course of several days, were limited as to what the three Government witnesses were authorized to say, and went quite well from the CIA's standpoint. Inevitably, they provided an opportunity for the CIA to explain its "Glomarization" position on the public record in even greater detail,[35] which was not a bad thing in that it strengthened the CIA's position all the more because it subjected that to what is called "adversarial testing." The common-sense basis for the Agency "neither confirming nor denying" the existence of "covert records" pertaining to UCLA was, in a word, manifest.

And based upon this, as well as the legal arguments presented, Judge Green eventually concluded that "to confirm or deny the existence of the documents at issue can reasonably be expected to result in the disclosure of intelligence sources and methods." This was the first adjudication ever to uphold a "Glomarization" position, and it was hailed out at Langley and even elsewhere in the Intelligence Community as such.[36] And it set the stage for the adjudication of the other such "university" cases that were on the litigation runway behind it.

The next two such cases were *Medoff v. CIA*, involving what one wag out at Langley unkindly called "Fairly Ridiculous University," and *Daily Orange v. CIA*, which arose from Syracuse University.[37] I soon found myself flying to Newark, New Jersey, to argue the *Medoff* case,[38] and then to Syracuse, New York, to argue *Daily Orange*. And when the ACLU took its "final shot" on this novel issue by appealing Judge Green's decision, I argued that appeal before the D.C. Circuit, as well. The stakes were highest in the latter argument, of course, but by that point I had presented oral arguments on the issue several times and was confident that I would prevail.

All three of these ventures were successful,[39] including a big victory from the D.C. Circuit in *Gardels*,[40] which left the "Glomarization" principle firmly established as a conceptual pillar of the Freedom of Information Act, for all time.[41] And that does not mean only for its use under Exemption 1 for classified information or Exemption 3 for protecting intelligence sources and methods. Rather, "Glomarization" is something that applies, at least theoretically, to any FOIA exemption. This is because, at the conceptual level, "Glomarization" involves protecting the "abstract fact" that can inchoately surround many items of exempt information -- with the "secret" often being the very fact that such an item exists.[42]

In the following years, "Glomarization" was readily applied to certain personal-privacy situations, particularly to the abstract fact that an individual was associated with -- and might be or have been the subject of -- a law enforcement investigation. What this meant is that at my urging, federal agencies such as the FBI were theoretically able to begin giving a "Glomarization" response to almost any third-party FOIA request that sought records about a named, living individual. The basis for this is the underlying idea that the mere acknowledgment that a criminal law enforcement agency holds records pertaining to someone could be expected to stigmatize that person (see Chapter Thirteen).

So therefore, not long after "Glomarization" was firmly established in the national security realm under FOIA Exemptions 1 and 3, it migrated over to Exemption 7(C) of the FOIA to provide enhanced personal-privacy protection in the law enforcement realm as well.[43] In September of 1982, OIP set forth the policy position that henceforth law enforcement agencies such as the FBI would "neither confirm nor deny" that they hold records on named individuals.[44] And this policy position was soon upheld in a series of litigation precedents, including several at the appellate level, that have been handed down consistently over the years.[45]

These decisions cover not only "Glomarization" employed under FOIA Exemptions 1 and 3 (as in *Gardels*) and the FOIA's personal-privacy exemptions (Exemptions 6 and 7(C)), they also extend to the "self-actuating" source-protection situation that can be covered by "Glomarization" under FOIA Exemption 7(D).[46] And today, "Glomarization" operating in conjunction with multiple possible FOIA exemptions[47] is a well-entrenched part of the FOIA landscape.[48]

CHAPTER EIGHTEEN
The FOIA's Exclusions

"I do know that the slickest way to lie is to tell the right amount of truth, then shut up."

-- Robert A. Heinlein, *Stranger in a Strange Land*, 1961

During the summer of 1979, literally in the middle of the night, it suddenly dawned on me what the solution to an unprecedented FOIA problem that I had encountered that day must be. And that single thought, once taken to its logical conclusions, led to the development of an analytical construct under the FOIA that ultimately was codified by Congress as a necessary part of the Act itself.

The problem that triggered this thought had to do with confidential source protection, which Congress had amended the FOIA just four years earlier to provide in abundance. Indeed, under FOIA Exemption 7(D), law enforcement agencies such as the FBI could protect the identities of their law enforcement sources (read: informants) both directly (i.e., by withholding their names and all identifying information about them) and indirectly (i.e., by withholding the entirety of all information provided by them in a criminal or national security intelligence investigation).[1]

This broad protection actually worked quite well in more than 99.9% of all confidential source situations. But that day, I was presented by the FBI (read: my biggest client, with the CIA and NSA running second and third) with an actual situation in which Exemption 7(D)'s source protections did not in fact provide a particular FBI informant sufficient protection -- one in which the leader of a terrorist cell (read: domestic terrorism) was attempting to use the FOIA to "ferret out" any FBI informant within his or her cell's midsts.

Yes, this was a real-life (read: life or death) situation. In this particular case, the Bureau had at great pains managed to infiltrate a domestic terrorist group (read: what we used to worry about most of all, but not as much immediately after 9/11), to very good effect, but in time the classic informant-infiltration dilemma had set in: The more successful the informant, the more voluminous and valuable the information that he or she provides, and the more suspicious the infiltrated group becomes (once that information is put to some "countermeasure use") that it might have been penetrated by what we might popularly call a "mole."

And in this case, that kind of suspicion had led that cell's savvy leader to take some truly innovative action. Knowing not only about the FOIA, but apparently also about the process of a first-party file subject giving consent for third-party FOIA disclosure, he (or she, for all I knew) had all of his or her cell members consent to the submission of individual FOIA requests to the FBI, returnable to the cell's leader, for access to any records that the FBI maintained on them.[2] This certainly threatened the secret identity of the informant (in a "Superman/ Clark Kent" sense), who of course had to provide such consent, lest he (or she, but not likely) dangerously stand out among the others.

These FOIA requests had just arrived when my Bureau friends brought this daunting problem to me (as if in the form of a giant turd, as I recall four decades later) and basically said: "Here, if you're so smart, you figure out how we get out from under this one!" And I did, although only as a short-term "solution" in that particular case, because I concluded that the only true solution to this problem required remedial FOIA legislation. In other words, the problem was so serious, and the FBI's position so analytically infirm, that an on-point legislative "fix" was warranted.

I called the form of this legislative solution an "exclusion," in order to clearly delineate it from a FOIA "exemption," from which it was quite distinct. At the time, I was the Civil Division's representative on a working group within the Justice Department that was working on developing a comprehensive legislative package of proposed FOIA amendments that the Carter Administration (read: Attorney General Benjamin R. Civiletti, at the recommendation of Associate Attorney General John H. Shenefield) planned to have introduced in Congress just before the end of (presumably) President Carter's first term.

Of course, that didn't quite work out as President Carter had planned (with the 1980 presidential election really not all that close), but we had prepared such a solid package of proposed FOIA amendments that it very viably carried forward to the law-and-order-oriented Reagan Administration (see Chapter Twenty-One) when it came in in 1981. And a major part of that legislative package was my favorite proposed FOIA provision, an "exclusion" for the FBI (or for any other federal law enforcement agency, such as the Drug Enforcement Administration ("DEA," to its pharmaceutical friends) that might need it).

Before going any further with this analytical tale, though, I should provide at least a few words about how an exclusion works -- especially because at at least first blush it is not so easy to grasp, much less believe (think: like "meteor burst technology" or "tempesting" in Chapter Twenty-Six). First, it is always based upon an existing FOIA exemption -- in this case, Exemption 7(D) -- and a firm premise of it is that all (read: absolutely all) records responsive to a particular type of FOIA request, received under particular circumstances (that might well change with the passage of time), would, if "processed" regularly for disclosure, be entirely exempt (read: in their entireties) under that exemption.

Then, and this is a key part, the request must arise in a situation in which the very acknowledgment of the existence of records responsive to it, as a targeted (read: usually targeted) FOIA request, would itself (as in this case) imperil a confidential source, at an "abstract fact" level. And, as a practical matter, all exclusions by definition proceed from the implicit premise that there are, in fact, some FOIA requesters "out there" who (not being as dumb as the FBI's favorite criminals of long standing, i.e., bank robbers) have the smarts, motivation, and initiative to patiently formulate the kind of FOIA requests that (we came to realize somewhat belatedly) make exclusions necessary.[3]

Now I realize that thus far this sure is sounding an awful lot like relatively mere "Glomarization" (see Chapter Seventeen). But this is *not* the same as "Glomarization." Why? Because by definition (at least how I defined it), an exclusion applies only in the exceptional situation in which "Glomarization" itself is simply inadequate to the task. In other words, if the FBI could possibly employ "Glomarization" to deal with this sort of problem, it surely would do so, without any need for the even more exotic mechanism that an exclusion is.[4]

So circling back as to the leader of that domestic terrorism cell, the question had been: Can't we just "Glomarize" our way out of this potentially deadly situation? The answer was no, because that would require the FBI's being able to establish a distinct "Glomarization category" (see Chapter Seventeen), one consisting of all third-party FOIA requests made with the consent of the individual subject -- which unfortunately was the only distinguishing characteristic of the problem FOIA request that was at hand.[5] Not at all viable.

Thus, with a "conventional" FOIA response out of the question, and even the extraordinary response of "Glomarization" unable to "do the trick," the only thing left was to boldly cover the problem with the explicit legislative authority to act as if the informant file did not exist. Yes, that it what an exclusion does: It gives the agency the statutory authority to lie. In other words, it allows the agency to lawfully go back to that terrorist cell leader and properly say that there are no records responsive to his or her request, just as it would be saying (presumably) in response to the requests for any existing records on the other cell members.

What is more, the use of an exclusion means that an agency is wielding a "sword as well as a shield." As to the latter, it is defending against the cell leader's "FOIA ferreting" attempt by shielding the informant from exposure. That part, for most observers, is intuitive. But what might not be so obvious to some is that in giving an exclusion response -- under subsection (c)(2), for example -- the agency actually is *misleading* the requester into believing that that informant is *not* one, and possibly even into concluding that there simply exists no informant in that cell at all. That is an exclusion's "sword."[6]

So back to our legislative process for amending the FOIA with a host of remedial provisions. I was given a leadership role in that process near the outset of the Reagan Administration, leading up to a "near-miss" with legislative success on it in May of 1982.[7] And by that time, after thinking the exclusion idea through thoroughly with respect to any other possible such situation, I actually had come up with two more exclusions, one "floating atop" Exemption 7(A) and another "inchoately surrounding" Exemption 1 in a particular type of situation. So I had added them to the Department's legislative package, knowing that it was time for solving all such potential problems at once.[8]

In time, of course (read: 1986), all three exclusions were enacted by Congress, just as I had formulated them (read: beginning with their first prototype) starting in 1979, and they became part of the FOIA, just as FOIA exemptions had in 1966 (see Chapter One) to begin with. And with that, I must say, came a measure of paternalism (see the Introduction) that can make government service all the more worthwhile.

But that was only the first step of this legislative process: I next had to personally explain the practical operation of these exotic statutory provisions to federal agencies, to the public, and even to members of my own staff within OIP, given the exceptional novelty and complexity of what we were dealing with.[9] I will put it this way, aphorismally speaking: It is one thing to achieve a measure of legislative reform, but it is quite another to successfully implement it. (Put that in *Poor Richard's Almanack*, Ben Franklin.)

* * * * *

As a lengthy aside, I should observe here that sometimes even courts can confuse the operation of an exclusion with the use of "Glomarization." A good (read: dangerously bad) example of this is the case of *Benavides v. DEA*, which has been (read: even to date) one of the few appellate decisions to deal with an exclusion, making it extremely precedential in 1992, and it was issued by the singularly authoritative D.C. Circuit Court of Appeals to boot.

That was a case in which an incarcerated FOIA requester[10] sought much information about two witnesses who testified against him at his trial and whom he therefore alleged were Government informants. In what actually was a very rare Exemption 7(D) "Glomarization" case, the D.C. Circuit panel hearing the appeal managed to muddle the difference between that species of "Glomarization" and the (c)(2) exclusion; it actually went so far as to declare that the district court had "erred in failing to consider the applicability of subsection (c)(2)."

In that panel's defense, it had casually relied upon some passages from the 1986 FOIA Reform Act's legislative history that actually *did* conflate the two things; they were incorrect, of course, and so was the D.C. Circuit's confused language in its opinion. And as such, that language threatened to potently derail the effective implementation of all of the exclusions, not just exclusion (c)(2). It badly needed to be fixed, if at all possible.

The problem (read: an underlying one) was that this very significant litigation case was atypically being handled by the local U.S. Attorney's Office, where the level of expertise applied to the case was not the same as if it were handled at Main Justice. So it was decided that, in a spasm of paternalism about the exclusion mechanism, I would take over the case for purposes of filing a panel rehearing petition, which I prepared with the terrific assistance of a brilliant fellow from the Appellate Staff of Main Justice's Civil Division by the name of Malcolm L. Stewart, who later went on to hold (as he still does) the highly esteemed position of career deputy solicitor general.

So Malcolm and I quickly put our heads together, under the standard tight deadline for such things, and laid out exactly why and how the panel had gotten things so terribly wrong on this important analytical distinction.[11] And to that same D.C. Circuit panel's credit, it did promptly issue a corrected new opinion "clarifying" itself, and allowing that it was doing so out of "concern that the precedents of this Circuit [not] become confused."

* * * * *

Back to legislation implementation. The key means of doing this was the preparation, issuance, and extensive distribution of something widely called "the Attorney General's Blue Book" on the subject, a soft-cover booklet that could be used for handy reference by anyone interested in any aspect of the 1986 FOIA Amendments. Such a guidance document had been issued by the Department of Justice for implementation of the 1974 FOIA Amendments in 1975 and for the initial implementation of the FOIA as originally enacted (and made effective) in 1967. So it was regarded as "traditional" (if three can make a "tradition") in the Federal Government, private sector, and FOIA-requester communities.

I prepared such a guidance publication, titled the "Attorney General's Memorandum on the 1986 Amendments to the Freedom of Information Act," to guide all agencies' implementation of the 1986 FOIA Amendments (known as the "FOIA Reform Act"), which addressed all of the law enforcement-related changes that were made to the Act, including the addition of the Act's three new exclusions.[12] It explained each exclusion in unsparing detail and took particular pains to carefully delineate their operation from that of "Glomarization." For implementation purposes, that undoubtedly was the most important part.[13]

And it also was important for any agency that might employ an exclusion to realize that, by their very nature, exclusions were designed to counter any attempt by a FOIA requester to use the Act as a means of "ferreting out" highly sensitive agency information, particularly in the form of "abstract facts." Each agency's firm grasp of the very concept of this -- exceptionally challenging as that was -- was my goal. Simply put, proper implementation of the exclusions absolutely required that.[14]

By the same token, however, I also had to warn agencies not to get "carried away" with this special new (and admittedly counterintuitive)[15] congressional authorization, lest Congress conduct oversight of its use, find the executive branch lacking, and repeal it the next time that the FOIA were to be amended.[16] Toward that end, by this formal memorandum the attorney general effectively ordered all federal agencies subject to the FOIA to not (read: absolutely not) even start breathing hard about possibly using an exclusion without first consulting with OIP. For the first couple of years or so, I handled all such consultations myself, but after that I had one of OIP's senior attorneys handle most of them; he firmly understood exclusions better than anyone else on OIP's 23-person attorney staff.[17]

Before leaving this part of the exclusion discussion, though, I must admit that this particular aspect of the FOIA's administration concerned me the most as I retired. Up until then, for more than 20 years, the process of agencies consulting with OIP before utilizing an exclusion had worked remarkably well. But I was quite concerned that this might not continue so effectively after my departure. And of the three exclusions, the one that concerned me the most, by far, was "exclusion (c)(3)" (see below), the one that provided exceptional statutory authority to the FBI. So I took pains to leave explicit instructions about this that I hoped would help rein in the worst instincts of the FBI.[18]

* * * * *

The first exclusion provision, which came to be known as the "tip-off" exclusion, was designed to operate in conjunction with FOIA Exemption 7(A). Of the three exclusions, it is the one that is the most frequently applied, by the widest potential range of federal agencies. It provides as follows:

Whenever a request is made which involves access to records described in subsection (b)(7)(A) and

(A) the investigation or proceeding involves a possible violation of criminal law; and

(B) there is reason to believe that (i) the subject of the investigation or proceeding is not aware of its pendency, and (ii) disclosure of the existence of the records could reasonably be expected to interfere with enforcement proceedings,

the agency may, during only such time as that circumstance continues, treat the records as not subject to the requirements of [the FOIA].

5 U.S.C. § 552(c)(1). Subsection (c)(1), like Exemption 7(A) itself, has a distinct temporal aspect. As such, it applies (or conversely does no longer) only so long as certain eventually changing circumstances exist.

This exclusion covers the situation in which a criminal law enforcement agency is conducting an investigation of a person, institution, or other type of entity that is not currently aware of that investigation's pendency and could be harmfully "tipped off" to it through ordinary FOIA processing of a targeted FOIA request.[19] Preventing such harm (e.g., a "tipped off" criminal's "covering of his tracks") is exactly what FOIA Exemption 7(A) is all about.

Exemption 7(A) covers law enforcement records or information the disclosure of which "could reasonably be expected to interfere with enforcement proceedings." At its most basic level, it permits agencies to withhold requested records where their disclosure could harm a law enforcement proceeding primarily through premature disclosure of evidence or other sensitive information. And it is well recognized that such disclosure could allow an investigation's subject or target to interfere with an ongoing law enforcement investigation or proceeding in a number of possible ways.[20]

Ordinarily, the basic protection afforded by Exemption 7(A) is amply sufficient to safeguard against any possible impairment of law enforcement investigations or proceedings through use of the FOIA. In order to avail itself of Exemption 7(A), however, an agency must routinely specify that it is relying upon that exemption -- first at the administrative level and then, if sued, in court -- even where it is invoking the exemption to withhold all responsive records in their entireties.[21] The difficulty, however, is that in those unusual situations in which the investigation's subject is as yet unaware of the investigation's existence, the agency's specified reliance upon Exemption 7(A) can "tip off" that investigative subject and thereby cause harm.

In such cases, even invoking Exemption 7(A) to withhold all details of an investigation during its pendency would not be sufficient to avoid potential interference, because the investigation's subject would thereby learn of its existence nonetheless and the very secret that is being protected would be divulged. As well, any person (or entity) who suspects that a federal investigation might have been launched against him or her or it regarding certain of his or her or its activities could try to use the FOIA to confirm that suspicion.

A carefully worded FOIA request is all that this would take. And an agency response invoking Exemption 7(A) would serve to confirm the existence of an ongoing investigation; conversely, any response that did not invoke Exemption 7(A) in withholding a law enforcement file would tell such a requester that his, her, or its activities (or perhaps those of some other entity named in the request) have thus far managed to escaped detection. So the (c)(1) exclusion was designed (I can attest) to afford necessary protection in such situations in which the "conventional" protection of Exemption 7(A) is inadequate to the task.[22]

The (c)(1) exclusion provides federal law enforcement agencies with a means of guarding against these dangers of "tipping off" an investigation's subject. It authorizes them, under these particular circumstances, to exclude their records of ongoing criminal investigations or proceedings -- records that would be withheld as entirely exempt from disclosure under Exemption 7(A) anyway -- from the very reach of a FOIA request.

As a practical matter, and as extreme as such a solution might seem, this is the only effective way to avoid the "tip off" problem that savvy users of the FOIA can pose. The (c)(1) exclusion permits law enforcement agencies to avoid having to disclose to investigative subjects a sensitive abstract fact (i.e., whether there is an investigation ongoing, or not) that would be revealed by the mere, ordinary invocation of Exemption 7(A).

Significantly, and most logically, this special protection is available only under the particular circumstances that are specified clearly in the exclusion's particular language, which provides fairly rigorous requirements for the exclusion's use. First, of course, the records in question must be those falling within the proper scope of Exemption 7(A) to begin with. Further, under the precise terms of this exclusion, they must relate to an "investigation or proceeding [that] involves a possible violation of criminal law." This "criminal" requirement alone is more than exists within Exemption 7(A) itself.[23]

Beyond that, though, the (c)(1) exclusion's language imposes two closely related requirements which go to the very heart of the particular harm that is being guarded against. Any agency considering whether it should employ the (c)(1) exclusion must consider whether it has "reason to believe" that the investigative subject in question is not aware of the investigation's pendency and then, most fundamentally, that disclosure of the very existence of the records in question "could reasonably be expected to interfere with enforcement proceedings."

Obviously, where all investigative subjects involved in an ongoing matter already are aware of an investigation's pendency, the "tip off" harm sought to be prevented through this record exclusion is not of concern. Accordingly, the language of this exclusion requires agencies to carefully contemplate the level of awareness already possessed by all investigative subjects involved as they consider employing it. Agencies must do so, as the statutory language provides, according to a good-faith, "reason to believe" standard, one that closely comports with the "could reasonably be expected to" standard that Congress utilized both within this exclusion and in the simultaneously amended form of Exemption 7(A).

This "reason to believe" standard for considering a subject's pre-existing awareness affords agencies much latitude in making such determinations. As the exclusion is phrased, this requirement is satisfied so long as an agency determines that it affirmatively possesses a "reason to believe" that any such disqualifying awareness does not in fact exist. In other words, an agency must have a reasonable belief of current subject unawareness, and that the mere invocation of Exemption 7(A) under all current circumstances could reasonably be expected to cause harm, for the (c)(1) exclusion to properly be employed.[24]

Where all of these requirements are met, and an agency reaches the judgment that it is necessary and appropriate to employ the (c)(1) exclusion in connection with a request, that means that the records in question are to be treated, as far as the FOIA requester is concerned, as if they do not exist. And where the excluded records are but a part of the totality of records responsive to a FOIA request, such as could be the case if there were a previous investigation, the request should be "bifurcated" and handled as if the other responsive records are the only such records in existence.[25]

And finally, where there are no such non-excluded records responsive to a request, as will be the case most often, the requester may lawfully be advised that no records responsive to his, her, or its FOIA request exist.[26] In other words, the existence of the current investigation (more likely than a "proceeding") will be shielded from the requester (and his, her, or its criminal compatriots) and the agency will get to wield the sword of misleading the requester as well.

The second exclusion, which was the one that I had originally conceived of in 1979, operates in conjunction with FOIA Exemption 7(D). Applying to a realm in which a response to a targeted FOIA request can literally be a "life and death" matter, it provides as follows:

> Whenever informant records maintained by a criminal law enforcement agency under an informant's name or personal identifier are requested by a third party according to the informant's name or personal identifier, the agency may treat the records as not subject to the requirements of [the FOIA] unless the informant's status as an informant has been officially confirmed.

5 U.S.C. § 552(c)(2).

This exclusion covers the situation described above in which a confidential law enforcement source (usually called an "informant") is in imminent danger of being "found out" by a dangerous group that he or she has infiltrated, which truly could cost him or her his or her life. It is serious business, indeed, as everyone on Capitol Hill who needed to hear my explanation of this proposed provision readily agreed.[27]

The (c)(2) exclusion is designed to protect against the possible use of the FOIA to discover the identities of confidential informants ("moles," if you will), which would be contrary to the protective policy of Exemption 7(D), just as the (c)(1) exclusion is aimed at maintaining the integrity of the policy underlying Exemption 7(A). It contemplates the situation in which a sophisticated requester could try to ferret out an informant in his or her or its organization by forcing a law enforcement agency into a position in which it could not ordinarily withhold records on a suspected informant except by relying on Exemption 7(D) -- which would itself confirm that the person whose records are sought is indeed an informant.

In the ordinary situation, Exemption 7(D), adequately allows a law enforcement agency to withhold all items of information necessary to prevent the identification of any of its confidential sources. As with Exemption 7(A), though, the mere act of invoking Exemption 7(D) in response to a FOIA request tells the requester that somewhere within the records encompassed by the scope of his, her, or its particular FOIA request there is some reference to at least one confidential source.[28]

Ordinarily, within the subject-matter context of the usual FOIA request, the disclosure of this abstract fact (i.e., the Bureau's use of Exemption 7(D)) poses no direct threat to any confidential source whatsoever. Within the context of a FOIA request that is specifically targeted at any files maintained on a named individual, however, the threat can be real and palpable. Generally speaking, informants at the

FBI have what are called "134" files (the use of which apparently has gravitated toward counterintelligence sources in recent years), regardless of whether they are what the Bureau calls "symbol-numbered" sources.

It is possible, for example, for an informant who has infiltrated a criminal organization or even a loosely affiliated terrorist group to come under suspicion by those around him or her, either specifically or more generally together with others. Those in control of that enterprise could seek to ferret out that source by requesting all law enforcement agency records that relate to him or her, as well as to any others similarly suspected, in any way. As a matter of routine policy, federal law enforcement agencies generally respond to such "third-party" requests for records on named individuals by neither confirming nor denying the very existence of responsive records, on personal-privacy grounds (see Chapter Seventeen), pursuant to Exemption 7(C), which leaves the source well protected.

However, in such a situation, the source could readily be forced to surrender any such privacy protection if compelled by the criminal organization or group to execute a privacy waiver (otherwise known as "written consent"), or else to make the request directly, but on the organization's behalf (i.e., with its return address). In either case, a law enforcement agency could find itself in the untenable position of having to respond to a valid FOIA request directly targeted at a named informant's informant files. To invoke Exemption 7(D) in response to such a request would be utterly useless.[29]

The (c)(2) exclusion is principally intended to address this situation by permitting an agency to avoid giving a response that would be tantamount to identifying a named person as a confidential source under such circumstances. So any criminal law enforcement agency is explicitly authorized to treat such requested records, within the extraordinary context of such a FOIA request, as beyond the FOIA's reach. And as with the (c)(1) exclusion, the agency has no obligation to acknowledge the existence of such records in response to such a request.

A criminal law enforcement agency forced to employ this exclusion must do so in the same fashion as the one in which it would employ the (c)(1) exclusion discussed above, except that in this case it is difficult to imagine that there could exist any non-excluded record that would have to be processed in response to such a targeted request. Thus, in the instances in which the (c)(2) exclusion needs to be employed, the requester very likely will receive just a disarming "no record" response.

And the third exclusion, which pertains only (read: potentially, but perhaps not quite only) to the FBI, works with respect to certain classified records that the FBI maintains regarding three types of especially sensitive records in certain exceptional circumstances. It provides as follows:

Whenever a request is made which involves access to records maintained by the Federal Bureau of Investigation pertaining to foreign intelligence or counterintelligence, or international terrorism, and the existence of the records is classified information as provided in [Exemption 1], the Bureau may, as long as the existence of the records remains classified information, treat the records as not subject to the requirements of [the FOIA].

5 U.S.C. § 552(c)(3).

This exclusion covers the situation in which one of these three types of FBI records -- foreign intelligence, foreign counterintelligence, or international terrorism -- could be exploited by a savvy first-party FOIA requester in order to learn a classified abstract fact. This is a somewhat narrower circumstance (but no less vital) than the ones covered by the two preceding exclusions.

The reason for this third exclusion is that sometimes, within the context of a certain FOIA request, the very fact that the FBI does or does not hold any record regarding a specified person or subject can itself be a sensitive abstract fact, properly classifiable in accordance with the current executive order on national security and protectible under FOIA Exemption 1. When this is so, however, as can be the case under Exemption 7(A) and Exemption 7(D), the mere invocation of Exemption 1 to withhold such information in certain contexts can provide a harmful signal to an adversarial requester. In other possible contexts, the furnishing of an actual "no records" response, even to a seemingly innocuous "first-party" FOIA request, can effectively compromise sensitive international activities.

As an example, a foreign agent could infiltrate the United States, adopt a unique "cover name," and then sometime later make a first-party request for any record that the FBI might have on him or her -- on the theory that if a responsive record does exist under that cover name at the Bureau,[30] that must mean that the counterespionage folks there are "onto" him or her. Conversely, the receipt of a "no records" response will be taken as a clear indication to the contrary. The rationale against allowing this is simple: The United States ought not be in the business of aiding foreign espionage in such ways.[31]

This exclusion obviously is more particularly focused than the other two, but it operates in much the same way. It recognizes the exceptional sensitivity of the FBI's activities in the areas of foreign intelligence, foreign counterintelligence, and the battle against international terrorism, as well as the fact that the classified files of these activities can be particularly vulnerable to targeted FOIA requests -- i.e., any request that in context is recognized as seeking to learn a classified "abstract fact."

The (c)(3) exclusion specifically authorizes the FBI to protect against such harm in connection with its records maintained in one of these three areas. To do so, it must of course reach the judgment, in the context of a particular request, that the very existence or nonexistence of responsive records is itself a classified fact, within that particular context,[32] and that it need employ this record exclusion to shield against its disclosure. Plus, in the example described above, being able to lawfully give that spy a "no records" response, a misleading one, is a considerable advantage for the FBI.[33]

So by the terms of this provision, too, the excluded records may be treated as beyond the FOIA's reach, with the requester receiving a "no record" response. But as with the (c)(1) exclusion, this remains so only so long as the abstract fact of their existence, within the context of that particular FOIA request, "remains classified information." Once that ceases to be so, the exclusion's applicability ceases also.

* * * * *

A few years later, the chairman of the House subcommittee holding oversight jurisdiction for the FOIA's governmentwide administration sent a pointed formal request to the Justice Department (read: to OIP) for extensive information on the exclusions' implementation thus far,[34] no doubt hoping to discover some implementation failure with so novel and complex an enterprise. And as might be imagined, we scrambled quite a bit to provide a full and timely response to that congressional request, even though it was something that we had anticipated.

Indeed, this was made much easier by the fact that we had kept careful records on that, including all of OIP's many exclusion-related consultations, from the very outset in 1986.[35] Once we confidently provided that detailed response, we never had any follow-up attention from that oversight subcommittee on that subject again.[36]

Nor had the Department of Justice ever encountered any administrative difficulty with the use of exclusions until after my retirement, when it surprisingly raised issues about that by attempting to add this delicate subject to its FOIA regulations a quarter-century later, in 2011. For some reason, OIP at this later time proposed adding a new FOIA regulation subsection, denominated Section 16.6(f)(2), that actually would have done nothing more than recapitulate what the Attorney General's FOIA Memorandum on the subject had already said 25 years earlier.

This unnecessary, inexplicably gratuitous action drew a flurry of unanticipated criticism, however, as if the operation of exclusions were being focused on by the public for the very first time. With the subject thus being "opened for public comment," in effect, by its proposed incorporation into the Department's FOIA regulations, members of the FOIA-requester community and others heavily criticized both the proposed regulation and the Department of Justice for attempting to do something new (read: as if it were new) that would impede both governmental transparency and accountability.

Most fundamentally, these critics reacted as if the regulation would *newly* authorize agencies to "mislead" FOIA requesters, without their recognizing that 25 years earlier Congress had already done exactly that to begin with, as the Attorney General's FOIA Memorandum had back then explained. And in an even loftier vein, they criticized the proposed regulation by going so far as to complain that it would undermine the government's legitimacy by "making deception an explicit rule of law." Again, they chose to overlook the fact that Congress had already done as much in enacting these extraordinary exclusions in the first place.

But, unduly daunted by such criticism, the Department failed to recognize the problem that it had caused for what it actually was (read: a self-inflicted wound) and therefore did not just drop this proposed regulation subsection altogether.[37] Rather, after a delay of almost a year,[38] it "doubled down," so to speak, by going ahead with the regulation and instead having agency criminal components (both within the Department and at other agencies) provide a special notification to all of their FOIA requesters that exclusions do exist (as if that hadn't been publicly known) and that, by implication, an exclusion might have been employed in their cases.[39] This, even though it was at the same time recognized that the use of exclusions is "quite limited."

*　*　*　*　*

Exclusion matters in FOIA lawsuits are handled according to some novel, but fundamentally logical, operating principles. First, is the fact that all judicial review of suspected exclusion determinations[40] must be conducted *ex parte* (read: without the participation of or, in this case, the full knowledge of the plaintiff or counsel) through *in camera* court filings (including an *in camera* declaration) that are submitted directly to the judge. Second, it is of course essential to the viability of the exclusion mechanism that the plaintiff in such a case (as well as any member of the public) not be able to deduce whether an exclusion was employed based upon how any case is handled in court.

To achieve that, it is crucial that the special *in camera* defenses of exclusion issues raised in FOIA cases be brought to bear not only in those cases in which an exclusion actually was employed and is in fact being defended. (Indeed, unlike with "Glomarization" (see Chapter Seventeen), the overwhelming bulk of cases in which an exclusion is claimed to have been used will not in fact be such a case.) And those defenses must be made with the utmost care, by both administrative-level agency personnel and Justice Department litigation attorneys alike.

For this, it is the Government's standard litigation policy and practice in the defense of FOIA lawsuits that wherever a FOIA plaintiff raises a distinct claim regarding the suspected use of an exclusion, the Government will routinely (read: no exceptions) and promptly submit an *in camera* declaration addressing that claim, one way or the other. Where an exclusion was in fact employed, the correctness of that action is justified to the court in that declaration, and where an exclusion was not in fact employed, the *in camera* declaration will simply state that fact, together with an explanation to the judge of why the very act of making such a submission, and then its consideration by the court, was necessary to mask whether that is or is not the case.

In either case, the Government will of course urge the court to issue a public decision that does not indicate whether it is or is not an actual exclusion situation. In effect, the Justice Department will ask those courts deciding exclusion-related claims to "Glomarize" the question of whether an exclusion was or was not utilized in a given case. Such a public decision by the court, not unlike an administrative appeal determination of an exclusion-related request for agency review, should specify only that a full review of the claim was undertaken and that, if an exclusion was in fact utilized, it was, and continues to remain, amply justified.

*　*　*　*　*

As can be seen from this exclusion exegesis,[41] the recognition of the need for, and the full development of, the exclusion mechanism was only a matter of time in the United States. In time, even if belatedly, other nations of the world (see Chapter One) will eventually have to develop their own exclusion-type mechanisms, as well as the related concept of "Glomarization," in order to provide necessary protection for some of their records as their FOIA requesters become increasingly sophisticated in making their own targeted requests.

CHAPTER NINETEEN
One Thing Again Leads to Another

"If at first you don't succeed, try, try again."

-- Robert the Bruce, King of Scots (from 1306 'til his death in 1329), exhorting his troops to victory over the English at the Battle of Bannockburn in 1314 and whose name appears on the four faces of the tower (i.e., "King/Robert/The/Bruce") at Dunfermline Abbey in Scotland's original capital

In short order, I found myself greatly enjoying both the substance and the process of what I was doing, strongly committed to my litigation caseload as well as to the FOIA as a burgeoning field of public policy and law. Simply put, the analytical challenges that both the FOIA and the Privacy Act presented, at this formative time of their development, were hard to beat. Indeed, this was so much so that when I suddenly was offered exactly what I had sought less than a year earlier, I actually turned it down.

Yes, in the summer of 1978, I was asked to become an Assistant United States Attorney ("AUSA," to Federal Government litigators) in the Civil Division of the U.S. Attorney's Office for the District of Columbia, where I would be handling a wide variety of civil litigation cases, even though I still did not yet quite meet its ordinary (and theretofore seemingly rigid) standards for length of litigation experience. But evidently, my careful handling of the case involving the FBI records compiled on Dr. Martin Luther King, Jr. (see Chapter Three) had so impressed the trial court judge in that case that he not only praised it in his written opinion, he also touted it to the supervisors in the U.S. Attorney's Office (one of whom later became a district court judge himself), who in turn promptly decided to immediately hire me away from Main Justice.[1]

Saying no to such an unexpected and highly flattering offer, and to the particular career path that had so recently seemed optimal for me, certainly was not easy, not at all. But doing so was a reflection of my new-found strong sense that government secrecy law, still a relatively new and fast-growing field of both policy and litigation that could be entered nearly on "the ground floor,"[2] was a career choice well worth committing to, even at the relatively young age of 26.

To be sure, there are those who believe it best to remain a generalist during at least the first few years of one's legal career, if possible, and I do agree with the value of such an approach in general.[3] But for some people, be they doctors or lawyers or academics, for example, a particular area of specialization and eventual strong expertise can be quite compelling early on -- and it can last a lifetime. In my case, the same type of judgment that I had quickly reached years earlier about working for the Department of Justice in the first place, as opposed to anywhere else, kept me committed to remaining within the secrecy field.

Sure enough, as things developed over the course of the next three years in the Civil Division, not to mention thereafter, this early judgment was confirmed at nearly every turn. Not long after declining to make this move, I had the portentous opportunity to add a very nice dimension to my litigation work with both policy development and written litigation guidance related to a new privacy law, the Right to Financial Privacy Act ("RFPA," to bank customers). And it even led to my litigating the first precedent-setting cases under that brand-new statute.

Enacted in late 1978 and made effective by Congress as of early the next year, the Right to Financial Privacy Act (RFPA) was a model statute that became the first of what then was expected to be a series of several such laws protecting privacy rights in certain types of private-sector records -- in this case, bank account records that no longer would be so freely available to third parties, particularly government investigators. Because I was asked to represent the Civil Division on a multi-component task force that was set up through the Deputy Attorney General's Office for the RFPA's implementation, I was able to literally "write the book" on this new law, in the form of a Civil Division litigation monograph and related interpretative guidance, becoming the leading expert on it by the time it took effect, then successfully defending the Government in the first half-dozen cases filed under it for good measure.

The RFPA, as we liked to call it, established a complex set of procedures for protecting the secrecy of "customer records," one that was imposed on banks and federal law enforcement agencies alike, in a way that was novel at the time.[4] It assured bank customers that the Federal Government would no longer be able to subpoena their records from any such "financial institution" without first meeting strict standards, most notably of having the customer's knowing consent, unless it was under exceptional circumstances, which in law enforcement situations often was the case.

As such, it was seen as the model for all future such remedial statutes planned by the Department of Justice to likewise provide such privacy protection for similar record types.[5] So from the very outset of its effectiveness in February of 1979, the Department placed a high priority on the RFPA's fair and effective implementation during the coming months and years. And that is where I came in, as the most vigorous member of the RFPA Task Force who necessarily was then preparing to defend the statute, and the Department's interpretation of it, in the face of inevitable challenges to its use in court.[6]

I use the word "interpretation" here because the RFPA, which was drafted by Congress somewhat hurriedly (as if that were remarkable any longer), contained several specialized terms of art (e.g., "financial institution," "customer," "account," and "access") that were key to its proper interpretation, as well as some ambiguous terms (e.g., "legal entity," "reasonably described," "financial record," "law enforcement inquiry," and "emergency access") that likewise required some interpretation for the statute to be implemented coherently.

So I prepared two lengthy guidance memoranda (yes, replete with footnotes) that addressed all of these points, as well as any others that I could think of, and set the stage for the RFPA's uniform and proper implementation in advance. I also wrote a detailed formal Civil Division document (Civil Division "Monograph Number 53," but who's counting) that specified exactly how RFPA court cases should be litigated once they arrived. This all made me the "world's living expert" on this statute right quick, and I started fielding all of the phone calls that came into the Department about it, even before its effective date of February 1, 1979, from federal banking agencies and law enforcement agencies, as well from the private sector, accordingly.[7] What this turned into was, in effect, a "warm-up" for the role that I was to play for the governmentwide implementation of the Freedom of Information Act (and, to a large degree, also the Privacy Act of 1974)[8] just a couple of years later.

Although the RFPA is relatively narrow in scope, pertaining largely to the law enforcement activities of the Department of Justice and its FBI in particular, it offered the opportunity to completely master it, literally from the ground up, and for someone such as myself to become the "go to" expert on it for anyone seeking 100% accuracy in response to any question about it. And for me, this quickly became a "trial run" for what I proved to myself (and to others, soon enough) I could do for the much larger subject area of the Freedom of Information Act.

This in turn led to my getting immediately involved in heavy-duty Carter Administration efforts to build on the RFPA by urging Congress to enact similar legislation for medical records (read: first), insurance records, and the records of other personal transactions. This legislative activity heated up greatly during the summer of 1979, and it actually looked like a medical record privacy bill that I helped draft would be Congress's next step -- yet at what seemed like the last minute, the bill suddenly failed. Indeed, it is a little-remembered fact of that era that Congress came very close to creating a nationwide medical privacy regime but that the legislative package for it abruptly fell victim to a schism within the Democratic Party: Senator Edward M. "Ted" Kennedy's preliminary political moves to challenge President Carter for the Democratic Party's nomination in the upcoming 1980 presidential election.

Yes, but for that happenstance, I believe, we would have had a 1970s version of the privacy protections that eventually were created as "HIPAA" (the Health Insurance Portability and Accountability Act, enacted in 1996) many years later. In fact, when I later (read: more than 16 years later) helped Clinton Administration appointees at the Department of Health and Human Services develop their HIPAA implementation regulations on medical privacy, I was surprised to learn that they knew so little of what had nearly pre-empted HIPAA so many years earlier. Yet this work on prospective legislation then dovetailed perfectly with something that, as it turned out, would occupy much of my time for decades to come: FOIA-amendment legislation.

Indeed, at about this same time (i.e., mid-1979), the Department of Justice was beginning to "gear up" on the development of legislative amendments to "reform" the FOIA. I was asked to play a leading role in this, as part of a team assembled by Associate Attorney General John H. Shenefield that took a very comprehensive look at the subject, most particularly with an eye toward the real-world difficulties that had been experienced by the Justice Department (read: especially at the FBI and the Department's Drug Enforcement Administration, or "DEA") as a result of the many broad, pro-disclosure changes to the Act that were made when an arguably overreactive Congress (read: acting also in haste) amended it not long after Nixon had resigned five years earlier.[9]

So we promptly began compiling a list of possible amendments to the amended FOIA that were suggested by the Department's various components.[10] We massaged this list heavily, as might be imagined, and also contoured it according to what would likely meet with judicial receptivity once such statutory provisions would inevitably be challenged or interpreted by an array of public-interest groups and FOIA plaintiffs' attorneys in court. As the *de facto* "chairman-cum-scrivener" of the group, I also threw in some additional amendment ideas of my own, thinking as creatively as I could.[11]

By the summer of 1980, our group's numbers had dwindled but we had a strong legislative package with which to go forward -- one that was fully endorsed by the FBI and was informally approved by the in-house FOIA lawyers at the CIA and NSA (clients of mine one and all), even though it was modulated by the fact that it was, after all, a Carter Administration proposal. This package contained several seemingly small but legally vital changes to the wording of Exemption 7 of the FOIA, the exemption that had been a major focus area of the 1974 FOIA Amendments.

These changes would afford much greater protection of confidential law enforcement sources of information (read: largely "informants"), which the FBI rightly referred to as "the lifeblood" of its investigative processes. They also greatly strengthened the Act's protection for individuals whose personal-privacy interests were implicated in law enforcement files, they significantly enhanced its protection of information regarding "ongoing or prospective" investigations or proceedings, and they broadened its coverage of law enforcement techniques.[12]

Additionally, they included a somewhat radical idea that a year earlier had struck me literally in the middle of the night (if such a thing is metaphorically possible) as a solution to an especially difficult confidential source-protection problem that the FBI had had under the existing law -- a provision that would "exclude" certain types of records, under carefully controlled conditions, from the statute's very reach. Most vital of all, in my opinion,[13] this was a "new species of FOIA animal," so to speak, henceforth to be known as an "exclusion," for rare but tangible circumstances in which even the exceptional "Glomarization" defense simply was not adequate to provide necessary nondisclosure protection. As it turned out, a total of three such exclusion provisions were accepted by Congress and enacted into law. (Chapter Eighteen is devoted entirely to these provisions.)

We refined this proposed FOIA-amendment package to the point at which it was formally approved by Associate Attorney General Shenefield in mid-1980. John Shenefield, who brought a distinct intellectual perspective to the subject of FOIA reform that in this case ran counter to the Carter Administration's more liberal views (read: he was not impracticably pro-disclosure), then enthusiastically recommended this legislative package to Attorney General Benjamin R. Civiletti, whom we all thought would be able to advocate it up on Capitol Hill as part of the Department's new legislative agenda once the 1980 election (read: President Carter's re-election) was over.

But when that election was over, we realized that Attorney General Civiletti would not be going anywhere except back into private practice. It also became clear that much would soon change greatly in the Federal Government and, more specifically, that our corner of the world concerned with the FOIA and government secrecy was likely to undergo large changes as well. And so it was that this crafted package of proposed amendments to the FOIA carried over to the next presidential administration (together with me, as its new formal shepherd),[14] to receive further intense consideration right away but not to become law for nearly six more years.

CHAPTER TWENTY
The Creation of OIP

"I was always interested in figuring things out. I'd do experiments, like combining things I found around the house to see what would happen if I put them together."

-- Alan Alda (née Alphonso Joseph D'Abruzzo), actor, director, and serial memoirist

The year 1981 certainly brought a new wave of conservatism to Washington, as opposed to Carter Administration "liberalism,"[1] one that admittedly did fit more smoothly with the interests of my principal FOIA litigation and legislation clients, the FBI and the CIA. The "Reagan Revolution" promised to sweep across the Federal Government with a quick and sure vengeance (read: or less than that in many cases, as that perhaps is a bit too strong a word) and the Department of Justice was at the center of much of that. Within days of the inauguration, new Attorney General William French Smith, who had been President Reagan's own personal attorney, took a strong hold of the Department and made it clear that he was planning to make some serious organizational changes.

One of the first of these changes was the reinvigoration of the very "sub-office" that I had worked in seven years earlier during law school,[2] which was renamed as the "Office of Legal Policy" and was to be headed by a new assistant attorney general, Jonathan C. Rose, a former White House aide during the Nixon Administration who notably was given "first among equals" status and authority among all of the Department's other assistant attorneys general. He also was given policy authority over the FOIA and the Privacy Act in the bargain.

At the time, apart from the FOIA litigation that was conducted and overseen by the Civil Division, and the free-lance policy and legislative work that I had been doing there (read: within my own sort of FOIA "node"), as well, there were two separate offices that primarily handled FOIA matters for the Department. They were the Office of Information Law and Policy ("OILP," for short) and the Office of Privacy and Information Appeals ("OPIA," for longer).

The former was that office that I had heard was being contemplated in 1974 when I had just happened to be on the scene (read: standing in a doorway) at the time (see Chapter Seven). Ultimately, OILP did not break off from the Department's Office of Legal Counsel ("OLC," forever) until much later, but by then it was exercising potentially powerful policy authority over all cabinet departments and agencies for the attorney general, on increasingly significant matters of governmentwide FOIA interpretation. As of the outset of the Reagan Administration, OILP was headed by a highly regarded OLC veteran, Robert L. Saloschin, who soon announced that he would retire after more than thirty-five years of federal service.

The other office, known to its friends as OPIA, had been created in the wake of the 1974 FOIA Amendments in order to handle the Attorney General's over-all administrative responsibilities for FOIA and Privacy Act matters *within* the Department -- primarily the adjudication of copious numbers of administrative appeals that were taken from denials of record requests made to the Department's many different components. Chief among those components was the FBI, which had experienced a deluge of such access requests in recent years, and had denied them all too regularly, contributing in turn to a fast-growing OPIA caseload of administrative appeals.[3] As of early 1981, as the Reagan Administration began, it was headed by the late Quinlan J. Shea, Jr., who had founded the office a few years earlier and was, to put it most delicately, someone known as not at all likely to enjoy any compatibility with members of the incoming administration.[4] Indeed, Quin left his position (for a senior one in another part of the Department) not long after Bob Saloschin retired from his. Both were career members of the Senior Executive Service.[5]

This is where I came in, though not quite as immediately as the Reagan appointees at the Department would have preferred. My work on FOIA reform legislation in the Carter Administration had become well known to the Reagan Transition Team,[6] and it was not long before I was carrying that forward with renewed vigor for Jonathan Rose and his new Office of Legal Policy ("OLP," to those in the Department) -- while juggling my litigation caseload at the same time, of course. In short, the Reagan Administration had good reason to have much confidence in me based upon my track record of both defending the FBI and the CIA in court and my handling of proposed FOIA legislation up to that time.[7]

So less than three months into the new Administration, while I was on an all-too-brief period of paternity leave, Jonathan called me at home one day to offer me Bob Saloschin's position as head of OILP, which he saw as a "perfect fit" given both my legislative work and the fact that I was already providing a good deal of interpretative policy guidance to FOIA officers at other agencies (not to mention to AUSAs) across the country as part of my particular litigation-related activities.[8] This was a bit of a shock.[9]

As flattering and promising as it was, however, I saw this offer as less than perfect -- because it would have meant giving up my very full docket of high-profile litigation cases,[10] to which I had become quite attached, as well as my well-burnished role as a government litigator in general, for as long as I were to hold such a new policy position, and I was even more attached to that. To my mind (read: narrow, even borderline-myopic) back then, FOIA litigation, and the nascent development of case law through it, was most important to me, case closed.

Even so, declining this offer was not easy, just as declining the one from the U.S. Attorney's Office 2½ years earlier had not been (see Chapter Three), and it surprised many family members and friends, but I had a strength of commitment to FOIA litigation, and to my pending cases in particular, that kept me from accepting it. Looking back at it all now, this probably was a mistaken (read: shortsighted) judgment on my part, because as it turned out, the potential import and impact of FOIA policy development over the coming decades, especially with the advent of "electronic records" issues and then the necessity of so many post-9/11 ones, would have been enough to keep me well occupied.

But as it fatefully also turned out, the person who was hired for this position (read: in my place) after I declined it lasted only a few months in it before she suddenly left the Department to become a law professor. This meant that, as of the late summer of 1981, the Reagan Administration was right back to "square one" on its need to appoint someone to handle the FOIA. And by that time, I had done even more good work for it on prospective FOIA-amendment legislation, work that evidently was highly regarded by the Department's political leadership. (It certainly helps to have a depth of expertise in a vital area that is greater than anyone else's.)

So to make a longer story shorter here, I will just say that a deal was struck: I agreed to leave the Civil Division (and almost all of my pending litigation cases), but only if Bob Saloschin's relatively small policy office (with six "slots") and Quin Shea's much larger appeals office (with 27 of them) were consolidated together into a single, strengthened office -- one that, as a "sweetener" for me, also would have a caseload of selected FOIA litigation cases that I would personally supervise.[11]

This negotiated arrangement was approved by Attorney General Smith, who upon meeting with me personally promoted me to the level of GS-15 on the spot, with the promise that a promotion to a career Senior Executive Service position (which is what Bob Saloschin had held, being more than thirty years my senior) would follow if all went well by the end of that presidential term. Being not yet thirty, I saw it as a unique opportunity that even I could not be single-minded enough to turn down.[12]

*　*　*　*　*

What the Department's consolidation of major FOIA functions involved, of course, was the delicate matter of exactly how to merge its two high-level FOIA offices, which had had a sometimes-uneasy co-existence over the years as they were headed by Bob Saloschin and Quin Shea. Very fortunately, though, Quin Shea's acting replacement was one of his two deputies (the other having been that short-term replacement for Bob Saloschin); the more senior of the two, Richard L. Huff, had been in that office for several years and was a quintessential career professional, a very talented, highly dedicated, and absolutely superb public servant.

Simply put, I knew Dick Huff well enough to be entirely confident that he and I could work very well together, even though he was (and still is) 8½ years older than me. And this time my judgment was not at all mistaken, because we wound up working exceedingly well in a unique partnership[13] that lasted nearly two dozen years. (But that's getting ahead of the story, which will be told largely in later chapters.)

In short, Dick and I became co-directors of this newly consolidated office -- which I promptly named the "Office of Information and Privacy" ("OIP," forever thereafter) after my old "Information and Privacy Section" in the Civil Division -- and together we greatly strengthened the Department's handling of the Attorney General's FOIA and Privacy Act responsibilities. The Office of Information and Privacy was born on a *de facto* basis on November 2, 1981, the day that I arrived from the Civil Division, and we soon had a full complement of 33 people[14] dedicated to the key policy tasks of annually answering hundreds and then thousands of "FOIA Counselor" calls, training FOIA personnel across the government, and developing our new policy-guidance publications, among other things that carried over from the two predecessor offices[15] or further developed as we went along.[16]

Dick, who at age 38 was far more experienced than was I and also was a Judge Advocate General officer (soon to be a full colonel) in the Army Reserve, held the title of "Director (Policy and Administrative Appeals)" and continued to concentrate primarily on supervising the adjudication of those surging numbers of appeals,[17] which was a major and increasingly challenging enterprise. And with the counterpart title of "Director (Policy and Litigation)," I supervised OIP's fast-growing docket of litigation cases (eventually to reach more than 500) and handled most of its governmentwide policy activity,[18] including extensive work on prospective FOIA legislation.[19]

This was ideal for me. I even managed to keep one of my pending Civil Division cases, a non-FOIA challenge to the authority of the Federal Mediation Board, that I was able to successfully brief and argue (read: even after moving to OIP) before a court of appeals. And it also allowed Dick to expand his own horizons, most especially in the area of training and lecturing, in which he greatly excelled.[20]

In sum, as that first year of the Reagan Administration came to a close, I found myself firmly yet comfortably committed to a career in government secrecy (read: or transparency, on the other side of the coin) administration, with more than enough continued litigation involvement to satisfy that strong professional bent, and with a very satisfying new focus on formally and (where necessary) forcefully guiding all agencies of the executive branch on the myriad secrecy questions that came up continuously. Indeed, I found the processes of analyzing these legal questions, and crafting the most effective governmentwide guidance on them, to be uniquely challenging and intriguing. As I described this aspect of FOIA work twenty-five years later in a *Legal Times* interview upon my retirement:

> [The FOIA presented unique] challenges that came up almost daily. One of the wonderful things about the position I held is that every single day held the prospect of bringing some new issue, or new potentially sensitive record, to be analyzed and addressed.

> With very limited exception, everything that the Federal Government does is reduced to a record, and any record can suddenly be "placed on the [FOIA] hook," as it were. So when I walked in each morning, I knew I could be dealing with a difficult legal issue in virtually any area of governmental activity -- and as much as I'll enjoy teaching law, it'll be hard to ever top that.

Yes, just as I had found at age nineteen that the Justice Department was the place for me, I found barely ten years later that governmentwide policy work on issues of government secrecy (read: sufficiently including litigation) was an area of legal specialization worth devoting an entire career to. There certainly was a great deal of room for an enormous amount of policy development remaining to be done in this area as of 1981 (see, e.g., Chapters Twenty-Two, Twenty-Three, Thirty-Three, Thirty-Seven, Thirty-Eight, and Forty-One), more than even I realized at first.

And I must say now that had I known then of the challenges that the coming decades would bring -- especially those resulting from the events of September 11, 2001 -- I think I would have felt all the more strongly about making that career choice.[21] But first, I had to survive the Reagan Administration.

CHAPTER TWENTY-ONE

The Reagan Years

"My fellow Americans, I am pleased to tell you today that I've signed legislation that will outlaw Russia forever. We begin bombing in five minutes."

-- President Ronald W. Reagan, quipping (and perhaps revealing his innermost thoughts) while testing a microphone before a scheduled radio address, August 11, 1984

Heading up governmentwide Freedom of Information Act policy for the Reagan Administration was not unlike being a successful crisis negotiator for a local police force. You had to try to talk someone out of jumping off a ledge or following through on some dastardly act every now and again, but at least you succeeded nearly all of the time. And I have to admit that I succeeded as well as I did during the Reagan Administration in no small part because by and large the Reagan appointees at the Department of Justice were keenly ideological but generally reasonable.

That is to say that they almost all had the intellectual honesty and personal integrity to engage in a merits-based discussion of an issue and not rest on the fact that they usually had the raw power to just do what they wanted. This certainly was true in the secrecy area and it stands in stark contrast to the "Bush II" Administration that began exactly twenty years later. (But that's getting ahead of the story, which will be told in great detail in Chapters Thirty-Six, Thirty-Nine, Forty-One, and Forty-Three.)

Actually, the above metaphor applies much more to the second Reagan term than it does to the first. During the first term, under Attorney General William French Smith from 1981 to 1985, OIP worked hard and well to develop many new and refined policies on a wide variety of disclosure (or, one might say, nondisclosure) issues -- on matters of personal privacy, business confidentiality, and a host of law enforcement-related problems, for example.

It is true that we sometimes struggled with Attorney General Smith's stuffy propensity to react to the FOIA's disclosure requirements with a stock utterance

-- "We surely never had to do that at Gibson, Dunn & Crutcher!" -- and some-times it took longer than it should have taken for him to recognize the difference between an agency operating under federal law and how things were at his old California law firm, almost comically so.[1]

Yet only once did we have to crawl out on that ledge to talk someone down from a position that was, one could say, "way out there." And on that issue -- which involved an intricate question of whether the disclosure provisions of the FOIA could be "trumped" by their "interplay" with the nondisclosure provisions of the Privacy Act -- Dick and I were able to persuade the Department's politi-cal leadership to not go ahead with that highly questionable position in actual administrative practice unless it first was firmly adopted by the courts -- which ultimately it was not.

Indeed, Congress explicitly outlawed the taking of that ill-advised position through special legislation enacted soon thereafter,[2] despite the fact that its adop-tion would have saved law enforcement agencies like the FBI enormous amounts of resources by wrongly cutting back on the FOIA's use by first-party requesters. In other words, it was a bad idea that should not have gotten as far as it did, all superficial "Reaganite" appeal notwithstanding, but at least it did not take hold. And it served to set the tone for OIP's hegemony over such issues for the next 25 years.

In fact, during that first Reagan presidential term, OIP enjoyed tremendous support from Reagan appointees, who fully respected our expertise, appreciated our work, and never once failed to talk something through if we thought that it was merited.[3] We even encountered surprisingly little difficulty when, in 1984, our fresh analysis of the law led us to conclude that the leading appellate court on FOIA issues, the Court of Appeals for the District of Columbia Circuit, had made an analytical error years earlier on what became the highly controversial issue of access to executive branch records by individual Members of Congress.

This subject constitutes the entirety of Chapter Twenty-Two, immediately below, as it was a truly "BFD" (read: "big friggin' deal") at the time. Indeed, of all the policy-development activities that OIP engaged in over the years, this one was perhaps the most significant in that it so directly involved (read: half-antag-onized) a coordinate branch of government.

To be sure, things did change a bit during President Reagan's second term. First, we had a new attorney general, Edwin Meese III, who certainly was a more activist conservative than his predecessor had been. Yet although he was another close personal and professional friend of the president, he seemed at least at first to have brought no fundamental misconceptions about the FOIA itself with him, though the very idea of government information disclosure was certainly not his cup of tea.

Soon enough, though, Meese became so embroiled in his own controversies (read: multiple investigations of his conduct and business relations with outside parties) that he paid hardly any attention even to what was the major FOIA development of his tenure: The culmination of seven years of Justice Department efforts to obtain what we called "comprehensive FOIA reform" through the 1986 FOIA Amendments -- which at the same time provided much-needed relief to law enforcement agencies from the "rough cuts" that had Congress had made in its Watergate-reactive 1974 FOIA Amendments and even gave FOIA requesters some relief from FOIA fees as well.

OIP pulled out all the stops in vigorously implementing these new statutory provisions through extensive policy guidance and special training programs, and when it came time to issue the major interpretive document on the subject, titled the "Attorney General's Memorandum on the 1986 Amendments to the FOIA,"[4] Meese signed it without changing a single word that I had written, including in his own foreword to it.

So by and large, even the tenure of Attorney General Meese ultimately left the FOIA realm relatively unscathed. Up through the time of Meese's abrupt departure in mid-1988, Dick Huff and I were concerned mostly with dampening the darkest instincts of his political team -- such as on FOIA fees, public interest fee waivers, and the growing prevalence of "surrogate" FOIA requesters -- which we were able to do with fairly consistent success as we awaited the arrival of a replacement attorney general and the next administration as well.

CHAPTER TWENTY-TWO
"Congressional Access" Under the FOIA

"Suppose you were an idiot. And suppose you were a [M]ember of Congress. But I repeat myself."

-- Samuel Langhorne Clemens (a.k.a. Mark Twain), 1835-1910

One of the things that I realized upon the Office of Information and Privacy's creation was the possibility that we might on some issues come to a different policy position than what had been established by our principal predecessor office, the Office of Information Law and Policy ("OILP," to its friends), which had existed from 1977-1981. I do not mean by this any policy difference stemming from mere philosophical differences between the Reagan Administration and the Carter Administration before it. Rather, I was concerned about the chance that we might discover that OILP had developed some policy incorrectly.

Well, this actually did happen, as it turned out, on a major FOIA-related policy that strongly reverberates to this very day: The process of "congressional access" to executive branch records and the proper legal contours of that access. Agencies provide information to Congress every day, in one form or another, which is nothing to be alarmed about per se. Indeed, this interrelationship between coordinate branches of government actually was the focus of the original efforts to enact a Freedom of Information Act in the mid-1950s.[1]

Through a range of different communications -- letters, briefings, document transmittal, telephone conversations, and even congressional testimony -- federal agencies routinely provide information either at congressional request or at their own initiative to all types of congressional recipients, sometimes formally and sometimes less so. And along a continuum, congressional recipients can range from committees and subcommittees to individual Members of Congress acting in their official capacities to those acting in their own personal capacities -- and from legislative majority to minority status thrown in for all three. In other words, the circumstances of congressional access to agency information can vary considerably from case to case.

The legal and policy issue involved in "congressional access" to agency records arises from the fact that the Freedom of Information Act contains a provision -- then in subsection (c) of the Act[2] -- explicitly stating that the Act "is not authority to withhold information from Congress." And the question is: Exactly what was meant by Congress when it used the term "from Congress?" Did it mean "Congress as a whole," "Congress through its committees and subcommittees," "Congress through its individual Members," or some combination thereof? And also for good measure, does the majority/minority distinction or the official/personal capacity one, or both, come into play?

Prior to OIP's creation in 1981, the prevailing view on this question (read: that of OILP) was based on a D.C. Circuit Court of Appeals decision, *Murphy v. Department of the Army*, that OILP said commanded the conclusion[3] that "Congress" in this context included all Members of Congress acting in their official capacities, especially what were then called the "ranking members" (i.e., the most senior members not in the majority) on congressional committees and subcommittees. This meant that agencies often did not employ FOIA exemptions to what were loosely referred to as "congressional FOIA requests."

But the *Murphy v. Department of the Army* decision dealt primarily with Exemption 5 of the FOIA and whether it could be applied to a record concerning the construction of a dam in Kentucky even though it was disclosed by the Army to a single Member of Congress in whose district the dam was located. The FOIA requester argued that Exemption 5 was "waived" by that disclosure (read: that the exemption was forfeited) even if it did apply.

The D.C. Circuit's opinion was written by District Court Judge Harold H. Greene, sitting by designation, who did not have the benefit of another panel member's wisdom because that circuit court judge, Harold Leventhal, died more than a month before the opinion was issued. In it, Judge Greene made it very clear that he fully agreed with Exemption 5's applicability to the record at issue, but that he preferred not to have to deal with the thornier issue of "waiver" in the case.[4] In lieu of that, he seemingly worked around that issue by declaring that the disclosure in question was, in effect, "authorized" by FOIA subsection (c).

The next year, OILP took the *Murphy* decision and, as sometimes is said, "ran with it." It said that *Murphy* "seemed to indicate" that individual Members of Congress were legally entitled to receive exempt records under FOIA subsection (c). Based upon that, it elaborated that this could include even a congressperson acting to "assist a constituent," which could of course have the effect of laundering citizen FOIA requests so as to compel disclosure of even exempt information. Further, as a matter of governmentwide agency policy guidance, OILP spoke of balancing the interests protected by an exemption to see if they "outweigh the Member's need in a particular case." And if that were not bad enough, OILP's published guidance also managed to muddle the issues of "waiver" and "discretionary disclosure" under the FOIA to a point at which it was almost beyond repair.

The following year, OILP was consolidated into the newly established Office of Information and Privacy, together with the larger Office of Privacy and Information Appeals (see Chapter Twenty). At that point, among a wide range of other activities, OIP began developing policy guidance on a series of FOIA-related topics, such as the protection of business information, personal privacy, fee waiver policy, the Privacy Act's relation to the FOIA, the expedition of FOIA requests, and copyrighted materials. And in addition to this forward-looking policy development, we also looked back at what OILP had said about the issue of "congressional access" under the FOIA based upon the *Murphy* decision.

Unfortunately, the more we examined the *Murphy* decision, together with the proper implementation of FOIA subsection (c) (later subsection (d)), the more we realized that it actually was incorrectly decided and therefore was a flawed foundation for OILP's policy guidance.[5] Yes, upon carefully analyzing this, OIP unavoidably concluded that the Department of Justice's policy position on the "congressional access" issue was incorrect and had to be replaced.

Now, it is quite a daunting thing for a federal agency to suddenly no longer follow an appellate decision, especially in a subject-matter area that holds strong, governmentwide significance, all the more so where the decision was issued by the court of "universal venue."[6] And in this case, the issue in question involved a coordinate branch of government, no less. But I had absolutely no doubt that what the Department had been advising its agency clients and both the House and Senate congressional staffs was just plain wrong -- and I felt a professional responsibility to act on that, no matter what the consequences.

The primary problem with *Murphy* was that, among other things, it only assumed the very conclusion that it ostensibly was trying to reason its way toward. It managed to do so by limiting virtually its entire analysis of the issue to just rebuttals of the arguments made about it, rather than examining the content of subsection (c) itself. Had Judge Greene directly considered the meaning of the words "from Congress" in the subsection, he would have had far greater difficulty so expansively construing those words to mean "any Member of Congress in his or her official capacity."

Further, Judge Greene completely misconstrued the Act's legislative history statements on the issue. He quoted the relevant part of the House report, but seemed not to grasp the fact that it actually equated individual congresspersons with mere FOIA requesters, which is the very opposite of what he held to be so. Likewise, the Senate report actually was to the same effect, rather than supporting the conclusion that he assumed, as is the fact that the Privacy Act's counterpart provision, 5 U.S.C. § 552a(b)(9),[7] stands directly contrary to what Judge Greene held for the FOIA. It came as no surprise, therefore, when the aberrational interpretation of subsection (c) that was employed by Judge Greene in *Murphy* was pointedly and persuasively criticized in a subsequent D.C. Circuit case, *FTC v. Owens-Corning Fiberglas Corp.*, in 1980.

This all led to OIP's issuance of an extensive analysis of the "congressional access" issue, detailing exactly what was incorrect about the *Murphy* decision, and explaining why it was necessary and appropriate that all federal agencies change their approach to it. We stated that from that point on, all agencies were required to respond to "congressional FOIA requests" as such only if they were made by a body of Congress (i.e., the House or Senate per se, which is rare) or by Congress through its committee or subcommittee structure (with proper jurisdiction over the subject matter), not by any single congressperson, whether in an official capacity or not.[8]

Beyond that, this interpretation of subsection (c) meant that we had to deal with the other big distinction that very often comes up in this area as a practical matter -- the majority party versus minority party one. Most formal congressional requests for access to agency records or information are made by congressional committees (read: or subcommittees, makes no difference). Agencies accept such requests as made by the committee when they are made by the committee's chairperson.

Requests made by the minority of a committee, however, including by its highest-ranking minority member, are on the other side of the proper subsection (c) line. OIP has long told agencies not to comply with such requests as if they are "from Congress," as a matter of both policy and practicality. To do so is to place all sensitive information at peril of being held subject to "waiver" in the context of any future FOIA request.[9]

In sum, this meant that: (1) "congressional access" requests made by a committee chairperson are honored as within the disclosure mandate of subsection (d) (formerly subsection (c)); (2) requests made by a committee's minority members (regardless of rank) are not; and (3) requests made by individual Members of Congress likewise are not given special subsection (d) treatment, regardless of being made in a Member's official capacity. This delineation and OIP's "congressional access" guidance have stood the test of time for nearly four decades now, despite the occasional attempt to overturn it by minority Members of one body of Congress or another from time to time.[10]

CHAPTER TWENTY-THREE
The Settlement Privilege

"Making Love Out of Nothing at All."

-- James R. "Jim" Steinman (1947-2021), sung by Air Supply, 1983

People who work with legislation know that it is only the exceptional broad legislative scheme (read: a comprehensive one like the FOIA or the Privacy Act, for instance) that contains no unanticipated gap, regrettable drafting oversight, or overlooked aspect of it that does not become apparent until after it is implemented. The Privacy Act has a number of these (see Chapter Fourteen). And the FOIA, for its part, has at least two such defects, one of which was realized only in the 1980s and the other of which (discussed in Chapter Eighteen) actually did not arise until after September 11, 2001. The former of these two has to do with the need for the protection of "settlement information."[1]

"Settlement documents" is the term broadly used for records that are prepared by litigation (or potential litigation) parties, sometimes for their own use alone but most often to be shared with opposing parties, as part of settlement negotiations. Many civil litigation cases are settled (not just criminal ones that are disposed of through plea bargains) and when this occurs, or merely is attempted, there are of course documents (or today, more likely email communications) that are exchanged between the parties for possible settlement purposes. And when one of those parties is a federal agency, the records of which are subject to potential FOIA disclosure, the question becomes: Can the agency, if it receives a FOIA request encompassing such records, withhold even any part of them on the basis of an applicable FOIA exemption?

The reason for an agency wanting to withhold settlement information has nothing to do with the case being settled.[2] Rather, in such a case the agency is looking forward to the *next* such case or cases in which a new private party to the same type of case would seek a litigation advantage in learning about the agency's thinking (and degree of settlement willingness) in the previous one. The Supreme Court presciently envisioned exactly this in 1982 when it decided the FOIA case of *Federal Trade Commission v. Grolier Inc.,* in which Justice William J. Brennan, Jr.'s concurring opinion recognized that the federal government each year defends "hundreds or thousands of essentially similar cases" in which opposing litigants would benefit from having advance knowledge of "on what terms they may be settled."[3]

The problem was that while "settlement information" under some circumstances might qualify for viable Exemption 5 protection by virtue of the "deliberative process privilege" or even the "attorney work-product privilege" incorporated into that exemption, in many instances such information cannot. And as the numbers of such instances grew as the use of the FOIA matured during the 1980s, this problem became more and more serious. Put another way, by 1985, agencies had received a growing number of FOIA requests in which "settlement information" had been "placed on the hook" without any clear means of protecting it from public disclosure, because it was widely believed that no "settlement privilege" actually existed.[4]

So OIP did what it was created to do: We researched the issue to within an inch of its life, verified that no "settlement privilege" had yet been recognized under the FOIA, but discerned that there indeed was a solid (albeit slender) basis for the recognition of such a privilege in other contexts. Then we prepared a formal written policy announcing a new "settlement negotiations privilege" applicable under Exemption 5 (or, less frequently, Exemption 4) of the FOIA, with full supporting detail, and advised agencies that they could begin applying it wherever need be.

What we had discovered in our "deep dive" research of this issue was that there were, indeed, two instances (admittedly, one stronger than the other) in which federal courts had in effect recognized a "settlement privilege" as part of a case's adjudication. Under the general law of "privilege" in federal jurisprudence,[5] it is something that is "judge made," meaning that a privilege does not exist until at least one federal court declares it to exist and applies it in a particular case.[6] So it was that these two precedents, together with the language of Justice Brennan's pragmatic concurring opinion in *Grolier*,[7] provided a firm basis for OIP's conclusion that a "settlement negotiations privilege" does in fact exist.

This legal conclusion, and the policy statement that announced it, provided the basis for much needed protection of the information exchanged between government agencies and party opponents over the following decades. In fact, it was not long before OIP itself successfully litigated this position, in a case by the name of *M/A-Com Information Systems v. United States Department of Health & Human Services*, in which Judge Gerhard A. Gesell[8] declared that it "is in the public interest to encourage settlement negotiations in matters of this kind and it would impair the ability of HHS to carry out its governmental duties if disclosure of this kind of material under FOIA were required."[9]

Thus, as was evidenced also on the "congressional access" issue discussed in the previous chapter, OIP was not at all timid about advancing its client agencies' interests, and seeking necessary protection for sensitive information, through aggressive policymaking as well as through litigation.[10]

CHAPTER TWENTY-FOUR
The "White Out" Case

"Any sufficiently advanced technology is indistinguishable from magic."

-- Sir Arthur C. Clarke, 1917-2008

Among the more than 500 FOIA and Privacy Act cases that I directly supervised at both the district court and court of appeals levels in my 25 years at OIP was one that hopefully will never recur in any form. Styled as *Simon v. Department of Labor*, it was handled by a then-junior member of OIP's 22-person attorney staff and it took a blatantly unlawful yet nonetheless sad turn about half-way through it.

Mark E. Nagle was that young attorney and his involvement with the *Simon* case turned out to be a springboard to bigger and better things in his career.[1] The FOIA requester in the case was a representative of a public interest group who was holding the defendant agency's "feet to the fire" by using the Act to obtain access to some highly sensitive records that the agency was loathe to turn over. The year was 1983 and the agency (actually, a sub-agency) was the Occupational Safety and Health Administration ("OSHA," to its friends), which was part of the Department of Labor.[2]

During those years of the Reagan Administration, OSHA was headed by a very conservative Reagan appointee, Thorne G. Auchter, who as one might expect was not a particularly strong foe of industries in implementing OSHA's regulatory responsibilities. Neither was Reagan's Secretary of Labor, the late Raymond J. Donovan, who went on to be indicted for larceny, fraud, and general mayhem but ultimately was fully acquitted, whereupon he was famously quoted as asking: "Which office do I go to to get my reputation back?"[3]

Mark and I never learned whether either of these political appointees (more likely the former) ever was directly or indirectly involved in OSHA's treatment of the requested records that we were defending. But we did know that these were highly sensitive records reflective of agency decisionmaking in some controversial areas. And our review of those records in "processed" form made us somewhat suspicious of how well our client agency had handled them.

This is where it needs to be made clear that when a Justice Department Trial Attorney defends agency action under the FOIA (or in any civil litigation more generally, for that matter) that litigator has a time-honored obligation to make sure that that action is properly defensible, at least by some minimal standard. And in FOIA cases, wherever the Justice Department determines that this is not so, that agency action will not be defended in court and the records in question will have to be disclosed. Under the law, with the Justice Department holding what is called "litigation authority," it is just that simple.

So it was that Mark and I ventured over to OSHA one afternoon in order to examine the withheld records "in the clear" (meaning in their original, "un-processed" form) in the midst of OSHA's somewhat disorganized FOIA office. And when we focused on one record in particular, and with particular care, we noticed that a key paragraph of that document actually extended further down the page on the original version than it did in the version that had been released to the FOIA requester. Sure enough, the released version gave the impression that that paragraph ended well before it actually did.

Mark and I stared at the head of the office long enough for it to be clear to him what we were discerning and it did not take long for him to crack: He himself had "processed" this document, he admitted, and as he looked at it in its released form he allowed as how he had deleted the information missing from it, but had used "white out,"[4] instead of a standard method of document redaction, in doing so. But that did not tell the entire story: He had also inserted a period partway through the paragraph, at the point at which the deleted lines appeared, which of course gave the false impression that the paragraph just ended there and went no further.

At this point, Mark and I had two responsibilities. First, as the litigators, we were obliged to immediately purge what could fairly be deemed a "fraud on the court" with (dis)respect to this document, "coming completely clean" with both the judge and our opposing counsel about what we had just discovered. Second, because one of OIP's responsibilities is to oversee the FOIA's administration throughout the executive branch, we had to take steps governmentwide to ensure that no federal agency had ever done such a thing -- or worse yet was now doing such a thing -- in the past.

Obviously, OSHA in particular and the Labor Department more broadly became "ground zero" in this review, but we reached out to all agencies on this and we emphasized that it was a "cautionary tale" being told for their possible benefit. As one might imagine, it right away became a highlight of OIP's governmentwide FOIA training programs in order to guard against such a thing ever happening again.[5]

In doing this, by the way, we declined to identify by name the miscreant OSHA employee. By the time we left his office (if not beforehand), he knew that what he had done was very wrong, potentially scandalous with the harshest publicity, and that it put his agency, its parent Department, and the Federal Government's entire FOIA program in an awful light. But we knew that under sound principles of law, or at least OIP's newly developed privacy policy, an employee at his level did not necessarily forego all personal-privacy interests in a case such as this. And we took into consideration the problems in his personal life that he remorsefully explained to us when we caught him.[6]

But this was hardly the end of this litigation case, as it also came to include a novel legal issue as well. I must first say that the opposing counsel in the case, a well-respected FOIA litigator, was understanding of what we described to him. It helped in this regard that he was very familiar with OIP's work, and with the reputation for trust and integrity that we had already established within the FOIA's "public interest" community during the previous two years, so he did not give us nearly as hard a time as he could have about our client's shameful actions.[7] But he did, once the more routine issues of the case were disposed of, proceed to seek some extraordinary relief that the Act permitted the court to grant in exceptional cases.

By this, I am referring to a little-known feature that Congress had added to the Act, at the behest of public interest groups, when it enacted the 1974 FOIA Amendments. As a special deterrent to intransigent agency behavior (which had all too often characterized the very early years of the FOIA's implementation), Congress pointedly provided that whenever a court "find[s] that the circumstances surrounding the withholding [in a case] raise questions [of] whether the agency personnel acted arbitrarily or capriciously with respect to the withholding" the court may refer the agency employee(s) in question for investigation of the action by the U.S. Civil Service Commission (later succeeded, for this purpose, by the Office of Special Counsel).[8]

Arguably, if any case deserved the shame of such a referral it was this one. Yet Mark and I had a professional duty to defend our client agency against so ignominious an outcome to the extent that we arguably could do so.[9] And this became a realistic possibility for us when upon a close reading of this statutory provision's entire language we found that it actually provided a basis for resisting such a referral in this particular case. Indeed, that provision stated that it could apply only if a court first "orders the production of any agency records improperly withheld."[10]

As it happened, due in no small part to the agency's egregious error, we had undertaken a top-to-bottom review of every bit of information that had been withheld in the case, according to strict Justice Department standards. And before the case reached a conclusion (let alone the judge doing so), OSHA had made a generous supplemental disclosure of all even borderline information that had been at issue. Therefore, when the case reached adjudication on its merits (i.e., as to the proper applicability of FOIA exemptions), the court granted summary judgment to the agency and had virtually no basis for ordering, in the words of the statute, "the production of any records."

This was a very technical defense, of course, one that seemed to ring hollow in the face of what OSHA had done, but it was enough to "do the trick": The Court issued a precedential decision to the effect that it lacked authority under the statute to make the misconduct referral that the plaintiff vigorously (and quite understandably) demanded be made. And when the case was over, inasmuch as the plaintiff public interest group ultimately shied from the expense of taking an appeal, Mark Nagle and I promised ourselves that we would never risk being in such a position in the future.

CHAPTER TWENTY-FIVE
The Spies Who Left Us

"If you can't love your country, you should at least do it no harm."

-- United States District Court Judge Ricardo M. Urbina, October 16, 2002

A relatively small part of what the Office of Information and Privacy does has to do with what is called the "Department Review Committee," or "DRC," for short, which is the mechanism by which the Department handles, among other things, FOIA administrative appeals that involve classified information.[1] One of OIP's two predecessor offices historically "staffed" the DRC's activities, through a small unit that was headed by an attorney supervisor. Ancillary to this, we had one of the greatest concentrations of highly classified documents within the Department (extending back many, many years) sitting in eight oversized safes that we maintained in a "back room" of our office.[2]

OIP's "DRC Unit" consisted of two supervisors (including one OIP deputy) and two paralegals, one of whom we rotated among three other areas of paralegal responsibilities in OIP, and a clerical support person as well. In the early 1980s, one of those rotating DRC paralegals was a young woman who quickly became OIP's sharpest and most capable paralegal among all others. Her name was Ana Belen Montes -- and in 1985, while working for OIP, she also became a spy.

Ana is of Spanish ancestry, tracing back to a particular region of Spain, and her grandparents immigrated to Puerto Rico before her parents came to the United States. Her father was a psychologist in the U.S. Army who settled with his family in Topeka, Kansas, and then in a Maryland suburb of D.C. After graduating from the University of Virginia, Ana came to work for one of OIP's predecessor offices (see Chapter Twenty) and then became a mainstay paralegal for OIP.

Evidently, Ana was recruited to spy for Cuba while attending the Johns Hopkins School of Advanced International Studies ("SAIS," to its students and faculty alike) in the evenings as she pursued a master's degree in (ironically) "foreign affairs." This was during her last year at OIP and she used this degree (atop glowing OIP recommendations) to obtain an intelligence analyst position at the Defense

Intelligence Agency ("DIA," to those with much of it) in the summer of 1985, where she could better pursue her new secret career.[3]

Everyone in OIP was quite sad to see Ana leave, as she was a lovely and extremely well-liked person even apart from how capable and intelligent she was. One of OIP's two longtime deputy directors, Margaret Ann "Peggy" Irving, in particular, was close friends with her, and she remained so even while Ana spent the next 16 years engaged in very active espionage. Peggy had not the slightest clue of this; no one did.[4] Yes, Ana was that good (read: very, very good) at concealing her true allegiance to Cuba and her secret feelings about its treatment by the United States.[5]

In time, Ana rose higher and higher within DIA's ranks -- specializing in Cuba, of course -- so much so that by early 2000, when Attorney General Janet W. Reno became embroiled in a highly publicized controversy over the status of a five-year-old Cuban refugee by the name of Elian Gonzalez, Ana was the senior Cuba expert at DIA (and perhaps of the entire Intelligence Community) who came over to Main Justice to brief Janet on it. And she did an excellent job on this, as always, which is part of how Ana maintained her cover.[6]

And all this time,[7] Ana was operating a "one-woman espionage ring" by sending large amounts of highly classified information[8] to the Cuban Intelligence Directorate in Havana, doing so through the use of sophisticated encryption and clandestine communications. For that, she had a short-wave radio built into a specially designed piece of furniture in her Cleveland Park apartment on Macomb Street, N.W.,[9] for receiving encrypted messages from Cuba, and she always used coded numeric page messages through public phones for transmitting them. Apparently, a nearby phone booth located at the entrance to the National Zoo on Connecticut Avenue was her favorite.[10]

Evidently, Ana succeeded in disclosing many high-value U.S. secrets in doing this, including the identities of four undercover U.S. operatives in Cuba, the location of a U.S. Army Special Forces camp in El Salvador that she herself had visited on behalf of DIA, and some items of information from other agencies of the U.S. Intelligence Community to which she had been given access (or had stealthily obtained access) through a high-tech information-sharing system.[11] Atop that, given the level that she eventually reached at DIA, Ana was actually able to influence national policy toward Cuba, in ways both small and large, which made her a "double-threat" as espionage agents go.[12]

This came to an end, however, in 2001. In the spring of that year, the FBI "cracked" a Cuban espionage ring operating out of Florida, which then led to it obtaining an indication that someone such as Ana might exist. In time, the fact that the FBI was looking to uncover such a person (read: a Cuban agent working out of Washington, D.C.) became known within the Intelligence Community and someone made a fateful connection to a previous (albeit relatively routine) suspicion of Ana.[13] (Such suspicions are aroused all the time in that line of work.[14]) This led to both her surveillance and a surreptitious search of her apartment, where some of the tools of her tradecraft were found.

Indeed, once Ana's secret short-wave radio was discovered, the FBI knew that it had her. But as often is the case in such counterintelligence operations, a high-level decision was made to not arrest her right away, but rather to keep her under very close surveillance in order to see what else might be learned about her tradecraft and possible involvement with others. This phase of the investigation went on for many months.

But then this abruptly ended with the events of September 11. Apparently, there was a sudden concern that Cuban leader Fidel Castro might have a "back-channel" to Iraqi leader Saddam Hussein that could be used to connect to Ana in a newly dangerous way.[15] So she was quietly "rolled up," as they say, at her desk, on Friday, September 21 -- which I learned about when I received a phone call at home that evening officially informing me of that as a former employer and setting the groundwork for the "after action" analysis that I knew would have to be done in order to see if Ana had compromised any classified information while she was at OIP.[16]

It perhaps goes without saying that everyone who knew Ana at the Justice Department was absolutely shocked by this development, no one more so than Peggy Irving. For a while, there were those who simply refused to believe that this was not just some big mistake. But then I obtained the indictment that had been lodged against Ana and knew that it was sadly true. She had betrayed her country not for any of the most common reasons -- "sex, drugs, and rock 'n roll," we used to say, meaning sex, drugs, alcohol, or money. No, it was for purely (read: not entirely pure) ideological reasons: Ana simply could not abide how the U.S. treated Cuba, not in her perception, anyway, and she became determined to counteract that, as best she could (read: very well), in the worst way.[17]

So just a few days after Ana's arrest, I had a long talk with Peggy, who had been providing comfort and other accommodations to members of Ana's family, and went through the particulars of the indictment with her, telling her that Ana should get good counsel as soon as possible, as the charges against her carried the death penalty. That is when Peggy informed me that an attorney had indeed been lined up for her, and she gave me his name.

Now, I will not be including this name here, for good reason, I think, because it just so happened that I knew this gentleman quite well from a case that I had personally handled in my Civil Division litigation days (see Chapter [excised]).[18] In fact, this attorney, who as I recall was a law professor at the time,[19] had been co-counsel against me on that case together with a young rising star in the legal community, whom I knew then as "Rick" Urbina. And the "kicker" was that, based upon his initial handling of that case, I did not at all have a high opinion of that senior attorney's legal abilities, far from it.

So I told Peggy that I strongly urged her to in turn strongly urge Ana's family to find other counsel for Ana, and I told her exactly why. I even suggested to Peggy that Ana's family try to cash in her government retirement funds if they were still available to her so that she could afford high-priced counsel.[20] And having recently seen how local attorney Plato Cacheris had succeeded in obtaining what seemed like an extremely favorable plea deal for Bernadette "Bonnie" Hanssen, the wife of Soviet "mole" Robert P. Hanssen, an FBI Supervisory Special Agent,[21] I suggested that he be contacted first, as a perfect candidate for the job.

And he was, both contacted and perfect. Plato Cacheris agreed to represent Ana and he negotiated a plea deal for her that was beyond compare, considering the circumstances. In October of 2002, after having been incarcerated for more than a year, Ana pled guilty to conspiracy to commit espionage and was sentenced to a 25-year prison term (including time served), followed by five years' probation and 500 hours of community service; no fine was imposed, as all her assets were taken from her.[22] And she was essentially banned for life from having free access to any Internet-connected computer.

At her sentencing, Ana looked ashen but resolute, fully composed. She never looked back at anyone in attendance, including her family members. She just sat straight up, staring only at the judge, with her face showing no sign of emotion. None. We all had hoped that she would give at least some indication of remorse for what she had done, through either her words or her body language, but she did not.

Rather, Ana made it clear to everyone, for once and for all, that she was totally, irrevocably unrepentant. She made a statement to the Court that left no doubt whatsoever about that:

> Your honor, I engaged in the activity that brought me before you because I obeyed my conscience rather than the law. I believe our government's policy towards Cuba is cruel and unfair, profoundly unneighborly, and I felt morally obligated to help the island defend itself from our efforts to impose our values and our political system on it. . . . My way of responding to our Cuba policy may have been morally wrong. Perhaps Cuba's right to exist free of political

and economic coercion did not justify giving the island classified information to help it defend itself. I can only say that I did what I thought right to counter a grave injustice.[23]

And in response, District Court Judge Ricardo M. "Rick" Urbina[24] lectured Ana about what she had done and about what she had just said: "If you cannot love your country, at least you should do it no wrong."

With time off for "good behavior," Ana should be eligible for release from prison very soon.[25]

* * * * *

Edwin Earl Pitts, on the other hand, was a far less sophisticated spy. He was known within OIP simply as "Earl," who together with many other Supervisory Special Agents[26] was part of an entire division of personnel within the FBI dedicated to handling FOIA and Privacy Act requests -- and, most importantly for present purposes, defending the FBI's withholding of records to OIP attorneys on administrative appeal.[27] For the Bureau's very large percentage of the roughly 2500 administrative appeals that OIP received each year, we would send OIP attorneys "across the street" to the FBI's Main Headquarters Building ("FBIHQ," when it opened in 1975) to examine what was being withheld and to make a recommendation as to whether that should be upheld on administrative appeal. Earl was part of that.

And for a stretch of time from the late 1980s to the mid-1990s, we all got to know Earl because year after year he would join his fellow Bureau comrades (no implication intended) and cross Pennsylvania Avenue to attend OIP's "Holiday Party,"[28] where much merriment would ensue. Earl quickly became a "regular' in the terminology of OIP's party-planning committee, one who seemed to know a good party when he found one.[29] Little did any of us know, though, that Earl had already found himself a different kind of party, a year-round one, when he signed up to work for the Kremlin in 1987.[30]

Earl began his FBI career in 1983 after a six-year post-graduate stint in the Army, where he served as a military policeman, rising to the rank of captain. He held a master's degree and a law degree, the latter of which was his strongest credential upon being hired.[31] In his early FBI years, he was stationed in two relatively low-cost-of-living areas in the Commonwealth of Virginia, but this changed greatly when he was transferred to New York City in early 1987. Unlike Ana Montes, ideology played no part in his decision to become a spy; it was all about money, or the lack of it, as he tried to support himself and his wife on a relatively small salary in a high-cost location.

Earl's position in New York was made to order for an FBI Special Agent willing to trade his professional allegiance for ready cash. He worked on FBI foreign counterintelligence investigations out of the New York Field Office, which meant that he was part of a longstanding cadre of FBI personnel who "kept tabs" on a constant stream of Soviet-bloc diplomats to New York City, many of whom actually were operatives of the KGB. Earl was intimately involved in the Bureau's surveillance of both known and suspected Soviet intelligence officers, including its identification, targeting, and reporting on them. In short, he was privy to a wide range of highly sensitive, and thus highly classified, FBI operations.[32]

But the cost of living and working in the New York City area on what was then only about a $30,000 annual salary (at the pay level of GS-12) soon got to him.[33] He also still had student loans to pay off, after all those years, and he suffered the humility of having to ask his father, who operated the family farm and drove a truck on the side, for a loan. It wasn't long before he started holding this against the FBI for its particular pay scales and the Federal Government in general.[34]

So Earl did something that U.S. intelligence agencies worry about all the time: He "self-recruited," by sending a letter to an official at the Soviet Mission to the United Nations in New York City whom he himself had surveilled.[35] In this letter, Earl made reference to some of that official's recent activities and sought an official meeting with him, which led to him being turned over to a high-level KGB officer (read: as his "handler"), who guided his espionage career. Little did Earl know (because he could not at the time) that that very Soviet intelligence officer would himself decide to "change sides" after the Soviet Union collapsed in 1991, whereupon he would turn Earl in. It was "spy vs. spy" in all its splendor.

Anyway, Earl worked as an active "mole" within the FBI for more than five years, first as an agent of the KGB (more formally, the "Union of Soviet Socialist Republics' Committee for State Security"), and then for its successor, the "Sluzhba Vneshney Rasvedi Rossii" ("SVRR," to its less violent comrades), the intelligence service of the Russian Federation. And he was quite a successful mole at that: He provided much information about the Bureau's inner workings and also some especially sensitive information on an FBI asset who reported to the FBI covertly on Russian intelligence matters.

In exchange for this, Earl was paid a grand total of $224,000 over the course of five years. The first two of those years were spent in New York City, but then the stakes got even higher when in August of 1989, he was promoted to the rank of Supervisory Special Agent based upon his "good work" (read: for the FBI) in New York City. And with that promotion came a welcome transfer to FBI Headquarters in Washington, D.C., where he was assigned to the Bureau's

Records Management Division (read: its FOIA shop) for the next three years,[36] leading to a purely legal position in the Bureau's Legal Counsel Division (read: the predecessor to its Office of General Counsel).

Earl continued his espionage activities even after leaving New York City for Washington, though evidently on a lesser scale, and he was successful in that he managed to remain undetected in both locations. At some point in 1992, the FBI later determined, Earl also managed to shift to what it later called a "dormant status," which meant that Earl was both an active spy and then a "dormant" one when he attended a half-dozen holiday parties at OIP. In his "dormant status," Earl in 1995 accepted a transfer to the Behavioral Science Unit at the FBI Academy in Quantico, Virginia, where his work was of less interest to the Russians.[37]

Consistent with Earl's success in remaining undetected in all of his covert activities, his downfall had nothing to do with what he did or did not do as a spy. Rather, it became inevitable only because his long-term KGB (and then SVRR) handler defected to the United States in the mid-90s. And with that, it was not long before the U.S. Intelligence Community (which includes parts of the FBI) learned through that Russian's debriefings that the FBI had had a mole in its midst, by the name of "Pitts," for several years. This caused much embarrassment within the Bureau, as might be imagined, accompanied as it was by the faint sound of J. Edgar Hoover "rolling over in his grave."[38]

Plus, there was the fact that by this point in time, i.e., 1995, Earl had been "out of the game" for about three years, with almost six years having passed since his espionage "heyday" in New York. So a decision was made that something creative had to be devised to fit these circumstances, not unlike what the Bureau did in the "Solo source" case with William Albertson in the 1960s (see Chapter Fifteen). And a "false flag" gambit was settled on as the perfect thing for the job, which gives Earl's sad tale even more depth.

A "false flag" operation is defined for this purpose as one in which someone pretends to be of an opposing nationality (e.g., Russian, not American), leading the victim to think that he or she is dealing with someone of that nationality, not the actual one. In this case, the FBI pretended to be Russian operatives who needed to "reactivate" Earl for (at first) just "a little bit" of assistance.

To do this, an FBI undercover agent visited Earl at his home in Virginia, persuaded Earl of his SVRR *bona fides*, and without much difficulty elicited from Earl a commitment to briefly come out of retirement. An initial payment of $15,000 in cash probably sealed the deal, inasmuch as Earl said that he could use the money, with a promise of more to come. This wound up stretching for a period of 16 months, with a series of payments totaling $65,000.

During that time, Earl provided personal information about fellow Special Agents, ideas about how the SVRR could recruit some of them (including a retired Special Agent who Earl said was "lonely"), and took several initial steps toward smuggling a SVRR (read: FBI) technical expert into FBI Academy facilities. Toward that end, he provided an FBI cipher lock combination, an FBI key, and his own FBI identification badge. He also stole a "STU III" handset device and left it at a "dead drop" to be picked up by the "SVRR."

The FBI's primary purpose in running this "false flag" operation was to confirm Earl's suspected (read: alleged) espionage activities during 1987-1992 and to try to get a better handle on exactly what he did for the KGB and then the SVRR back then. And, indeed, during the course of the operation, Earl made many, many incriminating statements concerning his prior espionage activities. With that, atop what Earl was documented doing during his 16-month "retirement" spree, the FBI had more than enough to arrest and prosecute him.[39]

And so it did. The charges against Earl and the maximum penalties upon conviction were: conspiracy to commit espionage, life in prison; attempted espionage, life in prison; communication of classified information by government officer or employee, ten years in prison; and conveyance without authority of government property, ten years in prison. And given the nature of his crimes, there was at least a possibility of his receiving the death penalty.[40]

At the time of Earl's arrest, in mid-December of 1996, Attorney General Janet W. Reno and FBI Director Louis J. Freeh held a joint press conference in which they tried to put the best face on this troubling development. Janet said that the whole episode showed the Department of Justice's willingness to carry out "the type of vigilant self-examination that the American people demand of all of our institutions." For his part, Louie Freeh ventured that "the success of the 'false flag' operation leaves no doubt about the continuing threat to national security that the defendant posed . . . but we must do a better job of finding spies before they do major damage."

Earl pled guilty, of course, and as part of his plea deal he received a promise from the prosecutors that they would seek a sentence of less than 25 years (i.e., a better deal that Ana's). That commitment was kept with a recommendation of 24½ years, however. And then in February of 1997, District Court Judge Thomas S. "T.S." Ellis III sentenced Earl to 27 years' imprisonment for good measure.[41] He was released from prison on December 20, 2019, after serving less time than that.

We talked about this at a weekly OIP staff meeting after Earl was arrested down at Quantico. This was still nearly five years before Ana would be "rolled up" in the wake of 9/11, and to us, then, it marked the first time (read: that we knew of) that OIP had had an actual spy "on site."[42] We all vaguely knew that potential espionage was part and parcel of the job that we did, especially in connection with OIP's ancillary national security classification-adjudication activity (read: through its "DRC" function) on behalf of the Attorney General. That was, after all, why we had a "cypher lock"[43] and those big, heavy safes. But Earl had made it become real.

★ ★ ★ ★ ★

Actually, one of us already had come close to having a spy "on site," only this was on the Main Justice Building's Sixth Floor, which also had been occupied by the FBI. Anyway, this was a spy of an entirely different ilk, but a highly successful spy nonetheless. Her name was Sharon Thomas and for more than a year she had worked as a secretary in the Civil Division's Information and Privacy Section and then had left that position, under somewhat mysterious circumstances, not long before I arrived in that section in 1977. It turned out that she had been "planted" there by a borderline cult of which she was a member, which was looking for "inside" FOIA litigation case information, as well as anything else that could be used by her organization, the Founding Church of Scientology.[44]

A bit of background: For decades prior to the late 1970s, the Foundation Church of Scientology had been locked in a veritable "death-grip" battle with the Internal Revenue Service (as well as its counterparts around the world), over its tax-significant claim to be a "religion." And toward that end, it had filed scores of FOIA requests and then more than a dozen FOIA litigation cases, many of which were being handled in a closely coordinated fashion by one particular Assistant United States Attorney in the Office of the United States Attorney for the District of Columbia and also by a relatively junior attorney in the Information and Privacy Section (read: "Unit," at first) at Main Justice.[45] Enter, from stage left, "Operation Snow White," which was an astonishingly wide-ranging Scientology "operation" that involved the infiltration of multiple IRS offices and the offices of those two Justice Department litigation attorneys.

Scientologist Sharon Thomas began her employment at the Department of Justice in Washington, D.C., on February 29, 1976. She was somehow assigned as an entry-level secretary in what was then called the Information and Privacy Unit of the Department's Civil Division, which at the time was handling several Scientology-initiated FOIA lawsuits. After becoming acclimated in that position, she stole (read: photocopied) some documents that were involved in a number of pending Scientology FOIA cases, which she purloined either after regular working hours and on weekends. Her *modus operandi* was to take all such documents to a "safe" photocopying machine on the Fourth Floor of the building (read: one that she thought would not be monitored), photocopy them there, and then return the documents to where she had found them.

This young Scientologist then met on a weekly basis with a Scientology "supervisor" in nearby Arlington, Virginia, who guided her on how to proceed. In time, she was instructed to try to obtain all files on Scientology (including attorney work product) from the office of the particular Justice Department attorney who was personally handling the unit's Scientology FOIA cases. She also was directed to be attentive to that attorney in the hopes that she might become his secretary, in order to have immediate access to all of his files.

Meanwhile, she was to try to overhear his phone and office conversations and make notes of any matter that she though relevant to Scientology. Apparently, she was able to do all of this without arousing the slightest suspicion and within four months after her arrival she succeeded in becoming that attorney's full-time secretary.[46] And when I arrived there as a Trial Attorney the following year, I learned that she also had succeeded in breaking into the Deputy Attorney General's Office one weekend to forage for Scientology-related information there.[47]

At the same, the other Justice Department attorney handling Scientology FOIA cases, Assistant United States Attorney ("AUSA," within DOJ) Nathan Dodell, also became a target of high-level Scientology attention. Nate was much older than his Main Justice counterpart; he was a grizzled veteran of that office by that time, by both tenure and temperament, and is now deceased.[48] And it was at about the same time that he was in open Court one day before a crusty Senior District Court Judge, former Chief Judge George L. Hart, Jr., and heard that judge wonder aloud whether the government should consider subpoenaing Scientology leader L. Ron Hubbard for a deposition.

That apparently caused great alarm back at Scientology headquarters in Los Angeles and Sharon Thomas was immediately notified to be on the lookout for anything she might detect about a possible decision by the Justice Department to take such an extraordinary step.[49] It also led to several increasingly risky, but initially very successful, attempts by other Scientology operatives to break into Nate's courthouse office.

This was greatly facilitated by the fact that -- in addition to courtrooms, judges' chambers, AUSAs' offices, and the like -- the federal courthouse in D.C. at the time also contained the District of Columbia Bar Association Library as an amenity for local attorneys. And it just so happened that Nate's office was located on the same floor of the building, directly across from the library's back exit. So these two aggressive Scientology agents decided to try to take advantage of that by saying that they were visiting the library for "legal research" and then using it to get directly to Nate's office for some after-hours research of a different kind.

And they were lucky at this, in that they were able to locate and duplicate a set of keys that Nate's secretary had left on her desk, without her realizing that this happened. They then gained access to Nate's office and quickly located several Scientology case files. In their first entry, they were able to photocopy about five inches of documents and return them, just as Sharon Thomas had done at Main Justice. And after a second entry, in June of 1976, that grew to more than a foot of documents, totaling more than 1000 pages. Many of these documents were in Nate's handwriting and constituted his strategy and other work product on the cases.[50]

All told, these document thefts at both Main Justice and the D.C. federal courthouse amounted to one of the largest infiltrations of the United States Government in history or, in the words of one media outlet, "the largest incident of private domestic espionage in the history of the United States." And they came to a halt only because one of the Scientology agents involved in the courthouse burglaries used his real identification when confronted by a courthouse security guard and then by the FBI. This led to a grand jury investigation, which apparently spooked the second covert operative (whom Scientology leaders tried to keep "under wraps" at their headquarters in Los Angeles) to escape from that custody, return to Washington, and (to the FBI) ultimately confess. And as it happened, this Scientologist was the very "supervisor" who had guided Sharon Thomas in her Justice Department "career."

So suddenly, the Federal Government had enormous investigation on its hands, one that took a great deal of time. Indeed, it was not until mid-August of 1978 that the "Operation Snow White" indictment came down, and it included a total of eleven defendants, of whom Sharon Thomas was one and the wife of Scientology head L. Ron Hubbard, Mary Sue Hubbard, was another. And the case went to trial, in 1979, with guilty verdicts all around.

Sharon Thomas, who on balance arguably had committed the least of these eleven Scientologists' sins, was not sentenced until mid-December of 1979, with the prosecutors recommending that she be given the maximum sentence of one year in prison for misdemeanor theft.[51] Yet when she received that sentence, six months of it was suspended, with five years of probation and a $1000 fine thrown in. Mary Sue Hubbard, by contrast, received a five-year prison sentence and a $10,000 fine. All eleven of them appealed, and in October of 1981, nearly six years after this all began,[52] the D.C. Circuit Court of Appeals upheld both the convictions and the sentences.

One final coda on this Scientology spy. I am sure that the Information and

Privacy Section Trial Attorney for whom she worked swore quite a bit (albeit in a Texas drawl, with only mild "cuss words") when he later learned about her and how she had fooled so many co-workers around her, especially him. But I know firsthand that he also swore she was "the best damn secretary [he] ever had."

∗   ∗   ∗   ∗   ∗

The fourth and final (read: or so we think) spy connected to OIP was someone who, like Ana Montes and Sharon Thomas, spied purely for ideological reasons, although unlike the latter, her motivation was geopolitical in nature. And she had been doing it for quite some time before her professional path crossed with that of OIP.

OIP had an attorney to whom I had assigned the responsibility of handling business-information issues under the FOIA, including those that were presented in proposed legislation. On one such issue during the early 1990s, she found herself working together with a particular Department of Defense attorney, a "working mother," and visiting her at her office at the Pentagon. The proposed legislation that they worked on resolved well enough, but the circumstances of that Defense Department attorney did not. Her name was Theresa M. Squillacote and it turned out that she was a spy -- initially for East Germany and then for the Soviet Union, the Russian Federation, Russia, and potentially South Africa.

Terry Squillacote, as she was known, was married to a man named Kurt A. Stand,[53] whose parents had fled from Nazi Germany and maintained strong ties with someone who over time rose high the ranks of East Germany's foreign intelligence service, known as the "HVA" and part of what was better known as "Stasi." In the early 1970s, Stand began working for that man as an HVA agent and about a decade later, Stand brought his wife Terry into his espionage, whereupon her involvement became so deep that she ended up having a highly emotional, long-term affair with that East German spymaster, one that lasted for more than 15 years.[54]

Terry Squillacote and her husband moved to Washington, D.C., at the HVA's suggestion and her handler suggested that she go to law school as well. After graduating in 1983, she used her father's connections to obtain a temporary attorney position with the House Armed Services Committee, from which in 1991 she obtained a permanent attorney position at the Department of Defense, where she soon rose to become the Director of Legislative Affairs in the Office of the Undersecretary of Defense for Acquisition Reform,[55] a position that provided her with access to the kind of valuable information that had always been sought by her East German handlers.

Of course, by that time East Germany as a Nation was nearly in a state of collapse. But nevertheless, her principal handler, the one with whom she had an ongoing romantic relationship, was adeptly able to "sign on" with the Soviet Union's KGB, whereupon she and her husband simply became KGB spies, with a relatively seamless transition.[56] This was jarringly interrupted, though, when that former East German handler was arrested by the newly reconstituted German Government in 1992.

Although she and her husband (perhaps for not exactly the same reasons) were confident that their handler would not "give them up,"[57] at this point they knew that the U.S. and its allied intelligence agencies were aware of some spies operating out of Washington and of some of the code words that they had used. Among other things, this made them interested in some possible espionage affiliation with kindred spirits in the Government of South Africa. In short, their commitment was more to the cause of communism than to (or against) any particular nation.

Toward that end, Terry Squillacote in 1995 began using an alias, "Lisa Martin," in making overtures to a South African Communist Party leader from whom she hoped to receive supportive correspondence to a post office box newly rented under the "Lisa Martin" name. What she did not realize, however, was that the FBI was in fact "onto" her and been surveilling both her and her husband since at least 1992.[58]

And as of 1996, the FBI initiated a "false flag" operation against them (shades of Earl Pitts's case) by pretending to be that South African Communist, so that they might induce her to admit to her past espionage activities. This came at a time of particular emotional vulnerability for her because that year marked the end (read: at his hand) of her romantic relationship with her original East German handler. This led to the two of them (read: Squillacote and Stand, together with their two children!) meeting with an undercover FBI Special Agent posing as a South African intelligence officer near the end of 1996 and then a second time in January of 1997.[59]

This continued until October of 1997, when they both were arrested by the FBI and a six-day search of their home uncovered a wealth of incriminating evidence, including a miniature camera, a Casio digital diary, and memory cards. In October of 1998, they were convicted of conspiracy to transmit information relating to the national defense, attempted transmission of national-defense information, and wrongfully obtaining national-defense information. In January of 1999, Squillacote was sentenced to a prison term of nearly 22 years, four years longer than that of her husband. Their appeals were denied by the Court of Appeals for the Fourth Circuit and then the United States Supreme Court in early 2001.

When we learned of this in OIP, we certainly were all shocked, especially the OIP attorney who had worked closely with her. (This was shortly after Earl Pitts was discovered, but still three years before we learned about Ana.) And of course we talked about it at no small length at our next weekly staff meeting. As best as I recall, though, the predominant reaction was tremendous sympathy for the fact that this convicted spy would be separated for so long from her growing children.[60] Apparently, in many views, this was not nearly as bad for her husband as it was for her.

And here is a coda (read: more of a postscript) for this OIP-related spy as well: Theresa M. Squillacote spent only 18 years in prison -- though the word "only" is more easily said by someone who is on the outside, not the inside, of a penitentiary -- which meant that she was released from prison in 2015. Then, in October of that year, having been disbarred, she nevertheless managed to establish a business called "Core Legal Support" in New York City, which to this day operates as a "research and consulting business" that she is careful to say does "not provid[e] legal representation or any direct legal services."[61] And in December of 2021, she petitioned the D.C. Board on Professional Responsibility and the District of Columbia Court of Appeals to restore her ability to practice law, based upon her attestations that she is "a different person" today and "just was struggling so much with mental health issues" for those 17 years.[62] But that was recommended against on July 26, 2022 in a 47-page ethics board opinion concluding that she "continues to display a lack of candor."

CHAPTER TWENTY-SIX
Thinking the Unthinkable

"I've been making a few rough calculations based on the effect of two twenty megaton bombs dropped on New York City in the middle of a normal workday. I estimate the immediate dead at about three million. I include in that figure those buried beneath the collapsed buildings. It would make no difference, Admiral Wilcox, whether they reached a shelter or not. They would die just the same. Add another million or two who will die within about five weeks."

-- Professor Walter Groeteschele, a character in *Fail-Safe*, a novel by Eugene L. Burdick and Harvey Wheeler, 1962

In the fall of 1982, in keeping with the Department's commitment to secure a precious career Senior Executive Service ("SES," to high-level employees) allocation for me sometime relatively soon,[1] I attended a two-week SES training program that the Office of Personnel Management ("OPM," to federal employees) conducted every year at the Merchant Marine Academy on Long Island's north shore.[2] There were about 40 of us, from a wide variety of federal agencies, and we went through a series of seminars, open discussions, and group developmental activities designed to prepare at least some of us for the possibility of holding positions of executive leadership down the road.

Almost all of the participants were men (yes, no women yet)[3] in their forties or fifties, who already had distinguished themselves in lengthy federal careers. One was still in his late 30s and I was just 30 myself.[4] And as it turned out, amongst this group was someone who served as sort of a "recruiter" for a covert government program, though no one knew it at the time.

Not long thereafter, I suddenly found myself drafted onto a secret team of Justice Department attorneys who were part of what was then a very highly classified, governmentwide program for ensuring the survival of our system of government in the wake of nuclear war. Referred to as the Federal Government's "Continuity-of-Government" program ("COG," to those within it), this consisted of a wide-ranging but entirely secret governmental structure that traced its roots to the 1950s and the advent of the Cold War. Today, if a residual version of it were to exist, it would likely be known as "shadow government."[5]

It now is no secret that the Federal Government had relatively rudimentary but solid plans for surviving a nuclear strike almost as soon at the Soviet Union developed the capability to accomplish that. The plans included the construction of an enormous underground facility into a mountaintop approximately 50 miles outside of Washington, D.C., near Purcellville, Virginia, one in which huge state-of-the art blast doors could protect its occupants from the effects of a nuclear exchange.

Built in 1959, and sometimes referred to as "Mount Weather," but more formally designated as the "Special Facility" (or the "Mount Weather Emergency Operations Center" or just the "SF," for short), this "underground city" contains more than a half million square feet of "safe space" and was the primary focal point of government continuity for the next quarter century. Briefly stated, the plan was for the president and his highest-level officials to be whisked there by helicopter in the face of an imminent Soviet attack, where they would then proceed to manage the operations of the Federal Government, to the extent it survived nearby and elsewhere, from that presumably safe location.

But, this all changed drastically with the advent of the Reagan Administration, for multiple reasons that just happened to coincide. First, as has been reported widely, Ronald Reagan by the second year of his presidency firmly made it known that he was not inclined to relocate to anything such as the Special Facility if need be; rather, he expressed his preference to "go down with the ship," so to speak, if it came to that.[6]

Second, the physical security of the Special Facility was increasingly called into question by U.S. intelligence estimates that the Soviets had by then developed a degree of accuracy in their telemetry that made the chance of a nuclear strike hitting dead center there much greater than in even the recent past. Atop that, it was by then believed that the Soviets also had developed a form of "earthmover technology" in its nuclear arsenal that imperiled even the deepest and strongest of our underground sites. In short, as of mid-1982, it was no longer believed by our military and intelligence experts that the SF was a "survivable site."[7]

This called for what we now might describe as a "reimagining" of our whole Continuity-of-Government concept, something that then had to be accomplished with the extreme urgency that such absolutely vital, life-or-death matters require. So it was that the heavy forces of the Federal Government, primarily at the Department of Defense ("DOD," to its service members) and also at the Federal Emergency Management Agency ("FEMA," to its many COG participants), were mobilized to design, develop, and most importantly "exercise" (read: practice) an entirely new substitute plan for what had been counted on to work since the 1950s if "the balloon went up."

What emerged from this critical need was a huge post-nuclear program that carried the utmost of national security classification back then but is no longer classified. Its new concept was that rather than the president, vice president, and perhaps the two congressional successors to the presidency[8] being safely ensconced at the SF, or anywhere else near Washington,[9] they would not survive a targeted nuclear attack (then most commonly predicted to be a "decapitation strike," most likely from an offshore nuclear submarine). Instead, some number of current cabinet officers (at least two) would be "dispersed" in advance to "super secret" locations around the United States, waiting there quiescently to serve as presidential successors as ensuing circumstances required.[10]

I became a relatively junior member of the COG program in 1983 (though as an attorney I was in a special category of it), representing the Justice Department as part of the program's "domestic node," and then advancing further to the point at which I was representing both FEMA and the Department of Defense as an "exercise controller" until after "the wall fell" and the program was discontinued, in effect, near the end of 1991.

During this "COG era," I came to devote about 10% of my time to it year-round and was "dispersed" in 1984, 1986, 1987, 1988, 1989, and in the spring of 1991, around the clock, for full weeks at a time. And by receiving multiple "battlefield promotions" during these exercise activities, I rose from being a neophyte member of the Legal and Law Enforcement Group, to the role of "nighttime attorney general," then to that of "daytime attorney general," then to deputy head of the domestic node, and ultimately to a deputy "controller" position for all four nodes (domestic, military, intelligence, and diplomatic).[11]

The program's domestic node consisted of expert representatives of all purely domestic federal agencies, including domestic law enforcement, and the idea was that these people (or their eventual "real world" counterparts) would in the event of a nuclear "laydown" have the wherewithal to function just as their agencies would and together reconstruct the Federal Government in the fullness of time in a viable post-nuclear environment. No easy task, to be sure. But everyone involved solemnly acted as if this were "real life," from the beginning of each exercise to nearly its end.[12]

A large responsibility of the Legal and Law Enforcement Group in particular would be to vet appropriate "PEADs" (presidential emergency action documents) for issuance by a new Acting President.[13] And in order to determine exactly who that might be -- which was recognized as absolutely essential to our constitutional form of government surviving such a disaster -- we had to very carefully examine the known facts of the particular exercise scenario in the light of all applicable legal authorities and then reach an unshakable legal conclusion about presidential succession that was beyond reasonable challenge.[14]

And it was that latter responsibility that, in the fall of 1987, led to what threatened to become a potential rupture in this Continuity-of-Government program. That problem arose when one of the former high-level officials brought in to play the role of a potential presidential successor[15] decided that he was not going to "adhere to the script," so to speak, and that he was set on becoming the Acting President in this scenario come hell or high water.

As it happened, he was playing the role of a cabinet officer who was indeed higher up in the line of succession than any other one "in play," but the scenario was unkind to him: It specified that his potential presidential survival node was "incommunicado," at least as of the outset of exercise play, which meant (read: to us) that his location might not have survived the nuclear exchange.[16]

So once we set up the Legal and Law Enforcement Group within the domestic node, as much as hundreds of miles away from any other node, and we saw that this wrinkle had been built into this exercise's particular scenario,[17] we quickly determined that under it the more junior successor had in fact survived and was in good enough condition to become Acting President as the law provided.[18]

But even after that successor was sworn in within the realm of exercise play, and the exercise proceeded accordingly, we suddenly received an "extremely urgent" communication from the theretofore-quiescent potential presidential node that announced its survival and aggressively challenged the legitimacy of the Acting President who had been sworn in.

At first, we all thought that this surely must have been some kind of a joke.[19] But something as serious as this, even within the realm of an artificial exercise, albeit one in which everyone should be acting as if it were the "real thing," ought to be no joking matter. Then we learned the actual, "real world" identities of the two former officials who were playing the roles of potential successor and principal advisor there: One had held not one but two cabinet posts in the past, under three different presidents; the other was less experienced and well known, but he would go on to hold a most senior position in the federal Intelligence Community.[20]

What's more, we began receiving increasingly aggressive, even threatening, communications from these two. We did have a lower-level Justice Department representative situated with them, who doubtless agreed with us, but we learned through "back channels" that she was entirely incapable of influencing them in any way.

It actually got so bad that the more senior Justice Department official (our group leader) who was serving as attorney general on the daytime shift began having heart fibrillations as he looked over the message traffic, including my polite but firm replies.[21] The next thing I knew, he was in a cordoned-off medical area hooked up to an EKG, where he was attended to by some of the medical doctors among our ranks. So I patriotically took over for him, serving as attorney general on both 12-hour shifts, and got even less sleep in the bargain.[22]

The head of the domestic node, himself a medical doctor as well as a commissioned officer in the Public Health Service within the Department of Health and Human Services, was appalled by this. He promptly shifted into "real world" mode and tried to get FEMA to take care of the problem, i.e., talk some sense into these two private-sector volunteers who the Defense Department had brought into the program.[23]

In time, cooler heads did prevail, the exercise proceeded to its full length unimpeded, and I wound up being promoted to the position of deputy head of the entire domestic node (even at the relatively tender age of 35 at the time) when an emergency vacancy in that position arose soon thereafter. (In a personal vein, I must admit that that was especially gratifying when I learned that no one in the program's history had ever come even close to making such a "leap" in responsibility, let alone at such a young age.)

In retrospect, I am still amazed by this series of events. While they directly led to my being drawn more heavily into FEMA's further program development over the next four years,[24] not to mention counterpart work that I did for DOD,[25] with my learning much more about the nature and potential sweep of the program in its entirety, I never could quite figure out exactly what had transpired, other than to chalk at least some of it up to human nature. As Lord Acton wisely observed, and I'm paraphrasing loosely here, of course, "Absolute power corrupts absolutely, even when it's all pretend."

CHAPTER TWENTY-SEVEN
"Third-Term Stuff"

"Three blind meese . . ."

-- English nursery rhyme and musical round (variant), 1609 (later the theme song of The Three Stooges)

So, just as I had found at age nineteen that the Department of Justice was the place for me, I found barely ten years later that governmentwide policy work on issues of government secrecy was an area of legal specialization potentially worth devoting an entire career (or at least a first one) to. Such issues by definition covered all aspects of government activity, as an overlay atop everything else.[1] Plus, there certainly was room for an enormous amount of statutory interpretation and policy development remaining to be done in this relatively nascent area of the law as of 1981.[2]

And had I known then of the challenges that the coming decades would bring to this area -- from scandals beyond my imagination to institutional machinations and most especially to the events of September 11, 2001 -- I would have felt all the more strongly about this career choice. But first I had to survive through to the end of the Reagan Administration, though it actually was not nearly as regressive as was most commonly thought.

This certainly was true in the government secrecy area -- just as it surprisingly was so even in the areas of civil rights and civil liberties, at first -- and it contrasts with the "Bush 43" Administration that began exactly twenty years later.[3] (But again, that's getting ahead of the story, which will be told in Chapters Thirty-Six, Thirty-Nine, Forty-One, and Forty-Three.)

Things did change when we had a new attorney general, Edwin Meese III, who did make a mark within about a year of his arrival from the White House when he saw one of OIP's *FOIA Update* publications and immediately jumped to the mistaken conclusion that the cover photo of an OIP attorney conducting a routine FOIA training class for federal employees instead depicted someone teaching FOIA requesters how to make more FOIA requests with which to beleaguer federal agencies. That, too, like Attorney General Smith's blunder (see Chapter Twenty-One) was so off-base as to be comical in its own way, except that the political appointee who stood between Meese and OIP at that particular time took literally months to screw up the courage to tell Meese how wrong he was (if he ever actually did so)[4] and we had to scramble a bit to circumvent Meese in the meantime.

It was at about this time that Dick and I revived an expression that we jokingly had used in referring to that extreme FOIA/Privacy Act "interplay" issue (see Chapter 21) that fortunately had never taken hold in the first Reagan term: "That's second-term stuff," we used to say -- meaning that the proposed policy was "so far out there," in our considered opinion, that no president (or, by extension, attorney general) would want to embrace it with his re-election still ahead. Only at this later point in time, in Reagan's second term, we had to revise our standard to be one of declaring something suitable only as "third-term stuff" -- meaning that it was unfit for any presidential term.

Little did we know at the time that our cynical joking about "third-term stuff" actually presaged what would threaten to become government secrecy policy not in Reagan's imaginary "third term," or in what we came to call the "Bush I" presidential term of President George H.W. Bush, but rather in what we were to come to refer to as "Bush III" -- the second presidential term of son George W. Bush beginning in January 2005, for which all that preceded it was mere prologue.

CHAPTER TWENTY-EIGHT

The Mystery Case

"There is a lurking fear that some things are not meant to be known."

-- Carl E. Sagan, astronomer, planetary scientist, cosmologist, astrophysicist, astrobiologist, author, and science communicator, 1934-1996

I first met Janet Reno under the most extraordinary of circumstances. It was in late March of 1993, not long after her belated arrival as our new boss, and I was at home on a Saturday morning hosting my parents on a visit for my mother's birthday. Something in the morning paper caught my eye[1] and after thinking about it for a moment I realized that a highly consequential thing likely was soon to happen. And with that realization, I knew that I had to try to do something to prevent it if I could.

So I excused myself from my family, hooked up to my Department-issued (but no less archaic) home computer,[2] and communicated to a political appointee in the Attorney General's Office that I needed to see her right away that afternoon. No, something such as this could not wait until Monday.

The thing that I had realized, and this will be described elliptically for reasons to be understood, was that there was a potential presidential nominee at the Department whom I knew had explosive information connected to his or her background file that, if he or she were to be nominated, would inexorably lead to a scandalous and highly consequential public disclosure through the Senate confirmation process. And he or she did not even know of this information -- that was no small part of the problem -- nor did anyone else, save for less than a handful of people within the Department.

The person with whom I had communicated was Nancy E. McFadden, a veteran of the legendary "war room" of the Clinton campaign, who had arrived at the Justice Department in the first wave during mid-January and was working very closely in support of the man who, during the Clinton Administration's early days, was serving as the *de facto* Acting Attorney General. Nancy and I had become well acquainted while we were working on several information-related issues during the Administration's first two months[3] and she already had good reason to trust my judgment, even if I was a Reagan/Bush Administration "holdover," after a fashion.[4] Unlike so many other incoming political appointees (especially in Republican administrations), Nancy had a palpable respect for the integrity and institutional knowledge of those who were there when she arrived.[5]

So Nancy readily agreed to meet me in her office that Saturday afternoon and I drove to Main Justice right away. And when I told her in general terms what I had stumbled upon, and that it involved someone whom I imagined would soon be nominated to a high-level Department position, she instantly took me down the hall on the Main Justice Building's Fifth Floor for me to tell the full story to the putative Acting Attorney General, whose name was Webster ("Webb") L. Hubbell.[6]

Webb was working out of a large office to one side of the attorney general's front office and adjacent conference room, with Attorney General Reno's office on their other side. I sat there with Nancy in front of his desk and when I was about to begin, Nancy quickly leaned over to me as if something had just occurred to her and she whispered, "Oh god, it's not Webb is it?" "No," I assured her, slightly amused by her sudden, if a bit delayed, utterance.[7] In point of fact, even during my brief time with her in her office, I had not yet told her which potential Department appointee it was -- let alone the fact that a Member of Congress was involved.[8]

But I surely then told the full, extraordinarily complex story to Webb, who sat there every bit as stunned as Nancy was and, in effect, readily confirmed to me that the potential presidential nominee I was concerned about would indeed be nominated (assuming that that would continue to be possible).

Webb was a former chief justice of the state supreme court in Arkansas who had been a partner in the famous Rose Law Firm together with Hillary Rodham Clinton and Vince Foster (then deputy White House counsel, soon to be deceased). Presumably, while also mayor of Little Rock and a close friend of the president, he had seen more than his fair share of tough problems, but he struggled at first with this one, involving as it did a delicate interplay of federal information statutes. He soon reached a point in his thinking at which he blurted out, "So how do we..." I finished his sentence for him by offering "...get out of the box?"

"Yeah," he agreed, "How do we do that?" As a true politician at heart, Webb was grasping for a practical solution to an exceptionally difficult problem. Fortunately, having had the advantage of a few hours to think about it, and much experience with such matters generally, I had an answer prepared for that question: I told him and Nancy that I thought there might be a way to solve the problem, mindful that I could not allow myself to be party to our doing anything unlawful for the sake of an expedient solution. And just as I finished explaining this idea to them, Janet Reno walked in.

Now I had not seen or heard her coming, as my back was to the side of the Attorney General's suite that her personal office was in. And there also was the fact that, even for a large person, she was making little noise as she padded toward us without shoes on. But Webb quickly introduced us, as I stared up at a woman who was at least six foot two in her stocking feet; she towered over me by several inches, it seemed, more than just four.

Webb explained to her that we had encountered "a bit of a problem" with a nomination -- he mentioned the nominee's name -- but that we thought we might possibly have a viable solution to it.[9] And then I repeated the remarkable story of what I happened to have learned in the past and how the nomination process would ordinarily lead to its wide disclosure on Capitol Hill, which stood to cause immense personal-privacy injury to the unwitting nominee, not to mention great embarrassment to a president who already had been stung by two failed nominees to be attorney general.

Of course, this was atop the consequences for the Member of Congress, who would be expected to resign from Congress about ten minutes after this explosive information were to reach the minority staff of the Senate Judiciary Committee if it were to do so. There really could be no doubt about that.

Once I uttered that last clause about failed AG nominees, candidly, I realized that it had hardly been necessary; Janet Reno was herself a politician, after all, and she didn't need me to point out what upon reflection I'm sure was obvious to her. But Webb soothed the edge off of this by somewhat theatrically (if that's even possible in a Southern drawl) taking pains to add, in what sounded like a low, conspiratorial voice, that for obvious reasons this all had to be handled on an extremely strict "need to know" basis.[10]

Janet looked at me (by this point, I was presumptuously if not also conspiratorially thinking of her as "Janet") and in her characteristic low-key way said that she certainly hoped that I would be able to take care of the problem, even if nothing like it had ever arisen before. I made some comment about my trying my very best and I assured her, just as I had assured Webb and Nancy right before she had walked in, that I "knew a guy," at the FBI, who was perfectly positioned to facilitate the solution that I had in mind.

For her part, Janet seemed very grateful for this possibility, just as Webb and Nancy had been, though she noticeably did not press me on exactly how "we" would make this work (which was quite unlike her, I later came to learn). So I left the Department's Fifth Floor that Saturday afternoon thinking to myself that I darn well better start working on this unprecedented mess bright and early Monday morning.

So here is the story, sanitized even after all these years for someone's (or several someones') protection: The rare circumstance underlying all of this was that many years ago, I had worked on an extremely delicate access issue involving a sitting Member of Congress. Oddly, he (or she)[11] had made a FOIA-cum-Privacy Act request for access to any information that was held by the Department on him or her in any possibly existing file. Such a request, though generally speaking not uncommon in those days, would naturally draw at least some special attention at the initial administrative level, simply by virtue of the type of requester who was making it.[12]

But this was no ordinary case in any respect, because there existed an extremely sensitive investigatory file on this congressional member, one that fully detailed the fact that he or she had come within a "hair's breadth" of being prosecuted for "affiliating" (shall we say) with the highest personal aide of an infamous Mexican drug lord. In fact, it was strongly suspected by both the FBI and the Department's Drug Enforcement Administration (known to its friends and especially its foes as "DEA") that this Member of Congress had been enjoying the fruits of that drug lord's bounty, so to speak, through this exceptionally close affiliation. What's more, it was a 100% certainty that no one within his or her professional orbit, nor more importantly within his or her family (assuming that he or she had one), had even the slightest idea that he or she had been effectively leading a double life (no exaggeration) in this way for several years.[13]

Indeed, the only reason that this investigation did not result in this person's criminal prosecution was that the investigation culminated in a failed "sting" operation for which there was a gross malfunction of surveillance equipment at just the wrong moment. In other words, he or she was saved by a mere technological fluke and had "gotten away with murder," colloquially speaking, as a result.[14] Yet there could be no doubt that this congressional member's career (among other things) would evaporate almost instantly if this heavily documented secret ever got out, which doubtless created considerable anxiety on the part of the Member.[15]

I had handled the administrative appeal that was filed on that FOIA/Privacy Act request personally, concluding that this requester actually was attempting to learn what the Department "had on" him or her regarding this, an effort likely born of that anxiety. Though the fact remained that he or she was taking a hellacious risk that if the Department actually *had* been onto him or her at at least some point in his or her pattern of criminal behavior, he or she was placing all that was dear to him or her in the hands of, and banking on the integrity of, the Department's FOIA officers, which in this case boiled down to me.[16]

So on that Monday morning, it was my good fortune to be able to immediately reach that "guy at the FBI," at which point I said to him the same thing that I had said to Nancy two days earlier: "I'm coming over to meet with you right away." Luckily, this FBI Supervisory Special Agent was a former agency client of mine; we had worked together on the one-of-a-kind FOIA and Privacy Act case a decade earlier that is recounted in Chapter Sixteen, and we had enjoyed a very solid professional friendship through which he knew that he could trust me implicitly.

By this point, more than a dozen years later, he had risen to be the head of the Bureau's "background investigation" team, which meant that he and his staff were in charge of conducting background investigations ("BIs," to them) on the Department's "PAS" ("presidential appointment/Senate confirmable") nominees. Typically, their background investigation reports went to the majority staff of the Senate Judiciary Committee, where they routinely were shared with the minority as well.

In this case, however, this FBI team chief readily agreed that taking the ordinary course would not end well for anybody. Fortunately, though, inasmuch as the nomination in question had not been formally made yet, his team had not yet undertaken the formal compilation of any information for possible inclusion in the prospective background report that we were so concerned about. And I offered him an analytical path that would support his not going out of his way to include such arguably collateral information in his report as part of its preparation.[17] Hearing this from me, and gathering that he had at least the tacit approval of the new attorney general, he proceeded in the way that I outlined and eventually that nominee was smoothly confirmed.

And no one else, to the best of my knowledge, has ever learned of the extraordinary investigative details that underlay this matter, let alone how "we" handled them as of that Saturday afternoon.[18]

CHAPTER TWENTY-NINE
Life Under Janet Reno

"Dammit, Janet!"

-- Richard Timothy Smith (a.k.a. Richard O'Brien), *The Rocky Horror Picture Show* (stage version), 1973, sung by Barry Bostwick in the 1975 film version

Though there had not been much of a change in the governmentwide administration of the Freedom of Information Act when the Reagan years ended and the presidency of George H.W. Bush began in 1989 -- in part because the new president had been Reagan's vice president for the previous eight years -- that was not at all the case when President William Jefferson Clinton came to town in 1993. After a rocky start at the Justice Department with two failed attorney general nominees (see Chapter Twenty-Seven), President Clinton finally settled in with a surprise nominee, Florida State's Attorney (read: for Miami-Dade County, not the university) Janet W. Reno, who turned out to be, hands down, the best attorney general I ever worked under (read: she certainly was worth ending a sentence with a preposition over).[1]

As I have said elsewhere, Janet Reno arrived in Washington, D.C., in the midst of an unexpected March snowstorm and soon found herself embroiled in a raging fire (read: the Waco conflagration), not to mention the congressional furor that almost immediately ensued. But she surprised just about everyone (read: President Clinton included) by acquitting herself quite nicely (read: being forceful as well as regretful) in a hostile congressional oversight hearing on Waco. (And this was even apart from the prominent fact that she was functioning as the Nation's first female attorney general.) In short, the Waco controversy turned out to be almost as much a positive as it was a negative for her.

Yet she received much criticism from even liberal news outlets at first. Most people, even those who worked at the Justice Department at the time, now forget that Janet came under sustained criticism from the left side of the ideological spectrum at the beginning of her tenure, especially from *The New York Times*, for example. It described her handling of the Waco catastrophe as itself a "fiery disaster," editorializing that it "could not be papered over by . . . her willingness to take the blame."

This criticism continued in some quarters all throughout her first year. At the same time, however, and quite paradoxically, Janet's background (read: child of the Everglades; mother used to wrestle alligators; both parents and brother were journalists; and near-champion kayaker who in her mid-fifties could out-paddle her young and athletic FBI security detail) eventually led to her enjoying almost "folk hero" status and, according to no less an authority than *The Washington Post*, made her into "a media celebrity of near-mythic proportions."

Within the Justice Department, we did not care so much about such things. But we did quickly came to respect Janet for her sharp intellect,[2] probing questions, and, not least, for how hard and well she worked. She wisely had rented an apartment just across Pennsylvania Avenue and down a couple of big blocks from the Main Justice Building, and it was not long before stories abounded of her loping (read: she was indeed six foot, two inches tall) on in to work, security detail on the move behind her, at some ungodly hour of the morning.

And in time, some of us came to learn that in doing so she sometimes under-medicated herself to the detriment of her personal fight against Parkinson's disease. Evidently, her prescribed dosage left her feeling at least a bit "groggy" in the morning, which she deemed incompatible with her work ethic. When she died of Parkinson's a few years ago at age 78 (read: a relatively young age for a female nowadays), many people wondered whether this self-sacrifice might have shortened her lifespan.

Yes, Janet Reno worked exceptionally long, hard, and well, not just for a political appointee (read: people who are, by and large, not exactly workhorses), but for anyone in that building (read: where many of us *were* known as workhorses). And she also was known for her staunch, sturdy brand of integrity, a rare commodity in Washington, indeed. She often said that her decisionmaking would be based on wherever the facts of the matter at hand, in combination with "the law," would take her.[3] Which sometimes meant that although she had been a politician in Florida (having run for state office many times) and surely did have political instincts, she would not necessarily do the most "politic" thing, even if that meant making her extremely difficult job all the more so.

Janet's relationship with President Clinton was a huge case in point. She began her tenure in Washington well knowing that she was not his first choice for the job, the others being women named Zoë, Kimba, Rya, and before them D.C. Circuit Court of Appeals Chief Judge Patricia A. Wald (see Chapter Twenty-Seven). And although she came from Clinton's part of the country, she most definitely was not a "schmoozer" (read: a geographic "mixed metaphor") like him. In fact, they were quite opposite: She was the farthest thing from a transactional rationalizer and stood as a woman of principle and virtue, one who would prove to be unbendable in the face of political pressure if it meant not doing what was just and right. Moralistic, yes. Overtly vengeful, no, but don't overlook the caveat.

So it is fair to say, especially in retrospect, that the two did not much "get along," not in the Southern "chummy" sense, anyway. In fact, I think that Clinton actually came to fear her, knowing what he did about himself, and kept her at arm's distance as a result. And he probably decided within himself early on that he might be "stuck" with her during his entirely first presidential term, yet surely not for the second. But that's getting ahead of the story.

Anyway, there was a woman during that first Clinton year -- whose name I will not mention here because she might still be "burrowed" into the Federal Government somewhere, even at an advanced age, and doubtless has suffered enough difficulties over the years due to her, shall we say, "sparkling personality" -- who arrived at the Justice Department in the spring of 1993 with the notion that she somehow would "take over" the Office of Information and Privacy. And the threat that she posed, which would have been bad enough just because it was at the beginning of a new presidential administration, was greatly enhanced by the fact that she had a close "mentor" at the White House (read: "rabbi," in other settings). That "White House official," we learned, was on her way to receiving a very high-level presidential appointment (though fortunately not at the Justice Department) and had an enormous amount of "clout."

At that time, I knew that I was "politically vulnerable," having served in a quasi-political-but-actually-career, high-visibility position for nearly 12 years (read: during three Republican administrations, counting both of Reagan's). As a matter of governmentwide personnel law, and as a career Senior Executive Service member (since 1984), I could not legally be moved out of my position until 90 days after the Senate's confirmation of a presidential appointee above me. But I figured that at any time as of about mid-May I could be told (read: nicely, of course) that I was too closely tied to the nondisclosure policies of the Reagan and Bush Administrations, that there were folks on "the other side of the fence" who were calling for my ouster (read: very true, at least in the case of one vengeful Democratic congressional staff member), and that I sure would make a fine immigration judge rather than continue in OIP.[4]

But I had, as they used to say in Wild West saloons, "a card up my sleeve" (read: more than one, actually): I had helped Janet Reno big-time with a problem that I had both identified and then solved for her within the span of one weekend in late March (see Chapter Twenty-Eight). And even as busy as she then was, Janet could not possibly forget such a thing in less than three months. So, to make a much longer story just a little shorter, I was able to arrange things so that OIP would continue on unimpaired, with that interloping political appointee being told to "cool her jets," and all would be right with the world.

Now, did Janet Reno ensure this result simply because she knew full well that I knew full well what a big "secret" I had handled for her -- even to the point of thinking that she (not to mention the Member of Congress involved) would suffer if I were to "leak" that secret in retaliation for being removed from my position? No, I do not think so, simply because I believe Janet herself would never do such a thing, so it might not even have occurred to her that I could. But without a doubt there were other, more "political" folks in the upper reaches of the Justice Department and at the White House, even during a relatively benign Democrat administration, who did think that way. To Janet, though, I think the greatest likelihood is that she thought of it as a favor, in return for one duly received, with hopefully no small measure of regard for competence thrown in for good measure.

So OIP went rolling along (read: with my career "trajectory," if that's what you want to call it, maintained), and the next major item on our agenda was the existing Attorney General's Memorandum on the Freedom of Information Act, which traced all the way back to what was issued by President Reagan's first attorney general, William French Smith, in May of 1981, a dozen years earlier. It needed to be replaced.

Indeed, once President Clinton was elected, I knew beyond a shadow of a doubt that that anti-disclosure edict was going to have to be superseded by a more liberal Clinton Administration one in order to usher in a new "pro-disclosure" policy of government openness under the Freedom of Information Act; it was only a matter of time. And I did not intend to waste any time.

So I started crafting a brand-new AG FOIA Memorandum long before the Clinton Administration began, by first devising a new substantive standard to govern FOIA exemption decisionmaking at the litigation level: "foreseeable harm." It just suddenly occurred to me that this novel standard, employed together with the concept of "discretionary disclosure," could best achieve the pro-disclosure "turn-around" that I knew the Clinton Administration would want to accomplish.[5] (Little could I have dreamt that after being established in the Reno FOIA Memorandum in October of 1993, this standard would be replicated in the Holder FOIA Memorandum in March of 2009 and then codified by Congress within the Act itself in 2016.)

To this, I added several other pro-disclosure elements such as FOIA backlog reduction, pending litigation reviews, FOIA regulation reviews, and a complete rethinking of all formats and standard language used by agencies in their processes of FOIA administration. Plus, there was a hortatory admonition that agencies cease erecting "unnecessary hurdles" that block FOIA requesters and instead treat them in a "customer-friendly manner." All of this, plus other such things, were consolidated into the Presidential Transition Team papers that were prepared by OIP in December of 1992 for the incoming attorney general.

And when Janet Reno signed this AG FOIA Memorandum on October 4 of 1993, it was exactly as I had crafted it, with one major exception: The first page of what I drafted was appropriated by President Clinton, who liked it so much that he (read: together with White House Staff Secretary John D. Podesta, Jr.) turned it into an unprecedented (albeit one-page) FOIA policy memorandum of his own. So it was that the draft's "procedural hurdles" and "customer-friendly" elements became Clinton's, while leaving Janet with plenty of progressive elements of her own.

Later on, we worked with Janet to institute two other big pro-disclosure policies: the issuance of public summaries of internal misconduct investigations (largely of AUSAs) conducted by the Department's Office of Professional Responsibility (see Chapter Thirty-Two), and a special provision for "expedited media access" under the FOIA that was overseen by the Department's Office of Public Affairs (see Chapter Thirty-Six).[6]

At OIP, we implemented the hell out of all of these new FOIA policies, especially the "foreseeable harm" standard, which we applied across the board at the administrative level as well as in all FOIA litigation. Ever supportive of this, Janet gave several key speeches at OIP's FOIA programs,[7] as well as before media groups and other members of the "FOIA Requester Community." And she went on to develop a reputation as "the queen of openness" over the course of the next seven years.[8]

CHAPTER THIRTY

The Other Secret Scandal

"You needle a Christmas tree in your life, fir sure."

-- Old Christmas saying

I once was on a C-SPAN interview program, at the outset of former Secretary of State Hillary Rodham Clinton's email problems (see Chapter Forty-Seven), where after making reference to the many FOIA-related scandals that we had had during the Clinton Administration I off-handedly said that two of those scandals (or potential ones) had not ever seen the light of day.[1] The interviewer did not immediately react to this (we were on live television), but then about 30 seconds later he did an abrupt pivot while in the middle of his next question and said: "Uh, can you speak obliquely to them at all, or no?" And for much of the remainder of this hour-long interview he tried to get me to identify the two things that I had been referring to.

In fact, one of them was the very thing that is described (read: incompletely) in Chapter Twenty-Eight, above. As to that one, I allowed as how it was of such nature that it probably would *never* be exposed. (Nor should it.) But in the case of the second one, I confessed that knowing Washington as I do, I was more than a little surprised that even so many years later it still had not come out. To be sure, I do not intend to alter that status quo here, but I think that I can convey at least the essence of this "scandal in the making," in this brief chapter, without permitting its exact circumstances to be discerned.

It all started, of course, at the beginning of the Clinton Administration, when so much was being done, so fast, in so many government locations, that expected White House controls on such things were not immediately applied.[2] This led to my receiving a call from the White House Counsel's Office about what it had focused on only belatedly as a big potential legal and policy problem for it. And it involved the question, as nearly all such government scandals do, of how to keep the details of -- and in this case even the very *existence* of -- this problem contained within the White House and to just a few people at the Department of Justice.[3]

Elliptically speaking, this problem had to do with the types of personal information that recently had been memorialized in writing about some new Federal Government employees who had had certain experiences the likes of which had not often before been seen. There were so many of them that, in the aggregate, they could understandably give the public a damaging impression.[4] In short, we all knew how the problem had arisen, and why it had arisen just then; the White House was just uncertain of how the hell to deal with it.

So I received that "emergency" call one afternoon,[5] to the effect that there was a "FOIA issue" that was unlike any that had been seen before and that the White House urgently needed assistance with it. Well, resolving such things had become no small part of my job, something that I regularly did on a priority basis. So I made it my business to do all necessary fact checking on it immediately and began preparation of a highly detailed, fully comprehensive written analysis of all aspects the problem, one that contained solutions (and in some cases alternative solutions) for each of them.[6] And after working through the night on this, and transmitting it electronically, I expectantly awaited the White House's response.

This response came very quickly, I must say, in the form of a grateful phone call from Assistant Attorney General for Legal Counsel Walter E. Dellinger III, who was known within the Department as someone who ought to be on the Supreme Court because he truly was a legal genius[7] and technically was the principal White House contact for advice given to it by the Department.[8] He told me that my analysis had been very well received, that it even had left no further question for the folks at the White House to pose (which was unusual), and that my recommended solutions to the problem were being applied to it "as we spoke."[9] And I held my breath for a while to see if this potential scandal really did evade detection by the news media and the public. It did.

CHAPTER THIRTY-ONE
Scandals du Jour

". . . the cover-up can be worse than the underlying conduct [read: crime]."

-- United States District Court Judge Royce C. Lamberth, ruling against the Government in *Association of American Physicians & Surgeons v. Hillary Rodham Clinton*, Civil No. 93-0399 (RCL), December 18, 1993

Sometime about half-way through President Bill Clinton's second term, I realized that my tally of scandals and like controversies during the previous six years had reached nearly two dozen, at which point it became too tiresome to maintain that list either in my frontal lobe or in paper form. That true fact, hyperbolic as it might sound, fairly well sums up much about the Office of Information and Privacy's institutional life (and my own) during the Clinton Administration.

The thing about scandals (read: just one of the things, actually) is that in modern times they invariably involve the creation, maintenance, and at least partial potential withholding of documents (read: records and information) that, once the scandal comes to light, others will want to see. In general, such others can be family members, co-workers, or other associates (speaking first on a small scale) or official investigators, the media, or even Congress (on a larger scale). And one way or the other, as so often is the case, there can be much controversy over whether, and if so to what extent, that disclosure will occur.[1]

Whenever such a controversy erupts -- and by its nature such a thing usually arises abruptly, with a "short fuse" -- it calls for the making of very precise and well-reasoned determinations as to what can or should be disclosed about it versus what information (read: or document portion) need not or should not. And over the years, OIP developed a well-earned reputation throughout the executive branch as the place to turn to when a controversy arises and the question is how to best handle it with respect to information disclosure.

In short, we knew where (and how) to best "draw the line" on the disclosure (or not) of sensitive information, based upon both legal and policy considerations. Now, did that make OIP quite popular, including with relatively new presidential administrations (read: once they came to realize it)? You bet it did. Did we "play that for all it was worth?" Yes, sometimes we did.

And did we sometimes pay a price for all of this by having to devote late and long hours under what could be hellaciously short deadlines that were attendant upon such things? Yes, we did. But we knew that when we so methodically "scrubbed" a lengthy report, a series of documents, or even a fact pattern that we were presented with in the abstract we were doing (read: almost always) what was "good for America," so to speak.

During the Clinton years, there were many reports that had to be very carefully scrubbed for disclosure (read: usually public disclosure, but sometimes disclosure to Congress), almost always on a time-sensitive basis: Waco, Ruby Ridge, the "Good O' Boy Roundup," the FBI Laboratory (i.e., including the allegations of whistleblower Frederic Whitehouse), many other law enforcement investigations, Waco again,[2] the White House Travel Office, the White House's personnel office, and numerous "Whitewater-related" things of all shapes, colors, and sizes.[3]

Usually, the primary substantive concern in these reviews was with personal privacy, under the Privacy Act of 1974 or otherwise, with law enforcement sensitivity coming in a close second. And usually, one or both of OIP's deputy directors would lead the largest and longest-lasting of these review efforts (with supervisory consultation support), which made it a very good thing that by the time the Clinton Administration rolled around they both had gained a ton of experience with such things.

In the Clinton Administration, this began almost immediately, because so did the scandals and "controversies."[4] Both "Travelgate" and the suicide of Deputy White House Counsel Vincent M. Foster (see Chapter Three) took place within the first six months, for instance, and there were other things that, as the saying goes, "never saw the light of day." There was First Lady Hillary Rodham Clinton's "Health Care Task Force" during 1993-1994 and Secretary of Energy Hazel R. O'Leary's "Radiation Disclosure Task Force"[5] at the very end of 1993 and into 1994,[6] the latter of which, truth be known, was largely a cover (read: diversion) for the "Whitewater" scandal (read: much more than one scandal),[7] which emerged publicly as of late 1993 (and internally sooner). And there were White House personnel matters that also required immediate attention.[8]

OIP was actively involved in all of these things, applying the law (read: both statutory and case law) to their handling and developing new policies wherever need be. And we were ever mindful of (and sometimes had to pointedly remind the "new folks" of) the old refrain that "the cover-up can be worse than the crime." More than once, it was that very bit of wisdom that made the difference between surgically cauterizing a scandal's wound through prompt yet precise disclosure and worsening it with what I would call "heedless stonewalling."

Fortunately, as characteristically prone as the Clinton Administration was to producing scandals of all stripes, and "controversies" that resonated widely, it also quickly grasped the value of delineated disclosure as an antidote to such ills. And without exception over its eight years, it respected the Office of Information and Privacy's ability to help deal with such things carefully and speedily in order to minimize public (and congressional) reaction to them. And this, too, caused OIP's already-sterling reputation to grow, and circle around on itself.

CHAPTER THIRTY-TWO
The "AUSA Smith" Matter

"Wise men say/Only fools rush in/But I can't help/Falling in love with you."

-- Luigi F. Creatori, George David Weiss, and Hugo E. Peretti, sung by Elvis
Aaron Presley, 1961

Early in the Clinton Administration, OIP took on an additional distinct area
of responsibility: Reviewing the proposed "public summaries" of employee misconduct investigations conducted by the Department's Office of Professional
Responsibility ("OPR," to its many friends). OPR had come into existence during
the Ford Administration as a vehicle of "post-Watergate" reform. Its mission
was to conduct internal Justice Department investigations of conduct by any
Department employee who "may be in violation of law, regulations or orders,
or applicable standards of conduct." Most commonly, these would be Assistant
United States Attorneys ("AUSAs" to their investigators) who were on the "front
lines" of the Department's prosecutorial efforts and in whom the public's trust
was most vital.

Realizing the importance of this self-regulatory function, together with the
Department's need to assure the public of its prosecutorial integrity in the first
place, Attorney General Janet Reno in 1994 called upon OPR to begin preparing
summaries of its dispositions of all of its cases for public consumption. (Their
issuance was to be purely a matter of "administration discretion," a concept that
I had advocated personally to Janet Reno for purposes of FOIA administration
(see Chapter Twenty-Nine)). And to determine what was or was not suitable for
public disclosure, she asked OIP to quickly review each such proposed "public
summary" before it was released to the public so that personal-privacy interests
and the Department's other interests would be properly protected within it.

OIP took this responsibility very seriously, as might be imagined, and we
spared no effort in discharging it as expeditiously as possible. So it was that many a
night I took home a recently received proposed public summary in order that OIP
might be able to "turn it around" as soon as possible.[1] Some cases were relatively

simple, but many were not, and some were exceptionally complex.

But in all such matters, we reviewed them both critically and scrupulously, inasmuch as OIP's information-disclosure perspective was not quite the same as that of the Department's "grizzled," longtime investigators and prosecutors, whose mindset usually was "we worked hard and well on this, so let's let the public see that." That mindset certainly prevailed in OPR, which as a former prosecutor herself (albeit at the state level), Janet surely had realized when creating this system.[2]

Sometimes we would focus on a proposed summary's mention of persons who were third parties to the conduct involved, people whom OPR tended to view as "collateral damage" -- i.e., if their privacy had to be sacrificed on the altar of "public interest," then so be it. OIP tended to view such people as being potential victims of public disclosure, because their very mention in a law enforcement file, especially a misconduct one such as what we were dealing with, could be quite stigmatizing for them, perhaps unnecessarily so (see Chapter Thirteen).

So we applied a "balancing of interests" that comported with what federal law enforcement agencies regularly did when processing FOIA requests for their files: We asked whether the degree of potential privacy interest invasion involved was outweighed by the public interest in disclosure of that information in that particular context and at that particular time.

OIP reviewed dozens and dozens of such proposed public summaries during the Clinton Administration. Typically, we would find portions of them that were questionable for inclusion to our minds, which led to follow-up discussions with the leadership of OPR, with whom we had enjoyed a very close working relationship over the course of many years. Sometimes, OPR explained why it had included the information at hand in that particular summary in a way that we found persuasive, sometimes not. Most often, we were able to persuade OPR that it had gone too far, in which case the proposed public summary would be revised accordingly and OIP would "sign off" on its issuance in its revised form.

The "AUSA Smith" matter, however, was not such a case. As a matter of fact, OIP and OPR were so far apart on it that whereas OPR said that it should be released in its entirety, OIP concluded that this was one proposed public summary that should not be issued -- an outcome that at that time would have been entirely unprecedented.

As had become sort of a pattern with such things, I received this proposed public summary by hand-delivery late one Friday afternoon, together with a brief message from OPR saying that it was aiming to disclose it at the beginning of the following week for some lame reason or other. I just glanced at it before heading home for the weekend, suspecting that I might be spending that weekend back at my office attending to it.

The situation was this: One hapless soul of an AUSA had found him- or herself in an untenable position[3] while in the midst of a criminal prosecution. The prosecution was going well, from his or her perspective, but a key witness still needed to be prepped for his or her testimony at the trial.[4] And for whatever reason, this genuinely had to take place in the AUSA's hotel room at what was nearly the "last minute" before the testimony was to be given. But as one thing led to another, as they say, this professional witness-preparation session somehow became a session of another kind.

Nevertheless, this witness did go on to testify, doing a "bang-up job" by all accounts, and the defendant was convicted based in no small part on that testimony. I cannot now recall exactly how OPR got onto this, but it did, and it imposed discipline on the AUSA accordingly.[5] And now, having done so, it wanted to take a step that was likely to further destroy his or her life (yes, he or she was married, with children), in the name of the general "public interest" in disclosure.

At least that is how I saw the situation as I began reviewing this proposed summary that Friday evening. OPR, as might be expected, viewed it as a report of a "job well done" by it in bringing this poor AUSA "to justice" (no pun intended). Put another way, it really, *really* wanted to make a full public disclosure. I, on the other hand, soon determined that there should be no public disclosure of the matter at all.

What is more, I learned at the beginning of that weekend that OPR's institutional "feeling" about this matter was such that it already had gone ahead and obtained the approval from the Deputy Attorney General's Office (sometimes known within the Department as "ODAG") for public disclosure to be made -- actually bypassing the ordinary process![6] This meant that, if OIP were going to oppose the making of that disclosure, I would have to persuade the key person in ODAG for such things, Senior Associate Deputy Attorney General David M. Margolis,[7] that what OPR was proposing to do was self-servingly wrongheaded[8] and would cause unwarranted harm.

Yet I felt both professionally and (not to sound too melodramatic) even morally bound to try to turn this around. And I decided that although I might well be able to do so with a meeting in ODAG, which would be the usual course of such things, there would be a much better chance of my doing so through a detailed written analysis.[9] So that is how, though I loathed having to spend time putting something in writing when mere "human dialogue" ought to suffice, I came to spend almost that entire weekend crafting an exhaustive explanation of why the Department should not damage this poor AUSA (not to mention his or her spouse and children) in this way.

Now while the contents of that memorandum remain confidential to this day, as they should, and I have spoken only elliptically of this matter here (hence this chapter's title), I can say that I am gratified to relate this story's happy ending: There was no issuance of this proposed public summary, not in any form nor to any degree, made by OPR that coming week. And somewhere there is an AUSA (or former one, most likely) who "dodged a bullet" on this by virtue of my not having, say, an out-of-town wedding to attend that weekend.[10]

CHAPTER THIRTY-THREE
Departing Officials

"Bye, Bye, Baby (Baby, Goodbye)"

-- Robert J. Gaudio and Robert S. Crewe, sung by The Four Seasons, 1965

One of the most intractable problems we ever had in a FOIA-related area was the one posed by the departure of Federal Government officials, usually high-ranking ones,[1] who unilaterally (or with the "blind eye" contrivance of their agency federal records officers) left Federal Government service by taking some of "their" records away with them.[2] Going back decades upon decades in time, there was very little attention paid to this particular phenomenon and there is little or no evidence (other than belatedly by myself and others at the Justice Department) of it being focused on as the serious problem it actually was.

Even after Congress enacted the Federal Records Act in 1950, high-ranking federal officials in particular used to "get away with" removing agency documents, either in "carbon copy"[3] or even "original document" form, upon their departure. To be sure, this is something that was far from universal, but it silently took place more often than it ought to have, with little notice by anyone (federal records officers or otherwise) and even less commotion.

I first became aware of this problem when Attorney General Griffin B. Bell left the Justice Department partway through the Carter Administration in 1979 and a few years later wrote a memoir of sorts titled *Taking Care of the Law*. In it, he recounted the story of a case involving a 12-year-old Hispanic boy named Santos Rodriguez who had been the victim of an alleged police brutality murder in Dallas, Texas. In 1978, during Bell's tenure as attorney general, this case became quite controversial when the Justice Department declined to bring civil rights charges in it.

The case was the cause of great friction between the Justice Department and the White House. It became well known at the time that President Jimmy Carter was apologetic toward the Hispanic community for what he said technically was the Department's declination decision and that he was uncomfortable with it.

This was not good, of course, in that it put President Carter publicly at odds with his attorney general and reflected badly on the Department in general and on Attorney General Bell in particular. And it also left it unclear who had actually made the declination decision, Attorney General Bell (including his Civil Rights Division) or President Carter.

In writing of this episode in his book -- seemingly seeking to "set the record straight," or even to "settle a score," perhaps -- former Attorney General Bell wrote from his own perspective (of course) and he managed to "slip in" part of a White House document that he obviously had taken with him from the Department when he left. He stated that President Carter had sent "a handwritten note" to him stating that "'[t]he Rodriguez case was/is very embarrassing to me. I hope you made the right decision. J.C.'"

My own "add on" to this vignette is that Judge Bell should never have relegated to himself the wherewithal to include the text of that presidential communication in his book.[4] (And I say this even with new-found sympathy for anyone writing such a book.) Even putting aside what the Federal Records Act (not to mention the Presidential Records Act) would say about this,[5] I can attest that had a Freedom of Information Act request come into the Department for access to that presidential note (or, more likely, for a *corpus* of agency records of which it was a part), it would not (at least not back then) have been disclosed to the public in response to that FOIA request. Such things were regularly withheld from disclosure under Exemption 5 of the FOIA, which former Attorney General Bell wrongfully managed to circumvent.

This in its own way was an extremely pointed example of the "departing official" problem, as compared to others in which no particular part of what is taken away is so specifically known to be FOIA-exempt. Such was perhaps the case with Attorney General William French Smith II, who was rumored, after the fact, to have taken away "11 barrels of records" when he departed from the Justice Department almost six years later, in 1985.[6]

But that was not the case with the Department of Justice's next attorney general, Edwin Meese III, whose controversy-ridden tenure ended three years later, in the summer of 1988.[7] Maybe just following what he had heard to have been Attorney General Smith's "lead" on this, Meese left the Department together with an enormous number of file boxes filled with papers of all types, perhaps thinking that this was all right, perhaps not.[8] And with such blatant overreaching, he was caught!

Yes, after his departure from the Justice Department, all of those boxes (which we presumed were intact) were removed from Meese's garage (some said at the time that his garage was "scoured" for them), where he had been storing them, and they were returned to the Department. Now here is where I must admit that I certainly ought to remember exactly how many boxes there were, because I was involved in their return from Meese. In fact, we stored them in my office (by which I mean in OIP's space on the 7200 Corridor of the Main Justice Building) for several months afterward.[9]

I do not recall that any of the "Meese papers" (as we were calling them) included classified information. In fact, I have a slight recollection that we had all of those boxes roughly screened for that, which was not entirely "kosher" under national security rules, but apparently no one in replacement Attorney General Richard L. "Dick" Thornburgh's Office was inclined in this embarrassingly woeful situation to call Meese at home to ask him about that. So we just assumed the best, thinking that even Meese would not knowingly include anything classified within his illicit tranche.

But all that changed big-time in early 2003, after Secretary of the Treasury Paul H. O'Neill, never known to be much of a "team player," was abruptly fired by President George W. Bush, reportedly for his unremitting "outspokenness." Not long afterward, O'Neill committed a "departing official sin" that far surpassed anything known to have occurred at any federal agency since the dawn of time.[10] And this involved a good deal of what was believed (at least by some of the good folks at Treasury) to be classified information.

It was learned that near the time of his departure, Treasury Secretary O'Neill developed a very close working relationship with a journalist and author named Ronald S. Suskind, with an eye toward Suskind writing a book in very close collaboration with O'Neill about his time as Treasury Secretary. For many years, Suskind had worked as a reporter for *The Wall Street Journal*, winning a Pulitzer Prize during his tenure, and had since moved on to writing books.[11]

For that book project, which began very soon after Secretary O'Neill's departure from the Treasury Department, O'Neill was interviewed heavily by Suskind, including about O'Neill's (shall we say) tempestuous relationship with President Bush and others in his Administration about the "run-up" to the U.S. invasion of Iraq in 2003. And this involved Suskind gaining access to sensitive Treasury Department information in more ways than one.

I became involved in this for three reasons. First, I happened to notice a reference in a *Washington Post* article from which I inferred that Paul O'Neill's departure from Treasury had involved what I suspected was improper information disclosure to Suskind. I remember calling over to alert the White House on this one weekend and learning that my concern was being relayed to the White House

Counsel (Alberto Gonzales) right away for close examination. (Little did I know.)

Second, I was contacted by those involved in this examination, because the realm of document removal by departing officials was recognized as integral to the administration of the FOIA. Any agency information that makes its way into the public domain through such a departure could readily be claimed to be no longer entitled to FOIA exemption protection, on the theory (more than a theory, actually) that any such protection has been waived. And waiver of exemption protection was a significant part of what OIP oversaw throughout the government under the FOIA.

Third, the Department of Justice had established itself as the leader among all federal departments and agencies in finally addressing this longtime "dirty little secret" subject area near the end of the Clinton Administration.[12] Indeed, after being concerned about this problem for many years, I had developed a formal process for dealing with it as far as the Department of Justice's records were concerned, and it worked well.

In 1999, with the strong and direct support of Attorney General Janet Reno, we formed a five-person, inter-component committee to handle such "departing official" matters formally and relatively routinely.[13] This involved developing a comprehensive process, supported by a newly created regulation,[14] through which high-level Justice Department officials who would like to take some documents (i.e., in "non-record" form) with them upon their upcoming departures from the Department can get an official ruling on the propriety of that, even down to a granular, document-by-document basis.[15]

The first official to whom this new policy was to be applied, at her own insistence, was Attorney General Janet Reno, near the Clinton Administration's end. Still at the height of her popularity (except, perhaps, with President Clinton and others at the White House),[16] Janet told our committee that in the back of her fertile mind she had the idea of writing a book about being attorney general someday (and had already received "feelers" from potential publishers about that), for which her having post-departure access to at least some documents could prove useful to her. But as it turned out, that did not come to pass, for reasons that I do not recall.[17]

Nevertheless, the fact that the Department of Justice developed such a forward-looking formal policy for this record-maintenance area became known throughout the executive branch and stood as a model for other departments and agencies to follow. I remember talking to folks from many agencies about this, including (most ironically) people whom I knew quite well at the Department of the Treasury. In fact, ironically, I recall Treasury beginning to develop its own policy for that based on the one that we had developed at Justice.

And circling back to Treasury: It was not known whether former Secretary O'Neill himself took any agency records with him when he left. That question quickly became secondary, however, when we learned that soon after his departure (i.e., when he was a mere private citizen), he managed to have a massive tranche of Treasury Department records delivered for his book partner Ron Suskind, as if that were pre-arranged.

The way in which O'Neill did this was by simply calling upon his former general counsel, David D. Aufhauser, to arrange this disclosure for him. General Counsel Aufhauser, who was an upright member of the D.C. Bar, had been a close aide to O'Neill who was chosen for his position not by the White House (which is not uncommon for cabinet department general counsels) but rather by O'Neill himself. Evidently, the strength of this personal relationship, too, played a role in this most unusual "departing official" fact pattern.

Indeed, it was further learned that General Counsel Aufhauser had gone ahead to make arrangements to have three disks (a single CD and two DVDs) filled with unscreened information from a main Treasury Department computer system for delivery either to former Secretary O'Neill or to Suskind directly, at O'Neill's request. And because of the abruptness of that process, *inter alia*, there arose very serious concerns about those disks containing classified information.[18] This necessitated an urgent analysis and attempted reconstruction of that information disclosure.

As best as I could determine from where I sat, there was some surprising reluctance at both Treasury and the White House to cross-examine either O'Neill or Suskind on exactly what had occurred. It was known that Suskind had obtained much information from O'Neill about his Bush Administration tenure, with particular focus on President Bush's first cabinet meeting and its alleged early emphasis on invading Iraq. But the exact contents of what had been delivered to Suskind remained largely unknown, with commensurate uncertainty about what Treasury might be able to do about it.

It was not long, though, before Suskind produced the expected book, titled *The Price of Loyalty: George W. Bush, the White House, and the Education of Paul O'Neill*, that detailed what evidently were many points of conflict between the White House and O'Neill and also leveled charges of overall "inattention" and of being "disengaged" at President Bush.[19] And with O'Neill's and Suskind's promotion of that book in a *60 Minutes* interview together on January 9, 1994, glimpses of documents were shown on camera (as opposed to *in camera*), one of which (evidently a classification "cover sheet") visibly bearing a classification legend of "Secret."[20]

With that, the folks at Treasury decided the very next day to just refer the matter to that department's inspector general for investigation. (This is a time-honored practice in Washington of "kicking it upstairs.") And the following month, replacement Treasury Secretary John W. Snow provided Congress with a thoroughly unsatisfying capstone assessment of this atypical[21] yet highly consequential "departing official" episode: "The Treasury Department recognizes that those documents were not properly reviewed before their release."

So today, one can only hope that agencies follow the Justice Department's lead on responsibly regulating the removal of non-record copies of agency documents by their departing employees, especially their "high-level" ones.

CHAPTER THIRTY-FOUR
Another Failure

"Success is the ability to go from one failure to another with no loss of enthusiasm."

-- Either President Abraham Lincoln (1809-1865) or Sir Winston Leonard Spencer Churchill (1874-1965), or neither

Many chapters above (see Chapter Nine), I wrote of what I deemed to have been an early failure in my legal career. Now I will admit to a second one,[1] which had far greater consequences, ones that persist even to the current day. I am speaking of my failure to have the Federal Government move toward universal acceptance of FOIA requests that are made in purely electronic form -- as an absolute right of FOIA requesters.

To fully appreciate this, one has to understand the entire development of "electronic records" under the Act. When the FOIA was enacted, of course, the very idea that records could exist in electronic form was still a decade or so away. Sure, there were federal databases in existence, some of which ultimately became of interest to FOIA requesters,[2] but the entire question of whether (and under what circumstances) the FOIA might legally apply to information in "newfangled" electronic form[3] was a novel one -- one that, after a while, increasingly plagued the processes of FOIA administration.[4]

This started with the question of whether electronic "things" were "agency records" subject to the Act in the first place.[5] During the 1980s, computer software became a big question in this regard; most agencies were inclined to view them as items of computer "hardware" (i.e., computer "tools") rather than as actually "vessels" of information.[6] The establishment of what I saw as the best policy answer to this question -- i.e., that software all too often contains information and therefore cannot be treated categorically as a mere "tool" (and thus as other than a "record") -- took many years.

A second "electronic record" question under the FOIA was whether a requester could compel an agency to retrieve requested information from a database according the particular parameters that the requester sought to be employed.

What this means is that while all databases have "retrieval software" through which agencies access "slices" of them for their own mission purposes, more and more sophisticated FOIA requesters were trying to have agencies alter their existing retrieval software for purposes of fulfilling their particular requests -- which the agencies almost all vehemently resisted as requiring "new programming."[7] In short, the FOIA embodied a time-honored principle (read: one well supported by prevailing case law) that an agency never had to "create a new record" in order to respond to a request, so this principle was clung to by agencies as a cherished bulwark against having to do that in the new computer realm.

A third such question was whether an agency could be compelled to produce a requested record (presumably an entirely non-exempt one) in a particular form of the requester's preference. This issue arose in two possible contexts: One was where the record already existed in multiple forms, but the form preferred by the FOIA requester was not the one in which that information was ordinarily produced by the agency. And the second was where the information did *not* exist in the preferred form, though producing it in that form was in fact technically feasible, but the burden of taking that whole new step would necessarily have to be incurred in order to satisfy the requester's preference.[8]

These issues became the subjects of a lengthy process of policy development by OIP -- from surveying agency attitudes and experiences on them to analyzing all positions taken on them to the development of "electronic record" principles for them to providing governmentwide policy guidance on them and to negotiating legislative reform on them. And then there was matter of developing detailed implementation guidance on the remedial provisions of law that Congress enacted. All told, this took more than eight years, most of which time was spent waiting for Congress to act.

Ancillary to these issues, and "behind them in line," so to speak, was the even more basic question of whether a FOIA requester could make a request, for any type of record or information and at any agency, in electronic form itself, rather than only in the conventional form of on paper, in a letter, as it always had been. Years earlier, OIP had yielded to "advanced technology" by deciding, purely as a matter of policy, that requesters should be permitted to make FOIA requests also by fax. Did Congress provide for that as a matter of statutory right? No. But agencies merely grumbled about this (read: some of them did) and they all eventually complied.

But the really big issue in this regard was whether agencies that in fact possessed the technological ability to do so should accept FOIA requests made *solely* through electronic means (read: email or, later on, through some sort of "web-based portal")? And, if so, whether all agencies should therefore develop the technological capability for that? (Remember: This was back in the late 1990s, when having such a capability was a BFD, especially for the smaller agencies.)

Well, I thought the answer to both of these questions should be a firm "yes." Frankly, as with the "software as a record" issue years earlier, I viewed this as something that was "only a matter of time" and I believed that the arguably liberal (read: and it was indeed sometimes argued about) Clinton Administration should be the one to "nail this down," even in the absence of legislative command, once and for all (read: before a less generous, shall we say, presidential administration came in behind it). And I had the idea that because there would be considerable resistance to such a policy shift at many agencies, as there had been on nearly every electronic FOIA issue up to that point, the best way in which to do so would be by establishing a "pilot program" (read: not at the FAA) at the Department of Justice in order to first show that accepting requests electronically would not really be so bad.

So this is what OIP made initial preparations to do -- to be a "do as I do" model for this. The problem with such a thing, though, is that it involved a structural change (read: not just my getting on the phone and exhorting component FOIA officers to "do what I say"), the type of thing that really would work best if I had high-level "buy in" (read: formal approval) from the Department's leadership offices, i.e., OAG, ODAG, and OASG.[9] This was particularly significant in that I aimed to have those very offices be the "tip of the spear" in this pilot program. Getting that, of course, required a bit of groundwork -- which required some time.

And this is where I made my mistake: I failed to leave enough time for doing this. Due to the press of other, more immediate things, I left this for the last year of the Clinton Administration and, worse yet, to its closing months. Had Vice President Albert A. Gore, Jr., won the 2000 presidential election (read: "won" better than he actually did), then it would not at all have been a problem: I would have just "carried things over," as I had done when Vice President George H.W. Bush came into office in January of 1989. But even after the election was "over" (read: in mid-December of 2000), I still thought that I would be able to set this pilot program up so that it would be well in place by mid-January of 2001, in which case it would have been too much "in the weeds" for the incoming Bush Administration to focus on it for months to come.

And I thought that I had this all arranged, through the good offices of a high-level political appointee who, although only recently appointed, seemed to be firmly "on board" with it. Only when "push came to shove" on it, she wasn't so firm after all. Then, almost before I knew it, we were so close to Inauguration

Day that even I had to admit that it no longer could realistically happen.

So it did not happen, not then and not during the entire two terms of the Bush Administration. And then not even during the eight years of the Administration of Barack H. Obama, when I was no longer there to shepherd it. And certainly not during the Administration of Donald J. Trump, who seemingly never met a regressive policy that he did not like. In other words, the fact that I failed to make this happen during the year 2000 (or in January of 2001) has meant that FOIA requesters still do not have the legal right (as a matter of governmentwide policy, if not by law)[10] to make requests electronically, even to this day, more than two decades later.[11]

CHAPTER THIRTY-FIVE
The "Whitewater Offshoot"

"I did not have sexual relations with that woman, Miss Lewinsky."

-- President William Jefferson Clinton at the White House, January 26, 1998

During the first year of the George W. Bush Administration, I was asked to enter a special appearance (read: as a formal advocate for the Department) in what could be called an "offshoot" of the Independent Counsel's "Whitewater" litigation. This was for purposes of the Department of Justice filing a very particular type of brief, under seal, in the D.C. Circuit Court of Appeals. I agreed, of course, and soon found myself working alongside Associate Attorney General David M. Margolis, who by that time already was widely regarded as a "legend" within the Justice Department.[1]

David had been a client of mine back in the very early 1980s when he was Chief of the Organized Crime and Racketeering Section of the Criminal Division (see Chapter Seventeen) and, after moving from there to the Office of the Deputy Attorney General during the first year of the Clinton Administration, he had become a mainstay of that office. By the late 1990s, he served as the Department's "liaison" with the D.C. Circuit Court of Appeals on Whitewater-related matters.[2] This meant that he was the Court's point of contact at the Justice Department for the "Whitewater" investigation and litigation handled by Independent Counsel ("IC," to boosters and detractors alike) Kenneth W. Starr[3] and then by his successor as Independent Counsel, Robert W. Ray.[4]

The reason for my being dragooned, so to speak, is that on May 18, 2001, Independent Counsel Ray had petitioned the D.C. Circuit -- actually, its "Division for the Purpose of Appointing Independent Counsels," which consisted of three circuit court judges appointed by the Chief Justice of the United States -- for an order permitting his filing of a certain document that he proposed to include in his final report on "Whitewater" matters.[5] And in turn, the Court had directed the Department of Justice to formally respond to that petition, the substance of which had to do with the possible applicability to that document of the Privacy Act of 1974.

In effect, the Department of Justice was being asked by Independent Counsel Ray, through the Court, to determine whether the Privacy Act stood as an impediment to what he was planning to do. And the fact that when it enacted the Privacy Act Congress formally vested governmentwide policy responsibility for it within the Office of Management and Budget (see Chapter Fourteen), not the Justice Department, did not slow either Independent Counsel Ray or the Court down one bit.

So I proceeded to analyze the question that was presented, which did not really hinge on the identity of the person to whom my brief obliquely referred as "the individual involved."[6] This analysis began with the first step of the Independent Counsel's planned action, filing the document in question with the Court together with his final Whitewater report, something that would be done "under seal." David and I (read: I) readily concluded that even assuming that the document was "covered" by the Privacy Act (read: "a record within a system of records retrieved according to an individual's name or personal identifier"), that action would not violate the Privacy Act in any way.

The reason for this is that the Privacy Act, in its subsection (b), prohibits the disclosure of protected information only "to any person, or to another agency." And on that point, the prevailing case law is clear: A court is not an "agency," nor is it a "person" within the Privacy Act's scope and meaning. And as for the fact that the intended filing would be "under seal," while this was not necessary to our conclusion, it bolstered it even further.

The next contemplated step was to determine what the Court could do with the document once the filing were made. This had two subparts, the Court's ordinary practice of affording access to such a document to any person named within it and its further practice of subsequently providing public access to it by lifting the seal. Our answer was the same for both prospective actions: It would not be constrained by the Privacy Act and its disclosure prohibition, simply because they do not apply outside of the executive branch, neither to Congress nor to the courts.

We next considered something that the Court had not explicitly asked our opinion about: The propriety of the Court disclosing the fact that some named individual had initially been determined to have exercised "poor judgment" but that the Independent Counsel subsequently determined that he or she had not.[7] On this score, we specifically deferred to the Court on what we described as the "balancing of public and privacy interests" that it should undertake in considering that.[8] To further aid the Court, though, we described for it a similar situation that, coincidentally, David and I together had confronted in the past.

In that case, one involving a "public summary" that the Department's Office of Professional Responsibility ("OPR," to both friend and foe) had prepared about one of its investigations, based on its finding that a Justice Department attorney had committed professional wrongdoing, that finding was overruled at a higher level. That ultimate determination was that the attorney's conduct only "raised possible concerns about [his or her] performance." And in that case, the Deputy Attorney General, in consultation with the Office of Information and Privacy, determined that no public summary of the matter should be made.

The Department's reasoning in that earlier case, we explained to the Court, was that it was not possible to draft an accurate OPR public summary in such a manner that its disclosure would not constitute an "unwarranted invasion" of the attorney's personal-privacy interests.[9] To go ahead with public disclosure in such a case, we advised, would be contrary to well-settled case law under both the Freedom of Information Act and the Privacy Act on the balancing of public and personal-privacy interests in such situations.[10] We said this even though we had already advised the Court that its actions were not constrained by the Privacy Act at all.

And here's the "kicker" that required more than a little finesse. We had determined within the Department that not only did we know of an existing basis for this question to arise between the Independent Counsel and the Court, we (read: the Department of Justice, on behalf of the executive branch) furthermore had an institutional interest of our own in the resolution of that question. So we had to protect that interest, and we did so with the following sentence:

"If the Court determines to publicly disclose the [document] as part of the Independent Counsel's Final Report, the Department of Justice respectfully requests an opportunity to seek leave to submit a proposed supplement to that Final Report in order to address a point of institutional importance to it."

And without going into too much explanatory detail here, I will just say that there were several more sentences that described the exact nature of the Department's interests and its concerns, which revolved around rules governing attorney conduct in relation to attorney "contacts with represented persons," and we adverted to the Department's "institutional interests that extend far beyond this particular case." Our bottom line was that "if the Independent Counsel's analysis on the above point of law is made public, the Department's should as well."

This certainly was ending a brief that was nice and helpful (almost gratuitously so) on a rough and pointed note, but we had no choice given the circumstances. And it all worked out well in the end, with both the Independent Court and the Court, so it was worth it.

CHAPTER THIRTY-SIX
Post-9/11 Detainees

"[T]he Constitution . . . is not a suicide pact."

-- Justice Arthur J. Goldberg, in *Kennedy v. Mendoza-Martinez*, February 18, 1963

One of the many consequences of the attacks of September 11, 2001 was the Federal Government's almost immediate campaign of searching for any and all possible other such potential terrorists on U.S. soil and "detaining" them for some period of time until investigations of them (and, in some cases, their known associates) were completed.[1] By early November, more than a thousand such persons were in such detention; even the exact number was a carefully guarded (read: enormous) secret.[2]

The reason for this secrecy was, in a word, fear -- fear that was partly well-grounded, but partly not. One has to remember that in the immediate wake of the horrific events of September 11, 2001, there was a strongly prevailing concern in the country that there would be (read: as a matter of when, not if) follow-up attacks of a similar nature. Probably not as large and dramatic, perhaps, but deadly attacks just the same. And this fear resonated throughout the Federal Government, from top to bottom, as reflected in President George W. Bush's admonition to Attorney General John D. Ashcroft: "Don't let this happen again."

This fear, and the accompanying resolve not to let it "happen again," drove all sectors of the Nation. The private sector had almost everyone on high alert for anything that seemed suspicious, anyone who seemed like he or she might be another terrorist living in our midsts.[3] People were very mindful of the fact that the 19 known 9/11 terrorists had been living in the United States while preparing their attacks and that they had escaped detection as such -- even by the flight-school operators who had instructed them without being suspicious that they wanted to learn take-offs and mid-flight maneuvers but not landings.

And in the government sector, especially among law enforcement personnel at the federal, state, and local levels, the sense of urgency and anxiety was even more profound. No one wanted to be the one who could have stopped another terrorist attack but failed to do so for lack of being vigilant or sufficiently reactive in his or her area of responsibility.[4] It certainly was a bad time to be Islamic or to look anything like the 9/11 highjackers.

This all inexorably led to suspicion being cast on hundreds of "terrorism suspects," of all manner and degree, during the months of September, October, and November of 2001. And the Federal Government led the way in questioning and incarcerating most of them, under the label of "detainees," without much regard for their rights and civil liberties, especially at first.[5] "The Constitution is not a suicide pact," was the refrain most often heard.[6]

With this, it was not long before some public-interest organizations began calling for a variety of things regarding these "detainees," many of whom were of questionable immigration status, as well as for their prompt release if they were not to be processed through ordinary immigration proceedings or charged with any crime. Among those things was their identification so that their relatives could locate them without further delay. And this issue of their public identification soon came to my desk for analysis, even before the first FOIA requests for that information landed. Up until then, everything about these detainees, including their total number, had been kept secret.[7]

More specifically, this "detainee information" consisted of the names of those who were detained, the locations of their arrest and detention, the locations of their current whereabouts, the dates of detention, the reasons for their detention, and the nature of the charges filed, if any, plus (read: for good measure) the identities of their lawyers (whether court-appointed or privately retained). And the detainees fell into three general categories: Persons held on immigration-related charges by the Department of Justice's Immigration and Naturalization Service ("INS" or "la migra," to undocumented persons), persons charged with federal crimes, and persons held on what were called "material witness warrants."[8]

The first of these categories was relatively large, the last relatively small. But for all of these categories, if they were to be spoken of as such, the Federal Government needed to determine what would be disclosed about them, including by Attorney General Ashcroft in public statements that he was expected to make about the "detainee situation." And that is where OIP's analysis came into play, first, last, and foremost.

So it was that I conducted a full-scale analysis of all detainee-related information in order to determine what could be withheld from the public (and, eventually, from the detainees themselves). At first, this was in the context of possible "affirmative" disclosure (read: without a FOIA request or anything else legally compelling it), primarily in media statements given by Attorney General

Ashcroft and a few others.[9] Soon, it became in context of both FOIA requests made by third parties (e.g., the media) and Privacy Act access requests made by (or on behalf of, with written authorization) the detainees.[10] And before long,[11] it was for purposes of defending the lead FOIA litigation case that was brought by a host of public-interest groups for a full range of detainee information.[12]

In mid-October, I created an outline of all of the information categories, disclosure issues, and my analytical conclusions on each, for all those in the Department's leadership offices -- the Offices of the Attorney General, Deputy Attorney General, and Associate Attorney General, plus the Office of Legal Counsel (for White House liaison purposes), and law enforcement components such as the FBI and the Bureau of Prisons -- who were working on detainee matters. This outline was circulated widely within the Department and, as I recall, to the CIA and INTERPOL (the "International Criminal Police Organization"), as well.

In short, I concluded that the Justice Department's ongoing investigation into the 9/11 crimes, and the subject of international terrorism within the United States more generally, provided a sufficient legal basis for the application of FOIA Exemption 7(A) to almost all detainee-related information in a broad-scale fashion. This meant that for at least the time being, any such information that could be linked to the substance of that investigation could be withheld on that basis.[13] As a general rule, however, this did not necessarily include any particular type of detainee information.

Consequently, we had to consider the personal-privacy interests of the detainees, starting with the FOIA rule that the mere fact that someone has been detained for a law enforcement purpose is a protectible abstract fact, not to be disclosed absent any overriding public interest in a particular case (see Chapter Thirteen). This seemed counterintuitive to many at the time -- i.e., that here was the Federal Government, having apprehended and incarcerated so many persons in secrecy, saying that it was withholding their identities in order to protect *their* interests. But that is what FOIA Exemption 7(C) provided, as a matter of both law and longstanding policy, and for any detainee who was a U.S. citizen (or lawful permanent resident), it is what the Privacy Act commanded.

* * * * *

An aside is in order here because to those of us in OIP, this was highly reminiscent of something that had occurred during the Clinton Administration when the Federal Government received FOIA requests for records concerning American journalist Terry A. Anderson, who was taken hostage by Hezbollah militants in Lebanon in 1985 and was held captive for nearly seven years. Upon his return, Anderson began a many-year quest to find out as much as he could about his captors, including through FOIA and Privacy Act requests, but was surprised (read: shocked and grossly disappointed) by the resistance that he met from both U.S. intelligence agencies and the Department of Justice. A big part of that was our standard FOIA policy of not disclosing information about a third party in a law enforcement context without that person's written consent. As a matter of policy, this applies to citizens of other countries even though the Privacy Act's mandatory nondisclosure provisions do not (see Chapter Fourteen).

Unfortunately, Terry Anderson came up against this obstacle in a most regrettable way: He made an early FOIA request to a Justice Department component (the name of which is sensitive but its initials are "D, E, and A") that was not known for its FOIA sophistication and had no idea who Terry Anderson was when it received his FOIA request. Nor did it read the content of his request letter with any particular care. So it just gave him its standard form response to any third-party request: It refused to confirm or deny that it had any responsive records (because Anderson had provided what names of his captors he thought he knew) and, worse yet, it suggested that he *go and obtain formal written consents from such persons* that would serve to waive their privacy interests and allow him to possibly obtain some information.

Well, this did not sit well with Anderson, with the media, or with anyone who relished criticizing the Federal Government's implementation of the FOIA. The problem was that the agency was entirely correct in the substance of this response, while at the same time the "optics" of such an action were, in a word, horrendous. All Anderson had to say to this was the obvious: He was a victim of militant international terrorism captivity who was being told by his Government that he had to seek the permission of his captors in order to learn what his Government knew about them. And of course it fell to OIP to handle this unique dilemma as best it could.

So we invited Terry Anderson into our office, together with his counsel and allied journalists, to first and foremost explain to him why he had received the affrontive response that was given to him -- something that I'm here to tell you is not easily explained. And to his credit, I think he sort of understood the general FOIA mechanics that we described, insofar as they went. But that was not enough for him to get past his blinding anger at what it had felt like to him to receive such a response in his case in particular.

This was exacerbated by the fact that, while trying to be totally open with him, we acknowledged up front that his captors, as foreigners, had no rights under the Privacy Act mandating nondisclosure. Indeed, the disclosure barrier was just a matter of standard policy, something to which we adhered as a matter of uniformity and even-handedness. And, frankly, this mattered to us more than a little as a matter of government integrity. In other words, it would be one thing if a political decision were made to have a policy exception in Anderson's favor, but quite another for him to receive favorable treatment unlike anyone else through ordinary FOIA processes.

As might be imagined, this did not go down well at all with anyone on Anderson's side of this controversy, people who didn't much care (read: at least not in this case) about the Federal Government being consistent and even-handed in applying the FOIA -- not if it meant such apparent disrespect to a returned captive American. And one of those people, as it turned out, was Attorney General Janet Reno.

Janet had arrived at the Department not long before this story "broke" and she read about it in the "Attorney General's News Summary" that was distributed to the Department's top officials, including all component heads, every day. We called them "the clips," and in those days they consisted of photocopies of news articles, bound together beneath a detailed table of contents, that our Office of Public Affairs staff literally worked through the night to produce each morning. (Remember: We had no Internet or World Wide Web until the mid-1990s, so this was the most efficient way in which to keep abreast of things that mattered to the Department and might even "pop up" during the day.[14])

Now even at this early point in her tenure, Janet already had good reason to have great respect for OIP (see Chapter Twenty-Eight), but she also was a politician, having been elected as the local state prosecutor for Miami-Dade County five times running, and she well understood the significance of "optics" in a law enforcement setting. And while she recognized the importance of government even-handedness, she also knew a bad-looking situation when she saw one. Plus, she had OIP telling her that Terry Anderson was being stymied only as a matter of *policy*, not law, as if begging her to intervene.[15] So she did just that.[16]

In the wake of the Justice Department's resulting change of its privacy policy for Terry Anderson in particular, he filed more than 50 FOIA requests with 11 federal agencies and received more than 3000 pages of records, which he used to write a book about his hostage experiences, titled *Den of Lions*. He also filed a FOIA lawsuit in 1994, which led to no significant further record disclosures. More successful was his suit against the Iranian government for his captivity; in 2002, he gained a multimillion-dollar settlement from frozen Iranian assets.[17]

* * * * *

So my conclusion was that a detainee's identity should remain secret unless and until he or she executed a written consent to his or her identity as such being publicly disclosed. Was this according all such persons the benefit of the Justice Department's standard privacy policy regardless of all post-9/11 sentiment? Yes, but it seemed to me to be the right thing to do, especially considering that many of the detainees (as U.S. citizens or LPRs) had the nondisclosure provisions of the Privacy Act (in a third-party access context) applicable to their information.[18] Accordingly, a process was begun for offering detainees that formal consent option, though to my recollection it was rather slow and cumbersome. And as I recall, a very large proportion of all detainees declined this offer.

Lastly, we had to consider the question of identifying the detainees' counsel. On this subject, I was most firm: There was prevailing FOIA case law saying that one's professional activities are distinct from one's personal life, meaning that the FOIA's privacy exemptions -- Exemptions 6 and 7(C) -- are applicable to the latter but not the former. I agreed with that as a matter of policy overall, as well as in the circumstances of this particular case. In my view, attorneys who plainly agreed to represent such detainees even in the context of an immediate post-9/11 environment knew what they were doing and could not reasonably have expected to have their identities shielded from public view. Moreover, there was a strong public interest in everyone knowing that, even under such exigent circumstances, these detainees were being provided with adequate counsel who could be contacted about their circumstances.

There was one possible exception to this: FOIA Exemption 7(F). That exemption, which I have described elsewhere as "like Exemption 7(C) on steroids" (see Chapter Forty), provides a basis for nondisclosure regardless of any public interest wherever someone's "life or physical safety" is involved. It was conceivable to me that such could possibly be the case for some of the detainees' attorneys, depending on the particular circumstances of their clients. So I made room for Exemption 7(F) applying to detainee counsel in any particular case in which its safety underpinning could be established,[19] but not as an across-the-board general rule.

So these were the rules and principles that OIP said should be applied to press statements, FOIA responses, and ultimately in the above-mentioned FOIA litigation case brought to challenge this new brand of government secrecy. That case, *Center for National Security Studies v. United States Department of Justice*, was filed in December of 2001, and it was adjudicated according to an informally expedited time schedule -- something that the plaintiffs had requested and the Department did not oppose.

The position that the Department took in this litigation hewed closely to what we had established administratively, but with one major exception: It continued to involve categorically withholding the identities of the detainees' counsel under Exemption 7(F). I strongly disagreed with this, so much so that although I had been asked to be the primary declarant in support of the Government's summary judgment motion, and was lined up to play that role, I ultimately declined to do so (yes, I could do that if I chose) and was replaced with a terrorism official in the Department's Criminal Division who was personally willing to support that position.

And when the district court decision was handed down on August 2, 2002, that Exemption 7(F) position was flatly rejected. The district court did so by reasoning, just as I had from the outset, that "Defendant's [Exemption 7(F)] rationale erroneously assumes that lawyers, like suspects or defendants, have an expectation of anonymity; they do not." Thus, neither Exemption 7(F) nor Exemption 7(C) (which had not been argued for the attorneys) was available for this attorney category.

Nor was either exemption found available for the identities of the detainees, as a categorical matter. Instead, just as OIP had recommended be used as a detainee "option" at the administrative level, the district court ruled that "detainees wishing to keep their name confidential may 'opt out' of public disclosure by submitting to the Government a signed statement requesting that their identities remain confidential." Otherwise, it declared, "the public's interest in learning the identities of those arrested and detained is essential to verifying whether the Government is operating within the bounds of the law."[20] Frankly, I well understood this "bounds of the law" concern, as I personally had seen and heard things that comported with it.

As to all of the information surrounding the detainees' apprehension and incarceration -- i.e., the locations of their arrests, detention, and current where-abouts, the dates of their detention, the reasons for their detention, and the nature of any charges filed -- the district court found that all such information was properly withheld under FOIA Exemption 7(A). Although this certainly was a wide-ranging application of that exemption, the district court ruled that the exceptional circumstances involved in the 9/11 attacks were "sufficient" to support such an approach in this case. To be sure, this was an exceptionally broad judicial acceptance of the applicability of Exemption 7(A).

Almost a year later, these rulings were partly reversed on appeal, with Exemption 7(A) ("on steroids," one might say) predominating across the board. In an opinion written by Circuit Court Judge David B. Sentelle,[21] a 2-1 panel of the D.C. Circuit broke new ground for the adjudication of FOIA cases involving Exemption 7. It declared that an "appropriate deference to the executive on issues of national security," which had long applied under FOIA Exemption 1, should be applied to law enforcement exemptions "in cases implicating national security."[22] And applying such an exceptional degree of deference to the Government's judgments of harm in this case meant that everything at issue in the case,[23] even the identities of the detainees' counsel, could properly be withheld under Exemption 7(A). This was a truly unprecedented FOIA decision.

Indeed, under the FOIA, there always has been a conceptual continuum running from law enforcement sensitivity at one end to national security sensitivity at the other; sometimes, when a law enforcement matter holds national security implications, the two can begin to merge. And in the wake of 9/11, which spawned a whole new realm of "homeland security sensitivity," that continuum gained a new middle ground. So the D.C. Circuit's decision in *Center for National Security Studies*, by holding that "the long-recognized deference to the executive" should be applied in the law enforcement context when matters of national security are involved, solidified that, for law enforcement (and, potentially, homeland security) FOIA cases, very much in the Government's favor.

And with the passage of time, even in the absence of major follow-up terrorism activity, this basis for broader law enforcement protection remains.

CHAPTER THIRTY-SEVEN
The Protection of Critical Infrastructure

"Fatherland [read: homeland security] without freedom and merit is a large word with little meaning."

-- Anders Chydenius, Age of Enlightenment philosopher, legislator, and grandfather of the FOIA, 1729-1803

After the horrific events of September 11, 2001,[1] as the world as we had known it instantly changed, so too did the world of government information policy, as well as the governmentwide administration of the FOIA within it. This included the immediate commencement of a wide-scale information-policy review by the Office of Information and Privacy ("OIP," even when we were overworked and dehydrated) together with the staff of the National Security Council ("NSC," to those inclined to confuse it with "NSA"), with whom I was to work very closely on such matters for more than the next five years.[2]

And just as we all soon came to use the term "homeland security" shortly after 9/11,[3] we also began heavily focusing on the identification, categorization, and protection of the Nation's "critical infrastructure" -- a term that few people knew of and one that I had encountered only in my Continuity-of-Government work (see Chapter Twenty-Six) before then.

This new term was used to describe the parts of the Nation's assets that could be seen as vulnerable to follow-up terrorist attacks -- such as the electric power grid; telecommunications systems; fiber optics networks; sewage systems; oil pipelines; transportation systems; elements of the federal banking system; airport radar control systems; satellite operability; bridges, tunnels, dams, and water supply;[4] and nuclear facilities, first and foremost.[5] It also included what were termed "weapons of mass destruction" (read: conventional weapons such as explosives, plus "bioweapons" such as anthrax and other toxins) that could be "weaponized" against the populace.[6]

As is indicated above, the protection of such things first involved their specific identification. This step was complicated more than a little by the fact that, it was estimated, no less than 85% of the Nation's critical infrastructure resided in the private sector. (In other words, had we been Russia, the task would have been far easier.) This therefore required, sooner rather than later and to no small degree, the cooperation of the individuals, businesses, companies, and corporations that owned such things and had proprietary control of the key information about them.

We called this "critical infrastructure information" (or "CII," to all those acronymically inclined), a term used very heavily after 9/11 (and only occasionally prior to then, mostly by the Federal Emergency Management Agency ("FEMA," to all thinkers of the unthinkable), in its Continuity-of-Government activities), in reference to a wide range of information. And information bearing such a label was to be "safeguarded" by a federal agency, which meant "within its four walls."

And atop that, we also had "PCII," which stood for "Protected Critical Infrastructure Information," the designation that was given to any CII that came to be verified as sufficiently sensitive upon its submission to homeland security officials from the private sector. Almost all such information, if submitted to the Federal Government voluntarily, readily fell within the protective scope of FOIA Exemption 4 under prevailing case law to begin with, as was advised by OIP. But again, the overwhelming bulk of all such information that never became the subject of a FOIA request still could be safeguarded and "controlled."

Such was the bedrock of what came to be known as "pseudosecrecy" in our post-9/11 information-policy environment. And before long, the most ubiquitous safeguarding label of all, as an umbrella sobriquet of sorts, was "SBU" -- the abbreviation of my policy memorandum's subheading of "Sensitive But Unclassified Information," which so many federal agencies used as the foundation for their own labels. Indeed, it came into widespread (read: very wide and spread) use (see Chapter Thirty-Eight).

This eventually became complicated and confusing, in many places and in many ways. And it developed into a huge impediment to information sharing among federal agencies (not to mention with state and local authorities), which by then had been declared to be a major policy objective by the Office of Homeland Security ("OHS," to those who thought the White House should be doing *something*) and its successor Department of Homeland Security ("DHS," to all those who cheered the creation of a new cabinet department, which certainly *was* something). In fact, that overall policy was labeled (no pun intended) as the vital "Information Sharing Environment" ("ISE," to those phonetically akin to DHS's "ICE") by Congress.[7]

Despite these concerns, however, it took several years for the entire Federal Government (read: not just me) to try to wrap its arms around the proliferation and use of safeguarding labels. In fact, it was not until mid-2006 that DHS, the Office of Management and Budget ("OMB," to budgeteers), and the new Office of the Director of National Intelligence ("ODNI," as odd as it sounds) combined forces, with advice solicited from the Department of Justice,[8] to try to tackle the problem by narrowing that use.

$$\ast \quad \ast \quad \ast \quad \ast \quad \ast$$

So back to "critical infrastructure." Remember that the tasks at hand were to identify, categorize, safeguard, and control information about it, for both what existed inside of the Federal Government (about 15% of it) and what existed within the control of the private sector (the other 85% of it).[9] And this was soon facilitated greatly by the measured use of safeguarding labels.

First but not foremost, the government-controlled 15% of the Nation's critical infrastructure pretty much took care of itself. There was no particular difficulty or controversy with it, except for two FOIA cases in which the requesters wanted to learn information that, upon analysis, would have permitted conclusions to be reached that could have aided a terrorist attack, in one instance, and the penetration of a security system in the other.[10]

But the information about the 85% of critical infrastructure that was in the private sector (and therefore came into the Federal Government's hands from the "outside") quickly became a "BFD" (read: a "big friggin' deal," though not exactly a safeguarding label itself). This was because, for the Federal Government to "identify" it as such, first and foremost, it had to be submitted to the Federal Government, voluntarily, by those who owned it (read: both the infrastructure item and the information about it). And then the next necessary step was for it to be verified by DHS as "sensitive" (read: "protected," as in "Protected Critical Infrastructure Information"), or not, upon its submission.

So DHS had to set up an elaborate mechanism and process by which both of these things could take place. It directed that such voluntary submissions be made to DHS in a certain form and fashion, and it labeled all such information as "CII," for "critical infrastructure information." Once verified by agency analysis as truly being of such sensitivity, it was then relabeled as "protected critical infrastructure information" ("PCII," to its corporate friends). As sometimes has been said, it seems that the Federal Government has never met a situation that it could not make more complicated.[11]

And it was not long before this very architecture of critical infrastructure information submission became hobbled by a fundamental question: Did it apply only to whatever information was submitted to DHS directly, or could it apply also to information that was submitted indirectly -- i.e., to another federal agency, which in turn then forwarded it to DHS? In my view, limiting this process to information submitted to DHS only (read: directly, not indirectly) made the most sense, as a matter of both simplicity and practicality.

Unfortunately, however, there were those in the private sector (read: businesses, corporations, and even whole industries) who sought to have the broadest possible scope of PCII applicability, for their own reasons. Primarily, they wanted to be able to shield through the *voluntary* CII process the very information that they otherwise were *required* to submit to other agencies. And their "water" on this, so to speak, was being noisily carried by a few relatively low-level political appointees in the Bush Administration.

* * * * *

Before going farther with this "direct/indirect" delineation, however, some background to it is necessary -- because this had to do with the Freedom of Information Act, at bottom, and how its business-information exemption, FOIA Exemption 4, operated under prevailing case law. About a decade before 9/11, the D.C. Circuit Court of Appeals, the leading circuit court for FOIA jurisprudence, ruled *en banc* that Exemption 4's protective scope was broad for voluntarily submitted information but relatively narrow for the vast range of business information that federal agencies require businesses to submit to them for either regulatory or procurement purposes.[12] And ever since, businesses have at every turn selfishly endeavored to have their "required" information submissions viewed as "voluntary" on one theory or another, so as to afford it the broadest possible disclosure protection in the face of FOIA requests (see Chapter Forty Six).

So at the birth of CII, corporate America had good (read: but not valid) reason to prefer having its business information viewed as "voluntarily" submitted rather than "required." Even better still, in addition to that, it also preferred that its CII information in particular receive "categorical" protection under a FOIA Exemption 3 statute if one could possibly be obtained by Congress to cover it.[13] Yes, corporate America wasn't missing a trick.

And that is when a group of government contractors -- big-time contractors, led by Raytheon Company[14] -- got together and aggressively made what amounted to an end run around the nascent CII system. They secured a secret "side meeting" with President Bush and actually got him to agree that he would get them such special statutory (albeit shamelessly duplicative) protection for their submitted information, as if there truly was much risk of their not submitting their CII information otherwise.[15] Yes, Bush was bamboozled on this, but no one ever accused him of being smart.

Now the reason that I am so clear on this now is that when it leaked out (read: internally, within the government, not publicly) that this had happened, I remember being surprised as well as greatly disappointed. Putting aside the fact that their purported non-submission of CII was a *total bluff* (read: given my familiarity with past activity, I knew this for sure), these companies were able to secure this commitment from Bush even though the type of information that they would be submitting was information that they could reasonably expect would be protected under existing law (i.e., Exemption 4); they just wanted to have 100 percent certainty about that (or perhaps their highly paid lobbyists just wanted to be able to say that they had accomplished something "significant").[16]

This led to an Exemption 3 provision for CII (read: PCII) finding its way into what was called the "Critical Infrastructure Information Act of 2002," as part of the massive homeland security legislation enacted that year. This new statute afforded broad, "categorical" Exemption 3 protection from FOIA disclosure for any information that businesses and other non-federal entities voluntarily provide to the Federal Government concerning their critical infrastructure vulnerabilities.[17] But at least it properly applied only to such information in the hands of DHS, which was a good thing.

DHS implemented this Exemption 3 statute as part of what it called its "Protected Critical Infrastructure Program," which it promptly established through proposed regulations.[18] These regulations were promulgated in "interim final" form, though, which meant that they became effective immediately upon issuance but were subject to revision upon their issuance as a "final rule" at some point in the future after another round of public comments. And they were the subject of much public comment after their issuance in proposed form in April of 2003.

* * * * *

So back to the "direct versus indirect" submission issue. To put it most simply, businesses wanted everything that they submitted, to any federal agency and in any context, here or there, old or new, to be categorized as CII and potentially PCII if sensitive enough. In their view, the new CII category should be treated as "oceanic," even if it meant that they were, in effect, exploiting it toward a ready nondisclosure end.

The Federal Government's new cadre of homeland security professionals (of which I ideally was a member only part-time), on the other hand, viewed this entire area of endeavor as already too complicated to begin with to risk adding another controversial layer to it.[19] We knew that the very heart of the CII concept was to allow DHS to gather such information for its homeland-protection purposes, which was best facilitated by its doing so with information submissions made to it -- both directly and distinctly, not through any intermediary agency.

But business lobbyists were relentless on this point, even after Congress was explicit in expressing its intent that the information flow to be protected should be only the flow that came into DHS and to DHS alone.[20] And then their political allies within DHS somehow managed to have its proposed regulations, when finalized, provide also for the submission of CII to other agencies as part of the new program. This was, of course, their ultimate "play" in their unrelenting efforts to obtain broad, "categorical" protection for all submitted business information.

It therefore was up to us to try to counter this move, which we did, though not entirely. This resulted in there being what were denominated as "revised" new "interim final" regulations (believe it or not) that spoke of "direct submissions," *but* the preamble to them nevertheless stated that DHS "anticipate[d] the development of appropriate mechanisms to allow for indirect submissions in the final rule." That is when I started describing this as the conflict that "just would not die." But die it did, when these regulations (and DHS's implementation of its CII program) finally came to rest without the inclusion of "indirect submissions."

And today, even with very little damage done to the Nation's "critical infrastructure" during what now has been more than 20 years, this "CII/PCII" program at DHS remains in operation, just as does the use of it continue through a "CUI Registry" at NARA. So the world of critical infrastructure protection, with its "alphabet soup" of safeguarding labels,[21] kept spinning, as I had to keep explaining how it all traces back to a memorandum heading that I thought I was using benignly when compensating for a sleepy-headed presidential science advisor in March of 2002 -- see Chapter Thirty-Eight, immediately below -- which is what spawned the whole new realm of "pseudosecrecy."

CHAPTER THIRTY-EIGHT
Pseudosecrecy

"[As to] sensitive but unclassified information related to America's homeland security, . . ."

-- White House/Justice Department memorandum dated March 19, 2002

Pseudosecrecy is a more-difficult-than-average concept that is a distinct information-policy outgrowth of 9/11. As noted above, it is the term that we used in order to describe the realm in which records of seeming sensitivity are "protected"[1] by a federal agency not from public disclosure, necessarily, but within its four walls, on a day-to-day basis, regardless of whether they are ever subject to an access demand such as a Freedom of Information Act request. And this "in-house" protection,[2] so to speak, is achieved through "safeguarding labels" that are placed (read: stamped, usually, but in some cases applied electronically) on those records, either after or at the outset of their creation.

Such safeguarding labels can be a tricky thing. To be sure, they play a legitimate role in ensuring that records so marked are not treated casually or otherwise without regard to their sensitivity internally (e.g., not just "left lying around" or maintained within information systems to which too many people are afforded access unthinkingly). But, human nature being what it is, they can easily give the false impression that their designation is equivalent to a determination that all safeguarded information is so sensitive as to be exempt from public disclosure under the FOIA -- yet it is not.

One way of looking at it is that pseudosecrecy determinations are made *en grosse*, on a rough and preliminary basis, by personnel who are not necessarily familiar with, nor particularly concerned about, legal nondisclosure standards. By contrast, FOIA exemption determinations are made for only a small percentage of safeguarded records, once FOIA requests for them are actually filed, by FOIA analysists who know how FOIA exemptions work. And only a percentage of all safeguarded records and information (albeit sometimes a large percentage, depending on the subject matter) is actually exempt from disclosure under the

FOIA. (So yes, this amounts to actually a small percentage of a small percentage of a whole *corpus*.)

Indeed, one of my biggest challenges after 9/11 was getting it through the heads of agency personnel that their use of a safeguarding label on a record absolutely does *not* mean that it would properly be withheld (either in part or in whole) in response to any FOIA request made down the road. And the most difficult such label to contend with in that regard, especially in reining in non-FOIA personnel at the Department of Defense ("DOD," to its *aides-de-camp*), was "FOUO," the rugged and ubiquitous label that stands for "For Official Use Only."[3] This was partly because "FOUO" existed, atypically, before 9/11 and certainly before the Department of Justice and the National Security Council began talking about "pseudosecrecy" at all.

Indeed, "FOUO" was used long before September of 2001 as a means of, in effect, "compartmentalizing" some of DOD's military information in sort of a low-key version of national security classification. The appealing advantage was that a "FOUO" designation (read: not a "classification") did not involve any of the cumbersome procedural requirements of national security classification; it just efficiently limited what was mostly internal access and dissemination. And in time, this appeal was recognized by some other federal agencies, which employed it with even greater abandon.

But as potent and potentially troublesome as "FOUO" was, in the post-9/11 world it soon became just the tip of a freezing iceberg of a whole host of such safeguarding labels. Indeed, by the year 2003, the nearly 100 agencies of the Federal Government had managed to create more than 100 such labels, with the world of pseudosecrecy expanding beyond any single person's imagination. And this all was jump-started, I have to admit here and now, by something that I did in March of 2002 just because the president's science advisor apparently failed to fully wake up before answering his home phone and speaking to *The New York Times* one Saturday morning.

Although this might sound unlikely, it nevertheless is true. On Saturday, January 12, 2002, as I recall, a *New York Times* reporter called Presidential Science Advisor Dr. John H. "Jack" Marburger III, waking him (read: well, perhaps not completely) with a question about the George W. Bush Administration's policy on protecting "sensitive information" now in a post-9/11 environment, particularly as regards what we had been calling "weapons of mass destruction."[4] And much as I hate being critical of someone who was the president of my own undergraduate university,[5] Dr. Jack Marburger really "screwed the pooch" in giving a response. Perhaps thinking only that it would be good to *have* such a policy, he clearly and unequivocally spoke as if one already existed -- only it didn't.

So early the next morning, when most presidential appointees were in church of necessity praying for their mortal souls, I received an urgent call from my principal "partner in crime" at the White House, who told me of Dr. Marburger's cotton-headed blunder, painfully described the internal White House reaction to it, and asked if we could possibly develop and finalize (read: issue authoritatively, in writing) such a policy on an "exigent circumstances" basis, so that it would actually exist as Dr. Marburger had said it did.[6] And, oh by the way, OIP would get all the organizational support it might need for such an endeavor (read: the White House would provide cover if anyone at Justice were to question it, which admittedly was not likely).

"Sure," I said, "the difficult can be done almost immediately, but the impossible usually takes a little longer." I estimated that if we did this right, it could be accomplished within about a month. But actually, it wound up taking a second month (read: until mid-March of 2002), as we subsequently decided that we wanted to have the White House chief of staff as a signatory to it as well, if at all possible. Then OIP would provide for its wide dissemination, using our excellent channels of long standing for that.

We titled this new policy "Action to Safeguard Information Regarding Weapons of Mass Destruction and Other Sensitive Records Related to Homeland Security," which went directly to the point. And as to classified or classifiable information, it first specified that:

- All departments and agencies should promptly "determin[e] the classification status of [their] records related to the development or use of weapons of mass destruction."

- "Government information, regardless of its age, that could reasonably be expected to assist in the development or use of weapons of mass destruction, including information about the current locations of stockpiles of nuclear materials that could be exploited for use in such weapons, should [be classified and] not be disclosed inappropriately."

- All departments and agencies should "[u]ndertak[e] an immediate reexamination of current measures for identifying and safeguarding all such [classified] information," including a "review [of such] records' management procedures and, where appropriate, their holdings of documents."[7]

Then, by contrast, we went on to address other sensitive (read: unclassified) information that "could be misused to harm the security of our Nation or threaten public safety," for which we required all departments and agencies to "consider the need [for] safeguard[ing it] on an ongoing basis."[8] And in doing so, so as to clearly delineate such information from the other information previously discussed, I used the heading of "Sensitive But Unclassified Information."

Well, here's the "kicker," so to speak: When I used that heading, it was only generically, as a means of delineation, nothing more. There in fact was no existing category of "sensitive but unclassified" information, by that name, nor did I intend there to be one.[9] And I maintain to this day that anyone reading that March 19, 2002 policy memorandum (which still remains in effect today) carefully would realize that. But that particular phrase nevertheless "took off like a rocket," as they say, from just about the moment that the memorandum was issued, and its progeny still live on today, in a world of "pseudosecrecy" that received an unintended boost that day.

Indeed, it was not very long afterward that "safeguarding labels" began blossoming in many fields of Federal Government endeavor, far beyond the basic "FOUO" and similar old labels at DOD and a few other agencies. Before we knew it, federal agencies were on their own developing and employing literally dozens of such labels under which they assiduously safeguarded and controlled wide varieties of information,[10] such as "SSI" ("Sensitive Security Information"), "LES" ("Law Enforcement Sensitive" information), and "NOFORN" (no foreign dissemination).[11]

To be sure, we did help that along more than a bit with the governmentwide safeguarding labels that we freshly developed, such as "SHSI" ("Sensitive Homeland Security Information," which I joked was used "only because 'Sensitive Homeland Information Technology' was already taken"). This meant information deemed to be sensitive and in need of "control" because of its potential for "use by terrorists for targeting, site selection, or any form of impairment of any part of the Nation's 'critical infrastructure.'"[12]

We also notably developed and widely employed the concept of "Critical Infrastructure Information" ("CII," to those in the know), which the White House Office of Homeland Security defined, expansively, as information pertaining to "systems and assets, whether physical or virtual, so vital to the United States that the incapacity or destruction of such systems and assets would have a debilitating impact on security, national economic security, national public health, or any combination of those matters" (see Chapter Thirty-Seven) and which OIP said could be withheld in the face of a FOIA request under FOIA

Exemption 2 (but see Chapter Forty-Six) if sensitive enough.[13] Regardless of its FOIA status, though, any such information could be safeguarded (not to be confused with withheld from the public, counterintuitive though that might be) under the rubric of "CII."

This was attempted only indirectly, however, through the formulation of a new rubric, that of "Controlled Unclassified Information" ("CUI," to those who had their fill of "SBU"). In an effort to "harmonize" the pseudosecrecy realm, the Bush Administration in 2008 eventually (read: after I had retired) morphed "SBU" into "CUI," leading to the creation of an entity called the "Controlled Unclassified Information Office" ("CUIO," to debt collectors) which is housed within the Information Security Oversight Office ("ISOO," to the litigation inclined) of the National Archives and Records Administration ("NARA," for the record) and to its use of something called the national "CUI Registry" of what by then were more than 140 safeguarding labels.

For all of its fanfare, though, and after all of that time, "CUI" was given no firm definition, which had been part of the problem with the unofficial "SBU" label to begin with. Even when this new regime was subsequently addressed in an executive order issued by President Barack Obama, in November of 2010, "CUI" still remained undefined, which left it to individual agencies to determine its scope and application. And to this day, the entire realm of "pseudosecrecy" remains an unresolved complication of the post-9/11 era.[14]

CHAPTER THIRTY-NINE
White House Visitor Logs

"Two things are infinite: the universe and human stupidity; and I'm not sure about the universe."

-- Albert Einstein, 1879-1955

A completely unique FOIA issue that came to a head during the second half of the George W. Bush Administration was the treatment of what became known as White House "visitor logs." This subject was never far below the surface when there was any reason for journalists or government watchdog groups to focus their attention on exactly who came to visit the president, the vice president, and/or their staffs during particular periods of time; they sometimes would ask whether there were any records of such visits.

The short answer is that such records were in fact kept by the United States Secret Service for the "clearance" of all people given access to the White House Complex and its grounds.[1] This was done through a records system that was long maintained by the Secret Service under acronyms such as "ACR" (the "Access Control Records System") and "WAVES" (the White House's "Workers and Visitors Entry System"). By any name, these systems documented the visits of all "outsiders" for ongoing protective service purposes more than just for administrative documentation purposes.[2]

The Secret Service, in turn, was part of the Department of the Treasury (later transferring to the Department of Homeland Security after that department's creation), where its records were subject to the Freedom of Information Act.[3] From time to time, it responded to FOIA requests for its "visitor logs," applying exemptions to any parts of them (read: as an exception, far from the rule) that held particular sensitivity.[4]

Thus, for several decades there was no question about the Freedom of Information Act's applicability to the federal records pertaining to those who entered the White House for one purpose or another.[5] From one administration to the next, the White House, the Secret Service, and the Department of Justice consistently recognized the records of White House visitors as "agency records" subject to both the FOIA and the Federal Records Act, not records of the "inner White House" itself subject to the Presidential Records Act.[6]

This changed radically during the second Bush Administration, which was particularly motivated to carve White House visitor logs out of the realm of the FOIA if at all possible.[7] Indeed, in mid-2006, the White House and the Secret Service executed a "memorandum of understanding" that designated all White House visitor records as "presidential." Through this, it suddenly took the self-serving position that the Secret Service did not have "control" over its visitor records (read: the touchstone for "agency record" status under the FOIA) so that they no longer were subject to FOIA access, and it maintained this position despite all district court precedents to the contrary.[8]

The legal status of White House visitor logs then came to a head in the fall of 2006, not long before the mid-term elections of that year, when what came to be known as the "Abramoff Scandal" broke. Indeed, during the run-up to those mid-term elections, with lobbyist Jack Abramoff's White House connections central to a growing lobbying scandal,[9] this issue boiled over. So *The Washington Post* not only filed FOIA requests for related "White House visitor" information, it brought a high-visibility lawsuit directly challenging the Bush Administration's position.

That change in longstanding FOIA practice was quite "transparent" in its own way, and it carried an odor redolent of the Abramoff lobbying scandal itself, which was not lost on the judge in the case. Indeed, District Court Judge Ricardo M. Urbina promptly ordered that the case be litigated according to an expedited schedule that plainly contemplated disclosures in time for the plaintiff to use them in newspaper articles written prior to the elections.

After Judge Urbina pointedly established such a timetable, however, the Bush Administration countered by seeking more time from the court of appeals. And it succeeded in obtaining an "emergency stay" of Judge Urbina's order, which had the effect of pushing the case beyond the time of the upcoming elections. With that, *The Washington Post* decided to abandon the case, which meant that the Bush Administration position on visitor logs continued to prevail through the remainder of the Bush Administration. But that was expected to last for only so long (i.e., until Bush 43 left office).

* * * * *

By any measure, when it came to secrecy across the board, the incoming Administration of Barack H. Obama had "an easy act to follow." Even beyond that, when President Obama famously declared that he was going to have "the most transparent administration" in history -- i.e., the very opposite of his predecessor -- the public's expectations became commensurately (read: exceedingly) high. And as regards the matter of White House visitor logs, every expectation was that this new Administration would of course return their FOIA status to what it had been before the Bush Administration so self-servingly altered it. As a colleague remarked to me: "I'd have put money on it."

Yet as it settled in during its first several months, the Obama Administration was less than forthcoming about restoring visitor log access under the FOIA, even in the face of growing public criticism that it was not implementing President Obama's transparency vision quickly or fully enough, on several fronts. In fact it actually resisted, seemingly reflexively, FOIA requests that were made (to the Secret Service) for the records of its own White House visitors, as well as those that had been "carved out" of the FOIA during the Bush Administration. And those requesters, nervous about it all, sued.

This led to a pile-up of FOIA litigation, most prominently a series of lawsuits filed by a single public-interest group, Citizens for Responsibility and Ethics in Washington ("CREW," to the people rocking the same boat), that originally sought to press the issue and move the Obama Administration away from the Bush Administration on it as quickly as possible. And there also were lawsuits brought by Judicial Watch, Inc., a government watchdog at the other end of the political spectrum. These FOIA suits provided a focal point for the new Administration.[10]

Then, behind the scenes (read: or so we learned later), the Obama White House began negotiating a secret settlement of all the FOIA cases that had been filed by CREW, which was very much to the White House's advantage in that it would avoid the possibility of a D.C. Circuit ruling against the lingering Bush Administration position that visitor logs were presidential records, not "agency records" subject to the FOIA. Yes, the Obama Administration had secretly adopted that position early in 2009, for the *very same* self-serving reasons that had motivated the Bush Administration before it.

And that "non-FOIA" position became a basis for the settlement of all of CREW's visitor log cases, which made it difficult to understand why on Earth CREW would agree to it. Then a likely answer was found in public criticism from Judicial Watch,[11] which alleged a conflict of interest inherent in the fact that one of the two co-founders of CREW, Norman L. Eisen, was the very person who negotiated that secret settlement for the Obama Administration. And soon enough, Norm was made "Vice President in Charge of FOIA" for the Obama White House. It certainly did appear that this had much to do with how it all turned out.

Indeed, in September of 2009, the Obama White House announced with much fanfare that it was establishing an "unprecedented" new disclosure policy for visitor logs whereby it henceforth would make unprecedented regular website releases of them -- albeit on what it maintained was a "voluntary" basis, *not* under the FOIA -- and with a routine time lag of three to four months. This included the settlement of all of the pending FOIA suits that had been brought by CREW, even though in its fine print the policy promised to respond to prospective visitor log requests only if it found them to be, among other things, sufficiently "narrow." And it more vaguely mentioned that it would not include in its releases any visitor log information that it deemed to be "particularly sensitive."

On one hand, of course, this could be viewed as a positive step insofar as it yielded the disclosure of far more visitor records than ever before in the past and because it did so automatically, without any FOIA request for them having to be made. That aspect of the new policy in and of itself, which was truly both unprecedented and ambitious, deserved some credit.

But hidden within this policy was the unattractive fact that its very "voluntariness" was premised on the Obama Administration's continuation of the Bush Administration position that visitor logs had been "carved out" of the FOIA, jurisdictionally, to begin with. In other words, if the FOIA were applied to these records as it had been for decades before the Bush Administration, the only thing "voluntary" about the policy would be that it involved automatic releases at regular intervals -- something that otherwise could readily be yielded by regular (e.g., monthly) FOIA requests without any difficulty. What a sham!

What this amounted to was a revised visitor log policy that, upon close inspection, actually had the following underlying negative characteristics:

Invisible Withholding. First and foremost, the Obama White House's use of a "voluntary disclosure policy," instead of FOIA compliance, meant that it could withhold from the public any visitor log it chose, whenever it chose, invisibly. Under its policy, any posting of those records could include all of them, 99% of them, or some lesser percentage of them for the time period involved -- the public would never know. Bluntly put, nothing prevented the Obama Administration from either improperly or mistakenly shielding such records from public view, silently, at any time. It is an axiom of good government accountability, not to mention basic administrative law, that such situations are strongly disfavored, to say the least.

No Specification. A further consequence of carving visitor logs out of the FOIA was that the Act's "specification" requirements need not be met. Through a series of FOIA amendments over the years, Congress had required agencies to specify the volume, location, and exemption applicability of information withheld under the Act. The Obama Administration's policy did nothing of the kind.

No Administrative Appeal. The Obama visitor log policy also fell far short of the FOIA regarding its administrative remedies, most particularly the requester's right to have a second, higher-level review of any information withholding on administrative appeal. Even if someone were to succeed in pressing the White House with a targeted request for specific visitor information, once it was withheld as "sensitive" that administrative response was final.

No Judicial Review. Of course, the primary legal effect of the Obama Administration's "voluntary" policy, and its embrace of the Bush Administration's underlying "not an agency record" position, was that its disclosure/nondisclosure actions on visitor logs became entirely (read: without exception) insulated from judicial review. The prospect of such review is essential to ensuring sound agency action, both as a matter of administrative law in general and under the FOIA in particular, and its absence greatly diminished accountability. No doubt that fact held strong appeal for the Bush Administration when it first took and then continued the underlying position, not to mention for the ostensibly much more transparent Obama Administration.

Pre-September 2009 Records. Also lost in the shuffle with the Obama Administration's policy were the records of White House visits during its first eight months, i.e., until the "new and improved" regime was set up. It was quite odd for the Obama White House to on one hand tout the value of its policy and on the other hand leave such a black hole to begin with. Even more oddly, this seemed to include visitor records from the Bush Administration as well.

Time Lag. Last, and relatively least, was the time-lag element of the Obama Administration's policy. Inherent in that policy's "voluntary" timetable was that visitor information was to be withheld from public view for a minimum of ninety days in all instances. This is a far cry from the twenty-working-day standard that the FOIA contains.

So if there had been an Abramoff-type lobbying scandal during the Obama Administration, there would have been absolutely nothing to prevent the White House from unilaterally withholding any visitor log evidence of questionable activity without any challenge by a public-interest group or -- and here's the most salient point -- even any *public awareness* that it was doing so. This was quite a remarkable position for a presidential administration that on the surface prided itself on standing for the very opposite when it came to government transparency and accountability.

Indeed, perhaps the most remarkable thing was not merely that the Obama Administration chose to follow the Bush Administration's extreme position on visitor logs at bottom. It was that it sought to obscure the very fact that it was doing so, shying away from anything that revealed its legal repudiation of the FOIA for all such records. This soon became most evident in the deceptive public insistence by the White House's "transparency czar" (as well as its "ethics czar," as if the two can go hand in hand), Norm Eisen, that there simply was "no need to make a FOIA request" for visitor log records under Obama. Or for anyone to "worry their pretty little heads about it," either.

This position, of course, blithely ignored all of the relative disadvantages that the Obama "system" held compared to standard FOIA access, which I knew Norm well understood as I pointedly questioned him about it at a program held by the Collaboration on Government Secrecy at American University's Washington College of Law in March of 2010. What it amounted to is that the Obama Administration not only failed to restore pre-Bush FOIA access in this vital area, it actually set up a regime of *less* access than had existed under Bush.[12] And what's worse, Norm Eisen flatly (read: transparently) refused to admit this, lest too much attention be drawn to his slyly devised slight-of-hand.[13]

In fact, time and again during the remainder of the Obama Administration, it actually pointed to its White House visitor log policy as evidence of its over-all transparency policy's implementation *success*, even going so far as to place it (among little else) in the "Freedom of Information Act" sub-category.[14] Call it a lack of "transparency about transparency," or worse, it was by any name far less than what was expected.[15]

More recently, under the Donald J. Trump Administration, there was a return to the categorical "no FOIA" policy of the Bush Administration (as surreptitiously continued under the Obama Administration), as well as a reversal of the Obama Administration's "automatic disclosure" practice for visitor logs. In other words, it was the worst of all worlds.

And as for how this FOIA issue will fare under the Administration of President Joseph R. Biden, the early indications are that there might well be a reversal of the Trump Administration position, but it is not entirely clear whether the Biden White House will acknowledge the FOIA's applicability to visitor logs in a full return to pre-2006 policy and practices. That remains to be seen.[16]

What also remains to be seen is exactly how the Biden Administration will treat the Freedom of Information Act and secrecy in general. Inexplicably, the Biden Administration entered its second year without a governmentwide FOIA policy memorandum being issued by Attorney General Merrick B. Garland,[17] nor did the Biden White House take any other such "pro-disclosure" step, despite being urged to do so by many greatly disappointed, and quite vocal, members of the openness-in-government community.[18] Indeed, with no such action taken within the Biden Administration's first year (read: in contrast to what nearly all other administrations have done), it joined the Trump Administration as the least attentive to the FOIA since the Carter Administration began issuing Attorney General FOIA memoranda in May of 1977.[19] This can only improve.

CHAPTER FORTY
DOD's "Sensitive Photographs" Case

"[This was] in a wartime situation, in the information age, where people are running around with digital cameras and taking these unbelievable photographs . . ."

-- Secretary of Defense Donald H. Rumsfeld, speaking of other photographs taken by U.S. military personnel at Abu Ghraib prison, as reported by *The Washington Times*, May 7, 2004

Of all the litigation cases that I was involved in during my career, the most vexing one (at least of the 21 of them that went up to the Supreme Court) was a post-9/11 case that did not come to fruition until after I had left the Justice Department. It involved a massive amount of Defense Department and CIA records pertaining to the presence of U.S. troops on the ground in Iraq during the early days of the U.S./Iraq War.[1] Within this huge record tranche, as it turned out, were many photographs that had been taken by the troops themselves, akin to the notorious ones that had been taken in a prison known as Abu Ghraib.

This FOIA case had been filed by the American Civil Liberties Union ("ACLU," to its faithful donors), which was known for its unstinting pressure in FOIA litigation cases (see, for example, Chapter Seventeen), in the Southern District of New York,[2] where per Justice Department tradition it was being handled by two very experienced (but FOIA neophyte) Assistant United States Attorneys ("AUSAs," to their parent organization), with whom I had several consultation discussions during the course of the case. For the court's part, this lawsuit had been randomly assigned to United States District Court Judge Alvin K. Hellerstein, who was not known to have tried many FOIA cases, if at all.

As I heard the story, these beleaguered AUSAs found themselves "behind the eight ball" in this case relatively early on, when that judge held his first "status hearing" in it in late 2004. It seems that Judge Hellerstein, who suffice to say here was not known within the U.S. Attorney's Office for having a "steady hand" in such matters, seized on the fact that the case's underlying FOIA requests had by that time not yet been responded to by the defendant agencies for more than 13 months (due to the sheer size and exceptional sensitivity of the records involved) -- and viewing the matter as he would a "discovery dispute" in ordinary litigation, he immediately established an onerous (not to mention impracticable) timetable for the agencies' FOIA "processing" and disclosure of the requested records to be completed.

This set off clanging alarm bells in both New York and Washington (as well in Virginia, I should add, where both defendant agencies' headquarters were located), because it meant, among other things, that the Government would be handling the case in an "under the gun" mode in which, history had shown, there was a much-greater-than-average chance of making rushed judgments that could greatly complicate it. And that turned out to be so within one small, but acutely sensitive, corner of this high-profile case.

I am referring here to a relatively small group of photographs, sometimes called the "Darby photos" (whether correctly or not) that had been taken by a U.S. service member "on the ground" in Iraq under, shall we say, the most unfortunate of circumstances that rendered them literally explosive in nature.[3] Simply put, DOD, the CIA, and the U.S. Attorney's Office for the Southern District of New York were in a quandary (which I'm told is the non-Korean version of "deep kimchi") over how these particular photographs should be handled in this FOIA litigation.

Everyone agreed that these photos should not (at least not at that time) be disclosed to the public because there could be little doubt of how that action -- including even the surrounding fact that this would be an official U.S. disclosure -- would be received by terrorist forces (or even younger potential terrorists) in Iraq (and elsewhere in the region, for that matter). But at the same time, no one could see how these photographs (there were about a dozen of them) could be defended as exempt from public disclosure under the FOIA.

That is the point at which I became more deeply involved. Early in 2005, I was asked to focus on this problem in a meeting held by the Office of the Joint Chiefs of Staff. At this meeting, it was explained to me exactly why these sensitive photographs had not been classified.[4] And I further learned exactly why we could not employ an Exemption 3 defense, despite the seemingly applicable nondisclosure provisions of the Geneva Conventions.

On the potential bright side, though, it was the case that these photographs had quite unusually been compiled by the Defense Department during its atypical "law enforcement investigation" of the conduct of its personnel. This meant, to my mind, that we potentially could employ one of the subparts of FOIA Exemption

7, which in general covered "investigatory records or information compiled for law enforcement purposes" (see, for example, Chapter Eleven). The problem thus boiled down to which Exemption 7 subpart (and which of its particular harms to be avoided), if any, could possibly apply.

After pondering this more than a little, I reached the novel conclusion that Exemption 7(F) in particular -- which as amended by Congress in 1986 protects law enforcement information the disclosure of which "could reasonably be expected to endanger the life or physical safety of any individual" -- could possibly be applied. By this point, I could see exactly what the photographs depicted, in context of daily life in that part of the world, and I could completely understand the expected consequences of their official disclosure.[5] Those consequences, I suggested, could reasonably be said to implicate the "life or physical safety" thrust of this exemption. At the very minimum, it was much more than just a "colorable argument," I advised them.[6]

I daresay that everyone left this meeting quite happy -- as were the AUSAs who were to advocate this new position before Judge Hellerstein (not that they had any illusions about how he would take to such a thing). The defendant agencies (DOD, actually) formally "processed" the photographs, labeled them (in a *Vaughn* index) as being withheld in their entireties under Exemption 7(F) and only that exemption, promptly notified the ACLU of this administrative development, and prepared the necessary affidavit(s)[7] for this position's advocacy in a partial summary judgment motion.[8]

We all waited to see if this would be successful, quite mindful that Judge Hellerstein seemed not inclined to accept any argument through which DOD might be able to block these photographs' disclosure. And . . . he certainly was not, as he made clear in a decision that showed him to be so resistant to protecting the photographs (not that he'd seen them, of course) that he was willing to grossly misinterpret Exemption 7(F) in order to do so.

Indeed, in September of 1985, Judge Hellerstein rejected what he termed this "eleventh-hour" argument[9] based upon his use of a misplaced "public interest balancing" analysis under Exemption 7(F). What made this analysis so flawed was that while the FOIA does indeed contain a "public interest" element within Exemption 7, it exists only under Exemption 7(C), not Exemption 7(F).[10]

So having unquestionably exhausted this new defense with Judge Hellerstein at the district court level,[11] the Government elevated it to the next judicial level on appeal.[12] It argued that public disclosure of these particular photographs could reasonably be expected to endanger the lives (and, *a fortiori*, safety) of many U.S. troops, other "Coalition forces," and even civilians in both Iraq and Afghanistan by inciting violence against (or, in the case of the civilians, in proximity to) them.

And it did so based upon the attestations of high-level military generals who said it was their expert judgment that these particular photographs were of such unique sensitivity that their official disclosure (for that is what a FOIA disclosure is, in the minds of many[13]) could be expected to inflame the passions of terrorists and potential terrorists toward the targeted (and/or collateral) deaths of U.S. forces and others in the region.[14]

This judgment was based in no small part on the then-recent "Koran flushing" episode in which at least 17 people were killed immediately after the publication by *Newsweek* of an article alleging that United States interrogators at Guantanamo Bay had flushed the Koran down a toilet in front of detainees. As it happened, the accuracy of that article subsequently was called into question, but not before U.S. intelligence officers were able to trace its publication directly to the reactions that involved those deaths.[15] So the Government had a distinct basis, even apart from that of an overall assessment, for concluding that the highly inflammatory nature of the photographs at issue could reasonably be seen as implicating the life and physical safety of those persons who were similarly situated.[16]

But on appeal, the Court of Appeals for the Second Circuit saw this very differently. To be sure, it did not accept Judge Hellerstein's flawed "public interest balancing" rationale for rejecting the applicability of Exemption 7(F).[17] (It certainly could not.) But after dispensing with that, it went on to focus on the "any individual" language at the end of the exemption instead. That language had been inserted into Exemption 7(F) as part of the FOIA Reform Amendments of 1986, when Congress acted to *broaden* the exemption's sweep by, atop another thing,[18] substituting that phrase for the narrower "law enforcement personnel" language that it had used in 1974.[19] (I know this because I'm the one who did it.)

Yet the Second Circuit, in a prolix and obviously outcome-oriented analysis of an exemption position that it first dismissively declared to be have been merely "raised as an afterthought,"[20] concluded that the words "any individual" were not broad enough to accommodate such circumstances. At bottom, it rested its ruling on the undeniable fact that these circumstances did not allow the Government to "point to any one individual and establish that he or she could reasonably be expected to be endangered," declaring that the Government "instead point[ed] to . . . a vast population," which in its view was just too "vast" to include "any individual," even under these particular circumstances. In other words, even though it could fairly be concluded that some people in Afghanistan (or Iraq) could be expected to be endangered, Exemption 7(F) was not available to protect them.

This decision, issued on September 23, 2008, nearly two years after the case was argued before the Second Circuit in November of 2006, left the Government with just one more judicial recourse before it would be compelled to make a FOIA disclosure. That step, asking the Supreme Court to take the case, required the authorization of the Solicitor General, who was expected to be a new appointee after the upcoming presidential election.[21] So the Government asked for, and was granted, an extension of its standard 90-day period in which to decide whether to file a *certiorari* petition in the Supreme Court. This allowed the "*cert.* decision" to be made by President Obama's incoming solicitor general, who turned out to be future Associate Supreme Court Justice Elena Kagan.

And Solicitor General Kagan did make that decision, after some deliberation that might or might not have included viewing the actual photographs. (The record is unclear on this point, which leaves me to guess that, in the rush of a newly confirmed solicitor general who had never before served in the Solicitor General's Office familiarizing herself with the job, she might not have taken the time to make the logistical arrangements to do so.) Indeed, on April 29, 2009, Solicitor General Kagan made that long-awaited decision and surprisingly -- very surprisingly -- it was to not seek *certiorari*.

Historically, such solicitor general decisions are invariably regarded as final (read: "case closed") ones, and in this case, once it was made, the AUSAs in New York accordingly advised Judge Hellerstein of it, in a formal filing, as was appropriate. Moreover, the White House Press Secretary even spoke of it as "final" from the White House podium. Only it wasn't.

Rather, in an unexpected and slyly belated move, DOD reacted to Solicitor General's Kagan's startling "no *cert.*" decision by prevailing upon President Obama to do what I was able to do four years earlier: He took a good look at the damn photographs![22] And what do you know, President Obama reacted to them by immediately declaring, on May 13, that they would not see the light of day while *he* was president if he had anything to say about it.[23] And he certainly did.

So it was that Solicitor General Kagan was forced to reverse her decision (a virtually unheard-of step that was highly embarrassing, of course)[24] and the full might of the Department of Justice (in this case, the Appellate Staff of the Civil Division, working hand-in-hand with the Office of the Solicitor General) set about preparing a petition for *certiorari* in the case.[25] That petition was filed with the Supreme Court on August 7, 2009, where it then enjoyed a series of stays issued by the Court to allow its due consideration of it. Effectively, three stays of *certiorari* consideration, in the form of the rescheduling of Court conferences, were issued in the case.[26]

The reason for all of this delay was that the Government was by then following an entirely separate path for achieving nondisclosure -- a purely (read: impurely, to some) legislative one. In July, the executive branch began pursuing an extraordinary "legislative fix" that would, in effect, provide unprecedented targeted protection for these photographs, and only these photographs, through a proposed new Exemption 3 statute covering them, one based upon a DOD "certification" of harm. This effort, which initially failed to pass Congress, ultimately won passage in late October, in a measure entitled the "Protect National Security Documents Act of 2009" ("PNSDA," to its amazed observers, especially the ACLU).[27] It thus appeared that the battle was over.

But rather than ending on this resounding note, this case continued in a procedural swirl under the exact terms of that remedial Exemption 3 statute. After that statute was passed, Secretary of Defense Robert M. Gates as expected issued a "certification" prohibiting (read: through Exemption 3) the release of the images that were subject to the ACLU's requests, which was a formal technical step that was required by the PNSDA for its intended implementation.

The Supreme Court then granted the government's *certiorari* petition and vacated the Second Circuit's challenged opinion in light of the subsequent congressional and executive branch actions.[28] On November 30, 2009, the case was remanded to the district court for further proceedings related to these and other documents in the case.

On remand in July of 2011, the district court first determined that the photographs were properly withheld pursuant to Defense Secretary Gates' certification under the PNSDA. However, that certification was set to expire on November 13, 2012, so a year later, in early November of 2012, with much of the rest of the case still pending, new Defense Secretary Leon E. Panetta issued a new certification, as the PNSDA presciently permitted. But Senior District Court Judge Hellerstein then was able to consider a renewed challenge to the withholding of the photographs, despite everything that had occurred.

And sure enough, in ruling on this "renewed challenge," on August 27, 2014, Judge Hellerstein held that "the 2012 Recertification, standing alone, was insufficient to meet the government's burden to justify its withholding the photographs from disclosure," because, he said, DOD had failed to provide evidence that Secretary Panetta had "evaluated the potential security impact of releasing each individual photograph." (In other words, he decided to be hyper picky about the wording of Secretary Panetta's declaration.) Judge Hellerstein then "generously" provided the Government with an opportunity to "create a record" to justify its "invocation of the PNSDA." Well, with any due respect to Judge Hellerstein, who by then was long past being called "Judge *Hell-on-Wheels*" by one and all, this was one hell of a note.

The case then carried on, believe it or not, for another *four* years. During that time, there were superseding certifications issued by three more secretaries of defense, based on the attested judgments of five more general officers, and several follow-up opinions were issued by the district court and the court of appeals. The opinions included Judge Hellerstein's prescribing the exact methods by which the Defense Secretary must make the prediction of harm, his intransigent application of the court of appeals' Exemption 7(F) opinion that by then *had been vacated*,[29] and his repeated rejection of the certifications (and supporting documentation) submitted by the Department of Defense in its efforts to fit into his increasingly "expansive" (read: restrictive) interpretation of the PNSDA's basic requirements for the photographs' protection.[30]

This time, atop all of the previous times, when Judge Hellerstein "expansively" provided the Government with an opportunity to meet his latest interpretation, the Government pointedly declined. (Manifestly, at that point, it had "had enough." I can't exactly confirm that, but I can't deny it, either.) This all led, eventually, to Judge Hellerstein entering final judgment against the Government on January 19, 2017,[31] having gone to even more convoluted lengths to order disclosure, whereupon the Government yet again appealed to the Second Circuit through a lengthy, up-to-date brief filed on June 30, 2017.

Finally, more than a year later, on August 21, 2018, the Second Circuit issued a rational order that reversed the judgment of the district court and remanded the case with directions for it to enter judgment for the Government.[32] Thus, the case (read: that part of it, at least) ended at last, after a tortuous and circuitous lifespan of 14 years, with no sensitive photographs having been disclosed. And to the best of my knowledge, as President Obama put it, they still have not "seen the light of day." Which in my humble opinion is exactly how things should remain.[33]

CHAPTER FORTY-ONE
Mug Shots

"You can never prepare yourself enough to see your mug shot."

-- Actress Tracey Gold, in her autobiography *Room to Grow*, 2003

Of all the issues that have been contested in FOIA litigation, the one that was the most challenging in its own unique way involved the FOIA status of what are commonly known as "mug shots," or more formally as "booking photographs," taken at the time of someone's arrest. This is an issue that remained under the surface of the FOIA landscape until it abruptly arose in a case decided by a circuit court of appeals in 1996.

Prior to then, there was scant controversy over mug shots taken at the federal level. What did exist, though, was a firm difference between how mug shots were treated by federal law enforcement agencies and their counterparts at the state and local law enforcement levels. At the latter, most states made their mug shots available to the public as a matter of course, never bothering to be concerned about possible personal-privacy protection. That is how, for instance, the mug shot of O.J. Simpson came to appear (with infamously different shadings) on the covers of *Time* and *Newsweek* in 1994, how Nick Nolte's mug shot became the subject of widespread derision in 2002, and how the website "thesmokinggun. com" became so popular.

At the federal law enforcement level, however, the consistent practice was to withhold mug shots under the FOIA, unless there was a specific public interest in favor of disclosure in a particular case. (This was OIP's firm policy position, after careful consideration of the issue.) When FOIA requests encompassed such records -- invariably at the U.S. Marshals Service, the FBI, or the Criminal Division of the Department of Justice, most often the former -- the withholding of mug shots under FOIA Exemption 7(C), on the ground that their disclosure "could reasonably be expected to constitute an unwarranted invasion of personal privacy," would be the default response.

Thus, as a matter of this longstanding policy, mug shots have been withheld from public disclosure on the basis of the significant personal-privacy interests in them -- the stigma of criminality, regardless of whether the person ultimately is prosecuted and convicted after arrest -- and the little if any legitimate public interest in their disclosure as a general rule.[1] This policy also recognizes that mug shots are taken at what are by definition one of the worst moments of a person's life, with an embarrassing appearance that arrestees invariably would prefer be forgotten, a preference greatly exacerbated by awareness of Internet-era dissemination.

This established practice at the federal level was disrupted, however, by the first appellate court to consider a mug shot under the FOIA. In 1996, in a case titled *Detroit Free Press, Inc. v. United States Department of Justice*, the Sixth Circuit Court of Appeals ruled that eight indicted persons awaiting trial on federal charges had *no* privacy interests in their mug shots.[2] Furthermore, it decided that, in any event, there were "potential" public interests favoring disclosure in the "balancing of interests" used under the FOIA's Exemption 7(C). Although this was a 2-1 decision, with a strong dissent, it was a singular one that received no further judicial review.[3] Hence, it had to be followed where it applied.

Yes, as the result of this appellate decision, the public disclosure of mug shots in response to FOIA requests became required within the Sixth Circuit's geographic boundaries -- Kentucky, Michigan, Ohio, and Tennessee -- though the Federal Government did not acquiesce to this ruling elsewhere. This made mug shots the only subject area under the FOIA -- ever -- in which a requester would get a different disclosure result according to the state in which he, she, or it was located.

Moreover, it led to a common yet no less anomalous practice of FOIA requesters around the country using surrogates located within those four states (usually cooperating media outlets, such as the *Detroit Free Press*) to obtain mug shots under the prevailing case law of the Sixth Circuit. And as it turned out, this awkward anomaly persisted for more than fifteen years, far longer than anyone (especially folks in the Solicitor General's Office) had anticipated. No one in the Department of Justice (at least within its long-term career ranks) was sanguine about this; we viewed it as a singular embarrassment for the Federal Government that such a situation existed.

Slightly half-way through that time period, however, there was a development in the United States Supreme Court that provided a basis for solving this problem. In 2004, the Court handed down a decision in an Exemption 7(C) case, *National Archives v. Favish*, that elaborated on the meaning and contours of Exemption 7(C) in a way that very arguably affected *Detroit Free Press's* analytical foundation (a phrasing that, believe me, is very kind). In short, the Supreme Court provided a basis for second-guessing the Sixth Circuit's problematic ruling of eight years earlier.[4]

So the Office of Information and Privacy began coordinating with both the Department's Civil Division and a local U.S. Attorney's Office in Michigan toward the goal of getting the mug shot issue back up to the Sixth Circuit, where it could be reconsidered by that Court *en banc*. That was clearly the way to go if we wanted to take on *Detroit Free Press* sooner rather than later (or if at all), and the Civil Division initially agreed.

But those efforts were abruptly curtailed by a Bush Administration political appointee who for some inexplicable reason did not want to see the Civil Division engaged in such an enterprise.[5] And that was barely discussed -- as such a thing ordinarily would be, with the full-throated participation, not to mention decisional imprimatur, of the Solicitor General. Rather, it was decided by fiat.[6] So *Detroit Free Press* continued to stand, and surrogate FOIA requests continued to be made, for several years more. And that is how the matter stood as of 2007 when I retired.

Years later, two different circuit courts of appeals finally considered the "mug shot" issue and explicitly rejected the Sixth Circuit's *Detroit Free Press* ruling. First, in *Karantsalis v. United States Department of Justice*, the Eleventh Circuit Court of Appeals in 2011 found a strong privacy interest in mug shots, calling them "vivid symbol[s] of criminal accusation." Then, a year later, in *World Publishing Co. v. United States Department of Justice*, the Tenth Circuit Court of Appeals likewise rejected *Detroit Free Press*'s reasoning, viewing a mug shot as a "vivid and personal portrayal" that warrants protection as a matter of personal privacy. This finally created a "conflict in the circuits" on the issue, which ordinarily is a strong basis (if not a requisite) for an issue's resolution by the Supreme Court, and the Solicitor General this time explicitly authorized the pursuit of such reversal.

In 2012, however, the Supreme Court surprisingly declined to accept the *Karantsalis* case for review, which relegated the issue to potential resolution by the lower courts and left the Sixth Circuit's *Detroit Free Press* precedent intact to yield even more disparate mug shot results. Although I had been retired from the Justice Department for more than five years by then, I still kept in close contact with my former colleagues there (read: I was sought out for advice) and therefore urged them to use this *certiorari* denial to trigger the very type of *Favish*-based challenge to *Detroit Free Press* that I had conceived, but which we had sadly failed to pursue, in 2005-2006.

This worked. In December of 2012, the Justice Department announced that it was no longer going to acquiesce to the *Detroit Free Press* decision within the four states that comprise the Sixth Circuit.[7] Rather, it finally took the position (more than eight years after the fact) that the Supreme Court's opinion in *Favish* seriously called into question the reasoning of that aberrational decision and that it should be reconsidered by the full circuit court. Toward that end, the Marshals Service pointedly withheld mug shots from *The Detroit Free Press* itself, leading to a case in which the lower-court result was of course a disclosure order under the Sixth Circuit's precedent. Then the Justice Department appealed this new *Detroit Free Press* decision to a Sixth Circuit panel, which we knew was bound by that circuit's 1996 decision as well.[8]

That worked even better than we had envisioned, because in August of 2015, a panel of the Sixth Circuit issued an opinion in this second *Detroit Free Press* case in which it unanimously "urge[d] the full court to reconsider" its troubling 1996 precedent, declaring that mug shots surely "convey the sort of potentially embarrassing or harmful information protected by" Exemption 7(C). In other words, this panel said, mug shots "capture how an individual appeared at a particularly humiliating moment immediately after being taken into federal custody [and are] an unmistakable badge of criminality." This sounded familiar, of course.

This was a perfect set-up for the Sixth Circuit to finally reconsider this issue *en banc*, which it indeed decided to do. And in July of 2016, a full *20 years* after the issuance of the split decision that started it all, the full Sixth Circuit Court of Appeals finally said what many of us in the Justice Department had long believed -- that that original panel decision was "untenable."

Briefly stated, the Court found that there is indeed a "non-trivial" privacy interest in mug shots. And it firmly agreed with the Department's "case-by-case" approach to determining the presence of any exceptional public interest that could possibly override such a privacy interest, rather than the "categorical" approach (read: always overriding) that *Detroit Free Press* advocated and the initial Sixth Circuit panel had adopted.

So today, order has been restored in the "mug shot" corner of the FOIA world. There is no longer any place in it where the result of a FOIA request hinges on where the requester lives (read: can "lay venue") -- although a party by the name of "AT&T" took a run at creating just that for business information a few years ago before being squelched by the Supreme Court (see Chapter Forty-Five). And, over time, more and more states have come into alignment with the Federal Government on their own "mug shot" policies, meaning that the personal-privacy interests in such photographs will perhaps someday universally prevail.

CHAPTER FORTY-TWO
Retirement Life

"A popular government without popular information or the means of acquiring it is but a prologue to a farce or a tragedy; or perhaps both. Knowledge will forever govern ignorance: And a people who mean to be their own Governors, must arm themselves with the power which [sic] knowledge gives."

-- Former President James Madison, Jr., letter to W.T. Barry, August 4, 1822

One of the advantages of having begun working at the Justice Department so young was that I reached possible "retirement" eligibility at a relatively young age as well. As much as I would greatly miss working at the Department (and more than 15 years later, I still do), the countervailing fact of life is that I always knew that someday I would end up teaching law -- and enjoying the hell out of it. So when the time came at which continuing to work for Alberto Gonzales (not to mention George W. Bush) was just too embarrassing to bear (see the Epilogue), I took the "retirement" plunge.

This meant that I went from working an average of 75 hours a week as of early 2007 to at first only about 60.[1] Luckily, the law school that I chose to work for -- the Washington College of Law ("WCL," which the faculty said stood for "wine and cheese in the lobby" or more succinctly "we cater lunch") of American University -- was not only just about a mile and a half from where I lived,[2] it was at that time looking to expand its curriculum into the area of government information law and policy, through its "Law and Government Program," which was then headed by someone destined to be a future congressman (not to mention "impeachment manager" in the era of Trump). Toward that end, the dean of the school brought me in in mid-2007 as a "Faculty Fellow in Law and Government," with the idea that I would design and teach both an elective class and a skills seminar, and also would create and run an academic "secrecy center" for the school, making WCL the very first law school in the world to do so.[3]

So it was that by the summer of that year, I had designed for immediate faculty approval both of those courses and also inaugurated what I named the "Collaboration on Government Secrecy" (or "CGS," to its many friends). As for the classes, I went on to teach them for 20 academic semesters over a period of ten years and to have more than 250 students, some of whom, I am proud to be able to say, went on to hold major positions in what we call the "Open Government Community."[4] Yes, being a proud professor is a little bit like being a proud parent, especially given that so many of those students entered a life of public service.

As for CGS, it was a most vibrant of academic centers. Among other things, we conducted a total of 24 full-day academic programs over the next seven years (from August of 2007 until the early fall of 2014), bringing into the school 220 different speakers[5] to address virtually every topic related to "government openness" on one side of the coin and "government secrecy" on the other. And as CGS expanded its activities and continued to grow, it gained a sterling reputation for excellence in the "Open Government Community" (and I daresay within the Federal Government, as well); it become the place at which International Right-to-Know Day was celebrated each year in the United States; it became a focal point of private-sector FOIA-related activity; and it provided unparalleled support of the Federal Government's nationwide FOIA administration.[6]

Most notably, as a vital part of CGS, we developed a massive website compilation of discussions, detailed outlines, and academic reference items within its subject areas. On it, we compiled links to just about every source item imaginable pertaining to the FOIA, including fresh descriptions of topic areas that we regularly added during the site's continuous development.[7] Indeed, CGS's hallmark in this academic enterprise was that its website was both scrupulously accurate and always up to date.

Unfortunately, for unavoidable personal reasons (i.e., a rapid decline in the health of my father),[8] I reluctantly concluded that CGS had to cease functioning after seven very fruitful years. I "ended its run," so to speak, but am pleased to observe that during its time, CGS become the model for four additional such academic centers or comparable transparency programs within the United States, in addition to one in Dundee, Scotland.[9] And as is shown in Chapter Forty-Five, its work even included its successful participation in an unprecedented case that was heard in the United States Supreme Court.

But I was able to continue teaching, with just occasional class rescheduling due to my father's continued decline in health, which meant that my students were still able to benefit from hearing Circuit Court Judge Patricia A. Millett's wisdom on oral advocacy even after she became a member of the D.C. Circuit in late 2013 (see Chapter Three). (This also pleased the school's dean immensely; each year, he made a big to-do about Pattie's appearance at the school.)

And I myself was able to benefit from what turned out to be a very smoothly graduated retirement transition from "full time" Justice Department work, to full-time academic work for the next seven years, and to my post-CGS teaching years for the following three. Now, five years farther down the "retirement" road, with this book in hand, I can strongly recommend striving for such a phased retirement approach.

CHAPTER FORTY-THREE
The *Gerlich* Corruption Case

"'Well, at least that's one thing I did right.'"

-- Former Counsel to the Associate Attorney General Esther Slater McDonald, quoting former Office of the Deputy Attorney General Chief of Staff Michael J. Elston in a deposition conducted on July 27, 2010 in *Gerlich v. United States Department of Justice*, Civil No. 08-1134 (JDB)

This is a story that will start at the very beginning, when in the summer of 1949 my mother and father, aged 17 and 19, respectively, decided that they would get married the following year. At that point, they had been dating for three years, precipitated by the fact that my mother's only sibling, her older brother, was my father's best friend. So they aimed toward having an October 1950 wedding, the arrangements for which included selecting a maid of honor and a best man.

This became complicated when both my mother's brother and my father's younger sister refused those roles. You see, he was over six foot tall and her height was, by her measurement, "four-eleven and three-quarters." And with such a height difference, they both felt that it would be much too embarrassing to be paired together as my parents had asked them to be at something so formal. (Plus, they didn't particularly like one another, they said, having learned this while growing up in the same close-knit neighborhood.)

Well, the outcome of this little episode was just what one might have predicted (in a movie-of-the-week screenplay or not): They ultimately did agree to be a "best man/maid of honor" couple, they then "hooked up" as might be said these days,[1] they were themselves married the following year, and they wound up having seven children. One of them, my "double-cousin" Mary, married a nice fellow named John Gerlich, and they had a son named Sean. The story then advances more than five decades in time.

In the fall of 2004, my cousin Mary asked me if I would help guide the career of that son Sean, by then a law student who had decided that he wanted to work as a law clerk at the Department of Justice during the following summer if he could.[2] So after talking to Sean for a while, I steered him toward a particular component of the Department, the Foreign Claims Settlement Commission, where I thought he would fit in quite well because I knew the head of that component well. And fit in well he did.

Then, in the fall of 2006, as I was preparing to retire,[3] Sean applied to the Attorney General's Honors Program for an entry-level career attorney position, stating his preference to work in that same part of the Department, which was his natural next step. With a strong recommendation from the head of that component, which Sean had, ordinarily it would have been a near-certainty that Sean would be accepted into the Honors Program and brought "on board" for that desired position.

But inexplicably he was not selected for the Honors Program. I learned of this only after the fact in late December, when Sean's mother Mary was visiting my father from out of state and hesitantly mentioned this to me during that visit because no one could understand what had happened. Neither could I, but I had an inkling that it was a mistake or improper in some way. So I promised Mary that I would certainly "get to the bottom of" whatever had happened, though I knew that it might take me a little longer to do so because as a retiree I would be inquiring from the outside.

It turned out that what had happened was that the Attorney General's Honors Program had been corruptly "politicized" in 2006. And the connection between this and my double-cousin's son, coincidental as it was, seemed devastating. And it became highly consequential -- for me and my family, for Attorney General Alberto R. Gonzales and his lawless "henchpersons" in this corrupt scheme, for the Department of Justice as an institution, and for, at bottom, the American taxpayers. So let's try viewing the background of this story from a different angle:

One of the responsibilities attendant upon being a "component head" at the Department of Justice is that of attending regular component head meetings, at which all 40 of us would gather together solemnly in a large, darkened room lined with lit candles along the sides and in perfect unison we would softly chant . . . No, that's not it; let me try this yet again:

There were three types of "component head" meetings at the Department of Justice, one for all of us at which the attorney general ordinarily would preside, with the deputy attorney general and the associate attorney general flanking him or her, to discuss current matters of Departmentwide importance. The second and third types were held more frequently (i.e., weekly, biweekly, or monthly) by the deputy attorney general or the associate attorney general, as the case might be, for the component heads on his or her side of the Department.

This was a criminal side versus civil side split, with the deputy attorney general overseeing the Department's criminal-related components and the associate attorney general overseeing the civil (read: much more polite) ones. The Office of Information and Privacy was on the civil side, which meant that it was organizationally located under the associate general, who held regular meetings (and a few irregular ones, if memory serves) for the component heads who worked under him.[4]

I begin with this particular background detail because it necessarily sets the stage for a foreboding conversation that I had with a fellow component head just days before I left the Department in January of 2007. That friendly fellow was the presidentially appointed chairman of the Department's Foreign Claims Settlement Commission ("FCSC," to its good friends), Mauricio J. Tamargo,[5] whom I had gotten to know quite well as we sat at component head meetings, sometimes waiting for them to begin. Although he was a presidential appointee who had worked for a very conservative Member of Congress, Mauricio was not nearly as ideological, let alone "political," as his Republican colleagues might have thought him to be.

Mauricio often had law students serving as summer law clerks in his component, and for the summer of 2005 he chose my nephew Sean Gerlich. Sean had done quite well, Mauricio had told me at the time, and all three of us (i.e., Sean, me, and no less Mauricio) expected that he would proceed to join the Department upon graduation, under the Attorney General's Honors Program, and go to work for that component on a permanent basis.

Then, at almost the same time, Mauricio invited me to lunch to celebrate my retirement. Neither one of us talked about Sean or what might have happened to him during that lunch itself. As for me, I had that inkling that what had happened was "political" somehow, even though there exists a very strong legal prohibition against anything such as that happening for a career civil service position. (Mauricio is such a gentleman that I did not want to corner him with such a question until he had a ready exit at hand.)

And that is exactly how it went: As he was leaving my car, just as I was about the ask him about Sean, Mauricio leaned over and expressed regret about what he said had "blocked" Sean; he said that he had been unable to do anything about it at the time and he gamely suggested that if Sean wanted to try again with the Department the following year he should avoid listing anything "ideological" on his resume if at all possible. I will admit that this was along the lines of what I had suspected, but to hear such a thing said out loud took me aback nonetheless. So that is when I began digging into this for my cousin and her son.

*　*　*　*　*

Of all the litigation cases that I handled during my career, one stands out as very different from the others, *Gerlich v. United States Department of Justice*. That big difference is that in every other case, I was working for the Department of Justice, defending the interests of the United States -- whereas in *Gerlich* I was working *against* it, in a singular and dare I say noble effort to take the Department, and by extension the Bush White House, to task.

The *Gerlich* case began, in effect, with the re-election of President George W. Bush, which brought about the "third Bush presidential term," or "Bush III," as some called it, in January of 2005. With that, there were several personnel shifts at the top of the Federal Government, not the least of which was that Alberto Gonzales left his perch in Bush's White House to become his second attorney general. For many reasons, though -- and I think he actually might agree with this if you were to ask him today[6] -- he should have stayed where he was (i.e., as Bush's White House Counsel) in the first place.

It very quickly became clear to those of us in the Justice Department that Attorney General Gonzales's arrival there was to be the harbinger of many changes in this "second George W. Bush administration," not the least of which was going to be a seismic shift in the culture and even the reputation of the Department.[7] As of January of 2005, the Department effectively became a "mere outpost" of the White House, with a Svengali-like character named Karl C. Rove over there pulling most of the strings.

Most infamously, this manifested itself during the fall of 2006 when those in the White House decided to fire more than a half-dozen United States Attorneys who had, in one way or another, proven insufficiently loyal to the conservative cause.[8] And even though such political appointees serve at the pleasure of the president and can be fired at any time for no reason at all, the way in which those termination communications were grossly mishandled within the Department, all at the same time, led to enormous controversy, especially when a very young Gonzales aide by the name of Monica M. Goodling proceeded to make things much worse.[9] The furor was deafening.

This led to Monica Goodling being subpoenaed to testify before Congress, where after detailing her role in the U.S. Attorneys debacle,[10] she witlessly went on to confess to having coordinated the improper handling of employment applications for career attorney positions in the Department as well (or as badly). This led to a lengthy inspector general investigation of exactly what she meant by that, which commenced just as I was trying to determine exactly what had happened to derail Sean's Attorney General's Honors Program application myself.

Before long, I learned that no fewer than 179 such applicants had been wrongfully "deselected" from the program, for purely (read: impurely) political reasons.[11]

These were brand-new attorneys we're talking about here, either directly out of law school or off of one-year or even two-year judicial clerkships, who in their prospective career attorney positions at the Department could pose no more than a negligible threat to the policy goals of the George W. Bush Administration before it ended. Yet the "Bush ideologues" wanted to "screen" many of them out (read: those with manifestly "liberal" credentials or with readily discernable such backgrounds[12]) from the Department nevertheless. And for these 179 young attorneys, with nothing to prevent this other than that it was both amoral and contrary to law,[13] they did so. This was confirmed in a formal inspector general report that partly documented this corrupt scheme but was not issued until late June of 2008.

Sadly, this scheme was nearly fool-proof, or so it seemed to the perpetrators of it. As it turned out, however, they made two mistakes: First, they were unaware of a little-known provision of a statute (read: subsection (e)(7) of the Privacy Act of 1974) that could be employed to challenge their scheme. And second, it appeared that they "deselected" one of my relatives. In other words, it seemed, they "screwed the wrong guy's nephew."

Ordinarily, Honors Program applicants submitted their applications to a central hiring office in the Justice Department, known as the Office of Attorney Recruitment and Management ("OARM," to those disarmed), which in turn forwarded them to the Department's components (usually including at least one of its large litigating divisions) for review, interview, and selection. Then, if all went well with the interview process (read: as it did with a very high percentage of the interviewees), the selected applicants received employment offers that were subject only to the successful completion of a background investigation and a drug test.

* * * * *

But Alberto Gonzales, operating through his "White House Liaison" Monica M. Goodling, set up a "political screening committee" that essentially hijacked this process. And they did so in complete secrecy. Headed by Office of the Deputy Attorney General Chief of Staff Michael J. Elston, it operated for the sole purpose of "deselecting" any Honors Program applicant who was deemed to be politically or ideologically "unsuitable." And those "suitability" determinations were made not merely on the basis of what the applicants submitted to the Department; rather, they were made heavily on the basis of "derogatory" information that could be gleaned from Internet searches undertaken on them according to special search algorithms that were provided by Monica Goodling in the Attorney General's Office.

Most significantly, those Internet searches routinely led to either printouts being attached to the applications or else annotations being made on them of what was learned "on screen." But what the perpetrators of this unlawful scheme did not realize is that by doing either of these two things, they were more than very arguably creating new "records" within the meaning of the Privacy Act, an action that triggered that law's protective provisions beyond the scope of the consent that was given when the applications were initially submitted.[14]

So I broke the news to Sean and told him that what the Department had done patently contravened century-old civil service laws that unfortunately provided no judicial remedy for him, but that I happened to know of a relatively little-known provision in the Privacy Act of 1974, its subsection (e)(7), that did provide an arguable basis for him to sue. And once I said that, atop my promise to his mother that I would pursue his case to the end, I had no choice: I spent the next four days working nonstop to prepare a Complaint that grew to be 243 paragraphs and 122 pages long that I managed to file in district court just before leaving for a vacation in the Canadian Rockies.[15]

That obscure Privacy Act provision, by the way, is tucked away in a part of that law known for establishing a set of "fair information practices." It says that a federal agency shall "maintain no record" reflecting an individual's exercise of his or her First Amendment rights "unless expressly authorized by statute," consented to by that individual, or "within the scope of an authorized law enforcement activity." Being exceptionally familiar with even the Privacy Act's obscure provisions, I immediately recognized that subsection (e)(7) was directly on point.

Indeed, in this case there was no express statutory authorization, there was no consent to maintenance of the results of such Internet searches, and although more than 95% of what the Justice Department does is for "authorized law enforcement" purposes, its everyday personnel practices, like those of any federal agency, are not. And there was little doubt but that the activities unearthed through the Department's Internet searching constituted the exercise of the Honors Program applicants' First Amendment rights.[16]

* * * * *

That freshly filed lawsuit captured much media attention, especially from journalists for whom I had been a source of secrecy-related analyses and quotes over the years. The lawsuit was noticed almost immediately by Washington-based reporters, which led to a series of telephone interviews on the case that I gave while not hiking up mountains in Canada. And it was less than a week before journalists such as Emma Schwartz of ABC News, Devin Montgomery of *Jurist*, Tony Mauro of *Legal Times*, Debra Cassens Weiss of the *ABA Journal*, and Eric Lichtblau of *The New York Times* covered the case and its underlying fact pattern at some length.

And as a result of this publicity, it was not long before I began hearing from many other unsuccessful Honors Program applicants who believed that they, too, had been victimized by the Department's corrupt hiring scheme. I politely heard them all out, took the time to carefully check out each of their stories, and found several that were quite compelling. They all asked me to represent them, just as I was representing Sean, by adding them to his lawsuit.

This raised a question or two for me, both personally and professionally. I had not hesitated before bringing suit on Sean's behalf, even though I had had no doubt that the Department -- through its Civil Division, where I had litigated from 1977-1981 (see Chapters Ten to Twelve and Fifteen to Sixteen) -- would fight the case "tooth and nail." (This was still the Bush Administration, mind you, which meant that the Justice Department would be defending its own wrong-doing.) I realized full well that by filing such a legal challenge, I was committing myself to countless hours of work in order to see it through.[17]

But adding additional plaintiffs to the case meant that I very likely would be obliged to pursue it as a class action, given that there were as many as 170 other similarly situated victims "out there" apart from Sean and those who had already contacted me. And that would have involved taking on professional obligations to not just Sean, whom I knew, but also to a range of putative plaintiffs even beyond the additional ones whom I had spoken with when they asked me to represent them. This made it close call in my mind, especially for the very practical reason that, as a retiree who did only "consulting" work on legal matters, I carried no malpractice insurance, which basically meant that I would be self-insured as to any such thing.[18]

However, I had to ask myself: Was I doing this just for Sean, or just because I had made a blind promise to his mother? The answer was no, I was doing it because the institution to which I had devoted most of my professional life, the United States Department of Justice, had been turned into a lawless instrument of *injustice* by Karl Rove, Alberto Gonzales, and their minions -- and I wanted to do my best to ensure that that never happened again. Yes, deterrence was my objective from the very start.[19]

So I agreed to add several additional plaintiffs to the case, thereby expanding the claims that were made in the Complaint, and took the position that all of the plaintiffs, as a group, stood as typical "class representatives" in what should be certified by the district court as a class action. And in doing so by means of an Amended Complaint,[20] I decided to go so far as to add an entirely new, more extreme type of claim, for what are known as "*Bivens*" violations, directly (read: with potential *individual* liability) against the five Justice Department officials involved.[21] This was a bold, almost unheard-of move, standing as it did on what admittedly was shaky legal ground, but I knew that it held the potential for having a big impact on the case. And it did.

These *Bivens* claims for violation of my clients' First Amendment rights named five individual defendants: Attorney General Alberto R. Gonzales; White House Liaison Monica M. Goodling; Office of the Deputy Attorney General Chief of Staff Michael J. Elston; Counsel to the Associate Attorney General Esther S. McDonald; and OARM Director Louis G. De Falaise. They were charged with working in concert to devise and implement the Department's scheme of unlawfully "deselecting" qualified Honors Program applicants on ideological and/or political affiliation grounds, with defendants Gonzales and Goodling as the scheme's overseers, defendant Elston as the ringleader, defendant McDonald as the "worker bee," and defendant De Falaise as the Department's overall hiring coordinator who sadly "cast a blind eye" at what the others were doing.

In response to these *Bivens* claims, all five named defendants lined up high-priced partners and associates at big law firms to defend them. Most prominent of these was former Acting Attorney General George J. Terwilliger III, who agreed to represent Alberto Gonzales but then abruptly withdrew from the case when he reportedly became upset about who would be paying his fees. This played out in public, bringing even greater publicity to the case, and it even became a matter of congressional controversy when Democrat leaders in Congress aggressively pressed the Justice Department to disclose all defendants' attorneys' fees in the case.[22]

So when the inevitable motions to dismiss the Amended Complaint (read: by the individual defendants and the Justice Department) were filed, briefed, and then argued before the Court in a consolidated hearing, I found myself walking into that courtroom and looking across at so many attorneys on the other side that they could not fit at the tables that were provided. Yes, I was the sole attorney for the plaintiffs and there were more than 30 of them (if you count Gonzales as one) on the defendants' side of the case.[23]

In their preliminary dismissal motions, the individual defendants argued that they were absolutely "immune" from individual liability for what they had done as government employees, and the Justice Department presented a "kitchen sink" array of defenses to the effect that the Privacy Act's elements for a damages claim were not satisfied under the case's particular facts. The former argument on the *Bivens* claims certainly had some merit (read: much merit, actually), but the Department's Privacy Act defense, in my view, did not.

Nevertheless, I continued to press the *Bivens* claims for all they were worth, with the hope that they would continue to distract (and detract) from the Justice Department's defense of the Privacy Act part of the case. And truth be known, I also had formed an alliance of sorts with a former litigation adversary with whom I foresaw the possibility of raising the *Bivens* issue up to the court of appeals and ultimately perhaps to the Supreme Court.[24]

As for the Privacy Act claims in the case, they rested on that little-known First Amendment-based "wrongful maintenance" provision of that statute,[25] together with my threshold legal conclusion that in its handling of Honors Program applications the Department's unlawful "screening committee" (read: Esther McDonald) had created new records (read: beyond the applications themselves) that unavoidably triggered the first factual requirement (read: arguably) for the Privacy Act's applicability. The second such requirement (read: again, arguably), by the terms of the statute, ordinarily was that the records in question be maintained in a formal "system of records."

The Justice Department's motion to dismiss devoted much attention to this second Privacy Act requirement, brazenly arguing that because of the unorthodox nature of the "screening committee" and its work, no system of records was ever established for it, and therefore (read: *ipso dipso*, as I call it) the Privacy Act simply did not apply. To this, I argued that it was "the height of chutzpah"[26] for the Department to create an unlawful screening process, fail to properly file the records of it, and then argue that by doing so it had relieved itself of otherwise-applicable legal obligations. This line of argument allowed me to brutally hammer home, over and again, the blatant, unprecedented wrongdoing that underlay the case.

I had the luxury of being so glib about this because I knew something that my Justice Department litigation opponents evidently had not yet discovered: The Privacy Act's "systems of records" element, while standing as a firm requirement for other damages actions under it, was not necessarily applicable to "wrongful maintenance" claims made under subsections (e)(5) and (e)(7).[27] In fact, there was solid case law interpreting the Act as not requiring that element in cases brought under subsection (e)(7) and also some case law suggesting that the same should hold true for subsection (e)(5).

As to my "creation of a new record" position, this threshold legal issue could be seen as the heart of *Gerlich* case. We (read: my clients and I) knew from the general findings of the inspector general's report that the screening committee operated by having paper copies of all applications printed out for its most junior member, Esther McDonald, to analyze first and then pass along to Mike Elston for all final "deselection" decisions.[28] And we knew that this process involved more than just viewing the applications alone in order to make those decisions. Indeed, it appeared that Esther McDonald had often conducted searches of the Internet, primarily through Google and MySpace pages, in order to glean what to her (and, we later learned, to Elston) was sufficiently "negative" to be injected into the process.

But the full details of this information injection were not yet known,[29] which meant that we needed to ferret them out through the discovery process if we possibly could. This process began with our making an enormous and wide-ranging request for the production of any documents that in any way touched upon what had taken place.[30] However, this initial round of discovery could not proceed until plaintiffs' Second Amended Complaint first survived the "motion to dismiss stage" of the case. This took more than a year, with much skirmishing between the parties, driven partly by the fact that the Justice Department made a significant error in answering our Second Amended Complaint in the fall of 2008.[31]

As it turned out, the heart of the Privacy Act part of the case did survive the dismissal motions and defensive arguments, despite extensive efforts by Justice's attorneys to prevent that,[32] although the *Bivens* claims predictably did not. With those claims nevertheless in mind, though, the District Court Judge John D. Bates referred to the case as "a dark chapter in the United States Department of Justice's history" and went out of his way to say that he "agree[d] that misconduct by senior government officials -- especially when it implicates the First Amendment -- is gravely serious and must not be condoned."

This encouraged me to shoot for the "holy grail" of anti-government litigation: Being able to depose the government officials who have personal knowledge of all the underlying facts of the case. I was able to make a strong case for that, given the Court's knowledgeably sympathetic view of the wrongful conduct involved,[33] and I decided that I would attempt to obtain something that had never been obtained before -- the compelled deposition testimony of a former U.S. Attorney General in a civil litigation case. Yes, I moved the district court for authorization to depose all five of the individual defendants named in the case, including Alberto Gonzales.[34]

Well, it should be no surprise to hear that all five of these defendants screamed like banshees over this. After all, they had just gotten clear of the case by having the *Bivens* claims against them dismissed, and now they had to face the prospect of my interrogating them at length (read: for up to seven hours, under the federal civil procedure rules) over wrongdoing that they certainly would rather forget having played a part in. So their attorneys "pulled out all the stops" trying to prevent the issuance of the subpoenas that I was preparing,[35] and then to quash them once they were issued and served. This even included having the Department wait until the very last minute before conveying by its silence that it would not officially try to stand in the way of my deposing Gonzales, especially in that by then I had already deposed the other three.[36]

Yes, the judge in the case, John Bates, by this point seemed to be more sympathetic to our side of the case than to the Justice Department, even though he was unmistakably pro-government and had for many years worked there.[37] And quite unexpectedly (at least by the defendants), he ruled in our favor on both the document-production discovery that we had long sought and our motion for full, unrestricted deposition testimony across the board. This ruling was an enormous development in our favor, one that I know surprised and even shocked all the attorneys on the case's other side. Although we might well have won the case without that testimony, it surely was a lot easier to do so once we had it.

This is because during the summer of 2010, the full picture of the case came tumbling out of these witnesses' sorry mouths. First up was Esther McDonald, who plainly was in way over her head to begin with.[38] She readily admitted that she had conducted Internet searches on many applicants, that she had used Google and MySpace repeatedly for this, and that whenever she found anything "negative" about an applicant online she would either note that adverse fact prominently on the face of the application or else print out what she had found and attach it to the application itself.

What Esther did not so readily admit was the full content of what Mike Elston told her after things started to "hit the fan" on what they had done. They had a meeting in his office, she said, at which he abruptly advised her to hire personal legal counsel but at the same time tried to relieve her concerns by letting her know that he had already destroyed all of the records of their screening committee's work. Actually, she admitted that twice, almost *verbatim*, as if she was trying to avoid saying something else. So I asked her what else he had said at that meeting. And she kept replying, in one way or another, that there was nothing more that she could recall.

Well, I asked Esther McDonald this question a total of *seven* times (we went back and counted them afterward) and by the seventh time, with both her counsel and Justice's counsel objecting "asked and answered" more loudly each time, she finally "remembered" that Elston had said one more thing to her about the record destruction: "Well, at least that's one thing I did right!"[39] At that, the

Justice Department's lead counsel promptly leaned over to his co-counsel, nearly falling to the floor, and stage-whispered: "She didn't just say what I think she said, did she?" Yes, she did, twice, and it was in the second time that she included the word "well."

And then I moved on to Monica Goodling, whose principal counsel John M. Dowd had sworn, in effect, that she would be deposed only "over [his] dead body." I kept looking for the hearse to arrive with it when the time for her deposition came, but all I saw was a frightened young woman who no longer had the refuge of power (read: through Gonzales and, at the White House, Karl Rove) and now was accompanied by only a junior member of John Dowd's law firm.[40]

Monica attempted to minimize her role in the corrupt affair, of course, but actually was persuasive on one point: She did not fully realize that the operation of the screening committee that she set up and oversaw was against the law. Nor did she know anything about the Federal Record Act's prohibition of what to her was casual record destruction, let alone about the requirements of the Privacy Act. What she did know was that she very much wanted to please her boss, whom she admitted might have been more than just Attorney General Gonzales,[41] and she made it quite clear that amazingly she had received little or no training in federal law or supervisory oversight from anyone, particularly Alberto Gonzales.[42] This was quite a sorry picture that she painted.

When I deposed Mike Elston, who like a death-row prisoner trudging to his execution seemed still unable to believe that such a thing was actually happening, I most keenly had in mind what I'd already gotten from the first two deponents, especially Esther McDonald, and that I did not want under any circumstances to allow him to "muddy" any of that up if it could possibly be avoided. There was no way that I was going to advert to his "one thing I did right" admission to Esther, nor even to that meeting more generally, lest he say anything that would encumber the use to which I planned to put that quote in both briefing and at oral argument.[43]

It turned out, though, that I did not have to worry much about him. He was indeed acutely hostile -- which sometimes comes with the territory when you accuse some people with wrongdoing to which they would rather not admit, though in his particular case it was just his defensive nature -- but the man sure did like to hear himself talk. And talk he did, without any seeming regard for the connection between what he was saying and the precise merits of the case. His irrepressible attitude alone was indictment enough, but it certainly was good when he witlessly allowed that he had been too "busy" to properly oversee what Esther McDonald was doing.[44] Most significantly, there was no mention (by either of us) of anything that he had said to Esther.

Alberto Gonzales was another story. By the time that I reached him, in September of 2010, I had learned so much from the first three deposition witnesses (not to mention from Lou De Falaise, informally) that I actually no longer had a burning legal need to gain anything more from him. But I knew that it would be an opportunity to learn just how it was that a young assistant like Monica Goodling could feel empowered to establish something as plainly unlawful as the Honors Program screening committee and then oversee its operation, seemingly free of any adult supervision, for months on end. Plus, one of my "poster child" plaintiffs, who was far from a child himself, had told me that he would consider the case won even if I could just force Gonzales to show up to be deposed.[45]

As it turned out, getting Gonzales deposed was not quite as simple as it was with the first three deponents in the Washington, D.C., area. This was three years after his forced resignation from the Justice Department and after a lengthy stretch of failing to obtain a "next step" position, let alone one fitting for a former attorney general, he had tried to get a faculty position at the Texas Tech Law School, with the aid of the Chancellor Kent R. Hance, who had deep roots in Texas Republican politics, having defeated George W. Bush for a House seat in the late 1970s. But doing that required faculty approval, which stirred no small amount of faculty opposition, so much of it that the attempt badly failed.

As a result of this, by the summer of 2010, Gonzales held a position at Texas Tech apart from its law school, one in which he did minimal teaching and also had the ersatz responsibility for overseeing the retention (read: not to be confused with recruitment) of minority students (read: Hispanics, mostly) at the university in general. This meant that if I were going to depose him (read: the second time around, in a sense) it had to be on his "home turf" in Texas, not in Washington, D.C.

So I proceeded to round up "the entire liberal establishment of Lubbock, Texas" -- all four of them -- to make arrangements for this big event. One of them was a Texas Tech law professor who had been the ringleader of the law school faculty's opposition to Gonzales there; another two were a husband-and-wife duo from the main university faculty who were atypically (read: for "Lubbock folk") embarrassed by his presence there; and the fourth one was a very pleasant surprise -- a nice lady who ran a court-reporter business in the center of town who said that she would provide her facilities and her own personal transcription services just for the opportunity to see Gonzales held accountable for something.[46]

And the other group of interested parties were the journalists back home in Washington who still had a hard time believing that this was actually going to happen and wanted to be the first to report it if it did. (Some of them had looked into it enough to be pretty sure that no other former attorney general had ever been forced to sit for a deposition, at least not in a civil litigation case.) I had one of my local helpers set up an open telephone line for this purpose and as I recall, the *Associated Press* (via *The Washington Post*) broke the story first.[47]

I must say that Alberto Gonzales did not disappoint in any way. He showed up at the appointed place and hour, straining to be convivial in his low-key (read: semi-somnambulant) way, and was far more dutiful than combative in his responses. (I don't think he knew how to be combative in such a setting; it was not in him.)

For nearly seven hours, even after his counsel attempted to shorten that time by claiming that "urgent plane reservations" had been made, we went back and forth on the whole sorry story, with him finally, grudgingly acknowledging: "I feel disappointment in myself" over what had happened; "I am disappointed that I didn't do things differently"; and "I, the attorney general, am ultimately responsible." That was tantamount to an apology and it of course became the centerpiece of the media's coverage of the enterprise.[48]

The court reporter later told me that the highlight for her came when I was trying to get Gonzales to acknowledge that as the head of the Office of the Attorney General itself he had an obligation to make sure that everyone on his own staff had been taught about their legal obligations under civil service principles, the Privacy Act, the Federal Records Act, and the like. He resisted this. So I asked him if the deputy attorney general had such an obligation for *his* staff, and he freely answered "yes." And then I asked him if the associate attorney general was so obliged to do that and he started to say the same thing until he abruptly caught himself and responded, "Oh, I know where you're going!" It took every ounce of civility for me not to reply: "Of course you now know where I'm going, you dolt; even that artificial tree in the corner of the room knew where I was going three minutes ago!" But I didn't, and he ultimately addressed what I was getting at.

And when he did, it became crystal clear that Alberto Gonzales was firmly afflicted of the belief that, as the attorney general, he was "entitled" to have a staff that already knew about such things, so he could just assume that that was so without bothering to be concerned about it. Did he ever take any step to verify or ensure that? No, not at all.

And also not according to Monica Goodling, who had already described for me how she and others on Gonzales's staff operated. In fact, her testimony and his lined up perfectly on this point. In short, she was allowed by him to operate in ignorance of such legal requirements; no one really cared.[49] This later allowed me to "paint a picture" in my briefs and oral arguments of an Attorney General's

Office operating with blithe disregard for such legal requirements and a young staffer like Monica being allowed to just "run rogue."

So at the end of the day (literally) with Gonzales, I concluded that he was obliviousness personified. Evidently, no one ever told him how the rules were different at the Justice Department than they were at the White House from which he came, and he in turn never "bothered his pretty little head" with such things as a cabinet officer, even as the friggin' Attorney General, for crying out loud! And my biggest take-away, having sat across the table for so many hours trying to deal with the limits of his mind,[50] was that I now well understood why he and George W. Bush had gotten along so well together: Each of them was too dumb to realize how dumb he was; it was a shared characteristic.[51]

* * * * *

So I marshalled all of this deposition evidence into a tidy narrative, close to the full story, of what actually had happened in the case. This sorry tale began with an attorney general who believed that he had absolutely no obligation to ensure that anyone on his staff, or on the staffs of his deputy and associate attorneys general for that matter, had any training in, or even any basic familiarity with, the obligations placed on all federal employees by the Privacy Act and the Federal Records Act (not to mention basic civil service rules). It continued with a young aide (Monica Goodling) who, lacking any meaningful supervision in her own office, was allowed to run rampant with a political screening committee at the White House's bidding, totally heedless of the civil service laws forbidding it.

And then there was Mike Elston, the most malign villain of the piece, who time and again proved himself capable of arrogance, deviousness, self-dealing, and irresponsible disregard for his obligations both as an attorney and as a government official. As for Esther McDonald, I almost (read: but not quite) felt sorry for her because she was so oblivious of the full legal effect of what she was doing that she was easily led by Elston (and also by Goodling, whom she knew personally) to produce the screening committee's most damaging results.

To all of this I added another category of vital evidence. It turned out that the document-production discovery that I had propounded back in the early days of the case struck pay dirt. Even the Department's principal counsel, by this time an exceptionally capable Civil Division Trial Attorney by the name of Brad P. Rosenberg,[52] was amazed to discover (no pun intended) that Esther McDonald's Internet search history in fact *could* be reconstructed (contrary to what Justice's inspector general had determined) and that some of it did indeed bear upon the case. When he finally had four boxloads of discovery documents delivered to my home, after much delay, he could not keep himself from acknowledging (read: elliptically, not directly) that I would find something of interest in there.

And so we did find out such a thing: Esther had indeed conducted actual Internet searches on at least two of the case's remaining plaintiffs[53] and there were in fact documents to prove it.[54] These documents, one of which actually contained both the plaintiff name "Daniel Herber" and a reference to "Green Party" on the same line, became vital support for the motion for summary judgment that I was preparing, as they fit very nicely with the deposition information that we had obtained.[55] That summary judgment motion was filed on May 20, 2011, together with supporting declarations, exhibits, and related deposition transcript excerpts.

But I did not stop there. I had a strong sense that the judge in our case, although aware of how "deplorable" (his word, as well as mine) the Department's misconduct was and sympathetic to how my clients were victimized by it, was most likely inclined to try to find a way by which to rule in the Department's favor if he possibly could. And the best analytical path for doing that, in my estimation, would involve pointing to the fact that the screening committee's documentation of its work -- the actual annotated or supplemented applications of my clients that I said Esther had worked on -- had been destroyed when Mike Elston had them placed in a "burn box."

This destruction was terribly wrong, to be sure, and it was a blatant violation of the Federal Records Act, but it had nevertheless taken place, arguably leaving my clients without essential evidence that they otherwise would have had in order to make their case. So I researched the principle of law that can be applied in such a record-destruction situation, called "spoliation of evidence." And I decided to become an overnight expert in this narrow, emerging legal area in order that I might take sufficient advantage of it so as to put my clients in the strongest position possible both in the district court and in a possible appeal.[56]

What I discovered was that the relatively new principle of spoliation had been addressed only obliquely by the D.C. Circuit, leaving me much room to argue that it applied to the record destruction that had occurred in our case. What this meant is that the evidentiary gap that had been created by Mike Elston's brazen use of a "burn box" for the working papers of the screening committee (read: the applications, as annotated and annexed by Esther McDonald) should not be held against the plaintiffs. Rather, with a "spoliation inference," sometimes called an "adverse inference" or a "negative inference," it would be held against the party that so callously destroyed those records, meaning that the Court (and, at trial, potentially a jury) would have to assume that my clients' applications were among those that Esther forwarded for deselection.

So I filed a novel "motion for spoliation sanction" atop our motion for summary judgment in order to pointedly press this legal position. The Justice Department's attorneys, in response, doubtless went scrambling through their library to learn more about spoliation (read: more than what I had chosen to put in my brief) and they came up with an argument against it, one that in my estimation was quite weak. And because I had had the foresight to raise spoliation in a distinct motion, I had a reply brief under the rules in which to point out just how weak their opposition was.

Then the time finally came, after more than three years of motions, briefs, declarations, depositions, document production, and much skirmishing, for District Court Judge Bates to deal with the arguments in our favor that I knew he could not easily ignore. And that did turn out to be so, because it took him nearly 30 pages to rule against us. But he gave us a shining silver lining within a transitory dark cloud by writing his opinion in such a way that it left no fewer than nine distinct pathways to reversal of it on appeal, at least three of which were "sure-fire winners" given the particular findings of fact that he made. To say that I was eager to write an appellate brief challenging that decision would be the proverbial gross understatement.

To make a long story somewhat less interminable, suffice to say that I put together a powerful opening appellate brief, all the more so in that I was able to integrate the spoliation arguments with the basic Privacy Act ones, even finding some recent case law that made our spoliation position all the more compelling. And after the Justice Department responded with what I saw as a "run of the mill, we should always win" opposition, especially on the case's new spoliation issue, I was able to "go to town" on it in a ripping reply brief that relied most heavily on spoliation as potentially the biggest key to the case.

*　*　*　*　*

At the court of appeals level, the Justice Department had assigned the case to a rising star on the Civil Division's Appellate Staff, Daniel Tenny, whom I learned from my former colleagues there had in law school earned the nickname "Tenny the Terminator." He was a pleasant enough fellow, whip smart, who seemed to believe that his case was much stronger than I knew it to be. I know this not only from how he acted, which of course could have been "just an act," but also by the fact that he actually went so far as to bring his mother to the oral argument.[57] Ouch.

We had drawn what I considered to be a balanced panel for the case. In the middle was Merrick B. Garland, later to be a Supreme Court nominee and then Attorney General, but as of that time recently elevated as the D.C. Circuit's Chief Judge. On the right was Circuit Court Judge Thomas B. Griffith, who had been appointed to that court by President George W. Bush, amid some controversy, and had a reputation for often going to some lengths to try to have the Government prevail. And on the left was Circuit Court Judge Judith W. Rogers, a Clinton appointee who had been on the Bench (both local and federal) for more than 30 years. She was the one D.C. Circuit judge whom I was sure would support the case's *Bivens* claims if we had taken them up on appeal.

But we did not really need a favorable panel, because John Bates had generously left us those nine distinct pathways to winning the case on appeal.[58] And after I had identified and then pressed all of them in our appellate briefs, the oral argument well reflected that. I was able to handle all of the panel's questions with confident reference to our briefs and I did not hesitate to remind each of the judges of the case's outrageous fact pattern, including the fact that even Judge Bates below had labeled the Justice Department's actions as "deplorable." It was challenging but fun.

When it was poor Daniel Tenny's turn, though, he was pummeled with questions from Judges Garland and Rogers, raising points about the Department's actions that were exceedingly difficult to defend -- and it showed. Even Judge Griffith, while trying to hold out a lifeline to Tenny, failed to succeed at that. And by the time that I rose to present a rebuttal, I was able to tick off the many weak points in Tenny's argument that made clear that the case was indefensible. No one leaving the courtroom that day (including, I daresay, neither Daniel Tenny nor his mother) thought that the case would not be won by the plaintiffs at long last.

So when the D.C. Circuit issued its decision in *Gerlich* three months later, it provided my clients and me with the victory that we had sought for more than 4½ years. It vindicated what we had been arguing about the unlawful creation of records all that time, it castigated the Justice Department's malefactors as having engaged in conduct that was "egregious and notorious,"[59] and it reversed the district court for having committed an "abuse of discretion." Most significantly, of the many possible pathways to reversal, it chose the one that was most favorable (read: to the plaintiffs and other future such victims of record destruction) of all.[60] This meant that the case will have a long-term impact as a deterrent to both blatant Privacy Act violations and callous record destruction. And that, as I've said above, by that point (read: with Sean no longer part of the case) mattered to me most.

The court of appeals' reversal left the case finally ready to be tried on its merits, with the only true remaining issue being the Privacy Act's requirement that for damages to be awarded the Justice Department's actions had to be found to be "intentional or willful."[61] As it turned out, the Department was loathe to take this issue to trial, especially given the adverse publicity that it had suffered with the court of appeals decision itself (publicity that I in no small part had engendered), so for the first time it was not at all sanguine about continuing the defend the case.[62] Far from it, in fact. This led to it proposing that we try to reach a settlement instead.

I had mixed feelings about this. As much as I looked forward to going to trial on what could be called the "*mens rea*" (read: degree of intent) issue, I had to admit that we had managed to obtain such rock-solid evidence on it (read: the McDonald/Elston conversations, for instance) that it would not be much of a trial. And I had clients who had waited a very long time for the case's conclusion and the money damages that they were due.[63] So Brad Rosenberg and I commenced negotiations on the terms by which we might settle the case, which was gratifying for my clients and me in that at long last we had the Justice Department "over a barrel," as is said.

This settlement-negotiation process, I must say, took much longer than anyone anticipated, more than a year in fact, largely because the Justice Department was now keenly sensitive to the case, and its attendant publicity, and evidently wanted to look as "least bad" as possible. My clients and I leveraged this, of course, toward dollar amounts that skewed to the uppermost end of what they had proven as having been adversely caused by their deselection. This yielded a nominal award of $2000 for Dan Herber, who did not have much in the way of actual damages, and a total of $50,000 for Matt Faiella, who had taken public-interest positions after his deselection before eventually becoming a government attorney at another federal agency. And I received ten times that total amount, $520,000 in attorney's fees and costs.[64]

Now this is where I should hasten to swear that I did not file this case for money, that I did not pursue it with any thought that it would lead to a fee award, and that my primary goal (beyond keeping a commitment made to my cousin Mary in front of my father) had long been shedding such public light on what the Justice Department had done, together with accountability and consequences, that it would deter anyone in the Department of Justice from even breathing hard about doing such a thing in the future. As I had stated in open court, I had been there at the time of the "Saturday Night Massacre" in 1973 (see Chapter Seven), I was appalled at how the Department was again corrupted 33 years later, and I idealistically wanted to do everything that I could to deter such a thing from ever happening again.[65]

As much as I thought I had achieved that, though, I did not even remotely envision the advent of anything like the Administration of President Donald J.

Trump within just a few years and what it could do to corrupt the Department of Justice so badly -- all deterrence, legal proscription, public opprobrium, and congressional reaction be damned.

* * * * *

As I caveated at the outset of this book, I did not intend to carry it forward into the era of the Trump Administration -- partly because I had no professional involvement with the Justice Department during it and partly because while I have no difficulty beginning to talk about the moron, I just find it hard to stop. But when it comes to the matter of deterring public corruption there, I have to observe that I never fathomed that the Department could be led by officials who, by their very natures (and that of their president), were simply beyond any meaningful deterrence (not to mention ordinary, normative, and even legal, constraints).

This was largely true of Attorney General Jefferson B. Sessions III, it was completely true of Acting Attorney General Matthew G. Whitaker, and it was very sadly and surprisingly true also of second-time Attorney General William P. Barr.[66] Slowly but unmistakably, they politicized the Justice Department beyond all "post-Watergate" norms, beyond the limits of law, and far beyond the bounds of its institutional integrity. Briefly put, by doing Donald Trump's sometimes maniacal bidding,[67] they turned the Department into something for which the deterrent effect of *Gerlich* was no match, far from it. Perhaps that effect will apply in the future, but during the Trump Administration, it never had a chance.

CHAPTER FORTY-FOUR
Secrecy at the World Bank

"Boy, those French: They have a different word for everything!"

-- Stephen G. "Steve" Martin, comedian, actor, and playwright, September 27, 2010

In mid-2010, while I was working "ass over teakettle" (as my sainted-but-some-what-profane mother used to say) on the *Gerlich* case (see Chapter Forty-Three), I was asked to serve on a "transparency tribunal" that was being established (under no small amount of duress) by the World Bank. This occurred against the backdrop of an enormous public scandal there,[1] one that shook that seemingly venerable institution to its very core[2] and led to a degree of transparency that (even in limited form) it had never before known.

Indeed, as transparency in government has grown enormously over the past few decades, it was only inevitable that this trend would begin to spread to in-ternational governing bodies as well. These consist not only of major interna-tional organizations such as the United Nations and the European Union, but also international financial institutions that likewise wield enormous influence, especially in the still-developing parts of the world.[3]

The ostensible leader among international financial institutions has long been the World Bank, sometimes referred to broadly as the "World Bank Group,"[4] which since World War II has provided loans to developing countries for the pur-pose of reducing poverty around the world. With more than 10,000 employees, mega-billions of dollars in assets,[5] and 189 member nations, it is regarded as the world's pre-eminent international financial institution by far.

During its first 60 years of existence, the World Bank was hardly known for its openness; in fact, it operated with a secretiveness that was quite traditional among international financial institutions. But this institutional culture became controversial when in 2005 Paul D. Wolfowitz began a brief two-year tenure as World Bank president, one curtailed by a personal scandal that made the Bank seem no different than many of the corrupt Third World governments with which it deals.

Wolfowitz was a former Reagan Administration and Bush Administration official perhaps best remembered for his pointed advocacy of the U.S. invading Iraq in 2001 even before September 11. As World Bank President, he paid lip service to the general idea of transparency, but it was discovered that he had had, and then covered up, an enormous conflict of interest involving a paramour on the World Bank staff, a high-level scandal that only worsened as he tried to deal with it. This set the stage for greater transparency about the World Bank's activities.

Wolfowitz's successor as World Bank President, Robert B. Zoellick, was unquestionably more liberal and reform-minded. And in the immediate wake of the Wolfowitz scandal, he saw the need for a major transparency initiative that would show the world that, despite the Bank's entrenched culture of secrecy, it was adopting transparency as one of its core values.

So on July 1, 2010, the World Bank announced with much fanfare the initiation of its new "Access to Information" policy, under which it said "[m]uch more information will be made available on key decisions made during project development and implementation . . . includ[ing] decisions of project concept review meetings, project supervision missions, and mid-term project reviews." Toward that end, it instituted a FOIA-like regime for its records and in Section 5 of its new policy set forth five specific "guiding principles" for it:

- Maximizing access to information.
- Setting out a clear list of exceptions.
- Safeguarding the deliberative process.
- Providing clear procedures for making information available.
- Recognizing requesters' right to an appeal process.

Under Section 24 of the World Bank's Access Policy, members of the public are permitted to submit written requests for records, including requests made by "electronic means," that indicate with "reasonable specificity" what is being sought. The Bank then promptly acknowledges receipt of the request and endeavors to provide a full response within 20 working days. Fees to requesters are relatively minimal and do not include any extra charges for commercial requesters.

A key feature of the Bank's policy is that it provides for two levels of administrative appeal: The first is to an "Access to Information Committee," which consists of Bank managers, and the second is to an independent tribunal named the "Access to Information Appeals Board" (or "AIAB," for short) which holds final authority for determining the applicability of the policy's access "exceptions" and, in the scheme of things, then ordering disclosure.

When the policy was initiated and first publicized in 2010, the Bank touted the establishment of the AIAB with much "pomp and fanfare," based upon the expertise of its members and the independence that we were to be given.[6] The Bank relied heavily on our professional standing and reputations in support of what it called the "public launch" and then the subsequent "roll out" of its new, remedial transparency policy.

The access exceptions, found in Sections 8-17 of the formal written policy, are in large part what might be considered ordinary ones on their face, akin to the "exemptions" in the FOIA, in that they protect personal information, financial information, information that is sensitive for security or safety reasons, and information "subject to attorney-client privilege." But they also contain (in Section 16) an extremely broad swath of protection for "deliberative information," one that explicitly encompasses even such things as statistics, audit reports, and information received from member countries or other third parties.

As to the latter, language contained in a footnote to the policy set forth a categorical approach to the effect that if "to the Bank's knowledge, the member country or third party concerned has not made the information public, then such information is considered to be deliberative." This is extremely broad, far broader than the counterpart protection for an agency's deliberative processes under Exemption 5 of the FOIA, for instance.[7]

Even more problematic, though, is language in the Bank's policy suggesting that a record might be withheld from a requester in its entirety simply because part of it falls within a disclosure exception -- which certainly would constitute a radical departure from the norm. Under the Freedom of Information Act, for example, it has long been established that an agency must "process" the requested records so as to withhold only the exempt information within them, and other nations of the world have uniformly followed suit on this.[8]

As written, however, the Bank's transparency policy contained what seemed to be a troubling ambiguity on that critical point. In the precatory language to the section (Section 3) that lists its disclosure exceptions, the following can be found:

> The Bank does not provide access to information whose disclosure could cause harm to specific parties or interests. Accordingly, the Bank does not provide access to documents that *contain or refer to* the information listed in paragraphs 8-17.[9]

On the other hand, in a more specific context (i.e., in Section 40 of the policy), it speaks of "the *information* requested" and of "the process for making the *information* available to the requester."[10] And most significantly (i.e., in Sections 20(a) and 20(b)), it plainly contemplates what certainly appears to be an ordinary document-redaction process in elsewhere specifying that the Bank will "take an approach to disclosing information" of "mak[ing] adjustments to [a] document" for purposes of withholding only the sensitive information within it.

This therefore became a major point of focus when the Bank's General Counsel Anne-Marie Leroy "rolled out" the Bank's new openness policy at an international transparency conference conducted by my academic center, the Collaboration on Government Secrecy ("CGS," to my students), at American University's Washington College of Law in September of 2010 (read: it was CGS's "Fourth Annual International Right-to-Know Day" program, which I had offered to Anne-Marie as a venue for her "roll out").[11]

After describing the policy in considerable detail, Bank General Counsel Leroy specifically addressed this "redaction issue" in responding to a question posed by one of the other program speakers and she explicitly reassured the audience that the Bank's policy "does contemplate redaction when necessary"; indeed, she went so far as to advise that anyone concerned about that "should look at, for instance, [Section] 20" of the policy, which she quoted in pertinent part as "contemplat[ing] redaction." Anyone in attendance at that program, or viewing the school's webcast of it, would take these comments as completely putting to rest this redaction concern.

However, it subsequently came to light (with not much digging on my part, inasmuch as I was on the "inside") that despite such official assurances, and to the astonishment of the Bank's potent "civil society" community,[12] the Bank had already issued a "policy interpretation" *to the very contrary*. In fact, under the heading of "redaction," that interpretive document purported to resolve the question in favor of gross *non*disclosure by stating as follows:

> Under the AI Policy, the Bank considers disclosure of documents in their original form. If a requested document includes restricted information, the AI Policy does not mandate the Bank to "redact" (i.e., "black out") restricted information in order to make the document acceptable for public access.[13]

Beyond the duplicitousness of this, such an interpretation and procedural approach to information disclosure is of course enormously consequential in that it permits the withholding of any document, no matter what its size or range of content, based upon the mere presence of a bit of sensitive information anywhere within it.[14] And by so doing, it not only broadens the scope of what is withheld immensely, it serves to greatly reduce the administrative burden of implementing any such disclosure policy commensurately.[15] This, I pointed out to the Bank during my time there, is "very much not good."[16]

It thus remains to be seen to what extent the World Bank will truly realize its promise of making its records freely available to the public through a FOIA-like disclosure regime.[17] If it does achieve this in a well-recognized way, it will be in a position to exert a unique influence over the still-developing nations of the world, especially in Africa, where there remains enormous room for transparency improvement, especially in relation to the corruption-laden extractive industries that have long run rampant there (see Chapter One).

And in time, if the World Bank's transparency regime proves successful (read: or at least successful enough, despite its flaws and transparently duplicitous underpinning), it even is possible that it will compellingly influence the United Nations, as the world's largest international governing organization, to follow suit.[18]

CHAPTER FORTY-FIVE
The Unprecedented
FCC v. AT&T Case

"We trust that AT&T will not take it personally."

-- John G. Roberts, Jr., Chief Justice of the United States, in *FCC v. AT&T, Inc.*, March 1, 2011

Anyone familiar with the Freedom of Information Act's exemptions knows that Congress created one (or two, actually) exemption for personal-privacy information and another distinct one to protect certain "business" information. This has proven to be an entirely workable delineation and, until the late 2000s, the two types of exemptions never mixed. That is, not until media conglomerate AT&T, Inc. took the unprecedented legal position in a litigation case that corporations actually do have "privacy interests" that can be protected as such under the FOIA. To the best of my knowledge, no one had ever even thought of taking such an extreme position before.

This case arose from an investigation conducted by the FCC's Enforcement Bureau of possible overcharges by AT&T for certain telecommunication services that it had provided to the Federal Government, during which AT&T furnished the FCC with numerous business records. After the matter was resolved (with the payment by AT&T of a half-million dollars), an AT&T competitor filed a FOIA request with the FCC for access to the entire investigative file, which is not an unusual use of the FOIA in the business world.

In response, the FCC of course withheld much of the AT&T-submitted information on FOIA Exemption 4 grounds (i.e., the FOIA's exemption protection for sensitive business information), which was not unusual either. And it also rejected a highly unorthodox argument made by AT&T that the FOIA's law enforcement privacy exemption, Exemption 7(C), should be applied to withhold other such information in the matter.[1] That argument was most unusual, to say the least.

Now ordinarily, the rejection of a business submitter's exemption argument would be challenged by it, if at all, in a "reverse FOIA" case in district court, with a possible appeal to the circuit court level looming beyond that. But in the exceptional procedural posture in which this case arose, involving a regulatory appeal to a circuit court directly as provided for by a specialized statute, the Third Circuit Court of Appeals was the court that considered it, because AT&T managed to obtain direct judicial review of the FCC's administrative decision in that court of appeals as if it were purely a regulatory matter.

And here is where things went completely off the rails. AT&T, having "staked out" its novel "corporate privacy" position before the FCC, managed to both raise it and prevail on it with a Third Circuit panel. It did so by arguing, *inter alia*, that it is deemed a "person" for litigation-claim purposes under a general statute called the Administrative Procedure Act ("APA," to its fans), so information submitted by it to the Government therefore is entitled, it contended, to broad "personal privacy" protection (not just narrower "business information" protection) under the FOIA.

Indeed, that panel of the Third Circuit completely "bought" AT&T's notion of "corporate privacy," with no fewer than a half-dozen analytical flaws and other errors in its reasoning. (I state this so unequivocally here because I pointed out each and every one of them in an *amicus* brief that I filed with the Supreme Court when the case reached there.) This ruling was totally unprecedented and was extremely broad in its inherent implications.

By the way, the word "unprecedented," which admittedly is sometimes over-used in such situations, is not an overstatement in this case. When the Third Circuit did this, at AT&T's behest, it truly did something never done before: It adopted the unheard-of notion (read: no more than a notion) that businesses have protectible "privacy" interests in addition to their business interests. The adverse ramifications of such a thing were wide and deep.[2]

This turned out to be the pivotal basis for what was perhaps the most important step in the case: The Solicitor General's decision to seek Supreme Court review even in the absence of any direct conflict in the circuit courts of appeals on the issue. As has been described above in connection with several FOIA cases to reach the Supreme Court (see, for example, Chapters Three, Eleven, and Forty), sometimes the "steepest hill to climb" in such cases is not persuading the Supreme Court to grant review of an adverse appellate decision, nor is it even winning the case on its merits once it gets there. Rather, it is persuading the Solicitor General to authorize the filing of a *certiorari* petition in the first place.

In this case, that climb was especially steep, given that the issue was narrowly cast and nearly every other circuit court in the country could be relied upon to come down on the right side of it. And although I had been retired from the Justice Department for three years by then (2010), I learned that there seemed to be little enthusiasm in the Office of the Solicitor General for "taking the case up." So the officials in the Department who were advocating that the Solicitor General do so enlisted my help in making a case for it.

Never shy about doing such a thing,[3] whenever I thought it was for a good cause,[4] I argued (read: informally, by phone) several things, but most importantly that the Third Circuit's anomalous decision held serious practical complications for the uniform administration of the FOIA.[5] Under it, for instance, any corporation registered in the State of Delaware could have brought a "reverse FOIA" lawsuit within the Third Circuit's geographic boundaries and authoritatively argued that information submitted by it for regulatory purposes was entitled to broad privacy protection under FOIA Exemption 6, or alternatively under its law enforcement record counterpart Exemption 7(C), not merely protection from ordinary competitive harm under FOIA Exemption 4, to block FOIA disclosure.

I also "sweetened the pot" a little by personally guaranteeing (read: for what it was worth) that the Government would definitely win on the merits of the case in the Supreme Court, with 100% certainty, if we could just get it up there. And in a spasm of "putting my own time and effort where my mouth was," I committed to filing an *amicus* brief on those merits through my academic center if *certiorari* were sought and granted. This, or some combination of things, ultimately carried the day with the Solicitor General, and the Supreme Court came down that way as well when it granted *certiorari*.

Then it was time for keeping my commitment. In November of 2010, on behalf of the Collaboration on Government Secrecy, I filed an *amicus* brief in the Supreme Court in support of the Department of Justice's position in the case, one that demonstrated every last flaw in the Third Circuit's decision. In short, this brief pointed out that (1) the Third Circuit had improperly ignored the FOIA's clear legislative history; (2) it had conflated the word "person" in the APA with the word "personal" in the FOIA; (3) it had mistaken the 1974 word "individual" in FOIA Exemption 7(F) as something that existed when the FOIA was enacted in 1966; (4) it had misconstrued the logical interplay between Exemption 7(C) and its predecessor exemption, Exemption 6; and (5) it had utterly underappreciated the impact of adopting the idea of "corporate privacy" in the "reverse FOIA" world, thus greatly distorting that realm of administrative law and practice. (The latter point was presented from CGS's (read: my own) unique perspective.) And of all of these points, it urged the Court to pay particular attention to the significance of Exemption 6, and its interplay with Exemption 7(C), in the case.

In response, AT&T did not labor greatly to try to defend the Third Circuit's decision. Rather, its position before the Supreme Court was one of very basic (read: third-grade level, to the FOIA *cognoscente*) statutory interpretation. It argued that, because the law often includes corporations in the definition of *personhood,* such as in the word *person* as defined within the APA, and because the FOIA was enacted by Congress as part of the APA, that "must mean" that the word *personal* in the FOIA's "personal privacy" exemptions, Exemption 6 and the later-enacted Exemption 7(C), "necessarily" includes AT&T and other corporations. Like the Third Circuit, it advocated a simplistic, if not unduly syllogistic, approach to the legal question that it had raised in the case.

In March of 2011, however, the Supreme Court issued a decision flatly rejecting this position, pointing first and foremost to the Third Circuit's total failure to take cognizance of "the difference between 'person' and 'personal.'" Emphasizing that the FOIA's privacy exemptions use the latter adjectival term, not the former noun, and that adjectives do not always mean the same thing as do their "corresponding nouns," the Court examined "the ordinary meaning of 'personal'" and found that it "ordinarily refers to individuals." Even further removed from the legal term *person,* the Court focused on the entire language used by Congress in both Exemption 6 and Exemption 7(C) and thus considered "the ordinary meaning of the phrase 'personal privacy.'"

Most significantly, it also recognized that Congress first used that phrase in 1966 in enacting the language of Exemption 6, where it "importantly defines the particular subset of . . . information Congress sought to exempt." And because "personal privacy" has always been properly understood to mean an "individual's right of privacy" in that earlier exemption (i.e., Exemption 6), that fact provided the key "context" for the Court to decide that "personal privacy" was intended by Congress to mean the same thing when it amended the FOIA to create Exemption 7(C) eight years later in 1974. So the Third Circuit's aberrational privacy decision was reversed, along the very lines that CGS had suggested.[6]

Notably, the author of the Court's opinion, Chief Justice John G. Roberts, Jr., did not use the case to address the limits of corporate personhood in the immediate wake of the Court's controversial decision in *Citizens United v. Federal Election Commission* the year before.[7] Rather, his opinion explicitly eschewed any consideration of constitutional privacy, stating instead that the statutory construction issue raised by the Third Circuit's novel FOIA interpretation "does not call upon us to pass on the scope of a corporation's 'privacy' interests as a matter of constitutional or common law."

And almost as notably, Chief Justice Roberts resoundingly concluded his opinion with the following ringing message: "We trust that AT&T will not take it personally."

CHAPTER FORTY-SIX
The *Milner* Case

". . . the bombs bursting in air . . ."

-- Future U.S. Attorney for the District of Columbia Francis Scott Key, 1814

A Supreme Court decision that ought to have an even bigger long-term impact than the *AT&T* decision as discussed in the chapter immediately above is *Milner v. Department of the Navy*, a "homeland security-era" case that arose under FOIA Exemption 2. Like so many other such FOIA cases discussed above, it has a long "backstory" that has to be recounted first; indeed, it was this very background that made *Milner* so potentially significant.

Milner's backstory went back nearly 30 years, to 1981, the year that the Office of Information and Privacy was created. In December of that year, the D.C. Circuit Court of Appeals issued an *en banc* decision[1] in a case dealing with the unduly opaque language of FOIA Exemption 2. Known as *Crooker v. Bureau of Alcohol, Tobacco & Firearms*, this decision established the delineation construct of what became known as "Low 2" and "High 2" for that exemption, with the former being a purely burden-based measure[2] and the latter more potently permitting protection of any "predominately internal" agency information the disclosure of which "would risk circumvention of law."

Although *Crooker* was adjudicated in the context of a "hard-core" law enforcement record -- the case involved a Bureau of Alcohol, Tobacco, and Firearms operational manual for its particular criminal surveillance[3] and SWAT-like techniques – once it came down, OIP almost immediately began advocating its application (read: extension) to other types of records and situations down a long situational continuum, from law enforcement manuals to other types of documents,[4] from criminal-enforcement to civil-enforcement situations, to non-enforcement records, and even to what were known as "crediting plans" used by agencies in their hiring processes.[5] In other words, we unabashedly and highly successfully stretched the hell out of *Crooker* for the next nearly thirty years,[6] until we "got caught," so to speak, when the *Milner* case arose and then reached the Supreme Court.

Milner was a very difficult case for the Government in that it involved factual circumstances that were more amorphous than most and it took the "anti-circumvention" principle of *Crooker* to its farthest reaches. It had to do with maps used by the Department of the Navy in storing "high explosives" (read: very high explosives) on a naval base in the State of Washington. The maps portrayed the magnitudes of entirely hypothetical accidental detonations that understandably were of strong interest to the local community.[7] Fearing that such specification of the explosives' location could lead to their being "weaponized" by terrorists (see Chapter Thirty-Seven),[8] and having been told by OIP that as a general tenet of post-9/11 information policy the broad "anti-circumvention" protection afforded by Exemption 2 was available to cover such potential harms, the Navy invoked "High 2" when it received the inevitable FOIA request for these maps.

It is an understatement to say that the naval base's neighbors did not take kindly to this. They reasoned that they, as much as Navy personnel, had a strong interest in knowing about the dangers posed by having these "high explosives" in their midst. So they sued in court, where they did not prevail either at the district court or the court of appeals levels.[9] Then they made a true "federal case" of the matter by petitioning for review of the lower courts' decisions by the United States Supreme Court.

I still remember the day that this request for Supreme Court review (called a "*certiorari* petition") was granted by the Court in June of 2010. Hearing of this, I called former colleagues still in the Department and told them that they best have a "remedial" legislative package prepared without delay.[10] This is because it was very clear to me (and some others) that the actual language of Exemption 2 (i.e., the "text" of it, as Supreme Court advocates call it) did not support its use this far down the continuum; in other words, it was now almost inevitable that the Supreme Court would reject this position and in doing so put an end to "High 2" within the next year.

And that is exactly what the Court did do in its *Milner* decision: It found that, as "High 2" then was being applied, it simply was too attenuated from Exemption 2's text,[11] and that "[b]y no stretch of imagination" could it be concluded that Congress actually intended such a thing. This was hard to disagree with, as I knew full well that we had "gotten away with murder" in our creative extensions of *Crooker* for at least 28 of the preceding 30 years, not to mention when it really counted, i.e., since 9/11.

But this did not mean that there still was not a great need for "High 2-like" protection across the Federal Government, especially in the "post-9/11" context.

Probably the most crucial -- or at least readily explainable -- example of this was (and remains) the government's continuing need to protect the "vulnerability assessments" that it regularly prepares, especially in the areas of "computer security" (or, now, "cybersecurity").[12]

To this must be added a continuing need for much of the "anti-circumvention" protection that was afforded in the wealth of "High 2" case law that came to exist after *Crooker* and until *Milner*.[13] Yet inexplicably, and to the great surprise and disappointment of federal FOIA officers across the Nation, there was no remedial response to *Milner* incorporated into the 2017 FOIA Amendments. This was extremely difficult to understand, as it was utterly contrary to what the Justice Department had done in such circumstances since the late 1970s.

The mystery of this reached a milestone of sorts when the Department of Justice finally admitted in public testimony before Congress that *Milner* had indeed presented problems for which there was an "urgent" need for a "legislative fix" of a "critical gap" in Exemption 2 coverage. But no adequate effort toward that has been made by the Department, not even by the Office of Management and Budget, which sometimes plays a role in such matters. So to date, this mystery remains, but by now I have given up worrying about it.[14]

* * * * *

Both the Supreme Court's decision in *Milner* and its decision in the *AT&T* case (see the immediately preceding chapter) were entirely clear and unambiguous, leaving no room for how they should be interpreted and applied. This cannot be said of all of the Supreme Court's FOIA decisions, however.

In March of 2001, the Court handed down a decision that at first blush seemed to severely limit the Federal Government's ability to protect some of its decision-making processes from public disclosure under the FOIA. The case was *Department of the Interior v. Klamath Water Users Protective Association*, and it dealt with the "threshold" requirement of FOIA Exemption 5 -- i.e., that the records in question first must be deemed "inter-agency or intra-agency memorandums or letters" before they can be considered for application of any of that exemption's "privileges," foremost among them the deliberative process privilege, the attorney work-product privilege, and the attorney-client privilege.

In *Klamath*, the Supreme Court unanimously held that this threshold requirement was not satisfied for seven records exchanged between the Department of the Interior and several Indian Tribes located in the Klamath River Basin, due to the Tribes' "direct interest" in the outcome of the agency's decisionmaking process involved. Consequently, the Court ruled that those records, which dealt with agency decisions on water allocation and had been withheld from competing water users under the attorney work-product and deliberative process privileges, must be disclosed.

In the lower courts, the Department of the Interior had at first prevailed in its Exemption 5 position. At the district court level, Exemption 5 was found satisfied in light of the agency's special "trust relationship" with the Indian Tribes involved, which the agency argued placed the Tribes in the position of being, in effect, an "outside consultant" to it. (We had through careful litigation management over the years shaped the implementation of Exemption 5's threshold language to include "outside consultants" within it.)

The Court of Appeals for the Ninth Circuit, however, ruled in a 2-1 decision that the Tribes' "direct interest" in the agency's water-allocation decisionmaking disqualified the records from Exemption 5 protection as a threshold matter. This ruling seemingly put an end to the Federal Government's long string of cases in which it had persuaded courts to accord a "pragmatic" interpretation to Exemption 5's threshold wherever the records in question arose from what we called an "outside consultancy."[15]

I was out of my office on medical leave when the Supreme Court's *Klamath* decision was issued and I returned to find that it had been taken as a broad-scale loss by the Department's Civil Division, at both Civil's trial court and appellate court levels; indeed, it already had been acquiesced to as such in more than one of the Civil Division's pending cases.[16] But upon my return, I very closely examined exactly what the Supreme Court had said (read: and had not said), in Justice David H. Souter's opinion for the Court, and I came to the more refined conclusion that the Court's ruling actually was not as broad as had been thought within the Government at first sight.[17]

Indeed, I quickly concluded that while the Supreme Court affirmed the Ninth Circuit's decision, it actually did so on a distinctly narrower ground, which made a considerable difference in how this new FOIA precedent was to be applied. In short, I recognized that although the Court had surely upheld that lower appellate court's adoption of a new "direct interest" exception to Exemption 5's longstanding "outside consultant" expansion in the case, it had done so only where, in the language of the Court, the outside consultant had been acting "at the expense of others similarly situated."[18] Yes, it took a very careful reading of Justice Souter's somewhat convoluted opinion to realize that nuanced point, but given the precise language that Justice Souter had used, that conclusion was inescapable.

So I immediately advised the Department's Civil Division of this, as well as the Office of the Solicitor General, and went about the business (which above all was OIP's governmentwide FOIA-policy business) of writing detailed policy guidance showing how this less onerous interpretation of Justice Souter's opinion was necessarily the correct one. This policy guidance was published by OIP in near-record time, given the circumstances, and for more than 20 years now it has stood the test of time.

CHAPTER FORTY-SEVEN
Hillary's Email Fails

"There is nothing there. There is nothing that should have been so controversial."

-- Former Secretary of State Hillary Rodham Clinton, speaking of her emails at an art exhibition at Despar Teatro Italia in Venice, Italy, September 10, 2019

"[A] half-truth is often a great lie."

-- Benjamin Franklin, 1706-1790

Another secrecy controversy that arose after my retirement from the Justice Department (but while I was teaching) was that of Secretary of State Hillary Rodham Clinton's unremitting fiasco (a "self-inflicted wound," one could say) with her utterly self-serving use of a personal email account at the State Department atop her even more secretive use of a personal computer "server" kept in the basement of her Chappaqua, New York, home. I was drawn into publicly commenting and writing about this by my colleagues at the Washington College of Law (and elsewhere) who, knowing my background and expertise, would ask me, in colloquial but no less pointed terms: "Is it possible that what she did was OK (or words to that effect)?"

The short answer to that question is no, it was *not* OK, not by a long shot. And as it happened, I was particularly well-positioned to know the full depths of that by dint of having worked with and for her (though indirectly) on FOIA-related matters during the Clinton Administration.

Actually, the first trigger for my involvement in media coverage of Secretary Clinton's burgeoning "email issue" was a request that I received from a well-known media outlet, *POLITICO*, to analyze her first major defense of her position on it at a hastily arranged press conference that was held at the United Nations on March 10, 2015.[1] It should be remembered that at the time, Secretary Clinton had not yet formally announced that she would be running for president in 2016, but her candidacy was by then a foregone conclusion. So when the news about her evident misuse of electronic mail communications during her State Department tenure "broke" on March 3, it resonated as a news story that threatened to derail her candidacy before it had even begun.

This is a tale that takes more than one twist or turn during the course of its unraveling. And it often turns on the exact meaning of particular words or phrases that have been used by Secretary Clinton in describing it -- words or phrases such as "allowed," "permitted," "opted," "chose," "vast majority," "captured," and (a nostalgic favorite) "it" -- which means that semantics, as well as law, policy, and administrative practice, are a very big part of it.[2] This in turn has led to no small amount of confusion, in many quarters, about what Secretary Clinton did, what she failed to do, and what she should have done with her electronic mail from beginning to end, both during and then subsequent to her State Department tenure. The primary purpose of this chapter is to remove such confusion.

Before proceeding further, however, it is most useful (read: necessary, actually) to focus briefly on the basic facts of this evolving controversy as they stood as of the time of that press conference on March 10. And lest anyone be inclined to think otherwise, the following facts are entirely beyond any dispute:

- Hillary Clinton began her tenure as Secretary of State on January 21, 2009, directly from her position as a U.S. Senator. As a senator, she had used a BlackBerry mobile device for sending and receiving electronic mail.

- When she arrived at the State Department, she ordinarily would have received a briefing or series of briefings from one or more career State Department officials about a variety of basic "nuts and bolts" administrative things -- such as ethics requirements, procurement restrictions, Federal Records Act obligations, Privacy Act prohibitions, and the like. Routinely, this would include at least some mention of the Freedom of Information Act,[3] although in Secretary Clinton's case this latter subject need have required only a relatively brief discussion, given her known familiarity with the FOIA during her eight-year tenure as First Lady during the presidential administration of her husband.[4]

- Nowadays (read: since the 2000s), for almost all new Federal Executive Branch employees at any other than the very lowest levels, this step would regularly include the establishment of an official government email account, together with the official issuance of computer equipment and/or a telephonic communications device to be used for all government business.

- In Secretary Clinton's case, however, she expressed a preference to use her existing BlackBerry device (and account), with which she was most familiar, and she continued to do so for at least her first two months at the State Department -- perhaps much longer.[5] In fact, there is evidence that she liked using BlackBerrys so much that she used 13 of them during her State Department tenure.[6]

- There then came a time, in about April of 2009, when she began sometimes using a State Department-issued telephone device for her communications as well. Note that this is not the same as using a State Department email *account* on that device. There is no indication that an official State Department email account was established for (or used by) her at that time or at any other time during her tenure.

- Rather, Secretary Clinton continued to use a personal email account on that device, then named "clintonemail.com," just as she had been doing (and also continued to do) with her BlackBerry device.[7] In short, no matter what device she used at any time, it was never connected to an official email account.

- In conjunction with this, and consistent with the fact that she had no State Department email account, and therefore had complete control over the email account that she *did* have, Secretary Clinton privately arranged to have all of her email communications, both official and personal in nature, "hosted" (i.e., routed through and maintained on) her own private server, one that was already in existence in the basement of her home in Chappaqua, New York.[8]

- The result of all of this -- i.e., (1) the absence of any *official* State Department electronic mail account, (2) Secretary Clinton's use of a personal email *account* instead of that, and (3) her use of a private *server* for this personal account -- was that all of her email communications, both outgoing and incoming, were entirely within her own personal control, not regularly connected to the State Department or accessible by anyone else under any circumstances.[9]

- On March 3, 2015, an article in *The New York Times* broke the story that the congressional committee that was investigating the "Benghazi tragedy"[10] had discovered that Secretary Clinton exclusively used her own personal electronic mail account rather than a government-created one, atop a personal email server, throughout her time as Secretary of State, and that her aides took no action to preserve the official-business emails sent through or received through her personal email account as required by law.[11]

- *The New York Times* also on that day reported that Secretary Clinton's "team" then insisted that she had "acted in the spirit of the laws governing email use." And on March 4, in the only other statement on the subject made by her or by anyone speaking on her behalf, Secretary Clinton issued a simple "tweet" that defensively (and safely ambiguously) said, "I want the public to see my email."

So, against this factual backdrop, we return to that crucial March 10 press conference at the United Nations Headquarters that *POLITICO* asked me to analyze.[12] Secretary Clinton spoke for only about 20 minutes at this key "explanation" session, first with a prepared statement and then time for some questions (but not as many as would be asked ordinarily). And it was noteworthy both for what she did say and for what she did not say that day, each of which held the potential to mislead her audience (and putative voters) to a very large degree.

Indeed, her opening sentence right away contained two words (italicized below) that were quite misleading at best and false at worst: "First, when I got to work as secretary of state, I *opted* for convenience to use my personal email account, which was *allowed* by the State Department."[13]

The word "opted," first and foremost, gives the false impression that incoming Secretary Clinton was specifically given a choice about how to use electronic mail for her official communications.[14] Yet there is no such "option"; no incoming federal employee is given such a choice with which to "opt."[15] Rather, *every* executive branch employee who has joined the Government since the advent of electronic mail (read: all employees at a level that requires it) has routinely been given an official email account to use -- every employee except for one, that is: Secretary of State Hillary Rodham Clinton. Her implication that this was not so was nothing short of deceptive.[16]

This was compounded, of course, by Secretary Clinton's tandem claim that her use of a personal email account rather than an official email account "was allowed by the State Department." The word "allowed" here -- much like her similar use of the word "permitted" elsewhere -- could mean either of two distinct things: First, it could mean that some State Department official, acting on behalf of the agency, specifically (as well as properly) authorized her personal email account's use. This undoubtedly is the meaning that Secretary Clinton wanted to convey.

Or it could mean that no one at the State Department -- ranging from the lowliest of tech staffers to the Under Secretary of State for Management -- prevented her from going ahead with use of her personal account in lieu of an official one, just as no one evidently prevented her from continuing to use her Senate-originated BlackBerry device and account for many months once she arrived at State in January.

This sense of the word "allowed," of course, conveys something that in some sense could have been literally true -- as in, no one tracked her down in the hallway as she left a meeting with her personal email device (connected to a personal email account) in hand to stop her. Common sense tells us that someone as powerful as an agency head (not to mention as a former First Lady) will be "allowed" to do pretty much whatever she damn well pleases unless she is stopped by a career agency official who has both the authority (read: gravitas) and the, shall we say, gumption to do so. There is absolutely zero indication of there having been any such gumption exercised in this case, not at any stage of it.[17]

The next key word in Secretary Clinton's press conference statement is one that actually was not spoken by her, as opposed to being heavily implied by her to apply to her situation. That word is "exclusively," as in "I was allowed to use my personal email account exclusively" -- i.e., all the time, in lieu of an official email account. Anyone listening to her statement that day, or reading a transcript of what she said later on, would tend to come away with the distinct impression that what was "allowed" or "permitted," in her words, was her use of her personal email account and that account *only*, to the exclusion of an official account at any time.

The major legal reason that this matters is because of a law called the Federal Records Act ("FRA," to those who obey it). This statute, which applies to all executive branch employees who are not within the "inner" White House itself (see Chapter Thirty-Three), requires the comprehensive documentation of the conduct of all official business, and it has long done so by regulating the creation, maintenance, preservation, and ultimately the disposition of federal records. When it comes to "modern-day" email communications, as compared to the paper memoranda of not so long ago, these messages now are themselves the very means of conducting much official business, by definition, and this is something that becomes even more so every day. So the FRA firmly applies to electronic mail, just as it has long governed records in paper form.

To be sure, this legal requirement cannot as a practical matter be slavishly absolute. When Obama Administration officials came into office in 2009, the Federal Records Act certainly allowed room for the occasional use of a personal email device and account for the conduct of official business where that was necessary -- such as where a secretary of state understandably must deal with a crisis around the world in the middle of the night when an official email device might not be readily at hand. This just makes sense.

But even then, in such an exceptional and only occasional factual situation, the FRA's documentation and preservation requirements still call upon that official (or a staff assistant) to forward any and all such exceptional emails (and perhaps also text messages just the same) into the State Department's official records system, where they would have been located (and readily locatable) ordinarily. Taking such a step ensures that such email messages can be used for future purposes.

The idea here is that a top agency official operating as best she can under exigent circumstances can make use of a personal rather than official phone device so long as the proper recordkeeping requirements of the FRA are met once things calm down. But this is a far cry from that official using that personal phone (and its underlying personal email account) for more than that.[18] And it is a much, much farther cry from an official using her personal email account *exclusively* -- i.e., for every working day and night of her tenure -- without bothering to obtain an official email account like everyone else. Make no mistake: That is exactly what Hillary Clinton did.

And then there is another thing that Secretary Clinton barely mentioned at her press conference -- her personal email "server," the computer equipment located in her basement that was connected to her personal email account.[19] While these two things certainly worked in tandem, with the former greatly amplifying the secrecy effect of the latter, they are two very distinct things (even though they often are conflated by those other than Secretary Clinton).[20] And the fact that Secretary Clinton had connected her personal email account to her private server was indeed contained in the March 3 *New York Times* article that blew the lid off of it all.

Yet Secretary Clinton did not at her press conference openly address the subject of her private server as a distinct problem -- i.e., one that had been specifically emphasized as such by *The New York Times*. Rather, she made only two off-handed references to it, as if its existence could be assumed by one and all and as if both its existence and its use scarcely mattered. She said: "The server *contains* personal communications from my husband and me, and I believe I have met all of my responsibilities and the server will remain private. . . . So, I think that [the] use of that server, which started with my husband, certainly proved to be effective and secure."

As for the first of these two references, notice that Secretary Clinton spoke as if the server's contents are all that matters, which is not the case. Moreover, in doing so, she employed what is a classic bit of imprecision, saying that something "contains" something, rather than saying that its contents *consist of* something.[21] The "contains" approach allowed her to truthfully state a true fact about her server as if that fact is dispositive of any question about it.[22] Manifestly, however, it is not.[23]

The second reference is almost as pernicious. Again, it speaks of her private server as if its existence is a foregone conclusion and then it speaks of its "use" as if the only issue about it has to do with the server's effectiveness and security. Yet no one listening to her press conference had any doubt about whether her server was "effective" -- actually, that was no small part of the problem to begin with. And as to whether it was "secure," that surely did become a matter of considerable concern later in time,[24] but as of that time that concern served only to distract from the real question of the server's "use." Why was that server used in the first place, one wonders? At no time during the press conference was that threshold question addressed.

And on top of this is the revealing fact that Secretary Clinton apparently felt compelled to bolster each of these two server-related statements with a reference to her husband, former President Bill Clinton, as if that should make any difference here. The fact that the server *contained* "personal communications from [her] husband" does not add any legal or moral justification to her having used that server to house official State Department communications, let alone serve as the sole repository of them. Neither does the fact that (as she heavily implied, so let's accept it as true) the server's "use" (in the only instance in which its any use is mentioned) "started with" him.[25] This, too, is utterly irrelevant to the propriety of what she did with that server once she started using it herself.[26]

Next, Secretary Clinton trotted out something that some people regard as a truly award-winning defense: Her "vast majority" approach. This gambit involves either speaking very quickly or writing very glibly (or both) about a controversial body of something (lawyers would call it the "*corpus*" of a case) with the blithe claim (or even a mere yet effective implication) that the "vast majority" of it is of a certain benign character so . . . therefore no one should worry their pretty little heads about the remainder of it.[27] It is as if whatever is so for *most of a corpus*, perhaps not much more than most of it, must be so for *all* of it as well.

In this case, which by its nature involved different categories of email messages, Secretary Clinton actually tried to "pull a fast one" by using this classic approach. Indeed, at her press conference, she made much of the fact that so many of her email messages were of a type (or in a category) that she evidently regarded as favorable to her. She also argued forcefully as follows: "Second, *the vast majority* of my work emails went to government employees at their government addresses, which meant they were captured and preserved immediately on the system at the State Department."[28]

Putting aside for the moment the deeper question of whether any such "capture and preservation" process actually occurred for *any* of her email messages (let alone for all of them), or even would have been viable for Freedom of Information Act search purposes in any event,[29] the question necessarily arises: "OK, Secretary Clinton, so please tell us about the 'unvast minority' of your official email messages that by definition do not fall into your 'vast majority' category -- what about them?"

There was no answer to this question at the press conference, unasked as it was, which of course is the goal of anyone trying to get away with talking merely about the "vast majority" of things in this way. And get away with it she did: No one asked Secretary Clinton about the "capture," "preservation," or very nature of whatever types of email messages she so evidently was not including within the "vast" confines of her statement.[30]

All she said about them (again, by dint of her exact phrasing) is that these messages were by definition other than "to government employees at their government addresses." All right, so could those recipients have been foreign governments, international organizations, or perhaps even lobbyists or their ilk? All we know, even if we were to accept (just for a moment) her claims of "capture and preservation" on their faces, is that they were not Federal Government recipients for which such steps could conceivably be viable.

This means, of course, that these email messages could have been sent to any recipient. Or, for all we know, some of them could have been *received from* any such person or entity, in which case Secretary Clinton's ever-so-confident categorical claim of "capture" is even more slippery. Moreover, we have no good idea of exactly how many (i.e., what percentage) of her emails (sent or received) fall within her "unvast minority" rubric.[31] Does "vast" mean 95% or could it mean only as little as 55%? No one knows, not even any State Department official (for FRA-related reasons that are discussed below), because she purposely tried to leave that as entirely unknown. And at least as of the time of her press conference, she did not just try to do this, she greatly succeeded.[32]

And Secretary Clinton likewise succeeded in other ways as well. One of them was through her use of the tiniest of words, but one that holds an enormous potential for purposeful vagueness and ambiguity. I speak here of the word "it," which when used in a clear, singular context is fully communicative and entirely benign. But if used in a context that includes multiple things, it can be abused (double meaning intended) to hide the truth of what is being referred to by anyone who has a motivation to skirt that full truth. And in this case, there are indeed multiple things, very distinct things, that could be contained within (or together consist of) the scope of that pronoun.

"Others had done it," is what Secretary Clinton defensively proclaimed on March 10. What is clear here is that she was referring to previous secretaries of state, especially former Secretary of State Colin L. Powell. What is not clear is exactly what conduct she was referring to, because of her careless (or perhaps care*ful*) use of the all-purpose word "it." "It" could refer to her use of a personal phone device tied to a personal email account. "It" could be her total failure to properly use an official State Department email account at all. "It" could be her use of a private server in connection with her personal email account. "It" could have meant any or all of those things.[33]

By this point in her press conference, it was well-established (read: admitted) that what Secretary Clinton "had done" was use her personal email device and a personal email account, plus her personal email server, to the exclusion of using the official State Department email system, exclusively -- i.e., for all of her official communications.[34] That was the true "it." And the actual fact was that no one had ever done *that*, at least not at the State Department (nor at any other federal agency as near as could be determined), before.[35]

Take former Secretary of State Colin Powell, for instance. His four-year tenure in that position preceded Secretary Clinton's by eight years and began in 2001, when the State Department's official email systems were antiquated and in many respects still developing. Reflective of that, Secretary Powell had used both a personal email account for some of his communications (on an ancient version of a PDA which worked over a phone line in his office at the State Department), and an official State Department account for others.

So Secretary Powell did not in fact use a personal account exclusively, as Secretary Clinton had done. Nor did he use a private server as she admittedly had done. Rather, he used only an antiquated America Online account, through a server maintained by that Internet service provider. This alone meant that none of his email messages were beyond the reach of congressional subpoenas up in the "cloud," whereas all of Secretary Clinton's were. The difference between the two was enormous.

Nor did former Secretary of State Condoleezza Rice, who immediately preceded Secretary Clinton, do anything that she did when it came to electronic mail. First and foremost, Secretary Rice did not use any "personal email account to conduct official business" during her tenure. That was the specific finding made by the State Department's Inspector General, about both Secretary Rice and previous Secretary of State Madeleine J. Albright (Secretary Powell's immediate predecessor) after Secretary Clinton falsely claimed that "[p]revious secretaries of state have said they *did the same thing.*" Yes, what she said about her predecessors was, in context of all of her words, condemnably false. And yet in her press conference, she claimed that to be so, over and over.

And then there is the matter of how Secretary Clinton handled the State Department's belated insistence that she "return" all of the work-related email messages that, after her departure as secretary of state, still remained in her sole possession.[36] In putative "compliance" with this, she had already relegated to herself the right to decide which ones of those retained emails were purely "personal" -- which she had already destroyed, she said, employing her self-serving idea that only she (or, worse yet, those working for her, undertaking a mechanical "keyword search" approach) could know which particular ones of those emails "could possibly be work related." This subject did draw some pointed questions at the press conference, for which she had some ill-considered answers.

About this, she said the following: "In going through the emails, there were over 60,000 in total, sent and received. About half were work-related and went to the State Department and about half were personal that were not in any way related to my work. I had no reason to save them, but that was my decision because the federal guidelines are clear and the State Department request was clear." To that, one first has to wonder what the hell was she doing with as many as 30,000 emails that were purely personal during her four-year tenure?[37] And what "guidelines" was she talking about? There were no such "guidelines."

And then she went on to claim: "For any government employee, it is that government employee's responsibility to determine what's personal and what's work-related." As a matter of law, however, this was patently untrue. FOIA officers do this, and Federal Records Act officers do this; employees alone should not. For example, a presidential appointee in Michigan once was castigated by a federal judge for insisting that he, too, could take it entirely upon himself to decide which records in his office were "personal" and which were not.[38]

And Secretary Clinton's defense of what she had already done (read: destroy half the records) went on: "I am very confident of the process that we conducted and the emails that were produced [and] have absolute confidence that everything that could be in any way connected to work is now in the possession of the State Department.... And I feel like once the American public begins to see the emails, they will have an unprecedented insight into a high [sic] government official's daily communications, which I think will be quite interesting." Neither of these two things, of course, was probative of the asserted correctness of the record destruction that she had already undertaken.

So then she was asked: "How could the public be assured that when you deleted emails that were personal in nature, that you didn't also delete emails that were professional, but possibly unflattering?" To which she gave this blunt, off-the-cuff reply: "Well first of all, you have to ask that question to every single federal employee, because the way the system works, the federal employee, the individual, whether they have one device, two devices, three devices, how many addresses, they make the decision." Untrue.

And to which she nonsensically added: "So, even if you have a work-related device with a work-related .gov account, you choose what goes on that. That is the way our system works. And so we trust and count on the judgment of thousands, maybe millions of people to make those decisions. And I feel that I did that and even more, that I went above and beyond what I was requested to do. And again, those [emails] will be out in the public domain, and people will be able to judge for themselves." *None* of this was true as a matter of law and practice under the Federal Records Act, at least not in the way she made it sound to be.[39]

So yes, Secretary Clinton's suggestion that federal officials can unilaterally determine which of their records are "personal" and which are "official," even in the face of a FOIA request, is laughable. Indeed, as the saying goes, "reality is not her friend."[40]

But on December 5, 2014, taking *de facto* control of the process, Clinton's lawyers had delivered 12 file boxes filled with printed paper containing more than 30,000 emails. In all, Clinton had withheld almost 32,000 emails deemed by her to be of a "personal" nature. And as to this, she claimed the following: "I provided all my emails that could possibly be work-related, which totaled roughly 55,000 printed pages, even though I knew that the State Department already had the vast majority of them. We went through a thorough process to identify all of my work-related emails and deliver them to the State Department." Yes, she had had a "process," all right.

What all of this amounted to, of course, except for the parts responding to unscripted questions, was a circumspectly crafted defense that upon close examination is highly misleading at best and manifestly deceptive at worst in nearly all of its key respects.[41] And the very fact that Hillary Clinton proceeded in this way on this subject, with words so readily identifiable as deceptive, itself revealed her deep concern for the vulnerability of her position.[42] Given that, the entire thrust of her press conference was: "Everything is fine, nothing to be seen here, so let's all just move along."[43]

Indeed, Secretary Clinton would not have had to resort to such depths of wordplay had she a more defensible case to make for her actions to begin with. So by erecting this multi-faceted defense in such a fashion -- and to no small success judging by the relatively minimal media coverage of the subject in the press conference's immediate aftermath -- she made her own credibility on such matters an open issue, even beyond the many issues surrounding her actions and inactions.[44]

* * * * *

So now we move beyond that press conference of March 10 and the multitude of deceptive statements made by Secretary Clinton at it. I wrote my analysis of them in a lengthy article for *POLITICO Magazine*, in which I was kinder to her than is this chapter in many respects, including the article's limited emphasis on her server problems and its total eschewal of the subject of classified information, not to mention that latter element's implications for possible criminal exposure.[45]

But even with these initial self-restraints, that article's in-depth critique of what she actually said about what she had done and had not done led to some follow-up media attention to the controversy. As did media focus on the element of national security classification. And in time, Secretary Clinton was forced to make additional public statements about her misconduct that at first held firm to the words of her press conference -- but then slowly began to retreat from them bit by bit -- such as:

- July 7, 2015, in a CNN interview: "Everything I did was permitted. There was no law. There was no regulation. There was nothing that did not give me the full authority to decide how I was going to communicate. Everything I did was permitted by law and regulation. I had one device. When I mailed anybody in the government, it would go into the government system." Nearly all of that was false.

- August 14, 2015: "I was permitted to and used a personal email." Half true.

- September 7, 2015: "What I did was allowed. It was allowed by the State Department. The State Department has confirmed that." Entirely false.

- September 9, 2015: Under the heading "Clinton Apologizes for What She Calls 'A Mistake,'" she gave an interview to ABC News's David Muir, admitting that her failure to use two separate accounts (i.e., including an official one) was "a mistake." Entirely true.

  She went on: "What I had done was allowed, it was above board. But in retrospect, certainly, as I look back at it now, even though it was allowed, I should've used two accounts. One for personal, one for work-related emails.

That was a mistake. I'm sorry about that. I take responsibility. And I'm try-ing to be as transparent as I possibly can to not only release 55,000 pages of my emails, turn over my server." Previously, she had told MSNBC's Andrea Mitchell that she was "sorry that this has been confusing to people and raised a lot of questions." Mostly true.

- February 6, 2016: In a debate with Senator Bernard "Bernie" Sanders, Clinton said that she had "absolutely no concerns about" an ongoing investigation focusing on classified information, claiming "I never sent or received any clas-sified material." But he, in turn, all too graciously let her off the hook. Untrue.

Then, as her presidential campaign progressed, Secretary Clinton asked others to speak on her behalf. First, spokesman Nicholas Merrill defended her use of her personal server and email accounts as being in compliance with the "letter and spirit of the rules." And her campaign spokesman Brian E. Fallon, Jr., spoke of the classification problem, saying: "She was at worst a passive recipient of unwitting information that subsequently became deemed as classified." Another Clinton campaign spokeswoman, Jennifer M. Palmieri, stressed that Clinton "was permitted to use her own email account as a government employee and that the same process concerning classification reviews would still be taking place had she used the standard 'state.gov' email account used by most department employees." None of this, as shown above, was true.

And then there was a spokesperson who also was personally embroiled in Secretary Clinton's records regime. Jacob J. "Jake" Sullivan reportedly either au-thored (215 of them) or forwarded many email messages containing potentially classified information that ended up with Hillary's other emails. She was said to be the author of messages that appeared on several email chains that subsequently not only were classified, they were labeled "Top Secret" by the State Department.

Sullivan had been Hillary's top foreign policy aide for years,[46] which meant that his communications with her were much more likely than those of others to involve national security information that, *at a minimum*, warranted expert review in order to determine its potential classification status.[47] So it should have come as no surprise to either him or Secretary Clinton that many of the messages with which they both were involved did receive classification designations once they were, after the "scandal" broke, properly reviewed.[48]

* * * * *

At this point, Secretary Clinton's "email scandal," as it by then was almost univer-sally referred to, began to transcend the realm of mere media coverage and became embroiled in multiple investigations -- and different types of them, at that. The first of these was an internal one that was conducted within the Department of State -- and it was long overdue.

On May 25, 2016, State Department Inspector General Steven A. Linick released an 83-page report that methodically contradicted almost everything that Hillary Clinton and her spokespersons had been saying about the scandal up to that point. No, it said, her self-serving email set-up was not "allowed" under the State Department's rules. No, she was not "permitted" to use a personal email system exclusively as she had. No, what she did was hardly just a matter of her "personal convenience." No, there is no evidence that any State Department attorney (other than perhaps Secretary Clinton herself) ever gave "legal approval" to any part of her own special email system.

No, everything she did was not "fully above board" or in compliance with the "letter and spirit of the rules," far from it. Yes, she was indeed required by the FRA to maintain all of her official emails in an official system for proper review, delineation, and retention upon her departure.[49] And yes, by the way, her private server equipment not only was noncompliant, it was in fact the subject of multiple attempted intrusion attempts (i.e., hacks), including by foreign nations.[50]

This was a damning blow, but it was in effect only a "civil law indictment" of Secretary Clinton, not a criminal law one. That distinction was important to her -- for obvious reasons -- as well as for accurate public perception, especially as any potential criminal aspect of what she had and had not done was to be based upon the ingredient of national security classification.

CIVIL LAW

When most people hear the phrase "violates the law," or "is contrary to law," or perhaps even the word "unlawful," they tend to think that the conduct being spoken of is a violation of some criminal law for which there are criminal penalties. But some laws and legal obligations are only civil in nature, for which there exist only monetary or administrative sanctions at most. Such is the case with federal records laws such as the Federal Records Act and the Freedom of Information Act, which govern the conduct of federal employees and officials, even that of former Secretary of State Hillary Clinton.

What's more, the civil sanctions provided in these laws can be applied only to people who *still remain federal employees* at the time at which their violation is discovered and acted upon. In other words, if you violate these laws and then leave government service quickly enough, you are beyond the reach of their penalties. This is reminiscent of a common refrain among political appointees during the latter part of the George W. Bush Administration, which was: "That's OK, because by the time anyone finds out about it, we'll be long gone."

The Federal Records Act is a decades-old federal law that governs such things as the creation, maintenance, preservation, and disposition of federal records, regardless of form or format, including electronic records such as electronic mail. Simply put, it tells those who work for the Federal Government that they must document their work and keep the resulting records safe during their tenures. Then, when someone leaves a federal position, the FRA requires that all such records be reviewed in conjunction with an agency records officer so that the agency (i.e., not the employee or his or her aides alone) can make decisions about which records should be preserved and which will be disposed of as unneeded. Then the employee is required to actually sign a document certifying that this has been done comprehensively and accurately, lest that not be the case.[51]

Any failure to meet these legal obligations, from the beginning of an employee's tenure to the end, is punishable with administrative sanctions up to and including dismissal. And the entire process, as a regulatory scheme existing by statutory command, is overseen by agency records officers, by an agency's chief records officer, and by the FRA experts at the National Archives and Records Administration ("NARA"), who hold ultimate responsibility for making sure that the FRA's requirements are properly administered.[52]

The importance of the FRA's proper implementation becomes quite evident when, for example, questions arise about the propriety of some agency activity (sometimes in full "controversy" or even "scandal" mode). Then the records pertaining to that activity need to be reviewed by an agency inspector general, by federal law enforcement personnel, or even by congressional investigators on behalf of a legislative committee. If all relevant records have not been properly preserved, then such inquiries are greatly impaired and sometimes the word "cover-up" is used.

Furthermore, the official availability of a federal agency's electronic mail communications is not just a matter of concern for purposes of the Federal Records Act only. It also makes an enormous (and highly foreseeable) difference to the proper implementation of the Freedom of Information Act (known as the "FOIA" to its friends, a group that evidently does not include Secretary Clinton). When a FOIA request is made to a federal agency, that agency has a legal obligation to search for all agency records responsive to that request's subject matter according to the terms of that request. But if a responsive record is not maintained in a readily searchable form or location, then the FOIA can readily be circumvented as a result.

That is because the starting point for handling a FOIA request is the search that an agency must conduct for all records responsive to that request's particular specifications. So any FOIA request that requires an agency to locate responsive email messages sent to or from that agency's head, for instance, is necessarily dependent on those records being locatable to begin with. And an agency simply cannot do that properly for any emails (let alone *all* such emails) that have been created, and are maintained, entirely beyond the agency's reach. Or as it sometimes is said somewhat cynically in the FOIA community, "You can't disclose what you can't find."

Indeed, in setting up her own personal recordkeeping regime, Secretary Clinton also managed to flagrantly circumvent the requirements of the Freedom of Information Act in the face of literally dozens of FOIA requests for access to her official records -- requests that she doubtless knew about, at least through her personal aides, yet blithely ignored. In so doing, she very arguably became the biggest "FOIA felon" (without having committed a "felony") in that Act's 50-year history.[53]

So these are the civil laws that Hillary Clinton so plainly broke or blatantly circumvented -- primarily the Federal Records Act and secondarily the FOIA -- in the growing, wide-ranging scandal surrounding her exclusive use of a personal email account, which was compounded by her use of a private email server, during nearly the entirety of her four-year tenure. Her misconduct violated the FRA from beginning to end, including through what appears to be her utter failure to meet any of the requirements placed on a departing employee.[54] This amounted to what can be viewed as the biggest, most consequential violation of the FRA in its history, as well as a circumvention of the FOIA the likes of which had never before been seen.[55]

Indeed, from her abject failure to properly ensure that all of her work-related emails were captured and maintained for recordkeeping purposes (not to mention responsibly restored after that initial failure), to her entirely unprecedented use of "private server" equipment, to her indulgently irresponsible supervision of her personal aides, and on down to her utter failure to follow any of the FRA's clear requirements upon her departure, Hillary Clinton self-servingly managed to elide all of these statutory commands like no one before her. And any requiem for "emailgate" should include full recognition of the fact that she so brazenly (read: and effectively) turned a blind eye to these statutes' legal requirements -- requirements that applied even though they carried no criminal penalties, nor any penalties at all for a since-departed federal official.

Yes, there were absolutely no penalties applicable to Hillary Clinton for any of this misconduct. The FRA, if violated, does provide a basis for some action being taken against a federal employee -- but only a personnel-type administrative action that simply does not work if the employee is "long gone." And as for the FOIA, in turn, it does contain a little-known sanction, in subsection (a)(4)(F)(1) of the Act, but there as well even it is available only as against someone who has remained in federal service. So what the public is left with, in the case of these key federal records laws, is a statutory scheme that is effectively toothless in many instances, especially in the cases of law-flouting political employees such as Hillary Clinton who seem to just do whatever they please and can get away with -- literally -- at least when it comes to civil laws.

NATIONAL SECURITY CLASSIFICATION

Then there is the matter of national security classification. The current executive order on that, which was issued by President Obama in December of 2009 (i.e., not long after Secretary Clinton's records regime commenced), continues the White House's traditional emphasis on protecting both "foreign government information" and information the disclosure of which could be expected to cause "foreign relations harm." Most significantly, these are historically broad categories that can easily be implicated through even indirect reference to serious international matters at a high level. So it is not at all easily imaginable that a 21st-century secretary of state could manage to spend four years in office without including at least *some* information in her official email traffic that *at the very least* called for a careful classification review.[56] Indeed, to even begin to think or suggest otherwise is pure folly.

The Department of State had a special procedure for this. It had an entirely separate (read: "firewalled") electronic mail system for use by any employee to send messages (and to receive like replies) that could possibly be deemed classified upon expert review. And this system naturally was used quite heavily for purposes of the State Department's "foreign relations" communications in compliance with its national security obligations.

In Secretary Clinton's case, given that the very nature of her position involved the *creation* and receipt of classified information (i.e., she was a veritable "walking source" of freshly generated foreign relations information), this unquestionably required her to use this special email system that is devoted to national security protection. But she simply did not do so, plainly as part of her scheme to use her own personal email account (in conjunction with her own private server) exclusively. And her failure to do so was not just occasional or inadvertent, it was damnably systemic.[57]

Secretary Clinton tried to defend this by pointing out that her emails were not marked "classified" when sent. None of her emails, she said, contained any "information marked as classified." What she left unsaid, however, was that she was the one who controlled this "marking" status of her emails, given that she sent them through her own system, not the State Department's. And there also was the highly inconvenient (read: for her) fact that she had signed a nondisclosure agreement that explicitly stated that classified material might be "marked *or* unmarked."

Indeed, the fact that Secretary Clinton bypassed the State Department's special system for classified or potentially classifiable emails[58] became a matter of possible criminal negligence. And this was especially so given that she did so, as stated above, *systemically*. In other words, her very email scheme itself appeared to have been a walking violation of criminal law.

CRIMINAL LAW

The criminal law part of this picture is the most acute one, and it is not an easy one for even experienced legal practitioners to bring into focus.[59] First and foremost, as is indicated above, it is based upon Secretary Clinton's handling, or rather her mishandling, of classified or potentially classifiable information. Once that element was added to picture, it became far more serious, and it led to the FBI conducting its own investigation of her misconduct, under the personal direction of FBI Director James B. Comey, Jr.

It also was clouded by the presence of two distinct legal *mens rea* standards for determining criminal culpability: "specific intent" and "gross negligence." Most crimes are "intent" crimes, with a prosecutor having to establish at trial the defendant's specific intention to act in violation of the law.[60] And at least some evidence of that intention is required before that defendant is charged to stand trial (e.g., is indicted) in the first place.

In this case, despite much supporting evidence of "intent,"[61] the FBI concluded that there existed insufficient "clear evidence" that either Secretary Clinton or any of her closely involved aides violated any of the applicable laws (e.g., pertaining to record removal, record destruction, or the protection of classified information) that required a showing of "intent." So those serious possible violations of law were "off the table," so to speak.

Yet there is also an applicable criminal statute, found at 18 U.S.C. § 793(f), that makes it a felony to mishandle classified information with "gross negligence." This particular statute thus does not hold a putative defendant's conduct to the hard-to-prove "specific intent" standard; rather, Congress has made it triggered by an individual's mere "gross negligence," due to the exceptional need to safeguard information of national security sensitivity.

It should be obvious to anyone that this is a far easier standard of criminal culpability for a prosecutor to satisfy at trial, as well as to use when determining whether to bring charges in the first place. In fact, it is this standard of conduct that is explicitly applied to federal employees when they sign, as Secretary Clinton did, the nondisclosure agreements that are handed to them when they are first provided access to especially sensitive national security information.[62]

But in a surprise (read: in more ways than one) public announcement on July 5, 2016, FBI Director Jim Comey abruptly declared that the FBI would not be "recommending" any criminal prosecution of Secretary Clinton whatsoever, including under the applicable "gross negligence" statute.[63] Notwithstanding all evidence to the contrary, he concluded that even this lesser statutory standard was not met in Hillary Clinton's case. Rather, he declared conclusively that she and the close personal aides under her direct supervision "were extremely careless in their handling of very sensitive, highly classified information," but that they somehow were not "grossly negligent" in doing so.[64]

This decision, unprecedented in multiple ways, surprised most interested observers, confounded many others, and raised a host of questions both legal and political. Most of all, for those who might wonder (be they attorneys or not) exactly how someone can be "extremely careless" about such very important things without being "grossly negligent," Director Comey offered little satisfying explanation of this, neither in his fifteen-minute announcement nor in his four-hour follow-up congressional testimony.

In fact, he did not even attempt to somehow draw an analytical line between the two terms. Rather, he spoke indulgently of Secretary Clinton's professed "un-sophistication" with classified matters ("It's possible -- possible -- that she didn't understand what a 'C' meant when she saw it in the body of an email like that."),[65] of the nature and history of Section 793(f), and of the perceived rarity of her case in relation to any other national security prosecution under a "gross negligence" standard. In other words, he was giving her the benefit of being unique; it was as if he were saying that her complex email scheme, unprecedented as it was, was simply too novel for such a high-level prosecution, that because she alone had had the "bright idea" of doing it, she should get away scot free.[66]

And no matter what anyone thought of any of this, Jim Comey's remarkable decision stood.[67]

* * * * *

In retrospect, it is painfully clear that Secretary of State Hillary Clinton could have avoided all of this -- every last bit of it, in both its civil and criminal aspects -- had she just eschewed her hubris-driven email chicanery and not tried to "beat the system" as she did. It would not have taken much, actually, when one thinks about it.

One need look no further than the fateful decision that brand-new Secretary of State Clinton made one day in early 2009, for whatever reason or reasons, not to "play by the rules." Even at that, Undersecretary of State for Management Patrick F. Kennedy should have stopped (rather than indulged and enabled) her from following such a plainly unlawful course.[68] Someone at the White House, likely knowing better, should have overridden her.[69] And at least one of her hyper-devoted, sycophantic personal aides (e.g., Cheryl Mills, who from her own White House experience definitely did know better)[70] should have protected her from her dangerously secretive self.

Indeed, all it would have taken was for her to act like any other State Department official, or any other member of Barack Obama's cabinet for that matter. First, when she arrived there, she would have had to begin using an official agency email account, one ending in "state.gov," for her basic official email communications. Patrick Kennedy and his staff would have set this account up for her, as he should have, regardless of her professed degree of technical proficiency or desire for singular expediency.[71] This having been done, as would have been ordinary and routine, Secretary Clinton would have had no occasion to involve a private email server in her State Department business.[72]

And then, if she were ever forced by exceptional circumstances to use her personal email account for the conduct of some official business (such as at 3 AM with some part of the world exploding somewhere overseas) her aides would have routinely retrieved those emails (both outgoing and incoming) for direct placement on State's official email system, through use of a regular State Department official email account, just as the Federal Records Act, proper State Department practices, and the fair administration of the Freedom of Information Act required. And here's the "kicker": Had she done so, she certainly could have kept her truly "personal" emails on her private server once they were properly generated through a personal email account, not her official one, if she so preferred.[73]

Then, throughout her tenure, Secretary Clinton would have had to just use the State Department's counterpart "classified system" for any email messages generated by her, sent to her, or forwarded by her that contained information classified or potentially classifiable on national security grounds. Inasmuch as one of those legal grounds is "foreign relations," and as Secretary of State she was the very voice of U.S. foreign relations policy, this would have involved at least some of her emails (read: many, actually) and would have allowed the State Department's classification experts to properly and routinely reach judgments about their classification sensitivity and act on them accordingly, wherever need be -- just as they did for everyone else (read: the "ordinary" folks) in the entire State Department.

And finally, just like other federal employees, she of course would have had to engage in an end-of-tenure process of organizing her files (read: having it done for her, with her input), including her official emails, for archival preservation when she left office in 2013. This would have been a relatively simple process, even for a cabinet official, because the vast bulk (read: a phrase that is apt here) of her truly personal emails during her tenure would not have been part of the official State Department system and would not have required review by anyone. Again, Undersecretary Kennedy and his staff should have helped her in meeting this "departing official" requirement rather than, as appears to be the case, irresponsibly ignoring it. Indeed, under the Federal Records Act, it was their responsibility, as well as hers, to ensure that this was done.

If all of this had happened, Secretary Clinton would not have violated the State Department's rules requiring necessary use of its special classified email system. She would not have placed any classified information at any type of risk on her private server. She would not have effectively circumvented the FOIA. And she would not have recidivistically violated the Federal Records Act from the outset and again at the end of her tenure in 2013 by failing to allow proper preservation of her official records.[74]

Plus, there would have been no inspector general's report to so bluntly "put the lie to" so much of what she had said in her attempted defense of her actions and inactions from the time of her original press conference to long after her statements could be credibly (even to her mind) maintained.[75] And perhaps most important of all, there would have been no embarrassing FBI investigation and damning FBI finding that, even if she arguably lacked prosecutable intent, she nevertheless had been "extremely careless" in her classified (read: and classifiable) email handling.[76]

* * * * *

A final note: When I began writing and speaking publicly about Hillary Clinton's email transgressions in March of 2015, there were some who said to me -- in person, by email, or even online -- that by so pointedly critiquing both her words and her deeds I was, in effect, aiding her eventual opponent should she win the presidential nomination. So I considered this at the time and then I considered it again once she and Donald J. Trump became their parties' respective nominees. By that later time, I had already written many articles on the subject, had appeared on several live interview programs (both TV and radio), and had been interviewed about it by numerous mainstream media outlets.[77]

But the reason that I continued with this, even writing a column about her for an online news outlet,[78] is that she persisted, intransigently, in saying (read: stating, not just implying) things about her email-related conduct that I knew to be flat-out false -- not as a mere matter of opinion, mind you, but as a matter of what I knew to be true as actual fact. Having spent my legal career being responsible for the fair and proper implementation of federal laws, I just could not stand silent as she boldly misstated, mischaracterized, and even touted her flouting of them.

Plus, I frankly found the notion of my own public assessment of her conduct having any tangible adverse effect on her candidacy to be somewhat far-fetched (or at a minimum, near-fetched). So that left me standing as perhaps her most acute critic on this subject (at least on the civil side), which was fine with me, especially inasmuch as I respected her unique accomplishments in so many other regards -- just not on this, where she was dead wrong, cleverly "got away with" something, and seemed too scared or stubborn to admit it even with the passage of time.[79]

Today, several years later, the "scared" possibility ought to have faded,[80] together with her presidential hopes -- although there are those who now say that "she might just run again," even if it were to mean challenging an incumbent president of her own political party (read: as Senator Edward M. "Ted" Kennedy did with President Jimmy Carter in 1979 (see Chapter Nineteen)).

And if that is so, then it might explain why former Secretary Clinton reacted as she did to the repercussions of the FBI's "Mar-a-Lago raid" of August 8, 2022, amid the Government's efforts to recover classified White House records, *inter alia*, that were wrongfully appropriated by former President Donald J. Trump in blatant violation of the Presidential Records Act and heaven knows how many potentially applicable criminal statutes as well. It did not take long before comparisons between the two of them were made and Clinton doubtless felt renewed heat about what she had done. (Some even weaker comparisons were made with small amounts of classified records that were found by President Joe Biden's personal attorneys during January of 2023 in an office used by Biden after he left the vice presidency.)

Unsurprisingly, her first line of defense to this was to complain about the very fact that she now felt forced to deal with the subject again: "I can't believe we're still talking about this ... I'm more tired of talking about this than anyone ... I'm sick about [sic] talking about my emails."[81] And next there was a response that contained multiple echoes of the past: "[T]he right is trying to make this about me again. . . . It's a witch hunt."

And then, perhaps due to such evident frustration, Secretary Clinton began going so far as to make wild claims about the classified information that was contained in her server. Over and again, she indignantly claimed that she had had nothing on her server that was classified: "The fact is that I had *zero* emails that *were* classified" (emphasis supplied).[82]

It is difficult to understand why she said this, as it inevitably led to headlines such as "Clinton Exaggerates Absence of Classified Information in Her Emails" from the Poynter Institute for Media Studies' PolitiFact Project, for example, atop a spate of other "Hillary Clinton Exaggerates" articles. This time, her bold claim of "zero" was belied by three separate investigations -- one by the FBI, one by the Justice Department's inspector general (whom I happen to know well and trust), and one by the inspector general at the Department of State.

And while their numbers varied somewhat due to differences in what they examined, they all found that no fewer than 110 emails on Hillary Clinton's home server contained classified information that was classified at the time they were sent or received (read: placed on the server), of which eight were at the "Top Secret" level or higher, with some labeled as "Special Access Program" materials.

So one has to wonder not only why Clinton set up such an email system in the first place, but why on earth she made such extreme, readily disprovable claims in the wake of the Trump debacle. I daresay that this leaves any rational observer concluding that on this particular thing (read: perhaps no others) she is just far too obdurate and prideful -- almost as a psychological imperative -- to ever admit that she was wrong. Badly wrong.[83]

CHAPTER FORTY-EIGHT
UFO Secrecy

"Sanitation worker A: 'Did you see that?'
Sanitation worker B: 'No, and neither did you, so shut up!'"

-- Two sanitation workers, after witnessing a Klingon ship commandeered by Captain James T. Kirk landing in Golden Gate Park, in *Star Trek IV: The Voyage Home,* 1986

Many years ago, during the "Star Wars missile-defense" era of the Reagan Administration, I received a call from a former client at the National Security Agency ("NSA," to its surveilees) at Fort George Meade, Maryland, who had risen two notches in rank since we had last spoken. "Dan," he or she said,[1] "I need to ask you a question without having asked you, if you know what I mean." Having been approached like this several times before, I gave my stock answer: "Sure, go ahead, [insert name], that's fine."[2]

This caller then proceeded to say that he or she had just come out of a "compartment-clearance pre-meeting" (which is held to ensure in advance that everyone expected to attend a prospective meeting holds the necessary national security clearances)[3] in which this person had been vetted to attend a very high-level, multi-agency meeting in which the primary question would be: "Can we lawfully withhold, other than through national security classification, records indicating physical interplanetary contact?" Odd as that phrasing might sound, it is exactly what was asked.[4]

Only mildly surprised, I resisted the urge to reply, "Gee, [insert name], what the hell do you think we developed 'High 2' for?" (See Chapter Forty-Six.) But I gave this person only a straight answer, given that we were on an open line and this was, after all, NSA that I was talking to -- and mindful also that this "professional friend" was taking more than a little risk in calling me on an open line about such a thing to begin with. So I said: "Yes, you possibly could, if this were part of an agency decisionmaking process (as it arguably would be), in which even a basic fact could fall within the scope of that deliberative process and thus be privileged under FOIA Exemption 5."[5] This colleague was grateful to hear this as well as for the coda that I added about how in such a context one could handle even a "targeted" FOIA request by carefully employing "Glomarization" (see Chapter Seventeen). And then I never heard another word about it.

Now I am a bit embarrassed to admit that I never followed up with this person on this, even though it would have been possible only in person or on what was back then a brand-new "STU-III" phone device (which automatically afforded encryption). Surely, I blithely thought, I would soon hear more about it, which I suppose we must chalk up to stellar naiveté on my part. So, sorry to say, this story's denouement is left to speculation.[6] (But anyone who is interested in the subject need only Google the relatively recent public disclosures of the Defense Intelligence Agency's "Advanced Aerospace Threat Identification Program" (see below), as succeeded by the "Unidentified Aerial Phenomena Task Force" of the Office of Naval Intelligence (see below) and then the Pentagon's "Airborne Object Identification and Management Synchronization Group" ("AOIMSG") (see further below) and even more recently by the Pentagon's newest such entity, the "All-Domain Anomaly Resolution Office" ("AARO").)[7] Or you could read on.

Of course, the subject of "UFO secrecy" is a highly complex, exceptionally challenging, and sometimes even political (not to mention, eventually, thoroughly commercialized) one. It has been identified, analyzed, studied, categorized, bureaucratically "committee'd," advanced, second-guessed, debated, debunked, explained, written about, explicated, critiqued, criticized, broadcast, and otherwise publicized in the United States for decades now, going back to at least 1947,[8] the year of both the claimed "UFO crash" (or crashes) near Roswell, New Mexico (in late June), and the "initial sighting" by aviator Kenneth Arnold of nine "flying saucers"[9] flying in what he said appeared to him to be a clear formation near Mount Rainier, Washington, not much more than a week earlier.[10] These two things together marked the dawn of the modern era of "UFO secrecy." And with that came a new, very particular brand of government secrecy.

* * * * *

So much has been investigated, reinvestigated, written, said, broadcast, rebroadcast, supplemented, amended, doubted, refuted, revisited, and updated about the "Roswell incident," with all of its implications and repercussions, that less than that need be said about it here.[11] A major exception to this is the little-reported (i.e., in the "mainstream media") *alleged* claim by German aerospace pioneer Dr. Wernher M. von Braun (who through "Operation Paperclip" was clandestinely brought from Germany to the United States at the end of World War II and then held high-level positions at NASA)[12] that he was asked by the Truman White

House to personally inspect the "Roswell debris," which was possible due to the fact that evidently he already was nearby at the "White Sands Proving Ground" testing captured V-2 rockets at the time.

As much as such a confluence of themes was a "ufologist's" dream -- especially as Dr. von Braun's alleged Roswell "debris descriptions" very closely matched those of U.S. Army Air Force Major Jesse Marcel's son (who claimed to have examined some such debris at age 11 when his father, the military's initial crash investigator, took it "home from work") -- this is a story that, to say the very least, is hardly free of doubt. Indeed, it has multiple conflicting (or now commercially competing) versions, depending on whom you ask.

Central players in the story include William W. "Mack" Brazel, the ranch foreman who evidently started it all off in late June of 1947 (some say as late as July 2) when he discovered some "crash debris" on his employer's ranch; patrons at a bar in nearby Corona, New Mexico, where Brazel reportedly first displayed some of the debris; George Wilcox, the local sheriff to whom he next took that debris; and Major Jesse A. Marcel, Sr., the local Army Air Force intelligence officer at Roswell Army Air Force Base (so named because the Air Force did not "split off of" the Army to become its own military department until three months later, in October of 1947), who evidently took some additionally discovered (read: by him, together with fellow intelligence officer Sheridan W. Cavitt) debris home with him to show to his wife and son.[13] (At first, the Air Force actually announced that it was an alien craft that had crash landed, which was "picked up" by the local newspaper and then circulated around the world (read: or perhaps galaxy), but then the Air Force quickly changed that story, with Major Marcel's seemingly witting acquiescence.)

In time, they all claimed (either directly themselves or indirectly through surviving family members) that the Air Force took complete control over all discovered debris, likewise took control over all "public relations" on it, and then firmly ordered everyone involved, and their families, not to speak of the incident, ever. This admonition, these families later publicly said, was so firmly and pointedly stated that it had truly made them fear for their lives. And many decades later, this was credibly reiterated by their surviving family members, friends, and neighbors almost without exception.

Major Marcel, who followed his orders in not speaking to the press,[14] received a promotion to the rank of Lt. Colonel later that year, and he did not speak to anyone other than his family about the incident until 1978. Then, he claimed that the debris had in fact been "otherworldly" and that he had, in effect, both reluctantly and unwittingly (not an easily conjured combination) been part of an official "cover-up." At that point, to "ufologists" around the world, this "confirmation" of a "cover-up," long suspected, resonated strongly in favor of there having been a true "flying saucer crash" -- and, by extension, of there having been alien beings on "the craft" that together with that vehicle were then reportedly transported to what became Wright-Patterson Army Air Force Base in Dayton, Ohio.[15] (Or, in subsequent speculation, taken for "reverse-engineering" to "Area 51.")

Superficially almost as credible, however, is the explanation that the entire incident was a creature of something called "Project MOGUL," a failed Top Secret military experiment operated out of nearby Alamogordo Army Airfield involving dozens of high-altitude neoprene balloons carrying microphones and foil reflectors intended for monitoring sonic booms from anticipated nuclear tests -- or was it "radio messages?" -- by the Soviet Union.

The support for this "conventional" explanation, to many, has seemed both strong and sound.[16] Most notably, this includes the fact that the MOGUL balloon flights (and crashes) were necessarily given "Top Secret" treatment by the military due to their connection to the Soviet Union. And the entire activity was not declassified until the 1990s, whereupon the Air Force belatedly identified it as the exact cause of the "Roswell crash." Could it be that Cold War tensions were so high even by 1947 that the Air Force deemed it preferable to have the world see this as alien activity rather than secretive spying on Russia? Perhaps.

So, so much for that, though admittedly there is so much "evidence" on each side of this seminal UFO mystery (including that the Air Force so abruptly changed the "official" story), which has grown and grown with the passage of time[17] and with the publication of several competing stories of "the Roswell incident" that up until this point one could have reasonably said that, until something further surfaces to tip the balance, you cannot easily reach a firm conclusion about it one way or the other. But with new analysis, I think that you can.[18]

One collateral postscript, though: In April of 2011, the FBI placed on its own "Vault" website a lightly expurgated "letterhead memorandum" ostensibly sent to FBI Director J. Edgar Hoover in March of 1950 that spoke of the Bureau having received informant information about "three so-called flying saucers [that] had been recovered in New Mexico," where "the Government had a very high-powered radar set-up." The document itself appears to be genuine,[19] but that of course is a far cry from concluding that its source information and full contents are accurate. Either way, on its face it does indeed corroborate some reports (read: only "reports") from 1947 that there were three, not just one, crashed objects involved (or at a minimum two crash *sites*).[20]

* * * * *

Ranking right up there with the assassination of President John F. Kennedy -- which remains, to many "students" of it, including myself, a crime still not solved in its entirety (see Chapter Forty-Nine)[21] -- the entire realm of "UFO secrecy" stands as one of the most profound and confounding mysteries of all time, with all of the deep emotion, belief, factual ambiguity, skepticism, disagreement, and controversy that one could ask for.

It has spawned generation after generation of "UFO enthusiasts," from gawkers who converge at the sites of sightings to more serious believers in alien visitation to serious scientists who study the subject objectively to members of the public who are just curious about it (or fascinated by it, in many cases).[22] This has amounted to nothing less than a cultural phenomenon (epistemologically and ontologically speaking) that gripped America more than 75 years ago (and the rest of the world not long thereafter) and has shown no sign whatsoever of abating since then.

It also has spawned a whole "cottage industry" of "UFO proponents" that began with paper handouts, pamphlets, articles, lectures, and books, and then with local radio broadcasts, but has taken on greater and greater sophistication with the advances of the "television age," all within the "mainstream media"[23] -- not to mention that "industry's" adaptation to the Internet and then to the realm of "social media" in increasingly sophisticated forms. And in time, it also became a popular area of study and data collection by academics, "quasi-academics," and other "UFO researchers," with analyses that compete not only with governmental assessments but also with one another, as there sometimes is a scramble to provide "expert" commentary when a significant new UFO sighting (or a series of them, which are called "flaps") occurs.[24]

Indeed, there are many who will readily trace for readers and viewers the long history of such "sightings,"[25] going back in time and folklore about as far as can be imagined, even as far back as needed to envision the presence on Earth of "ancient aliens."[26] And these sightings do not disappoint: In the United States, from the late 1940s onward, and then worldwide, across all continents, there have been initially spasmodic yet nonetheless ever-increasing experiential bases for focusing on the possibility that the Earth is being (or perhaps has been, or both) visited by extraterrestrial beings that use extremely (nay, even inconceivably) advanced technology to fly around in the Earth's skies[27] -- invariably without any visible means of propulsion -- at both low and high altitudes (including under water) and at speeds ranging from astronomically fast to "slow-moving" to "moving erratically" to "abruptly darting" to "zooming" to gliding to spinning in place to drifting to stationary[28] to slowly rotating and to a threatening hover.[29]

According to the most reliable of "UFO sighting" witnesses since 1947, these objects come in all sorts of shapes and sizes, from saucer-like to disc-shaped (most often smooth, metallic, and shiny, but sometimes a "dull pewter") to cigar-shaped to rod-shaped to bell-shaped to inverted bell-shaped to acorn-shaped to inverted bowl-shaped to dome-shaped to U-shaped to C-shaped to whistle-shaped to cone-shaped to can-shaped to cube-shaped to teardrop-shaped to egg-shaped to avocado-shaped to diamond-shaped to marquee-shaped to wedge-shaped to bullet-shaped to football-shaped to crescent-shaped to boomerang-shaped to banana-shaped to mushroom-shaped to carpenter's square-shaped to horseshoe-shaped to bat-shaped to jellyfish-shaped to tadpole-shaped (in China) to parachute-shaped to hoop-shaped to ring-shaped to delta-shaped to pyramid-shaped to helical-shaped to changing shape to flat to square to domed to round to circular to semi-spherical to fully spherical to "like a sphere encasing a cube" or "a cube encasing a sphere" to "like a spinning top moving against the wind" to "like a hole in a cloud" to "like a spiral" to "like a six-pointed star" to oval (with or without protruding antenna) to oblong to cylindrical to elliptical to rectangular to hexagonal to any such shape surrounded by an aura. And even to suspected intelligence-gathering balloons from China.

And further to those that (relatively recently) appear to be quite distinctly triangular (usually equilateral, but sometimes chevron-like, isosceles-like, right-angled, or with an elongated "V shape," possibly inwardly sloped on each side)[30] to drone-like to those that are described (most recently) as "Tic Tac-shaped," ranging in size from just a few feet in diameter to estimated sizes of "several football fields," and often moving slowly and then suddenly accelerating at hypersonic speed or even unheard-of speeds or anomalously maneuvering in the air (such as stopping to reverse course almost instantly, then instantaneously diving or making 90-degree turns or pivoting while moving side to side), unlike anything that could be possible within our understanding of the existing laws of physics.[31]

In darkness, they can appear bright or dim, luminescent or ephemeral, well-defined or "fuzzy" (even to the point of seeming "gaseous"), well-focused or "blurry," or blinking, flashing, flickering, sparkling, scintillating, glistening, glowing, pulsing, pulsating, or even "strobed," observed singly or together in a pattern or formation (sometimes one involving a perceived "mother ship" or a "whole fleet"), from "pinpoints of light" to "balls of light" to "beams of light" (including objects appearing to emit laser beams) to "streaks of light" (sometimes "zig-zagging") to "glowing orbs of light" to bright fireballs to (at low altitudes) blinding lights, halos, or auras. Some reports, particularly of triangular-shaped UFOs, describe those objects as translucent.

Their reported colors and hues cover most of the visible light spectrum, ranging from white to "pure white" to "bright white" to silver to "grayish-silver" to "silvery" (whatever that means) to "bluish-white" to white with a bluish tinge to gray to yellow to grayish-yellow to "bright amber" to "yellowish-orange" to pink to "pinkish-red" to "pinkish-orange" to orange to "orangish-yellow" to "orangish-red" to "burning orange" to fiery red (sometimes steadily blinking) to "reddish" to "reddish-orange"[32] to purplish to brownish-black to blue to green (sometimes alternating) to bluish-green to bluish-purple to bluish-black to black (in daylight) to ultraviolet to "mother-of-pearl" iridescence (or "shimmering") and to multiple combinations thereof, sometimes even changing colors in mid-flight. There even have been some "rainbow-colored" sightings, most recently an "oscillating" one seen over St. John's, Canada, in late 2020.

They reportedly have been viewed from the ground, from aircraft, from ships, and (in a few reported, but usually officially contested, cases) even by astronauts and cameras (either manned or unmanned, including from *Mir, Skylab,* and the International Space Station) up in orbit above Earth,[33] and perhaps even by the detection equipment aboard some satellites. They have been photographed, filmed, videotaped, "re-imaged," "infrared-viewed," audio-recorded, fabricated, and most recently captured even through "smart phone" digital recordings.[34] And while they most often are perceived to be silent, they have been known to emit "static noise," and in the distance sometimes they are heard to hum, especially when reported to have landed.

Yes, there have been scores of reports over the years, from all around the world, of such objects descending from the sky and hovering just a few feet off of the ground or actually landing on the ground for some period of time (often accompanied by dense fog), with a wide variety of reported consequences. Or of them crashing to the ground (usually unobserved, but sometimes after being seen "wobbling for a bit," or tumbling, or exhibiting some other type of aerial distress, as they were observed), but usually with little if any firm evidence remaining afterward, sometimes due to alleged intervention and comprehensive artifact removal by anonymous government (read: usually military) personnel.[35]

And beyond all human observers, reporting through their senses of sight and hearing (and in rare cases even smell), there are also now no fewer than hundreds of cases of such things being "picked up" on radar,[36] with equipment, both military and civilian,[37] of increasing sophistication over time, from basic bistatic radar to passive radar to "imaging" radar to infrared radar (or "FLIR") to "multi-role (or mechanical) electronic scanned array" ("MESA," to its mechanical operators) radar to "active electronically scanned array" ("AESA," to its more sophisticated operators) radar[38] to synthetic-aperture radar ("SAR," to Chinese epidemiologists) to space-based radar ("SBR," to military sabre rattlers) to "GEOINT radar" to something called "SPY-1 radar" to the next generation of radar that will be here before you know it.[39]

A primary factor in such UFO sightings (both reported and possibly not reported) is something that manifestly has existed from the very outset and has faded only slightly with the passage of time. It can be summed up in one word: ridicule. Yes, it appears to be another aspect of human nature[40] that people tend to ridicule others when those others are perceived to be different, weak, or ostensible believers in "unknown things," especially if those things happen to be thought of as "fringy" in some way. Consider the prototypical schoolyard bully, for example. He or she regularly "makes fun of" other children according to these particular characteristics, *inter alia*. And that behavior certainly seems to be universal, both around the world and throughout time.[41]

So, too, is it in any military group setting, a command structure,[42] or in almost any employment setting: The person who "stands out," in any significant way, runs the risk of being "teased" by others, in a way all too reminiscent of childhood, and potentially to a degree (and a consequence) that can be far more serious than anything in childhood ever was. (This is especially so given the fragility of adult reputations in some settings.) In short, employment positions and even entire careers -- especially in organizations such as military ones[43] -- can be adversely affected or even ended by such things.

Now add in the further UFO-related ingredient: What if the source of the "ridicule" is the fact that the person in question spoke of, wrote of, or (worse yet) officially "reported" a UFO sighting (or something of the kind)? As of late June of 1947, i.e., when news of Kenneth Arnold's "flying saucer" sighting started circling around the newspaper world, any such action would have drawn at least some culture-based reaction from grownups and children alike. And depending on the circumstances of the report, as well as the particular setting in which it was made, it could have had especially strong repercussions.

As one high-level government official is known to have phrased it: "You don't want the stigma of being the guy who saw a UFO."[44] (A softer word for this, perhaps, is "taboo," which I would combine with the word "optics" here.) Indeed, the annals of UFO reporting (or *non*reporting) are rife with examples reflective of this,[45] beginning in the late 1940s and continuing (albeit to a lessening degree) to the present day.

But that is not what matters most here. Rather, it is the *fear* of such ridicule, not to mention of ramifications beyond that, that can be the animating factor. In other words, the decision as to whether a UFO sighting report is made or is not made, to begin with, can hinge on this factor alone, as a matter of common sense and understandable self-preservation. Certainly, many pilots have feared "speaking out" about what they, together with their co-pilots, have seen. Air traffic controllers and other radar operators fear this as well, no doubt, to at least some degree. And this fear is not always of mere "teasing" by colleagues or even a heavier form of "ridicule." Sometimes, it has been expressed as a fear of being thought of as a sort of "fringe person" by one's peers, family, neighbors, associates, and even mere acquaintances, and suffering some consequence of that. This is serious stuff; no one takes such a thing lightly.[46]

So when one considers the volume of "UFO sightings" at a particular place, in a particular setting, and during a particular period of time, one must bear this factor of "human nature" (actually, both the ridicule and the fear) in mind. And this applies to sightings by military personnel (pilots or otherwise), by civilian pilots and cabin crews, by all stripe of radar personnel, by civilian authorities on the ground (such as local law enforcement officers and other first responders, who sometimes are no less stunned by what they observe than are pilots), and by just average members of the public (ranging from "credible" ones to persons facially lacking credulity), and from single individuals to groups pretty much the same.[47]

Far, far beyond (read: in perhaps a galaxy of that distance) any reasonable doubt, however, and as governments have consistently and credibly insisted over the years, the "vast majority" of such reported "UFO incidents" are not what they might be suspected to be (i.e., extraterrestrial), but rather are of natural origin, are something man-made (either by our Government or another), or are the result of some or another good-faith mistake, misperception, misunderstanding, or misidentification, as well as some outright hoaxes.[48] The big question, of course, the one that has persisted, seemingly intractably, for more than seven decades now, is: But what about all of the others -- i.e., the "unvast minority" of such reports?

To this must be added the widespread belief that UFO sightings have tended to "cluster" at locations associated with nuclear power, nuclear weaponry, and nuclear technology -- from early testing sites for the atomic bomb to nuclear power plants (with nuclear reactors),[49] ICBM silos, Strategic Air Command bases, nuclear-capable naval vessels, and even nuclear-powered satellites -- in short, the entire gamut of U.S. "nuclear triad" capabilities.[50]

People who focus on this pattern powerfully point out that the sudden dawn of reported UFO activity in the late 1940s[51] and early 1950s[52] coincided with the development of atomic (read: nuclear) power (not to mention the "nuclear arms race" between the U.S. and the Soviet Union) during the first of those two decades, a "correlation" that they maintain is "unmistakable."[53] (Those on the other side of this proposition, though, tend to attach primary significance to the word "reported" in that previous sentence.)

Yet over the course of this history, the idea that any government or its representatives would go to great lengths -- usually surreptitiously, often very elaborately, and sometimes even comically deceptively -- in order to keep such things "secret" is largely a modern, post-World War II contrivance, one that in this case no doubt was heavily fueled by intense Cold War-related anxieties[54] and competition.[55] And no small part of this picture (at least in the U.S.) has been the establishment and operation of Federal Government entities designed (purportedly) to "study" or "investigate" such things, with the assuring but sometimes no more than ostensible idea that this could lead to "the truth" about them -- rather than in fact serving as an effective means of "explaining away,"[56] demystifying, and even "covering up" actual inexplicable[57] UFO activity.[58] Thus was born true "UFO secrecy."

The primary case in point in the U.S. was the United States Air Force's "Project Blue Book," a large and durable "study" of this subject that began in 1952,[59] succeeded two others from the late 1940s,[60] and existed during the 1950s and throughout the entirety of the 1960s. Over the course of that nearly two-decade period of time, there also were two specialized Federal Government examinations of UFO activity, short-term entities known as the "Robertson Panel" in 1953 and the "O'Brien Committee" in 1965.

The former was something convened in secret by the CIA to support its institutional belief that the "UFO phenomenon" presented little or no national security threat and called for "greater debunking" so as to further educate the public along those lines. Its report remained entirely classified for many, many years; when declassified, it revealed that at least one scientist member of the panel concluded that an extraterrestrial explanation was the only possible conclusion for many of the cases analyzed, but he was overruled by the panel majority.

The latter was more of an ad hoc committee that recommended making greater use of universities in the scientific study of UFO phenomena, something that did eventually happen. And neither entity was the same as either "Majestic 12" (see below) or the "Interplanetary Phenomenon Unit," the latter of which is theorized (read: very speculatively) to have been established by General Douglas MacArthur in the late 1940s.

The general consensus (read: a more than fair conclusion) appears to be that Project Blue Book was used by the Air Force as a regular means of "explaining away"[61] (if not even debunking and suppressing) UFO sightings,[62] and thus managing public perception about them,[63] more than truly getting to the bottom of them.[64] And despite continually being beset with basic resource limitations (i.e., too few dollars to handle too many sightings), it operated somewhat successfully for almost two decades until running up against acute "internal" criticism from the Air Force's University of Colorado-based "Condon Committee,"[65] which issued a report in April of 1969 that recommended its discontinuation, something that did occur as of the end of that year.[66]

So as of the beginning of the 1970s, the United States Air Force had had four different entities studying UFOs (Projects Sign, Grudge, and Blue Book, as well as the Air Force-funded (but CIA-tinged) "Condon Committee"). This was in addition to two private-sector organizations, the National Investigative Committee on Aerial Phenomena ("NICAP," to its terrestrial subscribers) and the Aerial Phenomena Research Organization ("APRO," to its non-NICAP members),[67] which competed for a skeptical public's attention during the 1950s,[68] 1960s, 1970s, and in the case of APRO, into the late 1980s.[69] (The former, which was headed by retired Marine Corps Major Donald E. Keyhoe, ceased to exist as of 1980, while the latter lasted only until 1988.) Most recently, there is the Scientific Coalition for UAP Studies ("SCU," for short), which describes itself as "a think tank of scientists, researchers and professionals." Additionally, there is something called "MUFON," or "MUFON, Inc." (short for the "Mutual UFO Network"), which was established in 1969 mostly as an outgrowth of APRO, with chapters now in all states and more than 40 other countries, but which unfortunately is widely regarded as both commercial (despite its claim to be a "charitable corporation") and sometimes "unscientific," among other things, now. Nevertheless, it is quite active and often effective.[70]

* * * * *

During the 1970s, the Federal Government had no overt program for analyzing UFO sightings, even though they continued unabated.[71] If anything, in fact, they increased -- in numbers, range, and sophistication -- together with the technological advances that had been made by then in recording them, including through infrared radar, through something that was then called "over the horizon" radar capability, and something that was referred to as "sensor data collection." (These radar capabilities, as advanced as they were from what the military could employ at the dawn of the "UFO age" in the 1940s, were nothing compared to the advances in detection technology soon to come.)

On the ground, though, there emerged an entirely unique feature of "UFO secrecy," something that literally changed the landscape of it for the foreseeable future. This is "Area 51," of course, the "über-secret"[72] government facility, 4678 square miles in size, located about 83 miles north-by-northwest of Las Vegas,

Nevada, 30 miles south (only technically, because part of it is practically next door) of the little town of Rachel, Nevada, and proximate to Indian Springs airport, that has become the modern focal point for the public's UFO-related fascinations, suspicions, and activities, not to mention an inspirational source of unending cinematic fervor (with apologies to Roswell, New Mexico), initially on the basis of pure speculation alone.[73]

In operation seemingly as an U.S. Air Force base since the mid-1950s, it is known officially as "Groom Lake," which is also the name of a nearby salt flat that provides an excellent location (with an estimated four-mile-long runway) for the development and testing of highly advanced, experimental aircraft and weapons systems. Heavily blanketed with secrecy at the highest of levels, and favorably distanced from any surrounding civilization by barren hillsides, valleys, and wastelands, it was not officially acknowledged even to exist until August of 2013; tellingly, that acknowledgment came not from the Air Force, but from the CIA, and it came as the result (read: perhaps unintended) of a long-pending FOIA request.[74]

Although Area 51 initially was about as secret as anything that the United States Government had undertaken since the Manhattan Project in the early 1940s, at least on such a scale,[75] it was only inevitable that *some* information about it would "leak out" with the passage of enough time.[76] Significantly, Area 51 employs a massive workforce for construction, scientific analysis, physical maintenance, and who knows for sure what else; since the 1970s, many workers have been flown into and out of it from McCarran International Airport in Las Vegas, through an air carrier called "Janet Air" for some arcane reason (read: perhaps for "Just Another Non-Existent Terminal"), on a regular basis.

And by the late 1980s, Area 51 had become heavily beset with enormous environmental problems, resulting largely from hazardous waste disposal, that generated considerable environmental litigation -- including tort cases filed on behalf of workers who were exposed to that hazardous waste -- and related in-formation-disclosure attempts.[77] But this sometimes took a back seat to the fact that the entire region surrounding the Groom Lake area,[78] and in "flight lanes" beyond it, became known for a very high concentration of UFO sightings during that era, many of which were of high-speed and/or highly maneuverable aircraft in particular.

There is little doubt but that Groom Lake has been the primary military site for both the development and the testing of advanced and experimental aircraft for many years, together with new weapon systems,[79] and that it likely still is.[80] From the U-2 "spy plane" to its A-12 successor to the SR-71 Blackbird (and possibly now an SR-72) to the B-2 stealth bomber to other stealth aircraft (such as the newer F-35, or perhaps "Aurora") to the most sophisticated (and now semi-retired) F-117A Nighthawk, it apparently was something of a "home base" for such advanced aircraft for many years.[81]

Now whether it also is a location of alien remains (corporeal and/or mechanical), the "reverse engineering of alien technology," and even current alien "housing," as the more fanciful of UFO enthusiasts surmise, that remains to be seen -- or not, as the case may be.[82] (And as I have alluded to elsewhere (see Chapter Seventeen), I can neither confirm nor deny that it is the final resting place of the soviet submarine that was salvaged from the depths of the Pacific in 1974.) As for today, by dint of its topography[83] and with its secrecy still largely intact,[84] Groom Lake stands as probably the single greatest public-facing mystery within the realm of "UFO secrecy" overall.[85]

*　*　*　*　*

What had changed greatly by the mid-1970s, however, was the American public. The general distrust of government that was spawned by the "Watergate" scandal early in that decade greatly added further fuel to the UFO fires, as the public became less and less inclined to believe what the Federal Government was saying about UFOs insofar as it no longer was so readily willing to believe what the Government was saying about almost *any* subject -- just because it was the Government saying it. In other words, the public's predominant acceptance of the Roswell explanation of 1947, for example, was not so likely to fly after 30 years of overall public distrust as of 1977. And that is where the Freedom of Information Act, newly strengthened by Congress, very much came into play.

The year 1977 just so happened to be the year that I started representing the CIA in court. Most of my efforts on its behalf were devoted to the development of, and then the defense of, the delicate new "neither confirm nor deny" concept of "Glomarization" at that time. And no small part of that process involved the identification of clear "Glomarization" categories, in advance, so that the concept could be applied with integrity (and therefore gain judicial receptivity) to the types of "targeted" FOIA requests that (in certain subject-matter areas) we just knew were most likely to be received (see Chapter Seventeen). And a big item on this category list was UFOs.

In handling the CIA's first "Glomarization" cases decided in court, I worked shoulder-to-shoulder with two former "Cold Warriors" who had definitely "come in from the cold" (i.e., to the agency's general counsel's office) -- Deputy General Counsel Ernest Mayerfeld (see the Acknowledgments) and Associate General Counsel Launie Ziebell, the latter of whom was a gentle man even though he likely had killed with his bare hands while under cover two decades earlier. At least that was the impression that Launie gave me whenever the subject came up. (Launie was a few years older than my father, but we talked a lot.)

And Launie (as an attorney, mind you, not as a field intelligence officer) was involved in both JFK Assassination-related[86] and UFO-related searches for agency records responsive to requests made under the FOIA. He knew (because I told him so) that I had had a longstanding interest in both subjects -- the former also because I was by then also defending the FBI's position as to both its Dallas and New Orleans Field Office Kennedy Assassination files (see the Glossary) -- and he told me of the seriousness with which he had overseen (and in one respect was still overseeing, as of 1978) those FOIA searches. I could tell that he was taking that responsibility very seriously; the word "scoured" was used.[87]

Not long afterward, in response to continued public pressure on the CIA on the subject, and especially its treatment by *The New York Times*, CIA Director Stansfield Turner (then called "the DCI," for "Director of Central Intelligence"), an "old Navy man" who had been in President Jimmy Carter's class at the Naval Academy in Annapolis, suddenly took sharp notice (as if he he'd seen a ball of St. Elmo's fire off his starboard bow) of the threat posed to his agency by UFOs, though in doing so he didn't really have any physical threat in mind. So he declaimed within the CIA's leadership halls that he damn well wanted to know whether his agency actually was in the "UFO business" and that he wanted an answer to that question "toot sweet" (bastardized French, derived from "tout de suite," for "right away").

The unhappy task of responding to this very sensitive question, on behalf of the entirety of the CIA's organizational leadership, fell to another CIA "agency client" of mine, Don I. Wortman, who at the time held the position of CIA Deputy Director for Administration. Don was a vital deposition witness in the first "Glomarization" case to proceed to judgment, *Gardels v. CIA*, which I was then handling at the district court level (and soon in the D.C. Circuit Court of Appeals as well) (see Chapter Seventeen).[88] That deposition lasted much longer than anticipated, as Don was questioned closely by American Civil Liberties Union ("ACLU," to its Justice Department litigation opponents) counsel on the CIA's practices and procedures as they related to the covert versus overt CIA activities that were at the heart of that case.

Don was not a "Cold Warrior." Rather, he had joined the CIA for a two-year management stint after having served as acting commissioner of the Social Security Administration for almost a year. But he had an absolutely stellar reputation as a government manager -- as one who not only could "find where the bodies were buried" but also could bury one or two of his own where they would never be found by anyone else. (Actually, that is mostly rhetorical; Don was a very nice man.) As I prepared him as one of my three deposition witnesses in *Gardels*, I came to learn much from him about government administration in general and about the CIA's administration in particular. One could say that he was an excellent teacher as well as administrator. (I was only 26 at the time, and I appreciated it.)

So back to DCI Turner's pointed question. To answer that question, Don reviewed all of the CIA's existing (read: still existing) files and records on the subject of UFOs, at least as far as he could find them. I do not know whether he "built upon" what Launie had compiled for his own search purposes earlier; neither Launie nor Don ever told me that, as I recall. But this search enterprise doubtless was aided immeasurably by the fact that (as I heard it from Don) DCI Turner's exact question was about what the CIA was doing on UFOs, not what it perhaps *had done* in the (arguably) distant past.[89] (Remember, this is an agency that had just been "put through the mill" by Congress's Church Committee, in a spasm of "post-Watergate" cleansing; at that time, it supposedly was off to a fresh start under President Jimmy Carter and its staunch new ex-military DCI.)

Then, after reviewing all of these located records carefully (but, frankly, without much follow-up interrogation of the principal agency "players" who were still there, as I recall), Don concluded that he could give DCI Turner the assurance that he doubtless was looking for: That the Agency was (read: currently, *sub silentio*, which loosely translated in context meant "run silent, run deep" toward a sunken Russian sub) not involved in any effort to do research on UFOs, that it had no "UFO program" of any kind, and that its files held only "sporadic" items of UFO-related correspondence, just as one might imagine for such a sensational subject. True enough, but that of course also said nothing about what the Defense Department had been doing on the subject, through the Air Force and (secondarily) the Navy Departments, let alone what the rest of the "Intelligence Community" (especially NSA) might have been up to on it as well.

* * * * *

Now fast forward (again, no pun intended) to more recent years, with UFO sightings now taking place widely around the world,[90] and no less in the United States,[91] having grown ever more frequent and less spurious over the course of several decades,[92] bringing increasing pressure on governments to both address the "problem" and, perhaps even more importantly, relax their secrecy about it so as to lessen critical public mistrust.

And with this passage of more time (and also of many other nations' counterparts to our Freedom of Information Act),[93] citizens of the world began to question why at least some national government, especially the United States, had not "just come out and admitted that such things are real" already. Indeed, many other nations of the world joined in on this, with thousands upon thousands of sightings taking place within their borders, and with several other governments beginning to be less secretive than our own about what could be thought of as "the unknown."[94]

* * * * *

Then came the real-world, modern-day version of "the day the earth stood still" -- or at least "the day before." On December 16, 2017, seemingly out of the blue, *The New York Times* reported, and the Department of Defense officially confirmed, that its Defense Intelligence Agency ("DIA," to its secret admirers) had for several years[95] conducted a UFO "tracking" and investigation enterprise, named the "Advanced Aerospace Threat Identification Program" ("AATIP," to its nearest celestial neighbors), that had operated silently and secretly, entirely unbeknownst to the "UFO community," even for many years thereafter.[96]

AATIP, it was learned, was created to study "anomalous aerospace threats," a defensive-sounding new euphemism for UFOs, and, the Defense Department claimed, had been "disbanded" in 2012 for reasons not stated.[97] The official revelation of the very existence of this governmental activity, after decades of staunch Federal Government denials, sent shockwaves reverberating throughout the "UFO community" and even captured much mainstream media attention.[98]

Evidently, this development was connected to two highly sensational military UFO encounters, one off the west coast of the United States and the other off the east coast, that had occurred in 2004 and 2015, respectively. The first involved the USS *Nimitz* nuclear aircraft carrier (the head of a "carrier strike group"), which was accompanied by the USS *Princeton* guided missile cruiser and an E-2D Hawkeye "tactical early warning surveillance plane."

Two of its F/A-18E/F "Super Hornet" fighter jets made visual contact with a high-speed UFO off the coast of California during the afternoon of November 14, 2004.[99] With a completely clear blue sky, it was reported that all four of the airmen in the two jets were able to observe the object's "solid white color"[100] and its "smooth" oblong, "Tic Tac" shape as at first they traveled at comparable speeds.[101] During this time, they viewed the object as "mirroring" them and seemingly "jamming" their aerial radar.[102]

Then, when one of the fighter jets pursued the UFO, that object reportedly maneuvered in such a way as to suddenly appear behind that jet and in front of the other, which all four airmen[103] saw as a physical impossibility.[104] They then observed the object as it went from hovering at an estimated 80,000 feet to descending (without a sonic boom) at supersonic speeds and then coming to a complete stop at about 50 feet above the ocean.[105] At times, the object was observed as moving "erratically," as if "the laws of physics" did not apply to it.[106] Additional F/A-18s were vectored into the same area while the UFO was still there, with the same results; everyone reported seeing the same thing.

Most significantly, these observations were not only visual. Rather, this UFO also was detected by radar, on multiple systems used by the planes and ships below, including the highly sophisticated Hawkeye observation plane.[107] These instrument detections therefore were free of the subjectivity that is necessarily involved in mere visual observations; they made witnesses of the Navy's "ground personnel" as well.[108]

All told, dozens of military personnel aboard the various planes and ships in the *Nimitz* battle group were witnesses to these amazing interactions. Furthermore, what is called "gun camera footage" was taken of the object as well, featuring cockpit display data and infrared imagery, creating a record of the encounter that came to be known as the "FLIR1 video."[109]

A series of similar incidents took place off the coast of Florida involving the USS *Theodore Roosevelt* nuclear aircraft carrier and its "strike group," beginning on June 2, 2014 and culminating on March 19, 2015. The "marquee event" in this series of "sightings" (which mostly were only by radar) took place on January 20, 2015, when the same type of F/A-18 "Super Hornet" fighter jets (but a "generation" more sophisticated than its earlier version) encountered a high-speed UFO that reportedly maneuvered around them in the same way as the one encountered by the *Nimitz* strike force crew roughly ten years earlier. This time, though, what the pilots observed had not a "Tic Tac" shape but rather appeared to them to be "cubes,"[110] and each of the *Roosevelt*'s fighter jet pilots took care to capture video evidence of the encounter, through their "gun camera pod," in order to record the object's capability.[111]

These two videos, which included audio recordings, depicted the UFO flying at an altitude of about 25,000 feet and moving at such an extraordinarily high speed that it was difficult to "track" it at first, yet both pilots' automatic systems ultimately succeeded in doing so, with the same visual results. But even more dramatic was the fact that these videos were "narrated" by these two young Navy pilots, as they excitedly tracked the object's movements through the sky: *"Look at that thing! It's rotating! . . . What the @&%# is that thing? . . . Look at the flying!"* These became known as the "GOFAST video" and the "Gimbal video," for reasons that are largely but not entirely clear,[112] and were similar to the "FLIR1" or "Tic Tac" video made of the *Nimitz* encounter.[113]

So as of early 2015, there existed three such Defense Department videos that were of much more compelling quality than anything known to have been captured by any branch of the U.S. military before, each backed by senior military pilots and by highly sophisticated detection and recordation equipment "on the ground," so to speak, in these cases.[114] And as far as anyone has learned to date, the U.S. Government has no (read: zero) explanation for what might have been occurring within them. Apparently, this percolated for a while (and in the case of the *Nimitz* video, for quite a long while) before anything (at least within the public's view) came of it.

Then, as the Navy's young fighter pilots might say, "all hell broke loose" when all three of these UFO videos were inexplicably released into the public domain atop the Defense Department's surprise announcement of its Advanced Aerospace Threat Identification Program's existence in mid-December of 2017. And not long thereafter, the Defense Department went so far as to admit that the footage in each of these three videos was "authentic." This constituted the first time in history that the Department of Defense (or any comparable agency of any nation around the world, for that matter) had ever officially acknowledged the existence of "UFO activity" in such a way.

The reaction to this dramatic reversal in the U.S. Government's policy on public acknowledgment of the validity of UFO sightings (a nondisclosure policy that by late 2017 was more than 70 years old) was an only slightly muted version of shock and awe. It appears that no one in the public "UFO community" ever expected to see multiple, authenticated videos of a military UFO encounter, let alone any accompanied by a previously unknown Defense Department "UFO-tracking" program suddenly becoming known. The videos drew huge volumes of Internet traffic when they were posted online by several organizations, including *The New York Times*, and it is fair to say that the audio portions of the *Roosevelt* videos made a greater impact on the public than any record of any UFO sighting ever before.

* * * * *

The following years of 2018 and 2019 were "banner years" for UFO sightings, not surprisingly, with them coming so fast and furiously as to truly qualify for the word "surge."[115] Yet anyone who is familiar with what is now called the field of "ufology"[116] well knows that, quite apart from the circumstances of any particular case, the overwhelming bulk of UAP ("Unidentified Aerial Phenomena," to occasionally use this new alternative phrase) sightings are readily explainable, one way or the other. Plus, the primary point for these most recent years is that "sightings breed sightings" (as pointed out above), and it sure does seem that nothing can breed them quite like the dramatic events of December 2017, especially the audio parts of those videos.[117]

And then another governmental shoe dropped. On April 23, 2019, no doubt in reaction to what had occurred during the previous 16 months, the Department of the Navy took a big follow-up step: It established new "reporting guidelines and procedures" for use by its employees (read: both pilots and aircraft crew members, plus "ground observers," such as radar operators, seamen, and other flight deck personnel) in reporting all experiences with "unexplained phenomena," thereby formalizing the process by which all such reports are to be made and handled in the future.[118] What is more, it did so by taking the entirely unprecedented step of announcing this new regime publicly, with the express aim of "destigmatizing" the process for aircraft crew members (and their ground personnel) in the future.[119] This was characterized by some anonymous (but no less humorous) Navy personnel as a veritable "sea change" in how this entire subject was now being treated.[120]

But there still remained a noticeable gap in the Defense Department's treatment of UFOs or UAPs, no matter what they were called. No small part of its December 2017 "bombshell" announcements on the subject, which revealed that its Advanced Aerospace Threat Identification Program had existed for seven years in secrecy, was DOD's implicit assertion that it had no longer had such a program in operation since 2012. That did not seem right to many observers, who reasoned that if was necessary and proper for the U.S. to have such a program devoted to UFO sightings for seven years from 2005-2012, then something like it should have existed both immediately before and after that.[121]

Well, it was not long before *that* other shoe dropped or, to belabor the metaphor only slightly less, before the next logical step was taken. On August 14, 2020, the Defense Department issued a press release revealing that ten days earlier it had established a replacement UFO or UAP study organization, named the "Unidentified Aerial Phenomena Task Force" ("UAPTF," to its alien subjects), one designed to "improve its understanding of, and gain insight into, the nature and origins of UAPs" by investigating "unexplained aerial incidents" encountered by the U.S. military through detecting, analyzing, and cataloging UAPs that "could potentially pose a threat to U.S. national security."[122]

Most significantly, this new UAP study program was established within the organizational purview of the Department of the Navy (i.e., not the Air Force as in the past), as something that operated as part of the Office of Naval Intelligence ("ONI," to its staff of more than 3000).[123] So it remained to be seen what a UFO/

UAP study organization looks like and yields when operating under the auspices of the Department of the Navy, rather than the Air Force (or surreptitiously the CIA) going forward.

* * * * *

Now, after so many decades of consistently persistent "UFO secrecy," especially in the United States, one has to wonder: Why would the Department of Defense (or any underlying agency such as perhaps the CIA) so suddenly and sharply (not unlike the aerial maneuvers observed in some UFO sightings, actually) "reverse course" like this, making such things known to the public as never before? There are multiple possible answers to this very fundamental question (not unlike, again, the possible explanations of UFO sightings to begin with) depending upon one's degree of cynicism (again, not unlike how one views UFO sightings in the first place) and on one's willingness to speculate both inside and outside of the box.

The first possible explanation, of course, involves taking this remarkable series of developments entirely on its face, as nothing more or less than exactly what it purports to be (or exactly what the Government says it is), all of its history (not to mention human nature) notwithstanding.[124] This would mean that the Department of Defense (and in turn the executive branch of the Federal Government) now truly embraces a public posture of greater transparency, rather than of near-total secrecy, on this fraught subject, no longer to be so cynically probed and pressured regarding it, but by the same token no longer to enjoy the luxury of being able to shield itself from the necessary implications of the most challenging (and, let's face it, disquieting) UFO cases.

In turn, this could be because: (a) the Department of Defense (particularly the Air Force) has institutionally decided that "enough is enough" and that it is easier to be "open" rather than "closed" (the latter of which does, history has shown, take one hell of a lot of work, coordinated thought, and creative deception); (b) DOD has become acutely aware of the worldwide trend toward government openness on the subject and has opted to "join the party," so to speak, so as to not stand so idly (and, some might say, embarrassingly) alone on it; (c) the Federal Government (i.e., including the CIA) has decided that the major animating factors underlying its secrecy imperative *ab initio* (think: "from the get-go") -- i.e., the need to protect the security of its own advances in aeronautical capability in the face of the "Soviet threat" -- are just no longer what they used to be; or (d) either some combination of these three things or, perhaps, "none of the above."

The second possible explanation for these sudden developments is that this new-found openness is *not* genuine, that it is a calculated and carefully calibrated step taken for some reason, institutional or otherwise, that exists beneath the surface (not unlike USOs), such that nothing -- absolutely nothing -- done or said about it can be taken at face value. This would mean that the Federal Government has embarked on a whole new regime of "cover-ups," through new lies and boldfaced deception, one more proactive this time rather than reactive, and one that is even more risky (and fraught with potential for launching an astronomical degree of public distrust) than anything that it did in the 1940s through the 1990s.

In turn, this could be because: (e) the emergence of China on the world stage is now perceived, by both our military and civilian leadership, as posing just about as much a threat to the United States as the Soviet Union ever did; (f) the perceived need for "UFO secrecy" within the highest levels of the military and intelligence communities has become so acute in recent years that a "diversionary" approach, even one of such unheard-of magnitude and complexity, is now deemed worth employing; (g) the technology for detecting UFOs and analyzing all credible sightings is by now so advanced, sophisticated, and dispersed in the public domain that the military realistically can no longer hope to keep things as tightly wrapped as in the past (even when its commander-in-chief is very much that), creating a new need for some (read: limited) sort of "safety valve" disclosure; or (h) some combination of (or none of) the above.

Although these two possible basic explanations, seeming to be mutually exclusive of one another, would appear to cover the landscape (or "skyscape") between them, it also is possible that what is now going on here actually is most reflective of something "completely different."[125] Such a "something" could well be that, as so many fervent "ufologists" have suspected (nay, even ardently hoped for) for so long, the United States (or conceivably some other nation, as we are not the "center of the universe," at least not when viewed from space), actually *is* in possession of some truly verifiable "alien artifact" (ranging from "trace evidence" from a UFO landing at one end of the speculation spectrum[126] to full-on alien corpses and/or spacecraft at the other), at least as of now, if not harkening back to as long ago as the 1940s, and is, to state it simply, now acting accordingly. Much as such a thing might be very hard to believe,[127] one can only conclude that any unbiased analysis of the situation must at least admit of the possibility that such a thing might be so.[128]

And *if* it is so, world-shattering and portentous as that would be, then how should we consider what might have been the case with AATIP, its successor organizations UAPTF and AOIMSG, and their most recent reincarnation the All-Domain Anomaly Resolution Office ("AARO"), when looking at them through that new lens? To be sure, this is not an attempt to launch into some philosophical, geopolitical, or epistemological exegesis on the implications, ramifications, or even direct postulations of such a thing. But for present purposes here, if this is premised to be the case,[129] then at least a couple of practical observations (read: nonvisual ones) do logically follow.

First, there is the fact that proceeding from this premise would explain much. Consistent with the speculations of so many ufologists for so many years, it would mean that the driving force behind "UFO secrecy" in the United States has not been to protect our rapid advances in aeronautical technology since World War II, at least not alone. And it also would mean that the Cold War (at least directly, as well as not alone) was only an exacerbating (read: not the animating) factor in how to deal with something so historically monumental (think: a cinematic obelisk, posited to have existed nearly 20 years ago) and overwhelmingly significant to all of mankind (as well as to all of womankind, at least as of about 1970). Put another way, governmental behavior in light of such a thing would naturally be expected to be much, much different than it otherwise would be.

Second, such an actual reality (as redundant as that phrase sounds) would mean that governments might well be proceeding (as many ufologists have hoped for) out of some distinct new impulse of "human nature" that seeks to acclimatize the world's "public" to the very *idea* of extraterrestrials, bit by bit, with what could be called "soft disclosure," over the course of what now has been, in total, several generations.[130] It makes at least some sense that persons in positions of authority, acting out of fears of "worldwide panic" and of unknown other consequences,[131] might take extreme steps (i.e., up to and including deception, utter fabrication, and flat-out lying) in order to "ease into" any official announcement of the existence of alien life on Earth (not to mention to conveniently "kick that can" well down the road).[132]

And while it just cannot be reiterated enough that this all is based upon the seemingly fantastical premise that mature alien life actually is "out there" (as well as having been "down here" in the near-neighborhood of Earth),[133] the question then is: Was the extraordinary, totally unprecedented 2017 story of the Air Force's *Advanced Aerospace Threat Identification Program,*[134] together with its disclosed thrice-over "video evidence" of UFO or UAP maneuvering, and as supplanted now by the Navy's replacement UAPTF (not to mention DOD's AOIMSG" and its successor AARO) all just a major, entirely calculated part of that?[135] Could that possibly be the case?

One wonders also if there could possibly be any connection between all of this and the odd fascination of President Donald J. Trump with the creation of something that he confusingly called "Space Command" as actually a new branch of our military?[136] At the risk of foolishly trying to analyze Donald Trump's actions along any rational lines, one also could consider the following:

- **June 15, 2019.** Trump (unquestionably our most spacey president by far, to be most charitable) attempts to speak cogently to ABC News on the subject of UFOs: "I think it's probably -- I want them [the Navy pilots] to think whatever they think. They do say, and I've seen, and I've read, and I've heard. And I did have one very brief meeting on it. But people are saying they're seeing UFOs. Do I believe it? Not particular[ly]."

- **April 29, 2020.** Shortly after the release of the three AATIP UFO videos, (which White House staffers doubtless combined onto a single videotape for his convenience), Trump laughingly deems the footage to be "a hell of a video," and adds, "I just wonder if it's real."

- **June 14, 2020.** In an unprecedented acknowledgment for an American president,[137] Trump allows as how he has received a "briefing" on the subject of UFO sightings and then goes so far as to say: "I won't talk to you about what I know about it, but it's very interesting. . . . I'll have to think about that one."[138]

- **June 16, 2020.** Astrophysicists announce that "[t]here may be as many as six billion Earth-like planets (or "exoplanets") in our galaxy alone."[139] And this is beyond the possibilities of life within our own Solar System, such as on Mars -- where it is being sought most recently by NASA's Perseverance rover (together with its Ingenuity helicopter) and more recently by China's Zhurong rover -- and even on Pluto, where cryovolcanic activity associated with flowing water has recently been detected.[140] At the same time, NASA's newly deployed (read: launched in December of 2021 and operational as of July of 2022) James Webb Space Telescope, an infrared-based observatory, promises further discoveries in the search for interstellar life.[141]

- **August 4, 2020.** The Pentagon quietly establishes the "Unidentified Aerial Phenomena Task Force" ("UAPTF," to those who now call UFOs "UAPs") as a successor program to AATIP. It is organizationally located with the Naval Investigative Service ("NIS," to devotees) of the Department of the Navy, not within the Department of the Air Force as in the past.

- **September 16, 2020.** Air Force officials unofficially reveal the existence of a new fighter jet, designed and built using new digital engineering, which is said to be part of the Air Force's "Next Generation Air Dominance" ("NGAD," to all futurists) project. Built as a prototype, or "full-scale flight demonstrator," at Lockheed Martin's "Skunk Works" in Palmdale, California,[142] it is described as a "sixth-generation tactical aircraft" that has "already flown in the physical world, [breaking] a lot of records."[143]

- **December 2, 2020.** The Pentagon responds to the leaks of two classified intelligence reports on UAPs (from 2018 and 2020) that were widely distributed within the Intelligence Community through DOD's "Secret Internet Protocol Router Network" ("SIPRNet," to its routees) and "NSANet" (the NSA's official "Intranet"), saying that "DOD does not discuss publicly" such things. One report contained a photo of a silver, cube-shaped object that reportedly was taken by a Navy pilot using her mobile phone's camera when it was spotted hovering 30,000-35,000 feet above the ocean. The other report included a very clear photograph of an object described as a large equilateral triangle with rounded or "blunted" edges and large, perfectly spherical white illuminated areas in each corner, an image that was captured by an F/A-18 fighter pilot off the eastern coast of the United States in 2019 after the triangular craft emerged from the ocean and began to ascend straight upwards at a 90-degree angle.[144]

- **December 14, 2020.** President Trump spews a "tweet" suggesting that he "might declassify everything" before he leaves office (which he did indeed have the technical legal authority to do), prompting the public response that he should declassify "everything the Pentagon has on Roswell, other UFO incidents[,] and the findings of the UAP Task Force to date."[145]

- **December 16, 2020.** Former CIA Director John O. Brennan, speaking on a popular podcast, gives his own opinion that "some of the phenomena we're going to be seeing continues to be unexplained and might, in fact, be some type of phenomenon that is the result of something that we don't yet understand and that could involve some type of activity that some might say constitutes a different form of life."

- **January 8, 2021.** The Defense Intelligence Agency responds to a three-year-old FOIA request by releasing 154 heavily redacted pages that nonetheless disclose the existence of advanced technology reports on "Nitinol" (composed primarily of nickel and tin), described as a "shape-recovery alloy" (read: "memory metal") similar to what was claimed to be part of the debris at Roswell.

- **January 12, 2021.** The CIA is reported to have released an enormous trove of UAP-related records to a private-sector organization known as "the Black Vault," which in recent years has made many thousands of FOIA requests toward its purpose of becoming "the largest privately run online repository of declassified government documents anywhere in the world."

- **March 9, 2021.** The Department of the Navy formally acknowledges, through a response to a FOIA request, that "there is now a Security Classification Guidance document (at the Secret level) that addresses the UAP issue."

- **March 22, 2021.** Former Director of National Intelligence John L. Ratcliffe says that "satellites" have made "a lot more sightings [of UFOs] than have been made public." He elaborates that UFOs "have been picked up by satellite imagery; . . . [m]ultiple sensors . . . are picking up these things."

- **May 3, 2021.** Self-proclaimed AATIP "whistleblower" Luis Elizondo files a 64-page complaint with the Pentagon's inspector general alleging that top Pentagon officials are running a smear campaign to discredit him. Among other things, Elizondo claims that Congress's upcoming June deadline for the filing of a DOD report on its UFO/UAP knowledge is causing DOD to take such measures.

- **May 3, 2021.** The Department of Defense's inspector general announces that it will conduct an investigation "to determine the extent to which the DOD has taken actions regarding Unidentified Aerial Phenomena (UAP)." Reportedly, this step was taken under congressional pressure.

- **May 9, 2021.** The Navy releases a video from July of 2019 showing a dark, spherical UAP off of the coast of San Diego diving into the ocean near a U.S. "stealth ship" and not reappearing. The Navy pilot who filmed this says that from his vantage point, "[i]t splashed, it splashed!" A submarine search of the area was conducted but found nothing.

- **May 17, 2021.** On a late-night talk show, Former President Barack H. Obama first jests about the subject by saying that "when it comes to the aliens, there are some things that I just can't tell you . . . on air." Then he elaborates as follows:

"What is true, and I'm actually being serious here, is that there is footage and records of objects in the skies that we don't know exactly what they are. . . . We can't explain how they move, their trajectory. They did not have an easily explainable pattern. And so I think that people still take it seriously, trying to investigate and figure out what that is."

- **May 21, 2021.** At the end of a press conference together with South Korean President Moon Jae-in, a Fox News correspondent brought up Obama's comments in the form of a question: "President Obama says that 'there is footage and records of objects in the skies,' these unidentified aerial phenomenon [sic], and he says that 'we don't know exactly what they are.'" President Joseph R. Biden leaves the question unanswered.

- **May 27, 2021.** A video is released purporting to show a cluster of UAPs surrounding the USS *Omaha* off the coast of San Diego on July 15, 2019, with thermal imaging and sensor data supporting it. A radar screen is shown displaying several objects moving around the ship and at one point, an unidentified male is heard shouting "Holy shit! They're moving fast. . . . They're turning around!" One of these objects is seen to submerge, making it what is referred to as an "Unidentified Submersible Object" or a "trans-medium" UFO. At the same time, another released video shows three UAPs hovering over the nearby USS *Russell*, one with a distinct pyramid shape, but upon close analysis they appear to have conventional explanations.

- **June 3, 2021.** In an article titled "U.S. Finds No Evidence of Alien Technology in Flying Objects, But Can't Rule it Out, Either," *The New York Times* predicts that a highly anticipated Federal Government report to Congress will find "no evidence that aerial phenomena witnessed by Navy pilots in recent years are alien spacecraft, but [that the Defense Department] still cannot explain the unusual movements that have mystified scientists and the military." Also mentioned is the prospective report's focus on recent advances made by both Russia and China in the field of "hypersonics" (read: a field of exceptional future importance), although there is no evidence linking that, or any such advanced aeronautics developed by the U.S., to any of the more than 140 sightings studied.

- **June 25, 2021.** As mandated by Congress a year ago, the Office of the Director of National Intelligence ("ODNI," to those with creaky joints), in conjunction with the Department of Defense, submits a public report to the Senate Intelligence Committee on the recent activities and findings of DOD's UAP Task Force. Titled "Preliminary Assessment: Unidentified Aerial Phenomena," and only six pages in length (plus two administrative appendices), it covers just a selection of 144 UAP sightings since 2004 and finds that very few of them can be conclusively explained.[146] Possible explanations, it says, are: (1) ordinary items such as weather balloons mistaken for spacecraft; (2) atmospheric conditions, such as ice crystals; (3) aircraft designed by the United States Government or its contractors, which the report officially discounted; (4) such craft designed and operated by foreign adversaries, most prominently Russia or China, which the report also discounted; and (5) a category coyly labeled "other," by which it means, by process of deduction, "of alien origin," although the report is quick to point out that more information and study about it are needed.[147]

- **June 30, 2021.** A survey conducted by the well-known Pew Research Center shows that more than half of Americans, "(51%), say that UFOs reported by people in the military are likely evidence of intelligent life outside Earth" and that "[y]ounger Americans are more likely to believe intelligent life exists on other planets."

- **October of 2021.** Sailors aboard the amphibious assault ship USS *Kearsarge* (LHD-3) reportedly have an encounter with two car-sized "balls of light" seen to follow close behind the ship at about 200 feet above the ocean for several nights during a training exercise off the east coast. The *Kearsarge* reportedly deployed "anti-drone" weapons at them but observed that they were unaffected.

- **November 4, 2021.** The National Academies of Sciences, Engineering, and Medicine issue a ten-year report that places the search for extraterrestrial life as the scientific community's Number One goal for the next decade. Based on a survey of scientists worldwide, this 614-page report calls upon the nations of the world to build upon the "extraordinary progress" that already has been made on this in recent years.

- **November 10, 2021.** Director of National Intelligence Avril D. Haines, speaking at a forum titled "Our Future in Space" held at the Washington National Cathedral, provides further detail on her office's June 2021 "Preliminary Assessment: Unidentified Aerial Phenomena" report, adding that "[t]here's also the question of, 'Is there something else that we simply do not understand, which might come extraterrestrially?'" This is taken by the mainstream media as well as by the UFO community as portending a "seismic shift" in the government's official stance on the subject of UFOs. And in turn, the latest poll taken on UFOs (or UAPs) shows, according to a newly interested Member of Congress, that "the majority of people think that there is something going on" with such things.

- **November 23, 2021.** The Pentagon announces that yet another DOD entity will now be responsible for detecting, identifying, and assessing UAPs (read: "Airborne Objects"). To be known as the "Airborne Object Identification and Management Synchronization Group" ("AOIMSG," to those alienated by this sudden shift), this new office will replace the "Unidentified Aerial Phenomena Task Force," the successor program to AATIP that was established within the Department of the Navy's Office of Naval Intelligence on August 4, 2020, and it is now charged with "synchronizing" all Federal Government (read: including the Office of the Director of National Intelligence) efforts to detect, identify, and "attribute" airborne objects of interest.[148] It is to be located organizationally under the Defense Undersecretary for Intelligence and Security at the Pentagon, where it is feared by some ufologists that it will be only an oversight office, not an "operational" one as in the past.[149] And, in an entirely new such development, it will be overseen by something called the "Airborne Object Identification and Management Executive Council."

- **December 7, 2021.** The House of Representatives passes a lengthy bill titled the "National Defense Authorization Act for Fiscal Year 2022," which contains a provision calling for the Defense Department to undertake a range of specific UAP-related responsibilities (including as to "transmedium objects or devices") and to do so as a matter of congressional mandate. Most notably, under the bill, DOD would be required to file reports to Congress on any UAP incidents "associated with military nuclear assets, including strategic nuclear weapons and nuclear-powered ships and submarines," and to conduct "an assessment of any health-related effects for individuals that have encountered unidentified aerial phenomena." This legislation is approved as slightly amended by the Senate and signed into law before the end of the year.

- **April 6, 2022.** The Department of Defense releases 1500 pages of documents, including reports of UFO sightings involving serious health problems such as radiation burns, nerve damage, and feelings of electric shock, as well as perceived time loss. The documents are released in response (read: after four years) to a FOIA request.

- **May 2, 2022.** The *POLITICO* news outlet reports that "Members of the Senate Intelligence and Armed Services committees . . . receiving the latest secret briefings on UFOs say national security agencies still aren't taking seriously the reports of highly advanced aircraft of unknown origin violating protected airspace." These secret briefings, required by recent legislation, have reportedly left key Members of Congress and their staffs both "disappointed" and "frustrated" just four months after that legislation was enacted.

- **May 17, 2022.** The House Intelligence Committee's Subcommittee on Counterterrorism, Counterintelligence, and Counterproliferation holds a public hearing on the subject of UAPs, followed by a closed, classified hearing on the Pentagon's then-existing "Airborne Object Identification and Management Synchronization Group." This marks the first time that Congress has convened a public hearing on the "UFO issue" since the conclusion of Project Blue Book more than 50 years ago. In contrast to that, the Subcommittee's chairman warns in his opening remarks that "Unidentified Aerial Phenomena are a potential national security threat. And they need to be treated that way."[150] For their part, two high-ranking Defense Department officials emphasize that "it takes considerable effort to understand" UAP sightings and that it is a "delicate balance" to decide what is to be made public. What they testify to in the classified part of the hearing is not publicly disclosed.[151]

- **May 27, 2022.** Just ten days after the above congressional hearing, NASA reportedly confirms that it will be actively working in support of the new Airborne Object Identification and Management Synchronization Group. A NASA spokesperson says it is "evaluating how to provide our expertise in space-based Earth observations to improve understanding of Unidentified Aerial Phenomena (UAPs)," which could include both gathering firsthand eyewitness testimony of NASA employees and astronauts and a review of old archival photographs. This is a "first" for NASA, which has shied away from such things since its creation in the late 1950s and it is scheduled to continue until at least the spring of 2023.

- **June 2, 2022.** Amid zooming numbers of UAP sightings worldwide, footage taken from several angles at the Queen's Platinum Jubilee in London shows a mysterious circular object (read: non-royal orb) moving alongside Royal Air Force jets engaged in a "flypast" (read: "flyover") of Buckingham Palace. Queen Elizabeth II and most members of the royal family are standing on her balcony at the time but reportedly do not notice the white UAP streaking across the sky.

- **June 8, 2022.** Fairleigh Dickinson University releases a poll showing that more than one-third of Americans think it is "plausible" that extraterrestrials crash-landed at Roswell. "Roswell has become part of our national folklore," says FDU's poll director Dan Cassino. "This is not a fringe belief: if you ask your friends and neighbors, you're going to find people who think it's true."

- **June 9, 2022.** In a sudden development reflecting the tenor of the times, one that expands what it had announced just 13 days ago, NASA announces that it is "commissioning a study team . . . to examine unidentified aerial phenomena (UAPs) . . . from a scientific perspective."[152] (Such an effort should involve searching for both "biosignatures" and "technosignatures," as well as an exhaustive examination of NASA's imagery archives.) This effort is separate from what DOD is now doing and is expected to take about nine months to complete (i.e., the ordinary gestation time for the human species). NASA explains: "We have access to a broad range of observations of Earth from space -- and that is the lifeblood of scientific inquiry. We have the tools and teams who can help us improve our understanding of the unknown. That's the very definition of what science is. That's what we do."[153]

- **June 14, 2022.** In an interview on Russian television, Russian space agency Director General Dmitry O. Rogozin opines that some UFO sightings "can be attributed to aliens." He adds that the Russian Academy of Sciences is currently conducting studies of the subject. However, his credibility is questioned by Western observers given the bellicosity of other recent remarks by him regarding sanctions imposed on Russia during the war in Ukraine.

- **June 15, 2022.** Appearing on a late-night talk show, former President Bill Clinton says that during his presidency he "sent people to Area 51 to make sure there were no aliens [there]." He says he told them that "[w]e gotta find out how we're gonna deal with this because that's where we do a lot of our invisibility research. . . ." Clinton concludes by cryptically remarking that "[t]here's a lot of stuff we don't know."

- **July 12, 2022.** The James Webb Space Telescope ("JWST," to its amazing NASA designers) becomes operational, marking the next generation of the visual (read: largely infrared) exploration of the universe. Its greatly improved infrared resolution allows it to view objects that were too distant for the Hubble Space Telescope, including galaxies that were too many thousands of light-years away.

- **July 12, 2022.** The Senate issues a document that rebrands UFOs/UAPs as "unidentified aerospace-undersea phenomena," thus expanding the definition to include objects in space and under the oceans. This revised definition specifically includes "transmedium" objects that "transition between space and the atmosphere, or between the atmosphere and bodies of water." Most strikingly, this new definition of "UFO" excludes "man-made" objects.

- **July 14, 2022.** The House passes an amendment to the 2023 National Defense Authorization bill that would create a "secure system" within DOD for it to receive information about UAPs. The system also would serve as a mechanism to prevent unauthorized public reporting of classified military or intelligence programs (read: perhaps meaning more secrecy). Following an annual pattern,[154] the bill's next step is consideration by the Senate, perhaps as soon as August, and then a conference committee prior to final passage (or not) before the end of the year.

- **July 19, 2022.** CNN reports on the heightened interest in UFOs/UAPs on Capitol Hill in Washington, D.C. It declares that "[t]he seriousness with which Congress is now taking UAPs represents a massive shift" from even recent years. It concludes: "Congress has clearly woken up."

- **July 19, 2022.** The UAP/UFO group called "The Black Vault" releases to the public a trove of records that it says it obtained from NASA under the Freedom of Information Act. The documents include an internal invitation to a virtual event titled "Extreme Acceleration by UAPs and Sensors for Detection" that NASA had scheduled for October 6, 2020. This is further evidence of the seriousness with which NASA has been taking its role in UAP studies.

- **July 20, 2022.** A report by the Senate Select Committee on Intelligence on the Intelligence Authorization Act for Fiscal Year 2023 states: "At a time when cross-domain transmedium threats to United States national security are expanding exponentially, the Committee is disappointed with the slow pace of DoD-led efforts to establish the office to address those threats and to replace the former Unidentified Aerial Phenomena Task Force . . . To accelerate progress, the Committee has . . . renamed the organization formerly known as the Unidentified Aerial Phenomena Task Force [UAPTF] and the Aerial Object Identification and Management Synchronization Management Group [AOIMSMG] to be the Unidentified Aerospace-Undersea Phenomena Joint Program Office [UAPJPO]." Most significantly, it adds the following: "Temporary nonattributed objects, or those that are positively identified as man-made after analysis, will be passed to appropriate offices and should not be considered under the definition as unidentified aerospace-undersea phenomena." In response, a former Department of Defense staffer writes in an op-ed that this verbiage suggests that officials know that there are some UAPs not of this planet: "This implies that members of the Senate Intelligence Committee believe (on a unanimous, bipartisan basis) that some UFOs have non-human origins."

- **August 9, 2022.** A photograph described as "the best photo of a UFO ever taken" (read: maybe so, as it looks sharp enough to be a hoax) emerges in the U.K., 32 years after it was taken by two hikers near Calvine, Scotland, in the summer of 1990. Long known as the "Calvine UFO photo" (the name through which it can be Googled by all interested), it shows a crystal-clear, diamond-shaped aerial object. It was purportedly "lost" within the bowels of the British Ministry of Defense ("MoD," to the 1960s generation), after first being given to a local newspaper not long after it was taken. A former insider there says: "Somehow -- perhaps using a D-Notice [MoD secrecy order] or perhaps using some real-life Men-in-Black trickery -- someone at the MoD managed to extract all the photos and the negatives from the newspaper, who never got them back."

- **August 17, 2022.** At a town hall meeting held by NASA's Science Mission Directorate ("SMD"), its assistant deputy associate administrator for research (read: high enough) Dr. Daniel A. Evans promises: "We're going full force [on the UAP study] . . . This is really important to us, and we're placing a high priority on it." He elaborates that the study panel will consist of 15 to 17 people who will be "some of the world's leading scientists, data practitioners, artificial intelligence practitioners, [and] aerospace safety experts, all with a specific charge, which is to tell us how to apply the full focus of science and data to UAP."

- **August 19, 2022.** In a self-styled "event" called the "Big Phone Home," several "UFO activists," according to their website, "rally[] online to push for more transparency and accountability on these strange things seen in the sky and even underwear [sic]." The program includes speakers such as Professor Abraham "Avi" Loeb, of Harvard University; John Greenwald, Jr., founder of The Black Vault website; and ufologist Jane H. Kyle (known as "UFO Jane").

- **September 9, 2022.** The Department of Defense declares that releasing "any additional UFO videos . . . will [if done] harm national security" and that all of them now "are classified information." It states this partly in response to a Freedom of Information Act request made by The Black Vault, a relatively new UFO study group. Notably, in stating that "the videos contain sensitive information . . . and are classified and are exempt from disclosure," instead of refusing to confirm or deny that they exist, the Defense Department admits that UAP additional videos are in its possession.

- **September 23, 2022.** A part of the Federal Government that is known as the "National Intelligence Manager for Aviation" (or alternatively "for the Air Domain") and is sometimes referred to as "NIM Aviation," which is part of the "Intelligence Community" under the Director of National Intelligence, updates its official logo to include an image of a UFO. Serious or not, this is still reflective of the times.

- **September 28, 2022.** Amid growing speculation that the source of recent high-tech UAP sightings, if man-made, is China rather than Russia, NASA Administrator Clarence William "Bill" Nelson II expresses his concern that China is "very secretive" about such things. The advanced use of drones is particularly suspected. Indeed, as an even broader proposition, the increasing sophistication of drone technology now available to the general public (read: non-state actors) has made drones a greater and greater part of the UFO sightings landscape in recent years. Today, they are one of the first things suspected when conventional explanations are sought for UFO observations.

- **October 7, 2022.** The country's largest organization of government and private-sector technical experts in aerospace technology launches a project to study "unidentified aerial phenomena" after concluding that recent incursions by "mysterious" craft pose "a safety hazard to military and commercial aircraft." The American Institute of Aeronautics and Astronautics now has three committees, (1) to examine evident UAP technology, (2) to study how incursions affect pilot and passenger safety, and (3) to coordinate with government agencies and international researchers that also are focused on the topic. Called the "Unidentified Aerospace Phenomena Community of Interest," this group includes Lt. Ryan Graves, the Navy pilot who observed UFOs near the USS *Theodore Roosevelt* off the Virginia coast and then provided a closed-door briefing to members of national security-related congressional committees and their staffs in mid-2019, while still on active duty.

- **October 21, 2022.** NASA announces that a group of 16 people, including retired astronaut Scott J. Kelly (twin brother of Senator Mark E. Kelly), will spend the next nine months researching the information that is publicly available about UFOs/UAPs and how much more is needed to better understand unexplained sightings. The team, led by astrophysicist David N. Spergel, president of the Simons Foundation for advancing scientific research, will also consider how best to use all such information in the future. "Exploring the unknown in space and the atmosphere is at the heart of who we are at NASA," observes Thomas H. Zurbuchen, Associate Administrator of the Science Mission Directorate at NASA Headquarters. He goes on to say: "Understanding the data we have surrounding unidentified aerial phenomena is critical to helping us draw scientific conclusions about what is happening in our skies. Data is the language of scientists and makes the unexplainable, explainable." NASA says that the study will begin on October 24 and that a full report with the team's findings will be shared with the public in "mid-2023." In total, it is predicted to cost no more than $100,000.

- **October 31, 2022.** U.S. intelligence officials, through the Office of the Director of National Intelligence ("ODNI," to the intelligence cognoscente) deliver an updated report on UFO/UAP sightings to Congress, at least parts of which are expected (read: but not guaranteed) to be made available to the public very soon. It is submitted pursuant to the 2022 National Defense Authorization legislation that requires ODNI to provide an annual declassified update and a classified annex on the subject by October 31 of every year through 2026. This year's public report is expected to address recent unexplained sightings, including those of what some observers speculate are advanced Chinese drones or conceivably even China's new supersonic "J-20" jets. Once it is released by Congress in declassified form, it doubtless will stir up continuing controversy about the U.S. Government's ostensible new transparency approach to UAPs in recent years.

- **November 3, 2022.** More than a dozen federal agents from the FBI's Las Vegas Field Office and the Air Force's Office of Special Investigations ("OSI," to scared Nevadans), allegedly in "full riot gear," raid the home of notorious ufologist Joerg Arnu in the tiny desert town of Rachel, Nevada, the closest residential area to Area 51. Arnu, who operates a website labeled "Secrets of Area 51 Revealed" (reachable through dreamlandresort.com), claims that in a joint raid they pointed a gun at him and seized "laptops, phones, backup drives, camera gear" and a drone with which he makes overflights of Area 51 activity and facilities to post on his popular site. Arnu's home is one of a small group of residences clustered around a hotel in Rachel called the "Little A'le'Inn," on what is known as the "Extraterrestrial Highway," two hours north of Las Vegas and very close to Area 51's "back gate." A spokesman at nearby Nellis Air Force Base confirms that the raid did take place but offers no explanation for it.

- **November 9, 2022.** A new documentary titled "Moment of Contact" is released in the U.S. that depicts the mass sighting of nearly two dozen UFOs by both civilian and military witnesses in Brazil on May 19, 1986. It says that after these UFOs were viewed from the ground across the states of Sao Paulo, Rio de Janeiro, Minas Gerais, and Goiás, the Brazilian Air Force scrambled five fighter jets to intercept them. The documentary recounts that all five pilots became disoriented when they observed 21 bright objects "appear and disappear" while traveling at supersonic speed. It features a radio transmission by one of the fighter pilots to the control tower in which he yells "It's not an airplane, what is it?"

- **November 14, 2022.** A team of NASA researchers at its Jet Propulsion Laboratory in Pasadena, California, release a research report that postulates that "other civilizations, possibly several, have existed during the life of the Universe [sic]"; it does so, it says, "given a Universe stretching [across] approximately 92 billion lightyears and existing for nearly 14 billion years." But the report, titled "Avoiding the 'Great Filter': Extraterrestrial Life and Humanity's Future in the Universe," further postulates that one "existential disaster" or another may have "snowball[ed] quickly" into what it dubs the "Great Filter" of civilization destruction. It identifies the possible sources of such ultimate "grand scale" destruction as large-scale nuclear warfare, pathogens, impacts from asteroids, climate change, and artificial intelligence (AI), the latter of which it calls "Earth's first high-tech species." And as for the possible current existence of alien life, NASA's report concludes: ". . . the discovery of a planet-rich Universe has rendered less a question of whether aliens exist, but rather in the occurrence that they (statistically, at least) likely do, and are we *in a sufficiently stable position to receive such news.*"

- **December 16, 2022.** In the continued absence of a declassified version from Congress of this year's statutorily mandated ODNI report (see above), the Pentagon makes two high-level officials available for press interviews on the subject. Sean Kirkpatrick, director of the newly formed All-Domain Anomaly Resolution Office ("AARO"), says that he has received "several hundreds" of new UAP sightings, some of which might pose threats to U.S. national security. Elaborates Undersecretary of Defense for Intelligence and Security Ronald Moultrie: "In the absence of being able to resolve what something is, we assume that it [might] be hostile, so we have to take that seriously." Notably, these statements bespeak a new definition for the relatively new UFO acronym of "UAP": "Unidentified Anomalous Phenomena."

- **December 23, 2022.** President Biden signs into law the 2023 National Defense Authorization Act, which contains several provisions pertaining to UAPs and the operation of the Defense Department's new All-Domain Anomaly Resolution Office ("AARO," to those targeting UFOs). In addition to requiring an annual report to Congress on the subject by the Office of the Director of National Intelligence (which was submitted on October 31, 2022, but still has not been publicly released by Congress in declassified form), this law now requires an "Historical Record Report" that traces back to the 1940s. Initially, the "starting date" for this historical DOD investigation and report was set at January 1, 1947 (i.e., to include the Roswell incidents of July 1947), but this date was changed at the last minute to January 1, 1945, which is believed to be for the purpose of encompassing events recently reported to have occurred in San Antonio, New Mexico, on August 16, 1945 (with claimed military involvement soon thereafter). That date was just one month after the "Trinity" atomic bomb test was conducted 20 miles southwest of San Antonio, where a UFO was reported by local ranchers to have crash-landed during a thunderstorm near the Rio Grande. Recently, one surviving witness has come forward to say that he observed (with binoculars) soldiers from the nearby White Sands Proving Grounds load the crash debris onto a "huge flatbed truck," cover it with "blue tarpaulins," and take it away. Evidently, this recent report has been enough for Congress to make this last-minute change to call for an investigation of such "pre-Roswell" activity.

- **January 12, 2023.** The unclassified version of the "2022 Annual Report on Unidentified Aerial Phenomena" is finally published by the Office of the Director of National Intelligence after a months-long delay. It identifies (read: after a fashion) 171 newly reported UAP sightings that remain "uncharacterized and unattributed" upon initial analysis. "Some of these uncharacterized UAP [sic] appear to have demonstrated unusual flight characteristics or performance capabilities, and require further analysis," the report adds. In response, former Navy F/A-18 pilot and chair of the American Institute of Aeronautics and Astronautics' Unidentified Aerospace Phenomena Integration & Outreach Committee Ryan Graves observes: "We must stop unscrupulous speculation, break stigma, and invest in science to address this national safety threat."

- **February 4, 2023.** A high-altitude balloon is shot down by the U.S. Air Force after being observed traveling over North American airspace, including Alaska and Western Canada, for several days. Believed to be a Chinese-operated surveillance device, its wreckage is recovered off the coast of South Carolina and confirmed to be of terrestrial origin. Nevertheless, it triggers an "enhancement] of our radar," the Defense Department says, allowing it to "more closely scrutiniz[e] our airspace at these altitudes."

- **February 10-12, 2023.** Over the course of three consecutive days, three unidentified flying objects are detected over Alaska, Canada, and Michigan, where they are shot down by military forces. The first object, shot down over Alaska, is described in news reports as "the size of a small car." The second, downed over Canada's Yukon Territory, is described as "cylindrical." And the third, brought down off the coast of Lake Huron, is said to be "octagonal in structure." Together, and in such a short span of time, these four extraordinary incidents spark what the media call "UFO mania" in the U.S. and Canada.

- **February 16, 2023.** Taking an unprecedented step, President Joseph R. Biden addresses the Nation on the subject of the UAPs that recently were fired on and downed by U.S. military forces. Speaking for seven minutes from the White House, he calms the country by saying that he gave the order to fire at them "out of an abundance of caution" for our national security. "We don't yet know exactly what these three objects were," he acknowledges, "but nothing right now suggests they were related to China's spy balloon program or that they were surveillance vehicles from . . . any other country." And he explains the coincidence of three other objects atop the Chinese spy balloon as follows: "We don't have any evidence that there has been a sudden increase in the number of objects in the sky. We're now just seeing more of them partially because [of] the steps we've taken to increase our radar [capability]."

- **March 1, 2023.** In the wake of recent events involving UAPs over Canada, the Canadian Government announces that it has launched a national study of the subject to be conducted by the Office of the Chief Science Advisor of Canada. Entitled the "Sky Canada Project," it places emphasis on coordination with the U.S. and promises a report to the public sometime in 2024.

* * * * *

And all of this seems to be no less so regarding the closely related question of the possible existence of extraterrestrial life,[155] which of course holds the potential of being, inarguably, the biggest secret in human existence ever -- at least since that very first "caveman" and his three cavemates started things off (see the Introduction). Indeed, whole series of books and television programs have been devoted to this subject, with no small amount of focus on that cynical old belief that world leaders (and their dutiful underlings, buying into this down even to the lowest institutional levels) have concluded that when it comes to this, the general public "can't handle the truth" (with apologies to the play "A Few Good Men") and have acted accordingly. Perhaps so. In such a case -- i.e., once again, *if* all this were actually to be so -- it would seem to be a matter of secrecy not so much for the Department of Justice (at least not in the first instance), but rather more likely for NASA and DOD, ideally in that new order.[156]

On second thought, though, the Justice Department's involvement in this possible reality should not be given such short shrift. It is indeed conceivable that the state of the U.S. Government's knowledge of, and even experience with, alien life forms could reach a point at which, in the face of "targeted" FOIA requests (and FOIA litigation), there could be a need for careful legal representation of NASA's,[157] the CIA's, and/or DOD's interests in either blocking or limiting public knowledge of such things, for some valid reason and for at least some period of time. And in such a case -- i.e., *if* all of that were to become the case -- then the Department of Justice's involvement in such a new brand of secrecy would be paramount.[158]

CHAPTER FORTY-NINE
The Biggest Secrets Ever

"Three may keep a secret, if two of them are dead."

-- Benjamin Franklin, *Poor Richard's Almanack* (1735)

No book purporting to comprehensively address the subject of government secrecy would be complete without at least some attempt to assess the "biggest" secrets of all time. Doing so, of course, requires first dealing with exactly what that standard means. Does it mean the secret of the greatest magnitude? Is it the one that is most significant? The one with the most lives at stake? The longest-lasting?[1] The most effective? The secret most difficult for a government to keep? Does it matter that absolute secrecy was not achieved? Does it make a difference if absolute secrecy was not absolutely essential?

And must it be a secret that absolutely exists, as opposed to something that would be a secret only if it actually did exist? For example, the possible existence of intelligent alien life having visited Earth is only suspected, not known, and at that, it is suspected to be so only by some, not by most others. If those suspicions are in fact correct, though, and that "truth" actually is known with firm evidence by some within a government, then that is very arguably "secret number one" on any all-time government secrecy list.

But if such a thing does *not* in fact exist -- at least not yet -- then could it really be a secret at all? In that event, government records about UFOs, UAPs, and the like might be withheld from the public, for one reason or another, from one time and place to another, but not because any government is attempting to conceal the known existence of alien life. In other words, there might very well be no big secret there to hide, no matter how anything appears. On the other hand, though, because government secrecy can evolve over time,[2] at any given point in time there might exist some secret that is so deep and dark that the public has no inkling of it.[3]

The same is true for the two biggest assassinations of the 20th century -- that of President John F. Kennedy and of Dr. Martin Luther King, Jr., which were the subjects of what then were the most extensive law enforcement investigations ever[4] -- especially when one considers the work of the House Select Committee on Assassinations, which investigated both assassinations from 1976-1978, with a report covering both issued in 1979.[5] Even if based upon all of those investigations it is concluded that Lee Harvey Oswald and James Earl Ray were lone gunmen, then the "secret" in each case could well be that they did not act as such entirely alone -- meaning without the knowing assistance (read: conspiratorial involvement) of anyone else either before or after the fact.[6] But if that were not the case, if they indeed acted entirely alone and apart from anyone else, then there actually would be no such "secret" involved.[7]

Other "big secrets" are not complicated by such uncertainty.[8] There are no such doubts about the major military secrets that have been involved in a series of modern (read: in the last millennium) wars -- government secrets in the forms of covert diplomacy, cryptanalytic codebreaking, pivotal invasions or special forces raids, as well as the many secrets of the atomic age. Such secrets were spawned by the Revolutionary War, the Civil War, World War II, the Cold War, and most recently the Global War on Terrorism.[9]

Taking all of these secrecy elements into consideration, and balancing them against one another where need be, the following "top ten" list of historical government secrets is offered as at least a basis for debate and further discourse:

#1 D-Day. The Allied invasion of Normandy on June 6, 1944, known by the codeword "Operation Overlord" and most commonly as "D-Day," is the biggest secret of all time for several reasons.[10] First, the secret was uniquely multi-faceted, encompassing not only the "when" of it but the "where" of it as well; both aspects of the invasion had to be kept secret for a long time for it to succeed.[11] Had the Germans been able to prepare for it at Normandy rather than elsewhere (read: at Pas-de-Calais, the focal point of Allied deception[12]), and had they had precise knowledge of its timing, the Allied Forces' necessary foothold on the European Continent might never have been achieved, at least not before Germany either invaded England or otherwise brought it to its knees. And that would have inalterably changed the course of the war, even considering the subsequent availability of the atomic bomb. The fact that the Allied Forces were able to maintain the necessary secrecy in London and on England's southern coast[13] during the weeks, days, and hours leading up to the surprise landings was more pivotal and consequential than any military counterpart in all of history.[14]

#2 The Osama bin Laden raid. The most effective secrecy in modern U.S. history was maintained during the months, weeks, days, and hours preceding the deployment of SEAL Team Six to Abbottabad, Pakistan, on May 2, 2011. By that point, U.S. military and intelligence forces had been vigorously searching for Osama bin Laden for more than nine years, with minimal success. Then, in August of 2010, CIA analysts who had been tracking couriers known to have been used by bin Laden in the past detected a pattern of their visiting a place at the end of a dead-end dirt road on the outskirts of Abbottabad. This was known by only a few people within the "Intelligence Community" and when President Barack H. Obama was briefed on it, after asking the CIA to do everything it could to confirm bin Laden's presence at the suspected site as quickly as possible, he ended that briefing with the following order: "Don't tell anyone. Don't share this with anyone."[15]

By mid-December, after the CIA assessed there to be a very strong likelihood of bin Laden's presence at that location, the planning of a special forces raid on the compound began. That planning proceeded with the utmost of care and continued secrecy over the course of several months, with the military personnel who were chosen to direct and execute the raid being hand-picked for both their skill and their trustworthiness (read: demonstrated ability to be discrete). And within the White House and the Pentagon, no support staff was used, no record was made (read: any arguably applicable legal requirement to the contrary be damned), and every precaution was taken to prevent even the slightest whisper of what was going on to escape, as no one wanted the elusive bin Laden to "get spooked" and flee at any time, up to and including the very last minute.[16] This extraordinarily high degree of secrecy was absolutely essential to the eventual success of the special forces raid on bin Laden's compound.[17]

#3 The Breaking of the Enigma code. This was one secret atop another. The first, known as "Enigma," was the most secure communications code of its day, used by the German High Command during the first part of World War II. This code was the biggest secret of that war until it was "broken" by a team of highly specialized cryptanalysts who were gathered by the British Government on an estate known as "Bletchley Park" from 1939 through the end of the war. On July 9, 1941, at the very moment that the most sensitive (read: German naval) part the code was broken, the priority at Bletchley Park *instantly* shifted from one thing to another -- as can happen when a secret actually is that an original secret has itself been compromised. In other words, in this case the German secret was immediately replaced by an Allied secret -- i.e., that the Enigma code *had been broken*, with an imperative of preserving at all costs that new secret, such being the very nature of codes and codebreaking.[18] One could say that, in effect, it became a secret about the learning of a secret. And this new secret was kept for the duration of the war, greatly aiding England's (and the Allies') war efforts,[19] and in fact it was not fully disclosed the public for more than 30 years.[20]

#4 UFOs. Since the mid-1940s, if not by other names earlier, the subject of "flying saucers," "unidentified flying objects" ("UFOs," to most observers), or most recently "unidentified aerial phenomena" ("UAPs," to the U.S. military lately) has been a major source of suspected government secrecy for the past 75 years. This "secret's" ranking here is diminished, however, by the simple fact that such a thing might not actually exist (see Chapter Forty-Eight). On the other hand, though, is the strongly compelling factor that if UFO sightings and "deathbed confessions" mean that intelligent alien life (read: as visitors to Earth) *does exist or has existed*, and is actually known to exist or have existed by one or more governments, then this secret becomes the biggest one of all time, by far. Hence, it averages out at #4 on the list, with its significance slightly edging out its arguable unlikelihood.[21]

#5 The Manhattan Project. The secret development of the atomic bomb by a group of physicists in the New Mexico desert[22] during 1942-1946 is a well-known part of history today that was kept completely hidden from the public (including even the then-vice president) when it took place. According to the U.S. military, it was "more drastically guarded than any other highly secret war development," with no more than a few dozen people in the entire country knowing its full scope and import. One reason for such unprecedented secrecy was the fear that knowledge of it could induce Germany to accelerate its own nuclear projects, which actually were even more advanced than was suspected. While this secrecy was largely successful, it did become known after the fact (read: in 1950) that one spy, by the name of Klaus Fuchs, worked as a primary physicist at the Manhattan Project's main New Mexico compound. Thus, while total secrecy was not in fact achieved, it turned out not to be absolutely necessary for the secret enterprise to succeed.[23]

#6 Atomic secrets. Once the Manhattan Project produced the two atom bombs that ended World War II in the Pacific Theater in August of 1945, the world immediately entered the "atomic age," in which all of the technology, information, and knowledge pertaining to that was, in popular terms, held as "Top Secret."[24] Simply put, the U.S. manifestly had the technical wherewithal to "split the atom" and certainly had a strong interest in not sharing any information about that with others, at least not yet, so it proceeded to maintain the same level of secrecy about it that had characterized the Manhattan Project to begin with. And as that technology advanced even further to hydrogen bombs, plutonium bombs, and thermonuclear weapons of greater magnitude, there were more and more major and subsidiary secrets to be kept from falling into the hands of foreign powers -- most particularly the U.S.'s former ally, but almost instant adversary, the Soviet Union. Before long, the U.S. was working hard to protect its "atomic secrets" from highly skilled and well-placed Soviet espionage agents who became notorious for their effectiveness. And by the end of the 1940s, and well into the 1950s with the advent of what was called the "Cold War," this intensified and led to a secrecy regime that surpassed all others.[25]

#7 The covert American relationship with France. During the mid-1770s, including through the early stages of the Revolutionary War (formally referred to as America's "War for Independence"), it became clear to the revolutionaries that negotiating the assistance of France was going to be vital to that war's success. The Colonies' Continental Congress, which pre-existed the Declaration of Independence, had in 1775 established a "Committee of Secret Correspondence" to handle such sensitive diplomatic matters,[26] but that committee had many members. Benjamin Franklin, for one, had observed that "[t]hree may keep a secret, if two of them are dead,"[27] and most pointedly that "Congress consists of too many members to keep secrets." So future President George Washington made a decision not to inform anyone,[28] even members of the Continental Congress, of the pivotal negotiations that during late 1776 and throughout 1777 Benjamin Franklin undertook with France.[29] And France, as a result, began providing assistance to the Continental Army early on, but in an entirely clandestine manner. Indeed, there was a strong covert relationship between the new Nation of America and France that even pre-dated the formal treaties between the two that were signed on February 6, 1778. That secrecy was key to America winning the Revolutionary War.

#8 The JFK Assassination. As is noted above, this is a potential secret that might not actually exist. In other words, if Lee Harvey Oswald was indeed a lone gunman (which seems most probable in and of itself)[30] *and* if beyond that he actually acted without any co-conspiratorial instigation or support either beforehand or afterward (which seems much less likely), then there really is no secret here, unless you want to count the depths of Oswald's motivation.[31] But if this is not so, in any respect (read: even if only as regards Jack Ruby), then there is one helluva secret that persists here, one that would more than likely (read: though not necessarily) involve some arm of the Federal Government (most likely the CIA[32]), part of a local Texas government, perhaps the Cuban Government, or even the quasi-institutional structures of organized crime.

#9 The MLK Assassination. The same is true for the assassination of Dr. Martin Luther King, Jr., which occurred just four-plus years later (see Chapter Three). To be sure, the speculation about another gunman has been less intense here,[33] as has the theorizing about whether any others (read: especially instigators) might have been involved.[34] But as with the assassination of JFK, the secret involvement of anyone else would shock the country if it were true and were conclusively shown to be true, even if that did not include any government involvement, just some subsequent government awareness.

#10 Vatican secrecy. The first consideration here is whether "the Vatican," otherwise known as the "Holy See" or the Vatican City State, can be considered to be a "government." Historically, it has long been regarded as a sovereign entity under international law and in 1929 it became entirely independent from Italy by treaty.[35] As to its secrets, this is another case in which their particular subject areas are not entirely known, but any institution that for centuries has maintained a doctrine known as "Secretum Pontificium" is bound to be rife with them; without a doubt, there are secrets buried in the Vatican Secret Archive[36] that for centuries have not seen the light of day.[37] Most recently, the little-known anti-Nazi activities of Pope Pius XII both prior to and during World War II,[38] as well as the cover-ups of child abuse by Catholic clergy for many decades,[39] have solidified the Vatican's modern place on this "top ten" secrecy list.[40]

HONORABLE MENTIONS (IN NO PARTICULAR ORDER)

The Cuban Missile Crisis, most particularly the "secret codicil" to the U.S./Soviet deal resolving it that required the U.S. to remove its Jupiter missiles from Turkey. It was publicly announced that to resolve this nuclear standoff, the Soviet Union agreed to withdraw its missiles from Cuba in exchange for the U.S. pledging that it would not invade Cuba (as it had with the "Bay of Pigs fiasco" in 1961). What was not made public, and was kept completely secret for many years to come (read: until the late 1980s),[41] was that the U.S. also agreed that its Jupiter missiles located in Turkey (read: within striking distance of Moscow) would be removed as well.[42] There was an obvious political advantage to such secrecy.

The "**Venona Project**," a U.S. signals decryption counterintelligence program that was employed against the Soviet Union's intelligence apparatus from 1943 to 1980 (most heavily during the 1940s, including against "atomic spies" Julius and Ethel Rosenberg), which was kept secret even from Presidents Roosevelt and Truman and remained secret until 1995. Beyond its 37-year duration of secret operations and the total 52-year period of its secrecy, Venona's candidacy also is burnished by the fact that it yielded knowledge of Soviet espionage at the Manhattan Project in the mid-1940s and enabled the discovery of what is known as the "Cambridge Spy Ring" (Donald D. Maclean, Guy F. Burgess, Harold A. "Kim" Philby, Anthony F. Blunt, and John Cairncross), a long-term cadre of university-bred British spies, in the 1950s. And from a purely technical standpoint, the fact that it involved the painstaking analyses of extremely sophisticated, "double-encrypted" cryptographic systems (which used a "one-time pad"), without the aid of anything even resembling a computer, makes it a standout in secret cryptanalysis second only to what was achieved at Bletchley Park.

NSA telecommunications interception and surveillance during the 2000s and beyond (read: "warrantless surveillance"), which remained largely secret notwithstanding the revelations made by *The New York Times* in December of 2005, **and the subsequent unlawful disclosures made about that by former CIA employee and later NSA contractor Edward J. Snowden.** The disclosures made by Snowden in 2013 revealed, *inter alia*, NSA's longtime underwater cable interception in connection with U.S. allies such as Sweden, Norway, and France. The Kingdom of Denmark secretly aided this U.S. espionage effort, through an operation that it code-named "Dunhamme." On May 31, 2021, after further disclosures were made by official Danish sources, French President Emmanuel Macron demanded further details from Denmark and the United States. For its part, Germany joined Macron's demand, even though its own foreign intelligence service, the Bundesnachrightendienst, has aided those U.S. espionage efforts as well. (On another note, and I'm going to phrase this very carefully, I do not recall with certainty whether there was any connection between this particular activity and "Operation Ivy Bells.")

The origin of such secret telecommunications surveillance actually traces back to the second half of the Clinton Administration, when it was first employed against narcoterrorists largely in South America. Records of that activity were contained in the safes (read: "class six containers") that were maintained by OIP as part of its support of the attorney general's handling of her national security classification responsibilities.

Now the "flip side" of such U.S. surveillance secrecy, so to speak, is the use of "secret subpoenas" to obtain telecommunications information (read: phone call and email records) of U.S. journalists who are suspected to have been the recipients of national security leaks. Apart from such subpoenas being used during the Trump Administration (and continuing "on automatic pilot" into the early days of the Biden Administration), they were discovered to have been used even during the Obama Administration, for two months of records related to 20 telephone lines, in 2013, including records from major *Associated Press* bureaus and the home phone and cell phone records of individual journalists working there. As in other such situations, it was not just the fact that this was done, it was that it was kept secret both during and after it was done.[43]

The modern formula for "invisible ink," which was treated as "classified" from the time it came into active use for World War I until even as late as 2011. It is difficult nowadays to find a government secret that has stood as such for as many as 100 years. Vatican secrecy aside, perhaps the strongest candidates for this distinction are the royal wills in England that have been dutifully kept secret over the centuries. Currently, there is at least one such will that has remained secret since 1910 -- and most recently the will of Prince Philip, the late husband of Queen Elizabeth II, has been ordered sealed (in a hearing held in secret) for the next 90 years on the rationale that such secrecy is necessary to protect "the Queen's dignity." Recently, a British Government official, when pressed on the subject, acknowledged that the legal basis for this longstanding practice is "rather slender."

The U.S.'s "Ivy Bells" undersea cable communications interception operation, perhaps connected to the coterminous *"Glomar Explorer"* one. As is detailed in the chapter discussing "Glomarization," Chapter Seventeen, these two CIA operations occurred in close proximity to one another and might or might not have been connected. And if I knew that they were, through my handling of the *Glomar Explorer* FOIA litigation, I might still be barred from confirming that even more than 40 years after the fact.[44] (Yes, that is part of how national security classification can work.)[45]

The assassination of Robert F. Kennedy on June 5, 1968, for which Sirhan B. Sirhan has been jailed as a "lone assassin" ever since. Certainly no better than third on the list of 1960s assassinations, Robert Kennedy's murder has been the subject of much less public speculation over the past 50-plus years. But the fact remains that there is some credible evidence that Sirhan was subject to hypnotic manipulation at the time. Furthermore, a recent, more sophisticated acoustic analysis of an audiotape of the assassination concluded that 13 shots were fired, even though Sirhan's weapon had a capacity for only eight bullets (read: a compelling "fact" to be sure), and that the other five shots were fired from behind RFK (whereas Sirhan was in front of him), causing the four bullet holes that were found on the posterior side of RFK's body. And even though Kennedy's body was turned to his left to shake someone's hand at that fatal moment, there was an armed security guard alongside him (and therefore behind him when he turned) who bore him some animus. (This "rented" guard, Thane Eugene Cesar, had his gun drawn and it was never checked for firing during the investigation.) This ought to be enough to have raised reasonable doubt about Sirhan's guilt, or at least about his having been deemed a lone assassin.

Even Robert F. Kennedy, Jr., recently has said that he does not believe that Sirhan killed his father, and his sister, former Maryland Lieutenant Governor Kathleen Kennedy Townsend, has supported her brother's call for a reinvestigation of their father's assassination. In 2021, Sirhan was formally recommended for parole, but on January 13, 2022, that was rejected by California Governor Gavin C. Newsom, who has cited RFK as a political hero of his.

This brings up an ugly rumor: I know firsthand that in the 1970s it was believed by many folks at the Bureau that FBI Director J. Edgar Hoover personally commissioned a photographer to secretly photograph nearly every square inch of Robert Kennedy's dead body. This connects to the fact that there was much "bad blood" between the two, going back to the 1950s, which centered largely around the fact that RFK was a strong organized crime combatant and Hoover was an avowed organized crime denier. (He would rather his Special Agents chase "commies" or bank robbers than fight what he saw as a "losing battle" against organized crime). It also connects to the longtime rumors (read: since the 1940s) of Hoover's homosexuality, though they have never been confirmed. At a minimum, the corpse-photographs rumor is made plausible by Hoover's known psychological lust for power.

The clandestine Scotland Yard surveillance of the Crown Prince of Wales (later King Edward VIII and then the Duke of Windsor) together with Wallis Warfield Simpson during the mid-1930s, which culminated in the wiretapping of royal telephone calls by agents of MI-5 (and also by the FBI) on into the early 1940s. British intelligence agencies had long been greatly concerned about the royal couple's sympathies toward Nazi Germany. According to archived FBI records, the Duchess of Windsor in particular was suspected of sending secret messages to Germany about British activity. And the FBI, in coordination with the United States Secret Service, and with the encouragement of President Franklin Delano Roosevelt, greatly aided MI-5 with very active covert surveillance of the couple (read: through both "HUMINT" and "COMINT") during the many months that they spent in the United States. This severe royal intrusion was unprecedented in British history (read: utterly unthinkable to monarchists) and not just because the technology for it was relatively new. Indeed, the very fact of it was kept secret from the British public for nearly 80 (read: yes, 80) years.

The FBI's "Solo Sources," which were two high-level officials of the Communist Party of the United States who both so successfully spied against it (and the Soviet Union) that the FBI was able to secretly frame someone else for doing that. This rare episode of intense "spy vs. spy" maneuvering is discussed at length in Chapter Fifteen.

The Trojan Horse, though perhaps only a creature of mythology, which held an overnight secret that historically is said to have made all the difference to the outcome of the longstanding Trojan War. While the Trojan War and the ancient Greeks' siege against Troy are accepted as historical fact, the existence of the Trojan Horse itself is not *conclusively* documented through the epic poems of Homer and Virgil and other classic Greek literature. But like other things on this list, it's possible (read: even likely) existence is sufficient to qualify it for mention.

The Totten secret, which is the abstract fact that President Abraham Lincoln himself entered into a "secret contract" to personally receive covert intelligence about troop movements and other strategic conditions in the South. It is discussed at some length in Chapter One.[46]

CHAPTER FIFTY
Conclusion

"The liberties of a people never were, nor ever will be, secure, when the transactions of their rulers may be concealed from them."

-- Patrick Henry, 1736-1799

There are some things in life that, as long as I live, I am sure, I will never be able to completely understand.[1] The nature of "superconductivity," for instance; the intransigent case for "creationism" over Darwinian evolution; the functioning of "macroeconomics"; the strong appeal of the Broadway show *Hamilton: An American Musical*; and the psyche and inexplicable popularity (read: to some) of Donald J. Trump, who so very obviously is greatly psychologically impaired.[2] But my many years at the Department of Justice and the legal matters that I personally handled during those years have allowed me to acquire a firm understanding of the processes of government in general and of our Federal Government in particular, together with a bit of "human nature" thrown in for good measure. And some observations, many of which I am willing to share here, flow from that.

First, it certainly is true "what they say" about practical experience often being worth more than mere "book learnin'." My use of the "internship concept" -- not just once but thrice, actually, when you count my experience clerking for a federal judge and my time as a law student/law clerk at the Justice Department during 1973-1974 -- proved that for me. As did, in a comparable way, my earliest times as a fresh young government litigator as I gained knowledge and experience, as well as sheer skill, with extraordinary speed.[3] So I would tell all of my students, during my decade of teaching law later on that they should not substitute the substance of what I was teaching them from a lectern with the more valuable experience to be gained in the "real world."[4]

Speaking of which, my own experience also taught me the potential importance of "process" over "substance" overall. "Process *über alles*," I would say to my students (as well as to my own children as they became more and more sophisticated in their personal decisionmaking processes),[5] trying to prepare them for that "real world." Certainly, the realm of litigation is a quintessential example of this: Learning and advantageously applying the judicial rules of procedure (and thus strategies) governing case adjudication, I found, was indeed more than half "the battle." It is the very thing that, after my judicial clerkship, allowed me to be more successful than most of even my more senior Trial Attorney colleagues "right off the bat" during 1977-1978.

Another lesson learned is that, as an invariable rule, there is nothing in the world quite as dangerous as the second half of the second term of a Republican administration. This is so because, first and foremost, Republican political appointees tend to be not as experienced and capable (not to mention as dedicated) as Democrat ones as a general rule. And sometimes this is blatantly, even embarrassingly apparent.[6]

Now, this sounds like an awfully derogatory opinion to express so blithely, all the more so in that it marks a departure from the decidedly non-political approach that I brought to my government work and, hopefully, also to the tales told in this book (at least for the most part, I would like to think). But this is no less true, my experience tells me, and it stems largely from the simple fact that, statistically speaking, potential Republican appointees are more "well off" where they are positioned in the private sector beforehand than are Democrat ones; therefore, a Republican president has to "dig a little deeper" than a Democrat one in filling out his (or her) administration.[7]

To this, we must add that, as another general rule, the appointees in any president's second term are not quite as sterling as the ones of the first term (no matter how few of the latter have by then reached jail). This is sometimes best expressed in "A Team/B Team" terms, with an oft-snarky assessment of the latter, but we all know it to be true. And while this dichotomy might exist most evidently at the cabinet (and perhaps immediate sub-cabinet) level, to those of us in the career ranks of federal agencies it becomes increasingly evident as a second presidential term wears on.[8]

Which brings us to the *pièce de résistance*, the second half of a president's second term. My experience with this nearly began during the presidency of Richard Nixon (see Chapter Ten), but no more need be said about how that turned out.[9] This next encompassed the entire second term of President Clinton, including its second half, where there was so much going on that we scarcely had time to finish it all (see Chapter Thirty-Four). Nevertheless, there was to me a noticeable decline during those last two Clinton years, as best evidenced, perhaps, by Clinton's feverish pardon activity at the very end of his presidency.[10]

In January of 2005, when President George W. Bush began only the *first* half of his second term, he celebrated by shifting White House Counsel Alberto R. Gonzales to the position of attorney general of the United States,[11] thus perhaps easing some problem(s) within the White House but disastrously impairing the reputation, capabilities, and essential integrity of the Department of Justice in the bargain. This was so bad for the Justice Department that it laid the necessary groundwork for what took place near the end of the next year and then after January of 2007, in the second half of Bush 43's second term (see Chapters Forty-Two and Forty-Three).[12]

Another semi-gratuitous observation: The United States Department of Justice badly needs another deputy attorney general-level leadership position for proper, day-to-day "span of control" if nothing else. This has been true for a long time in my humble opinion, but never more so than in the wake of 9/11. In saying this, of course, I am mindful more than most that the other such Justice Department leadership position, that of associate attorney general, was created only a relatively short time ago (so recently that I myself remember it quite well in 1977). And that even once the Department (under Attorney General Elliot L. Richardson) came to realize that that leadership position was essential (i.e., in the fall of 1973), it took another 3½ years for that idea to firmly take hold.[13]

So one might ask, especially if that "one" were an OMB budget official: "If the Justice Department could get by with only one high-level leadership position below the attorney general until 1977, and has had the benefit of having added one then, then why does it need yet another one (tripling the number of such positions that it had until 1977) now? The first answer, I would say, is that the Justice Department was badly understaffed in this regard to begin with, particularly in comparison to the other senior cabinet departments.[14] The second is that the key legal/political position that the Department of Justice now holds, both in public perception and reverberations of newer "Trump-era" reality, has itself grown immeasurably in recent years. And the third reason (among others that the Department's budgeteers would mobilize to formulate) -- the very simplest one -- is 9/11. Having lived through the Department's post-9/11 existence for more than five years before retiring, I know firsthand that its leadership structure often has been overwhelmed. And that's on a good day.

* * * * *

As for government secrecy, I must say that it is alive but only partly well in the year 2023. Within the U.S. Federal Government, the very concept of it actually has developed *relatively* smoothly, if not always successfully, from the late 1930s to the 2020s -- though with several notable bumps and setbacks (e.g., espionage, leaks,[15] WikiLeaks, national security classification overuse, delayed declassification, black lists, black budgets, "black sites," "extreme rendition," secret drone strikes, war crimes, torture, "water boarding," cover-ups, privacy violations, White House obfuscation (in the Trump Administration, sometimes a euphemism for outright lying), and unlawful federal surveillance (in chronological order: physical, electronic, cyber, "emanational," and perhaps telepathic), along the way.[16]

But in our "modern" world (which looks less and less deserving of that sobriquet every day, despite the not-unamalgamated blessings of the "electronic revolution"),[17] with secrecy so heavily damaging the public's trust more and more as time goes by, one has to wonder whether our National Government (and those of other nations around the world) has not greatly overdone it with "secrecy" in recent years, even taking into account the enormous effects and exigencies of 9/11.

I, for one, am all in favor of secrecy's utility -- I've used it myself too many times (even in this book) not to be so -- but I am no more sanguine, by dint of experience, about the danger that it holds. And while such a danger is threatening enough when it is known, it is much more so when it is not. So I conclude here with the hope that those who follow me in this field of law and policy will recognize this danger as they proceed to build upon what already has been done in it by public servants such as myself.[18]

Epilogue

"Washington is too small to be a state, but too big to be an asylum."

-- Former EPA Administrator Anne Irene McGill Gorsuch Burford, in her autobiography *Are You Tough Enough?*, after a scandal doomed her career, 1986

It has now been more than 15 years since I retired from the Department of Justice,[1] and looking back from this distance of time, the biggest question for me is: "How the hell did I manage to accomplish so much over the course of my time there?" No small part of that question's answer lies in the "right place/right time" good fortune that I enjoyed so many times.[2] A second part of the answer is that I consistently worked exceptionally long and hard -- never once turning down a litigation case or shying from any opportunity to serve the public, even if in some unfamiliar way -- which gave me an enormous advantage. The very fact that I worked 75 hours per week on average during my last five-plus years, due to the unprecedented information-policy demands spawned by 9/11, speaks to this.[3]

But above all, I think, is the fact that I was working in a subject-matter area (including closely related ones) that at the time (i.e., the mid-1970s) was distinct and finite enough that it could be completely mastered -- so that I could develop truly unmatched expertise in it, which even early on gave me singular "guru" status,[4] both within and outside of the Federal Government, even internationally. Now all of this sounds extremely immodest, of course, but that cannot be helped.[5]

And to be sure, it doubtless is what can happen with many subject-matter experts, in all fields of endeavor, who manage to achieve "pinnacle status" in their chosen fields. But mine was one in which I was purely serving the public interest at every turn, which in turn spurred me to work harder and harder at it. Such is the nature of government service in general,[6] which is a good thing, as most civil servants are certainly not there for the pay.[7]

So I have very few regrets. As I have recounted here, two of them have to do with the "mug shot" issue (detailed in Chapter Forty-One) and with a basic "electronic record" issue (detailed in Chapter Thirty-Four). And a few more have to do with my utter failure to anticipate when someone might actually lie about something, even (or perhaps especially) about something important; the lesson learned is that some people actually will go so far as to tell a bold-faced lie if he or she (actually, two of each, in this case) feels the need to do so.[8]

Overall, though, it was, as they say, one hell of a run.[9]

Glossary of Terms

"Why did the spy cross the road? He didn't. He was never really on your side."

"My neighbor thinks I spy on her. I would tell her otherwise, but she's in the shower right now."

-- Two old spy jokes (nevertheless told by young spies), circa 1940s and 2010s, respectively

The entries that follow are listed not alphabetically, but not randomly either. In some instances,[1] they contain details that are somewhat beyond the scope of a book chapter, but they nevertheless are within the intended scope of the book.

FOIA (pronounced "FOYA," as in the phrase "It's good FOIA") -- the Freedom of Information Act, which was enacted in 1966, took effect on July 4, 1967, and has been amended by Congress several times since then. Its governmentwide implementation is overseen by OIP (and, to a lesser degree since 2009, OGIS).[2]

FRA -- the Federal Records Act, which is virtually coextensive in scope with the FOIA and governs the creation, use, maintenance, and disposition of federal records. Its governmentwide implementation is overseen by NARA, and it is what former Secretary of State Hillary R. Clinton violated (through use of her personal email account atop her private email server) throughout her entire tenure in that position. It provides for civil, not criminal, penalties for its violation, and only for employees who have not yet left federal service when their violations are discovered and acted upon.

PRA -- the Presidential Records Act, which is mutually exclusive in scope with the FOIA (and the FRA, likewise) in that it pertains to "inner" White House records (i.e., those of the president and his or her closest advisors). Its governmentwide implementation is overseen by the General Services Administration ("GSA," to those who need supplies), but the records covered by it come into the custody of the "presidential library system," which is operated by NARA. Any presidential administration's suspected failure to comply with this law, particularly as it is ending, can lead to prophylactic civil litigation. (And as currently may be seen in the case of former President Donald J. Trump's flagrant removal of even classified presidential records to his home at Mar-a-Lago, it also could lead to criminal litigation, i.e., prosecution.)[3]

"Inner" White House -- a colloquial term for the part of the Executive Office of the President that consists of "the president and his or her closest advisors," including both individuals and offices qualifying as such. Its records are not subject to the FOIA (at least not directly) and they are governed by the PRA, rather than by the FRA, for both recordkeeping and archival purposes. Examples are the Office of White House Counsel, the Domestic Policy Council, the White House Military Office ("WHMO," to its civilian friends), the Office of Administration ("OA," to its sympathizers, thanks to Vice President Dick Cheney), and the National Security Council ("NSC," to security buffs) (as of 1994). By contrast, entities such as the Office of Management and Budget ("OMB," or "inner White House wannabees" to their non-admirers) are not within this protective bubble and do have to respond to FOIA requests.

Privacy Act of 1974 (known simply as "the Privacy Act," by its many fans) -- the major companion statute to the FOIA that in large part overlaps with it, in small part seemingly conflicts with it, and for the most part works in tandem with it toward a rational result. It covers only United States citizens and those persons lawfully admitted for permanent residence ("LPRs," to their amigos). Its contents and operation are the subject of Chapter Fourteen. And it is not to be confused with any other statute (federal or state) that might sound like it or operate like it, such as the "Electronic Communications Privacy Act," the "Electronic Data Protection Act," the "Computer Fraud and Abuse Act," or the proposed "Data Privacy Act" (otherwise known to its many congressional supporters as the "Digital Accountability and Transparency to Advance Privacy Act," a second- or third-generation progeny of the eponymously named "USA PATRIOT Act").[4]

Right to Financial Privacy Act of 1978 ("RFPA," to its very close friends, who adhere to it "on account") -- a complex statute regulating the circumstances under which "bank records" can be obtained, or not, by federal law enforcement agencies. While in the Civil Division, I served as the principal interpreter and policy-development source for this new statute from early 1979 (when it took effect) until late 1981, taking responsibility for personally handling the first half-dozen cases litigated under it as a means of further guiding its implementation. This law was seen as a model for future ones planned by the Department of Justice to address similar areas such as medical records, insurance records, electronic fund transfer records, and the like, plans that never came to fruition once President Jimmy Carter lost his bid for re-election in 1980.

HIPAA (or the "Health Insurance Portability and Accountability Act of 1996," to its patient patients) -- a federal law that requires the creation and use of national standards to protect sensitive patient-health information from being disclosed without the patient's consent (and sometimes even knowledge). It came into being more than 15 years "after the fact" when medical privacy legislation prepared within the Justice Department during the Carter Administration in 1979-1980 ran afoul of presidential politics during that latter year.[5] It has been implemented at both government and private-sector levels by regulations issued by the Department of Health and Human Services ("HHS," to those with patients); for the typical person, it most commonly prohibits the disclosure of healthcare information without the specific consent (known as an "HIPAA authorization") of the individual patient.[6] (Tip: If you have aged or near-aged parents, become familiar with this.)

TSA -- the Trade Secrets Act, a criminal statute otherwise known within the Government as "18 U.S.C. § 1905," which very broadly encompasses "business information" and prohibits the public disclosure of such information by any federal employee, except as is "authorized by law." It is not an Exemption 3 statute under the FOIA, but it operates in tandem with Exemption 4 of the FOIA to bar any "discretionary disclosure" of information falling within that exemption, just as the Privacy Act can do in conjunction with Exemption 6 or Exemption 7(C).

"Reverse FOIA" -- a subject-matter area related to the FOIA's administration that focuses on the Act's "business information" exemption, Exemption 4, together with the procedural rights of the "business submitters" of that information[7] to federal agencies when "their" submitted information becomes the subject of a FOIA request.[8] It is largely based upon a presidential executive order, Executive Order 12,600,[9] and it involves an elaborate "administrative process" whereby businesses try but often fail to convince federal agencies that such information ought to be withheld as exempt under Exemption 4 rather than be disclosed.[10] Over the years, hundreds of such disputes have proceeded to court, in what is referred to as "reverse FOIA" litigation, where the Government usually (but with notable exceptions, all too often with McDonnell Douglas as the plaintiff) prevails.[11]

Antideficiency Act -- a criminal statute originally enacted in the late 19th century that prohibits the Federal Government's acceptance of "voluntary services" from any person or entity beyond what has been appropriated for by Congress. It is the reason why the Federal Government enters a "government shutdown" of some duration whenever Congress misses a deadline for passing a full-year or interim appropriations bill, something that has occurred with alarming frequency over the last four decades.[12]

The Protect National Security Documents Act of 2009 ("PNSDA," to its DOD friends) -- the statute hastily enacted by Congress in October 2009 to counteract the court-ordered public disclosure of certain DOD photographs taken by a service member "on the ground" in Afghanistan that both President Barack Obama and I viewed as too dangerously sensitive to be disclosed in response to a FOIA request.

Geneva Conventions -- a series of post-World War II multilateral treaties that in part regulate the public disclosure of certain information about prisoners of war and as such might qualify as an Exemption 3 statute under the FOIA. They are what the White House (read: Vice President Dick Cheney) in 2002 very controversially deemed to be "quaint."

Official Secrets Act -- the century-old law of the United Kingdom that makes it a criminal offense for any government employee, or by extension any media entity, journalist, or even private citizen sometimes to publicly disclose "damaging" information "relating to security or intelligence."[13] This law is characteristic of Commonwealth nations and in the U.K. has been amended or replaced four times since 1889, most recently in 1989. In one sense, it is akin to Exemption 1 of the FOIA and its underlying executive order on the classification of national security information, but in its broadest sense it stands contrary to the freedom-of-the-press principles embodied in our First Amendment.

FOIA Request -- the means by which a person, organization, or institution -- i.e., nearly "any person"[14] -- can seek access to "reasonably described" federal records maintained by (i.e., within the custody or control of) a Federal Executive Branch department or agency. This sometimes is referred to as the vehicle by which a record can be "placed on the hook" through the FOIA.

Redaction (or deletion, excision, or "blacking out") -- the process of withholding something from the released version of a requested record or information. This is a big part of what is sometimes referred to as FOIA "processing."

Search -- the process by which an agency locates records that at least initially appear to be responsive (by their subject matter) to the terms of a FOIA request.

Copying (or photocopying, duplication, or reproduction) -- a step taken for purposes of handling a FOIA request. This was definitely required in the old "paper world," but it might or might not be required for FOIA requests now handled entirely electronically.

AG -- shorthand for the attorney general.[15]

DAG -- shorthand for the deputy attorney general.[16]

ASG -- shorthand for the associate attorney general.[17]

SG -- shorthand for the solicitor general.[18]

Bureau -- a familiar form of "FBI."

Special Agent -- the title of the law enforcement officers of the FBI.

ASAC -- the Assistant Special Agent-in-Charge (i.e., second-in-command) of an FBI field office, of which there are currently 56.

"June files" -- records that the FBI improperly maintained apart from its Central Records System, making them isolated from records that are regularly located for disclosure in criminal discovery and, as of 1975, also shielded from disclosure in response to FOIA requests. "June files" pertaining even to the JFK Assassination existed in the FBI's Dallas Field Office as of March of 1978, where I came across them (read: incidentally, in an out-of-the-way place) while overseeing the search for all JFK Assassination-related records there. The FBI ceased using that designation thereafter.[19]

"See References" -- collateral file designations made by FBI clerks over the years within the Bureau's "main" subject-matter files in order to keep track of other subjects or persons of significant interest. These designations (sometimes called "cross references") were made through what the Bureau called "hash marks" -- i.e., penciled-in diagonal lines adjacent to secondary subjects (e.g., names) on the face of original paper records -- that led to those subjects or individuals being indexed as "see references" in the Bureau's Central Records System. Then, when a search for records responsive to a FOIA request was done, the "search slip" prepared for that request would list "main" files and "see reference" records separately, with the latter not necessarily included for processing the request.

This system became controversial in the very late 1970s and was challenged in the *Ramo* case that I took to trial in 1979 (see below). As a separate issue of law, it became the subject of a post-trial hearing at which the FBI's practice was defended by me (because the Bureau's legal position was at that time defensible), with a supplemental decision issued in the FBI's favor on September 21, 1979. Nowadays, the FBI's main FOIA-processing office, which bears the unfortunate name of "Record/Information Dissemination Section," or "RIDS," takes a more inclusive approach to "see reference" records.

"Call Detail" records -- records in data form produced by a telephone exchange or other telecommunications equipment that documents the details of a telephone call or other telecommunications transaction (e.g., text message) that passes through that facility or device. Such records contain various attributes of the call, such as time, duration, completion status, source number, and destination number, often referred to as routinely recorded "metadata." They are the automated equivalent of the paper "toll tickets" that in the past were written and timed by operators for long-distance calls in a manual telephone exchange. In the late 1980s, some federal agencies resisted including such information -- which they labeled as "mere metadata" -- in response to FOIA requests, but OIP determined otherwise and enforced its determination.[20]

"El Marko" -- the nickname used within the Bureau (as well as elsewhere) for the highlighter-type implement employed to "black out" exempt information on a page; used properly, a page portion would show as brown on a document original (meaning that it could still be read by a "processing" reviewer) but black once photocopied, especially (at one point in time) if on a Kodak copying machine.

"White Out" -- the generic name used within the Bureau for a liquid employed to cover exempt information on a page; its use, in lieu of an El Marko pen or its equivalent, can leave it unclear exactly what was redacted (see Chapter Twenty-Four). Very similar to the products "Wite-Out" and "Liquid Paper."

"Project Onslaught" -- a Herculean but largely misguided effort by the FBI during the summer of 1976 to deal with a suddenly skyrocketing backlog of pending FOIA requests in the wake of the passage (read: and February 1975 effective date) of the FOIA Amendments of 1974, which first made the FBI effectively subject to the Act. It involved bringing 300 FBI Special Agents in from "the field" to Washington, D.C., with battlefield-like training, so that they could themselves dispose of (i.e., handle, not discard) as many pending FOIA requests as possible.

FOIA Backlog -- the term used (sometimes imprecisely) to refer to the fact the many federal agencies or sub-agencies -- most particularly law enforcement agencies, agencies within the "Intelligence Community," and State Department-related ones -- routinely fail to handle their FOIA requests within the strict time limits of the statute,[21] thus resulting in "backlogs" of such pending requests. This problem has existed since at least the time of the 1974 FOIA Amendments and for the most part is born of too little agency resources being made available for ever-increasing numbers of FOIA requests, some of which are of enormous size and complexity. While several proposed solutions to this problem have been attempted here and there over the years, it appears to be an intractable one.

ASAP -- with its aptly temporal abbreviation, the American Society of Access Professionals, an association of FOIA-related personnel from agencies across the Federal Government, combined with members of what is known as the "FOIA Requester Community"[22] from the private sector, who together promote the implementation of the FOIA and similar statutes; foster improved relations between agencies and their FOIA requesters; and provide nationwide training opportunities apart from those provided by OIP. Formed by an ad hoc group of seven agency FOIA officers at an informal meeting in 1980,[23] this organization has existed continuously since then.

Handler -- the term used in the contexts of both domestic law enforcement sources (often, "informants") and national security intelligence sources for the agency representative who acts as the primary (and often sole) contact for such human sources as they operate "under cover," so to speak. It is well known that the source/handler relationship can be essential to the success of the source's activities and to the successful maintenance of his or her "cover," which in some situations can be a matter of life or death.

Name Check -- the process by which the FBI employs its vast electronic database of information about individuals (once kept on approximately 62 million index cards) for purposes of "checking out" prospective appointees of, and visitors to, the White House (and sometimes elsewhere). During the 1970s (if not also beforehand and afterward), the Bureau maintained a distinct staff of employees devoted to this function.

"Derog" -- the Bureau's shorthand for "derogatory information," which emanated from former FBI Director J. Edgar Hoover's penchant for using such information in his files (i.e., his "P&C" and "O&C" ones, meaning "Personal and Confidential" and "Official and Confidential," respectively) for leverage or even blatant blackmail purposes against the rich and powerful, including presidents.[24]

The Great Hall -- The three-story main auditorium in the Main Justice Building, which boasts a soaring balcony and a proscenium stage, as well as some unique distinguishing characteristics. Built in 1933, when Justice Department employees were paid in cash, it is flanked by "teller windows" that were maintained as part of the building's refurbishment in the mid-1990s. Prominently displayed on the stage are two cast aluminum Art Deco statues, each standing 12½ feet tall, on either side of the entrance to a backstage area in which intimate plays have been performed.[25] The statue located at stage right, formally known as the "Spirit of Justice," depicts "Lady Justice" (ordinarily shown with a sword, blindfold, and balanced scales) as a woman wearing a toga-like dress with one ample breast revealed and arms raised; it was affectionately nicknamed "Minnie Lou" long before I first saw it more than 50 years ago. In 1986, it was framed by a clever photographer as a backdrop to Attorney General Edwin Meese III as he raised a copy of the *Final Report of the Attorney General's Commission on Pornography* at the front of that stage.

During the tenure of Attorney General John D. Ashcroft, who was known for being more than a bit of a prude, a curtain was infamously installed blocking the view of "Minnie Lou." The Department's Office of Public Affairs announced that the cost of this censorship was "only $8000,"[26] but records that found their way to OIP showed that the actual cost was considerably more.[27] On the stage left side is a bare-chested male statue known as the "Majesty of Law"; during Ashcroft's tenure, it was "curtains" for him, too.

CPUSA -- the Communist Party of the United States of America, an official American political party, but one with heavy ties to the Soviet Union during the Cold War (and perhaps beyond).

Wiretap -- a mechanical surveillance method by which telephone conversations or even more modern telecommunications can be overheard, recorded, or interfered with by law enforcement authorities. Wiretapping can be authorized by statute under specified conditions or can be authorized by a judge, including judges on the Foreign Intelligence Surveillance Court, in cases involving national security, through what is called a "FISA warrant."[28]

Declaration -- the evidentiary vehicle by which a party in federal litigation establishes facts "on paper," i.e., without live testimony at a trial or evidentiary hearing. Formerly known as an "affidavit," this was in effect renamed by Congress in 1976, through a statute codified at 28 U.S.C. § 1746 that was aimed at permitting unsworn "declarations" to be used in lieu of "affidavits," which had had the cumbersome disadvantage of requiring notarization.

***Vaughn* declaration** -- the formal name universally used for the type of declaration that a defendant agency files in a FOIA lawsuit in order both describe the records (or record portions) being withheld from a FOIA requester and to justify, with reference to one or more (at least arguably applicable) FOIA exemptions, their being withheld. So called according to the name of the leading precedent on this FOIA-litigation requirement, *Vaughn v. Rosen*, 484 F.2d 820 (D.C. Cir. 1973). Coincidentally, the FOIA requester in that case was Robert Vaughn, who was a young "Nader's Raider" at the time. Robert went on to become the leading academic on the FOIA and related matters; he recently took professor emeritus status at the Washington College of Law of American University after a highly distinguished academic career spanning more than four decades.[29]

SES -- the Senior Executive Service, a personnel system created for high-level federal employees in the late 1970s. SES officials forego some aspects of job security in exchange for the prestige of being in the SES and the ability to earn relatively large performance bonuses annually.

CGS -- the Collaboration on Government Secrecy, the secrecy/transparency academic center that I established at the Washington College of Law within American University in Washington, D.C., as of August of 2007 (remaining in existence until September 2014). CGS was the first academic center of its kind at any law school in the world and its advisory board included such members as Carl Stern, Scott Armstrong, Stuart Taylor, Jr., Tony Mauro, Steven A. Aftergood, Sharon Bradford Franklin, Elizabeth "Liza" Goitein, and Professor Robert Vaughn.[30]

James Madison, Jr. -- the "founding father of freedom of information" and the author of the following seminal quote: "A popular government without popular information or the means of acquiring it is but a prologue to a farce or a tragedy, or perhaps both. Knowledge will forever govern ignorance: And a people who mean to be their own Governors, must arm themselves with the power which knowledge gives." (Media folks, in particular, just love this quote.[31])

Freedom of Information Day -- the annual celebration that is held in the United States on March 16, chosen because it is the birthday of President James Madison, Jr., who was our 4th president but more significantly for present purposes wrote of the importance of the public's access to government information. From 2008 through 2014, "FOI Day" was celebrated at American University's Washington College of Law, in a day-long CGS program regularly attended by more than 100 government personnel and members of the "FOIA Requester Community" alike. In other years, it has been celebrated at the National Press Club, where both Attorney General Janet Reno and I gave speeches on such occasions. "FOI Day" is ordinarily surrounded by several days of such revelry, known in the aggregate as "Sunshine Week."

International Right-to-Know Day -- the annual celebration of government transparency (sometimes referred to as the "right to know") that began in Europe and has proliferated worldwide. The date of this annual celebration, which has become fixed as September 28, organically arose from a meeting that several key European transparency activists held (reportedly in a local tavern, with drinks heavily flowing) in Sofia, Bulgaria, in 2002. From 2007-2013, the location of this celebration in the United States was American University's Washington College of Law, through an international program conducted by CGS.

"Survivor Privacy" -- the concept by which exceptionally sensitive information about a deceased person can be withheld from public disclosure notwithstanding that person's death, where its disclosure would harm the personal-privacy interests of a surviving family member (or, in the case of Dr. Martin Luther King, Jr., a "close associate"). This came into existence in February of 1978, on my own desk, in a case involving King's survivors and it ultimately was endorsed by the United States Supreme Court in a 2004 decision involving the 1993 suicide of Deputy White House Counsel Vincent W. Foster, Jr. (see Chapter Three).

Exemption 3 Statute -- a federal law (or comparable enactment) that calls for an agency *not* to disclose[32] certain specified (or criteria-laden) information, thus triggering the applicability of the FOIA's third exemption as a basis for the information being withheld as exempt from public disclosure under the FOIA. Commonly known examples are Rule 6(e) of the Federal Rules of Criminal Procedure (a grand-jury secrecy provision that was codified as a statute in 1976);[33] the "post-Watergate" law that requires secrecy for "tax return" information; and the statutory provision that mandates long-term secrecy for individually identifiable census information.[34] According to an extensive CGS analysis conducted in 2004 (and contrary to what the Federal Government still says), there exist only about 150 such statutes, if properly construed.

FOIA "Reading Rooms" -- the means by which federal agencies discharge their obligations to make certain records (i.e., basic records of agency functioning such as agency policy statements, administrative staff manuals, and final opinions issued in administrative case adjudications) "automatically" available for public inspection as required under the "non-FOIA request" part of the Act, known as "subsection (a)(2)."[35] Since the enactment of the Electronic FOIA Amendments of 1996, this has involved fewer and fewer "dusty old reading rooms" at agency headquarters buildings and the use of agency FOIA websites for this purpose instead. Most notably, those amendments expanded the scope of "reading room" records by requiring the inclusion of virtually any record, in disclosed form, that has been processed and disclosed three or more times under the FOIA (i.e., through a current FOIA request and two previous or subsequent ones), thus making that record a "frequently requested" one. It is fair to say that the use of FOIA reading rooms was revitalized (in electronic form) as of 1997.[36]

DEA -- the Drug Enforcement Agency, a component of the Justice Department that historically has had considerable difficulty in handling its FOIA requests.

United States Marshals Service ("USMS," to its "WitSec" protectees) -- the component of the Justice Department that handles judicial security, fugitive apprehension, prisoner transportation, witness protection (known as "witness security" or "WitSec" for short), and the like. This includes the taking and maintenance of "mug shots" of federal arrestees. Its creation in 1789 pre-dates that of the United States Department of Justice by 81 years.

Mug Shots -- the slang but universal term used by federal, state, and local law enforcement personnel for the photographs routinely taken of all persons arrested, immediately upon their arrest, for possible use thereafter. More formally referred to as "booking photographs," they are most commonly taken and maintained by the United States Marshals Service at the federal level. Generally speaking, state and local authorities favor their public disclosure, but on privacy grounds (except for their use in capturing fugitives) the Federal Government does not (see Chapter Forty-One).[37]

NRC -- the Nuclear Regulatory Commission, which ordinarily maintains an extensive FOIA website just chock full of items that are posted there (except during a brief unlawful period in mid-September of 2001), in some cases as required by law and in other cases as a matter of administrative discretion.

OMB -- the Office of Management and Budget, an entity within the Executive Office of the President ("EOP," to its career denizens)[38] that in recent decades has gained more and more sway over the more than 100 other agencies of the executive branch through the processes of budgetary control, management oversight, and blurred differences between its career and political appointees. Among its other problems, it houses the Office of Information and Regulatory Affairs ("OIRA," to its few friends), which holds (but from 1984 until 2017[39] poorly discharged) governmentwide policy responsibility for implementation of the Privacy Act of 1974, as well as (since 1987) oversight responsibility for the fee and fee limitations (but not fee waiver) parts of the FOIA.[40]

OA ("Office of Administration") -- another entity within the Executive Office of the President, one known to have been subject to the FOIA for decades until suddenly being declared (by Vice President Richard "Dick" Cheney) to be not so, for the transparent purpose of removing its "White House visitor logs" from the Act's reach. This occurred in 2006, in the midst of a lobbyist scandal that brought those visitor logs into prominent public attention.

Pseudosecrecy -- the name used by federal agencies (originally, the Department of Justice and the National Security Council) within a realm (one entirely ancillary to FOIA administration) in which agencies physically (or electronically) apply "safeguarding labels" to sensitive records for the purpose of protecting them *in situ*, i.e., within the agency's "four walls." While this has its place in ensuring, for example, that records so marked are not treated casually or otherwise without regard to their sensitivity internally, it all too often gives the impression that any record or record portion marked with a safeguarding label is therefore deemed to be exempt from disclosure under the FOIA. Bluntly put, it is not, and by now all agencies ought to realize that (see Chapter Thirty-Eight).

SBU ("Sensitive But Unclassified Information") -- an information-policy term that came into widespread use within the Federal Government after it was employed in a memorandum prepared by and issued by me, together with White House Chief of Staff Andrew H. Card, Jr., on March 19, 2002. Notably, information that is labeled "SBU" is not necessarily exempt from disclosure under the FOIA (see Chapter Thirty-Eight).[41]

SHSI ("Sensitive Homeland Security Information") -- so named because the term "Sensitive Homeland Information Technology" was already taken, this post-9/11 term came into use within the Federal Government regarding any information that is of "homeland security sensitivity" because of its potential for "use by terrorists for targeting, site selection, or any form of impairment of any part of the Nation's 'critical infrastructure.'" Something falling into this information category does not by virtue of that necessarily fall within the protective scope of a FOIA exemption (see Chapter Thirty-Seven).

Critical Infrastructure Information ("CII") -- the term used heavily since 9/11 (and only occasionally prior to then, mostly by FEMA) to refer to information about a wide range of possible targets of potential future terrorism, such as power grids, dams, nuclear facilities, elements of the federal banking system, transportation systems, telecommunications, water supply, and the like. In late 2001, it was estimated that 85% of the Nation's "critical infrastructure" is located within the private sector (see Chapter Thirty-Seven).

Homeland Security -- a term truly born of 9/11 (i.e., used not much at all before then), and reminiscent of the "homeland" theme of Nazi Germany, that pertains to the Federal Government's massive continuing efforts to avoid any recurrence of a 9/11-like terrorist event. It is the subject area of the 15th cabinet department, the Department of Homeland Security ("DHS," to those who are subject to its broad jurisdiction), which was created in 2002.

FOUO ("For Official Use Only") -- a "safeguarding label" overused by many federal agencies, most notably the Department of Defense, for information that might or might not be exempt from disclosure under the FOIA.[42]

DOD -- the Department of Defense, which despite what is said immediately above, has consistently had an outstanding FOIA (and Privacy Act) program over the years.[43]

UFO ("Unidentified Flying Object") -- a term used around the world since the late 1940s to refer to objects seen or otherwise detected in the sky (or at a low altitude of "hovering," or perhaps even "landed," or as high up as "outer space") for which there is no immediately discernable origin or explanation. Note that while this term effectively replaced the term "flying saucer" several years after the latter was coined in June of 1947 (and in turn was supplanted most recently by the term "UAP," for "Unidentified Aerial Phenomena"), it is not quite the same: A UFO or UAP could be nothing like what was popularly regarded as appearing to be a "flying saucer."

Ufology -- the colloquial term for the study of the entire realm of "UFO/UAP sightings," most often by persons who tentatively suspect at least some of them to be of extraterrestrial origin. According to recent polling, more than a third of Americans believe that UFOs are "real," compared to the 20% who believed that in 1996.

Ufologist -- a term sometimes used for someone who involves him- or herself in matters pertains to the sightings of UFOs by researching, studying, or even more casually analyzing or discussing them. It usually refers to someone who is a proponent of UFO validity (i.e., that they are in fact of extraterrestrial origin, at least in some instances), but it sometimes can refer to someone who remains a skeptic but is nonetheless actively open-minded on the subject. And the term can also be applied, sometimes *post mortem*, to someone who actively researches the subject but does so secretly, lest he or she become publicly stigmatized for doing so.[44] Some ufologists celebrate what they call "World UFO Day" annually on July 2, commemorating the putative beginning of the Roswell incident.

Uforia -- a state of mind or being that is characterized by intense interest in the subjects of UFOs (now "UAPs"), alien technology, and/or the possibility of mature alien life forms visiting (or having had visited) our atmosphere and/or our land and/or seas. A ufologist does not necessarily suffer from uforia, but he or she ordinarily does engage in ufology.

UAP ("Unidentified Aerial [or Anomolous] Phenomena") -- a more current term for "UFO" that means exactly the same thing. This term has been used in lieu of "UFO" with increasing frequency in this century and it now has been officially memorialized as part of the former "Unidentified Aerial Phenomena Task Force" ("UAPTF") as of 2020.[45]

USO ("Unidentified Submersible Object" or, more recently, "Unidentified Submersible Phenomena") -- a UFO once wet, i.e., one that has been observed or otherwise detected entering, leaving, or just "cruising around" in a body of water, at either shallow or great depths, and often at extremely high speeds. Sometimes referred to as "transmedium vehicles," or "waterborne UFOs," they have come within the attention of DOD's National Underwater Reconnaissance Office ("NURO," to its brainy friends), which left the "black world" in 1998 and among other things coordinates between the Department of the Navy and the CIA on underwater reconnaissance. This term sometimes is used in connection with suspected "underwater UFO sites," which are said to be believed to exist, either in general or in some locations in particular, by a minority of "UFO proponents." (Evidently, some things are just "too far out there" to be subscribed to by all ufologists universally.)

IFO ("Identified Flying Object") -- either a UFO once explained or something that was never "unidentified" to begin with. This term is not frequently used.

Spoofing -- the advanced electronic process by which U.S. personnel (suspected to be working out of Groom Lake, at least initially) allegedly create phantom radar and/or other electronic signatures of either a single UFO or a whole fleet of them with enough authenticity that even sophisticated observers (both human and mechanical) are fooled into regarding them as "genuine" UFOs.

AATIP ("Advanced Aerospace Threat Identification Program") -- an ostensibly unclassified but unpublicized investigatory effort within DOD to study UFOs or unidentified aerial phenomena ("UAP," to those in the know). The program was first made public on December 16, 2017, which came as a shock to the "UFO community."[46] It evidently began in 2007, under the auspices of DOD's Defense Intelligence Agency ("DIA," to its intelligent friends), with a

$22 million congressional earmark that expired in 2012, but it is not clear that this program actually expired quite so soon (read: as opposed to continuing to some extent at the Pentagon for as many as five more years).

UAPTF ("Unidentified Aerial Phenomena Task Force") -- the successor program to AATIP that was quietly established on August 4, 2020, in the absence of any known such government program or office. Most notably, it operates under the Department of the Navy's Office of Naval Intelligence ("ONI," to its soggy friends), not the Defense Intelligence Agency or the Department of the Air Force as had been the case in the past. DOD announced that it established the UAPTF "to improve its understanding of, and gain insight into, the nature and origins of UAPs. . . . The mission of the task force is to detect, analyze and catalog UAPs that could potentially pose a threat to U.S. national security."

Airborne Object Identification and Management Synchronization Group ("AOIMSG," to those alienated by the sudden shift) -- this office in November of 2021 replaced the "Unidentified Aerial Phenomena Task Force," the successor program to AATIP that was established within the Navy Department's Office of Naval Intelligence on August 4, 2020, and it was then charged with "synchronizing" U.S. Government activities in this area. It was located organizationally under the Defense Department's Undersecretary for Intelligence and Security at the Pentagon and was overseen by something called the "Airborne Object Identification and Management Executive Council." But as of July of 2022, it appeared that the Pentagon had once again renamed this organization as the "All-Domain Anomaly Resolution Office" ("AARO," to those in need of scorecards), in order to include "transmedium" (read: salty and wet) craft within its purview. (And the acronym "UAP" was subtly recast by the Pentagon as "Unidentified Anomalous Phenomena.")

Flap -- a term colloquially used to refer to clusters of UFO sightings, usually over a period of several days or even weeks. The most famous such episode occurred in the Washington, D.C., area over two two-day periods (i.e., two weekends in a row), July 19-20 and July 26-27, during the summer of 1952, which acquired the moniker "the Big Flap." It consisted of numerous "unexplained radar blips" reported by air-traffic controllers at Washington National Airport and nearby Andrews Air Force Base, as well; fighter jets were scrambled to protect the Capital, but to no avail. Just prior to this, *Life* magazine published an article headlined "Have We Visitors from Outer Space?," leading to an immediate spike in UFO sightings.

Other well-known "flaps" of UFO sightings have occurred in Farmington, New Mexico, in 1950; in England in 1967; in Piedmont, Missouri, in 1973; in Central Ohio in 1973; in Wales in 1977; in Brazil in 1977-1978; in Phoenix, Arizona, and in surrounding states in 1997;[47] in the Hudson Valley, New York, in 1983-1984; in Russia in 1989-1990; in Belgium in 1989-1990; in Topanga Canyon, California, in 1992; in Cardiff, Wales, in 2008; in Kansas City in 2011-2012; in Italy in 2018; and in Washington State in 2019. Sometimes, when a flap continues over an extended period of time, it is referred to as a "wave."

Acclimatization -- the term used to describe a process of attempting to inure a populace to something so profoundly shocking, so fundamental to the meaning of life, that its official disclosure would be expected to cause an unprecedented, both dramatic and traumatic, public reaction, up to and including sustained panic. In this particular context, we're talking about not just the existence of some form of life extraterrestrially, but potentially the existence of alien life forms capable of "visiting" Earth. In other words, it is an attempt to bring such knowledge, *if* it exists, to a "soft landing" within the public consciousness. Any sustained effort to "acclimatize" the public to such a thing necessarily involves a delicate amalgam of secrecy and transparency; as such, it is by its nature "paternalistic." What is more, if the United States Government had seen its way to "come clean" on the subject from the start, there would be no vast reservoir of deception standing to be tapped today. In other words, as technology writer Charlie Warzal put the point most recently: "In the unlikely event we [were to] learn that UFOs are proof of alien life and that this knowledge was withheld from the public for generations, public trust would implode."

Law Enforcement Sensitive -- a document-safeguarding designation usually abbreviated as "LES," this broad term applies to information that a federal law enforcement agency at least at first glance thinks might be exempt from public disclosure if sought under the FOIA. The possibly applicable FOIA exemption is Exemption 7 (through one or more of its six subparts), but it also should be remembered that a document labeled "LES" only might or might not (and all too often not) actually fall within that exemption.

FEMA -- the Federal Emergency Management Agency, which holds multiple disaster-related responsibilities, such as for the handling of hurricane-disaster responses for the Federal Government, which is generally well known to the public, as well as for domestic coordination of post-nuclear survival (read: "Continuity of Government"), which is not.

COG -- the abbreviation used for the Federal Government's Continuity-of-Government program prior to late 1991 (i.e., soon after the collapse of the Soviet Union) and perhaps beyond (see Chapter Twenty-Six). A subsequently used related term (albeit on a much smaller scale), in the wake of 9/11, was "shadow government."

Special Facility ("SF," for short) -- the formerly completely secret underground facility at Mount Weather in Virginia that was the centerpiece of the Federal Government's Continuity-of-Government plan from the late 1950s until approximately 1982.[48] Subsequently, it was used by FEMA for training and exercise purposes.[49] Its existence and location were a "worst-kept secret" until 1974, especially after the crash of a TWA jetliner near it on December 1 of that year.[50]

Decapitation strike -- a type of nuclear attack, feared by both sides during the height of Cold War tensions, that involves one side aiming to achieve a decisive advantage over the other by launching a pre-emptive, highly targeted nuclear strike on the other's capital only, presumably before any counter-attack could be launched. The most likely source of such an attack would be an off-shore nuclear missile-bearing submarine.

Nuclear triad -- the three primary means of nuclear warfare: By land-based missile (ICBM), from an aircraft bomber, and by missile launched from a submarine. ("Dirty bombs" need not apply.)

Post-Nuclear environment -- a term referring to the state of the world that would remain viable, to at least some degree, following a full-scale nuclear exchange. It would include the existence of EMP.

EMP ("Electromagnetic Pulse") -- a relatively little-known form of energy expected by scientists to be released widely through a full nuclear exchange, one that would severely impair the use of conventional communications means for a considerable period of time thereafter.[51] It also can result from an exceptionally high-magnitude solar flare and even could be weaponized by an extremely sophisticated, and belligerent, nation.[52]

Meteor burst technology -- the term for the extraordinary, science fiction-like means of long-range communication used by DOD for purposes of Continuity-of-Government exercises, because in actual post-nuclear settings ordinary communications would be impaired by EMP. Believe it or not, it involves "bouncing" digital information off of the tails (or, more precisely, the "ionized trails") of meteors, from point A to point B.[53] It actually works.

"Tempest" protection -- the means by which the Federal Government "hardens" computer hardware against the technological advance through which the audio signals produced by tapping a computer keyboard could be surveilled from outside of a building (hence yielding message content) merely through the interception of their vibrations off of a glass window or some other external surface. Such special precautions were taken with respect to all computer equipment used in COG activities.[54]

National security classification -- a process that has existed since the early 1950s by which duly authorized Federal Government "classification officials," who are designated in accordance with a series of presidential executive orders issued one after the other since 1940, to "classify" documents or information at varying levels of sensitivity requiring increasing degrees of protection. For many decades, the basic taxonomy of classified national security information has been at the following levels: "Classified," "Secret," "Top Secret," and then "Special Compartmented Information" ("SCI," to those who are cleared for access to it), for which special clearance processes (read: in a "Special Access Program") are established and maintained. The information and activities within a SAP or SCI activity are typically divided into various control systems and compartments and often further divided into sub-control systems and sub-compartments. The term "Control System" describes an umbrella security protocol for a specific subject.[55]

The current executive order on national security classification, Executive Order 13,526, was issued by President Obama on December 29, 2009, and even though such executive orders have been revised as a matter of policy in most new administrations since the 1960s, the Trump Administration atypically did not bother with the Obama national security executive order at all.[56] Neither did Trump aid the processes of declassification through some of his shoddy appointments to the under-performing Public Interest Declassification Board.

But the Biden Administration is currently preparing a wholesale review and revision in this area. That was stated in an internal memorandum of June 2, 2022 from the executive secretary of the National Security Council, which of course soon became known to the public. This year-long review marks the first such attempt to rein in the classification system in more than a decade, after what insiders and oversight authorities say has been frustratingly little progress since the Obama Administration took on the task. The Biden Administration review will also deal with the executive order governing "controlled unclassified information" that President Obama signed in 2010 but was also widely considered to have fallen short of the goal of forcing into public view more government files. (See Chapter Thirty-Eight.)

This all sprang from a presidential executive order (Executive Order 8381) that was issued by President Franklin D. Roosevelt on March 22, 1940 and set the series of such orders issued by nearly all presidents thereafter. (President George H.W. Bush did not issue one; rather, he just kept using the one issued by President Ronald W. Reagan, for whom he served as vice-president.) The National Archives and Records Administration estimates that government agencies create petabytes -- or millions of gigabytes -- of classified information each year.

Special Compartmented Information ("SCI," to those with higher than "Top Secret" clearances) -- information of exceptional national security sensitivity, above that of "Top Secret," which requires special treatment and handling in several respects.[57] First, such information is maintained and shared only within what are sometimes called information "silos," or more officially "compartments," of individually cleared persons, according to its specific subject matter. Second, each SCI compartment has an individually designated code name, such as (in a fictitious example) "Table Kettle," for which the abbreviation would be "TK." Third, due to the development of advanced surveillance technology, SCI is discussed only within the confines of a "SCIF" (see below). An example of SCI is the information contained in what are known as "black budgets" for "super secret" intelligence activities.

SCIF ("Special Compartmented Information Facility") -- a specially constructed part of a building that is shielded from external electronic surveillance through technology developed during the Cold War. The "compartmented" information that can be discussed there is by definition information that exists above "Top Secret" levels.

STU-III -- a type of secure telephone used as of the mid-1980s by national security agencies and offices through the Federal Government for especially sensitive conversations. They looked very much like large office telephones, but all conversations on them were automatically encrypted to prevent eavesdropping upon interception.[58] Today, secure video-conferencing is more commonly used.

PEADs ("Presidential Emergency Action Documents") -- draft documents that were carried by the Legal and Law Enforcement Group of a Continuity-of-Government team for review and potential implementation by an Acting President as soon as practicable after initial recovery from a nuclear exchange. One such document, it is publicly known (but the number of which I will not here disclose), would have formally suspended what is known as *"posse comitatus"* (sometimes expressed with reference to *habeas corpus*) thereby allowing the Federal Government to use military troops for domestic law enforcement purposes.

Presidential Succession Act of 1947 -- the law that establishes, beyond what is provided for in the Constitution (including its 25th Amendment), the order of succession to the presidency if both the president and any vice president (no, we have not at all times had one[59]) become deceased. This succession chain runs below the vice president through the Speaker of the House, the president pro tempore ("pro tem," for short) of the Senate, and then through all cabinet-department secretaries (read: born in the U.S.) in the order in which their respective departments were created. *Quiz*: At the moment that Lyndon B. Johnson was sworn in as president on November 22, 1963 (or as a practical matter for hours before then), who were the two men next in the line of presidential succession? Clue: Their last names began with the same letter, M, but one of them was missing a vowel.

Acting President -- the position held by anyone below the vice presidency who succeeds to the presidency; this title, and its concomitant authority, continues until the end of the original president's term. And it applies to the former speaker of the House and president pro tem of the Senate, though there does exist a constitutional question about whether the Presidential Succession Act of 1947 properly includes such congressional officers in the line of succession.[60]

"Avignon Papacy" -- the name used since the 14th century for the period (from 1309-1376) when seven successive popes resided in Avignon, France, rather than in Rome, Italy, during which time there were competing French and Italian claimants to the papacy. The modern-day counterpart would be having competing claimants to the U.S. presidency by surviving cabinet officers in a post-nuclear setting. The person who attempted to wield this name against me later became Director of the CIA (see Chapter Twenty-Six).

CIA -- the Central Intelligence Agency (sometimes familiarly referred to as "the Agency"), which was formed in the late 1940s as the principal organizational successor to the "Office of Strategic Services" ("OSS," to Nazi Germany and nascently the KGB), and which came into existence only after our Nation belatedly realized that the old-fashioned view of espionage (e.g., "A gentleman does not read another gentleman's mail.") just would no longer do in a modern world. Prior to 2004, with enactment of the Intelligence Reform Act of 2004, the CIA's director also wore the hat of "Director of Central Intelligence," by virtue of which he additionally had direct oversight of the 18 (then only 16) agencies (or sub-agencies) that make up what is known as the "Intelligence Community." This responsibility thereupon was given to the newly created position of "Director of National Intelligence" ("DNI," to his new friends) in a separate agency.

ODNI -- the Office of the Director of National Intelligence, which was created in 2005 and is headed by the Director of National Intelligence ("DNI"). The DNI now holds the governmentwide intelligence responsibility previously held by the Director of the CIA.

MKULTRA (or, to the *cognoscente,* "MK-Ultra") -- the CIA "mind control" program that operated in extreme secrecy from the early 1950s into the 1970s,[61] until it was made public by the Senate's "Church Committee" in 1975. Among other things, it involved human experimentation that was intended to develop drugs and procedures to be used in interrogations in order to weaken the individual and force confessions through control of the subject's mind. It was found that the program engaged in many illegal activities, including the use of U.S. and Canadian citizens as its unwitting test subjects.[62] It was the subject of pioneering FOIA requests filed in the mid-1970s, which became the subjects of contentious litigation with which I first became involved (read: collaterally) in 1978.

NSA -- the National Security Agency, the principal "SIGINT" ("signals intelligence") arm of the U.S. Government, which houses something called the "Central Security Service," a component that coordinates with cryptologic elements of the Armed Forces, within it.[63] Until the Federal Government became generally more "open" about such things, it sometimes was referred to as "No Such Agency."[64]

"Devil's Deal" -- an agreement reached in 1984 between the CIA and the ACLU (together with other public interest groups) whereby the CIA would receive what we called an "operational files" exception to FOIA applicability in exchange for a promise from the CIA that it would reduce its FOIA backlog commensurately. This deal was codified by Congress as the CIA Information Act of 1984, a stand-alone piece of legislation that, rather than amending the FOIA, instead became part of the National Security Act of 1947. In subsequent years, a series of other intelligence agencies (i.e., NSA, the NRO, and the NGIA) received such legislative treatment likewise. The premise of all such arrangements was that by definition they encompassed only records that would be exempt in their entireties on national security grounds under Exemption One of the FOIA anyway, so removing them from the FOIA's reach would not lessen what entered the public domain but would serve to free the agency to respond to other FOIA requests more quickly.[65]

Kryptos -- a large sculpture located on the grounds of the CIA's headquarters in Langley, Virginia. Since its installation in 1990, there has been much speculation about the meaning of the four encrypted messages that it bears; of these four messages, the first three have been solved, while the fourth message remains one of the most famous unsolved codes in the world.

"SIGINT" -- the shorthand for "signals intelligence," meaning information obtained by our intelligence agencies (particularly NSA) through electronic or other telecommunications means. Other such terms used by intelligence agencies include "HUMINT" (human intelligence derived from covert human intelligence sources);[66] "COMINT" (communications intelligence); "OSINT" (open source intelligence); "IMINT" (imagery intelligence, derived from collection assets such as reconnaissance satellites or aircraft); "GEOINT" (geospatial intelligence); "ELINT" (electronic intelligence); "MASINT" (measurement and signals intelligence); "TECHINT" (technical intelligence based on scientific and technical characteristics of weapons systems, technological devices, and other entities); and of course "LESSINT" (lesser intelligence, which unquestionably hit its utilitarian peak during the Trump Administration).

NRO -- the National Reconnaissance Office, which came into existence in 1960 as the Defense Department's arm for satellite-based intelligence activities,[67] but was entirely unknown to the public until its existence was mistakenly "leaked" through a Senate report in the 1970s and explicated in detail through a *New York Times* article written by national security journalist V. James Bamford in January of 1985.[68] And even then it was not until December of 1992 that this agency's existence was declassified and it left what is known in the U.S. "Intelligence

Community" as the "black world."

"Claw Back" -- a colloquially sounding but now formally accepted legal term for the act of regaining something of value (often, but not always money) from someone to whom it was mistakenly or improperly given. Within the government secrecy realm, it involves documents or items of information that a government agency mistakenly provided to someone, such as in an erroneous disclosure under the FOIA. The agency might then attempt to "claw back" what was disclosed, by asking the FOIA requester nicely to return it (in original, uncopied form) or else by seeking to have that ordered by a court through use of its "inherent authority." To the best of all recordation and recollection, the first such attempt was made regarding classified records, in 1981, and it failed (see immediately above).[69]

NGA -- the National Geospatial-Intelligence Agency (formerly known as the Defense Mapping Agency and subsequently as the National Imagery and Mapping Agency), which holds responsibility within the Department of Defense for the collection, analysis, and distribution of what is known as "geospatial" intelligence ("GEOINT," to those who are spatially inclined), in support of our national security. It was long believed within the Sangamore Road neighborhood of the NGA's headquarters that the telemetry used for potential nuclear strikes originated there.[70]

OSHA -- the Occupational Safety and Health Administration, which is a sub-agency of the Department of Labor.

FCC -- the Federal Communications Commission, one of several so-called "independent agencies" of the executive branch.

United States Court of Appeals for the District of Columbia Circuit -- often referred to simply as the "D.C. Circuit," this court is one of 13 circuit courts in the United States, though it is inarguably the most significant one. And most importantly here, it is the circuit of "universal venue" under the FOIA, which means that a FOIA lawsuit can be filed in its district court no matter where the requester is located (i.e., home or place of business), or where the defendant agency is located, or where the requested records are located. Therefore, as a practical matter, whatever the D.C. Circuit says about a FOIA issue must be adhered to by all agencies nationwide at the administrative level, even before a potential case gets to court.

En Banc -- a full court of appeals, not just a three-judge panel. There have been many appellate FOIA cases that have been heard *en banc*, mostly by the D.C. Circuit, whereas other circuit courts of appeals are traditionally more parsimonious about agreeing to sit as a full court.[71]

"Glomarization" -- the colloquial term[72] for the concept by which an agency neither confirms nor denies having any record responsive to a particular access request. Its name derives from the secret *Glomar Explorer* submarine-retrieval ship that was the subject of the first FOIA case to raise it, in 1975. After that case "washed out," so to speak,[73] the first half-dozen "Glomarization" cases to proceed to judgment were a series of so-called "university" FOIA cases (which I litigated between 1977 and 1981) in which the ACLU sought access to any records reflecting any CIA activity (i.e., either covert or overt) on particular American university campuses (see Chapter Seventeen).[74]

Exclusion -- a special FOIA-response defense created by Congress in 1986 (after being conceived by me in 1979) to cover three exceptional types of situations, two involving law enforcement and the third involving national security, in which only use of this unique statutory provision can avoid harm.[75] Much as it is difficult to say publicly, an exclusion effectively gives an agency the legal authority to lie (see Chapter Eighteen).

I&P -- the "Information and Privacy Section" of the Justice Department's Civil Division (in existence from 1975-1978).

OIP -- the Office of Information and Privacy, one of the roughly 40 (read: sometimes slightly fewer) distinct components of the Department of Justice. (In 1981, I was able to name OIP after the litigation section in the preceding entry, urological connotation and all.)

OPIA -- the Office of Privacy and Information Appeals (in existence from 1977-1981), one of OIP's two predecessor offices.

OILP -- the Office of Information Law and Policy (in existence from 1978-1981), the other OIP predecessor office.

OIPR -- the Office of Intelligence Policy and Review, which discharged the attorney general's foreign intelligence responsibilities (including the management of "FISA warrants") from 1978 until 2006, when it was absorbed into the Department's new National Security Division.

OPR -- the Justice Department's Office of Professional Responsibility, which undertakes misconduct investigations of Department attorneys and is the recipient of many "high profile" FOIA requests.

Public summaries -- the reports issued by OPR showing, to some degree of detail, the results of almost all of its investigations and disciplinary actions taken against Justice Department attorneys (most commonly AUSAs), beginning in 1994.

AUSA -- an Assistant United States Attorney in any of 94 federal judicial districts around the country.

OLC -- the Office of Legal Counsel within the Justice Department.

OLP -- the Office of Legal Policy within the Justice Department.

PRAO -- the Professional Responsibility Advisory Office, a small Justice Department component created in 1999 to resolve professional responsibility issues faced by Department attorneys, including Assistant United States Attorneys.

IG -- an inspector general, one of dozens across the Federal Government, 32 of whom are appointed by the president.

Special Counsel -- a designation roughly comparable to "Independent Counsel," but without specific congressional authorization. The first of these was former Senator John C. Danforth, who was appointed as special counsel for Waco matters (i.e., the investigation of ATF's and the FBI's handling of the "Branch Davidian" disaster in Waco, Texas, in 1993), and the second was former FBI Director (and Acting Deputy Attorney General) Robert S. Mueller III -- who was appointed by Deputy Attorney General Rod J. Rosenstein (then-Attorney General Jeff Sessions having recused himself from the matter due to an obvious (to most people, even if not to the president) conflict of interest) as a special counsel to investigate allegations of Russian interference in the 2016 presidential election and related matters. A third was Patrick J. Fitzgerald, who was appointed by Deputy Attorney General James B. Comey (then-Attorney General John D. Ashcroft having recused himself from the matter due to conflicts of interest) to investigate the public naming of covert CIA operative Valerie E. Plame. The fourth was United States Attorney John H. Durham, who was appointed by Attorney General William P. Barr to conduct a "counter-investigation" into the Mueller investigation of the FBI's investigation (of suspected Russian connection(s) to the 2016 presidential campaign) known as "Crossfire Hurricane." And more recently, Attorney General Merrick B. Garland on November 18, 2022, appointed former Criminal Division Public Integrity Section Chief John L. "Jack" Smith to investigate both former President Donald J. Trump's role in the January 6 insurrection at the U.S. Capitol and his astounding removal of classified White House records to his Mar-a-Lago home in evident violation of the Presidential Records Act among related criminal statutes. And then most recently, AG Garland appointed former Justice Department prosecutor Robert K. Hur to serve as a special counsel to investigate the handling of classified documents found (by Biden's personal attorneys) at a former office of President Biden and at his Delaware home in January of 2023.

ATF ("Bureau of Alcohol, Tobacco, and Firearms") -- a longtime enforcement arm of the Department of the Treasury that in 2002 was renamed the "Bureau of Alcohol, Tobacco, Firearms, and Explosives" (but is still known only as "ATF," for short). At that same time, as a relatively small part of a massive post-9/11 reorganization, it was "traded" by the newly created Department of Homeland Security ("DHS," to all), in a three-cornered deal with the Treasury Department and its component U.S. Secret Service, to the Department of Justice for the Immigration and Naturalization Service ("INS," to its friends; "la migra" to most others), along with a utility infielder, a future draft pick, cash considerations, and a player to be named later.[76]

Whitewater -- the name used for a series of related (and in some cases largely unrelated) scandals that plagued the Clinton Administration from November of 1993 (as far as the public knew) on (see Chapter Thirty-Five). The Whitewater Independent Counsel was former Solicitor General and D.C. Circuit Court of Appeals Judge Kenneth W. Starr, who had less famously interviewed prospective Justice Sandra Day O'Connor for her Supreme Court appointment, together with Assistant Attorney General Jonathan C. Rose, when Starr was a relatively young assistant to the attorney general in 1981.[77]

Health Care Task Force -- the inter-agency group (problematically including some nongovernment personnel) set up under the leadership of First Lady Hillary R. Clinton almost immediately at the outset of the Clinton Administration.[78]

It faced many difficulties, not the least of which were those posed by the FOIA and the Privacy Act, mostly the former.[79]

Janet W. Reno -- the 78th attorney general of the United States, who used her middle initial about as often as she would take her full Parkinson's disease medication dose during her tenure (March 11, 1993 to January 20, 2001). Janet was the Nation's second-longest-serving attorney general and the longest-serving one under a single president.[80] Within the Justice Department (if not the White House during President Clinton's second term), she was highly esteemed, good-naturedly feared, and (especially in the career ranks) much beloved.

Scandal -- a situation in which great public controversy arises over suspected criminality, misconduct, misdeeds, and/or gross mistakenness by an individual, a group of coordinating (ideally, not conspiring) individuals, or an institution (very often a government one); note that there might not be any actual wrongdoing involved. In the case of the Federal Government, there invariably are records memorializing or at least impliedly reflecting such a situation, sometimes thousands upon thousands of them, that are subject to public disclosure under the FOIA. Related to this is the adage that "the cover-up is worse than the crime," which means that there often are "cover-up records" (sometimes, believe it or not, even more than the underlying ones) to contend with.

Leak -- a descriptor of the process by which information (sometimes classified, but sometimes just "sensitive" on one basis or another[81]) leaves the protective confines of the Federal Government (or more broadly any other comparable institution) and enters the public domain, nowadays almost always irretrievably so.[82] It is the type of thing that often prompts a FOIA requester to contend that there has been a "waiver" of the Government's right to withhold any of that (or even closely similar) information. After a leak, there sometimes is a "leak investigation," which rarely succeeds.

Indeed, at the outset of the Reagan Administration a special high-level working group was formed to examine leaks of classified information and because I assisted in this enterprise I have a copy (read: a non-record copy) of its final report in my files. Titled "Report of the Intergovernmental Group on Unauthorized Disclosures of Classified Information" (Mar. 31, 1982), it acknowledges that "[l]eaks are extremely difficult to investigate," that "it is very rare for an investigation to identify the leak[er]," and that past investigations have been "almost totally unsuccessful and frustrating to all concerned."

Certiorari -- a Latin word literally meaning "to be certain of" or effectively "bring up the record of" a lower court for review. For present purposes, it is the writ (i.e., legal issuance) granted by the Supreme Court when at least four Justices agree, through the exercise of the Court's discretionary authority of judicial review, to hear a case on appeal from a circuit court of appeals (or very rarely from what is known as a "three-judge court"). The term is sometimes shortened, as in "*cert.* granted" or "*cert.* denied."

NSC -- the National Security Council, in the Executive Office of the President, at the White House. For a long while, it was deemed a "hybrid FOIA agency," with only half of it not subject to the FOIA, i.e., as to the activities of the National Security Advisor alone. In 1994, however, the pro-disclosure Clinton Administration counterintuitively declared as a matter of OLC/White House policy that the NSC was not subject to the FOIA at all. It defended that position in court and in 1996, in the case of *Armstrong v. Executive Office of the President*, the D.C. Circuit ruled that this is so.[83]

NARA -- the National Archives and Records Administration, which houses both OGIS and ISOO and is headed by the Archivist of the United States. Prior to 1985, NARA was known as the "National Archives and Records Service" ("NARS," to its Justice Department counsel, of which I was one) and was part of the General Services Administration ("GSA," to government vendors).

OGIS -- the Office of Government Information Services, at NARA, which has, *inter alia*, an ombudsman function for FOIA disputes. Beginning its operation in 2009,[84] it offers FOIA-mediation services and also holds some FOIA-related responsibilities that on their face can be seen as conflicting with those of OIP.[85]

ISOO -- the Information Security Oversight Office, a long-term entity (since 1981) located within NARA that, with substantive policy direction from the National Security Council ("NSC," to all), oversees the Federal Government's national security classification (and declassification) activities, a subject area that connects to Exemption 1 of the FOIA.

The National Archives -- most commonly means the National Archives and Records Administration ("NARA," to its many friends), which became an independent federal agency when it was wrenched from GSA in 1985, or perhaps refers to its headquarters building ("Archives I"), which is located due east of the

Main Justice Building between 7th and 9th Streets, N.W., in Washington, D.C.; there also is a massive "Archives II" facility located in College Park, Maryland.[86]

NASA -- the National Aeronautics and Space Administration, which faced unheard-of FOIA difficulties in the wake of the Space Shuttle *Challenger* disaster on January 28, 1986. (Sadly, another such NASA vehicle, the Space Shuttle *Columbia*, was lost on February 1, 2003.) Looking forward, NASA can expect to hit further difficulties, under the FOIA and in the court of public opinion, in connection with the UFO-related photographs and images that it captures.[87]

OPM -- the Office of Personnel Management, which handles personnel-related matters within the Federal Government, including governmentwide oversight of the Senior Executive Service ("SES"). (For some inexplicable reason, the Government has resisted any urge to rename it the "Office of Human Relations Management" thus far.)

Office of Special Counsel -- the entity to which a judge in a FOIA litigation case may under certain circumstances "refer" a FOIA officer for possible discipline purposes under subsection (a)(4)(F) of the Act. It was created in conjunction with the U.S. Civil Service Commission's break-up into the Office of Personnel Management ("OPM," to feds) and the Merit Systems Protection Board ("MSPB," to potential whistleblowers) in 1979; during the next decade, it was part of the MSPB, but in 1989 it became an independent federal agency. Very few FOIA personnel have been "referred" to it over the years.

Old Executive Office Building -- the ornate building located due west of the White House (i.e., between it and 17th Street). Built in 1888, and originally known as the "State, War, and Navy Building," it was renamed the "Eisenhower Executive Office Building" ("EEOB," if you want to sound modern), after our 34th president, in 1999. Not to be confused with the "New Executive Office Building" situated due north of it (i.e., across Pennsylvania Avenue and a half-block further down), which houses the Federal Government's "hubris factory," i.e., OMB.

LEAA -- the Law Enforcement Assistance Administration, now part of the Justice Department's Office of Justice Programs, which is one of the Department's current 39 distinct components. During the early 1970s, it housed the National Institute of Law Enforcement and Criminal Justice.

Capitol Hill -- either the part of the District of Columbia where the U.S. Capitol Building stands, or the building itself (more likely the latter). (Yes, the Capitol Building really does stand on a hill.)

Civil Division -- the huge litigating division at Main Justice, or (less commonly known) the part of a U.S. Attorney's Office that handles civil cases (more likely the former).

United States Attorney's Office -- the office located in each of the Federal Government's 94 judicial districts, where Assistant United States Attorneys ("AUSAs," to their spouses) handle some FOIA litigation cases "out in the field," in coordination with the Civil Division of Main Justice and OIP.

Main Justice -- either the main headquarters building of the Department of Justice, located between 9th and 10th Streets and Pennsylvania and Constitution Avenues, N.W., or the headquarters office and staff itself.

"Sovereign Independent State of the Southern District of New York" -- the name ever so lovingly used by the folks at Main Justice (and sometimes now on cable news programs, as well) to refer to the U.S. Attorney's Office for that judicial district in Manhattan. This nickname has been around for the length of recent memory, and now it probably will be used until the end of time.

One L -- a first-year law student (in general parlance only since about 1977).[88]

Law Review -- a legal journal traditionally published by most law schools that features both articles written by legal practitioners and student "notes" written by members of the law review's student staff. Membership on a law review's editorial board is viewed as a sterling credential by judges, law firms, and others who hire young attorneys.

Attorney General's Honors Program -- a special hiring program begun in 1953 and enhanced under Attorney General Robert F. Kennedy as a means of attracting "the best and the brightest" young attorneys to work at the Justice Department; it is the only means by which someone will be considered for an attorney position during the first year after graduation from law school (or upon completion of a one- or two-year federal judicial clerkship). It was corrupted under Attorney General Alberto R. Gonzales during the Administration of George W. Bush (see

Chapter Forty-Three).

JFK -- President John F. Kennedy, our 35th president, who was assassinated on Friday, November 22, 1963.[89] FBI records pertaining to this assassination and its multiple investigations were maintained at FBI Headquarters in Washington, D.C., as well as within its Dallas and New Orleans Field Offices; they have been the subject of numerous FOIA requests and many FOIA litigation cases over the years.[90]

RFK -- Robert F. Kennedy, younger brother of John, who was assassinated on June 6, 1968. His assassination, too, was the subject of many FOIA requests and also is not without controversy (see Chapter Forty-Nine).

MLK -- Dr. Martin Luther King, Jr., who was assassinated on April 4, 1968, was the target of intense FBI COINTELPRO activity, and his personal-privacy interests (or rather those of his surviving family members) were the subjects of much FOIA litigation, most particularly in *Lesar v. United States Department of Justice* (see Chapter Three).

COINTELPRO -- an FBI abbreviation for "counterintelligence program," this label applied to a series of covert (and often illegal) FBI activities to surveil, infiltrate, disrupt, and sometimes discredit certain American political groups, organizations, and individuals during the late 1950s, the 1960s, and the early 1970s, all under the personal direction of FBI Director J. Edgar Hoover. Targets included the Black Panther Party, the Nation of Islam, the American Indian Movement, the CPUSA, and Dr. Martin Luther King, Jr., in particular. This program was a secret one until 1971, when it was officially terminated, but it appears to have continued, in one form or another, for a few years beyond that (see Chapters Three and Fifteen).

"Bush I," "Bush II," and "Bush III" (otherwise known to many as "Bush 41" and "Bush 43") -- the presidential terms of President George H.W. Bush and of President George W. Bush, who had two terms.

9/11 -- shorthand for the horrific events of September 11, 2001, when terrorists crashed planes into each of the New York City Trade Center's "twin towers" and into the Pentagon in Northern Virginia. A fourth plane crashed near Shanksville (actually, within Stonycreek Township and Somerset County), Pennsylvania, where it is believed its passengers themselves brought it down by storming the cockpit after hearing of the other crashes. It is further believed that this plane was heading for the U.S. Capitol Building, due to the difficulty of hitting the White House (which is realistically possible only from the south).

"Outside Consultant" -- the term used for a nonfederal employee or entity with whom an agency consults as part of its deliberative-process decisionmaking under FOIA Exemption 5. His, her, or its work can be protected in the face of a FOIA request only in very exceptional circumstances (markedly more exceptional than was the case prior to 2001) (see Chapter Forty-Six).

WAVES -- shorthand for the "White House Worker and Visitor Entry System," the means by which visitors (including federal employees) to the White House complex, including the EEOB, are cleared for access by the Secret Service. Its records are now most commonly referred to as "White House visitor logs," and until Vice President Dick Cheney dictated otherwise in 2006, they were treated as records of the Secret Service, not of the White House, under the FOIA.

Vulnerability Assessments -- the documents prepared by an agency memorializing the results of its internal review of the security of a facility, system, computer database, or the like in the face of potential intrusion by a malign outside party. Sometimes prepared in accordance with the Computer Security Act of 1987, they are themselves vulnerable to FOIA requests (see Chapter Forty-Six).

Cybersecurity -- the processes of protecting against compromise of, penetration of, or any damage whatsoever to any part or aspect of an Internet-connected computer system by a malign actor.[91] This was a major focus of the Federal Government's security efforts prior to 9/11, but it was eclipsed by intense homeland security activity after then.[92] Today, with homeland security concerns fading and the technological means of "cyber attacks" acutely increasing, there has been another such reversal.

"High 2" -- a judicial creation (though one based upon an advocated concept) that permitted the applicability of FOIA Exemption 2 to "purely internal" information the disclosure of which "could reasonably be expected to allow circumvention of a law, regulation, or agency policy." It was in growing use for nearly 30 years (from 1981-2011), but was entirely vitiated by the United States Supreme Court's decision in *Department of the Navy v. Milner* in 2011 (see Chapter Forty-Six).

ACLU -- the American Civil Liberties Union, a public-interest group that is an especially aggressive user of the FOIA.

NGO -- a nongovernment organization. Roughly the same as a "public interest" group or part of what is called "civil society," this term originated in Europe.

Anders Chydenius -- a Finnish-born cleric and legislator who single-handedly succeeded in pushing the world's first freedom-of-information law through the Swedish parliament in 1766, exactly 200 years prior to the enactment of the FOIA in the United States.[93] Now known as the "great grandfather of the FOIA,"[94] he was strongly influenced by the relative enlightenment of the Tang Dynasty in 7th-century China (see Chapter One).[95]

ICIC ("International Conference of Information Commissioners") -- a gathering of the world's leading freedom-of-information (and in some instances also privacy) officials, nation by nation, for purposes of information exchange, relationship building, and much drinking with strong fellowship on matters of mutual official interest. I represented the United States at the one held in Manchester, England in 2006, at which I endeared myself to other commissioners by, *inter alia*, semi-wittingly "taking on" the commissioner from Germany, who was then known as "the bully of Europe."[96]

UCL (or "University College London," to its faculty, students, and friends alike) -- the university at which I was given a research fellowship upon my imminent retirement from government service in late 2006. Founded in 1826, it is London's leading university, with more than 13,000 staff and 142,000 students from 150 different nations.[97] I gave several presentations there in the following years and also provided consultation assistance to faculty and an academic staff that was heavily focused on the development and then the implementation of England's "Freedom of Information Act" (titled exactly the same as our own FOIA) during those years. It was these good folks who borrowed my phrase "It's good FOIA" for those purposes.

Attorney General's Memorandum on the FOIA -- a lengthy document prepared in pamphlet form in which an attorney general provided special definitive guidance on the implementation of the FOIA, or of a set of FOIA amendments, throughout the executive branch. The first such volume was issued upon the Act's enactment (and effective date) in 1967; the second addressed the FOIA Amendments of 1974; and the third addressed the FOIA Amendments of 1986.[98] This is not to be confused with the "Attorney General's FOIA Memorandum" (i.e., a statement of new FOIA policy) that often (but not always) is issued near the outset of a presidential administration.

Attorney General's FOIA Memorandum ("AG FOIA Memorandum," for short) -- a document issued by the Justice Department in a new presidential administration that sets forth its policy for the defense of FOIA litigation cases (and therefore for all agencies' FOIA decisionmaking at what is called the "administrative level") governmentwide; at a minimum, it establishes a new substantive standard for that, while ideally also addressing other pressing things such as large backlogs of FOIA requests, the correctness of FOIA correspondence, and the updating of agency FOIA regulations. The standard currently in effect[99] is the one specified by Attorney General Eric H. Holder, Jr., in 2009 (which he borrowed from Janet Reno's memorandum of October 1993); it uses a "foreseeable harm" approach, which carries with it the idea of "discretionary disclosure."[100] Looking back further in time (and skipping back over Janet Reno),[101] Attorney General John D. Ashcroft in 2001 established a "sound legal basis" standard; Attorney General William French Smith in 1981 spoke of "substantial harm"; and Attorney General Griffin B. Bell in 1977 established a standard of "demonstrable harm" required to be shown before an agency could employ an applicable FOIA exemption.

"Foreseeable harm" -- the FOIA litigation-defense (and administrative policy) standard first established by Attorney General Janet Reno on October 4, 1993, for use during the Clinton Administration. It calls upon both Justice Department litigators and FOIA personnel making decisions at the administrative level across the executive branch to consider whether the harm animating a FOIA exemption can reasonably be foreseen to occur upon disclosure in a particular case; otherwise, even if the information technically falls within an exemption, and so long as its disclosure is not prohibited by some other law (such as the one prohibiting disclosure of "tax return" information, for example), it ought to be disclosed as a matter of "administrative discretion."

During the Clinton Administration, this "pro-disclosure standard replaced the less "pro-disclosure" one (i.e., "substantial harm") that was used during the Administrations of Presidents Ronald W. Reagan and George H.W. Bush for the previous 12 years. In the Obama Administration, this Reno policy standard was revived for governmentwide use in its exact same form.[102] Based upon a total of nearly 15 years' experience with the "foreseeable harm" standard, Congress then codified it by legislative enactment in 2016, as new subsection (8)(A)(i)(1) of the Act (where it has lived a full and successful life ever since).

Settlement information -- the information generated for purposes of attempting to reach an agreement between the parties settling a litigation case or administrative claim that often is shared with an opposing party but invariably is kept confidential apart from any such sharing. It does not include a settlement agreement itself (see Chapter Twenty-Three).

Privilege -- the legal doctrine that provides a barrier to the use of certain testimony at a trial (i.e., through a "testimonial privilege"); to the obligation to provide information in what is known as litigation "discovery" (i.e., as part of the standard discovery-defense trio of "burden, privilege, or relevance"); or to the withholding of certain information under Exemption 5 (or in less common cases Exemption 4) of the FOIA (e.g., through the deliberative process privilege, the attorney work-product privilege, the attorney-client privilege, and/or the novel settlement privilege).[103]

State Secrets Privilege -- a unique litigation doctrine created by the United States Supreme Court in the early 1950s[104] in order to afford the Federal Government extraordinary litigation "shielding," both in discovery matters and even as to the maintenance of the very litigation itself, on a national security basis. As such, this privilege is like no other in that provides a basis for dismissal of a probing lawsuit, not just a basis for refusal to produce documents. Not to be confused with other "privileges" that exist, this doctrine bears a very close relation to the scope of "national security classification" under the FOIA's first exemption, Exemption 1. The State Secrets Privilege has been used by the Government with increasing frequency since 9/11, largely successfully.[105]

1974 FOIA Amendments -- the major set of revisions to the FOIA made in the wake of President Nixon's "Watergate" scandals, and his resignation, in 1974; these were entirely "pro-disclosure" changes. Among them was the replacement of the Act's original Exemption 7 -- which until then had "categorically" covered the entireties of all "investigatory files compiled for law enforcement purposes" -- with six new Exemption 7 subparts more specifically pertaining to confidential sources, law enforcement techniques, privacy, and such things. On the procedural side, these amendments among other things altered the Act's fee structure, added a sanctions provision, and provided for the award of attorney fees in cases in which a requester "substantially prevails." It also explicitly authorized courts to undertake "*in camera* inspection" in cases involving classified information under FOIA Exemption 1. All of these amendments became effective as of February 1975.[106]

1986 FOIA Amendments ("FOIA Reform Amendments") -- the major set of revisions to the FOIA made after more than seven years of "FOIA reform" efforts dating back to the Carter Administration. Largely a reaction to the impact of the 1974 FOIA Amendments, and thus somewhat Thermidorian in nature, these were roughly half "anti-disclosure" changes (regarding the Act's law enforcement provisions) and half "pro-disclosure" ones that heavily addressed the subject area of FOIA fees. As to the latter, the Act's entire fee structure was reformed, with many provisions aimed at easing the cost burdens on FOIA requesters in one way or another. And as for the former half of these amendments, among other things, a new "could reasonably be expected to" harm nexus was fashioned for Exemption 7 and three special "exclusion" provisions were created for careful use under highly exceptional circumstances. This remedial legislative measure became effective in October of 1986 for its law enforcement provisions and in April of 1987 as to its fee provisions.

1996 FOIA Amendments ("Electronic FOIA Amendments," sometimes referred to simply as "E-FOIA") -- the entirely procedural set of amendments to the FOIA that, it has been observed, "dragged the FOIA into the 21st century kicking and screaming." Addressing the subject of electronic records for the first time ever in the text of the statute, these amendments included several provisions pertaining to the processing of FOIA requests for records in electronic form. First, they did so by confirming existing general practices of treating information maintained in electronic forms as subject to the FOIA.[107] Second, they addressed the form or format in which a requested record is disclosed under the FOIA, requiring that "an agency shall provide the record in any form or format requested . . . if the record is readily reproducible by the agency in that form or format." Third, they addressed the "retrieval" issue that had plagued database searches for many years, by specifying that "an agency shall make reasonable efforts to search for records in electronic form or format, except when such efforts would significantly interfere with the operation of the agency's automated information system."[108] And lastly, they also addressed the subject areas of time limits (including by providing for "expedited access") and agency backlogs of FOIA requests, among other procedural provisions.[109]

2007 FOIA Amendments ("OPEN Government Act") -- a set of entirely procedural amendments to the Act that addressed the definition of the term "news media" in connection with fees and expedited access; the treatment of agency records that are maintained by government contractors; the recovery of attorney fees and litigation costs; annual reporting requirements; the computing and tolling of time limits for responding to requests; the tracking of requests; and new marking requirements for partially disclosed documents. Most notably, these amendments also created the Office of Government Information Services ("OGIS," to its many customers), within NARA, to provide mediation services, among other FOIA-related advisory support, to FOIA requesters.[110]

2016 FOIA Amendments ("FOIA Improvement Act") -- a set of amendments that completed the FOIA's "ten-year cycle" over a period of 70 years[111] with largely procedural modifications of the Act, one of which nonsensically duplicated an amendment already made 20 years earlier.[112] Like the FOIA amendments made in 2007, these amendments addressed such procedural matters as further limitations on the assessment of fees, new requirements for FOIA response letters, and the responsibilities of agency Chief FOIA Officers.

In the same vein, they also created a new "Chief FOIA Officers Council," expanded the responsibilities of OGIS, and added new reporting requirements for OIP, for OGIS, and for all federal agencies as well. And in the absence of OIP requiring this (as it had in previous years), these amendments specifically directed all agencies to review and update their FOIA regulations. They also specifically required OMB and OIP to "ensure the operation of a consolidated online request portal that allows a member of the public to submit a request for records under [the FOIA] to any agency from a single website."

In a substantive vein, the 2016 FOIA Amendments modified Exemption 5 of the Act by creating a unique "sunset provision" for the most commonly invoked privilege under it, the deliberative process privilege. They limited the applicability of that privilege under the FOIA by providing that it "shall not apply to records created 25 years or more before the date on which the records were requested." This was the first time in the history of the Act that Exemption 5 was amended and it was the first time in 30 years that any FOIA exemption (with the exception of a slight procedural revision of Exemption 3) was amended.

Most important of all, the amendments also codified the Department of Justice's "foreseeable harm" standard that governs the applicability of all FOIA exemptions, together with its twin concept of "discretionary disclosure." That pro-disclosure standard was created during the transition to the Clinton Administration for use by the attorney general in the Attorney General's FOIA Memorandum that eventually was issued in October of 1993. It was in effect, as a matter of firm governmentwide policy, during the Clinton Administration, during the Obama Administration (which adopted it in whole cloth), and by statute on into the Trump Administration (which out of ignorance or diffidence issued no replacement of the Attorney General's FOIA Memorandum). Thus, it became a cornerstone of the Act, first as policy, then as law. (And so the policy standard that I dreamt up for Janet Reno[113] during that December 1992 hike with my daughter is now enshrined in the Act itself as the legal standard governing all FOIA exemption decisionmaking for decades to come.)

"BFD" -- short for "big friggin' deal," which in turn is a stand-in for something else, just as the phrase "situation normal, all fouled up" ("SNAFU") is a stand-in for something else, as also is "FUBAR." The thing about the latter, though, is the uncertainty about its last letter -- it could stand for either "recognition" or "recall," take your pick.

Acknowledgments

"But ya got to have friends."

-- William Charles "Buzzy" Linhart and Mark "Moogy" Klingman, sung by Bette Midler, Track #2 of *The Divine Miss M* (1972)

I do have some people whom I need credit (or can blame) for the overall contents of this book. Certainly any of my family, friends, or former colleagues who read it (or parts of it) in completed draft form fall into the former category,[1] especially my in-house paramour Sharon, a trial attorney herself, who both encouraged and aided me during this book's preparation.[2] Among other things, she was quite proficient at noticing nearly all of my split infinitives, which I have a longtime tendency to very regularly write, and she also might have pointed out that no fewer than a dozen or more of the people on the below list were never exactly Justice Department employees themselves.[3]

But I also owe much credit and appreciation to all the men and women of the United States Department of Justice (and elsewhere) who worked so well and professionally with me on what is covered in this book: Richard L. Huff; Leonard S. Schaitman; Circuit Court Judge Patricia A. Millett; former Chief District Court Judge Royce C. Lamberth; Chief District Court Judge Beryl A. Howell; former Chief Circuit Court Judge Randall R. "Randy" Rader;[4] Circuit Court Judge Daniel P. Collins; Senior Circuit Court Judge and former Acting Solicitor General William C. Bryson; Senior Circuit Court Judge Alvin A. "Tony" Schall;[5] Senior Circuit Court Judge John M. Walker, Jr. (George W. Bush's uncle); District Court Judge Randolph D. Moss; District Court Judge Rudolph Contreras; District Court Judge Reed O'Connor; District Court Judge Lydia Kay Griggsby; Senior District Court Judge Sidney Stein; Senior District Court Judge John D. Bates; the late Senior District Court Judge Gerhard A. Gesell; the late Magistrate Judge (and later Federal Court of Claims Judge) Lawrence S. Margolis; former Magistrate Judge Deborah A. Robinson; former Solicitor General Seth P. Waxman; former Solicitor General Theodore B. Olson; former Solicitor General Donald B. Verrilli, Jr.; former Acting Solicitor General (now Solicitor General of New York) Barbara D. Underwood; Deputy Solicitor General (and former Acting Solicitor General) Edwin S. Kneedler; Deputy Solicitor General (and former Acting Solicitor General) the late Lawrence G. Wallace;[6] former Deputy Solicitor General (and later Chief Circuit Court Judge) Frank H. Easterbrook; former Deputy Solicitor General Kenneth S. Geller; Deputy Solicitor General Malcolm L. Stewart; former Assistant to the Solicitor General Harriet S. Shapiro; former Assistant to the Solicitor General Roy T. Englert, Jr.; former Assistant to the Solicitor General Lisa Schiavo Blatt; Assistant to the Solicitor General Anthony A. "Tony" Yang; former Office of the Solicitor General Executive Officer Carolyn M. Brammer; and former Principal Deputy Solicitor General (now Chief Justice of the United States) John G. Roberts, Jr.

And former White House Chief of Staff John D. Podesta, Jr.; former White House Associate Counsel (and later President of Oberlin College and now Pace University) Marvin Krislov; former Deputy Assistant and Deputy Counsel to the President Steven P. Croley; former Secretary of Agriculture Ann M. Veneman; former Assistant Secretary of State for Public Affairs Phillip J. "P.J." Crowley; former Director of the United States Secret Service John W. Magaw; former Archivist of the United States the late James B. Rhoads; former Archivist of the United States the late Allen Weinstein, former Acting Archivist of the United States Trudy Huskamp Peterson; former Food & Drug Commissioner (and fellow "soccer Dad," as our daughters played on the same team for a while) Dr. David A. Kessler; former Independent Counsel the late Jacob A. Stein; former Deputy Independent Counsel J. Keith Ausbrook; former Deputy Independent Counsel Bruce C. Swartz; former Deputy Independent Counsel Judith Bartnoff; former Associate Independent Counsel Mark Stein; Inspector General for Tax Administration at the Internal Revenue Service J. Russell George; and former Inspector General for DHS Richard L. Skinner.

As well as former General Counsel of the White House Office of Administration Bruce L. Overton; General Counsel of the Library of Congress Elizabeth A. Pugh; General Counsel of the National Archives and Records Administration Gary M. Stern; General Counsel of the Administrative Office of the U.S. Courts Sheryl L. Walter; former General Counsel of the National Archives and Records Administration the late Steven Garfinkel;[7] former General Counsel of the Administrative Conference of the United States (and later Professor at the University of Hull School of Law and Politics) Gary D. Edles; former General Counsel of the Merit Systems Protection Board Llewellyn M. Fischer; former General Counsel of the National Mediation Board Ronald M. Etters; former General Counsel of the Federal Emergency Management Agency the late Spencer W. Perry; former General Counsel of the Selective Service System the late

Henry N. Williams; former General Counsel of the Peace Corps and the White House Office of Administration Arnold A. Intrater; former General Counsel of the Consumer Financial Protection Bureau Meredith A. Fuchs; former Principal Deputy Legal Adviser of the Department of State James H. Thessin; former Deputy General Counsel of the Department of the Treasury Dennis I. Foreman; former Deputy General Counsel of the Office of Management and Budget the late Cecilia E. Wirtz; former Deputy General Counsel of the Commodity Futures Trading Commission the late Whitney H. Adams; Deputy General Counsel of the Federal Trade Commission John F. Daly; former Deputy General Counsel of the Administrative Conference of the United States David M. Pritzker; former Associate General Counsel of the Department of Homeland Security Hugo T. Teufel III; former Associate General Counsel of the Department of Housing and Urban Development John W. Herold; former Government Accountability Office Director of Information Management Issues Linda D. Koontz; former Senior Counsel of the Department of Commerce Thomas C. Barbour; former General Counsel of the House of Representatives Stanley M. Brand; and former General Counsel of the House of Representatives Douglas N. Letter.

Also former Deputy Attorney General and Acting Attorney General George J. Terwilliger III; former Deputy Attorney General Paul J. McNulty; former Deputy Attorney General (and later member of the "9/11 Commission") Jamie S. Gorelick; former Deputy Attorney General David W. Ogden; former Acting Deputy Attorney General, FBI Director, and Special Counsel Robert S. Mueller III; former Associate Attorney General, Acting Deputy Attorney General, and Ambassador Robert D. McCallum, Jr.; former Associate Attorney General and Acting Attorney General Peter D. Keisler; former Associate Attorney General Daniel Marcus; former Associate Attorney General John H. Shenefield; former Associate Attorney General (and later Circuit Court Judge) Raymond C. Fisher; former Acting Associate Attorney General (and later General Counsel of the Department of Homeland Security) Joe D. Whitley; former Assistant Attorney General Jonathan C. Rose; former Assistant Attorney General (and later Governor of Massachusetts) Deval L. Patrick; former Assistant Attorney General and Acting Attorney General Stuart M. Gerson; former Assistant Attorney General Lois J. Schiffer; former Assistant Attorney General Eleanor Dean "Eldie" Acheson; former Assistant Attorney General (and vice-presidential brother-in-law) Frank W. Hunger; former Assistant Attorney General J. Paul McGrath; and former Acting Assistant Attorney General (and later Federal Court of Claims Judge) Richard A. Hertling.

In addition, former Directors of Public Affairs Carl Stern, Bert Brandenburg,

Myron Marlin, Gina M. Talamona (acting), and Frank Shults (acting); former Chief of Staff to the Attorney General the late John M. Hogan; former Counselor to the Attorney General (and later United States Attorney, Senior Investigative Counsel for the January 6th Select Committee, and senatorial candidate in Missouri) John F. Wood; former Counsel to the Attorney General (and later Principal Associate Deputy Attorney General, Assistant Attorney General, Assistant to the President for Homeland Security and Counterterrorism, and now Deputy Attorney General) Lisa O. Monaco; former Assistant to the Attorney General (and later Associate Attorney General and Deputy Assistant Attorney General) Thomas J. Perrelli; former Assistant to the Attorney General Abbe D. Lowell; former Principal Associate Deputy Attorney General (and later Chief Circuit Court Judge and then Attorney General) Merrick B. Garland; former Principal Associate Deputy Attorney General (and later General Counsel of the Office of the Director of National Intelligence) Robert S. Litt; former Principal Associate Deputy Attorney General (and later Acting Associate Attorney General) William W. Mercer; former Associate Deputy Attorney General (and later Acting Secretary of the Treasury) Stuart A. Levey; former Associate Deputy Attorney General (and later Deputy Assistant Attorney General and Acting Attorney General) Robert M. "Monty" Wilkinson; former Associate Deputy Attorney General (and later Assistant Attorney General and FBI Director) Christopher A. Wray; former Associate Deputy Attorney General (and later Acting Assistant Attorney General) Roger B. Clegg; former Associate Deputy Attorney General (and later Deputy Assistant Attorney General) Grace Louise Mastalli; former Chief of the Criminal Division's Organized Crime and Racketeering Section (and later Associate Deputy Attorney General) the late David M. Margolis; former Associate Deputy Attorney General David S. Kriss; former Associate Deputy Attorney General B. Boykin Rose; former Associate Deputy Attorney General (and later Associate Counsel to the President and Member of the Interstate Commerce Commission) Gregory S. Walden; former Associate Deputy Attorney General Geoffrey R. Greiveldinger; former Associate Deputy Attorney General James L. Swanson; former Chief of Staff to the Deputy Attorney General (and later or earlier Chief of Staff to the FBI Director, Counselor to the Attorney General, Counsel to the FBI Director, and Acting Administrator of the Drug Enforcement Administration, *inter alia*) Charles P. "Chuck" Rosenberg; former Chief of Staff to the Deputy Attorney General Kevin A. Ohlson; and former Senior Counsel to the Deputy Attorney General Chad Boudreaux.

As well as former Counsel to the Deputy Attorney General (and later Deputy Attorney General and Acting Attorney General) Rod J. Rosenstein; former

Counsel to the Deputy Attorney General (and currently Special Inspector General for Pandemic Recovery Brian D. Miller; former Counsel to the Deputy Attorney General James A. "Mac" McAtamney; former Principal Deputy Associate Attorney General (and later Acting Assistant Attorney General) the late L. Anthony "Tony" Sutin;[8] former Counselor to the Associate Attorney General (and later Deputy Assistant Attorney General) the late Robert N. Ford; and former Counselor to the Assistant Attorney General for Legal Counsel (and later Assistant Attorney General for Legal Policy and subsequently Assistant Attorney General for Legal Counsel) Christopher M. Schroeder.

And also former Deputy Assistant Attorney General (and Acting Assistant Attorney General) Janis A. Sposato; former Deputy Assistant Attorney General Richard L. Shiffrin; former Deputy Assistant Attorney General William G. Shaffer; former Deputy Assistant Attorney General Irwin Goldbloom; former Deputy Assistant Attorney General Patricia M. Bryan; former United States Attorney Florence "Flo" Nakakuni; former United States Attorney Patrick M. McLaughlin; former United States Attorney the late Earl J. Silbert; former United States Attorney and later Chief Judge of the United States District Court of the U.S. Virgin Islands Wilma A. Lewis; former United States Attorney (and later DEA Administrator and Governor of Arkansas) William "Asa" Hutchinson II; former United States Attorney (and later Assistant Attorney General for the National Security Division and Under Secretary of Homeland Security for Intelligence and Analysis) Kenneth L. Wainstein; former Interim United States Attorney (and later Acting Assistant Attorney General, Deputy Associate Attorney General, and Deputy Director of the White House Office of National Drug Control Policy) Mary Lou Leary; former Principal Assistant United States Attorney (and later Acting United States Attorney, twice) Channing D. Phillips; former Director of the Office of Professional Responsibility H. Marshall Jarrett; former Director of the Office of Professional Responsibility the late Michael E. Shaheen, Jr.;[9] Inspector General Michael E. Horowitz; former Inspector General Glenn A. Fine; former Acting Inspector General Anthony C. "Tony" Moscato; former Special Master of the September 11th Victim Compensation Fund Kenneth R. Feinberg; former Director of the Bureau of Prisons Harley G. Lappin; former Pardon Attorney Roger C. Adams; former Pardon Attorney Margaret Colgate Love; former Chairman of the Foreign Claims Settlement Commission Mauricio J. Tamargo; and Ambassadors Robert M. Kimmitt[10] and Norman L. Eisen.

As well as the late Janet W. Reno;[11] the late Nancy E. McFadden;[12] the late Robert L. Saloschin;[13] the late Martin B. Danziger;[14] the late Donald J. Gavin;[15] the late Mary C. Lawton;[16] the late Dr. Steven R. Schlesinger;[17] the late John J.

"Jack" Keeney;[18] the late Ellen Lee Park;[19] the late Michael S. Bernstein;[20] the late Nathan Dodell;[21] the late Kathryn F. "Kitty" Harless;[22] the late Leo D. Neshkes;[23] the late Rosario "Ross" Cirrincione;[24] the late Larry L. Simms;[25] the late William J. Olmstead;[26] the late Mark M. Richard;[27] the late Claudia J. Flynn;[28] the late Barbara Allen Babcock;[29] the late Ernest ("Ernie") Mayerfeld;[30] the late James B. Jacobs;[31] the late William H. Harader,[32] and the most recently deceased Walter E. Dellinger III, the brilliant Acting Solicitor General and Assistant Attorney General for Legal Counsel with whom I worked closely on an especially sensitive White House scandal (read: an averted, never disclosed one) during the Clinton Administration (see Chapter Thirty).

And of course OIP Deputy Directors Miriam M. Nisbet, Margaret Ann Irving, Jean K. FitzSimon, and Kirsten J. Moncada (now Chief of the Privacy Branch of the Office of Information and Regulatory Affairs ("OIRA," to those who do not have affairs) of the Office of Management and Budget ("OMB," to needy agency budget officers who do)); former OIP Associate Directors Janice Galli McLeod and Tricia Sanders Wellman (now Executive Director of the National Counterterrorism Center ("NCTC," to its domestic and international adversaries)); former OIP staff attorneys Mark E. Nagle, Elizabeth Ross Withnell, Marina Utgoff Braswell (now Assistant United States Attorney for the District of Columbia), Philip A. Kesaris (now senior attorney at HUD), Charles J. "Chuck" Sheehan (now Deputy Inspector General of EPA), Fran L. Paver (now senior attorney at the SEC), Jennifer Ashworth Kendrick (now Assistant Counsel to the Inspector General of DHS), Kenneth D. Chasen (now Counsel to the Inspector General of the National Science Foundation), Kenneth A. Hendricks (now Chief FOIA Officer of the Antitrust Division), Marcy A. Toney (now Regional Judicial Officer for EPA), Kenneth J. Wernick, Michael H. Hughes, Cynthia H. Anderson, Laura A. Denk, Frank P. Menna, Philip J. Lindemuth, Benjamin N. Bedrick, Shannon V. Lane, Serafina M. Esposito Lobsenz, Wendy L. Weiss, Pamela S. Stever, Marion Lebron Silva (now deceased), Richard A. Cohn (now deceased), and Gerald B. Roemer (now deceased);[33] former OIP law clerks Alina M. Semo (now Director of the Office of Government Information Services ("OGIS," to its ombuds)), Garen J. Horst (now California Superior Court Judge); and Diane Brady Janosek (now Training Director of the National Cryptologic School at the National Security Agency); former OIP paralegals or "legal techs" Pamela A. Maida, Drema A. Hanshaw, Carmen L. Mallon, Charlene Wright Thomas, Bertina Adams Cleveland, Jeanne McLaughlin (now FOIA Public Liaison at the Federal Reserve Board), Lorraine Hartmann (now Appeals Officer at the State Department's Office of Information Programs and Services); OIP support personnel Priscilla A. Jones, Miriam R. Eubanks, Nakeitha D. Gilbert, Nisa C. Subasinghe (now Domestic & Guardianship Program Manager at the Maryland Administrative Office of the Courts); and of course OIP's best-ever paralegal Ana Belen Montes.

As well as Professor Emeritus Robert Vaughn; Professor Stephen I. Vladeck; Professor Jerome A. Cohen; Sensei (Professor) Maseo Horibe; Professor Robert Hazel, CBE; Professor Liu Wenjing; Professor Peter P. Swire; Professor Jeffrey S. Lubbers; Professor Stephen J. Wermiel; Professor James T. O'Reilly; Professor Jane E. Kirtley; Professor Corinne J. "Cori" Zarek; Professor Thomas M. Bondy; Professor Jason R. Baron; Professor I. Michael Greenberger; Professor Nancy Z. Boswell; Dean Erwin Chemerinsky; Dean Paul R. Verkuil; Dean Lucy A. Dalglish; Dean Charles N. Davis; Dean Mark H. Grunewald; Acting Dean Robert D. Dinerstein; the late Associate Dean Edward A. Potts; Associate Dean Alan B. Morrison; Dr. Louis Fisher; Dr. Harold C. Relyea; Dr. Sarah E. Holsen; former European Data Protection Supervisor Peter J. Hustinx; former Information Commissioner for the United Kingdom Richard J. Thomas, CBE; former Scottish Information Commission Kevin H. Dunion, OBE; former Chief Information Commissioner of India Wajahat Habibullah; former Information Commissioner of Canada John M. Reid; and former Information Commissioner (and Parliamentary Ombudsman for Public Administration) of Norway Arne Fliflet.

And also FBI Assistant Special Agent-in-Charge (and later Assistant Director) the late James M. Fox, FBI Assistant Director Thomas M. Coyle, FBI Assistant Director William F. Welby, FBI Deputy Assistant Director Thomas H. Bresson, FBI Special Agent-in-Charge Charles E. "Chip" Riley, FBI Special Agent-in-Charge Charles Matthews, FBI FOIPA Section Chief Emil P. Moschella, FBI Unit Chief John Hartingh, FBI Unit Chief James Bourke, FBI Unit Chief the late Parle T. "Tom" Blake, FBI Supervisory Special Agent Horace Beckwith,[34] FBI Supervisory Special Agent James King, FBI Supervisory Special Agent Bradley B. Benson, FBI Special Agent John H. Hawkes, FBI Special Agent the late John Paul Bokal, FBI Special Agent the late Wade M. Homesley, FBI Special Agent Jerry R. Donohoe, FBI Special Agent Michael German, FBI Supervisory Document Analyst William "Bill" Shackelford, and FBI Document Analyst Connie F. Ahrens.

Also William H. Leary, Thomas M. Susman, William G. Ferroggiaro, Freddi R. Lipstein, R. Craig Lawrence, Anthony J. "Tony" Steinmeyer, Wendy M. Keats, Mark W. Pennak, Howard S. Scher, William G. Cole, Michael E. Robinson, Steven I. Frank, Michael J. Singer, Peter R. Maier, Andrew M. Wolfe, Barbara L. Gordon, Linda A. Cinciotta, Rosemary A. Hart, Stuart Frisch, Jack E. Perkins, Warren Oser, Lt. Bernard Gattozzi, Vincent N. Micone III, Dennis G. Linder,

John J. "Jack" Farley, Nicki L. Koutsis, Bruce E. Titus, Barbara L. Ward, Paul F. Figley, Sandra Wein Simon, Mark J. Kurzmann, Thomas W. Hussey, JoAnn M. Dolan, Salliann M. Dougherty, Frederick D. Hess, Cary H. Copeland, Margaret A. Smith, L. Jeffrey Ross, James M. Kovakus, Nelson D. Hermilla, Stephen J. Csontos, J. Brian Ferrel, Geoffrey S. Stewart, Robert J. Roeder, Patricia Binninger, Elizabeth "Liza" Goitein, David M. Glass, Kathy Olesker Pounds, Professor June R. Carbone, former Missouri State Representative Susan E. Carlson, the late Linda Lance, the late Edgar H. Brenner, Ann S. Pepperman, Maurice Frankel, OBE, Helen Darbishire, Sarah Hutchinson, Andrew Ecclestone, Allan R. Adler, John Sanet, Claire E. Shanley, Miriam McD. Miller, Mary I. Ronan, Robert J. Ross, John N. Greer, Robert H. Moll, Danielle Bryan, Scott Amey, Ginger P. Quintero-McCall, Thomas S. Blanton, Amy A. Bennett, Kirsten B. Mitchell, Lauren Harper, Paul McMasters, Cindy S. Cafaro, Adina H. Rosenbaum, Janice L. Pesyna, Lucy Clark Dougherty, John W. Kropf, W. George Jameson, Dr. Edward Martin, Russell Salter, Nancy Griffin, and last but not least Justice Department litigation opponent Brad P. Rosenberg come most readily to mind, among countless other dedicated public servants who have worked (and in a few cases still work) with little or no public recognition at all.

Quiz Questions

"Sex, Drugs, and Rock 'n Roll."

-- *The Spectator* (British magazine providing "a weekly review of politics," established in 1828), 1971

QUIZ #1: Which former attorney general ("AG") came into the Department of Justice through the "Attorney General's Honors Program"?

ANSWER: Attorney General Eric H. Holder, Jr., who was an "Honors Program" hire in 1976.

QUIZ #2: Which former AG was closely related to a Supreme Court Justice?

CLUE: Think of President Lyndon B. Johnson's caginess.

QUIZ #3: Who was the worst attorney general?

ANSWER: The competition for that honor is quite stiff. In the first half of the 20th century, AG A. Mitchell Palmer made a bid for such recognition with his "Palmer Raids," through which he rounded up and deported thousands of suspected "radicals." During the 1970s, he was surpassed by the "Watergate" duo of AG John N. Mitchell, who went to jail, and AG Richard G. Kleindienst, who managed to evade jail. Then came AG Alberto R. Gonzales, whose middle initial reportedly stood for "retrasado" and probably was the most intellectually challenged person to hold that office in its 233-year history.[1] More recently, we witnessed the totally unexpected behavior of AG William P. Barr (who had very ably served in that position for more than a year during 1991-1993) while he served President Donald J. Trump's interests from early 2019 to late 2020. Suffice to say that there are many, including hundreds of appalled former Justice Department officials, who regard his second AG tenure as so irrational, irresponsible, and dangerously unredeemable as to have the award for "worst AG in history" retired in his honor.

QUIZ #4:   Which AG improperly removed the greatest number of agency records upon his or her departure from the Department? (With apologies to former AG Loretta E. Lynch and the memory of former AG Janet W. Reno.)

ANSWER: This competition for this distinction could be said to be a "photo finish," although one AG reportedly did so through the use of barrels (eleven), while another AG did so through use of conventional file boxes (more than a dozen). The former removal was achieved by AG William French Smith in 1985; the latter removal was at first achieved by AG Edwin Meese III in 1988, but then those boxes were seized from his home garage and returned to the Department, where they were held for safekeeping within the offices of OIP. This trifecta was completed with what was done by AG Griffin B. Bell (see Chapter Thirty-Three) and is akin to what was discovered to have been done by President Donald J. Trump when the National Archives and Records Administration had to retrieve 15 boxes of White House records that were removed by him to his home in Florida in violation of the Presidential Records Act.

QUIZ #5:   Which AG after law school co-founded a company called "Buy the Yard Concrete," defended "ready-mix concrete" manufacturers in court, and worked for a fraudulent "invention promotion firm?"

ANSWER: He was only an acting AG, but Matthew G. Whitaker, President Donald J. Trump's choice to temporarily succeed AG Jefferson B. Sessions III in November of 2018, fits this particular bill. There are those who argued that his appointment as acting AG was unconstitutional under the Appointments Clause of the Constitution, but a compelling case to the contrary was made at the time by Charles Alan Wright Chair in Federal Courts at the University of Texas School of Law (and former Washington College of Law Professor) Stephen I. Vladeck that Whittaker's appointment was indeed constitutional under the Federal Vacancies Reform Act of 1998. (Steve and I taught national security law together at WCL and my money's on him.)

QUIZ #6:   Which AG went on the be the United States Ambassador to the Court of St. James, the same position once held by JFK's father?

CLUE: He also is the only person to date to have held four cabinet secretary positions.

QUIZ #7: Which former Solicitor General of the United States sired a future senator?

CLUE: Think Utah.

QUIZ #8: Which former "Watergate" figure began his government career as a young Justice Department attorney?

CLUE: Remember when there was "a cancer on the presidency."

QUIZ #9: Which Justice Department employee was ineffectually accused of suddenly destroying extremely sensitive government files?

ANSWER: Helen W. Gandy, secretary to FBI Director J. Edgar Hoover from 1918-1972, who "carried out his wishes" upon his death.

QUIZ #10: How many FBI directors have there been?

ANSWER: There have been eight, with seven men serving as acting director since the death of FBI Director J. Edgar Hoover in May of 1972.

QUIZ #11: Of those seven acting directors of the FBI, which one was planned by the Nixon White House to be left "twist[ing] slowly, slowly in the wind?"

ANSWER: That would be L. Patrick Gray III, whose second-in-command W. Mark Felt, Sr., successfully persuaded him that he (i.e., Felt) was not "Deep Throat," which he actually was.

QUIZ #12: How many spies have worked within the Justice Department over the years?

ANSWER: No one knows for sure.

QUIZ #13: Which component of the Justice Department has a program so secret that it cannot respond to some of its FOIA requests in an ordinary fashion?

CLUE: It has nothing to do with "Glomarization," though this component would employ that if necessary in response to a certain type of request.

ANSWER: The United States Marshals Service ("USMS," to fugitives from justice), which houses the Department's "Witness Security Program" ("WitSec," to its "relocatees"). WitSec was created almost 50 years ago as a means of persuading organized crime members to testify against their criminal associates through their relocation with new identities, as well as with continued federal protection for them and often some members of their own families (i.e., certainly not their organized crime "families"). The program operates under authority of a specific statute, found at 18 U.S.C. § 3521, which explicitly protects the identities of program participants, as well as their new locations, and provides a basis for withholding information under Exemption 3 of the FOIA. However, while it is standard FOIA practice for an agency invoking Exemption 3 to specify for the FOIA requester the particular Exemption 3 statute that is involved, this usually is not possible in the case of this statute, lest the WitSec status of someone be compromised.[2] In such cases, the USMS coordinates with OIP as to the most appropriate approach to be employed. (Note: This question also implicates a part of the FBI that sometimes has reason to invoke the FOIA's "(c)(3) exclusion.")

QUIZ #14: How many times has an assistant attorney general at the Justice Department gone on to become attorney general?

ANSWER: Six (trick question), Tom Clark, Ramsey Clark, Ben Civiletti, Dick Thornburgh, and Bill Barr (twice).

QUIZ #15: Which former associate deputy attorney general went on to hold a cabinet-level position?

ANSWER: James H. Burnley IV, who was an ADAG from 1982-1983 (during which time he helped me with a "political matter," insofar as he was then acting as the Department's "political commissar" in coordination with the White House and OPM) and went on to become Secretary of Transportation in 1987. (In between those times, he participated in "COG" activities (see Chapter Twenty-Six).)

QUIZ #16: Which former associate attorney general went on to become a state governor?[3]

CLUE: He was fired by AG Dick Thornburg in January of 1989.

QUIZ #17: Which former AG made a FOIA request to the Department that was initially encumbered by the Privacy Act's protection of another person?

ANSWER: Attorney General Herbert Brownell, Jr., who was the AG from 1953-1957 and during the 1980s sought access to the Department's litigation files on the *Brown v. Board of Education* case -- which were Privacy

Act-protected files maintained under the name of an individual, lead plaintiff Linda Brown (together with her father Oliver Brown). We worked something out on this.

QUIZ #18: Which AG unwittingly allowed himself to be photographed abreast of "Minnie Lou" while holding up a copy of the "Final Report of the Attorney General's Commission on Pornography?"

CLUE: He is the only AG to have a "III" in his name, not to mention the only one to have several investigations of his conduct ongoing at any one time. (But he could "take incoming" better than anyone I've ever seen.)

QUIZ #19: How many former Justice Department officials wound up spending time in jail?

ANSWER: Not as many as ought to have, including a former AG.

QUIZ #20: How many FBI Special Agents have been convicted of espionage?

ANSWER: Three. Special Agent Richard W. Miller, Supervisory Special Agent Edwin Earl Pitts, and Supervisory Special Agent Robert P. Hanssen. Plus, FBI Intelligence Specialist Leandro Aragoncillo, who spied for the regime of a former Filipino president while at the FBI and prior to that in the Office of the Vice President at the White House.

QUIZ #21: How many spies have there been at the White House?

ANSWER: Very likely more than one.

QUIZ #22: Which AG has a middle initial for which there is no corresponding name?

CLUE: He is the only AG known to have been unable to find a new job upon leaving the Department. (Even former AG John N. Mitchell quickly snagged one in the prison laundry.)

QUIZ #23: Which AG was known to have mandatory prayer meetings for his staff?

CLUE: Until September 11, 2001, he continued his pattern of flying back to his home state almost every weekend.

QUIZ #24: Which AG had a mother who single-handedly built her own house?

CLUE: Her mother also navigated the Everglades.

QUIZ #25:   Which AG had a middle name that was the same as the last names of two other attorneys general?

ANSWER: Attorney General Alexander Mitchell Palmer.

QUIZ #26:   Which AG also served as Secretary of the Treasury and Secretary of War before also becoming Chief Justice of the United States?

ANSWER: Roger B. Taney, who succeeded John Marshall as Chief Justice.

QUIZ #27:   Which large component of the Department left it in the wake of 9/11?

ANSWER: Hardly anyone remembers its name anymore, but its initials were "INS."

QUIZ #28:   Which large component of the Department was transferred to it in the wake of 9/11?

ANSWER: The Bureau of Alcohol, Tobacco, Firearms, and Explosives (originally just the former three, hence still "ATF"), which came from the Department of the Treasury in exchange for a utility infielder, cash considerations, a player to be named later, and a future draft pick.

QUIZ #29:   Who was the first associate attorney general?

ANSWER: That was Michael J. Egan, a politician from Georgia closely allied with incoming AG Griffin B. Bell when appointed to the position in early 1977, more than three years after that position was first envisioned.[4]

QUIZ #30:   Which former assistant attorney general went on to become Chief Justice of the United States?

ANSWER: Actually, there were two of them, former Assistant Attorney General for the Civil Division Warren E. Burger and former Assistant Attorney General for the Office of Legal Counsel William H. Rehnquist.

QUIZ #31:   Which former assistant attorney general went on to hold a high-level position in the Trump White House?

CLUE: His bushy mustache was bright reddish in color, not white, back then.[5]

QUIZ #32:   Which former assistant attorney general went on to be a United States senator, winning seven terms?

ANSWER: Addison Mitchell ("Mitch") McConnell, Jr., was the Acting Assistant Attorney General for Legislative Affairs in 1975 before becoming a senator from Kentucky in 1985.

QUIZ #33: Which AG went on to become Chief Justice of the United States?
CLUE: His first name was the same as the surname of two Supreme Court Justices.

QUIZ #34: Which former deputy attorney general went on to become an Associate Justice of the Supreme Court?
CLUE: He played professional football for the Detroit Lions while attending law school.

QUIZ #35: Which former assistant to the solicitor general and deputy assistant attorney general went on to earn the nickname "Scalito" as a circuit court judge?
CLUE: The nickname worked, as he's now an Associate Justice of the Supreme Court.

QUIZ #36: Which former associate attorney general was not particularly well-liked by the Department's career officials and quickly earned the nickname "Rudy Kazootie?"
CLUE: A later nickname for him was "Mr. Mayor" (and more recently, "Trump Stooge").

QUIZ #37: Which FBI director was not fired by President George H.W. Bush because outgoing AG William P. Barr preferred to let the incoming Clinton Administration deal with his serious ethical lapses?
ANSWER: That was William S. Sessions, who ultimately was fired by President William J. Clinton seven months later, based on a series of severe travel and personal-expense abuses, although he staunchly denied any wrongdoing to the end (contrary to my personal knowledge).

QUIZ #38: Which president claimed to have "seen a UFO" prior to becoming president?
CLUE: He was "working for peanuts" at the time (1969), and it turned out to be only a "barium cloud."

QUIZ #39: Which incoming president wanted to know about UFOs more than almost anything else?

CLUE: It was in "second place" to "who killed Kennedy," on his priority list. And in third place probably was "where does a guy go to get . . . Lays potato chips around here?"

QUIZ #40: Which presidential chief of staff was (and evidently still is) a strong proponent of "ufology"?

CLUE: He used to speak at OIP's "Advanced FOIA" seminars.

QUIZ #41: What is the "official" mailing address for "Area 51," i.e., the one used by aliens?

ANSWER: "Cabins 1120-1151, Groom Lake, Nevada, Planet Earth (third planet from the relatively small star)."

QUIZ #42: To where is mail for Area 51 sometimes misdelivered?

ANSWER: Dugway Proving Ground, Utah, known as "Area 52."

QUIZ #43: Are Area 51 and Area 52 in the same state?

ANSWER: Yes, a state of confusion, as there is so much secrecy surrounding them. Otherwise, no, as the former is in Nevada and the latter is in Utah.

QUIZ #44: How many "UFO sightings" are unexplained?

ANSWER: About 10 percent of them, depending on your definitions of the words "sightings" and "explained."

QUIZ #45: How many people used to work at OIP?

ANSWER: Whenever someone asked, the standard reply was "about half," but the actual number ranged over the years from 33 to 50.

QUIZ #46: How many former members of OIP ("OIPers," to themselves) went on to become presidential appointees?

ANSWER: At least three. One became the U.S. Attorney for the District of Hawaii, one became the general counsel of GSA, and one became chairwoman of the FLRA. And a fourth one is too shameful (think Trump Administration) to be mentioned.

QUIZ #47: Which floors of the Main Justice Building were originally occupied by the FBI?

CLUE: They are the two uppermost ones, not counting the huge attic; plus, the "FBI Tour" took up much of the basement.

QUIZ #48: Has the Main Justice Building ever experienced a major flood due to its location?

ANSWER: Yes, the Main Justice Building is located atop an underground body of water known as "Tiber Creek," which until the mid-nineteenth century was an offshoot of the Potomac River, one that extended due east from the original Watergate area behind the Lincoln Memorial to nearly the foot of the Capitol, i.e., along what is now Constitution Avenue. For this reason, the Main Justice Building and its adjacent neighbors (i.e., the Internal Revenue Service Building to the west and the National Archives Building to the east) maintain pumps in their basements for use in heavy storms. On June 26, 2006, however, a lengthy storm brought so much rainfall to the Downtown D.C. area that the Justice Department's pumps were completely overcome, an electrical fire erupted, and flood waters rose nearly to the basement's ceiling. Unfortunately, the Department's basement cafeteria (its only one) had been completely refurbished not long beforehand and had to be rebuilt once the water receded.

QUIZ #49: Is it true that before the FBI moved across Pennsylvania Avenue in 1974 its standard tour included a view of a "Tommy Gun" (i.e., sub-machine gun) spray and John H. Dillinger's penis?

ANSWER: Yes and no. The "Tommy Gun" exhibition, which was the climax of the tour, continued even after moving over to the J. Edgar Hoover FBI Headquarters Building,[6] but it is possible that "Public Enemy #1" John Dillinger's "membership" in that club was misplaced during the move. Alternatively, it might now be stored away in one of the Smithsonian buildings or perhaps in the National Museum of Health and Medicine just outside of D.C. in Silver Spring, Maryland (formerly the Armed Forces Medical Museum), at the former Walter Reed Army Medical Center in D.C. Or it could be in Indianapolis, Indiana, where he was buried. (Recent plans to exhume at least the rest of his body on December 31, 2019, for the History Channel, were abruptly shelved.) There appears to be little or no truth the rumor that from

1934 until 1972 it occupied a preservative jar behind Hoover's desk. More substantial, in a creepy admixture of morbidity and prurience, is the rumor that Hoover had intrusive photographs of another body taken in June of 1968.

QUIZ #50: Is the Main Justice Building near where any president was shot?

ANSWER: Yes, yes, and not so much. Main Justice is bordered to the west by 10th Street, N.W., as is Ford's Theatre, two blocks to the north, where President Lincoln was shot and killed in 1864. Seventeen years later, in 1881, President James A. Garfield was assassinated at the Baltimore and Potomac Railroad Station (also known as the Pennsylvania Railroad Station), then located at the intersection of 6th Street, N.W., and what is now Constitution Avenue, three blocks due east of where the Main Justice Building now stands. One hundred years after that, on March 30, 1981, President Ronald W. Reagan was shot in an attempted assassination immediately after exiting the Washington Hilton Hotel, near the 1900 block of Connecticut Avenue, N.W., about 1.5 miles away. These were the only presidential shootings within Washington, D.C., although in November of 1950, two Puerto Rican pro-independence activists shot three members of President Harry S. Truman's protective detail during a gunfight outside of Blair House, on the northeast corner of 17th Street and Pennsylvania Avenue, N.W., where President Truman was residing during a White House renovation. President Truman famously stuck his head out of his second-floor bedroom window to see what all the gunfire was all about, but he was not shot at.

A personal note here: When he was shot, President Reagan was taken to George Washington University Hospital, where for security reasons (read: partly having to do with the building's configuration) he was placed in a room at the end of the hospital's maternity ward for his recovery. Eleven days later, my wife (and I) entered that ward for her to give birth to our first child, but due to a protracted period of labor (which turned out to be 29½ hours, for a 12 lb., 3 oz., 23½-inch-long baby) we were advised to walk loops along the corridors in order to help move things along. President Reagan was still there, however, which meant that we had to pivot around at his security stations as we walked. The next day, after our child was born, my wife had to warn me not to try to get back into the hospital as scheduled, because she could hear the heavy footsteps of Secret Service agents as they accompanied Reagan and his entourage down the hall for his departure. That was one time when all the special identification cards that I carried would have been good for naught. (Just another part of living in Washington.)

QUIZ #51: How many presidents have stood in the Main Justice Building?
ANSWER: Only six, because FDR was one.

QUIZ #52: Which president came to the Main Justice Building to, *inter alia*, celebrate my 50th birthday?
ANSWER: George W. Bush, except that he was there mostly to rededicate the building as the "Robert F. Kennedy Department of Justice Building," on what would have been RFK's 76th birthday as well.

QUIZ #53: Which president was born on the same day of the year as former AG Robert F. Kennedy?
ANSWER: President Joseph R. Biden, who also was born on November 20.

QUIZ #54: How many external exits are there from the Main Justice Building, not counting the two courtyard driveways?
ANSWER: Six, on the First Floor at the southwest, northwest, and northeast corners of the building, as well as mid-way between the latter two and mid-way along Constitution Avenue, plus the one at the top of the Eighth Floor attic stairway leading to the roof.

QUIZ #55: How many locations have housed the main operations of the Department of Justice since its creation in 1870?
ANSWER: Four. The Freedman's Bank Building, from 1870-1899 (floors 2-5); the Palmer House, from 1899-1917; an unnamed building at the corner of Vermont Avenue and K Street, N.W., from 1917-1934; and the Robert F. Kennedy Main Justice Department Building ("Main Justice Building") on the "Federal Triangle," between Ninth and Tenth Streets and Pennsylvania and Constitution Avenues, N.W., which opened in 1934. Additionally, various components of the Department (or parts of them) have been located in more than 50 D.C. locations over the years (in addition to "field office" locations around the country), including the FBI's Headquarters Building (still named after notorious FBI Director J. Edgar Hoover) located just north of the Main Justice Building. For instance, OIP has been located on two different floors

of the Main Justice Building and, at times during Main Justice Building renovations, in three other buildings (Todd, Flag, and New York Avenue) between Main Justice and the White House and it currently is located farther away, at 441 G St., N.W.[7]

QUIZ #56: What does the Main Justice Building have in common with Statuary Hall (technically National Statuary Hall) in the Capitol Building?

ANSWER: Both have an area where the domed shape of the ceiling conveys whispers from one end to another, as if magically. In Statuary Hall, just south of the Capitol rotunda, a semi-circular dome achieves this acoustic effect. In the Main Justice Building, there are places where a fully domed ceiling section causes the same effect, but on a much smaller scale. An example can be found on the building's 5200 Corridor, at its intersection with a transverse passageway.

QUIZ #57: What do you see if you are standing on the roof of the Main Justice Building?

ANSWER: You see a sea of predominately bright reddish-colored tiles covering the roofs of almost all of the buildings in "The Federal Triangle," which extends from the Federal Trade Commission Building (known as the "Apex Building," due to its acute angle at the "point of the triangle") at 6th Street to the east, all the way to the Commerce Department's Herbert C. Hoover Building at 15th Street to the west, and is bounded by Pennsylvania and Constitution Avenues, N.W. The heights of the buildings are uniform, so the effect is continuous. (The exceptions are the National Archives Building (now known as "Archives I") to the east and the tower of the "Old Post Office Pavilion" (which President Trump reportedly wanted to cover in taxpayer-funded gold leaf, as "second-term stuff"), the Ronald Reagan Building and International Trade Center, and the former "District Building" to the west.)

QUIZ #58: What did President Trump see immediately to the north of the Main Justice Building?

ANSWER: Potential competition for his "Trump International Hotel" (located in the "Old Post Office Building," two blocks away) once the J. Edgar Hoover FBI Headquarters Building was torn down as then planned.

QUIZ #59: Which two members of the "international transparency community" have an openness regime without the benefit of a disclosure statute?

ANSWER: Argentina and Tunisia.

QUIZ #60: Which two members of the "international transparency community" have an openness regime that began at the level of its prefectures?

ANSWER: Japan and China. (India has states and union territories, not prefectures).

QUIZ #61: Which member of the "international transparency community" has an openness regime that applies to its national legislature?

ANSWER: The Nation of Mexico.

QUIZ #62: Who are the 18 "lawgivers" (officially the "Great Codifiers of the Law") painted along the stairway and landing beneath the entrance to the Main Justice Building's Great Hall?

ANSWER: They are Sir Edward Coke, the Magna Carta, Sir William Blackstone, John Marshall, the Constitution, James Kent, Aemilius Papinianus, Justinian I, Thomas Aquinas, Oliver Wendell Holmes, Hugo Grotius, Jesus, Francisco de Vitoria, Socrates, Solon, Menes, Moses, and Hammurabi. (Extra credit if you recognized more than a dozen of them. Even more extra credit if you're there and happen to notice the "typo" in the words "Magna Carta.")

QUIZ #63: What lies behind the stage at the front of the Great Hall, just around the corner from "Minnie Lou"?

ANSWER: A small "staging area" for events occurring on the Great Hall stage (i.e., for VIPs such as the president who are brought forward to the stage and introduced with a flourish). In 1971, this space was used to stage the play "The Cage," about life in San Quentin Prison, which I attended.

QUIZ #64: Whose former Main Justice Building office (or suite of offices) became that of the Assistant Attorney General for Civil Rights in 1972?

CLUE: He would be "rolling over in his grave."

QUIZ #65: Was the Main Justice Building really the location of a "death trial" during World War II?

ANSWER: Yes, the federal criminal trial of eight "Nazi saboteurs" was conducted in a room on the 5200 Corridor of the Main Justice Building, a short walk from the Office of the Attorney General, during late July and early August of 1942. In mid-June 1942, eight German saboteurs entered the United States by submarine in two groups, one landing on the southeastern coast of Long Island, New York, and the other at Ponte Vedra, Florida. Both groups of men carried a supply of explosives, fuses, and incendiary and timing devices, but their operation was doomed to failure by their overall amateurishness and trepidation. Not long after they landed, the leader of the first group called the FBI in Washington and turned himself in; the other seven were located soon thereafter. On July 2, President Franklin D. Roosevelt issued orders that empowered a military commission to conduct the prosecution of the eight for capital crimes. That trial concluded on August 1 with a guilty verdict for all eight defendants, and the Supreme Court unanimously upheld the constitutionality of the process in a case named *Ex parte Quirin*. On August 8, 1942, six of the saboteurs were executed and two of them, including George G. Dasch, the defendant who had turned himself in, received prison sentences. To this day, a heavy metal historical marker on the outside of Room 5233 of the Main Justice Building reminds all hallway passersby of the unique trial that took place there.

QUIZ #66: Which former Assistant Attorney General for the Tax Division recused himself from a "JFK Assassination" FOIA case at the last minute in 1978?

ANSWER: That was newly appointed District Court Judge Louis F. Oberdorfer, who got this word to me just prior to the first status call in the case, with the explanation that he had just realized that he ought to recuse himself from it given that he had worked very closely with then-Attorney General Robert F. Kennedy in the wake of his brother's assassination.

QUIZ #67: Which "UFO group" has made the most FOIA requests over the years?

CLUE: It is either Citizens Against UFO Secrecy, Ground Saucer Watch, or (more recently) "The Black Vault."

QUIZ #68: Is it possible for a state to make a FOIA request to the Federal Government?

ANSWER: Yes, just ask the States of California, Texas, North Dakota, Florida, Massachusetts, or Pennsylvania, for example, or the City of Chicago, the Islamic Republic of Iran, or the British Airports Authority, as all of them not only have made FOIA requests, they have filed FOIA lawsuits against the Federal Government.

QUIZ #69: What is the most popular FOIA-related colloquialism?

CLUE: It is derived either from a submarine-retrieval ship or from the surname of a former "Nader's Raider" law professor.

QUIZ #70: How many FOIA exemptions are there?

ANSWER: Fifteen (trick question), considering Exemptions One through Six, Exemptions 7(A) through 7(F), Exemptions 8 and (just barely) 9, and the ever-popular but entirely imaginary "Exemption 10."

QUIZ #71: How many FOIA "exclusions" are there?

ANSWER: Not enough; there ought to be a fourth. (The need for that did not arise until after the events of September 11, 2001, at an inter-agency meeting led by me at the FBI Headquarters Building that focused on a particular type of "no fly" list in the context of a new non-classification policy.)

QUIZ #72: Which FOIA requester (and litigant) won two academy awards?

CLUE: She did not win them for acting as a FOIA litigant; rather, they were for *Klute* and *Coming Home*.

QUIZ #73: Which FOIA requester (and litigant) was a perennial presidential candidate?

ANSWER: Lyndon H. LaRouche, Jr., who ran for president eight times, from 1976 to 2004. A FOIA suit filed by one of his "followers," Edward W. Spannaus, led to the leading precedent on the operation of a statute of limitations under the FOIA, in a case argued before the D.C. Circuit by OIP senior attorney Philip A. Kesaris in 1987. LaRouche himself was later convicted of conspiracy to commit mail fraud, of mail fraud itself, and of conspiring to defraud the Internal Revenue Service.

QUIZ #74: Which FOIA requester (and litigant) performed more than a dozen songs at Woodstock?

ANSWER: Joan Baez, who has a legacy of "peace activism" that stretched back to the late 1950s. Because of her "FOIA activism," OIP in the 1980s began the practice of ostensibly hiring young law clerks only if they could identify who "Joan Baez" was; this long-term practice was seemingly discontinued in the late 1990s when it became clear that OIP would have no new law clerks otherwise. At that point, we began using Jane Fonda instead.

QUIZ #75: Which FOIA requester (and litigant) famously hailed from Hawaii?

ANSWER: That would be Congresswoman Patsy T. Mink (D-HI), who in 1971 sought access to records of underground nuclear testing in Alaska (believed responsible for tsunami activity in Hawaii), leading to the Supreme Court decision of *EPA v. Mink* in 1973. Other congresspersons who have filed FOIA requests include Lesley "Les" Aspin, Jr., James A. Leach, and George Miller III, and more recently Senators (now vice president) Kamala D. Harris, Sheldon Whitehouse, and Richard Blumenthal.

QUIZ #76: Which FOIA requester (and litigant) went on to become Archivist of the United States?

CLUE: An historian, he wrote a widely acclaimed book titled *Perjury: The Hiss-Chambers Case*, based partly upon more than 30,000 pages of FBI and CIA records that he obtained under the FOIA.

QUIZ #77: Which AG kept a large musical instrument in her office?

CLUE: It wasn't AG Loretta E. Lynch.

QUIZ #78: What was that instrument?

ANSWER: It was a steel drum, on which she played "Amazing Grace" for a group of us. She did so as therapy for the Parkinson's Disease from which she suffered. (Janet consistently undermedicated herself during her tenure because, she said, her Parkinson's medication diminished her effectiveness.)

QUIZ #79: What are the surnames of the first female AG, the first African-American AG (by way of Barbados), and the first African-American female AG?

ANSWER: Reno, Holder, and Lynch.

QUIZ #80: Which AG once sang a solo in the Main Justice Building's Great Hall?

CLUE: The song was a personal composition of his, "Let the Eagle Soar," and when I listened to this performance on a Sunday afternoon while standing on the Great Hall's back balcony with some other component heads, one of them, who shall remain nameless -- due to something informally known as the "component head privilege" -- blurted out: "If you see me start to climb up over this railing preparing to jump, please don't stop me!" (And yes, this was a political component head, not a career one.)

QUIZ #81: Which Republican AG not long before his appointment compared President Richard Nixon to a purportedly unknowing piano player in the lobby of a bordello?

CLUE: He easily won confirmation in 1974.

QUIZ #82: Which floor of the Main Justice Building (renamed the "Robert F. Kennedy Department of Justice Building" in November of 2001) initially housed the FISA Court?

CLUE: It was the one between the Fifth and Seventh Floors, not far from where the Civil Division's Information and Privacy Section was located during 1977-1978.[8] Subsequently, the FISA Court was relocated from the Main Justice Building to the E. Barrett Prettyman Federal Courthouse in Washington, D.C.

QUIZ #83: Which AG watched the arrests of "May Day" demonstrators from the small Fifth Floor balcony on the southwest corner of the Main Justice Building?

CLUE: This was on May 4, 1971, and this AG would go on to have a more personal connection with the word "arrest."

QUIZ #84: Which AG made good use of the private elevator located near the southwest corner of the Main Justice Building?

ANSWER: Many of them did, since the building was opened in 1934, but when AG Janet Reno was there, she for a time had three aides in the AG's Office with the first name "John," prompting some building denizens to observe that her executive suite had "three Johns and an elevator."

QUIZ #85: Was there another private elevator in the Main Justice Building?
ANSWER: Yes, there was one in the northeast corner of the building that was used by FBI Director J. Edgar Hoover until his death (and perhaps afterward) in 1972.

QUIZ #86: After whom is the First Floor conference room on the southwest corner of the Main Justice Building named?
ANSWER: Charles J. Bonaparte, AG from 1906 to 1909, who happened to be Napoleon's great nephew and created the Department's Bureau of Investigation, which grew into the FBI in the mid-1930s.

QUIZ #87: In which century was the Main Justice Building first planned?
CLUE: It was in 1899, so it wasn't the 20th century.

QUIZ #88: On what plot of land was the Main Justice Building constructed?
ANSWER: It was constructed during the early 1930s on a trapezoidal lot running from Pennsylvania Avenue, N.W., on the north, to Constitution Avenue on the south and from Ninth Street to the east and Tenth Street to the west. Because Pennsylvania and Constitutional Avenues do not run parallel to one another that far east, the shape of the building (which has three small internal courtyards) is not rectangular. It holds 1.2 million square feet of space, not counting the Eighth Floor attic.

QUIZ #89: How many elevators in total are in the Main Justice Building?
CLUE: It's somewhere between 28 and 30, counting the two private ones and the one that went to the FISA Court's courtroom.

QUIZ #90: Which AG did not use the traditional personal office for the attorney general?
CLUE: He used the very large "Attorney General's Conference Room" instead, where he could let his many children (nieces and nephews of the president) play and hide behind the curtains when they visited him there.

QUIZ #91: Which bit of leaked information holds the record for fastest circulation of a rumor within the Main Justice Building?

ANSWER: Bill Clinton's Oval Office exclamation (read: sometimes just short of an ejaculation) that "I'll smoke it later."

QUIZ #92: Which AG is known as "the Donald Rumsfeld of the Justice Department?"

CLUE: Rumsfeld served for two nonconsecutive tenures as secretary of defense, not unlike President Stephen Grover Cleveland during the period March 1885 to March 1897.

QUIZ #93: Which AG fired his associate attorney general and gave him only five minutes (i.e., from 11:00 to 11:05 a.m. on Monday, January 16, 1989) to argue against it?

HINT: This was on the Martin Luther King Day federal holiday (the first official one), but one of my deputies and I had a meeting in the Attorney General's Office that was scheduled for the odd time of 11:05 that morning. Do the math.

CLUE: The fired associate attorney general soon became general counsel of HUD, was nominated to the Court of Appeals for the Tenth Circuit (unsuccessfully), and became a two-term governor of the State of Oklahoma, serving at the time of the bombing of the Alfred P. Murrah Federal Building in Oklahoma City on April 19, 1995 (on the two-year anniversary of the conflagration that ended the FBI siege of the Branch Davidian compound in Waco, Texas, which secured AG Janet Reno's place in history when she forcefully and effectively defended her actions before the House Judiciary Committee).

QUIZ #94: Which AG came to that position directly after serving as a circuit court judge of a U.S. Court of Appeals?

CLUE: Upon stepping down from the position of attorney general "midterm," he took many records with him without authorization and then wrote a book titled *Taking Care of the Law* in which he improperly disclosed exempt White House-originated information (see Chapter Thirty-Three).

QUIZ #95: Which AG is said to have had a portion of the artwork near the ceiling of the Main Justice Building's Fifth Floor main library repainted because it sometimes "spooked" him late at night?[9]

ANSWER: Reportedly, AG Homer S. Cummings, who held the position during the building's earliest years in the mid-to-late 1930s, would sometimes work late at night, often in the building's main library just down the hall from his office on the Fifth Floor, where one of the library's Works Progress Administration-style murals (on an interior, north-facing wall, near the ceiling) contained a "spooky" image of a skull-like head -- one that actually looked a lot like the official portrait of AG Nicholas D. Katzenbach that was done three decades later, anachronistically speaking, for a deserved place (aesthetically, not in any way a reflection of the man) on the Department's "Wall of Shame." So AG Cummings, the story goes, had this image repainted with a bright-red, bank robber-style bandana covering its face. Hence, not only did this image presage that of a future AG in its original form, it also presaged the era of COVID-19 attire in its modified form.

QUIZ #96: What item sits in a place of honor in the middle of the "Great Courtyard" of the Main Justice Building?

CLUE: It was placed there on November 20, 2001, when the building was renamed for AG Robert F. Kennedy on the day that would have been his 76th birthday (and also was my 50th).[10]

QUIZ #97: Which of the quotations carved onto the exterior of the Main Justice Building was the favorite of AG Reno?

ANSWER: It is one on the eastern side of building, directly across from the National Archives Building: "The common law derives from the will of mankind, issuing from the life of the people, framed by mutual confidence, and sanctioned by the light of reason." She often used it in her speeches.

QUIZ #98: Where is the oldest classified (read: properly classified) record in America?

ANSWER: It is not known with complete certainty, but with the declassification of the World War I-era formula for "invisible ink" in 2011, a good bet is Fort Knox, Kentucky, where records about the security of the U.S gold reserves were created in the mid-1930s, likely classified on national security grounds in the early 1950s, and probably have not all been accessioned to the National Archives even today.

QUIZ #99: How many former secretaries of state did what Secretary of State Hillary Rodham Clinton did in her use of electronic mail?

ANSWER: Despite all of her repeated claims to the contrary, the answer is one, just her.

QUIZ #100: Which of these questions is the most difficult?

ANSWER: This one is, except for the next one.

QUIZ #101: Where is the typo hidden?

CLUE: Re-read the book, and I'm sure you'll find it.

Endnotes

"There are two typos of people in the world: those who proofread and those who don't."

-- Old proofreader joke (nevertheless told by young proofreaders), circa 1980s

PREFACE

1   In between my first "tour of duty" with the Department of Justice, as a teenage intern in 1971, and my time there as a first-year law student during 1973-1974, I finished college while working full-time for a law firm back on Long Island. Then, from 1974-1976, I had to finish law school, after which I went on to a judicial clerkship for the following year before rejoining the Department as a Trial Attorney in 1977. So it was that my 30-year career at the Justice Department spanned a total time period of more than 35 years.

2   The word "retirement" is placed in quotation marks here because I knew that I would not actually "retire" at such a relatively young age (i.e., 55). Having no interest in "cashing in" on my experience and litigation skills for a big boost in private-practice salary (beyond the six-figure pension that I would now be receiving), I planned to teach law for many years and I also had an idea for an academic center if I could find the right law school at which to build it (see Chapter Forty-Two). I most certainly did not plan to single-handedly litigate *against* the Justice Department (not to mention a veritable phalanx of "big law" firm attorneys) for an unexpected reward of more than a half-million dollars (see Chapter Forty-Three).

3   This opinion also was echoed by no less a personage than my friend Carl Stern, a former NBC News reporter who had covered the Department of Justice and "Watergate" for that network, had gone on to become the Justice Department's director of public affairs under Attorney General Janet W. Reno, and in 1996 became a distinguished journalism professor at The George Washington University's School of Media and Public Affairs.

4   The Department of Justice is organizationally divided into distinct "components" (back then a standard total of 40; currently numbering only 39) -- large ones such as the Federal Bureau of Investigation ("FBI," to its friends and enemies alike); relatively small ones such as the Office of the Attorney General (which shrank at least in stature during the tenure of Attorney General Alberto R. Gonzales); and many medium-sized ones such as the Office of Information and Privacy ("OIP," always), which I led. And as for those of us in charge of them, we were known within the Department, formally, as "component heads." At any given time, roughly 33 of them were political appointees (whom we sometimes referred to as "the temporary help"), such as the assistant attorneys general for the litigating divisions (i.e., civil, criminal, civil rights, antitrust, environment and natural resources, tax, and now national security), and a relatively small group of us were career appointees, who as such ordinarily "carried over" from one presidential administration to the next.

As of the time of my retirement in 2007, I was the most senior component head by length of service in the Department, needing only 22 more years to break the longevity record held by former FBI Director J. Edgar Hoover, who died still in that position at age 77. But as we used to say in New York City -- until the mid-1970s at least, when the fare finally went up -- that and a nickel will get you a ride on the Staten Island Ferry. (In 1997, due to political "deal," the fare was eliminated altogether.) Hoover and I, by the way, had something else in common: We both were appointed to head a Justice Department compartment at the ripe young age of 29. (As far as I know, and I do know a lot, we had absolutely nothing else in common whatsoever.)

During the 1990s, the Department had the benefit of having two older attorneys, octogenarian Herman Marcuse, who in the Office of Legal Counsel was the world's leading expert on the laws of the Trust Territories, and Ernest J. Brown in the Tax Division. As for "Professor Brown," as he was called by one and all because he held an emeritus chair at Harvard Law School, he had taught tax law to Attorney General Janet Reno in the early 1960s and came to the Department after retiring from teaching there in 1971. He did not retire (read: a second time) until 2001, at age 94.

5   During that year, I spent more time than I care to remember responding to media inquiries about what it had been like working underneath Gonzales -- not to mention President George W. Bush ("Bush 43," to all "Bushies") -- during the two years prior to my retirement. It was indeed a lengthy *Legal Times* interview published in April of 2007, at the behest of its publisher, that started this off, one in which I pulled no punches about how Gonzales had been harming the Department even more than the general public yet knew. One such thing led to another, and before I knew it I was hightailing it from CNN's local studios to C-SPAN, to NPR, to PBS and beyond for live interviews, as Gonzales even managed to worsen his own situation as we went along.

Candor compels me to acknowledge that I did so in no small part to gain publicity for my newly adopted law school, and for my new "secrecy/transparency" academic center there, the Collaboration on Government Secrecy, more particularly. Indeed, the Dean of the Washington College of Law at American University was quite transparent about the school's encouragement that I do so. In fact, he was most disappointed when my stepmother's emergency hospitalization kept me from appearing on what was then still thought of as the "MacNeil/Lehrer News Hour," live on PBS, one evening. (She was medevac'd by helicopter to Johns Hopkins Hospital in Baltimore with my elderly father in tow; I really had no choice.)

6   The University of Dundee (or, more specifically, Dundee Law School), in Dundee, Scotland, soon thereafter established the second such academic center, at the end of the next year. (There are by now several of them, including one established in 2009 at Yale.) I was invited to speak there several times and did so while traveling in the U.K. in conjunction with a fellowship that I held at University College London.

7   This book overall is designed be useful to students of law and secrecy, as well as those more generally interested in its popular subject matter. In the threatening context of current times, though, it also strives to issue a clarion call to the American public that it has a duty to require its democratically elected government to maintain standards of transparency consistent with the spirit of democracy -- in which the government holds its authority, granted by the people, only for the benefit of the people. As another Daniel surnamed Webster eruditely adjured the Senate in 1830, "It is, Sir, the people's Constitution, the people's Government, made for the people, made by the people, and answerable to the people."

8   This also necessarily includes at least some view into the operations of the White House during the Nixon, Ford, Carter, Reagan, George H.W. Bush, Clinton, George W. Bush, and even Obama Administrations. As for the Trump Administration, a new professional category of "psychiatric historian" will have to tackle that one.

9   Judge Wallach is deserving of a footnote all his own. A "close friend" of former Senate Majority Leader Harry M. Reid in Nevada, he was appointed as a judge on the Court of International Trade in New York City, from which he was eligible to sit by designation on federal district courts. In the late 1990s, the District Court

for the District of Columbia experienced serious workload difficulties, leading to Judge Wallach's assignment to some civil cases there, including a FOIA case, *Hemmings v. Freeh*, which was handled by one of my senior staff attorneys.

One day, that attorney returned from a status hearing before Judge Wallach quite upset by how she had been treated by him in open court. She said that not only had he mistaken what her client agency had done in the case, he had told her that she "ought to be spanked" as a result. This senior attorney, who was a particularly attractive woman, told me that she had no doubt of Wallach's sexist attitude toward her and that she was not looking forward to appearing before him again.

Hearing this, I immediately did three things: First, I ordered a transcript of that hearing, on an expedited basis. Second, I re-assigned the case to a male senior attorney (Kenneth D. Chasen), a shift that was gratefully appreciated by his female predecessor. Third, I took the extraordinary step of entering my own appearance as supervisory counsel for the government, so that I could personally explain to Judge Wallach why I had reassigned the case. And then I did so, in no uncertain terms, with the transcript in front of me in case there was any doubt in his mind about what he had said. In time, we won the case, after having to explain the applicable law to him more fundamentally than to a regular district court judge.

10   Just the same, I am mindful that, for some, some of this book's chapters might be read singly at times, in isolation from the others. The ones on Hillary Clinton, "UFO secrecy," and even perhaps the Privacy Act are examples. So I have included useful cross-references to either previous or subsequent chapters, whichever the case might be. In some chapters, there are both kinds.

11   As also is noted below, this stated sequence of course does not include the name "Trump" because, first and foremost, I had the good fortune of having left the Federal Government before it had the bad fortune of seeing him arrive. And as a purely academic point, had I not retired from federal service prior to 2017 (or as of his election in late 2016, actually), I certainly would have done so as soon as possible then. (Given that I retired partly out of embarrassment for working under "Bush 43," then *a fortiori* I would not for a moment have abided working under a president as dangerous, mendacious, and pernicious as Trump.) This is easy for me to say, of course, as someone who was retirement eligible as of late 2006, but I daresay that I would have engineered some form of "early" retirement had I found myself, like so many other poor souls, working within a Trump Administration while not yet eligible to retire. So one might say that my age relative to the "time of Trump" (as the era ought to be known and forgotten) was my final bit of federal service luck. (Yes, through the lens of history, the "Trump Era" ought to become known as a huge homonym, i.e., an immense national "error.")

12   One such "thing," as it happened, was the White House-drafted thing (read: a draft op-ed) that I was asked to "scrub" one Friday afternoon by future Supreme Court Justice Neil M. Gorsuch. As is described in detail in this book (see the Epilogue), Neil's proposal that we actually go ahead and effectively lie in that soon-to-be-published thing, lest someone in the White House become upset with him, is what spurred my decision over that weekend to retire.

PROLOGUE

1   At the time (i.e., the summer of 1975), no law firm in D.C. had surpassed the 100-attorney mark, with four of them holding firm somewhere in the 90s. Arnold and Porter, the firm for which I worked that summer, stood in the upper 90s; more important to me, though, was the fact that it led all other D.C. law firms with an exalted Summer Associate salary of $300 per week (see Chapter Nine).

2   By this I mean that there was so much information policy work to be done, with such urgency immediately after 9/11 (read: starting the "day after"), that I quickly found myself working more than 75 hours a week, especially in support of the new Office of Homeland Security at the White House (soon to become the Homeland Security Transition Office and then the Department of Homeland Security ("DHS," to its many new friends) itself.

3   I truly saw this as the best job in the world for a litigator and policymaker; the way that I had created it, it was "one of a kind" in the Federal Government.

4   Every now and again during those past two years (Gonzales had arrived at the Department in early February of 2005, at the beginning of George W. Bush's second presidential term) some senior career SESers at the Department would get together (sometimes over the phone) to compare notes on Gonzales and Bush, sessions that would usually end with mutual solace. No one had ever seen an attorney general quite like him, and that included the few of us who had worked under Attorneys General John N. Mitchell, Edwin Meese III, and (to a lesser degree) John D. Ashcroft. (And that was before Attorney General William P. Barr, who like Vice President Dick Cheney, so surprisingly "went over to the dark side.") We unfailingly agreed that, apart from any criminal activity, Gonzales was already the biggest continuous embarrassment that the Justice Department had ever seen. And that was before things got worse, much worse, with him.

And as for Bush, I saw him as very much of the same ilk. Indeed, when I had to depose Gonzales for several hours three years later (see Chapter Forty-Three), I came away from that with the clear and strong impression that, beyond anything else, he and Bush had one basic thing very much in common: Each one of them seemed to be too stupid (read: lacking in some form of intelligence) to realize just how stupid (read: of limited intellect, including any accompanying self-awareness) he is.

INTRODUCTION

1   Nearly all of the terms and concepts conveyed in this chapter and the chapters below became part of my courses at American University's Washington College of Law, where I taught secrecy law for ten years upon retiring from government service. Some, in fact, were further refined in class discussions during those years, as I always encouraged my students to try to disagree with me in order to stimulate discussion.

2   In such a very basic situation, the "information" involved is probably best thought of as "knowledge," i.e., what that person knows from what transpired. To those in the academic field of information science, the term "knowledge' is nearly identical to "information," but the former usually implies a degree of conscious awareness that the latter does not. When it comes to having and keeping a secret, referring to it as "knowledge" seems most apt, but these terms are easily used interchangeably, at least in this chapter. In later chapters of this book, for reasons that should be clear within them, the word "information" usually is the better choice.

On the other hand, when it comes to matters of espionage, for instance, sometimes knowledge is the coin of the realm. A ready illustration is the case of Ronald W. Pelton, a former intelligence analyst for the National Security Agency ("NSA," to its surveilees), who became so deeply in debt that he contacted the Soviet Embassy in Washington, D.C., in 1980 with the aim of divulging what he knew about highly sensitive NSA activities in exchange for money. No longer an NSA employee, he had no documents to hand to the Soviets, but he was possessed of an exceptionally good memory. So he basically sold that part of his memory, i.e., his "knowledge," for cash. Now this is rare, as espionage (or treason) goes, but there are those who fear a recurrence with our 45th president having left office, the only saving grace being that he certainly is not known for his attentiveness, much less for his retentiveness, when it comes to learning complex information.

3   As will be seen, "abstract" facts are a special breed of them that require acute awareness and special treatment for "secrecy" purposes. In a simple form, think of it this way: If a piece of paper contains writing that conveys the substance of a fact (e.g., "A former NSA employee was observed entering the Russian Embassy."), then there also is an "abstract fact" (i.e., that the FBI has the capability to make and record that observation) that inchoately surrounds those written words. And, to take this a half step further, if that piece of paper also contains a date or some other temporal reference (which can be thought of as significant "context" here), then that abstract fact is expanded, because it reveals an intelligence capability existing at a particular time.

4   I used to say to any of my students who thought a "secret" was born at this juncture that this was functionally no different than a situation in which one of them, alone in a hallway on the way to class, stumbles enough to bang his or her elbow against a wall. If that student were to then enter our classroom and tell no one of that "elbow bang," would that make it a secret? No, it would not. A true "secret" has to be more than that.

5   This of course brings up its own brand of "secrecy," having to do with what spouses or family members do and do not tell one another. As challenging a subject as that is, though, it does not involve government secrecy, which is the focus of this book. Likewise, there are other forms of "secrecy," sometimes denominated "confidentiality," that exist. A prime example of this is "business confidentiality," which can in some settings morph into government secrecy, primarily through the business-information protection of FOIA Exemption 4.

6   This is so because true "secrecy" requires an agreement -- or at least an understanding, even if only tacit -- between at least two people that they will keep certain information (one could think of it as joint knowledge) just between themselves. And analytically, there is what can be thought of as a sophistication continuum of such things: At one end of it is our situation with Cavemen #1 and #2; at the other end is the most sophisticated regime of governmental secrecy that can be imagined, perhaps the national security system that now exists in the United States. And in all the years that passed between them along that time continuum, modern-day governmental secrecy actually did not begin to exist in earnest until less than 250 years ago.

7   The word "secret" is well understood in English, as both a noun and an adjective, the latter being most similar to the words "clandestine," "surreptitious," and "covert." It derives from the Latin word *secretus*, meaning "separate" or "set apart," by way of Old French, and has been widely used in English for centuries. In the 20th century, it became most popularly known as part of the phrases "top secret" and "secret agent."

8   Such an approach runs long and deep in the secrecy world. Those who professionally guard secrets in interactions with others are trained to employ a range of techniques to accomplish that, up to and including outright, sometimes quite elaborate, lies. And beyond what they say or do not say, there also is the matter of how they act (which in this case truly is a double entendre). Intelligence officers who are in a "covert status" must act accordingly, virtually 24/7/365, in order to keep that basic secret from others.

    A recent example of such a person is former CIA case officer Valerie E. Plame Wilson, who worked under what is called "nonofficial cover" (i.e., as a "NOC") for more than a decade until she was "outed" as such by journalist Robert D. Novak in conjunction with Department of State official Richard L. Armitage and, allegedly, White House officials I. Lewis "Scooter" Libby and Karl C. Rove in 2003. This disclosure (or "exposure," actually), and the widespread publicity that it brought through a resultant "leak" investigation involving high-level government officials that was badly "politicized," led to her and her family receiving death threats, among other consequences. She was entirely a victim of this "leak" and, as is the case with almost all "leak investigations," her story did not end well.

9   This example illustrates the fact that some secrets, in some circumstances, are so delicate that even the slightest perturbation of the norm can imperil them. Such is often the case with "abstract facts," where the very existence or nonexistence of something is sought to be hidden.

10   Sometimes, in extreme circumstances, such a "stake" can be nothing less than someone's life. Most dramatically, this can be so with intelligence officers who work more or less "under cover" for the CIA, the Defense Department, or some other such organization. Another example is narcotics officers who do undercover work at the state or local levels of government. A third example, at the federal level, is FBI Special Agents who work undercover infiltrating domestic terrorist, militia, white supremacy, or suspected criminal "survivalist" groups, where they must pretend to be loyal members of those groups in order to survive themselves. Their secrecy, which is fundamentally the concealment of their true identities, can be a matter of life and death. A member of the Collaboration on Government Secrecy Advisory Board, former FBI Special Agent Michael German, twice experienced this.

11   This is akin to what is well known as "Murphy's Law," which my father learned full well during the 1950s while working as an airplane mechanic for a major airline. The way he would express it is that if a particular airplane part could at all possibly be "put in backwards," then sooner or later, somewhere and somehow, "some dumb schmuck going to do so."

12   This is something that would go on to plague governments, institutions, and individuals for millennia thereafter. "How do you deal with leaks," one might ask? "Never well enough," is the answer. And in modern times, as the problem took a quantum leap with the advent of something that came to be infamously known as "WikiLeaks," this was the subject of a day-long conference conducted by my secrecy (or transparency) center, the Collaboration on Government Secrecy, at American University's Washington College of Law titled "The Legal and Civil Policy Implications of 'Leaks,'" in 2013 (see Chapter Forty-Two).

13   I once described to my wife how I would use this example in class, with student volunteers playing the roles of Cavepersons #1 through #4. She gently allowed as how such a scenario, crude as it necessarily was, could be taken as at least a bit misogynistic by my students, especially the female ones. So, being the flexible and presciently "woke" professor that I was, I decided to explicitly own up to this very thing in future classes, as if doing so would make it all right (though more in my mind than in hers). What my wife did not then know was that when I called for volunteers for these roles, eight or nine times out of ten the most vigorous volunteers to be "Caveman #1" would be female. Which raises the question, perhaps: Was that a secret?

14   Or in the case of what is popularly seen as falling (but not necessarily crashing, in New Mexico or elsewhere) within the realm of Unidentified Flying Objects ("UFOs," to their observers) or "flying saucers," for instance, it could be something that is not fully "known," but is strongly suspected to exist on the basis of what thus far is limited available evidence. Either way, the basic elements of human nature apply to government secrecy very much through the 75-year-old realm of modern "UFO secrecy" that began near the middle of the 20th century (see Chapter Forty-Eight).

15   A case in point from relatively recent military history is the story of the sinking of the SS (or "HTS") *Rohna*, a borrowed British ship used to transport thousands of U.S. troops that was sunk by a German *Luftwaffe* bomber off the coast of Algeria on November 26, 1943, at the cost of more than 1000 American lives. The bomb used was an extraordinary "radio-guided glide bomb," an experimental one that Germany had developed as a precursor to the "smart bombs" of later years, called the "Hs-293." Because the Department of Defense did not want Germany

to know what the Allies had learned about that novel bomb's performance (read: it actually made a 90-degree turn) in the attack, it made a "snap decision" to keep the entire incident secret, even going so far as to swear the 1700 survivors to secrecy under threat of court-martial if they spoke of it. Meanwhile, the families of the dead service members were left to wonder about the fates of their loved ones, which became an enormous price to pay for the secrecy that was achieved. Inexplicably, this secret remained one for more than 20 years, until the fate of the *Rohna* and its passengers was finally declassified in 1967, shortly after the Freedom of Information Act became effective.

16   Or, as it often has been called, "the coronavirus," or COVID-19, or more technically, "SARS-CoV-2." For all anyone yet knows for sure, its threat might last even longer than the Cold War did.

17   The phrase "would . . . see" is used here in recognition of the fact that the full extent of a government secrecy regime will hardly be known to the general public. Indeed, the very "nature of the beast," as they say, is that nowadays people do not learn of even the "types" of some secret activities that their governments are up to until later in time, sometimes even long after the fact. Many post-9/11 activities such as torture, black sites, extreme rendition, Muslim profiling, and new forms, methods, and means of communications surveillance (not to mention their *exact* contours) have been unknown to the public until after the fact. Indeed, that very thing underlies the Freedom of Information Act, because without it, and its relatively short-term timeline (yes, I said "relatively" here), public awareness of such things would largely be left to the realm of historians -- not to speak ill of historians, of course -- who by definition have long timelines.

You might think that now in today's supercharged world of instant and widespread information dissemination (not to mention WikiLeaks distribution) very little can remain secret for very long. But you would be wrong. Our Federal Government can largely overcome this through strict "compartmentalization" -- the process by which it maintains information of exceptionally great national security sensitivity (i.e., well above that of "Top Secret") in what are called "information silos," or more officially "compartments," of such information that is shared with only those who are *individually* "cleared" for access to it according to its particular subject matter and each individual's "need to know." Such "special compartmented information" ("SCI," to those who are cleared for access to it) is handled according the strictures of "Special Access Programs" ("SAPs," to those who prefer the term) which greatly reduces any risk to its security.

On the other hand, it must readily be acknowledged that the very element of information-format "miniaturization" can serve to defeat this, in turn, in cases in which "cleared persons" choose to abscond with government secrets through the expedient of using thumb drives, CD-RWs, SD cards, little USB sticks, "downloading," "electronic copying," and the like. In other words, the relatively recent metamorphosis of the old-fashioned "paper world" into the electronic one for recordkeeping now in the "information age" has made espionage easier and secrecy security much more difficult to maintain. Just ask Chelsea E. Manning or Edward J. Snowden how relatively easy absconding with secrets was for them. (By comparison, it was a hell of a lot less laborious for them than it was for Daniel Ellsberg and his compatriot Anthony J. Russo, Jr., who photocopied the "Pentagon Papers" for hours on end, during multiple such sessions, in 1969.)

By the way, when I say "*exact* contours" three paragraphs above, here is an example of exactly what I mean: In 2004, a newspaper by the name of *The New York Times* came into possession of information that showed the existence and nature of a government communications surveillance program that was so sensitive at the time that *The Times* uncharacteristically acceded to the White House's plea that it not run the story. (This was reminiscent of something called the "Ivy Bells agreement" that had been reached between *The Times* and CIA Director William J. Casey (and some say also between President Reagan himself and *Washington Post* publisher Katherine M. Graham) for "nonpublication" of what was a longstanding U.S. undersea "cable tapping" -- and, necessarily, decoding -- capability in 1986.)

But in agreeing to withhold publication, *The Times* never agreed to continue to do so if in its judgment circumstances changed enough at some point down the road for it to go ahead. And, worse yet for the government, *The Times* never agreed to give any government agency any advance warning -- and thus the opportunity to inveigh against publication at such later time -- if it came to that. So what did *The Times* do? It waited about a year and then ran with the story, overnight. And in doing so, it happened to choose (intentionally or not, who's to say?) the night before a vital vote was set to be held in Congress on the reauthorization of the USA PATRIOT Act, which as a result was not then reauthorized.

But, wait for it, here's the key part of the story: The folks at *The Times*, as well as others who opposed that surveillance program, thought that that program (reportedly code-named "Stellar Wind") would necessarily have to be "shut down" once that story broke. What they didn't realize, however, is that during that year-long interval, the federal agency primarily involved (meaning "No Such Agency") silently went ahead and altered that program "just a bit," and even renamed it as well, so that it no longer was the exact same program as what *The Times* was divulging. (This allowed government spokespersons the latitude to speak as if "the program" was neither this nor that, even though everyone knew full well that it had remained virtually the same.)

But wait, there's still more: So, as it turned out in this prolonged exercise of high-stakes gamesmanship, first the government "won," then *The Times* "won," and then the government "won," which meant that the American public "lost." But then, as if that were not enough, President George W. Bush kept things going, in what now seems like a full-scale fit of "pre-Trumpian" pique, by deciding that whoever "leaked" the existence of this communications program to *The Times* in the first place ought to be ferreted out, prosecuted, and shot -- though not necessarily in that order. (As it turned out, the "leaker" was one Thomas M. Tamm, a somewhat hapless though patriotic fellow who worked the Justice Department's Office of Intelligence Policy and Review ("OIPR," when it received OIP's misaddressed mail) on Foreign Intelligence Surveillance Court matters and who, in an odd quirk, later asked me to represent him.)

And to do that, President Bush publicly declared, the government would first "cap" the list of people who held clearances for access to this particular security compartment and then "investigate" every "suspect" on that list. The moment I heard that, I knew that I had to do two things: (1) verify that the news accounts of this were true, i.e., that all of us on this compartment clearance list were actually now "under investigation" in order to satisfy President Bush; and (2) inform the "powers that be" both at the White House and within the Department that as a result of that every name on that list had instantly become Privacy Act-protected -- i.e., as the name of a person now under federal investigation -- and could not be disclosed by any federal employee without that employee (technically) committing a crime (i.e., under the Privacy Act of 1974). To be sure, "leak investigations" are never fun for anyone, and they rarely ever succeed, but this one was a new low.

18 A major example of the latter, for present purposes, can be found in the relatively recent proliferation of document "safeguarding labels" that are used by federal agencies in a variety of ways, within the realm of what most recently has been called "pseudosecrecy" (see Chapter Thirty-Eight). "For Official Use Only" ("FOUO"), "Sensitive But Unclassified Information" ("SBU"), and "Law Enforcement Sensitive Information" ("LES") are just three of dozens of such designations that agencies apply to their records (either by "stamping" them in paper form or achieving the same thing electronically), doing so so frequently nowadays that these labels often are mistakenly equated with solid legal grounds for keeping those records from the public -- "secrecy," in short. Yet they are not.

Indeed, agencies may properly use these designations as a means of safeguarding certain records *within their four walls*, but in fact they cannot use them, or their underlying rationales, as the sole legal basis for refusing to make such records public. Briefly stated, only the legislature (with aid of the courts) can create such legal prohibitions on, or exceptions to, public disclosure, all perceptions to the contrary notwithstanding. But when such "secrecy" mechanisms are reported to the public as if they are more than what they actually are, a public misperception of "overblown secrecy" is created (see Chapter Thirty-Eight).

A ready example of a huge misperception of government secrecy has to do with FOIA "reading rooms," including parts of agency websites that include "voluntarily disclosed" information. Immediately after 9/11 (and by this I mean hours, not just days, at some agencies), there began a highly reflexive process of "taking down" agency websites (or whole parts of them), lest the information posted on them be used by terrorists in what were expected (read: greatly and realistically feared) to be follow-up attacks. (Yes, that was the heavily prevailing fear at the time, that it would "only be a matter of time" before the next big foreign terrorist attack occurred.)

This led to a huge hue and cry from members of the public who mistakenly believed that most (if not even all) of the information thereby removed from public access was *required* to be available to the public on an agency website to begin with and therefore had been improperly removed from public view. (Within the realm of government information disclosure, or secrecy on the other side of the coin, there are many groups of people who stand ready to raise such a huge hue and cry whenever something at first strikes them as aggrieveable.) However, in this case, this just was not so.

Rather, the information "taken down" -- except in the case of one agency that took its entire website down, in its own mistaken belief that "DOD required this" -- was information that had been posted voluntarily, i.e., as a matter of administrative discretion, not because it was required by law to have been posted before 9/11 in the first place. So it was not "unlawful secrecy." (By the way, I had to threaten that overreactive agency -- which shall remain nameless here except that its initials are "NRC" -- to within an inch of its life in order to get that website "take down" rectified immediately.)

19 Notably, the word "harm" here ought not be thrown around loosely. In modern-day America, I suggest, it should mean harm cognizable under one or more Freedom of Information Act exemptions.

20 OIP began using this phrase immediately after 9/11 to advise agencies on how they should implement FOIA exemptions in 9/11's wake, most especially Exemption 2, which meant that some information that had been deemed insufficiently sensitive in the past would now warrant exemption protection. One of the things that we had to make sure agencies remembered, though, was that any such information (read: the exact same information) that had in fact already been disclosed to the public could not be withheld from a current FOIA requester, regardless of its new-found sensitivity.

The only perceivable exception to that was information that now appeared on a record in a different *context*, where that context difference actually made a difference to the information's sensitivity. In the world of government secrecy, context can matter a great deal in delineating sensitive from nonsensitive information, most especially with respect to matters of national security (though in this case of website contents, national security sensitivity was not involved).

21 Actually, the subject of chemical plants, their security, and their "downwind projections" if successfully attacked was the quintessential (read: sole) example of this until we experienced 9/11, one optimistically (as it turned out) referred to by us as posing a "worst case scenario" situation. Indeed, prior to then, both the Environmental Protection Agency ("EPA," to both its fans and detractors alike) and the FBI actively coordinated on this, under the auspices of an ad hoc group at Main Justice, as the only true precursor to what became a far more comprehensive post-9/11 analysis. (I was part of that 1990s coordination group, of course, and we all later looked back on it, through the lens of 9/11, as having been, to borrow a term, quite "quaint.")

22 Lest it be too quickly forgotten, the tenor of the times back then was extreme: It was widely feared that the next terrorist attack on U.S. soil was a matter not of "if" but of "when." And, human nature being what it is, this led to perhaps the greatest amount of American prospective ass covering since Pearl Harbor. In short, no one wanted to be the government official who in retrospect did not protect (or even "overprotect") something sensitive and thereby facilitated (arguably, at least) the next big terrorist attack.

23 Now this is a nuance that emerged subtly in our "worst case scenario" planning in the late 1990s. We slowly recognized that just as the perspectives of the government and the chemical-plant neighbors were diverged, so too could there be more than a slight divergence within the "neighborhood" community itself: Some wanted disclosure so that that they could decide whether to move away, while others wanted it because, on the "squeaky wheel" theory, it could best help them safely stay.

24 As is observed above and below, the fundamental aspects of human nature underlying government secrecy are proprietariness ("these are *my* records"); paternalism ("we know what is best for the citizenry"); and protectiveness ("we will do what is necessary to keep our people safe"). And to this should be added, in the context of "UFO secrecy," the natural resistance of government authorities to acknowledge the existence of something that they themselves cannot understand, much less control (see Chapter Forty-Eight).

25 A prime example of this in the United States during the 21st century, of course, is the "secret government surveillance" that continued even after the Bush Administration and *The New York Times* "squared off" on the subject during 2005-2007. It was in June of 2013, during the Obama Administration, that CIA contractor Edward J. Snowden notoriously leaked highly classified NSA information showing the existence of numerous global surveillance programs (read: of electronic data, email, and cell phone communications) that were employed within the United States (read: against U.S. citizens, not just those in other nations as was NSA's original warrant) and had escaped public notice until then. They necessarily involved the secret participation of major telecommunication companies whose key employees were sworn to that secrecy.

26 The use of the word "comprehensive" here, truth be told, is not entirely apt. No one volume could claim to cover "government secrecy" in all of its aspects, especially given how it has exploded as a subject since the dropping of the first atomic bomb (not to mention since 9//11). If nothing else, this book's treatment of this broad subject is necessarily contoured by the scope (albeit a wide one) of my own knowledge, professional experience, and subsequent discernment during the latter half of the 20th century and the beginning of the 21st. (And portions of it are adapted from previous articles, essays, and book contributions.) But within this scope, relatively little is left out.

27 As noted above, it is a memoir as well, with background going back farther in time. To no small extent, "you are where you came from," as the saying goes, and this certainly is true in my case.

28 This includes the high point of working from 1993-2001 for Attorney General Janet Reno -- the "queen of openness," as she was known -- under whom governmentwide policy on pro-disclosure implementation of the Freedom of Information Act reached new heights that unfortunately have not been matched (read: not even close) since then.

29 Secrecy means, above all, protecting vital national security interests -- war plans, details of troop movements, the identities of spies, methods of espionage, and the like. Anyone familiar with "James Bond" ("license to kill"), *Mission Impossible* ("the Secretary will disavow any knowledge of your actions"), and the genre of spy novels will recognize this. But government secrecy also means less dramatic yet nonetheless vital things such

as personal privacy; trade secrets and business confidentiality; protecting the identities of informants; avoiding "tip offs" to suspected criminals; and, sometimes, taking a step that otherwise could reasonably be expected to place the lives of people in jeopardy. Yes, sometimes the guardians of government secrecy, those who do their best to establish and maintain its precise contours, carry on their shoulders the weight of prospective injury or death if their judgments prove wrong.

By the way, does secrecy mean risking the ire of the general population? You bet it does. Can it mean running a risk of actually making things worse? Yes, it can -- especially in a scandal-laden situation in which the "cover-up" can easily surpass (and outlast) the "crime." Anyone who lived through the Clinton Administration, in which secrecy always seemed to automatically involve "cover-ups," should have a firm basis for recognizing this. Suffice to say that secrecy and politics make for a volatile admixture, in multiple respects, and that a solid understanding of one aids the successful practice of the other.

30   As is noted above, I do not include the Administration of Donald J. Trump in this sequence, for at least two reasons: First, although I was still teaching when Trump assumed the presidency, *inter alia*, in 2017, it is not as if I had any substantial professional involvement in what followed. (By contrast, I did indeed have much such involvement in matters arising during the Obama Administration (see Chapters Forty-Five and Forty-Six).) And second, Trump falls into a very distinct "Don't get me started!" category in my mind. Stated another way, I certainly know how to start writing about the malignantly narcissistic dolt, I just don't know how to stop.

31   Under the FOIA, there can exist a threshold jurisdictional issue of whether a requested record is an "agency record" within an agency's custody and control (which are the legal standards for determining that). For instance, a White House-originated record or one received from Congress, if subject to a contemporaneous reservation of control (read: at the time of transmission from such a non-FOIA entity), will not be subject to the FOIA. Nor would the records of a presidential transition team, under policy guidance issued by the Office of Information and Privacy in 1988.

32   All states and most U.S. territories have their own FOIA counterparts, with statutes of varying names and scopes. Some states, such as New York, Maryland, Virginia, and Connecticut, have become leaders in the field over the years.

33   Prior to enactment of the Freedom of Information Act in the mid-1960s, the only formal mechanism for the public to obtain federal agency records was the mere Administrative Procedure Act (of which the FOIA became a part), which was criticized as operating "more like a record-withholding law than a disclosure one." During the pre-1946 years, there existed something known to some as "gentleman's secrecy," which encompassed both agencies and the national media. Perhaps the two most prominent examples of that, which became known to the general public only long after the fact, were the true state of President Franklin D. Roosevelt's physical disability (read: his need to use a wheelchair) and the many affairs and dalliances (read: including through use of the White House swimming pool) of President John F. Kennedy. Apparently, it was an accepted understanding that no one in government or the media would speak of either one.

34   FOIA requests can be made by "any person," in the words of the statute, except that in a spasm of post-9/11 limitation on this Congress amended the Act to forbid foreign nations (or representatives of them) from seeking the records of the 18 United States "intelligence agencies."

35   Years ago, the phrase "formal written request" could be used freely here. Then came faxes, which OIP said (in 1989) agencies should accept as a matter of sound administrative discretion. Then came along electronic

mail, which to many FOIA requesters was a preferred medium but was not provided for by law, even through the 1996 Electronic FOIA Amendments (see Chapter Thirty-Four). Now, most (but not all) federal agencies will accept FOIA requests made in email form and many (read: far from all) agencies participate in a multi-agency Internet "portal" for FOIA request submission.

36   A key feature of the FOIA, and with one exception (see Chapter Forty-Four), of all other such laws world-wide, is the idea that a document, a document page, or even a portion of it should not be withheld from the public merely due to the presence of some exempt information within it. This is known under the FOIA as the "reasonable segregation" requirement, or the obligation of an agency to carve out for disclosure all "reasonably segregable non-exempt" information. The Act's language to this effect is found at the end of its list of exemptions, in subsection (b): "Any reasonably segregable portion of a record shall be provided to any person requesting such record after deletion of the portions which are exempt under this subsection."

37   The FOIA has nine disclosure exemptions, referred to as "Exemption 1" through "Exemption 9," but one of them, "Exemption 7," was divided into six subparts by Congress through the 1974 FOIA Amendments, making the total of 14. (Of course, some members of the FOIA community might say that this overlooks Exemption 10, the "we just don't wanna disclose it" exemption.)

38   Technically, the Act requires only that agencies "make available" the records sought, and in the FOIA's earliest days some agencies took the position that FOIA requesters therefore were not entitled to responses sent by mail. Ever since the 1970s, though, and with only a single obdurate exception (read: NARA, during the late 1980s, until OIP forcefully set it straight), agencies have recognized that mail delivery (sometimes even electronic mail) is, as a practical matter, the way in which this should be done.

39   In turn, this major procedural aspect of the FOIA has to do with the Act's several time deadlines, expedited access, and intractable "backlogs" of FOIA requests. FOIA backlogs have long been a huge problem area under the Act, with many causes, failed remedies, and points of extreme controversy. This stems from the fact that the FOIA's disclosure time limit was first set at a universally unrealistic 10 working days and then was "reformed" to be an only slightly less unrealistic 20 working days.

40   Apart from the realm of "FOIA requests," a separate other part of the Act deals with agency obligations to make "automatic disclosure" of certain records about the basic functioning of each agency (e.g., policy statements, as well as the disclosable (i.e., "processed") versions of what are called "frequently requested" records) through agency "reading rooms"). These obligations are set forth in subsection (a)(2) of the Act, while the regular "FOIA request" process is addressed in subsection (a)(3). With the passage of the Electronic FOIA Amendments of 1996 (sometimes referred to as "EFOIA"), reading rooms took on greater significance in the Act's administration, particularly with respect to what became known as "electronic reading rooms," which now exist as part of agency "FOIA Websites" (see Chapter Thirty-Four).

41   One of these other FOIA exemptions, Exemption 3, effectively incorporates into the Act separate disclosure prohibitions for some national security information (read: originated mostly by the CIA and NSA), tax-return information, grand jury information, and a variety of other types of information that are specific to one or just a few particular agencies.

One such "Exemption 3 statute" specifically protects information pertaining to the Department of Justice's "Witness Security Program," within its Criminal Division, in which some especially sensitive criminal informants are given new identities and relocated elsewhere in the country in order to keep them safe from former associates who otherwise would likely kill them. This program originated in the 1960s to protect a growing number of organized crime informants, but it has expanded to protect nearly 20,000 people, including former gang members and even some white-collar criminals. Its actions are highly secretive and its information is kept about as secret as anything held by the Department other than much national security information.

Consistent with this, OIP had to establish specially designed protocols for protecting such information in the face of targeted FOIA requests, which worked successfully and managed to keep "WitSec" cases out of court. Candor compels me to amend that statement, though, because we did hit a temporary problem in the spring of 2005, when the WitSec Program director, a rather dense fellow by the name of Steven J. T'Kach, inexplicably failed to follow these rules and unwittingly placed WitSec information in jeopardy of being disclosed. OIP had to, as the saying goes, "hit him with a two-by-four across the bridge of the nose" in order to straighten that all out.

By the way, the WitSec Program is part of the United States Marshals Service, a separate component of the Department that primarily provides security at federal courthouses and collaterally is responsible for the security of federal judges, several of whom have been the subjects of attacks over the years. So there exists a distinct realm of government secrecy connected to this function, which comes to the fore every time such an attack takes place, or even when post-*Roe* protesters congregate near the homes of sitting Supreme Court Justices, as recently has been the case.

A second exceptional position that we developed was for the protection of federal judges: We gave them special notice whenever personal information about them was contained in requested records and we invariably withheld any information that could be used to threaten their personal safety. Since 1979, four federal judges have been murdered, plus a federal judge's mother and husband, in attacks at their homes. Most recently, in July of 2020, a disgruntled litigant before District Court Judge Esther Salas in Newark rang her home doorbell, shot her husband, and killed their 20-year-old son Daniel. This led to the enactment of "Daniel's Law," a New Jersey statute that makes it a crime to publish the personal information of judges, prosecutors, and law enforcement officers, including their phone numbers and home addresses.

42   Another way of looking at the FOIA's exemptions is that they protect three basic sets of interests: personal-privacy interests; business interests; and several governmental interests, most prominently those involving law enforcement and national security.

43   It should also be noted up front that the FOIA does not apply to the judicial branch of the Federal Government, nor to Congress; each has its own rules for any public access to its records that it provides. Neither does it apply to records maintained within the "inner White House," i.e., those of the president and his or her close advisors. Every so often, it is suggested, publicly or privately, with one degree of seriousness or another, that Congress should make itself subject to the FOIA. (Senator Patrick J. Leahy, Jr., through his principal aide John D. Podesta, Jr., suggested that to me most seriously in 1991: "I'm willing to join forces with you to apply FOIA to the Congress.") Most likely, though, the entity at the other end of Pennsylvania Avenue (i.e., the "inner White House") would have to join the party as well.

Most recently, a novel legal theory on this has been advanced in a lawsuit filed on August 12, 2021 by a free-lance journalist seeking records pertaining to the January 6, 2021 insurrection that are held by Congress. This suit contends that there is a "common law right of access" to congressional records, a notion for which there is little, if any, support in law. I happen to know the attorney who agreed to file such a lawsuit (read: I knew him when he was an overly aggressive young law student) and I cannot say that I am surprised that he has done so.

And the FOIA applies only at the federal level and not to anything outside of the executive branch in any way. For example, the Smithsonian Institution adheres to the FOIA only insofar as it chooses to as a matter of administrative discretion, and a few other odd entities are like that as well. On the other hand, even an entity such as Amtrak, which is not a federal agency, has been made subject to the FOIA by dint of a statute enacted in 1997 that speaks of its receipt of "federal funding." Ironically, the Library of Congress also is subject to the FOIA, but only as to one distinct part of it -- the United States Copyright Office. And presidential transition teams, in and of themselves, are not directly subject to FOIA requests.

All states and most U.S. territories have their own individual freedom-of-information laws that operate at the state, and sometimes local municipal, levels. Most, but hardly all, of those laws hew closely to the federal FOIA for the most part -- and where they do not, no small amount of disappointment and even outright controversy can arise (regardless of whether hilarity ensues). A major area of potential controversy can exist when a state FOIA counterpart law is applied hard and fast to the records of a state university system. By and large, colleges and universities, particularly their ordinarily liberal faculties, are not well suited to be subjected to open-government laws.

44 OIP's training programs were for a time offered through the Department's Legal Education Institute ("LEI," when functioning well), which was a close cousin of the Department's Attorney General's Advocacy Institute, where I regularly gave a lecture to new AUSAs on the intersection of civil discovery and the Privacy Act for more than a dozen years. In the mid-1980s, however, LEI came to be headed by someone (named Susan Moss) who proved unable to reliably meet the challenges of institutionally hosting OIP's FOIA training programs, so OIP had to take it upon itself to do so. In time, this problem was rectified without any loss of training capacity.

OIP vigorously promoted proper FOIA administration by all federal agencies also through its past and current publications -- the *Freedom of Information Case List*, the "Short Guide to the FOIA," the "Justice Department Guide to the Freedom of Information Act," *FOIA Update*, and *FOIA Post* -- as well as through its "FOIA Coun-selor Service," which over the years has responded to more than 100,000 telephone calls from agency FOIA personnel seeking advice and assistance on the handling of their FOIA requests. It also regularly edited the "Citizen's Guide to Using the Freedom of Information Act and the Privacy Act of 1974," at Congress's request, when it was issued biennially.

45 Over the years, there has been much litigation over the exact contours of FOIA exemptions, as well as about its many procedural aspects. This is so much so that some private-sector attorneys even specialize in handling FOIA cases on behalf of aggrieved FOIA requesters. To date, there have been an estimated 9500 precedential court decisions issued under the Act, including 32 by the United States Supreme Court, one as recently as on March 4, 2021.

There is one noteworthy FOIA case that was never heard by the Supreme Court, even though *certiorari* was granted in it and it was scheduled for oral argument on December 8, 1999. That case, *Weatherhead v. United States*, involved information obtained from another nation (Great Britain, it was later disclosed) that very much wanted it to be protected under the FOIA as classified on foreign relations grounds. (The U.K.'s own FOIA counterpart had not yet been enacted by then.) And the Solicitor General, under intense pressure from the Department of State, had agreed to seek the Court's review of a rare court of appeals ruling that had ordered that classified information to be disclosed.

As I recall, it was over Thanksgiving weekend when the FOIA requester submitted a reply brief that revealed for the first time that he was in possession of a document that he received from a local British Consul that addressed the same subject. (It appeared that within the British Government, the "right hand" was totally unaware of what the "left hand" had been doing.) In response to this sudden revelation, the State Department immediately brought this new information to the British Government's attention, which then quite sheepishly decided to no longer insist on foreign relations confidentiality for the document at issue. This caused quite a scramble within the Office of the Solicitor General -- and among those of us who were assisting it on what was about to be the first such national security case to be decided by the Supreme Court in more than 25 years -- and it led to the dismissal of the entire case and the vacatur of the lower court's adverse opinion. Such a thing was unprecedented in the history of Supreme Court FOIA litigation.

This was not the only time that the U.S. Government went out on a limb under the FOIA for our favored-nation friends "across the pond." The most high-profile such case, as I recall, was that of John W. Lennon, who in his post-Beatle years became embroiled in a deportation dispute with the Nixon Administration based upon his heavy anti-war activities and a years-old conviction for marijuana possession in London. Years after his death, historian Jon Weiner sought complete access to his FBI files, consisting of 400 pages, leading to the withholding of two-thirds of them on national security grounds at the behest of the British Government, not unlike as in the *Weatherhead* case.

When Jon Weiner sued, the FBI prevailed at the district court level, whereupon OIP Deputy Director Miriam M. Nisbet defended his appeal to the Ninth Circuit, seeking to have the FBI's victory affirmed. When we "moot courted" her for that oral argument, we told her that at the first hint of any resistance from the court of appeals panel she should break into a rendition of "Let it Be." As I recall, Miriam returned from California saying that "behind the avocado curtain, the Ninth Circuit is a very dark place," and a loss followed. After a brush with Supreme Court review, the British Government ultimately agreed to have the FBI apply my "foreseeable harm" standard (see Chapter Twenty-Nine), under which almost all of the withheld information was disclosed.

46 Fully cited as *Department of Justice v. Reporters Committee for Freedom of the Press*, 489 U.S. 749 (1989), this Supreme Court decision is unquestionably the most significant FOIA decision ever issued in that it brought about a "sea change" for privacy protection under the Act (see Chapter Twelve). A little-known aspect of the case is that although the Court spoke of it as involving a request for relatively commonplace FBI "rap sheets" (i.e., criminal history records), it actually was a "Glomarization" case in disguise (see Chapter Seventeen).

47 Overall, when records are withheld under the FOIA, in whole or in part, more than 50 percent of the time the basis for nondisclosure will be personal privacy. Indeed, the protection of personal-privacy interests has long loomed large as a matter of Federal Government policy.

48 It is worth noting here that, unlike other government programs, even ones of governmentwide applicability, the FOIA is not a "line item" for budgetary purposes at almost all federal agencies. Rather, its funding falls under the heading of agency "administrative" activity, which means that each fiscal year the FOIA's implementation competes with many other agency activities for generally appropriated funds. Hence, another cause of FOIA backlogs.

49 There actually is a well-established ten-year cycle for this, going back more than seven decades (see the Glossary).

50 Despite what was envisioned when the FOIA was enacted, the vast majority of FOIA requesters are commercial entities or individuals seeking records about themselves. In fact, the use of the FOIA by commercial requesters came as a big surprise to Congress and even added a whole additional dimension to the FOIA -- what are known as "reverse FOIA" cases, in which businesses seek the *non*disclosure of information that is submitted by them to the Federal Government for one reason or another. And they all too often bring such lawsuits for one basic reason: When faced with a FOIA requester that seeks to obtain business information on one side, and a business seeing to prevent such disclosure on the other (read: meaning that a lawsuit is likely one way or the other), federal agencies tend to tilt in favor of the requester rather than the business submitter, and determine (read: threaten) to disclose the information, with the thought that a "reverse FOIA" suit would be less work to

defend. (Here's a "dirty little secret": Agencies most often do not much care one way or the other whether such information is disclosed; by and large, they truly are "mere stakeholders.")

Although a "reverse FOIA" case is not jurisdictionally founded on the FOIA, rather on another part of its parent Administrative Procedure Act that provides a milder adjudication standard than full "*de novo*" review, it is a challenging one to litigate nevertheless. Most often, they are based on FOIA Exemption 4, covering business information, but in a few instances over the years they have been based on claims of personal privacy under FOIA Exemptions 6 or 7(C), and in at least one case, a "reverse FOIA" claim was brought by a Savings and Loan company against the Federal Home Loan Bank Board under the "bank secrecy" exemption to the FOIA, Exemption 8. That case was readily disposed of, which I know because in 1979 I defended it. Perhaps the most unusual "reverse FOIA" case was one filed by a group of Native Hawaiians seeking to prevent disclosure of location information on ancient burial grounds on the basis of privacy under Exemption 6; that case, under the name *Na Iwi O Na Kupuna v. Dalton*, was unsuccessful in 1995.

In rare cases, "reverse FOIA" lawsuits can be based on an arguably protective provision of a separate statute, such as the Federal Insecticide, Fungicide, and Rodenticide Act. I litigated one such case in 1977, *Dow Chemical Co. v. EPA*, which involved my having to fly to Midland, Michigan, during a cold winter (read: the "edge of the Arctic Circle" is how I recall describing it) in order to defend a contentious deposition at Dow's headquarters and then file litigation papers in nearby Bay City. Most of all, I remember three things about that trip: (1) the sheer obnoxiousness of my opposing counsel toward my female client, (2) the fact that the per diem travel rate (read: for both food and lodging) in that place at the time was only $35, and (3) when I stopped for lunch in Bay City, I could taste an odd "flavor" not only in the water served there but also in a dinner roll as well. Years later, I thought back to that day upon the discovery of toxic chemicals in Bay City's tap water, which surely had absolutely nothing to do with the Dow Chemical plant just down the road. Right.

51   And as for the Trump Administration, suffice here to say that during it ordinary government disclosure issues gave way to so many extraordinary issues of government mistrust, outright falsity, and breach of the presidential normative structure that the old ideas of "controversy" seemed to be transformed almost overnight.

CHAPTER ONE

1   In a rough corollary to this, American Founding Father Benjamin Franklin pointedly observed in *Poor Richard's Almanack* that "[t]hree may keep a secret, if two of them are dead." In a sense, this 18th-century observation presaged the 21st-century, "WikiLeaks era." A modern-day counterpart is a 2012 statement attributed to National Security Advisor Thomas E. Donilon regarding the planning of the U.S. military operation against Osama bin Laden: "There is only one way in Washington to keep a secret: Don't tell anybody." That quite aptly makes the point, though it stands in tension with the nature of what a secret actually is (see the Introduction).

2   I can provide a "close-to-home" example of this from my own experience. To me, official authority carries with it personal responsibility for the people who work for you. It was this strong sense of responsibility that impelled me to immediately shut down my part of the Department of Justice once I spotted White House personnel being evacuated on September 11, 2001 (see Chapter Three). And that same feeling of paternalism and protectiveness led me to insist that I, not any clerical personnel, would open the office mail that had accumulated out of fear of anthrax exposure a few months later (see Chapter Thirteen).

3   Actually, the term "transparency" originated in Europe and was imported to the United States, where it has taken hold, especially since the beginning of the Obama Administration.

4   For nearly three decades now, openness-in-government advocates in the United States have celebrated "Freedom of Information Day" each year on James Madison's birthday (March 16), with remembrance of the following quotation from his writings:

> A popular Government, without popular information, or the means of acquiring it, is but a Prologue to a Farce or a Tragedy; or, perhaps, both. Knowledge will forever govern ignorance: And a people who mean to be their own Governors, [sic] must arm themselves with the power knowledge gives.

For the past two decades, the world has celebrated its counterpart "International Right-to-Know Day" ("IRTKD") on September 28.

5   Accordingly, OIP memorialized him in limerick form as follows:
A farsighted Finn named Chydenius
As enlightened as anyone seen; yes,
He invented the FOIA
Without being a lawyer:
The world's first transparency genius.

6   Chydenius's collected works are made available for study today by the Anders Chydenius Foundation in conjunction with Finland's Kokkala University Consortium and the Chydenius Institute. The former has compiled a wealth of information about him, which can be accessed through its homepage.

7   This point certainly resonated when I made it for the first time in China in 2009, while addressing the Inaugural Sino-American Conference on Rule of Law and Human Rights. Even the few Chinese scholars who had by that time begun to explore the very idea of government transparency had not yet uncovered that, so when I brought it up it became a source of considerable notice and palpable national pride.

8   It has been observed on *PBS* that "[b]ecause of its democracy and reputation for openness, Athens became a magnet for new thinking during the 5th-century BCE."

9   There is no question but that, generally speaking, secrecy is the necessary backdrop against which transparency emerges. And government secrecy began to be recognized as a formal concept in the 17th century; it was a minister to the King of France, Cardinal Richelieu (Armand Jean du Plessia, the Duke of Richelieu), who then most famously said: "Secrecy is the first essential in affairs of state."

10   This is memorialized in what today would be referred to as the "Congressional Record," 5 Anals of Cong. 760–62 (Mar. 30, 1796), and also in a D.C. Circuit Court of Appeals decision, *Halperin v. CIA*, which noted the existence of a "Committee of Secret Correspondence within the Continental Congress" during the Revolutionary War.

11   In something parallel to the circumstances of the present day, the Continental Congress paid at least lip service to its preservation of secrecy when, on September 6, 1774, it aspirationally passed a resolution stating: "Resolved, that the doors be kept shut during the time of business and that the members consider themselves under the strongest obligations of honor, to keep the proceedings secret until the majority shall direct them to be made public." On this point, however, Benjamin Franklin was presciently more realistic, saying that "Congress consists of too many [M]embers to keep secrets."

12   In *Totten v. United States*, the Supreme Court in 1876 held that "the existence of a contract of that kind is itself a fact not to be disclosed." It reasoned, quite presciently as it turns out, that this is because "[a] secret

service, with liability to publicity in this way, would be impossible." This became the underlying precedent for the Supreme Court's establishment of the "State Secrets Privilege" in the *United States v. Reynolds* case in 1953 (see the Glossary). And it was an underpinning of the FOIA concept of "Glomarization" that I began propagating almost exactly 100 years later in 1977 (see Chapter Seventeen).

13   On July 11, 2011, the National Archives and Records Administration made this official by displaying what it referred to as "newly declassified secret ink documents from 1918." Another unique locus of secrecy, since the 1930s, is the United States Bullion Depository (otherwise known as "Fort Knox") in Kentucky, where most of the U.S.'s gold reserves are stored amid much secrecy. Reportedly, that secrecy involves more than just site security. With the declassification of records pertaining to "invisible ink," it is possible that the U.S.'s oldest classified records now reside in the Commonwealth of Kentucky.

14   The first, of course, was the "Official Secrets Act," which was enacted by the British Parliament in 1889 and then greatly strengthened in 1911. In time, it came to apply in more than 40 Commonwealth (or former Commonwealth) Nations.

15   The work begun by the United States on cryptography, cryptology, and cryptanalysis in the late 1930s was preceded by that of the U.S. Cipher Bureau (otherwise known as the "Black Chamber") during the 1920s -- which in turn had its roots in work originally done by the top U.S. code-breaker, Herbert O. Yeardley, during World War I. Yeardley "broke" Japan's diplomatic code in 1921 and later wrote a book about it in which he revealed some cryptologic secrets. Much more damaging to U.S. code-breaking efforts, though -- and to U.S. espionage in general -- was the profoundly archaic attitude expressed by Secretary of State Henry L. Stimson in 1929 that "[g]entlemen do not read each other's mail." Stimson did more than just espouse this short-sighted view; he shut down the Cipher Bureau almost as soon as he became secretary of state.

16   These early U.S. intelligence activities and the heightened levels of secrecy that they required are well described in historian Joseph E. Persico's detailed treatment of the subject in his 2002 book *Roosevelt's Secret War: FDR and WWII Espionage*.

17   For an inside story of Bletchley Park secrecy and the breaking of the Germany's vital "Enigma" code (and the effective disabling of an estimated 20,000 "Enigma" machines), one could read F.H. Hinsley's 1993 book *Codebreakers: The Inside Story of Bletchley Park*, or else see the movie *The Imitation Game*, which was released in 2014 and was nominated for eight Academy Awards.

18   So, too, was the situation in the cases that spawned "Glomarization," the "we can neither confirm nor deny" defense that was first deployed to protect the secret retrieval of a sunken Soviet submarine in the mid-1970s (see Chapter Seventeen).

19   Friedman, who was nothing short of a legend in the field, actually might object to use of the word "cryptologist" to describe him, as he himself invented the term "cryptanalyst" in 1920 to serve in its place. My cyber-security daughter Emily, who has more than dabbled in this field, says that Friedman was correct. Friedman also had a hand in developing the Army's own counterpart to Enigma, called the "SIGABA" machine, which continued to be used by both the Army and the Navy even after World War II. It was used side by side with a voice encryption system known as "SYGSALY," otherwise dubbed "the Green Hornet" for the sound it would emit upon attempted interception.

He did all of this, history has only recently recognized, with the aid of his wife Elizebeth Smith Friedman, who deciphered enemy codes during both world wars and applied her unique skills against organized crime bootleggers in between. In fact, it was she who taught her husband the basics of cryptanalysis to begin with.

20   It is time for a side story on secrecy here, one that is spawned by both cryptanalysis and a "leak." It has to do with the Battle of Midway, at an early stage of World War II, where the U.S. Navy won a tremendous victory over the Japanese fleet that had hit Pearl Harbor. It was able to do so because it had "advance information" about the Japanese fleet's intended location, which was obtained through successful cryptanalysis of the Imperial Navy's operational code -- which was all well and good. But on the day after that victory, an article published in the *Chicago Tribune* spoke of it in a way that made it unmistakable even to uneducated readers that this success was due to the breaking of that Japanese code.

All hell ensued, in the Navy Department, the War Department, the White House, and even at the Department of Justice, which actually empaneled a grand jury to investigate the leak, thereby threatening the *Chicago Tribune* and whoever was the source of the story with criminal prosecution (read: "We'll start the trial and figure out whatever charges we can bring as we go along."). Well, it turned out that that source was a *Chicago Tribune* reporter embedded on a U.S. Navy ship at which a message was received from Admiral Chester W. Nimitz, four days before the battle, in which he carelessly predicted victory in it based upon the Navy's "advance information." It is not known whether this led to the World War II-originated warning "Loose Lips Sink Ships," but even if not, the true coda to the story is that, despite all of the fear and anxiety about this on the U.S. side, the Japanese were not "tipped off" to their code's compromise because they never heard of the article. They went on using the code, and the Allies kept on deciphering it, for weeks afterward.

21   Another example of this is the "Venona Project," a counterintelligence program initiated during World War II by the United States Army's Signals Intelligence Service ("SIS," to its brothers in arms) in February of 1943. Between then and until October of 1980, it decrypted and translated approximately 3,000 messages, and this work was so sensitive that the very existence of Venona was kept secret for more than 15 years after its work concluded. Eventually, the Freedom of Information Act (not to mention something called "mandatory declassification review") caught up with it, posing the legal question of just how long this activity had to be treated as still secret in order to serve a realistic government interest (see the Glossary).

22   This executive order (sequentially numbered 10,290) was issued on September 24, 1951. Prior to that, the only such wide-scale secrecy regime in the U.S. was the one established by Executive Order No. 8381 near the outset of WW II (i.e., on March 22, 1940), within the confines of the military only.

23   This law, the Atomic Energy Act of 1954, which is found at 42 U.S.C. § 2011 (as amended), establishes a separate national security secrecy regime for what today would be called "nuclear-related" information (see the Glossary).

24   The United Kingdom, for its part, has long had an "Official Secrets Act," which runs counter to government transparency. The U.K. eventually enacted a freedom of information law in 2000.

25   The details of Congressman Moss's singular efforts toward the FOIA's enactment are closely chronicled in the "Freedom of Information Pages" of the website maintained by the John Moss Foundation. Thus, another close parallel between Moss and Chydenius.

26   Symbolically, the Freedom of Information Act was signed into law on July 4 of 1966, the Nation's Independence Day, and it took effect exactly one year later, on a federal holiday.

27   Speaking of supporters, there also was a young "firebrand" Republican congressman named Donald H. Rumsfeld who wrote Lyndon Johnson an ardent letter in support of the bill (a FOIA-disclosed copy of which I have in my files) in which he urged that it be signed by Johnson despite whatever misgivings he might have about doing so. Looking back on it later, of course, this plea becomes redolent of irony of the first order.

28   The full quote is: "LBJ had to be dragged, kicking and screaming, to the signing ceremony. He hated the very idea of open government, hated the thought of journalists rummaging in government closets, hated them challenging the official view of reality."

29   Bill Moyers was even known to joke about this a bit by saying that the LBJ Ranch, which is where Johnson was staying at the time, and was dry and dusty most of the time, bore the "double tracks" of Johnson's boots from where he was "drug" from behind to the signing ceremony. He told me this story while we were sharing a "green room" prior to presentations that we were making at a media conference in 1997. And I in turn told him that, believe it or not, we both had worked for the same newspaper during 1967-1968. This had him stumped for only a moment. "You worked for *Newsday* back then?" he exclaimed. "Sure," I said, "I started there as a young paperboy in 1964 and happily plateaued at that level for several years." (He had become the *Long Island Newsday*'s publisher after leaving the White House while I was still at the opposite end of the newspaper's hierarchy, though I had worked my way up to "top news carrier" status by that time.)

30   Actually, the first official articulation of this came in 1998, when the State Department authorized an official United States "mission" in which a representative of the FOIA-requester community (William G. Ferroggiaro) and I traveled by bullet train up and down Japan, with the support of the United States Embassy in Tokyo, spreading the "gospel of transparency" (not that we called it that then) in order to spur the enactment of Japan's version of the FOIA two years later. From then on, it has been the explicit policy of the United States to strongly encourage the proliferation and refinement of FOIA-like laws around the world.

31   In fact, during its first 25 years, OIP hosted hundreds upon hundreds of representatives of other nations and international governing bodies who were interested in the adoption of their own versions of the Freedom of Information Act, using it as a working model, providing briefings on the operation of our statute, advice on the development, implementation, and further refinement of their counterpart laws. They came singly and in groups, in government delegations and academic ones, and with the full sponsorship of the Department of State. And they included national legislators who were responsible for drafting their new access laws, sometimes even negotiating their terms on OIP's conference room table.

    As a rule, these nations have built on the experiences of the nations that came before them, taking pains not to repeat any misjudgments, miscalculations, or legislative drafting errors that were made elsewhere. (I used to exhort them: "Be careful! Don't make our mistakes.") In some cases, these efforts involved many years of internal deliberation, much as took place in the U.S. between 1955 and 1966 when the FOIA was the subject of protracted consideration in Congress. By and large, they have done so with great success.

    And at the same time, OIP sent its experts around the world to do the same thing with presentations and on-site training sessions in China, England, Scotland, Mexico, Argentina, the Dominican Republic, South Africa, South Korea, as well as Japan over the years. It also participated in television broadcasts from Washington, D.C., that promoted government transparency activities in such other nations as Peru, Paraguay, Bolivia, Chile, and the Czech Republic.

32   Indeed, back then the word "transparency" was used, if at all, only overseas. This began to change only in the early 2000s, much as that might be hard to believe now.

33   The Office of Information and Privacy worked with nearly 100 nations and international governing bodies in the development, implementation, or improved administration of their own statutory counterparts to our Freedom of Information Act.

34   Well, that actually took until the next century, because Japan's national openness-in-government law was not enacted by its legislature (called the "Diet") for another 18 years, in total, and it did not come into effect until the year 2000.

35   This travel took me to many different "prefectures" (read: like the states in the U.S. or the provinces in Canada and China), where I learned that openness in government was both popular and well-developed at Japan's prefectural level (for instance, the Kanagawa Prefecture adopted such a law in 1982), mostly due to the strong influence of the local media there (read: just as in the U.S). The problem, I was told, was that Japan's national media still operated in a traditional "wine and dine" (read: cozy and readily coopted) relationship with the government at that national level; hence, there was little or no clamor for freedom of information in Tokyo as there had been in Washington in the 1960s. That took 18 years to overcome. (From my many meetings with Japanese delegations over the years, however, including those from academia, I knew that an equally large barrier was posed by the powerful business interests there, which were loath to risk any disclosure of their most sensitive business information.)

36   Intermingled with this, have no doubt, was the perceived greater need to curb corruption in all sectors of Chinese society, for which transparency (read: at least ostensible transparency) was by then a proven tool.

37   To me, it was quite notable that I found transparency to have developed first in the provinces of China, in nascent forms, just it had at the prefectural level of Japan a decade earlier. This is the opposite of what happened in the United States.

38   The second such event was held in Xiemen, China, in 2010, with follow-up discussions in Beijing (together with a side trip to Shanghai). And the third was held in Great Neck, Long Island, not far from my original home. (Unfortunately, my participation in a fourth one, back in China in 2012, was bungled when one of Jerry Cohen's assistants, Haini Guo, failed to make travel reservations in time after being stressed by Hurricane Sandy.) By the end of these sessions, I actually had heard the "D word" (read: "democracy") mentioned by some of the Chinese participants, which made it clear to me that to many of the Chinese, the lingo of economic expansionism was beginning to overtake the dogma of Communism.

39   One of the gratifying things about being part of such a high-level delegation is having the opportunity to work together with people whom you might not ordinarily meet. For example, I traveled twice to China with Second Circuit Court of Appeals Judge John M. Walker, Jr., who is a first cousin of President George H.W. (read: Herbert Walker) Bush. During the second trip, in a quiet moment (read: in the back of a darkened bus), he spoke with me about "young George" (read: President George W. Bush) from the perspective of an uncle who had seen him grow up (read: this is assuming that he ever really did). I will not repeat here what Judge Walker said to me about our 43rd president, not for lack of memory about it and not because it was so very sensational in its content (though it likely could have been). Rather, it is because doing so just would not feel right. I very much respect Judge Walker (who still sits as a senior circuit court judge) and I respected his cousin both as vice president and president, so I think I owe it to the both of them not to blithely pass along what I remember Judge Walker confidentially saying.

40   Another distinctive characteristic of the U.K.'s transparency regime is that it applies not just to the national government, but to all political subdivisions within it, right down to the granular level of its smallest village constabularies and individual medical units of its National Health Service.

41   More than any other, one such "campaigner," Maurice Frankel OBE of the U.K.'s "Campaign for Freedom of Information" starting in 1984, was most responsible for this eventual result, even more so than the British media.

42   This meant that the U.K.'s FOIA did not begin to take effect until 2005, not long after which one of its largest universities, University College London ("UCL," for short) developed a major research initiative on that and offered me a fellowship in the bargain. I spent much time in London during the following years, consulting also in conjunction with the U.K.'s Office of the Information Commissioner in Manchester. I remember one particular suggestion to them in 2006 (which was readily adopted) that they use the phrase "It's good FOIA!" to browbeat the British bureaucracy into the law's full acceptance.

43   Wales, too, administers the U.K. transparency regime on its own, as does Northern Ireland.

44   At one of our International Right-to-Know Day Celebration events during this time, CGS established its first-ever trans-Atlantic video conference "hook-up" with Scotland's Information Commissioner's Office, which became the forerunner of several more to come.

45   The highlight of this came, at least for me, when I learned of a new plan by the Scottish Government (not to be confused with the Office of the Information Commissioner there) to suddenly take a draconian view of document "processing" (read: withholding an entire page if anything on it was exempt) that I bluntly told them, in a speech to an assembled multitude, was pure "horseshit," which translated well). Soon enough, this aberrant policy was changed. (This speech, by the way was held in a long, rectangular building that bore the plain words "The Scottish Government" over its entrance.)

46   A prime example of this are the "extractive industries" that have long preyed upon the nations of Africa. Any use of government transparency against endemic corruption greatly threatens their interests.

47   As of 2003, the world began having a celebration of "International Right-to-Know Day" on September 28 of each year, for the purpose of recognizing and promoting the worldwide proliferation of government openness. In the United States, of course, the model for this, "Freedom of Information Day," is celebrated each year on March 16, which was chosen because it is the birthdate of President James Madison, Jr., regarded as the "Founding Father" of transparency in the United States. American University's Washington College of Law was the principal site in the United States for both celebrations from 2007-2014 (see Chapter Forty-Two).

When CGS began this in 2007, we barely were able to set up international telephone connections with coordinating government officials overseas, but we succeed in doing so for the first event with Wellington and Paris. As time went on, we managed to have full video-conference hook-ups with London, Scotland, Madrid, Oslo, Brussels, and two locations simultaneously in South Africa. And there also was a European information commissioner visiting Princeton University on that day whom we linked in as well.

48   More than one FOIA wag over the years has breezily suggested that we probably could get transparency to catch on in Antarctica as well if only we could find a way to keep the icy wind from making the pages stick together.

49   Indeed, it would seem to be only a matter of time before a majority of the more than two-hundred nations of the world will have formal openness-in-government regimes. Right now, several additional nations, including Ecuador, Russia, and El Salvador, are actively considering such legislation.

50   An overlay above the exemptions -- especially the ones protecting national security and personal privacy -- is the principle that sometimes an agency can neither confirm nor deny the existence of requested records without thereby impinging upon the interests protected by them; this has come to be known in FOIA jargon as "Glomarization," named after the clandestine submarine-retrieval ship *Glomar Explorer* used to secretly raise a sunken Soviet sub in the mid-1970s (see Chapter Seventeen). And at even a more abstract (read: exotic) level, the FOIA contains three provisions that I named "exclusions," for especially sensitive types of law enforcement or foreign intelligence records, used in very particular contexts in which even "Glomarization" is inadequate to the task (see Chapter Eighteen).

51   Hoover died in 1972, nearly five years after the FOIA became effective, but during that time it contained so broad an "investigatory files" exemption that the FBI was hardly touched by it.

52   Notably, England's historical Official Secrets Act was not an impediment to transparency efforts in these three Commonwealth nations as it was in the U.K.

53   I know this firsthand because, simply put, I was responsible for meeting with them, as well as for responding to follow-up questions that they had upon returning to their home countries. Overall, it was the academic visitors, especially the ones from Japan, England, and New Zealand, who had the most such questions.

54   A good example of this comes from Mexico, which has an excellent FOIA-like law and relies on civil society organizations to aid in its FOIA implementation. During its first year of that, one such group caught wind of corrupt conduct by Mexico's ambassador to France, who happened to be a cousin of Mexico's president. It seems that he was "double dipping" in his own way by both purchasing outrageously expensive furnishings for himself while padding the invoices so that he could pocket part of what he was so lavishly spending. When this "leaked out," after a fashion, the vast majority of Mexicans simply assumed that this would be "swept under the rug" (read: "debajo de la alfombra") and the offending official would escape any consequence. Well, to the contrary, he was fired almost on the spot, with much FOIA-disclosed documentation disclosed to his dishonor. This single case of FOIA effectiveness reverberated throughout Mexico, especially within its official ranks, to strong deterrent effect, and word of it spread internationally as well.
      A less blatant episode in the United States had a similar effect. I remember during the early years of the Reagan Administration being consulted on a situation in which a sub-cabinet-level official was suspected of abusing her official travel for personal purposes. When all of her official travel records were examined together for purposes of a FOIA request, a distinct pattern emerged. It turned out that she was regularly scheduling speeches on Fridays each week in the fall, in various locations around the mid-west -- locations that just happened to coincide with the away schedule for her son's college football team, of which he was a member. Now, there was nothing wrong per se in her wanting to see her son play, but she was doing it "on the taxpayers' dime" and was unmistakably concocting the need for these out-of-town speeches in the bargain. This, too, reverberated amongst the political appointees of the Reagan Administration, as a cautionary tale brought to them courtesy of the FOIA. And I would like to think that more than a few potentially corrupt "official" travel plans were curtailed by this as a result.

55   In China, despite its nature as a socialist state, transparency efforts began to take hold in the late 1990s, and they did so first at the local and provincial level. (This was quite like the growth of transparency in Japan, which began at the prefectural level and then "went national"; in the United States it was the opposite, with the states following the Federal Government.) Since 2008 (coincidentally not long before the Beijing Olympics were held), China has had a somewhat limited national transparency regime.

56   I say "haltingly" in the case of South Africa because over the course of many years (i.e., 2007-2014), it wavered between pro-disclosure and anti-disclosure policies, with the former seeming to prevail. The secretive interests of rich and powerful companies comprising the "extractive industries" in Africa carry much sway on government transparency, something from which even South Africa is not immune.

57   To date, the only nations of Africa with a viable transparency regime are Côte d'Ivoire, Guinea, Kenya, Liberia, Niger, Nigeria, Sierra Leone, South Africa, Tanzania, and Tunisia. Several other African nations -- most particularly Angola, Ethiopia, Ghana, Malawi, Mozambique, Rwanda, and Zimbabwe -- appear to have that goal within reach sometime in the near future. And in the Arab nation of Egypt, perhaps as a category of its own, freedom of information is potentially part of larger societal change.

58   There should be no doubt that the horrific events of September 11, 2001 and the implications of related terrorist activity have presented the greatest challenges to government transparency's continued growth and maturation, especially in the United States. In time, however, the effects of this may be less profound.

59   As it happened, I learned of this sudden diplomatic development even before the Obama Administration formally did, believe it or not. The day that it occurred (read: with many time zones taken into account), I was in a meeting with my fellow Access to Information Appeals Board members at the World Bank (see Chapter Forty-Four) and one of them -- Wajahat Habibullah, the former Chief Information Commissioner of India -- told me that he had to leave our session early in order to be part of some sort of "strategy meeting" at India's embassy several blocks away. (Wajahat is a "good guy," in my parlance, a quintessential civil servant who had survived more than one assassination attempt during his government career when he was chairperson of India's "National Commission for Minorities," which apparently is a thankless (not to mention dangerous) position over there.)

When he returned, "Waja" sat across the width of a long conference table from me, looked at me somewhat side-long in the eye, and whispered that he had just learned the most surprising news: India was about to abruptly back out of the Africa part of its arrangement with the United States, evidently due to last-minute diplomatic (read: perhaps not so diplomatic) pressure from China. Knowing from former colleagues who were still in the Government that this arrangement was something that the Obama Administration was very much counting on to support some of the president's yet-unfulfilled transparency pledges, I whispered back to Waja that his Nation might've "backed the wrong horse" in choosing China over the USA. (That was back when I thought President Obama had more clout on the world stage for such matters than it turned out he did.)

60   "BRIC" stood for "Brazil, Russia, India, and China," later to be "BRICS," with the additional of South Africa. These were countries at similar stages of newly advanced economic development that could conceivably become among the four most dominant economies in the world by the year 2050. Obviously, the alignment of India and Brazil with Russia and China was entirely disadvantageous to the United States and other "old-world" nations such as England and most of the European Union. The year 2010 could be seen as a "pivot point" for that.

61 In keeping with its emphasis on openness, the Open Government Partnership maintains an extensive website detailing its activities. Thus far, more than 75 nations have joined this coalition, some of which still do not have a FOIA. For the latter nations, enactment is the key goal; for the others, the goal is improved implementation.

62 The one enormous dark cloud in this metaphor, of course, is the presidency of Donald J. Trump, who in four long years managed to set back America's international relations by about 25 times that much. Suffice to say here that it likely will be quite some time until we all can calculate the damage that his presidency has done to the United States both domestically and internationally -- so I will not presume to predict the amount of such harm that has been done to transparency in particular. And if I were to do so, unfortunately, no small percentage of the U.S. population might be inclined to just label it as "fake news" anyway.

63 Truth be known, Sweden's initial transparency law was not very strong, just as the U.S.'s Freedom of Informa-tion Act was relatively weak at first, especially given the half-heartedness with which it was first implemented. That attitude on the parts of federal officials did diminish with the passage of time in the late 1960s and early 1970s, but that did not keep FOIA-requester resentments from festering until they boiled over in late 1974.

CHAPTER TWO

1 Some scholars blithely expound that there is "an inverse relationship between privacy and secrecy," but as a broad proposition this is untrue. To be sure, that can fairly be seen as so in a civil libertarian context, but within the realm of government secrecy, and its relation to privacy, it is unquestionable that the expansion of the latter means the expansion of the former.

2 Even in privacy's nascent antecedent strains, Warren and Brandeis took pains to connect them to government secrecy by using the case of King George III and observing about his "madness" (in the months before his death in 1820) that "if one of [his] physicians had kept a diary of what he heard and saw, the court[s] would not, in the king's lifetime, have permitted him to print and publish it." Thus, they recognized an early form of "executive privilege" as secrecy based on privacy.

3 Put another way, Warren and Brandeis argued: "Indeed, the elasticity of our law, its adaptability to new conditions, the capacity for growth, which has enabled it to meet the wants of an ever[-]changing society and to apply immediate relief for every recognized wrong, have been its greatest boast."

4 The early "technological advance" that threatened the right to be let alone was photography, which Brandeis in his later years acknowledged had been the very thing that spurred Warren to conceive their article. Brandeis, of course, went on to become an Associate Justice of the United States Supreme Court from 1916-1939, where in a famous dissent in *Olmstead v. United States*, he enshrined "the right to be let alone" in the context of constitutional law. And ironically, he is the author of the most famous quote ever on the broader subject of secrecy versus transparency: "Sunlight is said to be the best of disinfectants."

5 Prior to then, government secrecy pertained almost entirely to information generated by a government about government activities, not individuals (see Chapter One).

6 In fact, the protection of personal privacy quickly became one of the most complex and challenging of all secrecy areas. Broadly speaking, it involves (1) identification of the individual privacy interests that can be implicated in information, (2) the connection of such interests to a specific individual, and (3) due consideration

of whether those interests are overridden by any countervailing public interest in a particular case, if not "categorically."

7   This begs the question, of course, of whether (and if so to what extent) privacy is first and foremost enshrined in the U.S. Constitution. While the word "privacy" does not appear in the Constitution itself, it is said to exist within the Ninth Amendment's "penumbra" (covering "reproductive rights"), the Fourth Amendment (guarding against "unreasonable searches and seizures"), the Fifth and Fourteenth Amendments ("due process"), and the First Amendment (freedoms of expression and association). Significantly, Chief Justice John G. Roberts, Jr., at his confirmation hearing in 2005, endorsed this list and even added to it the lesser-known Third Amendment's protection against housing soldiers. So there is indeed at least some constitutional grounding for the protection of personal-privacy interests.

8   Privacy's importance is reflected in the fact that it is the subject of not just one but two exemptions of the FOIA -- Exemption 6, for information maintained in "ordinary" contexts, and Exemption 7(C), for the context of law enforcement records -- as well as an entire other federal statute, the Privacy Act of 1974 (see Chapter Fourteen). Another indication of its importance is the fact that among all the interests that are cognizable under the FOIA's many exemptions, personal-privacy protection is invoked (under Exemption 6, not even counting Exemption 7(C)) more frequently than any other.

9   There are two things about the *Reporters Committee* case that might escape the notice of the casual reader. First, it actually is a "Glomarization" case (see Chapter Seventeen), because the Department of Justice effectively did not disclose the abstract fact that the subject of the request (Charles Medico) had any "rap sheet" that could be disclosed to FOIA requester CBS News in the first place. (If such a record existed, it would have traced back more than 30 years, to the 1950s at the latest, and Medico lived well into the 2010s.)

Thus, the Supreme Court's *Reporters Committee* decision was very much akin to its 1982 FOIA decision in *Department of State v. Washington Post Co.* where that "Glomarization" element (read: neither confirming nor denying whether two Iranian officials had ever applied for U.S. citizenship) was likewise "hidden." And it also was akin to a 1984 case in the D.C. Circuit Court of Appeals, *Laborers International Union of North America v. United States Department of Justice*, in which the FOIA requester was seeking a disclosure "which could serve to confirm or deny the authenticity of" a leaked Criminal Division Organized Crime and Racketeering Section report on the involvement of labor unions with organized crime.

The second extraordinary thing about the case was something that did not come to light until the 20th anniversary of the Supreme Court's decision. In fact, the Collaboration on Government Secrecy celebrated that anniversary with a day-long symposium at which we revealed that the Library of Congress held the answer to the question of whether a "rap sheet" on Charles Medico did exist. He was still alive then, so I did not disclose that abstract fact, but I did describe how some of my students and I went there to review the papers of Justices Thurgood Marshall and Harry A. Blackmun in preparation for the symposium, only to discover that one of them had made a note of that pivotal fact upon reviewing an *in camera* submission. Doubtless that fact had escaped all notice when those papers were screened prior to being made publicly available. But out of respect for whichever Justice made this *faux pas*, I will not disclose that fact even though Charles Medico is now deceased.

We learned one other thing on that *Reporters Committee* "field trip": One of those two Justices (again, I'm not saying which one) included in his files a piece of paper from which we were able to deduce the preliminary vote that was taken in the case. It seemed that the late Justice Antonin G. Scalia cared more about that case's outcome than previously known, so much so that he "gamed the system" by voting with an initial majority so that (as the senior Justice) he could control the assignment of which Justice would write the Court's opinion.

Now anyone familiar with the Supreme Court's procedure on such things should be asking: How did he manage that, given that the late Justice William J. Brennan, Jr., was still on the Court then and certainly was senior to Justice Scalia? Well, a few of the symposium speakers and I were wondering about exactly that just before the symposium began until one of my faculty colleagues, Stephen J. Wermiel, suddenly snapped his fingers with a thought, raced up to his office, and hurriedly returned with the answer: Justice Brennan was rushed to Bethesda Naval Medical Center with a serious case of pneumonia before the *Reporters Committee* vote. As it happened, Steve was writing the definitive biography of Justice Brennan at the time, which afforded us the serendipity of so readily learning that question's answer. And my students, of course, were amazed at our academic proficiency.

10   The "balancing" of interests in privacy decisionmaking under the FOIA is the means by which courts give content to the term "unwarranted," which Congress used in each of the Act's two privacy exemptions -- i.e., disclosure that would be "unwarranted" under Exemption 6 or "clearly unwarranted" under Exemption 7(C).

11   Sometimes, an individual need not be named in a record in order to be "identifiable" for this purpose, such as when he or she is described as being within a sufficiently narrow setting. In one old case, *Harry v. Department of the Army*, identifiability was found among a close-knit group of ROTC cadets and in another, *Alirez v. NLRB*, the protected individual was part of a small group of co-workers. Indeed, courts have generally taken what is referred to as a "pragmatic approach" to determining identifiability under the FOIA.

A more extreme example of identifiability is something that took place in the late 1970s and 1980s when the Founding Church of Scientology waged a highly aggressive campaign against the Department of Justice and the Internal Revenue Service ("IRS," whether collecting back taxes or not) through FOIA requests and more nefarious means (see Chapter Twenty-Five). It actually went so far as to conduct handwriting analyses of IRS employees for purposes of "cross-matching" them and then to harass those employees (or in one instance take a step much worse) at their homes. When the IRS consulted with the Justice Department on this, we determined that under such extreme circumstances it could properly withhold handwritten notes and signatures under FOIA Exemption 7(C), which involved a novel view of identifiability as its foundation.

A second exceptional position that we developed was for the protection of federal judges: We gave them special notice whenever personal information about them was contained in requested records and we invariably withheld any information that could be used to threaten their personal safety. Since 1979, four federal judges have been murdered, plus a federal judge's mother and husband, in attacks at their homes. Most recently, in July of 2020, a disgruntled litigant before District Court Judge Esther Salas in Newark rang her home doorbell, shot her husband, and killed their 20-year-old son Daniel. This led to the enactment of "Daniel's Law," a New Jersey statute that makes it a crime to publish the personal information of judges, prosecutors, and law enforcement officers, including their phone numbers and home addresses.

12   As to "computerization," the Court explicitly recognized "the power of compilations to affect personal privacy that outstrips the combined power of the bits of information contained within." It should be remembered that this was in 1989, at a time when government databases were well established but "computerization" had just recently taken hold and the "Internet" (let alone the "World Wide Web" and its information-search capabilities) was still years away from widespread public use. Note that even seven years later, when Congress enacted the Electronic Freedom of Information Act Amendments of 1996, it still was so unfamiliar with the Internet that it instead used the awkward intermediate phrase "computer telecommunications means" to refer to it.

13   This technological advancement of "computerized information" in the second half of the 20th century was recognized by the Department of Justice as placing enormous amounts of additional information, much of it privacy related, in play for potential public disclosure: "Indeed," OIP said in its "Report on 'Electronic Record' FOIA Issues" issued in 1990, "through the tremendous power of 'computerization,' . . . file systems can be programmed

to achieve retrieval capabilities that far transcend anything even remotely possible within a 'paper' system. And as with 'computerization' in general, the ratio of effort to result in this regard can be exponentially less than in the conventional realm."

And as we moved into the 21st century, with hitherto-unimaginable private-sector information "just begging" for government use, such personal information became the subject of new government secrecy, even as to its very existence in government hands. The most recent example of this is "cell phone location" data, which are derived from "smart phones" and can be used by law enforcement agencies for "real-time tracking" of individuals and can be stored for prospective use as well. In July of 2022, the Department of Homeland Security ("DHS," even to those not feeling so secure) admitted to making "warrantless purchases of access" to such information. This is despite the fact that in June of 2018, the Supreme Court ruled 5-4 that the government needs a warrant to access (read: by what is called "compulsive process") a person's cell phone location history from cellular service providers, because of the "privacies of life" that those records can reveal. So now the question is whether this ruling, in *Carpenter v. United States*, 585 U.S. _____, 138 S. Ct. 2206 (U.S. June 22, 2018) (No. 16-402), can be readily circumvented by government agencies such as DHS through commercial acquisition.

14   As to such information, the Court adverted to the concept of "information privacy" and spoke favorably of an individual's "right to control" information about him. An adjunct to this fundamental concept, when it comes to privacy as part of governmental secrecy, is an individual's "expectation of privacy." Notably, this can arise when a government agency specifically "promises" someone that certain information furnished to it by him or her will be kept secret. The Supreme Court addressed this in the 1991 case of *United States Department of State v. Ray*, in which privacy protection was extended to several interdicted Haitian "boat people," buttressed by the admonition that "great nations, like great men, should keep their word."

15   The Court did so in recognition of the fact that the information in question, being more than 30 years old if it ever existed, "may have been wholly forgotten" by 1989. This presaged by many decades a concept that has recently arisen in Europe called the "right to be forgotten," which was embraced by the European Court of Justice in 2014 (see Chapter Thirteen).

16   Plus, the Court said that it could take the very fact that a FOIA request had been filed in the case as evidence of "practical obscurity": It reasoned that "if the [information at issue were] 'freely available,' there would be no reason to invoke the FOIA to obtain access to [it]."

17   The Court's "categorical balancing" approach had strong appeal in that it can both obviate unsatisfactory ad hoc results and greatly reduce administrative burdens. Indeed, the Court's use of the phrase "workable rules" for privacy determinations suggested as much. And when it comes to administrative burdens, in a novel recent case involving a request for "all data and information pertaining to the application and approval of the Pfizer Vaccine," *Public Health & Medical Professionals for Transparency v. FDA*, Civil No. 4:21-cv-01058-P (N.D. Tex. Jan. 6, 2022), the court ordered expedited FOIA processing *even if it impairs the efficiency and effectiveness of FDA doctors and scientists responsible for handling vaccine licensing.*

18   Indeed, this change in personal-privacy protection was so great and potent that the *Reporters Committee* decision was at the top of a coalition of media groups' "hit list" during the Clinton Administration, hoping to have it legislatively overruled. But even though longtime Attorney General Janet Reno came from a strong media background (both of her parents were journalists), she was never so entreated and *Reporters Committee* remarkably withstood her tenure. (I was prepared for this to be raised with Janet, in which event I expected

that she would be receptive to the idea, but surprisingly it never was. And I certainly never raised it with her; fortunately, as it turned out, I was able to not do so without failing in any obligation to her.)

As part of the 1996 FOIA Amendments, though, Congress made "findings" that purported to overrule the decision, but such a generalized legislative approach (read: through a minority committee report) was found by an appellate court to be legally insufficient in 1999. And then the Supreme Court itself implicitly rejected this attempted argument in its *Favish* decision in 2004.

19   While Warren, Brandeis, and subsequent scholars such as Professor Alan F. Westin, Professor Richard A. Posner, and Professor Charles A. Fried were true privacy pioneers, I do with all immodesty lay claim to two major features of privacy law: The conception of "survivor privacy" (see Chapter Three) and the original development and propagation of "privacy Glomarization" (see Chapter Seventeen). Even beyond that, I devoted much time and attention to the many permutations of privacy protection, as the law and circumstances required.

20   A substantial part of this has to do with what is called "data protection," which involves information maintained within the private sector and, most significantly, U.S. information transmitted to and through the European Union, where privacy values are held most acutely (see Chapter Thirteen).

21   This became obvious to all except to those who badly wanted to disclose information for their own purposes, a group that included inspectors general (see Chapter Thirty-Two), Justice's Office of Professional Responsibility, and two political appointees who wanted to have their own way regardless of what the applicable case law actually said. These two "hard-chargers" came from the White House ahead of Alberto Gonzales, settled into the Department's Office of Legal Counsel, and quickly developed a reputation among the career folks for heedless expedience. And in one particular matter, they challenged OIP's judgment about mandatory privacy protection, demanding a meeting at which the associate attorney general (for whom I worked) would preside.

So there we sat one dark afternoon, with my Privacy Act deputy Kirsten J. Moncada and I on one side of a table and with these two fellows -- Stephen G. Bradbury and, heaven help him, future Solicitor General Noel J. Francisco -- on the other side, refusing to confront every legal point that we made. Rather, with a flourish, they pulled out a copy of the *Reporters Committee* decision and proceeded to make an argument based on their interpretation of a part of the Supreme Court's opinion. Kirsten and I looked at one another and smiled, because we knew exactly which part of the opinion they were relying on, and how.

For a moment, I considered letting Kirsten have the honor of making the response to this defective argument, but I could not resist: "You obviously failed to read down to the bottom of that page," I said, "because if you had, you would have seen a paragraph in which the Court made it crystal clear that its actual holding was exactly contrary to what you're arguing." So they did, and then they understood, and then they abruptly rushed out of the meeting, declaring over their shoulders as they went that the issue would be "handled somewhere else." Well, Kirsten and I looked at Associate Attorney General Robert D. McCallum, Jr., and he looked back at us with a mixture of surprise and embarrassment, and the "issue" was never raised, in any forum, again.

CHAPTER THREE

1   This number has varied from time to time over the years, to as few as 37, now at 39, but during my time at the Office of Information and Privacy it most often stood at 40.

2   I immodestly take credit (or blame) for first using the phrase "It's good FOIA," but in my defense I should add that I subsequently managed to export it to the U.K. -- in exchange for the word "transparency" (see Chapter

One) -- in 2006, when England's information commissioner told me that he liked the sound of it and began using it to cajole British civil servants into acceptance of their own FOIA (which has the same name).

Several years later, newspapers in England used the British Freedom of Information Act in attempting to learn details about a big political subject, the British national debt. This information is contained in a register maintained by England's Debt Management Office but FOIA requesters were told that its contents are a "state secret." Government secrecy is no less prevalent in the United Kingdom than it is in the United States.

3   Notably, in order to trigger this "balancing process," all that is required is for there to be even the smallest bit of conceptualized privacy interest on that side of the balance, a "smidgen" in Scottish law and a "mere peppercorn" further south in England, as illustrated in the famous case of *Crowell v. Cross Alley, Ltd.*

4   In such cases, the "law" also included the Privacy Act of 1974, which in most cases added a mandate of nondisclosure atop the FOIA's privacy exemptions, meaning that an agency's use of the latter was not just a matter of judgment and discretion. In other words, once a privacy exemption was deemed applicable, it had to be applied.

5   In this case. like so many other FOIA cases when they are first filed in court, the defendant agency had not yet completed the "processing" of the requested records. When this is so, it is up to the Justice Department Trial Attorney defending the case to become involved -- sometimes very heavily so -- to determine exactly what information will be withheld, and defended, as exempt from disclosure.

6   It was clear to me from reading the FBI's MLK files that Hoover and his minions at the Bureau viewed King as a dangerous demagogue, one who threatened the very fabric of American society as they saw it. And the fact that he was hypocritical about his religious commitment and his family life served to compound this.

7   Stanley Levison was an American lawyer who was a close friend of King going back to the late 1950s and was an officer of both the American Jewish Conference and then the Southern Christian Leadership Conference with King. Most significantly, he was found by the FBI in the early 1950s to be a financial coordinator of the "CPUSA," the Communist Party of the United States, through the informant efforts of the Bureau's "Solo sources" (see Chapter Fifteen). Levison's alleged CPUSA activities were the primary (read: mostly the sole) legal basis for the FBI designating much of its files on King as classified on national security grounds.

This connection was so potent that on June 22, 1963, President John F. Kennedy personally warned King to sever all ties with Levison, whereupon King began circumventing that by communicating with Levison through an intermediary named Clarence B. Jones, one of King's attorneys, a step that ordinarily would work. This did not escape the FBI's notice, however, because it was already "tapping" Levison's phone, from which it learned of Jones. And then of course it began tapping Jones's phone. From this, the FBI learned for the first time of King's extramarital affairs, which incensed Hoover even more than even the original CPUSA connection had.

8   The very existence of COINTELPRO was a closely held secret until the program was exposed by a small radical group calling itself the "Citizens' Commission to Investigate the FBI," which used the Muhammed Ali/Joe Frazier "Fight of the Century" on March 8, 1971 as "cover" to burglarize an FBI satellite office in Media, Pennsylvania. From that office, they stole thousands of document pages on surveillance of the anti-war movement -- nearly every piece of paper that that office held, including those that mentioned COINTELPRO. I first learned about this from Collaboration on Government Secrecy Advisory Board Member Carl Stern, who covered that break-in as a young legal reporter for NBC News at the time. Carl told me of an irony in the matter: It turned out that Muhammed Ali himself was a subject of COINTELPRO surveillance due to his association with the Nation of Islam.

By the way, the perpetrators of this political crime were never apprehended, even though they mailed many of the purloined documents to newspapers around the country, leading to publication by *The Washington Post*. The FBI closed its investigation into the burglary in 1976 without ever getting even close to identifying them. Then, in 2014, more than 40 years after the fact and well beyond the expiration of the applicable statute of limitations, five of the eight members of the group stepped forward to identify themselves, including a husband-and-wife duo named John C. Raines and Bonnie Raines, with two others declining to divulge their identities. The eighth burglar, named Judi Feingold, came forward after she learned that the others had done so. More information about the group's members can be found directly by Googling the phrase "Characters of 1971." (Carl's picture is in there as well.)

9   It later was learned that Hoover made it a point to listen to every audiotape that the Bureau made of King's sexual activities. In retrospect, it is reasonably suspected that he did so for other than purely professional reasons.

10   The FBI reports on these activities were at a "granular" level of detail and even included the fact that at the Willard Hotel its listening devices were placed in lamps around the room. I recall there being no indication in these records that King ever realized (read: had even the smallest clue) that he and his paramours were being recorded. I remember sharing this with my wife at the time, telling her that the Bureau's surveillance coverage of King was so tight that he "couldn't take a leak without the Bureau being able to count the drops." (We had been married almost a year at that point and she was used to hearing such things from me.)

This latter observation, I should go on to say, serves to illustrate a common feature of secrecy, even government secrecy: People privy to secrets often tell them to their spouses or significant others. I'm not talking of classified information; government employees know better than to do that. But when it comes to secrets the disclosure of which is not prohibited by law, it is not uncommon for them to be shared within a marital bond. In my case, my wife was an attorney to whom confidentiality was part of her profession, and I shared many parts of my professional life with her, being entirely confident that they would go no farther.

11   What is stated here about King's infidelities (read: as opposed to what is *not* stated) consists of information that since the late 1970s has one way or another entered the public domain. Moreover, it is now more than 40 years since I first became privy to the details of King's infidelities and even the youngest of his three surviving children is now in her late 50s.

12   Twenty years later, the Supreme Court issued a solitary decision that did provide collateral support for the idea that FOIA nondisclosure rights are not extinguished upon death, albeit under Exemption 5. In *Swidler & Berlin v. United States*, in 1998, the Court extended attorney work-product privilege protection to client secrets in a post-mortem context on the basis of the decedent's own interest. The decedent in that case, coincidentally, was former Deputy White House Counsel Vincent M. Foster, Jr., whose death and family's "survivor privacy" interests are discussed below.

13   I do not recall being able to reach a conclusion back then as to whether the Bureau's conduct toward King was actually unlawful. At the time, there were rumors that Attorney General Robert F. Kennedy had been "blackmailed" by J. Edgar Hoover (with information, ironically enough, about his brother's relationship with paramour Judith Campbell Exner) into signing an authorization for the electronic surveillance of King. Fortunately, my opposing counsel in the case, James H. Lesar, did not make the argument (which later became quite popular with FOIA plaintiffs) that the FBI's underlying conduct was so unlawful as to negate the applicability of FOIA Exemption 7 (and thereby threaten the privacy of many individuals) for failure to meet its requirement of "law enforcement purposes."

This is not to say anything negative about Jim, who is a fine fellow as well as a consummate expert on the assassinations of both JFK and MLK. In fact, Jim had helped legendary trial attorney Percy E. Forman represent James Earl Ray at his trial. And speaking of Dr. Martin Luther King, Jr.'s putative lone assassin, I had occasion to directly communicate with James Earl Ray when he made a FOIA request of his own to the Justice Department and then brought a FOIA suit atop it -- seeking approximately 58 cubic feet of audiotapes, transcripts, logs, and other records pertaining to the FBI's surveillance of MLK during 1963-1968 -- in 1980.

Notably, his complaint in that lawsuit contained a routine assertion that he "resides at Brushy Mountain State Penitentiary in Petros, Tennessee." However, this was not long after he had escaped from that very institution and had been "on the run" with other escaped prisoners for three days. (Plus, this was the second successful jailbreak of which he was a part; Ray had previously escaped from the Missouri State Penitentiary by hiding in a prison truck used to transport bread from the prison bakery.)

So when I wrote the Department's formal "answer" to Ray's legal complaint, I responded to his assertion of where he "resides" by using the following almost entirely standard phrasing: "Deny, for lack of knowledge or information sufficient to form a belief as to the current truth of the allegation." Well, Ray must have had much time on hands at that point, because this bit of official sarcasm did not escape his notice. Indeed, he accompanied the service copy of his next court filing in the case with a side note letting me know that while he understood my response, he did not appreciate it.

14   I recall being keenly aware of the impact that disclosure of such details could have on King's family, with the emotional pain expected to arise from fresh publicity, especially as it was then still less than ten years after King's death.

15   The other King children were not much older, teenagers mostly, and all of them were minors at the time. It did not take much imagination to envision how information of such a sexual nature would be used on their school playgrounds, even if they were in private schools.

16   Furthermore, by that time, in early 1978, I was pretty much left on my own to handle my cases, due to growing turmoil in the Information and Privacy Section (see Chapter Ten) and the fact that I had the experience and skill to do so. Under ordinary circumstances, the advancement of such a novel litigation defense would have involved the participation of case reviewers up and down the supervisory chain. Once again, it was my good fortune that I could handle this novel legal issue as I saw fit.

17   An example of the latter was a copy of a card that the Bureau had sent to the King home, an ostensible "Father's Day" card from Newark, New Jersey, that was signed "Love, Chrissy." The Bureau thought it had reason to believe that King had fathered a daughter there.

18   After many hours of this process, I found that I had used the ammonia more than I had expected, as I strove to strike the exact right contour between what I withheld and what I released. This led to something else that I had not anticipated: blotter discoloration. You see, the desk that I was using dated back to the opening of the Main Justice Building in the mid-1930s, and it came with an old-fashioned desk blotter that was in fashion back then, when fountain pens were prevalent. And my such blotter was pristine, for some reason, just a stretch of billiard table-type green cloth bordered with diagonal bands of leather at each of its four corners.

So as I applied my ammonia on top of the brown ink of my El Marko pen, I found that for small restorations, just holding a swab above the lettering -- in other words, using just fumes -- would take care of it. But on the other hand, sometimes I used more ammonia than was needed and this led, I confess, to my spilling some of it or even touching it to the underlying blotter. In such cases, the ammonia immediately turned the blotter bright yellow. And spying this, and well knowing what case I was working on, some of my attorney colleagues took to calling it my "Martin Luther King Memorial Sex Life Blotter." (Yes, I was sympathetic to his family, very much so, but not so much to him.) We had another such saying, which applied to the utterances of both MLK and JFK: "The midnight masturbatory ramblings of fallen liberal leaders with feet of clay."

19   "Judge Brown" actually was Judge Gesell's secretary, Doris Brown, whom I got to know very well during my clerkship, as she was a close friend of my judge's secretary, Pat Karpen, just down the hall, and she was just tickled by the fact that so many of us referred to her as "Judge Brown." Very atypically, Judge Gesell employed only one law clerk instead of the regular two, which meant that Doris had more sway over his case management than did the secretaries of other judges.

20   Judge Gesell elaborated by saying: "There is no reason to question the bona fides of these deletions. . . . It is difficult, if not impossible, to anticipate all respects in which disclosure might damage reputations or lead to personal embarrassment and discomfort." *Lesar v. United States Dep't of Justice*, 455 F. Supp. 921, 925-26 (D.D.C. 1978). And on a more personal note, he added what every young litigator would like to hear: "The Court in this instance is impressed with the detailed nature of the affidavits submitted by both sides, the competence of Government counsel, and the apparent care with which the matter has been dealt with administratively. Thus reliance is placed on the Government's representations."

21   In most cases, a "win" at the district court level is the end of the case. But in federal court, the losing party always has the right to appeal, and in this case the plaintiff did just that. This led to the concept of survivor privacy being approved at this higher judicial level, as Judge Gesell's decision was entirely upheld. *See Lesar v. United States Dep't of Justice*, 636 F.2d 472, 487 (D.C. Cir. 1980) (recognizing survivors' privacy interests even in avoiding "annoyance or harassment").

22   This is a cardinal rule of case law development: Not going too far too fast with new fact patterns, lest a court impair a smooth line of precedential acceptance with an adverse decision based on improvident facts. One agency, the Department of Defense, "went rouge" on this when it tried to withhold murder-scene photographs of man killed twenty-five years earlier even though it was unable to demonstrate the actual existence of a surviving family member. *See Outlaw v. United States Dep't of the Army*, 815 F. Supp. 505, 506 (D.D.C. 1993). The lesson is that the use of "survivor privacy" logically requires reasonable certainty that a survivor actually exists to merit such exceptional protection.

23   *New York Times Co. v. NASA*, 782 F. Supp. 628, 631-32 (D.D.C. 1991). In this regard, the district court also adopted a viewpoint that applies to many "survivor privacy" situations -- that surviving family members have "reasonable expectations of undisturbed enjoyment in the solitude and seclusion of [their] own home[s]." This connects to the fact that some "survivor privacy" cases are by their nature so sensational that agencies (and courts) have to anticipate that disclosure will likely lead to a degree of media coverage that is itself highly intrusive on family privacy. (That certainly was very much so in the *Favish* case that is discussed immediately below.)

24   The D.C. Circuit Court of Appeals was one of these circuits, certainly, with both the King case and the *Challenger* one decided there. Then there also was the Seventh Circuit's acceptance of the concept in the *Marzen* case involving a deceased infant's medical records (see below).

25   I knew Vince only slightly, as I was in two meetings with him in what was then called the "Old Executive Office Building" adjacent to the White House. I came to know Webb Hubbell much better, as I worked directly under him in his capacity as Associate Attorney General (see Chapter Twenty-Eight).

26   Vince's secretary, Deborah Gorham, had brought him lunch from the cafeteria, as was the custom in the White House Counsel's Office. On his way out of the office, he offered another secretary the remainder of the M&Ms from his lunch tray. That second secretary was Linda R. Tripp, who most infamously later became the key confidante of White House intern Monica S. Lewinsky.

27   Vince had unexpectedly come under fire that spring for his handling of a controversy involving the White House Travel Office, which had been under investigation for alleged financial improprieties. Some staff members had been fired without proper authorization, with the alleged involvement of Catherine Cornelius, President Clinton's cousin, and in some of the media coverage Vince appeared to be the fall guy, while later investigations suggested that then-First Lady Hillary Clinton might have been the real culprit.

   Atop that, the botched nomination of Zoë E. Baird to become the Nation's first female attorney general also reportedly took a toll on Vince after two additional nominees also were forced to take their names out of contention due to similar personal controversies (see Chapter Twelve). And I also know firsthand that at least one issue raised by Hillary Clinton's healthcare task force, involving a statute named the "Federal Advisory Committee Act" ("FACA," to those who speak Yiddish), had been troubling him.

28   The initial investigation into the death was conducted by the United States Park Police because it evidently had occurred on federal parkland within its jurisdiction. The Park Police found no evidence of foul play, nor did any of the other four official investigations.

29   As so often happens under the FOIA, this reconstructed document itself came to be at issue in FOIA litigation. A case filed by *The Wall Street Journal* (read: under the name of "Dow Jones & Co.," its corporate parent), before future Supreme Court Justice Sonia M. Sotomayor (then a district court judge), raised the question of whether a photocopy of that reconstruction could be withheld from the public as exempt, which involved a balancing of public versus privacy interests. I was asked by the Associate Attorney General to consult in the case, prepared a detailed analysis of the issues and sub-issues involved, and formally concluded that a reasonable case could be made for applying Exemption 7(C) on a "survivor privacy" basis, as the Foster family strongly preferred. (The Interior Department had allowed "access" to the reconstructed note (read: viewing of it), just not that it be photocopied.) Judge Sotomayor balanced otherwise, however, and ordered the document disclosed. Years later, when she was nominated to the Supreme Court, media groups hailed that decision as a "good sign."

   By the way, some people wondered at the time how it was that Vince's note, as an internal White House document found within the Office of the White House Counsel, became subject to the FOIA in the first place. The answer is simple: It was given to federal investigators (including the Park Police of the Department of the Interior), became a part of their investigatory file, and was placed on the "FOIA hook" at that location.

30   Almost immediately, multiple conspiracy theories began to circulate about the abruptness and seeming incongruity of Vince's action, fed in no small part by the fact that he had been a law partner, close friend, and rumored paramour of the First Lady in Arkansas prior to the 1992 presidential election and had been seen by some as personally uncomfortable supporting the depth of her burgeoning White House controversies. The latter of these allegations turned out to be well grounded in fact, but there appears to be no evidence in the public domain to support the rumor contained in the former.

31   At this administrative level of this case, while advising the Park Police on how best to handle it, I came quickly to hold the opinion (and forcefully express it) that the "survivor privacy" principle should be applied. One of the images that I kept coming back to was that of Vince's then-89-year-old mother pushing a shopping cart up to the checkout line of her local grocery store only to be confronted by the image of her dead son staring out

at her from the cover of a tabloid magazine. Another was that of Vince's youngest child, then-13-year-old Brig, entering his classroom (where there was in fact a television mounted in an upper corner of the room) only to see his father's bloodstained face broadcast by Fox News.

32   Actually, there was a slight albeit inconsequential difference: The plaintiff in the *AIM* case in D.C. for some reason had sought only black-and-white photocopies of the photographs that were taken, while Favish in his California lawsuit sought what he called the "highest quality" color copies of them.

33   Allan Favish was an avowed "skeptic" of the repeated law enforcement investigations that had found Vince's death to be a suicide. He claimed that that he intended to serve an "overriding public interest" through his own further investigation of the circumstances surrounding Vince's death. One of the more outlandish conspiracy theories about that was that Hillary Clinton had had Vince killed elsewhere in Virginia in order to keep the secret of one or more of her actions and then had his body wrapped in a carpet and dumped on that parkland berm.

34   The threshold issue here was the "preclusion doctrine," a judicial principle holding that a party ought not be able to litigate the same issue twice, at least not in two cases involving the exact same "*corpus*"; this falls within the broader legal rubric of *res judicata*, which means literally that the "thing" is being presented for adjudication. Here, though, because the second person to litigate the substantive issue in the case was not exactly the same, even though the contested records were, it was a question of first impression as to whether Favish could do so, at least in the FOIA context. Given that the plaintiff in this second case had been the losing counsel in the first, the Government argued that the "privity" between Favish and his D.C. client should yield a preclusive effect, known as "collateral estoppel."

35   We had the D.C. Circuit accepting it, of course, as had the Seventh Circuit in a case involving the medical records of a deceased infant, *Marzen v. HHS*, 825 F.2d 1148, 1154 (7th Cir. 1987). But the Ninth Circuit's ruling against it was a major blow to its perpetuation. At best, it would now be a question of first impression for the Supreme Court, which could have decided that the FOIA's exact language (i.e., "personal privacy") afforded no room for survivors' protection -- thus leaving it to Congress to amend that language in order to protect such information or not.

36   This factor, probably more than any other, plays a primary role in the Supreme Court's *certiorari* decision-making. Because there are 13 circuit courts in the federal judicial system (i.e., the First through the Eleventh plus the D.C. Circuit and the more recently constituted Federal Circuit), there are times when one or more circuit courts disagrees with others on a distinct legal issue, which is the kind of issue that the Supreme Court then historically resolves. Of the 36 FOIA cases that the Supreme Court has accepted for review since the first one in 1973, most of them have involved a "circuit split." However, because under the FOIA the D.C. Circuit holds "universal venue" in FOIA cases (meaning that its decisions have widespread effects on agencies' FOIA implementation nationwide), no fewer than five appeals arising from that circuit have been accepted for review by the Supreme Court even in a conflict's absence.

37   The "we" here consisted of Assistant to the Solicitor General Patricia A. "Pattie" Millett, who now is a Circuit Judge on the Court of Appeals for the D.C. Circuit; longtime Civil Division Appellate Staff supervisor Leonard Schaitman, whose deep expertise and experience with appellate FOIA litigation by then went back more than 35 years; and myself, as the progenitor of "survivor privacy" more than 25 years prior and the "keeper of the flame" on it as a matter of sheer will and paternalism.

Pattie, by the way, left the Solicitor General's Office in 2007 to become head of the Supreme Court practice at the law firm of Akin, Gump, Strauss, Hauer, and Feld. Six years later, President Obama decided that he wanted to fill three vacancies on the D.C. Circuit, even in the face of resistance from the Senate, and he chose Pattie to be the "tip of the spear" in this effort (i.e., the first one of the three to be put forward). Unfortunately, when she was confirmed as the first of the three, which involved the invocation of "cloture" and the deployment of what was then called the "nuclear option," the final vote count in the Senate was such that her confirmation necessitated a modification of the Senate's filibuster rule (which had required 60 votes for many years), making all future appellate court appointments, including those to the Supreme Court, confirmable with only 51 votes. This "boomeranged" back around with the Supreme Court appointments of President Donald J. Trump, especially his second and third ones. (And as for his first one, see the Epilogue.)

38   The thinking underlying this is that Supreme Court Justices might view a *certiorari* petition as somewhat diffident if every effort had not been made beforehand to achieve the reversal sought. This is practically "gospel" in the SG's Office, probably because someone ran afoul of it more than a century ago. Consequently, it is the rare *certiorari* petition filed by the Solicitor General that is not preceded by such a rehearing petition being filed in the circuit court below.

39   Stated another way, there was no small amount of sentiment in the Solicitor General's Office that it would have been far better if Vince had killed himself in the privacy of his own home rather than in a public park where any passerby could have observed what the contested photographs depicted. (This school of thought did not include Pattie Millett, who made the initial "*pro-cert.*" recommendation to the SG.)

40   The Ninth Circuit was the most inhospitable of all of the circuit courts of appeals for the Government in FOIA cases; in the history of the FOIA, most of our biggest appellate losses came from there. And overall, during one documented stretch of time in the 1980s, the Ninth Circuit was reversed 26 out of 27 consecutive times in its cases that were taken up to the Supreme Court. (In fact, when OIP's deputy director Miriam Nisbet went "behind the avocado curtain" to argue an appeal there in 1991 -- one involving FBI investigatory records on John Lennon -- she came back saying that the Ninth Circuit was "a very dark place, indeed.")

41   This "Tenth Justice" idea is something taken quite seriously. And it is a big part of the explanation of why the ordinary success rate for certiorari petitions is about 5% while the Solicitor General's is more than 70%. And as for FOIA cases that reached the Supreme Court on the Solicitor General's petition, almost all were decided in the Government's favor. (Over the course of my Justice Department career and then beyond that, I had a hand in 21 of them, including two that reached the Court but then "washed out" on procedural grounds once there.)

42   The Solicitor General at the time was Theodore B. "Ted" Olson, a highly respected man (as SGs tend to be), who more than 20 years earlier had been the Assistant Attorney General for the Office of Legal Counsel and whose wife Barbara perished on the plane that hit the Pentagon on September 11, 2001. We hoped that he therefore was inclined to be sympathetic to the plight of a grieving family in the wake of a sudden, unexpected death.

43   Once again, this view was not held by everyone in the SG's Office in connection with this case. The person there who advocated most strongly for *cert.* authorization was Supreme Court advocate Pattie Millett, who went on to prepare all of the government's briefs (including the *certiorari* petition and the reply) and present oral argument in the case. In time, Pattie would hold the record for most Supreme Court arguments made by a woman.

44   Sheila Foster Anthony was Vince's older sister, who also came to Washington with the Clinton Administration in 1993. (She, Vince, and Clinton White House chief of staff Thomas "Mac" McLarty all grew up together with Bill

Clinton in Hope, Arkansas.) For two years, 1993-1995, she served as the Assistant Attorney General for Legislative Affairs under Attorney General Janet Reno and then she became a Member of the Federal Trade Commission, a position that she held for several years. Sheila Foster was married to former Arkansas Congressman Beryl F. Anthony, who also reportedly spoke with Vince about his depression shortly before he died. Sheila Anthony said in a public statement that: "Vince called me at my office in the Justice Department a few days before he died. He told me he was battling depression and knew he needed help. But he was worried that such an admission would adversely affect his top-level security clearance and prevent him from doing his job." For the record, the security-clearance form that so worried Vince, which is known within the Federal Government as the "SF-86," was modified in the wake of his death. (And of course I had a hand in that.)

45   This *cert*. decision was well supported by Senior Deputy Solicitor General Edwin S. Kneedler, who at that time was probably the smartest person in the building and whose approval was critical.

46   Something not widely known about *certiorari* petitions is that they do not focus heavily on the substantive merits of a case, i.e., the legal reasons why the court of appeals below was wrong and should be reversed. Rather, they primarily discuss the procedural issue of why the Supreme Court should agree to review the decision below at all (e.g., conflict in the circuits, importance of the issue, consequences of *cert*. denial, etc.) at that particular time.

47   It was no surprise when the media firmly reported that Pattie was under active White House consideration for elevation to the Supreme Court when Justice Antonin G. Scalia died suddenly in early 2016. That appointment, of course, eventually went to D.C. Circuit Court Judge Merrick B. Garland, who received no Senate consideration. But it can easily be conjectured that if instead Justice Ruth Bader Ginsburg had left the Court at that time, through death or resignation, Pattie would have been at least a front-runner to have replaced her. And even now, seven years later at age 59, she remains a viable candidate for the next opening or two.

48   I emphasize this not just in praise of Pattie, something on which I take a back seat to no one, but to contrast her with the typical advocate in the SG's Office, although almost all of them are of absolutely stellar caliber by definition. I worked closely with more than a dozen of them over the years, from 1978 to 2007 (and *sub silentio* beyond), and I can easily say that even the very best of them (i.e., Ken Geller, the late Larry Wallace, Ed Kneedler, Bill Bryson, and Malcolm Stewart, deputy SGs one and all) did not surpass Pattie when it came to closely collaborating with others.

Another note connected to Pattie, or about female judges in general: As of the summer of 1976 when I began my judicial clerkship, believe it or not there were only six female federal district court or court of appeals judges in the entire country, one of whom worked just down the hall: Senior Judge Burnita Shelton Mathews. One was two floors down, Judge June L. Green, before whom I would soon appear as a government litigator; one swore in LBJ, Senior Judge Sarah T. Hughes of Dallas; one would go on to a cabinet position under President Jimmy Carter, Shirley A. Hufstedler of the Ninth Circuit; plus Cornelia G. Kennedy of the Sixth Circuit; and the other was on the Bench of the Southern District of New York, Constance Baker Motley. Once the Carter Administration began the following January, that number would double and then triple mighty fast. But the first female Supreme Court Justice, Sandra Day O'Connor, was still almost five years away.

49   Pattie also made much of the "last words" audiotape in the *Challenger* case that had been decided in the D.C. Circuit. There was a certain kinship between a family member of a doomed astronaut hearing a loved one's last words and a Foster family member unwittingly viewing his or her loved one's face in death. When you get to the Supreme Court in a case, you point such things out for "maximum effect on the Justices," Pattie used to say.

50 Something else not widely known is how tight the dimensions are in the Supreme Court's courtroom, especially at the front of it where the Justices and counsel sit in surprisingly close proximity. The counsel tables are very near the Bench of the Court, with the lectern even closer, so advocates feel that the Justices are nearly "on top" of them. And immediately behind that is the first row of seating, which is reserved for members of the Supreme Court Bar. I've been a member of the Supreme Court Bar since 1979 (from back when the membership fee was only $50) and have attended many arguments, including with my law students in later years. And although in the scheme of things I never would have the opportunity to stand at that lectern to present an oral argument, I was able to do so once when moving the admission of one of my deputies in the 1980s.

51 There were some secondary issues in the case as well. First, there was the latent procedural issue of Favish's ability to bring this second suit for the photographs in California given that the exact same issue already had been adjudicated in D.C. The Government had grudgingly allowed that a second person or institution could do that sort of thing under the FOIA, as a general rule, but it had argued that because that second person in this case had been the losing counsel in the first, the "privity" between Favish and his client should yield a preclusive effect, known as "collateral estoppel."

The Supreme Court did not address this as an issue before it, however. Rather, it briefly undertook a factual recounting of the lower court's ruling on the issue and simply let it go at that. Indeed, Justice Kennedy's opinion for the Court simply noted that "the District Court held that the decision of the Court of Appeals for the District of Columbia did not have [a] collateral estoppel effect on Favish's California lawsuit brought in his personal capacity." So, with this not being a holding by the Court, the issue remains an open question.

On the other hand, the Court did address the related argument made by Favish on the "public interest" side of the balance, especially his blithe argument that his personal "skepticism" and "informed speculation" about the correctness of the five government investigations of Vince's death was sufficient to make a difference here. To that, Justice Kennedy said that "the requester must produce evidence that would warrant a belief by a reasonable person that the alleged Government impropriety might have occurred." In other words, he stated, "the requester must establish more than a bare suspicion in order to obtain disclosure."

Twelve years later, in what was not the least bit an uncharacteristic move, presidential candidate Donald J. Trump clambered onto Favish's "conspiracy" bandwagon, as part of his broader "anti-government" campaign, to declare that the Foster suicide was "very fishy" and to proclaim the Foster-related conspiracy theories to be "very serious." In effect, Justice Kennedy's opinion in Favish anticipated such a thing by presciently observing in Favish that: "Allegations of government misconduct are 'easy to allege and hard to disprove.'"

52 This phrasing of the Court's holding, specifically its use of the word "close," brings up a "side-issue" of survivor privacy that I had been grappling with as a matter of policy for many years. In OIP's training programs, sometimes a FOIA officer would ask me to tell him or her exactly who could reasonably be covered by the "survivor privacy" concept as a matter of policy, even if not as established in existing case law. I would tell them that certainly spouses (or their equivalent), children, mothers, fathers, grandparents, and grandchildren could be covered, and probably even aunts, uncles, and cousins as well, if the family bond were strong enough in a particular case. And then I would tell them that in fact I included even very close associates of Martin Luther King in that first case, although you can scarcely discern that from the courts' opinions.

I have little doubt but that someday there will come a case that tests the outer edges of the concept's coverage, probably one involving no surviving family but a friend or associate who would very much grieve the subject's death just as a family member would. At the other end of the spectrum, we once had a case involving a sexually transmitted disease medical report on a decedent that we decided to withhold in order to protect the privacy interests of a living paramour directly; in other words, we regarded such information as pertaining to her as well as to the decedent, given the unique nature of it.

53   Writing for the full Court, Justice Kennedy elaborated on this point, saying that Exemption 7(C) "requires us to protect, in the proper degree, the personal privacy of citizens against the uncontrolled release of information compiled through the power of the state."

54   He also cited the *Marzen* case involving the exceptionally sensitive medical records of a deceased infant. That Seventh Circuit decision, by the way, was decided under Exemption 6 of the FOIA, not Exemption 7(C), because it involved medical records, not anything to do with law enforcement. This was a reminder that the "survivor privacy" principle operates just the same under both of the FOIA's two privacy exemptions.

55   This did not mean, of course, that a survivor must formally object and intervene in the matter as the Foster family understandably went so far as to do in this case. As to that, Justice Kennedy noted that the Foster family even took the further exceptional step of submitting a "sworn declaration . . . oppos[ing] the disclosure of the disputed photos."

56   As is described above, this was nearly the basis for the case not reaching the Supreme Court at all, as there was considerable concern in the Office of the Solicitor General that this "public" element of the case too heavily compromised its fact pattern.

57   Notably, Justice Kennedy explicitly agreed that, as Pattie had argued, it was only proper in a case such as this for the Court to consider its facts "in light of the consequences that would follow were [it] to adopt Favish's position."

58   Thus did Pattie's "hook" have a big impact on the Court. Beginning a few years later, from 2008 to 2017, she would serve as a "guest lecturer" (even after she joined the D.C. Circuit) in my "Secrecy Controversies" seminar at American University's Washington College of Law, where I taught law for ten years upon retiring from the Justice Department. Keying in on the appellate advocacy part of this seminar, Pattie would give a 90-minute presentation (off the top of her head) on "the art of oral advocacy," in which she would always use the *Favish* case and this gruesome prison-cell example in particular -- whereupon she and I would routinely "battle" over who most deserved the credit for it. I can report that invariably I won this argument, because she definitely did.

59   As to the media, the Court recognized the Foster family's well-grounded fears of "intense scrutiny by the media." And pointing out that Vince's family members were invoking their own "right and interest to personal privacy," it also spoke of "the right of family members to direct and control disposition of the body of the deceased."

60   The Supreme Court's decision is styled *National Archives & Records Administration v. Favish*, 541 U.S. 157 (2004). Because the respondent Office of the Independent Counsel terminated its operations seven days before the decision was issued and transferred all of its records -- including the photographs that were at issue in the lawsuit -- to the National Archives and Records Administration, the Court substituted NARA as the primary petitioning party.

CHAPTER FOUR

1   All told, when viewed as individual presidential terms, I worked during eleven presidential administrations -- from Richard Nixon's first term to George W. Bush's last -- and under more than a dozen different attorneys

general, one of whom, Alberto Gonzales, was quite different indeed. Crudely put, I later got to depose him (see Chapter Forty-Three), though sadly not in a South American junta sense.

2   Admittedly, being born the first of five in a borderline-poor Catholic family placed me in a position of responsibility early on. As did the fact that my next-oldest siblings were more than five and six years younger than me, respectively, which meant that looking out for "the kids," as my parents and I spoke of them, was a role that fell naturally to me. This is what led to my managing their participation in Little League baseball (which was "big time" for kids on Long Island back then, much like youth soccer is today) from the time that they were nine and ten. And as for my next sibling, a sister who was born more than 12 years after me, I actually became her formal "Godfather," a role in the Catholic Church that ordinarily is held by adults, not pre-teenagers. By the time my youngest brother was born, while I was in college, I had taken on much responsibility within my family and had established a pattern of financial and other support that continued well into adulthood and on to this day.

Most recently, for example, I took my youngest brother to the U.K. with me, where we visited "the ancestral home of the Metcalfe clan," which is a castle built in the Yorkshire Dales centuries ago by a Metcalfe who was a hero of the Battle of Agincourt in 1415. (I previously had visited the last Metcalfe in the line of succession to own it and had obtained permission for my siblings to explore it together with me.) So first my brother John and I did so and then I brought my sister Mary over there to do so as well. Money is tight for both of them (always has been), so I cover things such as that.

3   As high school jobs went, I lucked out by working in the kitchen of a brand-new building, a retirement home that opened in early 1968. I was able to progress from sweeping the floors and running a state-of-the-art dishwashing machine to basic food-preparation tasks during what became my 3½-year tenure there. And after discerning that the non-clergy manager of that place was developing a Mafia-style skimming operation to defraud the nuns on a large scale, I was able to silently "blackmail" my boss, who realized that I alone among the kitchen staff had figured it all out and who was willing to nearly double my meager teenage salary "off the books" as a result. Nary a word was spoken between us about this at the time; there did not have to be. And as for the risk that I ran in being arguably complicit in this food-pricing scheme (misprision of a felony being the crime that it is), let's just say that I'm glad that the statute of limitations on that has long expired. I assume that such corruption is still rife in much of the food industry on Long Island today, even in places where the Mafia does not thrive.

In 2018, the Sisters of St. Joseph celebrated the 50th anniversary of the opening of that convent building and we determined that I was the only living survivor of that day. All of the nuns from back then, even the relatively few "young" ones, were deceased and the only other possible survivor was another student worker of my age who I knew had become a police officer in Kansas City as he'd always hoped but later took his own life with his service revolver. I was unable to attend the celebration due to a family obligation, so the sisters kindly shipped a parcel of remembrance items to me. In return, I considered informing them about their having been defrauded back them, but decided that no good could come of it now.

4   Speaking of resourcefulness, there also was the fact that the Brentwood School District repeatedly saw its resources strained beyond the breaking point during my school years there. That explosive growth of housing and families that had peaked during the mid-1960s yielded such things as "split sessions," "austerity" school budgets, and huge class sizes throughout that decade. The size of my high school graduating class of 1969 stood at well more than 1000 during most of its years, dipping just below that due to last-minute dropouts near the end of our senior year.

For those of us at the top of that class, the school left us largely to fend for ourselves, on the premise that we would be able to gain admission to at least some college somewhere if we could possibly afford it. Suffice to say that I'm sure that no one in my high school class even considered the possibility of applying to an Ivy League-level university, nor were the school's overburdened guidance counselors equipped to steer us toward any financial aid sources (for whatever existed back then) that might fund such an education even if we knew enough to pursue it.

5   Years later, I would realize that the seven B's that I received during that freshman year happened to equal the total number of B's that were received by my two children over the course of eight years of high school, eight years of college, and a combined total of six years of graduate school. Arguably, they made better use of this than did I.

6   I had concluded by then, even without a single role model in sight, that I was just born to become an attorney somehow, if that were at all possible. The way I put it is that even had I lived a century or two earlier, in poverty from the start, I would have felt driven to make every effort to practice law, rather than do anything else with my life. There are those who gravitate toward the practice of law casually, sometimes due to family background, a desire for riches, or by process of elimination with other careers. With me, it was a combination of analytical skill, writing and speaking ability, and a keen sense of right and wrong that made being an attorney inevitable. And within the legal field, government service is what compelled me most strongly.

CHAPTER FIVE

1   This hotel was the historic Dodge Hotel, located at the southwest corner of North Capitol and E Streets, N.W., which had been built 50 years earlier as one of the closest hotels to Capitol Hill. (The way D.C. is configured, the Capitol is dead center within its four quadrants, but nearby only the northwest one is heavily developed commercially.) We did our laundry in its dank basement, next to a line of open shower stalls that we soon learned carried a history of their own. As it happened (believe it not), some of the hotel's original staff were still there in 1971, African-American men of a certain age who regaled us with stories of how Lyndon Johnson got his political start on that very spot.

It seems, they said, that back in the early 1930s there was a political organization known as the "Little Congress," consisting of congressional staffers (all men, of course), the leadership to which future President Johnson strongly aspired. And because the vast majority of the voting membership of this group lived at that hotel, including Johnson, he is said to have done most of his electioneering for that position there. And much of that, we were told, was done by Johnson in that basement shower area; he was known to have "hung out" there, even to the point of sometimes taking several showers a day. To paraphrase Teddy Roosevelt in a rough way, Johnson might have spoken softly, but he evidently carried a big, er, stick.

2   A major feature of the Washington Semester Program was its affiliation with former White House Press Secretary George E. Reedy, a venerable Washington figure who had famously left that position due to his personal disagreements with President Lyndon B. Johnson over the escalation of the Vietnam War. George (as he asked us to call him) was known as a "war horse" of Washington journalism and politics who related many a "war story" to his wide-eyed students during his evening seminars. He went on to become dean of the journalism school at Marquette University and also wrote the seminal book *The Twilight of the Presidency*.

3   It is said that the true mark of a Washington intern is that he or she will almost immediately upon arrival start throwing around Capitol denizen terms such as "the Hill," enrolled bill, pocket veto, conference committee, constituent, cloakroom, filibuster, cloture, supermajority, quorum, mark-up, and even Ramseyer (a particular

document format in which all language changes are clearly shown), as well as precious Latin words and phrases such as *ultra vires, amicus curiae, inter alia,* adjournment *sine die, certiorari, stare decisis, verbatim, de facto,* and *pro forma* session. We were no different.

4   Two years later, though, I was proud to learn that the Justice Department finally was establishing a personnel category for academic interns, one modeled on what the proposal paperwork referred to as "the Metcalfe internship." Again, implausible but true.

5   I can still remember, more than fifty years later, walking the halls of all three House Office Buildings (Rayburn, Longworth, and Cannon, from west to east) and both of the Senate Office Buildings (Russell and Dirksen, because the Hart Office Building was not yet constructed), just to soak up the atmosphere there. From either side of "the Hill," one could take the congressional subway from both of the Senate Office Buildings and the Rayburn House Office Building to the Capitol Building and back, except during quorum calls or votes.

And in the Capitol Building itself, not only could one visit all of the "public" spaces designated as such, one could also venture without challenge elsewhere as well, so long as you were discrete and looked like you belonged there. (There were so many young staffers coming and going that it was not hard to fit in.) I remember slowly wandering through a sub-basement that was chock full of excess furniture soon after I arrived in town. (Today, the Capitol Building basement is "built out," with secondary offices there for all Members of the Senate.) It all was inspiring to me, as someone who had come to see and experience our national government.

6   Actually, back then the White House was not nearly as far beyond reach as it is today. Yes, there was a fence entirely around it, so there were no farm animals grazing on the North Lawn as in its early days, but in 1971 West Executive Avenue as well as East Executive Avenue were both wide open to pedestrians and the latter to vehicular traffic. The latter remains open to monitored pedestrian traffic still, having been closed to public vehicular traffic in the mid-1980s, but the complete public closure of West Executive Avenue in the mid-1980s allowed it to be used as a "primo" parking lot by Executive Office of the President employees as of 2017.

And the roadway south of the White House, a curved stretch of E Street between the South Lawn and the Ellipse, was open to vehicular traffic. In fact, I used to commute on it four times a week, with Fridays reserved for commuting by bicycle along G Street instead. That stretch of E Street was closed, unfortunately, due to security restrictions imposed in the wake of the Oklahoma City Bombing in 1995. Then it was opened up again, not long before 9/11, and it has been closed ever since. The White House's north side, which is bordered by a "due east-west" stretch of Pennsylvania Avenue between it and Lafayette Park, was also closed to vehicular (but not pedestrian or bicycle) traffic in May of 1995 and it has never reopened.

7   In fact, after I returned to Stony Brook to finish my college years and apply to law schools, I was very pleased to learn that my high-level supervisor at LEAA had taken it upon himself to write a letter to my pre-law advisor about my work, saying that I had quickly become "an integral and invaluable part of the [staff]," working as "a full member of [it] on an equal basis with lawyers, mathematicians, and social scientists." This was sent to the Washington, D.C. law schools to which I applied and played no small part in my receiving the scholarship that was granted to me by GW Law upon admission. (I include such detail because this internship experience at LEAA, even at the tender age of nineteen, played such a pivotal role in launching my career.)

8   In truth, I was able to very quickly develop a reputation for this among the staff, who soon began asking me to just "look over" something that they had written, often in haste, whereupon I was all too glad to oblige -- and to improve a draft more than could be expected. This alone made me quite popular there, with many a satisfied "client." One of them even joked that I could spot a period that had been mistakenly italicized, which

was somewhat odd in that we did not yet have word processors at the time. (Actually, such a thing can be done; it just requires use of the right font.)

9 That was one of my major lessons from my internship at Justice: If you work notoriously hard and well for senior colleagues in a professional setting, more often than not they will notice it, appreciate it, and be inclined to reward it, one way or the other, within the bounds of their power to do so. I recall making much of this point in one of the two major papers that I had to prepare for full academic credit on my internship experience.

10 Not that it was imaginable at the time, but this presaged how I would spend my 30th birthday ten years later, preparing to give a presentation on a Saturday (i.e., the next day) to a group of newly appointed United States Attorneys on the FOIA and especially the Privacy Act of 1974, because the latter, I told them, was a statute that could sneak up behind them and "bite them on the ass." Years later, I would begin to recognize the names of some of those in my audience that day, such as now-Senator Lindsey O. Graham, former Senator Jefferson B. Sessions III, former Governor Francis A. Keating II, and Senior Circuit Court Judge Stephen S. Trott. For the record, I think my 40th birthday fell in the middle of a week, not a Saturday, but I probably worked both Saturdays around it.

CHAPTER SIX

1 Although I'll admit that by that point I was taking courses largely according to which ones best fit my full-time work schedule, there was one course in particular that completely engaged my interest -- an anthropology course taught by a young protégé of famous anthropologist Laura Nader (Ralph Nader's older sister). For it, I did a "field study" of judicial dispute resolution by observing many days of proceedings in the local small claims court near where I lived. After a while, the presiding judge of that court noticed my presence and very kindly invited me into his chambers for some invaluable lessons on the processes of adjudication. Sadly, I was able to repay that favor only through a letter published in *Newsday* describing his kindness after he died in a freak accident (during a thunderstorm, his car was hit by a falling tree) soon thereafter.

2 The "draft lottery," as it was called, was a nationwide process used by the Selective Service System initially in 1969 and again in 1970 to determine the draft status of all American males born between 1944 and 1949 and then between 1950 and 1956, for purposes of annual military drafts conducted between 1970 and 1973. (Any number above approximately 190 was generally considered "safe," which meant that my draft number, number 98, was far from it.) This replaced the purely age-based military conscription system (which took "oldest men first," in the 18-25 age range) that until then had supplied U.S. soldiers for the Vietnam War. The draft itself actually ended after June 1973, the very month in which I became eligible for it.

3 Although I took this job primarily for the money ($200 per week was big money for a college student back then), it also afforded me considerable legal experience before I even began to attend law school. Having worked in a high-level setting at the Justice Department, even without much legal experience *per se*, I was able to function as an effective law clerk for this mid-size law firm with a busy litigation practice.

4 I never completely understood exactly how the school's Trustee Scholarship administrators managed to secure so lucrative a financial aid package for me, but as I all too often have been heard to say, "I'm glad that the statute of limitations must have run out on that by now."

5 The way that GW's National Law Center conducted its admission process back then (I later learned, when I "ran" registration for the school), as well as its financial aid decisionmaking, was to take an applicant's under-

graduate grade-point average, multiply it by a coefficient correlating to the "difficulty" of that school, add it to the applicant's LSAT score and then also to some less objective factor (such as impression made in an interview), and feed it all into an algorithm that predicted what the applicant's grade-point average would be through the first law school year. I was told later on that this system had predicted my second-in-the-class standing almost exactly. (For this system to be even more accurate, however, it would have had to have had some way of factoring in the fact that I spent almost the entirety of that first year working nearly full-time.)

6   Back then, a "draftee" was inducted for a standard two-year hitch, with virtually no say as to exactly where and how those two years would be served. But an "enlisted man," especially one who had college under his belt, could pretty much "write his own ticket" (as it was called) as to branch of service (except the Marines), "military specialty," and perhaps even location of service, at least at the outset. The "kicker," of course, was that enlistment involved three years of service, not just two. So it was a clear tradeoff for many young men, particularly those who had finished college: Be drafted for two years or enlist for three. In my case, even though I had law school admission, a very generous scholarship, and a fiancée waiting at home, the choice was clear: I made preliminary arrangements, as far back as in late 1972, to enlist in the Army if and when it came to that.

7   Coincidently, my father had had similar "close calls" with being drafted during the Korean War two decades earlier. In the spring of 1950, as that war geared up, he received his draft notice (at age 20) at a time when the military was not yet drafting married men. However, he was able to avoid induction at that point because he and my mother had already planned their marriage for later in that year; fortunately for them (and for me, I suppose), they could produce for his draft board a sworn attestation from their local parish priest to the effect that they had in fact previously scheduled their wedding by reserving the church for a specific date. (Apparently, that's how good Catholics did it back then, especially because they weren't "doing it" in any other way.)

The next year, though, with the Korean War greatly heating up, brought a tightening of this standard, such that only married men with at least one child were being excused. And once again, my father was able to provide documentation to his draft board showing that he in fact now met that higher standard -- which is why, to this day, I have an original photostatic copy of my birth certificate that was officiously stamped "Selective Service System, 35-20 Broadway, Long Island City, New York" on its obverse side.

I suppose it was my awareness of coming from a long line of draft dodgers (sort of) that animated my early devotion to public service in general and my commitment to serve the country through Continuity-of-Government leadership (see Chapter Twenty-Six) in the event of a World War III in particular, later on. In sum, rightly or wrongly, I do feel that I have repaid both my and my father's "debt to society" in this regard, even recognizing that several of my father's high school buddies were drafted and then never made it back home.

8   Richardson was (and still is) the only person to hold four cabinet-secretary positions in the Federal Government: secretary of health, education, and welfare; secretary of defense; attorney general; and secretary of commerce. (He also served as U.S. Ambassador to the Court of St. James (read: England) after resigning as attorney general.) A close second is former secretary of state, secretary of the treasury, secretary of labor, and OMB director (a cabinet-level position at the time) George P. Shultz, who despite all that lived to be 100.

9   The first of these was former Attorney General John N. Mitchell, who was sentenced to a lengthy prison term for his part in the "Watergate" scandal. Decades later, when speaking of one of his successors, former Attorney General Alberto R. Gonzales, I invoked AG Mitchell's memory by observing in 2007 that Gonzales was the only former attorney general who was unable to get a job after leaving that position because even Mitchell quickly caught on in the prison laundry.

10   Skipping ahead, I will note here that this was another "life lesson" that I passed on to my students during my subsequent decade as a law professor: Wherever possible in your early years, try to stay in at least casual touch with professional colleagues (and even key professional acquaintances) from your past, because you never know when the slightest shift in circumstances will lead to that connection redounding to your benefit. Many people do this (and perhaps some overdo it) under the general rubric of "networking" and it can be invaluable.

CHAPTER SEVEN

1   A word about that. In those days (if not also today), there was an American Bar Association standard to which all major law schools adhered: No first-year (and full-time) law student, no matter how strapped for cash, should carry more than 20 hours per week of employment. Right. Let's just say that I hope the statute of limitations has run on that by now also, because in that regard my second Justice Department tour of duty was about as kosher as my first.

2   By the words "work on" here, I do not mean to overstate my role. As the most junior member of the professional staff by far, I was asked to do nothing more than proofread this high-level document, as my reputation for doing that very well had preceded me. (It has always amazed me how so many highly educated, very successful attorneys struggle when it comes to proofreading their own work -- or the work of others, for that matter.) As I recall, I did a little more than that, by cross-checking section references and the like, enough that I felt invested in the enterprise and commensurately disappointed when Attorney General Richardson was repeatedly diverted from it once I was done.

3   The way in which the Justice Department is now structured, it is divided into two major parts: The deputy attorney general oversees the Department's criminal and law enforcement components, such as the FBI and the Criminal Division, while the associate attorney general similarly oversees the Department's dozen or so civil ones, such as the Office of Justice Programs (formerly LEAA) and the Civil Division. This focused "span of control" was not possible until the position of associate attorney general was created (see Chapter Ten)..

4   Vice President Agnew was a flat-out crook, we came to realize, and this ironically had nothing whatsoever to do with the intensifying "Watergate" scandal at the time. He was a crook when he started accepting payoffs for the awarding of government construction contracts while still the county executive in Baltimore, he was a crook when he continued taking such bribes as Governor of Maryland, and he became a threat to national security once he actually continued doing that from the White House upon becoming Nixon's vice president.

In time, we all came to learn that Attorney General Richardson and U.S. Attorney for the District of Maryland George Beall VIII had together been engaging in some delicate "Chinese formal dancing," for several weeks, in order to negotiate Agnew's plea (to only one felony charge) and resignation within a time frame that did not interfere (as had been feared) with the ongoing "Watergate" investigation of President Nixon. (Agnew had actually beseeched Speaker of the House Carl B. Albert to have the House impeach him -- yes, an impeachment beseechment -- on the belief that such a step would as a practical matter preclude his being indicted.) The next year, without delay, the Maryland Court of Appeals disbarred Agnew, describing him as "morally obtuse."

5   That first associate attorney general was Michael J. Egan, a close associate of Attorney General Griffin B. Bell, who was appointed by President Jimmy Carter in 1977. My most vivid memory of him was at a Justice Department holiday party near the end of that year when I was introduced to him with the utterance, "Look, *here's* a white male; who says we don't hire white males up here?" Those words were spoken by a semi-drunk though otherwise fully incompetent section chief who was defensive about the fact that of the eight young

attorneys she had hired into her section in recent months, four were female, two were African-American males, one was an Hispanic male, and then there was me.

6   Twenty years later to the day, i.e., on Wednesday, October 20, 1993, I sent an email to Justice Department Public Affairs Director Carl Stern asking: "Hey, Carl, do you remember where you were exactly 20 years ago tonight?" "You bet I do," he replied. "I was standing on the edge of the North Lawn worrying that we had a constitutional crisis on our hands. And Dan Rather was breathing even harder than I was." Rather, of course, was reporting the event for CBS News while Carl was doing so for NBC News.

7   A little-remembered fact is that between 1971 and 1977, Congress changed the observance of Veterans Day from November 11 to the fourth Monday of October. So Monday, October 22, 1973 was a federal holiday, which allowed a bit more "breathing room" after the events of Saturday night.

8   There was much speculation after the "massacre" that had Bork followed the lead of Richardson and Ruckelshaus in not firing Cox, then perhaps no one else down the line of succession in the Department would have done so, either. This thought usually was expressed with the responsibility ultimately falling upon a janitor in the building's basement, but some of my relatives opined that my own junior status could serve for this bit of frivolity just as well.

9   Yes, I distinctly remember hoisting gray mailbags from the floor to the AG's conference table at the time, just as I remember such mailbags accumulating near my office's front door in the wake of the "Anthrax scare" 28 years later (see Chapter Thirteen). And I recall the secretarial staff in the Attorney General's Office being quite agitated. After all, most of them had gone through abrupt transitions from one attorney general to another (read: Mitchell to Kleindienst and then to Attorney General Richardson) just months before, and now they faced the prospect of another attorney general, not to mention an interim period of unknown length working for Acting Attorney General Bork, who didn't exactly have a reputation for kind supervision. As a rule, such Department employees (all women, "to a man") were highly graded, exceptionally skilled administrative and clerical ones who had "career" status. But that did not mean that any of them could not be shipped somewhere else at a moment's notice, regardless of how solid her working relationship might have been with the attorney general who had just walked out the door. I came to feel their pain, as a future president would say many years later; when you're an even lower-ranking 21-year-old as I was, you can easily become attuned to the "ground floor" of political upheaval.

10   I unabashedly claimed at the time to have formed the best study group in the class, but only because our collective grades bore that out after each of the first two semesters. We went our separate ways after that and I dropped down to third in the class thereafter.

11   At the time, then-Senator Saxbe was widely applauded for having had the courage to say such a thing. (One might contrast this with the utter lack of such courage displayed by so many Republican senators during the presidency of Donald J. Trump.) I admired Senator Saxbe for his remark, which made it unfortunate when, more than 30 years later, I was contacted by his granddaughter, Darby Saxbe, who told me in no uncertain terms that she did not "appreciate" how I had "spoke[n] of" her grandfather in a published interview (given to *Legal Times* in 2007) on the subject of the "post-Watergate" Justice Department. So I went back and reread that interview and for the life of me could not see how what I had said could anger even the most loving of granddaughters, though it obviously had. I considered that Ms. Saxbe was a relatively young Ph.D. student at the time, in the field of clinical psychology, no less, so I contacted her to offer her a gracious apology, which is what she so obviously

needed, even though I knew not exactly what for. I figured that any granddaughter of a man who could make that trenchant "bordello" remark during the height of "Watergate" deserved no less.

12   By a wide margin, the largest funeral that I have ever attended was Elliot Richardson's, in January of 2000. It was held at Washington National Cathedral, where he was remembered as "a symbol of public virtue for a society on the edge of cynicism." Then-Attorney General Janet Reno was also among the more than 1000 people there.

13   Senator Saxbe's confirmation was delayed a bit by something that I had never heard of back then -- something that was called the "Ineligibility Clause" of the Constitution (sometimes mistakenly referred to as the Constitution's "Emoluments Clause," which is not the same). That constitutional provision prohibited presidential appointments from being given to Members of the House or the Senate if their salary and benefits (known very formally as their "emoluments of office") had been increased during the congressional term for which that current or former Member of Congress was elected. (Inflation was so high at that time that this definitely did apply to Senator Saxbe.)

But this is something that with a little time and effort could be circumvented. Indeed, the modern work-around for it, which was to become known as the "Saxbe fix," involved setting the appointee's executive branch salary and benefits at the same level as had existed for that person as of the outset of his or her most recent congressional term. This delay, which extended over the holiday season at the end of 1973 and into 1974, as I recall, figured into the departure plans of some of AG Richardson's direct appointees.

14   This office was going to be the Office of Information Law and Policy, which was soon to originate within the Department's Office of Legal Counsel, where it engaged solely in matters of governmentwide FOIA policy and, after becoming an independent part of the Office of the Deputy Attorney General in 1978, became one of the Office of Information and Privacy's two predecessor offices in 1981 (see Chapter Twenty).

And the attorney who was recruited for that (my "next-door neighbor," so to speak), was a very capable fellow named Jerry Clark, who could not bring himself to go ahead with it without a firm commitment of independence from Attorney General Saxbe himself. A while back, Jerry and I ran into one another at the holiday party of a public-interest group, where we reminisced about "old times," including the ironic fact that I succeeded him, in effect. As it turned out, I learned, Jerry had received a commitment of "total independence" in his handling of FOIA matters but Saxbe had almost immediately reneged on that in light of the anticipated legislative process for FOIA amendments (which meant assuming that Nixon would either be impeached and convicted or resign). Jerry went on to become a highly effective community activist in local D.C. politics instead.

CHAPTER EIGHT

1   The Hatch Act of 1939 is a law well known within the Federal Government because it prohibits career federal employees from engaging in many forms of political campaign activity. Because of it, I had to make sure that my Justice Department tenure and my formal work for Tom did not overlap.

2   Tom wanted to come down to Washington to familiarize himself with national issues before announcing his candidacy and thereby drawing the scrutiny of the media (which we then called the "press"). So I set him up in a relatively low-cost hotel near my law school on 20th Street, N.W., boarded his soon-to-be campaign manager in my small apartment a block away on 19th Street, and told him what I'd planned for him.

Just learning the layout of D.C. was an education for Tom. I can still recall standing with him on the corner of 18th and G Streets as we watched the demolition of the ancient YMCA building there, just a block or so from the White House grounds, and I explained that the "ghost of Walter Jenkins" was said to walk that old building's halls. (Walter W. Jenkins was a longtime aide to President Lyndon Baines Johnson who was arrested for "disorderly conduct" in one of that YMCA's bathrooms just a month before the 1964 presidential election. Once the *Washington Star* newspaper found out about it and published the story, Jenkins was forced to resign from his high-level White House position, to President Johnson's deep dismay. Then Johnson's opponent, Senator Barry M. Goldwater, harshly used that in his campaign, with the slogan "ALL THE WAY WITH LBJ, BUT DON'T GO NEAR THE YMCA.") Needless to say, there was far less tolerance of homosexuality (if "tolerance" is even the correct word) then than there is today.

3   Coincidentally, I had met a future lobbying partner of future Senator Breaux's a year earlier when representing Stony Brook at an academic conference conducted by the Center for the Study of the Presidency in French Lick, Indiana. He was a freshman Member of Congress, having been elected just months before, and I remember him as having been a Democrat. He was quite friendly to student attendees such as myself, and his name was Chester T. "Trent" Lott. (He was only 31 at the time, ten years older than myself, and the "Sr." at the end of his name came later.)

4   It is redolent of irony, of course, that this recollection comes at a time when President Biden's age is yet again an issue -- only this time, at "the other end," it could be said, of the time continuum. At age 79 (exactly nine years to the day older than I), he is now poised to hold the presidency from ages 78 to 82 (if not longer). Just imagine if Tom and I had forecast such a future for him when we met with him in 1974.

5   I even set up my own version of a Washington-style "political cocktail party," at the home of a much older law school classmate of mine, where Tom got to mingle with some political aides from recent national-level campaigns whom we gathered together for him. All of them, filled with that same anti-Nixon spirit, urged him to run and run hard.

6   For me personally, the process was quite an education in itself, both in electoral politics and in the nature of the work done on Capitol Hill. The congressional staff members with whom I had made contact made it strikingly clear to me that their work was done almost entirely on a partisan political basis, with the intrinsic merits of any issue taking second place much of the time. This was fine for then, as we were so heavily caught up in a strong anti-Nixon fervor, but I quickly learned from people on the Hill that a career spent working for Congress (or at least one launched there) is forever imbued with a partisan cast that seemed to me to be antithetical to what the Justice Department stood for. While there can be personal advantages to that, to be sure, I fortunately was able through this experience to decide early on that taking the "political route" to a legal career was just not my style.

Indeed, I've known many a contemporary who either got his or her start on the Hill or otherwise hooked up with a political star at or near the beginning of his or her legal career -- and this propelled them forward as nothing else could. Some became judges, some became lobbyists, and some joined law firms with an enormous "leg up." But never once have I looked at any of them with envy for what became of him or her with that special ingredient of "politics" involved. To the contrary, I tend to think that someone's accomplishments without that ingredient are more genuine and merit-based. Others will disagree with me on this, I am sure, but that's entirely fine by me. As is the fact that I earned far less in government service -- far, far less -- than I could have in private practice.

7   Tom and Al Gore became so close personally and politically that no less than a cabinet position was anticipated for him had *Bush v. Gore* turned out differently in 2000. Indeed, Tom played the role of opponent Jack Kemp in Gore's 1996 vice presidential debate rehearsals and until a conflict arose was set to play George W.

Bush in Gore's rehearsals for the 2000 presidential debates. A strong environmentalist like Gore, Tom in 2007 married former EPA administrator Carol M. Browner, a lady whom I must say is far more sophisticated than the flighty girlfriend Tom brought with him to our Washington campaign week in 1974.

8   As it turned out, I was able to wring a measure of recompense from Tom when he came to the Washington College of Law to speak for me, together with Senator Patrick J. Leahy (as fellow "Watergate babies," they declared), at one of my "Freedom of Information Day" programs in 2009. Tom was a lobbyist by then, having lost his congressional seat after being (unfairly, I thought) caught up in the "House Post Office" scandal, as a friend of Congressman Daniel D. Rostenkowski in 1992.

CHAPTER NINE

1   Longtime *National Law Journal* Supreme Court journalist and blogger (*The Marble Palace Blog*) Tony Mauro calls this the Court's "spillover period."

2   Justice Clark was succeeded on the Supreme Court by Justice Thurgood Marshall, who had been a Circuit Court Judge on the Second Circuit Court of Appeals. President Johnson, very much wanting to appoint him to be the first African-American Justice on the Supreme Court, managed to create a vacancy for that in much the same way as he had created room to appoint Justice Abraham "Abe" Fortas to the Court by persuading Justice Arthur J. Goldberg to leave it in order to become the U.S. Ambassador to the United Nations in 1965. And he nearly parlayed that latter appointment, as well, when he nominated Justice Fortas to succeed Justice Earl Warren as Chief Justice of the United States when Chief Justice Warren announced his retirement in 1968.

It was said at the time that LBJ very much wanted to appoint his longtime colleague and friend William Homer Thornberry to the Supreme Court before the end of his presidential term. (In late March of 1968, LBJ had announced that he would not seek a second full term.) Judge Thornberry had been the congressman who succeeded Johnson as the representative for the 10th congressional district of Texas when Johnson narrowly won his Senate seat in 1949 (ironically, with Abe Fortas's great help) and he had been a Circuit Court Judge on the Fifth Circuit Court of Appeals since 1965. Judge Thornberry was nominated by President Johnson for Justice Fortas's seat on the Supreme Court once he had nominated Justice Fortas to be Chief Justice.

However, once Justice Fortas stepped back from his nomination in October of 1968 due to sudden but nevertheless substantial ethics charges, Thornberry's nomination became moot and was withdrawn without a vote. Then, even more ethics charges (read: scurrilous ones against his wife, Arnold & Porter tax partner Carolyn F. Agger) forced Justice Fortas to resign from the Court altogether the following May. This meant that incoming President Richard M. Nixon had two Supreme Court seats (Warren's and Fortas's) to fill near the outset of his presidency. And just imagine: That all occurred without any severe breach of Senate norms.

3   The tenures of Justices Clark and Stewart on the Court overlapped for more than eight years, from October 4, 1958, to June 12, 1967.

4   Seven years later, coincidentally, that same Justice Department appellate lawyer, Tony Steinmeyer, and I again worked together -- this time as litigator and case reviewer rather than interloping law student and receptive Government counsel -- on a case that I argued before the Third Circuit Court of Appeals.

5   Coincidentally, the *Gautreaux* case was argued before the Supreme Court by the person under whom I had worked when he was the Acting Attorney General from late 1973 to early 1974, Solicitor General Robert H. Bork (see Chapter Seven). He went on, of course, to be a failed nominee to the Supreme Court himself in 1987.

6   Also coincidentally, I actually had the opportunity to briefly discuss this case with Justice Clark when he came to GW Law School in early 1976 to judge a moot court competition. As I presumed to hand him a copy of my published law review article, I brashly drew his attention to its theory that he wrote his Seventh Circuit decision with his unique knowledge of Justice Stewart's thinking in mind. Standing alongside his wife, amidst a crowd of other law students, he properly neither confirmed nor denied that that was so.

7   There is an exception to this assertion -- the case detailed in Chapter Forty-Three, in which I was awarded attorney fees of more than a half-million dollars.

8   It is no overstatement to say that, at top law firms in big cities, highly ranked "Summer Associates" are treated almost like royalty, with more emphasis placed on law firm outings -- such as dinners, parties, picnics, musicals, and the ballet -- than on the actual work we were doing. It was as if each big firm (of which there were about seven in D.C. at the time, each with -- believe it or not -- still slightly less than 100 attorneys in total) was trying to outdo the others, just to recruit a relatively small sliver of soon-to-graduate law students who were believed to constitute the best (read: potentially most lucrative) future of the legal profession. And this premise was indeed correct to some degree: Nearly all of the 14 other members of my "Summer Associate class" at Arnold & Porter that summer went on to do very well as attorneys; in my case, though, I was just lucky to be able to convince my relatives back on Long Island that "clerking at A&P" did not mean stamping the prices on cans of beans at the local supermarket. About half of them got that.

9   *Gideon's Trumpet* is a book written by *New York Times* journalist Anthony Lewis, who in 1964 wrote the second-most-likely book to have been read by a Washington law student (the first having been Joseph Goulding's *The Superlawyers*), which memorialized the *pro bono* assistance given to one Clarence Earl Gideon in the landmark case of *Gideon v. Wainwright*, in which the Supreme Court established the right to counsel in criminal cases in 1963. The law firm that handled that case before the Supreme Court *pro bono* was Arnold, Fortas & Porter; the attorney who argued it before the Court was future Associate Supreme Court Justice Abraham "Abe" Fortas.

Quiz: Can you name the last seven failed nominees to a seat on the United States Supreme Court? *Clue:* It's a trick question, doubly so, in that the "seventh" one (in reverse chronological order), Justice Abe Fortas, failed in his nomination to be elevated to another "seat" on the Court, that of Chief Justice of the United States -- leading to the withdrawn nomination of LBJ buddy William Homer Thornberry behind him (which in turn led to successive failed nominees Clement F. Haynsworth, Jr., and G. Harrold Carswell for that seat) -- and the putative "third" one, Douglas H. Ginsburg, actually withdrew when his prospective nomination "went up in smoke" before he could be nominated officially. *Answer:* Merrick B. Garland, Harriet E. Miers, "not Ginsburg," Robert H. Bork, Carswell, Haynsworth, Thornberry, and Fortas. (Note that this does not include John G. Roberts, Jr., whose nomination to an Associate Justice seat was withdrawn in favor of his nomination to be Chief Justice of the United States in 2005.)

Anyway, my best recollection of Justice Fortas was in looking (together with his wife Carolyn Agger) at a famous photograph of him bending over to the near-tipping point in front of an imposing (one might say "looming") Lyndon Johnson, which hung on the wall of his den, during an A&P party at their house in that summer of 1975. Ms. Agger (as she was most respectfully called) was an eminent presence at A&P, even though just a relatively young 66 at the time, and one had the distinct impression that she had shown off that iconic photograph (which revealed as much about Johnson as it did about Fortas, not to mention volumes about their relationship) dozens if not hundreds of times before.

10   This is because offers received by law students typically are extended far in advance. Hence, I knew that I would be working at A&P over the summer of 1975 back in the fall of 1974, when I received and accepted its offer. The same was so with my judicial clerkship for the 1976-1977 year; I "nailed that down," so to speak, more than a year in advance, i.e., in June of 1975.

11   Remember, this was in 1975, when such things still could fall through the cracks even at a major law school, especially one as disorganized as GW Law was at the time, and the Americans With Disabilities Act was still many years away. The thought of a sightless law student being left to fend for herself today is difficult to imagine. But back then, it might have been shocking but was not so surprising.

12   When I had "had" this professor for Administrative Law the year before, my classmates and I used to say that he "cruised at 20,000 feet and only rarely touched down for a landing."

13   In other words, I have to admit that I had a basis for suspecting that this scofflaw professor would fail to keep his commitment, as I knew of his irresponsible ways, but it never occurred to me to double-check him on the Brailling in advance. By the way, the competition for that "biggest failure" distinction was to become stiffer in later years. As is recounted in Chapters Thirty-Four and Forty-One, I suffered two further failures, one minor and one major, during the Clinton Administration and the "Bush 43" Administration, respectively.

14   Eventually, at age 37, Judge Gasch married the principal harpist of the National Symphony Orchestra (and the very first female member of it), who was responsible for my working on Saturdays; Mrs. Gasch practiced on that day of the week (even in semi-retirement) and Judge Gasch figured that he might as well go in to the office (together with yours truly, of course) on such days.

15   I did manage to get a big lesson in connection with a matter of criminal law, though. During my year with Judge Gasch, he presided over the trial of an AUSA who had foolishly (shades of Chapter Thirty-Two) gotten himself involved with a local prostitute who in turn managed to extricate herself from an undercover "sting operation" by informing on him. The FBI then proceeded to "sting" the AUSA, with several hundreds of dollars of "bribes," which he accepted unbeknownst to his supervisors (and certainly unaware that he was being vid-eotaped at the time).

His defense at trial was that he innocently "played along" with this (read: with his "sting") for fear that the persons with whom he thought he had been dealing -- FBI undercover agents pretending to him to be "dangerous Mafiosos" -- would otherwise harm his wife and family. The prosecution countered that he was indeed worried about his wife, all right; he didn't want her to learn of his illicit association.

Anyway, throughout the trial, this AUSA defendant consistently maintained a strict "choirboy" demeanor for the jury, consistent with his "long shot defense" story. As to the jury, I was sitting in the "law clerk's chair" alongside it, immediately across from the witness stand and perpendicular to Judge Gasch, a position from which I could observe the defendant's demeanor up close when he took the stand in his own defense. And in that position, I was able to observe this poor fellow when, during his testimony, his attorney approached him and quickly said something *sotto voce* to him with a file folder blocking anyone's view (read: except for mine) of his mouth. And the attorney's body, just few feet away from me, also blocked both the jury's view, as well as Judge Gasch's, of the defendant's face when he whispered a response.

But I saw his face, from my vantage point, clear as could be. And with it, that defendant's entire demeanor instantly changed, giving a picture of his true attitude, which shall we say was not angelic in the least. And this ploy worked, together with his "long shot defense," as he ultimately was acquitted by that jury, against what were said in the legal community at the time to be "seemingly impossible odds." He was, however, subsequently disbarred. And even though this occurred more than 45 years ago, with part of this story available on the public record, this poor former AUSA will not be named here, as it would serve no useful purpose and could in fact still be harmful.

16   There was another exception that proved the rule: When Judge Gasch sat "by designation" on a D.C. Circuit panel -- pursuant to a special statute, 28 U.S.C. § 292(a), that permits this -- he held the "writing assignment" for the panel on a criminal case. So I was able to draft a D.C. Circuit opinion in a case involving the issue of proper surveillance of a drug buy. Something roughly akin to that was a case on my side of his docket that was a special "three-judge-court" case (read: one in which the National League of Cities challenged the implementation of a federal statute that required exceptional three-judge-court adjudication), on direct remand from the United States Supreme Court and on which he sat together with fellow District Court Judge Barrington D. Parker and D.C. Circuit Court Judge Harold Leventhal. Although their decision was issued as a *per curiam* (read: unsigned) one, it was written by Judge Leventhal, who for my money was the smartest person in the building at the time, which meant that my input on behalf of my judge was limited to what I call "just a scrub."

17   Yes, that case did involve an issue that was ahead of Judge Gasch's time: gay rights. And it does little to breach the sanctity of what attorneys call the "chambers privilege" (another form of government secrecy to add to the list) to say that (as the opinion he eventually issued reveals) he just could not get his head around the idea of someone having anti-discrimination rights based on minority sexual orientation.

Which brings up something collateral to the subject of government secrecy: The fact that during the 20th century there was so much secrecy about sexual orientation. While this was not a matter of the government having secrets *per se*, it was about government employees -- sometimes high-level officials -- living in secrecy about being gay. And they did so out of enormous fear that their true sexual orientation could be used against them -- as during the "McCarthy Era" of the 1950s, when hundreds of homosexuals were ferreted out from within government ranks in the name of combatting communism as a matter of national security.

Unfortunately, this attitude was so extreme that the government (read: rationally) had to be concerned about the potential for such persons to be potently blackmailed into disclosing the sensitive information with which they had been entrusted. I myself became part of this when in 1992 I had to insist that one of our young attorneys "come out" to his family or else I could not lawfully approve his obtaining the security clearance necessary for him to work for us (see the Acknowledgments). (Just three years later, by the way, this security requirement was greatly relaxed, but not entirely.) Perhaps the day will come (though not likely within my lifetime) when such a thing will never be necessary.

CHAPTER TEN

1   Actually, there might be a misspelling in this text sentence in that some AUSAs might argue, especially while working in the middle of the night, that the word should be "humanely." (I, for one, pulled many all-nighters during my Justice Department career, which prepared me well for the ones required by the *Gerlich* litigation (see Chapter Forty-Three), as well as the many involved in the writing of this book.)

2   It nearly always seemed to astound my law school classmates and other peers how much responsibility a young attorney could be given in one of the litigation divisions of Main Justice. That certainly is true of government service overall, but for a new 25-year-old litigator such as myself, becoming a Trial Attorney at Main Justice was a doorway to tremendous opportunities.

3   In fact, the story on Capitol Hill was that these laws were connected to "Watergate" in more ways than one -- in that Congress had "hired up" with many legal staffers during the early summer of 1974 in anticipation of a Nixon impeachment trial. These were attorneys who suddenly, upon Nixon's abrupt resignation on August 9, were "all dressed up but with no place to go." So they worked on creating the Privacy Act, and on very heavily amending the FOIA, during the remainder of that session of Congress as a result.

The fact that two among this group of relatively young congressional attorneys were Bernard W. Nussbaum and Hillary D. Rodham, later to be President Clinton's first White House Counsel and his First Lady did not go unnoticed down the road. (One of the more remarkable things heard in Main Justice's hallways about Hillary Clinton was that while she might have been Bill's First Lady, she certainly wasn't his last. I repeat such scurrilous gossip here only because, frankly, I happen to know that she deserves no better, given her utterly disgraceful conduct with respect (or not) to her electronic mail, both during and after her tenure as Secretary of State in the Obama Administration (see Chapter Forty-Seven). Harsh? Yes. Too harsh? No, not given what she knowingly did.

4   Indeed, the "Watergate Era" served to usher in a period of much such reform, with new laws, new agencies, and a more sophisticated view by the public of its government's activities. Even the media was never again the same, with its new, "Woodward & Bernstein"-inspired bent toward investigative journalism. That distinct change in media orientation itself greatly fueled the growth of the Freedom of Information Act from the mid-1970s on.

5   In total, I actually had four distinct "tours of duty" at the Justice Department over the course of my career: The first was an internship that lasted for only an academic semester in 1971. The second was much longer, with me serving as a mere, though highly placed, law clerk during my first law school year; it was technically a part-time position, but I managed to turn it into nearly a full-time one. The third was my time as a Trial Attorney in the Department's Civil Division, first in its "Information and Privacy Section" ("I&P") and then, when the Civil Division was completely reorganized in late 1978, in what was named its "Federal Programs Branch," where I continued litigating for a total of exactly four years.

Lastly, there was the Office of Information and Privacy ("OIP"), where, seemingly lacking any personal initiative and imagination whatsoever, I spent more than the next 25 years. My primary reason for remaining in that position for so long was that it was, to me, "the best job in the world," as the saying goes. I thought so at the outset of my tenure there and I thought so when I left it. (And I left it, as is detailed in the Epilogue, only when a future Supreme Court Justice asked me to essentially lie.)

6   Suffice to say that there developed a tremendous, almost unheard-of schism in the Information and Privacy Section just before I arrived, with most of its attorneys strongly loyal to its longstanding deputy chief and only a few supportive of a controversial new section chief who surprisingly had been installed by Assistant Attorney General Barbara Allen Babcock soon after the Carter Administration began. I very much admired AAG Barbara Babcock and came to benefit greatly from working under her, but I soon realized that in appointing this new section chief from elsewhere in the Department, undoubtedly just because she was female, she had unwittingly made an awful mistake. And it wasn't long before she realized it.

Barbara actually took me into her confidence about this, meeting with me together with two of her deputies, even though I was relatively "brand new." Looking back, I think she did so because she trusted me as a needed source of information about what actually was going on in the I&P Section. And I recall one such meeting in which a firm consensus was reached that that section chief should immediately be removed, but Barbara did not go ahead with that because one of the meeting participants (read: not me) persuasively opined that upon receiving such news at that particular time, that section chief "might intentionally drive into a bridge abutment on the way home." (Although I happened to know where that section chief lived, and that in fact there were no bridges on her commuting route, I kept my own counsel on that.) So that section chief stayed on until she did more serious damage.

7   By the time that I began teaching in 2007, this term for a first-year law student had become entrenched in academia as well as elsewhere.

8   This had another significant effect, one that presaged what I would be doing later on in a more formal capacity: Finding myself in this position, and not being shy about sharing my expertise, I soon began guiding AUSAs around the country as they struggled with their own unfamiliar FOIA cases. To them, getting solid information about that law from an experienced "expert" in Washington was a big relief. And as word spread, more and more calls for such assistance came in, as well as from a growing clientele of FOIA officers at agencies across the executive branch, so it was as if in a relatively short period of time I had developed by own specialized legal practice.

9   I used to say at the time that my job extended "from assassinations to assignations" and then beyond. Years later, as the assignations mounted, this became more and more the case.

10   The details of these cases, among others, are discussed in later chapters (see Chapters Eleven to Twelve and Fifteen to Seventeen).

11   On this score, I distinctly remember one summer -- 1979, I believe -- in which I worked more than 90 days straight. (And this was without being able to, as one might today, "remote in" electronically.) My wife, too, worked those same days, as she was a busy litigator herself.

12   One might think about it this way: Imagine the most controversial of government activities, involving matters of the most acute sensitivity, and then imagine the records (even if only a few) that pertain to such a thing. Well, those records can be "placed on the hook" under the FOIA, either directly or indirectly, whether their sensitivity (or even their very existence) is actually suspected by a FOIA requester or not. And then, to deepen this, imagine further that the federal agency (or more likely, agencies) involved, greatly concerned about the very nature of these records (reflecting, as they do, the underlying activity), then acts to "cover up" these records (together with the facts underlying them), thus creating a whole new record layer, i.e., the records *of* the "cover up" itself. FOIA cases can be like this.

CHAPTER ELEVEN

1   Without "jumping the gun" too much on my descriptions here, I'll just say that this case ended up featuring prominently in the work of both other branches of the Federal Government, in ways that no one could have imagined at the time.

2   Howard was a very well-respected journalist from Connecticut whose wife, Sharon Nelson Abramson, represented him during most of the case. I met with them multiple times, as I recall, and found them to be considerably more amenable to reason than many other FOIA requesters-cum-litigants are.

3   This "name check" unit chief, coincidently enough, was named David F. Nemecek (read: "Nem-a-check"). And although he struck me as someone forlornly worried about keeping his job at the time, he actually rose to hold the titles of Section Chief of the FBI's National Crime Information Center and later Deputy Assistant Director of its Criminal Justice Information Services Division.

4   Their names, which have long since entered the public domain, in what might or might not have been a violation of the Privacy Act itself depending on the circumstances (see Chapter Fourteen), were as best as I can recall Cesar Chavez, Thomas Dodd, Joseph Duffy, Maurice Eisendrath, Richard Goodman (Doris Kearns Goodwin's husband), Fannie Lou Hamer, Reinhold Nieburh, Paul Schrade, Adam Walinsky, Lowell Weicker (the senator from Connecticut), and George Wiley.

5   It is not unusual to have a litigation case effectively drive an agency to take steps outside of the confines of the case itself. This certainly was so with respect (or not) to the FBI back then. I knew that the Bureau was going to have to take public relations steps (and perhaps congressional affairs ones, as well) that would be ancillary to my defense of the case in court. So I basically told it what to do. Such is the power that a Justice Department Trial Attorney can hold as to a client agency that has run afoul of the law.

6   It might seem to an outsider that I was wielding a surprising amount of "clout" over the Bureau's actions on such things. But that is what can happen in the defense of a case, especially a high-profile one in which a client such as the FBI has to "clean up its act."

7   Ironically, this process necessarily constituted a further "recompilation" of the derogatory information, for purposes of handling the litigation.

8   There was, of course, another privacy exemption in the FOIA, Exemption 6, which did not have a law enforcement-related threshold requirement, but that exemption was markedly narrower than Exemption 7(C), requiring a "clearly unwarranted" privacy invasion (see Chapter Eleven). Therefore, I viewed Exemption 6 as only a "back-up" defense to be raised in the alternative in the case.

9   Previously, in its original form, Exemption 7 had spoken of "files," with "records" being a subsequent refinement of that. Ultimately, Congress would amend Exemption 7 again to fix that with the word "information," based upon what was yet to happen in the *Abramson* case.

10   The fact that the Bureau had so blithely acceded to Ehrlichman's request(s), of course, was the genesis of the problem here, as was its entire "name check" system. But within the Bureau, that had long been swept away in the midst of the even larger problems that the FBI had faced as part of "Watergate." Needless to say, the very fact that the Bureau's longtime "name check" chief was still there, available to be interviewed by me many years later, spoke volumes in and of itself.

11   Actually, this would have been the third place. The first was when the Bureau gathered the derogatory information about these 11 people to begin with. (Most of it was mere bits of "Hooveresque" gossip and raw, uncorroborated "facts." But they nevertheless had the potential for embarrassing them -- or worse.) The second was when that information was culled from the Bureau's files and summarized for Ehrlichman. And the third, the "icing on the cake," so to speak, would be if the information were to be disclosed to the public through no fault of their own.

12   I had asked Special Agent Donohoe to do something "special" on the case, inasmuch as it seemed likely that we were going to need it. Jerry took every bit of the "derog" at issue and traced it back to its point of origin in the Bureau's files. And having done so, he was able to attest firsthand that it all was compiled, initially, for regular investigative purposes. I remember Jerry telling me this one afternoon and thinking that although compiling such sheer gossip (at worst) might have been "regular" in the Hoover days, I certainly hoped it would be such no longer.

13   The word around the courthouse was that Judge Richey was on the Bench in D.C. only because he was a close associate of Vice President Spiro T. Agnew back in Maryland when Agnew was accepting bribes for steering construction contract as county executive and then as governor. (That conduct evidently continued when he became vice president (see Chapter Seven).) More than once, in what is admittedly scurrilous gossip, I heard him referred to as having been Agnew's "bag man" at times. Knowing Judge Richey, this was not hard to believe.

14   One might think that if his side was the one that prevailed in the lower court, then that must give him a "leg up" in winning at the court of appeals level as well. This certainly is true in many types of cases, especially ones in which appellate courts use a limited "standard of review" to assess the lower court opinion. But FOIA cases are not typical (in so many ways) and ordinarily they can be decided either way on appeal, no matter how the lower court ruled.

15   The federal judge for whom I clerked, as described above, was a rare exception in that he was appointed by President Lyndon B. Johnson even though he was a life-long Republican and had even held an appointment as the U.S. Attorney for the District of Columbia from President Dwight D. Eisenhower. LBJ was looking for a Republican at the time so that he could say that he was "balanced" (see Chapter Nine).

16   I drew him for the appeal that I argued in my *Gardels v. CIA* case later on (see Chapter Seventeen), but that worked out much better for me, perhaps because, unlike in *Abramson*, Circuit Court Judge Edwards was not accompanied on the panel in *Gardels* by two "known liberals."

17   With all the talk of Ehrlichman's misconduct and the Bureau's complicity in it, this is not to overlook the FBI's own misconduct in gathering and recording the derogatory information in its original form in the first place. It is perhaps easy to skip over that as just "par for the course" within J. Edgar Hoover's FBI during his lifetime, but it constituted the foundational harm for what was to become exacerbated later.

18   This had gone on for more than five years, by the way, almost the entirety of Nixon's presidency.

19   At the time at which *certiorari* was being considered -- i.e., during the early months of 1981 -- I was still a Trial Attorney in the Civil Division and technically had no business advocating for something that my own division had formally decided not to recommend. But I had already developed enough of a reputation as a singular FOIA litigation force by that time that the Solicitor General's Office paid full attention to my recommendation anyway. (This is not how it works in everyday life, boys and girls, so please don't try it at home.)

20   Sometimes the progress of a case at the Supreme Court level takes much more time than people expect. The parties can seek, and are regularly granted, lengthy extensions of their time deadlines at both the *certiorari* petition stage and the merits briefing stage of a case. That certainly was the case in *Abramson*. And what it meant was that the appeal of a D.C. Circuit decision issued in October of 1980 was not heard by the Supreme Court until more than 14 months later. Looked at it another way, a FOIA request filed by Howard Abramson in 1976 for records of improper White House/FBI collusion going back to 1969, after being sued on in 1977, was not heard and decided by the Supreme Court until 1982. (And, as is seen below, it was not completely adjudicated until more than a year after that.) As long a history as this was, many FOIA cases over the years have had even longer ones.

21   The Supreme Court later explained: "Because this interpretation of the Exemption has important ramifications for law enforcement agencies, for persons about whom information has been compiled, and for the general public, we granted *certiorari*."

22   As noted above, John went on to become White House chief of staff under President Bill Clinton. Then among other things during the Clinton Administration, he played key roles on Hillary Clinton's Health Care Task Force (see Chapter Twenty-Nine), President Clinton's approval (read: partial absorption of) Attorney General Janet Reno's October 4, 1993 FOIA Memorandum (see Chapter Twenty-Nine), the White House's approval of the Justice Department's draft of the Electronic FOIA Amendments of 1996 (see Chapter Thirty-Four), and efforts made on gaining acceptance of something called "Public Key Infrastructure" ("PKI," to those in favor of it) which pertains to the use of digital signatures in an encrypted electronic environment, ultimately through something developed by the National Security Agency known then as a "Clipper Chip," over which there were fierce policy debates. Later on, John managed Hillary Clinton's 2016 presidential campaign.

23   Justice O'Connor's dissent was a big surprise, to say the least. I have observed above that the Reagan Administration official who recruited me from the Civil Division to form OIP in 1981 also that year traveled with then-Counselor to the Attorney General Kenneth W. Starr to Arizona to recruit her -- and that he would upon occasion sum that up by joking, at my expense, that he "batted .500" that year. Well, you can be sure that as soon as *Abramson* came down I handed him a copy of her dissent and suggested that perhaps he had had things backwards.

24   The Government had used the word "recompiled" to describe the second-level handling of the information by the Bureau given the statute's use of the word "compiled" to begin with. As it turned out, though, any of the three words was adequate to the task.

25   This afforded the Government great flexibility in what we called the threshold's "front end," to which the Supreme Court later added flexibility at its "back end," as well: In its decision in *John Doe Agency v. John Doe Corp.*, 488 U.S. 1309 (1989), the Court had occasion to consider records that had been created for routine audit purposes by a non-law enforcement agency but subsequently became sensitive within the context of an ongoing criminal investigation. It found that such records, too, qualify for Exemption 7 protection, which together with *Abramson* made it a case of the Government "having its cake and eating it, too."

26   The dissents in the case added little. Justice Blackmun's simply could "not escape the conclusion that the Court has simply substituted the word 'information' for the word 'records' in Exemption 7," which was both accurate and prescient (given what was about to happen in Congress afterwards). And Justice O'Connor's dissent approached the issue from the perspective of a legislator (which she had been in Arizona until just a year prior), saying that the majority had ruled as it did in "an effort to perfect the FOIA by judicial alteration." In both cases I say, yes, of course those criticisms are true, but that's what courts have to do sometimes to achieve justice, despite the arguable import of the words that Congress has (often loosely) used.

27   Actually, there was one other "final chapter" of the case itself: On remand of *Abramson* to the D.C. Circuit, Sharon Abramson managed to convince that Court that she and her husband had never conceded that there was a proper law enforcement purpose for the *original* compilation of the information to begin with. (She was right; I had hoped not to have to litigate that.) So that issue was litigated before Judge Richey and he ruled in the Government's favor on July 1, 1983. By that time, I had given up the case when I moved to OIP, so it was handled by Civil Division Trial Attorneys Barbara L. Gordon and Robin M. Stutman.

28   Actually, Congress adopted the very statutory words that were part of the FOIA-amendment proposal that traced back to the Carter Administration (see Chapter Ten), well before *Abramson* was decided.

CHAPTER TWELVE

1   "Watergate," of course, took its name from the Watergate office building in which Nixon's "plumbers unit" so infamously broke into the offices of the Democratic Party Headquarters in furtherance of Nixon's campaign for re-election in 1972. This name became incomparably unique in American culture, with its suffix "gate" appended to what seemed like every other comparable (or, more accurately, less than comparable) scandal thereafter.

Examples of this are "Billygate," involving President Carter's ne'er-do-well brother; "Irangate," which served as an alternate to the "Iran/Contra Affair"; "Troopergate," which described soon-to-be-president Bill Clinton's alleged use of state troopers to facilitate his alleged philandering when he was (allegedly) governor of Arkansas; "Nannygate," which scuttled the successive nominations of Zoë E. Baird and then District Court Judge Kimba M. Wood to be attorney general in January of 1993; "Travelgate," which referred to the treatment of White House Travel Office employees at the outset of the Clinton Administration; "Filegate," which had to do with the transfer of certain "BI" (read: "background investigation") reports from the FBI to the White House; "Passportgate," of which Clinton was, atypically, a victim; "Koreagate," a corruption scandal involving the Korea Central Intelligence Agency and several Members of Congress; "Bridgegate," in New Jersey; "Camillagate," in the U.K.; "Plamegate," which described the politicized leak of a CIA case officer's covert status; "Emailgate," which of course described former Secretary of State Hillary Rodham Clinton's email travails; and, most recently, "Pussygate," which came within a hair's breadth of aborting then-candidate Donald M. Trump's drive to an electoral-college victory in the presidential race of 2016. This craze perhaps reached its lowest point with "Gategate," a scandal over former National Security Council official Oliver L. (known as "Ollie" to his co-conspirators) North's reported improper procurement of a high-grade security gate for his driveway at his home in Virginia in the 1990s.

But yet another new low point was more recently reached with "Pizzagate," an utterly false "conspiracy theory" spawned by the fact that the "spearfished" emails of 2016 Hillary Clinton campaign manager John D. Podesta, Jr., showed a connection to a pizza emporium on upper Connecticut Avenue, N.W. (alongside my regular morning jogging route, coincidentally), which was taken by some deluded persons to indicate the existence of (in its mildest form) a human-trafficking and a child-sex ring, a "QAnon predecessor" story that members of the "alt-right" and some conservative journalists promoted to the point that an especially deluded man from North Carolina drove to D.C. one Sunday afternoon to "take over" the establishment (i.e., "rescue the children," in his mind) at gunpoint.

2   I was there, happenstancially, because the Justice Department official for whom I had worked as a teenage intern two years earlier, Martin B. Danziger, had been appointed by new Attorney General Richardson to head up a new criminal justice-oriented function (to be named the "Office of Criminal Justice," later the "Office for Improvement in the Administration of Justice," and ultimately the "Office of Legal Policy") as part of the larger Attorney General's Office, and Marty had brought me "on board" to work for him as I began my first semester of law school.

3   When the WSPF was finally terminated and custody of the documents was transferred to the National Archives, the latter began the processing of this FOIA request, which had basically been ignored by the WSPF. This was nine months after the Fund for Constitutional Government initiated its FOIA lawsuit and a year and a half after it had submitted its underlying FOIA request.

4   The Fund for Constitutional Government was founded in 1974, as a not-for-profit public-interest organization aimed at addressing issues of corruption in the Federal Government. It filed a FOIA request for wide swaths of WSPF records in November of 1975, long before the WSPF completed its work. Less than a year later, in September of 1976, it sued on its FOIA request in a case brought by the public-interest law firm of Dobrovir and Oakes.

William A. Dobrovir was a veteran public-interest attorney who was infamous at the time for having played a Nixon tape recording at a Georgetown cocktail party. He had represented Ralph Nader in a "Watergate-related" corruption case and had formed an organization named "Tax Analysts" with which he battled the IRS in FOIA litigation and ultimately reached the Supreme Court, where he won a rare victory against the Government in 1989. Andra N. Oakes, his partner, had strong ties to the world of investigative journalism in that she was the grand-niece of the longtime owner and publisher of *The New York Times*. And as of 1978, they were very ably assisted by a young associate of about my age by the name of Erwin Chemerinsky.

Erwin went on to become the most-cited academic in the country while teaching at Nixon's alma mater, Duke University School of Law, until he was recruited to be the founding dean of a brand-new first-tier law school, the University of California at Irvine, in 2008. At that point, our paths crossed again when we each were attempting to establish case law support for *Bivens* jurisdiction on behalf of our respective clients in the D.C. Circuit -- he, for outed CIA case officer Valerie E. Plame Wilson; me, for victimized applicants to the Justice Department's Honors Program (see Chapter Forty-Three). Small world. Erwin now is the dean of the University of California at Berkeley School of Law, otherwise known as "UC Berkeley."

5   These were what were known as (1) the investigation of "the 18½-minute tape gap"; (2) the ITT investigation; (3) investigations of corporate campaign contributions; (4) the "Townhouse" investigation; (5) the "Milk-Fund" investigation; and (6) the Hughes-Rebozo investigation.

6   This practical reality soon found its way into FOIA litigation cases, some of which involved an agency moving to dismiss based upon the requester's failure to pay applicable fees. In such cases, the FOIA requester would argue that he, she, or it did not properly owe any fee to begin with due to the agency's failure to waive any such fee. And, in turn, the agency would want to argue that, given the statute's requirement that it grant a waiver only on the basis of a (presumably known) record disclosure, it could not know what records (or record portions) would be disclosed through a particular FOIA request, and therefore it could not determine any "benefit to the public" from that, unless and until the requested records were "processed" for disclosure -- which an agency would not do, as a cardinal rule, without the requester's payment of at least a portion of a prospective copying fee. This dizzying spiral plagued not just litigation cases, but also the thousands of such disputes that arose at the administrative level.

Arguably the most extreme example of a fee dispute was the one that the Department of State had in mid-1978 with an inmate, aptly named Richard Armstrong (and just as aptly nicknamed "Red"), who made numerous FOIA requests premised on his view (read: not that he had much of one in his cell) that his incarceration constituted "human rights violations" that the State Department ought to swiftly investigate. A self-described "political dissident," he deftly zeroed in on the Assistant Secretary of State for Human Rights and Humanitarian Affairs, Patricia M. "Patt" Derian, and somehow found ways to get his FOIA correspondence directly to her desk on the State Department's Seventh Floor. This became a problem because he had the distinct habit of chopping off the first knuckle of a finger (read: his, an investigation confirmed) and including that in his FOIA correspondence (read: three separate times, no pun intended).

Well, this caused no small amount of consternation (read: outrage) all along the Seventh Floor over there and it was not long (after receipt of the second digit, as I recall) before the Justice Department received a high-level request from the Department of State (read: I will neither confirm nor deny that it was from Secretary of State Cyrus R. Vance himself) to see if "something could be done" about the situation. Now I am sure that some initial effort was made toward that end within the Justice Department's Bureau of Prisons, but as it turned out this inmate was being held as a guest of the State of Ohio (in its Lucasville prison), not of BOP.

So I was asked to handle a FOIA lawsuit that Armstrong had recently filed and to apply a "zero tolerance" standard to him. I made it known that this was certainly not going to include my curtailing his rights under the FOIA, no matter how "tipped off" the State Department was with this troubled fellow, but I did find a way to accomplish what was asked. It turned out that Armstrong still owed the Federal Government a small amount (read: a "meager sum" is how I forthrightly described it to the Court) of FOIA copying fees from one of his early FOIA requests, in the amount of $2.20, because the agency's duplication costs (read: for copying 272 releasable pages at 10 cents per page, given that records were not yet "digitized") of $27.20 were two dollars and 20 cents over its $25.00 regulatory threshold. (Back then, most agencies would routinely assume that their FOIA requesters "were good for" up to $25 in fees.)

This provided a basis for arguing that Armstrong had "reneged" on a commitment that he had made to pay such fees in full, which in turn (read: under the strict letter of that agency's relatively harsh FOIA regulations) provided a basis for us "shutting him off" from receiving any further "FOIA service" anywhere in the entire Federal Government. So I did that, I'm now almost too embarrassed to say, through a litigation-based communication to him that was worded in such a way as to definitely get the fingertip message across to him. (In a footnote in my dispositive motion, I pointed out to him that "substantial harm to governmental interests" was "threatened by the course of conduct undertaken by [him]," which is why he was experiencing "vigorous advocacy of [the Government's] position in this lawsuit.") This worked, and I daresay that if this poor fellow is still alive today, I would like to think that he still has at least seven intact fingers to work with.

Years later, we were able to use this precedent in the cases of the most prolific FOIA requester ever, Barbara Schwarz of Utah, who filed literally thousands of FOIA requests based upon the fanciful premise that she was the illegitimate daughter of Scientology Founder L. Ron Hubbard and was raised in a secret "submarine village" underneath the Great Salt Lake. As it happened, she failed to pay a FOIA fee that she owed to the Salt Lake City Field Office of the FBI, which gave us a legal basis for "shutting down" all past, present, and future FOIA requests filed by her until she made good on that debt (which we were quite sure she would never do).

So on September 14, 2001, as we were still very much in shock over 9/11, we sent a governmentwide policy memorandum to all federal agencies advising them of our conclusion that they need not expend any FOIA resources on Barbara Schwarz unless they heard from us otherwise. Then, we dealt with her litigation. Taking a nationwide approach to her deluge of FOIA lawsuits, OIP obtained an Order of Injunction against her filing any more of them, which was applied with great relief by dozens of federal agencies in district courts across the land.

7   The only real requirement placed on a FOIA requester by the Act (apart from what we used to say was "the price of a 20-cent stamp," which is what a stamp cost in the early 1980s) is that the requester must "reasonably describe" the records sought, which sometimes poses no difficulty whatsoever even in immense-volume cases. For instance, I used to sardonically remark back in the day that I could make a viable FOIA request for all records on the Fifth Floor of the FBI's Headquarters Building -- not the Fourth Floor or the Sixth, mind you, just the Fifth. Such a FOIA request would certainly "reasonably describe" the records sought within the statutory standard.

8   I must say that I had an excellent team of client personnel supporting me on this FOIA case. First, there was Steven Garfinkel, who was then the general counsel of NARS and went on to be the founding director of NARA's Information and Security Oversight Office ("ISOO," to all national security mavens); Steve and I became good friends. Then there was supervisor James Hastings, who went on to become the director of access programs at NARA. And lastly, there was Steven Tilley, who went on the become the chief records officer at the National Security Council before returning to NARA to be the chief of its JFK collection, among other positions, in 1993; when it came to "working in the trenches," that Steve was the one who best got things done.

As a team, they had overseen the agency's "sample processing" of the WSPF files, knowing that I might need to use that in an effort to protect them from the possible result that they feared the most: Having to process all three-quarters of a million pages just because Dobrovir and Oakes asked for that to be done. And anticipating the use of this number in court, they took a careful "Goldilocks" approach to it: "Not too hot, not too cold; just right." This is how they arrived at the number two -- two hours of "processing" time per page, for an average page. Although this might have seemed like a lot to some (read: Dobrovir and Oakes), I was confident that I could justify it to the Court.

9   I should mention that at the time (i.e., late 1977), there was precious little FOIA case law bearing upon this threshold legal question of putting voluminous records "on the hook" in any way. So I knew that litigating this issue in a "high public interest" setting could be an uphill battle. Indeed, it would not be until 1985 that the Office of Information and Privacy was able to issue policy guidance in specific support of agencies on this issue, reasoning based upon emerging case law that "[o]therwise, a FOIA requester could easily frustrate '[t]he interest underlying the duplication fee requirement' in 5 U.S.C. § 552(a)(4)(A) by not allowing the agency to 'defray' its actual duplication costs."

10   Actually, we had a second big advantage: I knew that once we litigated a small part of the case, whoever lost would want to take the case up to the court of appeals, which would take years. I figured that by then, which turned out to be the summer of 1981 in this case, the impetus for battling over the rest of the case would be long gone. And as it turned out, that was indeed so.

11   These were "early days" for FOIA litigation, which I suppose is what led Judge Flannery to observe that what the Government filed was "fairly complex." Far better that we dealt only with the "closing memos" of each investigation rather than the entire *corpus* of what was actually "on the hook" in the case.

12   It was calculated by Judge Flannery that we had handled only approximately .2% of total number of document pages requested. Actually, it was less than that, because he was working from a total of only one-half a million pages, whereas I knew that the true total was closer to three-quarters of a million pages.

13   Erwin, of course, went on the become one of the most-cited legal scholars in the land, the founding Dean of the University of California's Irvine School of Law, and the current Dean of the University of California's Berkeley School of Law. A fine fellow, he later (read: thirty years later) collaborated with me in connection with the *Gerlich* litigation (see Chapter Forty-Three).

14   The D.C. Circuit Court of Appeals is treated as the "leading circuit" for purposes of FOIA administration and litigation because its district court is the court of "universal venue" under the Act (see Chapter Three). As a practical matter, its precedents carry far more weight than those of any court other than the United States Supreme Court when it comes to the FOIA.

15   This is a formal process by which the chief judge of a circuit court can appoint a district court judge within that circuit to sit on a circuit-court panel if both so choose. Judge Gasch liked to sit on the circuit court once a year, taking the assignment to write an opinion in two of eight cases in a panel sitting, one each for his two clerks. This is how I had had the opportunity to write a D.C. Circuit opinion in a criminal law appeal during my clerkship four years earlier (see Chapter Ten) and it is how Judge Gasch came to sit on the D.C. Circuit panel hearing the *Fund for Constitutional Government* appeal in late 1980, with his opinion for the Court issued in mid-1981.

16   The grand jury secrecy issue in the case, on which the plaintiff so heavily labored both in its brief and at oral argument, was readily dispatched by Judge Gasch's opinion. After reviewing the nature of the underlying

statute -- in the form of Rule 6(e) of the Federal Rules of Criminal Procedure that was codified by Congress in 1977 -- and the information withheld under it, he readily determined that all of it fell within "the broad reach of grand jury secrecy."

17   What Judge Gasch concluded applied *a fortiori* to the identities of individuals who were mentioned in the files but were themselves never even targets of the investigation.

18   This is so even though the Supreme Court, in its landmark *Reporters Committee* decision eight years later, effected a "sea change" in personal-privacy protection (see Chapter Two). Nothing in *Reporters Committee* took anything away from the D.C. Circuit's privacy rulings in its *Fund for Constitutional Government* decision.

CHAPTER THIRTEEN

1   As will be seen, there is a distinct difference between an individual who is a "subject" of an investigation and one who is a "suspect" in it. The former is someone who is investigated, whereas the latter is someone whom an investigation shows to be truly implicated in a crime. In other words, as sometimes is said, "the subject designation leads to a police investigation, while the suspect designation results from one." And a "person of interest," well, is an ersatz term that improperly makes it sound as if an investigation's subject is actually a suspect. Two of the investigative subjects in this chapter, both completely innocent, were incorrectly branded with that label, one explicitly and the other almost so.

2   In most cases, this derives from the disclosure prohibition that is contained in subsection (b) of the Privacy Act of 1974, which was enacted at roughly the same time as Exemption 7(C) was created. Simply put, the Privacy Act has the effect of making an agency's invocation of Exemption 7(C) nondiscretionary for all individuals who are U.S. citizens or persons lawfully admitted to the U.S. for permanent residence (see Chapter Fourteen). And as a matter of both practicality and policy, this rule is followed for everyone (read: almost everyone) else as well.

By contrast, a law enforcement exemption that can lend itself to a discretionary approach in some instances is Exemption 7(A), which under prevailing case law usually is applied on a "categorical" basis without much attention to individual documents in a file, let alone document segments. I recall being asked one day in the 1980s to consult with a Criminal Division attorney who was serving as a "Special AUSA" in the murder prosecution of Green Beret doctor Jeffrey R. MacDonald in North Carolina. That attorney, Brian Murtagh, was dealing with the Government's obligation to disclose (read: as "*Brady* disclosure") exculpatory information from Justice Department files (including FBI laboratory paperwork) on one hand, and the applicability of Exemption 7(A) to thousands of document pages also requested by MacDonald under the FOIA, on the other hand. It was a high-visibility case particularly well suited to "non-categorical" record processing. As I recall (without disclosing what he said to me under the attorney-client privilege), the applicability of the FOIA in the matter also created a question about the timing of any disclosure.

And another area in which personal privacy blurs into the safeguarding of law enforcement interests is the protection of "whistleblowers" to the Securities and Exchange Commission ("SEC," to market timers). In very recent years, it appears, the SEC has placed a "blanket of secrecy" over its relatively new "tips" program by which its makes million-dollar awards to company insiders who "blow the whistle" on corporate fraud. This is a whole new realm of government secrecy that was spawned by the Dodd-Frank Act of 2010 and only now is beginning to draw media attention.

3   This guiding principle was perhaps best articulated by a political appointee whom I admired, Stuart M. Gerson, who was the Assistant Attorney General for the Civil Division under President George H.W. Bush and then

served as acting attorney general in the early weeks of the Clinton Administration (see Chapter Twenty-Eight). He said: "In my time, when something was before the grand jury or otherwise was [the subject of] a pending investigation, you didn't talk about it. And if there was no indictment, you didn't say a word about it ever again."

4   This brings to mind the lament of Reagan Administration Secretary of Labor Raymond J. Donovan, who after being publicly faced with corruption charges that proved to be groundless famously wondered aloud: "[Where] do I go to to get my reputation back?"

5   This is intentionally phrased broadly here so as admit of the possibility that in some cases someone outside of an agency will of necessity be told (or at least be permitted to infer) of such an investigatory interest in a particular person for purposes of obtaining pertinent investigative information. As a practical matter, a law enforcement agency "looking into" a matter will sometimes need to provide investigative information (e.g., the name of a suspect) in order to, *inter alia*, gain a potential witness's trust and cooperation. (In the law enforcement community, this is part of what sometimes is called "give to get.")

6   This entitlement, by the way, is not merely a matter of moral imperative or opinion. Rather, since the mid-1970s in the United States, it is a matter of law, given that it exists by virtue of the Privacy Act of 1974, which provides for criminal (read: misdemeanor) penalties and also civil damages in such cases of "wrongful disclosure" (see Chapter Fourteen). This readily came to the fore in the *Hatfill* case, discussed below, as well as in others of a similar nature.

7   There is one other basic privacy principle that connects to law enforcement information, but it is one that recently originated in Europe and has not quite "caught on" in the United States yet (read: perhaps not ever). That is something referred to as "the right to be forgotten," which essentially means that, with the passage of time (read: enough time, whatever that means), an individual whose adverse characteristics, conduct, or other circumstances was memorialized in a record (read: one used to be able to cover this with the phrase "in writing," but not anymore), is entitled to have that no longer see the "light of day" (read: even though our days are now lit by the Internet, where information is said never to die), as a basic right (read: sort of a perk of getting older).
In 1995, this "right" was enshrined in the European General Data Protection Regulation, where it now most often is called "the right of erasure," and it actually was determined to be a "human right" by the European Court of Justice in a case brought against Google in 2014. That case, *Google Spain SL, Google, Inc. v. Agencia Española de Protección de Datos, Mario Costeja González*, required Google to consider requests from individuals to remove any links to freely accessible website pages resulting from a search of their name. (My "Google daughter," who handles what Google calls "cyberprivacy" for it, has complained to me about that decision ever since.) In a turn-around, though, Google in April of 2022 quietly instituted a policy that now allows U.S. citizens to request removal from its "search results" of information identifiable to them.
This "right" has never been recognized in the United States (and I predict that it never will be) due its tension (to put it mildly) with the First Amendment to our Constitution. The closest it has ever come to that is the corollary concept of "practical obscurity" that the United States Supreme Court established in the landmark FOIA case of *Department of Justice v. Reporters Committee for Freedom of the Press* in 1989 (see Chapter Two). It is one thing for a search engine to follow such a rule but quite another to expect the U.S. Government to do so.

8   There is one particular exception that recently has drawn much attention: Public disclosure of police disciplinary files. This has arisen as an issue at the state and local law enforcement levels, of course, fueled by public pressure and media interest in the wake of the police murder of George Floyd in 2020 and the Black Lives Matter movement, among others. Two states, New York and California, now routinely disclose the records of

all police disciplinary investigations, with Virginia and Maryland now not far behind. The trend in this particular area certainly is in favor of less government secrecy, sensitive privacy interests notwithstanding.

9   I remember that it was much later determined that these letters had been dropped into a mailbox located at 10 Nassau Street, on the perimeter of the Princeton University campus, in which investigators found residual anthrax spores remaining even nine months after the fact. Coincidentally, my family was familiar with that exact mailbox because my wife had graduated from there, we often visited that campus, and my older daughter took her graduate degree there as well. We knew it to be almost directly across the street from the only post office in town.

10   Such was the case with a central mail facility used by the Department of Justice, for instance. In the Office of Information and Privacy ("OIP," always), our mailbags sat unopened for more than six weeks, as I recall, and as of mid-October all new incoming mail was diverted for irradiation in outlying facilities. Our mail service did not begin to be restored until well after Thanksgiving, when the first few irradiated envelopes began to arrive. And when it finally came time to open the bags of mail that we had stockpiled, I refused to allow our secretaries and clerical staff to do so. Simply put, I was just too uncomfortable with telling them to do that, so I did it myself on my own office conference table. I just told them that "that was why I got paid the big bucks."

We also had to give special guidance to all agencies throughout the executive branch on how to deal with the fact that "a series of escalating safety concerns about opening, handling, and even being in the proximity of mail led to [many] disruptions" in the FOIA's governmentwide administration. Titled "Anthrax Mail Emergency Delays FOIA Correspondence," this policy guidance advised that "[b]oth FOIA officers and FOIA requesters alike must accept that the unprecedented delays in mail delivery . . . have been caused by the anthrax mail emergency" and that they should further accept the fact that this of course "cause[s] corresponding delays in the administration of the FOIA."

11   The Leahy letter had been misdirected to a State Department mail annex in Sterling, Virginia, because a ZIP code was misread; a postal worker there contracted inhalational anthrax.

12   Only the *New York Post* and the NBC News letters were found; the existence of the other three letters was inferred because people at ABC, CBS, and American Media became infected with anthrax. There is absolutely no truth the rumor that at one point *The New York Times* claimed that it "must have" received such a letter, too, but that its employees are "a hardy lot immune to such things."

13   I remember speaking with one of Stephen Hatfill's attorneys, whom I had known for a while, at a media conference at which I was giving a presentation. This was right after the FBI went through a "pond draining" process up in Frederick, not far from where my parents lived. As I recall, I suggested to this fellow, who need not be named here, that there was a time not so long ago, certainly within my recent memory, that the Bureau was so "buttoned down" under J. Edgar Hoover (read: and in his wake, for many years thereafter) that it would never be so casual and sloppy as to publicly disclose the fact that any particular person was the subject of one of its investigations. Grossly violate civil liberties under such programs as COINTELPRO, yes. But jump the gun on publicly identifying one of its suspects, no. He told me that he could hardly believe it either. And we also agreed that in this case the blame could squarely be placed on Attorney General Ashcroft, who didn't seem to know any better and apparently did not care to learn. Further evidence of the latter came when in August of 2004 (which turned out to be a big month for Federal Government leaks), a New York physician by the name of Kenneth M. Berry was wrongfully identified to the public as "linked" to the investigation, under the label of "material witness."

14   In an exercise of at least minimal self-control, I have deleted the name of this law enforcement officer from the paragraph above, realizing upon reflection that its disclosure is not necessary to the story.

15   Notably, Senator Charles E. "Chuck" Grassley (R-IA) almost immediately "called Ashcroft out" on his self-servingly irresponsible use of this term, observing with political tongue in cheek that he certainly "appreciate[d] the [Justice Department's] candidness that [his fellow Republican former colleague's] action regarding Mr. Hatfill and his employment is unprecedented." Not long thereafter, a Northeastern University professor, James Alan Fox, also addressed this by observing that "'person of interest' was not part of law enforcement vernacular" until then.

16   Ashcroft, at his core, was a politician more than a law enforcement leader. He came to the Justice Department in early 2001 directly from the United States Senate, which showed almost immediately in the fact that he continued his senatorial pattern of flying back to Missouri nearly every weekend until it became more obviously impolitic for him to do so after 9/11. Prior to his arrival on the Washington scene, he had been elected as attorney general for Missouri (in 1976) and immediately after that served two terms as the state's governor (from 1985-1993), before being elected to the Senate (in 1994). And before all of that, he had served a term as Missouri's state auditor, going back to 1973, beginning his political career at the age of 30.

Speaking of which, the incoming "Bush 43" administration in 2001 saw the arrival of many young political appointees who had little if any experience in government. This of course did not set well with the Department's career officials, even unsurprising as it was, especially after 9/11 raised the stakes exponentially that year. In the Department's Criminal Division, for example, there was a staff meeting at which the age of a new aide to the assistant attorney general (a hard-nosed fellow by the name of Michael Chertoff) was brought up and a grizzled veteran of the division was heard to exclaim: "Thirty-one? I have underwear older than that!" Not long thereafter, three veteran Criminal Division career SESers learned on a Friday afternoon that they would be leaving their positions to become immigration judges as of Monday morning.

17   I knew Vic from one of my earliest cases, back when he was a young civil liberties lawyer in Alexandria, Virginia. In fact, he was the first "ACLU attorney" whom I ever met. I remember being quite impressed by him, by his character as well as by his litigation skill, which I suppose made him an early role model for me to emulate, though we wound up plying our common craft on "opposite sides of the fence," as they say. (By the way, who exactly is the "they" who keep saying all these things?)

18   Yet there is an additional, strange addendum to Dr. Steven Hatfill's unique story: In the year 2021, he resurfaced in the public eye as having worked as an "unpaid volunteer" (albeit with a ".gov" email address) for the Trump White House on its COVID-19 policies once the pandemic began. At one point, he said that he was working "seven days a week, ten hours a day" on COVID-19, primarily by advocating the "prophylactic use of hydroxychloroquine with zinc supplement." Then, after the presidential election, he shifted from his vigorous advocacy of that discredited treatment to advocating that the voting machines used in both Arizona and Nevada were "fraudulent," as part of the "fight" to overturn the election. In my view, he is entitled to such abnormalities given what his government put him through.

19   A particular type of public pressure develops when the public has an overriding imperative under current circumstances to feel safe, which is something that can weigh heavily on law enforcement authorities. And the best antidote for this is where there is determined to be only a single perpetrator (think: "lone assassin") and law enforcement agencies tell everyone that, not to worry, he has been caught! Anything short of that leaves fear.

20   I well remember being at Louie Freeh's swearing-in ceremony at the FBI Headquarters courtyard during President Clinton's first year in office in September of 1993. Afterwards, we all (read: fellow component heads, mostly) repaired to a large space in the building that each year served as the "overflow room" for OIP's biggest governmentwide training program (read: the Bureau's Main Auditorium held only 454 seats, so this room became necessary). This was the first time I had seen Bill Clinton up close and I recall being struck by how his hair had already changed, to mostly gray and wiry, during less than eight months in office. I was also struck by how "tightly wrapped" the new FBI director seemed to be up close.

21   Most particularly, these FBI Special Agents harkened back to two cases during the previous decade in which someone created a situation (in one case by setting a fire, in the other by planting a bomb) in which he could "save the day" an emerge as a hero. A "hero complex," it was called. They "latched onto" this, explicitly concluding that Richard Jewell might be such a person, i.e., that he "fit the profile."

22   There apparently is no small amount of controversy over whether the word "suspect" was used with (dis)respect to Richard Jewell or whether he was said to be "the focus" of the Bureau's investigation, which arguably is a somewhat "softer" reference. Either way, however, the result would be essentially the same.

23   In fact, there was an FBI Special Agent by the name of Thomas Shaw at the time, but this depiction is hardly firm evidence that he was involved in the case as the "leaker"; it much more likely is a fictitious name instead. Indeed, the real "leaker" in the Jewell case, to *AJC* reporter Kathy Scruggs, is on good information believed to be FBI Special Agent Donald H. Johnson, who was one of two agents who dealt with Richard Jewell and his mother Barbara "Bobi" Jewell at the beginning of their ordeal and could have served as the focal point of a Privacy Act lawsuit.

Given that Kathy Scruggs is now deceased like Johnson (read: they are equally dead), others speculate that the actual "leaker" could have been her boyfriend at the time, an Atlanta police officer, who might have learned of the Bureau's new-found suspicions "on the job" (read: through informal, indiscrete conversations). In either event, however, it would have felt just the same to Richard Jewell, whose identity (read: as inchoately surrounded by the "suspect" label) unquestionably left the discrete confines of law enforcement circles and then proliferated throughout the media domain.

24   Jewell was never officially charged in the case, but the FBI thoroughly (and very publicly) searched his home more than once, questioned his associates, investigated his background, and maintained 24-hour surveillance of him. From almost the outset, of course, his home was the site of a round-the-clock "stakeout" by members of the media, both print and TV, as well.

25   Richard Jewell was entirely innocent, of course. Eventually, it turned out the bomber was anti-government, anti-abortion extremist Eric R. Rudolph, who also planted three other bombs in the Atlanta area and in Birming-ham, Alabama, that killed two more people and injured over 100 others. Rudolph was not captured until May of 2003, nearly seven years beyond the time of the Centennial Olympic Park bombing, after spending more than five years hiding out in the mountains of western North Carolina with the help of "kindred spirits." He pled guilty to all four bombings in 2005 and is serving life in prison.

26   And Janet, being Janet, elaborated on this further: "I regret very much the leak that made him an object of so much public attention. I don't think any apology is sufficient when somebody has gone through what . . . Mr. Jewell has gone through. If I could see Mr. Jewell, I would apologize to him." Now I'm here to tell you, as a former Civil Division Trial Attorney, that if your agency head makes a public statement like that about someone who

might sue your agency for wrongful conduct, you start adding some zeros to the number in your head that you think the case could be settled for (read: admittedly ungrammatical as that might be, the point still is made).

27   Indeed, as with the other main characters of this chapter, the Federal Government's liability for "wrongful disclosure" under the Privacy Act of 1974 (see Chapter Fourteen) was palpable. It should be noted in this regard that the Privacy Act's most difficult hurdle for such a lawsuit is its "intentional or willful" *mens rea* standard. But that standard is defined in both that statute's underlying legislative history and its prevailing case law as meaning "only somewhat more than gross negligence." (I litigated more than one of the Privacy Act lawsuits that established this case law in the late 1970s, so this is still very much in mind for me.)

28   Irrepressible as ever, however, Leno later was heard to remark, in an obvious reference to the Jewells, that this was "the greatest week in trailer park history."

29   In the wake of the Richard Jewell case, what happened to him raised an important question internally within the FBI: Does the FBI have any responsibility to protect the privacy of an innocent man? At one point, this question was both raised and elided by one of the Bureau's top officials. His answer was no, the FBI has no responsibility to "correct information in the public domain." Such a response unfortunately shows a blatant ignorance of the responsibility that the Bureau, like any other federal law enforcement agency, has to protect raw investigative files and their contents, together with their "abstract facts," under subsection (b) of the Privacy Act of 1974 (see Chapter Fourteen). And when you come right down to it, it is perhaps my fault that Louie Freeh, as a fellow Justice Department component head, apparently "never got the memo" on that.

30   The other one, of course, was the transit system bombings that took place in London on July 7, 2005, which the British refer to as "7/7" (read: as their own version of "9/11"). All four of them were perpetrated by Islamic suicide bombers, in very close coordination, with three of them on moving Underground (read: subway) trains exploding within 50 seconds of one another and the fourth on a double-decker bus traveling through Tavistock Square in Central London about an hour later. This was during a weekday morning rush hour and together the bombings claimed 52 lives (not counting the four bombers) and left more than 700 wounded. The images of this carnage were most vivid at the surface explosion of the bus and its surroundings near Upper Woburn Place; the upper deck and the rear of the bus were demolished in the blast and several passers-by were injured as well.

Some of the 13 persons who died on the bus were foreign exchange students, owing partly to the proximity of University College London ("UCL," to its students and faculty) in that area. Coincidentally, Tavistock Square was the exact location at which I would spend much time during the next several years as part of a fellowship that I held at UCL and, on an even more personal note, my younger daughter Lindsay spent the spring semester of her junior year of college the next year studying neurobiology at UCL, where she was not far from that tragic location. In fact, due to that recent bus bombing, my wife and I spent more than a few hours deliberating her safety before we agreed that she should go.

31   During that time, the Bureau also managed to search Mayfield's home through what it calls "sneak and peek" entries, to wiretap his phones, and to plant listening devices in both his home and his office. (Mayfield and his family were under the impression that their house had been broken into at least twice, based upon shoeprint carpet patterns alone.) Due to lack of evidence, these Portland Special Agents did not seek ordinary wiretap authority, but rather were able to use a Foreign Intelligence Surveillance Act ("FISA," to its surveillees) warrant, which they based on the attestation that they had "probable cause" to believe that Mayfield was acting on behalf of a foreign terrorist group.

32   There actually was another side to this scale, however. On it were the facts that Mayfield did not have a current passport; that he had not in fact been out of the country since completing his military duty as a U.S. Army lieutenant in Germany during the early 1990s; that the Spanish law enforcement authorities had by then determined that the bombings were conducted by persons from North Africa; and that there was no evidence linking Mayfield with Spain or North Africa.

33   According to my younger daughter, psychologists sometimes will call this "confirmation bias," or a form of "cognitive dissonance." By whatever name, the Bureau ought to be conducting lectures on it at the FBI Academy in Quantico, Virginia, by now.

34   This is what I say not only was wrong, it was malignly so. And it is the only instance I know of in which a federal law enforcement agency (read: not to be confused with the CIA or some other intelligence agency, where such things are indeed done) has callously planned to commit a Privacy Act violation for the purpose of then leveraging that wrongdoing to its investigative advantage. Had Mayfield turned out to be guilty, of course, that would have been but a "blip on the screen," so to speak. But with his innocence, it resounded.

35   Actually, the FBI's three fingerprint examiners saw some differences within this "match" but, in what appears to have been an exercise of "group think" (read: "mutual confirmation bias"), they all rationalized them away. Allegedly all three of them were aware of Mayfield's Muslim faith when they conducted their analyses.

36   I do not now remember whether these agents (and their supervisor) were ever disciplined for what they did to Mayfield, but if they weren't, they certainly should have been, despite the degree of latitude that was accorded to FBI Special Agents in such activities in the immediate wake of 9/11.

37   In fact, it later came out that the Spanish law enforcement authorities had informed the FBI of this in a letter dated April 13, 2004, long before his eventual arrest on May 4. This fact, as might be imagined, became a key part of Mayfield's subsequent claim for damages.

38   True to form under the Bush Administration (and I mean this in the kindest way possible), the Justice Department filed several motions to have Mayfield's claims dismissed as a matter of national security, or based upon unspoken "national secrets," but these were readily denied by the Court and wisely not appealed.

39   I once had occasion to warn someone that "there are few things in life more dangerous than a retired trial attorney with time on his hands" (see Chapter Forty-Three), and this situation was somewhat akin to that.

40   These three cases had one more thing in common, something that partially explains why federal agents so doggedly adhered to their suspects' guilt for so long: Those case agents (all the way up to Ashcroft and Freeh) became "invested" in their being guilty, lest their extensive efforts have been for naught. Each of these suspects so strongly "fit the profile" that their investigators became blind to the possibility of their innocence and inured to violation of their privacy rights.

41   There also is a "privacy victim" who sometimes is mistakenly thought of as the subject of a government "leak," but that is admittedly debatable. That was a 33-year-old decorated former U.S. Marine named Oliver W. "Billy" Sipple, who received disabling wounds in Vietnam and had the further misfortune of possibly having had saved the life of President Gerald R. Ford when he was shot at from nearly point-blank range by would-be assassin Sara Jane Moore in September of 1975 at Union Square in San Francisco. Moore had already fired one shot that missed the president by only inches and quite obviously was preparing to fire again when Sipple dove

towards her and managed to grab her arm, deflecting it downward, just as the second shot was about to be fired. That bullet ricocheted off of the ground and hit a nearby cab driver, who was not seriously injured.

Not unlike Richard Jewell, Billy Sipple was hailed as a hero, all the more so in that this was the second attempt on President Ford's life within three weeks, the other being when Charles Manson follower Lynette A. "Squeaky" Fromme aimed a loaded gun at him in another part of San Francisco. This public acclaim was short-lived for Sipple, though, because only two days later, a *San Francisco Chronicle* columnist by the name of Herbert E. "Herb" Caen carelessly "outed" him as being gay, something that was well known to Sipple's circle of friends in San Francisco (which included burgeoning gay activist Harvey B. Milk, who had mentioned it to Caen) but not at all to his parents and extended family back in Michigan, a situation that was not uncommon (see the Acknowledgments). Soon Sipple was labeled by reporters nationwide as the "gay ex-Marine," whereupon his mother, who reacted no less negatively than the rest of his family, unfortunately told him that she was "disowning" him as a result.

These circumstances present what I think can fairly be called a "borderline" case. On one hand, the primary disclosure that caused Sipple harm was that of the *San Francisco Chronicle*, which disclosed "to the world" (read: to his folks back home in Michigan, not just to his San Francisco community) that Sipple was gay. But there also are journalists' reports that almost as soon as the near-assassination took place, Sipple actually pleaded with the Secret Service agents who were interviewing him about the incident not to release his name to the press. And thus, in a "proximate cause" sense that might be explored on a first-year law student's Torts exam, he could not have been "outed" as gay if no one "knew who he was" in the first place.

This element of the fact pattern makes it at least arguable that it actually was the United States Secret Service that disclosed the key "law enforcement information" about Sipple (read: that it was he who apparently saved President Ford's life) and thus provided the foundation for his being caused great personal harm. The weakness in that analytical conclusion, though, is that under these circumstances it was not as if the Secret Service had taken his name, placed it into a Privacy Act-protected file, and then callously removed it for dissemination.

Rather, the name "Oliver Sipple" was simply given to the Secret Service agents on the spot (read: orally) and was in turn given "from their heads" to clamoring reporters right then and there -- which is something that is very arguably not covered by the Privacy Act at all. (I have to admit that I myself would have argued this position on the Federal Government's behalf if defending such a case; in fact, I did so argue it in a case by the name of *King v. Califano* in the late 1970s; one could look it up (read: by simply Googling it), as they say.)

Plus who's to say that, if there were time for a calm analysis of the question, the Secret Service would not have concluded that there was "an overriding public interest" in the public learning that name under such extraordinary circumstances. (I might have reached such a conclusion myself, had I not still been in law school at the time.) So, with all of this said and done, you have the case of privacy victim Billy Sipple in this equivocating endnote, rather than in the text.

42   In addition to the two high-level military officers discussed below, others falling into this category include Defense Department contract employee Lawrence A. Franklin, who was convicted of orally passing classified information to agents of Israel in 2003. He was sentenced to 13 years in prison, but that later was reduced to only 10 months of house arrest after the Justice Department belatedly focused on the fact that his identity as a suspected spy was wrongfully disclosed in August of 1994. That same month, a DEA supervisor named Reginald Cheney was anonymously placed on administrative leave for (ironically) invading the privacy of individuals in a DEA database and was publicly identified by "government sources." And there also was the case of Senator Richard C. Shelby, who during that same month formally accused Justice Department prosecutors of "an abuse of public trust" when they reportedly disclosed to the media information about an ongoing investigation of him for (ironically again) allegedly leaking to the media items of classified information.

But at the same exact time, the Federal Government *was* sued under the Privacy Act by former FBI translator Sibel D. Edmonds, who alleged that she was the subject of "wrongful disclosures" in retaliation for her "whistleblowing" on the Bureau's dealings with Turkish nationals. Her Privacy Act "wrongful disclosure" lawsuit came atop others filed by Energy Department official Notra Trulock and Los Alamos scientist Dr. Wen Ho Lee, who ended up with a settlement in the amount of 1.6 million dollars. Large as that settlement was, it soon was dwarfed by a six-million-dollar settlement in a "wrongful disclosure" suit brought against the FBI and the State Department, *Stewart v. FBI*, for their leaking personal information about an international businessman.

OIP was consulted in almost all of these Privacy Act cases that went to litigation, as well as in many that did not, leading to their settlements. And after the spasm of such cases that occurred in the summer of 1994, atop those that had arisen previously, I decided to flex OIP's institutional muscles by comprehensively compiling all of these Privacy Act violations, and their consequences, into a single document that could be the basis for concentrated focus and remedial action.

Toward that end, I chose the beginning of President Bush's second term as the most propitious time for raising this. But I could not have been more wrong. My memorandum to the incoming attorney general, deputy attorney general, and associate attorney general, dated January 7, 2005, contained the pointed recommendation that the Department recognize and act on "the need for remedial Privacy Act training for its law enforcement components, most particularly the FBI." But with incoming Attorney General Alberto Gonzales running the show (ostensibly), it soon became clear that he (and therefore the Department) had little or no interest in preventing the type of violations that had occurred so many times. Indeed, as it later became even clearer (see Chapter Forty-Three), he was more interested in committing them.

43   While the exact source of the leak has never been conclusively and officially determined, there is little doubt but that it was somewhere within the FBI, perhaps an FBI Special Agent by the name of Humphries. The genesis of the leak, and for the FBI learning any of this to begin with, was its investigation of a "cyber-stalking" complaint that led to the door of Petraeus's paramour (see below). (And as it happened, the secret investigative technique that was used to prove this connection was novel at the time and will not be disclosed here.)

44   According to documents filed in court, Petraeus lied to FBI investigators in October of 2012, before he resigned from the CIA, by saying he had never given classified information to Paula Broadwell. These court documents went on to state that after resigning from the CIA the next month, Petraeus executed a security form attesting that he did not then possess any classified information, even though the notebooks in question (having been returned to him by Paula Broadwell) were still at his home. Upon issuance of a search warrant, the FBI subsequently went to his home and seized those notebooks from an unlocked drawer in Petraeus's study. So it was that "the hits just kept on coming" for General Petraeus.

45   In fact, this is one of the crimes to which another general, Lieutenant General Michael T. Flynn, pled guilty in 2017 after spending 22 days as President Donald J. Trump's National Security Advisor. The exact phrasing of this felony was "willfully and knowingly making false statements to the FBI." Like so many others, Flynn received a pardon from President Trump.

46   A previous example of such a thing, though, was the treatment given CIA Director John M. Deutch when it was discovered in 1997 that the desk and laptop computers kept at his home contained highly classified information related to covert action and that his computers were wrongfully connected to the Internet. Not unlike Petraeus, Deutch was allowed to plead guilty to a misdemeanor for "mishandling government secrets" and on January 19, 2001, he was pardoned by President Bill Clinton.

I remember this well because one evening years later, I read in *Newsweek* that a cabinet secretary was considering appointing Deutch to an advisory panel that I knew would involve his access to classified information.

I had remembered the fact that when Deutch's case had been belatedly referred to Attorney General Janet Reno for possible prosecution (read: a sheer formality at that point), she had formally recommended that there be a proper investigation to determine whether Deutch should retain his security clearance, and that such an investigation, titled "Improper Handling of Classified Information by John M. Deutch," resulted in the issuance of a report in February of 2000 that concluded, *inter alia*, that "John Deutch's continued suitability for access to classified information should be reviewed immediately." (I had not remembered that exact language, of course; I had to go look it up.) So I delicately raised this with the right people in the Justice Department and in turn the White House, lest that cabinet agency proceed in possible ignorance of this with what it was reportedly planning.

And if it sounds as if in so doing I was going out of my way to be unsympathetic to John Deutch, well, consider this: Years prior to that, when my younger daughter Lindsay was playing on a soccer team with FDA Commissioner David A. Kessler's daughter (yes, this is part of how Washington works), his wife Paulette told the other parents a "sidelines story" about how she and her husband had recently been at some function for Clinton Administration political appointees where she was approached by a man who without identifying himself awkwardly tried to make small talk with her and, after she explained to him that she was there as the wife of the FDA commissioner, asked her: "Well, how do you spend your time, little lady?" Well, Paulette admitted to us that she was somewhat taken aback by that, seeing as how this was during the 1990s not the 1960s and she was a University of Chicago-trained practicing attorney, but when she told her husband about the encounter later on, he said: "Oh, that's just John Deutch."

47   Most significantly, perhaps, the entire plea deal enabled Petraeus to avoid a potentially embarrassing criminal trial in which details of his affair doubtless would have been featured prominently.

48   In this regard, Petraeus was different than the typical law enforcement leak victim in that it was not just the *fact* of his being under investigation (sensational as that was) that was wrongfully disclosed; rather, it was also part of the *content* of what was leaked (read: his affair with his biographer) that damaged him as well. The Federal Government had a legal obligation (read: and a moral duty) to keep both of those secrets for him, at least for a while longer.

49   These things are not mere allegations, it should be emphasized: Broadwell admitted to them when she eventually was tracked down as Jill Kelley's "cyberstalker" and was interrogated by the FBI. However, all charges against her (which were potentially serious) were ultimately dropped, without much public explanation, though her evident disinclination to sue the FBI (and perhaps also the Department of the Army) for arguably violating her rights under the Privacy Act, like with Generals Petraeus and Allen, might well have had something to do with that.

This, by the way, is not the first time that all of this has been written about Colonel Broadwell (read: Major Broadwell, actually, as she was soon demoted for having classified information at her home). Although I personally learned of Broadwell's name and involvement directly from Jill Kelley (see immediately below), it already had been made known to the media through a suspected leak to ABC News even before any potential prosecution or formal action by the Army was taken against her, evidently in yet another Privacy Act violation. Yes, this whole affair (read: ahem) was studded with leaks galore.

50   I speak so extensively about Jill Kelley here because I came to know her (read: from a distance) when she repeatedly asked me to represent her in the fall of 2012. By that point in her saga, she had come to the legal conclusion (read: pretty much on her own) that she had been "badly mistreated" by the Federal Government and that her rightful remedy for that was a damages lawsuit under the Privacy Act of 1974. And in her own research of this, she came across the fact that I had been litigating a novel Privacy Act lawsuit on behalf of many newly

minted young attorneys who had been wrongfully "screened out" (read: "deselected" is what then-Attorney General Alberto R. Gonzales called it) from being hired through the Department of Justice's Attorney General's Honors Program, on political or ideological grounds (see Chapter Forty-Three). (In fact, after deposing Gonzales to within an inch of his life for nearly seven hours in 2010, I wound up prevailing in that lawsuit to the tune of $572,000.)

Anyway, Jill Kelley called me one afternoon to tell me that she had considered this, as well as information about my background that appeared on my faculty page (see Chapter Forty-Two), and that I just "had to" be her attorney for this Privacy Act lawsuit that she was planning. Well, I quickly gained several impressions of Jill (read: she very much insisted that we speak on a first-name basis), not the least of which was that she seemed not at all familiar with the basic concept of taking "no" for an answer. (I had many reasons for not agreeing to represent her, not the least of which being that in retirement I carried no malpractice insurance -- which I had not needed for that Honors Program case -- and I told her that right away.)

But I listened very politely to her during what evolved into a series of about a half-dozen such phone calls, as I recall, and I finally satisfied her by recommending some attorneys whom I thought might just take her case. And one of them did. So Jill and her husband sued the United States in 2013, alleging that either the Department of Justice (read: the FBI) or else the Department of Defense (or conceivably both) violated the Privacy Act by disclosing sensitive law enforcement information about them during the FBI's investigation of General Petraeus. In this lawsuit, they were represented by former Office of Management and Budget General Counsel Alan C. Raul, of the well-respected law firm Sidley and Austin, and their case became bolstered somewhat when FBI Special Agent Humphries attested that he believed that someone at FBI Headquarters, where Jill Kelley seemed to be regarded as a mere "femme fatale," had leaked her name in "a purposeful attempt to discredit both Mrs. Kelley and myself." (Yes, he too might have become a Privacy Act wrongful disclosure victim himself down the road, which was long and winding like so much else in the case.)

In the summer of 2015, remarkably, the Justice Department actually offered to settle the Kelleys's claims, but evidently their subsequent negotiations left them too far apart, with the Kelleys reportedly holding out for more than $4,000,000. And then by the following spring, continued "disagreements" between the Kelleys and their counsel apparently reached a boiling point at which the latter asked to withdraw from the case, citing (as many spouses do in divorce proceedings) "irreconcilable differences." And with that, in a fittingly odd denouement, the Kelleys inexplicably just dropped their suit.

51   This is the second time I've had occasion to use this glib phrase in this chapter alone. It brings to mind my failed effort to create and distribute such a memo two years before I retired in 2007, as mentioned above.

52   To close out this sad chapter, it should be noted that on January 22, 2013, General Allen was entirely cleared in a Defense Department misconduct inquiry. And he retired from the military two months later. In my view, he had the right under our privacy laws (read: Exemption 7(C) of the Freedom of Information Act and subsection (b) of the Privacy Act) to have been investigated toward that end without the public ever learning anything (read: not a damn thing) about it. Had he sued, General Allen's case for damages due to more than grossly negligent reputational harm would have been, in my humble opinion, very strong.

CHAPTER FOURTEEN

1   The citations for the two statutes are quite similar: The FOIA had been codified in 1966 at 5 U.S.C. § 552, so the Privacy Act was codified in 1974 at 5 U.S.C. § 552a, creating much room for confusion between the two.

2   The record is not entirely clear on this point, but the fact that the Justice Department had been corrupted during the Nixon Administration probably had something to do with Congress not wanting to entrust it with overseeing what was widely viewed as one of several Watergate remedies.

3   Under subsection (v) of the Privacy Act, OMB is designated as the agency responsible for the Privacy Act's governmentwide oversight. But historically that obligation has been honored more in the breach by OMB, leaving it to the Department of Justice (through OIP) to fill the gap with governmentwide guidance, training, and assistance to federal agencies as a function ancillary to its advisory role under the FOIA. In 2006, shortly before I retired, that role was shifted to the newly created Office of Privacy and Civil Liberties in the Department's Office of the Deputy Attorney General. Currently, it resides back at OMB where it ought to, in the very capable hands of the head of the Privacy Branch of OMB's Office of Information and Regulatory Affairs, former OIP Associate Director Kirsten J. Moncada.

4   It took some time and effort, but not long after the Privacy Act's provisions became effective on December 31, 1974, federal agencies began conforming their file systems and recordkeeping practices to fit its requirements, most particularly as to file system organization and record retrieval, such that after a while it was the rare part of any agency that had failed to do so. A notable exception to this, however, one redolent of irony, was the Office of the Independent Counsel for the investigation of the "Clinton Passport" matter -- i.e., the 1992 pre-election review of then-candidate Bill Clinton's passport file at the State Department in search of a letter rumored to exist that allegedly memorialized an effort by Clinton in the 1960s to renounce his U.S. citizenship in order to avoid the draft.

That office was headed by Independent Counsel Joseph E. diGenova, a former United States Attorney who was tasked with investigating whether any such search violated the law, most particularly the Privacy Act of 1974. Yet when I was asked by that office to consult with it on the Privacy Act's requirements, I learned that, amazingly, it had set up its own file systems and information-retrieval software in a way that did not comply with the Privacy Act itself. I remember Joe diGenova as being none too pleased to hear that, and not because he thought he had done anything wrong; the irony of that was profound.

Years later, in 2015, I sat behind a cramped table right next to Joe at a televised panel discussion that the right-leaning group Judicial Watch conducted on the subject of another Clinton's use and abuse of her email system, also at the Department of State. For my part, I was speaking "against the grain" in explaining how she had violated civil law requirements (read: the Federal Records Act and at least the spirit of the FOIA), but I declined at that time to suggest publicly that she might have violated any criminal statute (read: 18 U.S.C. 793(f)) (see Chapter Forty-Seven). Joe, on the other hand, grabbed that criminal thread and vociferously shook it to an extreme, as if to predict that Hillary Clinton would be "in handcuffs by sundown" for it, so much so that I could feel his leg vibrating with his anti-Clinton fervor. We both had come a long way in those intervening 22 years.

5   The Privacy Act's specific access exemptions include information classified on national security grounds, information on confidential sources who received express assurances of confidentiality, attorney work-product information, and confidential U.S. Secret Service information.

6   Significantly, the word "disclosure" in this context does not mean just disclosure to the public or disclosure outside the executive branch, as would be so under the FOIA. Rather, it includes disclosure to another federal agency and even disclosure *within* the agency that is holding the information. The latter is regulated through a "need-to-know" standard. Because even intra-agency disclosure is regulated, the Privacy Act calls for the use of strict security measures and training of agency personnel in order to protect the internal confidentiality of all Privacy Act-covered information.

7   Note that this says "retrieved," not "retrievable," which can make a big difference in the case of information held in database form, rather than in "old-fashioned" paper files. Nowadays, agencies are *able* to retrieve all sorts of information through searches conducted with "retrieval" computer software, but only the information that they actually do retrieve in the regular course of agency business, in that form, is Privacy Act-covered.

8   The terms "routine use," "systems notices," and "systems of records" (or "record systems") are highly technical terms of art created exclusively for the Privacy Act as part its unique recordkeeping requirements.

9   AUSA Convertino's case was a highly unfortunate one in which a very successful anti-terrorism prosecutor ran afoul of his supervisors on something (the merits of which do not matter here), was the subject of a disciplinary referral to the Justice Department's Office of Professional Responsibility, and then saw the abstract fact of that referral leaked to a reporter. Ultimately, former AUSA Convertino did not prevail in his "wrongful disclosure" suit because the reporter and his newspaper successfully raised the "reporter's privilege" as a barrier to pinning down which agency employee(s) made the disclosure.

10   Mike Isikoff and I, by the way, became professional friends under very unusual circumstances. It began on October 4, 1993, when Associate Attorney General Webster L. "Webb" Hubbell and I held a press conference as part of the "roll out" of Attorney General Janet Reno's big FOIA policy memorandum on the First Floor of the Main Justice Building and afterwards he surreptitiously followed me up to my office on the Seventh Floor (read: I turned around and he was there). He pressed me for further details on the subject, which of course was entirely fair (Mike was working for *The Washington Post* at the time) and I suppose I gave him the type of candid answers (read: direct, unstinting) that he was not used to receiving from a government official.

Skip forward about a month and there came a day (November 3, as I recall) that the Department issued (read: distributed to reporters in a room maintained for that purpose in its Office of Public Affairs) a government guidance memorandum telling agencies exactly how to handle FOIA requests for White House-originated information in the Clinton Administration. This was in fact a "regular" memorandum in that it replaced one that we had last sent around four years earlier, in the George H.W. Bush Administration. But that evening, I received an urgent call from Mike (read: I think he managed to reach me at home through the switchboard in the Justice Command Center) in which he declared that the timing of this memo was "highly suspicious" because it was issued by Webb Hubbell on the very same day that news of the Whitewater scandal (which certainly did involve Webb) broke into the public domain. Mike's theory (my word, not his) was that this memo was issued to distract the media from Whitewater, and he said he was about to write a story to that effect.

I can still recall, almost 30 years later, sitting at my kitchen table for more than an hour that evening trying over the phone to "talk Mike down" from what he so strongly suspected. I told him that what he thought just was not so, that there was absolutely no connection between the two things, and that he would be making an embarrassing mistake to go ahead with such a story. And I used a technique that I sometimes call "hitting him with a two-by-four across the bridge of the nose": "Mike," I said, "I have a big advantage over you on this: *I'm* the one who wrote the damn memo and I know firsthand why it was issued today!"

That did stop him cold, as intended, but it took a lot more explaining. I told him that I had started drafting that memo for the Clinton Transition Team the previous December, leaving blank spaces in it to be filled in once the new administration took shape. I told him that it had been sitting on my desk (read: on my computer, actually) as I coordinated its development with a buddy (Marvin Krislov, later president of Oberlin College) in the Office of the White House Counsel. And I told him that I'd given it to Webb in final form to initial just the day before.

To make this long story just a bit shorter, Mike eventually admitted (contrary to his cherished "investigative reporter instincts") that he believed me (which is where having a reputation for integrity certainly helps), so he therefore did not run the story. And we've been, as I say, friends ever since. Over the years, even into my retirement, he used me as a "sounding board" for his government-related stories and became a regular speaker at my Collaboration on Government Secrecy programs, including once while from "the road" on the way to the birthplace of International Right-to-Know Day in Bulgaria (see Chapter Forty-Two). I consider Mike to be a journalist *nonpareil*.

11   A disadvantage to this, however, is that a Privacy Act access request, much like a FOIA request, can take a long time.

12   Taking such a step has an analytical consequence: It involves the creation of a new "record" under the Privacy Act, one that is literally born subject to the Privacy Act's requirements and prohibitions.

13   For example, one public-interest organization, the Electronic Privacy Information Center ("EPIC," to those hooked up to it), recently called on Congress to go even further on matters of privacy by establishing an independent "U.S. Data Protection Agency." As proposed, in a Senate bill (S. 3300) introduced in the fall of 2020, it would protect from disclosure not only Federal Government information but also private-sector consumer information, an area in which the United States has blatantly fallen far behind Europe for more than 20 years now. In fact, the U.S. had already made two failed attempts to comply with European Union data-protection standards (in the form of Europe's "General Data Protection Regulation," or "GDPR"), with two weak plans called "Safe Harbor" and "Privacy Shield," the latter of which was rejected by the European Court of Justice in July of 2020.

   Over the course of my years at OIP, I grew increasingly concerned about this and talked with some of my colleagues in Europe about it, because neither the White House nor the two other executive branch agencies best situated to exert jurisdiction over such matters, the Federal Trade Commission or the Commerce Department, consistently did so. My own view is that the U.S. should establish a new federal agency to oversee both the Privacy Act and data protection, perhaps by amending the former to deal with the latter, in order to remedy longstanding deficiencies in both areas.

   On the other side of that coin, however, lies the deep-seated concern that involving a government agency in any new private-sector privacy regulation could lead to the use of such information for particularly popular (read: with the government) law enforcement purposes, such as anti-terrorism initiatives. That very concern arose in France in early 2021, where the tension between privacy protection and combatting terrorism is now especially strong.

CHAPTER FIFTEEN

1   Evidently, sometimes these cash "pick-ups" would take place within the United States, but sometimes not. In addition to his trips to Moscow, Morris also with his brother made trips to China, Eastern Europe, and Cuba.

2   Indeed, both the CPUSA in America and the Kremlin in Moscow held Morris Childs in great esteem, as he made no fewer than 52 secret trips to Moscow over the years. In 1977, in honor of his (i.e., Childs's) 75th birthday, Soviet Union General Secretary Leonid I. Brezhnev hosted a banquet in his honor at the Kremlin, where Brezhnev personally presented him with a medal, the Order of the Red Banner, for his services in couriering funds around the world for the Soviet Government. This involved his having face-to-face conversations also with Soviet Premier Nikita S. Khrushchev and China's leaders Mao Zedong (née Mao Tse-tung) and Chou En Lai. He also met with self-described Cuban President-for-Life Fidel A. Castro (long before Trump ever thought of the idea) in the Cuban embassy in Moscow and with Soviet Union General Secretary Yuri V. Andropov.

3   This was through a wide-scale initiative that the Bureau began in the early 1950s called "Operation TOPLEV," which was designed to recruit high-level American Communists as informants for it. Doing so was not quite as difficult for it as was recruiting foreign agents (known as "intelligence sources") for the CIA, largely because these were Americans, whose allegiance to begin with was only an ideological one, which can sometimes be merely ephemeral or transactional.

4   This "deal was sealed," so to speak, when Special Agent Freyman decided to provide Morris Childs with support for his heart condition. Freyman actually arranged, entirely on his own authority, for him to be treated at the Mayo Clinic in Rochester, Minnesota, where his health greatly improved. Afterward, Morris Childs even credited (read: privately) Freyman with saving his life.

5   In 1962, the Childs brothers' team even broadened to include Morris's new wife Eva, who played a vital role in both enterprises -- accompanying Morris in most of his 57 total CPUSA "missions" overseas and simultaneously aiding him in his "double-agent" work for the FBI. She became very well acquainted with the Bureau's tight-knit "handler" (or "case agent") team over the years, especially Special Agent Freyman and three others, forming lasting friendships.

6   In one dramatic such instance, apparently Morris happened to be at a meeting inside the Kremlin on November 23, 1963, when word arrived that Lee Harvey Oswald, who had defected to the Soviet Union from 1959-1962, had assassinated President Kennedy; upon his return, he was able to assure the FBI that the Soviets with whom he was meeting were absolutely stunned at the news and that it appeared that the USSR had had no hand in the assassination.

7   In the early years, Jack Childs was more useful to the FBI than he was in later years, when Morris became the principal "Solo Source" by far.

8   Who says FBI guys have no sense of humor? And back then, they definitely were all "guys." When I began absorbing FBI lore in 1977 (read: I spent a lot of time over there), J. Edgar Hoover had been dead for five years and the Bureau finally had begun hiring female Special Agents. One of them, FBI Special Agent Margaret "Maggie" Owens, who later gained a coveted "Legat" (read: "Legal Attaché") posting in London and then returned to FBI Headquarters as a congressional liaison, only to become embroiled in the Clinton Administration's "Filegate" scandal, was a friend back then. She told me that, sadly, one of the first female FBI Special Agents tragically died in a plane crash while returning to Washington on FBI business.

I remember also hearing (from male FBI Special Agents, this time) that one of the very first female Special Agents, in 1972, competed so hard and well at the FBI's Training Academy in Quantico, Virginia, that she surpassed most of her male classmates and as a mark of respect earned the nickname "Thunder Thighs." A dozen years later, I spent a week there, as part of a Continuity-of-Government activity (see Chapter Twenty-Six), and came away thinking that in addition to other amenities it certainly had a great pool.

9   Owing to the extreme sensitivity of their dual infiltration, only a very small group inside the FBI knew of the Childs's identities -- and the Bureau further minimized even that by keeping four Special Agents in its Chicago and New York Field Offices solely on Operation Solo for a dozen years or more. Reportedly the FBI allowed one, Special Agent Alexander C. Burlinson, to remain a Childs handler for a total of 24 years. Another, Special Agent Walter A. Boyle, stayed with them for 20 years. Yet another, Special Agent John Langtry (who was the "case agent" for Morris's brother Jack) put in 14. And their Supervisory Special Agent, James M. Fox, was with the Childs brothers for so many years (beginning in 1971) that Morris and his wife Eva thought of him as "family." (Jim

came to play a role in another of my cases, described in Chapter Sixteen.) Even the brothers' initial recruiter, Special Agent Freyman himself, remained their handler (or "case agent") for 13 years (including the year of the Albertson "coup"), until he retired. Never before in the FBI's history had it kept Special Agents on a single case for such protracted periods of time.

I need to add a special word here about another supervisory special agent who was, in his own way, involved in what the FBI sometimes called the "Solo operation." Michael Steinbeck was an FBI counterintelligence specialist who in time rose to the supervisory position of unit chief in its National Security Division. Because his activities linked so often to the classification work done by some of the attorneys in OIP (in connection with OIP's "Document Review Committee" ("DRC," to those who felt cleared) responsibilities), several of them thought that they knew Mike pretty well.

Then one day, they heard whispers "over at the Bu" that Mike had been diagnosed with a fatal disease, in the form of a "rare parasite" that he had mysteriously contracted somewhere in the Pacific. And then he died of AIDS, unable to come out as a gay FBI official even more than a decade after J. Edgar Hoover was gone. Professionally, the poor guy was as conservative as they come (read: very conservative, even for an FBI person), but it just goes to show that some people can live with enormous inner turmoil when their professional and private lives conflict.

10   This term clearly derives from the word "snitch," which is street jargon for "inform," as with a "law enforce-ment informant." And the "jacket" part of the term doubtless comes from the police slang word for an official criminal file folder.

11   I remember reading in the underlying files that Albertson was chosen for this role because he was, as far as the Bureau knew (which was a lot), one of the most capable and efficient of the CPUSA's high-level members. In fact, the FBI had been reading his mail and recording almost all the Albertsons's home telephone conversa-tions with wiretaps for years, just routinely. Years later, when news of this operation eventually became public, together with the astonishing story of the "Solo Sources," I remember that some journalist wrote a lengthy article about it with a Biblical-sounding title *Let Him Wear a Wolf's Head*. (Although I certainly read that at the time, it evidently is no longer in print.)

12   Of course, some of the Bureau's most experienced Special Agents assembled to shape the content of the "informant report" as realistically as possible, with words and phrases that the Childs brothers themselves had used in the recent past. They even concluded the report by asking for "a raise in expenses." Inasmuch as the FBI (unlike Nixon) did not electronically surveil itself, it is not known whether this merry band had pizza brought in to the Main Justice Building for this enterprise -- but if it did, one can be quite certain that any sauce spilled would have landed on shirts that were white.

13   Indeed, if one were to say that it was nothing short of miraculous that the delicate secrecy of the "Solo Sources" actually remained intact for nearly 40 years (i.e., from 1952 to 1991), unbeknownst to the public until Supervisory Special Agent Jim Fox first spoke openly (and reverently) about it at Morris's funeral, then the secrecy of the "Albertson operation" would have to be deemed "Vatican worthy" in nature. One might even say that the "double secrecy" of these two things, interconnected as they were, was "one for the books."

14   The two Solo Sources reported to their handler (who was still Special Agent Carl Freyman) that the CPUSA leadership's "party line" (pun intended) was that it had acted so swiftly on "irrefutable evidence" that it removed "every shadow of doubt" that Albertson was a duplicitous traitor to their cause.

15   The Childs brothers ought to be in the "Double-Agent Hall of Fame," because not only did Morris receive that Order of the Red Banner medal from Leonid Brezhnev in 1977, their joint work as spies for the American Intelligence Community was recognized on the other side of the Iron Curtain when they both were awarded the Presidential Medal of Freedom by President Ronald W. Reagan in 1987, in what doubtless could be seen as a case of President Reagan characteristically "poking the bear in the eye." (If this were today, with Russian President Vladimir V. Putin in charge, there might be concern about his having Morris Childs poisoned even on American soil.)

For Jack Childs, this award was posthumous, as he had died of natural causes in 1980. Morris Childs, the one who had had a serious heart condition going back to the late 1940s, lived in "double retirement" until 1991. He enjoyed a generous FBI "pension" in recompense for all that he had done. And within the hallowed halls of the FBI, at least, they together carried the clandestine title of "The FBI's Most Valued Secret Agents of the Cold War."

16   This included not only Moscow and its environs, of course, but also several Eastern European cities, Havana, and Peking -- a total of 57 overseas trips, sometimes for weeks at a time, from 1958 to 1982, the year of his retirement from both the CPUSA and the FBI.

17   It evidently was Jack Childs who remembered that Levison had been an active Communist Party member in the early 1950s before he (Levison) withdrew from that role. But for Jack Childs's memory of this, J. Edgar Hoover would not have had it as a predicate for wiretapping Levison, and in turn King, not to mention for classifying everything about Levison (and thus including Levison in relation to King) on what seemed like solid national security grounds.

18   Eventually, the Bureau learned that Levison and King had become well acquainted as far back as 1956, in New York City, with Levison over the next dozen years providing King with increasing amounts of political counseling, close friendship, and occasional financial support. Levinson outlived King, but he never learned that the Childs brothers were the ones that triggered the FBI's surveillance, including through wiretaps, of both him and King.

19   More than 30 years later, in 2007, Carl became a member of my secrecy center's advisory board at American University's Washington College of Law. He also had become the Justice Department's Public Affairs Director, as well as a good friend, by then (see Chapters Twenty-Nine and Forty-Two).

20   Recognizing the significance of this, Carl made sure that this document found its way to the ACLU, where it could be put to good use. And it was.

21   I recall thinking when I read this document that even the deletion of a mere name was not sufficient to provide adequate confidential source protection in this case. In other words, it would not have taken very much effort on the part of Carl or some other document analyst to (even in pre-Google days) search for any instance of a CPUSA member being expelled and then link it together with this document. In other words, the inexperienced (by definition) FBI FOIA "processor" should have deleted far more "context" surrounding the names in this document as well.

22   Such a thing was to happen in another of my FBI cases as well, during the summer of 1977, though it did not come to the fore until I began defending that case in 1979 (see Chapter Sixteen).

23   Albertson had died in 1972. His FBI file, however, very arguably pertained to his widow Lillian B. Lewis (a.k.a. Lillie B. Albertson) given that their lives in relation to the CPUSA, and hence the FBI, were so intertwined.

The author with his two oldest
younger brothers, 1962

The author with his father and
younger brothers, 1967

The author with his parents and
four siblings, 1973

The author with his mother
and future former wife
Debbie, 1977

The author with his four siblings, 1978

Former OIP paralegal Ana Belen Montes, released from federal prison on January 6, 2023

Ana's encryption/decryption "cheat sheet," as posted by the FBI

Attorney General Robert F. Kennedy (to whom the Main Justice Building was dedicated on what would have been his 76th birthday, which also was the author's 50th birthday, November 20, 2001) holding an informal meeting in his converted conference room, 1964

"Minnie Lou" (a.k.a. "The Spirit of Justice"), located on the stage of the Main Justice Building's Great Hall

Iconic photograph of the MLK Assassination scene, 1968

The author appearing on C-SPAN's *Washington Journal* program while declining to identify the two Clinton Administration scandals that never became public, March 17, 2015

Criminal Justice Class Hosts Speakers

The author giving a presentation at Brentwood High School, 1982

The author finishing a 10K at the Tidal Basin, 1984

Former FBI Special Agent and spy for the Soviet Union Earl E. Pitts

The author finishing a half-marathon at Jones Beach, Long Island, 1986

Metal plaque outside of Room 5233-5235 in the Main Justice Building (Courtesy of current Justice Department attorney Rosemary A. Hart)

Proceedings of the Nazi saboteur trial in 1942 (Courtesy of former Justice Department component head Linda A. Cinciotta, whose father was a court reporter for the trial)

The author with other Justice Department attorneys and AG Edwin
Meese III (standing as far from him as possible), 1988

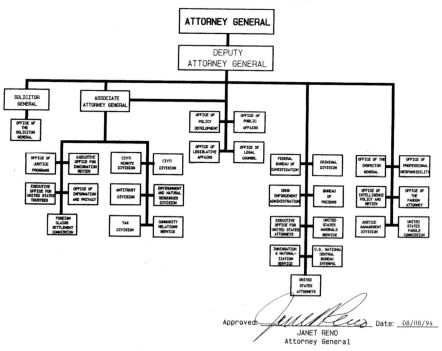

Department of Justice organizational chart, 1994

The author standing near the receding edge of Athabasca Glacier at the Columbia Icefields, Alberta, Canada, 1996. (Not shown: The "high tech" DOJ mobile phone used throughout the trip.)

The author with AG Janet Reno at a FOIA program in the FBI Main Auditorium, 1998

The author presenting a retirement gift to Information Security Oversight Office Director Steven Garfinkel, in suitably redacted form, 2002

The author when profiled by *Legal Times* upon his retirement from the Justice Department, 2007 *(Courtesy of* Legal Times *photographer Diego Radzinski)*

The author giving the keynote address at the Library of Congress's "25th Annual Forum on Federal Information Policies," September 12, 2008

The *Glomar Explorer* submarine-
retrieval ship

Deputy White House Counsel
Vincent W. Foster, Jr.,
Jan. 15, 1945-July 20, 1993

D.C. Circuit Court of
Appeals Judge Patricia A.
Millett with the author,
after speaking to his
class on oral advocacy on
January 29, 2014
*(Courtesy of the
Washington College of Law)*

Mug shot of Nick Nolte,
California Highway Patrol

Mug shot of Zacarias
Moussaoui, known as "the
20th 9/11 hijacker,"
Sherburne County, Minnesota,
Sheriff's Office

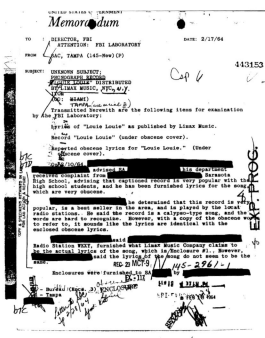

Redacted document as released by the FBI under the FOIA, showing FOIA exemptions applied and numerous internal markings and notations

Photograph of UFO sighted hovering over Gate C-17 at O'Hare International Airport on November 7, 2006

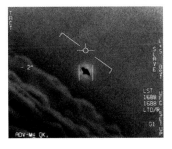

Snapshot from the "Gimbal" video taken by a U.S. Navy F/A-18 fighter jet off the coast of Florida in 2015, as authenticated by the Navy in 2017 and released to the public in 2020 together with "Flir1" and "Go Fast" videos of comparable "Tic Tac" UAP encounters in 2004 and 2015, respectively

U.S. delegation to the Sino-American Conference on Rule of Law and Human Rights, Xiamen, China, 2010, showing Professor Jerome A. Cohen, bottom row, far left, and Circuit Court Judge John M. Walker, Jr., next to him

Side view of Nappa Hall, "the ancestral home of the Metcalfe clan," Askrigg, England, taken in 2010 (but looking pretty much the same as when constructed during 1426-1459)

Senator Patrick J. Leahy together with Congressman Thomas J. Downey and the author at the Collaboration on Government Secrecy's Annual Freedom of Information Day Celebration, March 16, 2009 *(Courtesy of the Washington College of Law)*

The author with his grandson, 2019

National Archives Main Building, with adjacent Main Justice Building in background *(Roman Babakin/Shutterstock.com)*

24   The way in which the Bureau handled its recordkeeping regarding William Albertson (and his wife Lillie) was such that his "file" contained massive amounts of information about the Childs brothers, the document forgery, and the CPUSA. So the FOIA (and Privacy Act) case alone promised to be a lot to handle.

25   Ultimately, as anticipated, Lillie Albertson's claims did merge together into a single lawsuit. This alone made that case unique. As of that time, no one had ever filed such a "combination" case before. And I don't know that any has been filed since.

26   Anyone with knowledge of how the Civil Division ordinarily operated might well think that the opposite of this would be the case -- i.e., that the Torts Branch attorney handling the FTCA claim (in anticipation of a tort case arising from it) would just oversee the processing of Lillie Albertson's FOIA request (and handle any ensuing litigation on it). In other words, there was good cause for viewing the tort aspect of such an exceptional fact pattern as primary, with the FOIA aspect secondary.

And indeed, the principal director of the Torts Branch at the time, who ironically had been chief of the Civil Division's Information and Privacy Section until 1977, expressed no small amount of displeasure at this jurisdictional arrangement, even though he had been a self-animated mentor of mine for quite some time by then. Knowing him well (which wasn't difficult), I imagined (read: hoped) that he might have just seen it as a bureaucratic "turf" sort of thing.

27   I had previously been part of an inter-branch "shared-case" arrangement between what became the Civil Division's Federal Programs Branch and its Torts Branch when I agreed to take on the *Ramo v. Department of the Navy* case, which then went to trial in San Francisco, together with Torts Section (later Torts Branch) attorney Nicki L. Koutsis. In each of these two instances, it was my strong personal relationships (with Nicki and then Freddi) that made this professional arrangement so effective. (This is another litigation lesson that I passed on to my students years later: It can be very helpful if attorneys sharing responsibility for a case have, or can quickly develop, such a relationship of trust and high regard (see Chapter Fifty).)

28   William Albertson, his wife Lillie, and their family were ostracized by their friends as well as by their long-standing CPUSA colleagues, which constituted their entire world. No one believed him when he said that the discovered informant report must be a fake planted by the FBI to destroy him, nor did anyone at the CPUSA or the Kremlin ever figure out that the FBI had such a motivation (let alone the technical wizardry) to do so. (Ironically, the Bureau knew this through the continued informant reports of the two "Solo Sources" themselves, who of course remained at the CPUSA in perfectly good standing. Albertson died as the result of an accidental fall from a porch that broke his neck. (No, there was no foul play suspected; the Bureau had no reason to have him killed, even it ever did such a thing, and neither did the Kremlin.)

Most Americans, perhaps, would find it hard to imagine being pained at expulsion from a group as unpopular, even detested, as the American Communist Party was, but communism had been William Albertson's (and Lillie Albertson's) whole life. He lost his circle of friends, he lost his reputation, and he lost his profession (as it were). His family was shunned, even threatened, by those around them. As an example, a school took a scholarship away from his youngest child, on the theory that the "informant money" that he presumably received from the FBI should be sufficient for him. Tragically, Albertson held only menial jobs, in transient work, until he died in 1972, at the age of 61.

29   There are several possible threshold defenses to claims under the FTCA. Among them are "due care," "discretionary function," and (for law enforcement conduct occurring before 1974) "intentional torts." Plus, in a "national security" case such as this, the "granddaddy" of all defenses, the "nuclear option" as it were, was

the use of the State Secrets Privilege, which if invoked in this case would have precluded Lillie Albertson from having her claim even considered by a court on its merits.

30   This is where Freddi came in. Her role, as I arranged it, was to help me factor in the value to the Government of it being able to elide any risk of litigating Lillie Albertson's FOIA or tort claims at the appellate level, where the uniquely horrendous and emotionally compelling facts of the case could lead to the creation of what we called "bad law." ("Bad facts make for bad law," is what we would say.) I chose my proposed settlement figure of $100,000 partly with this in mind.

31   It must be emphasized here that, unlike other parties to civil litigation, the United States Department of Justice has a special obligation to "do justice" in a case, beyond what its client's own particular interests might be. Given the extreme circumstances underlying this pre-litigation matter here, this obligation weighed heavily in my judgment about it.

32   This belief about Lillie Albertson's amenability to settling was ultimately corroborated when she readily accepted, evidently without even making a counter-offer, the Government's eventual settlement offer in 1989. Then again, the fact that it was a considerably larger amount might have had something to do with that.

33   This was not hard to predict because I knew that the Bureau had not done a good job in processing these records for FOIA disclosure in the first place and that they were going to be "reprocessed" on administrative appeal, with liberal "public interest" standards, anyway. As it turned out, Lillie Albertson received more than 30,000 new or newly "reprocessed" document pages by the end of the case.

34   This problem became much more of one when AAG Babcock herself left the Department (to return to her tenured position on the faculty of Stanford Law School), whereupon she was replaced by someone who was, shall we say, less inclined by nature to be sympathetic to Lillie Albertson's situation. In retrospect, of course, it would have been easier if I had known to bring in Jim Fox.

35   This is because the "hard liners" did win out after I left the Civil Division, at least in the "short run." They resisted my proposed $100,000 settlement until the point at which, in exasperation, Lillie Albertson filed an FTCA lawsuit on her claim in 1984. Then, for *five years*, the Civil Division's Torts Branch did raise and maintain the State Secrets Privilege threshold defense, contending that the Federal Government could not contest the suit at all without compromising state secrets, and that hence the case should be dismissed; even to file a formal Answer to the Complaint, it argued, would irreparably harm national security. (There is a technical legal term for this: "bullshit.") And the Department argued that position through an *in camera* declaration, i.e., not on the public record, which I knew firsthand skirted the rules for using *ex parte, in camera* submissions. (For the record, by the way, the FBI's entire Solo files, totaling nearly 7000 document pages, were finally declassified in mid-2011 and early 2012.)

The District Court for the District of Columbia nevertheless flatly refused to dismiss the case on that basis, which was no surprise. Then, undaunted, the Civil Division took that decision up on appeal to the D.C. Circuit Court of Appeals, which in turn also rejected the state secrets defense, declaring (over a dissent by Circuit Court Judge Douglas H. Ginsburg that itself contained several "secret" pages that were left blank) that it was unconvinced that a lawsuit 25 years after the fact actually threatened current national security. This all amounted to an enormous embarrassment for the Torts Branch and for the (ir)responsible branch director in particular. And it led to a quick settlement of the case, with the rational involvement of the Solicitor General's Office, not too long thereafter.

36   At the time, this was very first lawsuit in which the Federal Government agreed to make a compensatory payment to a victim of FBI action, most particularly activity undertaken through its COINTELPRO program (redundant as that might sound). *New York Times* journalist Anthony Lewis (who had spurred my interest in civil liberties law 15 years earlier (see Chapter Nine) and had closely followed the Albertson saga), opined in an article titled "Abroad at Home; Rule of Law?" that "the outcome of the case is a victory for decency." Well, yes, relatively speaking, but for my money it would have been a helluva lot more "decent" if Lillie Albertson hadn't had to wait so long for compensation.

37   Later on, in the mid-1980s, I brought Freddi into the "Continuity-of-Government" program (see Chapter Twenty-Six) once I reached a leadership level within it from which I could do so. In time, I was able to do the same with three other Department attorneys whom I knew well and trusted, greatly strengthening the program's Legal and Law Enforcement Group, which by then I led.

CHAPTER SIXTEEN

1   This is the point at which I should acknowledge that I considered whether this plaintiff's gender should be masked -- by use of "his or her" -- in this chapter. Obviously, I decided against that. The reasons for that were threefold: First, a big part of this man's "story" is that he was a highly respected leader in his community during the 1960s; to say that this was a man, not a woman, does not add much to what anyone would imagine anyway. Second, the very use of "his or her" here would be taken by many or most observers to be an unrealistically hollow attempt to employ a pretense that a female could have been this longtime source. And lastly, even more than 40 years after the fact (not to mention more than 50 years after the informant activity), I remember exactly what (and how) the identification risk was for that person and am in a singular position to make an informed judgment on how this risk stands (read: for his surviving family members, including one in particular) today.

2   This was a good-faith but in this case misguided effort by the Bureau to use Special Agents from "the field" during the summer of 1977 to clear up as much of its huge "backlog" of pending FOIA requests as possible.

3   The truth was that this plaintiff's name appeared in the document a total of eight times and the inexperienced FOIA analyst responsible for deleting it succeeded in doing so only seven times. Yes, he failed to notice and delete it the eighth time it appeared. And then a FOIA supervisor who was responsible for double-checking that work failed likewise. I learned this upon examining the document in both its original and "processed" versions, as part of my basic fact-finding for purposes of handling the case. (And this was reminiscent, of course, of what had happened in the "Solo Source" case when a name was once overlooked, and not deleted, in the same way (see Chapter Fifteen).)

4   This meant me, of course, and whomsoever I chose to involve in the case for purposes of best handling it. At that point in time, after a recent Civil Division reorganization, I might not have had the remarkable autonomy that I enjoyed on the Martin Luther King "survivor privacy" case a year earlier (see Chapter Three), but I nonetheless had the wherewithal to move the case in the direction that seemed most just to me, bearing in mind the palpable risk that the case's very existence posed to the plaintiff. I intended to spare no effort in attempting to bring the case to its best possible conclusion, in "the interests of justice," as quickly as I could.

5   Only in this case, from these relatives' perspective, the word "mistaken" carried an entirely different meaning. To the Bureau, of course, it described the act of "under-withholding" in the rushed processing of records responsive to the reporter's FOIA request. But to this plaintiff's family, which was truly in the dark, it meant that the substance and import of the disclosure were grossly incorrect.

6   This explanation was made to this source's former handler, of course, not to me directly. Every attorney knows (or should know) the ethics rule that an attorney shall not communicate with a party opponent who is represented by counsel. Mindful of this, I had to consult with the Department's Office of Professional Responsibility ("OPR," to its close friends) in order to make sure that I was staying within proper ethical bounds under this case's unique circumstances. Even before doing this, I had researched Canon No. 9 of the American Bar Association's Ethics Code, as further explicated in its Ethical Consideration No. 75, about effectively engaging in such a communication through an intermediary -- in this case, the FBI handler. How I proceeded in this case was "blessed" by OPR.

7   After all, this informant had spent most of his adult life pretending to be strongly anti-government in his personal and professional orientation, and anti-FBI in particular, in order to maintain a clandestine posture that was most protective of what he actually was (or by a later point in time, had been) doing. His family and many friends knew him only that way. So he had no room to suddenly act any way other than utterly outraged by what, as it now appeared, "they did to him." (Yes, there's a "movie of the week" screenplay in there somewhere, one that would be sensationally animated by the uniqueness of this case, but you won't get it from me.)

8   When the FBI "runs" such a confidential source, it establishes what is known as a "134 file" that is maintained by a Special Agent "handler" for as long as the source remains alive (and in many instances even longer). In this case, fortunately, that "handler," Jim Fox, was still at the FBI. In fact, he had been a relatively young Special Agent when he began handling this informant and over the years had risen in rank (based partly upon his success with this informant, no doubt) to become the "ASAC" (i.e., the "Assistant Special Agent-in-Charge," or second-in-command) of the Bureau's San Francisco Field Office. And coincident with his Complaint's filing, this plaintiff had successfully reached out to that FBI official in a phone call.

Jim Fox, by the way, rose farther in the Bureau's hierarchy after helping me with this exceptional case. Eight years later, he was named an FBI assistant director and the SAC for the FBI's New York City Field Office (nearly the equivalent of a deputy FBI director), where he sent Mafia boss John Gotti to prison, did the same for the chief judge of New York State's highest court, and led the FBI's investigation of the 1993 World Trade Center bombing. Coincidentally, he also was heavily involved in another case that I would soon be handling, entirely unbeknownst to me at that time (see below). Jim died much too young at age 59.

9   I once (more than two decades later) told my children while sitting in a campus bar with them at Brown University (where they both did their undergraduate work) that that day was only the third time in my life that I ever was in an actual bar. The first had been when I was taken to one by two FBI Special Agents in Dallas, Texas, while I was there in April of 1978 to superintend the removal of the FBI Dallas Field Office's large collection of records on the John F. Kennedy Assassination (see the Acknowledgments) and the second was this meeting with Jim Fox.

10   Speaking of irony at this level, it turns out that, in the height of irony, Jim Fox was also the FBI's supervisory handler of "Solo" sources Morris and Jack Childs, going back to 1971. (Small world.) When we were meeting in that bar in 1979, I had no idea that this was so, nor should I have, because I did not start working on the "Solo Source" case until more than a year later (see Chapter Fifteen). Looking back on this now, and having learned of this huge coincidence only during the writing of this book, I wish that I had somehow been able to talk with Jim about his many experiences with the Childs brothers that day. And I wish all the more that Jim were still alive today.

11   I will admit that there initially was some hardline sentiment in Main Justice (certainly not in the FBI) that was less than fully receptive to this plaintiff's plight. (Litigators tend to be this way, even some government ones, and even some in the Department of Justice. (See Chapter Fifteen.) Such a "win at all costs" mentality, though, can be incompatible with an "act in the interests of justice" one.)

In this case, such a mentality even briefly afflicted a political appointee who stumbled across the case and spoke skeptically about it (albeit only within the Civil Division internally) before learning all of its facts. But in this case that attitude quickly shifted to the intellectual challenge of our trying to figure out how on Earth we were going to escape from this unheard-of dilemma. And on that score, I was largely on my own.

12   There is a solemn principle that animates much of what the Federal Government does under the Freedom of Information Act: "Great nations, like great men, should keep their word." This quotation comes from a dissenting opinion written by Associate Supreme Court Justice Hugo L. Black in a case involving Native American rights in 1960. We firmly adhered to this principle in FOIA exemption decisionmaking -- for law enforcement source protection under Exemption 7(D), for national security source protection under Exemptions 1 and 3, and where applicable even for personal-privacy protection under Exemption 6 (e.g., in a case before the Supreme Court involving the identities of interviewed Haitian refugees).

13   To the best of my recollection, the FBI had never as of that time revealed the identity of *any* confidential source, certainly not of its own volition, and not as compelled in a FOIA case. To be sure, there have been some cases in which a former source has *self*-identified as one, but the Bureau as a firm rule assures its confidential law enforcement sources (all the more so its national security ones) that it will never publicly identify them as such, even once they are deceased. (The rationale for this latter aspect of the rule is that someone could be "signed up" as a confidential source one day and then get hit by the proverbial truck the next day. Even in such a case, the safety of that person's surviving family could be jeopardized by public disclosure of his or her loved one's planned source activity -- and all sources are well advised of this for their own peace of mind.) Indeed, any system of law enforcement (or intelligence) source protection must be managed on an airtight, categorical basis so that the flow of vital information through it, and the subtly distinct underlying degree of source cooperation as well, is maximized.

14   It should be obvious to even the casual reader that the full details of this case, as well as the exceptional contours of its underlying circumstances, are not included here -- not unlike those of the "mystery" case that is recounted in only limited fashion in Chapter Twenty-Eight. To be sure, more than 40 years later the plaintiff/confidential source involved here is now deceased. But the need for protecting the secrecy of his former source status did not necessarily expire with him. Under the prevailing case law that establishes the precise contours of the FOIA's law enforcement source protection under Exemption 7(D), it is generally accepted that there is "no sunset provision" for this protection -- and over the course of my career I strongly advocated for full judicial acceptance of this view. Having done so, it would be awfully hypocritical of me to just abandon that principle in providing any greater specificity here. In short, and at the risk of committing open sanctimony, proper secrecy requires no less.

15   And while it might go without saying, I know full well (read: through Jim Fox) that in the end the plaintiff in this unprecedented case was quite happy, and appropriately relieved, when the case was disposed of without any harm. And my other "client" in the case, the top leadership of the FBI, felt that the Bureau had managed to dodge an extraordinary, entirely unanticipated bullet. Such is the satisfaction of a lucky litigator.

CHAPTER SEVENTEEN

1   This so-called "cover story" was that the *Glomar Explorer*'s manufacturer (purportedly a company run by billionaire Howard R. Hughes, such as the Hughes Tool Company or Summa Corporation) had built it for the purpose of mining manganese nodules on the ocean floor. Then, just as the *Glomar Explorer* was being deployed in mid-1974, this "cover story" became even more convoluted when Howard Hughes's headquarters were broken into and documentation of the Hughes/CIA connection (i.e., their collaboration on the "cover story") was reportedly stolen. (Among other things, this left it somewhat unclear whether a Hughes company had actually built the vessel or not. On the other hand, there is the fact that the very name "*Glomar*" does seem to be an amalgam of the name of Hughes's company "Global Marine, Inc." -- as in, "Glo-Mar.")

After both the CIA and the FBI were brought into that burglary's investigation (again, reportedly), and attempts were made to ransom that documentation (allegedly), their "burglary concerns" were allowed to fade. But the significance of this odd episode is that it allowed some hints of the *Glomar Explorer*'s true mission to seep, osmosis-like, into the public domain, most particularly to some folks at *The Los Angeles Times* and *The New York Times*, which were definitely not good places (from the CIA's perspective, ostensibly) for such seepage to be.

Now, although this is getting a bit ahead of the story, any consideration of this "cover story" and its attendant circumstances should include making room for the possibility that the entire (read: multi-layered) *Glomar Explorer* "secret" actually was itself a "cover story" for something further below the surface (pun intended), something called "Ivy Bells" (see the Introduction). For obvious reasons, or at least for reasons that should be obvious, I can neither confirm nor deny that this might be so.

2   The historical record is somewhat unclear on this point in that only the forward half of the submarine was "targeted" for raising and evidently not all of that was successfully raised. In any event, the Azorian enterprise was hailed (secretly, of course) within the government as a "great success." (I have a faint photocopy of a White House document dated March 19, 1975, in which Secretary of Defense James R. Schlesinger observed about it as follows: "This episode has been a major American accomplishment. The operation has been a marvel -- technically, and with maintaining secrecy." The original of this document was classified by none other than Dr. Henry A. Kissinger.)

3   Yes, it is true that a certain Intelligence Community demographic was weaned on this now-iconic feature of *Mad Magazine*, which has appeared there regularly now for more than 60 years.

4   Toward that end, the Department of the Navy (read: the CIA, actually) had to decide just what to do with the recovered part of the *K-129* once it was analyzed and its intelligence value was exhausted. As to current whereabouts of that partially recovered Soviet submarine, I can neither confirm nor deny that it was buried at what is now publicly known as "Area 51" in Nevada (see Chapter Forty-Eight).

5   For instance (read: relatively small instance), to the best of my recollection the code name "Azorian" did not become public at that time and entered the public domain only many years later. This stands as an example of the fact that some secrets, like a peeled onion, can have multiple layers to them -- especially secrets that are connected to espionage or to other foreign intelligence, counterintelligence, or international terrorism activities. It is no coincidence, by the way, that these latter three terms of art appear in the language of the "(c)(3) exclusion" that I paternalistically helped shepherd through Congress as part of the 1986 FOIA Amendments (see Chapter Eighteen).

Speaking of the FOIA's "exclusions," as distinct from its exemptions, there actually are three potential levels of FOIA "processing" in all: conventional, "Glomarization," and exclusions. The former is an ordinary case, in which exempt records or portions of them are plainly withheld from the requester (or not, in a case of discretionary disclosure). The latter is a very rare case in which the agency doesn't merely "Glomarize," i.e., refuse to confirm or deny any responsive record's existence; rather, it responds (with statutory authorization) as if existing records do not in fact exist (see Chapter Eighteen).

And within the "conventional" processing realm, there are two particular processing approaches for exceptionally sensitive information that should be mentioned. The first is called the "mosaic" principle, which holds that sometimes seemingly innocuous bits of information, when viewed together like separate pieces of a jig-saw puzzle, will reveal a damaging picture that warrants FOIA exemption protection, most often on the basis of national security classification. The second is called the "exacerbation of harm" principle, which holds that even after certain (read: usually privacy-sensitive) information is disclosed to the public, its further release and dissemination can cause harm above and beyond what already has occurred. Both were advocated by the Department of Justice beginning in the late 1970s and have since been recognized by the courts.

6   I had occasion to chat with Seymour Hersh at a Saturday morning media program, at which we both were speaking, three decades later. He seemed interested in picking my brain a bit about my years representing the CIA and I in turn was interested in learning more about the Agency's successful efforts to get *The Times* to hold off on the *Glomar Explorer* story. (Out of respect, I did not ask him, even at that late date, who or what had "tipped him off" to that story. He did, however, mention that at the time, he knew of the CIA's efforts only as "Project Jennifer.")

7   Coincidentally (or perhaps not), it was later suggested, as a somewhat extreme "conspiracy theory," that the *Glomar Explorer* retrieval itself might have been a "double-layered cover" for "Ivy Bells," which involved the secret "tapping" of ocean-bottom communications cables and was another clandestine CIA operation that, for it to gain its intended results, required complete Soviet unawareness of it.

Considering such a possibility for a moment, it must be said that it certainly does seem to be the case that a vessel of the *Glomar Explorer*'s unique capabilities could be used to tap a communications cable traversing the ocean floor for the purpose of intercepting communications carried by that cable. Yet at the same time, it might also be observed, one might think that if the *Glomar Explorer* enterprise actually *was* such a "double victory," then the world surely would have heard about that, one way or another, by now. Or perhaps not, considering that we're talking about the CIA here, as well as about a deeply (pun intended here) covert communications intercept that could conceivably still remain active. But if all of that were in fact so, meaning that there is a deep (pun intended again here) secret at play, then I could not say any more about it than is said here, not without breaching a continuing obligation to maintain the secrecy of what would in that event be continued classification.

8   By then, an incomplete and somewhat garbled version of the story had become public a few weeks earlier when *The Los Angeles Times* published an article about something that it referred to as "Project Jennifer." For whatever reason, that apparently did not have much impact at that time. Another name for the enterprise was "Project Matador." By any name, though, it was a remarkable success.

9   Reportedly (which is itself an irony when used here), the CIA, through the good offices of Director of Central Intelligence William E. Colby, convinced not only *The New York Times* and *The Los Angeles Times*, but also *Time*, *Newsweek*, *Parade Magazine*, *The Washington Post*, *The Washington Star*, National Public Radio, and all three major television networks to withhold the story. As such things usually do, this lasted only so long.

Ironically, Director Colby has his own turn with publication suppression when, after retiring, he wrote a book titled *Honorable Men*. When he submitted his draft of this book for "pre-publication review" by his former agency, his successor, Admiral Stansfield Turner, reportedly asked him to omit just a few names plus a single paragraph dealing with the *Glomar Explorer* episode. He did so, in the American version of the book. But in the French edition of *Honorable Men*, all of that information is retained.

10   There was a conceptual underpinning to this position, one that oddly enough had been provided by the United States Supreme Court in 1875 in a case involving a "contract for intelligence services" alleged to have been signed by President Abraham Lincoln during the Civil War (see Chapter Forty-Nine). The Supreme Court in that case observed that "the existence of a contract of that kind is itself a fact not to be disclosed [because a] secret service, with liability to publicity in this way, would be impossible." *Totten* is generally regarded as the first true "secrecy" decision of the United States Supreme Court and perhaps of any court of ultimate jurisdiction anywhere.

11   Yes, that nominal defendant in the *Military Audit* case was "Bush," as in future President George H.W. Bush, who at the time was serving as Director of the CIA. In time, he became a declarant in the case. Apropos of that, it should be noted somewhere in this chapter that the term "affidavit" was transitioned to the term "declaration" by a statute that took effect as of October 1, 1976. This took a while to completely "catch on" in both agencies and the courts.

12   In retrospect, it came to be seen that the Justice Department either underplayed its hand at this point, or underestimated Judge Gesell, or both, which led to much brinksmanship (to say the least) in how the case was handled. I remember carefully studying the give-and-take that had occurred in the *Military Audit* case when I defended the CIA in the *Gardels* "Glomarization" case two years later.

13   Mandamus is usually a last-resort procedural mechanism whereby a party seeks "emergency relief" from what it believes to be an entirely off-base, manifestly flawed district court order. Mandamus relief is rarely ever granted.

14   It was only subsequent to this that it was acknowledged that the CIA was involved in the *Glomar Explorer* operation. All along in this case, as well as in the companion case brought by Harriet Phillippi, the Justice Department had steadfastly maintained the fiction that the actual agencies involved -- most prominently the CIA -- were not publicly known and had never been officially acknowledged.

15   This is what I made widely known throughout the executive branch as the "*Phillippi* obligation" -- the requirement that before an agency tries to submit an *in camera* declaration it first submit a declaration explaining the agency's position in as much detail as is possible on the public record. Thus, the D.C. Circuit's decision in *Phillippi* stands as both the seminal precedent on this procedural point as well as the first decision anywhere to embrace the "Glomarization" principle, even if only in the abstract.

16   This itself was less than clear at the time. It sure appeared that some "*Glomar Explorer*" information had entered the public domain, to some extent, but there had been no official confirmation of any of it, certainly not at first.

17   Technically, his title back then was "Assistant to the President for National Security Affairs" and he supported the "neither confirm nor deny" position to the point of submitting a classified affidavit in the *Military Audit* case.

18   Actually, however, the secrecy surrounding the *Glomar Explorer* operation did not evaporate in its entirety. Upon the subsequent appeal taken by the plaintiff in the *Military Audit* case, the court of appeals in May of 1981 considered the possibility that the public *still* might not know the true purpose of the *Glomar Explorer* mission

and it suggested that the CIA might still have something to hide from the Soviets, even if only the abstract fact that it "has nothing to hide." That was a rare instance of "Glomarization" reaching a new level.

19   Yes, in truth the records sought in both *Phillippi* and *Military Audit* did indeed exist, as one might imagine to be the case with most, but not all, "Glomarization" cases. In fact, I recall one such case, involving matters of national security, in which the underlying secret was that there actually were no records responsive to the FOIA request. And the government prevailed at the appellate-court level in "Glomarizing" that abstract fact. Of course, I can neither confirm nor deny (read: identify) which case that was. But I can say that it involved . . . no, I'd better not.

20   It is relevant to note that at this time, the CIA was still very much reeling from the intense Watergate-driven scrutiny of its past and present activities, primarily through the efforts of the "Church Committee," but also through the emerging use of the FOIA "against it." As I was to discover soon thereafter, the good folks out at Langley were ill-prepared, by dint of nearly 30 years of unexamined secrecy, to adjust and calibrate their secrecy positions in light of changing transparency-related circumstances.

Stated another way, it took the "crew out at Langley" a while to wrap their collective minds around what full implementation of the FOIA actually meant for them. (This is with the sole exception of soon-to-be CIA Deputy General Counsel Ernie Mayerfeld, who had the intellectual firepower to "see around corners," as is said -- which might have kept him alive during brutal Cold War conflicts, but also later afforded him a grasp of the FOIA that none of his colleagues had.

21   This was a violation of the Act, of course, in that it then contained a "10-day deadline" for FOIA responses. But that was a legal obligation honored more in the breach back then.

22   Yes, by dint of my representation of the CIA in these initial "university" cases, I found myself in the position of developing how the Agency would implement the concept of "Glomarization" at the administrative level, which I would then defend in court. This put me in a unique position, to be sure, and presaged what I would be doing for decades thereafter.

23   This of course was even apart from the standard intelligence concern about the uses that foreign counter-intelligence services would be expected to make of any confirmation of covert CIA contacts at specific academic institutions by being able to "zero in" on those particular academic communities and their members. Such foreign counterintelligence measures would reasonably be expected to include a foreign government's special attention to its students returning from a period of study at those schools; a foreign government's refusal to allow its students to attend such American schools in the future; and, most significantly, a foreign government's curtailment of access and information to academics traveling abroad from an identified college or university.

24   In fact, the only exception to this, which at that point in time proved the rule, was of course the abstract fact of the very existence of a certain secret submarine-retrieval vessel during the mid-1970s.

25   Indeed, the key to this deftly devised approach was this very up-front dichotomization of all that the CIA did, together with its underlying records. I knew that if we were to have any chance of resisting the ACLU's clever FOIA targeting in court, we had to come up with a position that was at once both simple enough to make intuitive sense and universal enough that it could be implemented (read: and defended) with the utmost integrity.

26   Did that mean that we were in some (read: many) cases "Glomarizing" the existence or nonexistence of records that did not actually exist? Sure. But that's the "nature of the beast" with "Glomarization." What always had to be remembered, as an inescapable fact, was that any savvy requester could otherwise pierce the agency's secrecy by simple process of elimination.

27   Indeed, it often is surmised, in cases of national security "Glomarization," that surely responsive records do exist. But as noted above, this is not always the case, even for cases that proceed to litigation. And I am here to tell you that of the 125 academic institutions chosen by the ACLU to be "test cases" in 1975, many of them (without specifying how many) involved no covert CIA activity (as we defined it) and therefore no "covert records."

28   The *Gardels* case was filed in February of 1978, after preliminary negotiations between the Agency and American Civil Liberties Union ("ACLU," to its donors) counsel Mark H. Lynch. Mark was a very experienced litigator who had a well-deserved reputation for litigating in a straightforward manner, with exceptional integrity. He later went on to "do the devil's deal" with the CIA in 1984 (see the Acknowledgments and the Glossary).

29   I learned of this bizarre order, as I recall, at the close of business on a Friday afternoon and knew that it had to be responded to immediately (read: on Monday), given the illogic import and timing of what Judge Green was seeking. Even *the plaintiff*, well understanding what was involved, moved for the summary withdrawal of this order before too long.

30   No, I was not at all confident that Judge Green would grant reconsideration of her *in camera* inspection order. This was based on both my perception of how she was handling the case up to that point and also what I had learned of her weaknesses through my judicial clerkship. So despite the press of time, I concluded that it was necessary to anticipate her denial of that motion by simultaneously filing one in the alternative. In retrospect, of course, I was very glad that I did so, because otherwise we might not have been well-positioned to gain reversal of her order on appeal.

31   Frankly, at this point I was thinking that it was Judge Green who was "certifiable." At our first status call in the case, she seemed not to grasp the nature of it at all, which was partly my fault for not explaining it to her sufficiently monosyllabically as Judge Gasch had warned me to do. But beyond that, she also seemed "shaky on the Bench." Let's just say that this case was not her finest hour.

32   Attorneys are known for their ability to "think on their feet," or at least trial attorneys are, and this challenging little episode showed me that this could apply not only in court. Inasmuch as I was taken completely by surprise by Frank Easterbrook's questioning, having been blithely ignorant of its premise, I later viewed it as good "on my feet" training.

33   Jack Blake was a veteran of the Office of Strategic Services ("OSS," a CIA predecessor) who became one of the CIA's premier managers, serving as its Director of Logistics, Deputy Director for Administration, and acting Deputy Director of Central Intelligence. He was an excellent deposition witness for me on the CIA's behalf and died in 1995 at the relatively young age of 72.

34   A fourth CIA affiant, CIA Director of Personnel F.W.M. Janney, addressed the "overt record" part of the case, but those issues did not (in my view and eventually the Court's as well) rise to the level of warranting depositions. It should go without saying that the "overt records" were the easier part of the case to defend.

Speaking of defending the case, I would be remiss if I did not in this chapter recognize the extraordinary assistance that I received from National Security Council Executive Secretary and General Counsel (and future ambassador) Robert M. Kimmitt, who so very ably coordinated the deposition participation of NSC China expert Michel Oksenberg. Bob was a prince among men back then and it did not surprise me when he went on to become the U.S. Ambassador to Germany and then Acting Secretary of the Treasury.

35   This fit well with the D.C. Circuit's then-recent admonition in *Phillippi* that an agency seeking to rely on an *in camera* affidavit (later to be denominated a "declaration") must first justify its merits position on the public record "in as much detail as possible" there. Frankly, we went about as far as we thought we could with the specificity of our three public affidavits, for fear of running afoul of this new procedural rule, but as a practical matter there always is at least some bit more that can be said, from one angle or another, within the format of a deposition.

36   *Gardels* was followed especially closely because in it we survived an *in camera* inspection order that threatened to derail the concept's implementation. Indeed, had I not worked so hard to craft those two alternative motions over that weekend, and filed them immediately without the Solicitor General's authorization, there is no telling what further damage Judge Green could have done to this embryonic position.

37   There also was a somewhat belatedly filed "university case" involving the University of Pennsylvania, *Daily Pennsylvanian v. Central Intelligence Agency*. I did not have to travel to Philadelphia to argue that one, because after I filed a lengthy summary judgment motion in it the ACLU decided not to litigate the case further. Notably, though, *Daily Pennsylvanian* involved an entirely unique (read: redundantly speaking) issue on the "overt" side of the case -- a group of records that we said for good reason could not be identified. Those records, as I recall, pertained to the former CIA project infamously known as "MK-Ultra," a "super-secret" mind control experiment (see the Glossary) in which a particular University of Pennsylvania professor was involved.
  The fact was -- and we explained this to the Court in a supporting affidavit executed by a high-level CIA official -- that under the unique circumstances involved (think: an overarching factual situation), any disclosure of those records within the context of the particular FOIA request at hand would almost certainly bring about the exposure of that particular professor (see immediately below). And we had contacted him about this, learned that he was still employed on that campus, and that he had quite understandably requested complete, continued confidentiality. Unfortunately, I did not get the opportunity to litigate that challenging issue once the case was withdrawn. Later on, I learned, expurgated copies of those records were released into the public domain within what the CIA called a harmless "larger context." Go figure.

38   The oral argument in *Medoff* was most memorable for me because it was the first time in my career (read: amongst others yet to come) that I received such extended positive reactions to the advocacy of my legal position directly from the Bench. The judge in that case, the late Frederick D. Lacey, was known in Newark for his keen mind, his quick (sometimes unfiltered) wit, and his eloquence above all else. He immediately grasped what I was arguing and loftily observed: "What we learn as men we cannot forget as judges. I understand what goes on at college campuses. The moment this information [were disclosed] the pressures exerted on Fairleigh Dickinson administration would be enormous. 'We want the name of the man!' And eventually realism tells us the name would have to be disclosed." (I kept the transcript, of course.)

39   In a highly unusual way, the *Medoff* case was the most successful, because the judge, declaring himself struck by not only the logic of the CIA's case but also the "transparency" of the ACLU's FOIA request-making pattern, decided to take the unheard-of step of awarding "costs" in the case to be paid by the plaintiff. Usually, this would be a nonstarter in a case litigated by the Federal Government, due to the extremely limited availability

of costs to it. But it just so happened that the judge had earlier asked me to have a transcript prepared of one of our hearings (see immediately above), which my legal research showed actually qualified the CIA to recover the sum of $93 under the judge's order.

Needless to say, I decided to take the judge up on this, if for no other reason than to make it all the clearer to the ACLU that its approach in these "university" cases (which in my own opinion, I had to admit, was perfectly ethical, logical, actually quite clever) was going to be met with equal force on behalf of my client agency. So the CIA got another check photocopy to pin to Ernie Mayerfeld's bulletin board out at Langley (see the Acknowledgments) and I got "bragging rights" at the ACLU's further expense.

Now what could go wrong with something like that, one might ask? Well, I made the mistake of mentioning (read: slightly bragging about) this at my mother-in-law's next Passover Seder (read: one of the 40 Seders that I have "under my belt" in lieu of some, not all, fat cells), whereupon the entire clan of my wife's extended Jewish family (read: yes, the "whole mespokah"), before I knew it, took up a collection (using a yarmulke in lieu of a passed hat) for a countervailing donation to be made to the local ACLU. And I was asked, as the first member of the goyim to breach that Jewish family, if I intended ever to treat the ACLU like that again. My answer, of course, was that I could neither confirm nor deny that.

40 In *Gardels*, I drew what might be described as a "mixed" panel, with Circuit Court Judge Harry T. Edwards most prominently on the "left." And to be sure, the oral argument was all the more challenging by dint of that. But ultimately, the D.C. Circuit ruled quite conclusively in the CIA's favor, fully applying the "Glomarization" principle to our overt/covert delineation for "university" cases. And on the substantive question of protecting any linkage between its covert activities and any particular college or university, the D.C. Circuit explicitly recognized the importance of sometimes masking the "provenience" of information as part of the need to "keep foreign analysts in the dark." My favorite line from the decision is: "The CIA has the right to assume that foreign intelligence agencies are zealous ferrets."

41 This became completely so when the Supreme Court issued the most significant FOIA decision ever in the case of *United States Department of Justice v. Reporters Committee for Freedom of the Press*, 489 U.S. 749 (1989). Although the fact pattern in that case at first glance might seem to be a "conventional" one, it actually is a "Glomarization" case involving the abstract fact of whether a particular individual had a "rap sheet" maintained on him by the FBI. The Court upheld the Department of Justice's decision not to say so, one way or another, on personal-privacy grounds. Incidentally, this fact was inadvertently placed into the public domain (at the Library of Congress) when Justice Harry A. Blackmun allowed his donated judicial files to include information about the case from which it could be inescapably inferred, whereupon my students and I did so. (see Chapter Two).

By the way, the word "Glomarization," as a colloquial term of art (or bit of *lingua franca*, one could say), was not so commonly used in initial judicial decisions on the subject, nor necessarily in any immediately subsequent one. But beginning in the late 1970s, and all the more so after the creation of the Office of Information and Privacy ("OIP," to its confirmed friends) in 1981, I steadfastly (read: paternalistically) proliferated the term as a means of achieving shorthand clarity about it, in order to propagate its use wherever applicable in the federal FOIA community. This included, of course, use of other forms of the word -- a "Glomar" response or denial, "Glomarize," "Glomarizing," "Glomarized," and (a personal favorite) "Glomarizable," as well as "Glomarization." Over time, this has become arguably the second-most-used colloquialism in the FOIA universe, second only to "*Vaughn*" as both a noun and a verb, underscored or not, in relation to agency declarations (see the Glossary). (Think of it as like the case name "Miranda"; whether Ernesto A. Miranda liked it or not, his name became an active verb in American criminal law and procedure, as in to "*Mirandize*" a criminal suspect.)

42   One appellate "Glomarization" decision, involving someone who claimed publicly that he was a former CIA "contract employee," which CIA folks simply did *not do,* deserves special mention because it was in a category all its own. This was the case of someone who, if he in fact had been a CIA "contract employee," had a distinct administrative avenue open for him to pursue "personnel-type" claims internally, outside of the public domain. (I knew this, coincidentally, because I had handled two similar but entirely meritless cases, filed against the CIA and the FBI, as a Civil Division Trial Attorney in the late 1970s.) But for whatever reason (we never found out exactly why), this fellow chose to proceed under the FOIA, which was unacceptable to the CIA for good reason.

The case was handled by OIP senior attorney Elizabeth Ross Withnell, who with a lot of hard work and acumen prevailed at both the district court and court of appeals levels. And she did so despite the fact that during the course of the litigation, it came out that the plaintiff possessed a genuine letter from the Federal Government's Office of Personnel Management that actually made reference (albeit only implicitly) to his federal personnel status, something that took some creative lawyering for us to get around. But get around it we did, and then some.

In fact, the D.C. Circuit's decision in this case actually went so far in our favor as to say that the CIA was entitled to judgment regardless of this unfortunate "left hand, right hand" situation, doing so with expansive language (something that appellate litigators call "*dicta*") that subsequently supported some regrettable government overreaching in the post-9/11 context. Years later, when we discussed this case, my students and I agreed that in hindsight this "favorable" decision (read: favorable to the client agency) went too far and should not be exploited. (Notice that the case's name is not mentioned (read: propagated) in this endnote.)

But more recently, in August of 2021, that precedent was applied and even expanded farther (read: too far) by a D.C. Circuit Court of Appeals decision in the case of *Knight First Amendment Institute of Columbia University v. CIA,* which involved the difficult question of whether an official State Department acknowledgment at a press conference -- that "we" had no prior knowledge of *Washington Post* columnist, U.S. resident, but Saudi Arabian citizen Jamal A. Khashoggi's disappearance before his murder -- could be imputed to the CIA so as to preclude it from neither confirming nor denying the existence of any record reflecting that. This decision, authored by Circuit Judge Gregory G. Katsas (see Chapter Forty-One), is now "Glomarization's" new "high point," or its "low point," depending upon how one looks at it. (I know that the "national security" branch of the "FOIA Requester Community" very much looks at it the latter way, for which I feel partly responsible.)

43   A "wrinkle" that can arise in the realm of law enforcement "Glomarization" under FOIA Exemption 7(C) is something that I described as "Glomarization bifurcation" in giving law enforcement agencies guidance on it. This arises from the fact that even a law enforcement agency might possess a record pertaining to an individual that is not purely a "law enforcement" one in character and therefore cannot properly be "Glomarized" under Exemption 7(C). For FOIA policy guidance purposes, this was illustrated by a 1995 case in which two FOIA requesters submitted a third-party request to the United States Customs Service that in general terms sought any record on a named individual -- former presidential candidate H. Ross Perot -- but then went on to specify that the requesters were "especially interested in documents and records that pertain to [reported] offers by Mr. Perot to assist the Customs Service in the interdiction of illegal drugs." And toward that end, they even identified and described one particular document that they believed existed in that latter category. In a word or two, that latter document was not "Glomarizable."

Given such a request, the D.C. Circuit found the Customs Service's across-the-board "Glomarization" response to be inappropriate, observing that "records discussing offers of assistance may implicate a less substantial privacy interest than any records associating Perot with [any] criminal activity." In other words, part of this FOIA request was not so very sensitive and only part of it was. So OIP advised all federal law enforcement agencies to ensure that where necessary they "bifurcate" their FOIA responses in "Glomarization" situations, just as the CIA did in the "university" cases with respect to its categories of "overt" versus "covert" records, by carefully distinguishing between any law enforcement record responsive to a third-party request the very existence of which can be privacy-sensitive, and any extant non-law enforcement record that might also be responsive to that FOIA request.

And speaking of OIP guidance, there is yet another "wrinkle" that agencies -- this time, all federal agencies -- need to be alert to in connection with "privacy Glomarization." This has to do with record "referrals," the time-honored process by which an agency possessing a FOIA-responsive record that originated with another federal agency lovingly handles that record by simply forwarding it to that agency of origination for its direct response to the requester. (This used to be called a "kiss-off referral"; I'm not sure that it's called that anymore.)

Indeed, all agencies do this, back and forth, as a fundamental aspect of the FOIA's administration. The problem with that, though, is that when making such a referral it is routine practice for the agency to helpfully notify the FOIA requester of that development, lest the requester become confused about what is going on. But if an agency were to do so where that that record is to become part of a "Glomarization" *corpus* at the receiving agency (which can indeed happen), then the integrity of that "Glomarization" would be breached.

I never worried much about this happening in cases of potential national security "Glomarization," because intelligence agencies are quite savvy about such things and by nature look out for one another. But in the more mundane law enforcement context, the potential for a receiving agency suffering harm to the integrity of its "Glomarization" position in this way is quite palpable. So OIP had to advise all federal agencies, in both its training programs and in written guidance, that they needed to be alert to inadvertently doing this. And as a result, this problem arose only twice, as I recall, and in one of those two instances any harm was averted through a procedural maneuver.

44   In the September 1982 issue of *FOIA Update*, OIP stated: "[A]ll third-party requests for FBI records on individuals are met with the response that the requester must submit a notarized authorization from that person permitting the FBI to acknowledge the existence of any such records." Beyond consent, additional exceptions to this privacy "Glomarization" rule are where the individual subject of FOIA request is deceased or where the individual's law enforcement status has already become a matter of public record. Of course, the latter exception does not at all apply when the government itself wrongfully discloses that abstract fact (see Chapter Thirteen).

45   One of the very first appellate decisions to apply the "Glomarization" principle did so in a very rare circumstance in which the FOIA requester was effectively trying to use the FOIA to force an agency to "authenticate" a record. This was the *Laborers' International Union v. United States Department of Justice* case, which arose in 1982. That case was based on the fact that an extremely sensitive 65-page report on the relation of organized crime to labor unions, prepared by the "Organized Crime and Racketeering Section" of the Department of Justice's Criminal Division, was the subject of a leak. And the FOIA requester sought to have a copy of the document released under authority of the Act because it wanted to verify that the "draft" copy in its possession was authentic. So it attached that copy of the report to its Complaint.

This extraordinary FOIA case was handled by OIP attorney Fran L. Paver, who worked very closely with the chief and deputy chief of the Organized Crime Section in fashioning a novel defense for it. We concluded that the Department could neither confirm nor deny that it actually held a copy (or original) of the report identical to the one held by the plaintiff without causing harm cognizable under FOIA Exemption 7(C). (The harm underlying Exemption 7(C) was the fact that the report contained many names of individuals who were unprosecuted and therefore possessed privacy rights in not being officially associated with the report's subject matter.)

The foundation for the defense of the case was the candid admission that yes, this leak had in fact occurred and, further, that a true copy of the actual report was indeed "out there" in the public domain. But that was not to say that the version held by the plaintiff, and submitted to the Court, was the same as the original final document. In effect, we were "Glomarizing" the very fact of whether the two were indeed identical.

And atop that, we went so far as to say that had there been no leak we could have disclosed the report in expurgated form; because of the leak, however, even the most innocuous report segment could be used in an effort to authenticate any particular version, meaning that the report in its entirety was exempt. This seemingly extreme position was supported by both a public declaration and an *in camera* declaration by the section chief of the Organized Crime Section (with whom I was to work closely on a "Whitewater" case more than 20 years later, see Chapter Thirty-Five), as well as *in camera* submission of the actual final report itself.

The District Court, per Judge Thomas F. Hogan, who later became Chief Judge of the United States District Court for the District of Columbia, fully appreciated the logic of this defense. He referred to the report attached to the Complaint as "a draft of a report . . . which may or may not be part or all [of] an authentic copy of the [report] which plaintiff seeks to have disclosed." Then he observed that "[t]his presents a difficult situation because disclosure of any information, in itself innocuous, which would verify whether the draft in possession of plaintiff is an authentic copy of the [r]eport might amount to disclosure of the entire [r]eport."

Therefore, Judge Hogan concluded that if we took any other position in response to such a FOIA request, under these circumstances, it would "serve to confirm or deny the authenticity of the document held by plaintiff [thus causing] a significant invasion of the personal privacy of individuals mentioned therein as being subjects of a criminal investigation." And on appeal, the D.C. Circuit, after likewise reviewing the *in camera* declaration and the authentic report itself, reached the same conclusion. So it was that one of the earliest privacy-based "Glomarization" cases also involved this rare "authentication" issue, and to the best of my knowledge there has not been a case quite like it since.

46   Indeed, Exemption 7(D) can be made to order for "Glomarization" in some situations. Just imagine a FOIA (and/or Privacy Act) requester who takes the extraordinary tack of in some way or another incorporating the element of a confidential law enforcement source into his, her, or its request. There are many different ways to do this, but the common thread is that the requester posits the existence, or at least the possible existence, of a confidential source being involved in the subject matter of that request. I used to advise federal agencies that any such request is an inherently "self-defeating" one, because any acknowledgment of a record's existence in response to it (or denial of that, given the power of the "process of elimination") would be tantamount to saying something about the actual (read: not just "possible") existence (or nonexistence) of a related confidential source. (By the way, many lawyers, not just myself, just love to use the word "tantamount," because it can be so useful in communicating the nature of a dynamic such as this.) So, the only correct response to such a FOIA request is for the agency to "Glomarize" under Exemption 7(D) and say that the reason it has to do so is all the requester's fault. A very recent example of this is the D.C. Circuit's decision in *Montgomery v. IRS*, No. 21-5168 (D.C. Cir. July 19, 2022), in which it explained why it was appropriate for the IRS to "Glomarize" the possible existence of a whistleblower (read: a confidential source) in a particular case.

47   Theoretically, "Glomarization" can apply in conjunction with any FOIA exemption in the face of a carefully tailored FOIA request that probes into the suspected existence of exempt information. For instance, a FOIA requester might first make a simple request for a record that contains a recommendation properly withheld as exempt under the deliberative process privilege of FOIA Exemption 5 and then, after receiving a denial, follow that up with a request seeking disclosure of any record containing imagined recommendation X, or recommendation Y, and so forth. Only "Glomarization" can protect the content of the actual recommendation in such a context.

Another example can be found in one of the FOIA's law enforcement exemptions, Exemption 7(E), which protects law enforcement techniques, procedures, and guidelines in certain situations. Recently, the District Court for the District of Colombia (read: per my old friend Judge Royce C. Lamberth) upheld the FBI's use of "Glomarization" in conjunction with that less common exemption in the context of the Bureau's alleged communications with certain financial institutions in its investigation of the January 6, 2021, insurrection, *Judicial Watch, Inc. v. Department of Justice*, Civil No.1:21-cv-01216-RCL (D.D.C. July 20, 2022) (appeal pending).

48   It should be noted that, after the national security context and the law enforcement privacy one, the next most common use of "Glomarization" was in the area of general (read: non-law enforcement) privacy under FOIA Exemption 6. This is not always intuitively obvious, so when speaking in OIP's training programs, in academic settings, or elsewhere, I usually would use the following example to convey it:

Imagine that the Justice Department has an employee-assistance program (which it in fact does, under the acronym "EAP"), in which it provides counseling help to Justice employees who suffer from, for instance, alcoholism -- a sensitive personal fact, to be sure. And let us further imagine that a particular employee has in fact received counseling through the EAP, in which case that program certainly would maintain a file under that employee's name. Lastly, let's imagine that a co-worker hostile to that employee suspects that he is an alcoholic and further that he (i.e., the initial employee) has sought counseling from EAP.

Then that co-worker files a FOIA request to the EAP (which is part of a federal agency) seeking access to all records maintained by it under the name of that target individual. In this hypothetical, the EAP would indeed have a file responsive to that FOIA request, and it would be able to withhold virtually all portions of it on personal-privacy grounds under FOIA Exemption 6. But doing so would be small solace to the target employee, because it would necessarily be tantamount to disclosing the abstract fact that he or she has received counseling. (Else there would not be an existing file.)

So what does that employee-assistance program do? It establishes a "Glomarization category," in which it declares (sometimes even well in advance) that any FOIA request of that type will be met with a "we will neither confirm nor deny" response, as necessary to protect personal-privacy interests. And, just as importantly, that program must use that very same language in responding to any FOIA request seeking records on an individual who is *not* an EAP client, i.e., for whom there is no responsive file.

Now, the first question that I would receive about this hypothetical example would invariably be: "Why can't we just give a 'no records' response in such a case (read: the case with the non-client), as we would in any ordinary 'no records' situation?" The answer to that is simple (to me): Because of the "process of elimination" problem. By that I mean that any savvy FOIA requester (and, believe me, there are some out there) could just submit a series of such FOIA requests, seeking EAP records on, say, persons #1 through #10, with the latter being the requester's true target. So the unwitting agency would go ahead and respond by saying "no records, no records, no records," etc., for the first nine requests, and then have to say "we neither confirm nor deny" for the tenth? No, that would not at all work. So agency responses within any "Glomarization category" must be scrupulously consistent, lest that category fail.

By the way, much of the work that OIP and I did on "Glomarization" over the ensuing years was not just consulting on "Glomarization" cases filed in court, but consisted of working with client agencies to help them formulate such "Glomarization categories," in advance, for use in a consistent manner. I would use the phrase "Glomarization integrity" to describe how an agency must handle this exceptional defense with complete consistency in order to maintain judicial receptivity to it. Sometimes, however, an agency would screw this up, leading to anomalous and harmful judicial results. (This occurred twice after I retired.) It is, after all, the most intellectually challenging aspect of FOIA administration, together with the operation of "exclusions" (see Chapter Eighteen).

CHAPTER EIGHTEEN

1   We refer to this latter aspect of the exemption as the "bottom half" of Exemption 7(D). It is unique among all FOIA exemptions in that while four exemptions -- Exemptions 4, 5, 6, and 7 -- have what we call "threshold requirements," Exemption 7(D) has its own such requirement (i.e., "criminal" or "national security") deep within it.

2   Actually, there were two ways to do this. One was to have all cell members execute notarized consent forms allowing the cell leader to submit third-party FOIA requests for any FBI records about them directly. And the second was for the cell leader to order each cell member to make a first-party FOIA request and then hand over the response. You might think that the former could be defended against by the FBI having the informant's consent privately withdrawn, but that would leave the formal response in the informant's case looking different than those for the others -- unless the Bureau fabricated a response letter and in effect lied. This is the method that was used, at no small risk, in that first such instance in 1979.

　　　And in the second scenario, all a savvy cell leader would have to do is have the presence of mind to have each cell member use the cell leader's own address -- for the FBI's response to go to him or her directly, thus bypassing the "hand over" part, and the FBI could not lawfully provide a response that would not be telling. (The Bureau figured (and I agreed) that any cell leader savvy enough to be using the FOIA to ferret out possible moles in the first place would figure this part out, too.) And remember, any tell-tale difference could dangerously "tell the tale."

　　　To round out this analysis, just picture this: A "post-Watergate" congressional oversight hearing at which an FBI witness is asked the following question: "Tell me, has the Bureau ever lied in responding to a FOIA or Privacy Act request? And before you answer, please remember that you're under oath, so you damn well better not lie here and now."

3   Yes, it took more than four years after the effective date of the 1974 FOIA Amendments (i.e., February 19, 1975) for anyone in the Justice Department to realize that those amendments created such a vulnerability in "exclusion-type" situations. To this, some might say, "Well, four years isn't really all that bad, considering that the entire area of information policy was just exploding during that decade, to say nothing of the enormous government upheaval that the 'Watergate' scandal wrought."

　　　To that, however, I say that the Department should have done better. In other words, the fact that it took more than four years for us to recognize the problem, not to mention more than ten years for Congress to fix it (1986 being 12 years after the 1974 FOIA Amendments created Exemption 7(D)), was (to slaughter a metaphor) not anyone's finest hour.

4   Years (read: roughly 30 years, during 2007-2017) later, my students would tell me that this was the best way in which they could both grasp and remember (read: for at least their exams) the nature of an exclusion: "Where even 'Glomarization' is inadequate to the task." I used to see that regurgitated sentence on their examination papers a lot.

5   Furthermore, there is the fact that "Glomarization," by its very extraordinary nature, necessarily involves the specification of the particular FOIA exemption under which that position is taken. But the whole idea in this dire situation was for the informant's name and the subject of source protection (i.e., through citing Exemption 7(D)) to never come even close to connecting.

6   If I do say so myself (not that I'm shy about such things), I was proud of this "sword" aspect of an exclusion, though candor compels me to admit that I do not recall that occurring to me right away. Rather, I was focusing on the need for the "shield," which was most pressing at the time. But as it turned out, the Bureau was able

through some (unspoken) procedural maneuvering to defuse that first source emergency in 1979. And it was lucky not to have any other such situation arise within its informant universe until later on.

7   Truth be known, we actually thought that with the strong support of the Senate's FOIA subcommittee chairman Orrin G. Hatch (R-UT) and that of full Judiciary Committee Chairman Strom Thurmond (read: "Strum," to most Southerners, or "James Strom Thurmond, Sr.") (R-SC)), we had the Senate "locked in" on our bill and the House would just have to follow along -- with a counterpart bill and then reconciliation of the two bills in conference committee, of course.

But that was a miscalculation, mostly by the congressional affairs "tea-leaf readers" at the White House. In fact, it wound up being another four long years for this package to gain full legislative approval. And then, truth be known, that was only because a University of Maryland basketball star (Leonard K. "Len" Bias) precipitously died of a cocaine overdose, leading to a legislative juggernaut called the "Anti-Drug Abuse Act of 1986," of which our "FOIA reform" legislative package became a part.

8   When I did so, after trying to think through every possible circumstance imaginable that could be an "abstract fact" problem under the FOIA (which apparently no one had really done before), the truth is that I actually missed one, which became evident only 20 years later, when about a year and a half after 9/11 I was sitting in a multi-agency "no fly list" meeting held at FBI Headquarters. At that time, there was tremendous (read: extremely strong) pressure in the wake of the 9/11 after-action review (read: the Report of the "9/11 Commission") for agencies *not* to classify newly created "post-9/11-type" records unless absolutely (read: very absolutely) necessary. (This pressure might or might not still exist.)

As a direct result of this new non-classification policy, I learned, there was a secondary "no fly list" that had been created by the Bureau, the Department of Homeland Security, and several other participating agencies within the Intelligence Community that existed as an unclassified database at a "fusion center" that was being administered by the FBI. (More than that, I cannot say, perhaps for lack of recollection, but perhaps not; the word "secondary" here is a bit of a mask.)

Yes, it was "the law of unintended consequences" at play, something that potentially plagues all decision-makers, regardless of how far-seeing their intentions might be. And at this meeting, I learned further that there existed a single first-party FOIA request (read: one also made under the Privacy Act) that implicated that particular database just enough to be a problem -- because none of these agencies wanted to allow that FOIA requester to learn that he or she was on that list (which of course, in this case, he or she actually was). This, of course, struck me then as déjà vu all over again from 1979.

So as I sat there, I realized right away that this extremely rare, totally unanticipated (read: by me, first and foremost) problem had only one analytically correct solution: It needed an exclusion. Now as it happened, there were two complicating things about that. The first was that in the prevailing political environment at that particular time, seeking a legislative "fix" to this would have been very problematic, for more than one reason.

And second, this particular, singular FOIA request very soon "washed out" for other, only partly related reasons, which meant that we would not have had an actual (read: not merely hypothetical) example of the problem even if we had tried to fix it -- which would have been further complicated by the need to explain that problem on the Hill in what up there they call "executive session" (read: an "*in camera*-like" proceeding). Therefore, the best that I could do was to leave this as one of several legislative recommendations when I retired. And in doing so, of course, I labeled that fix as the new "(c)(4) exclusion," i.e., one too explosive to touch.

9   Additionally, there also was an instance in which I had to explain this to a Member of Congress at a congressional hearing in the 1990s -- and I recall being not at all sure that I succeeded. Even the chairman of the House subcommittee with oversight jurisdiction for the FOIA's governmentwide administration, Robert E. Wise,

Jr. (D-WV), kept confusing exclusions with "Glomarization" (a not-uncommon thing, unfortunately), even though that subcommittee had "led" the legislative impetus in the House for the exclusions' enactment. To be sure, that is little more than a corollary to the civics lesson learned in high school about Members of Congress being unfamiliar with (read: not bothering to read) their own legislative proposals, but in this case it was particularly disappointing.

10   A big part of the FOIA landscape since the mid-1970s has been its heavy use by prisoners, who with much time on their hands often seek to belatedly supplement the criminal discovery (read: information shared by the prosecution) that they had received at (or shortly before) their trials. Proclaiming their innocence, many inmates profess the need to find that one "smoking gun" (read: OK, bad metaphor) that "will" exculpate them from their crime. Over the years, hundreds of their FOIA requests have proceeded to litigation -- often filed on what is called a "*pro se*" and "*in forma pauperis*" basis, where some of them actually have led, including at the appellate court level, to quite significant court decisions. Within the FOIA's large law enforcement agency community in particular, such prisoner/FOIA plaintiffs' names as Crooker, Landano, Maydak, Antonelli, Julian, Manna, Jefferson, Krohn, Kuzma, Tanks, Lykins, Massey, Doyle, Willis, Hall, Pickard, McQueen, Sosa, Perrone, Biear, Stimac, Cox, Ferri, Durns, and Gasaway, as well as Benavides, are well known. This list even includes some names more widely known to the public, such as James Earl Ray, Eldridge Cleaver, Brett Kimberlin, and Leonard Peltier.

11   Although the most difficult type of brief to write can be one that tells a court that it went badly wrong, this was not so difficult an undertaking here as might be thought. Truth be known, the hardest part of this mission for us was complying with the D.C. Circuit's firm 15-page page limitation (which today of course is expressed in units of words, not pages). As I recall, this came down to the last of those 15 pages, where I had to "cheat" with a hyphenation in order to get the brief in under the wire.

12   Although very pressed for time, I did this single-handedly, including while with an arm in a sling, which was better than having a different body part there had I not been up to the task. There was no small amount of clamor for this issuance, especially in the federal law enforcement community, which was more than understandable. I did receive one useful suggestion on it from elsewhere in the Department, but in the end Attorney General Edwin Meese III, in whose name the document was issued, had only one small edit: I had misspelled the word "foreword" in one location.

    The main guidance part of this document is 30 pages long and contains (no surprise) 54 footnotes. It can be found simply by Googling: "Attorney General's Memorandum on the 1986 Amendments to the Freedom of Information Act." "Hard copies" of this soft-cover publication, even after more than 35 years, should be maintained in the FOIA offices of all federal agencies, especially those holding law enforcement responsibilities.

13   Ancillary to this, OIP also added a newly crafted "Exclusions" section to its annual "Justice Department Guide to the Freedom of Information Act" publication. This meant that every year, with "the *Guide*'s" governmentwide distribution, our message on the exclusions was being disseminated over and again.

14   As perhaps with any extremely broad grant of congressional authority, there is a tendency for aggressive folks in a federal agency to view it as a "solution in search of a problem," which come to think of it is one more instance of basic human nature rearing its head (see the Introduction). In this case, I had to fend off some agency FOIA personnel who were inclined to read these three new authorities and then seek FOIA requests to which at least one of them could be applied. I had an advantage in doing so, I admit, by virtue of authorship of them -- as in, "No, that is not what was meant when I wrote the damn thing!" Nevertheless, I do recall one agency,

which shall be nameless except that its initials are DEA, that carried its insistence to the point at which I had to go over there in person and talk some sense into it.

15 Without a doubt, the most difficult thing about a FOIA exclusion is the logical agency FOIA officer reaction to it: "Wait a minute, are you really telling me that Congress has authorized me to *lie*?" My response to that always was "yes, in effect, but that's only because Congress recognized that it is the only way to adequately protect an investigation, an informant, or a counterintelligence activity in the face of some exceptionally well-targeted FOIA requests under certain specified circumstances." A mouthful, for sure, but a necessary one.

16 As is noted elsewhere (see the Glossary), the FOIA has been amended on a regular "ten-year cycle" for decades.

17 This was OIP senior attorney Thomas J. McIntyre, who showed a very strong intellectual aptitude for this critical responsibility, even if amalgamated with other less appreciated traits. He went on to be the chief of the Criminal Division's FOIA unit, a perch from which he repeatedly (and sadly) embarrassed himself in attempting to disagree with OIP.

18 Frankly, the focal point of this concern was what I knew about the person at the FBI who as of then could be making exclusion decisions without what we sometimes referred to as "adult supervision." That Bureau official, David M. Hardy, came to the FBI in the early 2000s from the Navy Department, where he was already a "legend in his own mind." He became Section Chief of the Record/Information Dissemination Section ("RIDS," remarkably, to those who don't mind destroying records) of the FBI's Records Management Division, a position in which he was the FBI official declaring under oath what happened in a litigated case, and it was not long before it became increasingly apparent that he was not at all a good fit for that position. It wasn't just that his reliability was so much worse than that of his half-dozen predecessors, it was that it wasn't even close. It got to the point at which AUSAs and OIP attorneys had to build extra time into their briefing schedules in order to painstakingly doublecheck his declarations for accuracy and even integrity.

And courts began noticing his deficiencies as well. In one exemplary case, District Court Judge Cormac J. Carney sanctioned the FBI after finding that Hardy had misrepresented key facts to him. This caused him to observe: "Simply put, the Government lied to the court . . . Parties cannot choose when to tell the Court the truth." In another case, District Court Judge Amit P. Mehta refused to accept Hardy's attestation on a FOIA issue, saying that it "falls woefully short" and was "particularly inadequate." As of the time of my retirement in 2007, OIP was coordinating with the Deputy Attorney General's Office on a possible institutional solution to this problem, but with my departure apparently the momentum toward that was lost. I can only hope that Hardy did not get "carried away" with the (c)(3) exclusion once I was no longer there, because the nature of an exclusion's implementation is such that if he did, probably no one else would know it.

19 By the way, the word "targeted" here could mean several distinct but closely related things. Most commonly, it refers to the fact that some (read: a small percentage of) FOIA requests are purposely crafted to probe into an abstract fact -- most often the existence or nonexistence of something, at the "record" level and more importantly the substantive level underneath. And sometimes in order to recognize that an agency has to bring some external knowledge to bear on the situation.

20 The "classic" ways of doing so were first identified by the United States Supreme Court more than 40 years ago in a case by the name of *Robbins Tire*: Destruction of evidence, falsification of records, modification

of testimony, fabrication of alibis, intimidation of witnesses, relocation of assets, redeployment of resources, and the like.

21   The federal agency given the greatest leeway in the invocation of Exemption 7(A) is the United States Secret Service, which by necessity maintains the types of law enforcement records that sometimes cannot be described with particularity in FOIA litigation without causing harm. OIP worked very closely with the Secret Service to fashion especially broad-based responses to its most challenging FOIA requests, as well as to shape Exemption 7(A)'s evolving case law to accommodate its special needs. (Each year, OIP would receive special invitations to the White House Holiday Party (previously known as the "White House Christmas Party") as a result.) This close relationship became even more so in 1992 when John W. Magaw was appointed as Secret Service Director by President George H.W. Bush. John was the Legal and Law Enforcement Group member who kindly brought me a steak dinner as I was working a 24-hour shift as acting group leader (and then deputy team leader) when we were "underground" in a week-long Continuity-of-Government exercise in 1987 (see Chapter Twenty-Six). An excellent discussion of Secret Service secrecy is contained in a very recent book, *Zero Fail: The Rise and Fall of the Secret Service*, written by *Washington Post* reporter Carol D. Leonnig, who was another speaker at one of my Collaboration on Government Secrecy programs (see Chapter Forty-Two).

22   Nor would the possibility of "Glomarization" be of much help here. To "Glomarize" in conjunction with Exemption 7(A) would require the principle's use in all third-party FOIA requests and even first-party ones, including those made under the Privacy Act, as well -- because those are the types of requests that can probe into the abstract fact (i.e., the existence of a current investigation) that is needed to be protected. And if challenged in court, the notion of Exemption 7(A) "Glomarization" would be extremely complicated, counterintuitive, and quite difficult to defend.

23   Hence, any records of an ongoing matter that is purely civil in nature, although they could qualify for ordinary Exemption 7(A) withholding, cannot be excluded from the FOIA under exclusion (c)(1). However, the statutory requirement that there be only a "possible violation of criminal law," by its very terms, admits a wide range of investigatory files maintained by federal agencies, not merely those of criminal law enforcement agencies.

24   Additionally, the explicit language of this exclusion conditions its applicability so that it can be utilized "during only such time" as the above required circumstances continue to exist. This condition comports with the extraordinary nature of the protection afforded by the exclusion, as well as with the basic temporal nature of Exemption 7(A) underlying it. It means, of course, that an agency that has employed the exclusion in a particular case is obliged to cease doing so once the very circumstances warranting it cease to exist.

In other words, once a law enforcement matter reaches a stage at which all possible subjects are aware of its pendency, or at which the agency otherwise determines that the public disclosure of that pendency no longer could lead to harm, the exclusion is regarded as no longer applicable. And if the FOIA request that triggered the agency's use of the exclusion remains pending either administratively or in court at that time, the excluded records must then be identified as responsive to that request and processed in the ordinary course.

On the other hand, this is not so if by that point that FOIA request has been closed. An agency is under no legal obligation to spontaneously revisit a closed FOIA request already acted upon, even though records were excluded during its entire pendency. In such cases in which the (c)(1) exclusion was properly invoked, the records, by operation of law, simply were not subject to the FOIA during the pendency of the request.

25   Nearly the same as with "Glomarization" (see Chapter Seventeen), we had to deal with the possibility that the use of this first exclusion (but by their natures not the second or the third) could in some cases require

"bifurcation." By this, it is meant that it is entirely possible that "excluded" records responsive to a particular FOIA request could co-exist with other records that do not warrant exclusion treatment. For example, a law enforcement agency could have a delicate ongoing investigation warranting use of the (c)(1) exclusion, yet at the same time possess the records of an older investigation that does not. In such cases, the requester would see those latter records handled in an ordinary way, never learning that there were other, more current records that were not.

26   In either case, the requester will not learn of the existence of the excluded records, or of the investigation or proceeding that underlies them, through the agency's response to his, her, or its FOIA request. By the same token, sophisticated FOIA requesters should never be able to rely (even by process of elimination) on "no records" responses to carefully crafted FOIA requests to discern those instances in which no investigation is underway. In short, they will not know anything for sure, one way or another. This is part of the "sword" aspect of the exclusions.

27   Here is where I have to admit that when I dreamt up this exclusion in 1979, and then faithfully advocated it for the next seven years before its enactment, I never fully appreciated its import. Yes, I understood the world of undercover work in the abstract, but not completely. It wasn't until I spent some time chatting about "real world" undercover experiences with retired FBI Special Agent Michael German, who had gone undercover for months at a time among white supremacists and then right-wing militant groups, that I could vividly see what the (c)(2) exclusion can do. Mike is both a scholar and a gentleman, as they say, who now works as a Fellow of the Brennan Center for Justice at NYU School of Law's Liberty & National Security Program. And for several years, he graciously served as a member of the Collaboration on Government Secrecy's Advisory Board at American University's Washington College of Law (see Chapter Forty-Two).

28   And similarly, as with the (c)(1) exclusion, there is a slight temporal aspect of this exclusion as well: If ever it were to develop that the informant's status as an informant has been officially confirmed -- recognizing that "official confirmation" is a high standard, indeed -- this exclusion would no longer apply. This possibility is highly theoretical, though, because of the type of informant most likely to be involved and because it is very rare (read: occurring almost never, see Chapter Sixteen) for the Federal Government to officially acknowledge having such a relationship.

29   And as noted above, Exemption 7(D) "Glomarization," which does exist, is a total *non sequitur* to this situation, in that it logically applies only on the basis of the content of a FOIA request (i.e., in that it references source existence in and of itself), not based upon threatening external circumstances.

30   One of the footnotes to the Attorney General's Memorandum envisions that although this exclusion was manifestly created for use by the FBI, such records "might be maintained elsewhere, potentially in contexts in which the harm sought to be prevented by this exclusion is no less threatened." So in an extreme case, such as a "post-9/11" one, another agency of the Federal Government's Intelligence Community might possibly see fit to employ the (c)(3) exclusion, in coordination with the FBI and OIP, where necessary to avoid extremely serious (read: very extremely serious) harm. I am not saying that this ever has been done, mind you, but I am not saying that it hasn't, either.

31   A concrete, publicly disclosed example of this was a group of eight (read: or perhaps more, for all that is known) Russian spies called "illegals," who entered the United States at a young age as "sleeper agents" and transmitted sensitive information back to Moscow for decades. As part of a ten-year FBI investigation code-

named "Operation Ghost Stories," they were detected and were kept under surveillance until being rounded up as a group in late June of 2010. Very little is known publicly about how any of them was detected, or how for so many years prior to then they remained undetected, but it can be surmised that the (c)(3) exclusion was involved. I can neither confirm nor deny whether this particular activity by Soviet intelligence (read: the KGB) was known by the FBI in the 1980s when this third exclusion was added to the other two.

32   The element of "context" here is a key one, as it is also with some basic FOIA exemptions in many situations. In the case of personal-privacy protection, for instance, an agency is obliged to consider "full context" in order to determine exactly how much protection (read: of how large a portion of a record, in a redaction process) is warranted. By the same token, an agency is entitled to consider "full context" in determining how much nondisclosure is warranted for the protection of its own institutional interests.

33   And in doing so, of course, any "excluding" agency, just as a "Glomarizing" one (see Chapter Seventeen), must take great pains to ensure that all of its correspondence with its FOIA requesters is consistent with that throughout, so that no telling inference can be drawn anywhere. As I advised in Attorney General Meese's implementation memorandum: "It does little to shield sensitive abstract facts if an agency phrases its response in an exclusion situation in any way differently than usual."

34   After all these years, I have insufficient recollection of what the statistical content of this response was to recount it here. But I do have a clear recollection of once estimating for someone that I thought the exclusion ratio was at that time approximately 99% (c)(1), .5% (c)(2), and .5% (c)(3). And if there ever is a (c)(4) exclusion (see above), that should tally in at less than .5%.

35   All agencies making use of the exclusion mechanism must keep a secret record memorializing each such instance, with an eye toward both possible administrative appeal and, beyond that, defending a possible case in litigation. Such records must be made with clear delineations as to exactly which underlying records, of all those that might be responsive to the FOIA request, are encompassed within the exclusion's sweep. And more than that, all excluded records must be maintained, for the full length of either a pending FOIA litigation case or the FOIA's six-year statute of limitations, against the possibility that the need for exclusion (although in subsection (c)(2) cases, hopefully not the informant) expires.

What is more, because it is publicly known that exclusions exist and are there to be used, whereupon it can logically be surmised that agencies would create and keep such exclusion-related administrative records, the very fact of their existence necessarily receives "Glomarization" treatment. Or in exceptional such "second-generation" exclusion cases, these records could themselves need to be excluded in the face of a probing FOIA request.

One last such procedural consideration has to do with administrative appeals of FOIA denials. As a matter of policy, in order to maintain the integrity of the exclusion mechanism, agencies should accept any clear request for administrative review of the possible use of an exclusion and treat it as a distinct aspect of an overall administrative appeal. Unless the agency did in fact use an exclusion and did so incorrectly, the requester is advised that this aspect of his or her or its administrative appeal was reviewed and found to be without merit.

36   This was typical of that subcommittee chairman, Congressman Robert E. Wise, and also of his predecessor Congressman Glenn L. English, Jr., both of whom were served (read: not all well) by the same longtime congressional staffer.

37   There never was any need to incorporate the Meese Memorandum's guidance on exclusion implementation into the Department's FOIA regulations in the first place, else I would have done so back in 1987.

38   During this odd interim, and seemingly not knowing what to do with the problem that it had unwittingly created, OIP temporarily withdrew its proposed regulation, as if that would calm things down for at least that time being. It did not.

39   This is part of a noticeable decline in OIP's analytical proficiency in the years following 2007, such as was seen in its flawed congressional testimony on its claimed inapplicability of discretionary disclosure to the attorney work-product privilege under FOIA Exemption 5 in 2012. Also in that category were OIP's inconsistent positions (i.e., inexplicable diffidence, then alarm, then diffidence once again) as of 2011 on the need for remedial amendment of FOIA Exemption 2 (see Chapter Forty-Six), its inexplicable failure to recognize the significance of updating agency FOIA regulations in light of statutory amendments, its misleading claim of a "94.5% release rate" at the Department, and its false 26% backlog-reduction claims. This led to the chairman of the House FOIA subcommittee admonishing my successor as OIP director that in making such claims she was "living in a fantasy land."

40   From the beginning, we employed a broad, encompassing standard for determining that a FOIA plaintiff's claims have sufficiently implicated the exclusion mechanism to warrant giving his, her, or its case the full "exclusion treatment." We very consciously chose to "err on the side of inclusiveness" with such claims, lest any FOIA plaintiff (or, frankly, any judge) be able to say that we somehow impaired that delicate mechanism in any case. On balance, though, and with no small rhetorical flourish, I (read: Attorney General Meese, nominally) advised: "Such claims should neither be engendered nor ignored."

41   This word, of course, mostly rhymes with "come-to-Jesus," which is the type of meeting that OIP used to have to hold with especially intransigent folks at other agencies and sometimes even in the Justice Department's own components. More than any other type of government employee, it was military autocrats -- generals and admirals -- who thought that they could just ignore the law. Not one of them ever succeeded, however. Indeed, it was most fun telling them bluntly that they had to do what they had to do, period.

CHAPTER NINETEEN

1   That case was *Lesar v. United States Department of Justice*, 455 F. Supp. 921 (D.D.C. 1978), *aff'd*, 636 F.2d 472 (D.C. Cir. 1980), in which Judge Gerhard A. Gesell, upon ruling in the government's favor, went out of his way to observe that he was "impressed with . . . the competence of Government counsel, and the apparent care with which the matter has been dealt." 455 F. Supp. at 926. Little could Judge Gesell know that his ruling would trigger a landmark Supreme Court decision on the concept of "survivor privacy" more than 25 years later (see Chapter Three).

2   The phrase "on the ground floor" is not exactly apt here, as government secrecy and secrecy litigation in general were not new (read: roughly 25 years old by then), but I remember being mindful of the fact that FOIA litigation and its underlying case law were still in their infancy as of 1978, holding much potential for mastering that entire subject area in a relatively short period of time. And that is exactly what I proceeded to do.

3   In fact, I would advise almost any young attorney to if possible "sample" practicing law in different substantive areas before focusing, if at all, on any one area in particular. And I certainly advised that to my students over the course of teaching law for ten years (see Chapter Forty-Two). But at the same time, I told them to remain open to the possibility of zeroing in on a particular area of the law that they might recognize greatly appeals to them and then just going with that for a satisfying career. Not to overdramatize it, but it's a little like finding a spouse; for some people, it happens early in life (as in my case, at ages 17 and 23).

4   Prior to enactment of the RFPA, the Federal Government did not even have to tell bank customers that it was accessing their bank records, and customers did not have any right to prevent such a thing, so financial institutions usually (though not always) readily cooperated with the Bureau. The RFPA came about after the Supreme Court flatly ruled (in the case of *United States v. Miller* in 1976) that financial records are the property of the financial institution in which they are held, rather than the property of the customer. (This, of course, was back when such records were largely held in physical form, in one location, not "in the air," as we used to call it (read: in "the cloud")).

5   This included things such as medical records, insurance records, electronic fund transfer records, consumer-protection records, and the like. Of these, the extension of privacy protection to medical records was the next biggest priority, so a group of us started putting together a solid legislative proposal for that big area in late 1979. By the summer of 1980, this legislative package was completely ready to go, with great expectations. But it suffered a fatal wound when Senator Edward M. Kennedy, who was the chairman of the Senate Judiciary Committee at the time, suddenly decided to challenge President Jimmy Carter for the Democratic nomination for the presidency that year. And as for our plans for legislation regarding the other types of records, they, too, never came to fruition once President Carter lost his bid for re-election in 1980.

6   We believed that such litigation challenges were inevitable because by that time (read: the late 1970s), it seemed like just about every new thing that the Federal Government did was being challenged in court, at least in several "test cases," to start. (The enormous growth of "public interest" groups in the 1970s, which was or course fueled by "Watergate," had had much to do with that.) Hence the tremendous growth of the Justice Department's Civil Division, which had expanded into three branches (plus an appellate staff) the year before.

7   I also made it a point to handle the first half-dozen litigation cases brought under this new statute myself, even though they were spread out all over the country. This allowed me to compile a folder of my own litigation papers filed under the RFPA (together with copies of the successful results) for use by Assistant U.S. Attorneys ("AUSAs," in both Washington and beyond the Beltway) as "brief bank" models in all future such cases coming down the pike.

8   The Privacy Act was in a slightly different category because (a) governmentwide oversight for it was delegated by Congress to the Office of Management and Budget ("OMB"), not to the Department of Justice, and (b) OMB was actually doing a half-way decent job of that (read: relatively speaking) until about 1985. After that, at OMB's request and with OIP's "good government" agreement, the Justice Department (read: OIP) stood in for OMB on most Privacy Act-related matters, especially all governmentwide training. A big part of this was OIP's preparation of a detailed, case law-based treatise on the Privacy Act, which we began issuing in updated form, together with our "Department of Justice Guide to the Freedom of Information Act," each year. OIP senior attorneys Philip A. Kesaris and then Kirsten J. Moncada wrote, expanded, and then updated that treatise with painstaking care (not to mention meticulous review), and to universal acclaim.

9   In theory, we were undertaking this also on behalf of all other federal agencies across the full span of the executive branch. And we truly were faithful to that mandate. But one of the nice advantages (read: in addition to the burden) of being the "lead agency" for a statute is being able to "take care of your own" in such a process. And as far as the Justice Department's law enforcement components were concerned, we did just that.

10   Truth be known, we also "snuck in" a couple of amendments that were advocated at the last minute by other federal agencies, such as our good friends at the CIA.

11   These included an expanded version of my "exclusion" idea through which I tried to envision all conceivable needs for it but failed to anticipate the "no fly lists" that came into existence two decades later in the wake of 9/11 (see Chapter Eighteen).

12   Among all others, "source protection" was our biggest-ticket item, because in "breaking down" the Act's original Exemption 7 into subparts such as Exemption 7(D) in 1974, Congress (read: "theory-based" Democratic staffers in both the House and the Senate, lacking much real-world experience in how federal law enforcement actually works) had enacted a subpart for that that left much to be desired. So this was to be a correction for that, with the hope that it would not lead to any Thermidorian "re-correction" by any future Congress down the road. (Yes, the FOIA would become subject to that sort of thing eventually, but not with respect to Exemption 7(D).)

13   I will confess to being more than a bit paternal about what I labeled as "exclusions," as their very concept was something that had dawned on me during the summer of 1979. In short, there can exist some circumstances in which, given the nature of a particular FOIA request, the nature of any responsive records that might be held, and the nature of the surrounding fact pattern, an agency cannot handle a FOIA request in a conventional way without "tipping off" the requester (or someone else similarly situated) to a situation that cannot be disclosed to anyone without harm to a law enforcement or counterintelligence activity. And such situations can be extreme enough that even the agency's use of the exceptional "neither confirm nor deny" defense is unavailing (see Chapter Eighteen).

14   Decades ago (read: now five of them), the father of a young fiancée of mine, who was like a father to me, gave me a bit of sage, albeit somewhat cryptic, advice that I've never forgotten over the years. While I was still in my teens, he passed along this wisdom: "You'll find that life surprises you," he said, "sometimes, one thing will just lead to another." That certainly did hold true throughout my early years at the Justice Department. And he followed that advice with something even more cryptic: "Remember, you never know what you don't know." (By the way, that young fiancée went on to medical school while I attended law school in a different state (read: of confusion, sometimes) and I went on to marry and/or live with two trial attorneys (in succession, mind you) more than 40 years apart.)

CHAPTER TWENTY

1   That certainly is what everyone called it back then, and for a long time since, with people who were not "moderates" or, worse yet, "conservatives" being rightly (read: "leftly") referred to as "liberals." Today, I think, the latter are too widely labeled "progressives," which to me sounds a bit too moderate. I don't know quite how that shift in nomenclature occurred, much less when, but one day not long ago I suddenly realized that I had failed to "get the memo" on it.

2   This was the "Office of Criminal Justice," which was established within the Office of the Attorney General and then the Office of the Deputy Attorney General during 1973-1974. In the immediate wake of the "Saturday Night Massacre" back then (see Chapter Seven), these organizational lines blurred.

3   Indeed, the numbers of these administrative appeals, by which FOIA requesters are afforded second-level review of FOIA requests denied (in whole or in part) by the Justice Department's various components, soon increased to beyond 2,000 and then 3,000 per year and even 4,000 per year, constituting a daunting FOIA workload in and of itself.

4   Not to mince words here, Quin was nothing short of an avowed socialist. I had always admired him (a) for his known willingness (read: outright eagerness, at times) to "speak truth to power," (b) because he immediately saw my own potential, and (c) for the little-known fact that he had hired OPIA (later OIP) paralegal Ana Montes (see Chapter Twenty-Five) just because he met her at a bus stop one day and was struck by her appearance.

5   The Senior Executive Service, very often referred to as the "SES," is a category of high-level Federal Government officials that was created by Congress in 1979 in place of the "GS" levels of GS-16, GS-17, and GS-18, the very top of the career ranks. This change, especially as it has been implemented by agencies under the direction of the Office of Personnel Management ("OPM," to those who are favored by it), had the effect of "tightening" those three "supergrade" levels and placing a much greater premium on agencies receiving an allocation for any additional SES "slot."

For instance, once Bob Saloschin and Quin Shea left their respective positions, their SES allocations just disappeared -- and in order for them to be regained a new allocation had to be obtained from OPM -- for reasons that were never made entirely clear. In time, I went on to obtain the equivalent of a Ph.D. in OPM's arcane rules for this, which led to my regaining Bob Saloschin's "SES slot" and becoming the Federal Government's youngest-ever career SES member in 1984. Each year, I'm asked by OPM to serve on an SES performance board and am told that this record still stands.

6   I later learned that the Reagan Transition Team's scrutiny went deep enough that it also included my work on the Right to Financial Privacy Act (see above), as well as some of the more high-profile litigation cases that I had handled.

7   It is worth noting that, atypically, the Justice Department's new political leadership had no idea whatsoever where I stood on any political or ideological spectrum at that time. Had anyone asked me -- Jonathan, to begin with, or Attorney General Willian French Smith during my appointment session with him later on -- I would have honestly said that I sure did not vote for Ronald Reagan (read: it later turned out that I voted for no successful presidential candidate from McGovern in 1972 all the way until Obama in 2008) and would have most accurately described my own leanings as very liberal to moderate (read: somewhat more moderate than my wife, who was a self-described socialist), tempered more than a little by my government orientation.

This was a time, by the way, during which ideological "litmus tests" were being applied more than ever before, given both the Reagan Administration's especially sharp departure from the ideological orientation of the Carter Administration and, quite frankly, the newly acquired inclination of Republican administrations to do so. Within the next year, for example, this became extremely clear to OIP (read: Deputy Director Miriam N. Nisbet, most particularly) in its FOIA processing of the initial personnel paperwork of the Department's second-level political appointees: That was a somewhat "incestuous" group who all recommended one another as to their conservative *bona fides*, with Federalist Society and Heritage Foundation affiliations being the gold standard. I distinctly remember thinking back then that, although my position was not quite a political appointment per se (read: I had made sure of that), it certainly was close enough to one, due to its governmentwide policy nature, that I was glad that such "vetting" (read: ideological, not just professional) apparently was overlooked in my case.

In retrospect, I have to say that that was yet one more instance of my getting lucky in one way or another during my career. Once again, as had begun when I first managed to get a Justice Department internship at the National Institute of Law Enforcement and Criminal Justice of the Department's Law Enforcement Assistance Administration ten years earlier (see Chapter Five), I luckily "fell through the cracks." That sort of thing does happen within a government sometimes.

8   And the fact that I was only 29 at the time apparently did not slow any of the Reagan folks at the Department (or at the White House, in the less likely event that I was vetted there) down one bit. It is possible that neither Jonathan nor Attorney General Smith focused at all on my age; with more than five years of litigation experience behind me, they might well have assumed that I was older.

9   As it happened, I was not the only prospective appointee then being recruited by Jonathan. I later learned that he and a young aide to the attorney general by the name of Ken Starr traveled to Arizona together to recruit Sandra Day O'Connor for a far more significant position at around the same time -- which allowed me to kid Jonathan that he batted at least .500 for that season. (And it was not long before Jon turned that around on me, saying the same thing when he and I were among Reagan appointees, which was much of the time.)

10   During the previous three-plus years of the Carter Administration, I had quite methodically acquired and developed an unparalleled docket of cases (see Chapters Three, Eleven-Twelve, and Fifteen-Seventeen) to which I felt a certain "loyalty," as quaint as that might sound. Although some of these cases had concluded by then, there remained others that I very much wanted to see through.

11   This was a rare arrangement by which I would train and oversee all OIP attorneys in their handling of such cases, at both the district court and appellate court levels, as if they were AUSAs, and would transmit their court papers for filing by the local U.S. Attorney's Office. A big part of this scheme was that in reviewing all litigation filings (including letters), I committed to read (read: myself, without exception) every single word that OIP's attorneys wrote before anything was placed in final form. Was I committing to do an enormous amount of work on this, including much that had to be done at home at night? Yes, I was, especially as our total docket grew past 500 cases by the time that I retired.
But I had outstanding assistance from OIP's deputy director (Miriam Nisbet) and its soon-to-be associate director (Margaret Ann "Peggy" Irving) in meeting this personal litigation-review responsibility. And this allowed OIP to recruit an exceptionally high-caliber attorney staff because we could say to applicants that we singularly offered our attorneys an extraordinary breadth of legal experience, consisting of administrative adjudication, policy development and dissemination (read: providing governmentwide training), and part-time litigation as well.
OIP hired a total of exactly 75 new attorneys during my 25 years there, in addition to those who were there to begin with in 1981, and only one of them stated (read: shyly, but we wanted her to speak her mind) a personal preference against engaging in all three of these things. On one hand, she was not one of the 75 newly hired, as she was already there when OIP was born in 1981. On the other hand, she is the only OIP alum to have gone on to become a United States Attorney. (And it was terrific that she flew in all the way from Hawaii for OIP's 25th anniversary celebration in November of 2006.)

12   As noted, not a single Reagan appointee in the Department ever asked me if I was a registered Republican, as they surely all were, or a Democrat, as most Carter Administration attorneys were. To be sure, this was to be a career appointment, not a political one; I had made sure of that. But the fact of the matter was that I was a registered Independent, which best comported with my view of federal service. This remained so until the George W. Bush Administration, when I decided it was time to register as a Democrat after all.

13   One of the keys to this was that I knew how much Dick enjoyed training, in no small part because he had been doing so much of it in his Army Reserve role as a leading Judge Advocate General, so I helped him develop an extensive regime of FOIA training that we provided to all agencies of the executive branch. And he, in turn, knew of my passions for litigation, legislative work, and policy development. So it was that I wound up creating

more than 90% of OIP's written output and editing all of it, apart from the letters by which he adjudicated administrative appeals.

14   That number grew and grew over the years, until it reached as high as 50 at one point. Dick was known to recount in our training sessions that someone once walked through our offices and inquired, "About how many people work here?" "About half," he would say as his reply. (Yes, humor was no small part of how we operated.)

15   The other things, of course, included adjudicating thousands of administrative appeals each year, which was a major enterprise, especially as their numbers increased greatly during the 1980s. Also a "growth industry" was overseeing the implementation of the Privacy Act within the Department; representing the Department at public programs held on government-access subjects; assisting the Civil Division and its appellate staff with its FOIA and Privacy Act litigation; supporting the Office of the Solicitor General likewise; generally advising and guiding all federal agencies on uniform and proper FOIA implementation (read: an enormous category); and any other collateral or ancillary mischief that we might from time to time get into. Plus, commenting on all FOIA-related legislative proposals and the like.

16   OIP issued three major publications as part of its governmentwide FOIA policy activities: (1) *FOIA Update* (later "FOIA Post," in successor electronic form), a regular update on new FOIA-related developments, including new policy guidance; (2) the Freedom of Information Case List, an annually updated list of all FOIA litigation decisions (as well as related ones) that were of any precedential value; and (3) most popularly, the "Justice Department Guide to the Freedom of Information Act," a detailed treatise on both the Act's substantive and procedural provisions that at its peak was updated each year and consisted of 1127 pages and 4119 footnotes. The latter, which began as the "Short Guide to the FOIA" and grew to the point at which it no longer could be called that, soon became known as the "FOIA Guide" -- or as the "FOIA Bible" -- to many.

17   The annual numbers of such appeals hovered at about 2100 in the very early 1980s but then increased dramatically to more than 3000 before too long. Adjudicating them was still the primary responsibility of OIP's attorneys and the full-time job of almost all of its growing ranks of paralegals. Atop that, we began the practice of hiring night-time law students to work full-time for us during the day, which also became a pipeline for hiring the very best of them as attorneys upon graduation. Lastly, we pioneered within the Justice Department the hiring of "part-time working mothers," beginning with three of them in 1984 who shared two "slots" (which is what "full-time equivalents" or "FTEs" were called in those days); the majority of them (read: we eventually hired a total of six, as I recall) went on to become some of our very best attorneys. OIP's total staff jumped from 33 in 1981 to nearly 50 by the late 1990s.

18   Most predominantly, this meant producing almost all of OIP's written work on policy issues and other matters of governmentwide guidance, as well as taking the lead on in-depth legal analysis.

19   Among other things, OIP also had two other major responsibilities: (1) it is responsible for the adjudication of what we called "initial requests," i.e., the FOIA and Privacy Act requests received *ab initio* for records of the Attorney General's Office, the Deputy Attorney General's Office, the Associate Attorney General's Office, and those of other leadership offices of the Department, including OIP; and (2) it staffs the Department Review Committee ("DRC," to those inside of a "SCIF"), which makes decisions on matters of national security classification on behalf of the Attorney General.

20   Right away, OIP greatly expanded the Department's FOIA training activities, within its new governmentwide scope of responsibility, and it was not long before we were collectively giving more than a hundred training

presentations each year. Dick carried the heaviest part of that load, with great distinction, while I was also more likely to speak to media groups, to public-interest groups, and to other members of the "FOIA Requester Community" that were on the "outside" of government, especially as ancillary to my activities on FOIA-amendment legislation.

21 This of course premised that I subsequently would further choose to "make a career" (read: the first and major one) of it by remaining in the Justice Department for more than 30 years. The latter choice, many long-term government employees will tell you, is one that can sort of "sneak up" on you; before you know it, fifteen or so years have passed, you still think you have the best job in the world, and you realize that you are in it for the "long haul" -- which fortunately, in the Federal Government (read: if you began federal service before 1983), need be only until you reach age 55 in order to retire.

CHAPTER TWENTY-ONE

1 Though this is entirely anecdotal, it is not at all apocryphal. Attorney General Smith certainly did view the FOIA in that way, at least at first, and I can attest that he was heard to exclaim such a thing without humor.

2 This was in 1984, when Congress enacted the Central Intelligence Agency Information Act, which in part amended subsection (q) of the Privacy Act of 1974 to unequivocally provide that the Privacy Act cannot serve as an Exemption 3 statute under the FOIA.

3 On reflection, though, I realize that this is not completely true, as we once had to deal with an absolutely horrendous Reagan patronage appointee (read: actually, he was worse than that), who later actually went on to become a Michigan state supreme court justice (even chief justice, eventually), with whom we had an enormous, seemingly intractable policy disagreement (read: he was either unable or unwilling to follow the law). I very vividly remember sitting calmly in front of his desk (coincidentally in the very room that I had ended up occupying as a law clerk in 1974), in bike shorts (as it was a "casual Friday"), with my legs crossed (which I later was told might have been part of what "set him off"), and challenging both his legal acumen (read: which is way too strong a word to use in his case) and his policy wisdom, to his face, a thing to which he plainly had grown unaccustomed.

His response was to yell and scream and to then storm out the back of his office behind his desk (again, coincidentally through the very doorway from which I had overheard that conversation about the incipient creation of OILP back in 1974), which ironically led to the disagreement being resolved in OIP's favor by default. I hereby confess that I did so partly because that asshole (read: an utterly apt and near-universal characterization) had earlier that day thrown another temper tantrum in his office that had brought OIP's deputy director to tears (read: yes, so this was direct payback for that). This same political appointee, by the way, somehow got it into his head that he definitely would be "carrying over" from the second Reagan Administration to the first Bush Administration in early 1989. Quite embarrassingly (read: to him, for sure, but also to his few underling allies in the Department), he did not. And no, he is not named here, because his family has suffered enough.

4 This was something known to Congress and the "FOIA-requester community" as the "Blue Book," so called because of its cover's pale blue color. The first of these was issued by Attorney General W. Ramsey Clark in June of 1967 upon the FOIA's enactment, for which the color was chosen by someone unknown, and the second had been issued by Attorney General Edward H. Levi in February of 1975 to guide the implementation of the 1974 FOIA Amendments. Hence, there was every expectation that Attorney General Meese would issue one on the 1986 FOIA Reform Amendments as well. Meese did not know this, of course, at least not at first, but I certainly did, and I took the responsibility of writing it very seriously.

CHAPTER TWENTY-TWO

1 The Freedom of Information Act was conceived not in the caldron of media and public-interest group efforts to obtain information from federal agencies, as one might imagine, but rather in the frustration of congressmen who were stymied by executive branch officials of their *own* political party -- i.e., Republican Members of Congress unable to get information out of the Eisenhower Administration (see Chapter One). Thus, a backdrop to public access to agency records has always been that of congressional access to agency records, with the two sometimes intersecting, in one way or another, less than neatly. And once the Privacy Act was enacted, in 1974, it entered into the mix, so to speak, in a way that complicated things even further.

2 Former subsection (c) subsequently was "renumbered" as subsection (d) when Congress created the three FOIA "exclusions" as new "subsection (c) in the FOIA Amendments of 1986 (see Chapter Eighteen). You can blame that on me; I thought they'd look better that way -- i.e., exemptions in (b), exclusions in (c).

3 The D.C. Circuit (together with the District Court for the District of Columbia beneath it) is known within the FOIA realm as the court of "universal venue" under the Act. As is described elsewhere (see Chapter Three and the Glossary), this means that its rulings on FOIA issues must be taken by agencies as "the law of the land" at the administrative level, because any FOIA challenge could be filed in D.C.

4 The court of appeals in *Murphy* was affirming a district court decision that was in the Army's favor as well, though that decision addressed only the applicability of Exemption 5 and the basic question of whether there had been waiver.

5 As it happened, OILP's misconception of the D.C. Circuit's *Murphy* decision was just the first of three such misinterpretations made by parts of the Justice Department on FOIA issues. The second was the Civil Division's initial misapplication of the D.C. Circuit's *en banc* decision governing Exemption 4 in *Critical Mass Energy Project* in 1992 (see Chapter Forty-Six). And the third was the Civil Division's misreading of the Supreme Court's *Klamath* opinion on the operation of Exemption 5's threshold requirement in 2001 (see Chapter Forty-Six).

6 As noted above, this was all the more significant in that we were arguably "flying in the face" of the leading judicial circuit for the FOIA, which was antithetical to the usual policy approach under the Act.

7 At the end of a long, hard day, we sometimes would joke that this particular statutory provision, given its potency, was not so "benign."

8 It also was not without significance that several FOIA requests from individual Members of Congress had been litigated by then, including requests unquestionably made in a Member's official capacity, without it ever having been held that such requests qualified for special access under subsection (c).

9 And if any of the information disclosed to a "minority" committee member happens to be covered by the Privacy Act, then such a disclosure can be deemed a criminal violation of that statute as well as a basis for agency civil liability. This is so because the Privacy Act's disclosure prohibition has an exception for disclosures to congressional committees themselves (see Chapter Fourteen). The one fact pattern that presents difficulties in this regard is that of an agency witness testifying before a congressional committee in "open session."

 It is generally agreed that the witness can disclose Privacy Act-protected information in response to a majority committee member's questioning, but perhaps not if the questioner is a minority committee member. The Office of Management and Budget ("OMB," to Privacy Act subjects), which has jurisdiction over the Privacy

Act's governmentwide administration, has never clearly addressed that question.

10   I must confess that I often found it quite amusing over the years to see an incoming minority in one body of Congress or the other just rail against this guidance, as if it were a violation of birthright, even though just a month earlier, when it was in the majority, it thought that OIP's guidance was just fine and dandy. This happened at least a half-dozen times during my tenure, always to little consequence.

Apart from that, there is one particular public interest group, the Project On Government Oversight ("POGO," to its friends, of which I am one), that has doggedly resisted OIP's guidance on this issue, from almost the outset in 1984. Now I do like and respect the folks over there, led by POGO Executive Director Danielle Brian, but they have never offered any analysis to the contrary, much less a cogent one. And most recently, in congressional testimony given in March of 2022, they appear to have finally retreated to the position that Congress should "clarify" this issue with an amendment to subsection (d)'s language (what they call "a simple fix") instead.

CHAPTER TWENTY-THREE

1   It should be emphasized at the outset this this does not include a final settlement *agreement* itself, for it has long been the rule that the terms of an agreement, which very often include the payment of taxpayers' dollars, should be made known to those who are "footing the bill," as it were. The one known instance in which this was *not* the case stands as the exception that proves the rule. That was the case of the Space Shuttle *Challenger* disaster, which claimed the lives of seven astronauts, four of whom were not military personnel, in 1986.

When the families of those four brought administrative wrongful death claims against both NASA and the primary shuttle contractor, Morton Thiokol, a settlement was reached, one memorialized in a government document (i.e., a settlement agreement) that has never been publicly disclosed. The public was made aware of the aggregate facts that the payments totaled approximately $3,000,000, were paid over some period of time, and that Morton Thiokol contributed approximately 60% of that amount.

But NASA (which was extremely sensitive about *any* public disclosure in the wake of that emotion-charged disaster) made a public announcement to that effect without disclosing the settlement agreement itself. And amazingly, no one to date has ever filed what would be a successful FOIA request to obtain it. Do I know the exact amounts involved? Sure, as do several other former government employees, I imagine. But do I have any warrant to disclose them here? No, quite to the contrary.

2   After all, the nature of the situation is that this type of information typically is being shared with the opposing party to begin with, and any FOIA request seeking what has not been shared most likely would not be processed before that case has reached completion anyway.

3   Justice Brennan also cautioned that information disclosure connected to prior litigation "can cause real harm to the interests of the attorney and his client even after the controversy in the prior litigation is resolved."

4   OIP had been told by numerous parties, including some within federal agencies, that there was just no such thing as a "settlement privilege" and that this was just a belatedly discovered "loophole" in the statute that would have to await FOIA-amendment legislation for it to be fixed.

5   We are speaking here of a "discovery privilege," not necessarily of what is known in the law of evidence as a "testimonial privilege." The latter stands as a barrier to the use of evidence in court (i.e., as a matter of "admissibility"), and it includes what are popularly known as the spousal or marital privilege, the doctor-patient privilege, the therapist-patient privilege, the priest-penitent privilege, and of course the attorney-client privilege. There is a rule of evidence governing admissibility of "settlement information," Rule 408 of the Federal Rules

of Evidence, which prohibits the use of "compromise negotiations" (i.e., settlement offers or statements made in furtherance of negotiating settlements) to prove the validity of, or the amount of, a claim that is in dispute. The existence of a "settlement negotiations privilege" under the FOIA, within either Exemption 4 or Exemption 5, is collaterally supported by Rule 408.

And as to the term "privilege," there also has emerged something in recent years called the "reporter's privilege," a qualified (read: limited) privilege recognized by some courts and even state statutes in the U.S. as founded in the First Amendment. Under some circumstances, it can protect the identities of journalists' confidential sources (read: often a good thing) but also can be used to shield a journalist from having to testify in a civil suit involving a "leak" (or otherwise wrongful disclosure) to that journalist of sensitive (even Privacy Act-protected) information. (And in a criminal investigation of a "leak" where the recipient is a journalist, there is the uncomfortable fact that the reporter claiming the privilege is by definition the only witness to what is, after all, a crime.)

I was involved in such a case after I retired, when I agreed as a consultant to analyze a fact pattern involving a federal prosecutor whose career was seriously damaged by a wrongful agency disclosure of personnel information about him, and by subsequent publication of it, and to provide a sworn statement memorializing my professional judgment on the matter. However, that prosecutor's efforts to obtain from the journalist the identity of his unlawful source were prevented by a broad "reporter's privilege" application in court, even though the prosecutor ultimately was fully vindicated as to the falsity of the information wrongfully disclosed and published about him (see the Glossary).

By the way, the subject of journalists' confidential sources, whether involving "leaks" or not, is a tricky one for them. On the one hand, journalist groups tend to decry the government's use of confidential law enforcement sources, often pressing reflexively and vigorously against their protection under FOIA Exemption 7(D). But on the other hand, without blinking an eye, they will cry to the heavens about any law enforcement effort to obtain the identities of their own sources.

I pointedly raised this contradiction in a speech to a media audience at the Freedom Forum on Freedom of Information Day in 2006, shortly after I decided to retire. In so doing, I even went so far as to label this as an "inherent conflict of interest" that journalists have when it comes to source protection. But I regret to say that I made little or no headway on this, as media groups tend to think that the First Amendment (about which they feel quite proprietary) matters more than the lives and physical safety of those who speak in secret to the FBI. And I daresay this will never change.

6   Although this recognition might occur at the level of the United States Supreme Court -- as was the case with the "attorney work-product privilege," which was found to exist in the well-known case of *Hickman v. Taylor* in 1947 -- it can occur at any judicial level.

7   Justice Brennan also pragmatically observed that federal agencies "have an acute interest in keeping private the manner in which they conduct and settle their recurring legal disputes."

8   This was the same district court judge who years earlier had boosted my litigation career by explicitly praising my handling of the Martin Luther King Assassination FOIA case (see Chapter Three). The fact that he was regarded as the most intelligent judge on the D.C. District Court (thus not including Judge Harold Leventhal on the D.C. Circuit Court of Appeals) was of course entirely coincidental.

9   This was a case decided under Exemption 4 of the FOIA, rather than Exemption 5, which was a reflection of the fact that the former exemption actually contains the word "privileged" within it. This made no difference, however, to the privilege's application for the first time in a FOIA context.

10   Not too many years later, the settlement privilege was firmly recognized at the appellate-court level as well. In *Goodyear Tire & Rubber Co. v. Chiles Power Supply, Inc.*, the Court of Appeals for the Sixth Circuit adopted the privilege and declared: "The public policy favoring secret negotiations . . . leads us to conclude that a settlement privilege should exist." It also comports with something called "settlement mediation" protection for "alternative dispute resolution" proceedings under a statute found at 28 U.S.C. § 652(d), as well as with "dispute resolution communications" between a neutral and a party under 5 U.S.C. § 574(j), in conjunction with FOIA Exemption 3.

CHAPTER TWENTY-FOUR

1   OIP hired Mark in March of 1982, as one of its first new attorneys, and it was not long before he showed me that he truly had "ligation in his blood." Three years later, I told the chief of the civil division of the local U.S. Attorney's Office (coincidentally, the same man whose offer I had turned down myself in the summer of 1978 (see Chapter Three) and who later became chief judge of that district court) that he ought to hire Mark to litigate full-time -- his litigation skills were that good -- and very soon OIP had lost one of its best young attorneys. (This happened again several years later when OIP Senior Attorney Marina Utgoff Braswell greatly impressed me with her litigation abilities and her extraordinary work ethic; she has been a "star" litigator in that U.S. Attorney's Office ever since.)

Making good on the promise that he had shown me, Mark ultimately went on to become the chief of that office himself, an SES-level position, which was a remarkable rise for someone who was so mediocre a player on OIP's softball team. (Yes, over the course of many seasons of softball on the Ellipse and the Mall, we especially liked trouncing opponents such as the Office of Legal Counsel, whose attorneys were so nerdy (with the notable exception of centerfielder Paul P. Colborn) that it was hardly a fair contest. And no, there is no truth to the rumor that OIP regularly hired its law clerks based on their ability to serve as "ringers" for this purpose; there was in fact only one such hire, and she played second base for us while hitting over .300.)

All told, by the way, OIP hired exactly 75 attorneys during my tenure and 16 of them (by last count) went on to hold SES positions across the span of the Federal Government. (And several former OIP paralegals and law clerks did as well.) One went on to become a politically appointed agency general counsel, one an inspector general, one a senior NSA official, one a United States Attorney, and one became the head of OGIS, for example.

2   This is just as the FBI is a part of the Department of Justice, though this fact is little known within the general public and sometimes conveniently forgotten even by FBI personnel. Most cabinet departments have sub-agencies; the Justice Department itself is divided into 40 (read: sometimes slightly fewer) distinct components, one of which is OIP.

3   This quote actually was put to good use in OIP's governmentwide training programs. We used it to remind all agency FOIA personnel that the fact of investigation (or even subsequent prosecution) should not be viewed as dispositive of someone's privacy rights. In other words, the subject of an investigatory file must of course be presumed innocent unless convicted and is entitled to have his or her personal-privacy interests treated accordingly. Many years later, this principle became a major part of a unique FOIA controversy that developed over "mug shots" (see Chapter Forty-One). This likewise is so as to internal agency disciplinary matters.

4   Technically (and commercially), this clerical product is "Wite-Out," the registered trademark for the brand of correction fluid originally created for use with "originals" and sometimes photocopies (as in this case) in the "olden" pre-word processor days. A similar product known as "Liquid Paper," was famously invented by the mother of Robert Michael "Mike" Nesmith, of the group The Monkees, in the 1950s.

5   And I would have liked to be able to say that, as far as I knew, such a thing never did happen again. But that was true only until I received an email message from a researcher on the subject of "paraphysics" in mid-March of 2021 complaining about the Defense Intelligence Agency ("DIA," to current UAP devotees) having done something very much akin to that, under cover of the following technical explanation: "Our redaction tool removes original text with pixel-replacement, ensuring the redacted content is permanently removed, thus eliminating the need for 'black out.'" This of course stood directly contrary to language that Congress added to the Act, in the concluding paragraph of its subsection (b) in 1996, which provides that "[i]f technically feasible, the amount of the information deleted, and the exemption under which the deletion is made, shall be indicated at the place in the record where such deletion is made."

Now, I remember working in close coordination with both DIA and NSA when developing OIP's "secret" governmentwide guidance in 2003 on counteracting the very *opposite* -- a newly discovered capability among some FOIA requesters to "read through" the electronic "blacking out" of FOIA-disclosed records through mere "cutting and pasting" (see Chapter Thirty-Four), Now, my days of protecting agencies from requesters being able to electronically overcome proper redaction are past, so one can only hope that my successors at OIP (or perhaps at OGIS) are capable of carrying this weight after me. Indeed, such redaction protection has become all the more crucial with advances in technology, because in addition to guarding against redaction circumvention through basic cutting and pasting as in my day, agencies now have to deal with new tools such as something called "Edact-Ray," which can allow requesters to "extract" such "latent" information as glyphs, "hidden fingerprints," and "CVE numbers" from some redacted segments. As one expert once told me: "It's hard to securely redact something as complex as a PDF."

And when I say "secret," above, I mean that by the mid-1990s OIP's governmentwide policy guidance was almost always disseminated electronically, which meant that it was automatically available to the public as well. The two exceptions to this were guidance given on the subject of redaction, and its possible circumvention, where the nature of the beast was that we wanted to arm agencies with the knowledge of what FOIA requesters could do to overcome redaction under some circumstances without engendering or facilitating that circumvention in any way. The second such "secret" guidance had to do with the mechanics of non-electronic redaction and it was disseminated to agencies in oral form through OIP training programs and in consolidated written form in 2001.

6   This gentleman was immediately removed from his position, at OIP's insistence, and not long afterward he retired. I do not include here any further reference to his personal problems, other than to observe that they were manifest and were the type of problems that one could well imagine led him to do what he had done, presumably under pressure. And beyond making sure that the Justice Department's political leadership was alerted to what we had found going on at a sister cabinet agency, for whatever that was worth, we did not pursue the possibility that this man had done what he did only under some untoward pressure from the political appointees at his agency.

7   This was an especially big relief for us because we knew that this attorney, Eric R. Glitzenstein, had served as a law clerk to the very district court judge who had the case and therefore had that advantage in litigating it. Later on, he and I served on a panel (together with Chief Circuit Court of Appeals Judge Patricia A. Wald) at an American Bar Association program celebrating the 25th anniversary of the enactment of the FOIA.

8   This provision is found in subsection (a)(4)(F) of the Act, 5 U.S.C. § 552(a)(4)(F). As of 1983, it had not yet been imposed on any agency employee by any court, despite the likelihood that in at least some cases that might well have been warranted. Now over the years, some people have asked whether there is any other type of penalty that can be imposed on miscreant FOIA personnel. The answer is "yes," because federal judges have inherent power to issue "sanction" orders in cases of extreme misconduct. One example of this is what occurred in the

2000 case of *Jefferson v. Reno*, when an agency (read: component of the Department of Justice, unfortunately) known as "EOUSA" ("Executive Office of U.S. Attorneys," to its sometime detractors), blatantly violated a court order requiring that wrongfully destroyed records be reconstructed and provided to their FOIA requester. The component FOIA officer responsible for this fiasco had personal problems, just like the OSHA FOIA processor in the *Simon* case, and charitably she is not named here.

9   I do confess to being somewhat conflicted about this. On one hand I had this duty to the client agency (put aside the offending employee, who most certainly was not my client), but on the other hand it would have been of even greater deterrent effectiveness in OIP's training programs to be able to warn that an agency FOIA officer actually had been "placed on a hook" for such misconduct.

10   5 U.S.C. § 552(a)(4)(F)(1). Again, this sanction provision was still so relatively esoteric as of 1983 that very few people working on FOIA issues, either inside the government or outside of it, had paid much attention to it. Later on, Congress enhanced this sanction mechanism by enacting a provision of the Whistleblower Protection Act of 1989, codified at 5 U.S.C. § 1216(a)(3), that allowed any FOIA requester to seek an Office of Special Counsel investigation of agency FOIA action even without a court order. This provision of law, too, was scarcely utilized, which frankly surprised us at the time. In the future, I would advise FOIA requesters to pay closer attention to it.

CHAPTER TWENTY-FIVE

1   While such administrative appeals from classified-record denials by the Department's components (largely the FBI) constituted the vast bulk of the DRC's work, it also acted on the attorney general's behalf with respect to other national security classification decisions, such as those made in matters of civil or criminal discovery. The DRC's membership consisted of the Department's top national security experts, whose expertise and judgment were called upon for collective action; the DRC's "institutional knowledge," which operated as key elements of administration, resided primarily within OIP's "DRC Unit" supervisor and staff.

2   This became a major logistical consideration when, in the mid-1990s during a complete refurbishment of the Main Justice Building, OIP left it for quarters that we were able to "build out" to our specifications in a building three blocks east of the White House. (It was from there that I saw White House staff members running north across Pennsylvania Avenue in their stocking feet on September 11, 2001 (see Chapter Thirty-Six).) Because of the sheer weight of those special safes, we had to have the floor beneath them certified as sufficiently load-bearing before we could move in.

And speaking of that refurbishment, an unfortunate casualty of it was the "wall of shame" that one could visit on the Main Justice Building's Seventh Floor, just around the bend from where OIP was located at the time, at the "back door" of the offices housing much of the Civil Division's Appellate Staff. The back story for it is the fact that, like some other federal agencies, the Justice Department had long commissioned official portraits (read: paintings) of its attorneys general, going back to the late 1780s. By tradition, incoming attorneys general, deputy attorneys general, associate attorney generals, solicitor generals, and assistant attorneys general got to choose one such portrait to hang in either their personal office or their conference room. For example, Attorney General Janet Reno had the portrait of Attorney General Robert F. Kennedy, showing him walking with his head slightly down and his hands in his pockets, hanging in her personal office, across from her steel drum.

Anyway, the "wall of shame" was a special collection of such official portraits, consisting of those of the "Watergate duo" of John N. Mitchell and Richard G. Kleindienst; Attorney General W. Ramsey Clark, whose portrait might have been hung there just because it looked so much like Lee Harvey Oswald; Attorney General Nicholas D. Katzenbach, whose portrait was so jarringly abstract as to perhaps lead the way for that of his immediate successor; Attorney General A. Mitchell Palmer, known for the infamous "Palmer Raids" during the "Red Scare" of 1919-1920, which probably was an unfair reason for his placement on "the wall"; Attorney General Edwin Meese III, who was the subject of more scandals and investigations than any other attorney general but could "take incoming" better than anyone I ever saw; and now presumably Attorney General Albert R. Gonzales and Attorney General William P. Barr, who might get a second portrait for his second tenure, though for now these portraits (i.e., the ones since Attorney General Eric H. Holder, Jr.) are just photographs, and at least one of them of Bill Barr should be on "the wall" soon enough. Many Justice Department employees who worked in the Main Justice Building knew of this wall.

3   Remarkably, Ana was not polygraphed as part of DIA's clearance process. I remember that because two former OIP attorneys went on to legal careers at the CIA and both of them were polygraphed over there, yet Ana was not.

4   I have to place myself in this category as well. While she was at OIP, Ana always seemed to me to be the model government employee, strongly dedicated to her work and entirely patriotic. Even after she joined DIA, I would see her occasionally at Peggy's house and as she would describe the general nature of her work I had not the slightest suspicion about her. In retrospect, I think it fair to say that she had a true gift for such deception. Her track record on that score certainly shows that.

5   Indeed, at the time of her sentencing 17 years later, *The Washington Post* crowned her "the most adept Cuban spy to infiltrate the U.S. military." (That certainly was the correct word for Ana: adept.) And to the *Miami Herald*, the paper of record for Cuban-American affairs, she was "the most damaging spy you've never heard of." And even in the wake of such spies as Aldrich H. Ames, Jonathan J. Pollard, and Robert P. Hanssen -- not to mention the Rosenbergs and Benedict Arnold -- she has been regarded as "one of the most damaging spies in U.S. history."

6   I think it might just be part of human nature to not be suspicious of those who do excellent work. That certainly was so in the case of the Justice Department secretary whose story is told later on in this chapter. And I've heard of the same thing being said about some better-known long-term spies such as Alger Hiss, Harold A. "Kim" Philby, Robert P. Hanssen, and Whittaker Chambers. In Ana's case, it was just part of who she was -- or who we thought her to be.

7   At one point, it was thought that Ana might have held the modern-day record for longest continuous espionage activity, at more than 16 years, but this has been challenged by some who point to the case of FBI Supervisory Special Agent Robert P. Hanssen, who was a Soviet and then Russian "mole" for a span of 22 years. However, a closer looks shows that Hanssen's espionage actually occurred in several "cycles," with several years between them. If there are prizes given out for such a thing, the Department of Justice tends to hold the award ceremonies within the walls of its own prisons.

8   None of this information was in the form of DIA documents, printouts, or photocopies of them, nor did Ana ever "download" any database information onto a transportable computer device. Rather, she simply used her excellent memory; her "downloading" took place when she arrived home at night and "typed up" what she had memorized during the day. For a spy operating into the 21st century -- and unlike Edward J. Snowden and Chelsea E. Manning, for instance (see Chapter Fifty) -- she certainly was "old school" in this regard.

9   Notably, Ana did bill the Cuban Government for some "expenses" incurred in her espionage work, but she did that work unpaid, which sets her apart from most spies against the United States, including several mentioned in this chapter.

10   Ana also made use of something known as a "numbers station," which is a short-wave radio station that broadcasts only a continuous series of formatted numbers in order to facilitate communications with intelligence officers (or spies) operating in foreign countries. She used what is called the "Atención" station of Cuba and was able to receive coded messages directly from Cuba on it. Although "numbers stations" originated more than 100 years ago, they remain in use today.

11   So much for using compartmentalization to minimize the security vulnerability of intelligence information. This particular system became a focus of much "after-action" analysis after Ana was detected.

12   Prior to Ana's sentencing, and plainly in an effort to influence it, an undersecretary of state by the name of John R. Bolton publicly opined that Ana's work in her "day job" contributing to Cuba policy might even have led the Clinton White House to take a more benign view of Cuba than it otherwise would have. She was no ordinary spy.

13   Afterward, one counterintelligence official echoed the words of many others: "We only really catch the dumb spies, and the only reason we caught her is because we got lucky."

14   It later was learned that, true to her roots at OIP, Ana had made a Freedom of Information Act request to DIA for access to her own "background investigation" file, which is not an uncommon step to take for both spies and ordinary employees alike, and that some information was released to her in response. She probably thought that if she had been under serious suspicion she might be able to glean an inkling of that from whatever would be disclosed. On the other hand, after her arrest, she said that about a week prior to that she finally detected that she was being closely surveilled, yet she did not flee.

15   According to public statements made by prosecutors, Ana had been or was about to be made privy to highly secret information about the U.S.'s impending invasion of Afghanistan in October 2001, which the U.S. military certainly did not want to risk her passing on. Of course, she presumably could not have learned that information had she not been kept in "surveillance mode" in the first place.

16   As it turned out, it was determined that she had not done so, even though our risk assessment showed that the timing would have made that possible. There was little doubt that Ana was recruited at SAIS, from which she graduated in May of 1985. And she left for DIA just a few months later. So with access to OIP's safes through her DRC role, she could have stolen (read: photocopied) some of their contents. But at the time, there was no information in there about Cuba (or about Nicaragua, which was a fleeting area of interest to her at the outset), so it was determined that she did not do so. Someday, I might have the chance to ask her about whether she ever considered doing so, given that OIP's 50th anniversary party is now less than ten years away. (I'll still be in my 70s for it and Ana will be not yet 75.)

Ana also was the subject of comprehensive, in-depth damage assessment conducted by the Office of the National Counterintelligence Executive ("ONCIX"). To do this, the ONCIX organized what it called a "Montes Damage Assessment Team," which issued a report titled "Review of the Actions Taken to Deter, Detect and Investigate the Espionage Activities of Ana Belen Montes" on June 16, 2005. This assessment was undertaken at the request of the House Permanent Select Committee on Intelligence and was released to the public (as opposed to those of us involved) only in heavily redacted form. This document essentially was used within the

Intelligence Community as an object lesson for coping with, as Ana was regarded to be, "the prototypical spy," one of the best (read: at it) ever.

17   Ironically, Ana came from a very patriotic family. Her brother and sister, Tito and Lucy, were both FBI employees. And as I recall, her sister-in-law, who like her husband was also an FBI Special Agent, was involved in bringing down the Cuban spy ring in Florida that had provided the lead to Ana being discovered. That spy ring, called the "Wasp Network," had more than a dozen members infiltrating Cuban exile organizations and U.S. military bases in Florida. After the FBI identified some of its members, it surreptitiously searched their homes and uncovered secret "crypto keys" on their laptops that were being used to decipher their communications with Havana. This led to wiretaps being placed on their phones.

   At the time, Lucy Montes was working as an FBI language analyst in Miami, translating wiretaps and other sensitive communications, and she translated wiretapped conversations of the Wasp spies that allowed the Bureau to conclude that Cuba had a high-level mole somewhere within the U.S. Intelligence Community. In time, the search for this person narrowed down to Ana.

18   Although that litigation case is featured above, it is not identified as involving this attorney in its early stages. Nevertheless, out of an abundance of caution, I will not identify that case in this context.

19   Yes, anyone interested in doing so could perhaps figure out who he was, especially in these days of Internet searches, but including his name (or even that case) here would serve no particular purpose. And given my relative professional assessment of him and his replacement on Ana's case, it would cause at least some damage to his reputation -- unnecessarily so.

20   Looking back on this today, I do not know for sure whether this crossed some ethical line for an attorney working for the Federal Government. If it did, then I suppose I was unthinkingly reckless in doing something that aided Ana. But she was facing the death penalty at the time and Peggy, whom I'd known as both a friend and colleague for more than 20 years by then (read: my wife and I held an engagement party for her at our home), was absolutely shattered by Ana's utter betrayal, as well as beside herself in coping with Ana's family, especially Ana's mother. And it did not help things that Peggy's husband adamantly refused to accept the fact of Ana's guilt even in the face of incontrovertible proof.

21   Cacheris had represented both husband and wife, in effect, in that part of the plea deal was that she received his "survivor pension." More significant than that was that she avoided any prosecution even though it was established that she learned of her husband's spying before he was finally arrested, prior to at least one of the deaths that were attributed to his espionage. In the espionage prosecution realm, having a death on your account is a major factor, one that usually "ups the ante" on the sentence and can lead to the death penalty being sought.

22   The FBI determined that Ana atypically accepted no money from Cuba for what she did, only reimbursements for some expenses. But as a high-level government employee living a modest lifestyle, she made more than a comfortable living.

23   Upon her arrest, Ana was heard insisting that she had the "moral right" to provide classified information to Cuba, presaging what was later said by spies such as Snowden and Manning.

24   In another one of those "small-world" coincidences that every now and again (read: in this case three times, counting Ana's unnamed original counsel in tandem with his previous co-counsel, Judge Urbina) do happen, I

once found myself chatting with a woman a little younger than myself at a holiday party who as it turned out knew Ana before she was a spy or even on the staff of OIP. She had been a college classmate of Ana's in the late 1970s and had even shared a house with her while they attended an academic program abroad. She told me that she had not been surprised to learn of Ana's espionage because she knew her back then to be very strongly principled and generally unforgiving of U.S. foreign policy. And she was certain that she was never contacted as part of Ana's background security investigations (including any "re-ups" that were done) when Ana was at either the Justice Department or DIA. If nothing else, this illustrates both the value and the limitations of such background investigations.

25   Before I retired, it occurred to me that I might write about Ana's story someday. So after a full-scale "component head" meeting in late 2006, I started chatting with a fellow component head, Federal Bureau of Prisons Director Harley G. Lappin, about the prospect of my visiting her at the place of her incarceration, which originally had been in Virginia. An amiable sort, Harley immediately said that he might be able to set a visit up for me, assuming of course that Ana herself was agreeable. But then I learned that she had been relocated to a prison in Fort Worth, Texas, which seemed a bit far to travel for such a thing at the time. And speaking of time, the most up-to-date information at the time of this writing is that Ana will finish serving her 25-year sentence (with credit for time served before sentencing and much time off for "good behavior" after it) on January 6, 2023. If that timing were better, in relation to the publication timetable of this book, she perhaps could have been interviewed for it. But that was not to be.

26   The title "Supervisory Special Agent" was used at the Bureau to distinguish its more senior Special Agents (usually at the GS-12 level and above) who were not just "street agents" or agents relatively new to the Bureau. This delineation also reflected the Bureau's basic "two-track" career path for its Special Agents: On one track, a Special Agent was subject to moving with his or her (originally only his) family to a new FBI field office as frequently as every two years, but with built-in advancement potential. (Inside the Bureau, it was said that, in additional to being on this advancement track it was particularly helpful for a rising Special Agent to have a "rabbi" on his side, i.e., a more senior friend or mentor who could "look out for" him as he progressed in his career.) On the other track, a Special Agent could opt not to subject his family to such moves, in which case he ordinarily could remain in the same field office for most or even all of his FBI career; it was much more difficult for one to become a "Supervisory Special Agent" in this static track. Earl Pitts held that title at FBIHQ as of 1989, having moved there from the New York Field Office (and Virginia) beforehand.

27   At any point in time back then, the Bureau had literally hundreds of its personnel devoted to FOIA matters -- e.g., initial record searching and "processing", defending administrative appeals, and creating detailed "*Vaughn* declarations" for the defense of its FOIA cases that proceeded to court. This number varied greatly, however, due to such things as new appropriations (on the "plus" side) and the secretive "draining" of FOIA personnel for other "exigencies," which happened over and over again. At one time in the mid-1990s (under Janet Reno, of course), this number approached a full one percent of the total workforce.

28   When this party originated in an OIP predecessor office in the late 1970s, I am sure that it was called a "Christmas Party." And I'm certain that it was still called that during OIP's first Christmas season after its creation in 1981. That name probably lasted throughout the Reagan years, at least, and sometime thereafter it succumbed to "political correctness" with substitution of the word "Holiday." Though I have been told that I have a phenomenal memory for most things (meaning the most important things), I cannot for the life of me recall when we changed this name. But I certainly recall Earl Pitts.

29   OIP's two deputy directors at the time had joined the Department in the largest of OIP's two predecessor offices in 1978 and, shall we say, together had themselves a rather large "following" among the predominantly male FOIA personnel in the Department's components. So for that reason among others, OIP's annual "Holiday Party" was known far and wide and was very well attended, including by officials at the Department's highest levels. When Janet Reno sauntered by one year, and stayed longer than anyone expected, we knew that OIP had fully hit its stride.

30   This generic term is used here, rather than the "Soviet Union," because it is pretty clear that Earl worked for the USSR starting in the late 1980s and probably continued for at least a bit past its formal dissolution in December of 1991.

31   "Back in the day" at the FBI, which meant during the longtime (read: 47-year) tenure of Director J. Edgar Hoover, there was an enormous chasm between being just any old FBI employee and being a Special Agent. And the only way in which those ranks could be entered was if the applicant (or advancing existing employee) had either an accountancy degree or was an attorney admitted to the bar, mostly the latter. This carried forward for many years after Hoover's death in 1972.

32   Ironically, part of Earl's job in this position was to assess the likelihood that newly arrived Soviets might be vulnerable to recruitment as "double-agents" against their home country. This brings to mind the expression "physician, heal thyself," of course.

33   To make ends meet, Earl and his wife Mary rented a small cottage in Greenwood Lake, N.Y., which gave him about a two-hour commute to his office in New York City each way, day after day. Back in the day, the KGB had an English acronym to indicate what motivates a spy. Rather than "sex, drugs, and rock 'n roll," its intelligence agents used to say that it was "MISE," which stood for "money, ideology, sex, and ego." The latter element includes the deeply psychological "thrill" that some spies experience; I see it as the counterpart to the American version's "rock 'n roll."

34   Although it can be difficult to be sure of someone like Earl's complete motivation, it seems reasonable in this case to conclude that he developed an enormous rage against what he saw as the unfairness of being placed in such financial straits by his government. Having known Earl scarcely at all, I'll venture the opinion that, in Earl's mind, this factor simply operated as a rationale by which he justified his actions (read: proposed action, in his initial decision to "cross that Rubicon") to himself.

35   This, by the way, is one of the reasons why the FBI (or the CIA, if overseas) maintained (read: still maintains) continuous surveillance on many Soviet embassies and related diplomatic residences, both inside and outside of the United States (see the Introduction and Chapter Forty-Eight). Some potential spies have been known to simply "walk in" to these establishments in order to offer their services. And the other primary route, which is what Earl followed, is to simply send a letter instead -- which is why the Bureau uses "mail covers" in the United States (read: its interception of incoming mail) to guard against such contacts.

36   Earl held a "Top Secret" security clearance in New York City and much of his work product there was classified at the "Secret" level (read: on the continuum from "Confidential" on up). When he began working on Freedom of Information Act matters, however, he also was granted access to Sensitive Compartmented Information ("SCI," to its users) through a "code-word" clearance that he sometimes needed in order to do that job.

37   Earl is one of just a few spies whose tenure as such spanned both the Soviet era and that of Russia alone. By all accounts, however, that shift did not seem to affect what he did much at all.

38   At the time, Earl Pitts was only the second FBI Special Agent (and the first supervisory one) ever known to have sold out his country, after Special Agent Richard W. Miller (and before FBI Supervisory Special Agent Robert P. Hanssen, of course). Special Agent Miller had been arrested for espionage in 1984, after being detected through routine FBI surveillance of Soviet intelligence operatives, a job that he himself had held at one time, much like Earl Pitts. He, too, faced heavy financial difficulties (read: he was a Mormon with eight children) and he provided classified documents to KGB operative Svetlana Ogorodnikov, with whom he was having a sexual relationship, for $65,000 in gold and cash -- thus ticking off both the "sex" and "money" boxes on the espionage scorecard (and perhaps the "alcohol" one, as well).

Miller initially faced life in prison, but his ultimate sentence (after his third trial) was for only 20 years -- and even that was due to the persistence of a young federal prosecutor by the name of Adam B. Schiff (later chairman of the House Intelligence Committee). Of that, though, he wound up serving a term of only 13 years before his release in 1994, at about the same time as his KGB paramour Svetlana.

In later years, no other FBI Special Agent has joined Miller, Pitts, and Hanssen in this infamous group (read: none has been detected as such), but there was someone in a different category of the FBI, Leandro Aragoncillo, who in September of 2005 was arrested on charges of conspiracy to commit espionage and transmitting more than three dozen classified documents (at the level of "Secret") to current and former high-level Philippine officials. Aragoncillo worked as an FBI Intelligence Analyst only from July 11, 2004, to September 10, 2005, but prior to that, from July 1999 to April 2002, he served in the Office of the Vice President as a staff assistant to the vice president's military advisors (read: mostly for Vice President Cheney). He evidently gathered and leaked classified information on the Philippines from both of these two positions. (Perhaps deflecting a bit, the FBI labeled Aragoncillo as the first known case of espionage in the history of the White House, at least until it was occupied by President Donald J. Trump, of course.) In 2007, he was sentenced to ten years in prison.

The FBI did suffer an espionage failure of another sort when it took the responsibility of surveilling a CIA case officer named Edward Lee Howard, who was suspected (read: with little doubt) of spying for the KGB in the mid-1980s. The Bureau kept him under surveillance at his rural home near Santa Fe, New Mexico, and even wiretapped his phone. He devised a plan, however, that allowed him to escape: First, he ambled over to a member of the FBI surveillance team and said that he was ready to talk but needed one more day to confer with an attorney. Then, as his wife drove them back to their home from a casual appointment elsewhere, and with the surveillance team in tow, he jumped from their car as his wife rounded a sharp corner and left a dummy in the passenger seat that fooled his followers. It was several days before the ruse was discovered, long enough for him to make it to Albuquerque, New York City, Helsinki, and then Moscow, where he died at age 50 in 2002.

39   In a case such as this, as was the case with FBI Supervisory Special Agent Robert P. Hanssen later on, there inevitably will be focus on the possible complicity of a spouse, even if only in the form of possessing some knowledge of what was going on, the likelihood of which is greater when the espionage is rooted in money, not sex or "rock 'n roll." In this case, atypically, Earl's wife Mary secretly contacted the FBI near the outset of the 16-month "false flag" period. She worked at the Bureau in a clerical position and stated that she placed patriotism above her marriage. (It probably helped that they had no children.) When Earl was finally arrested, the FBI took pains to specify that she was not a defendant in his case. They are now divorced.

40   By all accounts, Earl cooperated with investigators freely in his debriefings upon his arrest. Given the evidence against him, he had no reason not to do so and every reason to do so. And when he was asked the standard question of whether he was aware of any other spy within the FBI, he reportedly said that he was not -- but

that he had a suspicion about someone, Supervisory Special Agent Robert Hanssen. Evidently, and inexplicably, this was not acted on, and Hanssen's espionage continued for another four years, until he was exposed due to the efforts of a special FBI/CIA mole-hunting team. Hanssen was convicted of selling U.S. secrets to the Soviet Union and then Russia for more than $1.4 million in cash and diamonds over a 22-year period (1979-2001), which the FBI attributed to the fact that he took pains to keep his identity hidden from both the Soviets and the Russians. As a high-level counterintelligence official, he was the most dangerous FBI spy ever.

41   At Earl's sentencing, Judge Ellis explained his upward departure from the prosecutors' recommendation thusly: "There are folks in every veterans hospital and on grave markers from here to Europe to Asia [who] you have dishonored. . . . You did it in part out of simple greed."

42   There is an old (read: well, it can't be *that* old) espionage joke that is sometimes told within the Intelligence Community, with more than a touch of gallows humor: How many spies does it take to screw up a "dead drop"? No, no, not that one; I mean this one: How many spies have you had at your agency? Answer: None that we know of yet.
      In addition to Ana, Earl, and Sharon Thomas (see below), of course, there were at one time eight other spies at Main Justice. They sat together in Room 5233, where they were tried as "Nazi saboteurs" in 1942. And six of them suffered a fate worse than anything meted out to their three named successors (see the Quiz Questions, below).

43   A "cypher lock" was an added measure of security that we used even inside of the secure Main Justice Building. One would have to get past that even to get in proximity of our safes. Don't be fooled, however. We're talking here about a part of the building (i.e., its Seventh Floor) that originally had housed much of the FBI, from the time of the building's construction in 1934 to when the Bureau's headquarters building across the street was finally ready for occupancy in 1975. (This square city block was a giant hole when I first worked at Justice in 1971; it took a long, long time to finish, especially for a structure that now only a short 48 years later (to me) is deemed "obsolete.") Because of that, as reconfigured, we had a "drop ceiling" above us. It did occur to us that the special "cypher lock" could be easily circumvented through that.
      Also, there is the fact that when my oldest daughter Emily, the computer-genius math whiz, was only about eight years old, she visited my office one Saturday afternoon and the next thing we knew, she was in the area containing the safes. Evidently, in a way that no amount of torture could force her to reveal, she managed to defeat the lock by entering a correct sequence of signals. This could have been just a matter of pure luck, of course, but she did it very quickly, just as she manipulates Rubik's cubes; from then on, she referred to it as OIP's "psycho lock."

44   I suppose that to my small list of items that I do not think I will "never understand" (see Chapter Fifty) I should add "Scientology," which to my mind is so patently illogical that, even taking basic "human nature" into account, it is difficult to imagine any thinking person becoming so "swept away" by it.

45   As is discussed in greater detail elsewhere (see Chapter Ten), the very nature of government litigation is such that new or still-junior attorneys often will be assigned to handle cases that one might think are so significant as to warrant handling by far more senior and experienced colleagues. But a number of factors -- including limited resources, large caseloads, and heavy turnover as young attorneys advance elsewhere -- can conspire to obviate that as a general rule.

46   According to the indictment eventually filed in the matter, Sharon Thomas "was given money to purchase some 'sexy' clothes for [this purpose]." By noting this, I do not in any way intend to intimate that that had

anything to do with her selection as this attorney's personal secretary. In fact, I know this attorney well, as well as his wife, and know that he is of such character as to resist the blandishments of such charms. Lest anyone think that perhaps this young infiltrator somehow used her "feminine wiles" to be chosen as the secretary of the very attorney who was "ground zero" for Scientology FOIA litigation coordination at that time, I can attest that that attorney is about the "straightest arrow" you would ever want to meet.

47   What I did not learn then, because it apparently was treated as a shameful secret even within the Justice Department, was that evidently Scientologists also managed to steal documents from the office of the Information and Privacy Unit's unit chief at the time. He has been identified elsewhere in this book, in far from flattering terms, so he is not identified by name here.

48   I knew Nate very well during my clerkship at the District Court for the District of Columbia, then as a litigator in the Civil Division of Main Justice, and later when I supervised litigation at OIP (see the Acknowledgments). In that latter role, I attended regular monthly staff meetings at the Civil Division of the United States Attorney's Office (not to be confused with the larger Civil Division at Main Justice) and Nate always seemed to have some wise words for me. Late in 1984, after I had lost more than 100 pounds that I had gained while sitting on my butt writing and editing, he quipped that he barely recognized me but still thought that my authoritative opinions on FOIA matters carried "a lot of weight." In a similar vein, there was another AUSA whom I regularly saw at those meetings, Barbara "Biz" Van Gelder, who was even quicker with a quip; she took evident joy at these staff meetings in lobbing rhetorical bombs to the front of the room.

49   It is extremely rare in FOIA cases for the Government to seek, let alone obtain, discovery of anyone associated with an opposing party. I was able to do it once, but it was on an exceptional attorney fee issue. The fact that Judge Hart even suggested that on the record constituted a radical departure in FOIA litigation.

50   A secondary purpose soon developed for these repeated break-ins: These Scientologists simplistically posited that if they could find enough personal information about Nate they could "render him harmless" through blackmail or some related means. As to that notion, I say: They just didn't know Nate.

51   She also had been charged with conspiracy and burglary but, to both abuse and mix two metaphors, that evidently got "lost in the shuffle" as the prosecutors (to her good fortune) had "bigger fish to fry."

52   Actually, this was so only for Sharon Thomas's time at the Justice Department. She had begun her espionage there in early 1976 but had infiltrated the Coast Guard prior to that. And Scientology's "Operation Snow White," in a broader sense, was born and implemented many years before that.

53   The two of them met at the University of Wisconsin, where they both were well known as "campus radicals." They married in 1978, which is what brought Terry Squillacote into the realm of German espionage to begin with. Their ideological commitment to socialism is illustrated by the fact that they named their two children Karl and Rosa, after German Communist "martyrs" Karl Liebknecht and Rosa Luxemburg.

54   To aid their espionage, this husband-and-wife team, together with a third co-conspirator, received much support from the HVA in the form of extensive training in such things as detecting and avoiding surveillance, receiving and decoding messages sent by short-wave radio from Cuba (shades of Ana Montes), the use of codewords and phrases, using a miniature camera to photograph documents, and removing classified markings from documents. They also received large sums of money that were mostly denominated as "travel expenses." This all was arranged by their East German handler. Evidently, Terry Squillacote and her husband Karl had the

type of spousal relationship that was not an impediment her long-distance, and long-term, relationship with that East German.

55   When this rapid rise at DOD is viewed in conjunction with her academic achievements -- e.g., Dean's List as an undergraduate, a 3.9 GPA in obtaining a Master's Degree in European History, a law degree, and then a Masters of Law degree -- it becomes clear that, like Ana Montes, Terry Squillacote's espionage activities were greatly aided by both a strong work ethic and very high intelligence.

56   At this point, she and her husband began using "micro cameras" and Casio digital diaries with interchangeable memory cards. They all (read: including the KGB) began communicating with one another by exchanging memory cards.

57   As it turned out, he was released after a relatively short period of incarceration, for reasons never made clear.

58   It later came to light that the FBI was given multiple big "leads" to detecting them in the files of the HVA and its sister intelligence services when they were made available to western intelligence agencies subsequent to the collapse of the Soviet Union. This certainly rang true to me because I remember being visited by a foreign diplomat from the former German Democratic Republic in the early 1990s who, after receiving a briefing on FOIA implementation, suddenly produced a laminated, highly detailed schematic of what he said were repositories of "Stasi files," as if that were of interest to me. I politely accepted that "gift," of course, and promptly sent it over to my former clients at the CIA.

59   All told, the FBI conducted 550 consecutive days of surveillance on the two, over a span of more than three years.

60   Reportedly, her son Karl was only 14 at the time and had long suffered from severe physical disabilities resulting from what is known as Kinsbourne's Syndrome, a rare form of encephalitis, and she also had a daughter who was then about 12. Coincidentally, Terry Squillacote also had severe physical deformities, including a missing right leg (below the knee), a clubbed left foot, and the absence of fingers on one hand.

61   And she is open (read: not completely, but only by dint of artful phrasing) about her past, saying: "I am a currently unlicensed attorney. I spent 18 years inside [a] federal prison on espionage-related charges, arising from an undercover agent pretending to be from Nelson Mandela's new government and prior contact with the former East Germany. I regret my past conduct but believe [that] with the passage of time and significant rehabilitation efforts I am able to offer reliable, comprehensive professional services."

62   Oddly, there is no indication whatsoever that Squillacote has ever sought any leniency based upon the severity of her own physical deformities. That itself is remarkable, as is reflected in the counterpart case of *Kennedy v. Festvelt*, and it certainly speaks well of her.

CHAPTER TWENTY-SIX

1   The Senior Executive Service was a personnel system created by Congress in 1979 to encompass what previously were the top civil service grades, GS-16, GS-17, and GS-18. One feature of this system was that agencies could not unilaterally promote their employees to the top-most levels. Rather, they could do so only with the approval of the Office of Personnel Management ("OPM," to personnel staffs) and only within a limited number of career SES "slots" allocated to each agency. So any promotion or career appointment above the GS-15 level involves a multi-step process: (1) the individual has to be selected by the agency; (2) he or she has to be found

individually qualified for the position by OPM; and (3) the agency has to have a current career SES "slot" available for the appointment. I was appointed to the SES in 1984 and retired at the ES-5 (formerly GS-18) level.

2   This was located in Kings Point, New York, not far from where I had worked full-time for a law firm during my last two years of college and only about a 30-minute drive from where I had graduated from high school 13 years earlier. Serendipitously, this allowed me to pay a weekday visit to my old school, where I was invited by its principal to give two lectures on the value of higher education, with subtext conveying the value of not being limited to Long Island.

3   It was no secret that there were relatively few women in the Federal Government's executive ranks at that time. And despite the "women's movement" of the 1970s (of which my wife was a part), there was only slight expectation that this would change much at all under President Reagan. In fact, I can still remember a time when I was able to count on two hands and a foot (and by name, as I knew them all) the full complement of female career SESers in the entire Justice Department. That was in the early '90s and the number was 13.

4   I had the feeling during this program that I was standing out amongst this group, not just because of my age but because I was able to participate very actively in the program's interactive sessions. This was due in large measure to the fact that so many of the fact patterns that were covered, especially in the developmental activities, involved matters of law, or at least had legal implications. And of those, a good proportion raised potential issues of constitutional law, as one might expect in a program designed to cover our governmental system. Yes, I had a distinct advantage, not only as an attorney but also in that I had been a longtime student of that subject.

5   This term came into vogue, and the public's perception, in the immediate wake of the horrific events of September 11, 2001. Some smaller semblance of COG came into service then, relabeled "Continuity of Operations" (or "COOP"), with the most public awareness of it revealed by a few journalistic accounts of some high-level officials spending time in "an undisclosed location." Reportedly, on that fateful day, the senior leadership of Congress fled to the Federal Government's underground "Special Facility" at Mount Weather, Virginia. I used to spend weeks at a time there.

6   The fact that President Reagan was by then more than 70 years old (our oldest president as of then) might have had something to do with this, but those of us in the COG community mostly attributed it to a cowboy-like desire (reminiscent of the Slim Pickens character in the movie "Dr. Strangelove") to directly command our nuclear forces in a counter-attack against the Soviets down to the very last possible moment.

7   This was reflected in President Reagan's issuance of two national security directives ("NSDDs," to those interested in national security matters): NSDD 47, titled "Emergency Mobilization Preparedness," issued on July 22, 1982, and NSDD 55, titled "Enduring National Leadership," issued on September 14, 1982, the latter of which remains partly classified.

8   Those congressional successors are, in turn, the Speaker of the House and the President Pro Tempore (sometimes shortened to "President Pro Tem") of the Senate (usually the longest-serving senator in the majority). This is not provided for in the Constitution, but rather in the Presidential Succession Act of 1947. Beyond that, the presidential line of succession reaches down through the cabinet (for those cabinet secretaries who, unlike Secretaries of State Henry A. Kissinger and Madeleine J. Albright, were born in the United States) in the order of the creation of their cabinet departments.

9   What the public (and even Congress itself) came to realize only much later on is that it never was "the plan" that Members of Congress, including even the Speaker of the House and the President Pro Tempore of the Senate, would be co-located with the president at the Special Facility. Rather, in the late 1950s the government secretly built a so-called "underground bunker" (but one not completely underground, as it occupied what was called the "West Virginia Wing") both beneath and alongside the historic Greenbrier Hotel in White Sulphur Springs, West Virginia, to house as many Members of Congress as could make it there "in time." (Today, however, there is good reason to think that Congress provided its own such facility, of a sort, at the bottom level ("level 3") of the Capital Visitor Center when that was constructed (with a three-year delay and massive cost overruns) in 2008.)

In fact, it was not until this facility's existence was made known by enterprising *Washington Post* reporter Tad Gup in April of 1992 that even Congress officially learned of this secret plan, inasmuch as "the locals" there (read: the relatively few who knew of it) made it a matter of patriotic pride not to let this secret slip out. (There are other examples of secrets not being divulged by a local populace in comparable circumstances, but not many. Nowadays, in the age of the Internet, "24/7 news," and communications at one's fingertips, such a thing would scarcely be conceivable.)

A third such facility, known as the "Raven Rock Mountain Complex," was built in the area of Gettysburg, Pennsylvania, not far from the Maryland border, in the very early 1950s. Carved out of the Blue Ridge Mountains at Blue Ridge Summit, it was conceived as a nuclear bunker for use by the military services in the event of war and for a while was secretly known as the "underground Pentagon." It was effectively replaced by the Special Facility in the early 1960s and, as far as the public knows, has been used by Department of Defense components only for secondary purposes since then. A fourth similar facility, known as "Mount Pony" near Culpeper, Virginia, was built in 1959 for the Federal Reserve Board's use (e.g., stockpiling cash) and now is used by the Library of Congress for its long-term storage purposes. And a fifth such facility, unconfirmed by the National Security Agency ("NSA," to its surveilees), has been added to the longstanding NORAD complex at Cheyenne Mountain, Colorado.

10   The necessary premise for this plan, of course, was that any nuclear exchange would be preceded by at least some period of escalating tensions between us and the Soviets (or any other nuclear power, such as Pakistan, for example) such that the plan's activation would be possible just before Washington was destroyed. Hence, when we began to "exercise" this plan, doing so involved the real-world dispersal of many people to undisclosed locations around the country, at considerable expense. As a matter of fact, the entire COG plan, involving as it did four nodes of government activity and multiple "successor nodes," plus a cadre of "control" personnel, with such activity taking place year after year, was "godawfully expensive," but perhaps this was just a few drops in the bucket of a big "black budget," especially in the Reagan years.

11   This latter role afforded me the opportunity to work with several Cold War veterans who had a wealth of experience in the matters with which we were dealing. One of them, senior CIA official Charles E. Allen, served as the chief exercise "controller" and was responsible for adjusting the contours and flow of "exercise play" as we went along, including what he called "ramping things up" where in his judgment it would be best to do so. In a word, I found Charlie to be amazing at this. I like to think that I do not impress easily, but Charlie impressed me enormously and I felt honored to serve as one of his two deputies in 1991.

12   I vividly recall spending more than ten hours straight in a conference room full of dedicated senior COG members (mostly from State, DOD, and the CIA, some of whom were former ambassadors) in 1991, who dutifully stayed "within role" for that entire time, as if it were all real. I had rarely seen such dedication firsthand.

13   It is relevant to Trump Administration events, without saying too much here, to note that a primary focus of PEADs, as would reasonably be expected, was the related subjects of martial law and *posse comitatus*, having to do with the potential use of military forces for domestic law enforcement purposes. The legal members of our Legal and Law Enforcement Group had to be well versed on such things.

14   The principal legal authority on presidential succession (apart from the Constitution and its 25th Amendment) is a statute called the Presidential Succession Act of 1947, 3 U.S.C. § 19, which in section (d) sets out the line of succession (below the two congressional successors, who in our scenarios never made it out of D.C.) through the heads of the departments of the cabinet, one that hews to the date on which each department was created: State, Defense, Treasury, Justice, Interior, Agriculture, Commerce, Labor, Health and Human Services, Housing and Urban Development, Transportation, Energy, Education, Veterans Affairs, and most recently Homeland Security.

Thus, if in the real world (and its mirror-image "exercise play") the Secretaries of Agriculture and Commerce, say, were the only two to survive as dispersed, and this was solidly verified by the Legal and Law Enforcement Group (headed by the presumptive acting attorney general), then we would validate that Agriculture Secretary as Acting President of the United States, and he or she would be sworn in as such, serving at least until the end of the pre-nuclear president's presidential term. From that moment, regardless of any new-found status of anyone higher up in the succession line, that would stand.

15   For perhaps obvious reasons, current cabinet members were not regularly used for this purpose. So the role was played by someone who had once held responsibility at such a high level but was no longer in federal service. This included, for example, a future vice president, his administration's national security advisor, and at least three other future cabinet members. Evidently, this role did not lack for volunteers.

16   The "nuclear exchange" part of each exercise's scenario was not just described in written materials for us; rather, it was communicated graphically. Each time, as an exercise began, we all gathered to view a big video map of the United States that was suddenly "lit up" with red dots and then larger and larger red circles by which this exercise's particular "laydown" was depicted.

By the time this ended, for example, the State of South Dakota usually was entirely eclipsed, on the rationale that it contained so many missile silos that the Soviets would target them on a priority basis in the hope that in so doing those sites would be destroyed before the launching of their own payloads.

17   By this time, including in the less sophisticated doomsday exercises that had taken place prior to the Reagan years, the government had developed many basic fact scenarios for this purpose. So it was not entirely surprising to find such a wrinkle in 1987.

18   It should be added that by "condition" I mean not just alive, as a survivor, but also of such fitness, in mind and body, that he or she was comfortable serving as the Nation's new president at that time. In our view, this included, again within the exercise's factual parameters, surviving in a location that still offered adequate physical security for a president and, even more importantly, still maintained sufficiently secure and robust "coms" for this purpose. It is worth noting in this latter regard that any post-nuclear environment would almost certainly be constrained by severe "EMP" (electromagnetic pulse) problems, meaning that conventional communication means would be far from reliable.

So in a science fiction-like solution to this, the Defense Department had developed what was known as "meteor burst technology" by which communications could be transmitted, believe it or not, by being converted into electronic signals that actually could be "bounced" off the tails (read: ionized trails) of meteors and down to a precise location for reception. (Yes, this is real; you could look it up just by Googling it, if you like. Some people hear the term as "*media* burst technology," but those are mostly people who were working in the press office of the Trump White House.) Therefore, we actually used this phenomenal means of communication (in "real world" fashion) to communicate with other COG sites in all of our exercises. And we used only "tempested" word processors, which means that they were certified by the National Security Agency as safe from any surveillance penetration by audio-keystroke interception through the vibration of a building's exterior surfaces, especially those made of glass. (Yes, one could look that up, too.)

19   As serious as this kind of enterprise was, it must be confessed that some lightheartedness was inevitably resorted to by its participants in order to relieve the pervasive tension involved. After all, we were continuously speaking and acting as if this all were in fact "the real thing." Add severe sleep deprivation to that, especially for some of us, over a week's time, and you have a prescription for at least some clever wordplay, at the very minimum. For example, there is a two-time cabinet secretary who probably has no idea that her surname was abused when cases of real-world food poisoning suddenly erupted at her node in 1991.

20   Though one of these former officials is now deceased, neither one of them need be identified here. I certainly would not want to be identified in this context if it were me.

21   I had explained as best I could that under the particular language of the applicable statute, succession to the presidency is not allowed for anyone "under disability to discharge the powers and duties of the office." 3 U.S.C. § 19(d). And being incommunicado, as specified in this exercise scenario, and thus being unable to communicate with a traumatized American populace as its new commander-in-chief, is surely a "disability" in anyone's book. But these two officials simply did not want to hear this, either in their exercise roles or in their real-world ones, and after I told them "no" for the third time they went so far as to accuse the Legal and Law Enforcement Group leader, and in turn me, of promoting a "treasonous Avignon papacy" given that they had made clear their intention not to stand down.

22   One of my favorite memories of that hectic time was of turning around to find that one of the Legal and Law Enforcement Group's law enforcement members had placed a steak dinner on my workspace, knowing that I hadn't been able to break away for a meal in more than 24 hours. That kind benefactor was John W. Magaw, a member of our group from ATF, who later went on to become the head of ATF and then was appointed Director of the United States Secret Service. The next time I saw John, he was walking alongside President Clinton's limousine as it moved slowly along Pennsylvania Avenue during the January 1993 inauguration parade.

23   This was the "back channel" that yielded the names of the two high-level people involved; as I recall, the price for obtaining this information was that our incapacitated group leader and I had to suffer their counter-request for our names and "real-world bios," presumably as a form of attempted intimidation (not that it worked).

     At this point, I remember thinking that this would be an exquisitely effective way to "test" the COG system on such a pivotal thing -- i.e., to apply maximum pressure on the acting attorney general to see if he or she would buckle on the matter of legal succession. I actually said to myself, and to others, that this is how I would design the exercise play if I wanted to do that. But no, once we learned the identities of these two would-be despots, we concluded that this was just a matter of their personalities running amok. (Plus, we soon enough learned through a "real world" conversation with worried exercise "controllers" that their scenario writers actually had not yet thought of throwing such a further wrinkle at us (logical though it would have been).

24   There were several more exercises and much more development of the COG program during the following years, and I was asked to devote so much time to them, with days on end at FEMA (not to mention program

contractor facilities), that it sometimes felt as if I had two jobs, not one. This reached a high point when in 1991 I was asked to serve as one of two deputy "controllers" of the entire exercise that was conducted then -- i.e., overseeing all four primary program nodes, as well at the successor ones. This certainly broadened my perspective, over the course of a nonstop 110-hour week, even though by then (i.e., mid-1991) it was imagined that this most active COG program would soon be ended as simply no longer necessary in light of the Soviet Union's collapse.

And not long thereafter, it was. But through this last exercise, I had the privilege of working directly with several "grizzled veterans" of the Cold War, mostly from DOD and the State Department, who explained from their perspective that the COG program had greatly succeeded in its mission in that the Soviet Union was permitted to learn just enough about it for it to serve as a strong deterrent to nuclear war. And so, it worked.

25   DOD was of course the all-encompassing bureaucratic umbrella under which the entire COG program necessarily operated. For its part, it nicely sent me a written commendation of my "exceptional assistance," both during our exercises and in the developmental work undertaken between them, but that document was so detailed that I could only view it, and only in a "SCIF" (i.e., a "sensitive compartmented information facility") on the Sixth Floor of the Main Justice Building. Presumably it is still there, or perhaps it is in the (declassified accessioned files of the National Archives by now.

CHAPTER TWENTY-SEVEN

1   The way in which I would phrase it to friends and family is that holding this position meant that when I woke up each morning I knew that during the coming work day I could be presented with (or discern the existence of) a legal issue arising from the subject matter of any record that was held by the executive branch of the Federal Government, bar none. (Well, there was one exception -- information concerning nuclear materials, which was covered by its own federal nondisclosure law.) This meant that I could find myself involved in, and resolving disclosure issues about, most anything that the Federal Government did.

2   Noteworthy in this regard was the fact that while the FOIA had been in existence for about fifteen years by this time, it was limited in its strength and therefore not yet heavily utilized, relatively speaking, during most of that time -- i.e., from its effective date in July 1967 to its pro-disclosure reform in 1974 (which was not effective until September 1975). Indeed, the statute did not effectively apply to the FBI, much less the CIA, until just a few years before the Reagan Administration began. Thus, it was still rife with even the most basic legal questions requiring both governmentwide policy and case law development, especially as to its law enforcement exemptions and intelligence-agency protections.

3   After President George H.W. Bush's son became president in 2001, many of us in the Justice Department took to referring to their terms as "Bush 41" and "Bush 43," respectively. Then, when Bush the Younger managed to actually win a second term (notice the use of the phrase "actually win" here), those presidential years sometimes were referred to as "Bush I," "Bush II," and "Bush III."

4   This, of course, was that same political appointee who yelled and screamed as he fled from me out of the back exit of his office.

CHAPTER TWENTY-EIGHT

1   During those years, with so many secrecy-related news stories "breaking" overnight, I made a point of reading The Washington Post every morning without fail, even on weekends. In some cases, this allowed me

to take action on something the moment I walked in the door at work; in others, it would prepare me for an inevitable phone call or meeting request on some new subject. In this case, it gave me crucial information that I was able to act on, at first, from home.

2   Back in those days, you had to be a very senior official of the Department to have it issue you a specially designed computer configured to allow remote access to your office computer system. And what you got for your trouble was a clunky beast of a thing that was less reliable than the newer system that my 11-year-old daughter used. But it was good for "stand-alone" work, and for the occasional emergency communication to Main Justice, even if I had to ask my computer-savvy daughter (who now handles computer security and privacy for Google) to help me make a connection with it every now and again. This early computer (called a "DG-1") was especially useful on weekends, but it had a "dial-in" connection to Main Justice that was so fragile it could be interrupted by any incoming call -- meaning that I had to type quickly lest some scheduling call from, say, my other daughter's soccer team wipe everything out.

3   For instance, there already had been much information-policy activity created by challenges to the "Health Care Task Force" that First Lady Hillary Rodham Clinton headed up from the Administration's very first days. Helping her White House "clients" (which included Deputy White House Counsel Vincent M. Foster) with this, Nancy had already consulted with perhaps the smartest person in the building (Deputy Solicitor General Edwin S. Kneedler) on that and based upon his work with me over the years he had recommended me to Nancy as someone whom she could, and should, rely upon for multiple reasons.

4   This is probably a good juncture at which to point out that, as a general rule, high-level career officials, especially those working in vital policy areas, are often viewed by incoming political appointees as perhaps not truly "career." This is understandable, if for no other reason than because political appointees sometimes manage to "burrow in" as nominal career ones as an administration ends, and even apart from that the political sympathies of the career ranks can hardly be presumed. So looking at it from the perspective of an incoming political appointee such as Nancy, scrambling at the very beginning of a new administration, you cannot be confident of the objectivity and even the reliability of the high-level career officials whom you encounter until you have some basis for being certain of this. One has to have a very strong instinct for "sizing up" the career folks with whom you have to work, or else you can use the technique of finding a very high-level person whose judgment you can trust and then asking for that person's candid opinion of those people. Nancy, to her credit, had both of these things working for her in my case.

5   A person of great integrity herself, Nancy went on during the Reagan Administration to become general counsel of the Department of Transportation and then deputy chief of staff to Vice President Al Gore, and then upon returning to her native California she served as Governor Jerry Brown's righthand and chief of staff from 2011-2018. Sadly, she died of ovarian cancer in 2018, at the young age of 59, and both President Clinton and Hillary Clinton spoke at her funeral.

6   During a presidential transition, ordinarily the deputy attorney general or some other high-level Justice Department official carries over from the outgoing administration until a new attorney general is confirmed. In this case, outgoing Attorney General William P. Barr left on Inauguration Day (though he returned ignominiously later) and anticipating the imminent confirmation of Zoë E. Baird to the position, President Clinton named Civil Division head Stuart M. Gerson to serve as Acting Attorney General (because Zoë knew him) during what was expected to be only a very brief interregnum period. But this unexpectedly turned out to be a period of more

than six weeks, and it was during this time that Webb, as a close Clinton confidante, acted as our *de facto* attorney general.

7   As it later turned out, Nancy was more prescient in this question than she realized: Years later, Webb coincidentally became embroiled in the Whitewater investigation, through which it was discovered that, astonishingly, he had as managing partner of his law firm been embezzling huge sums from it over the course of many years. Those of us who worked with and for him during his 13-month tenure in the Department were shocked by this, but we sardonically observed that at least he didn't commit any crime while he was with us.

8   Looking back, I am amazed (and, I confess, more than a bit flattered) that Nancy reacted so decisively in her office given that I had told her only the general nature of my concern, without any such details. She must have been able to tell from the look on my face (not to mention the "emergency" nature of my contact with her) that this sad tale was grave enough for me to tell it to her and Webb together.

9   Webb's liberal use of the word "we" immediately put me in mind of that old, politically incorrect Lone Ranger joke that ends with Tonto's punchline: "What you mean 'we,' white man?" But I fully understood what Webb was doing, and I certainly did not at all mind having him doubly in my debt.

10   I had told Webb and Nancy that there were only an extremely few people within the Department who knew anything about this, much less who were in a position to "connect the dots" with something that had happened several years ago. To the best of my knowledge, there were only two of us in a position to do so and as it turned out the other person never came even close to doing any such dot connecting. Of necessity, I subsequently had to tell the secret to two other people at Main Justice, career employees who worked for me, and I "put the fear of god into them" about the absolute secrecy that was now required. It was the type of secret that OIP regularly handled, but this one in particular was especially fragile for a further reason that I cannot divulge.

11   It should be apparent that I have taken great pains not to disclose anything here that would allow discernment of the identity of the Member of Congress involved, starting most fundamentally with the use of dual pronouns and the nonidentification of the particular body of Congress to which that person belonged or perhaps still belongs. Simply put, this person (and his or her family, if one existed) was entitled to protection of the underlying facts, as a matter of both law and policy, regardless of how inculpating those facts were. This has necessarily required limiting the depth of this story, lest its full details be recognized by anyone other than that Member of Congress him- or herself. (If upon reading this, that current or former Member of Congress would like to contact me to discuss "old times," that would be alright with me -- assuming that he or she is still alive, that is.)

12   Members of Congress have in fact used the FOIA many times over the years, on an individual basis, beginning with Representative Patsy Mink in the early 1970s with a FOIA request that travelled all the way up to the Supreme Court in 1973. Indeed, "courts have long entertained FOIA actions brought by [M]embers of Congress." *Maloney v. Carnahan*, slip op. at 5 (D.C. Cir. Aug. 8, 2022) (Millett, J., concurring in denial of rehearing en banc). But it is quite rare for a Member of Congress to make a *first*-person access request, i.e., one for records pertaining to him- or herself, where the access provisions of the Privacy Act can apply.

13   Yes, the circumstances were such that for some period of time this description was apt. I pass no moral judgment on the Member of Congress involved; it was not my role to do so, let alone allow any such judgment to influence my work. Rather, what I held was a responsibility to protect this pathetic miscreant, no matter how

or why he or she had escaped justice, because the law, most particularly the Privacy Act, required it. And at even an analytical level, I likewise held a responsibility to safeguard the abstract possibility that a confidential law enforcement source was involved, in which case we would have invoked FOIA Exemption 7(D) in lieu of an overlapping Exemption 7(C) in order to cover that.

14   It should be understood that the investigators and potential prosecutors here naturally were working toward having the strongest case possible given the exceptionally high-profile subject of their investigation. And that when their elaborate "sting" operation so ignominiously failed, they apparently lost their zeal for moving forward with the case. Sometimes, in the law enforcement world, things just work out that way.

15   Nevertheless, as an unprosecuted person, even this sitting Member of Congress had the right to nondisclosure of this information. It is a longstanding and well-established principle of our legal system, as ultimately enshrined in FOIA case law, that someone is always entitled to have his or her case tried in court (read: not in the court of public opinion) and that even the fact that someone was specifically considered for public prosecution -- as a bare, abstract fact -- should never be publicly disclosed by any law enforcement personnel involved in an underlying investigation. As someone who took a back seat to no one in enshrining this principle within the FOIA's new Exemption 7(C) in litigation precedents created during the late 1970s and early 1980s, I stand behind this principal no matter how egregious the attendant circumstances might in some cases be. (See Chapter Thirteen, for example.) Indeed, the only exception to this of which I am aware -- and it is an exception that proves the rule -- is the extreme case of long-term Hezbollah captive Terry Anderson, whose captors' identities, in the absence of Privacy Act applicability, were atypically disclosed to him (see Chapter Thirty-Six).

16   We might never know exactly why this Member of Congress did what he or she did, at either the underlying-event stage or the FOIA-bound stage of this sad story; it is a mystery in more ways than one. As it happens, speaking of "flukes," I happen to know quite well a relative of this person and, if he or she is still alive, I theoretically could try to learn this mystery's answer through him or her. But to do that, even now, would be to disclose even to a single person the abstract fact of what this Member of Congress did, which the Privacy Act, at least in spirit (read: because as a retired federal employee it no longer applies to me), admonishes against (see Chapter Fourteen). (That last part, by the way, is a giant loophole in the Privacy Act's protection, one that ought to be addressed by Congress sooner rather than later.)

17   We did not dwell on the fact that, left to its own devices, the Bureau would have routinely included this highly sensitive, even explosive information in its report. The point is that doing so or not was within the realm of reasonable administrative discretion, given how the Bureau had long operated, and even the majority side of the Senate Judiciary Committee was not being deprived of anything that truly mattered to what was before it -- the fitness of the nominee *vel non*. Rather, the information at hand here instead bore on the *security* interests of the Department in relation to the nominee, something more fitting for Attorney General Reno to decide. That Saturday afternoon, whether she fully realized it or not, she effectively did.

18   In an interview broadcast live on C-SPAN many years later, I was asked about a "secret scandal" that (see Chapter Thirty) I had referred to as such. Well, this chapter was about that entirely secret scandal. I did not say much more about it on live TV that day, but I knew that with a bit of time (i.e., not off the top of my head on TV) I ought to be able to safely craft a limited version of it that would preserve the personal-privacy interests of the individual(s) involved -- even though, technically, I was under no legal obligation *per se* to do so, just a moral one. This chapter is exactly that.

CHAPTER TWENTY-NINE

1   These were 14 attorneys general all told: Mitchell, not Kleindienst, Richardson, Saxbe, not Levi, Bell, Civiletti, Smith, Meese, Thornburg, Barr, Reno, Ashcroft, and Gonzalez (plus two "actings," Robert Bork and Stu Gerson). And this was under eleven different presidential administrations: Nixon I, Nixon II, not Ford, Carter, Reagan I, Reagan II, Bush 41, Clinton I, Clinton II, Bush 43 Part I, and Bush 43 Part II. (Although I worked for the Federal Government under President Ford and during the tenure of Attorney General Levi, it was at the courthouse as a judge's clerk, not at the Department of Justice.)

2   Less well known about Janet Reno was that she was at the top of her class in high school, majored in the then-unladylike field of chemistry at Cornell, and then was one of only 16 females in her class of 500 at Harvard Law School. She might not have gone on to a sterling clerkship credential with a federal judge, but she was no mere "state-level political hack" or intellectual lightweight. Far from it.

3   Janet's most oft-repeated refrain was "I will follow the facts and the law," which bespoke her firm resistance to political influence in any official decisionmaking.

4   Truth be known, there eventually were several immigration judges who were shifted from their SES policy positions, though mostly in the Bush 43 Administration. I knew all of them well.

5   No small part of its viability (and thus durability) is its use together with what we called its "twin concept" of discretionary disclosure -- but by any name, it has served to constrain the unnecessary use of FOIA exemptions and to maximize public disclosure unlike any other such thing ever devised.

6   There is a dark secret here that never before has been told. In 1989, the Supreme Court issued a landmark FOIA decision, *Department of Justice v. Reporters Committee for Freedom of the Press*, that became the bane of the existence of media groups, leading to several failed efforts by them to overturn it (see Chapter Two). But when Janet Reno arrived as AG in 1993, I wondered whether that might mark the beginning of the end of that Supreme Court precedent. Janet, had she focused on this, certainly could have (and I do believe would have) acted to effectively overturn *Reporters Committee* as a matter of administrative fiat. But I never raised this, nor did anyone else in or outside of the Department, for the nearly eight years that she was the AG -- and believe me, I would have known. So the epitaph on this dead letter is that it was an opportunity negligently missed by the media community by inexplicably not pressing the fact that she had "printer's ink in her blood."

7   A highlight of this, sardonically speaking, was when we arranged for Janet to speak at our biggest govern-mentwide program of the year, which we held at the FBI's Main Auditorium, where we had a capacity for 454 agency FOIA personnel, with an "overflow room" that could seat another 100. The demand to hear her was so great that we also made use of Main Justice's Great Hall, with a video feed that Bureau technicians set up to literally "beam her" across Pennsylvania Avenue. Mid-way through her presentation, however, I received word that this link had been broken. It appeared that a low-level staffer in the Department's Office of Public Affairs had unwittingly given permission for a television program transmission (for Geraldo Rivera, no less) that somehow interfered with our video hook-up. Did I tell Janet that her speech was being interfered with? Not that I recall.

8   I promised at the outset of this writing process that I would strive for giving "balanced" presentations of the matters discussed. In order to keep this promise, I must add here that, as time went by, Janet was not always so pro-disclosure in her orientation. For instance, I can recall her vetoing any disclosure of Solicitor General's Office records in a particular case, where the applicability of Exemption 5 was far from clear, much less any reason for

not making a discretionary disclosure. In all fairness, I should acknowledge that this is part and parcel of what I have seen to be a universal characteristic of all new presidential administrations: They don't mind so much making disclosures of the old records that existed when they arrived, but after a while the records requested more and more become new ones that they themselves created. Hence, a presidential administration cycle in which all of a sudden even "progressive" administrations start to say, "Oh, no, not with *our* records."

CHAPTER THIRTY

1   The phrase "light of day" is one that I used during an hour-long television interview that I did for C-SPAN in March of 2015. The program was called "Washington Journal" and it was hosted by longtime C-SPAN interviewer Pedro Echevarria. At one point in that interview, in response to a caller's question, I made reference to two scandals that after many years still had not seen that (read: "the light of day"), without saying much more about them. Well, this turned out to be more than Pedro could bear, because just a couple of minutes later he suddenly did a "double-take," interrupted himself, came back to that reference, and asked me to please tell him anything further that I could possibly say about that.

Briefly put, I obliged him to a limited point on the first matter, allowing that I actually was not really surprised that its secrecy remained intact even after nearly 22 years, given how few people actually knew of it. But as for the second secret Clinton Administration scandal, I said that it indeed was surprising to me that such a thing had not ever leaked out, at least to some extent, during all those years. (A video of the entire interview can be viewed by just Googling my name (sans middle initial) together with "C-SPAN"; Pedro's pivot can be found at the 20.15 mark.)

2   In other words, things were "falling through the cracks left, right, and center," according to a putatively career person in the Executive Office of the President.

3   There was one other agency involved, one that ought not be identified here. While this agency was necessarily involved in the genesis of the problem, it was less involved in its solution.

4   Note that this was during "early days" of the Clinton Administration, when "damaging impressions" due to scandal did not yet abound.

5   Nearly every call from the White House was an "emergency" one during the first six months of the Clinton Administration, which felt more like twelve months to many of us. The only thing that ever matched that in my experience was the six-month period immediately following 9/11.

6   The key to such a written analysis, I would tell my students many years later, is formatting it in predominately outline form, so that the reader can easily follow each legal determination, together with its consequences and recommendations, at a glance.

7   I have personally known a number of "true geniuses" in my life and the late Walter Dellinger surely was one of them; it is a loss to the country that he was unable to follow what once seemed to be an inevitable path to a seat on the United States Supreme Court. Some others are Edwin S. Kneedler, who served as the Acting Solicitor General of the United States in 2009 (after having been the senior career deputy solicitor general since 1993); the late Mary C. Lawton, a career Justice Department official who was Founding Director of its Office of Intelligence Policy and Review ("OIPR," to its "FISA warrantees"); and Stephen I. Vladeck, a brilliant young law professor with whom I taught a national security course at the Washington College of Law. (Speaking of my older daughter Emily, she has worked at Google for about a dozen years now, on such matters as cybersecurity

and what Google calls "cyber privacy." Yes, she is carrying on the family privacy tradition, and whereas I would tell her during my many "Continuity-of-Government" absences (see Chapter Twenty-Six) during her childhood that I could tell her where I was going but then would have to kill her, she now turns that around against me whenever I probe too closely into things that Google treats as proprietary.)

8   The Office of Legal Counsel ("OLC," to both friend and foe), held as one of its high-level responsibilities the duty of providing the White House with necessary legal advice. Effectively, I had been contacted outside of regular channels on this exceptionally urgent problem.

9   Walter also kindly wondered aloud why it was that I was not working for him directly in OLC, to which I modestly replied that I was too expensive for him.

CHAPTER THIRTY-ONE

1   So one might think of this chapter's subject as information-disclosure "controversies," as well.

2   The second Waco report was issued by former Senator John C. Danforth, who served as the Department of Justice's second special counsel from 1999-2000. The first special counsel, by the way, was former U.S. Attorney Robert B. Fiske, Jr., who undertook the initial "Whitewater" investigations, at the behest of Attorney General Janet W. Reno during the first half of 1994, before he was supplanted by Independent Counsel Kenneth W. Starr. I worked closely with Special Counsel Fiske's staff in "scrubbing" his draft report on the suicide of Deputy White House Counsel Vincent W. Foster, Jr., which was issued on June 30, 1994.
Anyway, back to Special Counsel Danforth's report on the Waco conflagration. He was appointed to that position by Attorney General Janet Reno to essentially reinvestigate the Waco siege, with focus on the FBI's role in it, most particularly its alleged use of gunfire and pyrotechnics on the scene just prior to the fire. Special Counsel Danforth's final report almost completely exonerated the FBI, although its treatment of some FBI personnel, including one of its counsel, blatantly violated the Privacy Act in at least one instance. (I had scrubbed the draft of this report, at Janet Reno's request, but with their intransigent rush to finish their work was unable to prevent Danforth's staff from going forward with it, privacy problems and all. This was a thoughtless mistake that should have been avoided.) Danforth's final Waco report was excoriated by one former attorney general, Attorney General W. Ramsey Clark, who called it a "whitewash," which apparently was not a mere reference to the color of Special Counsel Danforth's hair.

3   "Whitewater" started as a "land deal gone bad" in Arkansas involving Madison Guaranty Savings & Loan Bank in the late 1970s and, with both legal and political complications, eventually metastasized into federal investigations of such things as the "Monica Lewinsky affair," the suicide of Deputy White House Counsel Vincent M. Foster (see Chapter Three), a White House scandal nicknamed "Travelgate," another one called "Filegate," and even the private embezzlement by future Justice Department Associate Attorney General Webster L. "Webb" Hubbell at Hillary Clinton's Little Rock law firm (see Chapter Twenty-Eight). It was the subject of extensive inquiries by the Senate Special Whitewater Committee, the House Banking Committee, one Special Prosecutor (Robert B. Fiske, Jr.), and two successive Independent Counsels (Kenneth W. Starr and Robert W. Ray). It also triggered the impeachment of President William Jefferson Clinton in 1998, followed by his subsequent acquittal by the Senate in 1999.

4   The first such thing, as far as I knew, was the extraordinary problem that is described, albeit in anonymized form, in Chapter Twenty-Eight. It involved my recognizing a prospective situation, analyzing it, coming up with a solution, and then implementing that solution so as to avoid any whiff of that scandal ever escaping into the

public domain (read: to Congress, actually, which so often is one and the same). And it all worked: To this day, with Attorney General Janet Reno and Deputy Associate Attorney General Nancy E. McFadden now deceased, only four former Department of Justice employees, myself included, are aware of what happened.

5   I was a member of both of these task forces, but for the former one I also served as its resident privacy expert, which led to a greater review workload. The "lead" Justice Department official for Hillary Clinton's Health Care Task Force for most of its existence was a very capable Duke Law professor named Christopher H. Schroeder, who came to the Department together with Walter Dellinger. I found Chris to be quite proficient at conducting effective meetings on subjects that were, after all, sometimes too novel to readily wrap one's arms around them.

At one such meeting, in October of 1993, the Justice Task Force members received a briefing from the White House's Task Force staff on what was currently being envisioned. This was the first time that any of us heard of the "individual mandate" (read: compulsory insurance to be obtained by all) and it immediately raised a big question in my mind: "Have you folks run the 'mandatory' aspect of this past the Office of Legal Counsel for a constitutionality check?" I politely (but truth be told disingenuously) asked. "Uh, we're very confident of that," is what I heard in reply. A few months later, at a gathering of Fellows of the National Academy of Public Administration ("NAPA," even to those of us who eschewed red wine), I raised the same question. I even used the example of "Unabomber" Theodore J. Kaczynski, who lived in a remote mountainside shed and wandered down into a small village only a few times per year. "Can we viably insist that enrollment include even such a person?" I more pointedly inquired.

Years later, of course, this very requirement, when carried over to "Obamacare," presented so serious a constitutional issue that it not only reached the Supreme Court, it caused Chief Justice John G. Roberts, Jr., to engage in nothing less than lexical gymnastics in order to preserve that law for a slender majority (read: and also the country). While it might be difficult to respect the transactional view of the word "tax" that he engineered toward that end, I think we must respect Chief Justice Roberts's social-policy objective. I must say that this did not surprise me, by the way, because I had worked closely with John Roberts (a neighbor before he joined the Court) on a pair of census-based emergency FOIA cases when he was the principal deputy solicitor general in the very early 1990s and had found him to be brimming with integrity, as well as towering intellect, back then.

6   When it came to "task forces" -- inter-agency groups of subject-matter experts -- they invariably raised secrecy issues of one type or another, often more than one, and as of the beginning of the Clinton Administration they seemed to suddenly abound. Prior to then, as best as I recall, we had only the Vice President's Task Force on Regulatory Relief, for which OIP developed "reverse FOIA" procedures in June of 1982 (see Chapter Twenty-One and the Glossary). Then there were the health care and radiation task forces described above, in 1993 and 1994, each of which had its own secrecy and privacy issues to be dealt with. The beginning of the George W. Bush Administration brought the vice president's energy task force, which carried with it multiple "agency record" FOIA issues. And there also was the less-well-remembered Blackout Task Force that investigated the August 14, 2003 electricity blackout that cut power to 50 million people, mostly in the Northeastern U.S. and Canada. I recall suddenly becoming enmeshed in the latter as I filled in for the Information Security Oversight Office (as it was between directors at the time) to provide leadership on matters of national security classification.

7   I say this so freely because I was on the ground floor of the "radiation fallout scandal" that erupted in late 1993 over the suddenly confirmed fact that the U.S. Government had used American citizens as guinea pigs in human radiation experiments from the mid-1940s into the early 1970s -- as there immediately arose privacy and other disclosure issues (read: both to the public and to Congress, as so often is the case) about the records of those activities. I was there at the large White House strategy meeting on how to deal with all of this that Hillary

Clinton attended. And I also was privy to the earliest rumblings of concern at the top of the Justice Department about the difficulties that became known as "Whitewater" (see Chapter Thirty-Five).

Yes, the Clinton White House, monolithic yet amorphous as it was, was more than happy, anthropomorphically speaking, to have Energy Secretary O'Leary carry weeks of news cycles on the human radiation experimentation scandal rather than having the media focus on Whitewater-related things in January of 1994. Thus did the Clinton Administration's first year (which felt like seven, whether one was dogged or not) end with one scandal replacing another.

8   There also were other like matters in which OIP's role was primarily to review investigative reports on things of great controversy, such as the FBI's handling of the Waco conflagration in 1993, its 11-day Ruby Ridge siege in late 1992, ATF's "Good Ol' Boy Roundup" in 1995, and the FBI Laboratory scandal in 1997. In these situations, as in many others, the larger questions addressed were two-fold: (1) what should be released to the public? and (2) what should be released to Congress? To be sure, there often was a distinct difference between the two, one that had to be crafted quickly and with precision.

CHAPTER THIRTY-TWO

1   I shared this responsibility with my partner Dick Huff, of course, but played the primary analytical role in meeting it, as was the case with many other things that OIP did. Doubtless, as is illustrated by the case described in this chapter, OPR was surprised (read: perhaps disappointed) with how expeditiously we were able to do so.

2   As wisely created (and yes, OIP had a heavy hand in drafting its organic document), this new system allowed for each public summary, in the form in which it was proposed to be made public, to be made available to each subject of the investigation (which could be more than one person) for review together with his or her attorney, so that objections, requests, or other input could be received by and considered by OPR (as well as OIP) in advance. In the particular case discussed in this chapter, as best as I can now recall, the AUSA was so mortified by what he or she had done that nothing significant came out of that process.

3   "Oh, is that what they're calling it these days?" OPR itself was known in the Department for its pithy synthesis of what underlay almost all of the employee misconduct cases that it looked into: "Sex, drugs, or rock 'n roll." Only it would hasten to substitute "money" for the latter.

4   Notice the double "his/her" masking here. This serves to obscure not only "AUSA Smith's" gender but also that of the witness, in order to provide a further bit of protection. Every day, across the Federal Government, FOIA personnel exercise exactly this type of judgment in order to provide fulsome protection of personal-privacy interests, in full contexts, under the FOIA's two privacy exemptions. To do this, they have to be forward thinking, lest the import of even a small detail allow an especially savvy FOIA requester -- or a knowledgeable insider with whom some of the disclosed information might already have been shared -- to figure out the identity of the person involved.

5   This new type of decision about issuance of the public summary of an OPR matter should not be confused with Department's decision about how to discipline an offending employee. Those underlying decisions were made by OPR (subject to review in the Deputy Attorney General's Office) before a proposed public summary was even prepared by OPR.

6   I would be lying if I did not promptly say here that this alone was enough to impel me to work throughout the weekend on this case. OPR had never done such a thing before -- it turned out that it truly, but not entirely

innocently, had gotten its internal wires crossed -- and I wanted to make damn sure that it never happened again. It just so happened that this occurred with the exceptional case in which I concluded that no public summary issuance should be made.

7   David was an old litigation client of mine from back in the very early days of the Reagan Administration, when he was Chief of the Criminal Division's Organized Crime & Racketeering Section (see Chapter Seventeen) and he also was to play a prominent role in my handling of a "Whitewater" litigation matter in the D.C. Circuit (see Chapter Thirty-Five) much later on.

8   By this phrasing here I do not mean to impugn the well-deserved reputation of OPR, one that it enjoyed as nearly without blemish until it blatantly leaked highly sensitive investigatory information in a case called *Pilon* years later. It was headed by longtime career public servant Michael E. Shaheen, Jr., for more than 20 years by that point, and its deputy was Richard M. Rogers, who had gotten his Justice Department start in the Department's FOIA administrative appeals office in the mid-1970s and as such was well known to OIP. Plus, they both were former clients of mine.

By the way, the "self-serving" characteristic that I describe here is one that I consistently perceived as likewise afflicting the Department's Inspector General Office, as well as other inspector generals' offices across the Federal Government. It was a very powerful tendency toward broad public disclosure of their work in order to show, in short, how well they performed. In other words, they were rightly proud when they "nailed" someone and wanted to "hang him (or her) out to dry," the more publicly the better. In 1998, I had the opportunity to make a FOIA and Privacy Act presentation to all presidentially appointed inspectors general ("IGs," to their friends in Congress, at least), which at that time numbered 29, as I recall, in a White House conference room where I bluntly stated this observation; I received no more than nominal "pushback" on it because, I think, they all knew it to be true.

Lastly, it should be noted that "independent counsels" and "special counsels," by whatever name and statutory authorization, tend to be this way as well. Waco Special Counsel John C. Danforth, for example, ran roughshod over the privacy interests of more than one person when he issued his public report in 2000 (see Chapter Thirty-One). And one independent counsel, who ironically was charged with investigating a Privacy Act violation, himself violated the Privacy Act, systemically, in the very way in which he structured his office to begin with. He is not named right here, but he is still quite active in the current political environment, notoriously so; I had the experience of sitting next to him at a panel presentation on the Clinton email scandal while he palpably vibrated with anti-Clinton fervor (see Chapter Forty-Seven).

9   Putting something in writing holds the advantage that such a thing (especially in email form) can be just "zapped over" to others in the Department if need be. Yes, in a case such as this, I would have done so if need be. Being a component head with a strong reputation does have its privileges.

10   And that, I would tell my students many years later, is how things in government, even significant things, can pivot to one result versus another, sometimes.

CHAPTER THIRTY-THREE

1   I once made the mistake of referring to "high officials" in this context, forgetting that that similar term could accurately be used only for White House officials (and their staffs) during the Clinton Administration.

2   Here's where I have to confess that I initially wrote this sentence by saying "*home* with them." But then I remembered the infamous case of former Secretary of State (and before that "Assistant to the President for National Security Affairs," i.e., "National Security Advisor") Dr. Henry A. Kissinger, who in 1976 had enormous

volumes of "his" State Department records (in duplicate, technically "non-record" form) shipped to the private New York estate of then-Vice President Nelson A. Rockefeller for further personal disposition through the Library of Congress. Inevitably, this raised the legal issue of the status of these removed federal records under the Freedom of Information Act, which had to be resolved in 1980 by the United States Supreme Court.

3   In a spasm of either nostalgia or old age (depending upon whom you might ask), I can remember that when I first started litigating in the Justice Department's Civil Division in 1977, long before the ubiquity of word-processing equipment in government offices, my memoranda would be typed by my secretary -- on a "modern" electric typewriter, of course -- by using what were called "carbon sets." These were prepackaged sets of typing paper (four sheets to a set, as I recall), with carbon paper placed between them -- so that the top sheet in each set would be a pure white "original" and it would be followed by duplicate sheets, of different colors, behind it.

Yes, we did have photocopy machines back then, most often "Xerox" ones (trademark be damned), but they were not regularly used for such memoranda. Rather, even as recently as in the early 1980s, the Justice Department was still using what probably had seemed like a great innovation decades earlier (read: carbon paper, hence "carbon copy," the genesis of "cc"). And if such a memorandum was removed upon an official's departure back then -- barring the exceptional effort of photocopying thin, inky "carbon copies" page by page -- it would be taken in "carbon copy" form. And it was not very long before then that any "photocopying" would not at all be available as an alternative, because it did not yet exist.

4   Griffin Bell was surely not the first attorney general to "bend the rules," such as they were, about the removal of official records from the Justice Department. Attorney General Elliot L. Richardson did just that, albeit under extreme circumstances, as he was being fired by President Richard M. Nixon in what became known as the "Saturday Night Massacre" in October of 1973.

He had his executive assistant John T. "J.T." Smith II remove (only temporarily, under exigent circumstances, mind you) several sensitive "Watergate-related" files from his office in the Main Justice Building to his home, where they were kept in his attic for safekeeping. I met J.T. only briefly during our overlapping tenures there, as I knew his wife as a fellow first-year student at my law school.

5   The Federal Records Act of 1950, which was amended by the National Archives Records Management and Records Administration Act of 1984 (Public Law 98-497) and is found primarily at 44 U.S.C. chapters 29 and 31, governs the proper maintenance and disposition of federal records, federal "non-record materials," and what it calls "personal papers" -- a list that specifically excludes "extra copies of documents preserved only for convenience of reference." (The best way to think of this, I suggest, is that document "originals" must remain on site but "non-record" copies of them might qualify for removal.) Its primary significance here is that it requires all federal employees -- regardless of level -- to go through a review of his or her work records upon leaving government service, which presumably would encompass most "record removal" circumstances. The Presidential Records Act, enacted as a "post-Watergate" reform, applies similarly to the handling of most White House (and some Executive Office of the President) records.

6   Why barrels? I do not recall. In fact, I have no recollection of having seen any barrels just lying around in Main Justice at the time. One would think that someone engaged in such an enterprise would try to be less conspicuous about it, but the sad fact of the matter is that in early 1985 Attorney General Smith was probably not much concerned about what he was doing in that regard, as he easily did so with no consequence. (It took the tenure of one more attorney general for *that* to be so.)

7   Among his other contretemps, Meese was the subject of multiple independent counsel investigations, which made his removed "personal" files of greater official concern.

8   It is indeed difficult to "get into the mind" of the official actor in a situation such as this, which certainly was the case with Attorney General Meese. This is something that is of course quite comparable to what the FBI and current Attorney General Merrick B. Garland have had to face in 2022 with the many boxes of records (covered by the Presidential Records Act, just as would be the case under the Federal Records Act) that evidently were so blatantly and wrongfully "removed" from the White House by outgoing (nay, even boisterous and unruly) President Donald J. Trump.

9   One of OIP's senior attorneys, Thomas J. McIntyre, had just recently risen in seniority to the point at which he was entitled to have his own office; soon enough, however, he had a roommate again, only it was in the form of Meese's boxes, which filled nearly half of his office. I recall Tom clamoring now and again during the coming months to be relieved of this "unwelcome roommate" situation. Poor Tom.

10   Actually, I have to offer a technical caveat to this assertion before going any farther. We should not over-look the removal and destruction of so many (though not all) of FBI Director J. Edgar Hoover's "Official and Confidential" ("O&C," for short) and "Personal and Confidential" ("P&C," for short) files (see the Glossary) from his home (read: in order to burn them), which was accomplished by his longtime secretary-cum-"executive assistant" Helen W. Gandy, who starting on the day of his death (i.e., during the night of May 1-2, 1972), began attending to "his" files.

Miss Gandy (as she was universally known), continued to do so until May 12, when she removed more than 30 file *drawers* of files from the Main Justice Building to the basement of Hoover's home, where she continued her "file work" from May 13 until July 17. This is not quite the same as what Paul O'Neill and no fewer than three attorneys general did later, of course, but it certainly is competitive. And here's a brief postscript: Twenty-five years after this, when one of OIP's senior attorneys handled a FOIA case that involved the remains of Hoover's "O&C" files, we knew that the *corpus* of that case was much smaller than it ought to have been.

11   I was personally familiar with Suskind's work because his Pulitzer was won for a series of articles that he wrote about the struggles of an inner-city high school student in Washington, D.C., who despite his odds strove for the Ivy League and then, after succeeding, had to make a challenging adjustment at Brown University. This led to a best-selling book, *A Hope in the Unseen*, which in 1998 described college life at Brown as it chronicled that minority student's efforts to "fit in." Later that year, my older daughter Emily gained early admission to Brown, so that book was well read in my family. (And four years later, my younger daughter Lindsay began her Brown years as well.)

12   In a coincidental example of just how "longtime" this problem had been, one of the secrecy areas addressed later in this book (see Chapter Forty-Eight) includes an unmistakable "departing official" episode going back as far as the mid-1950s. That official was Air Force Major Edward J. Ruppelt, who was the head of the Air Force's "Project Blue Book," an early government study of what were then called "flying saucers," who wrote a pioneering book about that in 1956 after retiring from government service.

Major Ruppelt, who historically is credited with coining the term "unidentified flying object" ("UFO," for short) to replace the term "flying saucer," was the director of "Project Blue Book" (as well as its predecessor, "Project Grudge") for more than two years, during which time he had complete access to all of its files. His book, titled *The Report of Unidentified Flying Objects*, read like an official government report and claimed to reveal "many details" taken from those files, as "complete official accounts." It contained several lengthy passages, some of them in *verbatim* quotation form, from which one could only conclude that he was divulging the contents of government records that he had self-servingly taken with him, in one form or another, upon his retirement. And there is no historical indication today that anyone batted an eye about this back then when that book was published.

13   The four other members of this formal committee, named the "Department Document Committee," consisted of career designees from the Department's Office of Legal Counsel, Office of Legislative Affairs, and Justice Management Division (with a very capable back-up designee), and a political designee from the Office of the Attorney General. In addition, we had executive secretariat support from OIP's long-term Privacy Act expert (its Associate Director Kirsten J. Moncada) and administrative support from one of OIP's top-notch paralegals. We all worked together quite well.

14   This took the form of a document signed by Attorney General Reno that is known as DOJ Order 2710.8A, "Removal and Maintenance of Documents" (1999). It was issued in accordance with the predecessor to NARA Bulletin 2000-03 (May 16, 2000) and it was supplemented by a series of "working principles" that we fully developed by August of 2000.

15   For lower-level Justice Department employees, a counterpart process for this is conducted by agency records officers and their designees under the procedures of the Federal Records Act, as overseen governmentwide by NARA. This is one of the critical things that Secretary of State Hillary Clinton evidently failed to do as part of her long-lived email scandal, known perhaps forever as "Emailgate" (see Chapter Forty-Seven).

16   It was an "open secret" within the Department that, by the end of his first term, President Bill Clinton regretted that he had chosen Janet as his attorney general (in the hurried wake of "Zoë, Kimba, and Rya"), because she turned out to be too much of an individualist for his liking and, more specifically, she had authorized new areas of independent counsel investigation that plagued him.

I well remember sitting in relatively small component head meeting in December of 1996, after Clinton had just won re-election, when a senior political appointee somewhat jocularly questioned Janet about her "plans for the New Year" -- meaning whether she might soon be leaving given Clinton's increasingly naked suggestions that she "might" do so. As it happened at that meeting, she had arrived late and took a seat close to me. And I still recall the steely look on her face as she allowed as how that was "*not* going to happen." (She stayed on as attorney general for another four years, of course, until Clinton himself left office.)

17   As it did turn out, we developed our working principles by "processing" the records of a former principal associate deputy attorney general as a "sample set"; coincidentally, they were the records of now-Attorney General Merrick B. Garland. To the best of my knowledge, these principles are still in use today.

18   When I was consulted by the Treasury Department on this odd "departing official" problem, the Justice Department had just recently established its formal policy governing this process, with standards and procedures that other agencies could follow. And I knew that folks at Treasury were familiar with Justice's policy, procedures, and regulation (in the form of a "DOJ Order") on this. I also knew that someone at Treasury had presciently attempted to replicate what we had done, in time to cover the O'Neill case, but that a draft memorandum toward that end had not yet been issued in final form. Consequently, as of the time at which all of this transpired, Treasury's General Counsel's Office still "had no defined process for reviewing the records to be removed."

19   It is clear from reading Ron Suskind's book that Paul O'Neill certainly harbored much resentment of President Bush's management style, a conclusion that greatly informed any assessment of how he, Suskind, and David

Aufhouser managed to achieve their exceptional "departing official" disclosure in this case. By the way, perhaps O'Neill's most pointed characterization of "Dubya's" decisionmaking, as he saw it, is that he "was like a blind man in a roomful of deaf people."

20   By this time, it was believed that approximately 140 (out of an estimated 19,000) pages of documents delivered to Suskind should have been withheld as classified on national security grounds. If so, this would have made the "Bamford" disclosure that is discussed in the Glossary pale by comparison.

21   Yes, the Paul O'Neill episode certainly was quite atypical, as "departing official" stories go, but so were the circumstances of Secretary of State Hillary Clinton's departure from her cabinet department ten years later. In her case, of course, the record "removal" occurred literally throughout her tenure, on a daily basis, rather than all at once. And a common element with Paul O'Neill's situation, it appears, was a compounding failure to comply with the time-of-departure records-preservation requirements of the Federal Records Act (see Chapter Forty-Seven).

CHAPTER THIRTY-FOUR

1   This is not to say that there were not other, relatively smaller ones. One could point to, for instance, my failure to settle the *Albertson* "Solo Source" case before leaving the Civil Division in 1981 (see Chapter Fifteen) or to my similar inability in 1995 to persuade the Civil Division to settle an OPR case called *Pilon* before it went ahead with a misguided appeal -- which ended up costing the Treasury hundreds of thousands of dollars combined. Or to my failure in 2006 to get the Justice Department on a better policy and litigation footing (read: reversing its "circuit acquiescence" position) on the "mug shot" issue before retiring, something that took several more years to be rectified after that (see Chapter Forty-One).

2   A case in point was the National Library of Medicine's "Medical Literature Analysis and Retrieval" database ("MEDLARS," to its users), to which a company sought FOIA access during the early 1970s. That database actually went to litigation, in a case that ultimately was decided by then-Ninth Circuit Court of Appeals Judge Anthony M. Kennedy in 1976 called *SDC Development Corp. v. Mathews*.

3   Also entering this category, in time, were things such as electronic mail, text messages, and the "metadata" that surround them. As a matter of firm policy, we determined that any such thing generated on a government device is an "agency record" subject to potential FOIA disclosure. (Likewise are messages generated on personal devices if they pertain to government business and are used as such.) And as for "metadata," we first dealt with that in 1997, when it became a potential issue in connection with "call detail" information stored by government telephone systems; OIP declared that to be in the "agency record" category, with the grudging concurrence of OMB (see below).

Over the years, this view became accepted worldwide as to electronic mail, but not so universally as to text messages. For example, on July 18, 2022, *Washington Post* reporter Carol D. Leonnig reported that most United States Secret Service Agents still do not regard (or therefore treat) their work-related text messages as "agency records" subject to public disclosure. This is wrong, and Secret Service supervisory personnel should pay a price for not ensuring that their employees comply with the Federal Records Act for even such seemingly ephemeral things -- *especially* text messages sent and received prior to, during, and immediately after the January 6, 2021 insurrection.

And more recently, it was learned in early August of 2022 that the text messages and call records on the cell phones of key Defense Department officials were "wiped" (read: not "with a cloth," see Chapter Forty-Seven) soon after the insurrection. So on August 3, 2020, the Defense Department belatedly (and transparently pomp-ously) "reminded" all of its personnel that record retention (specifically including text messages) "is a solemn responsibility and legal obligation for all federal employees, civilian and military." Chapped "lip service," to be sure.

On the other hand, in reaching an issue that was never presented to OIP during my tenure, as described below, the D.C. Circuit Court of Appeals ruled that "Internet browsing histories" are categorically not "agency records" subject to the FOIA, unless in a particular case they are "used" -- and thus "controlled" -- by an agency. Indeed, agency "control" over a record in question has long been recognized by the courts as the key touchstone for determining that record's legal status.

4   One particular species of electronic record, distinct from all other types, consists of what is known as "call detail information." This is a form of "metadata" surrounding telephone calls that is produced by a telephone exchange or other telecommunications equipment, most often automatically. It contains information about a call -- such as time, duration, completion status, source phone number, and destination phone number -- but nothing about the content of the call (read: words spoken) itself.

Federal agencies began possessing "call detail" information, in paper and then database form, during the 1970s and FOIA requesters began seeking access to them in the 1980s, meeting much resistance. This all came to a head in June of 1987, when OIP took on the issue (read: took on the agencies that insisted that these were not "agency records" subject to the Act), convened a meeting on it that included both GSA and OMB, and decided on behalf of the entire Federal Government that "call detail" records are indeed agency records within agency "control" under the FOIA. After that, we guided agencies that received such FOIA requests on how to redact (read: on privacy grounds mostly, but also sometimes to protect agency deliberative processes) them most efficiently.

And speaking of redaction, we learned in 2001 that some agencies' paper redaction techniques actually were insufficient to protect their withheld information in the face of advanced technology. So we immediately advised all agencies that they should carefully examine their "blacked out" document segments to ensure that their content remained secure. We summarized this problem by telling them the following: "Simply put, if you can discern any [underlying] lettering or differential markings whatsoever on a page that [you have] prepared for release -- including by holding that page up to a bright light -- then you cannot confidently release that page to a FOIA requester." This was one of only two governmentwide FOIA policy memoranda that we did not immediately make public.

Nearly 35 years later, the D.C. Circuit Court of Appeals considered whether a similar type of record, the "internet browsing histories" on federal agency computers, constituted "agency records" subject to the FOIA. In a surprising decision issued on August 20, 2021, *Cause of Action Institute v. OMB*, it held that agencies make "insufficient use" of browsing histories (and allow employees to delete them) for them to qualify as within agency "control." The commonality with "call detail" records is that in this case, likewise, an internet browser "automatically generates" the data. Had this precedent existed back in 1987, which is like positing a time warp in that "browsing histories" certainly did not even exist back then, I would have found it more difficult to decide (and enforce) the status of "call detail" records as I did.

5   By that time, of course, it was well settled that the Act applied to government-held documents within agency control in conventional form -- i.e., traditional paper records, microfilm, and even microfiche, as well as tape recordings, movies, and photographs. By the same token, though, it was likewise well settled that the FOIA could not be made to apply to physical objects, such as the gun used to assassinate President John F. Kennedy, pieces of equipment, some solid museum material, paintings, and sculptures This latter point actually came up when in 1990 the CIA erected a sculpture known as "Kryptos" near the entrance to its New Headquarters Building in Langley, Virginia, that reportedly contained four encrypted messages in physical form.

Only three of these codes have yet been solved, leaving the fourth one as one of the most famous unsolved codes in the world. For those who enjoy cryptography (such as my computer-engineer daughter, who devoured the subject when very young), this object (read: its complete solution) has become a bit of a holy grail. In 2013, an American cryptologist used the FOIA to learn from NSA that several of its employees, relishing a challenge, had made attempts to solve the fourth Kryptos code. While she did receive special CIA permission to make "rubbings" of the sculpture, there is no record of her attempting to "make a FOIA request" for it. Along with other physical objects in the Federal Government's possession and control, it would be difficult to imagine an agency FOIA officer making a "copy" of it for mailing.

6   By the early 1980s, the Supreme Court had necessarily begun to treat the FOIA as applicable to "information," rather than the "records" of which the statutory language spoke (see Chapter Eleven). It was based upon this that we inveighed upon Congress to amend that archaic statutory language, through the 1986 FOIA Amendments, to say "records or information" instead (see Chapter Eleven).

7   In both public speaking and in OIP's governmentwide training programs, I used to refer to this issue as one of "how to slice the bologna," in order to convey the very nature of database retrieval, which animated this issue. On all such "electronic record" issues, which heavily involved technical computer "things" that I was not initially equipped to handle, I had the advantage of being able to rely on the expertise of my daughter Emily, who was born in 1981 but by 1989 had more computer expertise than I will ever have. That expertise now benefits the company for which she has long worked, Google.

8   Usually, this all had to do with database-retrieval and production processes, but sometimes it was just a matter of a requester simply preferring one conventional form over another -- e.g., paper versus microfilm or microfiche.

9   This meant the Office of the Attorney General, the Office of the Deputy Attorney General, and the Office of the Associate Attorney General. And it helped that the FOIA requests made to all three offices were handled by the Initial Request Unit of OIP.

10   Could such a right have been established legislatively in the FOIA amendments of 2007? You bet it could. But the Department of Justice failed to seek that, among other of its FOIA-related failures during that time (see Chapter Forty-Six).

11   What does now exist, as a distinct yet still incomplete step in that direction, is the use of "portals" for making FOIA requests. This is an idea that was pioneered by the Environmental Protection Agency in 2012, without the support of my successor at OIP. It nevertheless caught on, and it was used by some other agencies, though this notably did not include the Department of Justice. And there the matter sat. (As with other such shortcomings, such as OIP's inexplicable non-reaction to the Supreme Court's *Milner* decision (see Chapter Forty-Six), there is no good explanation for this.)

Then, in 2016, in the FOIA Improvement Act, Congress amended the FOIA again on its regular ten-year cycle and this time it finally addressed the problem, sort of. It commanded that:

"The Director of the Office of Management and Budget, in consultation with the Attorney General, shall ensure the operation of a consolidated online request portal that allows a member of the public to submit a request for records under subsection (a) to any agency from a single website."

Still, however, this did not prompt immediate action from either OIP or the Office of Management and Budget ("OMB," to those who think it means "Often Mysteriously Busy"). Indeed, it was not until mid-February of 2019 that OMB sent a memorandum to all federal agencies saying that they had until mid-May of that year to provide to OMB a *plan* for how they intend to achieve "full interoperability" for such a portal. From 2016 to 2019 (or later) and even at that, only a "plan."

Today, fewer than two dozen federal agencies participate in anything resembling an "on-line portal" for FOIA requests. And most significantly, what I was trying to achieve for FOIA requesters in 2000-2001 -- their legal ability to file a FOIA request electronically *as of right* -- still has not been achieved, notwithstanding that it is now more than 20 years, and two FOIA-amendment cycles, later.

CHAPTER THIRTY-FIVE

1   David had most prominently solidified this status at a congressional hearing. Not long before that, he had suffered a massive heart attack (David was relatively lean, but smoked like two chimneys) while in his Justice Department office; his secretary heard a noise emanating from there and rushed in to find him flat on the floor. It was later determined, legend had it (and David confirmed it to me), that David had actually "died" while taking a mid-day nap on his sofa (which was a large and quite comfortable one, as I recall), but then he had had the good fortune of rolling off of it onto the floor, where the impact restarted his heart pumping.

So when David arrived on the Hill to testify before the Senate Whitewater Committee surprisingly soon thereafter, he naturally was asked by Committee Chairman Alphonse M. D'Amato whether he was "comfortable." And without missing a beat (read: another one), David replied: "Well, I make a good living." This was a reference to an old Vaudeville joke, of course, and one could say that it "brought down the House." David died at the young age of 76 of one heart attack too many, in 2016, after 51 years of Justice Department service ("But who's counting?" David would say).

2   The position of "Independent Counsel" had an irregular history over the years. The model for it was that of "Watergate Special Prosecutor," the position held successively by Archibald Cox, Jr., Leonides "Leon" Jaworski, and finally Charles F.C. Ruff back in the 1970s (see Chapter Seven). Then Congress enacted a law that allowed the naming and supervision of independent counsels by the attorney general for many years, until mid-1994, when that authority was eclipsed by a successor statute.

The next incarnation was that of non-statutory independent counsels, who were appointed and then overseen (read: at least theoretically) by a specially designated panel of three circuit court judges. Ultimately, when that system fell into disuse (read: when the successor statute was allowed to expire in 1999), the Department of Justice promulgated a regulation (read: one that I had a hand in drafting) providing for the attorney general's appointment of "special counsels," of which Robert S. Mueller III was one. All told, there have been 17 independent counsels (two of whom are publicly unknown, as they were appointed and operated in total secrecy) and six special counsels (including Robert B. Fiske, Jr., a "pre-regulatory" one who often is mistakenly thought of as having been an independent counsel as he immediately preceded Independent Counsel Ken Starr in 1994) over the course of the past forty-nine years.

3   After serving as the "Whitewater" independent counsel for more than four years, to either fame or disdain depending upon who you are talking to, the late Ken Starr resigned from that position in September of 1998 to return to a private life of both teaching and practicing law.

4   As Ken Starr's formal successor as of October of 1999, Independent Counsel Ray continued the work that Independent Counsel Starr had begun (not to forget that of Special Counsel Fiske, before Starr) for another 2½ years, finishing off the White House Travel Office investigation, completing what was called the "White

House files controversy" investigation, and "wrapping up" the "Whitewater" investigation in general. He held the responsibility of preparing and issuing the final reports of the Office of the Independent Counsel, as well.

5 I will largely refrain from providing any sort of a "lest it be forgotten" endnote on what "Whitewater" was all about. In my book (pun intended), any scandal significant enough to lead to a presidential impeachment (which "Watergate," by contrast, technically did not) should be familiar enough for decades to come so as to not require that. Suffice to say here that what began as the investigation of an Arkansas land deal gone bad, combined with a suspicious suicide by a White House official (see Chapter Three), "grew like Topsy" (read: or "like crazy" or "like a weed," to be less politically incorrect) and became the biggest amalgamated scandal of the Clinton Administration, which believe you me is really saying something, as the competition for that distinction (like Clinton, one might say) was quite stiff (see Chapter Thirty-One). And this all was grossly catalyzed, of course, by a nubile (read: or zaftig, as she is Jewish) White House intern who had left California for Washington, D.C., with the full-throated declaration that she was going to bring her "presidential kneepads" along with her (read: figure it out).

One side note, however: The "affair" between President Bill Clinton and Monica S. Lewinski, which began during the first extended government "shutdown" period in mid-November of 1995, was kept secret by them for well more than two years (read: giving a modern-day cast to the phrase "government secrecy") until they were "outed" by her close confidante Linda R. Tripp, who had secretly recorded conversations between the two (read: Lewinsky and Tripp) that included Lewinsky's admissions about various forms of sex (read: not intercourse, as Clinton himself was hard-pressed to explain) that she had had with her president (read: one who better would have been president of France rather than the United States).

And in turn (read: as in "one bad turn deserves another"), Linda Tripp herself later became the victim of a leak when she worked at the Department of Defense and two of its officials -- Assistant Secretary of Defense for Public Affairs Kenneth H. Bacon (aptly titled as such) and his deputy Clifford Bernath -- conspired with a former journalistic co-worker of one of them (read: Bacon, as best as I recall) to wrongfully disclose particularly sensitive background information about her (which will not be recounted in full here) that resided in her Defense Department background-investigation file. The former co-worker was Jane M. Mayer, then of *The New Yorker* magazine, and the leak was a flat-out, "intentional and willful," violation of Tripp's Privacy Act rights.

I happened to learn of, and become involved in, this last piece of the story because that "Tripp leak" was duly investigated by the Defense Department's Office of Inspector General, which formally requested consultation assistance from me on the Bacon/Bernath/Mayer fact pattern and how the Privacy Act operated in relation to it. (Again, inasmuch as OMB had abrogated most of its responsibility for overseeing the Privacy Act, I was in the "who ya gonna call" box for that.) I told the Defense Department Inspector General that with all my years of working with the Privacy Act (see Chapter Fourteen), I could hardly imagine a more pointedly blatant violation of it than what had transpired at DOD. (Linda Tripp had responded "no" to a question on her Form 398 (read: the DOD counterpart to OPM Form 86), which was belied by some derogatory background information found elsewhere in her file. In other words, the damaging information had to be ferreted out and correlated in order to be used in the way in which it was.)

So the Defense Department's Inspector General issued a report formally "rebuking" both Bacon and Bernath for so blatantly violating Tripp's Privacy Act rights and she received a payment of nearly $600,000 in settlement of her inevitable Privacy Act lawsuit against DOD. Then when it came time for Secretary of Defense William S. Cohen to weigh in on the whole sad matter, he waffled rather than making a strong statement of deterrence: He went no farther than to say that Bacon's and Bernath's actions were a "serious lapse of judgment" that was "hasty and ill-considered." He seemed to not "get" the pointedness and seriousness of what his people had done.

And for his part, Bacon said: "It certainly never occurred to me that the Privacy Act would preclude disclosing how a public figure recorded a public arrest record on a security clearance. . . . I don't think that I performed unlawfully." Neither did Bernath, who went even further to declare: "My actions were not only legal, but also ethical and correct." So once again, we had some high-level Federal Government officials (arguably up to and including a cabinet secretary) who "didn't get the memo" as far as the Privacy Act's prohibitions were concerned.

6   The primary "individual involved" with that document was not directly identified in the Court's order, but doing so was unnecessary. The Court knew that we knew that that individual was none other than Monica Lewinsky. And our responsive brief identified her only in its heading: "United States Department of Justice's Response to Independent Counsel's Ex Parte, In Camera Petition for Order Permitting Sealed Filing of Summary of Special Counsel's Investigative Report as Part of His Final Report Regarding the Investigation of Monica Lewinsky and Others." And of course, also in the case's caption: "In re Madison Guaranty Savings & Loan Association (regarding Monica Lewinsky and Others)."

7   Without getting into any detail on this aspect of the matter, we had reason to believe that the Court had a basis for being concerned about this. So we extended our warrant, so to speak, in order to address it with what we believed would be useful information.

8   In doing this, I have to confess, we presumed to remind the Court that it held a distinct statutory authorization to make any disclosure, to anyone, that it considered "appropriate."

9   Indeed, in such a case, if a summary were to reflect the fact of OPR's misconduct filing, then it necessarily would disclose both the existence and details of an initial finding of wrongdoing concerning a named individual that was not ultimately adopted, and in fact was reversed, by the Department.

10   In addition to case law at the district court level, we brought to the Court's attention three solid precedents decided by appellate courts, two of which were handed down by the D.C. Circuit itself.

CHAPTER THIRTY-SIX

1   It should be observed at the outset of any discussion of post-9/11 detainees that, more than 20 years later, 17 of them remain incarcerated in the American military prison at Guantanamo Bay in "indefinite law-of-war detention" and are neither facing military tribunal charges nor being scheduled for release. It has been hinted, partly through leaked but not declassified documents, that the explanation for this lies in some 9/11-related "secret" that is connected to such remaining detainees. If so, then one can only hope that it pertains to something other than these detainees' treatment at the hands of their CIA interrogators.

2   I do not know whether this number has ever been publicly disclosed, but I recall that as of the second week of November 2001 it stood at 1189.

3   Indeed, the public's new post-9/11 mantra was "see something, say something," which probably had not resonated so vibrantly since the fear of Japanese-Americans on the West Coast during World War II.

4   This is not to overlook the fact that, as with any major crime, federal law enforcement authorities were investigating whether other co-conspirators of the hijackers who did not perish on the four 9/11 planes remained at large. A prime example, of course, was Zacarias Moussaoui, a French citizen who was located through his "flight school" activity in Minnesota (resulting in a five million-dollar reward for his flight instructor), was accused of being "the 20th hijacker" even though he was arrested a month before 9/11, and ultimately pled guilty to a variety of related crimes at one time or another during his protracted trial. Among other things, he was charged

with lying to the FBI when he might have prevented 9/11 by telling what he knew about some of the 19 actual hijackers. In short, he represented himself, acted bizarrely, and repeatedly said that he wanted to die for the sake of al-Qaeda. He was sentenced to life in prison without the possibility of parole and currently resides in the Federal Government's "Supermax" prison ("ADX," to its confinees), located near Florence, Colorado.

Moussaoui also became the subject of a FOIA issue that came to OIP. After his sentencing in the federal courthouse in Alexandria, Virginia, where he had been held during his trial, Moussaoui remained in the custody of the U.S. Marshals Service for transport to his place of incarceration through the Justice Prisoner and Alien Transportation System ("JPATS," to its travelers, but more commonly called "Con Air"). Inexplicably, even though he had spoken of suicide several times during his trial, Moussaoui was placed on a JPATS plane all by himself, well before the planned departure time, and was not continuously (read: not even close to continuously) observed by the U.S. Marshals who were accompanying him. This latter fact became clear when he was found unconscious in his seat, evidently having had banged his head so furiously and repeatedly onto the surface in front of him that he had nearly killed himself by the time he was discovered.

So the Marshals revived him, called for medical attention, and for some reason decided to photograph him in a way that most graphically displayed his injury. And those two photographs, when they came to me, depicted a bruised area of his head that made one wonder how it was that he had survived. You see, Moussaoui has what can fairly be described as a large head, little hair, and a forehead that, in effect, extends toward the very top of his cranium. And that entire area was one massive dark bruise, from top to bottom and side to side. This was an enormous problem for the Marshals Service, which is a component of the Department of Justice, and it wanted to say (in the face of a "got wind of" inquiry from a major media outlet) that these photographs should not be disclosed, on the basis of Moussaoui's personal privacy.

Now there was no doubt that these photographs (which were nearly identical) were in effect "medical records" about Moussaoui, as well as law enforcement records about the activity of his official transport. But the very idea of withholding them from the public on that basis was beyond the pale. Indeed, they fit squarely within the exception that we had always maintained for our "mug shot" policy -- i.e., where the appearance of the arrestee photographed showed the treatment that he or she had received upon arrest and thereby served an overriding public interest warranting disclosure (see Chapter Forty-One).

I did not yet know the results of an internal investigation into the matter, but that was of no matter to me: I told the Marshals Service that OIP definitely would not support withholding these photographs in the face of a FOIA request (read: either a targeted one or one seeking such records in general) and that if the director of the Marshals Service wanted to discuss it further, well, my phone number was 514-FOIA. The "kicker" to the story is that I never heard of this again. Nor is there any public record that I can now find about the episode at all. Lord only knows how they fended off that reporter.

5   This is not to suggest that their detentions and associated interrogations were necessarily unlawful in any case; they might or might not have been, especially at the outset, for all I knew for sure. What I do now remember knowing is that by the month of November, the Department of Justice had succeeded in exercising dominion over all such detainees, even those maintained in state or local incarceration facilities, so that their treatment could be made uniform and, more importantly, so that their interrogations could be best coordinated.

6   I have heard this aphorism attributed to 1964 Republican presidential candidate Barry M. Goldwater, or even to President Abraham Lincoln, but apparently the phrase "suicide pact" was first used in this way by Associate Supreme Court Justice Robert H. Jackson in a dissenting opinion written by him in 1949. (And no, it was not in the *Korematsu* case involving Japanese-American internment.)

7   There was one possible exception to this, depending upon the timing and other circumstances involved: As time went by, many of the detainees availed themselves of their right to counsel and some of those attorneys spoke publicly (read: not anonymously) about their clients.

8   This last category became merged with the other two as a practical matter, especially through judicial pronouncement of the breadth of Exemption 7(A).

9   Ashcroft's public statements about detainees were guided by a document titled "draft talking points," which was derived from the analytical outline that I created. In short, he declined to say anything publicly that I thought could properly be withheld in response to any third-party FOIA request. And he also had to be careful not to say anything about any individual detainee who might hold Privacy Act rights barring disclosure.

10   Inasmuch as the Privacy Act of 1974 applies only to U.S. citizens and persons lawfully admitted to the U.S. for permanent residence, it held limited applicability to this group of detainees. But any "authorization" that a detainee executed, which in effect was a "privacy waiver," was significant to the processing of any third-party FOIA request.

11   The timing on these detainee FOIA requests was accelerated by the fact that OIP, together with the Department's Office of Public Affairs, decided to grant "expedited processing" (read: faster-then-usual processing of the requests) in all of them. This is something that we did under strict statutory and regulatory standards.

12   In addition to the lead plaintiff, the Center for National Security Studies, these groups included the American Civil Liberties Union, the Electronic Privacy Information Center, the American-Arab Anti-Discrimination Committee, the American Immigration Law Foundation, the American Immigration Lawyers Association, Amnesty International USA, the Arab-American Institute, the Asian-American Legal Defense and Education Fund, the Center for Constitutional Rights, the Center for Democracy and Technology, the Council on American Islamic Relations, the First Amendment Foundation, Human Rights Watch, Multiracial Activist, *Nation Magazine*, the National Association of Criminal Defense Lawyers, the National Black Police Association, Inc., the Partnership for Civil Justice, Inc., the People for the American Way Foundation, the Reporters Committee for Freedom of the Press, and the World Organization Against Torture.

13   There is an unstated premise here that should be stated. Based upon what the U.S. military and our intelligence agencies were saying at the time, we were assuming (read: because we could not safely assume otherwise) that al-Qaida operatives and sympathizers were closely monitoring the status and circumstances of all detainees as best as they could. This was especially so, we imagined, for those detainees who actually were affiliated with al-Qaida in some way, even if not as to the 9/11 attacks themselves. So there was a reasonable concern that some of the detainee details could enable this by providing at least some pieces of a "roadmap" to the U.S.'s ongoing investigation. Truth be known, we did not yet know with certainly which details could do so.

14   More than once each year, on average, I would find myself called to a meeting on some sudden "emergency" that I would not have known anything about but for first reading something about it in that morning's News Summary (sometimes, they were produced both in the early morning and the late afternoon). I would scan them each morning, making good use of their table of contents, and then read them more completely at home each night. And I'll confess to annotating them whenever the mood struck me, both irreverently and sometimes even scatologically. This once created a bit of a scare when one of my deputies took an annotated summary home with her to read and left it outside near her pool where a visiting political appointee nearly read it. So much for secrecy there.

15   This was a gray area, as might be imagined, and all I can say is that OIP communicated to Janet exactly where things stood on the issue so that she could make a fully informed decision on it. We were not at all surprised that she decided to put this fire out (read: better than at Waco, which had just blown up in her face) rather than continue to stand on what could so easily be viewed as a mere technicality.

16   This is one of only three times that OIP was overruled by an attorney general during the initial 25 years of its existence. The first had to do with a description of certain political circumstances pertaining to the nomination of Associate Supreme Court Justice Sandra Day O'Connor in 1981. The attorney general at the time, William French Smith, wanted to withhold most of it, thinking that the applicable standard should be the same as at his old law firm; he was heard to remark: "We never had to disclose anything like *that* at Gibson, Dunn, and Crutcher!"

Attorney General Smith was right, of course, about what private law firms disclose. But he was wrong about what federal agencies disclose when compelled to do so under the FOIA. In this case, FOIA Exemption 5's deliberative process privilege didn't quite cover the information in question -- much as he would have liked it to -- and he was told so. But the Department wound up withholding it under Exemption 5 anyway. And it never went to court, so the determination stood. This was "early days" for OIP; I would like to think that had the timing been different, the result would have been different, too.

The second time, like with the Anderson matter, was one in which OIP was of the opinion that the information in question should be withheld as exempt, on personal-privacy grounds, but only as a matter of policy as the Privacy Act did not in that case apply. Yet the Department's political leadership had what seemed to be a blatant political reason for having the information disclosed; one needed only to connect the dots to information already within the public domain to see that. The information was disclosed, with OIP's tacit acquiescence rather than over its objection, but that was a distinction without much real difference, so I count it as OIP having been overruled. And this time, there was some follow-up; the disclosure became swept up on a congressional hearing at which the Department took a "hit" for what it did.

So all told, there were only three such situations, which I maintain is a pretty darn good track record for an office that formulated and implemented policy on a governmentwide basis. And this allowed me to boldly say, when speaking at media FOIA gatherings and the like, that of the rare instances in which this happened, the result was in favor of disclosure two times out of three, which to most observers certainly seems anomalous. Or as Jack Nicholson's character as president in the movie "Mars Attacks!" proclaimed after the Capitol was destroyed: "[We] still have 2 out of 3 branches of the Government working . . . and that ain't bad!"

17   Moving much farther forward in time, in a post-9/11 setting, the horrors of that day spawned another unique circumstance that stretched the FOIA to its limit: The "death scene" photographs of Osama bin Laden after he was killed by U.S. special forces in 2011. They depicted graphic post-mortem views of bin Laden's corpse that in my view (as a retiree being consulted on it) could properly be redacted so that most of the photograph's contents could be disclosed without any harm. Then-CIA Director Leon E. Panetta agreed with this; he actually made a public statement to the effect that the photos could be disclosed in their entireties. But President Obama, not unlike how he reacted to other highly sensitive photographs two years earlier (see Chapter Forty), ultimately overruled such views and determined that not a single bit of the 59 photographs and videos would be disclosed.

18   There are those who say that the measure of a society should be how it treats people during the worst of times, which is a variation of the well-known saying of Fyodor M. Dostoyevsky that "[a] society should be judged not by how it treats its outstanding citizens but by how it treats its criminals."

19   I remember there being some talk of this being pursued with some of the detainees' attorneys, i.e., among those who did not self-identify through the media, but I cannot now recall anything coming of it. Over time, as the year 2001 turned into 2002, what was initially a pre-FOIA analysis became a formal FOIA one and then just a few months later (read: by May of 2002) became a matter of defending FOIA litigation.

20   So some of the information requested was ordered disclosed by the district court, by no later than 15 days from the date of the decision, but this did not occur because the Government moved for, and was granted, a "stay" of that disclosure order pending appeal. This procedural step is entirely commonplace in FOIA cases; else the Government could never appeal a district court loss without the issue becoming moot. In fact, it is a major thing (read: a three-alarm fire) when a district court does not stay a FOIA-disclosure order that it has issued. Resort to the court of appeals, on an "emergency" basis, is needed in such situations. And in those rare cases in which a disclosure order is not stayed at the court of appeals level, immediate relief has to be sought from the United States Supreme Court, in the form of a petition filed with the "Circuit Justice" for that part of the country, who rules on the stay request alone. Over the years, only a few such "Circuit Justice" stays have been sought and in one case, originating in California, such a stay was denied and the contested information had to be disclosed.

21   I knew Judge Sentelle from having chatted with him at the Solicitor General's holiday parties over the course of many years. He always attended, it seemed, and was as jovial as can be. He once told me that he greatly admired one of his colleagues on the D.C. Circuit, Circuit Court Judge David S. Tatel, who lost his sight as a young attorney and was able to accomplish so much despite that handicap. The two were polar opposites ideologically; Judge Sentelle is about as conservative (read: pro-government, at least in FOIA cases) as the day is long.

   Coincidentally, both of them were on this panel. Judge Tatel filed a lengthy dissent, the type that makes you suspect that it was first written as a majority opinion, but one that failed to gain a second judge's vote. And in it, lest there be any doubt, he made clear that until then courts "ha[d] never held that such heightened deference is also appropriate in Exemption 7 cases." Also, for the record, he had a thing or two to say about the case's "attorneys' identities" issue that became eclipsed by the extraordinary breadth of the panel majority's Exemption 7(A) ruling. He observed that the Government "claims to be withholding the attorneys' names for their own good," which was an unduly paternalistic way to treat such grown professionals, and he also noted that "[the] Government completely fail[ed] to substantiate its concerns about releasing attorneys' names." So much for the argument that I refused to go along with.

22   Judge Sentelle actually went so far as to state that the "same deference" is owed under Exemption 7(A) as had been applied for more than a decade under FOIA Exemption 1. Most notably, in a 1982 opinion written for her judge sitting on the D.C. Circuit by one of OIP's early attorneys, Marcy A. Toney, this was calibrated as "the utmost deference."

23   Specifically, the panel majority accepted the Government's judgment that the requested disclosure "would give terrorist organizations a composite picture of the government investigation" and thus enable them to impede it through "counter-efforts."

CHAPTER THIRTY-SEVEN

1   Today, with American COVID-19 deaths having surpassed 3000 per day, some people forget (or are young enough that they never knew) the impact of the 2,977 deaths in New York, Virginia, and Pennsylvania that day, much less the many that followed among those who worked through the rubble of those disasters, particularly

in New York City. When my wife Debbie worked for the September 11th Victim Compensation Fund, where the claimants were the family members of those who died but also included some survivors of the Pentagon with horrible burns, she would bring their stories home sometimes. Those of us who worked in homeland security-related areas tried to never forget those in whose memory we were working.

2   Much of this work was done in conjunction with William H. Leary, who was Senior Director for Records and Access Management at the National Security Council ("NSC," to those in the Intelligence Community) and who served as Special Advisor to the Assistant to the President for National Security Affairs and as Chair of the Information Security Classification Appeals Panel. Bill and I had worked closely together on many matters prior to 9/11 and became sort of a "dynamic duo" on governmentwide information policy immediately after it.

3   I remember first hearing the term employed in the post-9/11 context in mid-September of 2001 and thinking that it smacked of how the Nazis referred to "the homeland" under the Third Reich. But the term stuck in America anyway, big time, as it came to denote the Federal Government's massive continuing efforts to avoid any recurrence of a 9/11-like terrorist event.

Thus, the focus was on what could be called "transnational terrorism," as opposed to the forms of "domestic terrorism" that animated Oklahoma City bomber Timothy J. McVeigh, Centennial Olympic Park bomber Eric R. Rudolph (see Chapter Thirteen), "Unibomber" Theodore "Ted" Kaczynski, Boston Marathon bombers Dzhokhar and Tamerlan Tsarnaev, and "Anthrax Killer" Dr. Bruce E. Ivins (see Chapter Thirteen). As to that, as time goes by, this focus seems to have shifted to organized (read: instead of "lone wolf") domestic terrorist groups such as the militaristic, anti-government ones that manifestly took part in the January 6, 2021 storming of the U.S. Capitol. Today, such groups have reached the point at which the threat that they pose warrants infrastructure protection with regard to them as well.

This was confirmed when FBI Director Christopher A. Wray testified before the House Judiciary Committee on February 5, 2020 and, for the first time since 9/11, identified domestic terrorism as as great a threat as foreign-born terrorism. And he has said that it is the "fastest-growing" of all terrorist threats. This perhaps marked the end of the post-9/11 era's focus on terrorism arriving from overseas.

4   A concrete example (no pun intended) is what is known as "Tunnel Number Three," the most recent addition to the major piping systems that transport water from Upstate New York into New York City. It terminates in a chamber located more than 60 feet beneath Central Park, with an entrance that is hidden from the public, lest the security of the City's water supply be easily compromised.

5   Sometimes the sensitive information about such things is plain, such as the locations of installations or facilities, but sometimes it is more subtle, even as simple as a number. I can recall a Freedom of Information Act case, for instance, in which the only information at issue was the number of terrorists that was estimated to be required to overcome the security of a particular nuclear facility. That case went up to a court of appeals, where the Government prevailed, and the number was not publicly disclosed. I will say here only that that number was somewhere between 5 and 55. (For all I know for sure, that number could still be applicable and conceivably could still be classified.)

6   Another subtle aspect of anti-terrorism vigilance was the recognition that some infrastructure information could be critical because it could be used for site-selection and "targeting" purposes. This is something that we successfully argued in two early post-9/11 FOIA cases, *Coastal States Delivery Corp. v. United States Customs Service*, a case in California involving the pattern of inspecting cargo containers, and *Living Rivers, Inc. v. United*

States Bureau of Reclamation, a case in Utah involving "inundation maps" that showed the points of greatest dam vulnerability.

7   This happened against the backdrop of much *post-mortem* analysis of exactly "what the hell went wrong" with 9/11, most particularly with the use of vital intelligence information and especially with regard to the *sharing* (or not) of such information between the FBI and the CIA (or between the CIA and the FBI, depending on who was saying it). The major 9/11 *post-mortem*, of course, was that which was provided by the National Commission on Terrorist Attacks Upon the United States ("9/11 Commission"), which among other things spawned a forceful and almost faddish emphasis on information sharing among Federal Government law enforcement and intelligence agencies within the newly named and widely adverted to "information-sharing environment." But problems arose when this soon bumped heads against necessary information protection, especially when it led to less national security classification. The special protection needed for different types of "no-fly" lists became a quintessential example of such problems (see Chapter Eighteen).

What is more, though it might not have been well known to the public at the time (much less remembered at all today), there was a very strong and immediate post-9/11 sentiment in Congress (and elsewhere) that the U.S.'s governmental structure of having the CIA handle foreign intelligence matters and the FBI handle such matters domestically -- in addition to its basic, cop-like law enforcement responsibilities -- had had a harmful causative effect in that god-awful disaster. Given the discovered facts of pre-9/11 federal activity (or inactivity, as the case often was), this was a relatively easy case to make.

Those who were of this view, and wanted to make a change so that 9/11 might "never happen again," pointed to the United Kingdom's governmental structure, where Scotland Yard handles basic law enforcement, MI-6 handles purely foreign espionage and analysis activity, and MI-5 handles matters of domestic terrorism and the like. In short, there was a big push, largely behind the scenes, to replicate that in the U.S., certainly at the institutional expense of the FBI. But that did not happen, mostly due to the character and staunch perseverance of FBI Director Robert S. Mueller III, who was sworn in as FBI director (against his wife's wishes, which I happen to know firsthand, as I overheard her speak of it while in the Deputy Attorney General's Office) just seven days before 9/11 (and just one month after prostate cancer surgery) and was properly hell-bent on seeing it through.

I can still remember sitting in the "component head section" of the Justice Department's Great Hall for a 9/11 memorial program at which Director Mueller was to speak and realizing that the fellow sitting to my left (read: physically, not ideologically) was the FBI's deputy director, Thomas J. Pickard, Jr. We chatted while we waited for the program to begin and, not being shy when talking about an organization that used to be my biggest client as a Trial Attorney (see Chapter Three), I asked him about the intense post-9/11 pressure that I knew the Bureau had been receiving to cleave into an "MI-5 type" entity. "No," he replied, it had just been decided that that was not going to happen, and before I could follow up by asking why and how, he added, while pointing at Bob Mueller on the stage beneath the infamous "Minnie Lou" statue, ". . . entirely because of that man up there." So much for that.

8   This took place during my last year before retirement and consumed no small part of my time that year. I remember going to meeting after meeting about this effort and thinking that much of it sounded unrealistic to me. Perhaps this was because it was by then a second generation of homeland-security "specialists" who were coordinating it (in two cases, actually a third), but perhaps it was mostly due to the fundamental intractability of the problem. My primary purpose was to remind everyone involved of the distinction between safeguarding and FOIA withholding, which seemed necessary more than I thought it ought to be.

9   Notably, as it got up to speed on infrastructure protection, DHS (read: beginning with its predecessor OHS, not to mention the transition office between the two) became aware of a basic reality -- that if it wanted to adequately protect the infrastructure of the Nation, it had to deal with the fact that 85 percent of it was "out there" (read: not just "beyond the Beltway," but beyond the Federal Government's immediate reach as well) in the private sector. And that made the good folks at DHS quite uncomfortable.

"How can we protect an infrastructure that we can't even wrap our arms around?" they wondered. "Well, we need to get information about the infrastructure from the private sector so that we can begin to wrap our arms around it and therefore protect it from the target selection, penetration, and attacks that we're worried about," was the only answer -- at least as to the infrastructure that is truly "critical" and the information about it that is deemed "sensitive."

10   The former case involved a map that showed the particular parts of a dam that were most vulnerable to attack (read: as to both attack efficacy and "downstream effect"), while the latter involved statistics that showed which West Coast ports were most susceptible to successful shipments of illicit weaponry.

11   Actually, this glib reference is not entirely fair here. When one proceeds from the premise that foreign terrorists might attack parts of the Nation's critical infrastructure, and that we want to prevent that as effectively as possible, then this inexorably leads to learning both where and how best to do so. And the CII/PCII process is a reasonable way in which to accomplish this, at least if one accepts the further premise that we want to be all-encompassing in this effort, lest a foreseeable target be overlooked by "us" but not by "them."

12   "We live in a highly regulatory society," I used to say to my students as we began class coverage of Exemption 4 and its affiliated area of "reverse FOIA." That was not always so, of course, as Federal Government regulation of the privacy sector did not take strong hold until the New Deal era of the 1930s and then it expanded further during the 1970s.

Indeed, Chief Justice William H. Rehnquist culinarily observed in a 1979 FOIA decision (*Chrysler v. Brown*) that the many new regulatory agency names born of the New Deal amounted to "alphabet soup." He spoke of both eras by venturing that "[t]he term 'alphabet soup' gained currency in the early days of the New Deal as a description of the proliferation of new agencies such as WPA and PWA. The terminology required to describe the present controversy suggests that the 'alphabet soup' of the New Deal era was, by comparison, a clear broth."

But with that, the amount of "business information" submitted to the regulatory agencies of the Federal Government (even apart from what is submitted for government procurement purposes) is immense. And as we often would say, every "business submitter" thinks that everything it submits to an agency is highly proprietary and should be withheld from public disclosure under the FOIA without any doubt.

13   For anyone who might be wondering why business-interest proponents (read: lobbyists) would try to get unduly broad PCII applicability *and* Exemption 3 coverage at roughly the same time, the answer lies in the fact that such folks (read: lawyers, mostly) are big believers (as am I, actually) in taking what we used to call a "belt and suspenders" approach to such things. In other words, if an analytical path seemed viable but was none-theless even slightly in doubt, then adding an alternative path toward the desired outcome was only prudent, inconsistent as it might on its face seem. In this case, the idea that PCII protection might apply even to any required submissions ordinarily made was very much in doubt, given than it amounted to (in my view) gross overreaching contrary to rational congressional intent.

14   At the time, my older daughter Emily had just joined Raytheon as a steppingstone into the field of cyber-security between her first position out of graduate school (with a federally funded research and development

center) and her current one with Google, where she has handled cybersecurity and then "cyberprivacy" for nearly a dozen years. When I told her at the time about how her company had been aggressive in this way, and to this end, she said that she was not the least bit surprised; Raytheon apparently had a reputation for such things internally as well.

15   The "bill of goods" sold to President Bush was that this new exemption protection was "essential" in order to encourage the voluntary submission of CII. There was absolutely no evidence to support such a notion, however.

16   Again, this was a further, closely related example of the "belt and suspenders" approach described above. Indeed, the D.C. Circuit's *en banc* decision in *Critical Mass* had made Exemption 4 protection for voluntarily submitted business information a near-certainty (see Chapter Forty-Six), which is certainly something that President Bush did not understand.

17   This statutory provision, titled "Protection of Voluntarily Shared Critical Infrastructure Information," defined its scope as information that "reveal[s] current vulnerabilities of systems, installations, infrastructures, or projects relating to national security." This law also contained a provision that makes it a criminal offense for any federal employee to "knowingly . . . disclose[] . . . any critical infrastructure information [that is] protected from disclosure" under it, without proper legal authorization. In this respect, it is akin to the Privacy Act of 1974 and the Trade Secrets Act (known as "18 U.S.C. § 1905"), both of which likewise contain criminal penalties for wrongful information disclosure (see Chapter Fourteen).

And for good measure, the Critical Infrastructure Information Act also specifically provided for the continued protection of all such information even if it is shared with a state or local government in the course of DHS's activities. To cover that circumstance, it specifically mandates that any critical infrastructure information now exempt under the FOIA "shall not, if provided to a State or local government . . . be made available pursuant to any State or local law requiring disclosure of information or records," while at the same time also expressly guarding against "waiver of any applicable privilege or protection provided under law." This statute thus explicitly provides for the "pre-emption" of state freedom of information laws by federal law with respect to any question of whether there should be public disclosure of such information. Quite a secrecy regime, indeed.

18   Part of this program, which likewise derived from the same part of the Homeland Security Act, involved implementation of a series of statutory provisions aimed at promoting the free flow of CII within and among government agencies (read: federal, state, local, and even foreign) for effective homeland-security purposes. Among other things, these statutory provisions called upon DHS to develop procedures by which it would "identify and safeguard homeland security information that is sensitive but unclassified." Yes, that ubiquitous "safeguarding label" that began life as my mere memorandum heading (see Chapter Thirty-Eight) wound up being codified in legislation.

19   For instance, we knew that DHS's implementing regulations already were going to have to address the fact that "mandatorily submitted information" at one federal agency sometimes might be identical to information that is voluntarily and separately submitted to another, i.e., to DHS under its CII program, with the two submissions properly treated differently under the law. What must be remembered is that the same industry information can exist in two counterpart forms, identical in whole or in part, and that any information can be submitted to multiple federal agencies on entirely different tracks.

20   Indeed, Congress did so through two provisions. The first, titled "Independently Obtained Information," spoke to the fact that federal agencies routinely obtain business information that might fall within the definition

of "critical infrastructure information" as part of their everyday regulatory processes; it made clear that "nothing in [the CII legislation] shall be construed" to apply to such submissions. And on the obverse side of that coin, the second such provision made clear that the voluntary submission of CII information "shall not be construed to constitute compliance with any requirement to submit such information" elsewhere, such as through those everyday regulatory processes.

21   For one of my CGS programs, I had my student assistants prepare an exhaustive compilation of these labels, which we distributed to an audience that was surprised at how many there were -- more than 150 as of that time. Previously, I had used such a compilation for purposes of the FOIA Officers Homeland Security Information Group that OIP established for regular inter-agency meetings on such things not long after 9/11.

CHAPTER THIRTY-EIGHT

1   Here the word "protected" can mean two different things: Ordinarily, it means having a FOIA exemption applied to agency information, resulting in that information being withheld from public disclosure. In the pseudosecrecy realm, on the other hand, it means "safeguarded" within the executive branch (read: or "controlled") without regard to whether it would be exempt from any FOIA disclosure. This can be highly confusing to all concerned, so OIP consistently strove to drive home this distinction in both agency and private-sector guidance programs.

2   Actually, this protection is not only "in house," because it significantly carries forward (read: at least in theory) when such records are shared with another agency (federal, most often, but sometimes state or local, or even foreign) or find their way into other government hands by some other means.

3   I must admit to carrying this frustration with me to the U.K. when giving a speech over there in 2006, because England's Information Commissioner pithily summarized what I'd said, in part, as "FOUO is phooey for FOIA."

4   Officially, the term "weapons of mass destruction" was defined as "chemical, biological, radiological, and nuclear weapons," including "stockpiles of nuclear materials." Information pertaining to radiological and nuclear weapons is classified under a special statute, the Atomic Energy Act of 1954, not a presidential order on national security classification.

5   That was the State University of New York ("SUNY") at Stony Brook, to which I commuted for seven semesters, having spent one more as a Justice Department intern in Washington, D.C. (see Chapter Five). Dr. Marburger was president there for 14 years during the 1980s and early 1990s, well after I graduated.

6   This is not an uncommon thing, of course, as people have been "covering" for such official misstatements in this way probably since the beginning of time, or close to it (see the Introduction). In Jack Marburger's case, he was a scientist and an academic, not a politician or anything near an experienced government official, and sometimes such people will speak to reporters (read: "on the record," unless wisely, anticipatorily, and explicitly "off of the record") before thinking through what they are about to say.

7   All departments and agencies were ordered to report the results of their reviews to the White House through its Office of Homeland Security, the precursor to the Department of Homeland Security, which was then located within the Executive Office of the President. They were given 90 days to do so.

8   Further, we directed that "federal departments and agencies should not hesitate to consult with the Office of Information and Privacy, either with general anticipatory questions or on a case-by-case basis as particular matters arise, regarding any FOIA-related homeland security issue."

9   When questions arose later about this phrase and its intended meaning," I was well-positioned to address them, as the phrase originated entirely with me. And nothing was intended other than delineation from classified information, for guidance clarity, not realm building.

10   Years later, I had one of my students compile a list of all safeguarding labels still used for non-classified information and she found 114 of them, including Chemical-Terrorism Vulnerability Information ("CVI"), Confidential Business Information ("CBI"), and Critical Energy Infrastructure Information ("CEII").

11   Other big examples are Nuclear Security-Related Information ("SRI"), Information Systems Vulnerability Information ("ISVI"), Personal Privacy Information ("PII"), Protected Personal Privacy Information ("PPPI"), Controlled Technical Information ("CTI"), Official Use Only ("OUO"), Limited Official Use ("LOU"), and Protect as Restricted Data ("PARD").

12   On the other hand, in a nod to openness, we at the same time at least paid lip service to the value of scientific integrity by cautioning that "[t]he need to protect such sensitive information . . . should be carefully considered, on a case-by-case basis, together with the benefits that result from the open and efficient exchange of scientific, technical, and like information."

13   A valid way of looking at this is that some information, even if of a type previously released under the FOIA, could be viewed as having taken on new and heightened sensitivity in the light of 9/11. A simple example of this was the architectural plans and utility schematics of federal buildings, which were often viewed as non-sensitive prior to 9/11, but not after.

14   Indeed, the most recent government characterizations of the pseudosecrecy realm, after what are now more than two decades of its existence as such, are that it is "vastly overcomplicated" and "exponentially more complex" than it ever needed to be. So much for my use of "simple" delineation language in a 2002 governmentwide policy-guidance memorandum.

CHAPTER THIRTY-NINE

1   This encompassed the White House's "eighteen acres," which included the former State, War, and Navy Building to the west along 17th Street (which in the late 1930s was renamed the "Old Executive Office Building" ("EOB," to historians) and then in 1999 was again renamed the "Eisenhower Executive Office Building" ("EEOB," except to us old hands who reflexively still call it the "Old EOB")). This building has housed the offices of the White House Counsel, the National Security Council staff, and several large conference rooms as well over the years, beginning with the Carter Administration.

2   An example of this can be found in the story of the investigation of Vice President Spiro T. Agnew's continued receipt of Maryland-based construction contract payoffs even after he became vice president in 1969. Many of the payoffs, believe it or not, were made hand-to-hand by visitors to Agnew's Second Floor office in the Old EOB from 1969 though through 1971. Federal investigators were able to use what were then called the Secret Service's "Appointment Record" logs in order to corroborate the exact dates on which those payoffs were made.

3   Records that are purely "White House records," by contrast, particularly those that are part of what we called the "inner White House," are not subject to the FOIA; rather, they are governed by the Presidential Records Act ("PRA," to excited presidential archivists), a "post-Watergate" law that provides for the delivery of all such records to each president's eventual library within the "presidential library system," which is administered by the National Archives and Records Administration ("NARA," to its patrons). Generally speaking, access to a record (in its original form) will be governed either by the FOIA (more precisely, the Federal Records Act) or the PRA, not both.

The Presidential Records Act is self-implemented by "inner White House" staff, who are required by it to maintain and preserve virtually all of their records for proper disposition at the end of each presidential administration. Over the years, there have been several instances of White House personnel falling short in meeting this requirement here and there, but the most infamous such situation was the attempt by the Reagan White House not to preserve any of the electronic mail contained in what it called its "PROFS" computer system as the two-term Reagan Administration ended in January of 1989. This effort, however, was successfully countered through litigation brought by future Collaboration on Government Secrecy Advisory Board Member Scott Armstrong on behalf of the National Security Archive, with assistance from the Public Citizen Litigation Group.

Most recently, concerns about possible gross PRA noncompliance arose and then became heightened during the Trump Administration, based upon reports of President Trump's personal recordkeeping habits and also the use by members of his family of "screenshots," which do not include metadata for such communications. In November of 2020, the same National Security Archive, together with two historian groups, filed a lawsuit similar to the one filed at the end of the Reagan Administration, but one much broader in scope, to guard against any widespread attempts by Trump Administration White House staff to simply ignore the PRA's prohibitions and requirements, as it had ignored so many other laws, legal obligations, and presidential norms of behavior in the past. And then Donald Trump himself violated the PRA in spectacular fashion with his removal of presidential records to his new home at his Mar-a-Lago club in Palm Beach, Florida.

4   An example of this could be logs showing visits by prospective Supreme Court nominees prior to an official nomination announcement; a president could have good reason to keep such a visit secret for at least some period of time. Another could be a log showing a visit by a lobbyist who now is caught up in one scandal or another; there could be "good reason" there, too, but it would not necessarily be good.

5   A singular exception to this occurred at the very end of the Clinton Administration in January of 2001. As President Clinton prepared to leave office, White House lawyers proposed the transfer of the Clinton Administration's visitor records from Secret Service control to the White House, so that they would be part of the Clinton Presidential Library, where they now reside.

6   In 1993, for example, I wrote a governmentwide policy memorandum for the attorney general that delineated "White House records" from "agency records" under the FOIA in such a way as to explicitly include visitor logs in the latter category, not the former. To the best of my knowledge, that memorandum remains in effect even today.

7   This change for White House visitor logs ran parallel to one made, evidently at Vice President Cheney's insistence, for the White House's Office of Administration ("OA," to its Executive Office of the President customers), which played an administrative role for the Secret Service's visitor logs. Created during the Carter Administration, this office had always been regarded as subject to the FOIA; indeed, it had responded to FOIA requests for more than two dozen years and had sought consultation assistance on them from OIP on several

occasions. But one day in 2006, Vice President Cheney woke up, had a healthy breakfast, and declared that the Office of Administration was no longer subject to the FOIA.

By the way, I say "a healthy breakfast" here because I know firsthand a little about Cheney's health from our mutual participation in "Continuity-of-Government" activities during the late 1980s (see Chapter Twenty-Six). During one such activity, in 1988, we found ourselves standing side-by-side at bathroom urinals, where we briefly chatted about the number of heart attacks he'd already had at that point and some of the measures that he had to take as a result. (We'd already had some interaction during the program activity.) He certainly seemed amiable back then, not at all a devotee of the "dark side" quite yet.

8   This position was extended even beyond the White House Complex. Not long after the "memorandum of understanding" was executed, counsel for Vice President Cheney formally took the position that visitor records for the vice president's official residence (located on the grounds of the Naval Observatory, alongside my commuting route on Massachusetts Avenue, N.W.) were "subject to the exclusive ownership, custody and control" of the Office of the Vice President.

Speaking of this official residence for the vice president, such a thing did not exist until the mid-1970s; prior to then, vice presidents lived wherever they chose. President Harry S. Truman, for example, lived on upper Connecticut Avenue, N.W., adjacent to a park where I would take my children when they were very young, as we lived just a few blocks away. He actually continued to live there as president for a while, giving former First Lady Anna Eleanor Roosevelt the same type of courtesy that President Andrew Johnson extended (read: extending for five weeks) to former First Lady Mary Todd Lincoln in 1865. As of the 1980s, this building was still known in the neighborhood as "the Truman Building."

Anyway, it was in 1974 that an official residence for the vice president was established, at the house that had long been occupied by the chief of naval operations at One Observatory Circle. This was during the vice presidency of Gerald R. Ford, who did not occupy it as he soon thereafter became president. And the next vice president, Nelson A. Rockefeller, preferred to live in his own, more luxurious home. So the first vice-presidential occupant was Walter F. "Fritz" Mondale, who lived there with his family during the late 1970s until 1981.

Skipping ahead almost 20 years, as it was about to be occupied by Vice President Cheney, the residence's main entrance was the subject of nightly gatherings of his supporters; as I would drive home every night, at the intersection of Massachusetts Avenue and Reno Road (known as "Observatory Circle"), I would see and hear them loudly chanting "Get out of Cheney's house! Get out of Cheney's house!" The object of their jeers, of course, was Vice President Albert A. Gore, Jr. (This, too, is part of living in Washington.)

9   Jack A. Abramoff was a lobbyist convicted of a wide-scale fraud scheme that involved White House officials, a sitting congressman, congressional aides, and several Native Americans tribes. As part of this, he allegedly had more than 300 meetings with White House personnel during the George W. Bush Administration, including ten with senior Bush advisor Karl C. Rove. As the investigation into his lobbying activities grew, so did the significance of White House visitor logs pertaining to it.

10   CREW had been the most active public interest group on this issue by far. It was founded in 2003 by future Obama appointee Norm Eisen and Melanie Sloan as a nonprofit liberal watchdog organization. And it had filed a total of four visitor log FOIA lawsuits, including two that had been victorious and were pending on appeal.

I was most familiar with CREW as one of the Department of Justice officials deposed by it in connection with the Department's high-level settlement of tobacco litigation in the early 2000s. My deposition ended on a high note when CREW executive director Melanie Sloan lost her composure at some of my answers and objections to her questions. (Those objections were made by me, rather than by Civil Division counsel, because by that point of the deposition I was essentially defending myself.) We had had to call in the magistrate judge overseeing the case to rein in counsel for both sides, which resulted in the deposition being curtailed along contours that I had suggested.

11   More recently, the most active such FOIA requester has been Judicial Watch, which filed a series of its own FOIA lawsuits for White House visitor records and was a very aggressive FOIA litigator. Fully aware of what was going on between the White House and CREW, it filed a FOIA request in August of 2009 for all visitor records since Obama took office, When the White House continued the Bush Administration position that the FOIA did not apply, it brought suit on what was by then a clear Obama Administration position, but it did not prevail in court.

12   Indeed, not once did the Obama Administration openly admit that it had exploited the Bush Administration's efforts to take such a step backward.

13   After conceiving, setting up, and then attempting to tout and defend this plainly deficient "visitor logs" system, Norm moved on to other things, becoming the United States Ambassador to the Czech Republic, befitting someone who had served on the Harvard Law Review's editorial board alongside a young Barack Obama, and he later became a consultant to the House Judiciary Committee for Trump impeachment purposes. He then moved on to be a fellow at the Brookings Institution.

14   Officials in the Obama Administration tried to claim credit for being the first administration to release White House visitor logs, but this was patently false; such releases (read: largely partial ones) were made by the Secret Service long beforehand.

15   And speaking of such expectations, it also was expected by the openness-in-government community that the Obama Administration would restore the "FOIA agency" status of the White House's Office of Administration, a step that seemed to be a "no brainer" for the immediate implementation of its touted transparency policy. Yet this never happened. In fact, the Obama White House even took a formal regulatory step in the opposite direction for that office, in a "tin-eared" move that actually (read: inadvertently, but no less incompetently) took effect during "Sunshine Week" in 2009.

16   Regrettably, the Biden Administration already has failed in one particular respect -- his White House has thus far refused to release visitor logs for "virtual meetings," which POLITICO points out is the "primary mode of interaction until the coronavirus pandemic eases." On May 8, 2021, it did release its first batch of records disclosing physical visits by official guests, returning to the minimal disclosure practice that was set by the Obama Administration (as heavily criticized above) but then was ditched in favor of no disclosure whatsoever by Donald Trump. In this release, the White House disclosed some visits during President Joe Biden's first 12 days in office. However, it pointedly declined to disclose the identities of any of his visitors (read: official ones) at either of his two homes in nearby Delaware, to which he travels quite regularly and thus far has spent more than a quarter of his time. Reportedly, the Secret Service stated in April of 2022 that it had "no records" of any visitors there and reiterated that again in late September, with the White House saying that releasing any such records "would amount to an unnecessary intrusion into the president's private life." Unfortunately, a decision written by then-Chief Judge of the D.C. Circuit Court of Appeals Merrick B. Garland in 2013, Judicial Watch v. United States Secret Service, seems to support such a position -- as a matter of law, but not of good policy.

17   This made Attorney General Garland only the second attorney general to fail to issue a formal memorandum setting out his administration's governmentwide FOIA policy within its first year. (The first, of course, was in the Trump Administration, which never bothered with any such thing during its four years.) This unfortunate fact

spurred the openness-in-government community to write a second letter to the White House (the first was ignored) calling for such action. And even more seriously, it led to a rare bipartisan, bicameral letter of criticism from Congress in February of 2022. Evidently, it took such pressure to yield what in previous years would have been an ordinary step.

18   No small part of this, sorry to say, are calls for my old office (read: OIP), to take a more active and effective role in overseeing governmentwide FOIA administration. It has been more than 15 years since I left that office and I have been embarrassed by its performance many times in the years since then.

19   Finally, on March 15, 2022, Attorney General Garland did issue such a memorandum, which reiterated "the foreseeable harm standard" that had been initiated by Attorney General Janet Reno in October of 1993 (see Chapter Twenty-Nine) and replicated several elements of her policy guidance.

CHAPTER FORTY

1   This is not to overlook the U.S.'s 20-year war in Afghanistan, which in some respects is indistinguishable from the one against Iraq. I had occasion to hear President George W. Bush speak of both wars together at DAR Constitution Hall and will never forget it. In September of 2005, he decided that he would personally address all career Senior Executive Service members (read: in the D.C. area) because his father had done so more than a dozen years earlier. So I soon received a personal invitation to the event.

When I arrived there, however, I immediately noticed the presence of many young-looking attendees, including some with atypically short haircuts, and it soon became clear that Bush had not invited *all* career SES officials as his father had done. Rather, he had instead invited all of the political SES members (read: his own appointees, either directly or indirectly) and just the "top 15%" of the career SES. (How the White House determined that small group is something that I never learned, even though I apparently was part of it.)

Once inside, and sitting close to the stage because I had arrived early, I was treated to an unvarnished speech from Bush, uninhibited by the facts that there were absolutely no media present and that he evidently also thought that his audience was overwhelmingly "his people." This was about a month after Hurricane Katrina had overwhelmed New Orleans, so he started off by referring to that and actually repeating his highly criticized praise for FEMA Director Michael D. Brown. "Brownie did a heckuva job," he exclaimed, in his casual, frat-boy style, to the shock of only a minority of us. He then shifted to the number-one issue in America -- the maintenance of three wars: against Iraq, in Afghanistan, and something that the White House was then calling the "GWOT," the acronym for the "Global War on Terrorism."

And this is when the heart of this story reared its ugly head. Bush started talking (read: extemporaneously, not from a script) about Iraq and Afghanistan, especially the latter. He praised our Armed Forces stationed over there, of course, and then he promised that their "good work" would soon be done. At that point, he described that work as necessary to "spread democracy" around the world. Yes, he actually spoke as if the people of Iraq and Afghanistan inherently needed democracy (read: impliedly a superior form of government) and it was our responsibility to provide it to them. And yes, he sounded as if he were a European missionary hell bent on con-verting a native population to Christianity. And I was close enough to see the unmistakable gleam of religious zealotry in his eyes. And as I said above, I will never forget it.

2   Yes, this U.S. Attorney's Office was indeed referred to within the Main Justice Building as the "Sovereign Independent State of the Southern District of New York," and it traditionally enjoyed having a singular authority among all other such offices in the Justice Department hierarchy. I can recall, for example, an exceptionally challenging (and high-profile) FOIA litigation case during the early days of the Carter Administration in which

this tradition was sorely put to the test; that organizational battle was resolved only when the Civil Division of "Main Justice" (of which I was then a part) agreed to that case being shared -- i.e., being handled on an admittedly cumbersome "50/50" basis -- between the two competing offices.

3   Apropos of this, I wondered how on Earth it was that U.S. servicemembers, this far into our presence in Afghanistan and Iraq, felt free to so indiscriminately take photographs of literally anything within their view and then, for instance, send them home for whatever further distribution of them might then occur. Didn't they receive strict instructions not to do such things, along with their mess kits and compasses, for instance, when they first arrived? Then I had an opportunity to put this question to one of OIP's staff attorneys, who had just returned from a mobilized reserve tour of duty in Iraq, where her military job, coincidentally, was to lead a "photography unit" for several months.

"Surely, you knew of such logical constraints having been placed on servicemembers, right?" I probed. "Don't call me Shirley," she replied, "my name is Jennifer. And no, there were no such universal constraints." (Jennifer's first name is real, but her last name is not given here because she was young enough at the time that she could still be an officer in the Army Reserves today and I do not want to take any chance of compromising that position.)

4   This is something that I already had surmised, based on what is referred to as "public source" information. Nevertheless, I will not recount it here.

5   Years later, when studying this case, my students would try in all sorts of ways to get me to tell them the "real secret" of what it was about these particular photographs that made them so sensitive as to warrant these extraordinary measures -- from my Joint Chiefs of Staff meeting to the advocacy of the novel Exemption 7(F) argument to DOD's "end run" with President Obama to the gamesmanship with the Supreme Court and to the pursuit of a "legislative fix" -- in order to keep them from public view.

And I would tell them that it certainly was a very extraordinary thing, indeed, and I would even invite them to guess what it might be (not that these inquisitive young folks really needed to wait for such an invitation). Fortunately, none of them ever did guess correctly, so I never had to take extreme measures on it. (No, I do not mean having anyone killed; just maimed a bit would be sufficient.)

By the way, a key part of the fact pattern on this is that the photos were never classified, so I had (and still have) little residual obligation to maintain this secret at that time. (This is a point at which I should emphasize that an oath to protect the secrecy of information classified on national security grounds extends beyond one's government tenure.) But I did, thinking it best. And I continue to do so here, because there is good reason for maintaining this secrecy even today.

6   To be sure, the Joint Chiefs would have accepted even a mere "colorable" defense here with open arms and perhaps even shouts of glee at that point. And it does not disclose too much to say that their greatest concern was in avoiding any situation in which the U.S. would be making an official disclosure of these photographs *right then*, for fear of the consequences of such a disclosure. In other words, they were looking to solve the problem that was at hand.

7   Technically, under a law passed by Congress in 1976, these actually were "declarations." And in this case, they were submitted by very high-ranking generals.

8   The legal question in the case thus became: Whether FOIA Exemption 7(F) applies to exempt these photographs from disclosure because their public release could reasonably be expected to endanger the life or physical safety of any individual, where the individual is unidentified except as a member of a large threatened group.

I now will proceed to address this issue, and recount the convoluted procedural history of its adjudication, in what some might regard as almost nauseous detail. But I daresay that there has never been anything quite like it, and without the full story (read: almost) being told here it likely would be "lost to the ages," so I will give an accounting of it that leaves hardly anything other than the actual "secret" of it out.

9   Discussion of a point of law is warranted here, lest one get the impression that what we did with Exemption 7(F) was procedurally infirm in any way. In point of fact, the FOIA permits exactly what we did, because it provides for what is called "*de novo* review" by district court judges. This means that, unlike in other cases litigated under the Administrative Procedure Act (of which the FOIA technically is a part), whatever happens at the "administrative level" underlying a FOIA case in court (with the exception of cases involving FOIA fees or presenting a "reverse FOIA" situation) simply does not matter.

This is turn means that a defendant agency in a FOIA litigation case can modify existing defenses, can take new positions regarding them, or even add new defenses (such as a "new exemption") well after case has begun. In theory, of course, that means that an agency should not be penalized in any way for doing so, but that did not stop Judge Hellerstein from viewing Exemption 7(F) pejoratively in this way.

10   In this exceptionally complex case, this particular ruling eventually was merged together with other parts of the case and formed part of the basis for disclosure orders issued by the district court in June 2006.

11   It was very clear, especially to the AUSAs handling this case directly in the U.S. Attorney's Office, that bringing this glaring error to the attention of Judge Hellerstein would be futile. As part of his rejection of Exemption 7(F) as a defense, he oddly declared that "[o]ur nation does not surrender to blackmail, and fear of blackmail is not a legally sufficient argument to prevent us from performing a statutory command." *ACLU v. Dep't of Def.*, 389 F. Supp. 2d 547, 575-79 (S.D.N.Y. 2005). We never did figure out exactly what he meant by that.

12   In order to do such a thing, by the way, it ordinarily is necessary for the Government to obtain, from either the district court or the court of appeals, what is called a "stay" of any disclosure order that, once obeyed, would effectively "moot out" a case. Because the Government (read: DOD) was hell-bent on not disclosing these photographs, it would have pushed this "stay" issue all the way up to the Supreme Court if necessary. (Over the years, there unfortunately have been several such FOIA cases in which emergency Supreme Court stays (by a single Justice known as a "Circuit Justice") were made necessary by the intransigence of lower courts.)

13   It should be noted that this was a key factor here. From the perspective of an observer in that part of the world, what is disclosed to a requester under the FOIA (and hence to the public, in any third-party request) is an "official" disclosure, no different than, say, a DOD press release. The fact that the disclosure was *compelled* by U.S. law is of no moment. Such is the environment in which harm judgments under the FOIA sometimes must be made.

14   In December of 2006, shortly after this case was argued before the Second Circuit Court of Appeals, and shortly before my retirement, future Acting Attorney General Peter D. Keisler took me to lunch to thank me for what I had done in devising the novel Exemption 7(F) defense in the case. Based on how the oral argument before the Second Circuit had just gone, he had an inkling of the panel's flat resistance to it, and he was almost apologetic that the Civil Division (of which he was the assistant attorney general at the time) seemed to have failed to succeed with it. I of course thanked Peter for his kind gesture, but I optimistically assured him that, based on my experience with so many Supreme Court reversals of troublesome circuit court FOIA opinions

over the years (seven as of then, with two others yet to come), I believed that the Court would see the issue our way (so long as it also saw the photos), if it were to come to that. Peter is another prince among men.

15 In short, these reactions included the burning of American flags, attacks on both U.S. installations and relief organizations, and scores of injuries to U.S. personnel and related local citizenry in Afghanistan.

16 Related to this, the Government also pointed to, in the words of the court of appeals, the "risk that the enemy would seize upon the publicity of the photographs and seek to use such publicity as a pretext for enlistments and violent acts." To my mind, the greatest risk lay in how they would be viewed by young males.

17 Neither did the Second Circuit seriously question any of the underlying judgments about the harms (i.e., deaths and injuries, *inter alia*) that were expected to flow from these particular photographs' disclosure.

18 That other thing, of course, was Congress's enactment of the more refined "nexus" language of "could reasonably be expected to" cause harm instead of "would" cause harm under this particular exemption. This legislative change clearly lessened the Government's burden of showing potential harm under Exemption 7(F) and it should have made it easier for us to prevail in this case. Except, as it turned out, it didn't.

19 Not long after the FOIA's 1986 amendments were enacted, the attorney general issued guidance to all federal agencies explaining the amendments' scope. In it, the attorney general (nominally) explained that Congress's expansion of Exemption 7(F) to "encompass 'any individual' is obviously designed to ensure that no law enforcement information that could endanger anyone if disclosed . . . should ever be required to be released" under the FOIA. (OK, so I'm quoting myself here.) In light of that "clear authority" to withhold records "endangering any person," the attorney general instructed that "agencies should take pains to ensure that they withhold any information that, if disclosed under the FOIA, could reasonably be expected to endanger someone's life or physical safety."

20 Yes, this Second Circuit panel was guilty of the same sin as Judge Hellerstein's -- supporting its adverse decision by anticipatorily (and improperly) denigrating the Government's timing in making an Exemption 7(F) argument in the first place. Here is a good "rule of thumb" for interpreting judicial opinions: If the judge(s) evidently feels the need to do such a "bolstering" thing, especially at the beginning of an opinion's legal analysis, then that bespeaks a lack of confidence in the adjudication of the substantive merits of the case, which at the appellate level, especially with a ruling against the Federal Government, often reflects a telling effort to "*cert.* proof" that case.

21 Remember: President George W. Bush was then concluding his second (and hopefully last) presidential term, so no matter who won the 2008 presidential election (i.e., either Barack H. Obama or the other guy), there would definitely be a new solicitor general appointed relatively soon.

22 Evidently, neither District Judge Hellerstein nor the Second Circuit panel that upheld him undertook *in camera* inspection of the photographs at issue, nor is it publicly known whether Solicitor General Kagan did so either. (I know, but I'm not saying.) In my view (no pun intended), this was a critical oversight. If ever there was a case that cried out for such an examination, this was it.

23 Beyond its rare (and perhaps totally unprecedented) novelty in the annals of judicial proceedings, this decision by President Obama was viewed as somewhat of a "man bites dog" story in that he had declared on his first full day in office that he intended to "usher in a new era of open Government." Indeed, the progression

from the Administration of George W. Bush to that of President Obama was widely viewed (at least as of those "early days") as a giant step in the direction of more transparency and greater FOIA disclosure. Yet here was President Obama blatantly (as well as belatedly) interjecting himself into a FOIA lawsuit, far outside of the ordinary processes for such things, with a determination that ran in the opposite direction.

The President explained his decision by saying that it was based on his determination that "the most direct consequence of releasing [the photographs] . . . would be to further inflame anti-American opinion and to put our troops in greater danger." Remarks Prior to Departure for Tempe, Ariz., Daily Comp. Pres. Docs., 2009 DCPD No. 00359 (May 13, 2009). He further stated that "it was [his] judgment, informed by [his] national security team, that releasing these photos would . . . endanger[] [our troops] in theaters of war," and that "the lives of our young men and women serving in harm's way" provide "a clear and compelling reason to not release these particular photos." Remarks at the Nat'l Archives & Records Admin., Daily Comp. Pres. Docs., 7-8 (May 21, 2009). I concur.

24   I do not recall learning whether this action was unprecedented; remember, I had retired more than two years earlier and was still involved in the case, from afar, only through contacts with the Department's appellate attorneys and perhaps a former client at the Defense Department. (I neither confirm nor deny whether this included Deputy Solicitor General Ed Kneedler.) I do remember thinking that Solicitor General Kagan certainly was off to a bad start in that role, but then again it obviously did not stand in the way of her appointment to the Supreme Court two years later.

25   In between, the Government had routinely asked the Second Circuit to consider rehearing the issue *en banc*, but that petition almost as routinely was denied. And after the Government made an initial determination not to seek *certiorari*, the Second Circuit issued its "mandate" on April 27, 2009, which meant that the case was ready to return to the district court for the photographs' ordered disclosure.

The Government subsequently moved the court of appeals to "recall" its mandate, explaining that President Obama and his top national security advisors (somehow, they didn't mention me) had determined that release of the photographs would create an unacceptable risk of danger to U.S. military and civilian personnel. Significantly, that motion, which was granted on June 7, was supported by the public and classified declarations of both Lt. General David H. Petraeus, the Commander of U.S. Central Command (and coincidentally a major subject of Chapter Thirteen), and Lt. General Raymond Odierno, the Commander of the Multi-National Force-Iraq.

Based on his insurgency expertise, "extensive experience in Iraq," and information obtained as Commander of U.S. Central Command, General Petraeus concluded that producing the photographs would "endanger the lives of" U.S. military and civilian personnel by "fueling civil unrest" that would "caus[e] increased targeting of U.S. and Coalition forces." General Odierno similarly expressed his professional judgment (based on years of command experience in Iraq and discussions with senior Iraqi leaders) that "the release of these photos [would] endanger the lives" of United States military and civilian personnel and its Iraqi partners, and that the Multi-National Force-Iraq would "likely experience an increase in attacks" in retaliation. General Odierno added that "[c]ertain operating units are at particular risk of harm from release of the photos," including members of certain 15-to 30-soldier training teams who execute small-unit patrols that are more vulnerable to insurgent attacks and who live in Iraqi-controlled installations without the protections available to most soldiers.

26   In the Supreme Court, with the Government as the petitioner, the case was styled *Department of Defense, et al. v. American Civil Liberties Union, et al.* (No. 09-160).

27   This entirely unprecedented (as far as the FOIA as concerned) legislative remedy was enacted as Section 565 of the Department of Homeland Security Appropriations Act, 2010, Pub. L. 111-83, Title V, § 565, Oct. 28, 2009, 123 Stat. 2184-85.

28 558 U.S. 1042 (2009). It should be noted that, as a procedural matter, the Supreme Court was not *required* to vacate the Second Circuit's adverse Exemption 7(F) opinion, as not doing so would not technically have affected the photographs' protection. So the very fact that it did so, with the issuance of what is known to Supreme Court practitioners as a "*Munsingware* order," was significant in more than ways than one: It removed a precedential opinion that was highly adverse to the use of Exemption 7(F) by the Government in the future and it vindicated the judgment that I had conveyed to then-Assistant Attorney General (later Acting Attorney General) Peter Keisler over lunch three years earlier. (By the way, the order of *vacatur* issued by the Court flew in the face of the ACLU's plea that the Second Circuit's interpretation of Exemption 7(F) be "left intact" so that it would be available "should another [such] controversy arise." Rather, that opinion is null and void.)

29 In order to "cover" the case as safely as possible in light of Judge Hellerstein's persistent quarrel with the Government's compliance with the PNSDA, the Government had continued with an alternative Exemption 7(F) argument before the court of appeals. In doing so, it pointed to what then was a recent D.C. Circuit decision on Exemption 7(F), *EPIC v. United States Department of Homeland Security*, 777 F.3d 518, 523 (D.C. Cir. 2015), that stood directly contrary to the reasoning and outcome of the Second Circuit's vacated opinion on that exemption, thus creating a clear "conflict" for potential Supreme Court review (see Chapter Eleven, for example).

30 No, Judge Hellerstein never gave up, it can fairly be said -- even to the point of his then holding, in a new interpretation that transparently mirrored that of the Second Circuit in its vacated opinion, that the PNSDA actually required the Secretary of Defense to "consider each photograph individually, not collectively." (At this point, the story goes, a brilliant attorney from the Appellate Staff of the Civil Division was heard late one night lamenting the course of this litigation by softly singing: "Seems to me, we got to solve it individ-u-ally. And I'll do unto you what you do to me." Yes, he was a young rascal, indeed.)

31 It is worth noting that this "photographs" issue was but a part of this massive case, which involved, as mentioned at the outset, an immense amount of DOD and CIA records. Such is the price paid by a government that, paradoxically, proclaims to embrace transparency yet engages in activities that breed enormous public distrust.

32 *ACLU v. DOD*, No. 17-779, 2018 WL 3977021 (2d Cir. Aug. 21, 2018). From the time that Judge Hellerstein held his first status hearing on the case in 2004 to its ultimate denouement in 2018, more than 14 years had passed, requiring the sustained efforts of many high-level government officials, as well as by the litigation forces that were often consumed by the case, especially the beleaguered AUSAs of the Southern District who, after all, had to "live with" Judge Hellerstein on a day-after-day basis. I myself was glad that I was officially involved in the case for less than two of those 14 years, but I will confess to being "consulted" on it more than I had ever imagined after I retired. (Such consultations, by the way, are proper under certain circumstances.)

33 This unavoidably brings up the potential question of how long something adjudicated as exempt under the FOIA, i.e., as "properly withheld" in the semi-transmogrified language of the statute, can and should remain "withheld." In one sense, we've already seen an answer to that question in another case involving photographs, i.e., the second FOIA lawsuit for access to the "death-scene" photographs of Vince Foster (see Chapter Three, describing the *Favish* case), in which a second FOIA request could have led to disclosure despite the fact that the first one did not.

Ordinarily, then, a second FOIA request for these photos, especially one for which the requester "lays venue" within a different judicial circuit (see Chapter Three, for an example), could lead to disclosure even though the first one did not. In this particular case, however, the prevailing legal basis for nondisclosure was a statutory disclosure prohibition, which is immutable unless subsequently changed by Congress. So in this somewhat unusual situation, someone reading this today could not just "run right out" with a new FOIA request seeking a different result as Allan Favish did in the *Favish* case.

Along those same lines, though, a fair question would be: Does this mean that the public will never, ever get to see these photographs? Well yes, it does mean that, unless Congress rescinds the law or until the underlying circumstances change so as to preclude an up-to-date "certification," which would be akin to the harm contemplated under Exemption 7(F) dissipating over time. Fifteen years ago, I would have imagined that that would be the case by now. But I would have been mistaken.

CHAPTER FORTY-ONE

1   The only exceptions to this policy are when a mug shot is used for purposes of capturing a criminal suspect who is at large (e.g., a fugitive on a Ten Most Wanted poster) or where there is an issue about the treatment of the suspect at police hands, in which case the photograph could serve an overriding public interest in documenting the suspect's physical condition at the time of arrest.

2   As it turned out, though, not all of the eight were prosecuted, much less convicted.

3   The Solicitor General did not authorize the filing of a *certiorari* petition in *Detroit Free Press* because not only was there no conflict in the circuits on the issue, this was the sole appellate decision to deal with mug shots under the FOIA at that time. It also was believed in the Solicitor General's Office that the case law on this issue would develop quickly enough to make waiting viable and therefore worthwhile. Time proved this to be a mistake, one that seemed to be unduly influenced by a political employee.

4   The Supreme Court's *Favish* decision (see Chapter Three) undercut the Sixth Circuit's *Detroit Free Press* ruling in more ways than one, providing a perfectly viable basis for the Justice Department attempting to overrule it by simply taking another "mug shot" case up to the *en banc* level. The very fact that *Favish* modified Exemption 7(C) case law on both sides the exemption's "balance" greatly facilitated this.

5   That political appointee was Deputy Assistant Attorney General Gregory G. Katsas, who seemed to take a constant "don't rock the boat" approach to his Justice Department service (which should sound familiar) and accordingly went on to become a deputy White House counsel during the Trump Administration and then an appointee of President Donald J. Trump to the D.C. Circuit Court of Appeals. There is every reason to believe that he just did not bother to understand that such a litigation course was part of how for decades we strove to shape the development of FOIA case law in such a circumstance. Even his "own people" in the Civil Division were distressed that he wouldn't listen to this from them. Greg's callow, self-serving handling of the *Detroit Free Press* issue put him very much in league with Neil Gorsuch as well (see the Epilogue).

6   Ordinarily, the Department would handle something such as that collegially, with a meeting that included the key participation of the Office of Solicitor General. That did not take place in this case, however, and the decision to back down from the *Detroit Free Press* challenge suffered greatly for it.

7   This was the first step of the litigation course that I had formulated and initiated years earlier. It set the stage for what the Department so belatedly then did in litigation.

8   The way precedential jurisprudence works is that district courts within a judicial circuit are bound to follow the "law of the circuit" once it is clearly enunciated at the court of appeals level. And subsequent court

of appeals panels are likewise bound by the holdings of prior panels, except in the exceptional circumstance in which a distinguishing factor can be found. Only if a circuit court decides to "go *en banc*" on an issue can a panel decision, such as the 1996 *Detroit Free Press* one, be overturned. Unless it is overturned by the United States Supreme Court, that is.

CHAPTER FORTY-TWO

1   Indeed, this is the number of hours per week that I had calculated having worked on average from September 12, 2001 to the day that I retired in early 2007, over a span of more than five years. This was culminated with my having worked four "off" days (i.e., weekends, New Year's Day, and the day commemorating the death of President Gerald R. Ford), as well as three additional days that were actually *ultra vires* because my retirement had already taken effect. As may be discerned, I very much wanted to get as much work completed as possible for a transition after my departure. (Though the latter might well have been a violation of something known as the "Antideficiency Act," here's hoping that the statute of limitations has by now run on that, too.)

2   The Washington College of Law (which has since moved to Tenley Circle in Northwest D.C., was at that time located on Massachusetts Avenue, N.W., less than a half mile from the District/Maryland line. My neighborhood, known as "Wood Acres," was where "Mass Ave" (as we called it, with apologies to the good folks in Cambridge, Massachusetts) ended. (Chief Justice John G. Roberts, Jr., lived there, too, when he worked at the Justice Department.) This was a relatively easy commute for me, one that I could make by bike once a week (on "casual Fridays"), down what is known as the "Crescent Trail" (an old railway line) alongside the Potomac River.

    This commute also worked out well when my older daughter Emily worked downtown as a "computer jock" during high school. We would drive home together whenever our schedules allowed, and as we hit the intersection of Reno Road and Mass. Ave. we would regularly wave in support to an older gentleman who religiously manned that corner (the northeast one, in front of the Catholic Church's Apostolic Nunciature) without fail, rain or shine, even in winter, where he protested the Vatican's treatment of abused altar boys such as himself; Emily nicknamed him "Pope Guy" and it must be said that he certainly was "well ahead of his time."

    Indeed, the only rush-hour time that he ever was not at that corner was during the second half of November 2000, when large crowds would displace him each night as they massed together to yell "Get OUT of Cheney's house!" Yes, that intersection was also the main security entrance to the Vice President's Residence (on the grounds of the Naval Observatory), where Vice President Albert A. Gore, Jr., was awaiting the outcome of what became the *Bush v. Gore* case in the United States Supreme Court.

3   Being the first in the world at this certainly held more than a bit of cachet for WCL, which over the years had cultivated a reputation for "public interest" academic excellence, being located in Washington, D.C., and all. This was the "big idea" that I brought to the university, one that I had formulated while still working at Justice.

4   One, for instance, Hannah H. Bergman, holds the title of "Information Policy Counsel" at the National Archives and Records Administration. Another, Elizabeth M. "Liz" Hempowicz, is the director of public policy at a premier government "watchdog," the Project On Government Oversight ("POGO," to its many "public interest" friends). And a third is Asheesh S. Bhalla, formerly deputy attorney general for the State of Nevada in charge of transparency matters statewide and now Executive Director of Nevada's State Infrastructure Bank.

5   As this list of CGS program speakers grew, I would begin to tell some but not all of them that, say, my phrase "100 different speakers" by that point meant that some of them were "very different," indeed. These speakers included a senator, three congressmen, four federal judges, five international FOIA commissioners, the general

counsel of the World Bank, a political appointee who soon thereafter became the Solicitor General of the United States, several White House officials, more than two dozen fellow law professors, the deans of several law or journalism schools, and many veteran "open government" journalists such as Carl Stern, Scott Armstrong, Michael R. Isikoff, Josh Gerstein, and Carol D. Leonnig of *The Washington Post*.

6   In recognition of this, CGS was twice invited to testify before Congress as part of its oversight of the administration of the Act. In turn, each year, the principal congressional staff members (read: House and Senate, majority and minority) for this subject area would gather at CGS's annual "Freedom of Information Day" program in mid-March to participate in our "congressional forecast" panel discussion.

7   I say "we" in this description because, from beginning to end, CGS always had somewhere between three and eight student assistants (whom we called "Dean's Fellows," for some reason no longer remembered), who to their credit worked both hard and well to support our website's constant development and to keep it accurately up to date. In turn, most of them received both letters of recommendation from me and even more active help in their efforts to find legal positions (often in the "government openness" field) upon graduation. There were a total of 21 of them over the years and one of them, for example, went on to become the principal FOIA officer at a major federal agency.

8   Sadly, my father, who was only 22 years older than me but smoked for more than 75 years, suddenly became chronically ill to the point at which he required several hospitalizations, emergency hospital trips, and close monitoring as of the summer of 2014. And as the eldest of his five offspring and the only one living near him, it was up to me to head to his side at a moment's notice whenever need be. I therefore could no longer safely schedule any CGS program event that required my presence (which they all did) as of that time, and I had to have the school put CGS into an archival status from which, with my father's further declining health, it never recovered.

9   There is a funny thing about this, one that I believe has thus far largely escaped academic notice: It actually was not so long ago (i.e., just 20 years) that the word "transparency" was scarcely used in the United States. I know this because in 2002 I spoke at a government openness conference in London, where I gave "the Brits" several points of advice for the upcoming implementation of their own Freedom of Information Act. And in writing about that upon my return, I wrote of the U.K.'s nascent freedom-of-information efforts by parenthetically saying: "or 'transparency,' as it is called overseas." In other words, as of that relatively recent time, the word "transparency" was so barely used in the United States that I felt that I had to explain it. Now, of course, it has more than taken hold here; in fact, it now has an even broader application, one that in its shorthand use regularly includes the private sector. Indeed, nowadays it seems as if public discourse just would not be the same without the word transparency's widespread use.

CHAPTER FORTY-THREE

1   Although this term today can confusingly mean a range of things, back then in the heavily Catholic community in which my parents and their siblings lived, this meant little more than that they were "going together," in their parlance. Stated another way, their seven kids came later.

2   As we got older, I stayed in touch with all of my double-cousins, especially after they lost both of their parents at early ages and my own parents looked out for them when they were young. In fact, Mary and I had even run the *Newsday* Long Island Half-Marathon together a couple of times in the mid-1980s, with her siblings Eddy and Lynn, as I was training for the full Marine Corps Marathon.

3   As noted elsewhere (see the Preface and the Epilogue), I had decided to retire the previous March as a matter of principle when asked to go along with a proposed White House statement that was 180 degrees from what was true, but I had to wait until after I turned 55 near the end of that year. This enabled me to devote several months to "winding down" my long Justice Department tenure, so that I could leave OIP in early 2007 with relatively little undone.

4   I use the word "him" here because all of the associate attorneys generals for whom I worked (14 in number) were male (which was more of a coincidence, I think, than anything else, as the Department has had four *deputy* attorneys general over the years who were female). While the position was created in 1977 (see Chapter Seven), there was not a female associate attorney general until slightly more than 40 years later, when the position was slightly filled by Rachel L. Brand, who resigned somewhat abruptly after only eight months in the position and now works for Walmart.

5   Mauricio's full, proper name is "Mauricio J. Tamargo-del Portillo." He was a three-time presidential appointee who held that position for more than eight years.

6   Today Gonzales can be found at Belmont University College of Law, a Christian institution not accredited until 2013, where he finally landed many years after leaving the Department of Justice in disgrace. Initially, when he was forced to resign as attorney general in the summer of 2007, his reputation was so damaged that he failed to find a new position. (Many folks joked that he was the first attorney general ever to be unable to get a new job after leaving the Department, because even former Attorney General John N. Mitchell quickly caught on with the prison laundry.) As is described in more detail below, he eventually landed an embarrassing sinecure position at a relatively small university, where I "hunted him down like the dog he was" to depose him in his home state of Texas.

7   In my experience (and there was a great deal of it at top levels of the Justice Department), many Republican appointees seem to actually disdain the very process of governing, as if they (as opposed to Democrat appointees) do not particularly care whether most things (i.e., apart from the agendas that they really care about) are done successfully, much less properly. This assertion is a broad generalization, to be sure, and is readily criticizeable as such, but it is no less true as a general rule.

There are notable exceptions, of course, such as Associate Attorney General Robert D. McCallum, Jr., under whom I worked for several years before he left to be the Ambassador to Australia; he had been part of the "skull and bones" society together with his Yale classmate George W., and as such he had his own "power center" independent of the prevailing one around Alberto Gonzales. Another such exception was Paul J. McNulty, who had very ably served the Department during the first Bush Administration (i.e., that of "George H.W.") and then came back as deputy attorney general in George W.'s first one; he quite memorably managed to squelch the loud and blustery actions of the vice president's son-in-law (who is not really worth an endnote) when he (the son-in-law) attempted to roughly interfere with the work of my office. (Note that I do not name him *per se* here, out of respect for his wife only.) And then there was Jonathan C. Rose, of course, who so graciously secured my career SES position when I was still at the tender age of 32 (as recounted in Chapter Twenty); a veteran of the White House at a tender age himself, Jon did indeed care about getting things "right."

8   The reasons for this varied somewhat among them, but the most common one by far was failure to bring cases promoting the conservative agenda on elections and voting, at least in the eyes of White House hench-person Karl Rove. Rove, lest it be forgotten, served a highly manipulative function for both President Bush and Vice President Cheney and had a "Teflon" reputation for avoiding potent scrutiny of his actions. His principal

contact at the Justice Department was Monica Goodling and he doubtless was heavily involved in both her U.S. Attorney scandal and her creation of an unlawful "screening committee" for the hiring of career employees. Rove left his White House position in the summer of 2007, at about the same time that Alberto Gonzales was being forced out of his position at Justice.

9   Speaking of "worse," on May 7, 2007, the *National Journal*'s "Inside Washington" column reported that it actually was Goodling who ordered drapes to be placed over the partially nude Art Deco statue named the "Spirit of Justice" (but known widely as "Minnie Lou") in the Justice Department's Great Hall during John D. Ashcroft's tenure as Attorney General. At the time, the Department's Office of Public Affairs (where Goodling then worked) claimed that those drapes cost only $8000, but my office handled documentation showing that the true cost actually was greater.

10   The Justice Department's scandalous treatment of its own political appointees around the country sprang from the immature grandiosity of young political aides operating without ordinary supervision at high levels within the Department, but it was badly compounded by the painful immaturity of Alberto Gonzales, who proved his unfitness for the position of attorney general from the very first press conference that he attempted to hold on the scandal. Eventually, after he repeatedly performed no less poorly at congressional hearings as well, this led to his forced resignation in disgrace by the late summer of 2007.

11   I was shocked to learn that in Sean's application year the Attorney General's Honors Program had been corrupted, on political and ideological grounds, on orders from the White House and the Attorney General's Office itself. Put simply, the Bush Administration's most conservative ideologues wanted to prevent any "liberals" from joining the Justice Department and they found an effective, albeit utterly unlawful, way in which to do so.

12   As it turned out, the word "discernable" here meant "background information" that could be learned from improperly recorded Internet searches for the political counterpart to what the FBI would call "derog" (see Chapter Eleven).

13   The laws governing the Federal Government's career hiring go back to the late 19th century with a statute known as the "Pendleton Act," followed by the Civil Service Reform Act, which sets forth a series of merit-system principles that currently prohibit what the Department so blatantly did. The problem, and this is where a case such as *Gerlich* comes in, is that such laws are not self-enforcing and provide no legal remedy (read: a waiver of sovereign immunity) for anyone aggrieved under them.

14   As a matter of law, the Honors Program applicants consented to the Department's use of their applications for its legitimate hiring purposes. (By contrast, had they been applicants for political rather than career positions, they would have been required to go further by consenting to the Department doing just about anything whatsoever.) Once a "new record" was created, however, through either annexation or annotation, the Honors Program applicants' consents very arguably no longer applied. Hence (although it is getting ahead of the story), one result of the *Gerlich* lawsuit was that federal agencies learned that they could no longer treat career applicants the same as political ones in the hiring process. Nor can they do what hiring personnel in the private sector do -- "vet" their applicants through Internet searches.

15   Fortunately for Sean (and later for others similarly situated), my 30-plus years of handling litigation had left me so adept at it that I was able to do such things under short deadlines literally (read: figuratively) "in my sleep." (Which my wife at the time said she could confirm.) To that should be added my own bromide that "there are few things more dangerous than a retired litigator with time on his hands." Not that I actually did have

so much time on my hands, given both my teaching load and the fact that the Collaboration on Government Secrecy was then "taking off" at the end of its first year (see Chapter Forty-Two), but I made the time for this case by working almost as long and hard as I had during my last five years at Justice (read: post-9/11) prior to my "retirement."

16   To be sure, I took the position that when these young attorneys awoke and started breathing hard each morning, they were "exercising their First Amendment rights" within the meaning of this broad Privacy Act phrase, and this was supported (albeit not conclusively) by analogous case law. Ultimately, the Justice Department's litigators did not seriously contest this point of law, although they contested just about everything else.

17   Unspoken in all of this is that I would be handling the lawsuit single-handedly, up against a team of first-rate litigators that the Department typically assembled for such a case, not to mention high-level supervisors at one end of the team and virtually unlimited support personnel at the other. (And this is not to mention the private-practice litigators.) Having "been there, done that" myself, I had no illusions about that but was entirely comfortable (read: immodestly confident) with it nonetheless.

18   When it came to Sean, of course, I was not the least bit concerned about this; he was family and that was that. But as for other named plaintiffs, I had to rely on an explicit understanding (read: agreement) about such things. Did it mean that I was running at least some slight risk? Sure. But I did not foresee even the slightest chance of my committing even arguable malpractice in this area of law.

19   Indeed, deterrence became a running theme in the case, one that I would advocate over and again, both in court and in the media interviews that I gave about it. I would point out that the corruption of the Attorney General's Honors Program was the first such high-level Justice Department wrongdoing since the Nixon Administration, which meant that it had been more than 30 years since something such as it had occurred. Having been at that level of the Department back then (albeit as a lowly law clerk) at the time of the "Saturday Night Massacre" (see Chapter Seven), I wanted to do my part to try to ensure that something like that did not recur in another 30 years. (Little did I know that it would be only another ten.) Self-ennobled and perhaps a bit naïve, that is the attitude that I brought to the case. And added to the mix was that I knew I had the sophisticated litigation skills to handle such a challenge, even entirely on my own.

20   Actually, I amended the original Complaint twice in the case, first in mid-August to add additional plaintiffs and the *Bivens* claims, and then again in mid-November in order to incorporate shameless efforts made by the Justice Department in mid-September to dissuade additional "deselectees" from asking to join the case. So the case proceeded under plaintiffs' Second Amended Complaint, which was insufficiently answered by the Department of Justice.

21   A *Bivens* claim is one made based upon a decades-old Supreme Court decision that first recognized the viability of an individual's Fourth Amendment-based suit against Federal Government officials in their personal capacities. Handed down in 1972, the decision created an implied cause of action for the violation of at least some constitutional rights, but it was one that developed very slowly under judicial limitations over the years. By the time the *Gerlich* case was filed, the Supreme Court's *Bivens* jurisprudence left no more than a slight opening for such redress of First Amendment violations, but it was enough to command much attention from both the Justice Department and the five agency wrongdoers who were made individual defendants, potentially "on the hook" for money damages, through the filing of the Amended Complaint. (A dozen years later, the Supreme Court effectively overruled *Bivens* entirely, in a 6-3 decision, *Egbert v. Boule*, No. 21-147 (U.S. June 8, 2022).)

22   According to news reports, once it became public knowledge that George was representing Gonzales in the case at taxpayers' expense, the chairmen of both the House and Senate Judiciary Committees immediately seized on that and demanded that the Justice Department "describe the terms of the fee arrangement[,] . . . disclose whom in the department approved it and on what basis[,] . . . [and] say whether the department has agreed to cover the legal expenses of other officials named in the lawsuit." Evidently, George was none too eager to be representing Gonzales in the first place, let alone amid such inter-branch warfare. As near as I can tell, his successors in this role were none too happy about it either.

23   I had a big advantage with these numbers in that they did not intimidate me one bit, even though these opposing counsel plainly expected that they would. The most extreme case of this was with the principal counsel for Monica Goodling, a notoriously aggressive litigator by the name of John M. Dowd, who right off the bat in the case sent me an "over the top" letter telling me that his client was being persecuted and that I would personally regret it if I did not immediately drop the case against her. What he did not know was that I had a close personal friend who also was a professional friend of his and that I therefore knew full well what his aggressive blustering was all about. We even had a good laugh about it during a bike ride to Haines Point one day, with me joking that if you looked up "pit bull" in the dictionary you'd find two pictures and the second one would be of the dog.

Later on, long after Monica ultimately was deposed in our case (read: much to his chagrin), Dowd gained even more notoriety (read: not at all the good kind) when representing President Donald J. Trump in connection with the Special Counsel's investigation of Russian collusion through retired General Michael T. Flynn. Among other overly aggressive bumblings, he left the infamous "heads up" voicemail for Flynn's attorney (blatantly seeking coordination from a potential witness), whereupon Trump very publicly let him go for a stated lack of confidence in him. Sad.

Many times during my career as a Justice Department litigator I found myself singly up against several attorneys on the other side of a case, who usually thought that the odds favored them, which was not uncommon for a Justice Department Trial Attorney. Yet in my four years of directly handling litigation in the Civil Division, I was lucky to have never lost a case. In this case, I was glad to see that the lawsuit had had such an enormous impact. And my young clients were very happy to see the publicity about their victimization that the case's very existence continued to attract.

24   This former litigation adversary was Erwin Chemerinsky, who as a young attorney had helped Bill Dobrovir in litigating the *Fund for Constitutional Government* case in the late 1970s (see Chapter Twelve). He had gone on to "make something of himself," as they say, by becoming the most-cited law professor in the land as a professor at Duke Law School and then being appointed Founding Dean of the University of California at Irvine School of Law in 2008. It was at that time, just as the *Gerlich* case was revving up, that Erwin represented former covert CIA case officer Valerie Plame Wilson in her *Bivens* lawsuit against White House official I. Lewis "Scooter" Libby, Jr., and others, for their role in her being publicly "outed" from her covert status.

Erwin and I had consulted with one another on the viability of *Bivens* claims in his lawsuit and mine, and in the summer of 2008, he was considering taking Valerie Plame's case up to the Supreme Court, where the only completely reliable vote for a *Bivens* claim would be Justice Ruth Bader Ginsburg. For my part, I was envisioning a possible appeal to the D.C. Circuit, where at least one of the circuit judges, Circuit Court Judge Judith W. Rogers, had signaled a strong receptivity to a *Bivens* claim, most particularly in the Privacy Act context. Ultimately, Erwin took his D.C. Circuit loss on the issue and sought review of it by the Supreme Court, but his petition for *certiorari* was denied. That did not happen until June of 2009, by which time the *Bivens* claims in *Gerlich* had long served their purposes.

25   Actually, there were two Privacy Act provisions that I thought applied to the facts of the *Gerlich* case. In addition to subsection (e)(7), the Act contains a similar "fair information practices" provision, in its subsection (e)(5), that more broadly requires agencies to maintain records used "in making any determination about any individual with such accuracy, relevance, timeliness, and completeness as is reasonably necessary to assure [sic] fairness to the individual in the determination." Because that legal obligation is so generally stated, I chose to include it in the case but not place primary emphasis on it. As it turned out, both subsections ultimately stood as grounds for our winning in the eyes of the D.C. Circuit.

26   The classic definition of this Yiddish word, of course, is that of the teenager who murders both his parents and then throws himself on the mercy of the court as an orphan. With 40 in-law Passover Seders under my belt (read: not just avoirdupois), I tend to deploy Yiddish freely.

27   This is the juncture at which I should emphasize that the Privacy Act is an exceptionally complex statute, one that was cobbled together by Congress within a short period of time (see Chapter Fourteen) and for the most part can be fully understood only with reference to its case law. In other words, expertise with this statute makes a very big difference. And the leading expert on the Privacy Act was (and doubtless still is) Kirsten J. Moncada, a former OIP associate director to whom I assigned that responsibility when she began at OIP in 1989. I daresay that Kirsten is the only person on Earth who knew the Privacy Act and its proper implementation better than I did as of then; she singlehandedly prepared OIP's "Privacy Act Overview" treatise for many years, and I reviewed it.

28   There was a third ostensible committee member, an AUSA who was on detail to Main Justice and participated in a limited way, and only under duress. I informally interviewed him, with opposing counsel's consent, of course, and concluded that he was a person of integrity who did not act with anything near the sheer malice and irresponsibility that the other two, especially Elston, brought to the scandal. So he is unnamed here.

29   As I phrased it at oral argument, the operation of the screening committee was a "secret enterprise" that operated in complete secrecy and remained "shrouded in silence" at the time.

30   The trick to doing such a thing, not unlike in making some FOIA requests, is to make the production demand broad enough that it leaves nothing of potential value out, but not so broad as to engender a fair response that it is "overbroad" and "unduly burdensome." I used to tell that to my students, together with the admonition that in making such a request "in the dark" (read: at least partly so) you don't want to exclude something valuable to your case that you might not know exists. To be sure, not an easy balance to strike.

31   This stemmed from the fact that I had noticed the Justice Department's failure to include what is known as an "affirmative defense" in its Answer to the Second Amended Complaint as is required by the federal civil rules. It eventually explained this as an "oversight by counsel."

32   Of all the barriers that the Justice Department tried to erect to the *Gerlich* claims, the most extreme one was its argument that the application copies that Esther McDonald forwarded on for deselection were "functionally the same" as what had been sent to her. The Department's supervisory attorney on the case, John Tyler, even stood up in court and declared that what she had added to them was just "innocent stuff" that (he mistakenly assured the Court) held no legal significance.
    When I heard this, I knew it to be false (read: not within the realm of any reasonable characterization), which mostly made me disappointed in John. He then went on to contend that the Justice Department actually was "duty bound" to find out such information about its job candidates, which of course was not at all true in the case of

career employees; therein lies the substantive difference between career and political employees, or the difference between vetting applicants in the private sector versus doing so in a Privacy Act-governed federal agency.

I had known John Tyler since he was a summer law intern himself in the Department's Civil Division many years beforehand and had never heard of him mischaracterizing anything in court or overzealously "cutting corners" like that. My best guess is that, like many busy government litigators, John had not had sufficient time to prepare for that argument, which would mean that this was not entirely intentional on his part. I remember wanting to think the best of him, because he truly is a very solid attorney of excellent demeanor and character, but what he claimed in court (read: twice) made that difficult.

33 It was obvious to me that Judge John Bates' conservative, pro-government bent was a large barrier to the plaintiffs prevailing in their claims, but at the same time I knew that he, too, cares deeply about the reputation and integrity of his former agency. Indeed, he went out of his way to criticize what the Department had done, multiple times and in multiple ways. So I saw broad discovery as a way in which he could at least give us the means by which we could expose the Department's corrupt conduct to the fullest. And that is how it turned out, though I think we succeeded more than he had in mind.

34 Under prevailing case law of long standing, whether such discovery is allowed is a matter left to the district court judge's "sound discretion," yet with a heavy presumption against depositions being allowed for high-level government officials (read: even former ones). But I had hammered away at the exceptional corruption involved in the case when pressing the *Bivens* claims and, as recounted above, at oral argument had labeled it a "secret enterprise" that without full discovery would remain "shrouded in silence" forever. Evidently, that carried the day with Judge Bates, who pointedly observed that the case involved "extremely troubling behavior from high-ranking Department of Justice officials."

35 There was one exception to this: Lou De Falaise. I had known Lou for more than 25 years at that point. As one of many freshly minted United States Attorneys, he had been in my audience when I briefed them all on the FOIA and (ironically) the Privacy Act on that Saturday in late November 1981 (see Chapter Twenty) and I had sat in countless meetings with him when he followed being a long-term U.S. Attorney with a lengthy stint in the career ranks at Main Justice. I knew that he was not a schemer like Monica Goodling was and I knew that he was not self-servingly arrogant and malicious (read: and drunk with power) like Mike Elston was. So I negotiated an agreement with his attorneys, and with the attorneys at Main Justice as well, that I would not formally depose him but would instead just sit down with him for a quiet little chat about what he knew.

And the key point, especially as I had a fiduciary duty to my clients, was that I personally trusted Lou and was confident that I need not place him under oath in order to get straight answers from him. In further deference to Lou, I will not divulge exactly what I learned from him, except to reiterate that the phrase "cast a blind eye" fairly characterizes it. Stated another way, Lou had his feet in both the political and career realms within the Department, and I gathered that this sometimes could be difficult for him. So as much as he was blameworthy in a general sense, I do not think that he acted with the venality of the case's other named defendants, especially Elston and Goodling (and of those two, especially Elston).

36 In scheduling these depositions, I "worked my way up" (read: as TV detectives do against organized crime) from McDonald to Goodling to Elston and then to Gonzales, whom I had to hunt down in Lubbock, Texas, where he had finally landed a political patronage job at Texas Tech University (read: not to be confused with its law school), of all places.

37   John was a Vietnam War veteran who had come to the Department as an AUSA in the early 1980s and with a powerful intellect rose to be chief of the Civil Division of the U.S Attorney's Office (not to be confused with the much larger one in Main Justice). But he then vacated that position (turning it over to my former staff attorney Mark Nagle, who as described in Chapter Twenty-Four "had litigation in his blood") in order to become a top aide (alongside future Supreme Court Justice and inveterate beer lover Brett M. Kavanaugh) and eventually deputy to Whitewater Independent Counsel Kenneth W. Starr.

I knew John as a neighbor as well as a Justice Department colleague; our children attended school with one another, we served together as volunteers at school functions, and he lived adjacent to the local elementary school on the route that I jogged along most mornings. Although John is as conservative as the day is long, when he was appointed to the district court by President George W. Bush in 2001, I thought that he was an excellent choice (read: an exceedingly smart, pro-government judge). I just never thought that I'd draw him as a judge on a case that I was litigating against the Justice Department.

38   Esther McDonald carried the title of "Counsel to the Associate Attorney General," but frankly that was a joke. I happened to have known very well the Department's first senior attorney to hold that title, the late Robert N. Ford, who transferred over to Main Justice to hold it just as I was receiving that unexpected offer from the U.S. Attorney's Office, where he was the civil chief, in the summer of 1978 (see Chapters Three and Ten). Bob and his successors in that position were light years ahead of Esther, who had been practicing law for less than two years when she was given it; even the Department's inspector general characterized her as "a junior attorney new to the Department" when he described her blithe wrongdoing. Such was the way that political appointments often went in the Justice Department during the George W. Bush Administration, especially in Bush's second term (see Chapter Fifty).

39   It was clear to all who were there that Esther McDonald had been prepped to not say anything that might help the plaintiffs' case if she could possibly avoid doing so. And she made a valiant effort toward that, but one that was shameful for an attorney. Esther Slater McDonald reportedly became the subject of disciplinary proceedings for her misconduct in the case. For her part, Monica Marie Goodling was publicly reprimanded by the Virginia State Bar on May 10, 2011; in the predicate for that, the Fourth District Section II Subcommittee of the Virginia State Bar ruled on March 14, 2011 that she "commit[ted] a criminal or deliberately wrongful act that reflects adversely on the lawyer's honesty, trustworthiness or fitness to practice law." And Michael J. Elston, who has claimed to be a member of four state bars, reportedly has been the subject of multiple disciplinary complaints only to the Virginia State Bar. As for Alberto R. Gonzales, his consequences included the pain of having to be deposed by me for nearly seven hours (which I wouldn't wish on anybody), to the point of abject apology, about his actions, his inactions, and those of his lawless subordinates.

On the other hand, Esther did disclose something else that was quite remarkable and became very helpful to us in the long run. In describing her dealings with Elston, and with relatively little prompting, she recounted a hallway conversation in which he praised her Internet searching to date and even went so far, she said, as to say that they ought to "institutionalize" her Internet-search methods for all career hiring Departmentwide. I concluded on the spot that she spoke of this so freely because (a) she saw it as exculpatory of her, and (b) she did not understand the Privacy Act well enough to realize that this was damning evidence of the Department acting in a manner that was "intentional or willful" (read: in satisfaction of a key Privacy Act element) in what she and Elston were doing. And so I continued to question her accordingly.

Some people (read: mostly my students) have wondered why I didn't just flat-out ask Esther McDonald whether she conducted Internet searches on any of the plaintiffs once I had her under oath. (Even the D.C. Circuit panel that eventually decided the case recognized this chosen tack.) The answer to that is two-fold:

First, Esther had right away given a rehearsed speech about having very little memory of what she did for the screening committee with regard to any particular applicant. More important, though, was something born of the old lawyers' adage about "never ask[ing] a witness on cross-examination any question to which you don't already know the answer."

While I am not a true devotee of using that as a flat, general rule, I did think that it would have been very easy for Esther to respond to such a question by saying that by then (i.e., nearly four years after the fact) she had absolutely no recollection of doing that for any of the named plaintiffs in particular but that she seriously doubted that she actually did so. In fact, as the district court subsequently observed, Esther made "repeated offers to have her memory refreshed by the plaintiffs' [actual] applications," all of which I purposely ignored. Sure enough, the Justice Department's appellate counsel later attempted to make something of the fact that I asked neither Esther nor Mike Elston such questions, but he was rebuffed by Court of Appeals Chief Judge Merrick B. Garland, who at oral argument endorsed my approach by saying that "[a] reasonable juror doesn't ask what questions might have been asked at [a] deposition." So I advised my students not to ask any risky question of a deponent or witness unless they absolutely had to.

When talking with my students about this (after I advised them of my new "seven-question" rule for pressing a witness on instinct), I explained that when one is conducting a deposition in a case like *Gerlich* (or defending one, for that matter) one must always have in mind how any statement on the record could be used by the other side in prospective briefs and/or oral arguments, either offensively or defensively, either to make a point or to "muddy one up." So in sitting across from Esther McDonald at that deposition table (which had been provided, by the way, by my good friends at the Project On Government Oversight ("POGO," to its very many friends) courtesy of their terrific Executive Director Danielle Brian, another CGS Advisory Board member), I had to continuously envision what she predictably might say in response to any question that I asked her and how that could be used by my opposing counsel in the case later on. And I had to do this even though I knew that, even at the end of a long day, my opposing counsel might attempt to ask any such question on cross.

40   In one of those amazing "small world" coincidences in life, I recently learned that Monica is one of my next-door neighbor's best friends and even was the maid of honor at her wedding. I imagine that we will one day meet again, but I did not offer her an opportunity to read what I've written about her in advance.

41   Quite notably, as I recall, Monica Goodling did not at any point attempt to throw Alberto Gonzales "under the bus," as they say, even though under the circumstances she unquestionably could have done so. When I subsequently deposed Gonzales, I kept waiting for him to do the honorable thing and return the favor, but he failed to do so. On a personal level, I thought the contrast spoke volumes.

42   Nevertheless, Monica admitted, "I crossed the line of the civil service rules . . . I believe I crossed the lines. But I didn't mean to." Such was her resort to the last refuge of a caught transgressor.

43   Putting myself in my opponent's shoes, which I would tell my students is almost always worth doing, I realized that there was only so much that I could do in that regard. In other words, even if my direct examination was crafted in such a way as to skirt that point, the opposing counsel could always get Elston to go as far as he could to dispute it on cross. But he didn't, nor did Elston himself have the presence of mind to bring it up. (Note that there's a premise there.) So that entire quotation rings out loud and clear, to great effect (read: twice, actually), in the court of appeals' decision.

44   In that vein, Elston made it clear that he considered it to be the responsibility of only those *other* than himself to be concerned about the particular requirements of basic administrative statutes such as the Federal

Records Act and the Privacy Act. In other words, he manifestly was more concerned with how he made himself look than with what might serve his agency's liability interests. Elston would have made a great hostile witness for us if the case had proceeded to trial. I would rank him as a D- deposition witness from his agency's standpoint but an A+ one for any plaintiff bringing suit against it.

45   This plaintiff, Daniel J. Herber, was a remarkable one in several respects. First, he was in his mid-thirties, having had a career in politics before going to law school. This was because at age 21, he won election as the youngest-ever member of the LaCrosse, Wisconsin, City Council. Better yet, for our purposes, he ran as a candidate of the Green Party, a fact that was publicized through Internet news coverage of that feat that remained on line when Esther McDonald was doing her "derog" Internet searching in the fall of 2006. The only negative factor with him was that once he was "deselected" for the Honors Program, he secured a high-paying attorney position in the private sector and therefore had only limited damages to claim.

46   The *Gerlich* plaintiffs and I owe a big debt of gratitude to this generous person, Cathy C. Sosebee, on Mac Davis Lane, in that she not only provided her well-appointed office facilities to us and spent all day personally transcribing the deposition (read: rather than have someone who worked for her do it), she ultimately decided, after hearing Gonzales speak, to provide her transcription (read: an original and multiple copies) to us free of charge. So if you ever need transcription services in that dusty, tornado-prone part of Texas, she more than deserves your business.

47   *Associated Press* investigative reporter Pete Yost won this race, as I recall. Pete had covered Gonzales closely for many years and he wanted to be the first to report his "further fall," as he put it. Pete told me that he had good reason to believe that Karl Rove viewed Gonzales as a "patsy" for what the White House wanted to accomplish in Bush's second term. (In Russia, the term would be "useful idiot.") Others were Jason A. Leopold, then of *Truthout* and later *BuzzFeed News*; Evan Perez, then of *The Wall Street Journal* and now of *CNN*; Marisa Taylor of *McClatchy Newspapers*; John Hudson, then of *Atlantic Wire* and now of *The Washington Post*; Josh Gerstein of *POLITICO*; Ashby Jones of *The Wall Street Journal*; Mike Scarcella and Zoe Tillman of the *Legal Times*; and Carrie Johnson of *The Washington Post*.

48   Or as I told the *Legal Times* at the time, "I think everyone in the room realized that, in his own limited way, he was at last being apologetic for what had or had not taken place."

49   And far less was any concern that the screening committee's principal worker, Esther McDonald, had been given any training on Privacy Act rules down in the Associate Attorney General's Office. She corroborated this in her deposition testimony, just as Monica Goodling did in hers. As for Mike Elston, he managed to leave unclear the extent to which he firmly knew of the Privacy Act and Federal Records Act prohibitions that he had violated. (He doubtless knew of the civil service ones, but he just did not care.) Fortunately, I did not need to prove his "state of mind" on this; his documented actions, including his hallway conversation with Esther, spoke loud and clear on what could be called the "*scienter*" element of the case.

50   Gonzales himself spoke to this: "Obviously everyone is smarter in hindsight. In hindsight you wish you would do some things differently." Yes, you do, Alberto, but only if you did some things wrong in the first place.

51   To be sure, it is not at all polite to refer to someone as "dumb." Some might say that this holds especially for high-level officials such as the president and the attorney general, where at least respect for the office is due. But I think the public record on Bush (read: even the nonpartisan one) is sufficiently well established, notwithstanding some inevitable spurts of native intelligence, to support such a characterization of him. And as

for Gonzales, I have to say, as probably one of the few professionals who ever spent that much continuous time with him, especially one on one, that he comes across as the least intellectually capable government official, at any level, that I have ever met. And that's saying something.

52   Brad was a breath of fresh air among the dozens of attorneys on the other side of this case. In time, he came to function as my principal opposing counsel and I came to know him as a man of principle as well. In short, having worked with and against untold numbers of opposing counsel during my career, I became entirely certain of Brad's integrity and professionalism, just as I was entirely sympathetic to the fine line he was walking within the role that he had to play in the case. (It was Brad who practically fell out of his chair when Esther McDonald finally uttered Mike Elston's "one thing I did right" admission at her deposition.) And having served in that Civil Division Trial Attorney role myself for several years, I was able to well recognize and respect the quality of his work.

53   Unfortunately, I learned something else through this tranche of discovery documents, something that took me very much by surprise: My nephew Sean had not been deselected by the Department's screening committee. In fact, he had not even been selected in the first place, due to the way in which he had electronically filled out his application. This meant that Mauricio was mistaken about what he had surmised and then told me about Sean, and it meant that I was proceeding on an incorrect assumption when I filed the lawsuit to begin with. Yes, had the case not attracted other qualified plaintiffs during its first month, it would have been subject to ready dismissal on its own. But this did not mean, as a matter of law, that the case was subject to dismissal at this later point just because its original foundation was gone, far from it. (To the Justice Department's credit, it did not attempt to advance such an argument.)

But it did mean that I had to break the news to Sean (and to our family) about what had been learned about his case, and to do that I felt that I needed to verify "with my own eyes" that this was true. Fortunately, Brad Rosenberg understood this full well and, as a professional courtesy, arranged for me to have special access to Sean's putative "unselected" file so that I could see for myself exactly how Sean had gone wrong. Then, when I gave this news to his mother, my cousin Mary, I was able to say that I had verified with 100% certainty that Sean actually did not qualify to be part of his own case.

54   This was flatly contrary to what the Department's inspector general had found; he had concluded that there simply was "virtually no written record" of Esther McDonald's screening committee work. Worse still, he had explicitly stated that "we were unable to reconstruct what information McDonald obtained from the Internet." So much for inspector general reports in comparison with court-ordered discovery.

55   There also was counterpart information in the records of Esther's Internet searches about plaintiff Mathew J. Faiella, in the form of publicity about his personal efforts against military recruitment on the Cornell University campus while he was a law student there. No such information was found about a third plaintiff, James N. Saul, which complicated his claims by comparison.

56   I had barely even heard of "spoliation," frankly, and knew not much more about it than that it often was mistaken for "spoilation," which is a distinctly different thing. But as it happened, the very next day, while attending an adjunct faculty meeting at my law school, I bumped into an old friend who used to teach for me in my Advanced FOIA seminars when she succeeded John Podesta on the staff of the Senate Judiciary Committee. Beryl A. Howell had moved to the United States Sentencing Commission by then, was teaching a Legal Ethics course in her spare time, and actually had just written a legal article on the subject of spoliation (of all things), which made for several large coincidences heaped upon one another. Needless to say, I pumped Beryl for all she

was worth on the subject that evening, to which she was quite agreeable given what I was doing it for, and that happenstance sent me along the road to mastering that area of law. (Beryl, by the way, soon was appointed to the United States District Court for the District of Columbia, where she very quickly advanced to be its chief judge, as position that she holds to this day.)

57   I learned this only because she sat down to speak with me while he was occupied elsewhere with the counsel check-in process. She told me that she was very proud of her son and I allowed in return that I certainly thought she should be, based upon both his reputation and my own dealings with him. All that time, though, I kept thinking that I didn't think I would bring my mother to one of my oral arguments unless I was quite sure that the argument would go well. I suppose I should add that I felt sorry for her in that she was about to be badly disappointed.

58   Whether this had been witting or unwitting, I'll never know for sure. But I do know that John Bates is more than smart enough to not do anything without realizing it.

59   Not once, but twice, the court of appeals' opinion quoted Mike Elston's boast (per Esther McDonald in her deposition) that as to his record destruction, "at least that's one thing I did right." That was nice.

60   The court of appeals did so by explicitly extending its nascent spoliation precedent in a case named *Talavera v. Shah*, 638 F.3d 303, 311 (D.C. Cir. 2011), to make it easier for plaintiffs to make use of it for "negative spoliation inferences" wherever "future litigation was reasonably foreseeable to the party who destroyed relevant records" or where there is "a reasonably foreseeable . . . investigation" involved. So we not only made new law on the Privacy Act through the case, we advanced the developing law of spoliation as well.

61   The court of appeals had effectively acknowledged the plaintiffs' satisfaction of every other Privacy Act element required for them to prevail in the case, with the arguable exception of an "adverse effect," which is the Privacy Act's version of "causation." But in its zeal for reaching a settlement, the Department apparently lost focus on this requisite and it never arose as a possible additional issue for trial.

62   One might wonder about the Justice Department's continuing to defend the case even after President Bush's tenure gave way to that of President Barack H. Obama. The answer lies in the bureaucratic nature of litigation in the Department. Ordinarily, civil suits against the Government are defended routinely at the non-political level, where a change of presidential administrations does not call for any change in litigation posture. In *Gerlich*, the case initially was elevated up several levels, given the political nature of what was being defended.

But then, with the departure of the "Bush folks," the *Gerlich* case proceeded as if on "automatic pilot" under the supervisory authority of a Branch Director in the Civil Division. That person was Joseph R. "Jody" Hunt, who was regarded as more "political" than career, something that was borne out when he became a personal aide to Deputy Attorney General Lawrence D. "Larry" Thompson and then went on to be appointed the Assistant Attorney General for the Civil Division. As a practical matter, unless he took the initiative to change the Department's posture on the case, which he evidently did not, it would remain unchanged. He carried over from the Bush Administration to the Obama Administration and to the very end of the case.

63   This was particularly so for plaintiff Matt Faiella, whose career was most heavily derailed by what the Justice Department had done to him.

64   There was some question (read: at least in my mind) as to whether the circumstances of my representation qualified for attorney fees (which the Privacy Act allows), in that such fees ordinarily are awarded to a prevailing

party as reimbursement for a fee that is owed. As noted above, I never intended to charge any *Gerlich* plaintiff a fee, under any circumstance, nor did I petition for an award of attorney fees at any time. Rather, it was the Department of Justice that designated an award of fees and costs in the settlement that it initiated and zealously pursued so as to not have to take the case to trial.

65   Indeed, once the case was over, I issued a public statement about it that spoke of its deterrent value: "The fact that the Government was ultimately forced to pay more than a half million dollars should serve as a strong deterrent in years to come against the type of corruption that, even for the George W. Bush Administration, was especially deplorable."

66   I have to confess that until he rejoined the Justice Department for a second AG tenure, I had always liked and respected Bill Barr -- and not just because when we chatted at Paul McNulty's farewell party in December of 1992 folks nearby remarked at how much (at that stage of our lives and with similar glasses) we resembled one another. He was generally regarded as a "straight shooter" by the Department's career officials during that time and I don't recall a bad word being said against him back then, even though I do tend to recall such things.

So I tried to give some comfort to my friends and former colleagues when he came back, assuring them that he was "not nearly as bad" as they feared. Well, was I ever wrong about that, just as I was likewise wrong about Dick Cheney in whole, Jim Comey in part, and to a much lesser extent Rod J. Rosenstein, all of whom I knew professionally and thought I knew well enough to assure my family, friends, and colleagues that they would be better appointees (read: or an electee, in Cheney's case) than it was feared they would be. Indeed, one could say that I batted only one-for-five on such things, with my only "hit" being Chief Justice John G. Roberts, Jr., whom I knew best of all when we were at the Department together. While the jury is still out on him, of course, he has already proven himself to be very much the type of Supreme Court Justice (read: possessed of sterling character, brilliant pragmatism, and institutional fealty) that I predicted he would be: Conservative as all hell, but brimming with integrity, both personal and institutional.

Cheney, by the way, was my biggest miscalculation. After spending time with him in "Continuity-of-Government" activities during the late 1980s (see Chapter Twenty-Six), I had concluded that he seemed to me to be just about the most capable government official that I'd ever personally worked with. This was before he traveled over to the "dark side," however, with examples too numerous to recount. Jim Comey was someone whom I knew better, and his impeccable reputation as deputy attorney general made it easy to predict the exceptional integrity with which he would lead the FBI. So how do I explain that he so badly mishandled the Hillary Clinton email investigation (see Chapter Forty-Seven), not to mention the fact that he himself unlawfully emailed his Trump notes to his law professor friend Daniel Richman (who in turn expectedly shared some of them with *The New York Times*) in New York City? I cannot, unless Comey was blackmailed or otherwise personally threatened (read: with threats to his family) into giving Hillary such exceptionally tame treatment. And as for Rod, all I can say is that I don't think anyone who knew him expected him to become so aligned with Trump through Bill Barr, not even as a matter of mere acquiescence.

67   The history of the Trump Administration will be rife with applicable examples of this, but for present purposes the Department's shameful complicity with "the big lie" -- that the 2020 presidential election was "stolen" from Trump and until he left office (and even now thereafter) everyone should have acted accordingly -- will suffice. I remember it being said after President Nixon left office that there was much to do in order to restore the integrity of the Department, and I said (and wrote) as much myself in the wake of Attorney General Alberto Gonzales's tenure, but those dark days were nothing compared to the damage to the Department (read: its reputation, its normative structure, and its employee morale) caused by Trump. If back in the mid-1970s one

could have said that Attorney General Edward H. Levi "had his work cut out for him" in restoring the Justice Department to what it once was, then Attorney General Merrick B. Garland has an even more significant job to do in doing so now. And there ought to be no "government secrecy" about that.

CHAPTER FORTY-FOUR

1   It may be observed that scandals (see Chapter Thirty-One) certainly have a way of spurring major reform, including efforts toward greater transparency, especially if compounded by "cover-up" activity. (It is an old adage in the U.S. and elsewhere that "the cover-up usually is worse than the crime.") Such was very much the case in the United States when the "Watergate" scandals of the Nixon Administration led both to extensive pro-disclosure amendments of the Freedom of Information Act and to enactment of the Privacy Act of 1974. Similarly, it was the "SARS Crisis" in China during 2002-2004, and the widespread loss of public confidence in what government officials did and said about it, that most spurred the development of government transparency at provincial and then national levels there.

2   It sometimes is said that as scandals go, there is nothing like a good old high-level corruption one to shake an institution up, especially if it contains the added ingredient of sex. And in Paul Wolfowitz's case, there were generous portions of hubris thrown in as well, both in what he did and how he thought he could brazen it through when it came to light.

3   Such international financial institutions (often referred to as "IFIs") include the International Monetary Fund, the European Investment Bank, the Asian Development Bank, the African Development Bank, the Inter-American Development Bank, the Islamic Development Bank, the European Bank for Construction and Development, and the World Trade Organization. The first three of these have begun developing transparency regimes for their records. And there also is the European Union, which holds government openness as one of its core values and has had its own FOIA-like regime for its own records as of 2001.

4   The World Bank (or "Bank") formally consists of the International Bank for Reconstruction and Development and the International Development Association, whereas the "World Bank Group" consists of those organizations plus the subsidiary International Finance Corporation, Multilateral Investment Guarantee Agency, and International Centre for Settlement of Investment Disputes. For present purposes, it is the former that is subject to the Bank's transparency policy.

5   In 2020 alone, the Bank distributed more than 77 billion dollars through its programs worldwide (read: no small chunk of change).

6   The first Access to Information Appeals Board members, who served two-year terms, were Wajahat Habibullah, former Chief Information Commissioner of India; Olivier Schrameck, former ambassador and magistrate of the French Council of State; and myself (who at one point was asked to be acting chairman of the AIAB). The current appeals board members are Rosemary Agnew, the Scottish Public Services Ombudsman; Carole Excell, Acting Director of World Resources Institute's Environmental Democracy Practice; and Miriam McIntyre Nisbet who was my deputy at the Justice Department from 1982-1994 and was Founding Director of the Office of Government Information Services ("OGIS," which became successful) thereafter.

Miriam was the best OIP deputy director we ever had, but we lost her when I was overly generous to the Acting Archivist of the United States, Trudy Huskamp Peterson, in the spring of 1993. I had barely known Trudy as a client, though she knew me better by reputation, but at the beginning of the Clinton Administration, she found herself in the midst of a series of conflicts and controversies plaguing the National Archives, so she came to my office one day and asked for help in dealing with them. I wanted to help her and was so sympathetic to what her agency was going through that I offered her Miriam (think: "eldest male child") for a three-month inter-agency "detail" (read: at a tremendous loss to OIP) that inevitably was extended several times as Miriam did what I knew she could do over there: She soared. The culmination of this saw me sitting at the Archivist's desk, which is in the northeast corner of the building's Second Floor (you can see its atypical windows from the outside), as I drafted the terms of Miriam's transfer there, which included an SES-like position for her (read: an "SL" one that can readily lead to the SES), that we had negotiated for her. Miriam went on to obtain a full SES position at the Archives and later became the director of UNESCO's Information and Society Division in Paris and then (at my urging) Founding Director of OGIS back at the National Archives.

7   To be sure, this is not just a matter of misinterpretation or corrupted implementation as are some other items below; this excessive "deliberative process" policy is set forth firmly and unambiguously in Section 16 (at pages 6-7 & n.11) of the Access Policy itself.

8   In fact, of the more than 100 other FOIA-like regimes worldwide (see Chapter One), not a single one goes so far as to protect records *en grosse* in such a way. As the exception that proves the rule, Scotland flirted with doing so as a matter of new policy in the late 2000s, after experiencing the heavy burden of standard FOIA "processing" for several years, but then (after I gave a condemnatory speech on the subject over there through my fellowship at University College London in April of 2010) it thought better of it. Stated another way: No one familiar with the processes of "government transparency" anywhere in the world would imagine that a new transparency policy would not, at least in actual practice, provide disclosure of all non-sensitive portions of a requested record through some process of redaction.

9   Thus, after speaking first of "*information* whose disclosure could cause harm," the access policy then states that the Bank "does not provide access to *documents* that contain or refer to" such information. This inexplicable shift is unmistakable.

10   More fundamentally, the Bank's policy states at the outset (in Section 6) that "[t]he Bank allows access to any information in its possession" that is not on a list of exceptions.

11   I confess to having done so despite already having serious doubts about the integrity of the Bank's intent and activities on its new policy, and it was not long before those doubts proved out. Even apart from the substantive problems that soon came to light, there was a separate one that -- there's no other word for it -- absolutely astonished me. On the day that the two other Board members and I began receiving our introductory briefings on the Bank's operations, we were shown a video demonstrating the Bank's work combatting poverty worldwide. Then, directly after viewing that graphic depiction of poverty in its most dire form, the three of us were taken for an introductory lunch at a nearby restaurant that we were told was favored by Bank officials. (I used to live just two blocks away, but was unfamiliar with it.)

I then was appalled to see two Bank vice presidents at this lunch (including Anne-Marie) proceed to order meals for themselves that included *appetizers priced at $33 apiece*. I must say that after living and dining in Washington for nearly fifty years (inflation notwithstanding), I still have yet to encounter any other instance of a restaurant offering a $33 appetizer at lunch, let alone one ordered by World Bank officials immediately after addressing the subject of world hunger! Lord only knows what the World Bank's budget must be like (not to mention its expense auditing) in order to accommodate such a thing. (Note: In order to be on the safe side of my confidentiality agreement with the Bank as a former official, I checked with no less than the World Bank's president before revealing this here.)

12   These folks did not learn about this from me. I had executed a standard nondisclosure agreement upon becoming a member of the Bank's Access to Information Appeals Board, which prohibited me from publicly disclosing any adjudicative matters coming before the Board, and I held to that obligation. But multiple "watchdog" groups that monitor the Bank's activities attended the CGS program and were alerted to the issue accordingly. Bluntly put, Anne-Marie should have considered that -- among other things, such as that CGS videotaped all of its programs -- before she either brazenly or incompetently said what she said in public that day.

In the same vein, it became evident to all three of us Board members that Leroy actually had attempted to hide the most controversial parts of the draft Board procedures that she asked us to bless, including non-redaction, by withholding the latest draft of it from us until after business hours. And when we looked into this, we learned that this shameless effort was facilitated by her having her principal assistant (read: Lisa Lui, an attorney) flat-out lie to us about a key part of that process. That perhaps is part of the reason why she is no longer there.

13   At present, this document is no longer publicly available on the Bank's website. However, I do retain a copy of it.

14   By contrast, for example, the United States' FOIA contains a diametrically opposite provision that was added to it as a "post-Watergate" reform just to make sure that no federal agency ever attempts to "over-withhold" a record merely due to the existence of some exempt portion within it. This provision, which is known as the "reasonable segregation" language at the end of the FOIA's exemption section, commands that "[a]ny reasonably segregable portion of a record shall be provided to any person requesting such record after deletion of the portions which are exempt under this subsection."

15   Taken together, this extreme document-processing policy, atop an exceptionally broad deliberative process-protection policy, stand in stark opposition to the first of the Bank's stated five "guiding principles," i.e., that of "[m]aximizing access to information." In fact, it suggests the existence of an unwritten sixth "guiding principle" governing the Bank's FOIA-like regime: The minimization of administrative burden to the maximum extent possible.

16   Although it took some time for this to sink in, the Bank finally recognized its persistent (read: pernicious) error on redaction in an official ruling on June 11, 2014. And with Scotland having seen the error of its ways (read: a proposed "anti-redaction" policy), this leaves the world free of the notion of non-redaction (see Chapter One).

17   Thus far, the public's initial use of the Bank's transparency policy has been relatively light, at the rate of fewer than 500 properly received requests per year, leaving much room for future consideration of its effectiveness.

18   This possibility was raised during the Bank's "roll-out" conference for the new transparency regime at the CGS program referenced above. Even if it remains so flawed, the very existence of the World Bank's groundbreaking transparency regime could become influential as to other such international organizations.

CHAPTER FORTY-FIVE

1   AT&T brazenly contended that the FOIA's privacy exemptions, in this case Exemption 7(C), should be applied where necessary to protect the interests of a business, a corporation, or any other "artificial entity."

2   Indeed, had the Government not taken the Third Circuit's aberrant decision up to the Supreme Court for reversal, that would have created the second anomalous situation in which FOIA requesters (and in this case, "reverse FOIA" plaintiffs) would receive different results depending on where a case was filed. The other such

anomaly was in the case of "mug shots," where it ultimately took 20 years for an aberrant Sixth Circuit Court of Appeals decision to be resolved (see Chapter Forty-One).

3   This was not unlike what I did in getting a *certiorari* petition authorized almost 30 years earlier in the *Abramson* case when I lobbied for it directly with the Office of the Solicitor General (see Chapter Eleven).

4   Not long after retiring, I had taken to using the saying (of my own devise) that "there are few things in life more dangerous than a retired trial attorney with time on his (or her) hands." Now, this was in 2010, when I was more than 100% busy with teaching, running the Collaboration on Government Secrecy, and preparing for depositions in the *Gerlich* case (see Chapter Forty-Three), but my invented aphorism still applied. I found this to be an enormous advantage gained from my 75-plus-hour weeks between the times of 9/11 and my retirement more than five years later: If I needed to work more than that in order to get something worthwhile done, then I could do so without feeling much strain.

5   This was the Office of Information and Privacy's bailiwick, so to speak, as a major area of its responsibilities was to guide the development of FOIA case law in such a way as to facilitate the smooth, uniform administration of the Act (see Chapter Forty-One). Yes, I was carrying OIP's water here, partly for old times' sake and partly because OIP's bucket was by then known to be quite leaky.

6   Notably, this line of reasoning utilizing Exemption 6, which the Court put to such good use in its opinion, was advocated in CGS's *amicus* brief only. It had always seemed like an obvious argument to me.

7   *Citizen's United* was a case dealing with the issue of whether a nonprofit corporation has the same right to fund political campaigns as a "person." In this controversial decision (so much so that it led Justice Samuel A. Alito, Jr., to noticeably mouth the words "not true" at President Barack Obama's description of it during the State of the Union Address in January of 2010), the Supreme Court ruled 5-4 that corporations, either for-profit or nonprofit, have the same right as a "person" to financially support political campaigns.

CHAPTER FORTY-SIX

1   The term *"en banc"* is oddly enough a French (not Latin) one that refers to a circumstance involving the full complement of active judges on an appellate court, not just the three-judge panel of it that ordinarily hears a case.

2   As conceived in *Crooker*, "Low 2" was the very opposite of "High 2" in that it was not at all based on any harm resulting from disclosure; rather, it merely shielded an agency from the sheer burden of responding to requests for information so mundane that agencies ought not be bothered by them. In making this odd and somewhat forced delineation, the D.C. Circuit implemented both the House and the Senate reports from the mid-1960s, which espoused completely divergent views of what Exemption 2 was all about. So blame Congress for this one.

3   Today, this would include the full breadth of video-surveillance technology employed by law enforcement agencies, together with sophisticated facial-recognition software, through a once-secret video-analytic facial-scanning system known as "TrapWire."

4   Candidly, there was one type of document that, in one form or another, presented a particularly difficult challenge under *Crooker*. These were documents specifying or otherwise reflecting the quantitative standards used by law enforcement agencies in deciding which conduct is prosecutable and which is not. Yes, there are

standards built into criminal statutes that regulate public conduct, but as a practical matter the standards that actually matter are those used by prosecutors for possible criminal prosecution.

A good example in the 1980s and 1990s was possession of marijuana. At different times and in various jurisdictions, prosecutors would have policies of prosecuting cases in which certain amounts of marijuana were involved, but would let smaller amounts "slide." But they would not want those "tolerance levels" to become known (or too widely known) in the community for fear that many unlawful marijuana users would use that knowledge to stay "just under the line," so to speak. However, on the other hand, such exact levels can fairly be seen as "secret law," which is strongly antithetical to the Freedom of Information Act's spirit, even if not the letter of the law.

In my view, "secret law" is the stepchild of authoritarian regimes, not democracies, and certainly not liberal democracies that take pride in government openness. So, as a matter of policy (even in Republican administrations), I admonished federal law enforcement agencies not to get carried away in applying *Crooker's* "High 2" protection whenever an issue about "secret law" arose. Over the years, OIP applied an informal "balance" in such cases, which stood as a singular exception to *Crooker's* expansive application. And at the same time, we also inveighed against any agency effort to create "secret law" simply by having a "draft" policy document, never finalizing it, and nevertheless using it while withholding it as "predecisional" under FOIA Exemption 5. (Yes, IRS, it's mostly you that I'm talking about here.)

5   The most vital application of this new "anti-circumvention" protection -- at least until 9/11 came along -- was its use for what in the 1980s became known as "vulnerability assessments," most often prepared for agency computer systems pursuant to the Computer Security Act of 1987. Just imagine that you are the new secretary of a cabinet department, perhaps one quite well-versed in the computer-security regimes that were used where you came from in the private sector. Not long after your arrival, you get your standard top-level "administrative matters" briefing from your department's top career officials -- where their institutional knowledge is passed on to you about such things as government procurement, government ethics, the Federal Records Act, the Antideficiency Act, the Privacy Act, and the Freedom of Information Act (yes, I'm speaking of you, Hillary Clinton, see Chapter Forty-Seven) -- and one of the questions that you ask is this: How recently has the department undertaken a top-to-bottom assessment of its databases' vulnerabilities to computer hacking? Crickets.

So as that meeting ends, you order that such an assessment be done right away. Then imagine that your department's top computer-security people soon come to you in a follow-up meeting to report both good news and bad news on that: They found three types of weaknesses, the first of which was so minimal that it already has been fixed. That's the good news. Second, they discovered a type of weakness that could not be fixed immediately, but now that they have a handle on it, it should be fixed within a few weeks. In Washington, this also counts as good news. But the bad news is that a third category of computer vulnerability discovered in your department's system(s) is so severe and so resistant to ready repair that not only cannot it be fixed within the near future, it will require a supplemental congressional appropriation of additional funds to support such a major undertaking and therefore will continue to exist as a hacking vulnerability for quite some time to come.

Next, imagine that, after you regain your composure, you learn that your people have of course created a highly detailed "vulnerability assessment" document that lays all of this out, which is something that institutions do tend to do. Then imagine that your department's FOIA office soon thereafter receives, either in a targeted effort or not (it really makes no difference), a FOIA request that encompasses that very document. How does your department protect that document from public disclosure and from its potential use against it by sophisticated computer hackers? At OIP, we regarded such a document as a "quintessential High 2" record.

6   This included, most notably, "High 2's" very prominent use in the wake of 9/11. As a big part of OIP's immediate post-9/11 policy-development activities, we urged all federal agencies to consider using *Crooker's*

"anti-circumvention" coverage in looking at their FOIA-requested records through what we called "a new, post-9/11 lens." While we took pains to emphasize that agencies ought not "get carried away" with this (human nature, after all, being what it is), this became a major part of homeland security-related policy under the Act over the course of the next decade.

7   Most specifically, these maps were so sophisticated that they showed the radial distances that potential blasts would travel. They were exactly the types of maps that a terrorist would want to view while planning a "weaponizing" (read: one using a "weapon of mass destruction" available on site, rather than having to be brought in) attack. (Remember, as has been said before, this was still within the first decade post-9/11, when the possibility (read: likelihood, to some) of such attacks was still foremost on many minds).

8   It is perhaps easy by now to forget (or for younger generations, to never learn) that there was much such fear in the wake of 9/11, even a decade later. The FOIA request at issue here was filed barely two years after 9/11, in 2003, when the conventional wisdom within the Federal Government was that it really was only a matter of time (i.e., "when, not if") before at least some semblance of such a horrific thing would happen again. The fact that this really has not recurred, to date, does not detract from the rationality of what was then the "tenor of the times."

9   Such was the strength of the *Crooker* line of authority that we had established -- even the *Milner* facts passed muster under it in those two courts.

10   When I retired in 2007, one of the things that I left behind on a "wish list" of prospective FOIA amendments – remember, I had been working on FOIA amendments for nearly 28 years by then -- was the codification of "High 2." The FOIA had been amended on several 10-year cycles by then -- roughly ten years after its 1966 enactment (though two years early, due to "Watergate") in 1974; at the 20-year mark in 1986; after another ten years in 1996, to be followed by a series of amendments made later in 2007 (one year delayed, due to the issuance of the only FOIA executive order in mid-2006) -- and if this decades-long pattern held, the next set of amendments were due soon.

I never learned quite why "High 2" enshrinement was not achieved through the 2007 FOIA Amendments -- I was no longer in the Department by then, teaching law at American University -- but from what I was able to gather, it was the result of incompetent oversight. Had that been achieved in 2007, of course, the *Milner* case would not have been a problem -- hell, at the Supreme Court level it would not even have *existed* after Congress had acted -- and "High 2" protection would most likely still exist today.

11   The Court's word for this actually was "disconnected." Given our history of bold-faced "High 2" expansion under *Crooker*, this was generous.

12   My older daughter Emily, who was handling cybersecurity for Google at the time, was (perhaps naïvely) astounded to learn that the Supreme Court's *Milner* decision had left the Federal Government's "cyber" vulnerability assessments themselves vulnerable to FOIA disclosure. To be sure, many such documents can properly be classified, in whole or in part, on national security grounds. But many cannot. This concern alone should have animated remedial government action as soon as *Milner* was handed down. But it did not.

13   Just a few examples of this can suffice: Vulnerability assessments of all kinds, of course; guidelines for undercover agents; security techniques; audit criteria and guidelines; military rules of engagement; information detailing prison security measures; records pertaining to aviation watch lists and other watch lists; information pertaining to border security; homeland-security and critical infrastructure information; and guidelines for

protecting government officials; and even the numbers of cargo containers regularly inspected by customs agents at a particular port of entry.

14   This has not, however, prevented me from formulating the following language for any proposed amendment of Exemption 2 today: "matters . . . (2) of predominantly internal governmental significance the disclosure of which (A) would undermine the personnel rules and practices of an agency, (B) would expose the cybersecurity or computer security vulnerabilities of an agency, or (C) would risk harm to a government facility, system, or other national asset that is of critical importance to homeland security." One can only hope.

15   Yes, this was another major instance in which we very deliberately moved to "shape" the law. Another one, of course, was with the extremely broad application of Exemption 2, which worked for nearly three decades before the Supreme Court's *Milner* decision ended that. A third exemption-based one was with the threshold requirement of Exemption 7, where we enjoyed support from both Congress and the Supreme Court in broadening it (see Chapter Eleven).

16   This was sadly reminiscent of what the Civil Division had done about a decade earlier when the D.C. Circuit issued an *en banc* decision in a case called *Critical Mass Energy Project v. NRC*, which involved a subtle interpretation of the word "confidential" in FOIA Exemption 4. The key part of that court's ruling was its division of commercial information submitted to the Federal Government into two mutually exclusive categories: information that was required to be submitted and information that was submitted "voluntarily," with the latter receiving broader protection from disclosure than the former.

But as to the question of "voluntariness," the Civil Division (left to its own devices for a while) all too readily bought into the self-serving position espoused by government contractors that everything submitted by them was in the highly protected "voluntary" category, simply (or, better stated, simplistically) because a contractor's decision to bid on a contract to begin with was itself a "voluntary" one -- so . . . ipso dipso (as we sometimes would say), the entirety of any contract bid would, now under *Critical Mass*, they said, be entitled to full, categorical protection.

Well, this analysis simply did not stand up to reason, once we pointed out its flaw -- i.e., that a careful reading of the court's majority opinion made it crystal clear that it was focused on the "voluntariness" of the information submission not of any underlying process *participation* -- and the Civil Division actually had to withdraw positions that it had hastily taken in two pending cases. It was an embarrassment for the Department, surely not the Civil Division's finest hour, and OIP had to act immediately with the issuance of a detailed analysis of the *Critical Mass* decision and practical guidance for its governmentwide implementation. (This was followed up years later with respect to the Supreme Court's Exemption 4 decision in *Food Marketing Institute. v. Argus Leader Media*, 139 S. Ct. 2356 (U.S. June 24, 2019) (No. 18-481)). And as much as I truly hated criticizing the part of the Department in which I had "cut my teeth," so to speak, as a new Trial Attorney years earlier, there was just no way, as to either *Critical Mass* or *Klamath*, that this could be otherwise.

17   In other words, in all due immodesty, I was saying that some of the Department's best "FOIA minds" had been misreading this Supreme Court opinion in my absence.

18   Such was the situation in the *Klamath* case, in that the Tribes were of necessity competing with all other water users in what was, in effect, a "zero sum game." In other words, because there was "only so much water to go around," the Tribes' "consulting" with the Interior Department, which was actually advocacy of their interest at its unvarnished bottom, was indeed undertaken "at the expense of others." In time, even agencies such as the Office of the U.S Trade Representative, for example, began to recognize the fact that what it freely

called "multilateral" trade environments ran afoul of the Supreme Court's *Klamath* standard, when properly understood and applied, while "unilateral" ones did not.

CHAPTER FORTY-SEVEN

1   The location of this press conference seemed to be largely happenstantial in that Secretary Clinton was attending a women's rights conference at the U.N. Headquarters that day and (apart from an eight-word "tweet") had not herself responded to the allegations of the *The New York Times* article in the full week since it had appeared. The fact that it was held there, though, allowed Clinton to control the event's setting, including its ending point, through friendly U.N. staff.

2   To those who might think or say that "mere semantics" are too slender a thing to form the basis of a conclusion in a matter such as this, I say that such a view is about as wrong as wrong can be. Words matter, even when thrown around loosely in public discourse nowadays. And they matter especially to attorneys, who are trained to recognize that a legal obligation can easily depend upon the use and meaning of a single one of them. In fact, the law books of decided cases are replete with instances in which this is so and Secretary Clinton, being quite "learned in the law," well knows this.

Moreover, as a litigator by profession (which means that she used words particularly carefully both in court and in writing litigation briefs), she also knows that many words and phrases, in many contexts, can effectively convey a meaning that is "shaded" at best and downright misleading or even deceptive at worst. (Successful politicians, by the way, are also adept at this. What we have in Hillary Clinton, though her 15 years as a corporate litigator are rarely recalled, is a professional litigator turned politician who is doubly so.)

In other words, sometimes employing a word or phrase will leave the reader with an impression that is not entirely accurate, or perhaps not accurate at all. Attorneys do this all the time, particularly skilled ones and especially those who craft litigation briefs, in order that they might maximize their clients' interests within the rough bounds of "truthfulness." And those who are sufficiently experienced at doing this (read: borderline linguistic chicanery) can readily recognize when it is being done by someone else; it almost instantly "jumps out" at you. You might say that it's a variation of the old saw "It takes one to know one."

Well, I am here to tell you that Hillary Clinton is a master at this, born of many years of both legal and high-level political experience, as well as from having a keen native intelligence for such things. (Or, as the saying goes, she proved herself to be too smart by half.) So this has to be borne in mind in considering her exact words, when formulated and uttered in defense of her actions and inactions in a highly charged, high-stakes controversy such as this.

3   At the Department of Justice, for example, this takes place every time there is a new attorney general (except, perhaps, when a deputy attorney general succeeds to the position, as Attorney General William P. Barr did in November of 1991). And I can attest firsthand that such basic briefings do routinely include the requirements of the FOIA, the Privacy Act, and the Federal Records Act.

4   This is something that I happen to know firsthand, by the way, from my handling of White House-related FOIA matters -- including one in particular for which I met with Associate White House Counsel Cheryl D. Mills (later Clinton's chief of staff at the State Department) there, who served as an intermediary for the First Lady on a FOIA matter in which she herself was involved.

5   In fact, there was an iconic photograph of Clinton using her BlackBerry while wearing sunglasses on a military plane in 2011 that prompted a recordkeeping official in her office to inquire about whether she had been

assigned a "State.gov" email address. (Evidently, she continued to use her BlackBerry even after April of 2009.) Yet even that occurrence did not lead to her obtaining and using such an official account.

6   Apparently, when Clinton first took office, she requested a government BlackBerry similar to the one that the National Security Agency had just put together for President Obama. When that request was rejected, she kept using her own BlackBerry, which she frequently lost or misplaced, according to the FBI. And then, the story goes, she began buying replacement BlackBerrys on eBay (believe it or not) because she liked older models that BlackBerry (through its licensees) had long retired. (Yes, this was an enormous security vulnerability.) Notably, neither Clinton nor her lawyers were able to provide her old BlackBerrys to federal investigators. It is unclear what happened to them, although one aide to Bill Clinton, Justin Cooper, reportedly told investigators that he smashed at least two of those devices with a hammer when they were being replaced.

7   It is unclear whether Clinton might have still been using a Senate-hosted email account and server when she first began working at State. If so, it makes no difference to the analysis, because it is entirely clear that at some early point in her State Department tenure, she began using (read: exclusively) both her personal email account and her personal server. However, it does appear that the first seven weeks of her State Department email activity were completely "lost," without any attempt at restoration, due to her unorthodox email handling. This paled alongside of her other email "sins," however.

8   This server was located in Secretary Clinton's Chappaqua home from January of 2009 (or even earlier, if used by her husband in his capacity as a former president) until June of 2013, when it was handed over to a small Colorado-based company with no government security clearances named Platte River Networks, which took over administering it and moved it to Secaucus, New Jersey; it is not clear why. However, it is clear that for the first two months of its relevant use -- January of 2009 through March 29, 2009 -- it was not secured with a "TLS certificate," which meant that all information transmitted through use of it was unencrypted and was vulnerable to both interception and subsequent hacking. By the time the server was the focus of any official attention, it had been moved to the control of a company known as Datto, Inc., which provided "data backup service" for Clinton's emails and subsequently gave the FBI the associated hardware for investigation.

9   Part and parcel of this set-up was the fact that Clinton's email communications were not accessible by anyone else even "in the cloud," as some might put it. Beyond the fact that her emails were routinely insulated from the State Department to begin with, she notably did not use a conventional Internet service provider -- such as Google's "Gmail" -- to store and manage her database of these emails. Had she done so, as so many others have, her emails would have been no more subject to State Department access (and by extension to potential public access through commonly made FOIA requests), but they certainly would have been subject to any third-party subpoena issued for them, most particularly by Congress.

10   As so often is the case with such things, it sometimes takes a tragedy of some sort to bring an ongoing government deficiency unavoidably to the fore. Such was the case here when the death of U.S. diplomats at our Embassy in Benghazi, Libya, cast light on Clinton's whereabouts at particular times.

11   Oddly enough, this seminal New York Times article placed primary emphasis on Clinton's use of her private server rather than on her more fundamental threshold use of a personal email account in lieu of an official one. Perhaps the server's basement location made for a more sensational story; perhaps the server, as a clunky piece of computer equipment, was seen as an interesting novelty; or perhaps The New York Times, proficient as it is, simply did not appreciate the significance of a government official's use of a personal email account. Whatever

the reason, this article failed to focus on Clinton's threshold mistake of proceeding to use her personal email account in lieu of a standard official one (not to mention the State Department's special official one for currently or potentially classified information).

12   This analysis of Secretary Clinton's March 10 statements formed the foundation of the article published in *POLITICO Magazine* titled "Hillary's Email Defense Is Laughable," with the subtitle of "I Should Know -- I Ran FOIA for the U.S. Government," on March 16, 2015 (read: on annual "Freedom of Information Day," just six days after Clinton's press conference), which in turn became a foundation for media coverage of the subject thereafter. It most easily can be found simply by Googling "Hillary" together with the word "laughable."

13   This statement, right off the bat, gave a grossly false impression, through these two key words that were used and a third one that was missing. Clinton's use of "opted" strongly implied that she actually had a choice under the Federal Records Act; she did not. And her accompanying use of the word "allowed" likewise suggested that what she did was permissible as a matter of law. It was not. It obviously was "allowed by the State Department" in the sense that it did proceed to happen; no one physically prevented her from doing it by tackling her in the hallway or some such thing. But that does not mean that it was *properly* allowed, which is what she repeatedly implied.

The missing word, of course, is "exclusively." Officials were not absolutely barred from *ever* using their personal email accounts. But again, that is a far cry from what she falsely implied -- that the law and regulations at any time allowed the use of a personal email account *exclusively*. She never should have been using a personal email account exclusively for her email correspondence, in lieu of an official email account, in the first place. That is the key ingredient that made her email setup contrary to policy, practice, and law. And that, in turn, is what made her press conference defense so transparently shameful.

14   It is noteworthy that this "opted" dynamic did immediately work for her in that right away it was readily accepted by her first questioner in the press conference's Q&A part.

15   This is true of previous secretaries of state as well. Clinton became enamored of pointing to Secretary of State Colin L. Powell as a "precedent," yet he did not use a personal email account exclusively, as she had (see below), far from it. (With the passage of time, though, she would be able to point to a "sequel" to her misconduct in the form of White House Chief of Staff Mark R. Meadows, who in December of 2021 was discovered to have used "a personal cellphone, a Signal [i.e., encrypted] account and two personal Gmail accounts for government business."

16   At the press conference, she very defensively said: "And when I got there, I wanted to just use one device for both personal and work emails, instead of two. It was *allowed*. And as I said, it was for *convenience*. And it was my practice to communicate with State Department and other government officials on their .gov accounts so *those* emails would be automatically saved in the State Department system to meet recordkeeping requirements, and that, indeed, is what happened."

Again, she used "allowed" here, without further explication, and added the element of "convenience" to the "simplicity" cited earlier. Tellingly, she did not say that this all was *only* a matter of convenience, as other people might, which leaves the question of whether any other motivation might have been at play. In that regard, she did admit to having an awareness of "recordkeeping requirements," just not necessarily a complete one. Further, in speaking of "those emails," she ignored the fact that a FOIA request for "her emails" would not in fact capture them, her implication to the contrary notwithstanding.

17   Far from "gumption" (the colloquial version of which could be any of several words, such as "stones"), the term that is most apt in this case, from beginning to end, is "cast a blind eye." In short, there were career State Department officials who knew full well exactly what Clinton (and the Department) were required by law to do in this case, and they certainly knew what she *was* doing (i.e., it should have been obvious on the face of every email message that she sent), yet this was by everyone's uniform account of the matter utterly ignored.

18   Of course that personal phone device is to be used for personal communications, to which the Federal Records Act by definition does not apply. Indeed, that is what it's there for. This presumes, of course, that the official does not "cross the line" between "personal" and "official" communications in any instance -- at least for email communications (i.e., records), putting aside any "metadata" record of an ephemeral telephone conversation.

19   Using this private server meant that unlike the multitudes who use a Gmail account, for instance, Secretary Clinton was able to keep her communications entirely "in house," even more deeply within her personal control. No "cloud" for posterity, or chance of Google receiving a congressional subpoena, not for her. No potentially pesky "metadata" surrounding her communications or detailed server logs to complicate things. And absolutely no practical constraint on her ability to dispose of any official email of "hers," for any reason, at any time, entirely on her own. Bluntly put, when this unique (read: truly "one of a kind") records regime was established, somebody was asleep at the switch, at either the State Department or the National Archives and Records Administration (which oversees compliance with the Federal Records Act) or both.

20   This is something that, with the passage of time, has all too often become mistakenly conflated with Clinton's personal email account, as if her private server, not her personal account, was the primary problem involved. It was not. The personal email account, in lieu of an official one, was very much the primary problem; her use of a private server atop that, especially one insulated from any Internet service provider "host," then *compounded* that problem -- with the tandem effect being total secrecy entirely within her sole control. Nevertheless, most recently (read: in connection with former President Donald J. Trump's emerging "Mar-a-Lago records" scandal), what seems to be most remembered for purposes of comparison is only her malfeasance in using a private server, which of course is an element not present in Trump's case.

21   In a case such as this, the speaker says "contains," which can easily be true, but the listener (or reader) tends to take that as meaning "consists of" (read: "consists *entirely* of"), which in this case certainly is not true. Sadly, some lawyers do this type of thing all the time, telling themselves that they are safely within the bounds of truthfulness while achieving a false impression that maximizes their clients' interests. Hillary Clinton is nothing if not highly adept at protecting such interests, especially when those interests are her own.

22   Clinton also applied a close variant of this approach to the matter of her non-preservation of emails: "At the end, I chose not to keep my private personal emails -- emails about planning Chelsea's wedding or my mother's funeral arrangements, condolence notes to friends as well as yoga routines, family vacations, the other things you typically find in inboxes." Did this imply that what she disposed of was only what she so specified? Yes. Does it mean that there might have been other, unspecified "private personal emails" likewise disposed of? Yes, it meant that, too.

        Furthermore, Clinton went on to bolster this dodge with the self-serving observation that "[n]o one wants their personal emails made public, and I think most people understand that and respect that privacy." Now, who could disagree with that, at least in general? Just note that it proceeds from (and in effect self-validates) her premise that what she destroyed unquestionably consisted of truly personal content in its entirety. Unfortunately (though perhaps not for Hillary Clinton), because of the records scheme that she managed to establish for herself, no one will ever know that for sure, leaving it to be rightly doubted.

23   And speaking of her words being "dispositive," Clinton at the same time deftly staked out her position that "the server will remain private." Faulty as this brazen claim was, such smooth aggressiveness is a hallmark of an adept attorney as well.

24   At this early stage, with Clinton barely even mentioning her private server, there was very little focus on how secure the information housed on it was, especially in the face of expected intrusions by America's foreign adversaries. (At that time, any thought of political hacking of it, whether in conjunction with WikiLeaks or not, was still many months away.) But for purposes of the magazine article, I consulted with my family computer-security expert, my computer engineer daughter who had handled cybersecurity at Google for several years by that time; she took one look at the purported security configurations of that "home-brewed" set-up and found them to be so irresponsibly vulnerable that she could scarcely believe they were real.

25   It is entirely plausible that this server equipment was placed in the basement of the Clintons' Chappaqua, New York, home originally for President Clinton's use as a former president. So no one has ever suggested that Hillary Clinton went out and purchased a server for the purpose of keeping her official email messages entirely within her control. Evidently, she did not have to do so, because one already stood (or was already "stood up," in computer tech parlance) in her basement. But this matters not one whit to the impropriety of what she did.

26   During the Q&A session, Clinton continued to rely on this "husband" point as well as on the "security" one, tying them together to achieve a deflection about the server's physical (and any other unstated) security: "Well, the system we used was set up for President Clinton's office. And it had numerous safeguards. It was on property guarded by the Secret Service. And there were no security breaches." In sum, it was the very existence and use of her server for official State Department activity that mattered as of the time of her press conference, not its full contents, nor its Secret Service-guarded security.

27   Clinton even used this formulation in yet another, self-aggrandizing way: "[A]fter I left office, [I] provided all my emails that could possibly be work-related . . . even though I knew that the State Department already had the vast majority of them."

28   It should not be overlooked that this claim in and of itself is a conflated overstatement. Clinton's category of "government" correspondents actually consists of two subcategories, those in the State Department and those in other federal (or even foreign) agencies: "[It] was my practice to email government officials on their [S]tate or other .gov accounts so that the emails were immediately captured and preserved." It is a huge question as to whether all of her communications with State Department persons actually were "captured and preserved," but there is little doubt about the fate of all of her "government" communications elsewhere.

Moreover, even if such an email to or from a non-State Department government employee *were* actually captured and preserved -- one sent or received by a Department of Defense official, for instance -- there is just no way, as a practical matter, that it would be reachable through any FOIA request (or any congressional access request, for that matter) for her records (or for a certain type of them) that was subsequently made to the Department of State. Anyone with more than a passing familiarity with how the FOIA works, a subcategory that certainly included Clinton by then, would know full well that this was so -- and agencies would be able to take advantage of it, by virtue of her "personal account" system, while feigning innocent ignorance of this consequence even if forced to acknowledge its existence. (As of the time of her press conference, of course,

Clinton was still at the "attempt to elide the existence" stage of her defense on this.)

29   Having strained for credit based upon her "vast majority" formulation, Clinton spoke as if she selflessly opted not to exclude what even she herself could not be certain had been "captured" by the State Department's record system through others. As it turned out, the State Department subsequently announced that no such automatic capturing had in fact ever occurred.

30   It should be remembered that we are not talking about communications that are frivolous or in any way disregardable here. Rather, by virtue of Clinton's own words, we are talking about her "work emails," which is about the only thing that we truly know about them. That is hardly a characteristic that lends itself to ignoring these "minority" emails as negligible, is it?

31   This must be fewer than 50% of them, one must fairly assume, else they would not be apart from a "majority." No "email critic" of Clinton (relatively few as they are) has suggested that she might have been lying about this being a majority of her emails. It is a fact, however, that how she set this all up means that we have to take her word for it. Even that is contrary to the thrust of the FRA.

32   Here's one way of looking at it: Had I myself written this statement for her, being worried about neither truthfulness nor my mortal soul, I would have been proud of its craftsmanship.

33   And it also could have meant (as is discussed below), her complete failure to use a special "fire-walled" computer system that is maintained by the State Department for the transmission (or receipt) of classified information -- or of any information that is of such sensitivity on its face that it might be *classifiable* and therefore warrants expert classification review.

34   And the word "all" here truly does mean all, because Clinton had no other means of electronic (or telephonic) communication. Remember: She preferred to use, and usually did use, only one such device, not two.

35   Speaking of something that she said was *unprecedented*, Clinton claimed that she "took the unprecedented step of asking that the State Department make all [her] work-related emails public for everyone to see." This disingenuously resorted to undeserved credit-claiming. The fact that her "step" was "unprecedented" flowed only from the fact that her entire recordkeeping scheme *was itself unprecedented* (to say the least) to begin with.

Further, this claim deceptively implied that the State Department's next step would be to disclose the entirety of what she recently sent to it. Indeed, the word "all" here is transparently designed to make one think that no part of this record trove would be withheld from the public, on the basis of one FOIA exemption or another -- which is inconceivable. Indeed, if none of her work-related email communications contained any highly sensitive information, then she would be guilty of substantive dereliction of duty, which no one thinks is so.

36   As it happened, the State Department claimed that it did not as an institution learn of Clinton's unofficial email set-up until long after she had departed the agency. Under the circumstances, it is difficult to accept this as true.

37   That very number, which just rolled off her tongue, is itself astonishing. As a practical matter nowadays, almost all federal employees send and/or receive personal email during the work day. But that many? I supervised a staff of several dozen federal employees for more than 25 years, including "email-heavy" years into the 2000s, and if I had learned that one of them had been engaged in as many as 30 personal email communications per work day, day after day, I would have wondered how she was performing her job.

38   Years ago, I consulted on this case in which a presidential appointee -- who shall remain nameless though not blameless -- after becoming caught up in an especially controversial matter, intransigently declared that all of the records on a credenza behind his desk were "personal" and thus were beyond the reach of the FOIA (and that of the agency FOIA officer, whom he physically prevented from going back there). This official was severely rebuked by a federal judge after it was found that he was, in no small part, quite mistaken about both things; the judge's opinion was so pointed that we used the case regularly in our FOIA training programs.

39   To be sure, it is not at all uncommon for the average federal employee on a day-to-day basis to bear the initial responsibility of "separating the wheat from the chaff" under the Federal Records Act, as well as when that employee departs from federal service. Even relatively high-level employees such as myself (as an ES-5 in the Senior Executive Service) often are able, as a practical matter, to determine such things, just as I did when I retired from the Justice Department more than 15 years ago. But I certainly could not have taken with me the sole copy of any agency-generated document, nor could I have properly stymied any pending FOIA request -- not even for a record in my office that I was convinced was 100 percent "personal."

40   For example, at the Justice Department we had a very formal process to govern things that departing officials sought to "remove" (see Chapter Thirty-Three). In accordance with the FRA, no federal agency, much less a cabinet department, should have operated without such a process, especially for a politically charged cabinet head.

41   This means that Hillary Clinton was guilty of deceiving the public (with a malign intent inferred) -- even before any inspector general inquiry or FBI investigation began looking into her wrongdoing -- and all it takes is a close, knowledgeable analysis of her actual words to convict her of that. That itself is not a crime, of course, except on the campaign trail. And the very fact that she "doubled down" on this issue with those words speaks volumes, in more ways than one.

42   I cannot tell you how many times during the eight years of the Clinton Administration I heard someone say, "The cover-up is worse than the crime." For those of us who knew what most of the alleged information "cover-ups" actually were, even if not always the full extent of each "crime," I can tell you that this often was very true, even if not always so (see Chapter Thirty-One). In fact, the exact phrasing of the public explanations given, with their sly connotations versus evident denotations, can make all the difference.

43   Beyond what Secretary Clinton actually dared to say at her press conference were some things that largely went unaddressed, including the official sensitivity of her emails and specifically whether any part of them might have warranted classification on national security grounds or even special handling as "Sensitive But Unclassified" information (see Chapter Thirty-Eight). The former category, as it turned out, provided a basis for potential criminal liability even though the latter did not.

44   Some people have wondered whether Hillary Clinton actually realized the risk that she was running -- to both her credibility as a candidate and her integrity as an attorney -- in taking such a deceptive approach. Judging by her past practices together with her husband during the Clinton Administration, perhaps she didn't. In other words, she might not have looked beyond the "fix" that she was so badly straining for. And as someone not exactly known for critical self-analysis, she might have convinced herself all along, from her initial BlackBerry usage to the end of her State Department tenure, that what she was doing and not doing with her emails was "good enough" and should simply be accepted as such by one and all, based upon her word or words alone. One thing, though, seems entirely clear: She apparently thought that she had put this dangerous matter to rest,

for the remainder of her nascent (soon to be burgeoning) presidential campaign, by holding a "once and for all" press conference as she did. Time surely proved her wrong about that, too.

45   This is a distinction worth pointing out early on. Almost everything that I wrote and said about Hillary's email wrongdoing by this point had to do with the words she spoke, their implications regarding her clear violations of the Federal Records Act, and her blatant circumvention of the Freedom of Information Act -- in other words, her trampling over civil laws. Even when participating in a webcast program (billed as a "special educational panel discussion") held by longtime institutional Clinton foe Judicial Watch on March 31, 2015, with former U.S. Attorney Joe diGenova vibrating alongside me at the very thought of her being criminally prosecuted, I still refrained from saying anything about her potential criminal liability without knowing more. It was not until later, when the element of classified information was added to the stew, that I began addressing the criminal side of her fact pattern, an area in which I admittedly hold only incomplete legal expertise.

46   Indeed, in the Administration of President Joseph R. Biden, Jake Sullivan currently holds the position of National Security Advisor. Evidently, his affiliation with Secretary Clinton and his involvement in her "email scandal" did not dampen his career prospects, even though Fox News certainly attempted to do so when it reported in January of 2021 that "he was a central figure in the email scandal that rocked the final days of Hillary Clinton's presidential campaign in 2016." There also is the fact that during the Obama Administration Sullivan served as the principal national security advisor to then-Vice President Biden.

47   An example of this reportedly was a Benghazi-related email chain that he sent to or through Clinton's unsecured personal server, which raised concerns both at the FBI and within the broader Intelligence Community.

48   Long after the fact, in October of 2019, the State Department concluded that 38 then-current and former Clinton staffers, including Sullivan, were "culpable" in the violation of internal security procedures regarding her official records. However, it also somehow concluded that there was "no persuasive evidence of systemic, deliberate mishandling of classified information." It is difficult if not impossible to reconcile the two.

49   As for her FRA violations, the report made clear that "Secretary Clinton should have surrendered all emails dealing with Department business before leaving government service, and because she did not do so, she did not comply with the Department's policies under the Federal Records Act."

50   Not at all taken unawares by what the IG found, I commented publicly as follows: "This report unsurprisingly finds gross violations of the Federal Records Act's requirements by then-Secretary Clinton and her personal staff, not to mention inexplicably poor oversight by State's top records-management officials as they simply let her do as she pleased. . . . Even taking a charitable view, it serves as an indictment of Ms. Clinton's conduct on the civil side of her ledger, documenting misconduct that would surely lead to dismissal were she still employed there."

51   And when that employee is a supervisor, not to mention the head of an entire agency, she is naturally obliged to ensure that those who work for her comply with the FRA's requirements as well. In this case, Secretary Clinton committed a series of further FRA violations when she permitted (or, worse yet, specifically authorized) several members of her State Department staff to make official use of her personal server, at a minimum casting a blind eye to what they did in that regard as well.

52   Accordingly, there is a procedure by which the chief records officer of any agency can raise any question with NARA's experts about how to handle a particular situation. By all accounts, the State Department never did that at any point in Hillary Clinton's case.

53   Or stated another way, she will forever be remembered as the biggest FOIA scofflaw in American history -- simply by virtue of her grossly successful evasion of it at such a high official level -- even though the competition for that honor is quite stiff. And who gets to proclaim her the winner of that "competition? I do, I daresay, as someone with more years of experience with FOIA decisionmaking, litigation, and critical analysis (i.e., more than 45 now) than anyone else. Plus, I was joined in this condemnation by my old friend former Chief District Court Judge Royce C. Lamberth, who lambasted Clinton in December of 2018 by calling her email scheme "one of the gravest modern offenses to government transparency [ever]." And also by another personal acquaintance (she and my wife worked for the same small law firm during the early 2000s), then-District Court Judge Ketanji Brown Jackson, who in July of 2017 spoke of "the facts and circumstances surrounding Secretary Clinton's extraordinary and exclusive use of her [private email account]," which she proclaimed were "indicia of bad faith."

54   Under the FRA, she was specifically required to maintain all official emails in an official system for proper review, delineation, and possible retention upon her departure. These end-of-tenure requirements are an important part of the FRA's proper implementation, all the more so for a cabinet-level official. In fact, at the Justice Department, as noted above, we created a formal process to govern anything that departing officials sought to "remove" (see Chapter Thirty-Three).

    The first official to whom this policy was applied, at her own insistence, was Attorney General Janet Reno, at the end of the Clinton Administration. This stood in stark contrast with the sad case of Attorney General Edwin Meese, who was so overreaching upon his departure that we had to scour his garage in Virginia to retrieve more than a dozen boxes of records that he wrongfully took with him in violation of the Federal Records Act, among other things. One cannot help but wonder about how Secretary Clinton's departure process was handled, if at all.

55   In this case, which is truly unprecedented, no matter what Secretary Clinton would have one believe, she managed successfully to insulate her official emails, categorically, from the FOIA, both during her tenure at State and long after her departure from it -- perhaps forever. "Nice work if you can get it," one might say, especially if your experience during your husband's presidency gives you good reason (nay, even highly compelling motivation) to relegate unto yourself such control if at all possible.

56   Similar to this, though of less concern, is the matter of what since 9/11 has been universally called "Sensitive But Unclassified" information, which pertains to the labeling and safeguarding (read: special "control") of anything that an agency chooses to give special handling on one sensitivity basis or another. As the primary author (in March of 2002) of the seminal White House/Justice Department memorandum on this particular subject (see Chapter Thirty-Eight), I am sensitive to the fact that the State Department regularly uses record designations (such as "Nodis" and "Noforn," for instance) within this realm that would readily have been deemed utterly incompatible with Secretary Clinton's "personal email account/private server" scheme had there been proper attention to it.

57   Indeed, there is no evidence that Secretary Clinton paid any attention whatsoever to the prospect of any of her email traffic being reviewed by agency classification experts for a proper determination of its possible classification. Such a review is part of the agency's official, "fire-walled" communications system, as it is employed systemically, but that was a system that she successfully evaded.

58   Despite Clinton's tepid defense on such matters, it was ultimately found that no fewer than 110 of the emails on her private server contained classified information (including eight email chains at the "Top Secret" level), not to mention the many others that contained *potentially* classified information that properly warranted expert review. (The fact that these two numbers are smaller than the counterpart numbers thus far involved in former

President Donald J. Trump's "Mar-a-Lago" scandal does not in any way absolve Clinton. And what certainly does the opposite is her utterly fantastical claims of "zero" for herself in comparison to Trump as of September 2022 (see below).)

59   Before going forward, a candid delineation is in order. I am an expert in many parts of civil law and in civil litigation procedure, but I claim no particular expertise in the field of criminal law. Accordingly, in my public speaking and writing about Hillary Clinton's email scandal, I have consistently taken pains to make this distinction clear. However, I nevertheless maintain that the following analysis of Clinton's criminal vulnerability is no less correct.

60   Ordinarily, the FBI would merely be the investigator of a suspected crime, with "Main Justice" being the prosecutor, but in this case Attorney General Loretta E. Lynch inexplicably (read: even aberrationally) announced that she would just defer to Jim Comey, so in effect he wound up playing the prosecutorial role. There is no firm evidence to support the suspicion that this highly unusual arrangement had anything to do with Attorney General Lynch's unorthodox "tarmac meeting" with Bill Clinton at that time, but that suspicion remains.

61   It was found, for instance, when forensic experts examined Hillary Clinton's personal email server and undertook a reconstruction of it, that there were "several thousand work-related emails that were not in the group of 30,000" that she had returned to the State Department. Plus, most significantly, more than 100 email messages sent through her server contained information that was classified "*at the time they were sent*," including some that were designated "Top Secret" at the highly classified "Special Access Program" level. (The investigation found 110 emails in 52 email chains containing information that was classified at the time it was sent or received; eight chains contained "Top Secret" information, the highest level of basic classification; 36 chains contained "Secret" information; and the remaining eight contained "Confidential" information.) And as for her vaunted security precautions, even Jim Comey pointedly declared that "it is possible that hostile actors gained access to Secretary Clinton's personal email account." In other words, despite what she has said, these are the established facts of the matter.

As for the "Special Access Program" information, sometimes referred to as "SAP" (or "SCI"), it exists within subject-matter "compartments" at above the "Top Secret" level. For example, when I worked in the "Continuity-of-Government Program" in the 1980s and early 1990s (see Chapter Twenty-Six), almost all information pertaining to it was treated with SAP protection, which included our being "read in" and "read out" of aspects of it.

62   This applies, I can say firsthand, both when a national security clearance is first granted and when someone is "read into" a new SCI ("Special Compartmented Information") compartment. Anyone who has ever received a national security clearance (during at least the past 60-70 years) knows this.

63   Inexplicably, Director Comey framed the issue as whether there was "clear evidence that Secretary Clinton or her colleagues *intended* to violate laws governing the handling of classified information." However, as noted above, "intent," which is the high standard applicable to other statutes, was not the very standard (read: it was unintentional "gross negligence") that was properly applicable in this case.

64   According to a Majority Staff Report of the Senate Committee on Homeland Security and Governmental Affairs titled "The Clinton Email Scandal and the FBI's Investigation of It" (Feb. 7, 2018), Director Comey "repeatedly referred to [Clinton's] behavior as 'grossly negligent' in his original drafts of his public statement [but t]hat phrase was subsequently edited to [be] 'extremely careless,'" making all the difference in the world under section 793(f). This factual assertion, while authoritative, might or might not be true.

65   Actually, the height of her *faux* unsophistication came when she was asked about the emails that had disappeared from her server *en masse*: "Wiped?" she exclaimed. "What, like with a cloth or something?"

66   On this latter point, many criminal defendants prosecuted for such crimes -- such as former CIA Director John M. Deutch; Retired U.S. Army General and former CIA Director David Petraeus; former CIA officer Jerry Chun Shing Lee (also known as Zhen Cheng Li); former CIA contractor Reynaldo Regis; former U.S. National Security Adviser Sandy Berger; FBI Special Agent James Jay Smith; Kendra Kingsbury, an employee at the FBI's Kansas City Field Office; Retired Lieutenant Colonel Benjamin Pierce Bishop; Army Major Jason Brezler; Marine Corps Sergeant Ricki Roller; Air Force Staff Sergeants Arthur Gonzales and Arthur Gaffney; Air Force Senior Airman [sic] Reality Leigh Winner; Navy code technician Scott J. Chattin, former Navy radio operator Henry Spade, Navy Chief Petty Officer James McGuiness, Naval Reservist Bryan Nishimura, and U.S. Navy reservist Bryan Nishimura; former defense contractor and sailor Weldon Marshall; U.S. Defense Department employee Asia Janay Lavarello; former NSA analysts David W. Griffith and his wife; former National Security Agency senior executive Thomas A. Drake (not to be confused with former Justice Department attorney and whistleblower Thomas Tamm, who as noted elsewhere asked me to represent him); former NSA employee Elizabeth Jo Shirley; and former NSA contractor Harold Martin -- doubtless would take issue with him.

67   I knew Jim Comey well enough when he was the deputy attorney general to believe that he would handle the Clinton matter much differently than he ultimately did. But I was very wrong (read: very, *very* wrong) about that. First and foremost, I do not understand how he so anomalously came to play the roles of both investigator and prosecutor in the case. I cannot explain why he was so indulgent of Hillary Clinton, as if she truly deserved such special treatment. And even as a non-practitioner of criminal law, I cannot fathom how her conduct was not seen as even worse than "grossly negligent," let alone at least that, in light of all of the circumstances involved. As I used to tell my students, "some things in your professional life will be inexplicable, and they might sadden you."

68   Kennedy, who unquestionably knew better, could do no better than offer the following lame excuse: "I was told she had a personal BlackBerry for keeping in touch with her family. . . . It did not strike me as abnormal to get emails from the secretary of state on evenings or the weekend from her personal BlackBerry. . . . I had no reason to know that these were not being recorded somewhere." The fact that it was *his job* to know such things, at least at the cabinet level, apparently never weighed him down. This itself was indefensibly damning.

69   It was conclusively determined by investigators that Clinton did indeed have some email communication with the White House, including with President Obama in particular, and that it should have been apparent on the face of those emails that they did not originate from an official State Department account. This led to nothing, however, except for White House embarrassment when it was discovered and made public. According to *POLITICO* in September of 2016: "It's been known since last year that Obama and Clinton corresponded occasionally via her private account, but the White House has insisted [that] Obama did not know [that] she relied on it routinely and exclusively for official business." In the true sense of the word, that's incredible. In the words of President Obama's press secretary at the time, "he was not aware of . . . how Secretary Clinton and her team were planning to comply with the Federal Records Act." Now *that* certainly was true.

70   I knew this full well, having met with Cheryl Mills at the White House, one-on-one, on a FOIA issue that involved Hillary Clinton. I recall that Mills' "take-away" from that meeting was to go back to Clinton to give her my advice and to get answers to more FOIA-related questions.

71   Given Clinton's oft-repeated claim that what she did was "approved" or "permitted" or "authorized" by someone, congressional investigators ultimately wanted to learn if Kennedy "approved Clinton's plan to use private email and why he did not step in to stop it," according to *POLITICO*'s Josh Gerstein. Despite that logical investigative focus, no one at the State Department ever stood up to take responsibility for that.

72   In other words, the fact that she and former President Clinton maintained a so-called "home brew" server in the basement of their Chappaqua home would have been wholly irrelevant to any official matter.

73   Indeed, this would have afforded her the benefit of insulating her purely personal emails from the realm of a commercial email service provider, and thus from the potential grasp of any congressional subpoena, just the same. Put another way, she need not have intermingled her official and personal communications in order to achieve this. Any truly knowledgeable "computer person," let alone a FOIA expert, could have told her so. That makes this sorry tale a tragedy as well.

74   And she therefore would not have had to engage in what became a highly controversial process of delineating her official emails from her purely personal emails at State Department request during the summer and fall of 2014. There would have been no question about how she performed such a delineation and eradication in 2015, about how she somehow managed to have more "personal" emails than "official" ones during her entire tenure despite being one of the busiest officials in government (a potent question in and of itself), or about why she chose to "return" her official emails in paper rather than readily searchable electronic form. None of that would have occurred.

75   She also would have been spared the harsh indignity of officially being told that, no, what she did actually was *not* allowed as she so intransigently kept insisting, nor would it ever have been had she ever bothered to ask.

76   In fact, as "get out of jail" cards go, what she received from Jim Comey was far from ideal, as it was heavily amalgamated with some (albeit non-actionable) culpability. And it also provided the foundation for the damage that she suffered several months later through the Bureau's handling of the email messages that it coincidentally found on the laptop of former congressman Anthony D. Weiner, the husband of her closest aide Huma M. Abedin. There can be no doubt but that Abedin suffered greatly through this entire scandal, probably acutely so, but this does not relieve her of the culpability that she willingly absorbed as Clinton's closest State Department aide.

77   A primary example of this was an hour-long appearance on C-SPAN's "Washington Journal" in March of 2015, which can be located simply by Googling "Metcalfe" and "C-SPAN" together.

78   I was asked to write a series of columns about Hillary Clinton's "email travails" by media entrepreneur Dan Abrams, who featured them in his *LawNewz* online publication. Each one engendered a range of comments, mostly about the foolhardiness of what she had done.

79   The closest that Clinton ever came, as near as I can tell, is in an interview on September 8, 2015 in which she first intransigently reiterated her persistent defense and then went a bit farther: "What I had done was allowed, it was above board. But in retrospect, certainly, as I look back at it now, *even though* it was allowed, I should've used two accounts. One for personal, one for work-related emails."

80   A counter-argument to this, though, is that the record-destruction actions of the Trump White House that were discovered by NARA late in 2021 first drew fresh parallels to what Clinton did, albeit in Trump's violation of the Presidential Records Act rather than the analogous Federal Records Act. For instance, in early August of

2022, the Justice Department publicly focused on the evident record-destruction practices of former Trump White House official Peter K. Navarro, whose emails, the Department has said, should have been preserved for residence in the National Archives. This in turn led to much social-media activity under the hashtag "But Her Emails" (though soon thereafter, believe it or not, Hillary Clinton actually was fundraising by selling "But Her Emails" hats on her "Forward Together" website). Indeed, on the basis of this alone, it suddenly remained to be seen whether Clinton had truly put all of this behind her.

And then, less than a week later, "all hell broke loose" with the FBI's "Mar-a-Lago raid" -- its recovery of over 13,000 records (including dozens of highly classified ones) that Trump improperly removed from the White House -- which greatly intensified the "whataboutism" comparisons to Clinton's record practices. Among other things, this led to Trump raising all sorts of fantastical defenses, such as his claimed ability to declassify records "even by thinking about it." Such a claim was firmly rejected by an appellate court in the case of *New York Times v. CIA* in 2020, which derided it as something that lacked "actual declassification." (That decision, by the way, was written by Senior Circuit Court Judge John M. Walker, Jr., the cousin of President George H.W. Bush who travelled with me to China as part of U.S. delegations in 2010 and 2011 (see Chapter One).)

81   The full quotation here is as follows: "I'm sick about talking about my emails, but I do think it's important to remember at the end of the day, after two parts of an FBI investigation, two separate State Department investigations -- one under Tillerson and one under Pompeo, so the Trump years -- they did not find one piece of paper of any kind *marked* classified. Zero." Of course, anyone familiar with Clinton's semantic chicanery of several years ago might wonder why she spoke of "paper" when she knows full well that the information under investigation existed in electronic form.

Now, it can easily be imagined that if Clinton were to try to wrest the nomination for the presidency from President Biden in 2024 (shades of Ted Kennedy and Jimmy Carter in 1980) -- or compete for it if he were not to seek reelection -- she would have such enormous difficulty defending her "zero" classified information claim that she might be forced to employ such a transparent, hair-splitting approach once again. If that were to come to pass, it could not be said to be a surprise.

82   The use of the word "were" here should not escape attention. Could Hillary Clinton be playing word games with this, reminiscent of Bill Clinton's infamous deposition reply (i.e., "it depends on what the meaning of 'is' is")? It is not inconceivable, given her own track records for such things, that she is taking the position that, in the absence of any classification marking sufficient to alert her, the timing of classification could be an "out" for her. Just a thought.

83   Indeed, as recently as September 10, 2019, Clinton summed it all up by saying: "There is nothing there. There is nothing that should have been so controversial." And so many of her closest allies, mostly Democrats and "progressives," support her in this revisionist history, so much so as to make an accurate, stringently analytical recounting of her email travails all the more important with the passage of time.

By the same token, in another more recent statement, one quoted in the January 20, 2022 issue of *The New Yorker*, Clinton came quite close to making an admission about her own emails when commenting on those of another: ". . . [I]f I were [on a congressional investigating committee], I'd take a close look at Trump's emails. Given how hard he tried to keep them from being released, those must be some emails." Really. And in what might likewise have been in an unguarded moment, Hillary Clinton summed up her email approach (read: her intent) by openly instructing: "I don't want any risk of the personal being accessible."

CHAPTER FORTY-EIGHT

1   Yes, this is one of those situations in which it is best not to disclose the gender of a person, in order to provide an additional measure of anonymity for reasons that should be clear.

2   This chapter contains an even greater endnote-to-text ratio than any other chapter of this book, which is truly saying something. The reason for this is that perhaps more than any other subject area, "UFO secrecy" calls for heavy historical treatment, with as much supporting detail as possible included, so as to present as balanced picture of it as possible.

3   Such national security "clearances" exist at multiple levels. Beyond the primary "Top Secret," "Secret," and "Confidential" levels for access to basic "classified" information, there exist numerous "compartments" for what sometimes is called a Special Access Program ("SAP," to those in need of bludgeoning) or "special compartmented information" ("SCI," to denizens of that realm), with a "compartment" being something that a "cleared person" is "read into" on a particular "need-to-know" basis. So someone holding a "Top Secret" clearance, for example, could be cleared (and "read into") two closely related SCI compartments, but not a third. Careful records are maintained regarding who has been cleared for exactly what. And being "read into" an additional compartment can be a quite formal step.

I can vividly remember, for instance, being "read into" an especially sensitive new compartment more than 40 years ago in a large ceremonial room at the Original Headquarters Building of the Central Intelligence Agency ("CIA," to the public, or "the Agency," to its insiders) out at Langley, Virginia, with a large array of metallic gold stars spread across one wall. (This was in the late 1970s, so there were not nearly as many as there are now.) They were the CIA's "Intelligence Stars" memorializing its lost intelligence officers and they later were moved from that interior room to a wall at the front lobby of the CIA's current headquarters building (called its "New Headquarters Building") when it was constructed in the early 1990s.

While this new place of honor for the CIA's "Memorial Wall" affords much greater visitor access to this impressive display (yet made them vulnerable to dishonor when used as a backdrop by a new president on January 21, 2017); there is nothing quite like getting briefed on something "extremely secret" (which is hardly a term of art) in front of such a solemn display. By the way, I still remember the code words for that compartment (as I should) and am aware that one of them, but not the other, somehow "leaked out" since then. (I know this because I have heard it used on television here and there, most prominently on "The West Wing." And that is the television program, coincidentally, that used the Office of Information and Privacy's colorful "Department of Justice Guide to the FOIA" volume to "dress the set" just outside of its portrayed Oval Office.)

4   I specifically remember my caller saying "interplanetary," whereas today that word might be "intergalactic."

5   Had we ever withheld a "pure fact" on such a rationale? Yes, we had, but only exceptionally -- and when push came to shove (as it once did in an environmental law case), not easily. But if ever there were a situation in which to be analytically creative, I opined, this would be it.

6   One possibly corroborative bit of such speculation comes from a former executive assistant to the CIA's top leadership named Victor Marchetti, who publicly said in 1974 that he thinks the United States Government has engaged in "ultra secret" contacts with extraterrestrials, based upon what he said he "heard" while working at high levels of the CIA, i.e., that NSA had received "strange signals" believed to be of extraterrestrial origin. Marchetti was a disgruntled former CIA official, not to mention an unsuccessful FOIA requester, so there are reasons to be skeptical of this claim. But he could be right about this.

If so, then what Marchetti says atop my own very indirect "evidence" is in turn supported (albeit also very indirectly) by a Brookings Institution research report commissioned by the National Aeronautics and Space Administration ("NASA," to those who look up to it) during the early 1960s that concluded that any public disclosure of such extraterrestrial contact would be "dangerously disruptive," inasmuch as throughout human history superior civilizations tend to demolish inferior ones, often quite violently. Titled "Proposed Studies on the Implications of Peaceful Space Activities for Human Affairs," this Brookings Institution report dramatically warned that an official announcement confirming the existence of intelligent extraterrestrial beings could have "disastrous consequences" for human civilization -- and it therefore spoke of the need to control public perceptions about the possibilities of alien life.

7   Never shy about renaming its UFO-related organizations, the Pentagon in July of 2022 came up with the name "All-Domain Anomaly Resolution Office" ("AARO," it says) ostensibly to encompass UFOs that are submerged in water or deemed "transmedium." This was done by an unorthodox "amendment" of DOD paperwork that makes it clear that AARO will henceforth (read: perhaps until the next such change) be DOD's "focal point" for UAP matters.

8   This is not to discount the reports by U.S. airmen of what they called "foo fighters," strange "flying lights" (read: luminous balls of light), near the border of Germany and France during the late stages of World War II. There is some credible evidence to the effect that such things were in fact one of two types of aerial devices designed in secret by German engineers before the war's end. If that is so, though, no government, neither Germany nor the United States, has ever confirmed it, even though the United States' post-war "Operation Paperclip" enterprise -- for the absorption of rocket scientist Wernher von Braun and his fellow scientists from Germany's Peenemünde Army Research Center, who developed the U.S.'s seminal Redstone rocket as a descendent of Germany's V-2 rocket -- should have yielded that knowledge, at least by now.

In the same time period (i.e., August of 1944), but different in character, a Royal Air Force crew returning to the east coast of England from a reconnaissance mission over Europe reported being persistently "shadowed" by a disc-shaped UFO that then accelerated away at a high speed. This appears to be the only such aerial UFO sighting made prior to the end of the war. On land, however, there was a report, singularly sourced, of a UFO crash near Cape Girardeau, Missouri, in April of 1941. If true, which is doubtful, this was a Roswell-like event that preceded it by several years.

And there were reports of a UFO crash back in 1936 in the Black Forest near the village of Freiberg in south-western Germany. The story goes that a disc-shaped object was taken to nearby Wewelsburg Castle, where the Germans reverse-engineered its propulsion system under the oversight of Nazi SS leader Heinrich L. Himmler, who used the castle as a base of operations until World War II. From this, it is said, Germany developed first a disc-shaped flying object called the "Haunebu," which reportedly employed some form of "anti-gravity" force and might have been the source of the "foo fighter" sightings described above, and also the V-2 rocket and something called the "flying wing." Not hardly likely.

There also were post-war reports of things called "ghost rockets," which were observed beginning in early 1946. These sightings, which always were in daylight, occurred primarily in Sweden, and in Scandinavia more generally, and were taken quite seriously for a time and then just faded away by the end of that year. (However, there appears to be absolutely no truth to the rumor, circulating stratospherically at the time, that the phrase "scanning the skies" for UFOs originated with this particular location of early UFO activity.)

Even less substantial were newspaper reports from California of "mystery airships" at the end of the nineteenth century; inasmuch as neither the aircraft nor cannabis industries had gotten off the ground by then, these sightings were largely viewed as just artifacts of the "yellow journalism" of the times. And speaking of California, there always is the old story of what was derisively called the "Battle of Los Angeles," which was reported to have taken place in February of 1942 when more than a thousand artillery shells were fired into the sky by jittery troops in San Bernadino, California, who saw lights that they mistook for enemy planes; characteristic of later years, the military evidently misled the public as to what that was all about. Decades later, memoranda purportedly written by President Franklin D. Roosevelt and classified as "Ultra Top Secret" surfaced as seeming corroboration of this. If such FDR memos truly were written by him, then they would cast a whole new light on this incident.

9   Truth be known, Kenneth Arnold never actually described any of the nine objects that he observed as "saucer-shaped" or resembling a "saucer" per se. Rather, he repeatedly described them as looking like "pie plates." It was "the press" (or "the media," in today's parlance) that found the word "saucer" more to its liking for convenient reference. (But for that matter of journalistic convenience (read: contrivance), I suppose, we'd have been talking about "flying pie plates" for the past 75 years.)

So in a way, Kenneth Arnold originated the term "flying saucer." As for the term "UFO" (later to morph into "UAP," see below), credit for its origination goes to writer and retired Marine Corps Major Donald E. Kehoe (in an odd quirk, Charles A. Lindburgh's former manager), who first used it in writing in 1953. A very early "ufologist," Keyhoe had written an article titled "Flying Saucers Are Real" that had appeared in the January 1950 issue of *True* magazine and helped launch what later came to be known as "UFO fever" in the United States.

And an amateur photographer in Phoenix named William Rhodes captured two images of a UFO that were published by the *Arizona Republic* on July 9, 1947. Then, when Kenneth Arnold saw that newspaper article and the two photos, he reportedly said, "That's exactly what I saw." Rhodes later claimed that he was then visited by two government agents, who intimidated him and began what some today call "the greatest cover-up in U.S. Government history."

If the Rhodes photographs were the first ones taken of a UFO (save for one perhaps taken as long ago as in 1870 at Mt. Washington in New Hampshire), then the first "video" of UFOs was perhaps taken by another amateur photographer, Navy officer Delbert C. Newhouse, when he was vacationing in Tremonton, Utah, on July 2, 1952. He and his wife claimed that they saw 12 shiny craft high in the sky and what they filmed supports that. After years of studying this film, the Air Force weakly announced that it might have been taken of "high-flying birds." Just as weak was the Air Force's explanation of the sudden disappearance of First Lt. Felix E. Moncia, Jr., while performing an "air defense intercept" of an unidentified object over Lake Superior on November 23, 1953. Sometimes referred to as "the Kinross Incident," this involved solid radar evidence but the Air Force inconsistently passed it off as a case of "pilot vertigo."

10   Curiously, these two seminal events marking the very outset of the "modern UFO age" occurred only days apart (i.e., on June 14 and in late June or early July 1947, depending on who you go by), with nothing of comparable magnitude occurring (at least in the U.S.) during the centuries before then. (This Roswell time frame, by the way, stems from the discovery of the "crash debris" by rancher "Mack" Brazel on the J.B. Foster Ranch, not when he eventually reported it to Sheriff George A. Wilcox three weeks later and 70 miles away in Roswell, much less the time of the subsequent handling and publicizing of it by the Air Force in early July.)

In the midst of this, there was reported to be a third such "UFO event," centered on Maury Island in the Puget Sound, on June 21, 1947, which likely was one of the most serious UFO hoaxes ever, in that it led to an actual military plane crash with two fatalities. There also were reports, utterly unverified and perhaps likewise hoaxes, of even earlier "UFO activity," in January of 1947, taking place in Antarctica, of all places, in connection with an ambitious U.S. Navy expedition code-named "Operation Highjump" that was headed by Admiral Richard E. Byrd, Jr. -- who is said to have written a "classified diary" of the expediation that speaks of an "inner earth" -- and was shrouded in secrecy. Whatever the truth of these latter two episodes -- or even of the former two, actually -- it certainly does seem, all the more so in retrospect, that 1947 was truly some sort of watershed year.

And as to Antarctica, which covers more than five million square miles, it is indeed regarded as an ironic "hot spot" of UFO-related activity, especially during the last twenty-five years. For instance, there are credible reports dating to the 1990s of military pilots being ordered to bypass a particular area there for no explicable reason, leading to the suspicion that a large "hole in the ice" at that location is not a natural feature and is instead part of some secret activity. To such things, ufologists add the fact that few places on Earth are as conducive to secrecy as is Antarctica. (A primary such other place, of course, is the depths of the oceans, which raises the subject of "Unidentified Submersible Objects," or "USOs," sometimes referred to as "transmedium" craft.)

11   It should be noted, though, that the Roswell story actually died down by the end of the 1940s and remained well in the background of ufology until it was re-ignited by UFO researchers, most particularly nuclear physicist Stanton T. Friedman, in the early 1980s. Once Friedman began writing and lecturing about the Roswell incident, it took off like a rocket and has been in orbit ever since. (Further evidence of this can be found in the huge "75th Anniversary Celebration" held in Roswell in early July of 2022.)

It should also be noted that in 1947, the Roswell Army Air Force Base was the home of the Air Force's "509th Bombardment Group," otherwise known for some reason as the "509th Composite Group," which was tasked with the operational deployment of nuclear weapons. Two years earlier, that group had prepared and launched the planes that dropped the atomic bombs on Hiroshima and Nagasaki to end World War II. It was our military's (and the world's) only "atomic" military unit at the time.

12   Perhaps the second-most valuable Nazi scientist was Austrian inventor Viktor Schauberg, who was the progenitor of the Nazis' most exotic devices and craft. After being heavily debriefed, he could have remained in the U.S., working for NASA alongside von Braun, but he chose to be repatriated to Austria instead.

13   According to Major Marcel's son, Jesse A. Marcel, Jr., some of the debris that his father brought home -- consisting of thin, flexible pieces of metal -- behaved as a "shape-recovery" alloy, sometimes referred to as "memory metal," which if twisted or even "crumpled" would quickly return to its original shape. Young Marcel's mother eventually corroborated this as well. This also connects to more recent accounts of a "meta-metal" called "Nitinol" that is now acknowledged to exist.

14   Indeed, it was at a press conference held on July 8 that Major Marcel knelt down alongside General Roger M. Ramey (who had taken control of the entire matter) for the iconic photograph of Marcel holding in his hand what Ramey then said was merely debris from a "fallen weather balloon." Auspiciously, though, what General Ramey was holding in his hand at that moment was a folded-up piece of paper that evidently contained his notes for the event. Decades later, with modern forensic analysis tools and photographic enhancement, parts of this document (which appears to be a telegram) purportedly have been found to contain the phrases "aviators in the 'disc' they will ship" and "victims of the wreck" -- although the discernment of these words is far from clear. This has recently become perhaps the most compelling evidence on its side of the Roswell controversy.

15   Among the reports, speculation, and military denials of the Roswell incident stands the well-established fact that *something* was shipped to Wright-Patterson as part of it. One has to wonder why the military would take such a step for recovered debris if it were merely mundane in nature.

16   Part of this support is a sworn statement by Marcel's fellow officer Sheridan Cavitt, who also retired as a Lt. Colonel, given in an official interview in 1994. He stated that what he and Marcel recovered "consisted of a reflective sort of material like aluminum foil, and some thin, bamboo-like sticks." He said that he thought at

the time that what they discovered was "a weather balloon." On the other hand, his wife reportedly stressed to his interviewer "on the side" that he was faithfully speaking under the constraints of a "secrecy oath." So go figure: Like much of the "evidence" of Roswell, this could be viewed one way or the other.

17   For example, it was just a few years ago that small metal fragments discovered near the purported "crash site" (read: if there was only one, not two or even three) were subjected to modern scientific analysis and found to contain unexpected amalgams of metallic elements, most inexplicably selenium and molybdenum. In itself, this proves nothing, of course, but that sort of finding does serve to keep the controversy alive. As do reports that the suspected Roswell crash was accompanied by radar detection at Roswell Army Airfield, without any record being made of that.

18   I belatedly must add here, though, that upon further analysis I myself have reached such a firm conclusion, one that necessarily encapsulates virtually the entire "UFO question." In the past, I had always viewed the answer to that question as hinging on the credibility and plausibility of UFO sightings alone; in other words, were the things reportedly observed in the skies, in the aggregate, sufficient by themselves to answer that question, or not? And I answered that question, for myself, by concluding that there was no more than a 5-10% chance of UFOs "being real." And then while in the course of researching and writing this chapter, that percentage for me rose to 25%, 40%, and then 50%.

But I now believe that an analysis of UFO sightings in and of themselves is not the most effective way to approach this cosmic question. Rather, it is with careful consideration of the firsthand testimony of the literally dozens of witnesses to U.S. military involvement in claimed UFO landings (read: crashes, mostly), and their aftermaths, beginning with the Roswell crash(es) in 1947. *Simply put, there are just too many people, mostly from the military, who now have come forward to soberly report nearly identical things about the existence and contents of alien craft to disbelieve all of them.*

The best compilation of such descriptions that I know of is contained in book titled *Roswell, The Ultimate Cold Case: Eyewitness Testimony and Evidence of Contact and the Cover-Up* by Thomas J. Carey and Donald R. Schmitt (New Page Books, 2020), Chapters 12-14, which lists more than a dozen with the shared characteristic of seeing "little bodies," or the like, consistently with "large heads and eyes." Among the most compelling of these is that of Lt. Walter G. Haut, the Air Force public relations officer who issued, and then was ordered to retract, the official Air Force press release at Roswell. In an affidavit executed shortly before his death, Haut described being taken to a hangar in which he saw a damaged spacecraft and several small alien bodies with large heads. He also stated that there were not only one but two crash sites in the Roswell area, with the Air Force using one as a diversion from the other.

Indeed, many of these descriptions are "deathbed confessions" from former military personnel like Walter Haut, who honored a government secrecy oath well into their old age, one for as long as 70 years (the length of his specified "vow"). (Another, Lt. Col. Philip J. Corso, also went so far as to describe the transfer of alien technology to the private sector (as described below).) Some did so out of fear, the fear that unquestionably was imposed on nearly the entire Roswell community, for example, with a fervor born of whatever the military might have found. Some did so as a matter of military honor and the bond that they shared with their comrades. And one, who claimed to have been a "CIA agent" operating under the cover name "Agent Kewper," asserted that he feared for his life but wanted to state before he died that he saw alien bodies at "Site 4" south of Area 51.

19   Having seen many such FBI "LHMs" over the years, and having close familiarity with their characteristic markings and routing notations, I have no difficulty believing that this particular document is not an elaborate hoax. In legal terms, that makes it probative but not conclusive as to its sensational contents.

20   Perhaps the most well-known proponent of the multi-craft version of the "Roswell crash" was Stanton Friedman, the nuclear physicist who said he interviewed more than 100 "witnesses to the story" and single-handedly popularized it through publications and hundreds of lectures during the 1980s and 1990s. (In fact, as noted above, there was very little publicity of the "Roswell Incident" after 1947 and prior to 1980.) He contended (with some others) that not only one but two alien craft crashed in the Roswell area, the second one closer to the much smaller village of Corona, New Mexico. Some have placed that second crash site in what is called the Plains of St. Augustine.

21   Like many others, in my youth I devoured the books that were written about the Kennedy Assassination (read: JFK, not RFK), including the House Assassinations Committee report that was issued in late 1978 -- when I was already working on two Kennedy Assassination FOIA cases (see Chapter Ten). Indeed, earlier in that year, I had visited Dealey Plaza when I traveled to Dallas in order to oversee the relocation to FBI Headquarters of all FBI Dallas Field Office records pertaining to the JFK Assassination -- because I was handling that FOIA case back in Washington, including the lengthy file that the Bureau's field office had compiled on Jack L. Ruby (née Jacob Leon Rubenstein). I've always regarded the evidence of Lee Harvey Oswald being the lone *gunman* in Dealey Plaza to be most compelling, but I will never believe that Oswald was able to act as he did without underlying coordination from others, very possibly from "organized crime," in no small part because of the background and actions of his murderer, Jack Ruby.

On the other hand, a competitive one, there is compelling evidence, in both FBI files and extensive CIA ones, that Oswald was very much entangled with the CIA in conjunction with his defection to the Soviet Union, his involvement with the Fair Play for Cuba Committee in New Orleans, and his visit to the Cuban Embassy in Mexico City in the fall of 1963. To that must be added evidence that Oswald had had a CIA "handler" during much of 1963, under the suspected supervision of notorious spymaster James Jesus Angleton, in connection with a KGB-related CIA operation known as "Project Tumbleweed."

Indeed, there was much sharing of records on Oswald between the FBI and the CIA both prior to and immediately after November 22, 1963, as well as much controversy over "who saw what, and when?" That is why I reacted immediately when an FBI document reviewer (over whose shoulder I was looking) proposed that we not include a particular memorandum (as a "duplicate") in our tranche of records that we were bringing up to FBI Headquarters from the Dallas Field Office in March of 1978.

That document was indeed a duplicate of one that we'd already included, except for one thing: That particular copy of it bore the initial "H," which we verified was a notation signifying that it was read by FBI Supervisory Special Agent James P. Hosty, whose relations with both Oswald (who had formally accused him of harassing his wife Marina) and his CIA counterparts (with whom he had "cross-blaming" disputes even before the assassination) that I knew were especially controversial. So we not only included that document version for a properly complete record, we also used that as example of what would make any other document a "non-duplicate" for our search-and-retrieval purposes. And years later, I used that example, plus another one in which a margin notation was merely an exclamation point, for governmentwide policy guidance on what can make a version of a document a different or "new" record under the FOIA.

22   Here's a story about someone who is fascinated by the subject: In 1993, when I was working closely with Associate Attorney General Webster L. Hubbell (see Chapter Twenty-Eight), Webb told me a tale about his close friend Bill Clinton. He said that when Clinton first arrived at the Oval Office on January 21, 1993 (after a long night of "partying," no doubt), he turned to an aide and declared that he wanted to know two things, right away, most of all: He wanted to know "who killed Kennedy?" And he wanted to know "if UFOs are real." And

Webb knew this to be true, he said, because Clinton told him that himself. So because Webb, in turn, told that to me, I know it very solidly, albeit secondhand.

Plus this is nicely corroborated by a statement that former President Clinton made about the subject of UFOs four years after the end of his presidency, in Hong Kong in 2005: "I did attempt to find out if [the Government had any records of extraterrestrial beings, but] . . . if there were, they were concealed from me, too." And as a postscript, he coyly added: "I am almost embarrassed to tell you that I did try to find out." Yes, accord to Webb, he certainly did, but he failed.

Then, in turn, four years after the end of his own presidency, former President Obama said very much the same kind of thing when he was questioned on the subject of UFOs in a televised interview on November 30, 2020: "Certainly, I asked about it." Evidently agreeing wholeheartedly with President Clinton, he also pointedly said that "[t]here are times where prying information out of the bowels of an agency can be challenging."

Now zoom over to former Clinton White House Chief of Staff John D. Podesta, Jr., who used to teach for OIP at our Advanced FOIA seminars and then went on to "make something of himself" serving President Clinton, President Obama, presidential candidate Hillary R. Clinton, and President Joseph R. Biden, *seriatim*. In 2002, when speaking of UFOs at the National Press Club, John very forcefully said: "I think it's time to open the books on questions that have remained in the dark on government investigations of UFOs. It's time to find out what the truth really is that's out there. We ought to do it, really, because it's right; we ought to do it because the American people quite frankly can handle the truth; and we ought to do it because it's the law [presumably meaning the FOIA]."

Now that very last part, about the law, is at least a bit debatable, but a president certainly has the power to declassify anything that has been classified on national security grounds, and John spoke of that also to KLAS-TV during a Hillary Clinton campaign stop in Las Vegas (known as a "hotbed" of UFO activity) in 2016: "[M]ore attention and more discussion about unexplained aerial phenomena can happen without people who are in public life who are serious about this being ridiculed." As for Hillary Clinton herself, she boldly proclaimed what she would do if she won the presidency: "Yes, I'm going to get to the bottom of it."

A year earlier, John publicly stated that his biggest regret from his times working in the White House for both President Clinton and President Obama was "not securing the disclosure of the UFO files." (But it was not for lack of trying.) "People want to know what the Government knows. And they ought to know what the Government knows," he has said. This is a remarkably pro-disclosure statement from such a high-level government official, making John a singular force in what ufologists refer to as the "UFO debate."

And speaking of such disclosure, when more than 20,000 pages of John's email messages were publicly disclosed by WikiLeaks after the successful "phishing" of his email account during the run-up to the 2016 presidential election, there were some UFO-related emails in that tranche, including ones sent to him by Apollo-14 astronaut Edgar D. Mitchell, the sixth man to walk on the moon and a firm UFO "believer," in January and August of 2015, as well as another in October of that year with the subject line, "Important things." Someday, perhaps, John will elaborate on this.

23   And in turn, there is a "counterforce" to these proponents, initially called not just "skeptics" but full-on "debunkers," that weighs in heavily with a wide variety of Earthbound explanations for UFO sightings -- ranging from swamp gas ("iridescent" or otherwise) to ionized gas (either charged by solar wind or generated by the intersection of two or more laser or maser beams) to temperature inversions to atmospheric phenomena to light phenomena to visual phenomena (such as the "parallax effect" and "camera lens flares") to reflections (including of headlights or campfires) to searchlights to "aeronautical anomalies" to the aurora borealis to Venus, Jupiter, and other celestial bodies to asteroids to meteors to "vaporizing meteorites" to "meteor bolides" to "shooting stars" to the moon to "sun dogs" to solar flares (known as "coronal mass ejections") to St. Elmo's

fire to ball lightning to "earthquake lights" to "atmospheric gaseous electrically charged buoyant plasmas" to "plasma-related fields" to all sorts of types of flares (including "burn-off" ones from oil rigs) to Chinese fire lanterns to upper-atmospheric lightning to high-altitude ice crystals to cloud formations (of all types) to launched "barium clouds" to reflective birds to "high-flying geese" to large hailstones to weather balloons (e.g., the second Roswell explanation, though "weather" need not be part of it) to "probe balloons" to dropsondes to metallic balloons (deflating or otherwise) to modern drones (submarine-launched or otherwise) to "drone swarms" to "drone clusters" to helicopters to blimps (such as the Goodyear Blimp or dirigibles, if you're old enough to worry about "the humanity" of it all) to zeppelins to "near-neutral buoyancy-rigid hull airships" to other rigid airships to all types of satellites (including Starlink and SpaceX ones, viewed either during launch or during deployment) to missile tests to missile launches (failed or not) to decades-old "upper rocket stages" to other "space debris" (sometimes called "space junk") to advanced military aircraft (both U.S. and Soviet) such as the U-2 reconnaissance plane, the SR-71 Blackbird, the B-2 stealth bomber, the even stealthier F-117 Nighthawk, and even the very newest "TR-3B anti-gravity spacecraft" (with its "warping of gravity through plasma") to ever-popular (and sadly realistic, especially when computer-generated) hoaxes to mirages to "space jellyfish" to other "optical illusions" to hallucinations to individual psychological impairment or "histrionics" and even to long-distance diagnoses of "mass hysteria" -- leading to much vibrant controversy (if not actual conflict) as each side energetically seeks and proclaims its own "truth." (And as to the latter of these "explanations," the question fundamentally comes down to whether these sighted objects are "real" physical things or rather some types of figments of the mind. Evidently, they (read: at least some of them) are in fact the former.)

The Blackbird (also known by the code name "SR-71"), it should be noted, was a long-range, high-altitude, high-speed (think on the north side of Mach 3) reconnaissance aircraft that was developed at Lockheed Martin's cutting-edge "Skunk Works" facility (officially known as its "Advanced Development Programs," or "ADP," to its best customer, and previously known as "Lockheed Advanced Development Projects") in Palmdale, California, during the 1960s and operated for more than two dozen years, largely out of "Area 51" (or "Groom Lake," as those in government most commonly call it). It was developed under the umbrella code name of "Project OXCART" (which is why that name appears so often in UFO documents of the time) and is believed to be the first plane to have had complete "stealth" capability.

During its decades of extraordinary testing and operation, the "SR-71 Blackbird" without any doubt was responsible for countless numbers of properly reported UFO sightings (perhaps reflective of the fact that it was originally intended to be painted silver, not black), which makes it a major part of the "explicable" (i.e., versus "inexplicable") side of the UFO ledger. And it should be recognized that *its own* secrecy, for understandable reasons given its importance to the U.S.'s secret waging of the "Cold War," inevitably became part of "UFO secrecy" overall -- and it did so in a way that only the best spy novelists could imagine.

24   An excellent candidate for being viewed as the most unusual and unquestionably unique UFO ever sighted is 'Oumuamua (Hawaiian for "scout" or "messenger"), the first known interstellar object ever detected in our Solar System and perhaps the "ultimate UFO" thus far. First spotted on October 19, 2017 as it was already exiting our Solar System (because it had entered it against the backdrop of the Sun), it is a long, thin, relatively flat, somewhat cigar-shaped metallic rock appearing to be like a skyscraper (perhaps an oblate spheroid, with a length-to-width ratio of 6:1), dark reddish in color, possibly icy at its core, that has been observed tumbling end over end on a rough hyperbolic trajectory at over 100,000 miles per hour that took it on a path between the orbits of the Earth and Mars.

At first, it was seen as an exceptionally elongated asteroid or perhaps a comet. Then, closer observations revealed that it was actually accelerating, but not gravitationally, as if something were pushing it on an irregular trajectory or it was being piloted. Astronomers and other planetary scientists still aren't sure why, but they gathered enormous amounts of data about it and are continuing to analyze all of it. Recently, no less a luminary than Professor Abraham "Avi" Loeb, who is the longest-serving chair of Harvard University's Department of Astronomy, has bravely (read: and highly controversially) stated his belief that 'Oumuamua "was created by an intelligent civilization not of this Earth." It thus holds the potential for bringing the "UFO debate" to a firm conclusion before anything else.

25   It is fair to say that almost anyone taking the "long view" of UFO history over these past 75 years would conclude that the numbers of UFO sightings (not to be confused with their "quality") certainly do correlate with the occurrence of high-profile, highly publicized UFO-related events. In other words, publicity seems to breed sightings (witness the almost immediate "flap" of sightings after June 1947), which in turn bring more publicity. A unique spiral? No, not really, but an evident spiral nonetheless.

26   There is an entire realm of "ufology" that now embraces and builds upon the premise that the Earth was visited by otherworldly beings in ancient times, thus explaining such things as the erection of enormous stone figures on Easter Island, the visible-from-above "Nazca Lines" in Peru, the depictions of "spacemen" in petroglyphs and pictographs around the world, and even the many pyramid structures of Egypt, Mexico, and Central America. As there has never been much government secrecy about such things, this subject area is left for others to explore. And with that, sightings during the subsequent time periods leading up to what can be characterized as "the modern era" (i.e., during and after World War II) are not dwelled upon either. The invention of photography in the mid-19th century, and especially "motion pictures" in the 20th century, provided much for governments to be secretive about.

However, there is another category of sightings that deserves mentioning -- mass UFO sightings. Depending upon one's definition of how many observers it takes for a sighting to be a "mass" one, there certainly have been several over the years that fall into that category. The sightings in rural Wisconsin on December 1, 2022 and in Kecksburg, Pennsylvania, on December 9, 1965, surely qualify for that, as do the Washtenaw County, Michigan, sightings in mid-March of 1966, the Lake Michigan sightings of March 8, 1994, the "Phoenix Lights" sightings of March 13, 1997 (which involved thousands of witnesses), the "Hudson Valley" sightings during 1983-1986, the sightings of a huge craft by dozens of townspeople in Stephenville, Texas, in 2008, the sightings by both civilian and military observers in Brazil in 1986, and the remarkable one at Ariel Elementary School in Harari, Zimbabwe, on September 16, 1994. (Nearly 18 years later, dozens of the 62 students who as children aged 6-12 said they all saw a "silver disc" with a bottom row of blinking lights land amongst the school's perimeter trees for about 15 minutes behind their playground were gathered to relive the event as adults for the documentary film *Ariel Phenomenon*. Several reported seeing a humanoid figure, with classic size and appearance, briefly standing nearby. That report is similar to the circumstances of the recently released documentary *Moment of Contact* about UFO activity in Brazil, including a series of comparable contact experiences with an alleged military cover-up thrown in for good measure, as reported by local citizens in the small town of Varginha during January of 1996.) So do some sightings as far back in time as the 16th century, such as ones in Nuremberg, Germany, on April 14, 1561, and similar ones in Basel, Switzerland, in 1566, each of which reportedly was witnessed by thousands of people. Both of these sightings were memorialized in contemporaneous woodcut depictions that survive to this day.

Of all of these, the 1965 sightings in Kecksburg stand apart because they involved not just a sighting in the sky (of an object making a sharp turn) but also a crashed craft that reportedly was observed by many townspeople on the ground in a ravine. In fact, dozens of local residents saw its fiery but relatively soft impact in the midst of nearby woods and several more, including volunteer firefighters, gathered around it immediately. They reported a bell-shaped or acorn-like craft, copper-colored at the top and with a metallic band or collar around it containing "raised symbols" that appeared to them to be like hieroglyphics, all bathed in an eerie blue light. Then almost before they knew it, state police and military forces with searchlights moved in, abruptly declared the entire area to be "restricted" (even from the local firefighters), and ordered all of the townspeople to leave. Nevertheless, several residents reported being able to get close enough to the military operation to observe the object being loaded onto a flatbed truck, covered with a tarp, and taken away. And a minority of witnesses reported seeing a "humanoid figure" removed from it and placed into a large box. Four days later, the Air Force announced that it was "only a meteor," which was later officially said to have been a "cover" for a crashed Soviet satellite.

27   This is not to overlook "USOs," or "Unidentified Submersible (or 'Submerged') Objects," or more recently "Unidentified Submersible Phenomena" or "transmedium" craft, which are akin to UFOs, only wetter. This refers to unidentified objects (or vehicles) capable of operating both under water and in the air (read: hence "transmedium"), according to observations of them made in the air (i.e., of them entering or exiting the ocean) or detections of them made beneath the ocean's surface. While they are relatively few, such observations have been made for many years and most recently they have increased in both numbers and complexity, especially with the detection by advanced military systems of what have been described as "non-cavitational, extremely fast-moving objects within the ocean." One such sighting, claimed to have been made by a Russian nuclear submarine in July of 2009, was of six disc-shaped objects traveling under water (and in formation, no less) that were observed (both by sonar and then also visually through a periscope) leaving the water at high speed. On the other side of this coin, many such sightings that have been made in the coastal waters off Sweden have been attributed by Sweden to Soviet/Russian submarine intrusions.

This category of sighting has been associated with what are believed by some (read: a minority of) ufologists to be "underwater bases" at a variety of locations where USOs reportedly have been observed entering and/ or exiting the water, most often near shores. A prime location for such conjecture is the Baltic Sea, where in Stockholm Harbor alone many USO sightings have been reported, including one involving hundreds of witnesses and Sweden's military forces in October of 2014. Then there is what is known as the "Baltic Sea Anomaly," a rock-encrusted structure or formation that reportedly (read: it has been well photographed and this is what some people think) looks like some sort of ancient "sea craft."

Two other such speculated locations are off the shores of Cuba and Southern California. The first, now dubbed the "Lost City of Cuba," is a 1.2 square mile area off Cuba's west coast, where undersea explorers at a depth of 2000 feet came within sonar range of what appeared (read: to some, especially upon the use of unmanned underwater photography) to be the ruins of an ancient submerged city. This was 20 years ago, but Cuba has yet to bring enough technology to bear to analyze this theory further.

The other is a recently discovered oval-shaped cliff area near the California coastline that to some observers appears to be an unnatural (read: and therefore intelligently designed) ocean formation. At a coincidental depth of 2000 feet and approximately three miles in width, this site is less than 100 miles (as the saucer flies) from Vandenberg Air Force Base, which is the launch and landing home of SpaceX and also the site of many secret ballistic missile tests. A related area of suspected USO activity, characterized by "magnetic anomalies," is proximate to (read: slightly north of) Catalina Island.

And then of course there is the "Bermuda Triangle," an area extending north from Cuba and Puerto Rico and east of Florida to Bermuda that during the 20th century was said to "mysteriously" cause ships and planes to "disappear" in it due to "inexplicable navigational disruptions" and "electromagnetic interference." Like no small part of the "UFO mystery," however, this has involved heavy commercialization and much "evidence" that cannot withstand scrutiny.

In a similar vein (of lava, perhaps), recent years have seen a growing series of sightings of UFOs that have been perceived to be entering (or in even more common instances, exiting from) volcanoes. Most of these sightings have been in Central America or South America, in countries such as Chile (which appears to have the most UFO sightings in the world), Costa Rica, Colombia, and Peru. To them should be added Canada, Iceland, Indonesia, Japan (Mount Fuji), and Italy (Mount Etna, most prominently), with the latter being a bit of a "hot spot" most recently. (Another long-term "hot spot" in Italy is Mount Musine, which is near Turin.)

By far and away, though, the greatest numbers of volcano/UFO sightings have been in Mexico, especially at the volcano Popocatepetl ("El Popo," to locals) near Mexico City. (I've been there, only a half-day's drive from Mexico City, back before its glaciers melted.) Still a highly active volcano, it is situated within an area of constant seismic activity, which means that it is subject to the presence of "earthquake lights," making that a possible explanation of any UFO activity. That having been said, though, there is no denying the fact that over the past five years in particular, more and more objects (and after dark, lights) have been both observed and photographed seemingly entering or exiting this volcano.

Within the United States, there have been such sightings in Hawaii, California (at Mount Shasta), and Washington (at Mount St. Helens and Mount Adams). And perhaps the oddest sightings in this broad category are those that have been made above a "supervolcanic hot spot" (read: both an ancient and active caldera) in Yellowstone National Park, which lies mostly in Wyoming.

28   And for those unidentified objects that are reported to be "stationary," especially at high altitudes, sometimes the biggest question is whether they were at all rotating, which apparently is a big factor to physicists in assessing UFO provenience.

29   There is another reported UFO characteristic, one that sometimes arises as part of daylight observations and the photography of light-colored clouds. This characteristic, in a category unto itself, is "cloaking," which in this context means creating the perception that an aerial object either has taken some action to render itself invisible (anthropomorphically speaking) or has managed to "hide" within or behind (from an observational aspect) one or more clouds. This is the stuff of science fiction, of course, with no apologies to the "Star Trek" franchise, but then again, aren't UFOs that in the first place?

30   Of these five triangular configurations, the most common one by far, especially in recent decades, is the equilateral one, which is observed typically at night, usually with white lights at their three somewhat rounded vertices and sometimes with a red or orange light in their middles. Appearing to be rigid structures rather than disconnected groups of lights, these sightings are most recently referred to as "black triangles" by ufologists, who sometimes go so far as to suggest that these craft might achieve "triangulated data recording" through sensors contained within their three vertex lights.

Consistent with that speculation, these "black triangles" are invariably reported to be completely silent and are almost always reported to be both exceptionally large (i.e., much larger than conventional aircraft or even "conventional UFOs," oxymoronically speaking) and also exceptionally slow-moving, with an airspeed not much above basic "hovering" and an altitude that often is surprisingly low (e.g., seeming "to float on air"), but also the capability of instantaneously moving away at supersonic speed. And an even greater bit of speculation is that, from the beginning, they actually have been the most sophisticated form of U.S. aircraft in existence (whether "reverse engineered" with "alien technology" or not), such as that which now reportedly carries the code name "TR-3B." The most well-known sightings of such UFOs have been in Iceland in 1977 (where a Navy officer aboard a nuclear-powered U.S. submarine photographed one through a periscope diving into the sea); in Hudson Valley, New York, during 1983-1986; in Belgium in 1989-1990; in England in 1993-1995; in and around Phoenix in 1997; in Southern Illinois in 2000; in Tinley Park, Illinois, a suburb of Chicago, in 2004; in Rochester, Michigan, in 2014; in Louisville, Kentucky, in 2018; in Moab, Utah, in 2019; in Nevada in 2019; and in Pasadena, California, in 2021. Atop that, there were more than 200 such sightings reported during the first half of 2020 in the U.S. alone.

And before all of this, there was a seminal sighting of a large triangular object, described as "silvery" in color, that was made repeatedly during a massive NATO exercise in the North Sea called "Operation Mainbrace" during September of 1952. Reportedly, hundreds of American and British seamen observed this object and it also was detected on radar. It is said that a military investigation of the incident was undertaken, leading to a report that for some inexplicable reason has ever since remained classified (making it an excellent target for FOIA requests).

31   This is a common element of many UFO sightings: Estimated or sometimes even measured speeds and/or rates of acceleration that have "G-forces" strong enough to be fatal for any human occupant in the observed craft. On the other hand, there have been recent reports from trained military observers of UFOs seeming to remain completely motionless for several seconds at 10,000 to 30,000 feet in the air.

32   In recent years, apart from the "traditional" white and silver, the most common color reported seems to be somewhere between "orangish red" and "reddish orange," with "glowing orange orbs" (as with orbs in general) gaining in popularity. And as for color combinations, there is a distinct recent trend toward white lights at the vertices of "black triangles," sometimes with a single red light in the middle.

33   The most well-known astronaut UFO "witness," thus far, is probably Edward Eugene Aldrin, Jr., known to the world as "Buzz," who was the second man to walk on the moon. Now in his 90s (and the namesake of an elementary school just across the street from where this is being written), Aldrin is one of only a dozen men who have done so (no women yet); only three others, one of whom is former Senator Harrison H. Schmitt of New Mexico, are still alive as of this writing. A former fighter pilot himself, and also an aeronautics engineer, Aldrin is reputed to have observed (and reported) a UFO during Apollo-11's approach to the moon in 1969, but this might well have been only "space debris" and is far from confirmed. He also spoke of seeing a UFO during his Gemini-XII mission in 1966.

By contrast, back on May 15, 1963, during the final Mercury mission, Astronaut L. Gordon Cooper, Jr., reported seeing a "bright green glowing object" that he said "buzzed" his capsule during his solo flight (and reportedly also was tracked by NASA), an early sighting that NASA did not immediately suppress (but neither did it allow Cooper to talk about it upon his return). And on June 4, 1965, Astronaut James A. McDivitt on Gemini-IV observed a "can-shaped" UFO that, atypically, became the subject of an official NASA report. These sightings were discussed favorably (which does not mean that they are genuine) in what became known as the "Condon Report," issued in 1969. Thereafter, Apollo-XII, too, was the source of such "UFO sightings," as was the Soviets' space station Salyut-7 (on two occasions, the second by six cosmonauts) in July of 1984.

And then there was the Space Shuttle, which flew from April 12, 1981, to July 21, 2011, with two shuttle disasters, *Challenger* on take-off in January of 1986 and *Columbia* upon re-entry in February of 2003. In between those two disasters, Space Shuttle *Discovery*, on mission STS-29, reportedly was involved in a UFO "sighting" unlike any other before or since. On March 13, 1989, *Discovery*'s mission pilot, Col. John E. Blaha, was recorded as saying the following to Houston ground control: "Houston, this is Discovery. We still have the alien spacecraft under observance [sic]."

Although this brief conversation is said to have been transmitted through a secret NASA "bypass channel," it was recorded by a ham radio operator listening in on behalf of the "Goddard Amateur Radio Club," a group founded in 1969 by employees of the NASA Goddard Space Flight Center in Greenbelt, Maryland, which apparently monitors all NASA missions. This group promptly made this recording public, whereupon NASA did not deny the recording's authenticity; it just claimed that in saying this Colonel Braha was referring to something else. (Notwithstanding NASA's mere deflective denial, it is always possible that this somehow was a ham radio hoax.)

By far and away, though, greatest potential for astronaut-related UFO sightings lies with the International Space Station ("ISS," to its multi-national inhabitants), which was launched on November 20, 1998, is expected to remain operational until at least 2030, and has been manned primarily by U.S. astronaut and Russian cosmonaut crews, with astronauts from 17 other nations (in coordination with the European Space Administration), including Belgium, Brazil, Malaysia, Kazakhstan, the Netherlands, Sweden, and the United Arab Emirates, as well. Over the years, it has been the venue of many reported UFO encounters (particularly during 2005 and 2016, and most recently in August of 2020 by Russian Cosmonaut Ivan Vagner), none of which has been officially confirmed by NASA or any other space agency, but often suspiciously accompanied by unexplained "video interruptions" (read: abrupt ones) of transmissions that are quite telling.

Perhaps the single greatest source of UFO "sightings," however, are the non-human ones that are automatically made by cameras, both motion and still, even though they are made alone (i.e., without accompanying observational testimony). Indeed, such "photographic evidence of UFOs," ufologists maintain, actually should be regarded as superior in that it is not tainted by human subjectivity as it is being made. More than a dozen known cameras are operational on the International Space Station at any given time, including a "live stream" of both internal and external views that is regularly sent back to the United States. So both in the past and going forward during the next decade (regardless of whether Russian participation is impeded by the Russia/Ukraine War), these cameras offer the best vantage point for photographed "UFO sightings."

34   This latter recording mode has most frequently been used by observers on the ground, of course, but there now have actually been instances of military pilots capturing UFO images through use of their personal cell phones within their cockpits; at least two of those became public in 2020.

35   Both the "landing" and "crashing" species of such things, as well as some of the "hovering" ones, can quickly verge into what is popularly now known as "close encounters" of some kind (e.g., with either humans, in claimed "abductions," or seemingly dissected animals), which for a "UFO sighting" crosses a line that will remain intact in this book (even though many of the people who claim to have been subjected to "alien abductions" tell stories that are strikingly similar to one another). Far better for others to venture beyond that line, as many do, with varied results.

36   This is of course not the only equipment on which a UFO might be "picked up." Even as early as the mid-1950s there were reports -- some facially spurious, some otherwise -- of "radio signals" or "radio codes" from purported UFOs being detected by just ordinary folks with what were then widely known as "ham radios." These constituted only a tiny sliver of UFO reports overall, but they had considerable impact at the time.

37   Not to be forgotten in this mix are astronomers, meteorologists, and planetary scientists (as well as those who work with them), who sometimes are military personnel but far more often are civilians, perhaps academics. They are professionals at having "eyes on the sky," it is said, and have long played (i.e., back through time, even before 1947) a big role in UFO identification.

38   Evidently, at least when it comes to radar systems used by the most advanced fighter jets, it is the AESA system that is the most advanced, such that UFO detections can be made through use of it that would not otherwise be possible.

39   Notably, the percentage of all reported UFO sightings during the 1950s and 1960s that were determined to be "unknown" or "unexplained" usually hovered at no more than ten percent, in the Air Force's estimation, and reportedly averaged about eight percent. Evidently, this was regarded as a "significant percentage" by both the Air Force and its "science consultants."

40　The other aspects of human nature identified in the Introduction, of course, are paternalism, protectiveness, and proprietariness. Another, perhaps less fundamental aspect of human nature is, crassly putting it, "ass covering," which certainly also applies to the realm of UFO sightings, especially in military settings.

41　It is not intended here to delve too far into the realm of the psychological; my younger daughter, for one, would say that she spent nine years of higher education toward her Ph.D. in order to do that. But at the same time, neither one of us is likely to enter into a "schoolyard bully" discussion without observing that it is perhaps the least dangerous psychological affliction of our 45th president, everything being relative, of course.

42　This is where yet another aspect of human nature can rear its ugly head: No one likes to be wrong, and people tend to not like admitting that they were wrong, especially those in authority, who often don't think that they need to do so. This can manifest as either official resistance or "disinterest," which certainly characterizes much of the military's historical attitude toward UFO sightings and investigations, both across the board and in individual cases.

43　It is credibly said that in 1955, President Dwight D. Eisenhower's Secretary of Defense, Charles E. Wilson, gave orders to the military that for any UFO information to be released to the public, it had to make a "constructive contribution" to "national security." For decades, those "marching orders" certainly seemed to be followed.

44　Indeed, the word "stigma," strong as it is, can readily apply here, just as it does to the association of an individual with a law enforcement investigation (see Chapter Thirteen). Given how "people are about such things," this, too, seems to be part of basic human nature. And it is broad enough to encompass the closely related word "taboo."

In the modern-day history of UFO sightings and government (mis)handling of them, the idea of UFO "stigma" most prominently arose during the 1950s, most particularly in context of the military, of course. In fact, a recently declassified Top Secret report shared with the Australian Government in the 1970s traced the concept to the CIA, which as noted elsewhere was greatly concerned about the overloading of military communications during a "flap" such as the one in Washington, D.C., in the summer of 1952. It soon became "career suicide" to seriously report such things -- and not only in the military. Both pilots in the skies and first responders on the ground, in cities and towns both large and small, were affected by it as well. And as for federal employees, such as both air traffic controllers and Federal Aviation Administration personnel, an amendment to the National Defense Authorization Act for Fiscal Year 2022 provides special new protection for any such person reporting "any event relating to unidentified aerial phenomena."

45　For those working within the Federal Government (which includes both military personnel and, as a practical matter, many civilian contractors) this has even been expressed as fear of "getting our clearances pulled." Such a fear is realistic, not fanciful, in that a national security clearance is based partly on an assessment of the individual's "stability" -- and in this particular subject area there certainly is a particular risk as to that. In other words, if you report a UFO, expressing any perceived "belief" in it, you "must be crazy," in a true "Catch-22" sense, in which case you no longer can be trusted to be in the position from which you reported the UFO in the first place. Or something like that.

46　What is more, even scientists can have this fear, such as those asked to consult on UFO sightings already reported. It is said that "in space, no one can hear you cry," but in academia, one's professional reputation can be "everything," yet lost in the blink of an eye, because it doesn't take much for it to become tinged with controversy or even mere embarrassment through a connection to "UFOs and such things." Over the years, there reportedly have been many scientists who were afraid to speak about the subject of UFOs because they feared being thought of within academic circles as taking seriously a subject that so many others view as a utterly frivolous.

47   Of all potential UFO sighting "reporters," though, it is hard to imagine a greater *fear of ridicule* -- or of worse than that, such as retribution -- than that which exists in the military. This surely explains the observed reluctance of military personnel to even speak of the subject of UFOs (or to "speak up," in a group setting) for most of the past 75 years, even where the potential military speaker was not actually under orders (direct or indirect) to be silent on it. Further, it has been a recognized part of "military culture" (not that someone who "evaded" the draft (see Chapter Seven) is the best expert on that) that one should even go so far as to actually voice criticism (whether genuine or not) whenever others so speak.

There is, however, a countervailing fear that can come into play -- the fear that UFOs (i.e., the more credibly detected ones) constituted evidence of a Soviet threat to the Nation. This fear was very much part of the picture during the length of the Cold War (i.e., from late 1946, arguably, to 1991) and no doubt many of the people who reported UFO sightings during that span of time (and who otherwise might not have done so) did so out of fear that failing to do so (even in a "borderline" case) could be dangerous, if not also unpatriotic. And to round this off, it must be added that as fear of the "Soviet threat" diminished over time, some people replaced that in their minds with fear of the possibility of an "alien threat." (Today, perhaps one needs to add China, if not also Trump, to this fearsome mix.)

48   The history of "UFO hoaxes" is long and varied, as might be imagined, with most of them readily confirmable as such -- but with some of them ultimately residing in the category of merely "suspected hoaxes," and with yet a smaller subset doomed forever to be strongly contested by "both sides of the question." An example of the latter is the "McMinnville UFO photographs," which all agree were taken by a couple named Trent alongside their Oregon farmhouse in 1950. On one hand, they certainly look to be genuine photographs (two of them) of an alien spacecraft at very low altitude (assuming that one knows what such a thing looks like), but to many skeptics they seem to be a deliberate hoax created by a model suspended from adjacent telephone wires.

49   This includes the U.S.'s first plutonium-production facility in Hanford, Washington, not far from Kenneth Arnold's seminal "flying saucer" sighting in 1947. Could that and the Roswell atomic bomb connection be a mere coincidence?

50   Those who firmly believe this to be true generally regard this "UFO activity" as a suspected "surveillance and reconnaissance effort" that in at least one known instance (on March 16, 1967 at the Malmstrom Air Force Base near Great Falls, Montana) reportedly involved the disabling of the electronics at a missile silo, with missiles there going "off-line," and with a reddish-orange, oval-shaped UFO seen hovering above the gate to the facility. Not to mention several government-acknowledged instances in which there were UFO sightings at the U.S.'s nuclear facilities in Los Alamos, New Mexico, and Oak Ridge, Tennessee, at times when the background radiation counts there became inexplicably elevated.

All of which means that if one truly does believe this to be so, then the conclusion that UFO sightings overall actually pose an astronomically large national security threat to the United States (and to Earth, actually) does logically follow. And such UFO "believers" are quick to find palpable corroboration of this also in any sighting-related deployment of military personnel (or even in almost any UFO-related Federal Government activity at a more institutional level), especially as to anything that smacks of any arguable federal, state, or local (far more likely the former) "cover-up."

51   Indeed, it was less than two years from the dropping of the first atomic bomb over Japan on August 6, 1945 to the "Roswell/Flying Saucer" period in June of 1947. (Or even if counted from the "Trinity" bomb test of July 16, 1945, in Alamogordo, New Mexico, it was still less than two years.)

52   In July of 1952, for instance, *Look* magazine, a mainstream media outlet, published an article titled "Hunt for the Flying Saucer" in which it spoke of a "secret Air Force investigation," under its "Air Technical Intelligence Command," of more than 800 UFO sightings in the areas of "vital atomic installation sites."

53   To this pattern within the U.S. must be added an unconfirmed report of a sustained UFO sighting in June of 1948 over the Soviet Union's primary ballistic missile test site, known as Kapustin Yar, near Volgograd (formerly known as Stalingrad) in the remote Astrakhan region of Russia. Some ufologists have gone so far as to refer to it as the "Russian Roswell."

54   These anxieties took many different forms: The perceived vulnerability of the U.S. air-defense network to penetration by incoming missiles mimicking UFOs; the fear that the Soviets might use UFO sightings to overload our Air Defense warning system such that it could not distinguish real targets from phantom UFOs; and a concern that UFO sightings could pose an indirect threat to national security by overwhelming standard military communications, overloading emergency reporting channels, and even swamping Air Defense systems with reports at critical times. There even was concern that the Soviets would attempt to use the growing "UFO phenomenon" for purposes of psychological warfare, a concern that apparently made the Air Force more inclined at rare times toward an intermittent policy of greater public disclosure (i.e., "acclimatization") in order to minimize the risk of panic.

55   It must be remembered here that during the late 1940s and early 1950s, the United States was undergoing a period of unique domestic and international pressure, in multiple respects. First, it had been required by the fateful confluences of history to pivot immediately from World War II to a new war, albeit a "cold" one, against the Soviet Union -- something that was exacerbated acutely by the new "atomic age" and its growing threat of nuclear war, which arose almost immediately. This very arguably loomed larger than even the bilateral threats posed by World War II. Second, there was the sudden need for the development and integration of an entire "Intelligence Community," beyond the relatively narrow confines of pre-war cryptology and the wartime activities of the Office of Strategic Services ("OSS," to officers of Hitler's SS) in resemblance of Great Britain's longtime such agency, known as MI-6.

This all was not accomplished without creating intense competition, inevitable friction, and even outright conflict among the emerging parts of that realm, most particularly the CIA, NSA, and certain parts of the military, including the Air Force, as they went through what colloquially could be called "growing pains" in the process. (In the Air Force's case, this "growing" involved its gaining its autonomy from the Department of the Navy (and to some degree from the Department of the Army) in the first place, something that apparently has continued in the form of inter-service rivalries and tensions up to the present day.) And as far as UFO sightings were concerned, the most intense competition was between the Air Force and the CIA -- something that played out only behind the scenes for a long time, as the latter had the "political clout" to declare its involvement in the subject to be a threshold (read: abstract) classified fact in and of itself (see Chapter Seventeen). Is this another example of "human nature" operating at the "macro-institutional" level? Yes, it certainly is.

56   "Project Blue Book," of course, is foremost among such things. It went a long way toward this through the 1950s and 1960s.

57   The word "inexplicable" seems to be absolutely key here. A former high-level government official, responding to a pointed question, once put it very bluntly: "We don't like what we can't explain; it's embarrassing." This is perhaps another precept of human nature, an off-shoot of "paternalism" perhaps, or possibly one connected to a no less fundamental human "desire to control." Whatever one chooses to call it, there can be no doubt but that it has animated government responses to UFO sightings quite heavily, especially as advances in science have made them more, not less, difficult to explain.

58   This smacks of both the "paternalism" and "proprietariness" elements of human nature that are identified in this book's Introduction. Can any greater, more consequential manifestation of them be imagined than in the context of any reality-based "UFO secrecy"?

59   At about the same time (i.e., in late 1952 and January of 1953), the relatively new Central Intelligence Agency "got itself into the game," so to speak, by sponsoring a four-day meeting of scientific experts who were known to themselves (and within the CIA) as the "Robertson Panel." Evidently, this effort was partly intended to "oversee" the then-nascent work of the Air Force on the subject, was partly undertaken in response to a huge "flap" (yes, that's what they were calling it back then) of UFO sightings over Washington, D.C., during the summer of 1952 (which had dangerously overloaded government telecommunications systems), and existed partly to flex the CIA's institutional muscles on the subject. But an overlay to all of this, as far as the CIA was concerned, was undoubtedly its interest in protecting the existence of the U.S.'s growing fleet of highly advanced spy planes from the early 1950s on, in which it had a heavy hand, indeed.

60   The first of these Air Force studies was originally known as "Project Saucer," which really wasn't such a good idea, so it was quickly renamed "Project Sign," which operated (mostly as a benign sighting-collection effort) informally near the end of 1947 and officially throughout 1948 and into early 1949. It was precipitated largely by Air Force General Nathan F. Twining, who was tasked to study the "flying disc situation" in July of 1947, very soon after the sighting made by Kenneth Arnold and the reported crash at Roswell. Twining, who was head of the Air Material Command and later went on to become chairman of the joint chiefs of staff, wrote a brief report in September of 1947 stating his view that "[t]he phenomenon is something real and not visionary or fictitious."

        Then, after not much more than a year, and amid rumors that it was leaning way too much toward an ex-traterrestrial explanation for the government's taste, Project Sign was renamed "Project Grudge" (for a reason lost in the mists of time), another relatively short-lived enterprise, which operated more or less haltingly from 1949 to late 1951 as a branch of the Air Force's Air Technical Intelligence Center ("ATIC," to those who like to "kick things upstairs"), which later included the Air Force's "Foreign Technology Division" at Wright-Patterson Air Force Base in Dayton, Ohio.

        "Project Grudge" operated as a cynically alleged "debunking machine," issued a lengthy report on the subject in 1949, and was the direct predecessor of Project Blue Book (after a brief interregnum period) when that project was created in March of 1952. During that interregnum period, the Air Force launched something that it lightheartedly (at least one can hope) named "Project Twinkle," an investigation in New Mexico of numerous, seemingly credible sightings of "green fireballs," which eventually fizzled out with a natural explanation. And at the same time, it also created something called "Project Stork," which gave birth to the idea of gathering experts in various scientific fields in one place, in this case at the nearby Battelle Center of Ohio State University, to analyze the most difficult UFO sightings together, with strong emphasis on standardizing the reporting process; it was created in early 1952, was fueled mightily by the Washington, D.C., "flaps" of that summer, but then was discontinued by the end of that year.

        The year 1952 also marked the first time that a sighted UFO was captured in motion on film. In July of that year, a Navy photographer vacationing with his wife in Utah filmed nearly a dozen white objects, high in the sky, that appeared to be like the ones observed by Kenneth Arnold in 1947. Both the Navy and the Air Force studied this film at length and came up with no credible explanation for it.

61   A major exception to this was the 1964 "landing" sighted by police officer Lonnie Zamora in Socorro, New Mexico, near the White Sands Missile Range, the Archuleta Mesa, and the small town of Dulce. Project Blue Book investigators took this sighting very seriously and, after analyzing it fully, reached the atypical conclusion that it could not be explained. The Archuleta Mesa, by the way, is itself the site of numerous UFO sightings over the years.

62   Project Blue Book is by far the most well-known Federal Government entity designed to study UFOs to date (perhaps with prospective apologies to the four programs established successively by different parts of the Department of Defense (at first, secretly) during the past 15 years (see below), the latter of which might well overtake Project Blue Book in time). And as such it has been much written-about, talked about, and even dramatized on television (including in a recent "series") over the years, so there is little need to dwell on it at any length at this point, except perhaps to make the point that its work has almost zero credibility (read: reliability and integrity, given its blatant shortcomings) in the minds of many, myself included.

Suffice to say here that under the leadership of both Dr. J. Allen Hynek and Major Edward J. Ruppelt, the latter of whom wrote a book about it in 1956 after retiring (see Chapter Thirty-Three), Project Blue Book was the public face of the Air Force's "handling" of UFO sightings, explanations, and controversies (sometimes with "disinformation") for nearly two decades until being "done in" by the Condon Committee's critique of it in 1969. In 1976, six years after it was shut down, the Air Force reportedly turned over all of Project Blue Book's files to the National Archives and Records Administration, which has made them available for public inspection (at its Archives II facility) with only very limited restrictions (e.g., for the names of some individuals involved) ever since.

63   Such purposeful management of public perception about UFOs appears to have been a large (perhaps predominating) part of the U.S. Government's approach to the subject from almost the outset in the 1940s. Some say that this was no more than a paternalistic but no less realistic recognition of the populace's capacity to greatly "overreact" to such things -- even to the point of panic -- which arguably called for extreme measures simply for the sake of public safety. Others point to the fact that, as a matter of basic human nature -- again, as a societal macrocosm (see the Introduction) -- no government is immediately (if ever) comfortable with the thought of publicly admitting that there exists something so potentially Earth-shattering yet so inexplicable that it just cannot figure it out. (Hence, we have not merely fear of the unknown here, but fear of the very fact that there *is* such an unknown.)

64   Perhaps the best example of this is an alleged UFO "crash" near Kingman, Arizona, in mid-May of 1953. Reportedly, Federal Government officials sent a team of about 40 scientists to the crash site to investigate, upon being forced by the military to swear an oath of lifetime secrecy (something that is not so easily enforced in the case of civilian personnel). Two of them, a metallurgist and an engineer, are said to have broken their silence nearly 20 years later to describe parts of the episode, and it was said that Project Blue Book had taken over the investigation of the entire matter.

Nothing is known to have come from it, though, except there were further allegations that its "cover up" was connected to something called the "Majestic 12 Special Studies Group" ("MJ-12," to its dozens of adherents) and to its "SOP" manual for the military's handling of such UFO events. There is a widespread belief, however, including even by some ufologists, that the very existence of "Majestic 12" was a hoax created through fabricated documents, the authenticity of which is thus an analytical pivot point. In fact, it can fairly be said that "Majestic 12's" existence itself is a point of controversy perhaps rivaled by only Roswell itself within the "UFO community."

But if "Majestic 12" actually did exist, as a group assembled by Secretary of Defense James V. Forrestal in 1947 to oversee the Federal Government's handling of UFO activity, then it would have been connected to anything found at the alleged crash site(s) at Roswell, as well as to anything believed transported from any crash site (such as Kecksburg, Pennsylvania) to Wright (later Wright-Patterson) Air Force Base ("Wright-Pat," to military insiders) in Ohio, home of the Air Force's Foreign Technology Division, reportedly in the base's "Hangar 18," for what the Air Force called "back engineering," with the aid of a metallurgical company named "Battelle Memorial Institute." (Today, ufologists point to the large numbers of UFO sightings proximate to this Air Force base as "corroboration" of this overall theory.)

The speculation about all of this was heightened when Defense Secretary Forrestal suffered a mental break-down in 1949 (after heated disagreements over UFO policy, it is theorized) and reportedly died by self-defenes-tration after being admitted to Bethesda Naval Hospital as suicidal and then inexplicably being placed in a room up on its 16th floor. And the "MJ-12" group, if it existed, would have continued through the Administration of President Dwight D. "Ike" Eisenhower and on into the Administration of President John F. Kennedy, in coordination with CIA Director Allen W. Dulles.

65   Dr. Edward U. Condon was a highly respected physicist at the University of Colorado and a former Director of the National Bureau of Standards. He agreed to conduct an 18-month study of the subject for the Air Force, which evidently was in turn acting under tremendous pressure from the CIA, although that latter agency's involvement in UFO matters apparently was then still a classified abstract fact (see Chapter Seventeen), at its insistence, and remained so for many years.

66   Behind the scenes, it is said, the Air Force and the CIA had been locked in some sort of institutional "death match" over the Federal Government's "handling" of UFO matters for nearly two decades by then, with the Air Force playing "little cousin" to its ostensible Intelligence Community "friends." Sometimes, it must be said, such bureaucratic rivalries can lead to unanticipated transparency, as was the case with the competitive rivalries (read: blame shifting) of the CIA and the FBI in the wake of 9/11 (as detailed by the 9/11 Commission), but in this case all indications are that the very opposite occurred: UFO secrecy prevailed, and even flourished, with the passage of time, just as the CIA preferred.

67   By all reports, the driving force behind APRO, and a true "ufology pioneer," was an Arizona housewife by the name of Coral Lorenzen, who compiled, analyzed, catalogued, and cross-referenced UFO sightings from around the world beginning in the early 1950s. Over the course of more than 30 years, she documented literally thousands of sightings that otherwise went unpublished due to the tenor of the times.

68   Apparently there once were at least two more such organizations at the time, a local one in the early 1950s called the "California Committee for Saucer Investigation," the existence of which might have been more a function of the State of California than anything else, and a short-lived one named the "International Flying Saucer Bureau" during 1952-1953. There also were reports of such organizations operating locally in Wisconsin and New York at that time. But although there were dramatically increasing numbers of UFO sightings in the State of Texas during the early-to-mid-1950s, beginning with what are known as the "Lubbock Lights" in 1951, no such organization was formed there.

69   By then, there was another private-sector player on the field, a small organization by the name of "Ground Saucer Watch," which was founded in the late 1950s but became most active during the mid-1970s, especially when it began making (and suing on) Freedom of Information Act requests. (I recall it having made an impact at the Justice Department when I became a litigator there in 1977.) Its place then was taken by another group called

Citizens Against UFO Secrecy, which made even more sophisticated use of the FOIA (especially FOIA litigation) against both the CIA and NSA in the wake of the liberalizing, "post-Watergate" FOIA Amendments of 1974. Its efforts, in turn, began to fade during the 1990s, but the FOIA remains available today as a tool for combatting UFO secrecy; it just has to be wielded expertly.

70   MUFON also is connected to a fellow named Scott C. Waring, an educator in Taiwan who operates a dramatic website called "UFO Sightings Daily." Over the decades, several other "UFO groups" have sprung up, only to relatively quickly disappear. The Center for UFO Studies was in that category; it was headed by Dr. J. Allen Hynek, the well-respected astronomer of Project Blue Book fame, but it remained viable for not much longer than he did. (Dr. Hynek died in 1983.) So, too, was something called the "Fund for UFO Research," which existed from the late 1970s until the late 2000s. More recent "UFO groups" have included such organizations as the National UFO Reporting Center ("NUFORC," to its old friends, as it actually traces back to 1974); the "Scientific Coalition for UAP [Unidentified Aerial Phenomena] Studies"; something called "UFODATA"; the newly formed National UFO Historical Records Center in Albuquerque, N.M., now the largest U.S.-based repository of UFO-related archives; and the "To The Stars Academy," which maintains a public-facing database of UFO sightings that it calls a "Virtual Analytics UAP Learning Tool" (or "VAULT," to its users), known commonly as "the Vault" (with the "UAP" standing for "Unidentified Aerial Phenomena," the more modern version of "UFO").

Of course, any UFO/UAP-related research information that is housed within a private-sector, purely non-governmental entity such as, say, Bigelow Aerospace, would not ordinarily be subject to FOIA disclosure under prevailing case law. Indeed, one "hot rumor" in the ufology world is that a DIA Director by the name of Vice Admiral Thomas R. Wilson reportedly admitted the existence of a secret U.S. Government alien spacecraft crash retrieval program, as well as the use of private contractors (read: including an aerospace corporation) to "hide" alien technology development from the reach of both Congress and the FOIA.

However, I must point out that there is a little-known and even less utilized provision in the FOIA that was added to the Act as subsection (f)(2)(b) in 2007 and defines a "record" as follows: "[A]ny information described under subparagraph (A) that is maintained for an agency by an entity under Government contract, for the purposes of records management." Inasmuch as Bigelow Aerospace is (or at least once was) a contractor of the Defense Intelligence Agency, a clever FOIA requester could theoretically use this "new" FOIA provision to place any government-originated information that is maintained for it by Bigelow "on the hook," so to speak, by challenging the "purposes" for which it is maintained. To the best of my knowledge, no FOIA requester has ever done this, and I do not know why.

71   The distinction between "overt" and "covert" must always be borne in mind in such a context. Not only could it make a difference in this particular case, I know from my own experience with using it (see Chapter Seventeen) that it can be a primary basis for delineating between different categories of files, records, and information for purposes of "Glomarization" under the Freedom of Information Act.

72   The use of this secrecy term here is rhetorical, not technical. However, there are indications that some parts of the Federal Government have employed the terms "Ultra Secret" and "Cosmic Secret" (and even "Über Secret") for some compartments of UFO-related information. And it stands to reason that *if* a government were to maintain information of alien origin, it certainly would give such information a compartmented classification level all its own.

73   A major focus of this speculation, from almost the outset, is that Area 51 has been the primary site in recent decades for the "reverse engineering" (or "back engineering") of alien craft. This narrative posits, of course, the very existence of alien craft to begin with. But the discovery of one does not prove the existence of the other.

74   Notably, this long-overdue revelation came only after the CIA had been effectively forced to take that step by a Freedom of Information Act request that had been made eight years earlier, in 2005. That FOIA request compelled the declassification and disclosure of some CIA records that had inadvertently mentioned the facility by one its "cover" names in 1992. All things being equal, the FOIA can be the best tool for piercing the secrecy of such a thing. (Tip: The Federal Government realizes this. It is why its "red hat" exercises sometimes posit the receipt of certain "targeted" FOIA requests in order to prophylactically plan against them -- with "secrecy techniques" -- including through the possible use of "Glomarization" since 1977 (see Chapter Seventeen).)

75   This is with all due apologies to "Operation Overlord" in June of 1944, otherwise known as "the invasion of Normandy," which historians say proceeded in total secrecy, despite all German efforts to determine the "where and when of it" beforehand (see Chapter Forty-Nine). As absolutely secret as that was, though, that secrecy needed to last for only a matter of weeks beforehand. By contrast, the Manhattan Project and Area 51 (or Groom Lake) remained entirely secret enterprises for much longer periods of time (see Chapter Forty-Nine), with the latter's secrecy not necessarily curtailed like that of the former. (Perhaps the desert locale has something to do with that.)

And speaking of such remote locales, it should be mentioned that there is another, quite similar, and perhaps even *more* secretive one in the adjacent state of Utah that has come to be known informally as "Area 52." Located about 85 miles southwest of Salt Lake City, this large expanse (covering an estimated 1250 square miles) is officially known as "Dugway Proving Ground" and long has been believed to be a military (read: mostly Army, with elite private contractors) site used for the testing and storage of chemical, biological, and radiological weapons going all the way back to the early 1940s. In recent years, its observable (read: aboveground) facilities have expanded, as near as can be discerned.

Long suspected to be undergirded by extensive tunneling, as part of vast underground facilities, Area 52 is the place to which NASA brought its Genesis "Solar Wind" space probe down for a controlled crash landing after its parachute failed in September of 2004 (thus revealing that NASA even had that capability). To many ufologists, it is suspected to be where alien technology (assuming that it exists) now is "reverse-engineered" -- as the successor location to Wright-Patterson Air Force Base (read: and then after Area 51) -- and also where the most advanced U.S. aircraft are now developed and tested. In recent years, not unlike with the "flight lanes" that are proximate to Area 51, it has been the locale of large numbers of UFO sightings -- including some "black triangle" craft sometimes seen flying even in broad daylight and by many accounts seeming to disappear. And to that must be added a laser-like "beam" that has been seen emerging from Area 52, heading due skyward, in the middle of the night.

In sum, we now have what appears to be a clear "reverse-engineering" progression over the years, from Wright-Patterson to Area 51 to Area 52, with site "S-4" (see below) remaining somewhere in the mix. And to those occupying the most extreme "wing" of ufology, Area 52 is where alien technology (again, assuming that it exists) is most actively integrated into advanced military aircraft and where there might even be a "spaceport" of sorts. If so, then the intense public focus on Area 51 might well someday yield to its numerical successor one state over.

76   As George Orwell presciently wrote (in *1984*, in 1949): "If you want to keep a secret, you must also hide it from yourself." In this case, the nature of the beast is that there were just too many "yourselves" involved to expect complete secrecy to hold forever. But give the Air Force (and its confederates) credit: It held for a very long time, arguably for more than 30 years.

77   Some of those attempts were made in connection with environmental law cases that in the mid-1990s were defended by the Department of Justice's "Public Lands Division" (or just "Lands Division," for short, renamed the "Environment and Natural Resources Division" in 1990), which invoked the "State Secrets Privilege" (read: a

barrier to the maintenance of lawsuits against the Federal Government that involve matters of national security) in conjunction with national security classification. The folks over there (i.e., on the Second Floor of the Main Justice Building) regularly consulted with OIP on such issues, especially insofar as the plaintiffs in those cases, as well as many other "UFO enthusiasts," were by then heavily using the Freedom of Information Act in efforts to learn whatever they could about what they referred to as "Area 51" at the same time. Without going into too much detail here, let's just say that the Justice Department managed to "hold the line" on the secrecy of Area 51 (not to mention Area 52) on behalf of its nominal Air Force client. Yes, we worked hard at that.

At the same time, however, there is a distinct fact about the use of the Freedom of Information Act at Groom Lake that now has entered the public domain: A former research supervisor there, who previously had been a high-level military officer and was able to specify holding what I know firsthand to have been a particularly high-level, compartmented clearance, has described personally taking steps designed to "evade FOIA requests" that were made for what would be Groom Lake's most sensitive research and development records. His favorite such gambit, as he has described it, is the prophylactic use of a "cover name" for such records -- for example, filing them under the heading "Advanced Theoretical Physics," which is a search term that he ventured "never would be guessed" by FOIA requesters. Such is the type of "secrecy technique" that can be used in timely anticipation of receiving FOIA requests.

78   This wide region extends for hundreds of miles in almost all directions and includes the Nevada Test and Training Range, the Tonopah Test Range, Nellis Air Force Base, and heaven knows what else. Something that is claimed to fall within this latter category is a facility referred to as "Site 4" or "Sector 4" or "S-4," which is said to exist about 10-15 miles south-by-southwest of "Area 51," near Papoose Lake, as a site for the "reverse engineering" of alien craft. Even the less far-fetched claims made about this site, which include use of a purported "anti-gravity" or "anti-matter" element with the atomic number of 115 (now recognized as element "Mc"), originally called "ununpentium" but later named "moscovium," border on the fantastical and for now should be left at that (or at least to reruns of *The X-Files* television program).

But there is the fact that a self-described "Site 4" whistleblower, Robert S. "Bob" Lazar, claimed in 1989 that he worked there "reverse engineering" (or "back engineering," in his parlance) alien technology. Even if his more extreme claims (e.g., nine hangars holding nine alien craft and propulsion through the "time dilation refraction" effect under what is known to physicists as "Snell's law") are taken with commensurate grains of salt, his detailed stories about working at Area 51 and "Site 4" are sufficiently plausible as to raise reasonable doubt about the government's flat denials of them. And they are supported by at least two others who have said similar things: Benjamin R. Rich, the long-term director of Lockheed Martin's Skunk Works known the "father of stealth tech-nology," and Lt. Col. Philip J. Corso, former chief of the Pentagon's "Foreign Technology Division," who made a deathbed statement about the Government giving alien technology to the private sector for "development." (He explained that much of the reason for this is that it took that beyond the reach of the Freedom of Information Act. This, too, is a "secrecy technique for evading FOIA requests.) In his deathbed video statement, he said that the word "foreign" in the name of his division actually meant "extraterrestrial."

Support of his claims has also come from SR-71 pilot David Freehoff, former Air Force officer James Goodell, and author Thornton D. ("TD") Barnes, all of whom have well-established employment backgrounds at Area 51. And then there is the case of a former CIA officer who said (on videotape) shortly before his death that he and his boss were sent to Area 51 on behalf of President Eisenhower in 1960 and that they were taken to a facility "thirteen to fifteen miles" away that they learned was indeed called "S-4." (In a series of interviews, he went by the names of "Anonymous" and "Agent Kewper," but his actual name was later learned to be Oscar Wayne Wolff.) Much of what he described was corroborative of claims made by Lazar.

And circling back to the "fantastical," I suppose that any comprehensive survey of the UFO "skyscape" arguably should include what is claimed to be another means by which UFOs are "seen" -- something that is called by some "remote viewing." This is described as "the practice of seeking impressions about a distant or unseen subject, purportedly sensing with the mind." And it has been applied, with notably inconsistent results, to the field of UFO observation. Something that is especially difficult to believe, it is a "pseudoscience," at best, one most accurately relegated to the realm of the "paranormal."

79   Over the years, the United States has seemed to devote almost as much attention to the development and testing of new weapons systems as it has to the development and testing of advanced aircraft. A primary new weapon system operating currently is something called the "Netted Emulation of Multi-Element Signature against Integrated Sensors" platform ("NEMESIS," to those who are acronymically inclined), a highly sophisticated radar "spoofing" system (read: one in which "phantom sightings" are created in order to distract, confuse, and profoundly confound any adversary) unlike anything ever seen before. NEMESIS first emerged in the Department of the Navy's Department's Research, Development, Test & Evaluation Budget Item Justification documents in its budget proposal for the 2014 Fiscal Year, which it released into the public domain in April of 2013.

Developed by the Office of Naval Research ("ONR," to its unsinkable colleagues) in conjunction with DARPA (the "Defense Advanced Research Projects Agency," of Internet fame), NEMESIS was said to be capable of generating viable "false targets," realistic-looking "false signatures," and highly effective decoys that increase the number of potential targets with which an adversary would have to engage. These false targets would "mimic the RF emissions and radar returns of real platforms" and include infrared decoys and "concepts and capabilities to simulate the computer network activity of deployed forces." The system even includes the use of underwater "high-fidelity acoustic decoys," radio emulators, and something called "Distributed Decoy and Jammer Swarms" ("DDJS," to its "swarmees"), through advanced "drone swarm" technology, guided by artificial intelligence ("AI," to those most intelligent) and the Navy's "Miniature Air-Launched Decoy" ("MALD-X," to other "swarmees") system. Now that's a mouthful.

Purported to having been both developed and tested primarily at Groom Lake, NEMESIS has been referred to reverently as a "System of Systems" ("SoS," without much irony) and as the evolutionary "next great leap" in electronic warfare. Apropos of that, an offshoot of NEMESIS is something called "LEAP" (or "Long Endurance Advanced Off-board Electronic Warfare Platform"), which is a distinct decoy system, together with a system code-named "LOCUST," which is a highly deployable "swarming drone" capability, and what are called "Nomad" drones -- low-cost, single-use, rotary-wing devices that provide enormous flexibility.

In other words, NEMESIS and its ilk together constitute an entire electronic warfare "ecosystem" -- and an almost entirely secret one at that. And related to that, as if any more is needed, in what appears to exist purely in the form of software "architecture," is something called the "System of Systems Integration Technology and Experimentation" ("SoSITE," to its programmers) program, which according to DARPA's wordy budgetary explanations "seeks to develop and deliver systems architecture concepts for rapid integration of new U.S. technologies as they are developed, without requiring significant re-engineering of existing capabilities, systems, or systems of systems."

All of which raises the following (im)pertinent question, of course: If our military actually has developed such sophisticated capabilities of "spoofing" opposing aircraft, with the ability to "project" anything from single planes maneuvering in "other-worldly" fashion to whole "phantom fleets," with an electronic mastery beyond anything until recently imagined, then might it possibly be testing that against our own aircraft, thereby generating "artificial" sightings by Navy fighter jets, for instance, in the bargain? And if a branch of our military has in fact been doing so, at at least some point or points in the relatively recent past, would not its "system testing" be enhanced if its own pilots and their ground support personnel were not "in the know" about it? And if that actually were so, then couldn't that explain some or even all of the recent fighter jet experiences with "UFOs," not to mention certain allegations that uniformed Air Force officers "strong-armed" Navy flight-data records from Navy ground personnel in 2004 (see below)? If so, then that degree of Air Force supremacy *vis-a-vis* the Navy would mark its high point because, as of 2020, it became clear that the Navy is now "on top" (see below).

80   Many other things are alleged (read: not at all officially confirmed) to exist as part of "black projects" operating out of Groom Lake. Even putting aside the more fantastical such claims (e.g., of "stored alien remains"), they include a range of "advanced electromagnetic warfare" techniques, across what is now called the "electromagnetic spectrum" -- "EMS," to those who are highly charged about "reverse engineering" (increasingly called "back engineering") of all kinds. (These latter terms, by the way, do not necessarily apply just to speculated "alien technology"; they include the analysis of highly effective Russian MiGs during the Vietnam War.)

And despite popular conceptions to the contrary (including by incoming President Bill Clinton, as described above), the very nature of national security "compartmentalization" at its highest levels (i.e., within some particular "information silos") appears to be such that keeping officials even as "high up" as a president in the dark about the true nature of a black project's activities, at least until a point of "push comes to shove" is reached with sufficient focus, actually is possible. Indeed, one could pragmatically argue that some Members of Congress -- through the appropriations power, as a practical matter -- have greater leverage than even a president for prying the most sensitive "black project" information loose.

To some, perhaps even many, this might sound like heresy within our constitutional system, especially given the development of the modern presidency and its focus on singular presidential power in the nuclear age. It is difficult to imagine a president holding the power to "push the nuclear button" on one hand, yet not being able to immediately see whatever he or she might want to see even in the darkest recesses of our National Government on the other. It seems like a whole new dimension of "secrecy."

But consider this: A president serves for no more than eight years (consecutively), perhaps for only four, and conceivably for even less in the case of resignation, assassination, or successful impeachment. And once a president leaves office, he or she carries whatever knowledge was gained (i.e., absorbed and retained, then not forgotten) during his or her presidency for the rest of his or her life. In the case of former President Jimmy Carter, for example, this has turned out to be more than 42 years since the end of his term in office thus far. (Born on October 1, 1924, President Carter left office on January 20, 1981, and has been a paragon of moral rectitude ever since.)

So what if we were to have a president who leaves office not like President Carter, but rather utterly awash in serious legal difficulties, surprising financial woes, and perhaps also psychological problems the likes of which have never before been seen (think Nixon, only far worse). And let's just say that, as a key part of this hypothetical, this president had a demonstrated track record in office of being, in the views of many, less than upright in his or her character, less inclined than most (read: anyone else, actually) to respect presidential norms of behavior (up to and including truth-telling), and more susceptible than most to the blandishments of malign foreign actors -- or, to put it bluntly, of foreseeably being predisposed to "monetize" what he knows. So the question is: Would we as a Nation want such a former president to have had all of our Nation's deepest national secrets readily available within his or her (assuming there is one) "frontal lobe"? Compartmentalization, even from a president, can anticipatorily guard against this hypothetical situation if ever it were to occur, thus giving "government secrecy" a slightly newer meaning than ever before.

81   There is little doubt but that to at least some extent over the years the U.S. Government has taken advantage of the public's interest (and partial belief) in UFOs to effectively camouflage its development of advanced aircraft for military and intelligence purposes. The sightings near Area 52 doubtless have been no small part of that.

82   Something similar to this that already has been seen is "RAF Rudloe Manor," an enormous facility that has been called "the British Area 51." Located in southwestern England in the County of Wiltshire, and close to the small market village of Corsham, it consists of 2.2 million square feet of caverns, chambers, and tunnels connected to the quarry from which stone was mined for ancient Roman baths. Britain's Ministry of Defense ("MoD," to its rockers) has acknowledged that the manor house and its underground facilities were the center of its UFO investigation activity during the 1950s, but through its Air Force Provost and Security Services it has kept mum (especially to those with mothers) on what has gone on there since then. (It's counterpart in Australia is an American satellite-surveillance base known as "Pine Gap," about a dozen miles from the town of Alice Springs, that has operated for decades in total secrecy.)

And not unlike Area 51, Rudloe has at least one other heavily guarded facility, known as the "Corsham Computer Center" (or "C.C.C" in its partially punctuated signage) located "within tunnel distance" nearby. And on its other side, likewise connected to it by tunnels, caverns, and originally a quarry lake, is England's version of our "Special Facility" (see Chapter Twenty-Six), Burlington Bunker. Built in the late 1950s on top of an underground quarry with limestone caves, its purposes was to house the top leadership of the British Government, together with England's Royal Family, in case of nuclear war, until it was deemed no longer needed as of 1991. That area (i.e., the County of Wiltshire) is the home of Stonehenge, other henges, and similar rock formations. It also has been a "hot spot" of UFO sightings for decades.

In a similar category is the nearby Town of Glastonbury, home of the elevated historical site known as the "Glastonbury Tor" (or "St. Michael's Tor," which is how it was labeled when I first ascended it nearly 45 years ago). Rising to an elevation of 518 feet, it is surrounded on all sides by a concentric downhill progression of seven deep terraces, the origins of which are a mystery, and it is topped by the ruins of "St. Michael's Tower," as restored in the early 19th century. Glastonbury, and the Tor (meaning steep hill) in particular, has been described as a UFO "hot spot" for many years.

83   There is one key element of secrecy that even Area 51's exceptionally remote topography does not provide: Protection from satellite surveillance. This has led to much speculation about the existence of expansive underground facilities at this site, including tunneling that can support underground rail capability. This would permit advanced aircraft (or anything else) to be developed entirely underground and then tested at night.

84   One particular departure from this is the recent claim by a known Groom Lake employee that he participated in something called "Project Palladium" there during the mid-2000s, which he says involved using "radar-spoofing technology" to engage in the "electronic warfare" technique of "spoofing" radar operators, both ground and aerial, into thinking that "phantom" detections were real ones. By all accounts, such a thing is entirely plausible. "Project Palladium was a long-term CIA program designed to study and interfere with Soviet radar; in the early 1960s, it had deployed radar-spoofing systems and submarine-launched balloons carrying metallic radar reflectors in order to stimulate and probe Cuba's Soviet-made air defenses.

85   By all appearances, including ostensible "shoot to kill" security protocols surrounding the entire area (read: certainly sufficient to withstand the Internet-spawned "Storm Area 51" event on September 20, 2019), the Groom Lake facilities continue to serve their largely secret purposes, which presumably would include the next generations of military aircraft, spacecraft, and accompanying weaponry, such as the suspected new "TR-3B Black Manta" surveillance craft, rumored (read: not yet even close to officially confirmed) to use highly pressurized mercury accelerated by nuclear energy to produce a form of "plasma" that creates a "field of anti-gravity" around the ship that in effect warps "space time" in some astonishing, truly surreal way. (Note that this articulation of such a process, whether or not involving the use of "reverse-engineered alien technology," in and of itself "crosses a scientific line," so to speak, and should be regarded as such.)

One the other hand, though, the development of propulsion systems through some use of plasma and electromagnetic fields is something that has been credibly tied to research done at Groom Lake. (The fact that plasma constitutes the most abundant form of ordinary matter in the universe, as well as more than half the volume of human blood, might be just coincidental.) And plasma has been credibly identified within the mainstream scientific community as a "fourth state" of matter (read: solid, liquid, gas, and plasma) that is theorized to occupy much of the known "voids" of the universe as what is now called "dark matter," which is known to exist only because it has a very strong gravitational signature in the "bending" of light and might actually be "the glue that holds the universe together." Which leads, inevitably, to the more theoretical existence of "dark energy," which if it exists would have an anti-gravity force (read: one that is repulsive, as magnets can be) and would cause not only the universe's expansion, but that expansion's acceleration. It is only logical to consider the composition of deepest space, as it is most recently theorized to exist, in conjunction with the conjectured mechanics of inter-stellar (read: and then Earth-bound) space travel.

86   As I recall, the focus of this was the fact that Lee Harvey Oswald had visited the Soviet Embassy in Mexico City not long before the assassination, where he was of course photographed by an intelligence agency (or by one of its contractor personnel), in this particular case against the backdrop of a street-facing metal fence. The concern was that the angle from which Oswald was photographed (as measurable from that geometric backdrop) could be used to determine the exact location from which such photographs were routinely taken. Thus, that photograph, in the Agency's view (no pun intended), constituted, in its entirety, a protectible "source or method."

87   I remember Launie telling me that he thought the best way for his agency to deal with these two high-profile subjects was to be both honest and unstinting in favor of disclosure (the latter being my word, not his), lest the CIA suffer harm from being perceived otherwise somewhere down the road. At the same time, though, Launie had sufficient cynicism (born of experience, no doubt) to realize that given the tenor of the times and the very nature of these subjects, no matter how many records he located, no matter how much information contained in them were to be disclosed in response to FOIA requests, and even no matter how much that information turned out to be unremarkable in its content, most FOIA requesters (and the public at large) were going to believe that some form of "cover up" was at hand. Anyway, anyone who knew Launie could see that while seemingly mild-mannered, he could be firm and demanding if need be. So I have a firsthand basis for having no doubt that what the CIA located (and came forth with) on both of these subjects was accurate and comprehensive as of that time. (Launie, like so many others, died too young, at age 70, in 1995.)

88   In fact, Don was one of two CIA deputy directors to be deposed in that case (together with an academic expert from the National Security Council ("NSC," to those who could keep things straight between it and NSA)), the other being John F. Blake, who served as Acting Deputy Director of Central Intelligence as well. During his deposition "prep," as well as thereafter, John Blake and I never spoke about UFOs or anything of the kind. Don Wortman died recently, at the age of 92.

89   As I recall, Don said that his formal formulation of DCI Turner's question was simply: "Are we in UFOs?" This was a reasonable interpretation, everyone thought, given that Turner's obvious concern was a political one -- i.e., could he be "bitten on the ass" (which I think Don said is how Turner put it) for anything happening "on his watch," which is something that old Navy officers rightfully do worry about.

90   A prime example is Cardiff, Wales, which during the summer of 2008 experienced an unremitting "flood" of UFO sightings, not unlike the "flap" that occurred in the area of Washington, D.C., during the summer of 1952.

91   Noteworthy examples are sightings in Phoenix, Arizona (the "Phoenix Lights") in 1997; Tinley Park, Illinois, in 2004; Bakersfield, California, in 2007; Lake Tahoe, in 2007; O'Hare International Airport (Gate C-17) in November of 2006; and San Juan International Airport in 2013 (a videotaped "tumbling" object that briefly submerges and then splits into two identical objects, also tracked on radar). The O'Hare case in particular involved many dozens of witnesses, nearly a dozen different photographs, and what seemed to be concerted efforts by the Federal Aviation Administration ("FAA," to its fair-weather friends) and United Airlines to "cover up" the sightings of a large, metallic-looking disc that was observed and photographed by many people as it hovered over one gate and then suddenly ascended vertically into the sky, "punching a hole" into the clouds. This also involved a Freedom of Information Act request that was filed by the *Chicago Tribune* and bedeviled the FAA just before I retired. (No, I cannot disclose what it asked me.) The O'Hare and San Juan sightings, together, constitute what is regarded as the most compelling pair of airport sightings in the U.S. in this century. There also have been several such airport sightings in China, the most well-known being at Xiaoshan Airport in Hangzhou on July 7, 2010.

92   Something else that became more frequent as of the 1970s was what came to be known as "cattle mutilation" cases, in which field animals are found with body parts mysteriously "excised," seemingly bloodlessly, with near-surgical precision. This phenomenon, which is essentially in the same category as "crop circles" (or crop "formations") posits that aliens operating at night are responsible for what is found in the morning. Most prominent examples of crop formations are designs made in fields of wheat and barley north of Stonehenge and in nearby Avebury that could be fully discerned only from above. Investigative reporter and filmmaker Linda Moulton Howe is probably the most ubiquitous ufologist to study this, primarily through her 1980 documentary "*Strange Harvest*," but as with mutilation cases, this subject is complicated by the fact that there are less sensational possible explanations for such things. Crop formations are most commonplace in England, increasingly so since the 1970s, and the most compelling actually appear to contain binary code. This fits with ufologists' belief that they are a means of alien communication, and for all anyone knows for sure, they might be.

And as for Stonehenge itself, it is the most famous "stone circle" in the world and, among other things, boasts astronomical alignments to both solstices and both equinoxes. Located on Salisbury Plain in Wiltshire, England, just a couple of miles from the small town of Amesbury, it has drawn amazed visitors (including myself, several times) and also draws UFO theorists who seemingly would like nothing better than to connect it to UFO activity. But there really have been no credible UFO sightings exactly there.

93   When "the age of the UFO" began, only Sweden and its geopolitical descendant Norway had a freedom-of-information law (one tracing back to the year 1776, believe it or not), but by 1967 the United States Freedom of Information Act was in effect and by 1974 our FOIA was heavily amended such that it was fully available for use in "finding out" about UFOs. And then during the next three decades the openness-in-government concept literally "exploded" throughout the world; it was not long before the list of nations "with a FOIA" started approaching 100 (see Chapter One).

94   In the early days of reported UFO sightings, the United States certainly was their principal location, but other nations soon joined the "UFO club": Sweden, Great Britain, Canada, and France led the way. Then, as passing decades took us to the present time, they were joined by such other nations as Argentina, Australia, Belgium, Brazil, Chile, Denmark, Finland, India, Italy, Japan, Mexico, New Zealand, Norway, Peru, South Africa, Spain, Uruguay, and even Russia. And all of these countries, with the possible exception of Argentina, eventually adopted policies of "openness" (read: at least ostensible transparency) for their sightings records at the national level. As for the other four South American nations on this list, plus Mexico, it has been observed that the people of Latin America are much more tolerant of "the unknown" than are people from other parts of the world, and this evidently has affected their attitudes toward UFOs.

In Chile, for example, there is a strong cultural orientation toward extraterrestrial life, as well as a spate of UFO sightings, such as the mass sightings of what is known as the "Santiago UFO" on August 17, 1985, which was filmed for nearly an hour when a live TV program was broadcasting nearby and shifted over to it. And more than in most any other nation of the world, many of these sightings have been proximate to such things as mines, power plants, water-treatment installations, and the like.

The Chilean Government has been notably receptive to these sightings, especially the many that have been reported from its military craft (including, in one recent case, a navy helicopter with a lengthy FLIR video showing a UFO with a long cylindrical "discharge," akin to glyphs found on a nearby desert floor), and its ground personnel, with a unique spirit of "openness" about them. This is evidenced also by its creation of a major UFO study organization, the "Committee for the Study of Anomalous Aerial Phenomena" ("CEFAA," en español), which has existed since 1997. All told, Chile is now at the forefront of UFO receptivity worldwide.

The "counter example" to this, of course, is not just the United States (until perhaps very recently) but also the United Kingdom, where its very strict "Official Secrets Act" has reigned for more than 130 years (though tempered somewhat by its own "Freedom of Information Act" as of 2000). England has had more than its share of intense UFO sightings -- which it has long called "Unidentified Aerial Phenomena" ("UAPs," to most blokes), and which its "Defence Intelligence Staff" ("DIS," to more serious blokes) studied under the auspices of what it called "Project Condign" -- most prominently one in Rendlesham Forest outside the gates of Royal Air Force Base Bentwaters (leased to the U.S. Air Force) in late December of 1980, which involved the reported landing of a triangular craft, several military witnesses, a contemporaneous audio recording, radioactivity findings, and even a claimed physical contact with the landed craft by a soldier (Staff Sgt. James Penniston) who said that he touched it in a place where hieroglyphs were on it. (Thirty years later, Penniston claimed that he telepathically received a coded message in "ones and zeros" that, as later translated by computer experts, suggested a "time travel" origin rather than an alien one. As is sometimes said in Brooklyn, New York, "Ya' pays yer money and ya' takes yer chances.")

And that episode continued the next night with strange colored lights (read: both in the sky and as laser-like beams to the ground), scorch marks, and triangular indentations reportedly encountered by a military search team led by the RAF Bentwaters deputy base commander, Colonel Charles I. Halt, who used a tape recorder to memorialize his search and recorded a similar experience. Notably, planes and resources at that base provided support during the Cold War for the United States Strategic Air Command and reportedly (but never confirmed officially) the U.S. used the base for the storage of nuclear weapons.

"Rendlesham," as it is widely known by ufologists in shorthand (read: much like "Roswell"), is widely regarded as England's most famous UFO/UAP incident, as it also included an extensive alleged "cover-up, though it competes for that honour with one that took place over the skies of nearby Woodbridge and Lakenheath Royal Air Force Bases more than two decades earlier, from August 13 into August 14, 1956. That incident involved some reportedly outmaneuvered British fighter jets, a C-47 cargo plane, extensive radar tracking (including from a third RAF facility, Bentwaters, albeit through relatively primitive radar equipment and with newly trained radar operators), ground personnel viewings, and pilot observations of an object traveling at what were estimated to be unheard-of speeds.

Records of such sightings are maintained by England's Ministry of Defence ("MoD," to its Carnaby Street friends); they have been the subjects of increasing pressure in recent years for disclosure under England's own Freedom of Information Act, which came into effect only near the beginning of this century. In 2013, this pressure led to the MoD announcing that it had just transferred almost all of its UAP files to Great Britain's national archives (read: for storage, not necessarily for immediate disclosure), but that 18 documents, suspected as pertaining to the two Rendlesham incidents primarily, were held back. In time, no doubt, such pressure will yield more and more UAP file disclosures by British authorities. But for the time being, this unexpected step by the British MoD has held more promise than delivery.

95   It is not clear exactly when AATIP began its operations. Some reports have it operating for five years, from 2007 to 2012 (or longer), at a total cost of 22 million dollars. Other reports peg its commencement to September of 2008, or even later. Either way, it was a total surprise when its existence was disclosed.

96   The origins of AATIP are not quite so clear. Evidently, there once existed a rather mysterious UFO-related military organization named the "Advanced Aerial Weapons Systems Applications Program" ("AAWSAP," to those who can remember it), which after about nine months (a well-recognized gestation period at the Pentagon, apparently) then progressed to eventually become AATIP. In between, it is said, there was work done by a private-sector organization, Bigelow Aerospace Advanced Space Studies ("BAASS," to those who think this sounds a bit fishy), which in turn appears to be connected to a notorious place called the "Skinwalker Ranch" in northeastern Utah, recently owned by billionaire Robert T. Bigelow, a ufologist extraordinaire, and more recently owned by Brandon Fugal, a multi-millionaire interested in testing paranormal phenomena.

97   It turned out that AATIP had been established with the strong support of then-Senate Majority Leader Harry M. Reid (D-NV), who reportedly took great pride in this accomplishment. On the surface, at least, it appears that AATIP officially wound down in 2012 when Senator Reid's "congressional earmark" for it ran out. Former Pentagon insiders, though, insist that AATIP actually continued on, in one form or another, for at least five more years.

   And at at least one point in time, according to AATIP's "Defense Intelligence Reference Documents" ("DIRDs," to DOD nerds) released under the FOIA in early 2022, it explored the viability of such things as "traversable wormholes, stargates, and negative energy . . . high-frequency gravitational wave communications," and "the manipulation of extra dimensions." According to these documents, AATIP even considered blasting a tunnel toward the center of the moon, by using thermonuclear explosives.

98   A focal point of this attention was a DOD intelligence officer by the name of Luis D. "Lue" Elizondo, who retired abruptly in October of 2017 and claims to have been AATIP's director for several years, something that is not entirely free of dispute. It is fair to say that he is an enigmatic figure within the realm of ufology; at times, he seems to freely divulge UFO-related DOD information, but at others he abruptly shifts to an unforthcoming posture under the shield of his "security oath." Based upon what he says he knows from the "inside," Elizondo predicts that longtime government secrecy will soon hit a "critical mass," forcing the disclosure of more and more information as time goes by. (I'd say that "the jury's still out" on him.) Another former "insider" is Christopher K. Mellon, who served as Deputy Assistant Secretary of Defense for Intelligence and worked together with Elizondo on UFO investigations after they both left the Government.

   Since 2017, Elizondo has been so peripatetically involved in media coverage of the subject that some ufologists speculate that rather than being a true "whistleblower" he actually is the tip of the spear on a long-term acclima-tization effort by DOD, leading to an "end game" of complete, or near-complete, UFO disclosure. Whether that is so or not, Elizondo certainly has cast his lot with former Blink-182 front man Thomas M. DeLonge, his UFO-related entity "To the Stars Academy of Arts and Sciences," and Nevadan aerospace entrepreneur Robert T. Bigelow. And in so doing, he has claimed familiarity with "meta metals" (sometimes referred to as "meta-materials") that are said to have unusual "isotomic ratios." (Former White House Chief of Staff John D. Podesta's emails, leaked through WikiLeaks in 2016, contained UFO-related communications to and from DeLonge.)

   As for media attention, the journalist who has been most active on this subject, and for the longest time, is KLAS-TV investigative reporter George T. Knapp in Las Vegas, who has been reporting on UFOs, in one form or another, since the 1980s. He was the first to report, in the late 1980s, on what later became confirmed to be "Area 51." He learned of AATIP (though not by that name) before any other reporter, although it was *The New*

York Times that broke the AATIP story. Knapp has been the "go-to" journalist on UFOs, UAPs, AATIP, and its successor entities ever since. In fact, in June of 2022, he "outed" Dr. Travis S. Taylor, who had secretly served as "chief scientist" for successive UAP task forces in DOD while at the same time appearing on television programs as an astrophysicist interested in ufology.

99   At the time, the Department of the Navy apparently referred to UFOs by another name, "Anomalous Aircraft Vehicles," a name that does not appear to have stuck.

100   The word "reportedly" is used here because the Air Force officially denied that this had taken place and continued to do so for more than a dozen years.

101   One of the pilots, Commander David Fravor, the commanding officer of the *Nimitz*'s "Strike Fighter Squadron 41," reported that he saw a white oval, cylindrical, or "Tic Tac"-shaped object about 40 to 50 feet in length with no visible means of propulsion, loft, or exhaust. (Actually, it might have been a Navy fighter pilot in another plane, Lt. Commander Chad Underwood, who coined that phrase.) This "Tic Tac" descriptor, which probably was more accurate than the "saucer" one of 1947, particularly resonated with the public once the Defense Department released videos of these sightings, some with full audio, years later.

102   This aspect of an aerial UFO encounter is exceptional, to say the least, and it adds a distinct new dimension that is a function of the advanced technology built into modern planes. In time, perhaps, it might become more commonplace.

103   This included the Weapons System Officer of the second plane, Lt. Commander Jim Slaight, who corroborated that the object ultimately left their field of vision and was out of sight in a "split second."

104   During this time interval, this object was observed as engaging in a strange "tumbling" motion, even "rotating," and as exhibiting unheard-of performance capabilities. These characteristics were to become increasingly common in following years.

105   Apparently, there was some uncertainty about whether the object went so far as to break the ocean's surface at any point. Over the years, as a relatively minor chord of UFO-sightings activity, there have been reports of some UFOs being observed as "transmedium," meaning water-bound. In time, such reports increased.

106   Commander Fravor elaborated by saying that the object "had no plumes, wings, or rotors, and outran our F-18s." And then he added: "I want to fly one!"

107   Evidently, at the time of this sighting in late 2004, the *Nimitz* had just recently received a newly developed "integrated air defense system architecture," known as a "Cooperative Engagement Capability" ("CEC," to the Hawkeye crew), which provided higher-fidelity radar telemetry data through its NIFC-CA architecture and was being fielded on a strike-group level for the first time aboard the *Nimitz* and the rest of its flotilla.

108   On the *Princeton*, its chief radar operator, Kevin M. Day, was operating the Navy's most sophisticated radar system at the time, the "Aegis Spy-1," and it showed multiple UFOs flying in formation, descending to an altitude of 28,000 feet, and then "hovering" near the Navy planes before suddenly accelerating away at an estimated 24,000 miles an hour. "It was the most humbling experience of my life," he observed.

109   This UFO was recorded with an infrared "gun camera pod," known formally as an AN/ASQ-228 "Advanced Targeting Forward Looking Infrared" ("ATFLIR," to video fans) system. The video footage of it was recorded by

Lt. Commander Underwood; evidently, the audio portion of this video was stored separately and for some unknown reason was not included. And as if that mystery needed deepening, it was further reported that two uniformed Air Force officers soon thereafter arrived on the *Nimitz* and on the *Princeton* and managed to brusquely confiscate the Hawkeye hard drives, much "radar data" from the Hawkeye, the *Nimitz*, and the F/A-18s, and all voice data and "CEC data" stored on magnetic tapes, with it all never to be seen again.

110   One of these pilots drew a distinction about this unusual cube shape: He said that it appeared to him that the cube was "inside a sphere," rather than the other way around. Either way, this configuration became the third-most intriguing UFO shape, after the "Tic Tac" and triangular ones. And to this should be added the "orb" configuration, which has become increasingly more commonplace (read: among sightings overall) in recent years. In some such instances, they might be explained as flares or drones.

111   These two Navy pilots were Lt. Ryan Graves, of "Strike Fighter Squadron 11," who provided a "closed-door" briefing to members of national security-related congressional committees and their staffs in mid-2019, while still on active duty, and Lt. Danny Accoin, who expressed his amazement that the object they saw had "no distinct wings, no distinct tail, [and] no distinct exhaust plume." In fact, infra-red sensors have shown such objects to be inexplicably cold.

112   The best explanation for the latter is that a "gimbal" is a structural configuration that allows for an object's rotation around a single axis, such as in a gyroscope or an inertial navigation system. In the case of the "Gimbal video," the object's perceived rotation is a key element; in fact, no fewer than four "geometric reconstructions" of this rotation established it as perhaps the best evidence yet of alien flight. And as for the "GoFast video," the reason for that name is more self-evident.

113   The only credible terrestrial explanation for these sightings was that they were of "hypersonic drones" manufactured and controlled by the U.S., Russia, or China. But even putting aside the public relations weakness of this theory, there is the fact that these sightings involved absolutely no observable exhaust or vapor trail, nor were they accompanied by the sonic booms that also would be expected. This leaves only an extraterrestrial possible source.

114   A similar incident occurred in early 2007 when American radar operators at Lakenheath Air Force Base in Suffolk, England, tracked an unknown object moving in the nearby sky. Two F-15 fighter jets from the Air Force's 48th Fighter Wing tried to intercept the object and together tracked it as climbing in altitude while ground radar tracked it as well. One of the pilots obtained a clear visual sighting and could describe it only as looking like a "rock." The Air Force denied this UFO encounter until a local "ham radio" operator announced that he had been able to record the pilots' conversations with one another as they tried to get a closer look at it.

115   This was a worldwide surge as well, with increased numbers of sightings in Belgium, Canada, England, Germany, Israel, India, Italy, Mexico, and the Philippines. The two states that led the way in the U.S. were California and Florida. More than two dozen nations, such as Brazil, Australia, China, Japan, Chile, Denmark, New Zealand, France, Russia, Spain, Sweden, Uruguay, and even Vatican City, have also conducted studies of, or are currently studying, UFOs. For its part, France created a Study Group and Information on Non-Identified Aerospace Phenomenon (known by the French acronym "GEIPAN") in 2014, Japan established what it calls a "Space Operations Squadron" in 2020, China created what it calls an "Unidentified Air Conditions [sic] Task Force in 2021, and Italy has begun to take a leading role in encouraging international cooperation on the subject. Of all such other nations, the most extensive, systematic such efforts are being made by China.

116   The use of the word "field" here is not to suggest that the study of UFOs and their sightings is thus far recognized as anything other than a "pseudoscience" at best (though NASA has recently emphasized the word "science" in connection with its new involvement). Most "ufologists," even when in the throes of "uforia," do recognize that the Federal Government's recent change of course on what it now calls "UAPs" does not take this subject that far yet (with emphasis on the word "yet"). Someday, almost regardless of how the recent UAP "flaps" play out, there might well be a recognized academic field of study for this, one perhaps called something along the lines of "UAP phenomenology." Until then, a private organization by the name of the "Scientific Coalition for UAP Studies" has recently sprung up. And some well-known individuals, such as England's Prince Philip, Duke of Edinburgh, have upon their death become known as secret "ufologists."

117   It should be mentioned briefly here that there exists some discrepancy about exactly when these videos were released into the public domain, and by whom. It appears that as many as four entities played a role in that -- the Defense Intelligence Agency ("DIA," to one of OIP's former paralegals), *The New York Times*, KLAS-TV in Las Vegas, and a recently formed private-sector, for-profit organization called the "To The Stars Academy of Arts & Science" ("TTSA," to its wary friends), the latter of which speaks on its website of its "mission to shed light on the noteworthy problem of UAPs through the collection and distribution of highly credible evidence that can be researched by academic and scientific communities," partly through an "unidentified phenomena" database that it refers to as "The Vault," and appears to have operated in some degree of coordination with the Federal Government.

Regardless of this, though, what is clear is that as of 2020 all three videos are well ensconced in the public domain (i.e., readily available online), that if they ever were classified on national security grounds they no longer are, and that they repeatedly have been officially verified by the Department of Defense as "authentic" in their available form. All three of them (as well as, presumably, any future such records) can readily be found in the Naval Air Systems Command's "FOIA Reading Room," a Department of the Navy website.

118   In true bureaucratic fashion, the Navy Department quickly developed a reporting format pursuant to SECNAVINST 5720.42 for this purpose. Notably, the Navy at the same time recognized that such new, formal-ized reporting was important also to addressing what now appears to be regarded as "increased hazards to aviation safety."

119   One former government official, for instance, applauded the Navy Department's "new position to address this issue in a serious manner" and to do so "without the distraction of the social stigma that this phenomenon seems to attract."

120   This was most aptly characterized as "an unprecedented and dramatic shift from the U.S. Government's long-held company line that there is nothing to the whole UFO phenomenon."

121   This reasoning, of course flew in the face of the fact that AATIP's existence in the first place was largely (if not entirely) due to Senator Harry Reid's idiosyncratic support of it in the form of a "congressional earmark," rather than it being a product of conventional DOD budget processes. But as of mid-2020, with all that had happened during the previous two-and-a-half years, the argument in favor of having a "replacement UFO office" located somewhere within the Defense Department (i.e., within the Department of the Air Force or within the Department of the Navy) nevertheless had some force.

And there is always the possibility that, as some suspected, DOD actually *did* have such a program up and running after its AATIP program nominally ended in 2012, one that had greater and greater Navy (read: no longer Air Force) involvement after the Navy's *Nimitz* and *Roosevelt* sightings. Somehow, the Senate Select Committee on Intelligence seemed to think that this was so, because it voted on June 23, 2020 to have such a DOD program file a detailed report with the committee on its activities within six months of that date, which later was extended to a full year (see below). (Reportedly, Acting Chairman of the Senate Intelligence Committee Senator Marco A. Rubio (R-FL)'s main fear was that China, Russia, or some other adversary of the United States, such as Iran, might have made some kind of "technological leap," putting the U.S.'s national security at great risk.)

122 In addition to using such expansive language, the Defense Department's press release also spoke of guarding against "any incursions by unauthorized aircraft into our training ranges or designated airspace . . . includ[ing] examinations of incursions that are initially reported as UAP when the observer cannot immediately identify what he or she is observing." Even folks with high draft numbers know that the word "incursion" is "military speak" for an invasion or, at the least, an "attack." So the question arises (not unlike a UAP on a vertical ascent): Is this meant to imply the possibility of some foreign power (i.e., China or Russia) being behind the recent Navy sightings?

Or as a third imaginable possibility, could the word "incursion" have been used (twice) to direct (read: misdirect) public attention away from the possibility that what the Navy's pilots encountered off the *Nimitz* and the *Roosevelt* actually was the handiwork of Groom Lake "spoofers," operating with an exceedingly high degree of sophistication and success in such new "electromagnetic warfare" techniques? A fourth possibility is difficult to imagine. Actually, I lied: There is indeed a fourth possibility, but it's actually just another version of the third: Rather than Groom Lake's "spoofers" being responsible here, it could conceivably be Groom Lake's aeronautical engineers, with an aviation "breakthrough" so immense that our military has decided to keep it under wraps and display it in unwitting "training" circumstances at the same time. And if that *were* the case, then the possibility of "reverse-engineered alien technology" being involved logically follows.

123 ONI is the Nation's premier source of maritime intelligence, the oldest member of the "United States Intelligence Community" (which now has a total of 18 members), and it is headquartered at the National Maritime Intelligence Center just outside of Washington, D.C., in Suitland, Maryland.

124 Indeed, this would have been the default public attitude in America prior to World War II, with government agencies proceeding with great confidence that their "word" was accepted by an overwhelming majority of the American populace. That public trust in government eroded over time, as we now know, suffering its biggest body blow then to date with President Richard M. Nixon and "Watergate." What little of it remains now, entering the 21st century's third decade, unfortunately was vulnerable to further gross erosion during the unprecedented, sadly preposterous Administration of President Donald J. Trump.

125 No allusion is intended here to anything "Pythonesque." Rather, so serious a subject as this calls for more somber focus than one might give to, say, a deceased parrot, or a minister with a pronounced ambulatory affliction.

126 At the "high speculation" end of this continuum is the belief that actual alien spaceship crashes have graced the U.S. Government (and/or some other national government) with "useful debris." This would of course support a novel "sightings theory" that at least some of the objects observed or detected are neither entirely alien nor entirely Earthly in origin. In other words, it would hold these objects to be Earth-made (presumably by the U.S., though not necessarily), but with "good old alien parts" (including raw metal and/or technology). Again, this is said here just to "cover the landscape," or the skyscape, as it were.

127   In this vein, there also are the increasingly credible rumors of a mysterious "exotic" metal, metal alloy, polymer, material, or highly manufactured "meta-material," possessed of unusual "layering" with extremely thin layers of bismuth, magnesium, and at least one other element or isotope said to derive from an extraterrestrial source, the existence of which was secretly briefed to individual Senate committee members, including Senator Reid, in October of 2019. In fact, a recent partnership announced among the U.S. Army's "Combat Capabilities Development Command Ground Vehicle Systems Center" (a potential initialism in search of an acronym), the To The Stars Academy through what it calls its "ADAM Research Project," and a company known as "Tru-Clear Global" is believed (read: not officially confirmed) to focus on this.

128   Make no mistake: This discussion is not to be taken as an attempt to advocate in favor of this premise, nor to suggest a belief in the absolute certainty of it. Rather, its inclusion here is largely born of the belief that a balanced, all-inclusive view of that is necessary to a proper analysis of it. Stated another way, any discussion of this subject should contain such balance if it is to establish and retain its intellectual integrity. And to do so it should, in my opinion, be rationally bounded by the fundamental fact that, at bottom, "we don't know." We truly do not know for sure the validity of Roswell, we do not know what actually happened in Rendlesham Forrest, and we just do not know "what is out there." Not for sure, not yet.

129   There is a phrase for such a premise: The "extraterrestrial hypothesis," most commonly referred to as "ETH." This premise was most intelligently propagated during the 1960s and 1970s by French astronomer and author Jacques F. Vallee. An antecedent of it was the writings of author Charles H. Fort, who in 1919 spawned the adjective "Fortian" to describe such views.

130   The additional premise for this, and indeed the very timeline "pivot point" here, would be that the big discovery or discoveries that are posited do go back in time for several decades. It is entirely possible, of course, that this is not so -- i.e., that initial reactions to UFO sightings were no more than that, that only later on did a new reality emerge to change things (perhaps even not quite so distinctly at first), and that the "acclimatization" possibility suggested here (as admittedly one highly speculative possibility atop another, with the first one being, in 1940s American parlance, "a doozy") applies only to the past few years or so, i.e., with the change of U.S. posture manifested through its sudden disclosure of both the very existence of AATIP and its accompanying fighter jet videos.

   No part of the Federal Government leaves the "black world" easily; the experience of the National Reconnaissance Office ("NRO," to its near-Earth neighbors) shows that. That large organization not only existed in secrecy, as a satellite-origination and maintenance agency, it had a "black budget" that was truly astronomical in size, which reportedly led to it "squirreling away" literally billions of dollars over the years, much to the surprise and chagrin of DOD, *inter alia*. As it happens, the NRO's longtime general counsel, E. Page Moffett, is yet another former "agency client" of mine, from back in the early days of FOIA litigation when he worked for, and I represented in court, the CIA; Page and I spoke at length not long ago at about both the "old days" and the more recent ones when his agency (which was created in 1961) emerged from the "black world" in September of 1992.

131   If that were so, especially so long ago, then it truly would exonerate at least some government agencies and officials (i.e., those who were "in the know," most likely limited to a relatively small "compartment") from their many public relations sins of the past. For instance, the U.S. Air Force could say that in its "cover-up" efforts it was just trying to prevent the mass panic expected to follow any official revelation that "the aliens have landed." In England, recently released government documents show Prime Minister Winston Churchill ordering a UFO sighting be kept secret in order to prevent what he, too, called "mass panic." (Support for this can be found in a government-sponsored study document known as "the Brookings Report," which in 1960 warned of "the

consequences of discovering intelligent extraterrestrial life.") Indeed, the implications of such a revelation would travel backward as well as forward in time.

132 And it is here, in connection with the idealized possibility of populace "acclimatization," that another aspect of human nature rears its head: No government authority (or single person, for that matter) wants the responsibility of conclusively announcing the existence of something that cannot be understood, much less controlled -- particularly something that, once disclosed, would erode the very foundations of mankind's traditional power structure, including its theological underpinnings. So . . . some good, old-fashioned "can kicking" has an appeal, especially if deployed in conjunction with some incremental "soft disclosure."

133 On the other hand, of course, if the reality of the situation actually is that Earth has *not* been visited by alien travelers (even in unoccupied vehicle form), and there truly is no such thing "out there," then the decades-long handling of the subject (read: possibility) by national governments, particularly in the U.S., its itself a fascinating case study of human behavior. And an enormous part of that is the existence, and operation of, government secrecy.

134 It should go without saying that if I were to have been consulted on the logical contours of the current and prospective secrecy of such a thing before I retired in 2007, I could not properly disclose anything about that here. (Indeed, the most that I could do is write a book chapter that only skirts to the edges of it.) It should be noted that the duty to preserve the secrecy of still-classified information does not expire once a government employee (or any equivalent government contractor personnel) leaves government service. Atop that, there is what could be viewed as a moral obligation not to do so, one that can be felt to be heightened if the information in question is "compartmented," i.e., classified and protected at an even higher level than "Top Secret" as part of a "Special Access Program." So, in the archaic words of old-time testification: "Further your affiant sayeth not."

135 And if this *were* actually so (just to keep the speculation ball rolling a bit more), it certainly would comport with some perceived hints here or there that (with apologies to a beknighted British author) some purposeful "acclimatization" is indeed "afoot." It could well be, as has been observed, that "disclosure is a process," especially for questions of the deepest and most profound nature, in order to prepare the populace for what only a relatively few in government might actually know.

136 Yes, as much as it sounds like something from a 1950s-era science fiction movie, Trump's "Space Command" (read: "United States Space Force," actually) is something that, according to Trump (who adamantly kept using that name), did then exist and was indeed a new (read: sixth) separate branch of the U.S. military. By whatever name, it was established on December 20, 2019, through the efforts of the White House's revived National Space Council ("NSpC," to its undercapitalized investors), which was chaired by Vice President Michael R. Pence during the Trump Administration.

Pence was an avowed "space junkie" (read: since childhood) who readily accepted this responsibility from the very outset of the Trump Administration and immediately had his Domestic Policy Director, Daris D. Meeks, draft a presidential executive order, Exec. Order 13803 (June 30, 2017), in order to re-establish (read: "revive") the National Space Council, which had lain dormant since the beginning of the Clinton Administration in 1993. Coincidentally, Daris is my next-door neighbor (yes, this sort of thing seems to happen all the time in Washington) and I recall him regaling me with tales of how two increasingly aggressive staff members of the National Security Council persistently tried to derail his work, in a typical Washington "turf war," because the NSC had assumed jurisdiction over all such matters in the rare bureaucratic vacuum that had long existed. (And within the Defense Department, this was equally so for the Department of the Air Force's claimed dominion over space.)

But Daris prevailed in this battle, ultimately because Pence flatly refused to back down, not unlike his admirable refusal to accede to the Secret Service's attempt to have him "get in the car" (read: flee the site of his constitutional responsibilities) in the relative safety of a Capitol garage on the afternoon of January 6, 2021. (And in a rare "double coincidence," Daris's wife Cindy is a very close friend of Monica M. Goodling, the personal aide of Attorney General Alberto R. Gonzales who figured so prominently in his Honors Program corruption scandal (see Chapter Forty-Three).)

In turn, the Space Council's revival led to the development of the U.S. Space Force as part of Daris's single-handed implementation of that executive order's provisions. Indeed, it was at the Space Council's first meeting that Vice President Pence announced the Trump Administration's intent to work with Congress on the Space Force's creation, with the Space Council serving as a vital forum for the legislative effort. Finally, on December 20, 2019, after no small amount of legislative wrangling and last-minute maneuvering by the Air Force, the "Space Force" was born. Reportedly, this required the strong personal urging of President Trump, who on more than one occasion seemed to confuse it with something previously existing known as the "Air Force Space Command." (Not to mention the 1953 television program "Space Command" that presciently starred the late actor James M. Doohan, who went on to "Beam me up, Scotty," "dilithium crystals," and "Cap'n, I think she's gonna *blow!*" fame on *Star Trek* and its progeny a decade later.) Most significantly, the Biden Administration, in its first month, announced that the Space Force had President Biden's "full support," and he promptly dispelled Trump's confusion by referring to it explicitly as "Space Force." Another month later, this government entity was firmly reiterated as such, as something that is allied with, but not part of, the Department of the Air Force.

Officially known as the "United States Space Force," it is a "fully unified combatant command" (read: the sixth branch of the military) that focuses on space as a war-fighting domain and is most responsible for military operations in outer space. Its signature product thus far (read: as far as is publicly known) is the X-37B "space plane," which was most recently launched on May 17, 2020, is entirely robotic, and as a "reusable platform" can linger in orbit for as long as 780 days; much secrecy has surrounded this Space Shuttle-like vehicle since it was first launched in 2006. Beyond that, the maintenance of a space-based laser weapon system, one that could counter an Earth-based missile attack on a satellite, appears to be a primary objective. And on January 11, 2007, when China first tested a satellite-destruction capability on one of its own disused satellites, successfully, this became an enormous priority for the United States.

As for the "Space Command," it was something set up within the Air Force in 1982, where it dealt with such things as space-based laser systems, "satellite warfare," and the effects of space-originated electromagnetic pulse. Primarily, though, it operated a clandestine "manned spaceflight engineering program" (read: aimed to-ward having military troops on DOD-controlled space shuttles). That novel program, dubbed "Project Horizon," was established entirely apart from NASA, but it became incrementally less vital over time as the imagery sophistication of the National Reconnaissance Office grew (read: through something called "Project Corona"). It existed alongside "Project MOL" (standing for "Manned Orbital Laboratory"), it secretly trained 32 astronauts and 134 support personnel, and it was permanently scuttled (or so DOD says) in the wake of the *Challenger* disaster. Space Command continued to operate for several decades, until its existence was called into question by the creation of "Space Force."

These days, by the way, more and more sophisticated laser weaponry is being developed by the Raytheon Technologies Company in McKinney, Texas, as well as elsewhere. High-energy lasers can shoot down drones, current laser-weapon technology can reach satellites from the ground, NASA satellites are now being built with sophisticated laser capability, and we can look forward to the prospect of having laser-armed satellites shooting at one another in space and ground targets (if not also "alien intruders") sometime soon.

And on the subject of satellites, by the way, they are by definition more vulnerable than might be thought. A GPS satellite, for instance, emits time-coded signals that are triangulated with two others, but a fourth satellite is required for perfect accuracy; any one of the four can be disabled remotely by "controlled space debris," which can be created by four nations (including India) now.

Russia reportedly has created a "satellite killer" that operates co-orbitally. Germany is said to be developing a co-orbital device that could grasp and fix satellites, but it could threaten satellites also. And beyond physical threats, cyber attacks on satellites can be launched as well. Lastly, there are satellites that are designed just to "spy" on other satellites. For the past eight years, Russia has undertaken that with its Cosmos 2491 and Cosmos 2054 satellites, the U.S. is presumed to do likewise, and reportedly China is developing that capability as well. It's truly "Spy vs. Spy" in orbit around the Earth.

137   Also in the year 2020, former President Barack H. Obama was closely questioned on the subject of UFOs in a televised interview conducted by the host of *The Late Show with Stephen Colbert* on November 30. Tellingly, when asked whether he, as president, had asked if there exist Federal Government files on the subject, he replied: "Certainly, I asked about it. Can't tell you. Sorry." Subsequently, though, former President Obama had more to say on the subject.

Indeed, on June, 2021, in a podcast interview with journalist Ezra Klein, Obama went far deeper into the possibility that alien life has visited Earth. When asked "how his politics would change if he found out that aliens exist," he replied:

> It's interesting. It wouldn't change my politics at all. Because my entire politics is [sic] premised on the fact that we are these tiny organisms on this little speck floating in the middle of space. . . . When we were going through tough political times, and I'd try to cheer my staff up, I'd tell them [about] a statistic that John Holdren, my science adviser, told me, which was that there are more stars in the known universe than there are grains of sand on the planet Earth. . . . Well, sometimes it cheered them up; sometimes they'd just roll their eyes and say, "oh, there he goes again."

Obama went on to say that he hopes that if alien life were discovered, it would remind Americans (and presumably their fellow Earthlings) of their "common humanity":

> We're just a bunch of humans with doubts and confusion. . . . We do the best we can. And the best thing we can do is treat each other better because we're all we've got. And so I would hope that the knowledge that there were aliens out there would solidify people's sense that what we have in common is a little more important. . . . But no doubt there would be immediate arguments like, well, we need to spend a lot more money on weapons systems to defend ourselves. . . . New religions would pop up. And who knows what kind of arguments we get into. We're good at manufacturing arguments for each other.

138   This is something that he said to his son Don, Jr., in a purported "Father's Day interview" hosted by his presidential campaign. It is not clear whether that circumstance made this interview any more or less credible.

139   Remarkably, it was not long before this that the very first such "viable planet" was discovered through NASA's Kepler probe on July 23, 2015. Then, less than a year later, NASA disclosed the existence of as many as 2300 "habitable-zone planets" in our galaxy, or now more than 4770 survivable (read: in what is called the "habitable zone" or sometimes the "Goldilocks Zone") "exoplanets," which soon thereafter jumped to an estimate of "perhaps six billion."

The first "exoplanet" discovered anywhere, in 1992, was found orbiting the star "Pegasus 51" (and thus named "51 Pegasi b") at a distance of 50 light-years from Earth. Thereafter, there were Kepler 36 b and, most prominently, exoplanet K-2-18 b. Currently, the closest known exoplanet is "Proxima Centauri b," four light-years away, with more yet to be discovered by NASA's successor to its Kepler and Hubbell missions, called its "Transiting Exoplanet

Survey Satellite" ("TESS," to NASA's romantics), which was launched in April of 2018. And that, in turn, now has been followed up by the "James Webb Space Telescope" ("JWST," named after former NASA administrator James E. Webb, who led the agency during most of the 1960s) in 2022.

The progression here is quite striking, but according to a mathematical formula known as the "Drake equation," it is within the realm of reasonable calculation. And all of this ties into what is called "SETI research" ("search for extraterrestrial intelligence") through the continuous radio telescope scanning of our galaxy, which began as a brief study under the name "Project Ozma" in the mid-1960s. SETI was established by Cornell University astronomers Frank D. Drake and Carl E. Sagan, among others, who greatly enhanced its place in the public imagination, though it must be added that it would take a radio signal approximately 25,000 years to reach our nearest intergalactic neighbor, the "Canis Major Dwarf," even traveling at close to the speed of light. But this fact did not deter another nation, China, from quickly constructing an even larger SETI-like facility, known in English as the "Five-hundred-meter Aperture Spherical Radio Telescope" ("FAST," to its builders) in southern China in 2016. (Of course, if a signal were to originate within our Solar System, such as from a comet near Jupiter known as "67P/Churyumov-Gerasimenko," then the time element would be much more viable.)

A parallel area of research focuses on "galaxy clusters," which in turn are perceived (read: through the most far-reaching earthbound telescope arrays) as "great walls" or even a combined "web of filaments" in deep space. Such "galaxy cluster" conglomerations (sometimes referred to as "super clusters") are believed to be held together not by forces of gravity (like with other structures such as gaseous, elongated "space clouds"), but rather by something that astronomers now refer to as "dark matter" -- or, in an ever-faster expanding universe, "dark energy." Especially considering that there exist as many as an estimated two trillion galaxies in the "observable universe" alone, and that almost all of the stars that comprise them likely have planets, this complexity adds to the possibility (read: probability) of their being life (read: perhaps intelligent life) elsewhere in the universe, which in turn speaks (read: at least arguably) to the "UFO question."

As for exoplanets themselves, perhaps the most promising ones in the search for extraterrestrial life are a cluster of them recently discovered within proximity to an "ultra-cool" dwarf star named TRAPPIST-1, in the constellation Aquarius. Seven exoplanets have been discovered there, with as many as six of them deemed within the "habitable zone." In particular, TRAPPIST-1e, which is a rocky one, is now regarded as the likeliest candidate for life on an exoplanet and it is expected that the Webb Telescope will soon focus on this possibility. This must be viewed in light of the fact that the best current estimate is that the universe contains no fewer than a hundred billion trillion stars -- but who's counting? And speaking of which, it has most recently been calculated that life on Earth took 541 million years to reach its current stage of development (read: having irrational Republicans as well as Democrats), viewed against the background of the universe's estimated age of 13,800 billion years.

140   Such activity also has been detected on Pluto's moons, as well as on what is known as the "dwarf planet" Ceres, which at the same time is viewed as the Solar System's largest asteroid. And when it comes to planetary moons, Pluto's are not alone in this respect; for instance, water vapor "plumes" have been detected on one of Saturn's moons, Enceladus, which is regarded as the single-most important detection of its kind.

141   A big part of this is the search for "exomoons," which are theorized to orbit some exoplanets, just as do the more than 150 moons that orbit six of the eight planets within our own Solar System (read: no longer counting Pluto, or any such "dwarf planet"). Right now, no confirmed exomoon has yet been detected -- either through inference from a gravitation effect on its exoplanet or through an interruption of light during transit, including from exoplanetary rings -- but a handful of candidates have emerged, such as one now known as "Kepler 1625 b," which is believed to be Earth-like and presumptively habitable. Such bodies are regarded as prime candidates for containing extraterrestrial life.

142 Notably, this includes Lockheed Martin's secretive "Helendale Radar-Cross Section Measurement" facility in the Mojave Desert, which is located near its Skunk Works headquarters.

143 This reportedly stemmed from a secret DARPA-led project called the "Aerospace Innovation Initiative," intended to develop "new air dominance platforms" through use of new digital-design technology that is said to be "lowering overhead for production and assembly." Which in turn brings up the very role that DARPA has played, and certainly continues to play, in the development of advanced, even "futuristic" aircraft.

The newest such thing, the TR-3B "anti-gravity" craft, is said to be a DARPA-connected creation, as are such other exotica as "directed-energy weapons," "particle beams," "zero-point energy" (sometimes called "Near Zero Power," or "N-ZERO"), and "drone swarms" guided with artificial intelligence (read: evolving computer programs that could conceivably become "self-aware"). It is clear by now that DARPA plays a central, perhaps even primary, role in our military's technological advancements (including the development of artificial intelligence for drone purposes) and that it should be viewed as such by Congress, by the public, and through future Freedom of Information Act requests (read: hint). This is one area of governmental activity that in my view has been "under-FOIA'd" to date.

144 The other such report included a photograph of a silver, "cube-shaped" object that was observed by a Navy pilot as "hovering" or completely motionless at an estimated altitude of 30,000 to 35,000 feet above the Atlantic Ocean in 2018. This photo was reported to have been taken from within the cockpit of an F/A-18 fighter jet through use of the pilot's personal cell phone. Yes, the realm of UFO sightings seems to have come down (or perhaps up, depending on your point of view) to something like this.

145 Three years earlier, on November 23, 2017, Trump seemingly took a reckless step in this direction when in a speech to U.S. Coast Guard personnel he blurted out that the F-35 Joint Strike Fighter then under development by the Air Force was going to be "invisible" (read: not just to radar, as stealth technology allows, but to the naked eye as well). "The enemy cannot see it," he freely boasted. And he even repeated as much in July of 2018 and August of 2020. Now, given that this was Donald Trump speaking, it is entirely possible that he was misunderstanding (and misstating) the operation of anti-radar stealth technology. But it also might be possible that, given the "reverse engineering" claims of Area 51 whistleblower Bob Lazar and the claimed properties of what are called "meta-materials," what Trump was irresponsibly disclosing was not far from the truth.

146 Former White House Chief of Staff John D. Podesta, Jr., reacted to the issuance of this report by observing that it "probably opened up more questions than it answered. . . . I think we'll learn a lot more. The Government has an obligation not to hide it." Former Director of the CIA John O. Brennan, who would have had access to related records, stated that it shows that "we must keep an open mind [because t]he absence of evidence is not evidence of absence." John Podesta has long been a strong proponent of UFO research, if not a full-blown ufologist himself, so much so that in 2010 he wrote the forward to a book titled *UFOs: Generals, Pilots and Government Officials Go on the Record*. It is said that he and former First Lady Hillary R. Clinton share views on this subject.

147 Toward that end, the report declared that "[t]he UAPTF intends to focus additional analysis on the small number of cases where a UAP appeared to display unusual flight characteristics or signature management." And some news reports about the report speak of a classified version of it, consisting of 17 additional pages, that remains secret. Notably, but perhaps just because of the limited nature of the sightings included, the report makes no mention of traditional government explanations such as optical illusions, hallucinations, and "mass hysteria."

148 As near as can be determined, the geographic sweep of this detection and assessment activity is limited to what the Pentagon calls "Special Use Airspace" ("SUA," to DOD's most litigious friends), areas in which the U.S. military (read: the Air Force and the Navy, mostly) operates regularly.

149 Actually, this development has led to a split of opinion on the parts of ufologists: Some see it as a genuine "culmination" of their decades-long efforts to drag the U.S. Government into the sunlight on the subject of UFOs/UAPs, while groups such as the Mutual UFO Network remain highly skeptical given the government's history of using such governmental entities (read: Project Blue Book, for example) to control and cover up, rather than shed light on, UFO/UAP activity.

150 In turn, Rep. Adam B. Schiff (D-CA), chairman of the full House Intelligence Committee, called the hearing's subject "one of the world's most enduring mysteries."

151 The two government witnesses were obviously careful not to say anything that revealed classified information in the open hearing, but Undersecretary of Defense for Intelligence and Security Ronald S. Moultrie at one point abruptly responded to a question posed to the other witness about any activity "underwater" by saying, "I think that would be more appropriately addressed in closed session." Such a reflexive interjection can itself be pregnant with an implication.

152 This was announced at a "media teleconference" held with only a few hours' notice, atypical for NASA, at which it reiterated what has become its "go-to" caveat about UAPs, that "[t]here is no evidence UAPs are extra-terrestrial in origin."

153 Well, researching UFO/UAPs is not what NASA used to do. But its announcement made it clear that it would no longer be "shying away from reputational risk."

154 Toward that end, the Senate's Select Committee on Intelligence cleared a bill in early August that explicitly addresses "Unidentified Aerospace-Undersea Phenomena."

155 This could of course broadly mean any life detected by Earth-originated means, including the smallest of micro-organisms or even, by extension, the "building blocks of life" in, for example, the soil of Mars, where more and more "rovers" are sent as the years go by. Rather, however, what is meant here is any discovery of fully formed alien beings capable of traveling from their place of origin to Earth (or, for purposes of the near future, Mars or the moon). The connection between the latter and UFOs is that the existence of intelligent alien life could readily be inferred from the existence of any solid, indisputable evidence of an alien craft.

156 Since the beginning of modern "UFO secrecy" in the 1940s, the principal Federal Government players regarding it have naturally been DOD's Department of the Air Force and, most recently, its Department of the Navy, not to mention the CIA (operating mostly behind the scenes). Yet there also is NASA, which until very recently has been strangely quiet on the subject, except for providing the occasional "debunking" explanation for alleged sightings by its astronauts. Most recently, though, NASA seems to have finally awoken to such things, most particularly the "sightings" that now come in on its "live feed" from the International Space Station ("ISS," to watchers of live feeds).

There also has come to exist another potential source of UAP photographs, only this time in the private sector. SpaceX, founded by entrepreneur Elon R. Musk, is a "space transportation" company that has launched dozens of manned and unmanned vehicles into space during the past decade, including two successful crewed missions in 2020. On December 8, 2020, at the launch of another SpaceX rocket in Boca Chica, Texas, a "yellowish orb" UAP was photographed seeming to hover over it. While on one hand SpaceX's many Starship spacecraft can themselves now be the source of others' UAP sightings (including a recent one in New Zealand), it is perhaps only a matter of time before SpaceX will be reporting sightings photographs of its own.

157   As compared to seemingly darker corners of the Federal Government -- most particularly, the Departments of the Air Force, of the Navy, and of Defense more generally, plus of course the CIA and NSA on behalf of the "Intelligence Community" -- NASA has left a relatively faint footprint on the UFO firmament over the past 60 years. (NASA came into existence only as of October of 1958, when it succeeded the longstanding "National Advisory Committee for Aeronautics" ("NACA," to old-timers), which had operated since 1915 with a far smaller budget and a much narrower mandate.) This seems surprising, at first glance, and at second and third glances as well, given that NASA's mission, especially as it has evolved, certainly overlaps the realm of ufology in more large ways than one.

Indeed, there are many who say that NASA has artfully managed to insulate itself from UFO controversies, much like the CIA has largely succeeded in doing since the early 1950s. The big difference, they say, is that the CIA has done so by wielding the broad brush of national security classification (applied at the highly effective "abstract level"), whereas NASA does not indulge in so transparent a secrecy regime and, it is said, wields a delicate air brush, where necessary, instead.

In other words, NASA is widely regarded by ufologists as "casting a blind eye" to what has been seen by its personnel, to what is detected by its equipment, to what is viewed by its cameras, and to what is imaged and then interpreted on, for instance, the surfaces of Mars now as well as the moon. Right or wrong, there apparently are literally hundreds if not thousands of NASA-generated images that to many eyes appear to be possibly indicative of either current or past extraterrestrial activity on many celestial bodies, yet have elicited from NASA "nary a blink."

A very concrete example of this is an image of the surface of Mars that was taken by NASA's Mariner 9 space probe in 1971, yet for some unexplained reason was not released to the public (as was routine for other such photographs) for nearly 45 years! This photograph shows a formation of stones, on a circular mound, that bears an uncanny resemblance (perhaps due to sheer pareidolia) to two sites on Earth, one of which (the other being Stonehenge) is an area situated within Dugway Proving Ground (i.e., the presumptive "Area 52"). (Photos of the three sites can be seen by Googling "marshenge.") The point here is not the plausibility of the three sites actually being connected to one another; rather, it is *what on Earth* possessed NASA to withhold such a photograph from the public for so long -- or even in the first place? Surely, there are plenty of folks at NASA smart enough to realize that the very act of doing so with such a photograph automatically lends credibility to any theory about it -- as in, "there must be something to it, else NASA would not go out of its way to so atypically withhold it." As the saying unfortunately goes, it's not exactly rocket science that we're talking about here. So here's to predicting that NASA will find itself playing a larger and larger role within the realm of "UFO secrecy" (read: growing transparency) in the future -- all the more so if it ever makes such an inexplicable mistake again.

158   Of course, the potential for the White House taking a "political" approach to such a thing would be palpable (if not potentially risible), so one can only hope that, in such an event, the presidency would have been restored to a better semblance of what it had long been by then.

CHAPTER FORTY-NINE

1   Due to the difficulty of establishing and maintaining government secrecy, even through the use of a "compartmented" national security classification regime, the length of time that a secret is maintained is a major

consideration. And some secrets exist in "layers," which means that an aspect of them might "leak out" but their cores remain intact thereafter. The secrecy of the *Glomar Explorer* (see Chapter Seventeen) is a case in point.

2   This brings up another particular characteristic of secrets, even big ones: They might erode, due to changes in events and circumstances, with the passage of time. UFO secrecy certainly falls into this category; in just the past five years it has changed markedly, with the possibility of its complete alteration always looming on the horizon (see Chapter Forty-Eight). Vatican secrecy, too, is no longer what it once was, due to public pressure. So, too, with government surveillance, which is fueled by rapid technological advances. And while almost all of the other secrecy realms on the list (both lists, actually) are static and time-bound, there is always the possibility that any of the three assassinations (most likely JFK or RFK, not MLK) will take some new turn.

3   For an example of this, one need only think back to the time when "splitting the atom" was entirely unknown to the general public and no more than a theoretical possibility to a small circle of putative nuclear physicists. In time, due to the confluence of science and geopolitics, this secret became reality and exploded onto the world stage.

In a similar vein is the adventurous suspicion in some quarters that the U.S. military has been able to establish a vast network of transportation tunnels, ranging nearly from coast to coast, through the use of "thermonuclear tunneling technology," developed by DARPA since the 1970s, that involves the "melting" of rock debris into a form of glass. There is indeed some evidence to support such a fantastic possibility, but even if it is so the secrecy of it thus far remains largely intact.

4   This is no longer so, given that two subsequent investigations that began in September of 2001 probably surpassed them. The first of these was of 9/11 itself, which was indeed a law enforcement investigation. The second was the "Anthrax" investigation, which lasted until 2008 (see Chapter Thirteen). And then there was the FBI's "Unabomber" investigation, which was exceedingly extensive and lasted from 1978-1998.

5   The Assassinations Committee concluded that there was a "high probability" that others were involved in the Kennedy Assassination and a "likelihood" that others (read: at least James Earl Ray's brothers) were involved in the King Assassination as well. The Committee used the word "conspiracy" (which might or might not have involved anyone within any government) in both cases. So if that congressional committee was correct, which might or might not be so, then there are secrets attendant upon each assassination. And of all four such possibilities (read: JFK and MLK, before or after), the greatest probability, based upon a clear-eyed view of existing evidence, lies with Oswald's pre-assassination involvement with the CIA.

6   In Oswald's case, this would include the suspected "conspiracy assistance" of his own assassin, Jack L. Ruby. The House Assassinations Committee could find no direct evidence of an organized crime conspiracy through Jack Ruby, but it found nothing that precluded that either, especially given Ruby's long (read: since the late 1940s) and deep connections to "the Mob." As for Oswald's involvement with others before the assassination, the passage of time has yielded much more information about his activities in Mexico City, his pro-Cuban activities in New Orleans, his contacts with at least one agent of the Soviet Union, and even about the suspicion that he might have been impersonated in recorded conversations.

The primary suspect in all of this is the CIA, which it now appears destroyed several Oswald files (read: in several distinct CIA sections) in order to "cover up" its extensive interest in him prior to the assassination. As for whether anyone at the FBI has done likewise, my best answer to that is that while the Bureau did attempt one small such thing in its Dallas Field Office, something that I detected and prevented in 1978, there is no credible evidence of it having done anything like what the CIA is now known to have done (see Chapter Forty-Eight).

7   To be sure, the Kennedy and King Assassinations are each in its own way a quintessential example of how supposed "secrets" can derive from conspiracies that are suspected to exist, especially those involving an untrusted government. Psychologists have long observed that it is part of human nature, at least for some people, to think along such lines. Indeed, a recent issue of *Psychology Today* (Dec. 2020) made the point that this stems from "the desire for understanding and certainty" and "the desire for control and security." Thus, any conspiracy-born "secrecy" must be viewed with no small amount of skepticism in this light.

Perhaps the most quintessential example of this is the persistent theory (even after more than 75 years) that German dictator Adolf Hitler did not die in his bunker as Soviet troops approached in April of 1945, but rather escaped Berlin with the aid of German secret agents and was able to live for another 17 years with the secret support of the Government of Argentina. This has been fed by the fact that the forensic evidence of Hitler's death is weak at best, creating an unsatisfactory degree of uncertainty about it. In other words, if "nature abhors a vacuum," then conspiracists, as a general rule, abhor uncertainty. And whatever the truth, government secrecy all too often thereby thrives.

8   On the first day of my "Government Information Law and Policy" class, after identifying the distinct types of "secrecy" that there are, I would boldly claim that every student in the class had contact with at least one of them -- "family secrecy." I would ask for a show of hands by all who had at least one big secret in his or her family, and when a pair of hands remained unraised I would ask that student: "What makes you so sure that there really isn't one in your family, one that has just not been made known to *you*?"

9   This latter term might be unfamiliar to many, but it actually was the name officially applied to post-9/11 military and intelligence activity during the Administration of President George W. Bush. Perhaps the next such war on this list will be a "space war," with high-energy lasers capable of disabling satellites from the ground, co-orbital "killer satellites threatening them and ground targets from low-altitude orbits, and cyber attacks on both satellites and their ground control stations. There already exists much secrecy about such things.

10   As can be the case with such things, there is competition for this "number one" position, but it is not from any other item on this "top ten" list. Rather, it is from the theoretical possibility that there might exist a secret that is so dark and deep that its very existence as such is unknown, even as to its subject-matter area. In that way, it would be different than the two assassination items below, in that in those cases the existence of a secret is within a known factual setting that causes it to be suspected or surmised. The same is so with the "UFO" item on this list, because there is ample reason today to think that such a thing might possibly be real.

But consider this: If one were making such a "top ten" secrecy list, say, 100 years ago, or 250 years ago to be sure, then the "secret" existence of intelligent alien life (apart from anything in the form of angels and other such religious "beings") certainly would not be an item found on that long-ago list. So, too, is it with the possibility of some comparable "unknown secret" existing today.

11   In fact, the invasion's secrets had to be kept for a day longer than planned, due to bad weather on the original landing date, June 5. Yes, the largest amphibian assault in history, once mounted, had to kept in stasis, surreptitiously, for 24 hours.

12   A landing at Calais was so compelling because invading from Dover to there would have meant taking the shortest route by far (read: a span of only eight miles), so much so that the Germans even continued to believe in the prospect of a further invasion at Calais for several more weeks after the Normandy landing. And the secret of the Allied deception for Normandy's invasion was even more elaborate than was revealed at the time. Code-named "Bodyguard" overall and "Operation Fortitude South" in part, it was designed to completely mislead

Germany into believing that the invasion would take place elsewhere, even to the point of thinking that it would be led by General George S. Patton, Jr., with a phantom amphibious force operating out of Dover. Toward that end, a sub-operation code-named "Quicksilver" was set up under Patton with a dummy army, dummy landing craft, and dummy radio transmissions and signals traffic as well. And nothing leaked out from all of that.

13   By early June of 1944, literally thousands of military and civilian personnel knew most or all of the invasion's secrets. But even with Germany's intense espionage efforts aimed at learning the intended invasion site, it could not learn its location; the beaches of Normandy were so unsuspected that on the morning of D-Day, Hitler reportedly believed that what was happening there was only a "feint" and that the "real invasion" was about to take place somewhere else, north of the Seine River. Other members of Germany's High Command were entirely certain that the landing point would be at Calais.

And Germany's most successful general, General J. Erwin Rommel, upon whom Hitler relied to thwart any invasion, was so convinced that it would occur later in time that on D-Day he was far away from the coast celebrating his wife's birthday -- and even by the evening of June 6 he still believed that the "real" invasion would come at Calais. In incalculable number of Allied lives were spared due to this extraordinarily successful deception-cum-secrecy.

14   And atop the Allied forces that landed in France by sea was a fleet of nearly 10,000 planes, many bearing troops who parachuted behind enemy lines. Among this fleet was a type of aircraft used in warfare for the first time -- British gliders carrying both troops and heavy armaments without making a sound, under the code name of "Operation Deadstick." In a way, they were the first "stealth" planes, and as one historian has put it: "Gliders can get closer to enemy lines undetected. The key to the entire operation was surprise. Everything about it was shrouded in secrecy."

15   At that point, very few people at the CIA and within the White House's national security apparatus knew that this site had been detected. So this presidential order meant that this fact would be kept secret from anyone else in government -- from the secretary of state, from the attorney general, and from even the secretary of defense and the chairman of the joint chiefs of staff -- until almost the last minute. This is the best way, in Washington, to guard against leaks.

16   After the fact, the commander of the Neptune Spear special forces operation, Four-Star Admiral William H. McRaven, observed: "I've been in this business for . . . 27 years, and I'd never been involved in anything as secret[,] as compartmented as this." Even at that, though, he stressed that "[y]ou can't expect to hold onto a secret forever."

17   Indeed, in the annals of military secrecy, it would be extremely difficult to find anything that matches, let alone surpasses, the sustained secrecy of Operation Neptune Spear.

18   This is depicted most vividly in the 2014 movie *The Imitation Game*, which dramatizes the sacrifice of a British cargo ship, the imminent attack of which was learned through a deciphered Enigma message (consisting of intelligence that as code-named "Ultra") for the very sake of maintaining the secrecy of the cracking of the Enigma code. In reality, this appears to have been the case with the German firebombing of Coventry on November 14-15, 1940, which Prime Minister Winston L. Churchill is said to have permitted to take place without warning to its residents in order to likewise preserve Enigma secrecy; this very fact itself became a secret that was kept from the public in turn.

19   Estimates made at the time were that the breaking of the Enigma code shortened World War II in the European Theater by as much as 1-2 years.

20   This was greatly aided by the existence of the U.K.'s Official Secrets Act, which was invoked very heavily for all Bletchley Park personnel to great and long-lasting effect. Under it, the full story of the breaking of the Enigma code at Bletchley Park was not made known to the public until the 1990s.

21   The use of the word "unlikelihood" here admittedly suggests that the chances of actual existence are less than 50/50. On reflection, however, and especially in light of the most recent U.S. Government evidence of and receptivity to UAP sightings, this assessment seems too low (see Chapter Forty-Eight).

22   While the primary site of the Manhattan Project was very near Los Alamos, New Mexico (read: in a tiny municipality called Otowi), and included what was known as the "Los Alamos Laboratory," its support personnel were also situated at several other key locations around the country, most particularly Oak Ridge, Tennessee; Hanford, Washington; Chicago, Illinois; New York City; and Berkeley, California.

23   As it turned out, Klaus Fuchs did not spy for Germany. Rather, his allegiance was to the Soviet Union; he supplied some atomic bomb information to it before the war ended and then much more afterward, from both Los Alamos and England, to which he returned in 1947. He was discovered to be a Soviet spy through a U.S. counterintelligence program known as "Venona" (see below), the secrecy of which was maintained when he was brought to trial in England and sentenced in 1950 to only 14 years' imprisonment because the Soviet Union was still legally an ally of Great Britain at the time. And in 1946, the Manhattan Project's Director, Major General Leslie R. Groves, Jr., had revealed to Congress in an executive (read: non-public) session that a British physicist by the name of Alan Nunn May had passed information about the Manhattan Project to Soviet agents. Nunn had worked for the British "Tube Alloys" project in Canada that was connected to the Manhattan Project. He was tried and convicted of espionage in a British court and sentenced to ten years of hard labor.

24   Another, more unique phrase applicable to such information is "born secret," meaning that no affirmative national security classification action was required; once it came into existence, it was "secret" *ab initio*. This concept was tested in a case in which I played a slight role when it was filed by the Justice Department on March 8, 1979, a case that was styled *United States v. Progressive, Inc.* -- in which we attempted to obtain a court order preventing *The Progressive* magazine from publishing an article titled "The H-Bomb Secret: How We Got It, Why We're Telling It" that revealed the design for the creation of a hydrogen bomb -- based in part upon the "born secret" provision of the Atomic Energy Act of 1954. The defendant magazine and its editors responded that such an order would constitute a "prior restraint" contravening the First Amendment, but the district court on March 9 issued a TRO (temporary restraining order) in order to preserve the status quo until further briefs and affidavits could be prepared.

Then, on March 28, after the district court heard extensive oral argument and was able to consider a wide range of classified and unclassified affidavits, it granted a preliminary injunction against publication, following the Supreme Court's World War II "troop movement" precedent of *Near v. Minnesota* that recognized "grave national security concerns" as warranting a prior restraint. In turn, the lawyers for the other side moved to vacate that decision on the reiterated ground that all of the sensitive information in the article was "already in the public domain," which the court denied on June 15, before the case could proceed to full trial.

So next *The Progressive*'s aggressive lawyers sought appellate review of the district court's decision (a dubious procedural step inasmuch as the case was then still in an interlocutory posture), but that was denied by the Court of Appeals for the Seventh Circuit. At that point, the preliminary injunction stood in effect, as an unprecedented bar against the article's publication, which was exuberantly celebrated as a first-of-its-kind litigation victory on the Third Floor of the Main Justice Building (something I know because I was there).

But over at the Energy Department's Headquarters Building, that celebratory mood was short-lived, because the agency "clients" over there soon saw a wave of efforts by additional publications, such as *Scientific American*, *The Daily Californian*, the *Madison Press Connection*, *Fusion* magazine, and the *Milwaukee Sentinel*, to publish some or all of the same information, making the maintenance of the government's classification position untenable. (To a litigator, this is known as handling a case with a foundation of "shifting sand.") So in mid-September, the Justice Department agreed to have the preliminary injunction (which had stood firm for nearly six months at that point) vacated. And in the end, *The Progressive* published the article in its November 1979 issue and, despite some of the Energy Department's direst of predictions, thermonuclear war did not ensue.

25   The United States eventually established an entirely separate system for the safeguarding of such information, under the provisions of Atomic Energy Act of 1954. Under it, the categories of Top Secret Restricted Data, Secret Restricted Data, Restricted Data, Formerly Restricted Data, and "Critical Nuclear Weapon Design Information" ("CNWDI," to those who know how to speak "CNWDish") were established to protect any information that "reveals the theory of operation or design of the components of a thermonuclear or fission bomb, warhead, demolition munition, or test device."

And any such information that either directly or indirectly reveals the "design, manufacture, or utilization (including theory, development, storage, characteristics, performance, and effects) of atomic weapons or atomic weapon components and nuclear explosive devices" was denominated as "Weapon Data" and had even further special protections. Access to all such information was made subject to a "Q clearance" (read: apart from national security clearances created by presidential executive orders), which remains in effect to this day. (For example, when my former wife began a clerkship for the administrative law judges of the Nuclear Regulatory Commission's Atomic Safety and Licensing Board Panel in 1976, she was given a "Q clearance," but only after her background teaching English and French in Japan was investigated to the point of her friends over there telling her that they were interviewed by "American Forces.")

26   Through this secrecy committee, the Continental Congress was said to have placed "great importance" upon "total secrecy in intelligence matters." But the tenor of the times was such that this was not entirely realistic, as the British were nearby, Loyalists abounded, and spies were "everywhere."

27   This was in his famous *Poor Richard's Almanack* publication in 1735. Franklin was truly ahead of his time in many ways.

28   It is said that George Washington, Thomas Jefferson, and Alexander Hamilton were so concerned about having their correspondence read by others, most particularly postal clerks, that they sometimes wrote in code. And code is indeed a distinct form of government secrecy.

29   Franklin's appointment as America's negotiator with France was probably America's first "state secret." Even though it was publicly known (read: at least in France) that Franklin was in Paris at the time, it was not known that he met repeatedly and always surreptitiously with the Comte de Vergennes, France's foreign minister, to inch France closer and closer into a crucial military alliance. Then, once the Revolutionary War was won, there was the matter of secret negotiations between America and England leading up to the dispositive "Jay Treaty."

30   This is not to suggest that the Warren Commission Report on the assassination was not replete with errors, including about such major things as Oswald's gun, its "magic bullet," Oswald's background, the medical

examination of President Kennedy's body at Parkland Memorial Hospital, and its autopsy at Bethesda Naval Hospital. But none of these questionable things, among others, has conclusively established the involvement of a "second gunman," despite the strenuous continued efforts of many "conspiracy theorists" over the years.

31   To that must be added, of course, the full nature of Jack Ruby's motivation in preventing Oswald's complete interrogation.

32   The CIA is the most likely candidate for this suspicion for several reasons, not the least of which were Oswald's extensive dealings with it (read: more than the Federal Government wanted to be known) during 1963 (see Chapter Forty-Eight). In fact, it later became known that President Lyndon B. Johnson had internally wielded the prospect of "World War III" in order to gain intergovernmental support for the simple "lone assassin" explanation, in order to calm an agitated public, which would have been undercut by anything other than "covering up" what the CIA knew.

This same sort of need to quell public reaction to a presidential assassination existed during the then-unprecedented manhunt for assassin John Wilkes Booth in the wake of Abraham Lincoln's death nearly 100 years earlier, in April of 1865. There are those who believe that it was not Booth who was killed 12 days later in a barn at Garrett's Farm, but rather that it was a former confederate soldier and Booth look-alike, James William Boyd, who inexplicably had been brought to the Washington, D.C., area by order of Secretary of War Edwin M. Stanton. Undoubtedly, it was in the strong interest of the succeeding Andrew Johnson Administration that Lincoln's assassin be successfully hunted down and face justice. The question is whether it was the right face.

This pivots on the true identity of the person with whom Booth was riding when he visited the house of Dr. Samuel A. Mudd, Sr., to have his broken leg treated on his way out of Maryland. An inconvenient fact of history is that Dr. Mudd later firmly identified this person not as co-conspirator David E. Herold, but as a much younger man, Edwin Hynson -- and if so, then perhaps it wasn't Booth who was at Garrett's Farm with Herold when the latter surrendered and Booth presumably was shot to death, but rather was look-alike James Boyd. Then, even beyond many questions raised as to the accuracy of the Booth autopsy, there also is some evidence (read: far from conclusive) that Booth actually eluded the manhunt for him and survived after the Garrett Farm raid. At this point, it is difficult to conclude with any objective certainty that Booth died at Garrett's Farm as history recorded.

33   At his trial, Ray at first pled guilty and then said that he had done so only because he thought (mistakenly, as it turned out) that he needed to do so in order to avoid the death penalty. When he tried unsuccessfully to withdraw his guilty plea, he contended that he had become involved with others (read: primarily with someone named "Raoul") who were primarily responsible for Dr. King's death.

34   However, this is not at all to say that no questions remain about Ray's travels (i.e., to Canada and then Great Britain) immediately after the assassination. It still remains a complete mystery, for instance, how someone of his background and station in life managed to obtain a fake passport to make such a journey.

35   Consistent with this, the reigning Pope is considered to be both a religious leader and a "head of state." So if at any time he is actively considering resigning, as Pope Benedict XVI anomalously did in 2013, then any such secret preparations are by definition a "state secret."

36   So named for more than a thousand years, this secret archival collection was renamed the "Vatican Apostolic Archive" in 2019 (why then, is uncertain). It consists of approximately 53 miles of shelving's worth of documents going back to the eighth century.

37   For example, the papacies of Popes Stephen VI, Sergius III, John XII, Boniface VIII, Leo X, and Paul IV -- over the years 896 to 1559 -- were replete with dark scandals and deep secrecy alike.

38   The Vatican Secret Archive has only recently disgorged documents showing both the range of Pius XII's sustained diplomatic work against Hitler in the 1930s and early 1940s (including his personal involvement in three internal German plots to kill him) and the depth of his knowledge about (and seeming indifference to) the Holocaust as of the summer of 1942. The fact that such documents were kept secret for so long only deepened the controversy over the nature of his tenure, but the truth (read: as now well documented) is that he continuously collaborated with a longtime friend, Bavarian book publisher Josef Muller (a.k.a. "Joey Ox"), in both taking and supporting covert actions against Adolph Hitler and the Nazi regime. And as to the Holocaust, it is now documented that he repeatedly received dire warnings, beginning in the 1930s, that if he were to speak out against such Nazi atrocities, Hitler was just vindictive enough to immediately visit them upon the Catholic bishops of Germany, as well as their congregations. All told, it now appears that Pius XII got a "bad rap," one that, but for extreme Vatican secrecy (read: including "secrecy about secrecy"), could have been mitigated decades earlier.

39   Few "cover-ups" have been as pernicious, pervasive, and sustained as the Catholic Church's historic handling of its predatory priests. In Germany alone, independent investigators recently determined that no fewer than 3677 young boys were abused by Catholic clergy there between the years 1946 and 2014; more than half of these victims were 13 or younger and a large percentage of them were serving as altar boys at the time. In a report issued on January 20, 2022, many of these cases were laid at the feet of retired Pope Benedict XVI, who as former Cardinal Joseph Ratzinger held jurisdiction over such matters in Munich and was found to have covered them up by failing to discipline (at a minimum) the bishops who shielded their priests. He actually summed up his secret actions and inactions by saying "the Lord forgives me" -- which sadly brings to mind the expression "nice work, if you can get it!"

And speaking of "cover-ups," it now appears that for decades the Vatican covered up the circumstances of Pope John Paul I's death after the end of his pontificate of just 33 days in 1978, ostensibly because his body was discovered in his bed by a nun, but possibly because he was a victim of foul play due to his view of Mafia-related corruption. Yes, secrecy works best when it can exist in layers.

40   And as a bastion of such secrecy, the Vatican is of course highly vulnerable to serious "leaks," such as the publication in 2012 of internal Vatican letters written to the Pope evidencing million-dollar corruption in contracting. They were stolen by the Pope's butler, who was sentenced to a prison term for "aggravated theft" but spent it within the Vatican's walls due to fears that in an Italian prison he might be "pressured" to leak further secrets. Reportedly, this led to the exceptional resignation of Pope Emeritus Benedict XVI (read: the first to do so in more than 700 years), although the abuse of altar boys in his home country of Germany undoubtedly had much to do with it.

Four years later, another leak scandal arose, with the nickname "VatiLeaks." It involved two journalists who coaxed internal documents from a high-level monsignor by the name of Lucio V. Balda, who was convicted and jailed (read: again, within the Vatican) for theft. He is said to be the highest-ranking Vatican official ever to be arrested, but considering all the secrecy, intrigue, and geopolitical maneuvering that existed in the Vatican during the previous two thousand years, that is difficult to believe.

On the other hand, in May of 2008, in a spasm of what might have been pure public relations, the Vatican officially acknowledged the possible existence of alien life, a position of shocking openness that contrasts sharply with its secrecy on such things in the past (see Chapter Forty-Eight). This announcement, made by Jesuit Father Jose Funes, director of the Vatican Observatory and a scientific adviser to Pope Benedict XVI, was seen by many as a forward-looking, albeit quite atypical, attempt to "get ahead of the curve" on the "UFO issue."

41   The depth of this secrecy can be seen in the fact that only a handful of President Kennedy's close advisors were told of it; not even Vice President Lyndon B. Johnson knew of Kennedy's secret. And scholars who long afterward listened to secret recordings of the deliberations (made secretly by Kennedy) say that Secretary of State David "Dean" Rusk and Secretary of Defense Robert S. McNamara even lied to Congress in order to protect it.

42   But as for the secrecy of the Kennedy Administration's internal deliberations during the crisis, evidently that was not ironclad: It was later concluded that the Soviets got the idea of insisting on the Jupiter missiles' removal from an article in *The Washington Post* written by columnist Walter Lippmann, who was privy to part of those deliberations. So this story contains both secrecy and a leak.

43   And as for the possible future of secret telecommunications surveillance, there now exists an amazing "telephone cracking" product, made by an Israeli cybertechnology company called "NSO Group," that apparently has the capability of "attacking" a smartphone device not only by obtaining its full contents (read: emails, call records and logs, social media posts, user passwords, contact formation, GPS data, pictures, videos, sound recordings, and browsing histories) but also by remotely enabling (read: "turning on") its camera feature and its audio receiver (thus allowing "real-time surveillance" of more than mere telecommunications) without the owner even being aware of what is going on. And here's the "kicker": It can do so even if the smartphone is turned off.

My daughter who handles cybersecurity for Google tells me that thus far both the domestic and international testing on this has shown that this software, known as "Pegasus," can work on I-Phones (i.e., Apple phones) but not Android (i.e., Google) ones. In mid-September of 2021, in the wake of reports of it being used against dissidents in Saudi Arabia under the name "Forcedentry," Apple issued a system "patch" intended to counteract it. Subsequently, in July of 2022, it introduced something that it calls "Lockdown Mode," which it says will block "Pegasus intrusion" for its IPhones, IPads, and Mac computers, though as of this writing that remains to be seen.

While there appears to be no evidence yet of Pegasus or its "zero click" technology being wielded by any government user in the United States, that might be just a matter of time. (In fact, it was most recently reported that in early 2021 the FBI gave serious consideration to deploying Pegasus and similar spyware called "Phantom" for "testing" purposes but then went no further with such plans.) For the time being, though, it reportedly has not been used by either Israel or any member of the "Five Eyes" intelligence-collection alliance of the U.S., the U.K., Canada, Australia, and New Zealand. Yet on June 15, 2022, it was reported that a U.S. defense contractor is in negotiations with NSO Group to purchase access to Pegasus capability. (Contrary to this, however, is a more recent news report (read: on July 8, 2022) of use of such technology by the national police force of Canada.)

And in a much more troubling vein, it not long ago came to light that the FBI in mid-2019 obtained a version of Pegasus called "Phantom," which it possessed for more than two years for what it insists was "testing" purposes only (at a cost of a reported five million dollars) before it (read: the privacy and constitutional experts at Main Justice) determined that its use could (read: an understatement) "raise Fourth Amendment concerns." (Ironically, at least to me, the very existence of this high-tech FBI flirtation was revealed to the public only through the filing of a FOIA request.") The Bureau swears up and down that it has not gone any farther with this, but . . . ? (As is noted above, I represented the FBI in court for many years -- it was my biggest client -- so one could say that I not only know where many of its "bodies are buried," I buried a few of them myself.)

This does remind me of a time in the late 1990s when OIP was belatedly consulted by the FBI on a communications surveillance system that it had developed, something that it actually had named "Carnivore." This was back at a time when the Bureau's approach to such things was to not take privacy into consideration during their development; rather, it let the engineers run rampant to the limits of their capabilities and then asked about privacy (and Privacy Act) implications only after the fact. (Google, I happen to know, took a similar approach to its problematic "Streetview" enterprise years later.) So there we were, my Privacy Act deputy Kirsten J. Moncada and I, standing with our jaws dropped as our FBI friends demonstrated what they had built. Suffice to say that we could not let them go forward with that system without first making some privacy-driven modifications. Plus, I urgently inveighed upon them to change the damn name of it as soon as possible; I suggested calling it something such as "fuzzy puppies."

44   An "Ivy Bells" operation was disclosed in part by Ronald Pelton, an NSA analyst arrested in 1985 and convicted of espionage. In Bob Woodward's book *Veil*, it is said that Pelton sold such a secret to the Soviets in 1980 (something that was incompletely disclosed by Pelton at his trial in 1986).

45   Speaking of clandestine operations bearing the code name "Bell," there also were the secret Defense Department "operational tests" conducted in collaboration with NASA during the Apollo-14 through Apollo-17 lunar landings called "Chapel Bell." Evidently based upon a seismic experiment undertaken by Apollo-12, during which the moon was detected to be "ringing like a bell," such secret tests were undertaken to determine whether the moon contains "spacious voids" that could explain such a seismic result. Although they were conducted in the early 1970s, the results and true details of these tests remain classified on national security grounds even to the present day. Question: What if NARA were to receive a FOIA request for them?

46   Notably, all but one of these areas of big government secrets are entirely (or at least very largely) historical ones, with the final chapter(s) of "UFO secrecy" yet to be written. To provide some temporal balance to this, I will add what is known as "Havana syndrome," a sudden constellation of symptoms ranging from "disorienting" to "debilitating" -- severe headaches, dizziness, impaired vision, nausea, vertigo, tinnitus (read: "ringing in the ears"), hearing loss, memory loss, confusion, "brain fog," other sustained "neurological issues" such as "clear disturbance of brain function" and even "severe brain damage" -- that were first experienced by U.S. and Canadian embassy staff at home or in hotel rooms in Cuba in 2016. In Havana, 25 out of 25 diplomats examined were found to have suffered "objectively determined neurological impairment." Some of these effects have been long-term.

   This afflicted a total of 26 Americans and 14 Canadian diplomats by 2018, a number that reached a total of 95 Americans and their family members by the next year and rose to more than 200 by late 2019, with a perplexing mix of inexplicable sensory experiences and physical symptoms that were described as caused by "attacks." An investigation by the FBI during that year was hampered by the fact that the State Department declined to disclose -- *even to the FBI* -- the identities of the victims, based upon invalid privacy barriers; its actual concern, remarkably, was its fear of possible "leaks," a fear that drives action (or inaction) in Washington more that the public realizes. This is part of the heavy criticism aimed at the Trump Administration's State Department for its inadequate handling of the entire matter, including its suggestion that what had been going on was nothing more than "psychogenic." (That attitude formed the basis of a lawsuit brought in December of 2021 by a State Department employee who was stationed in Guangzhou, China in 2017.) By contrast, the Biden Administration has sworn that it will "leav[e] no stone unturned" in getting the bottom of this "as swiftly as possible."

   In late 2019, a secret Centers for Disease Control study concluded that they "thus far have not identified a mechanism of injury," which had no small impact when this report was disclosed (read: with proper privacy redactions) under the Freedom of Information Act in early 2021. Recently, such injuries have been reported also in Russia, Australia, India, Poland, Georgia, Taiwan, Kyrgyzstan, Uzbekistan, Tajikistan, China, Austria, Colombia, Northern Virginia, Berlin, and Washington. More recently, the Biden State Department has focused on 20 cases reported by U.S. personnel in Vienna, the second-most-commonplace location after Havana. And most recently, it has been concerned with two serious cases of "Havana syndrome" in Hanoi, Vietnam, so serious that they delayed a trip there by Vice President Kamala D. Harris. And in early 2022, there were belated reports by two

Trump-era homeland security officials and a senior public-relations official who claimed to have experienced such symptoms while working on the White House grounds. As the numbers grew, a medical specialist described such symptoms as "[o]rganic responses; you can't fake them."

Speculation about the cause of what by early 2022 became more than a thousand such cases has centered around what experts variously call "an acoustic attack," a "sonic attack," a "microwave attack," or a "directed energy" attack, "through use of a concentrate beam of electromagnetic energy" or "pulsed, radio frequency (RF) energy." They think (but frustratingly are not certain) that these are created through use of some sort of sonic weapon (perhaps one aimed at diplomats' electronic devices), or some form of advanced microwave technology that causes injury within victims' inner ears. A recent panel of experts convened by the CIA found it "plausible" that such attacks could be caused by a portable device, most likely an ultrasound one, but these experts could not explain such devices' seeming effectiveness indoors.

To date, an incomplete January 2022 CIA report notwithstanding, this extraordinary mystery has not been solved and whichever government is responsible -- be it Cuba, Russia, or somebody else -- has done a spectacular job of maintaining its secrecy. (The best guess here is Russia, especially as CIA Director William J. Burns in November 2021 pointedly warned it about facing "consequences" if it ultimately is found to be responsible for what the U.S. now calls "anomalous health incidents" ("AHIs," for short). (Notice how governments have a tendency to reduce some things to benign-sounding names (and acronyms) in order to minimize them.) As yet, there has been no warning given to China.)

And as of mid-2022, with the number of reported cases exceeding 1000, the State Department and the CIA, under recent legislation known as the "Havana Act," began making dozens of six-figure compensation payments to verified "Havana Syndrome" victims. -- all without any acceptable explanation of what has occurred. Amazingly, the secrecy of it has been maintained for more than six years.

CHAPTER FIFTY

1   Another thing that can be added to this list, relatively lighthearted as it is, is how it seems lately that words and phrases in the English language can so readily transmogrify from one meaning or usage to another, proliferating with what seems like lightning (read: electronic) speed. A prime example is the phrase "begs the question," which actually means evading a subject, not raising it. Similarly, the phrase "fraught with" has suddenly devolved down to something merely being "fraught." And then there is the word "incredible," which until not long ago meant only "unbelievable," but now is popularly misused as a routine superlative; as with "fraught," its evolution seems here to stay.

Subjunctively speaking, unfortunately, there likewise is the use of "may" (which bespeaks empowerment) in lieu of "might" (which is conjectural); this is a substantive difference that precludes clarity all too often. Plus there is "gut wrenching" becoming confused with "heart rending," "hone in" being mistakenly used instead of "home in," and "insure" being used instead of "assure" or "ensure" (the latter of which actually is underutilized). This is not unlike the persistently mistaken use of "implied" and "inferred"; a speaker implies and a listener or reader infers, not the other way around. Then there is ambiguity-laden word "since"; it ordinarily refers to a subsequent period of time, but lately it has come to be used as a sometimes-confusing synonym for the word "because." Likewise abused is "including" (in all its forms) which until very recently meant some but not all of the items involved; lately, it often is used to reference a complete list, as if it means that nothing is left out. And somewhat akin to this is the recent abuse of the word "none," which is a word of singularity, not plurality; in other words, its usage should be "none has," not "none have."

Lastly (read: not actually, as there doubtless are more) is the misuse of "further" and "farther," "who" in lieu of "whom" (which does sound olde-fashioned), "that" instead of "which" (the former of which is limitive while the latter is descriptive), "that" instead of "who," "their" instead of "he" or "she" (when not in deference to a pronoun-averse person, the plurality/singularity ambiguity notwithstanding), and an old favorite: The misplacement of the word "only," which should directly precede the thing that is being limited. And speaking of splitting infinitives, to wisely do so in pursuit of clarity is no vice. Perhaps the "granddaddy" of them all is the near-ubiquity of the phrase "in terms of" as a poor and inexplicable replacement for "regarding," "as to," and "in relation to."

2   My younger daughter diagnosed Trump as suffering from malignant narcissism, among other things, within the first month of his taking office.

3   It certainly has been my own experience that the very earliest years of a professional career afford the biggest payoff for time and effort expended; in other words, that investment yields greater developmental rewards (even exponentially so) than it would just a few years later down the road. I think of it as not unlike a small child's ability to learn a second, or even a third language while still young; a child is able to process languages with far greater facility, and much more quickly, than an adult. So, too, is a brand-new attorney able to "soak up" more, both substantively and procedurally, in the first two years of law practice, say, than in the next five -- *if* that young attorney takes full advantage of that through the investment of boundless energy and a maximal work ethic. So this is one of the lessons that I would take pains to impart to my students, in addition to teaching them secrecy law and oral advocacy, before a semester drew to a close.

4   Among the other "real world" lessons that I taught them were about the importance of what I call "human dialogue" instead of voicemail, email, or (worse yet) text messaging; the correctness of the civics lesson learned in high school about Members of Congress being unfamiliar with (read: not bothering to read) their own legislative proposals; and the potential value of professional colleagues (as co-workers, or co-counsel in the case of litigation attorneys) becoming good friends who can be relied upon through "thick and thin," as the saying goes. To that, I would invariably add the Office of Information and Privacy's official motto: "Information is power; conserve it."

5   Sometimes one daughter would even go so far as to warn the other: "Look out! Dad is double-checking whether or not we had a 'good process' in making a decision on [this or that]." Or one of them would say to me: "It didn't quite work out as I'd hoped, Dad, but at least I had a 'good process.'"

    When it comes to decisionmaking, here is where I have to make the seemingly outlandish claim that I have never had any difficulty making any decision at any time of my life. Not even once, believe it or not, because I have always been able to analyze a fact pattern quickly, completely, and proficiently -- leading to a decision in which I had total confidence. For example, my wife and I decided to get married just four days after our first date. (The fact that we didn't get divorced until 41½ years later speaks to that.) And with only a single exception -- involving a financial decision that we made "on the fly" while in the thrall of Disney World's Magic Kingdom -- I have never regretted any decision I've ever made. To me, that counts as being exceptionally fortunate.

6   Relatively recent examples of this are FEMA Director Michael D. Brown, White House Counsel and failed Supreme Court nominee Harriet E. Miers, and Office of Special Counsel Director Scott J. Bloch. More recently, during the Administration of Donald J. Trump, examples abounded, including COVID-19 quack Dr. Scott W. Atlas; Postmaster General charlatan Louis DeJoy; HHS COVID-19 coordinator and former dog breeder Brian E. Harrison; "chief scientist" at the Department of Agriculture Samuel H. Clovis, Jr., who was not any type of "scientist"; HHS COVID-19 "science advisor" Paul E. Alexander, who also was no scientist; Ambassador to the European Union Gordon D. Sondland, whose incompetence spoke for itself; U.S. Agency for Global Media ("Voice of America")

head Michael Pack, a blatantly partisan and incompetent appointee; and Acting Attorney General Matthew G. Whitaker, who made a mockery of his bizarre appointment.

7   "You could look it up," as they say: The average income level of a first-term Republican appointee is markedly greater than that of a Democrat counterpart. In the legal field, for example, more of the former are already law firm partners or corporate executives, rather than mere law firm associates, law professors, politicians, and leaders of "public interest" organizations. For the most part, people on both sides of the partisan divide learn and, if pressed, admit this.

8   One thing that becomes quite evident is that political employees even at the lower levels begin thinking about their next positions and act accordingly. From near the end of a first presidential term to the middle of a second one, this takes the form of openly aspiring to that ultimate appointment before a president leaves office. For example, I remember a particular activity during the second half of the second Bush Administration that involved 11 such appointees who behaved badly for this evident reason. Nine of them, as I recall, received the next appointment that was desired. The other two ran out of time.

9   Much the same could be said about the latter years of the Reagan Administration, during which malefactors such as National Security Council official Oliver L. North were allowed to run rampant.

10   That certainly was not the "best hour" of then-Deputy Attorney General Eric H. Holder, Jr., given how he handled the pardon application of a wealthy fellow named (ironically) Mark Rich (née Marcell David Reich). I greatly admired Eric (his stance in what later became known as the "Operation Fast and Furious" scandal when he later became the attorney general during the Obama Administration notwithstanding), but I happened to know the Department's Pardon Attorney (Roger C. Adams) fairly well (even shared a bathroom with him for a stretch) and had a basis for being surprised and disappointed about what Eric Holder did on that and how he did it.

Apropos of this, I will share another story: About a week after President Clinton left office, while walking along Pennsylvania Avenue I happened to bump into a fine lady who for the previous eight years had been the Assistant Attorney General for the Office of Legal Policy, the Justice Department component that was the successor office to the one in which I had worked (as part of the AG's Office) as a law student more than 37 years earlier (see Chapter Seven). Eleanor Dean Acheson ("Eldie," to one and all) is the granddaughter of legendary Secretary of State Dean G. Acheson, and she even had "gone to Wellesley with Hillary," we used to say. I remember Eldie telling me then that, on Inauguration Day eve, very few Clinton appointees such as herself managed to get much sleep at all that night because neither did President Clinton, as he stayed up all night long racing to act on a backlog of pardon applications and other last-minute legal items. In short, the Clinton Administration came to a close just as it began -- frenetically.

11   With this shift, there almost immediately developed a new characteristic of decisionmaking that was employed almost uniformly by political employees: Decisionmaking by "consensus." This took advantage of what could be called "email technology," with electronic distribution "groups" created to deal with distinct matters, and it allowed decisions to be made with no one person taking responsibility for something that was done (or not done, as the case might be) by "the group." Time and again, Bush political appointees, especially under Gonzales, blatantly availed themselves of this approach and I was able to discern this (sometimes only after the fact) by examining email messages closely. As far as I'm concerned, it fits perfectly with the axiom that Republicans don't care so much about the process of governing; they want the power, but not the responsibility.

12   The major disaster of the second half of Bush 43's second term, of course, was Alberto Gonzales's gross mishandling of the Administration's United States Attorneys, all of whom had been appointed by President Bush, served "at the pleasure of the president," and lawfully could be fired at any time without reason. But when Gonzales and the White House (mostly the latter) decided that they wanted to replace several of them together at the same time in late 2006, they inexplicably left it to low-level political underlings to "break the news."

To say the least, those conversations and their follow-ups did not go well at all, as most of those U.S. Attorneys reacted quite strongly to both the substance of what they were being told and the disdain with which they were being told it. This led to enormous controversy and adverse media coverage even though, again, these were political appointees who could be fired at will.

A focal point of all this, as the putative "coordinator" of these high-level firings, was a very young assistant to Attorney General Alberto Gonzales by the name of Monica M. Goodling. Clearly "in over her head" in this enterprise, she struggled to limit the damage as best she could, which wasn't very well. Then, to make matters worse, she was subpoenaed to appear before the House Judiciary Committee, where her counsel rashly negotiated a grant of immunity for her that undercut her right to invoke the protections of the Fifth Amendment. So under congressional questioning, she broadly admitted that not only had she been involved in this U.S. Attorneys debacle, as the Justice Department's "White House Liaison," she also had personally overseen the politicization of the hiring of many career employees, which was both unlawful and unprecedented in the Department's history (see Chapter Forty-Three).

This led to an Inspector General ("IG," to its subjects) investigation into that additional admitted aspect of what Goodling had done, including the unlawful politicization the Attorney General's Honors Program for the hiring of newly minted attorneys, something that she brazenly oversaw in conjunction with the White House (i.e., Karl C. Rove, who held the title of Senior Advisor and Deputy Chief of Staff there) and with the implementation assistance of shameless political acolytes lower down in the Department, including one who then was serving as the deputy attorney general's chief of staff and seemed to be intimidated by her.

And that in turn led to the precedent-setting case of *Gerlich v. United States Department of Justice*, which challenged their corrupt scheme to reject Honors Program applicants for such career position on purely political or ideological grounds. (This was another classic case of political officials saying among themselves: "Don't worry, we probably won't get caught. But if we do, by then we'll be long gone.") I litigated this case singlehandedly on behalf of such victimized young attorneys; it ultimately cost the Government more than a half-million dollars in damages and attorney fees. (In August of 2010, despite the false bravado of her counsel, I deposed Goodling for several hours, to the point of tears, about what she had done (see Chapter Forty-Three).)

13   Much of the blame for this, I can say from firsthand experience, can be laid at the feet of former Vice President Spiro T. Agnew, oddly enough (see Chapter Ten).

14   The Department of State, for instance, has a deputy secretary of state and no fewer than six under secretaries. The Department of Defense similarly has a deputy secretary and also five under secretaries. And the Department of the Treasury has a deputy secretary and three under secretaries. Even the relatively lowly Department of Agriculture (which stands below the Department of Justice in the line of presidential succession) also has a deputy secretary and six under secretaries. I realize that such arguments do not necessarily carry the day on such matters, either with OMB or with appropriations committees in Congress, but I think a new presidential administration would be well advised to consider them.

15   As to "leaks," it is worth adding here that the subject of government secrecy also involves what could be termed "judicial secrecy" -- the long-held principle that the judiciary should maintain secrecy about its internal deliberations, its unannounced activities, and both the nature and the timing of its upcoming decisions. Indeed,

the United States Supreme Court, in particular, is renowned for this. But I can recall at least five instances within the span of my professional lifetime in which there have been shocking departures from this. The most general one was the exceptional access to the Supreme Court's inner workings that was given to Bob Woodward and Scott Armstrong for their book *The Brethren: Inside the Supreme Court* during the late 1970s; this came in the form of ostensible "off-the-record" interviews (read: leaks, actually), largely from the Court's law clerks, that were unprecedented at the time. (Disclosure: Scott is a friend; we began as "sworn enemies" on very opposite sides of the fence in the early 1980s and ended up with him being a valuable member of my Collaboration on Government Secrecy Advisory Board (see Chapter Forty-Two).)

Other leaks, notably in advance of major Supreme Court decisions, have also been attributed to Court employees and coincidentally three of them have involved abortion decisions. The first, in 1972, revealed the Court's internal wranglings over whether the historic *Roe v. Wade* case would be "held over" to another Court Term so that new Justices William H. Rehnquist and Lewis F. Powell, Jr., could participate in it. What appeared to be full details of the procedural maneuverings by Chief Justice Warren E. Burger, Justice Harry A. Blackman, and Justice William O. Douglas were laid bare in an unsigned *Washington Post* article that was attributed to anonymous "informed sources" and was wholly unprecedented at the time.

Then, when the Court's landmark decision in *Roe v. Wade* was nearly ready to be announced in 1993, Supreme Court clerk Larry A. Hammond "leaked" it to a *Time Magazine* reporter under a timetable that he thought would not involve a premature public disclosure. However, because *Time* was a weekly publication and the Court's decision was unexpectedly delayed, news of it appeared on newsstands several hours before it was ultimately announced by Justice Blackmun. At the time, Chief Justice Warren E. Burger was quite angry about that and sought to find and fire the leaker. Larry immediately confessed to Justice Powell, for whom he worked, and then to Chief Justice Burger, but the Justices forgave him as having been "double-crossed" by the altered timing (pun intended), so no formal punishment was administered and his legal career proceeded unimpaired.

Indeed, not many years later, in 1977, I had occasion to consult Larry on a fact issue that arose in one of my litigation cases. Larry had been a member of the Watergate Special Prosecution Force and I was defending the main FOIA case involving its records (see Chapter Twelve). By that time, he was a political appointee (read: a deputy assistant attorney general) in the Justice Department's Office of Legal Counsel and was ensconced in Room 5233-5235 on the Main Justice Building's Fifth Floor, coincidentally the "double room" in which the eight Nazi saboteurs were tried for espionage in 1942 (see the Glossary and Quiz Question #65). (Another coincidence (or irony) with Larry Hammond is that three more years later, while serving as the acting assistant attorney general for the Office of Legal Counsel, Larry issued a formal legal opinion to the effect that in leak investigations government employees can be "requir[ed] . . . to submit to polygraph [read: lie detector] examinations." Larry A. Hammond, Acting Assistant Attorney General, Office of Legal Counsel (Feb. 22, 1980).)

In 1979, ABC News Supreme Court correspondent Tim O'Brien obtained a "scoop" with predictions of the outcomes of several decisions that were on the verge of being issued. Chief Justice Burger immediately launched an investigation to find the "leaker," whereupon the *Associate Press* reported (through a compounding leak) that Burger suspected that it was someone in the Court's print shop. Shortly after, a Government Printing Office employee involved in setting type for the Court's rulings was transferred to a different division. That staffer, who was not publicly identified (not even through a leak), denied leaking any information, but nothing more was done or said about it.

Then there was the most dramatic (and arguably traumatic) Supreme Court leak ever, also in an abortion case, the one that overruled *Roe v. Wade*. On May 2, 2022, *POLITICO* published a leaked first draft of a majority opinion written by Justice Samuel A. Alito, Jr., in *Dobbs v. Jackson Women's Health Organization* that evidently had been circulated within the Court in February 2022. My good friend Josh Gerstein, senior legal affairs reporter for *POLITICO*, obtained this "mega-scoop" but of course has not disclosed how or from whom. A press release from the Court confirmed the leaked document's authenticity and Chief Justice John G. Roberts, Jr., condemned the leak as a "betrayal of the confidences of the Court" and it was called a "bomb at the Court," "the equivalent of the Pentagon Papers leak." The leaked draft of the proposed majority opinion, unprecedented as such, sparked a tidal wave of abortion-related protests, with such turmoil also spreading to the Court itself. Even Justice Clarence Thomas, not known for his verbosity (or his self-awareness, apparently), actually said: "You begin to look over your shoulder. It's like kind of an infidelity [sic], that you can explain it, but you can't undo it." On June 24, 2022, the Court issued its decision, with the majority opinion authored by Justice Alito, overruling *Roe*.

And in the wake of this unprecedented leak, a former anti-abortion leader named Robert L. "Rob" Schenck claimed in mid-November of 2022 that in 2014 "he was informed ahead of time" of the outcome in *Burwell v. Hobby Lobby Stores, Inc.*, 573 U.S. 682 (2014), a case involving religious rights in the context of contraception. In a recent letter to Chief Justice Roberts, this evangelical minister reportedly said that this occurred after two conservative allies of his had dinner at the home of Supreme Court Justice Samuel Alito and his wife. To this it must be said that Justice Alito has denied this implication and that, although the Justice most directly involved in this second recent "leak" was coincidentally the same, it cannot be assumed that it actually occurred. As for the leak of Justice Alito's draft opinion in *Dobbs*, it is easier to surmise a motive for that on the other side of that issue rather than on his. In any event, speculating about the source of that singularly "unsolved" Supreme Court leak will be left to others.

Lastly, it is worth noting that while all of the above Supreme Court "leaks" were manifestly born of ideological, political, or policy-related motivations, only one (save for, arguably, Woodward and Armstrong) was made with a commercial motive in mind. That came more than a century ago when a longtime law clerk to Justice Joseph McKenna named Ashton F. Embry was found to have leaked the outcomes of several business-related cases to Wall Street traders in 1919 so that he and they could "short" related stocks and turn a quick profit -- "insider trading," under the laws of today. Embry was charged with "defrauding the United States" but was not brought to trial due to problems with a key witness. He did, however, resign his position and turned to a career as a baker.

16   OK, so I made that last one up. (At least I think I did.) The point, of course, is that the technological underpinnings of secrecy over the past 85 years have advanced so far and so fast during that time that it is dizzying even to government professionals, all the more so for mere members of the public. Just consider the process of "tempesting" keyboarded computer equipment in order to thwart the "vibrational" surveillance that is described in Chapter Twenty-Six. I daresay that most people would not have believed that without actually seeing it as I did, no different than with the "meteor burst communication" method also described in that chapter (which some people understandably still do not believe). So, what is suggested here in this recounting is could "telepathic surveillance" really be so far behind? (See, by comparison, the MKULTRA experiments conducted by the CIA in the 1950s, 1960s, and early 1970s, as described in the Glossary.)

17   One very problematic byproduct of this "electronic revolution" is the fact that information is now readily available, and transportable, with the stroke of a keyboard and the use of media as small as thumb drives and the like -- which is highly detrimental to secrecy. Put another way, no longer does stealing secrets require the complete theft of the paper documents on which they are recorded (for example, the theft of more than 1000 documents from an FBI office in Media, Pennsylvania, in 1971), or the cumbersome page-by-page photography of documents (such as what "James Bond" often did, "high-tech" as it seemed), or the photocopying of classified records on site for later removal (for example, what Daniel Ellsberg did with what became known as the "Pentagon Papers" in 1969). More recently, by contrast, one might consider the case of young Reality L. Winner, who at age 25 stole a "top secret" intelligence report about Russian interference in the 2016 election from her NSA contract employer by just photocopying it and tucking into her pantyhose before mailing it to the media.

And, of course, one need look only at the successful espionage of Army Cpl. Chelsea E. Manning in 2010, of NSA contract employee Edward J. Snowden in 2013, and the corporate espionage of the unknown person who in 2016 leaked more than 11 million documents from a Panamanian law firm used by clients for purposes of money laundering and tax evasion. In other words, the days of simply locking a classified document in a "Class 6 container" (i.e., a security-certified safe) are now over. Both the Manning and Snowden leaks were made to WikiLeaks.

An even more recent example is Joshua A. Schulte, an employee in the CIA's Operations Support Branch, who is being prosecuted for disclosing to WikiLeaks a veritable trove of information about CIA hacking methods (an entire new realm of government secrecy), known as "Vault 7," which is said to have represented the single largest leak of classified information in the Agency's history. Schulte stands accused of being a disgruntled employee who was in a position to abscond with nothing less than thirty-four terabytes of data (or more than two billion pages' worth) of operational secrets in electronic form -- and stealthily doing so. That should stand as the modern-day record for such things, at least for a while.

18   As melodramatic as it might sound, I sometimes saw myself and my colleagues as shepherds of a secrecy "legacy" that in the United States was born in modern form only 80 years ago and has needed nurturing (and sometime reigning in) ever since. My modest contributions to this, largely in the form of "exclusion" conceptualization and "Glomarization" propagation, have helped perpetuate this legacy (within the realm of legitimacy) for the second half of this period, and now it is time for others to carry it forward.

EPILOGUE

1   At the other end of the age continuum, there is one more observation or recommendation that I should make, having to do with retirement. Many people retire, at one age or another, in a "full stop" fashion. Even such retirees who have hobbies and other such interests find it difficult to end their working lives so abruptly, which is how it invariably was for generations before mine. It is far better, however, that full retirement be "phased in," if at all possible. Here again, I was lucky to do so with teaching and running an academic center for seven years and then, with my father's health failing, shifting to just teaching for the next three (see Chapter Forty-Two). And then there came this lengthy book project, which I have thoroughly enjoyed. So it is based upon my own experience that I make this recommendation.

I should say that I also was lucky in that I was not tempted to continue on at the Justice Department beyond turning 55. To be sure, at that point I still viewed my job as "the best in world" and for several years had been working for a first-class Republican appointee, Associate Attorney General Robert D. McCallum, Jr., who had an excellent reputation that was well deserved. But one Friday morning in March of 2006, I was asked to participate in a matter in which a significant part of the Department's position was aiming to be -- there is no other word for it -- false. Briefly put, someone in the White House had decided that it would be a good idea for an op-ed piece on the subject of government transparency to be prepared for publication in *USA Today* during "Sunshine Week," and a draft of that soon arrived for my review.

In Robert McCallum's absence, I was asked by one of his deputies to review it for accuracy, among other things, and I was able to make a few corrections and substantive improvements to it. But I drew a line at even attempting to "improve" a Defense Department-related paragraph within it that actually was incorrect by a full 180 degrees. In other words, it sought to take credit for something for which the Bush Administration in fact held blame.

Knowing what the facts of the underlying matter actually were, I flatly refused to endorse (read: even touch) that paragraph, pointedly noting that the political appointee who had asked me to do so did in fact, to my own certain knowledge, know exactly what was true and not true as well. I suppose I can take some small satisfaction in that the false part of that "final draft" was eventually replaced with something that was at least arguably true, but that's hardly the point. By that time, over the weekend, I had taken a shower and decided to retire.

When I first spoke publicly about this, in March of 2007, I did not name the young political appointee who had, in effect, asked me to abet a lie. Perhaps I should have, because he was Neil M. Gorsuch, whom I later learned was at that time anxiously awaiting a prospective White House appointment to the Tenth Circuit Court of Appeals -- which did come through for him a few weeks later. It was quite obvious to me that Neil was extremely reluctant to "rock the boat" with anyone at the White House at all, even if it meant publishing something that he personally knew was in no small part untrue. And even if it meant insisting that I "go along" with him on something that he knew that I knew that he knew was false.

2   I have counted no fewer than two dozen distinct junctures at which I had such good luck over the course of those years -- some more crucial than others, of course. My students sometimes asked me if such a thing is "pure luck," or perhaps something else. After thinking about this for a while, I concluded that the best answer is that it is the kind of luck that can occur only if one is putting himself (or herself) "out there," working very hard, to begin with. In other words, the more a young student or professional "stretches" him- or herself into new situations, with new challenges, even (or perhaps especially) when they are unfamiliar ones, the more likely that such a thing will occur. And when it does, the key factor is that it be taken full advantage of, with as much hard work and time invested as possible.

3   Certainly, there are thousands upon thousands of federal employees, at all levels, who work "exceptionally long and hard" for their agencies and I do not gainsay that. But that is one thing. Becoming known as someone who can be relied upon to expend as much energy as is necessary to meet a responsibility -- or to help someone else to do so -- is something else.

4   This sounds like more extreme immodesty, of course, but if I had a nickel for every time someone called me a "FOIA guru" over the years, I'd have more than enough to buy a cup of coffee -- even a grande latte at today's prices.

5   To bastardize what is sometimes said about paranoia: Just because I did so well doesn't mean that I'm being immodest about it.

6   By the way, I recoil from use of the word "bureaucrat" when speaking of civil service employees, because I take some personal umbrage at the way in which that word now is often "thrown around." The now-ubiquitous "Urban Dictionary," regrettably, defines it in current popular culture by going so far as to say that it means "one who works by fixed routine, without exercising intelligent judgment." To this, I say: Wrong! That definition would make the word insulting. So on behalf of civil servants both across the country and around the world (except for in the U.K. and its Commonwealth nations, where career government employees are by tradition well respected, if not also well paid), let me say that the way in which this word often is used (and abused) just . . . sucks.

7   Please make no mistake in this regard: Civil servants as a general rule have their eyes open about the "trade-offs" involved in government employment, and when they sign on (or, day after day thereafter, stay on) they make a conscious choice, one utterly incompatible with complaining about it afterward. I certainly had my eyes wide open, right from the outset, having worked at the Justice Department twice before. But I also knew that as a government attorney I could earn sufficient income to raise a family, which is all that I really cared about on that score. (To be sure, having a wife who also was a Trial Attorney helped.) Plus, there was a retirement system that, as things turned out, has been worth its weight in gold.

And in my case, I was exceptionally fortunate because I became a career member of the Senior Executive

Service at the age of 32 (the youngest ever as of then), which meant that at least I started earning at nearly the top of the government pay scale early on. (Each year, OPM asks me to serve on a review panel for the selection of career SESers to receive presidential-rank awards, and each year the folks there tell me that as far as they know this record still stands; I figure that eventually at least some hotshot young scientist will break this record, though it has stood for close to 40 years thus far.)

8   To bring things full circle here, I probably should conclude that the list of applicable "human nature" tendencies identified at the outset of this book -- i.e., paternalism, protectiveness, proprietariness (tinged with hubris), and ass covering (see the Introduction) -- deserves one more entry: deceitfulness. Sadly, that can be part of the picture as well, especially when someone (or some institution) is in "cover up" mode. By the way, I do not mind so much being lied to as I do mind seeing someone employ a lie in a blatant attempt to avoid looking bad, or perhaps in a self-serving effort to gain, to secure, or to not ruin the chances of receiving a prospective political appointment or affiliation. In my experience, competent and secure people do not even think about doing such a thing, but sadly too many political appointees do.

9   One more thing in retrospect is that perhaps the biggest decision that a long-term federal official makes is the decision about when to retire, which can be both a personal and a professional one. As I approached age 55, the minimum full-retirement age for most federal employees in my civil service category, I knew it was entirely possible that (as my wife then openly feared) I would just "die at my desk" sometime in my late 80s in my same position (i.e., prone, to work hard) after a career spanning nearly seven decades. (I actually knew a couple of gentlemen -- much older than myself, of course, one at Justice and one at State -- who had done just that, even though their retirement benefits maxed out after slightly less than 42 years of service.) I even was aware that in doing so I arguably would long surpass the record held by J. Edgar Hoover as the longest-serving Justice Department component head (47 years and change), for whatever that would be worth.

But I had made a firm personal decision years before (in the late 1970s, actually) that I would not in the near term teach law, or write, or agree to any such thing as a part-time "side venture" that would diminish my ability to say that I was devoting nothing less than 100% of my time, energy, and talent to my government respon-sibilities. In other words, I never wanted anyone to be able to say that, but for whatever else I was doing "on the side," I could have done a better job on something at Justice. I did know people about whom that could be said and I was determined not to become one of them, no matter how lucrative or otherwise appealing any extracurricular teaching, writing, or speaking gig might be.

Yet I just knew all along that one day I would devote myself to teaching law, which meant that I had to retire at some point while still relatively young enough to do that. So when Neil Gorsuch so cowardly asked me to disregard what was true for him (and by extension for the White House) in March of 2006 (see the Epilogue), I decided that age 55 would be my "jumping-off" point (though I had not quite attained that age yet), which after all did leave me with many years for teaching, writing, speaking, consulting, public-interest advocacy, *pro bono* counseling, and all-around mischief-making thereafter. And in that sense, I enjoyed that as my final "right place/right time" Justice Department experience.

GLOSSARY OF TERMS

1   This is especially so with footnotes (or endnotes), which are a singular way of including further detail in a book such as this. "Read them or not at your peril," a proponent of footnotes might say, though he or she might say it in the text.

2   Additionally, it should also be added (in a triple redundancy generously authorized by the division of redundancy division) that there is one part of the FOIA -- that of fees and fee limitations, but not "fee waivers" -- that was placed within the jurisdictional purview of the Office of Management and Budget ("OMB," to its many detractors) by Congress in 1986.

3   And as a frightening coda to this evident abuse of classified information by Trump, it was reported on November 18, 2022 that during a crisis with Iran in August of 2019, he actually "tweeted" a classified image from a high-level U.S. spy satellite (called a KH-11). Such a thing allows foreign adversaries (read: Russia and China, if not also Iran) to learn the exact contours and surveillance capabilities of our satellite arsenal, with resultant harm to U.S. national security.

4   In the 1970s, Congress also enacted two other openness-in-government laws, the Federal Advisory Committee Act ("FACA, to government advisors) in 1972, to provide for disclosure of "advisory committee" records, and the Government-in-the-Sunshine Act ("GISA," to even young folks), in 1976, which is essentially an "open-meetings" law for the formal meetings held by the commissioners of independent regulatory agencies. The latter also narrowed Exemption 3 of the Freedom of Information Act for the first of several times.

5   Yes, this sudden turn of events was both surprising and disappointing, because those of us who had worked on crafting that legislation foresaw not only easy passage of it in the 96th Congress, but also legislative receptivity to a series of similar such bills down the road (see Chapter Nineteen).

6   During mid-1996, an HHS team led by Acting Assistant Secretary of Health and Human Services for Planning and Evaluation Gary E. Clayton undertook a comprehensive process (of which I was a part) for the development of HIPAA regulations that became binding both within governments and within the private sector (i.e., all medical facilities) nationwide.

7   Actually, the submitters of business information in "reverse FOIA" situations were often the same companies that were the FOIA requesters of their competitors' information, in what became a "tit-for-tat" business environment by the mid-1970s. We used to say that this spawned a "cottage industry" of making FOIA requests for, and objecting to the disclosure of, business information under the FOIA, one of which "reverse FOIA lawyers" were the primary beneficiaries.

8   Such matters often involve another statute, the Trade Secrets Act (or 18 U.S.C. § 1905), which operates in tandem with FOIA Exemption 4 to prohibit any "discretionary disclosure" of business information.

9   This executive order was created by OIP in 1987 and was based upon governmentwide guidance that was issued by OIP five years earlier under the auspices of the Vice President's (read: George H.W. Bush's) Task Force on Regulatory Relief.

10   Theoretically, under prevailing case law, a "reverse FOIA" matter could involve a FOIA exemption other than Exemption 4; all that is required is for someone to have an "outside interest" that is arguably protectible under a FOIA exemption and is placed at risk by a FOIA request. Thus, a personal-privacy interest, protectible under FOIA Exemption 6 or FOIA Exemption 7(C), can be the basis of a "reverse FOIA" case, but a big difference is that in Exemption 4 contexts the party in interest will of right receive advance notice of any disclosure contemplated in response to a FOIA request, while in the Exemption 6/Exemption 7(C) context he or she will not -- due largely to the impracticability of providing such notice to countless such persons. (The FOIA's two privacy exemptions, combined, are the most frequently invoked exemptions of the Act.)

There have been rare exceptions to this, however, such as in a case (*Ricchio v. NARA*) in which I provided a courtesy notification to former President Richard M. Nixon; my unsuccessful litigation opponent in that case, a very capable and friendly fellow named Seth P. Waxman, went on to join the Justice Department and become Solicitor General. Nixon was not the only former high-level "Watergate" figure to try to make use of the FOIA in "retirement." Another was his co-plaintiff in *Ricchio*, former Attorney General Richard G. Kleindienst, who phoned me directly one morning to "chat" about the case (which as an attorney he knew he could not properly do) and provided me with a line -- "call me Dick" -- that apparently I've not forgotten.

And then there was a FOIA lawsuit brought by former White House Chief of Staff (and principal Nixon henchperson) Harry Robbins "H.R." Haldeman who sought to obtain records created by him during his White House tenure that he claimed were being held by the General Services Administration ("GSA," to those federal employees who wanted new desks), in that they reposed at the National Archives and Records Service, which was still part of GSA at the time. I well remember being polite to "H.R.," through his counsel, but he picked the wrong guy (as well as the wrong time, as this was in 1978 and 1979, not long after "Watergate") to litigate against; he did not get what he most wanted.

11   A "reverse FOIA" case is just what it sounds like: Whereas in a "straight" FOIA case a FOIA requester is asking the court to order the defendant agency to disclose information, a "reverse FOIA" plaintiff is asking the court to order the defendant agency to *not* disclose information.

12   There have been no fewer than nine such shutdowns since 1980, lasting for a cumulative total of 86 days. Initially, they began occurring at the very beginning of a fiscal year (i.e., as of midnight on the morning of October 1), but with the advent of "continuing resolutions," they now can occur at almost any time of the year. It was during one such budgetary interregnum period that President Bill Clinton first "hooked up" with White House intern Monica S. Lewinsky (reportedly near the Oval Office) in November of 1995. (Note: The phrase "hooked up" will not be defined in this Glossary, neither in the Clinton/Lewinski context nor otherwise.) Trivia question: What media expression was spawned by Monica Lewinsky's first principal counsel on a Sunday morning two years later? Answer: "The full Ginsburg," i.e., appearing on all five major television interview programs on a single Sunday morning; he was the first person to do so.

13   The U.K., of course, had its own nomenclature for its secrecy regime, the most charming of which was the category "most secret." That label was applied to many of the documents generated during World War II, some of which were classified as such as early as the late 1930s and remained in that status until as late as 2015.

14   The hedge here is made necessary by the Intelligence Authorization Act for Fiscal Year 2003, Public Law 107-306, which in a section titled "Prohibition on Compliance with Requests for Information Submitted by Foreign Governments," expressly precludes any covered "intelligence agency" from disclosing records in response to any FOIA request that is made by or on behalf of any foreign government or international government organization. By its terms, it prohibits disclosure in response to requests made by such other-than-U.S. governmental entities either directly or indirectly through a "representative." 5 U.S.C. § 552(a)(3)(A), (E)(ii) (as amended). This means that for any FOIA request that by its nature appears as if it might have been made by or on behalf of a non-U.S. Government entity, a covered agency may inquire into the particular circumstances of the requester in order to properly implement this prohibition.

This FOIA amendment is something that, as proposed within the House Permanent Select Committee on Intelligence ("HPSCI," to Hill staffers) in 2002, was in my view a transparently emotional reaction to 9/11, in that many House Members, particularly HPSCI Chairman (and future CIA director) Porter J. Goss, yearned to "get at least something done" that year as a 9/11 response. (It was a bad idea.) This free-standing legislative proposal was circulated widely within the executive branch, in an entirely above-board fashion, and given the magnitude of the agency push-back that we were able to coordinate for it, by late September of 2002, I thought that we had managed to block it.

But then, literally in the middle of the night on October 3, 2002, Chairman Goss, with an assist from White House staff member David S. Addington (who had worked at HPSCI and by then was a close aide and co-conspirator of Vice President Dick Cheney), had this provision abruptly "pushed through" toward House passage as part of the Intelligence Authorization Act for Fiscal Year 2003 (and it was based upon a misleading underlying legislative report, at that), much to the surprise of the chairman of the House subcommittee that held jurisdiction over the FOIA. (OIP soon thereafter conducted an interview with that subcommittee chairman, Congressman John Stephen ("Steve") Horn, who openly regretted this, admitting that "it certainly should have been considered through the regular [legislative process] rather than as an obscure provision buried in an intelligence authorization bill.") Then, with no such provision contained in the counterpart intelligence authorization bill that had worked its way through the Senate (because this particular FOIA-related effort had been made in the House only), the two counterpart authorization bills proceeded to "reconciliation" in a conference between the House and the Senate -- first in mid-October and then again after Congress reconvened for an extraordinary "lame duck" session in mid-November. This FOIA-amendment provision was retained by the House/Senate Conference Committee and then was passed by both Houses of Congress -- even though the committees and subcommittees holding jurisdiction over the FOIA in neither the House nor the Senate had considered amending the FOIA through it. At the end of it all, what became the 2002 FOIA Amendment was most charitably characterized by Chairman Horn as a "bypass [of] the normal legislative process."

The only agencies affected by this FOIA amendment are those that are part of, or contain "an element of," what the Government refers to as the "Intelligence Community." As defined in the National Security Act of 1947, this consists of the Central Intelligence Agency; the National Security Agency; the Defense Intelligence Agency; the National Geospatial-Intelligence Agency; the National Reconnaissance Office; certain other reconnaissance offices within the Department of Defense; "the intelligence elements of the Army, the Navy, the Air Force, the Marine Corps, the Federal Bureau of Investigation, the Department of the Treasury, the Department of Energy, and the Coast Guard [or, by statutory succession, of the Department of Homeland Security]"; the Bureau of Intelligence and Research in the Department of State; and "such other elements of any other department or agency as may be designated by the President, or designated jointly by the Director of [National Intelligence] and the head of the department or agency concerned, as an element of the "Intelligence Community." There were 16 such agencies or sub-agencies comprising the "Intelligence Community" as of that time; now there are 18 of them.

15   Within the Office of the Attorney General in recent times, there ordinarily are no career employees (other than perhaps support staff who might or might not "carry over" at each AG's discretion), which creates a large potential for the lack of key institutional knowledge, as became quite evident during depositions conducted in the *Gerlich v. United States Department of Justice* case in 2010 (see Chapter Forty-Three). Although an attorney general like Janet Reno (or currently Merrick B. Garland) can compensate for this somewhat by having regular contact with Justice Department officials who hold that institutional knowledge, this is a weakness built into most federal agency hierarchies. In the U.K., by comparison, this is overcome as a matter of culture and tradition. That is just one relative advantage of a parliamentary system.

16   The Office of the Deputy Attorney General is known by the abbreviation "ODAG," a term that within the Department is very commonly used. Within that office are specially designated "associate deputy attorneys general," abbreviated as "ADAGs," who are predominantly "political" appointees but ordinarily have one or two career officials (who carry broad institutional knowledge) among them. One ADAG, invariably a political one,

will be designated as the "principal associate deputy attorney general," or "PADAG," for short. (Any further title extension along these lines would require relocating the Justice Department across the Potomac River to the Pentagon.)

17   The Office of the Associate Attorney General, the idea for which actually originated in 1973 (I was there) but was not implemented until 1977 (see Chapter Seven), ordinarily holds two or three "deputy associate attorneys general" ("DASGs," for short), one of whom is designated as the "principal deputy associate attorney general" (or "PDASG," for short); these are almost always political appointees. On more thing: When the ASG position was created during the Carter Administration, the oversight responsibilities for that position were divided from those of the DAG such that there was what became a traditional oversight "split" -- with the DAG overseeing the Department's criminal (or criminal-related) components and the ASG overseeing the civil ones (such as OIP). This did vary, however, during the second term of the Reagan Administration when the two positions "flipped" in order to accommodate replacement appointees.

18   Since 1977, the solicitor general has been the fourth-ranking official in the Department of Justice; prior to that (such as during the "Saturday Night Massacre" in 1973) he had been third in rank. Within the Solicitor General's Office, "staff attorneys" carry the title "Assistant to the Solicitor General" and are predominantly career attorneys; as a firm general rule (I can recall only three relatively recent exceptions), only they, as well as the Justice Department's political appointees, can make oral arguments before the Supreme Court. The current senior deputy solicitor general, longtime friend of FOIA litigation Edwin S. Kneedler, has made more than 150 of them.

19   It later came to light that at some point in the 1980s, the FBI began the practice of adding a "zero" to the serial numbers of some documents, which it sometimes withheld from criminal discovery as "zero files." It is unknown whether such documents were improperly kept apart from FOIA searches as well. More recently, with the advent of electronic file storage, the FBI maintained certain information on what it called an "I-drive" (and later on an "S-drive") which for a time had to be searched separately to locate requested information. Other types of FBI information kept separate from its Central Records System were "ELSUR" (read: electronic surveillance) administrative records -- i.e., no less than 48 linear feet of 3x5 index cards, arranged alphabetically, listing the names and identification details of everyone overheard in conversations recorded through the FBI's electronic surveillance) -- and "bulkies" (i.e., oversized paper file items that we discovered in a little-used area of the FBI's Dallas Field Office in 1978). (Over the years, many of those who believed that they were the subject of FBI investigations -- especially involving use of electronic surveillance -- have sought to prove that through FOIA requests; the most recent example is George Michael "Micky" Dolenz, Jr., who in August of 2022 filed a FOIA lawsuit against the FBI seeking full disclosure of its file on "the Monkees.")

20   This governmentwide policy-development process was complicated by the fact that in June of 1987 it was discovered by many agencies that their "call detail" recordation systems were automated in such a way that it would be more costly *not* to maintain such data than it would be to just continue letting their systems continue compiling it. Nevertheless, OIP insisted that any such data that was compiled be encompassed within responses to FOIA requests.

21   Originally, the Act required agencies to respond to FOIA requests within "ten working days." In 1997, this deadline was doubled to "20 working days," but to very little avail. Many members of the "FOIA Requester Community" have long contended that, with the devotion of sufficient administrative resources, any agency could reduce its FOIA backlog to zero, at least in theory. This is utterly unrealistic, however. All one has to do

is posit a situation in which an agency (most likely a relatively small one) manages to maintain a "zero backlog" all year long, but then, as the result of some controversy or another, suddenly receives even just one new FOIA request that happens to be of such magnitude and complexity (e.g., involving hundreds of thousands of sensitive document pages) that it would not be humanly possible (even with virtually unlimited agency resources, which itself is unrealistic) to handle it right away. By the next month (i.e., 20 working days later), that agency will have a FOIA backlog, without question. And because agencies ordinarily handle FOIA requests on a "first in, first out" basis, that backlog will soon encompass the FOIA requests (albeit even if relatively small and simple ones) that are next in line.

22   By this time, not so very long after the effective date of the 1974 FOIA Amendments, the increased use of the Act brought about a somewhat amorphous coalition of various individuals, groups, and organizations that could be thought of as constituting a general "FOIA Requester Community," one that grew larger and larger through time. And they soon realized that they shared one big common goal: Prying information out of the seemingly unyielding hands of "federal bureaucrats" who were, truth be known, sometimes very much on their side.

They included public-interest groups, such as the Public Citizen Litigation Group, the Government Account-ability Project ("GAP," to its whistleblowers), and the National Freedom of Information Coalition; media groups, such as the Reporters Committee for Freedom of the Press, the National Newspaper Association, the American Society of Newspaper Editors (recently renamed "News Leaders Association"), the First Amendment Center, the Foreign Press Center, participants in the Media FOIA Summit, the Freedom Forum, and the Society of Professional Journalists ("Sigma Delta Chi," to its sweethearts); environmentalist groups, such as the Sierra Club, the National Wildlife Foundation, the Environmental Defense Fund, the Nature Conservancy, and the Natural Resources Defense Council; "good government groups," such as the Project On Government Oversight ("POGO," to its many admirers), People for the Ethical Treatment of Animals ("PETA," to its furry friends), and Common Cause; research institutions, such as the National Security Archive; librarians, through the American Library Association ("ALA," except to those born in Alabama); historians, through the National Coalition for History and the American Historical Association; assassination investigation experts, such as James H. Lesar and Harold Weisberg; authors, such as Allen Weinstein (later to become Archivist of the United States); journalists, such as Jack Taylor, of the *Daily Oklahoman*, Nina Totenberg, of *National Public Radio* ("NPR," to its calm listeners), Ronald B. Kessler, Carol D. Leonnig, and the late George E. Lardner, Jr., of *The Washington Post*; researchers, such as Susan B. Long, of Syracuse University; professors, such as the late William H. Harader, Director of the Center for Governmental Services and Professor of Political Science at Indiana State University; American Bar Association leaders, such as Thomas M. Susman; media lobbyists, such as Paul McMasters and Tonda Rush; attorneys in private practice, such as Burt A. Braverman, Patrick J. Carome, and Eric R. Glitzenstein; treatise writers, such as James T. O'Reilly; "trade publication" editors, such as Harry A. Hammitt of *Access Reports* and Evan D. Hendricks of *Privacy Times*; civil liberties advocates, such as Mark H. Lynch, of the American Civil Liberties Union ("ACLU," to its contributors); private-sector national security experts, such as Morton H. Halperin and Allen R. Adler of the ACLU; scientists, such as Steven Aftergood, of the Federation of American Scientists; and frequent FOIA requesters such as Scott Armstrong, David C. Vladeck, and the Founding Church of Scientology.

That latter organization, by the way, quickly became quite proficient at attacking (read: not an overstate-ment) both the Internal Revenue Service ("IRS," to its fiscal correspondents) and the Department of Justice in connection with its FOIA-related activities. In fact, for a while, it posed the biggest threat as a FOIA requester that the Federal Government had at that time ever seen (see Chapter Twenty-Five).

23   This meeting was held in December of 1980 at the Department of Health and Human Service's headquarters building, owing to the fact that two of ASAP's seven founders worked there, and I was present in an anticipatory

"observer" capacity only. (In my view, there is a potential conflict of interest inherent in a government official who works on governmentwide FOIA policy participating as an officer or representative of such a government-related, but essentially nongovernmental, organization.)

24   For example, it is said that one cloudy afternoon, as Hoover and Attorney General Robert F. Kennedy were walking across Pennsylvania Avenue together, Hoover leveraged his knowledge of Judith Campbell Exner's simultaneous relationship with both JFK and Mafia chieftain Sam Giancana in order to obtain RFK's approval of wiretaps on MLK. It is a well-accepted fact that Exner was one of JFK's mistresses for about two years from 1960-1962, that she visited him even at the White House several times after he became president, and that she served as some sort of "go-between" between JFK and "the Mob," allegedly about CIA plans to assassinate Fidel Castro. (Note that both Castro and the Mafia were involved in suspicions about JFK's own assassination.) Exner, who by then was represented by longtime assassinations expert James H. Lesar, later made good use of the FOIA in efforts to obtain all FBI records about her, including in a case in 1978 that established a precedent on FOIA time limits in the Ninth Circuit Court of Appeals.

Jim Lesar, who earlier had been counsel to James Earl Ray, was the litigator of the major FOIA lawsuit for records on MLK's Assassination (see Chapter Three) and came to my retirement party at the Justice Department in late 2006 bearing gifts (i.e., several tape recordings of JFK Assassination interviews that he and longtime JFK Assassination expert Harold Weisberg, a former OSS officer during World War II, had recorded) from his organization, which is called the "Assassination Archives and Research Center" and still operates today with Jim as its president. At the time, that organization's headquarters was located in the National Union Building, a 19th-century structure at 918 F Street, N.W., situated diagonally behind Ford's Theater, where its southwest corner window overlooked the spot in the alley where John Wilkes Booth's horse was tethered in wait for Booth's escape north through that alley after his assassination of President Abraham Lincoln. That building still stands today.

25   I remember seeing one on a Saturday afternoon during my internship in 1971.

26   Even this claimed amount was more than the original cost of the two statues combined, which was $7275 (although that was in 1933).

27   In May of 2007, not long after her consequential congressional testimony (see Chapter Forty-Three), the National Journal's "Inside Washington" column reported that it was Monica M. Goodling who ordered the curtain (sometimes referred to as "drapes") to be placed in front of "Minnie Lou," thus preserving Ashcroft's deniability in that sensitive matter.

28   The "FISA Court," as it is most commonly known, oversees requests for surveillance warrants against foreign spies inside the United States by federal law enforcement and intelligence agencies, usually the FBI or NSA. It operated "just down the hall" on the Sixth Floor of the Main Justice Building from its inception in 1978 for almost 35 years in almost complete secrecy. As of 2013, only two of its decisions had been made public, with all else kept secret. Since then, many of its decisions have been published, with heavy national security redactions, and they are subject to potential review by the Foreign Intelligence Surveillance Court of Review. Someday, such a case might be taken up by the United States Supreme Court.

29   And Robert's surname, like other enduring bits of FOIA jargon, has lived on to actually become an active verb, one used by FOIA personnel every day and all around the country -- as in "Oh, I need to get back to my office quickly after this lunch because I have to *Vaughn* a whole bunch of documents this afternoon."

30   In full measure, CGS was a nonprofit, nonpartisan educational project devoted to openness in government, freedom of information, government transparency, and the study of "government secrecy" in the United States and internationally. Its mission was to, among other things, foster both academic and public understanding of these subjects by serving as a center of expertise, scholarly research, and information resources; promote the accurate delineation and development of legal and policy issues arising in this subject area; conduct educational programs and related activities for interested members of the academic and openness-in-government communities; and become the premier clearinghouse for this area of law both in the United States and worldwide. It engaged in no lobbying activity per se, but did provide its expertise at congressional request, including through congressional testimony. It also filed an *amicus curiae* brief in the United States Supreme Court.

31   For my part, I would regularly speak to media groups, including at their annual "National Freedom of Information Conference," where I would directly engage with their concerns and discuss privacy and access issues from the government's perspective. They would have media coverage of their own conferences; for instance, in 2004, this bore the headline "Access Faces Formidable Foe in Privacy Fears." This was perhaps because I "summed up the issue in three phrases: 'conflict of interest,' 'commonality of interest,' and 'contradiction of interest.'" The first one had to do with the fact that information is the "life blood" of journalists, which makes them hardly disinterested in the operation of the FOIA. The second recognizes that journalists, like law enforcement and intelligence agencies, need confidential sources and strive mightily to protect them. This, in turn, creates a contradiction when journalists myopically fight against source protection under the FOIA. Indeed, I found it to be only the exceptional journalist -- Mike Isikoff, then of *Newsweek*, Margaret Talev, then of *McClatchy* News, and Jennifer Lafleur, then of the *Dallas Morning News*, were good examples -- who would not do so.

32   Thus, the first requirement of an Exemption 3 statute is that it stands as a disclosure prohibition.

33   Rule 6(e) prohibits the disclosure of "matters occurring before a grand jury," but permits federal courts to authorize disclosure in exceptional (read: usually historical) cases. As of 2021, however, the Department of Justice is advocating that such "6(e) orders" be subject to a 50-year waiting period.

34   For instance, the information collected during the 1950 census was just recently made public, after being kept secret for 72 years.

35   The difficulties often encountered by agencies in meeting such obligations, especially since enactment of the Electronic FOIA Amendments of 1996, have led to their sometimes being referred to by the sobriquet "(a)(2) Brute." As a matter of policy implementation, OIP began regularly monitoring agency website compliance with these obligations in early 1997.

36   Although this is a reference to the Electronic FOIA Amendments of 1996, they did not become effective until one year later, in 1997.

37   This is something about which I have long held strong personal convictions, because I know how often mug shots are taken of arrested persons who are never criminally charged, or have charges dropped, or are otherwise exonerated without even a trial. And mugs shots typically depict a person at one of the worst moments of his or her life.

38   Located organizationally within the Executive Office of the President ("EOP," to its friends at the Secret Service), OMB is subject to the FOIA, unlike some other EOP entities (e.g., the Council on Environmental Quality;

the NSC; and the Office of Administration, which after 30 years of responding to FOIA requests was abruptly declared otherwise by the Bush White House in 2006) that are not.

39   OMB finally made a long-awaited improvement of its Privacy Act oversight capability when it hired former OIP Associate Director Kirsten J. Moncada to be the chief of the Privacy Branch in its Office of Information and Regulatory Affairs that year. Simply put, no one (read: by far) is more capable of serving in this role than she is; I regarded her as "an eleven on a scale of ten."

40   Housed in the New Executive Office Building ("NEOB," to those who care to go there) north of the "Old EOB" (i.e., across Pennsylvania Avenue and up half a block), it is invariably reputed, by no later than the middle of each new presidential administration, to operate a huge "hubris factory" in that building's basement. This impression is no doubt conveyed by the large banner hanging over its entrance, which reads, "Hubris R' Us."

41   In an attempt to "harmonize" the subject area known as "pseudosecrecy," the George W. Bush Adminis-tration in 2005 morphed SBU into "CUI" ("Controlled Unclassified Information"), leading to the creation of the "Controlled Unclassified Information Office," which is housed within ISOO (and, in turn, NARA), and to its use of a "CUI Registry" of more than 100 "safeguarding labels."

42   One of the biggest challenges after 9/11 was getting through the heads of agency personnel that their use of a "safeguarding label" on a record absolutely does *not* mean that it could properly be withheld (either in whole or in part) in the face of a FOIA request somewhere down the road. And the most difficult label to contend with in that regard, especially in reigning in DOD non-FOIA personnel, was "FOUO." I must admit to carrying this frustration with me to the U.K. whilst giving a speech over there in 2006, because England's information commissioner pithily summarized what I'd said, in part, as "FOUO is phooey for FOIA."

43   Indeed, from the tenure of FOIA attorney Bob Gilliat in the 1970s to those of chief FOIA officers Charlie Talbott, Will Kammer, and Jim Hogan thereafter, DOD's FOIA leadership has been nothing short of superb over a span of nearly 50 years.

44   A prime example of this is Prince Philip, Duke of Edinburgh, who died on April 9, 2021, at age 99. Soon after his death, it was revealed by royal aides that he was "a lifelong UFO enthusiast," in secret, and that he had amassed a large collection of books on the subject. It was reported that he was "so intrigued by flying saucers [that] he founded a secret spotters club and ordered his [military aide] to investigate UFO sightings . . . but he remained nervous about attracting ridicule for his 'crank hobby.'" Now, with the death of Queen Elizabeth II on September 8, 2022, more might be released to the public about this.

45   One might even say that the terminology line was crossed when the Government issued an official report on June 25, 2021 that pointedly used "UAP" in lieu of "UFO" in a way that seemed permanent (see Chapter Forty-Eight). Perhaps this change will help take the stigma and ridicule (and in turn the fear of ridicule) out of "UFO" sightings. (Though the even more recent official substitution of "Anomalous" for "Aerial" in "UAP" might cut in the other direction.)

46   Also shocking was the later revelation that AATIP actually was preceded for many months by something else, a Defense Department entity called the "Advanced Aerospace Weapon System Applications Program" ("AAWSAP," or "awe sap" to those few who knew of it) which for some undisclosed reason was renamed as AATIP. And this was before it was renamed three more times.

47   The "Phoenix Lights" sightings were most phenomenal. Thousands of people looking to the skies from Henderson, Nevada, to Tucson, Arizona, and mostly over Phoenix on March 13, 1997, saw a triangular pattern of lights (read: as many as six), or in some cases a solitary light, moving slowly and sometimes hovering, which led to much photographic documentation, in two sessions two hours apart. Although there was an Air Force base nearby, the flights of military planes did not provide a ready explanation, though it is possible that what was observed was an experimental U.S. aircraft based hundreds of miles away. Nor did the military's insistence that they were "just flares." For several reasons, if there were to be compiled a list of the "top ten" most consequential UFO sightings, the "Phoenix Lights" would be on that list.

48   Another similar facility named "Raven Rock," which was more DOD-oriented, was built near Gettysburg, Pennsylvania, prior to the Special Facility but fell into relative disuse over the years. It had a brief resurgence immediately after 9/11 when it served as the "undisclosed location" that housed Vice President Richard B. "Dick" Cheney apart from President Bush for a period of weeks. There were jokes back in Washington that of the two, he would be the primary target.

49   Apropos of that, I know firsthand, the particular configuration of the Special Facility allowed COG personnel training for the Marine Corps Marathon to run up and down its dual switchbacks early in the morning.

50   A personal remembrance is in order here: On that fateful day of December 1, 1974, I was on Long Island preparing to return to D.C., as it was the Sunday after Thanksgiving that year. But it was so extremely windy that day that I uncharacteristically made a sudden decision not to fly as scheduled, taking a crowded train out of New York City instead. Two planes crashed that day, one at Mount Weather (read: near the "Special Facility"), the other near West Point.

51   The Government first confirmed the existence of nuclear-related electromagnetic pulse in July of 1962, when it launched a nuclear warhead into space in an operation called "Starfish Prime." When that warhead was detonated over the Pacific, 250 miles up in space, it created an EMP effect that impaired communications for hundreds of miles around Hawaii. The next day, NASA launched a communications satellite by the name of "Telstar 1," which fell victim to "Starfish Prime's" EMP just a few months later, along with about a third of all satellites then in orbit.

52   Of all the nations of the world, the one said to be most likely to harness and weaponize EMP is China, which just adds to a long list of potential international threats.

53   More than any other single thing that I encountered during my career, this was, hands down the most difficult thing to believe. (Stated another way: I think I might have believed that Lee Harvey Oswald acted entirely alone or that J. Edgar Hoover was not a closeted gay man before swallowing this.) But I have seen it in operation with my own eyes -- and, as that anonymous plurality is wont to say, "you can look it up." By the way, though, this subject can be great fun at parties and other social gatherings; you can both astound and amuse your friends and family with it.

54   Did this make our hardware more "clunky" and difficult to use? Yes, it did. But it was a price that we had to pay in order to deal with the "real world" aspect of what we were doing. (Implicit in this, of course, was the "unspoken secret" that if the COG system were to be needed for activation while it was still being refined, then those of us who were "exercising" and still developing the system would be asked to be dispersed with it. It is for that reason, personally speaking, that a close family friend of mine, based upon the barest allusion to this,

kept her rural cabin in the Adirondack Mountains heated all winter for me, just in case my wife and children had to flee to it upon my possible dispersal.) Nowadays, I imagine, this has been improved.

55   The five known control systems for classified SCI information are: Special Intelligence ("S.I."), the control system for communications intelligence and communications intercepts; Talent Keyhole ("T.K."), for intelligence gained through space-based imagery; ("IMINT"), signals ("SIGINT"), and measurement and signature ("MASINT") intelligence; Klondike ("KDK"), the control system for geospatial intelligence; the HUMINT Control System ("HCS"), for intelligence gained through or involving human sources; and Reserve ("RSV"), the control system used by the National Reconnaissance Office ("NRO"). These are just the known active control systems. The Office of the Director for National Intelligence ("ODNI") acknowledges that more control systems remain unnamed "due to their sensitivity and restrictive access controls."

56   There is an additional national security information-protection regime, separate and apart from "classification," that governs the handling and nondisclosure of information pertaining to "atomic weapons" or "special nuclear material." In a unique piece of Cold War legislation, Section 224 of the Atomic Energy Act of 1954 criminalizes the communication, transmission, or disclosure of what is called "Restricted Data" to any person "with intent to injure the United States or with intent to secure an advantage to any foreign nation." The term "Restricted Data" is defined as information related to the design, manufacture, or utilization of atomic weapons or the production or use of special nuclear material.

57   A primary, categorical example of this is found within the realm of "Glomarization," where most of the information whose existence can neither be confirmed nor denied without causing national security harm is of this degree of sensitivity (see Chapter Seventeen). Another category is records so sensitive that they cannot be described even in an unclassified way. A very recent example of this is some of the documents that were wrongfully removed by departing President Donald J. Trump to his Mar-a-Lago home; when they were recovered by NARA, they could not be publicly inventoried because of their extreme sensitivity.

58   STU-IIIs are no longer in use today, however, as they have been replaced by what is called the "STE" ("Secure Terminal Equipment") and other comparable equipment that use the more modern "Secure Communications Interoperability Protocol" ("SCIP," to its conversants).

59   Cases in point: Nixon, immediately after Vice President Spiro T. Agnew resigned in October of 1973; Ford, immediately after he succeeded to the presidency in August of 1974; Johnson, immediately after he succeeded Kennedy in November of 1963; and Truman, upon FDR's death in April of 1945. The latter two presidents did not have a new vice president during their first (partial) terms, but the former two did (Ford himself and Nelson A. Rockefeller).

60   A little-known fact is that any congressional officer who succeeds to this position, even for a brief time only, must simultaneously resign from his or her congressional office.

61   The maintenance of decades-long secrecy about so large a program is no easy feat. A more modern-day counterpart, but with far greater impact, is something called "Crypto AG," an ostensible Swiss company through which the CIA has surreptitiously sold rigged encryption systems to foreign governments since the 1970s, in what the CIA itself has secretly called "the intelligence coup of the century." These systems all contained hidden vulnerabilities in the form of algorithms that allowed clandestine access by the CIA in conjunction with the NSA to all communications made through them. As of 2020, after more than 40 years of highly successful operation

as "Crypto AG," under a rubric code-named "Thesaurus" and then "Rubicon" that goes all the way back to World War II, this intelligence activity appears to be coming to an end.

62   MK-Ultra's techniques included the covert administration of high doses of psychoactive drugs, especially LSD, as well as electroshock, hypnosis, sensory deprivation, sexual abuse, and other forms of what today we would not hesitate to denominate as "torture." Its most infamous experimentation victims were future author Ken Kesey, who while working as a hospital aide volunteered to be dosed with a chemical known as "LSD-25," and an army chemist named Frank R. Olson who (unlike Kesey) had never taken LSD until he was covertly dosed with it by a CIA supervisor and a week later plunged to his death from the window of his hotel room. Kesey, of course, went on to write the novel "One Flew Over the Cuckoo's Nest," which drew heavily upon his experiences while working at that hospital. (And despite any and all rumors to the contrary, there is nothing to substantiate suspicions that Harvard Professor Timothy F. Leary volunteered for this part of the program on a subscription basis.)

   A secret CIA "project" akin to this was something called its "Stargate Project," which it began together with the Defense Intelligence Agency ("DIA," to its alphabetically challenged friends) in 1972. Best labeled as a "paranormal" effort, it involved individuals chosen for their ability to enter a trance-like state and achieve (read: seemingly so) what is called "remote viewing" of certain things elsewhere, or even elsewhere in time. Reportedly, one project subject succeeded "seeing" the location of a lost Soviet spy plane in 1976. Until this project was eventually cancelled and properly declassified in 1995, it was known (read: within the CIA and DIA only) by the secret code names SCANATE, GONDOLA WISH, STARGATE, GRILL FLAME, CENTER LANE, PROJECT CF, and SUN STREAK. Over the years, FOIA requesters have riddled the CIA (and secondarily DIA) with access requests made under all such names.

63   It also houses an entity called the "Office of Tailored Access Operations" ("TAO," to Chinese philosophers), sometimes referred to as "Computer Network Operations" or "S32," which is a cyber-warfare intelligence-gathering operation that focuses on computer systems used by foreign entities. Its existence was disclosed through a leak by Edward J. Snowden in 2013 (see Chapter Twenty-Five), which identified an "attack program" called QUANTUMSQUIRREL and a technique referred to as QUANTUM. When it comes to "attacks," though, it seems that nothing has been more effective than the infamous "computer worm" known as "Stuxnet," which was developed jointly by the United States and Israel for highly successful use against Iran's nuclear program, exploiting what are called "zero-day" vulnerabilities. This entire area of endeavor is most effective so long as it remains secret, which makes "cyber warfare" a relatively recent new government secrecy category.

64   For a stretch of time during the late 1970s and very early 1980s, this agency was my third-biggest client, after the FBI and CIA, in that order. NSA benefits under the FOIA from having a categorically protective shield from it -- contained in section 6 of the National Security Agency Act of 1959, 50 U.S.C. § 3605 (formerly at 50 U.S.C. § 402 note)), sometimes referred to as "section 6 of Public Law No. 86-36" -- pertaining to its "organization, functions, activities, and personnel." This statute triggers FOIA Exemption 3 as a basis for nondisclosure.

65   This "deal" was truly extraordinary in multiple respects. It was struck primarily between CIA Deputy General Counsel Ernest Mayerfeld, a litigation client of mine, and Mark H. Lynch, of the ACLU, one of my fiercest litigation opponents, and I supported it on behalf of the Department of Justice. Despite their ideological and institutional differences, Ernie and Mark personally came to terms on this novel legislation, codified at 50 U.S.C. § 3141, which caused no small amount of controversy within the ACLU and, to a lesser extent, in some corners of the CIA.

66   Above all, the protection of "HUMINT," and the extreme secrecy required for that, can be an intelligence agency's greatest priority. In October of 2021, for example, the CIA took the extraordinary step of sending a "Worldwide Stations and Bases" cable urging all of its field agents to "take greater care in handling human sources" in light of recent losses suffered in Iran, Pakistan, and China. This cable even took the unprecedented step of specifying the numbers of intelligence sources killed by foreign intelligence services. (I had never thought I'd ever see such a thing.)

67   It is publicly known that the NRO operates the Federal Government's reconnaissance satellites and provides satellite intelligence to several government agencies, such as signals intelligence ("SIGINT") to NSA; imagery intelligence ("IMINT") to the National Geospatial-Intelligence Agency ("NGA," to hyphen fans) (formerly known as the Defense Mapping Agency and then as the National Imagery and Mapping Agency); and measurement and signature intelligence ("MASINT") to DIA. Related to this is geospatial intelligence, or "GEOINT," which is of course within the purview of the NGA.

68   James Bamford, an attorney and former naval intelligence analyst, was well respected within the Federal Government as someone who knew NSA "inside and out" -- which is to say that he knew the inside of it even from outside of it. In 1981, it was suddenly discovered that two years earlier a high-level Justice Department official (in its Criminal Division) has mistakenly released more than 250 pages of records that Bamford had requested under the FOIA (having to do with no less sensitive a subject than a secret Justice Department investigation of illegal domestic eavesdropping by NSA), even though they had been classified on national security grounds. The Department (and others in the "Intelligence Community") determined that the documents had been "improperly declassified," had been released to Bamford "by error," and now required "reclassification" at the "Top Secret" level. (Remember, this was in 1981, when such things were unheard of, but it was during the brand-new Reagan Administration, after all.)

Therefore, it was decided by some "powers that were" that somebody had pay a visit to Bamford in order to explain the situation with these documents and "insist" that he return them. (The exact words to be used, as I recall, were along the lines of: "It therefore is your duty and obligation as a citizen of the United States to return this information to the Department of Justice.") A hapless young attorney was dispatched to convey this message and presumably retrieve the documents, perhaps thinking that all he had to worry about was bringing a briefcase large enough to carry them.

Well, it didn't quite work out that way, as Bamford was aware of a provision in the then-current national security executive order that stated that once a document had been declassified it could not thereafter be "reclassified." So rather than this going down in the annals of government secrecy as the first time that an incorrectly declassified document was successfully retrieved after its mistaken disclosure, this went down as merely the first time that a federal agency attempted to recover a FOIA-disclosed document on the basis that the disclosure had been made by it "in error."

By the way, this is the same Justice Department attorney who was well-known within parts of the Department for saying that he'd sometimes walk into a bar, put his left hand in his pocket, and then remove it without his wedding ring. Even more so, he had a habit in the very early 1980s of sitting on a bar stool while claiming to be a returned "Iranian hostage," which he said usually garnered him both free drinks and female attention. He need not be named here, as he might well still be married (his wife was quite rich, as I recall), but his initials were "GES."

In the wake of this visit, Bamford was threatened with prosecution under the Espionage Act. As a result of Bamford's defense to this threat, President Ronald Reagan changed the national security executive order to explicitly provide that once a document has been declassified it still can be reclassified. This could not legally be applied to Bamford *ex post facto*, so he was free to keep what was disclosed to him and to publish much of it in his book *The Puzzle Palace*, which also described NSA's "Minaret operation," in which anti-Vietnam War protesters such as Jane Fonda, Dr. Benjamin Spock (in pre-Vulcan days), and of course Dr. Martin Luther King, Jr., were placed under electronic surveillance.

69   More recently, such "claw back" attempts have been made in a handful of cases, with the Federal Government being successful in four of them (one involving social security numbers) and roundly unsuccessful in the most recent case, *Sierra Club v. EPA*, 505 F. Supp. 3d 982 (N.D. Cal. 2020), in which the Court surveyed the first four cases before denying any "claw back" in the one before it. Since then, a controversy has arisen over the mishandling of emails by former White House trade official Peter K. Navarro, which might well lead to a further judicial precedent.

70   For decades, the NGA's principal facilities were located less than a mile from my home in Bethesda, Maryland, as a primary target site in the event of a nuclear exchange.

71   Sometimes quite significantly, when a circuit court does decide to rehear a case *en banc*, that very decision automatically vacates the panel decision below. And once a FOIA issue is decided *en banc* by the D.C. Circuit, it becomes the "law of the land," in effect, unless and until the Supreme Court (including through the vehicle of some other case) either directly or indirectly overrules it (see Chapters Three, Eleven, and Twelve).

72   This term is used also in its verb form (i.e., to "Glomarize") and in its adjective form (e.g., a "Glomarized" response), as well, and it sometimes is less elegantly called a "Glomar defense." "Glomarization" theoretically can be employed atop almost any FOIA exemption, but it is most commonly used to protect national security secrecy, in conjunction with FOIA Exemption 1. It also is used quite often (every day, in fact) by federal law enforcement agencies (predominately the FBI) to protect personal privacy interests under FOIA Exemption 7(C) in the face of third-party requests (see Chapter Seventeen).

73   Actually, there were two such cases, the companion cases of *Phillippi v. CIA* and *Military Audit v. CIA*, which arose in the D.C. Circuit Court of Appeals at about the same time. Of the two, the D.C. Circuit's decision in *Phillippi v. CIA*, 546 F.2d 1009 (D.C. Cir. 1976), articulated what not long thereafter became widely known as the "Glomarization" concept (once I propagated it as such).

74   There was one atypical early "Glomarization" case, *Weberman v. NSA*, 490 F. Supp. 9 (S.D.N.Y.), *rev'd & remanded*, 646 F.2d 563 (2d Cir. 1980) (table cite), summary judgment granted, 2 GDS ¶ 82,067 (S.D.N.Y. 1981), *aff'd*, 668 F.2d 676 (2d Cir. 1982). The FOIA request in that case concerned a Kennedy Assassination record that, if it existed, would necessarily have borne a connection to Cuba, and its very existence or nonexistence was in context of the request reflective of possible NSA telecommunications capabilities. This was explained to the district court judge in public filings, unsuccessfully, and the district court not only ordered the NSA to "confirm or deny," it refused to permit the agency to prove its case with a more detailed explanation *in camera*.

Upon appeal, however, the Second Circuit Court of Appeals reversed that disclosure order and ordered the district court judge to read the agency's classified affidavit *in camera*. Once that judge did so, he ruled in the agency's favor, thus upholding "Glomarization." Being familiar with the nature of the case, from a consultation standpoint, I can say only that this case was unique in multiple respects.

75   These three "exclusions," which can be referred to as "(c)(1), (c)(2), and (c)(3)," address three very exceptional situations in which records responsive to a particular type of FOIA request actually might or might not exist, but the context in which the request is made does not as a practical matter allow the agency to make even a "Glomarization" response (i.e., to neither confirm nor deny the existence of responsive records) in order to

protect that highly sensitive abstract fact. Based upon a problem that I identified by as a theoretical one in 1979, and solved by congressional enactment seven years later, these record "exclusions" (i.e., distinct from the Act's 14 exemptions) cover relatively rare circumstances that can arise with ongoing law enforcement investigations, with the handling of confidential law enforcement sources, and with certain foreign intelligence, counterintelligence, or international terrorism matters -- with their underlying FOIA exemptions being Exemption 7(A), Exemption 7(D), and Exemption 1 of the FOIA, respectively. (Actually, a fourth such situation was identified internally in the context of post-9/11 "no fly lists," and their underlying databases, in 2003 (at a time when there was a strong policy imperative against greater national security classification), but this has not yet been addressed by Congress. At some point, there might well be a need for that, though; until then, it can be thought of as the prospective "(c)(4) exclusion," i.e., too "explosive" to be handled quite yet.

76   In all seriousness, the Justice Department was nothing short of ecstatic about "losing" INS, the management of which had bedeviled ODAG for what seemed like decades by that time and which at DHS then went on to fame and glory once it was broken up into the "U.S. Citizenship and Immigration Services," the "U.S. Customs and Border Protection [Entity]," and the "U.S. Immigration and Customs Enforcement [Entity]."

77   During that same year, as it happened, AAG Jon Rose was principally involved also in my appointment to my position in OIP, which allowed him to joke, in baseball parlance, that he batted .500 that year.

78   According to the Task Force's "Charter" (a copy of which I still have), it was announced by President Clinton on January 25, 1993, established as of March 17, 1993, and set to conclude on May 30, 1993. It was chaired by First Lady Hillary Rodham Clinton and intended "to recommend to the President as promptly as possible a proposal for comprehensive health care reform legislation to be enacted by Congress."

79   I handled privacy matters for the Task Force, which afforded me an inside view of its activities, both its successes and its failures. One of its successes, albeit a belated one, was the White House's formal reservation of "control" over all members' Task Force-related records (including my own) for the purpose of taking them beyond the reach of the FOIA -- something that I had to persistently urge until it finally was accomplished by then-White House Staff Secretary John D. Podesta, Jr.

80   Janet was second only to Attorney General William Wirt, who held the office for more than 11 years in the early 19th century, but only because he stayed on through the full terms of both President James Monroe (1817-1825) and President John Quincy Adams (1825-1829), two successive presidents.

81   A recent example of this is information disclosed by Natalie M. Edwards, a Treasury Department official who leaked what became known as the "FinCEN Files" (read: highly sensitive "suspicious-activity reports") to reporter Jason A. Leopold in late 2017. The leaked reports included those pertaining to the financial transactions of Trump campaign manager Paul J. Manafort, Jr., and they became the basis of a series of *BuzzFeed* articles. Atypically, nowadays, this leak was in the form of more than 2000 paper document pages. Edwards confessed once she was tracked as the leak's source through Leopold's news articles and the case against her was readily made through emails sent to and from Leopold, copies of which she unwisely (read: against her interests) maintained. In June of 2020, she was sentenced to six months in jail.

An even more recent leak case was that of former service member Daniel E. Hale (a claimed descendent of Nathan Hale), who took classified documents pertaining to U.S. drone warfare activity in Yemen home from his duty station. He was convicted of violating the Espionage Act of 1917 through a "whistleblower-type" dis-closure of those documents to a friendly journalist, which he said he did as a matter of "conscience." Hale was sentenced to 45 months in prison by a judge who told him, "You could have been a whistleblower . . . without taking any of these documents."

82   For more than a decade now, an entirely new dimension of leaks, and potential for dissemination of leaked information, has existed in the form of the organization known as "WikiLeaks." Founded by Australian activist Julian P. Assange, it came into prominence in 2010 when it electronically disseminated the military and diplomatic information stolen by Army "whistleblower" Chelsea E. Manning. The subject of an international arrest warrant, Assange took refuge in the Embassy of Ecuador in London in 2012, but Ecuador withdrew his asylum there in 2019, whereupon he was confined in a London prison on charges of having "jumped bail" in 2012. On December 10, 2021, England's second-highest court ruled that he can be extradited to the U.S. to face charges that he violated the Espionage Act of 1917 (in an unprecedented indictment of a "publisher" brought by the Trump Administration) by aiding the theft of classified information. That extradition might now be imminent.

83   *Armstrong* was a 2-1 D.C. Circuit decision, but it was a dispositive one, as the Supreme Court denied *certiorari* in the case. There have been attempts to overrule this result legislatively, but to no avail.

84   Actually, the legislation creating OGIS was enacted in 2007, but was not implemented in that regard by the Bush Administration. Only after the Obama Administration focused on it did NARA begin preparations for OGIS to be established. Once I received advance word of this, I reached out to my former deputy Miriam M. Nisbet to persuade her to consider leaving her high-level position as Director of UNESCO's Information Society Division in Paris in order to return and become OGIS's founding director. Once Miriam agreed to leave Paris (for which her husband Michael might never forgive me), OGIS formally came into existence.

85   The relationship between OGIS and my former office OIP was, to say the least, somewhat "fraught" from the outset. Miriam knew my successor at OIP quite well, having supervised her for more than a decade within OIP, so she was able to deal with her very effectively on anything that overlapped between the two offices, in a way that heavily favored OGIS as it asserted its new jurisdiction. Suffice to say that had I not retired two years earlier, things would have been quite different. Assuming that OGIS even would have come into being if I were still there, Miriam and I would have worked hand-in-hand to smoothly integrate OGIS into the realm of governmentwide FOIA administration, to the greater advantage of FOIA requesters.

86   This also could be a mistaken reference to the "National Security Archive," a nonprofit entity formerly housed at the Gelman Library of George Washington University that was created by then-*Washington Post* journalist (and former "Watergate" investigator) Scott Armstrong in 1985; this "archive" is an exceedingly frequent FOIA requester that has enjoyed no small amount of success in such matters over the years. In 1986, the Office of Information and Privacy took public notice of the fact that Scott Armstrong had filed more than 2000 FOIA requests and spoke of the new National Security Archive's "avowed" purposes, with the aim of encouraging agency coordination of his FOIA requests, whereupon Scott Armstrong took great umbrage at this attention. This led to a meeting at which he "roared like a lion but left as a lamb"; Scott and I became good friends and he later served as a member of the Collaboration on Government Secrecy's Advisory Board for seven years.

87   Though it is viewed by the American public as a benign civil agency, NASA in fact began collaborating with the Department of Defense on a secret space program in the late 1950s with the design of a "one-man space shuttle" that could be used for intelligence purposes. This craft, projected to be called the "Boeing X-20 "Dina-Soar," was abandoned upon the end of the Kennedy Administration. Thereafter, however, when the full space shuttle came into being, NASA secretly allowed it to be used for many military/intelligence operations,

with heavy DOD payloads, DOD-sponsored experimentation, and, under the secret rubric of something called "Project Onyx," the deployment of orbiting radar stations.

And in the same militaristic vein, there is some credible speculation -- based partly on the claimed discoveries of an infamous Scottish computer hacker named Gary McKinnon in the early 2000s -- that NASA has collaborated with DOD on a project code-named "Solar Warden" to create a defensive military posture in space. McKinnon, who suffers from Asperger syndrome, says he began searching for evidence of NASA "airbrushing" UFO-related photographs in 2001 (read: prior to 9/11), which led him deeper and deeper into NASA's files, an activity for which he was tracked down and arrested in London. In 2012, the British Government declined to permit his extradition to the United States for prosecution, nor was he prosecuted in Great Britain. As a capstone to all of this, McKinnon has claimed that what he learned about NASA from his hacking led to his belief in both "anti-gravity" and what is called "free energy."

88   As best as I can recall, this name for a first-year law student was not used until it was popularized by author Scott F. Turow in his first book, titled *One L*, in 1977. By the time I began teaching, 30 years later, its use was ubiquitous.

89   Kennedy was not the first American president to be assassinated, of course -- Presidents Lincoln, Garfield, and McKinley preceded him in such dastardly death -- but surprisingly it was not until President Kennedy's assassination that the Federal Government, and the United States Secret Service in particular, truly "got up to speed" on comprehensive presidential protection. Almost immediately, the Defense Advanced Research Project Agency ("DARPA," to its scientists) was tasked to "red hat" the subject of potential presidential assassination (read: imagine any way in which it could be done) with countermeasures to be developed accordingly. Its work was known, or not, as "Project Star" (security, threat, analysis, and research) and for its two-year duration in the mid-1960s it operated in extreme secrecy; even its very existence was not made known to the president.

Hence, an era of special security secrecy began, encompassing such things as Air Force One, Marine One, and the presidential limousine. As to the latter, we even established specially broad protection under Exemption 7(A) of the FOIA to shield its protective details. And the White House grounds, including its ostensibly secret bunkers and other facilities dug underneath the north end of them in recent years, were comprehensively covered as well. It is fair to say that today, matters of presidential secrecy are among the most closely guarded secrets that the United States has.

90   As well, Congress in 1992 enacted the "President John F. Kennedy Assassination Records Collection Act" (codified at 44 U.S.C. § 2107 note), which provided that all JFK Assassination-related records maintained by the Federal Government be identified and then "processed" for inclusion in a special collection of such records made available for public inspection and copying at the National Archives. This novel disclosure mechanism for Kennedy Assassination records is distinct from the Freedom of Information Act; it was enacted by Congress due to the heightened publicity over the assassination that resulted from the Oliver Stone-directed film, *JFK*, which was released in 1991.

91   According to the Metcalfe family cybersecurity expert, who has handled such matters at Google for more than a decade, a more complete definition would include reference to the three cybersecurity "pillars," known as "confidentiality," "integrity," and "availability" (but never abbreviated as "CIA").

92   One of the most well-known anecdotes of September 11, 2001 involved National Security Advisor Condoleezza Rice and National Security Council anti-terrorism expert Richard A. Clarke. Reportedly, at the moment that the second World Trade Tower was struck (making it clear that it was terrorism rather than an accident), Rice yelled

out "Clarke!" (He was several blocks away at the time.) Prior to the beginning of the Bush Administration, during the late 1990s, Richard Clarke's primary focus was on cybersecurity and, for a time, infrastructure protection. It was in that regard that he invited me to a large inter-agency gathering at the White House Conference Center, which is located on the western perimeter road of Lafayette Square (or "President's Park"), named Jackson Place, just north of the White House. And as he held forth before his audience, I noticed that he started verging into the significance of the Freedom of Information Act to his subject and then the next thing I knew he was calling me up to the stage to continue his narrative on cybersecurity and the FOIA. No, he and I had not planned such a thing, nor had his staff even mentioned it as a possibility. Yet I had no choice but to extemporize as best I could within the flow of his program -- which I did, evidently to everyone's satisfaction. Yes, Richard Clarke was a high-energy hard-charger, brilliant as hell, but a bit of a loose cannon as well.

93   This was remarkably similar to the near-singlehanded role played by Representative John D. Moss (D-CA), a relative "backbencher" in the House, who almost by force of will commanded the first legislative hearings on possible enactment of the FOIA; this was in late 1955, nearly a decade after congressional enactment of the foundational Administrative Procedure Act ("APA," to those who can remember not to pronounce it as "Procedures") in 1946 and nearly a decade before Congress's enactment of the FOIA itself in mid-1966. The FOIA thus boasts a near-perfect ten-year cycle for "years ending in six": APA enactment in 1946, to the dawn of underlying legislative activity on it in December of 1955, to its enactment in 1966, to its major amendment in 1974 (two years "early," some say, due to "Watergate"), to further major amendment in 1986, to further major (this time, "electronic") amendment in 1996, to further major amendment in 2007 (delayed one year, by the Bush 43 Administration's issuance of a first-of-its-kind executive order on the FOIA in 2006), to further major amendment in 2016. Heaven help us all when the year 2026 rolls around.

As for Congressman Moss, his legacy is further burnished by the fact that he said: "Our system of government is based on the participation of the governed, and as our population grows in numbers it is essential that it also grow in knowledge and understanding, . . . We must remove every barrier to information about -- and understanding of -- government activities consistent with our security if the American public is to be adequately equipped to fulfill the ever more demanding role of responsible citizenship."

94   And as such, he is most deserved of another near-award-winning limerick that was crafted in his honor: "I learned of a man named Chydenius/who was a transparency genius/While not yet a lawyer/he invented a FOIA/and was termed by the 'Urban Dictionary' a 'penius.'"

95   You have to believe that I used this obscure factoid when visiting China as part of a U.S. delegation in 2009 and 2010 (see Chapter One). Our delegation's goal was partly to foster the development of a freedom-of-information regime over there, counterintuitive as that might seem, so any bit of historical kinship such as this was well used and well received.

96   The story was this: Whilst in the midst of giving a plenary presentation at that conference, I suddenly became aware of a persistent noise that was emanating from the third row. It was the commissioner from Germany, Peter Schaar, who was carrying on a loud and rather animated cell phone conversation, without regard for what I was doing on the stage. So I did what Americans (as opposed to more genteel Europeans, I suppose) are known to do: I stopped my presentation, bent down to stare at him, and (after a moment or two without any response) asked him if he knew how distracting his conduct was. I must admit that I truly thought that such a question, in such a situation, would lead him either to end the phone conversation or to remove himself from the auditorium in order to continue it. But he did neither, as least not quickly enough to suit me.

So I followed this by pointedly suggesting to him that he "take it outside," by which I meant the phone call, of course. Well, that rebuke apparently was understood by nearly everyone else present to mean that I was inviting this rather barrel-chested gentleman to do something such as meet me in the alley behind the building, or the like, in order to settle the matter right then and there. Evidently, Peter did get the message by this point and he promptly slinked his way out of the auditorium, supported by his two assistants, perhaps to reinstate his call.

It was only the next day, when I was down (or, in Londoner-speak, "up") in London to speak at a private-sector follow-up conference, that I learned amid much backslapping by the English commissioner that that cell phone call had actually been one placed *by* Peter (i.e., not one reluctantly received by him) and that he was indeed known as a brazenly inconsiderate bully ("the bully of Europe," I was told) by his peers. And that all present were "thrilled" that I had faced him down. Nevertheless, he somewhat sheepishly (albeit only indirectly) expressed some regret about the episode later on, whereupon I overly graciously let him know that all was forgiven.

97   Most notably, UCL was ranked 10th in world among all universities, a level attained only after I had been affiliated with it for a few years, which was a fact that I would readily point out to its faculty (and to my younger daughter, who spent her "semester abroad" there) upon occasion.

98   Implementation of the Electronic FOIA Amendments of 1996 was achieved through a series of guidance issuances prepared by OIP instead, and no such formal, high-level memorandum was issued by the Department upon enactment of further FOIA amendments in 2002, 2007, and 2016.

99   Remarkably, the Administration of Donald J. Trump never issued a replacement FOIA memorandum, which is only consonant with its chronic indifference to such government processes. In fact, even through the end of its fourth year, the Trump Administration was noticeably silent on the subject. As longtime FOIA advocate (and First Amendment attorney) Kevin M. Goldberg observed: "The Trump Administration's inaction and silence on FOIA speaks volumes. For him, public records and open governance are certainly not priorities, seemingly nowhere on his radar. I'm not sure Trump [even] knows how to spell FOIA." In fact, only one thing is known for sure: The numbers of new FOIA litigation cases, in which disgruntled FOIA requesters seek relief from the courts, increased dramatically after Trump took office.

100   Notably, this very litigation and policy standard eventually was codified into law, nearly *verbatim*, within the 2016 FOIA Amendments, as new subsection (8)(A)(i)(I) of the Act. And it has thereafter been applied in FOIA litigation as a viable requirement on agencies that potentially provides some exemption relief to requesters. My own feelings of paternalism about this are broad and deep.

101   In total, there have been six such issuances: In May 1977, May 1981, October 1993, October 2001, in March 2009, and then in March 2022. In addition to the Trump Administration not bothering at all with this (thus paradoxically leaving the pro-disclosure Holder Memorandum in effect), the George H.W. Bush Administration simply carried forward with the AG's FOIA Memorandum that was in effect during the Reagan presidency. And as is alluded to above, Eric Holder used the exact same standard (i.e., of "foreseeable harm") that we had fashioned for Janet Reno 15 years earlier, as did Merrick Garland for Biden (belatedly).

102   This was accomplished through the Attorney General's FOIA Memorandum issued by Attorney General Eric H. Holder, Jr., on March 19, 2009. In between the Clinton and Obama Administrations, an intervening, only moderately pro-disclosure standard (i.e., "sound legal basis") was established through the Attorney General's FOIA Memorandum issued by Attorney General John D. Ashcroft in 2001, the latter (which like the Reno FOIA Memorandum also was predominately drafted by myself) made explicit reference to "discretionary disclosure."

103   An additional privilege fully recognized only relatively recently is the "presidential communications privilege," which is similar to yet weaker than the deliberative process privilege. It can apply to records that "reflect presidential decisionmaking," in the words of the D.C. Circuit Court of Appeals in a 1997 decision named *In re Sealed Case,* and therefore "affords greater protection against disclosure." It, too, can be applied to FOIA-requested records under Exemption 5, yielding broad swaths of presidential secrecy, but there have been few cases in which that has been done thus far.

104   The genesis of this unique judicial creation was a case by the name of *Reynolds v. United States*, in which the surviving family of a military pilot sought government records regarding his death in the crash of a "secret" high-altitude military plane during the height of the Cold War. Not only did the Government withhold any and all records pertaining to the plane, the plane flight, and the plane crash, it also argued that even the continued *maintenance* of such a lawsuit threatened disclosure of information that had been classified on national security grounds. Accepting this argument, and creating the "State Secrets Privilege" to accommodate it, the Supreme Court ordered the case dismissed. The academic criticism of this categorical litigation privilege has sometimes been referred to as "the rap on *Reynolds*" -- including at a CGS academic program that was devoted to it in the fall of 2009, which featured a presentation by a future Solicitor General of the United States defending the Obama Administration's surprisingly conservative positions on it.

105   In March of 2022, for example, the Supreme Court addressed this privilege in a post-9/11 torture case involving a "black site" reportedly located in Poland, *U.S. v. Zubaydah*. The Court markedly expanded the privilege's scope by holding that it can include even information "already publicly known" where official government confirmation of it is at issue "because the Government has not confirmed or otherwise officially acknowledged [it]." In so ruling, the Court drew parallels to the "official acknowledgment doctrine" that underlies the concept of "Glomarization" under the FOIA (see Chapter Seventeen).

106   In addition to multiple-part FOIA amendments such as this, the FOIA has been the subject of a singular amendment several times. First, there was a technical amendment of it in 1978, necessitated by the reconstitution of the U.S. Civil Service Commission, for the language of the FOIA's sanctions provision. Then there were successive narrowing amendments of FOIA Exemption Three in 1976, 2007, and 2009. Lastly, the Act was amended in 2002, in an emotional reaction to 9/11 by some congressman, including a future director of the CIA, to narrow its availability to foreigners. In sum, the FOIA has been amended a total of nine times, in 1974, 1976, 1978, 1986, 1996, 2002, 2007, 2009, and 2016.

107   While these amendments effectively "punted" on the exact legal status of computer "software" under the Act (remember, this was way back in 1996), they nonetheless broadly encompassed information maintained in electronic form toward that end. (Today, there no longer is much question but that software is indeed a vessel of information -- and hence a "record" -- rather than a mere tool used for manipulating information.)

108   These provisions can be found in subsections (a)(2), (a)(3), (a)(4), and (f)(2) of the Act, 5 U.S.C. § 552(a)(2), (a)(3), (a)(4), and (f)(2).

109   A personal word about these amendments is in order. This package of "electronic" FOIA amendments originated in groundwork that the Justice Department began for it in early 1989, almost as soon as the Reagan Administration ended. First, OIP undertook a governmentwide survey of agency experiences and viewpoints on the major "electronic record" issues, which was a first for FOIA-policy development, and then it gathered representatives of all executive branch agencies to discuss the results. Based upon these results, it then issued

an extensive report on the subject titled the "Department of Justice Report on 'Electronic Record' Issues under the FOIA," which in turn led to this area of law and policy becoming a large part of Vice President Gore's "Reinvention of Government" initiative, sometimes called the "Vice President's National Performance Review," which sponsored an "Information Infrastructure Task Force" ("IITF," to its participants in 1994), broadly charged with examining a wide range of telecommunication and information policy issues related to the development of what was known as the "National Information Infrastructure."

As a result, a major IITF working group was launched in early spring of 1994 to focus on FOIA electronic record issues with an eye toward legislation development and potential enactment. Chaired by me, this working group crafted a package of several dozen "electronic record principles" to guide the further crafting and acceptance by Congress of electronic record amendments to the FOIA. This policy groundwork took proposed legislation form during the summer of 1994, when the Senate unanimously passed S. 1782 in August.

However, this proposal was not at all considered by the House during the remainder of that year, nor during 1995, leading to the Senate's reintroduction of the measure, as S. 1090, in April of 1996. Finally spurred by this, the House subcommittee with jurisdiction over FOIA matters held hearings on the subject in general in mid-June of 1996, resulting in a commitment by the House subcommittee's chairman to hold a further hearing later in the year at which the provisions of the Senate bill would be formally considered.

At this point, I had to make a go/no go decision on a long-delayed family trip "out west," looping through national parks, the Canadian Rockies, the California coast, and more national parks for several weeks. My family and I had had to postpone this trip in the summer of 1994, due to the IITF working group's activities, and then again in the summer of 1995, due to OIP's relocation from the Main Justice Building for purposes of its entire refurbishment. On the other hand, I had worked on all FOIA-amendment legislative matters since 1979 and had taken the lead on them for the Federal Government since 1982. So before planning to go ahead with this rescheduled trip during the summer of 1996, I took the extra precaution of double- and triple-checking through the Justice Department's legislative affairs office that there would be no activity on proposed FOIA legislation in Congress while I was gone. And after those folks double-checked with "the Hill," I was assured that all would be quiet that summer.

Well, these assurances were enough to get us only as far as South Dakota before I received an emergency call, in the darkness of Badlands National Park, saying that the House leadership had abruptly decided to begin working on its own FOIA-amendment bill and that it intended to complete that work (i.e., conclude all negotiations on it) by August 25, i.e., before my return to Washington. Fortunately (or not, depending upon which member of my family you asked, and when), I had been issued a "state-of-the art" but nonetheless very clunky "mobile phone" (remember, this was back in 1996) to cover any such emergency and was able to make use of it wherever there was adequate phone reception coverage (which in 1996, in the wilds of the northwest and west, there often was not). As it turned out, I spent more than 110 hours on that phone (as billing records later showed) taking and making calls for the negotiations of the final provisions and wording of this rushed House bill. A highlight was when my 11-year-old daughter had to moderate a conference call between the FBI and DOD on that phone early one morning in Glacier National Park while I made use of a cabin phone to cajole a key lobbyist in a nearby room. (She now professionally treats patients under such stress.)

110   Prior to these 2007 FOIA Amendments, Congress also amended the Act in 2002, to preclude any "Intelligence Agency" (now numbering 18) from disclosing records in response to any FOIA request that is made "by or on behalf of" any foreign government or international governmental organization. Such a provision is not at all readily implemented, but that was beside the point; rather, this amendment was largely a reaction to 9/11 by a few Members of Congress who (abetted by the Cheney/Bush White House) wanted to at least "do something" as a legislative response.

111　This cycle began in 1946 with the enactment of the Administrative Procedure Act (of which the FOIA was to become a part), continued with the commencement of Congress's consideration of such a statute in December 1955 (just a tad early), led to the FOIA's enactment in 1966 (with a one-year effective date), continued on with the major FOIA amendments of 1974 (two years early, due to "Watergate"), got back on temporal track with the FOIA amendments of 1986, continued on track with the Electronic FOIA Amendments of 1996, followed on with the FOIA amendments of 2007 (one year delayed, due to the issuance of a novel executive order on the Act), and culminated right on time with the major amendments made in 2016. One can only hope that the year 2026 will see the remedial amendment of Exemption 2 by at least the 15th anniversary of the 2011 *Milner* decision (see Chapter Forty-Six).

112　In 1996, when Congress amended the Act to require the affirmative public disclosure (in electronic reading rooms) of "frequently requested" records whenever further "requests" are made for them, OIP advised all federal agencies that this requirement was of course triggered when a third request (i.e., the original one, plus two more such FOIA "requests") was received. Nevertheless, Congress in 2016 inexplicably chose to reiterate this requirement by saying that it applies to records "that have been requested [a total of] 3 or more times."

113　Actually, it came into being as part of OIP's transition papers, at a time when I thought the new attorney general would most likely be former Chief Circuit Judge Patricia A. Wald, who ended up declining the position near the end of December. Then, until literally the eve of Inauguration Day, we thought that it would be Zoë E. Baird, whom I knew because she coincidentally had been the judge's law clerk during a FOIA trial that I had in a case called *Ramo v. Department of the Navy* in 1979 . Then, after Zoë suddenly had to withdraw due to her "Nannygate" difficulties, it was District Court Judge Kimba M. Wood, whose nomination likewise was soon withdrawn due to (believe it or not) a similar "Nannygate" problem. (Then word circulated within the Department that President Clinton was about to nominate District Court Judge Rya W. Zobel, which would have completed the time-honored team of "Zoë to Kimba to Rya," a double-play combination reminiscent of "Tinker to Evers to Chance.") Then, finally, we were set with Janet, and all was well.

ACKNOWLEDGMENTS

1　A few people stand apart for special recognition in this book's preparation for publication. The first is Mary Ellen McGlone, who selflessly volunteered to read almost the entire first draft, catching numerous typos and making many helpful suggestions along the way. The second is another Mary, my sister and goddaughter Mary Elizabeth Hall, an author and longtime editor herself, who somehow managed to read nearly every word I wrote in order to tell me exactly where and how I was going wrong, never once shying away from splitting a "hair space" or "giving it to me straight." And the third, of course, is my senior production editor Brandon Coward, together with his top-notch supervisory editor, who likewise dedicated themselves to taking my electronic version of "scribblings" and turning them into the professionally produced book that this is. I am grateful to one and all. And I am grateful for the strong support and encouragement of prolific author Ronald K.L. Collins as well.

2　The sole exception to this is this book's unsparing analysis of the "email scandals" of former Secretary of State Hillary Rodham Clinton. This traces back to the many times during the presidential election year of 2016 that I pointedly critiqued Secretary Clinton's actions, inactions, and public statements on that subject from an expert legal standpoint, which Sharon feared could possibly hurt Clinton's candidacy. I, on the other hand, viewed my written criticisms as potentially no more harmful than the fact that I cast a write-in ballot for Joe Biden in Virginia that year.

In any event, I continued to say in 2016 what was true about Hillary Clinton's State Department tenure and do no less now in Chapter Forty-Seven of this book (read: whether she again seeks the presidency in 2024 or not). The only difference is that at this point in time this might hold implications for someone who was Clinton's deputy chief of staff for much of her tenure and was by all accounts heavily involved in her distribution of classified or "classifiable" information: Jacob J. "Jake" Sullivan, who now has the role of the president's national security advisor, was deeply enmeshed in what Hillary Clinton's did and did not do.

3   Unsurprisingly, I am firmly of the view that government employees receive too little appreciation of the quality of their work and the dedication with which they do it. So I have taken this opportunity to be commensurately inclusive of them, as well as to recognize the contributions of non-government folks.

4   Randy is an old friend, going back to the early days of "FOIA Reform" legislation in 1981. He worked for Senator Orrin G. Hatch (R-UT) back then, as a counterpart to John D. Podesta, Jr., the principal aide to Senator Patrick J. Leahy (D-VT), who now serves as president pro tempore of the Senate. He also is the judge for whom my young brother-in-law clerked when he graduated from law school, an outcome that previously had been in some doubt due to what we established to have been inaccurate allegations of cheating during college.

5   Tony was an officemate from 1977, who unquestionably was the most polite and gracious of the half-dozen that I had during my Civil Division days, the most remarkable one being one Milton Smith, who snored so loud during the middle of the work day that my wife Debbie could hear it when she telephoned me. As it turned out, Tony was a former college roommate of Attorney General Richard L. Thornburgh's "right-hand" man, Robert S. "Robin" Ross, Jr., whom Tony and his wife Sharon had allowed to stay in a spare bedroom when he first arrived in Washington. Tony soon became a counsel to Thornburgh and later was appointed to the Court of Appeals for the Federal Circuit.

6   Larry Wallace was a legend in the Office of the Solicitor General who had been there for more than a decade before I first got to know him in 1978. He argued 157 cases before the United States Supreme Court, more than any other government attorney ever and he also holds the record for the most cases argued before the Court in the 20th century. (Deputy Solicitor General Ed Kneedler has now argued more than 150 cases, which puts him within striking distance of Larry.) My strongest memory of him was that by the 1980s he no longer subjected himself to moot courts in preparation for his oral arguments, despite the strong custom in the SG's Office for holding one or even two of them. Rather, he held "meetings" for that, in which we all respectfully gathered around his desk to discuss the case at hand; typically, those of us on one side of his desk could barely see those on the other, let alone Larry, because his desk was entirely covered with a giant mound of papers, briefs, and law books, as was his fashion. Larry died at age 88 in 2020.

7   Steve was one of my first clients, in a big "Watergate" case going back to 1977 (see Chapter Twelve), and over the years he became both a close professional colleague and a good friend. He rose from being the chief counsel of the National Archives and Records Service to general counsel of the successor National Archives and Records Administration ("NARA," to its many friends), and then to be the second and longest-serving director of NARA's Information Security Oversight Office ("ISOO," even to those who do not sue), from 1980 until his retirement in 2002. Steve and I held similar, coordinating positions for most of our careers, which mirrored that fact that we both held Trustee Scholarships at our law school, albeit six years apart. Steve was one of the most capable, effective, and dedicated federal officials I ever came to know. And that did not end with his retirement; because his wife Tillie was not ready to retire when he did, he went on to a second career teaching in the Montgomery County school system for several years thereafter.

8   Tony's was a very sad story. He held a series of political appointments in the Department during the Clinton Administration, including Principal Deputy Associate Attorney General under Associate Attorney General Raymond C. Fisher, in which he was greatly admired for his intellect and amiable. almost spiritual, manner. In 1999, he left the Justice Department to help found the Appalachian School of Law in the small former coal-mining town of Grundy, Virginia, in the state's southwest corner not far from Tennessee. He said that he was going "to teach law to the sons and daughters of coal miners" in a place where he could "do much good." Not surprisingly, Tony soon became the school's dean.

His tenure ended very tragically, though, when three years later a very troubled student went on a shooting rampage at his law school, killing Tony, another professor, a 1L student, and wounding three others. That student, a 43-year-old naturalized U.S. citizen from Nigeria, was at that time in the process of being discharged from the school for academic reasons for having received too many failing grades.

An irony of the situation is that Tony had generously allowed this student to come back to the school and repeat his first-year classes. But the student had failed again, irreparably "flunking out"; evidently, it was just learning this that put him over the edge. After initially being found mentally incompetent to stand trial, he received three life sentences and an additional 28 years without the possibility of parole. And the case inevitably became a cause célèbre in the nationwide "gun control" community.

9   It begs noting that one of the consequences of reaching a leadership position at an exceptionally young age (29, in my case) is that all of your peers are older than you (in most cases much older) and they start dying off after not so many years. Hence my efforts to pay due tribute to so many of them in this book.

10   I first worked with Bob when he was a member of the National Security Council ("NSC," within the "Intelligence Community") staff and counsel to the National Security Advisor in the late 1970s, as he very ably helped me prepare a high-level NSC official, China expert Professor Michel C. Oksenberg, to be deposed as a defendant's witness in the *Gardels* "Glomarization" case (see Chapter Seventeen). He went on to become Ambassador to Germany, Deputy Secretary of the Treasury, and Acting Secretary of the Treasury.

11   Janet Reno arrived in Washington from Florida on March 12, 1993, in the midst of a heavy snowstorm that made her wish she'd packed warmer clothes, but she soon felt the heat from the Waco conflagration that threatened to engulf her. My second-favorite story about Janet was of her playing her steel drum for me across from the official portrait of former Attorney General Robert F. Kennedy, which she would do as therapy for her Parkinson's Disease. The song was "Amazing Grace," and she certainly had that to spare.

12   Nancy McFadden was a grizzled veteran of the famous Clinton campaign "War Room" when she arrived at the Justice Department on Inauguration Day, 1993, helping *de facto* Acting Attorney General Webster L. Hubbell bring order to the chaos that resulted from President William J. Clinton's series of failed attorney general nominees (see Chapter Twenty-Eight). She later was the "right arm" of Governors Joseph G. "Gray" Davis and Edmund G. "Jerry" Brown, Jr., in California, where she died of cancer way too young at age 59.

13   Born in 1920, Bob Saloschin was a veteran of World War II, where he served as a Navy "flying boat" navigator in the Pacific, jumping from one Japanese-held island to another and supporting the invasion of Iwo Jima. He returned to the U.S. as a lieutenant commander in the Naval Reserve and completed law school in 1947. Bob joined the Justice Department in 1958 and served 20 years in its Office of Legal Counsel. This led to his developing an expertise in a new law called the Freedom of Information Act, which in turn led to his chairing the Justice Department's Freedom of Information Committee, a small group that gathered periodically to discuss difficult FOIA issues, as of early 1970. Bob sure did like to "discuss."

In 1978, Bob was named founding director of the Department's Office of Information Law and Policy (known as "OILP"), which was established to discharge the Attorney General's responsibility under the Act to encourage its uniform and proper administration throughout the executive branch. In this role, he established the Department's *FOIA Update* publication, which served as a vehicle for FOIA policy development and dissemination until it was succeeded by its website version, *FOIA Post*, in the year 2000. Sometimes seeming too scholarly by half, Bob led OILP (which was a predecessor to the Office of Information and Privacy) for the next 2½ years (see Chapter Twenty).

Bob retired soon after the beginning of the Reagan Administration in 1981, after 35 years of federal service, and for years thereafter came to all of OIP's annual holiday parties without fail, as well as to its 25th anniversary celebration in November of 2006 when he was in his mid-80s. Although more than three decades older, Bob was unfailingly good to me both before and after I succeeded him and he even invited my wife Debbie and me to dinner at his home, together with Department legend Mary C. Lawton, where he and his wife Neita showed us the hot tub that they had just had installed in their garage -- a "sparage," they called it. Bob died in February of 2015 at age 95, as the longest-lived FOIA maven to date.

14 No one was more responsible for launching and nurturing the start of my Department of Justice career than Marty Danziger, a senior Department executive whose good fortune became mine as well as time went by. Marty had been a "star" prosecutor in the office of New York County District Attorney Frank S. Hogan during the early and mid-1960s, gaining national attention for his stellar work. So after "getting [his] ticket punched," as Marty would say, he came to Washington as an executive assistant in the enforcement arm of the Department of the Treasury in 1967 and moved on to fight organized crime at the Justice Department before being named the Director of the National Institute of Law Enforcement and Criminal Justice within the Department's Law Enforcement Assistance Administration in 1969.

And that is where I met Marty when I talked my way into being a teenage intern for his office in the fall of 1971 (see Chapter Five). (Marty had just turned 40 at the time; I was 19, going on 20.) Not only did he generously recognize my surprisingly good work, he told me when I left that he would certainly keep me in mind for future positions if I could manage to attend law school, if at all, in D.C. And then during the summer of 1973 when he was tapped by new Attorney General Elliot L. Richardson to set up a special sub-office in what became the Office of the Attorney General, and I had managed to afford law school in the meantime, he brought me on board as the most junior member of his professional staff (see Chapter Seven).

Then, the following spring, amidst the repercussions of what we called "the Saturday Night Massacre," when Marty had to leave the Department because he had been "too close" to Elliot Richardson, he became executive director of the United Mine Workers Welfare and Retirement Fund (a temporary sinecure position). And he again hired me, this time to revamp the Fund's administrative appeals procedures, which dovetailed well with both my decision to leave the Department in order to work on the congressional campaign of future Representative Thomas J. Downey (D-NY) and my need to continue to earn as much as I could notwithstanding that. Marty and I kept in touch for many years after that, until he died in a tragic bicycle accident in 2002.

15 I came to know Don quite well during my judicial clerkship, as he and a team of his attorneys in the Department of Justice's Tax Division were defending a series of Freedom of Information Act cases on my judge's docket. They had just completed the prosecution of the largest criminal tax-fraud scheme in U.S. history in Chicago and Don regaled me with vivid stories about the professional life of a Justice Department Trial Attorney. And when I became one of those myself, Don would pick my brain in return about how to best handle the FOIA abuse of both the Tax Division and his client agency (the Internal Revenue Service) by the Founding Church of Scientology.

16   Mary was a true legend at the Justice Department as a deputy assistant attorney general in the Office of Legal Counsel and then founding director of the Office of Intelligence Policy and Review ("OIPR," to its many friends), which administered the Foreign Intelligence Surveillance Act of 1978 ("FISA," to its many subjects, as in "FISA warrants"), and where she represented the Government before the Foreign Intelligence Surveillance Court ("FISC," to its rotating judicial members). Possessed of a towering intellect and embodying utter integrity, she died far too young, at age 58, of a pulmonary embolism.

Mary "took a shine" to me at an early stage of my career as our professional paths inevitably crossed and it was not long before we collaborated on a key policy memorandum dealing with the use of surveillance against domestic terrorist groups within the permissible bounds of the Privacy Act. I found that in addition to her unmatched acumen, she had a natural talent for balancing law enforcement needs with the protection of civil liberties, which is the very fine line that we walked in crafting this Departmentwide policy. This inevitably received renewed attention in the immediate wake of the bombing of the Murrah Federal Building in Oklahoma City on April 19, 1995 (the two-year anniversary of the Waco conflagration).

In fact, I was participating in a meeting on this very subject, chaired by Janet Reno's Chief of Staff John M. Hogan, when Janet returned to Washington from speaking at the Oklahoma City memorial service. As soon as she arrived at the Main Justice Building, she came directly to the conference room where we were meeting, still visibly affected by what she had just experienced. I still remember her passionately making the point for us all that "things are seen very differently outside the beltway," which was her way of emphasizing her view that domestic terrorism was a growing threat not limited to isolated individuals such as Timothy J. McVeigh. And as a result, I was motivated to find a bit more leeway within the Privacy Act in aid of the FBI's undercover law enforcement activities against domestic terrorism. (Years later, I came to know an FBI Special Agent -- as a vital member of the Collaboration of Government Secrecy's Advisory Board -- who successfully infiltrated two hard-core survivalist groups under our slightly updated policy (see Chapter Forty-Two).)

Mary lived just a few blocks from my home, alongside the Crescent Trail in Bethesda, where she was well known within the local community. My wife and I got to know her socially, where her intellect shone through as it did professionally at the Department, but we joined many others in concern about the impact of her heavy smoking, which I think carried over from the intensity of her responsibilities. When Mary died suddenly in October of 1993, we were shocked but not completely surprised, as she had literally dedicated her life to the Department. Right away, I recommended the creation of a new attorney general's award, for "career service," in her honor, and it has been bestowed annually ever since.

17   Steve Schlesinger had an intellect and mild personality that probably made him better suited for academia than the "rough and tumble" of bureaucratic agency politics (much as I dislike using that term). He had been the head of the Justice Department's Bureau of Justice Statistics for five years before accepting a political appointment at Main Justice during the George H.W. Bush Administration, one that placed him in temporary organizational alignment with the Office of Information and Privacy and allowed it to work together with him on potential FOIA legislation. Steve moved on to become the director of the Statistics Division of the Administrative Office of U.S. Courts for more than a dozen years before he died at the young age of 68 in 2002.

18   Jack Keeney already was a true legend in the Justice Department by the time that I first met him in the early 1980s, as Principal Deputy Assistant Attorney General (and periodically Acting Assistant Attorney General) in the Department's Criminal Division. He began at the Department in mid-1951, a few months before I was born, and by the time he retired in 2010 he was the Justice Department's oldest employee and also was the longest-serving career federal prosecutor ever in the United States. Ten years prior to that, the Justice Department named one

of its buildings (1301 New York Avenue, N.W., in Washington, D.C.) after him, an honor rarely if ever bestowed on a living person.

Jack was a strong believer in grand jury secrecy, which brought us together as allies when a particularly controversial issue on that subject arose in the FOIA context in 1983. He was not at all shy about disagreeing with his colleagues in the Criminal Division, and agreeing with OIP, on the status of what we called "intrinsic documents" under Rule 6(e) of the Federal Rules of Criminal Procedure for purposes of the FOIA; together we conspired to modify his division's litigation manual to memorialize what we believed to be correct on that score.

19   Ellen Lee was a legal pioneer, the first female assistant chief (and then deputy chief) of the civil division of the U.S. Attorney's Office in D.C. and a longtime law clerk to the first female federal district court judge in the country, District Court Judge Burnita Shelton Matthews, whose chambers were two doors down from where I clerked in the federal courthouse. She joined the U.S. Attorney's Office in 1956 and was a mainstay of that office until her retirement in 1989. As deputy chief, Ellen Lee was instrumental in coordinating the filing of all litigation papers of the Office of Information and Privacy (in what amounted to more than 500 cases all told) during the 1980s. In 1985, we featured her photograph on the cover of *FOIA Update,* together with her boss, future Chief District Court Judge Royce C. Lamberth. Her funeral in Old Town, Alexandria, in 1990 became a *de facto* reunion for, *inter alia,* the dozens of AUSAs (read: Assistant United States Attorneys) who worked with her and for her.

20   Mike Bernstein and I had a friendship outside of the Justice Department as well as within it, in that we met when two of our children started carpooling together to a summer camp in the mid-1980s. (Our other two children were the same age as one another also.) Mike was a veteran "Nazi hunter," part of the Justice Department's Office of Special Investigations, of which he became an assistant deputy director shortly before his untimely death. In addition to sharing children-related activities such as swimming with our wives and children at our local pool, Mike would call me at work from time to time with secrecy-related questions that were raised in his international work.

This ceased on December 21, 1988, however, with the bombing of Pan Am Flight 103 over Lockerbie, Scotland. Mike was returning on that flight from Vienna, Austria, where he had been negotiating with the Austrian Government about the deportation of a Nazi war criminal from here to there. Over the course of his career, Mike was personally responsible for the Department's deportation of seven former Nazis, and the Criminal Division dedicated a library in one of its satellite locations to him the following year. His boss, three levels up, was Criminal Division Deputy Assistant Attorney General Mark Richard (see below), who presided at the dedication and also spoke for the Department at a ceremony honoring Mike that was held at the Israeli Embassy (which, coincidentally, I could see from my bedroom window). Mike's wife Stephanie became a leader in the Flight 103 survivors group and honored him at her subsequent wedding to a fellow rabbi, which my wife and I attended.

21   Nate Dodell was a longtime Assistant United States Attorney ("AUSA") in the Civil Division of the U.S. Attorney's Office for the District of Columbia who handled several of the first Freedom of Information Act lawsuits ever filed, some of them by the Founding Church of Scientology. I came to know him well during my clerkship at the District Court for the District of Columbia and then as a litigator in the Civil Division of Main Justice. When Scientologists decided to infiltrate the Justice Department in order to steal inside information about their many pending FOIA cases in the mid-1970s, it was Nate's office that they broke into (see Chapter Twenty-Five). Nate was a one-of-a-kind type of guy who in his private life took on the D.C. Bar establishment in a quixotic but highly principled quest to lower bar dues. He died in 2018 at age 85.

22   Kitty Harless was one of the great "unsung heroes" of the Justice Department, someone who worked tirelessly on vital administrative matters that would be noticed only if they were not so expertly handled by her. Although small of physical stature and increasingly crippled by multiple sclerosis, she came to the Office of Information and Privacy's rescue time and time again as we fought "the bureaucracy" together whenever need be. Indeed, she was perhaps best known for figuring out how to "work around" the archaic rules and practices of the Justice Management Division. And yes, she knew where most of the "bodies were buried," having conspired to bury more than a few of them herself.

23   Leo Neshkes had already been working as a FOIA specialist for a while when I first met him in 1978. An attorney, he had "stood up" the FOIA office of the Department's Antitrust Division, was the Department's longest-tenured "component" FOIA Officer, and as such was part of a group of us who in 1979 began to plan what eventually became the 1986 FOIA Amendments. Everyone liked Leo, which made it even sadder when he developed brain cancer in the late 1980s. But Leo bravely fought what we all knew was a terminal disease, continuing to work for several years in spite of it, his head shrouded in fabric, his intellect intact.

  Leo died at the young age of 45 in late 1994, and near the end of his life he inspired me to create an Attorney General-level "FOIA Officer Award" within the Department, of which Leo was the inaugural recipient. So I was able to share this news with his wife Marcia at his funeral. It was only small comfort, to be sure, but not long thereafter Marcia came to the Department to receive it for Leo posthumously, together with her two sons, and in OIP we felt that we had done the best for Leo that we could.

24   Ross Cirrincione was the very heart and soul of the American Society of Access Professionals ("ASAP"), having served as both its president (for three separate terms) and resident "town crier" for many years. His "day job" was being the head of the FOIA office at the Department of Health and Human Services, but his specialty was using his booming voice to bring to a close many an ASAP training session when the time was right. Although he was a couple of decades older than me, Ross relied heavily on my career advice at a critical juncture for him, which I'm happy to say (for the both of us) worked out very well.

25   I knew Larry Simms only briefly when he was a political deputy assistant attorney general in the Department's Office of Legal Counsel during the late 1970s, where he occupied the "double office" in OLC that had served as the location of the "Nazi saboteurs" trial in 1942 (see Quiz Question #65). He had worked together with Bob Saloschin, under Assistant Attorney General Antonin G. "Nino" Scalia, on White House-related FOIA issues and I consulted him to tap his expertise on such an issue (read: Watergate Special Prosecution Force-related) that arose in one of my litigation cases (see Chapter Twelve). He was a friendly "Southern boy" who had more than enough intellectual firepower to overcome that in Washington, D.C.

26   Bill Olmstead was the Associate General Counsel of the Nuclear Regulatory Commission and had been deeply involved in the legal field of administrative law for many years by the time I came to know him in 1995. He was a mainstay of my "Electronic Record FOIA Working Group" during that year, which was created as part of the White House's Information Infrastructure Task Force to develop the legal and policy principles that guided our development of the Electronic FOIA Amendments of 1996 (see Chapter Thirty-Four). Bill was our working group's resident expert on both the current and imminent workings of the Internet at the time; the first time that I heard of the "World Wide Web" was from Bill, as he patiently schooled our group about something that, alone among us, he could foresee having a large effect on the administration of the FOIA in the not-too-distant future. He was 100% right, of course, and at his funeral in 1999, I remember conveying that to his wife and adult children.

27   Mark Richard was a deputy assistant attorney general (and, for a time, acting assistant attorney general) of the Department's Criminal Division from 1980 until his death in 2009, where he was the division's principal overseer of all of its international work (i.e., on counterterrorism, law enforcement treaties, extraditions, and the like), including its Office of International Affairs and its Office of Special Investigations (i.e., the Department's "Nazi hunters"). As a devout Jew, he took particular interest in the work of the latter, including its prosecution of Sobibor death camp guard John Demjanjuk, known to Holocaust survivors at the Treblinka concentration camp as "Ivan the Terrible." (I had a connection to this, as one day I found Demjanjuk's son-in-law, Edward Nishnic, filming away with a "60 Minutes" camera crew in OIP's entrance area -- whereupon I promptly covered the camera lens, told them to "pull the plug" on their equipment (not wanting to afford them even any "B-roll" footage on their way out), and escorted them from the building.)

Mark and I talked about this when we first shared sleeping quarters in an underground bunker as part of a "Continuity-of-Government" exercise in 1986. The following year, as we began serving as "daytime attorney general" and "nighttime attorney general" in these exercises, it was Mark who (as is described in Chapter Twenty-Six) suddenly found himself hooked up to an EKG in a medical area with heart fibrillations due to the stress of what we were dealing with. Mark was a true "institution" in the Department, relied upon over the course of several decades for handling many of its most difficult situations; for instance, Attorney General Janet Reno relied a great deal on him during the final days of the "Waco crisis" in 1993 (see Chapter Twenty-Nine). Mark was 12 years older than me and he died young, after beating and then succumbing to esophageal cancer, at age 69. I personally relied on him for his wisdom, depth of experience, and humanity.

28   Claudia was another career component head at the Department who died much too young. She was the director of the Department's Professional Responsibility Advisory Office ("PRAO," to its professional clients), which was created in 1999 to resolve professional responsibility issues faced by the Department's attorneys, mostly AUSAs. In 2002, her office became engulfed in a controversy created when one of her staff attorneys disagreed with the FBI's interrogation treatment of "American Taliban" John Walker Lindh in Afghanistan, gave legal advice to the contrary, and became extremely dissatisfied with how the entire matter was handled by the Department.

This led to that attorney "leaking" this information to a veteran journalist (Michael R. Isikoff, of *Newsweek* at the time) and to a personnel action against that attorney (taken by Claudia, over the attorney's loud objections) that in turn led to a Privacy Act lawsuit filed by that attorney against the Department. Because of the novelty of this suit (not to mention its high-profile nature), I was brought in to consult on it, including through the design of the case's defense and the review of the Department's prospective court filings.

Then, as if this fact pattern was not already complicated enough, this staff attorney's "story" was told in an issue of her university's alumni magazine, which I read because coincidentally both of my children attended that same university -- as did Claudia herself. I remember Claudia telling me that she was very glad that this article did not connect her by name to the case, despite her being a fellow alumnus, inasmuch as it was an entirely one-sided, and therefore badly skewed, account.

That Privacy Act suit was adjudicated in the Department's favor, with the court's rejection of all of that staff attorney's legal claims. Years later, I was compelled to point this out at an academic program held at my law school when that attorney -- who by then was claiming pristine "whistleblower," not "leaker," status and had failed to mention that fact, among other things. (As Claudia had died of cancer by then, she was not available to correct that attorney on the facts, so I did it for her, which appeared to bring tears.) But I will not name that attorney here, effectively "returning the favor" that Claudia had been done in not naming her in the Brown University alumni magazine article.

29   Barbara Babcock was the new Assistant Attorney General for the Civil Division when I joined it in 1977 and she, too, took a quick liking to me. She selected me for a newly formed advisory committee of young Civil Division attorneys; she confided in me about her difficulties with a new section chief (see Chapter Ten); she invited me to be part of her "moot court" for the presentation of oral argument before the United States Supreme Court in the landmark case of *Chrysler v. Brown*; and she placed me in precocious charge of coordinating "reverse FOIA" litigation nationwide after the issuance of the Supreme Court's decision in that case. (Unlike Mary Lawton, Barbara died in her early 80s this past year.)

30   Ernie was one of the last old "Cold Warriors" at the CIA. When I came to know him in 1977, he was chief of the litigation staff (soon to be deputy general counsel) in the CIA's General Counsel's Office, one who assumed the mantle of protecting his agency from the growing "threat" posed by the Freedom of Information Act. (I can recall seeing on his bulletin board a photocopy of a check in the amount of $188,000 (a down payment) written to the Agency by former case officer Frank W. Snepp III, as the result of litigation challenging his publication of his book *Decent Interval* in 1977 in violation of the specific nondisclosure agreement that the CIA required for its officers. (Ernie, with the full backing of CIA Director Stansfield Turner, pressed the Justice Department to pursue that.) Less than a year later, I was able to present him with another check for his bulletin board, one for $93 in court costs that we received in a hard-fought victory for "Glomarization" (see Chapter Seventeen).

    Hardened as he was, however, Ernie was able to make a 25-year-old Trial Attorney feel supported like no other such "grizzled veteran" could. I still remember him clambering aboard a 7 a.m. shuttle to Newark, New Jersey, to help me prepare for a court hearing in one of the first CIA "Glomarization" cases (*Medoff v. CIA*) that morning. (He was filling in for a CIA staff attorney, the late Lee S. Strickland, who was not up to the job.) You couldn't ask for a better agency client, especially one who had worked as an intelligence officer throughout Europe, employing his native German (as well as unspoken other skills), during the height of the Cold War in the 1950s. And as the driving force behind the controversial "devil's deal" that gave the CIA categorical protection of its "operational files" through legislation enacted in 1984 (not to mention of what was known internally as "MH/CHAOS," in the face of "NSDD 84"), he made a mark that would make any old "Cold Warrior" proud.

31   Jim was one of my "fellow travelers" when he and are were part of the U.S. delegation to the Inaugural Sino-American Conference on the Rule of Law and Human Rights in Nantong, China, in 2009, and follow-up conferences in Xiamen, China, in 2010, and in New York in 2011. Jim was a leading scholar in criminal justice who taught law all around the world. That did not stop him, however, from memorably sighing aloud to me, after we'd just travelled too many flight-delayed hours to arrive at an airport in China at four a.m., that "we're getting too old for this shit."

32   Bill Harader was a pioneer of sorts, in that he was the first member of the academic community to come to Washington for purposes of advancing the understanding of the FOIA. When I was still a Trial Attorney in the Department's Civil Division in the late 1970s, Bill would literally "fly into town" from his position as Director of the Center for Governmental Services and Professor of Political Science at Indiana State University in order to run a two-day training program (at which I spoke every year) for the Office of Personnel Management's Government Affairs Institute (which reportedly considered renaming itself during the Clinton years), before an audience of more than 100, at the end of every summer. After nearly a dozen years of this (it began in 1978), Bill was a FOIA institution. Tragically, though, while he was flying his plane on a standard pilot-recertification flight in December of 1988, he put the plane into a routine "pull out" maneuver but for some unknown reason was unable to pull out of it. (Inasmuch as Bill had a very good sense of humor, we jested that we renamed Exemption "Low 2" in his memory.)

33   Gerry worked for OIP for several years, first as a "full-time law clerk" while attending law school at night (OIP employed several law clerks in this category, with great success), and then as an attorney upon graduation. (We managed to elide "Honors Program" constraints for Gerry and several others in that category.) Gerry made no secret of the fact that he was gay (not to people who knew him in Washington, including those of us who attended his wedding), but we knew him well enough also to know that he was not "out" to his family, who were back on the family farm in Nebraska.

In order to take that next step of hiring him as an attorney, however, we had to comply with a higher level of security requirements, which unfortunately (but quite rationally) meant that we had to insist that Gerry "come out" to his family, lest he be vulnerable to potent blackmail efforts based upon his existing circumstances. (Yes, this is a real thing, not at all a "function of the times" type of thing; one needed only imagine any malign acquaintance of Gerry's acting to leverage him into disclosing classified information, with increasing pressure over time, given such circumstances.) So he did so, understanding the necessity of it.

At that time (i.e., in 1992), Gerry's HIV condition had progressed to the point at which he was slowly dying of AIDS, which to his enormous credit affected his work in only one instance: In September of 1993, Gerry was mugged by several assailants while walking home at night in his "safe" D.C. neighborhood (near Meridian Hill Park), resulting in several photocopies of court decisions that he was carrying (for purposes of updating his part of our annual "FOIA Guide" publication) becoming bloodied almost as much as Gerry was -- for which we had to take special precautions.

Two years later, Gerry's medical condition deteriorated to such a point that we encouraged him to take a special "disability retirement" that was newly available to him for his own sake. Then, seemingly miraculously, Gerry's medical team found a particular chemotherapy "cocktail" that worked so well for him that it improved his condition greatly, so much so that we could "unretire" him (just imagine the paperwork that *that* can entail in a government bureaucracy), which we promptly did in the summer of 1996. Sadly, this remission did not last nearly as long as we had hoped and Gerry died, at age 32, the following year.

Although Gerry was buried back home in Nebraska, of course, a special memorial service was held for him in Washington, D.C., which his parents attended, as well as hundreds of people from both the Justice Department and the local LGBTQ community (most particularly his friend Vince Micone, who was a dynamo at arranging such things). Meeting his parents for the first time, I was able to express my condolences not only for Gerry's death but also for the fact that I had forced Gerry to "come out" to them. They seemed to understand and accept this, perhaps partly because I was supported by a tall, rather imposing figure by my side. Yes, Attorney General Janet Reno spent much time comforting Gerry's family that evening, and the following year she authorized the Justice Department's "Gerald B. Roemer Community Service Award" for outstanding contributions to the LGBTQ community, which has been given out each year since then.

34   Horace Beckwith was a Supervisory Special Agent in the Bureau's FOIA shop whom I got to know very well when I worked on both the King and Kennedy Assassination FOIA cases in the mid-1970s. He oversaw the Bureau's document analysts on both of those teams and did a terrific job under difficult circumstances, even accompanying me to Dallas in March of 1978 to search for and remove Kennedy Assassination records from the Dallas Field Office (see Chapter Forty-Eight). During that trip, Horace told me that he had headed the team of New York City Special Agents (read: "Squad 47") that had been accused of conducting illegal break-ins (read: "black bag jobs," in Bureau parlance) in pursuit of the Weather Underground. The "tenor of the times" by then was against Horace and he was being investigated toward possible dismissal. I remember sending Horace a "hang in there" postcard from London when I was there in late September of that year and I made sure that the FBI's leadership was aware of how helpful he had been on my cases. A few months later, FBI Director William H.

Webster reversed a dismissal determination and allowed Horace to finish out his FBI career (he was only 46 at the time, 20 years my senior) in peace.

QUIZ QUESTIONS

1   This is not only a fair synthesis of public opinion on Gonzales' performance during and after his tenure, it is one born of my firsthand experience with him, including through nearly seven hours of deposing him (in a non-South American junta sense, alas) in the *Gerlich* case (see Chapter Forty-Three), where he was, in a word, characteristically dumb. To those of us who were there, including the *pro bono* court reporter, he seemed even less intellectually capable than the president who appointed him.

2   Indeed, the secrecy of this program is so strong that none of the more than 8500 witnesses or their nearly 10,000 family members who have been protected under it and followed its rules has been killed.

3   If this question were to be misunderstood as "assistant attorney general," then at least one answer would be Massachusetts Governor Deval L. Patrick, who used to sit across the table from me at "component head" meetings when he was the assistant attorney general for the Civil Rights Division during the mid-1990s.

4   Mike Egan, an amiable southern gentleman, graciously suffered the awkward blandishments of a Civil Division section chief at an office holiday party when she dragged me over to him and both loudly and a bit drunkenly exclaimed, "Look! Here's a white male. Who says we don't hire white males?" (As of that time, that section chief's section had hired an exceptionally large cohort of eight young attorneys during the first year of the Carter Administration, only one of whom was a white male.)

5   John R. Bolton was not at all well-regarded at the Justice Department when he was an assistant attorney general in charge of its Office of Legislative Affairs ("OLA," to those on the Hill) and then its Civil Division. First, at OLA, he was known to shy away from scheduled meetings if he thought that they might be politically damaging to him. (I can attest to that firsthand given how he "bailed" at the last minute from a meeting that I ended up conducting in order to cover for him.) And when he subsequently took charge of the Civil Division, Bolton became notorious for his unduly harsh treatment of a senior Trial Attorney in the Torts Branch who was on a medically extended maternity leave. In fact, his surname became so synonymous with such ruthless behavior by a Department official that she (and others who followed) were said to have been "Boltonized."

6   The FBI Headquarters Building, named for J. Edgar Hoover, was constructed during the early 1970s but was not completed until September of 1975, more than three years after Hoover's death. Before he died, though, Hoover was heavily involved in many of its construction details, even to the point of personally selecting a chandelier for what was to be his personal dining room in the new building. According to a recent source who divulged the following information for purposes of this book, this extravagant furnishing unlawfully exceeded Government Services Administration parameters, cost in excess of $15,000 (in 1971 dollars), and was installed secretly by the building's prime contractor, Blake Construction Co. Even worse is the fact that at about the same time Blake Construction Co. also served as the "middleman" for the illicit funding of extensive remodeling work done on Hoover's residence in Washington, D.C., including updated plumbing, at no expense to him. Yes, such corrupt activity was conducted in complete secrecy back then, not to see the light of day until now, more than 50 years later.

7   Perhaps the most significant Justice Department location was one that never came to be. I can remember hearing at a Department meeting in the early 1980s of a plan to purchase land along the north side of

Pennsylvania Avenue in order to construct a massive "expansion" Justice Department building adjacent to the Federal Courthouse, which would have featured a skywalk between the two buildings over an intervening park. Unfortunately, the plan stalled at the budget stage and the Nation of Canada, which owned the land at the time, succeeded in building its embassy there, the address of which is 501 Pennsylvania Avenue, N.W.

8   It also was the location of the "Justice Command Center," a Sixth Floor complex of conference rooms and telecommunications equipment that serves as the Department's primary "Sensitive Compartmented Information Facility," or "SCIF."

9   Speaking of getting spooked in the dark, this reminds me of the time that I had a gun pointed at me in the dark. That was in 1977, when the federal judge for whom I clerked was presiding over the trial of 12 Hanafi Muslims who had simultaneously taken over three buildings in downtown D.C., leading to a long siege, two deaths, and numerous injuries among 150 hostages. Due to the exceptional sensitivity of the case, including serious threats to disrupt the trial, the U.S. Marshals Service put extraordinary security measures in place, which unbeknownst to those of us in Chambers included having an armed deputy U.S. marshal placed in the courtroom long before each day's session began, waiting in the dark. So when I entered that courtroom to place something on the judge's chair for the day's proceedings, I was surprised to find myself looking down the barrel of a Glock pistol held by someone who knew not who I was in that darkness. And I've evidently never forgotten that experience.

10   And it was just steps from there that, on Saturday, September 15, 2001, I was placing my bicycle on a bike rack near the east driveway entrance to the courtyard when I heard a familiar voice calling out, "FOIA Guy!" It was Senator Orrin G. Hatch (the once and future chairman of the Senate Judiciary Committee), who knew me well from our work on FOIA-amendment legislation but never could quite remember my name. (Not so good for a politician, but Hatch was more into ideology than "retail politics," anyway.) He had been dropped off there, outside of the building's security gates, to attend the very first meeting on the development of the bill that became the USA PATRIOT Act. So I "badged him in" and showed him the way down a First Floor hallway to where I knew the meeting was taking place, albeit tentatively. I suppose it could be said that that legislation, which was highly controversial in more ways than one, got off to a somewhat slow start that day.

About the Author

Daniel J. Metcalfe joined the faculty of American University's Washington College of Law in 2007 as a Faculty Fellow in Law and Government upon retiring from a career in government service that began at the United States Department of Justice more than 50 years ago. As an adjunct professor of law there, he taught courses in government secrecy law for ten years and served as executive director of the school's Collaboration on Government Secrecy, the first such academic center established at any law school in the world.

A 1976 honors graduate of the National Law Center at The George Washington University, where he was a law review editor and attended on a full academic scholarship, Metcalfe worked at the Justice Department both as a teenage intern during college and as a law clerk in the Office of the Attorney General during law school. In 1981, after a federal judicial clerkship and four years as a Justice Department Trial Attorney, he was appointed to the position of founding director of the Justice Department's Office of Information and Privacy, one of the 40 components of the Department, where he served as the Federal Government's principal expert on transparency policy and related litigation during seven presidential administrations.

For more than a quarter-century in that position, he guided all federal agencies on the interpretation and governmentwide administration of the Freedom of Information Act ("FOIA"); directly supervised the defense of more than 500 FOIA and Privacy Act lawsuits in district and appellate courts; testified before Congress on FOIA-amendment legislation; authored Attorney General FOIA policy memoranda for successive presidential administrations; and met with representatives of nearly 100 nations and international governing bodies as they considered the development and implementation of their own government transparency laws. He also served as a principal advisor to the Department of Homeland Security on matters of post-9/11 information policy and likewise advised the Office of the Director of National Intelligence and senior staff of the National Security Council. During 2006, he held primary responsibility within the executive branch for guiding the governmentwide implementation of Executive Order 13,392 (Dec. 14, 2005), the first (and still only) executive order ever issued on the FOIA.

Dan Metcalfe was appointed to the career Senior Executive Service in 1984, the youngest Justice Department attorney then and since to hold such a position, and he now serves on Senior Executive Service evaluation panels for the Office of Personnel Management. As an adjunct professor at WCL, he regularly taught an elective course on government information law and policy during the fall semester, a professional skills seminar on oral advocacy titled "Secrecy Controversies" during the spring semester, and he also taught a seminar on national security secrecy law together with former WCL Associate Dean Stephen I. Vladeck (now holder of the Charles Alan Wright Chair in Federal Courts at the University of Texas School of Law). He is the author of several publications, including *Amending the FOIA: Is it Time for a Real Exemption 10?*, 37 Admin. & Reg. L. News 16 (Summer 2012); *From FOIA Service to Lip Service: The Unexpected Story of White House Visitor Logs*, 36 Admin. & Reg. L. News 3 (Spring 2011); *The Nature of Government Secrecy*, 26 Gov't Info. Q. 305 (2009); *Sunshine Not So Bright: FOIA Implementation Lags Behind*, 34 Admin. & Reg. L. News 5 (Summer 2009); and most recently *Forget the Hacking, One Decision Likely Cost Hillary Clinton the Presidency*, LawNewz (Jan. 2, 2017), and *Here's Why President Obama Should Absolutely Not Give Hillary Clinton a Pardon*, LawNewz (Nov. 13, 2016).

Additionally, he authored chapters for the volume *Research Handbook on Transparency* published in 2014, as well as a lengthy op-ed for *POLITICO Magazine* in 2015 titled "Hillary's Email Defense Is Laughable" that became a foundational legal analysis for media coverage of the Clinton email scandal thereafter. During 2015, he made several live television appearances, including on C-SPAN's "Washington Journal," to critique the legal and policy defects of former Secretary of State Hillary Rodham Clinton's handling of official electronic mail records in relation to her varied public utterances both during and after her tenure.

Beginning in 2008, Metcalfe served as sole counsel for the plaintiffs in a class action lawsuit filed on behalf of 179 applicants to the Attorney General's Honors Program who were, as found by the Justice Department's Inspector General, improperly "deselected" from consideration for entry-level career attorney positions on political or ideological grounds during the tenure of Attorney General Alberto R. Gonzales in 2006. This case, Gerlich v. United States Department of Justice, Civil No. 08-0034 (JDB) (D.D.C., filed June 30, 2008), marked the first time that an Attorney General of the United States has been deposed after leaving office, and it presented novel issues of Privacy Act liability, Federal Records Act applicability, and spoliation of evidence due to the improper creation and use of Internet-based records that subsequently were destroyed in the Office of the Deputy Attorney General at the direction of political appointees. After the court of appeals ultimately ruled in the plaintiffs' favor, establishing a new rule of adverse evidentiary inference for wrongful record destruction by a federal agency, *Gerlich v. United States Department of Justice*, 711 F.3d 161 (D.C. Cir. 2013), the Government readily settled the case for more than a half-million dollars in damages, attorney fees, and costs.

In 2010, Professor Metcalfe was appointed as a member of the World Bank's Access to Information Appeals Board, an independent tribunal empowered to make final decisions on appeals taken under the Bank's newly established worldwide information disclosure policy, together with board members from India and France holding final authority to order the public disclosure of World Bank records. In 2009, he was a member of the U.S. delegation to the Inaugural Sino-American Dialogue on Rule of Law and Human Rights in China, followed by further dialogues in Xiamen and Beijing in 2010 and in New York in 2011, and he has given dozens of presentations on international transparency around the world, including in representing the U.S. at the International Conference of Information Commissioners in Great Britain.

On behalf of the Collaboration on Government Secrecy, he testified before both the House Committee on Oversight and Government Reform and the Senate Committee on the Judiciary as an expert on governmentwide FOIA administration and the proper implementation of new FOIA policy; he organized and presented two dozen day-long academic programs on openness-in-government subjects; and he submitted a successful *amicus* brief on a novel FOIA issue heard by the United States Supreme Court. In 2012, in recognition of his work for the National Academy of Public Administration as the world's leading expert on government transparency and related litigation, he was elected as a Fellow of the Academy.

More recently, he served as a legal expert for coverage of Hillary Clinton's "emailgate" controversies by media outlets such as CNN, *The L.A. Times*, *LawNewz*, *The N.Y. Post*, *POLITICO*, *The Hill*, and World Radio; became a columnist for *LawNewz* on federal record issues; presented legal and policy analyses at a televised program titled "Hillary Clinton's Email Scandal" conducted by prolific FOIA-requester organization Judicial Watch; spoke on comparisons between FOIA implementation in the U.S. and in the U.K at the Office of the Information Commissioner in St. Andrews, Scotland; served as a principal contributor to the privacy encyclopedia *Privacy Rights in the Digital Era;* and advised congressional staff on proposed provisions of what became the FOIA Improvement Act of 2016.

Professor Metcalfe also has held positions as an Honorary Senior Research Fellow at University College London; as a formal consultant to the Administrative Conference of the United States upon its re-establishment in 2010; as a member of the Advisory Committee to the American Bar Association's Standing Committee on Law and National Security; as an unofficial advisor to the American Society of Access Professionals ("ASAP"), for which he received its President's Award for Distinguished Public Service; and as a contributing editor of the *Administrative Law & Regulatory News* publication of the American Bar Association's Section of Administrative Law and Regulatory Practice, for which he received its outstanding service award in 2014. Last, but perhaps not least, in 2007 he was inducted into his high school's 50th Anniversary Hall of Fame as an inaugural member.

INDEX

Brentwood School District, 488n4

The Brethren: Inside the Supreme Court (Woodward and Armstrong), 703n15

Brezhnev, Leonid I., 523n2, 526n15

Brezler, Jason, 646n66

Brian, Danielle, 427, 558n10, 624n39

Bridgegate, 506n1

British Freedom of Information Act, 478n2

Broadwell, Paula, 106, 518n44, 519n49

Brown, Doris, 481n19

Brown, Ernest J., 450n4

Brown, Jerry, 577n5

Brown, Michael D., 608n1, 700n6

Browner, Carol M., 497n7

Brown University, 530n9

Brown v. Board of Education, 69

Brzezinski, Zbigniew K., 128

Burdick, Eugene L., 191

Bureau of Investigation, 710n14

Bureau of Prisons, 232

Burford, Anne Irene McGill Gorsuch, 379

Burger, Warren E., 69, 79, 85, 703n15

Burlinson, Alexander C., 524n9

Burns, William J., 699n46

Burwell v. Hobby Lobby Stores, Inc., 704n15

Bush, George H.W., 3, 127, 197, 203, 225, 469n39, 510n3, 576n3

    Administration, 205, 450n8, 522n10, 725n101

    appointed John Magaw, 547n21

    Military Audit case, 534n11

    Texas Republican politics, 282

Bush, George W., 3, 5, 15, 29, 284, 287, 450n5, 452n4, 456n17, 487n1, 576n3, 611n21, 627n62

    addressed some career SES members, 608n1

    Administration, 111, 196, 199, 225, 226, 227, 248, 249, 250–51, 265, 274, 318, 450n8, 457n25, 499n13, 516n38, 554n10, 580n4, 583n6, 606n9, 607n11, 607n12, 612n23, 628n65, 691n9, 701n8, 705n1, 715n41, 722n84

appointed John Bates to district court, 623n37

"bill of goods" sold to, 602n15

first cabinet meeting, 221

and John D. Ashcroft, 230

"no FOIA" policy of, 254

"not an agency record" position, 253

"outspokenness" of, 219

policy goals of, 274

policy on protecting "sensitive information," 245–46

political appointees under Alberto Gonzales, 701n11

re-election of, 273

second term of, 197, 376–77, 611n21, 702n12

U.S. invasion of Iraq, 219

Bush v. Gore, 496n7, 615n2

business confidentiality, 453n5

Byrd, Richard E., Jr., 651n10

C

Cacheris, Plato, 180, 565n21

Caen, Herbert E., 517n41

Calais, 691n12

California Committee for Saucer Investigation, 667n68

Cambridge Spy Ring, 371

Camillagate, 506n1

Campaign for Freedom of Information, 470n41

candor compels, 450n5, 461n41

Canis Major Dwarf, 686n139

Cantor, Eric, 106

Capitol Building, 55, 411, 413, 490n5

Carey, Thomas J., 653n18

Carney, Cormac J., 546n18

Carome, Patrick J., 712n22

Carpenter v. United States, 476n13

Carter, Jimmy, 3, 218, 340, 485n48, 672n80

    Administration, 118, 127, 128, 137, 153, 155, 157, 158, 165, 217,

reorganization of, 529n4

senior Trial Attorney in, 77

started litigating in, 586n3

Supreme Court's *Klamath* decision, 302

Torts Branch, 116, 527n26, 527n27

Trial Attorney in, 117, 284, 501n5, 504n19

"voluntariness," 635n16

Civiletti, Benjamin R., 155

Civil Service Reform Act, 618n13

Clark, Jerry, 495n14, 497nn2–3, 498n6

Clark, Richard C., 67

Clark, Tom C., 69, 70

Clark, W. Ramsey, 556n4, 562n2, 582n2

Clarke, Arthur C., Sir, 173

Clarke, Richard A., 724n92

Clayton, Gary E., 708n6

Cleaver, Eldridge, 545n10

Clemens, Samuel Langhorne, 165

Clinton, Bill, 3, 15, 41, 42, 203, 227, 287, 376, 514n20, 518n46, 648n82

Administration, 198, 206–14, 220, 225, 232, 304, 371, 450n8, 459n29, 484n44, 499n13, 501n3, 505n22, 522n10, 524n8, 581nn1–6, 583n6, 605n5, 642n42, 683n136, 701n10

affair with Lewinski, 593n5, 709n12

alleged use of state troopers, 506n1

on Area 51, 356

"dirty little secret," 220

impeachment of, 582n3

Janet Reno's relationship with, 204–05

Lynch's "tarmac meeting" with, 645n60

OIP during, 210–12, 213

passport issue, 521n4

regrets for choosing Janet Reno as attorney general, 588n16

second term of, 210

statement about UFOs, 655n22

Task Force's "Charter," 721n78

Clinton, Hillary R., 41, 199, 208, 482n27, 521n4, 583n7–584n7, 636n2, 637n9,

641n31, 687n146, 721n78. *See also* Hillary's email issue

BlackBerry device, 305, 306, 308, 636n5–637n6, 642n44, 646n68

campaign stop in Las Vegas, 655n22

departure from cabinet department, 589n21

email travails, 506n1, 647n78

guilty of deceiving public, 642n41

Health Care Task Force, 211, 505n22, 577n3, 583n5

insulated official emails, 644n55

personal email "server," 309–10, 637n8, 637n11

"precedent" in Colin Powell, 638n15

public statements about email issue, 315–16, 638n16

responses to allegations, 636n1

statements given by, analysis of, 638n12

Sullivan affiliation with, 643n46

tenure as Secretary of State, 305

Clovis, Samuel H., Jr., 700n6

Coastal States Delivery Corp. v. United States Customs Service, 599n6

Codebreakers: The Inside Story of Bletchley Park (Hinsley), 466n17

cognitive dissonance, 516n33

Cohen, Jerome A., 25

Cohen, William S., 593n5

COINTELPRO, 38, 121, 412, 478n8, 512n13, 529n36

Colby, William E., 533n9

Collaboration on Government Secrecy (CGS), 267–68, 293, 474n9, 615n5

"Freedom of Information Day" program, 615n6

programs, 523n10, 603n21

collateral estoppel, 486n51

Collins, Ronald K.L., 728n1

Comey, James B., Jr., 321, 322, 628n66, 645n60, 645n61, 646n67, 647n76

Committee for the Study of Anomalous Aerial Phenomena (CEFAA), 676n94

Committee of Secret Correspondence, 369

International Ladies Garment Workers of America, 67

International Monetary Fund, 629n3

International Right-to-Know Day (IRTKD), 268, 465n4, 470n44, 470n47, 523n10

International Space Station (ISS), 660n33

Interpol, 102, 232

invisible ink, 372

Irangate, 506n1

IRTKD. *See* International Right-to-Know Day

Irving, Margaret Ann, 178, 179–80, 565n20

Isikoff, Michael R., 522n10, 616n5, 725n28

Islamic Development Bank, 629n3

Ivins, Bruce E., 98, 599n3

"Ivy Bells" operation 125, 372, 455n17, 532n1, 698n44

J

Jackson, Ketanji Brown, 644n53

Jackson, Robert H., 595n6

Jae-in, Moon, 352

James Webb Space Telescope (JWST), 357, 686n139

"Janet Air," 338

Janney, F.W.M., 536n34

Jaworski, Leonides, 592n2

Jay Treaty, 19

Jefferson, Thomas, 694n28

Jefferson v. Reno, 562n8

Jewell, Richard A., 99–102, 104, 105, 109, 514n22–515n29, 517n41

    and *The Atlanta Journal-Constitution,* 101–02

    candidacy for "perpetrator," 100

    labeled as "Olympic Park Bomber," 99

    obtained savvy counsel, 101

    out-of-court settlement with NBC, 101

    "profiled" by FBI agents, 100

John Doe Agency v. John Doe Corp, 505n25

John Moss Foundation, 23, 467n25

Johns Hopkins School of Advanced International Studies, 177

Johnson, Andrew, 606n8

    Administration, 695n32

Johnson, Carrie, 625n47

Johnson, Donald H., 514n23

Johnson, Lyndon B., 23, 54, 69, 468n27, 489n1, 496n2, 498n9, 504n15, 695n32, 697n41

Jones, Clarence B., 478n7

JPATS. *See* Justice Prisoner and Alien Transportation System

Judicial Watch, Inc., 251, 521n4, 607n11, 643n45

Judicial Watch, Inc. v. Department of Justice, 542n47

Judicial Watch v. United States Secret Service, 607n16

Justice Prisoner and Alien Transportation System (JPATS), 595n4

K

K-129 (submarine), 532n4

Kaczynski, Theodore J., 583n5, 599n3

Kagan, Elena, 260, 612n24

Kammer, Will, 715n43

Kapsa v. CIA, 129

Karantsalis v. United States Department of Justice, 265

Karpen, Pat, 481n19

Katsas, Gregory G., 2, 539n42, 614n5

Katzenbach, Nicholas D., 562n2

Kearsarge (ship), 353

Keating, Francis A. II, 491n10

Keisler, Peter D., 610n14, 613n28

Kelley, Jill, 106–07, 519n49, 519n50–520n50

Kelly, Scott J., 360

Kemp, Jack, 496n7

Kennedy, Anthony M., 47, 48, 589n2

Kennedy, Cornelia G., 485n48, 486n51, 487n57

    on Exemption 7(C), 487n53

Kennedy, Edward M., 154, 551n5

Kennedy, John F., 4, 41, 53, 459n33, 713n24

Marine Corps Marathon, 716n49

Markman, Stephen J., 3

Marshall, Thurgood, 85, 474n9, 497n2

Marshall, Weldon, 646n66

Martin, Harold, 646n66

Martin, Stephen G., 289

Marzen v. HHS, 483n35, 487n54

Mastalli, Grace Louise, 423

Mathews, Burnita Shelton, 485n48

Mauro, Tony, 276, 497n1

May, Alan Nunn, 693n23

Mayer, Jane M., 593n5

Mayerfeld, Ernest, 339, 425n30, 535n20, 538n39, 719n65, 736n30

Mayfield, Brandon, 102–04, 105, 109

    arrested by FBI, 103–04

    claim for damages, 516n37

    FBI apologized to, 104

    linking with Spain or North Africa, 516n32

    Muslim faith, 516n35

    religious beliefs of, 102–03

    search of home of, 515n31

McCallum, Robert D., Jr., 477n21, 617n7, 705n1

McCarran International Airport, Las Vegas, 338

McDivitt, James A., 660n33

McDonald, Esther S., 277, 279, 280, 281, 284, 285, 621n32, 622n36, 623n39–624n39

    "Counsel to the Associate Attorney General," 623n38

    "derog" Internet searching, 625n45

    records of Internet searches, 626n55

    screening committee work, 626n54

    training on Privacy Act rules, 625n49

McFadden, Nancy E., 198–99, 200, 202, 424n12, 577n4, 577n5, 578n7, 583n4

McGill, Anne Irene, 379

McGlone, Mary Ellen, 728n1

McGuiness, James, 646n66

McIntyre, Thomas J., 546n17, 587n9

McKenna, Joseph, 704n15

McKinnon, Gary, 723n87

McLeod, Janice Galli, 4–5, 425

McMasters, Paul, 712n22

McNamara, Robert S., 697n41

McNulty, Paul J., 617n7, 628n66

McRaven, William H., 692n16

McVeigh, Timothy J., 599n3

Meade, Fort George, 327

Meadows, Mark R., 638n15

measurement and signature intelligence (MASINT), 719n67

Media, Inc., 43

Media FOIA Summit, 712n22

Medical Literature Analysis and Retrieval, 589n2

Medico, Charles, 474n9

Medoff v. CIA, 129, 134, 537n39

    oral argument in, 537n38

Meeks, Daris D., 683n136, 684n136

Meese, Edwin III, 163–64, 196–97, 218–19, 452n4, 545n12, 556n4, 563n2, 587n8, 644n54

    Memorandum's guidance on exclusion implementation, 549n27, 549n33

    subject of multiple independent counsel investigations, 587n7

Mehta, Amit P., 546n18

Mellon, Christopher K., 677n98

Merchant Marine Academy, 191

Merrill, Nicholas, 316

Metcalfe, Daniel J., 36, 62

    agreed to leave Civil Division, 159

    awarded scholarship at George Washington University, 58–59

    became junior member of COG program, 193

    career member of SES, 706n7–707n7

    Civil Division litigation days, 179–80

    conversation with Mauricio Tamargo about Sean Gerlich, 272

    family history, 270

    first meeting with Janet Reno, 198

Novak, Robert D., 453n8

NSA's official Intranet (NSANet), 350

NSO Group, 697n43

Nuclear Security-Related Information, 604n11

Nussbaum, Bernard W., 501n3

O

Oakes, Andra N., 89, 90, 91, 93, 507n4, 509n8

Obama, Barack H., 3, 15, 251–53, 260, 262, 367, 607n13, 611n23, 612n25, 627n62

    Administration, 226, 250–54, 308, 372, 450n8, 457n25, 459n30, 464n3, 472n59, 501n3, 607nn11–16, 722n84

    cabinet, 323

    executive order issued by, 248

    national security classification, 320

    policy on visitor logs, 250–53

    reaction to death-scene photographs of Osama bin Laden, 597n17

    transparency vision, 251

    on UFOs, 351–52, 655n22, 685n137

    U.N. speech, 30, 31

    vacancies on D.C. Circuit, 484n37

    wars under, 30

Obamacare, 583n5

O'Brien, Tim, 703n15

O'Brien Committee, 336

Occupational Safety and Health Administration (OSHA), 173–76

O'Connor, Sandra Day, 85, 485n48, 505n23, 505n26, 554n9, 597n16

Odierno, Raymond, 612n25

Office of Attorney Recruitment and Management (OARM), 274

Office of Criminal Justice, 552n2

Office of Government Information Services (OGIS), 629n6, 722nn84–85

Office of Homeland Security (OHS), 239, 452n2, 603n7

Office of Information and Privacy (OIP), 35, 207, 234, 265, 449n4, 469n33, 501n5

analytical proficiency, recent decline in, 550n39

ancillary national security classification adjudication activity, 185

annual "Holiday Party," 567n29

attorneys, 188, 190

"Christmas Party," 566n28

Civil Division to, 85, 109, 119

during Clinton's second term, 210–12

"congressional access" issue, analysis of, 168–69

creation of, 157–61, 165, 166

delegations of foreign visitors to, 24

Department Review Committee (DRC), 177, 525n9

exclusion-related consultations, 148

expanded Department's FOIA training activities, 555n20

during first Reagan presidential term, 163

FOIA Update publications, 196

"high public interest" setting, 509n9

implementation of Privacy Act of 1974, 108, 111

information disclosure, 214

information policy review by, 238

Janet Reno takes over, 205

new "Exclusions" section added by, 545n13

policy guidance by, 167

"Privacy Act Overview," 621n27

promoted FOIA administration, 462n44

proposed public summaries, 213–14

publications, 555n16

public summary, 229

representatives of other nations, 468n31

responsibilities of, 174, 555n19

on settlement negotiations privilege, 171

staff within, 139

statutory provisions, 164

training programs, 462n44, 591n7

Office of Information Law and Policy (OILP), 157, 158, 165, 495n14

  Murphy v. Department of the Army decision, 166–67

Office of Intelligence Policy and Review (OIPR), 456n17

Office of the Joint Chiefs of Staff, 257

Office of Legal Counsel (OLC), 158, 582n8

Office of Legal Policy (OLP), 158

Office of Management and Budget (OMB), 108, 240, 551n8, 557n9, 591n11–592n11, 708n2, 715n39

Office of Naval Intelligence (ONI), 328, 345, 347, 354

Office of Naval Research (ONR), 671n79

Office of Personnel Management (OPM), 191, 553n5

Office of Privacy and Civil Liberties, 521n3

Office of Privacy and Information Appeals (OPIA), 157–58, 167

Office of Professional Responsibility (OPR), 207, 213–16, 229, 530n6, 584nn1–6

Office of Public Affairs, 207, 595n11

Office of Special Investigations (OSI), 361

Office of Strategic Services (OSS), 536n33, 664n55

Office of Tailored Access Operations, 718n63

Office of the Associate Attorney General, 711n17

Office of the Attorney General, 449n4

Office of the Deputy Attorney General (ODAG), 215, 710n16, 721n76

Office of the Director of National Intelligence (ODNI), 240, 352–53, 360, 362

Office of the Independent Counsel, 593n4

Office of the National Counterintelligence Executive (ONCIX), 564n16

Official Secrets Act (UK), 384, 466n14, 471n52, 676n94, 693n20

Official Use Only (OUO), 604n11

Ogorodnikov, Svetlana, 568n38

Ohio State University, 129

OILP. *See* Office of Information Law and Policy

OIP. *See* Office of Information and Privacy

Oklahoma City Bombing in 1995, 490n6

Oksenberg, Michel C., 133, 537n34

Old Executive Office Building, 481n25

O'Leary, Hazel R., 211, 584n7

Olmstead v. United States, 473n4

Olson, Frank R., 718n62

Olson, Theodore B., 484n42

Omaha (ship), 352

ONCIX. *See* Office of the National Counterintelligence Executive

O'Neill, Paul, 219, 221, 587n10, 588n19–589n19, 589n21

One Observatory Circle, 606n8

Open Government Community, 268

Open Government Partnership (OGP), 31, 473n61

Operation Deadstick, 692n14

Operation Fortitude South, 691n12

Operation Ghost Stories, 549n31

Operation Highjump, 651n10

Operation Mainbrace, 660n30

Operation Neptune Spear, 692n16, 692n17

Operation Overlord, 669n75

Operation Paperclip, 22, 650n8

Operation Snow White, 187, 570n52

Operation Solo, 113, 524n9, 525n9

Operation TOPLEV, 524n3

OPIA. *See* Office of Privacy and Information Appeals

OPM. *See* Office of Personnel Management

Order of the Red Banner, 523n2

O'Reilly, James T., 712n22

Organized Crime Section, 540n45, 541n45

Orwell, George, 669n76

Oswald, Lee Harvey, 366, 524n6, 562n2, 654n21, 694n30

  dealings with CIA, 695n32

  files on, 690n6

visited Soviet Embassy in Mexico City, 674n86

Outlaw v. United States Dep't of the Army, 481n22

Owens, Margaret, 524n8

P

Pack, Michael, 701n6

Palmer, A. Mitchell, 563n2

Palmer Raids, 563n2

Palmieri, Jennifer M., 316

Panetta, Leon E., 107, 261, 597n17

Parker, Barrington D., 500n16

Partnership for Civil Justice, Inc., 595n12

"Passportgate," 506n1

Patriot Act, 456n17

Patton, George S., Jr., 692n12

Paver, Fran L., 425, 540n45

PEADs. *See* presidential emergency action documents

Pearl Harbor, 21, 458n22

Peenemünde Army Research Center, 650n8

Pegasus, 697n43

Peltier, Leonard, 545n10

Pelton, Ronald W., 452n2

Pence, Michael R., 683n136

Pendleton Act, 618n13

Pentagon, 36, 188, 350, 362

    Airborne Object Identification and Management Synchronization Group, 328, 347, 355

    All-Domain Anomaly Resolution Office, 328, 650n7

    Foreign Technology Division, 670n78

    officials, 351

Pentagon Papers, 455n17

People for the American Way Foundation, 595n12

People for the Ethical Treatment of Animals (PETA), 712n22

Peretti, Hugo E., 213

Perez, Evan, 625n47

Perot, H. Ross, 539n43

Perry, Philip J., 3

Persico, Joseph E., 466n16

Peterson, Trudy Huskamp, 629n6

Petraeus, David H., 104–06, 107, 518n44, 519n48, 612n25, 646n66

Pew Research Center, 353

Philby, Harold A., 563n6

Phillippi, Harriet Ann, 125, 534n14

Phillippi v. CIA, 126, 127, 128, 534n15, 535n19, 537n35, 720n73

"Phoenix Lights" sightings, 716n47

Pickard, Thomas J., 600n7

Pitts, Edwin Earl, 181–85, 566n26, 566n28, 567n32–569n42

    as active "mole," 182

    arrest of, 184

    cooperated with investigators, 568n40

    FBI career, 181–83

    pled guilty, 184

    promoted to Supervisory Special Agent, 182–83

    "Top Secret" security clearance in New York City, 567n36

    worked for USSR, 567n30

"Pizzagate," 506n1

Podesta, John D., Jr., 85, 505n22, 506n1, 626n56, 687n146, 721n79

POGO. *See* Project On Government Oversight

political cocktail party, 496n5

POLITICO, 703n15

POLITICO Magazine, 315, 355, 607n16, 638n12

Pollard, Jonathan J., 563n5

Poor Richard's Almanack (Franklin), 365, 464n1, 694n27

Pope Benedict XVI, 695n35, 696n39, 696n40

Pope John Paul, 696n39

Pope Pius XII, 370, 696n38

"Portland Seven," 103

Portland Special Agents, 515n31

Posner, Richard A., 477n19

in post-9/11 information-policy environment, 239

Public Citizen Litigation Group, 712n22

Public Health & Medical Professionals for Transparency v. FDA, 476n17

Public Health Service, 195

Public Key Infrastructure (PKI), 505n22

Pulitzer, Joseph, 1

"Pussygate," 506n1

The Puzzle Palace (Bamford), 720n68

Q

QUANTUMSQUIRREL, 718n63

Queen Elizabeth II, 372, 715n44

R

radiation fallout scandal, 583n7

RAF Rudloe Manor, 673n82

Raines, Bonnie, 479n8

Raines, John C., 479n8

Ramey, Roger M., 652n14

Ramo v. Department of the Navy, 527n27, 728n113

"rap sheet" information, 34

Ratcliffe, John L., 351

Rather, Dan, 61, 494n6

Ratzinger, Joseph, 696n39

Raul, Alan C., 520n50

Raven Rock Mountain Complex, 573n9

Ray, James Earl, 366, 480n13, 545n10, 695n33, 695n34, 713n24

Ray, Robert W., 227–28

Rayburn House Office Building, 490n5

Raytheon Technologies Company, 684n136

Reagan, Ronald, 3, 157, 162–64, 203, 526n15, 553n7, 554n8, 572n3

    Administration, 137, 139, 158, 159, 161, 165, 173, 192, 196, 199, 205, 450n8, 471n54, 577n5, 701n9, 726n109

    issuance of national security directives, 572n7

    patronage appointee, 556n3

second term, 192, 197

    "Star Wars missile-defense" era of, 327

    Transition Team, 158, 553n6

Record/Information Dissemination Section (RIDS), 546n18

Reedy, George E., 489n2

Regis, Reynaldo, 646n66

Rehnquist, William H., 85, 601n12, 703n15

Reid, Harry M., 450n9, 677n97, 680n121

Rendlesham Forest, 676n94

Reno, Janet W., 49, 101, 178, 184, 198, 200, 203–07, 234, 408, 449n3, 450n4, 519n46, 562n2, 567n29, 582n2, 583n4, 644n54 , 721n80

    arrived as AG in 1993, 580n6

    arrived in Washington, D.C, 203

    attended funeral of Elliot Richardson, 495n12

    fight against Parkinson's, 204

    FOIA administration, 213

    FOIA Memorandum of 1993, 505n22

    FOIA policy memorandum, 522n10

    "folk hero" status, 204

    and pro-disclosure policies, 206–07

    relationship with Clinton, 204–05

    signed FOIA Memorandum, 207

    signed "Removal and Maintenance of Documents," 588n14

    supported inter-component committee, 220

    working for, 458n28

Reporters Committee for Freedom of the Press, 474n9, 476n18, 477n18, 477n21, 595n12, 712n22

Revolutionary War, 19, 366, 369, 694n29

Reynolds v. United States, 726n104

Rhodes, William, 651n9

Ricchio v. NARA, 709n10

Rice, Condoleezza, 312, 723n92–724n92

Rich, Benjamin R., 670n78

Rich, Mark, 701n10

Richard Jewell (film), 100

Susman, Thomas M., 712n22

SVRR. *See* Sluzhba Vneshney Rasvedi Rossii

Sweden, 18

> government transparency in, 19
>
> initial transparency, 473n63
>
> "openness-in-government" law, 14
>
> U.S. ally, 371

Swidler & Berlin v. United States, 479n12

Syracuse University, 129

System of Systems Integration Technology and Experimentation (SoSITE), 671n79

T

Taking Care of the Law (Bell), 217

Talavera v. Shah, 627n60

Talbott, Charlie, 715n43

Tamargo, Mauricio J., 272, 617n5

Tamm, Thomas M., 456n17

Tatel, David S., 598n21

Tavistock Square in Central London, 515n30

Taylor, Jack, 712n22

Taylor, Marisa, 625n47

Tenny, Daniel, 286, 287

"Tenth Justice" idea, 484n41

Terwilliger, George J. III, 277

testimonial privilege, 558n5

Texas Tech Law School, 282

Texas Tech University, 622n36

Theodore Roosevelt (aircraft carrier), 343, 344, 360, 680n121, 681n122

The Price of Loyalty: George W. Bush, the White House, and the Education of Paul O'Neill (Suskind), 221

Third Reich, 599n3

Thomas, Clarence, 704n15

Thomas, Sharon, 185–88, 569n42

> time at Justice Department, 570n52

Thompson, Lawrence D., 627n62

Thornberry, William Homer, 497n2, 498n9

Thornburgh, Richard L., 219

Thurmond, Strom, 544n7

Tilley, Steven, 508n8

Tillman, Zoe, 625n47

T'Kach, Steven J., 461n41

Toney, Marcy A., 598n22

Totenberg, Nina, 712n22

To The Stars Academy of Arts & Science (TTSA), 680n117

Totten v. United States, 19, 374, 465n12

Town of Glastonbury, 673n82

Trade Secrets Act, 602n17, 708n8

Transiting Exoplanet Survey Satellite (TESS), 685n139–686n139

TRAPPIST-1, 686n139

TrapWire, 632n4

Travelgate, 582n3

Trial Attorney, 77, 177, 284, 376, 449n1, 478n5

Tripp, Linda R., 593n5

Trott, Stephen S., 491n10

Trulock, Notra, 518n42

Truman, Harry S., 22, 328, 371, 606n8

Trump, Donald J., 12, 26, 324, 326, 350, 486n51, 607n16, 628n66, 648n83, 687n145, 700n2

> abuse of classified information by, 708n3
>
> Administration, 226, 254, 255, 288–89, 372, 450n8, 451n11, 459n30, 464n51, 513n18, 574n13, 614n5, 628n67, 647n80, 681n124, 683n136, 684n136, 698n46, 700n6, 725n99
>
> connection with investigation of Russian collusion, 620n23
>
> electoral college victory, 506n1
>
> impeachment of, 607n13
>
> international relations during, 473n62
>
> "Mar-a-Lago" scandal, 645n58
>
> popularity of, 375
>
> "Space Command," 348–49, 683n136, 684n136
>
> violation of Presidential Records Act by, 325, 605n3

Trustee Scholar status, 70–71